CAMBRIDGE CLASSICAL TEXTS AND
COMMENTARIES

EDITORS
J. DIGGLE   N. HOPKINSON   H. D. JOCELYN
M. D. REEVE   D. N. SEDLEY   R. J. TARRANT

34

ARATUS: PHAENOMENA

ARATUS
PHAENOMENA

EDITED WITH INTRODUCTION,
TRANSLATION AND COMMENTARY
BY

DOUGLAS KIDD

*Emeritus Professor of Classics, University of Canterbury,
Christchurch, New Zealand*

CAMBRIDGE
UNIVERSITY PRESS

PUBLISHED BY THE PRESS SYNDICATE OF THE
UNIVERSITY OF CAMBRIDGE
The Pitt Building, Trumpington Street, Cambridge CB2 IRP,
United Kingdom

CAMBRIDGE UNIVERSITY PRESS
The Edinburgh Building, Cambridge CB2 2RU, United Kingdom
40 West 20th Street, New York, NY 10011-4211, USA
10 Stamford Road, Oakleigh, Melbourne 3166, Australia

First published 1997

Printed in the United Kingdom at the University Press, Cambridge

Typeset in Baskerville and Greek New Hellenic

A catalogue record for this book is available from the British Library

Library of Congress cataloguing in publication data

Aratus, Solensis.
[Phaenomena. English]
Phaenomena / edited with introduction, translation, and commentary
by Douglas Kidd.
p.   cm. – (Cambridge classical texts and commentaries; 34)
Includes index.
ISBN 0 521 58230 x (hardback)
1. Constellations – Early works to 1800.   2. Planets – Early works
to 1800.   I. Kidd, D. A. (Douglas Alexander).   II. Title.   III. Series.
QB802.A713   1997
881'.01–dc21   96-44962 CIP

ISBN 0 521 58230 x hardback

AO

FOR
MARGARET

CONTENTS

CONTENTS

FIGURES

PREFACE

Thirty years ago, when I discussed with the late Professor Brink my thoughts about doing some work on Aratus, I was inspired by his immediate suggestion that I should undertake an edition of the *Phaenomena* with full introduction and commentary, in view of the growing interest in Hellenistic poetry and the lack of a major edition of this poem. I was fortunate again several years later to have the benefit of his advice and encouragement in response to my sending him a sample of commentary on a hundred lines. At the same time he passed on to me a list of helpful comments from Professor Sandbach. Over the last eight years I have benefited from a wide range of critical comments from Professor Reeve, who also suggested additional material to clarify parts of the scientific background, and put forward new interpretations of the text for me to consider. The lively interest he has shown in all aspects of this widely ignored poem has been very rewarding and helpful. I am also indebted to Professor Diggle for a long list of critical comments and additional references that I would otherwise have missed. This highly innovative poem has been a victim of many misunderstandings, and only selected problems have been adequately discussed in the journals and brief commentaries. I have therefore set out at some length the interpretations and preferred textual readings of different scholars before giving my own conclusions and preferences. I owe a great deal, of course, to those few of my contemporaries who have written on Aratus, most particularly to Jean Martin for his work on the history of the text (1956) and his valuable edition of the scholia (1974). Finally I am deeply grateful to the Cambridge University Press for accepting my typescript and patiently dealing with its many problems.

Christchurch, NZ, July 1996   D. A. K.

xi

BIBLIOGRAPHY AND ABBREVIATIONS

Periodicals are abbreviated as in *L'Année Philologique*, Greek and Latin authors generally as in LSJ and *OLD* respectively.

I. THE *PHAENOMENA*

(a) Editions

Aldus
Aldus Manutius Romanus, Ἀράτου Σολέως Φαινόμενα μετὰ σχολίων, with Julius Firmicus, Manilius, the *Aratea* of Germanicus, Cicero and Avienius, the *Sphaera* of Proclus (Venice 1499).

Ceporinus
Jacobus Ceporinus, Διονυσίου Οἰκουμένης περιήγησις, Ἀράτου Φαινόμενα, Πρόκλου Σφαῖρα, *cum scholiis* Ceporini, Gr. et Lat. (ap. Joannem Bibelium, Basiliae 1523). The Latin translation is not by Ceporinus, but is an anonymous version adopted by him.

Morel
Guillaume Morel, Ἀράτου Σολέως Φαινόμενα καὶ Διοσημεῖα, Θέωνος σχόλια, Λεοντίου μηχανικοῦ περὶ Ἀρατείας σφαίρας (Paris 1559).

Stephanus
H. Stephanus, *Poetae graeci principes heroici carminis et alii nonnulli*; pp. 288–317 Ἀράτου Σολέως Φαινόμενα (Paris 1566).

Grotius
Huig van Groot, *Syntagma Arateorum* (Leiden 1600).

Fell
John Fell, Ἀράτου Σολέως Φαινόμενα καὶ Διοσημεῖα, Θέωνος Σχόλια, Ἐρατοσθένους Καταστερισμοί (Oxonii 1672).

Buhle
Johannes Theophilus Buhle, *Arati Solensis Phaenomena et Diosemea, graece et latine ad codd. mss. et optimarum edd. fidem recensita* (vol. I, Lipsiae 1793).

Matthiae
F. C. Matthiae, *Arati Phaenomena et Diosemea, quibus subiciuntur Eratosthenis Catasterismi. Dionysii Orbis Terrarum Descriptio* (Francofurti ad Moenum 1816).

Voss
Johann Heinrich Voss, *Des Aratos Sternerscheinungen und Wetterzeichen*, übersetzt und erklärt (Heidelberg 1824).

xii

BIBLIOGRAPHY AND ABBREVIATIONS

Buttmann — Philip Buttmann, *Arati Phaenomena et Diosemea cum annotatione critica* (Berlin 1826).

Bekker — *Aratus cum Scholiis recognovit* Immanuel Bekkerus (Berolini 1828).

Koechly — *Arati Phaenomena et Prognostica rec.* A. Koechly in *Poetae Bucolici et Didactici* ed. Duebner (Paris 1851).

Maass — *Arati Phaenomena recensuit et fontium testimoniorumque notis prolegomenis indicibus instruxit Ernestus Maass* (Berolini 1893; *ed. sec. lucis ope expressa* 1955).

Mair — G. R. Mair, *Aratus with an English Translation*, in *Callimachus Lycophron Aratus* (Loeb, London / New York 1921).

Zannoni — Giuseppe Zannoni, *Arato di Soli, Fenomeni e Pronostici*, introduzione, traduzione e note (Sansoni, Firenze 1948).

Martin — Jean Martin, *Arati Phaenomena*, introduction, texte critique, commentaire et traduction (La Nuova Italia, Firenze 1956).

Erren — Manfred Erren, *Aratos Phainomena*, Sternbilder und Wetterzeichen, griechisch–deutsch, mit 23 Sternkarten von Peter Schimmel (Heimeran, München 1971).

(b) Commentaries and translations

Ach. *Isag.* — Achilles, Ἐκ τῶν Ἀχιλλέως περὶ τοῦ Παντός, ed. Maass, *Comm.* 22–75.

Arat. Lat. — *Aratus Latinus* ed. Maass, *Comm.* 174–306.

Avien. — Avien(i)us, *Les Phénomènes d'Aratos*, ed. Jean Soubiran (Budé, Paris 1981).

Cic. frr. — Cicero, *Aratea, Fragments poétiques*, ed. Jean Soubiran (Budé, Paris 1972) 158–95.

Erren *PAS* — Manfred Erren, *Die Phainomena des Aratos von Soli*: Untersuchungen zum Sach- und Sinnverständnis (Wiesbaden 1967).

Germ. — Germanicus, *Les Phénomènes d'Aratos*, ed. André Le Boeuffle (Budé, Paris 1975). D. B. Gain, *The Aratus Ascribed to Germanicus Caesar* (London 1976).

Hi. — *Hipparchi in Arati et Eudoxi Phaenomena commen-*

	tariorum libri tres ad codicum fidem recensuit Germanica interpretatione et commentariis instruxit Carolus Manitius (Teubner 1894).
Maass *Aratea*	Ernestus Maass, *Aratea* (Berlin 1892).
Maass *Comm.*	E. Maass, *Commentariorum in Aratum Reliquiae* (Berlin 1898; repr. 1958)
Martin *HT*	J. Martin, *Histoire du texte des Phénomènes d'Aratos* (Paris 1956).
Martin *SAV*	J. Martin, *Scholia in Aratum Vetera* (Stuttgart 1974).
Schol. Germ.	A. Breysig, *Scholia in Germanici Caesaris Aratea* (Berlin 1867) 55–238.
Schott & Böker	*Aratos Sternbilder und Wetterzeichen*, übersetzt und eingeleitet von A. Schott mit Anmerkungen von R. Böker (München 1958).
Sphaer. Arat.	Leontius, *De sphaerae Arateae constructione*, ed. Maass, *Comm.* 560–7.

2. TEXTS RELEVANT TO THE ASTRONOMY AND WEATHER SIGNS

Anon. Laur.	*Anon. in cod. Laurentiano* 28.32 (*saec.* xv), fol. 12, ed. M. Heeger, *De Theophrasti qui fertur* Περὶ σημείων *libro* (1889) 66–71.
Aristarchus	*On the Sizes and Distances of the Sun and Moon*, ed. T. L. Heath, *Aristarchus of Samos* (Oxford 1913) 351–414.
Arist. *Mete.*	Aristotle, *Meteorologica*, ed. H. D. P. Lee (Loeb, Cambridge, Mass. / London 1978).
Autol.	Autolycus, *De sphaera quae mouetur, De ortibus et occasibus*, ed. G. Aujac, *Autolycos de Pitane* (Budé, Paris 1979).
Catast.	[Eratosthenis] *Catasterismi*, ed. A. Olivieri (Teubner 1897).
CCAG 8.1	*Excerpta ex cod. Par. 2229 descripsit* F. Cumont, *Catalogus Codicum Astrologorum*, vol. 8.1 (Bruxelles 1929) 137–40.
Cleom.	Cleomedes, *De motu circulari*, ed. H. Ziegler (Teubner 1891).
DK	*Die Fragmente der Vorsokratiker*, edd. H. Diels and W. Kranz (6th edn, Berlin 1951–2).
D. S.	*De signis, Theophrasti opera quae supersunt omnia*,

	ed. F. Wimmer, vol. 3 *Fragmenta* 6 (Teubner 1862). *Theophrastus, Enquiry into Plants and Minor Works on Odours and Weather Signs*, with an English translation by Sir Arthur Hort, vol. 2 (Loeb, London / New York 1916) 390–433.
Euc.	Euclides, *Elementa* ed. J. L. Heiberg (Teubner 1883); ed. E. S. Stamatis (Teubner 1969). *Phaenomena* ed. H. Menge (Teubner 1916).
Eudox.	Eudoxus, *Phaenomena* and *Enoptron*, ed. F. Lasserre, *Die Fragmente des Eudoxus von Knidus* (Berlin 1966).
Gem. *Cal.*	Geminus, *Calendarium*, post *Elementa* ed. Manitius pp. 210–33; ed. Aujac pp. 98–108.
Gem. *Elem.*	Geminus, *Elementa Astronomiae ad codicum fidem recensuit, Germanica interpretatione et commentariis instruxit Carolus Manitius* (Teubner 1898; repr. 1974). Géminos, *Introduction aux Phénomènes*, texte établit et traduit par Germaine Aujac (Budé, Paris 1975).
Gp.	*Geoponica siue Cassiani Bassi scholastici de re rustica Eclogae*, ed. H. Boeckh.
Hyg.	Hyginus, *De astronomia*, ed. André Le Boeuffle (Budé, Paris 1983).
Johannes Lydus	*Liber de Ostentis et Calendaria graeca omnia*, ed. Curtius Wachsmuth (Teubner 1897).
Man.	Manilius, *Astronomica* with an English translation by G. P. Goold (Loeb, Cambridge, Mass. / London 1977).
Manetho	*Apotelesmatica*, ed. H. Koechly (Teubner 1858).
Max.	Maximus, Περὶ Καταρχῶν, ed. Arthur Ludwich (Teubner 1877).
Pap. Wessely	O. Neugebauer, 'Über griechische Wetterzeichen und Schattentafeln', *Sitzungsberichte der Wiener Akademie der Wissenschaften*, phil.-hist. Klasse Bd 240 (1962) Abh. 2.29–44.
Posid.	Posidonius, edd. L. Edelstein and I. G. Kidd (2 vols., Cambridge 1988).
Ptol. *Alm.*	*Claudii Ptolemaei Opera quae extant omnia*, vol. 1 Μαθηματικὴ Σύνταξις, ed. J. L. Heiberg (Teubner 1957). *Ptolemy's Almagest*, transl. and annot. by G. J. Toomer (Duckworth, London 1984).

BIBLIOGRAPHY AND ABBREVIATIONS

Ptol. *Phaseis*   *Eiusdem opera*, vol. 2 Φάσεις Ἀπλανῶν Ἀστέρων καὶ Συναγωγὴ Ἐπισημασιῶν, ed. Heiberg (Teubner 1907).

Ptol. *Tetr.*   *Eiusdem opera*, vol. 3.1 Ἀποτελεσματικά, edd. F. Boll et Ae. Boer (Teubner 1957).

Sphaera   [Empedoclis] *Sphaera* = Ἀπλανῶν ἄστρων σφαῖρα, ed. Maass, *Comm.* 154–69.

Theon Smyrn.   Theon Smyrnaeus Platonicus, *De astronomia*, ed. E. Hiller (Teubner 1878).

3. OTHER TEXTS

A. fr.   S. Radt, *TrGF*, vol. 3 Aeschylus (Göttingen 1985).

Antim.   B. Wyss, *Antimachi Colophonii reliquiae* (Berlin 1936).

Bion & Moschus   A. S. F. Gow, *Bucolici Graeci* (OCT, Oxford 1952), pp. 131–67.

CA   *Collectanea Alexandrina*, ed. J. U. Powell (Oxford 1925; repr. 1970).

Call.   R. Pfeiffer, *Callimachus* (Oxford 1949, 1953; reissued 1985); G. R. McLennan, *Hymn to Zeus* (Rome 1977); F. Williams, *Hymn to Apollo* (Oxford 1978); N. Hopkinson, *Hymn to Demeter* (Cambridge 1984); A. W. Bulloch, *The Fifth Hymn* (Cambridge 1985).

Cleanthes   *CA* pp. 227–31; Neil Hopkinson, *A Hellenistic Anthology* (Cambridge 1985), pp. 27–9.

E. fr.   A. Nauck, *TrGF* (2nd edn, Leipzig 1889).

FGE   *Further Greek Epigrams: Epigrams before A.D. 50 from the Greek Anthology and Other Sources* ..., ed. D. L. Page (Cambridge 1981).

FHG   *Fragmenta Historicorum Graecorum*, ed. C. Müller, 5 vols. (Paris 1861–70).

GP   *The Garland of Philip and Some Contemporary Epigrams*, edd. A. S. F. Gow and D. L. Page (Cambridge 1968).

Greg. Naz.   *Sancti Gregorii Nazianzeni Carmina Selecta*, ed. E. Dronke (Göttingen 1840).

HE   *The Greek Anthology: Hellenistic Epigrams*, edd. A. S. F. Gow and D. L. Page (Cambridge 1965).

Hes. fr.	R. Merkelbach and M. L. West, *Fragmenta Hesiodea* (Oxford 1967).
Nic.	*Nicander*, edd. A. S. F. Gow and A. F. Scholfield (Cambridge 1953).
Orph.	*Orphicorum Fragmenta*, ed. Otto Kern (Berlin 1922).
PMG	*Poetae Melici Graeci*, ed. D. L. Page (Oxford 1962).
Sapph., Alc.	*Poetarum Lesbiorum Fragmenta*, edd. E. Lobel and D. L. Page (Oxford 1955).
S. fr.	S. Radt, *TrGF*, vol. 4 Sophocles (Göttingen 1977).
SH	*Supplementum Hellenisticum*, edd. H. Lloyd-Jones and P. Parsons (Berlin / New York 1983).
SVF	*Stoicorum Veterum Fragmenta*, ed. H. von Arnim (Leipzig 1903).
TrGF	*Tragicorum Graecorum Fragmenta*, edd. B. Snell, al. (Göttingen 1971–).
Tzetzes *Chil.*	*Ioannis Tzetzae Historiarum Variarum Chiliades*, ed. Theophilus Kiessling (Leipzig 1826; repr. Hildesheim 1963).

For fragments of iambus and elegy, reference is to M. L. West, *Iambi et Elegi Graeci ante Alexandrum Cantati* (2nd edn, Oxford 1989).

4. GENERAL WORKS

AAC	*L'astronomie dans l'antiquité classique*, Actes du Colloque tenu a l'Université de Toulouse le Mirail 21–23 octobre 1977 (Paris 1979).
Allen	Richard Hinckley Allen, *Star Names: their Lore and Meaning* (New York 1963).
Aujac *Str.*	G. Aujac, *Strabon et la science de son temps* (Paris 1966).
Aujac *Zodiaque*	G. Aujac, 'Le zodiaque dans l'astronomie grecque', *Revue d'Histoire des Sciences* 33 (1980) 3–32.
Autenrieth	G. Autenrieth, *A Homeric Dictionary*, translated by R. P. Keep, rev. I. Flagg (Oklahoma 1958).
Bernhardy	G. Bernhardy, *Wissenschaftliche Syntax* (Berlin 1829).
Bickerman	E. J. Bickerman, *Chronology of the Ancient World* (London 1968).

BIBLIOGRAPHY AND ABBREVIATIONS

BKT	*Berliner Klassikertexte*, herausgegeben von der Generalverwaltung der Kgl. Museen zu Berlin (Berlin 1904–).
Boll *Sphaera*	F. Boll, *Sphaera. Neue griechische Texte und Untersuchungen zur Geschichte der Sternbilder* (Leipzig 1903).
Chantraine	P. Chantraine, *Grammaire homérique* (Paris 1958–63).
Chantraine *MHG*	P. Chantraine, *Morphologie historique du grec* (Paris 1945).
CHCL I	*The Cambridge History of Classical Literature*, vol. 1 *Greek Literature*, edd. P. E. Easterling and B. M. W. Knox (Cambridge 1985).
Cobet	C. G. Cobet, *Variae Lectiones*, 2nd edn (Leiden 1873).
Cook	A. B. Cook, *Zeus: a Study in Ancient Religion*, vol. 2 (Cambridge 1925).
Defradas	J. Defradas, Review of Martin, *REG* 70 (1957) 275–7.
Denniston	J. D. Denniston, *The Greek Particles* (2nd edn, Oxford 1954).
Dicks *EGA*	D. R. Dicks, *Early Greek Astronomy to Aristotle* (London 1970).
Dicks *GFH*	D. R. Dicks, *Geographical Fragments of Hipparchus* (London 1960).
Diggle *Phaethon*	J. Diggle, *Euripides, Phaethon* (Cambridge 1970).
Diggle *Studies*	J. Diggle, *Studies on the Text of Euripides* (Oxford 1981).
Edwards	G. P. Edwards, *The Language of Hesiod in its Traditional Context* (Oxford 1971).
Et. M.	*Etymologicum Magnum*, ed. T. Gaisford (Oxford 1848; repr. 1962).
Fehling	D. Fehling, *Die Wiederholungsfiguren und ihr Gebrauch bei den Griechen vor Gorgias* (Berlin 1969).
Ferrari	W. Ferrari, 'Cicerone e Arato', *SIFC* 17 (1940) 77–96.
Frieseman	H. Frieseman, *Collectanea Critica* (Amsterdam 1786).
Frisk	H. Frisk, *Griechisches etymologisches Wörterbuch* (Heidelberg 1960–70).
Gaisford	T. Gaisford, *Poetae Graeci Minores*, vol. 3 (Oxonii 1820).

Gilbert	O. Gilbert, *Die meteorologischen Theorien des griechischen Altertums* (Leipzig 1907).
Goodwin *GG*	W. W. Goodwin, *A Greek Grammar* (London 1894).
Goodwin *MT*	W. W. Goodwin, *Syntax of the Moods and Tenses of the Greek Verb* (London 1899).
Greenler	R. Greenler, *Rainbows, Haloes and Glories* (Cambridge 1980).
Guthrie *HGP*	W. K. C. Guthrie, *A History of Greek Philosophy* (6 vols., Cambridge 1962–81).
Hainsworth	J. B. Hainsworth in *A Commentary on Homer's Odyssey*, vol. 1 (Oxford 1988).
Harrison	J. E. Harrison, *Themis, a Study of the Social Origins of Greek Religion* (Cambridge 1912).
Hattink	C. J. Hattink, review of Martin, *CR* 8 (1958) 28–30.
Heath	T. L. Heath, *Aristarchus of Samos* (Oxford 1913).
Heeger	M. Heeger, *De Theophrasti qui fertur* Περὶ σημείων *libro* (Lipsiae 1889).
Hermann	G. Hermann, *Orphica* (Lipsiae 1805).
Hilberg	*Der Princip der Silbenwägung und die daraus entspringenden Gesetze der Endsilben in der griechischen Poesie* (Wien 1879).
Honigman	E. Honigman, 'The Arabic translation of Aratus' *Phainomena*', *Isis* 41 (1950) 30–1.
Hopkinson *HA*	Neil Hopkinson, *A Hellenistic Anthology* (Cambridge 1988).
Hutchinson *HP*	G. O. Hutchinson, *Hellenistic Poetry* (Oxford 1988).
Irigoin	J. Irigoin, *Histoire du texte de Pindare* (Paris 1952).
James	A. W. James, 'The Zeus Hymns of Cleanthes and Aratus', *Antichthon* 6 (1972) 28–38.
Jermyn	L. A. S. Jermyn, 'Weather-signs in Virgil', *Greece and Rome* 20 (1951) 26–37, 49–59.
Kaibel	G. Kaibel, review of Maass, *Göttingische gelehrte Anzeiger* n. s. 1 (1893) 937–61.
Kastner	W. Kastner, *Die griechischen Adjective zweier Endungen auf -ΟΣ* (Heidelberg 1967).
K–B	R. Kühner and F. Blass, *Ausführliche Grammatik der griechischen Sprache* (Hanover 1890–2).
Kerényi	C. Kerényi, *The Gods of the Greeks* (London 1951).

Keydell   R. Keydell, review of Martin, *Gnomon* 30 (1958) 581–4.

K–G   R. Kühner and B. Gerth, *Ausführliche Grammatik der griechischen Sprache* (Hanover/Leipzig 1898–1904).

Kiefner   G. Kiefner, *Die Versparung: Untersuchungen zu einer Stilfigur der dichterischen Rhetorik am Beispiel der griechischen Tragödie, unter Berücksichtigung des* σχῆμα ἀπὸ κοινοῦ (Wiesbaden 1964).

Kirk   G. S. Kirk, *The Iliad. A Commentary*, vol. 1 *Books 1–4* (Cambridge 1985).

Kramer   B. Kramer, *Kölner Papyri*, Bd 4 (Opladen 1982) 144–50.

Lasserre   F. Lasserre, *Die Fragmente des Eudoxus von Knidos* (Berlin 1966).

Le Bourdellès   H. Le Bourdellès *L'Aratus Latinus. Etude sur la culture et la langue latine dans le Nord de la France au VIIIe siècle* (Université de Lille III, 1985).

Leumann   M. Leumann, *Homerische Wörter* (Basel 1950).

LfrgE   B. Snell and H. Erbse, edd., *Lexikon des frühgriechischen Epos* (Göttingen 1955–).

Lobeck *Par.*   C. A. Lobeck, *Paralipomena Grammaticae Graecae* (Lipsiae 1837).

Lobeck *Phryn.*   C. A. Lobeck, *Phrynichi Eclogae Nominum et Verborum Atticorum* (Lipsiae 1820).

Lobeck *Proll.*   C. A. Lobeck, *Pathologiae Sermonis Graeci Prolegomena* (Lipsiae 1843).

Lobeck *Rhem.*   C. A. Lobeck, Ῥηματικόν, *sive Verborum Graecorum et Nominum Verbalium Technologia* (Regimonti 1846).

Loebe   V. Loebe, *De Elocutione Arati Solensis Poetae* (diss., Halle 1864).

Lombardo *AW*   S. Lombardo, 'Auriga reoriented: a note on constellation forms and Greek artistic imagination', *The Ancient World* 2 (1979) 107–9.

LSJ   *A Greek–English Lexicon*, edd. H. G. Liddell, R. Scott, H. Stuart Jones, R. McKenzie (9th edn with Supplement, Oxford 1968).

Ludwich   A. Ludwich, *De Hexametris poetarum Graecorum spondaicis* (Halle 1866).

Ludwig *Hermes*   W. Ludwig, 'Die Phainomena Arats als hellenistiche Dichtung', *Hermes* 91 (1963) 425–48.

BIBLIOGRAPHY AND ABBREVIATIONS

Ludwig *RE* W. Ludwig, 'Aratos', *RE* Supplementband x (1965) 26–39.

Maas P. Maas, *Greek Metre* (English translation by H. Lloyd-Jones, Oxford 1962).

Manitius C. Manitius, *Hipparchi Commentaria* (Leipzig 1894).

Maxwell-Stuart P. G. Maxwell-Stuart, *Studies in Greek Colour Terminology* (Leiden 1981).

Monro *HG* D. B. Monro, *A Grammar of the Homeric Dialect* (2nd edn, Oxford 1891).

Neugebauer *ESA* O. Neugebauer, *The Exact Sciences in Antiquity* (2nd edn, New York 1969).

Neugebauer *HAMA* O. Neugebauer, *A History of Ancient Mathematical Astronomy*, 3 vols. (Berlin / Heidelberg / New York 1969).

Norden E. Norden, 'Beiträge zur Geschichte der griechischen Philosophie', *Jahrb. für classische Philologie*, Suppl. 19 (1893) 365–462.

Norton *Norton's Star Atlas* (16th edn, 1973).

OLD *The Oxford Latin Dictionary*, ed. P. G. W. Glare (Oxford 1968–82).

O'Neill E. G. O'Neill, 'The localization of metrical word-types in the Greek hexameter. Homer, Hesiod and the Alexandrians', *YCS* 8 (1942) 102–76.

Opelt I. Opelt, 'Alliteration im Griechischen? Untersuchungen zur Dichtersprache des Nonnos von Panopolis', *Glotta* 37 (1958) 205–32.

Ovenden K. Ovenden, 'The origin of the constellations', *JBAA* 71 (1960–1) 91–5.

Palmer L. R. Palmer, *The Greek Language* (London 1980).

Pasquali G. Pasquali, 'Das Prooimion des Arat', Χάριτες *Friedrich Leo* (Berlin 1911).

Pollard J. Pollard, *Birds in Greek Life and Myth* (London 1977).

Polunin & Ever. O. Polunin, *Trees and Bushes of Europe*, with drawings by Barbara Everard (London 1976).

Polunin & Hux. O. Polunin and A. Huxley, *Flowers of the Mediterranean* (London 1967).

Porter H. N. Porter, 'The early Greek hexameter', *YCS* 12 (1951) 3–63.

RE *Pauly's Realencyclopädie der classischen Altertums-*

xxi

BIBLIOGRAPHY AND ABBREVIATIONS

	wissenschaft, edd. G. Wissowa et al. (Stuttgart / München 1894–).
Regenbogen	O. Regenbogen, *RE* Suppl. VII, 1412–15.
Rehm	A. Rehm, *Parapegmastudien* (Abhandlungen der Bayerischen Akad. d. Wiss., phil.-hist. Abt., neue Folge, Heft 19, 1941).
Richardson	N. J. Richardson, *The Homeric Hymn to Demeter* (Oxford 1974).
Ronconi	A. Ronconi, 'Arato interprete di Omero', *SIFC* 14 (1937) 167–202, 237–59.
Roscher	W. H. Roscher, *Ausführliches Lexikon der griechischen und römischen Mythologie*, Bände I–VI (Leipzig/Berlin 1924–37).
Royds	T. F. Royds, *The Beasts, Birds and Bees of Virgil* (Oxford 1914).
Sandbach	F. H. Sandbach, *Plutarch's Moralia*, vol. 15 *Fragments* (Loeb, Cambridge, Mass. / London 1969).
Schmidt	M. Schmidt, 'Zu Aratos', *Philologus* 9 (1854) 396–400, 551–5.
J. Schneider	J. G. Schneider, *Griechisch–Deutsches Wörterbuch* (Leipzig 1819).
O. Schneider	O. Schneider, *Callimachea* (vol. 1, Leipzig 1870, vol. 2, 1873).
Schwabl	H. Schwabl, 'Zur Mimesis bei Arat', *WS* Beiheft 5 (1972) 336–56.
Schwyzer	E. Schwyzer, *Griechische Grammatik* (München 1939–71).
Shipp	G. P. Shipp, *Studies in the Language of Homer* (2nd edn, Cambridge 1972).
Solmsen	F. Solmsen, 'Aratus on the Maiden and the Golden Age', *Hermes* 94 (1966) 124–8.
Spitzner	F. Spitzner, *De Versu Graecorum Heroico, maxime Homerico* (Leipzig 1816).
Stanford	W. B. Stanford, *The Odyssey of Homer* (London 1950–4).
Stinton	T. C. W. Stinton, *'Si credere dignum est*: some expressions of disbelief in Euripides and others', *PCPS* n.s. 22 (1976) 60–89 = *Collected Papers on Greek Tragedy* (Oxford 1990) 236–64.
Thiel	R. Thiel, *And There Was Light: the Discovery of the Universe*, translated from the German by R. and C. Winston (London 1958).

Thompson	D. W. Thompson, *A Glossary of Greek Birds* (2nd edn, Oxford 1936).
Traglia	A. Traglia, *SCO* 15 (1966) 250–8.
Ungnad	A. Ungnad, 'Babylonische Sternbilder oder der Weg babylonischer Kultur nach Griechenland', *Zeitschrift für die Deutsche Morgenländischen Gesellschaft* 77 (1923) 81–91.
Veitch	W. Veitch, *Greek Verbs Irregular and Defective* (Oxford 1887).
Vlastos	G. Vlastos, *Plato's Universe* (Oxford 1975).
Waerden *AHES*	B. L. van der Waerden, 'Greek astronomical calendars', *AHES* 29 (1984) 101–30.
Waerden *EW*	B. L. van der Waerden, *Erwachende Wissenschaft*, Bd 2 *Die Anfänge der Astronomie* (Basel/Stuttgart 1968).
Waltz	P. Waltz, 'Τροπαὶ Ἠελίοιο. Notes sur Odyssée xv 404', *Revue des Etudes Homériques* 1 (1931) 3–15.
West *GM*	M. L. West, *Greek Metre* (Oxford 1982).
West *Th.*, *Op.*	M. L. West, *Hesiod Theogony* (Oxford 1966); *Works and Days* (Oxford 1978).
Wilamowitz *HD*	U. von Wilamowitz-Moellendorff, *Hellenistiche Dichtung* (Berlin 1924).
Wilkinson	L. P. Wilkinson, *The Georgics of Virgil* (Cambridge 1969).
Wyatt	W. F. Wyatt, Jr, *Metrical Lengthening in Homer* (Rome 1969).

In the Introduction and Commentary I have also used the following astronomical abbreviations: ER (evening rising), ES (evening setting), MR (morning rising), MS (morning setting).

INTRODUCTION

I LIFE OF ARATUS

Ancient evidence for the life and works (other than the *Phaenomena*) is provided mainly by four Vitae preserved in Aratean MSS, with a version of Vita III in the Latin of *Aratus Latinus*, and a fifth Life in the Suda s.v. Ἄρατος. For the text and full discussion see J. Martin *HT* 137–95, for the text alone *SAV* 6–21. An earlier edition of the four Vitae without the Suda version is that of E. Maass *Comm.* 76–9, 323–4, 146–151, 324–6, and Maass has a full discussion of the lost works in *Aratea* 211–48. W. Ludwig in *RE* Suppl. x (1965) 26–30 gives a brief critical review of the information provided by the five Vitae.

The Vitae are sometimes contradictory, and contain obvious and probable errors, but where most or all agree they suggest a common origin. Martin (*HT* 196–202) plausibly ascribes this to Theon of Alexandria, a grammarian of the first century BC, who is named as the author of Vita III by Triclinius in cod. Ambrosianus C 263 inf. (*SAV* 14).

There is general agreement that Aratus came from Soli in Cilicia (cf. Call. *E.* 27.3 ὁ Σολεύς), that his parents were Athenodorus and Letophila, and that he had three brothers, Myris, Caliondas and Athenodorus. He is said to have studied under the grammarian Menecrates of Ephesus, the philosopher Timon, and also Menedemus (Suda), and in Athens with Persaeus (Vita IV) under Zeno (III). His date is expressed roughly by reference to the reigns of (κατά, ἐπί) Ptolemy Philadelphus (III, IV) and Antigonus Gonatas (I), and more precisely by his association with close contemporaries (συνήκμαζε, συνήκμασε, σύγχρονος, συνεγγίζων κατὰ τοὺς χρόνους), Alexander Aetolus (III, IV, Suda), Dionysius of Heraclea (II), Antagoras of Rhodes (Suda). Other poets also named are Philetas (II, IV), Callimachus (III, IV), and even Menander (IV). But very little is known about Philetas, there is no evidence that A. ever met Callimachus

3

(K.O. Brink, *CQ* 40, 1946, 13–14), and Menander was a generation older. A. must have spent several years in Athens, associating with other poets and philosophers, especially Stoics, and may well have become acquainted then with the circle of Menedemus in Eretria. He had already made a name for himself as a poet before the year 276, the only reliable date we have for his career, when he was summoned by Antigonus, who had himself been a student in Athens, to his court at Pella, along with the Stoic Persaeus, Antagoras of Rhodes, and Alexander Aetolus (Vitae I, III, IV, Suda). Antigonus had finally claimed his kingdom, strengthened by his defeat of the Gauls at Lysimacheia in 277, and his invitation to A. was probably linked with the king's marriage to Phila, half-sister of Antiochus II of Syria, about the end of the following year. This is apparently the year indicated by the reference in Vita I to Olympiad 125 (erroneously 105 in IV, 124 in Suda), to which is added καθ' ὃν χρόνον ἤκμασεν ὁ Ἄρατος. If we may think of A. as having been in his mid-thirties by this time, his birth could be tentatively placed about 310.

Vita I also gives us the legend of how A. came to write the *Phaenomena*, τοῦ βασιλέως Εὐδόξου ἐπιγραφόμενον βιβλίον Κάτοπτρον δόντος αὐτῷ καὶ ἀξιώσαντος τὰ ἐν αὐτῷ καταλογάδην λεχθέντα περὶ τῶν φαινομένων μέτρῳ ἐντεῖναι καὶ ἅμα εἰπόντος ὡς "εὐδοξότερον ποιεῖς τὸν Εὔδοξον ἐντείνας τὰ παρ' αὐτῷ κείμενα μέτρῳ." Vita III, however, after telling how Antigonus provided the theme, δοὺς τὸ Εὐδόξου σύγγραμμα καὶ κελεύσας ἕπεσθαι αὐτῷ, goes on to refute the opinion that A. merely copied Eudoxus and was no μαθηματικός himself, a misconception best known from Cic. *De orat.* 1.69 *si constat inter doctos hominem ignarum astrologiae ornatissimis atque optimis uersibus Aratum de caelo stellisque dixisse*; cf. *Rep.* 1.22. The story of Antigonus' command may have been inspired by some fulsome expression of gratitude on the part of the poet to

his patron for his encouragement, imitated perhaps by
Virgil in *G.* 3.41 *tua, Maecenas, haud mollia iussa.* Martin suggests (*HT* 172) that the legend was invented by A.'s critics.
At least the story suggests that the *Phaenomena* was written
at Pella in the years following 276, although A. had probably started to think about it during his sojourn in Athens.
Vita 1 also derives from an unnamed source (τινές) the
tradition that A. later went on to the court of Antiochus in
Syria to work on a recension of the *Iliad,* Vita III Δωσίθεος
δὲ ὁ πολιτικὸς ἐν τῷ πρὸς Διόδωρον ἐλθεῖν φησιν αὐτὸν
καὶ πρὸς Ἀντίοχον τὸν Σελεύκου καὶ διατρῖψαι παρ'
αὐτῷ χρόνον ἱκανόν. Hence Gow in *HE* p. 104 suggests
that Meleager's οὐρανομάκευς φοίνικος (3974–5) may have
been chosen with reference to A.'s residence in Syria. If
the sojourn in Syria is true, it may have been a short one,
since the Suda notice records that after A. went to Antigonus συνῴκει τε αὐτῷ καὶ παρ' αὐτῷ ἐτελεύτησε. This
suggests that A. died before Antigonus, that is, before 239.

II THE *PHAENOMENA*

(a) Structure of the poem

A. 1–18 Proem: hymn to Zeus as beneficent father-
god, who designed the constellations as a
guide to the changing seasons (1–14), invocation of Zeus and the Muses (15–18).

B. 19–461 The constellations and how to recognise
them.

19–26 The rotating sky, its axis and poles.

26–62 The northern circumpolar constellations: Bears (26–44), Dragon (45–62).

63–90 The Dragon's head group: the
kneeling figure (63–70), Crown (71–3),
Serpent-holder and Serpent (74–87), Claws
(88–90).

559–732 Simultaneous risings and settings: the time of night, to be estimated by observing the stars on the horizon (559–68), stars that rise and set simultaneously with the risings of the Crab (569–89), the Lion (590–5), the Maiden (596–606), the Claws (607–33), the Scorpion (634–68), the Archer and Capricorn (669–92), the Water-pourer (693–8), the Fishes and the Ram (699–711), the Bull (712–23), the Twins (724–32).

733–757 Days of the month (733–9) and times of the year (740–57).

D. 758–1141 Local weather signs observable in natural phenomena and the behaviour of birds and animals.

758–777 Second proem, on the weather at sea and the value of learning the signs.

778–908 Celestial signs, from the appearance of the moon (778–818), the sun (819–91), the Manger (892–908).

909–1043 Miscellaneous signs of weather conditions: of wind, from birds and natural phenomena (909–32); of rain, from natural phenomena, birds and animals (933–87); of fair weather, from clouds, stars, lamps and birds (988–1012); of storm, from stars, clouds, birds and domestic life (1013–43).

1044–1103 Seasonal signs: from vegetation (1044–63), of winter from farm life, of drought from comets (1064–93), of summer from birds (1094–1103).

1104–1141 Local signs of bad weather from animals.

E. 1142–1154 Conclusion: a summing-up of the principal lessons.

For the modern view of the poem's structure (cf. note on

733–757) see K. Schütze, *Beiträge zum Verständnis der Phainomena Arats*, diss. Leipzig (1935); J. Martin, *Arati Phaenomena* (1956) pp. xxi–xxiv; W. Ludwig, *Hermes* 91 (1963) 429–38.

(b) The Hesiodic genre

The *Works and Days* is in the first place a model for the *Phaenomena* as a whole. The genre is didactic epic; its form consists of a proem, development of a main theme, and a conclusion. The basic theme is the problem of how to prosper in contemporary life. Hesiod explains the presence of human troubles by reference to myths, and urges a morality of just dealings and hard work, then gives practical advice on farming and sailing, with instructions on the calendar and weather signs. The *Phaenomena* follows a similar overall plan. The basic theme is still a concern with problems of contemporary life, and practical instruction is given on astronomy and weather signs for the benefit of farmers and seafarers. But A. aims to improve on Hesiod in many ways, so bringing his genre up to date. The structure of the poem is more clearly organised, and the development from one section to another is more intelligible. With the growth of science the natural world is better understood, and Zeus is now a helpful rather than a hostile god.

Many of the minor themes of the *Phaenomena* are derived from the *Theogony* as well as from the *Works and Days*, and are meant to be recognised as such by Hellenistic readers, who are also expected to appreciate the ingenuity with which the source material is often differently treated. Both Hesiodic proems give pre-eminence to the Muses and then celebrate Zeus. A. gives the priority to Zeus, who is significant for the whole poem, and invokes the Muses only for the sake of the epic tradition. Hesiod's Zeus is celebrated for his power over men, A.'s new Zeus for his helpfulness to men: see notes on 1–18.

Myths are used by A. to relieve the technical description of the constellations, and several of these are drawn from Hesiod. From *Th.* 477–84 comes the story of the infant Zeus hidden in a cave in Crete (*Phaen.* 31–5). A. deliberately recalls Hesiod's Διòς μεγάλου διὰ βουλάς (465) with his Διòς μεγάλου ἰότητι (71), ἐς Λύκτον (477) with Λύκτῳ (33), and ἄντρῳ (483) with the same word in the same *sedes* (34). The *Theogony* also provides a mixed source for A.'s myth of the Horse (216–24): φασι gives a sly hint of Hesiod, Ἵππου κρήνης is taken from *Th.* 6, and the choice of πηγαῖς for 'water' suggests the naming of Pegasus in *Th.* 281–2. A. himself does not name the Horse, nor does he give it the power of flight, as Hesiod does in 284. The names Doris and Panope (658) are chosen from *Th.* 250.

The myths that link the *Phaenomena* most clearly with the *Works and Days* are those of Dike (*Op.* 213–85) and the Ages (109–201), which A. combines in 98–136. His ἄλλος λόγος (100) points back to Hesiod's ἕτερον λόγον (106), which introduces the myth of the Ages there. For Dike see note on *Phaen.* 105. For A.'s variations in the characteristics of the successive Ages, and omission of the Heroic Age, see notes on 96–136, 107 θέμιστας, 108 λευγαλέου τότε νείκεος, 109 διακρίσιος, 110 αὔτως δ' ἔζωον and ἀπέκειτο θάλασσα, 112 βόες καὶ ἄροτρα, 113 μυρία πάντα and δώτειρα δικαίων, 115 ἀργυρέω, 118 ἐξ ὀρέων, 123–6, 129–136 and 130. The departure of Dike to the sky (133–5) is modelled on that of Aidos and Nemesis in *Op.* 197–201, with the difference that these abandon men completely, whereas Dike remains at least reassuringly visible.

A major theme of the *Works and Days* is the star calendar, which gives the background for important times of the year in the section 383–694. Hesiod uses the system of risings and settings (see note on *Phaen.* 265), referring to the Pleiades (383–4, 572, 615, 619), Sirius (417, 587, 609), Orion (598, 609, 615, 619), Arcturus (566, 610) and the Hyades (615); his reference to Orion and Sirius in 609 is,

9

however, to a culmination at dawn. He also mentions the solstices as a time reference in 479, 564, 663. A. is mainly concerned with the entire annual movement of the constellations and bright stars, and their use as a guide to the time of night as well as the time of year, but he makes a point of alluding to the use of Hesiod's stars at their risings and settings, the Pleiades (264–7, 1066, 1085), Sirius (332–6), Orion (309–10), Arcturus (745), the Hyades (172–3); he also adds to the list the Goat and Kids (157–9). In associating the (morning) setting of the Pleiades with the beginning of winter and time for ploughing (266–7) he points back to *Op.* 384 and 616. A. also mentions the solstices three times (286, 499, 508).

Other passages on the farmer's year that are reminiscent of Hesiod are 514 εἴαρος ἱσταμένοιο (*Op.* 569), 733–9 (*Op.* 765–82), and weather signs (see note on 758–1141). The *Phaenomena* concludes by summing up the lesson on learning the signs throughout the year (1142–54), whereas *Op.* 822–8 sums up only the section on days.

(c) The Stoic element

While the character and language of the proem are clearly Hesiodic, its content strongly reflects the cosmic beliefs of the contemporary Old Stoa, especially as they are expressed in Cleanthes' *Hymn to Zeus*. The traditional sky-god Zeus is now presented as the life-giving force that pervades the whole cosmos (*Phaen.* 2–5; Cl. 1–2, 4–5, 11–13), and since we are a part of the cosmos and derive life from that force, we can still describe Zeus as the father of men (5, 15; Cl. 34). This god is also envisaged as a rational providence that directs everything for the best (5–9, 11–13; Cl. 2), and can therefore be seen as a benefactor of men (5, 11–13, 15; Cl. 32–4). For the purpose of the *Phaenomena* the most significant act of the cosmic Zeus was to establish in the sky constellations and bright stars to be used as guides to the climate of the ever-changing year (10–13). From time to time throughout the rest of the poem A. reminds the reader of this beneficent Zeus, e.g. in 265 Ζεὺς δ' αἴτιος, referring to the most important of all seasonal risings and settings, those of the Pleiades, and in 771 Ζεύς· ὁ γὰρ οὖν γενεὴν ἀνδρῶν ἀναφανδὸν ὀφέλλει, a general restatement of the helpfulness of Zeus.

But Zeus in the *Phaenomena* appears in a variety of different characters (see note on 1 ἐκ Διὸς ἀρχ.). Already in the proem the epithet ἤπιος (5) suggests an anthropomorphic god of the traditional religion, and is chosen because A. wishes to contrast the new Zeus with the angry god of the *Works and Days* (47). Similarly in 426 Διὸς παρανισσομένοιο he is the traditional weather-god responding to human prayers, while elsewhere he can relentlessly send frost (293), storm (886) or rain (936). In other contexts he is the Hesiodic mythological god (31), is slyly hinted at (99), is associated with the Goat and Kids (163–4), and related to Cepheus through Io (181). Again Zeus as the sky itself (224, 259, 756) can suggest both the primitive god and the Stoic god, and in the phrase ἐν Διὶ πατρί (253) these two extremes are amusingly merged with the mythological god who is known as the father of Perseus.

Wherever Zeus is named, however, there may be an intended reminder of the god of the proem, and the proem's essential message, his establishing of reliable signs for the benefit of men, is illustrated in detail throughout the remainder of the *Phaenomena*. Hence B. Effe, *Dichtung und Lehre* (1977) 40–56, basing his argument on the repeated reference to the signs and the insistence on their usefulness, suggests that A.'s higher purpose was to promote the religious dogma of the Stoics, by showing how the celestial phenomena communicate to men the wonder of the divine providence. But his case is somewhat overstated; see E. J. Kenney, *CR* 29 (1979) 72. In addition to the criticisms made by Kenney several others may be worth considering.

Night (408–10) may certainly be seen as equivalent to Zeus as a giver of signs, but her anthropomorphic distress over human suffering is not a characteristic of the cosmic god; cf. 159. The reference to planetary periods (458–9) does not suggest to me the Stoic theory that associated the cosmic cycle with the Great Year (*SVF* 2.596, 599): the point here is that these long and incompatible periods are of no use for any practical measurement of time (see note ad loc.). In 768–70 the reluctance of Zeus to tell all is not appropriate to the perfection of the cosmic god, whose signs must be firmly established for all time, and therefore can only be true for the sun, moon and fixed stars. The subcelestial signs which follow are not so reliable, and A. is obliged to make a concession to Hesiod and reality, and present Zeus more as a traditional god who may possibly be persuaded to change his mind. It is significant that all references to Zeus after 777 are expressed in traditional weather phrases (886, 899, 936, 964), and that in the poem's conclusion (1142–54) Zeus is entirely ignored.

A.'s higher purpose is literary rather than philosophical. He uses the Stoic concept of a rational god as a contrast to Hesiod's Zeus, thus bringing out the progress of the Greeks' civilisation and understanding of the natural world. He also, of course, gives a display of his artistry and ingenuity in making such technical material from prose sources compatible with the demands of Hellenistic poetry.

III THE ASTRONOMY AND WEATHER SIGNS

(a) Astronomy

(i) Earlier poetry

The night sky was a familiar and impressive sight to the ancient Greeks, and astronomy became a theme for poets long before it evolved into a science. Homer established as significant constellations and stars the Pleiades, the Hyades, Orion and the Bear (Σ 485–9), also Bootes (ε 272–5), the Dog (X 26–9) and Hesperus as the evening star (X 317–18). Hesiod added to this stock of poetic lore the calendar of risings and settings, the names Sirius and Arcturus, and the solstices (*Op.* 383–621, 663; see above pp. 9–10).

Lyric and dramatic poets developed these star themes for a variety of purposes: (*a*) to represent the night sky as a whole by means of a few notable constellations (E. *Ion* 1147–58, *Or.* 1005–6); (*b*) to suggest the time of night by the position of a constellation (Sapph. 104a; fr. adesp. 976 *PMG*), E. *IA* 7–8, *Rh.* 529–30); (*c*) to associate stars with the time of year (Alc. 347(a), 5–6, A. *Ag.* 5–6); (*d*) to invent a new metaphor (Alcm. 1.60–3, Pi. *N.* 2.10–12).

Presocratic philosophers speculating on cosmological problems followed Hesiod in adopting the hexameter as an appropriate medium for expounding astronomical theories: cf. Parm. frr. 8–11, Emped. frr. 27–9, 41–2.

(ii) Meton and Euctemon

The astronomy of the *Phaenomena* is limited to what was required for estimating the time of year or month or night, for the purpose of predicting weather conditions. The traditional system of risings and settings (see note on 265) involved a small number of bright stars and easily recognisable star-groups. But a precise measurement of the year had not been achieved until Meton and Euctemon c. 430 BC devised a more rational method of reckoning the days by months according to the passage of the sun through the zodiacal constellations. They are credited with the invention of the 19-year cycle (see note on 753), and may also have invented the parapegma, an inscription on stone for public use, listing risings and settings on key dates for the whole year, together with notes on the weather to be expected. Holes were drilled in the stone against the lines of the text, so that a peg could be moved from day to day to keep the calendar up to date. See A. Rehm, *Parapegmastudien* (1941), and for succinct accounts Dicks *EGA* 84–5, Neugebauer *HAMA* 587–9. The name parapegma was later given also to written calendars of this kind, well illustrated by the anonymous collection appended to Geminus' *Isagoge*, which includes one entry attributed to Meton, 46 to Euctemon, 11 to Democritus, 34 to Callippus, 4 to Dositheus and 60 to Eudoxus. Ptolemy, *Phaseis* pp. 14–65 Heiberg, records a similar parapegma for the Egyptian year, with 84 entries for Eudoxus, the largest number after the 158 ascribed to 'the Egyptians'.

(iii) Eudoxus of Cnidus

We have no precise dates for the life of Eudoxus, but he is said to have flourished in the 103rd Olympiad (368–365), and to have died at the age of 53 (Apollodor. ap. D.L. 8.8.90), apparently some time after the death of Plato (Plin. *Nat.* 30.3). For a full list of sources and discussion of biographical details see Lasserre 3–10 and 137–47, Dicks *EGA* 151–89.

Eudoxus studied geometry with the Pythagorean Archytas, and, after a short visit to Athens at the age of 23, spent sixteen months in Egypt with the priests at Heliopolis, where he made observations of stars and may have written a calendarial work entitled *Octaeteris*. He then founded a school of his own at Cyzicus, where, with the benefit of a good observation point (σκοπή), he made further observations of stars, which probably formed the basis of his *Phaenomena*. In the course of a second and longer visit to Athens, he had the opportunity to discuss his astronomical work, especially his mathematical model of planetary movements (cf. Arist. *Met.* Λ 8, 1073b), with both Plato and Aristotle. Finally Eudoxus retired to Cnidus, where he was held in great honour, and continued his researches with the help of a σκοπή on a hill outside the city, from which he was able to sight Canopus on the southern horizon (Posid. fr. 204 E–K). It was here perhaps that he wrote his second book on the constellations and celestial circles, called *Enoptron* ('mirror of the sky'), which was in some respects a revision of his *Phaenomena*: cf. Hi. 1.3.7 on the summer tropic.

Eudoxus was probably the first to attempt a mathematical description of the celestial sphere (Dicks *EGA* 153). The sphericity of the sky was deduced in the fifth century, probably from the changing altitude of stars observed by travellers as they moved north and south from the familiar night sky of the Mediterranean world. By the end of the century the sphericity of the earth had also been inferred, and fourth-century philosophers established the classical system of a rotating spherical cosmos with a stationary spherical earth at its centre: cf. Pl. *Phd.* 108e, *R.* 616b, *Ti.* 40b, Arist. *Cael.* 297a–298a.

In his *Phaenomena* Eudoxus described the geometry of this cosmos, with its axis and two poles (cf. Arat. 21–6), and the 48 Greek constellations. He identified the particular stars in the latter by reference to the parts of the figures, in the absence of any system of co-ordinates such as those later introduced by Hipparchus. If the figures are easy to recognise, the system is workable, but in most cases the figure imposed on a star-group is arbitrary, and there is sometimes an uncertainty about which star is meant, e.g. in the figure of the Charioteer (note on 156–166), and in Eudoxus' complicated guide to its position (fr. 29) κατέναντι δὲ τῆς κεφαλῆς τῆς Μεγάλης Ἄρκτου ὁ Ἡνίοχος ἔχει τοὺς ὤμους λοξὸς ὢν ὑπὲρ τοὺς πόδας τῶν Διδύμων. See note on 161 and A.'s attempt to simplify the directions. Eudoxus sometimes uses geometry to clarify a star's position, e.g. fr. 33 (see note on 184, with A.'s version and the comment of Hipparchus).

That A. derived the astronomical material in 19–732 from Eudoxus is illustrated at length by Hipparchus (1.2.1–16), who makes this point because there are many who have disputed it. To prove his case he quotes parallel passages to be compared with 49–54, 91–2, 96–7, 69–70, 74–5, 147–8, 143–5, 161–2, 174–6, 184–7, 188–9, 197–8, 206–7, 229–30, 246–7, 248–9, 251–2, 254–6, 279–81. All these he quotes from the *Phaenomena*, but he later shows that in 498–9 A. has followed *Enoptron* in preference to *Phaenomena* (1.2.22). On the other hand in 712, on a point on which the two works disagree, he expresses his uncertainty as to which should be followed: see note ad loc.

The tradition of A.'s dependence on Eudoxus sometimes presents him as being himself ignorant of astronomy (cf. Cic. *De orat.* 1.69). The origin of this theme is probably Hi. 1.1.8 τῇ γὰρ Εὐδόξου συντάξει κατακολουθήσας τὰ Φαινόμενα γέγραφεν, ἀλλ᾽ οὐ κατ᾽ ἰδίαν παρατηρήσας ἢ μαθηματικὴν κρίσιν ἐπαγγελλόμενος ἐν τοῖς οὐρανίοις προφέρεσθαι καὶ διαμαρτάνων ἐν αὐτοῖς. What Hipparchus means is that A. was not a professional astronomer, and is not to be used as a scientific authority, as the popularity of the poem suggests he was by many readers. There is, however, no reason to suppose that he did not understand the basic astronomy required for his poem, and that he was not familiar with most of the constellations he describes. As far as we can judge from the fragments, Eudoxus gives a purely objective description of what is there, whereas A. describes the stars and their movement almost entirely from the point of view of the observer.

A. shows a certain degree of independence in his selection and omission of details, and in some cases the difference may be seen as a deliberate correction of Eudoxus. Most interesting is his lack of any reference to a star at the north pole: see note on 24. Similar is A.'s assumption that the solstitial and equinoctial points are at the beginning of the relevant zodiacal constellations, not in the middle, as Eudoxus assumes (see note on 151); cf. Hipparchus' comment (2.2.6) that, in the section on simultaneous risings, the assumption that a rising means the beginning of a rising suits A.'s division of the zodiac better than that of Eudoxus (see note on 569–589). At 524 A.'s choice of stars in the Horse that lie close to the equator seems to correct Eudoxus. On the other hand A.'s divergences from Eudoxus are sometimes in error: see notes on 84 and 578. In many lines where A.'s handling of the material is different from that of Eudoxus, this can be explained purely as poetic variation (e.g. 50–4), but in 160–2 A.'s guide to the position of the Charioteer is simpler and clearer than that of Eudoxus (see notes ad loc.), and this may be a deliberate clarification based on A.'s personal observation of the sky.

There is a tradition recorded by Cicero, on the authority of C. Sulpicius Gallus, that Eudoxus had the use of a star-globe (*Rep.* 1.22): *dicebat enim Gallus sphaerae illius alterius solidae atque plenae uetus esse inuentum, et eam a Thalete Milesio primum esse tornatam, post autem ab Eudoxo Cnidio ... eandem illam astris quae caelo inhaererent esse descriptam.* The association of a globe also with Thales gives one little confidence in Gallus' authority, and indeed there is no evidence that such an artefact existed in the fourth century. Certainly there is evidence for a kind of armillary sphere (see notes on 494, 526, 530–1), designed to illustrate the celestial circles; cf. Pl. *Ti.* 36b–c. But the only hint of an artificial sphere is the leather dodecahedron to which Plato compares the earth in *Phd.* 110b, on which Ti. Locr. 98e aptly comments ἔγγιστα σφαίρας ἐόν. Eudoxus did not have a system of co-ordinates, which would have been essential for any attempt to represent the fixed stars accurately on an artificial globe. Hipparchus, in comparing his own star positions, arrived at by the use of co-ordinates, cites the text of Eudoxus and makes no mention of a globe. The first accurate star-globe was probably that ascribed to Hipparchus himself by Ptolemy (*Alm.* 7.1.fin.). The solid globe attributed to Archimedes in Cic. *Rep.* 1.22 was designed for public display, and the constellations on it were probably represented not by stars, but by the popular figures, like those on the Farnese globe. The most accurate sphere available to A. for checking the stars was still that of the night sky.

(iv) Attalus of Rhodes

Attalus was a contemporary of Hipparchus (Hi. 1.1.3 ὁ καθ' ἡμᾶς μαθηματικός), probably older, since he had produced an edition of the *Phaenomena* with a commentary (1.3.3) before Hipparchus wrote his own commentary. His *floruit* may therefore be placed about the middle of the second century BC. Hipparchus quotes numerous passages from Attalus, as he discusses problems to which they have some relevance. These passages, together with the comments of Hipparchus, have been published by Maass *Comm.* pp. 1–24, and they are also usefully discussed by Martin *HT* 22–7. For my own comments see notes in the Commentary on lines to which reference is made below.

Attalus, whose commentary is described by Hipparchus (1.1.3) as the most painstaking of the earlier commentaries, regards the *Phaenomena* as an authoritative work on astronomy, and his aim is to show how A.'s descriptions are in agreement with the observed stars. He therefore prefers to support A. as far as possible against critics, but there are some passages on which he does disagree or find some fault with A. The aim of Hipparchus is to correct the errors he finds in both A. and Attalus, for the benefit of those who read the poem mainly as a guide to the constellations (1.3.2–4).

(v) Hipparchus of Nicaea

The only reliable dates we have for the life of Hipparchus are those of his own stellar and lunar observations recorded by Ptolemy in the *Almagest*: the earliest date is 147 and the latest 127 BC. His active period as an astronomer may therefore be placed in the third quarter of the second century. The known sites of his observations were in Bithynia and Rhodes; there is no clear evidence that he ever made observations in Alexandria. For a full account of his work see Neugebauer *HAMA* 274–343, and for a useful summary G. J. Toomer, 'Hipparchus', *Dictionary of Scientific Biography* xv, Supplement 1 (1981) 207–24.

Hipparchus' main achievements were in stellar astronomy, and were based on a desire to determine the positions of the fixed stars with the greatest possible accuracy. These were his catalogue of the fixed stars, and his discovery of precession, the slow westward movement of the solstitial and equinoctial points relative to the fixed stars, which he estimated to be at least 1° per century. He also refined the known length of the (tropical) year to $365\frac{1}{4}$ days minus 1/300 of a day. His only extant work, however, is his *Commentary on the Phaenomena of Aratus and Eudoxus*, and its survival is due to the popularity of Aratus.

Hipparchus addresses his *Commentary* to a friend Aeschrion, who has expressed an interest in A.'s astronomy. He says that the actual meaning of the poem is not very difficult to follow: ἁπλοῦς τε γὰρ καὶ σύντομός ἐστι ποιητής, ἔτι δὲ σαφὴς τοῖς καὶ μετρίως παρηκολουθηκόσι, and that his sole concern is with the accuracy of the astronomy, τίνα τε συμφώνως τοῖς φαινομένοις ἀναγέγραπται καὶ τίνα διημαρτημένως (1.1.1–4). He deals first with some of the northern constellations and stars on the tropics and equator, with special reference to Eudoxus, and the question of the latitude of the observer, with special reference to Attalus (1.2–3), then more fully with the northern constellations and with the sky at the rising of the Scorpion (1.4–7), the southern constellations and the celestial circles (1.8–10). At this point he departs from A. and discusses the stars on the arctic and antarctic circles, and those on the colures (1.11). Book 2.1–3 is devoted to the stars that rise and set simultaneously with the risings of successive signs of the zodiac. Here he makes two preliminary statements, one that he will treat the signs as exact twelfths of the ecliptic, the other that he will assume that when A. refers to the rising of a sign, he means the beginning of its rising (see note on 569–589). The first is the basis of many of the errors that Hipparchus finds in A., because A. is referring to the visible constellations. Hipparchus is writing for readers who are interested in mathematical astronomy, and are familiar with his division of the ecliptic into 360°, with 30° to each sign.

Whether the *Commentary* was written before or after the star catalogue is uncertain, but it is valuable in that it illustrates some of the advances in mathematical astronomy since Eudoxus. Most relevant to the understanding of Hipparchus' criticisms of A. is the greater accuracy with which he defines the positions of stars in 2.4–3.4. Only four stars are familiar enough to be designated solely by name: Ἀρκτοῦρος (2.5.7), Κύων (2.1.18), Προτρυγητήρ (2.5.5), Στάχυς (2.5.12). Normally the position is given merely by reference to a recognisable part of the figure, e.g. 2.5.1 ὁ ἐν τῇ κεφαλῇ, ὁ ἐν τῷ δεξιῷ ποδί (β ζ Bootis).

Another innovation in the astronomy of Hipparchus is his use of the 360° system to express angular distance. He defines it in explaining how far north a star in Bootes lies (2.2.25): ἔστιν οὗτος ὁ ἀστὴρ βορειότερος τοῦ ἰσημερινοῦ κύκλου μοίραις κζ' καὶ τρίτῳ μέρει μοίρας, οἵων ἐστὶν ὁ διὰ τῶν πόλων κύκλος μοιρῶν τξ'. He uses various fractions of a degree, but not a subdivision into 60 minutes. This example is equivalent to the modern 'declination' of a star. For southern declinations cf. 1.10.20. The complement of the declination is the polar distance, which Hipparchus uses frequently, similarly measured in degrees; cf. 1.8.17 ὁ μὲν γὰρ δεύτερος μετὰ τὸ στῆθος σφόνδυλος (τοῦ Σκορπίου) ἀπέχει ἀπὸ τοῦ νοτίου πόλου μοίρας νθ', ὅσας καὶ ὁ Ἀρκτοῦρος ἀπὸ τοῦ βορείου πόλου (see also note on 405). Hipparchus is also a very competent textual critic. He quotes about 250 lines of the *Phaenomena*, some more than once, occasionally discusses variant readings, and refers to all available copies of the poem. His comments on readings that are astronomically significant are particularly important for the establishment of the text. See Maass *Aratea* 66–117, and my commentary *passim*, e.g. on 69 μέσσῳ ... καρήνῳ, 90 ἐπιδευέες, 467 ἀπλατέες, 479 μέγα μείονες, 541 ἀποτείνεται αὐγή, 693 μέσον, 713 λήγοντι.

(b) [Theophrastus], *De signis*

Among the transmitted works of Theophrastus is one entitled Περὶ σημείων ὑδάτων καὶ πνευμάτων καὶ χειμώνων καὶ εὐδιῶν, edited by F. Wimmer, Theophrastus III 6 (1862), and A. Hort, Theophrastus, *Enquiry into Plants* II (Loeb 1916, with Wimmer's text). For a full discussion see M. Heeger, *De Theophrasti qui fertur* Περὶ σημείων *libro* (1889), and for a concise critical account of the main problems O. Regenbogen in *RE* Suppl. VII (1940) 1412–15. In antiquity a Περὶ σημείων was attributed to both Aristotle and Theophrastus. For the former cf. Arist. fr. 250 Rose Ἀνέμων θέσεις καί προσηγορίαι· ἐκ τῶν Ἀριστοτέλους περὶ σημείων, Ael. 7.7 Ἀριστοτέλους ἀκούω λέγοντος ὅτι ἄρα γέρανοι ἐκ τοῦ πελάγους ἐς τὴν γῆν κτλ. (see note on 1031), D.L. 5.26 Σημεῖα χειμώνων α'; for the latter cf. D.L 5.45 Περὶ σημείων α', Procl. *in Ti.* 3.286A Diehl ἐν τῇ Περὶ σημείων βίβλῳ φησὶν ἐκεῖνος (sc. ὁ Θεόφραστος).

The subject-matter of *D.S.* is in keeping with the interest in the natural world shown by the Peripatetic school, but the character of the writing does not entirely support its attribution to either Aristotle or Theophrastus. In his introduction the author only vaguely acknowledges his use of authoritative sources (παρ' ἑτέρων οὐκ ἀδοκίμων λαβόντες) as well as his own observations (1). On risings and settings of stars he betrays an inadequate knowledge of astronomy by giving a confused explanation: he understands a setting as occurring ὅταν ἅμα συνδύνῃ τῷ ἡλίῳ τὸ ἄστρον, i.e. a 'true' setting, and a rising as occurring ὅταν προανατέλλῃ τοῦ ἡλίου τὸ ἄστρον, i.e. a 'visible' rising (2). The main part of *D.S.* is arranged in sections according to weathers as predicted by the various signs. But the arrangement is not strictly observed. The section on rain (10–25) includes also some predictions of wind, storm, drought and fair weather, and an intrusive passage on the critical phases of the lunar month (12) gives weather signs of a completely different character. The section on wind (26–37) also has predictions of rain, drought and storm, and ends with a very different slant, an exposition of the various wind directions, similar to that in Arist. *Mete.* 2.6. Similarly the section on stormy weather includes predictions of rain, snow, wind, fair weather, cold, drought and heat, and there is a hint of astrology in a reference to the planet Hermes (46). Even the short section on fair weather has some predictions of storm (50–4). A brief conclusion (55–7) adds miscellaneous seasonal signs, the flowering of the mastich, weather conditions that allow a long-range forecast, a reference to comets as stars so named by the Egyptians (presumably the Alexandrian Greeks), and finally an obscure sentence about star risings. *D.S.* is therefore not a well organised account of weather signs, and Heeger (22) sees it as put together by a careless collector of excerpts.

A comparison of A.'s signs with those in *D.S.* shows that, while the poet does seem to derive the majority of his signs from the material preserved in *D.S.*, he also has many that do not appear in the extant work. These are : 796 a third-day moon's reddish disc, 802 a third-day sign valid for the whole month, 812 and 815–17 multiple haloes, 822–3 dark marks on the sun's disc, 838–9 black and red marks on the sun, 841–4 sun's rays concentrated or overarched with clouds, 845–7 light cloud rising before sunrise, 847–9 a thick belt of cloud before sunrise, 851–3 clouds at sunset after rain during the day, 859–60 rays dark or slightly dark, 905–8 one Ass faint, the other bright, 941 star halo, 1060–1 squill flowering (from Theophr. *HP* 7.13.6), 1118–21 snow on cornfields, 1104–12 sheep capering or dawdling, 1118–21 cows lowing continuously, 1122 goats eating evergreen oak leaves, 1123 sows tossing straw (from Democr. 147), 1137 mice, 1138 a crab on shore, 1140–1 mice tossing straw.

A.'s source for his weather signs must therefore have been a fuller work, containing the material in *D.S.*, but also much more. Heeger (25) attributes it to an anonymous Peripatetic, Regenbogen (1414–15) identifies it as the Περὶ σημείων ascribed to Theophrastus, and assigns the extant *D.S.* to the Alexandrian period. For later collections of weather signs see note on 758–1141.

IV LANGUAGE, STYLE AND THE HEXAMETER

(a) Language

The language of the *Phaenomena* follows largely the mixed poetic dialect of the Homeric poems, updated by a freer use of Attic forms and a regular use of the augment (see note on 375). Contracted vowels occur (I give the line numbers for single occurrences) in ἀγινεῖ, ὑπερανθεῖ (1060), ἀγινεῖν (68), ἀμνηστεῖν (847), ἀητεῖται (523), αἰωρεῖται, δινεῖται (478), νεῖται (407), κολυμβᾷ (952), ἀναστρωφῶσιν (1069), ὦσιν (903), βοῶντε (1023), ἐπαφώμενος (93), συῶν (1072). A. achieves variety with different dialect forms of the same word. e.g. ἀγείρωνται (976) and ἀγέρωνται (1118), ἀεί (14), αἰεί and αἰέν, αἰ and εἰ, ἀλῶα acc. (941) and

ἀλωή nom., ἀνδράσι and ἄνδρεσσι (732), βέβληται (330)
and βεβλέαται, βορέαο, βορέω and βορῆος, γόνασι and
γούνασι, γούνατα and γοῦνα, Διί, Διός and Ζηνί (275),
Ζηνός (823), εἰς and ἐς (see note on 995), ἑλίσσομαι and
εἰλίσσομαι, κέονται (451) and κέαται (492), μία and ἰή
(813), μόνος (612) and μοῦνος (1003), ὅλος and οὖλος, ὄρεος
and οὔρεος (912), ὀρώρη (978) and ὤρορε (764), πεπτηότα
(167) and πεπτηῶτα, πολλοί and πολέες (19), ποσί, ποσσί
and πόδεσσι, φάος and φόως (796), -εφήμισαν (221) and
-εφημίξαντο (442), gen. sg. -ου and -οιο, dat. pl. -αις and
-ῃσι. For epic diectasis see note on 27. πίσυρες occurs
twice, ποτί only in ποτιδέγμενος (1090). The instr. suffix
-φι is used as dat. in ἶφι (588) and αὐτόφι (980).

For Homeric parallels see the Commentary *passim*. In
many cases an apparent imitation has no particular significance for the context in the *Phaenomena*, but frequently,
and especially when an uncommon word draws attention
to it, A. seems to have in mind a line from a similar context, e.g. 36 ἐπίκλησιν καλέουσι (Σ 487 of the Bear), 152
κελάδοντες (β 421 of winds), 423 δεινὴ ἀνέμοιο θύελλα (ε
317 of storm at sea), 585 ὀψὲ δύοντι (ε 272 of Bootes), 638
ἑλκῆσαι πέπλοιο (λ 580 of Tityus), 733 οὐχ ὁράᾳς; (ρ 545
of a portent), 783 λεπτή (Ω 1–5 acrostic), 912 κορυφαί
(Μ 282 of mountains), 969 τιναξάμενοι πτερὰ πυκνά (β
151 of eagles), 1004 κεκλήγοντες (Ρ 756 of bird-cries).

In other instances the context of the Homeric passage
provides overtones that enhance the significance of the
Aratean word or phrase. Thus παλίνορσος (54), of the
Dragon, recalls the simile of the snake in Γ 3, with the adj.
cleverly transferred from the man to the snake. Similarly
with ἐμμενὲς ἤματα πάντα διώκεται (339), of the constellation of the Hare, A. recalls the simile of the two dogs
pursuing a hare in Κ 361, and thus seems to emphasise the
eternity of the sky-figures' movement. In 209 πέλεθρα recalls Φ 407 and λ 577, of Ares and Tityus, and thus suggests the heroic proportions of the celestial Horse. The

simile of the key and bolts in 190–3 similarly gives a heroic stature to the relatively small figure of Cassiepeia by its reminiscence of M 455–6. Cf. 642 ἀναρρήξασα and the frightening effect of the earthquake in Υ 62–3; 646 περὶ χθονὸς ἔσχατα φεύγειν with its overtones of Achilles' pursuit of Hector in Χ 157–63; 656 ἀρνευτῆρι and the amusing reminiscence of Homeric tumblers and divers in Π 742, Μ 385, μ 413; 748 ἀμείβεται of the sun's passage from sign to sign and the imaginative suggestion of the horse-leaping acrobat in Ο 683–4; 1009 κείουσιν of the birds recalling Α 606 κακκείοντες of the gods, and 1118 μυκηθμοῖο the cattle on Achilles' shield (Σ 575) and the cattle of the Sun (μ 265).

A.'s frequent use of rare Homeric words suggests that this was a deliberately contrived feature of his poetry. The following words, for example, reflect ἅπαξ εἰρημένα in Homer: ἀνέφελον (415), ἀπολείβεται (222), ἀσταχύων (150), αὐτονυχεί (618), αὐχενίην (698), γλήνεα (318), δεδοκημένῳ (559), δεῖμα (629), εἰνοδίην (132), ἔννυχος (580), ἐπέκοπτε (639), ἐπικέκλιται (486), ἐπικλείουσι (92), ἐπιλάμπεται (55), ἐσφήκωται (441), ἡμιτελής (215), θέναρ (485), ἰθύντατα (44), ἰλήκοι (637), ἰσώσασθαι (658), κακοεργόν (131), κατελείβετο (218), κόρυμβα (686), κουρίζοντα (32), μαργαίνουσαι (1123), μέσφα (599), μετανάσται (457), νειόθεν (234), νωθής (228), νωχελέες (391), παραβλήδην (535), πλειότερος (644), πόριες (1120), προγένωνται (706), προκυλίνδεται (188), πρύμνηθεν (348), πυριβήτεω (983), ῥάχιν (572), σταθμόνδε (1119), τείρεα (692), τοξευτής (306), ὑπόβρυχα (425), ὑποφῆται (164).

A. is also innovative in his use of language, creating new forms, new words, and new meanings for established words. The prefixes are new in the adjectives ἀμφιέλικτος (378), εὐάστερος (237), πολυγλαγέος (1100), πολυρρόθιος (412); in the verbs ἐπιλευκαίνονται (927), μετασκαίροντα (282), συνασταχύοιεν (1050). More frequent is the development of new suffixes, one of the commonest being -αῖος,

e.g. ἀμαξαίης (93), βορραίη (893), γαληναίη (765), Κυλληναίη (597), ὁποσταίη (739); cf. other adjj. ἀχείμεροι (1121),
βουλύσιος (825), ὀπίστερος (284); the adv. γενεῆθεν (260);
the nouns ἀνωνυμίη (146), δενδρείοιο (1008), κεράατος
(174); the verbs ἀδρανέων (471), βιβαιόμεναι (495), διχαιόμενον (495), τεξείεσθε (194).

New words, mostly compounds, appear to have been
devised for technical purposes, as in the description of
constellations, e.g. ἱππούραια (438) for the tail part of the
equine half of the Centaur, possibly ἱπποτάφηρος (664)
for the double figure itself, ὑπωμαίων and ἰξυόθεν (144)
for precise identification of stars near the Bear, μεταβλέψειας (186) for directing the eye of the observer towards
other stars. Some new words are there for the sake of
variation, picturesqueness, literary or linguistic interest,
e.g. ἄρραντοι (868), εἰναλίδιναι (918), ὁμηλυσίη (178),
ὁππῆμος (568), ὀρύχοιεν (1086), περιδνοφέοιντο (876),
πυριλαμπέος (1040), πυρώτερα (798), τριτόωσαν (796).

It is also characteristic of A. to extend the range of
meaning of words, either to suit the novelty of his subject-
matter or for the sake of variation. See notes on ἀμειβόμεναι (1020), ἀμφαδόν (64), ἐοικότα (168), κερόωσι (780), κομόωντες (1092), ὀχῆς (1069), σκιόωνται (600), τριπλόα
(1051), φθίμενος (809), φθίνοντος (514), ὡραῖος (1075).

(b) Style

In deriving much of his subject-matter from technical
works written in prose A. introduced a new problem into
the composition of didactic epic, but it was a challenge
that must have appealed to the ingenuity of Hellenistic
poets in their general quest for novelty. A. uses a complex
technique of imitation and variation. Sometimes he makes
a point of keeping close to the language of his source, as if
to bring out the basically practical aspect of the poem, but
even then he varies the words in a number of subtle ways.

The simplest is a purely linguistic variation, as in 920, a close paraphrase of a clause in *D.S.* 34 (presumably the same in the source followed by A.). Here A. changes the word order, varies πρὸς κορυφῆς with ἐν κορυφῆσιν, ὄρ-ους with ὄρεος, and ἂν μηκύνηται with μηκύνεται, but retains νεφέλη intact. In 91–2 A. paraphrases Eudoxus word for word, beginning with ἐξόπιθεν δ᾽ for ὄπιθεν δέ, and ending with the same name Ἀρκτοφύλαξ, but for τῆς Μεγάλης Ἄρκτου he gives the alternative name Ἑλίκης, for the prosaic ἐστίν the livelier φέρεται, and he adds ἐλάοντι ἐοικώς to relate the conventional human figure to the name Bootes at the end of the line. In 147 A. is more concise than Eudoxus, leaving it to be understood that οἱ refers back to the Bear, but in 148 he expands a little, because the Lion is the most important of these three constellations, and the next seven lines are devoted to it. The unparalleled ὀπισθοτέροισι draws attention to the importance of this line.

In most cases A. amplifies with greater freedom, as in 248–55. Here the essentials are in Eudox. fr. 35: the shoulders of Perseus close to Andromeda's feet, his right hand pointing to Cassiepeia, and his left knee to the Pleiades. Eudoxus is simply describing the relative positions of stars, but A. chooses to present the group as dramatic figures in a romantic relationship (γαμβροῦ, πενθερίου), brings out the heroic stature of Perseus by adding line 250 with περιμήκετος ἄλλων, and 252–3 with ἴχνια μηκύνει, and makes the setting picturesque with κλισμὸν ... δί-φροιο and κεκονιμένος. He also enhances the scene with the rare words ἐπωμάδιοι and ἐπιγουνίδος, the figurative ἐν ποσίν, and the different levels of meaning discernible in Διὶ πατρί.

A.'s ingenuity in versifying mathematical conceits may be seen in the following: 184–5 an equilateral triangle, 234–6 an isosceles triangle, 497–9 the ratio 5 : 3, 513–14 the equinoxes, 525–8 an armillary sphere, 541–3 a regular hexagon inscribed in a circle, 553–4 the horizon bisects the ecliptic, 753 the 19-year cycle. We do not have Eudoxus' version of any of these passages.

Word patterns, involving antithesis, balanced phrasing and chiasmus, are regular features of A.'s composition, and it is noteworthy that these occur in many extended passages, where they mark off an interesting digression from the strictly technical message of the poem. Lines 36–44, for example, make play with the two Bears in contrast, Cynosura and Helice, and their association respectively with the Phoenicians and the Greeks. This short digression is a piece of ring composition, which allows the poet to pick up the thread of his exposition at the end of it. A longer episode is 96–136, where the framework is marked by ὕπο σκέπτοιο Βοώτεω Παρθένον and Παρθένος with the punning πολυσκέπτοιο Βοώτεω. Within the episode the three Ages are arranged in a pattern of fourteen lines for the Gold (101–14), the same for the Silver (115–28), and eight for the Bronze, merging into the framework at 136. See note on 101 ἐπιχθονίη.

A more complex pattern is that of 367–85, the digression on the origin of the constellations (see note ad loc.). The framework is provided by the stars below the Hare, and within it is a chiastic arrangement of themes leading up to a central one and then back again in reverse order to the framework. For shorter chiastic passages see 216–23 (note on 221), 304–7 (note on 303), 413–16 (note on 413), 988–93 (note on 991), 1013–16 (note on 1013). In several of these passages the patterning is rather strained and confusing, so that the writing lacks the clarity that is appropriate to didactic poetry. Cf. the pattern of antitheses in 50–4 on the intertwining of the Dragon with the two Bears, the contrived antithesis of the half-set Crown added in 572, the word-play with different kinds of rising and setting in 750, the triple ἤ in 842–3, the series of contrasting or balancing pairs in 1007–9, the addition of a second antithesis within the second clause of the first antithesis in 1019–20.

Another feature of A.'s style, which has been responsible for misunderstandings, is his occasional use of a long periodic sentence, designed to give some special emphasis to the theme it contains. One is the passage on the Bronze Age and the ascension of Dike (129–36), with balanced protasis and apodosis of four lines each and a variation of clause structure within the two halves. Another is 420–9, in which the miseries of life at sea are highlighted. This is constructed in two contrasting conditions, one short and one long, each with its own apodosis, but the two are so closely related that it is reasonable to regard the whole as one sentence. The second part has a complex structure and carries the more important theme. More difficult is the passage on the Milky Way (469–79), and even the punctuation is debatable. Here we have two conditional clauses of four lines each and a short apodosis of three lines. The purpose of this long sentence is to enhance the impressiveness of the spectacle as described in the two protases.

Most of these passages are elaborations of or digressions from the basic subject-matter. Hipparchus finds that A.'s exposition of the actual astronomy is straightforward, concise and lucid (1.1.4): ἀλλὰ τὸ μὲν ἐξηγήσασθαι τὴν ἐν τοῖς ποιήμασι διάνοιαν οὐ μεγάλης ἐπιστροφῆς προσδεῖσθαι νομίζω· ἁπλοῦς τε γὰρ καὶ σύντομός ἐστι ποιητής, ἔτι δὲ σαφὴς τοῖς καὶ μετρίως παρηκολουθηκόσι. But he adds as a caveat that the charm of poetry is liable to make readers uncritical of the sense (1.1.7): ἡ γὰρ τῶν ποιημάτων χάρις ἀξιοπιστίαν τινὰ τοῖς λεγομένοις περιτίθησι, καὶ πάντες σχεδὸν οἱ τὸν ποιητὴν τοῦτον ἐξηγούμενοι προστίθενται τοῖς ὑπ' αὐτοῦ λεγομένοις.

While A. is normally concise, he sometimes accumulates words of similar sense for special emphasis, e.g. 20 πάντ' ἤματα συνεχὲς αἰεί (eternal star movement), cf. 339; 303

29

κείνης ὥρης καὶ μηνὸς ἐκείνου (dangerous time for sailing); 1045 πάντη ... πολλὸς ... αἰεὶ παπταίνει (constant alertness); 1049 ἄδην ἔκπαγλα περιβρίθοιεν ἀπάντη (excessive crop); 1070 πάλιν αὖτις ἀναβλήδην (frequent repetition). Anaphora for minor emphasis is common, and for variation in lists of phenomena, e.g. 2–3 μεσταὶ ... μεστή, 7– 8 λέγει, 73–4 νώτῳ (in transition), 102–3 οὐδέ ποτ', 125 καὶ δή, 131–2 πρῶτοι, 141 δεινὴ ... δεινοί, 144 εἷς, 200 τοίη, 239 ἔτι, 367 ὀλίγῳ ... ὀλίγῃ, 458–9 μακροὶ ... μακρά, 481–2 ἐν δέ (cf. 503–6, 518–21), 571 τοί, 572 δύνει (cf. 601), 573 ἥμισυ, 577–8 κατάγει, 587 εὖ, 615 αἰεί, 677–8 πάντα, 685–6 οὐδ' ἔτι, 802–3 πάντη ... πάντα, 890–1 ἑσπερίοις ... ἑσπερόθεν.

Alliteration in the *Phaenomena* sometimes reflects Homeric usage: compare, for example, 297 with P 674 and μ 233, 449 with X 33 and P 521. Frequently A. seems to use it to draw attention to an interesting phenomenon or event or emotional situation, e.g. the Phoenicians' use of Cynosura (39), the beneficence of Dike (112–13), the departure of Dike (128), the creation of Hippocrene (220), men in terror at sea (297), the multitude of stars all alike (377), ubiquity of signs from Zeus (772). The commonest alliterative consonant is π, and it is used in a variety of contexts; e.g. it is equally effective in rough seas (297, 772) and flat calm (991). It is therefore probably unwise to assume that the sound of this consonant is ever meant to suggest any natural sound, and the same may be true also of other alliterative consonants, even of κ in 449, of the pecking raven. See I. Opelt, *Glotta* 37 (1958) 205ff. D. Fehling, *Wiederholungsfiguren* (1969), esp. 12–13, 78–9, maintains that alliteration in Greek cannot be regarded as a deliberate figure of speech. It does seem, however, that certain words, like πάντα and πόντος, attract alliterative words to a line, whatever the subject-matter.

Rhyme plays an occasional part in the *Phaenomena*. Disyllabic rhymes in successive lines are clearly deliberate

in 190–1, 266–7, 634–5, 888–9 and 1115–16, producing a
Hesiodic effect in imitation of *Op.* 1–2, 383–4, 471–2, 517–
19, 672–3, *Th.* 5–6, 226–7, 241–2, and other pairs mostly
in lists of names. In A. the pairs cited are each within the
same sentence, whereas 394–5 is not, and this rhyme may
not be significant. The latter is true of most monosyllabic
rhymes, e.g. 901–2, 911–12, but 1062–3 are balanced in
both sense and structure, and the end-rhymes are part of
the pattern. More frequent in A. are disyllabic internal
rhymes, which look back to Homer (see note on 360) as
well as Hesiod (*Op.* 179, *Th.* 242, 959). For such rhymes A.
uses mostly Homeric -οιο (360, 435, 634, 693, 831, 876,
925), but also develops a rhyme that underlines the astronomical antithesis of rising and setting, in -οντες (571),
-οντα (617), -οντι (821, 1147). The noun–adj. rhyme in -ῃσι
(619) is more uncommon and is perhaps modelled on
Φ 239. A. also has an unusual Hesiodic imitation with
internal rhyming in successive lines in 813–16 (see note
ad loc.).

A. relieves the solemnity and repetitive nature of his
subject-matter also with lighter touches of dry humour
and verbal wit. The constellations and their movement
round the sky are impressive natural phenomena and are
expounded seriously, but the constellation figures are
named by men, and their quaintness leaves them open to
some degree of amused comment. Thus in 275 A., who has
already introduced the Bird in 273, now confirms the name
ironically with ἤτοι γάρ, as if it were surprising that there
should be a Bird in the sky. In 582 κορέσηται personifies
Bootes, and sch. comment χαριέντως εἶπεν. In 652 it is
something of a fantasy to suggest that it is the two Bears
who, similarly personified, prevent Cepheus from being
completely circumpolar. Cf. 696–7 of Night not finding
room (χαδεῖν) for other stars.

There is more scope for humour when a star-group is
outshone by the mythical personality after which it is

named. In 100 εὔκηλος φορέοιτο the verb applies to the stars, but its mood and the adj. refer to the goddess, and it is amusing to think of the goddess circling round the sky. Sometimes Homeric overtones can make a passage even more humorous. In 654–6, where Cassiepeia is pictured going down head first, her embarrassing position is brought out by οὐ κατὰ κόσμον, and made even more amusing by the simile of the tumbler (see note ad loc.). Similarly A.'s comparison of the sun to an acrobat (748 ἀμείβεται) is rather witty, and so is the juxtaposition of Κρητῆρα and φθάμενος in 603, which recalls the amusing episode in Ψ 778–9.

In the long section on terrestrial weather signs much play is made with the use of heroic language in describing small creatures and objects from everyday life, because they also are important in the scheme of things. Thus frogs are πατέρες γυρίνων (947), and domestic hens ἀλέκτορος ἐξεγένοντο (960); see Hutchinson HP 227–8. Earthworms are found πλαζόμενοι (958; cf. π 64 of Odysseus), the scampering of mice is compared to ὀρχηθμοί (1133; cf. N 637), and τρίποδος πυριβήτεω (983) recalls Ψ 702.

A. appears to be making a witty reference to Call. H. 1.8 by placing εἰ ἐτεὸν δή immediately before Κρήτηθεν (30–1), and ὕδροισιν ὄνειαρ (746) makes an amusing contrast to the solemn expression of the beneficence of Zeus in 15 and 761. For puns see notes on 2 ἄρρητον, 313 ἄηται, 900 ἄφαντος ὅλη (cf. Υ 303), 1023 ὀψὲ βοῶντε (cf. 585 and ε 272).

Two other mannerisms are discussed in notes on 21. One is the anticipatory use of the demonstrative article in introducing a new noun, so that the reader is kept guessing until the reference is made clear, often in the next line. The usage is Homeric, but seems particularly suited to the techniques of written poetry.

The other is the use of αὔτως in a variety of unusual senses.

(c) The hexameter

A.'s hexameters present a blending of Homeric usage with some of the stricter conventions of the Hellenistic poets, and this gives a certain individuality to his handling of the metre. I have made use particularly of O'Neill (*YCS* 8, 1942), Maas *GM* (1962), West *GM* (1982) and Hopkinson *Callimachus, Hymn to Demeter* (1984).

The third-foot caesura is predominantly masculine. Eight lines have no caesura in the third foot (201, 263, 398, 494, 502, 547, 804, 973), three of these having proper names. Elision at the caesura is rare: 10, 986, 1113, and three instances of particles, which are hardly significant.

Elision of adjectives, nouns and verbs is limited in the Hellenistic period (West *GM* 156). A. elides (I omit conjectural readings) μέγα, πάντα, ἄπαντα; πατέρα, δυωδε-κάδα, σῆμα, σήματα, γούνατα; ἐπιτροχόωσι, ὑπείκωσι, γίνεται, δύεται, θλίβεται, συμφέρεται, τρέπεται, γίνοιντο, ἐγένοντο, ἐπάσαντο, ἐπύθοντο, ἐφράσατο.

Bucolic diaeresis in the sense of a word-break after a fourth-foot dactyl occurs in about 50% of the lines; cf. 47% in Homer, 50% in Theocritus' epic group, 57% in A.R, 63% in Callimachus, 74% in Theocritus' bucolic poems and 79% in the Ἐπιτάφιος Βίωνος (West 154). Some long sequences are 5–14, 58–65, 219–25. The incidence is less frequent in the last 250 lines.

At the beginning of a line word-type −−−∪ occurs only twice (see note on 416). O'Neill (128) notes that A. avoids the combination of words shaped −∪ and ∪− in that position. There are thirty instances, however, of which thirteen have a preposition as the second disyllable.

Hilberg's Law (the tendency to avoid a word-end after a contracted biceps in the second foot) is not observed in 49, 111, 345, 653, 743, 954. In all these instances the second foot is a disyllabic word. Naeke's Law (the tendency to avoid a word-end after a contracted biceps in the fourth foot) is not observed in 29 lines, 14 having disyllabic words, 15 trisyllabic.

Words of shape – – after the masc. caesura (Hopkinson 53) are frequent in A. (123) compared with Hes. (87), Theoc. (66), A.R. (64), *Od.* (57), *Il.* (41), Call. (22): see O'Neill 141.

Hermann's Bridge (an undivided fourth biceps) is absent in 72 lines. Words ending with the fourth trochee include two quadrisyllables (660, 737), four trisyllables (58, 515, 824, 1068), five disyllables (585, 634, 855, 903, 1023), and sixty-one monosyllables: see O'Neill, Tables 13, 12, 5, 1. Maas 91 and West *GM* 155 suggest that the effect is mitigated in some instances by elision (634, 657, 827, 903, 1039), in others by a word-end at the fourth princeps (e.g. 71, 174). Pairs of closely related monosyllables often produce the effect of a bridge, e.g. γε μέν (13 times), δέ οἱ (8 times), τὰ δέ (6 times), δέ μιν (5 times). Other instances may be explained as Homeric imitation, e.g. 186, 585, 657, 1023 (see notes ad locc.).

Hiatus after a long vowel in princeps is frequent, occurring 38 times after η, 9 after ω, 7 after ου, 6 after οι, 5 after ει, 4 after αι, once after ευ. Hiatus after a long vowel in the third biceps occurs in 106, 787, 942, and in the fourth biceps in 753, 859, 918. Lines 106, 787, 918 and 942 have hiatus both before and after ἤ. The biceps is contracted also after a hiatus in 44, 122, 518, 587, 628, 679, 773, 940, 989. After a short vowel A. allows hiatus at the main caesura in 951, at the fifth trochee in 45, and between feet in 686, 962 *bis* (this line actually has three hiatuses), and perhaps 1133.

Digamma is generally ignored in εἴδωλον, εἰπεῖν, ἕκαστος, ἐλ(εἰλ)ίσσω, ἑσπερ-, ἰδεῖν, observed in ἑ, ἑοῖ, Ἑλίκων, ἴκελος, and sometimes observed in ἔοικα, ἔργον, ἴσος and enclitic οἱ.

Lengthening in the princeps position follows Homeric usage (West *GM* 38) with first syllables in ἀείδουσα (1000,

1023), ἀνέφελος (415, 826, 858), ἀπονέονται (1032), δύεται (309, 627), δυόμενος (840, 853), πάρειπών (764), ὕδωρ (see note on 219); short vowel + ν before initial vowel (76, 706), + ς (984, 1100); short open vowel before λ- (719, 1112, 1124), μ- (624, 940), ν- (852, 977), ῥ- (662), χ- (1019; West 156), hence perhaps before κ- in 34 (cf. κ 42, 141, though these occur at caesurae).

There are 159 *spondeiazontes* (13.8%); I omit 966 as doubtful. Their frequency per hundred lines increases up to the fifth hundred, then falls away and increases again to reach a maximum of twelve in the last hundred. Clusters of three occur in 419ff. and 953ff. (see note on 955), and pairs at 32, 158, 229, 387, 455, 564, 615, 744, 754, 873, 926, 932, 1123 and 1133. The great majority end in a quadri-syllable (if two words are read in 217 and 221, they may be regarded as a quadrisyllabic name), seventeen end in a tri-syllable, nine in a six-syllable word, two in a monosyllable (see note on 408), and one in a pentasyllable (see note on 186). All but nine have a dactyl in the fourth foot, the exceptions being 230, 262, 447, 497, 506, 744, 811, 887 and 1030.

Four-word lines total 45, and 18 of these are σπονδειά-ζοντες. The combination of the two features is often impressive and seems designed to enhance the importance of the subject-matter (e.g. 159, 455, 565, 609, 901), or the position of the line at the end of a section (757) or subsection (73, 325, 401) or sentence (412, 1121); see notes on 412, 548, 1000, 1134. Four-word lines occur occasionally in Homer; there are 17 and 8 respectively in the first 1150 lines of the *Iliad* and the *Odyssey*. But they do not appear to have been composed with any stylistic effect in mind. Hesiod has 16 in the *Theogony*, 9 in the *Works and Days*, and there are 13 in the *Aspis*. But both *Th.* 1 and *Op.* 1 are four-word lines, and make an impressive opening.

The sequence of three out of four on Heracles in *Th.* 315–18 also seems contrived, and *Op.* 68 makes an effective concluding line. Most striking of all is Hesiod's three-word line in *Op.* 383 (see West ad loc.), which A. does not attempt to imitate, but the idea of developing the four-word line probably originated in Hesiod. A.R. 1 has 41 instances, Callimachus 13 in *H.* 1–4 and 6, Theocritus 11 out of 742 lines in the epic group.

Final monosyllables occur in 26 lines, mainly following Homeric usage with particle and pronouns, also πρό (309, 866, 870), χρή (434, 860, 907, 995), νύξ (408, 470, 695), and, in apparent imitation of the ending in -ξ, the novelty of Αἴξ (679), γλαύξ (999), γνύξ (591). As in Homer, bucolic diaeresis doses not always precede a final monosyllable.

V CONTEMPORARY AND LATER POETS

(a) Relations with contemporaries

There is no evidence for thinking either that A. did or that he did not visit Alexandria, but it is clear that his *Phaeno-mena* was well known and admired there, and that he himself was familiar with the new principle of λεπτότης in poetry promoted by Callimachus. He implies this in the striking acrostic of ΛΕΠΤΗ in 783–7 and the anaphora of λεπτή in 783–4, a passage describing the slender and sharp outline of the new lunar crescent as a good weather omen, contrasted with the blurred appearance that portends bad weather; see note on 783. There may even be a hint of the same contrasting principles in such phrases as ὀλίγη μέν, ἀτὰρ ναύτῃσιν ἀρείων (42) and παχέα κρώζουσα (953).

Callimachus reciprocates with the epigram that praises the style of the *Phaenomena*, λεπταὶ ῥήσιες, Ἀρήτου σύντονος ἀγρυπνίη (27.5–6). Cf. Leon. Tar., *AP* 9.25 = *HE* 2573 γράμμα τόδ' Ἀρήτοιο δαήμονος, ὅς ποτε λεπτῇ φροντίδι δηναίους ἀστέρας ἐφράσατο, and Ptol. Rex, perhaps Philadelphus (*CHCL* 1, Part 4.62), Vita 1 p. 10 Martin = *SH*

712 = *FGE* 314 in an epigram on poets who have written on astronomy, ἀλλ' ὅ γε λεπτολόγος σκῆπτρον Ἄρατος ἔχει. The influence of Callimachus' *Hymn to Zeus*, which was probably composed in the 280s (*CHCL* 1, Part 4.10), may be seen in *Phaen.* 30–5. The birth of Zeus is a theme essential to the hymn, but A. has introduced it to highlight the importance of the Bears; see note on 30 εἰ ἐτεὸν δή. A. shares with C. an interest in aetiology. He inserts a highly patterned digression on the origin of the constellations in general (367–85), brief etymological notes on the names Ἄμαξαι (27), Βοώτης (92–3), Ἀητός (313–15) and Σείριος (331–2), explanations of how the Bears, Ariadne's Crown and the Maiden came to be in the sky (131–5, 71–3, 134–6), why the Phoenicians used Cynosura for navigation (39–44), the origins of Hippocrene (216–23), the Plei· ades as a weather sign (265 Ζεὺς δ' αἴτιος), and the myth of Orion and the Scorpion (637–47). A.'s humorous questioning of the ancestry of the Maiden (98–9) recalls Call. *H.* 1.5–7, and his apology for telling a story disrespectful to a goddess (637) may have been the inspiration for Call. *H.* 5.56.

In astronomical topics it is reasonable to suppose that C. is following A. Fr. 191.54–5 Ἀμάξης . . . ᾗ πλέουσι Φοίνικες imitates 39–44, fr. 2.1 ἴχνιον ὀξέος ἵππου takes up A.'s new myth in 216–21, fr. 75.35 refers to the MR of the Dog in 331–5 (but also Hes. *Op.* 587), with χαλεπήν borrowed from 314, and a modern dog-name substituted for Sirius. Fr. 110.59 Μινωίδος refers to Ariadne's Crown in 71–3, and *E.* 18.6 Ἐρίφων δυομένων to 158 and 679–82. The latter occasion is the ER about the end of September, but C. makes it a setting, as poetically more suited to the idea of drowning in the sea. Similarly fr. 269 ὁππότε λύχνου . . . μύκητες recalls A.'s weather sign in 976.

In the later *Hymns* other imitations of A. may be seen; e.g. 5.27 ἔρευθος ἀνέδραμε, of Pallas, recalls 834 of the sun, and the tripartite line in 6.5 was perhaps suggested by

1092, as Dr Hopkinson notes. In other instances C. appears to have had in mind both Homer and A.; e.g. οὐχ ὁράᾳς; in 2.4, ρ 545, and *Phaen.* 733 all refer to a kind of portent, and παλιμπετές in 3.256, ε 27 and *Phaen.* 1032 are all in a context of returning home.

The *Argonautica* and the *Phaenomena* have a common base in their Homeric language, and many similarities derive from that, rather than from imitation of one by the other. For example the lines on stormy weather at sea in 1.1203 and *Phaen.* 423 look back to Z 346 and ε 317, the door-and-key passages in 3.822 and 192 have sources in M 454–6 and φ 47–50, and ἄκρα κόρυμβα (2.601 and 686) originates in Ι 241, though in this case it is probably significant for A.R. that A. has used it in his description of the constellation Argo.

In contexts of earth, sea and sky Apollonius occasionally produces a line with an obvious Aratean character, although not intended to reflect any particular line in the *Phaenomena*, e.g. 1.108, 499–500, 4.848. Other instances show imitation of a particular Homeric line varied with a recognisable Aratean word. For example 3.745, on sailors watching the Bears and Orion, recalls ε 271–4, but Homer's Ἄρκτος is replaced by A.'s Ἑλίκη (37), and similarly 4.261 τείρεα πάντα τά τ᾽ οὐρανῷ εἰλίσσονται is almost a quotation from Σ 485, but the verb is very frequent in A. (265, 368, al.).

More clearly Aratean are a few technical passages using risings and settings of stars as signs of bad weather. In 1.1202 the (evening) setting of Orion, and in 3.225–6 the (morning) setting of the Pleiades, are probably drawn from both Hes. *Op.* 615–16, 619–21 and *Phaen.* 309–10, 1085. But in 2.1099 Arcturus as a sign of rain is not Hesiodic: it is implied for the first time in *Phaen.* 745.

Apollonius occasionally imitates other passages in A. with a variation that adapts the original to a new context. In 1.85 he takes δύσιές τε καὶ ἀντολαί from *Phaen.* 62, where A. refers to points of settings and risings of stars along both horizons; but he switches the reference to sunsets and sunrises, meaning west and east in illustration of geographical distances, and he replaces μίσγονται with μεσσηγύς (which has a similarity of sound) and ἀλλήλῃσι with an appropriate verb. At 1.725–6 the rare μεταβλέψειας is taken up from 186–7, where A. is giving directions for finding one constellation by moving one's line of vision northwards from another. The new context is a hyperbole that makes Jason's brilliant cloak more blinding to look at than the rising sun; and the verb is ingeniously moved back to a position which allows the fourth foot to be unbroken.

In 3.138 περιηγέες εἰλίσσονται is borrowed from 401 (also a four-word line), where the reference is merely to a circle of stars, but the hint of celestial phenomena gives a certain cosmic significance to the golden ball of Eros. At 3.957–9 Jason is compared to the Dog-star rising in brilliance, like Achilles in Χ 26–9, but here the name Sirius has overtones of destruction from Hes. *Op.* 587 and *Phaen.* 331–2. In 3.1002–4 there is a reference to Ariadne's Crown among the constellations as in *Phaen.* 71–3, but instead of giving the credit to Dionysus, Jason in his speech names Theseus as the hero with whom Ariadne left home, so ironically foreshadowing his later desertion of Medea. At 4.997 φαίης κεν ἐοῖς περὶ παισὶ γάνυσθαι recalls *Phaen.* 196, but with a change of context from lamentation to joyful welcome. The creation of the spring at Lake Triton by means of a kick (4.1446) imitates *Phaen.* 218–20 on the origin of Hippocrene.

In Theocritus the name Aratus (with short first syllable) appears as addressee in *Id.* 6 and as a friend of Simichidas in *Id.* 7. For arguments against the probability that this Aratus is the poet see Gow 2.118–19. There is no hint of Aratean themes in 6 or in the latter part of 7, nor any suggestion that this Aratus is a poet.

In 17.1 it is possible, and I think likely (see note on 1), that T. has 'quoted' the opening phrase of the *Phaenomena* and followed it with an invocation of the Muses to suggest that his eulogy of Ptolemy is worthy of the grander style of epic. There are no other Aratean phrases in the rest of the poem, nor are there any other non-astronomical borrowings in the rest of the Theocritean corpus. Minor similarities are not significant, and 25.226 γλώσσῃ δὲ περιλιχμᾶτο γένειον (cf. *Phaen.* 1115) is in a poem of doubtful authenticity.

But T.'s astronomy reflects some Aratean themes, mainly risings and settings of stars associated with changes of weather. In 7.53–4 the context requires a time of year towards the end of the sailing season when storms can be expected to occur. T. gives two stellar references. The first is ἐφ' ἑσπερίοις Ἐρίφοις, the evening rising of the Kids about the end of September, the only entry for this star-group in the Greek calendars, and noted by A. in 158 and 682; see notes ad locc. Gow suggests that ἑσπερίοις is taken from *Phaen.* 1065 ἑσπερίων, of the Pleiades, but that refers to a setting, not a rising. The source may well have been Euctemon's calendar for 28 Sept. Ἔριφοι ἐπιτέλλουσιν ἑσπέριοι (Gem. *Cal.* Libra 3). The second reference is χώρίων ὅτ' ἐπ' ὠκεανῷ πόδας ἴσχει. Euctemon dates Orion's ms at Scorp. 15 = 9 Nov. A. does not refer to the time just before Orion's setting begins, but notes the completion of the setting about a month later (309–10). The poets are not concerned with exact dates, and the two references mean roughly the month of October.

Id. 13.25 refers to the (morning) rising of the Pleiades in May, a familiar sign since Hesiod (*Op.* 383) of the beginning of summer weather, and A. alludes to it in 265–6. T. adopts the old name Πελειάδες (see note on 254–267), perhaps as more suited to a rural setting, and again there is no verbal echo of A. In line 50 the simile of the meteor, with its significance as a sign of strong winds, recalls the weather sign in *Phaen.* 926–32, though A. has meteors in showers. T. seems to have had in mind also the Homeric simile in Δ 75–7 of Athena's descent, together with Homeric ἤριπεν (cf. N 389). The following κουφότερ' ... ποιεῖσθ' ὅπλα has a parallel in *Phaen.* 421, but it is difficult to decide whether either is an imitation of the other.

Id. 22 has a brief allusion to risings and settings of constellations (8–9), in which δύνοντα καὶ οὐρανὸν εἰσανιόντα imitates A.'s internal rhyme in 617 and elsewhere with the same participles (see note on 360). In line 21 the pl. Ἄρκτοι suggests A. (27, 48) rather than Homer (Σ 487 Ἄρκτον), and in 21–2 the Manger and Asses group as a weather sign is certainly derived from A. (898–908 for bad weather, 996–8 for good). T.'s Ὄνων τ' ἀνὰ μέσσον ἀμαυρὴ Φάτνη directly imitates Ὄνοι μέσση δέ τε Φάτνη (898), ἀμαυρή interprets 892 and 893, εὔδια is Aratean (802, and frequently in other cases).

(b) Latin poets

Latin poets, other than the translators, show the influence of A. especially in non-technical star-lore. The themes and phrases most frequently imitated illustrate a somewhat limited range of familiar passages, on which see the relevant notes in the Commentary. These are *Phaen.* 1 beginning with Zeus; 36–9 Helice preferred by Greeks, Cynosura by Phoenicians; 108–9, 131 the absence of war in the Golden Age, and consequently the wickedness of swords; 110–11 similarly the absence of ships implying the wickedness of seafaring; 164 the Olenian epithet of Capella; 219–21 the origin of Hippocrene; 733 the much imitated οὐχ ὁράᾳς;

There is not much originality in these imitations, but several cleverly turned versions of less familiar lines are to be found in particular poets, e.g. V. *G.* 1.303–4 on ships entering harbour (*Phaen.* 345), and *G.* 2.483–4 the modest

recusatio (460); Hor. *C.* 3.6.46–8 on increasing decadence
(123–6); Ov. *Fast.* 5.532 apology for a discreditable story
(637); Man. 1.686 on Cassiepeia setting (654); Juv. 14.289
nearness of death at sea (299). See also E. Courtney, *Frag-
mentary Latin Poets* (Oxford 1993), 149–50 on M. Cicero,
179ff. on Q. Cicero, 221–2 on C. Helvius Cinna, 308–9 on
Ovid's *Phaenomena*.

Most remarkable of all is Virgil's use of Aratean material on weather signs in *G.* 1.351–460. The *Phaenomena* had
already been translated into Latin verse by Cicero and
Varro Atacinus, as had other Greek poems by other Latin
poets, but Virgil here is treating A. in much the same way
as A. treated his prose source on weather signs, though
with much more freedom, variation and personal involvement. Lucretius appears to have done this with his Epi-
curean sources, but Virgil's innovation consists in using a
poem in this way. The themes in these 110 lines, with a few
exceptions, are all Aratean, and a close comparison of the
corresponding passages will reveal the difference in both
arrangement and development.

G. 1.351–5 gives a brief proem on the establishment of
divine signs (*Phaen.* 10–13), 356–9 roaring sea and mountains (909–12), 360–4 sea-birds flying landwards (913–17),
365–7 meteoric showers (926–9), 368–9 light objects floating (921–3), 370–2 lightning and thunder (933–7), 372–3
sailors trim ship (421), 373–4 being forewarned (973–4),
374–5 cranes (1031–2), 375–6 cows sniffing (954–5), 377
swallows flying round a lake (944–5), 378 frogs (946–7),
379–80 ants (956–7), 380–1 rainbow (940), 381–2 rooks
(963–6), 383–4 sea and lake birds (942–3), 385–7 birds
splashing (951–3), 388–9 crow on beach (949–50), 390–2
lamps and snuff (976–80), 393–4 fair-weather signs (990–
1), 395–7 clear stars and moon (1013–15), 399–400 pigs
(1123), 401 low cloud (988–9), 402 night owl (999–1000),
410–14 rooks at home (1003–9), 424–6 moon and sun signs
(773–6), 427 crescent moon (780–1), 428–9 dull crescent

(785–7), 430–1 reddish moon (784–5), 432–5, fourth-day moon (782–4), 438–40 sunrise and sunset (819–21), 441–4 markings on sun (822–4), 445–8 divergent rays (828–31), 450–3 dark or red sun (834–7), 454–6 dark and red sun (838–9), 456–7 no night for sailing (287–8), 458–60 sunrise or sunset (825–7). Non-Aratean topics occupy 398–9, 404–9, 415–23, 436–7, 449.

VI SCHOLIA AND COMMENTATORS

(a) Scholia

The primary tradition of the scholia is represented by cod. Marcianus 476 (M) and those of its descendants that include scholia in full or abridged form; see Martin *SAV*, Praefatio. They are the result of various stages of development from the Alexandrian collection ascribed to Theon; cf. Edinburgensis (E) fol. 58 γένος Ἀράτου Θέωνος Ἀλεξανδρέως (*SAV* 14), Laurentianus 28.44 fol. 43 ἐκ τῆς εἰς τὰ τοῦ Ἀράτου Φαινόμενα Θέωνος ἐξηγήσεως ἐκλογαί (*SAV* xxx). This Theon was most probably the first-century BC grammarian, son of Artemidorus; he contributed to the scholia on A.R. and Nicander, and probably to those on Theocritus (Gow 1.lxxxii). In the fourteenth century Triclinius' edition of the scholia made use of Planudes' work on them (*SAV* xxix–xxxiii).

The E scholia are derived from a copy of M, and have been revised by Planudes, who has also added a number of marginal notes expressing agreement or disagreement with either the poet or the scholiast. Most of these notes occur in the astronomical part of the poem and make use of Hipparchus' criticisms, e.g. fol. 78ᵛ, sch. 62 (P. agrees with Crates on what A. means by the mingling of settings and risings) οὕτως καὶ ἐμοὶ δοκεῖ· οὐ γὰρ τὸν κύκλον φησὶν ἔνθα ὁ ἥλιος διερχόμενος ἐπισυνάπτει τὴν ἀνατολὴν τῇ δύσει, ἀλλὰ τὸν ὁρίζοντα ἔνθα μίσγεται τὸ ἀνατολικὸν καὶ τὸ δυσικὸν μέρος τοῦ οὐρανοῦ; fol. 79, sch. 70 (P. corrects A. in accordance with Hi. 1.2.6) οὐχὶ τοῦ δεξιοῦ ποδὸς ἀλλὰ τοῦ ἀριστεροῦ· ἠγνόηται τοῦτο τῷ Ἀράτῳ; fol. 85, sch. 185 (P. deletes part of a scholion describing the triangle as equilateral, and substitutes a correction to make it isosceles, as in Hi. 1.5.19) οὐκ ἀληθεύει δέ· τὸ γὰρ μεταξὺ τῶν ποδῶν τῶν τοῦ Κηφέως διάστημα ἔλαττόν ἐστιν ἑκατέρου τῶν πρὸς τὴν οὐρὰν διαστημάτων.

Planudes' revision of the scholia consists mainly of omitting what seems superfluous or rewriting what could be better expressed; e.g. in sch. 1 he omits the reference to Plato's *Laws*, and in place of οἵ κε μάλιστα τετυγμένα τῶν ὡρῶν σημαίνοιεν ἀνδράσιν he writes οἵτινες τετυγμένα τῶν ὡρῶν σημαίνουσι τοῖς ἀνθρώποις.

There is also a secondary tradition of scholia descending from edition Φ of Aratus in the second or third century. Evidence of this is found occasionally in M, more frequently in what exists of the Salmanticensis (Q) scholia, and most especially in Scorialensis (S). This edition is notable for its use of material from the *Catasterismi*, not itself the work of Eratosthenes, but a simplified and rearranged version in which the constellations are in the order adopted by A., this being most convenient for helping the reader to identify them. The work is apparently designed as a manual for the benefit of readers of the *Phaenomena*. It appears to have been also a source of the Greek text translated into Latin in the scholia on *Germanici Caesaris Aratea* (ed. Breysig) and *Aratus Latinus*. A few similar scholia are to be found in Vat. gr. 1087, and these are included in *SAV* (pp. 93, 107, 143, 149, 151 bis, 220, 251, 253, 281).

(b) Commentators

The commentators on A. are of two kinds, grammarians and astronomers (μαθηματικοί), and sometimes both are

involved in comment on the same topic, e.g. in sch. 23, where the former are dismissed as being ignorant of astronomy.

A.'s contemporary the grammarian Crates is named in sch. Germ. and *Arat. Lat.* 1 as interpreting Zeus as the sky (*SAV* 45–6), in sch. Arat. 62 as explaining this problem with reference to κ 86, and in 254 as reading ὑπογουνίδος in the sense of ὑπωμίδος. These notes may have come from his work on Homer, not from a commentary on the *Phaenomena*. His pupil Zenodotus of Mallos, who may have written a commentary, is cited in sch. 34 as taking δίκτος to mean δίκταμνον.

There is no evidence that Eratosthenes wrote a commentary on A., but he may have been inspired by that poem to compile his work on mythology, which would inevitably have included astral myths; cf. sch. Hom. K 29, on Erigone, ἱστορεῖ Ἐρατοσθένης ἐν τοῖς ἑαυτοῦ Καταλόγοις, and sch. Arat. (S) 97. The myths ascribed to him in sch. 225 (on the Ram) and 403 (on the Altar) most probably came from the later Καταστερισμοί (see above p. 44).

The name of the scholarly Aristarchus appears only twice in the scholia, at 28, where the scholiast rightly rejects his idea that the Bears' heads are turned towards their own loins, and at 254 for his interpretation of ἐπιγουνίδος in the Homeric sense of 'thigh' (see note ad loc.). The comments of Aristarchus were probably taken from his works on Homer. By the second century BC the *Phaenomena* was already being read as if it were an astronomical textbook, and the commentaries of Attalus and Hipparchus, especially the latter's, were written to explain and correct the poem from this point of view (see above pp. 18–21). In the process of assessing A.'s astronomy Hipparchus also had occasion to decide on textual problems, and to consult all available copies of the poem; see above p. 21. On astronomical points his evidence for the text must be considered seriously, but variants that are not

significant astronomically carry no special weight, e.g. 280 φαίνων, 382 λάμπεται, 557 τάνυται.

A contemporary of Hipparchus was Boethus of Sidon, a Stoic, who wrote a commentary on the *Phaenomena* in at least four books; cf. Vita 1 Βόηθος ὁ Σιδώνιος ἐν τῷ πρώτῳ περὶ αὐτοῦ, Gem. 17.48 Βόηθος ὁ φιλόσοφος ἐν τῷ τετάρτῳ βιβλίῳ τῆς Ἀράτου ἐξηγήσεως. Little is known about the content of this work. In sch. 62 Boethus is said to have suggested a solution for the problem of that line, but the sch. does not say what the solution was, only that the same was proposed by an Aristyllus, perhaps the contemporary of A., whose observations of fixed stars were used by Hipparchus (Ptol. 7.1). According to Gem. 17.48 he supported the view that winds and rain are to be explained by natural causes. Cicero's title *Prognostica* appears to have been derived from Boethus' use of the term προγνώσεις (*Div.* 2.47).

In the first century BC Aratus became popular in Rome, as is evinced by Cinna's epigram (fr. 11 Morel), the translations by Cicero and Varro Atacinus, and imitations in Virgil and other poets (see above pp. 41–3). Posidonius is cited on parhelia in sch. 881, and on the origin of comets in sch. 1091. Vita III makes reference to a work περὶ συγκρίσεως Ἀράτου καὶ Ὁμήρου περὶ τῶν μαθηματικῶν. The author's name is omitted there, but that of Posidonius can be supplied from the Latin version of Anon. II 3 (*SAV* p. 5).

His pupil Diodorus of Alexandria, a contemporary of Cicero, is mentioned in two Latin versions of line 1 (*HT* 30–1, *SAV* 48–9). On the question of whether Zeus here is the god of mythology or that of the philosophers his view is that the former can be reconciled with the latter. On 224 he reads ἔνδιος and, with reference to κ 450, he interprets it as μεσημβρινός; on 254 he reads ὑπογουνίδος in the sense of κνήμη, in view of Hipparchus' criticism of A.'s ἄγχι here (see note ad loc.). Macr. *Somn.* 1.15.5 records his

explanation of the Milky Way. Diodorus was therefore probably the author of a commentary on the *Phaenomena*, which may have been revised in a more popular form a generation later by Eudorus of Alexandria, a philosopher of the Academic school. He considered the stars to be living bodies (Ach. *Isag.* 13, p. 40 Maass), and had something to say about the origin of the constellations (Anon. II 3, *SAV* p. 4).

Geminus of Rhodes lived for some time in Rome, probably in the third quarter of the first century BC. His Εἰσαγωγὴ εἰς τὰ φαινόμενα was probably written in response to a demand for an elementary handbook on astronomy. It covers a wider range than is required for the understanding of A., but much of it would have been helpful, and indeed he quotes five difficult technical passages, on which his exposition could be used as a kind of commentary. These are 177–8 (14.8), 497–9 (5.24), 537–40 (7.7), 554–8 (7.13) and 733–9 (8.13); in 17.46 and 48 Geminus commends A.'s practice of relating weather changes to natural causes.

After the establishment of Theon's collection of scholia (see above p. 43), many other scholia appear to have been added from time to time, mostly without reference to an author. But three names stand out, because all are quoted for their views on weather or weather signs, and in most cases the name is added at the end, preceded by οὕτω(ς). Eight scholia come from Plutarch's Αἰτίαι τῶν Ἀράτου Διοσημιῶν (ed. Sandbach, *Moralia* xv, Loeb 1969). Plutarch's aim is to suggest natural causes for both the signs and the weathers predicted. The topics are the greater reliability of the sun (820), concavities in the sun (828), divergent sun-rays (829), fire being hard to light (1035), flowering of the mastich (1045), fruiting of evergreen oaks and mastich (1047), sympathy between different plants (1058) and why birds fly in from the islands (1098).

Sporus is quoted three times. In sch. 541 he gives what is essentially a paraphrase of 541–3, but the text is somewhat confused; in sch. 881 his comment is a description of what appears to be happening rather than an explanation of what causes a parhelion; in sch. 1093 he uses Aristotle's theory of exhalation to explain comets. We learn from Eutocius' commentary on Archimedes that Sporus came from Nicaea, and that he compiled a collection of notes entitled Κηρία, perhaps the Ἀριστοτελικὰ Κηρία mentioned in another work by Eutocius (Martin *HT* 205). Leontius, Περὶ κατασκευῆς Ἀρατείας σφαίρας 3, p. 562 Maass, refers to him as Σπόρος ὁ ὑπομνηματιστής. On the strength of possible clues in Gellius and Leontius, Martin suggests a date for Sporus in the second century (*HT* 206).

An obscure Apollinarius is introduced twice in the scholia: in 1057 he proposes a far-fetched derivation of λοχαίη from λοχῆσαι, in 1068 he comments on the creative impulse initiated by moisture in both animal and plant life. Ach. *Isag.* 19, p. 47 Maass, names Apollinarius as one of several astronomers who worked on solar eclipses at different terrestrial latitudes. His date thus lies between those of Theon and Achilles, presumably in the first or second century.

Achilles was a grammarian, probably of the third century (cf. Maass *Comm.* p. xvii, Martin *HT* 132). He wrote an introduction to cosmology (ed. Maass *Comm.* 27–75), which was apparently used as an introduction to the *Phaenomena*, since in Vat. 191 it is given the heading Τῶν Ἀράτου Φαινομένων πρὸς εἰσαγωγὴν ἐκ τῶν Ἀχιλλέως Περὶ τοῦ Παντός. It is a collection of material from a great range of poets and philosophers, including Aratus, but most of the forty topics are not relevant to the *Phaenomena*. Lines are quoted to illustrate a topic, and are not normally discussed; an exception is a comment which refutes a mistaken interpretation of 61–2 (p. 71). This work was clearly not written as an introduction to Aratus; cf. *HT* 131–2.

VII TEXT AND MANUSCRIPTS

(a) Transmission of the text

In view of the immediate appreciation of the *Phaenomena* in Alexandria (cf. pp. 36–41), there must have been several copies there derived from Aratus' own text, and at least one was no doubt preserved in the great Library for posterity. But we know that by the second century BC some commentators had suggested emendations, and that Hipparchus had corrected some of these. His own criticisms of Aratus certainly had some influence on the later development of the text (cf. pp. 212–13, and the apparatus criticus *passim*), and other variant readings presumably had their source in later commentaries.

In the late first century BC the grammarian Theon of Alexandria is likely to have been the editor of a text (cf. p. 43 on scholia), which became the standard edition in subsequent antiquity, and ultimately the basis of the medieval manuscript tradition represented by M and its descendants. The secondary edition Φ (cf. p. 44), which made its appearance probably in the late second or early third century, bringing with it new scholia and other accompanying material (cf. Martin *HT* 38–57), also introduced new variants into the text. These form a branch that leads to the eighth-century *Aratus Latinus* and the fifteenth-century Scorialensis, though widespread contamination has been responsible for their appearance also in other MSS. They are very evenly distributed throughout the poem, as will be obvious from the apparatus criticus.

(b) Papyri

The Aratus papyri show an interesting range of variant readings. One new reading is almost certainly correct (950), another is a *hapax* (927), others are of interest because they support a reading that has been dismissed as an error, or agree with an ancient quotation against the MSS or with a single manuscript against M and S, or anticipate a modern conjecture. See Martin *HT* 210–18.

Π1 = P. Hamb. 121 (ii¹ BC), 480–94. Line 482 confirms τὰ M Hi. against τε A and edd., correctly in view of A.'s frequent use of the def. art.

Π2 = P. Berol. 7503 + 7804 (i AD), 642–5, 684–802, 855–83, 922–934. Line 713 ανμενει supports ἀμμένει M, 717 ουρο[ν is an Egyptian form of οὖλον (Wilamowitz ad loc.; Diggle comments that ρ/λ is a common phrastic confusion), 722 τεσ]σαρες comes from a gloss on πίσυρες, 723 anticipates ἐπιτέλλεται Voss, 736 agrees with ἐπισκιάει Geminus, and anticipates ἄγουσα Buttmann, 744 agrees with πολυκλύστου E, 749 with ὄγμον S, 750 with ἐμπλήσσει D, 758 τωι confirms the dat. form of this adv. in A., 866 agrees with φανήμεναι Stob. and A, 927 επ[may agree with ἐπιλευκαίνονται Philoponus, but cf. Π5. *BKT* v.1 (1907) 47–54.

Π3 = P. Brit. Mus. 484E (i AD), 944–57. Line 944 supports μάλα δείλαιαι Plut., 950 κύματος is attested only here, but gives the right sense in the context (see note ad loc.), 953 πολλή agrees with S against M, predating the probable divergence of Φ from the Alexandrian edition.

Π4 = P. Oxy. 15.1807 (ii¹ AD), sch. 895–901, text 914–33. Line 897 sch. επικεκλιται is the reading in A, 901 εγγυς αλληλων (cf. sch. MKA 899) paraphrases ἀλλήλων αὐτοσχεδόν, 923 ἐπιπλώωσι agrees with K, on 927 επι[see Π5, 930 αλλοις agrees with S, correction αλλοι δ with M.

Π5 = P. Köln 4.185 (ii¹ AD), sch. 909–32, text 914–33. The text has the same source as Π4, and 927 επι[λευκα]νθ[ω]σιν probably indicates the reading to be supplied in Π4, perhaps also in Π2. Above the line a variant]ωνται is presumably λευκαίνωνται, but whether the prefix was ἐπι- or ὑπο- there is no way of telling; the sch. paraphrases with οταν λευκα[.

Π6 = P. Vindob. G.40603 (II–III AD), 542–50. Line 542 ending agrees with ὑποδράμῃ A and some MSS of Cleomedes, 543 with περιτέλλεται E, S.E. and Cleom., 545 with δ' ἐπὶ V and Plut. *ZPE* 49 (1982) 69–71.

Π7 = P. Brit. Mus. 273b (IV AD), 741–53, 804–14. The first passage is also included in Π2, where rather more of the text is extant. For 749 ογμον and 750 εμ]πλησσει see Π2. Line 811 κυ]κλωσωνται agrees with A and Stob.; the line after 812 has only the ending of 814]δε γαληνης, and should probably be supplemented with τῇ μὲν ἰῇ ἀνέμοιο, μαραινομένῃ, since the loss is most easily explained by haplography; cf. the omission of 814 in Π8. A marginal note at 811 beginning αι καλουμεν[αι probably explains the nature of haloes according to Aristotle (see my note ad loc.). H. I. Bell, *CQ* 1 (1907) 1–3.

Π8 = Vindob. G.29776 (IV AD), 746–56 verso, 810–20 recto. In 752 a marginal note συμφωνει explains συναείδεται, 814 is omitted, probably by haplography due to the repetition of ἀνέμοιο in mid-line. In 819 and 820 marginal notes εκ της ανατολης and εκ της δυσεως probably explain ἑκάτερθεν. J. Lenaerts, *Chronique d'Egypte* 43 (1968) 356–62.

P. Berol. 5865 (IV AD) is a fragment of a papyrus codex containing scraps of lemmata and scholia on lines 146–217 and 294–349; for a full commentary see M. Maehler, *APF* 27 (1980) 19–32. The scholia show the usual explanatory comments on language and star positions, but their main interest lies in the presence of constellation myths, which link them with edition Φ.

P. 1 fr. A on 147–8 suggests the apotheosis of the Twins granted by Zeus because of their brotherly love, which prompted Polydeuces to share his immortality with Castor; cf. sch. (Vat. 1087) and sch. (S) 147, Hyg. 2.22. ὁ δὲ Λέων οὗτός ἐστι[probably introduces the myth of Heracles and the Nemean lion (cf. *Catast.* 12), and the association of the Crab with Hera presumably points to the myth in *Catast.* 11

on how the crab that attacked Heracles while he was fighting the Hydra was rewarded by Hera with a catasterism.

In 2 Fr. A on 167 the name Europa and the verb κατεστήριξεν must refer to the Bull as another catasterism created by Zeus; cf. sch. (M) 167, *Catast.* 14. In 4 Fr. B the Horse and Medusa are named in a note on 205 or 215, a reference to the catasterism of Pegasus, son of Poseidon and the Gorgon; cf. sch. (S) 215 and Hyg. 2.18.1. In 9 fr. B a note on 348 hints at the voyage of the *Argo*; cf. sch. (Vat. 1087) 348.

I am obliged to Dr R. Dilcher, University of Tübingen, for kindly informing me of a small scrap of papyrus which he has prepared for forthcoming publication in the Oxyrhynchus series. It is part of a hypomnema, and contains a mixture of lemmata from *Phaenomena* 452–55, which agree with the transmitted text, and explanatory notes which show some verbal agreement with scholia. The script suggests the second half of the second century. The fragment adds nothing to our knowledge of the text, but is interesting as an example of a hypomnema.

(c) *Aratus Latinus*

The *Aratus Latinus*, so named by Maass, is a Latin version of the *Phaenomena* by an anonymous author in France, composed probably in the first half of the eighth century (Le Bourdellès, *L'Aratus Latinus*, p. 15), and revised in the second half (ibid. p. 69). The only printed edition is that of the original text by Maass, *Comm.* 175–306, based mainly on codd. Parisinus lat. 7886, saec. ix, and Bruxellensis 10698, saec. xii. The text is incomplete, some 85 lines, singly and in groups, being omitted.

The Latin of this translation is often nonsensical, and has therefore been described as barbarous; cf. Maass ibid. xxxvii, Martin, p. xviii of his edition. But Le Bourdellès (149–50) has set it in the context of its own time, when no

Byzantine scholars frequented France, and scribes had only a book knowledge of Greek grammar. It was customary then to write Latin equivalents word for word above the line in Greek texts, and sometimes the Latin was later made available by itself. If this were the case with the *Arat. Lat.*, that would explain the curious character of its Latin.

The translation is basically word for word, and sometimes the Greek is simple enough for the Latin to have been intelligible in this way, e.g. 12 *ipse enim haec signa in caelo adfirmauit*; but the Latin can also be correct when the Greek is understood and a freer translation attempted, e.g. 514 *postquam recesserit aestas* representing the gen. abs. φθίνοντος θέρεος. More often, however, the words have been identified, but not the overall meaning, e.g. in 48 *Arcturus* is confused, as often, with Arctus, *obseruantes* identifies the Greek verb, but not the sense required here, and the pl. is not in accord with *Arcturus*, *oceanum* is acc. because that makes a possible sense with *obseruantes*, and epic -oio is unfamiliar.

Misreading of words is very common, e.g. 204 *prodigia* for πάντ' ἤματα misread as φαντάσματα, 372 *iubentes* for κέλευθα, 508 *fidicula* for ἥλιος misread as χέλυς, 603 *extendens* for ἔκτανε, 818 *permanet* for ἐπὶ μηνί (ἐπί = *per*, μηνί read as μένει), 965 *narrantes* for ἰρήκεσσι read as εἰρηκ-, 1023 *prohibet* for κολοιοί (κωλύει), 1148 *ursina* for ἄρκιον (ἄρκτον).

Wrong division is occasionally a problem: 62 *occasu erit* for δυσι|εστε, 372 *ex quibus uersus est* for ἐξ|είης στιχό|ωντα. Unrecognisable Greek words are sometimes merely latinised: 12 *honophrem* (ὡρά|ων ὄφρ' ἔμ|πεδα), 579 *campes* (καμπή). Unfamiliar words may be simply omitted: 48 κυανέου, 310 ἐπ' ἰξύν, 656 δύετ' ἀρνευτῆρι, 671 γυῖα, 675 ἠῷου, 1119 βουλυσίῳ; 291 is reduced to *ueniet* only, 1039 to *et lucernae*. It is possible that some of the completely missing lines were omitted for the same reason.

Some words that are difficult to explain as translations may not be translations at all, but conjectures substituted for the purpose of giving an appropriate sense to the context. In 592 *ueluti* replaces ἤμενος after *nox* for νύξ (591), which is a misreading of γνύξ. Diggle plausibly suggests that ἤμενος is misread as ἢ μὲν ὡς. In 621 *spiculum Sagittae* takes the place of ῥύτορα τόξου, because the latter word is misinterpreted as the constellation Arrow, and ῥύτορα is not understood; in 808 σημαίνει διχόμηνον is replaced by *significationem peruentat*, the verb being introduced to complete the *donec ad ipsam* clause begun in 807; in 825 βουλύσιος ὥρη is replaced simply by *orbem*, a noun that will make sense after *si autem ipse purum non habuerit*; in 1023 *uigilans* takes the place of ἀείδουσα as an appropriate part. after *nocte* (νύκτερον), and *luscinius* is added as a suitable bird name, now that 1022 ends with *cum se uexat cornicla*.

A restructuring of 1028–30 seems designed mainly to bring together ξουθαί and μέλισσαι, but the rearrangement is confusing and the essential meaning is lost: *neque ergo a foris ueniunt, nisi magnam hiemem sentiant, sed et fuluidae apes, quae ceram gignunt, ipsius mellis opus se inuoluuntur.*

There are also a few additions to the text in the form of brief explanatory notes: after 42 *a nauigantibus obseruatur* (sc. Cynosura) is added *maria enim conturbat*, as if it were a weather sign; after 258, on the Pleiades, *has et Vergilias uocant*; in 579, after *Arctophylax, id est Arcturi custos*. On a larger scale relevant myths and a count of stars are added after each constellation. They are closely related to those in *Catast.* 1–44, similarly omitting the Claws and including the planets and the Milky Way; cf. Martin *HT* 65.

Despite the difficulties inherent in the understanding of this text, it is still possible to see in many places the Greek reading behind the Latin, either directly or by inference from a recognition of the source of an error in the Latin. In the first category are 15 *gaudium*, 187 *magni*, 341 *sectatur*, 475 *subsistens*, 962 *quando*; in the second are 237 *urbium* (confusion of πολύς and πόλις), 664 *sepultoris* (wrong division of ἱππο|τάφηρος), 977 *austrum* (confusion of νότιος 'wet' and νότιος 'south'), 1069 *masculos omnes* (reading ἄρσενα with πάντα.).

It is therefore possible to assess the affinities of *Arat. Lat.* with extant Greek MSS which offer variant readings, and it is of particular interest that *Arat. Lat.* frequently agrees with S against M, e.g. in 97, 157, 184, 300, 645, 655, 659, 671, 784, 846, 961, 962, 965, 1034, 1121 (see my apparatus criticus, and for a fuller range of readings that of Martin). Such readings are shown by Martin to be evidence for the edition he designates Φ and dates to the second or third century AD (*HT* 69–72, 289).

(d) Planudes and Triclinius

Towards the end of the thirteenth century the Byzantine scholar Planudes revised not only the scholia (see above pp. 43–4), but also three passages of the text on celestial circles: 481–96 on the northern tropic, 501–10 on the southern tropic, and 515–24 on the equator. Criticism of A.'s choice of stars to define these invisible circles goes back to Hipparchus; cf. notes on 483, 484, 488, 493, 505, 516, 521. Planudes may have been influenced also by the Latin translators, who occasionally 'corrected' A. on points criticised by Hipparchus. But this complete rewriting of 32 lines reveals a new attitude of scholars to classical texts that goes far beyond emendation; cf. the interpolated line 613.

In Baroccianus 109, fol. 167ʳ, a scribal note τοῦ Τρικλινίου opposite the third Planudean line presumably identifies the author of a longer note in the bottom margin. Here Triclinius explains that Planudes has substituted these lines of his own because the circles in A. are inaccurately positioned on the celestial sphere, and he has therefore followed Ptolemy's very accurate globe: ἰστέον δὲ ὅτι ἡ τοῦ Ἀράτου σφαῖρα οὐκ ἀκριβῶς ἔχει πρὸς τὴν θέσιν τῶν κύκλων ἐκτεθειμένα τὰ ζῴδια, ἡ δὲ τοῦ Πτολεμαίου λίαν ἠκριβωμένως ἐκτίθεται. ταύτη γοῦν τῇ τοῦ Πτολεμαίου σφαίρᾳ ἑπόμενος ὁ σοφὸς Πλανούδης κατὰ τὴν ἐκείνης θέσιν ἐκδέδωκε τοὺς παρόντας στίχους, ἐναλ⟨λ⟩άξας ὅσα μὴ καλῶς εἴρηκεν ὁ Ἄρατος. διὸ οἱ ἐντυγχάνοντες ταύταις, καὶ μάλιστα τοῖς περὶ τούτων λεχθεῖσι παρὰ ἀμφοτέρων, ἔχουσιν ἀκριβῆ τὴν περὶ τούτων κατάληψιν, ἀμφοτέρους [ἐπὶ τούτοις] εὑρίσκοντες ἐπὶ τούτοις συμφωνοῦντας. (I take the last phrase to mean that both Aratus and Ptolemy are in agreement about the function of the celestial circles.) Cf. Martin *HT* 250, L. Reynolds and N. Wilson, *Scribes and Scholars* (1968) 182 and plate VI. It appears that Planudes worked out relevant stars by following the circles inscribed on a Ptolemaic star-globe. He did not presume, however, to rewrite A.'s lines on the ecliptic, because that circle still ran through the constellations of the zodiac.

Planudes' lines appear first in the Edinburgensis (E), (*a*) 1–8 in the bottom margin of 98^r, 9–16 in the top and right-hand margins of 98^v; (*b*) 1–6 in the bottom margin of 98^v, 7–11 in the top margin of 99^r; (*c*) 1–8 in the bottom margin of 99^r, 9–14 in the top margin of 99^v. They are then copied with a few variants in the other Planudean MSS (those listed in Martin *HT* 254–5, with the addition of Harvardensis Typ. 18). I quote the text of E with one correction, (*a*) 9 τροχοῦ (for τοχου) from Vindob. phil. philol. 341.

(*a*)   ἐν δέ οἱ ἑσπομένου Διδύμων τὸ μέσον καθορᾶται,
ἐν δέ τοι Ὑάδες ἃς ἀνέχει λοφιῆς ἔπι Ταῦρος,
γλωχὶν Πληιάδων, ἤ γ' ἐς βορέην σκοπιάζει.
Ἰχθύος αὖ κεφαλὴ βορεωτέρου ἐστὶν ἐν αὐτῷ.
Ἀνδρομέδης κεφαλὴν δὲ καὶ Ὀρνίθειον ἀθρήσεις   5
ῥάμφος ὑπὲρ κύκλοιο βορειοτέρης ἐπὶ χώρης,
μικρὰ βορειοτέρης, καὶ ἀπόστασιν ἄμφω ἐς ἴσην.
ἐς μέσον ἀμφοτέρων δ' Ἵππου γόνυ μᾶλλον ἐκείνων
ἄγχι τροχοῦ κέκλιται καὶ μικροῦ δεῖν ἐν ἐκείνῳ.
τοῦ τ' ἐν γούνασι δεξιτερὸς διατέμνεται ὦμος   10

καὶ πολυπλεθροτάτου μυκτὴρ Ὄφεως Ὀφιούχου
αὐτοῦ τ' Ἀρκτούρου ἀριδείκετος ἐς πόλον ἀστήρ,
αὐτὰρ ἔπειτα λεοντέη ὀσφύς, ἔπειτα δὲ χαίτη,
εἶτα δ' Ὄνων ὁ βόρειος ἐπόψια σήματα κύκλου.
Καρκίνον ἐς μῆκος γὰρ ὅλον τροχαλὸς διαμείβων   15
δοιὰ μὲν ἐς νότον, ἓν δὲ βόρειον ἐς ἄντυγα λείπει.

(b) ἄλλος δ' ἀντιόωντι νότῳ νότι' Αἰγοκερῆος
τέμνει, καὶ στροφάλιγγα μέσην Ὑδροχεύμονος ὑγροῦ,
οἷς ἅμα Κήτεος οὐραῖον νοτιώτατον αἱρεῖ
καὶ πόδα προσθίδιον νότιόν τε θοοῖο Λαγωοῦ.
μεσσάτιός τε Κύων ἀπομείρεται ἔνθα καὶ ἔνθα.   5
εἶτα δ' ἀκροστόλιόν τε καὶ ἱστίον Ἀργόος ἄκρον
σχίζει, καὶ κεφαλὴν Κόρακος βορέηνδ' ἀπολείπει.
αὐτὰρ Ὕδροιο δίεισιν ἀειρομένης ἄκρον οὐρῆς,
Ἀντάρεως τ' ἔχεται, τὸν Σκορπίος ἴσχει ἐν αὐτῷ
ἀστέρα παμφανόωντα. καὶ οὐδὲ σύ, Τοξότα, φεύγεις,   10
ἀλλὰ καὶ ὑμετέρην κεφαλὴν διὰ μέσσον ὁρίζει.

(c) σῆμα δέ οἱ Σύνδεσμος ὃς Ἰχθύας εἰς ἓν ἐλαύνει,
ἐν δὲ γένυς μεγάλη μεγακήτεος ἔπλετο Κήτευς
καὶ μέσον Ὠρίωνος ὅπη ζώνη κατὰ μῆκος
ἐκτέταται, καὶ Ὕδρου πρώτη καμπὴ κρυεροῖο.
Παρθενικῆς δ' εἴδωλον ἔπειτα διάνδιχα τέμνει   5
λοξὸν ἀπὸ Πτέρυγος λαίης ἄλλην ἐπὶ πέζαν.
εἶτ' Ὄφεως μεγάλοιο, τὸν ἀμφοτέραις Ὀφιοῦχος
δραξάμενος κατέχει, καμπὴν πρώτην μετὰ κόρσην.
οὐρὴν δ' ἀκροτάτην καὶ δεξιὸν ἀνέρος ὦμον
οὐ πολὺ πρὸς βορέου ἀπολείπεται, ἐς μέτρα δ' ἴσα   10
Αἰετὸς ἐκτανύσας δ' ὠκύπτερον, ἐς νότου οἶμον
δεξιτερὸν κύκλοιο παράπτεται. Ὑδροχόος δὲ
αὐτοῦ ἔχει κεφαλὴν ἐπὶ κύκλου· τῶν νεπόδων δὲ
ὃς νοτιώτερός ἐστι διχάζεται, ἀλλ' ἐπὶ μῆκος.

(e) The manuscripts

Fifty MSS of the *Phaenomena* are known to date, and all are
fully described or briefly reported by Martin in *HT* 229–62
and *SAV* iii–xxxiii. Fell (1672) had the use of two Bodleian

MSS (presumably Barocciani 78 and 109), Buhle (1793) the Vaticanus Barberinianus gr. 43, Vratislaviensis Rehdigeranus 35, and readings from the Mosquensis (now Charecovensis Univ. 369). He notes the existence of other MSS, which he was unable to use, naming in particular a codex Parisiensis, apparently 2403 (A), a Scorialensis with scholia (S), two Matritenses, and a fine Laurentianus written in 1464 (Gregorian 1465). Voss (1824) refers frequently to MSS in Moscow, Vienna, Breslau, the Pfalz (now Palatinus 40), and others unnamed. Bekker collated fourteen, which were used by Buttmann (1826), including Marcianus 476 (M), Vat. 1307, Casanatensis and seven Parisini, and provided a critical apparatus in his own edition (1828).

Maass was the first to attempt a classification of the MSS, first in *Hermes* 19 (1884) 92–122, and then in his edition (1893). He began with M and Vat. 1307, established the latter as a copy of the former, and postulated as the source of M a scholarly edition of late antiquity. The rest of his MSS he set out in groups consisting of fifteen with scholia and ten without scholia. For his apparatus criticus he chose in addition to M only Par. 2403 (A) and Par. 2728, presumably because these two offered a large number of readings differing from M, and he presented all other variants under the *siglum* for *recentiores*, an arrangement that gave no indication of the affinities of individual MSS. He shunned the labour of collating all his MSS, and assumed that neither A nor Par. 2728 had its source in M or any other known MS (Maass p. xxi). In fact the former proved to be a descendant of M and the latter a copy of S.

Martin's thorough investigation of the MSS in *HT* (1956), and his use for the first time of Scorialensis, have shown that S represents a tradition that diverged from the Alexandrian text in the second or third century (edition Φ), when the new material on constellation myths was added to the original scholia (see above p. 44). This edition was also shown to have been the model for the *Aratus Latinus* in the eighth century (see pp. 52–5). In the tenth and eleventh centuries, when Byzantine scholars were actively searching for older copies of the *Phaenomena*, it seems that texts were discovered of both the Alexandrian tradition and that of edition Φ, and the two traditions experienced mutual contamination in subsequent copies of the poem. Thus M sometimes agrees with *Aratus Latinus* (L) against S, e.g. 26 ἔχουσαι (*habentes*), 341 διώκει (*sectatur*), 349 ἄχρι (*usque ad*), 498 ὑπέρτερα (*super terram*), 914 περιπολλὰ (*prae multitudine*); both M and S agree with L in 187 μεγάλοιο (*magni*), 467 ἀπλανέες (*sine errore*), 475 ὑποστὰς (*subsistens*); but M and S agree against L in 15 θαῦμα (*gaudium*), 327 ὑπὸ (*super*), 417 βορέαο (*uentum*), 471 νεόμηνι (*bipartita luna*), 506 ἀγαυοῦ (*leuioris*).

The extant MSS are thus seen to form two branches, but the ancestry of each is mixed. S and its three copies are all that we have of one branch; the other consists of M and all the rest. But in constructing a text it is not possible to ignore the rest because they are descendants of M, since contamination is also widespread among the later MSS, and in this period it includes scribal errors and emendations as well as readings from other MSS. Martin has classified the bulk of the MSS in nine groups designated by the letters a to i, but the groups are based on evidence largely external to the text of the *Phaenomena*, such as scholia and texts which serve as an introduction to the poem or as appendices at the end of it. But the readings are not necessarily consistent throughout any one group, and it would be misleading to give the group letters in a critical apparatus. This is true even in the most obvious group, that of the Planudeans (g). Some MSS have eluded classification, because they have affinities with several groups. Par. 2403 (A) is the sole occupant of Group c (*HT* 240–1), but it has affinities with Par. 2841 (D), Casanatensis (C)

and Vat. 1910 (V). Vat. 199 (N) has affinities with Groups c
and d (245), and Vat. 121 with several groups (262).

I have not included a stemma, since that would have been
of little help in choosing the best readings for the text.
Contamination has brought many good readings into late
MSS; e.g. 1142 κατόνοσσο appears in Y (end of fifteenth
century), but not in the primary MS of its group, P (early
fourteenth). For understanding of the history of the text
Martin has generously provided stemmata at many stages
in his *HT*, for the background material as well as for the
extant MSS. In my apparatus criticus I cite M, E and S in
every instance, M and S because they are the primary
MSS in the two branches of the text, E because it has not
been available for any previous edition, and is important
as the primary Planudean MS. The other eleven are cited
solely for variant readings not found in M, E or S, and
each is the earliest instance known to me.

I have collated M and E from the manuscripts, C, H, N,
T, V, Y from microfilms, A, D, P, Q, S from photocopies,
and have also used photocopies of M, E, C, H, V for reference. Readings of K are taken from Buhle.

(f) Manuscripts cited in the apparatus criticus

M: Venice, Marcianus 476, end of eleventh century or
beginning of twelfth.

Contents: Aratus with scholia and Lycophron with scholia. The Aratean scholia are followed by a series of supplementary texts: περὶ τοῦ
ζῳδιακοῦ κύκλου (the ecliptic), a brief letter of unknown date to an
unknown Julian criticising those who wrote superfluously elaborate
notes on the *Phaenomena*, περὶ τῶν Φαινομένων Ἀράτου, and some
brief astronomical notes. These have been printed in the same order by
Martin *SAV* 529–44.

The scribe who copied the whole MS has written at the
top of fol. 31ʳ κἀνταῦθα συνήθροισα λεξικοῦ λέξεις Νική-
τας οὐλάχιστος τῶν διακόνων. Nicetas was identified by
E. Scheer, *Rh.Mus.* 34 (1879) 281 as the deacon of St Sophia

who later became metropolitan of Heraclea. The MS was given to the Basilica of St Mark by Cardinal Bessarion in 1468 (Martin *HT* 229–31).

E: Edinburgh, Nat. Library of Scotland, Adv. MS 18.7.15, last decade of thirteenth century.

Contents: Cleomedes (fols. 1–54), a note on the Julian calendar (54ᵛ), Aratus with scholia (fols. 73–126), preceded by Anon. ΙΙ 1 προοίμιον (Maass *Comm.* 102ff.), Vita ΙΙΙ, and ἀστροθεσίαι ζῳδίων (Maass *Comm.* 181–277). For a fuller description see I. C. Cunningham, *Scriptorium* 24 (1970) 367–8.

The poem is divided into four sections. The first is denoted by the subscription after line 450, at the foot of fol. 95ᵛ, ἕως ὧδε τὰ τῆς ἀστροθεσίας; the second is introduced with a sub-title at the top of fol. 96, before line 451, περὶ τῶν ἐν οὐρανῷ κύκλων; the third has a sub-title περὶ τῶν ἀντικαταδύσεων καὶ συνανατολῶν written at the top of fol. 100ᵛ before line 545, but presumably intended to refer to 559, which introduces the new topic and begins with an uncial Ο. The fourth section has the traditional beginning at 733, and is introduced by ἀρχὴ τῶν διοσημειῶν at the foot of fol. 106ᵛ (Cunningham's reference is incorrect). The poem as a whole is rounded off with τέλος τῶν Φαινομένων Ἀράτου at the foot of fol. 126.

The writing of the text is scholarly. Main divisions and many sub-divisions, even items of a few lines among the weather signs, are introduced with an uncial letter, and new themes frequently start on a new page; cf. lines 15, 137, 167, 179, 254, 300, 338, 353, 359, 443, 451, 733, 799, 880, 933, 956, 960, 1031.

Metrical errors are comparatively rare, so that 909 σήματα δέ τ' comes as a surprise. Several variants which appear here for the first time may well be Planudes' emendations; cf. 49, 82, 249, 474, 523, 627, 691, 746, 846, 908, 935, 966, 1119, 1124, 1130, 1141.

E is a descendant of M, as is proved by the break in sch. 152 between καὶ τὸν ὄρτυγα (*SAV* 156, 3) and ἐτησίαι ἀπὸ

(157, 4). The text has the same omissions as M in 233 (ἔτ'), 281 (πτέρυγι), 763 (τά), and the same unmetrical readings in 435, 538, 834, 980. But the descent comes through some other MS. Where readings of E differ from those of M, they sometimes agree with readings found in Vat. 1307 and rarely elsewhere, e.g. 32 ποτὲ, 134 ἔπτατ' ἐπουρανίη, 793 ἦ τ', 837 ἐρευθέα, 918 εἰναλιδῖναι, 1049 μὴ μὲν.

E is the primary MS of the Planudeans, Martin's Group g (*HT* 247–55), which should include also the Harvard MS, Typ. 18, reported in *HT* 258–9, since this has Planudes' lines on the celestial circles substituted for the original text. E also shows an influence on its near contemporaries Par. gr. 2403 (A) and Vat. gr. 1910 (V), both of which have incorporated in the text Planudes' interpolated line 613. The presence of *catasterismi* among the introductory texts also points to some link with edition Φ. This link is also illustrated by readings which differ from M and agree with S and *Aratus Latinus* (L), e.g. 157 δοκέει (*uidetur*), 234 ἐστάθμηται (*ponderatur*), 284 τάνυται (*tenditur*), 735 ὅτε (*quando*), 809 δέχεται (*suscipitur*), 1034 μελαινόμεναι (*nigris*), 1121 ἐμπλήσεσθαι (*satiari*).

S: Escorial, Scorialensis Σ III 3, late fifteenth century.

Contents: Nicander, *Th.* and *Al.*; Aratus with scholia; Orphic *Argonautica*; Apollonius, *Argonautica*. Two Aratean texts precede the scholia: Vita IV and a fragment of a scholion on why A. began with Zeus (*SAV* 44–5). After the scholia are half of the letter to Julian (*SAV* 533, 1–9); two iambic trimeters, Ἄρατος ὧδε λήξας παννύχων πόνων (cf. Call. *E.* 27.4) νέοις τράπεζαν προύθετο πλήρη λόγων; five notes mostly irrelevant to Aratus (*SAV* 556 no. 1, 543 no. 4b, 541 no. 3, 556 no. 2, 557 nos. 3 and 4).

Part of S (including the *Phaenomena*) was written by Antonio da Milano in Crete (fol. 175), and a copy of it, Par. gr. 2728 (Maass's C), was written in Crete by G. Gregoropoulos, late fifteenth century. Martin reports that the Apollonius in S was copied from a MS of c. 1280–1300, and thinks it probable that the latter also contained the *Phaenomena*. He goes on to suggest that an earlier source was a MS of the tenth or eleventh century closely related to M (*HT* 231-4).

S differs from M mainly in having textual readings and scholia that descend from edition Φ. In other respects they share a common heritage, including errors and omissions; cf. apparatus criticus 140, 332, 401, 479, 555, 691, 744, 806, 838, 890, 929, 977, 1147.

Among the scholia on fol. 42ʳ there is a diagram of a circle enclosing a regular hexagon, with the sun outside the circumference; cf. note on 542.

H: Vatican, Vat. gr. 1307, end of eleventh or beginning of twelfth century.

Contents: Lycophron with scholia; Aratus with scholia (*HT* 231).

The text frequently has ten lines to a page. The last three lines and the corresponding scholia are missing. The text frequently differs from that of M, anticipating E most notably in such cases. Where it differs from M, E, S, it usually agrees with A, C or T; in errors it agrees mostly with A and C. Martin notes that the text is almost identical with that of two manuscripts in Group e (*HT* 246).

D: Paris, Bibl. Nat. gr. 2841, thirteenth century.

Contents: Aratus with scholia; Hephaestion, *Apotelesmatica*.

The text breaks off at line 811, the scholia at 497. The text of the poem is rich in scribal errors, but D is the earliest manuscript with the correct reading in 80 καὶ τῇ καὶ τῇ. Traces of edition Φ occur in 128 πάμπαν D, S (*Siluanus = Pan* L), and in 234 ἐστάθμηται D, S (*ponderatur* L). D and Par. suppl. gr. 652, fifteenth century, constitute Group b (Martin *HT* 239-40).

A: Paris, Bibl. Nat. gr. 2403, end of thirteenth or beginning of fourteenth century.

Contents: anonymous texts on cosmography and metrics; Tzetzes on poetic genres; Aratus with scholia; Proclus, *Hypotyposis*; Lycophron; Nicander; Pindar, *O.*, *P.* and part of *N.*; *Odyssey* to ω 309. The Aratean part includes introductory texts from M (*SAV* 535–44) and the scholion on why A. begins with Zeus (44–5).

Martin classifies A by itself as Group c, since no other manuscript is closely related to it (*HT* 240–1; cf. J. Irigoin, *Histoire du texte de Pindare* (1952) 264–6).

A has numerous readings that differ from M, E, S, and, though the majority are errors or otherwise unacceptable, there are still many good readings available, especially in the second half of the poem. The text has affinities with C, V and K, sometimes also with E, e.g. the interpolation of Planudes' line 613, which suggests that the date of A is perhaps after rather than before the end of the century.

C: Rome, Biblioteca Casanatense 356, end of thirteenth or beginning of fourteenth century.

Contents: Dionysius, *Periegesis*; Aratus with scholia; Hesiod, *Theogony* and *Shield*. The Aratean part concludes with the letter to Julian and the περὶ τοῦ ζῳδιακοῦ κύκλου from M (*SAV* 533–4 and 529–32).

The pagination of C is close to that of M, but it is not a direct copy. It has some affinities with H, including traces of edition Φ, e.g. 65 πόνος (*dolor* L), 427 παραστράψῃ (*coruscare* L); absence of Planudean 613; unmetrical φαίνεται (143), κικλήσκουσιν (245), πείθονται (420). For readings that differ from M and H it is most closely related to A. Other characteristics worth noting are the absence of a division of the poem after 732 and the omission of 1138–41. This is the primary manuscript in Martin's Group f (*HT* 246–7).

V: Vatican, Vat. gr. 1910, end of thirteenth or beginning of fourteenth century.

Contents: Lycophron (incomplete); Hesiod, *Works and Days*, *Shield*; Aratus with scholia, text to line 642, scholia to 290; Dionysius, *Periegesis*. The Aratus is preceded by Vita IV and introductory texts as in A and in the same order.

This is the primary manuscript in Martin's Group d (*HT* 241–4).

The text of V has affinities particularly with A, and

includes line 613. But after a new scribe takes over on fol. 73 at line 286, variants appear that are peculiar to V, some of them perhaps emendations prompted by a scholion or similar source, e.g. 312 γυμνός (sch. 311 μόνος), 328 οὐ μὲν for ἀλλ' οὐ (to avoid the repetition of ἀλλά?), 390 transposition of ἰχθύος and κήτεος (sch. 389) with metrical adjustment, 400 ἐπὶ for ὑπὸ (Hyg. 2.27 *ante huius pedes*), 421 δὲ for τε, 475 ἐπιστάς (sch. 469 παρεστηκώς); there are also readings from Hipparchus that are elsewhere ignored, e.g. 491 ἄμ' (1.10.10), 521 γούνατα κεῖται (1.10.20), 585 οἱ (2.2.17).

The text of V has affinities particularly with A, including line 613.

K: Kharkov, Charecovensis Univ. 369 (olim Mosquensis Synod. gr. 223), early fourteenth century.

Contents: Aratus with abridged scholia; Cleomedes. The scholia are followed by the περὶ τοῦ ζωδιακοῦ κύκλου and the letter to Julian (*SAV* 529–34).

A collation of the text of K by C. F. Matthaei was published in *Lectiones Mosquenses* (1779) and used by Buhle in his edition (1793). Buhle also had available a copy by H. C. Helm of the scholia, and printed these along with his text. The K scholia are now included in Martin's *SAV*, but I have been unsuccessful in attempts to obtain a copy of the text from the University of Kharkov, and have relied on the readings cited by Buhle in his notes.

Martin has assigned this manuscript to Group d. The text is closely related to A and V, but has acceptable variants of its own, of which four are probably correct (418, 789, 923, 979). The poem is divided into three parts or 'books', the breaks being noted after lines 450 and 732 (Buhle 1.xii–xiii, Šangin, *CCAG* xii, 1936, p. 91, Martin *HT* 242–3, *SAV* ix–x).

N: Vatican, Vat. gr. 199, fourteenth century (Martin *HT* 245).

Contents: Libanius, Plutarch, Lucian, Aristotle etc.; Aratus without scholia; Cleomedes. On the last page of the *Phaenomena* (fol. 16) are eight crudely drawn figures representing the constellations of Leo, Libra, Virgo, Sagittarius, Corona Borealis, Canis, Eridanus and Argo; cf. the illustrations based on Vat. gr. 1087 in Roscher VI, 898–9. These are followed by passages from the *Catasterismi*, and a περὶ τοῦ ζῳδιακοῦ κύκλου, but not the same as in M.

The text of the *Phaenomena* lacks 1–106, 703–75, 835, 954. Line 138 comes before 137, 743 before 742, 1009–32 are inserted before 917, with 1027 after 1032. Lines 1137–42 remain as in M. This manuscript is difficult to classify because of the absence of introductory material and scholia, but readings that differ from M tend to agree most frequently with A.

P: Heidelberg, Universitätsbibliothek, Palatinus gr. 40, first half of fourteenth century, perhaps before 1325 (Martin *HT* 235–6, 238; Irigoin 232).

Contents: Sophocles, *Aj.*, *El.*, *OT*; Pindar, *O.*, *P.*; Dionysius, *Periegesis*; Lycophron; Oppian, *Hal.*; Aratus without scholia; *Iliad* book II and *Iliad* complete; Choeroboscus περὶ τρόπων. The *Phaenomena* is preceded by Vita IV and part of the περὶ τῶν Φαινομένων Ἀράτου (*SAV* 535–8, line 7 Φάτνη).

This is the primary manuscript in Martin's Group a. The text of P, where it differs from M, is most closely related to C and V. Lines 540, 843–912, 991–2 and 1137 are omitted, 613 is included, 827 is written after 831, 980–1 are fused into one line by haplography, reading πομφόλυγες, μὴ δ᾽ ἦν θέρεος μέγα πεπταμένοιο.

T: Modena, Biblioteca Estense α τ 9 14 (olim II B 14), fifteenth century, probably 1460–70 (Irigoin 386; Martin *HT* 255–6, 259).

Contents: Aratus with scholia; Homeric hymns; Hesiod, *Theogony* and *Shield*; Lycophron; Pindar, *P.* and *N.* Aratus is preceded by Vita IV and introductory texts as in M, but in a different order: *SAV* 535–9, but with title Ὑπόθεσις τῶν Φαινομένων Ἀράτου, 541–3 nos. 4ª and 4ᵇ, 541 no. 3, 544 no. 5ᵇ, 539–41 no. 2, 543–4 no. 5ª, and 44–5 the scholion on why A. begins with Zeus.

This is the primary manuscript of Martin's Group h. The text has many interlinear glosses, especially in the first hundred lines. The Planudean line 613 and the authentic line 619 have been omitted and subsequently added *inter lineas*, 1137 comes after 1141. The text agrees frequently with C, E and A against M, and many readings also descend from H, e.g. 396 ἀπήωροι, 436 ὤμοις (ἄλλοις M), 464 πλανωμενάων, and others shared with other manuscripts. The Aldine edition is based to a large extent on this manuscript (*SAV* xii–xiii).

Q: Salamanca, Biblioteca Universitaria, Salmanticensis M 233 (olim 1, 2, 13), mid-fifteenth century (Martin *HT* 259–60, A. Tovar, *Catalogus Codicum Graecorum Universitatis Salamantinae*, 1963, 55–8).

Contents: Aeschylus, Vita, *Pr.*, *Eum.*, *Th.* 1025–43; Aratus to line 963 with scholia to 155; 'Letters of Phalaris'; Gregory Cor. *De dialectis*; Hephaestion, *excerpta Tricliniana*; Triclinius, *Metrica*; Platonius, *De comoediarum generibus*; Homer, *Vita Herodotea*; Homeric Hymn 25; Doxopater, '*Prolegomena*'; Aphthonius, *Progymnasmata*; Ptolemy, *Geogr.* 7.5.2.

This is the primary manuscript of Martin's Group i. The only subdivision of the text is at 732, after which two lines are left blank. Line 340 is omitted, 613 remains interpolated. There are numerous scribal errors occurring only here; other readings that differ from M agree with various manuscripts, but no general affinity with any of these is apparent. On the importance of the surviving scholia see Martin *SAV* xv–xxi.

Y: Vatican, Vat. gr. 1371, end of fifteenth or beginning of sixteenth century (Martin *HT* 236–7).

Contents: short hermetic and geometric texts; Aratus without scholia; Theocritus; Orphic Hymns; Aristophanes, *Plutus*. The Aratus is preceded by Vita IV and introductory texts as in M, but in the order *SAV* 535–9 no. 1, 541–2 no. 4ᵃ ... τοὐναντίον, 539–41, no. 2, 543 no. 4ᵇ, 544 no. 5ᵇ, 541 no. 3, 529–32.

This manuscript belongs to Group a, and is therefore closely related to P. Line 1137 is omitted, but 540 is not.

Many errors in P are corrected in Y, by direct substitution in the text, by addition above the line, or as a marginal variant. Some of the corrections are of recognisably Planudean origin, e.g. 49 ὑποτέμνεται, 54 ἐκ δ᾽ αὐτῆς, 65 οὐδέ τινι, 165 ἀγλαή, 234 ἀμφοτέραις, 966 δίους γε. The rare reading κατόνοσσο (1142), which is not in P, may have had its source in edition Φ (see note ad loc.).

TEXT AND TRANSLATION

SIGLA

Papyri

Π1	P. Hamb. 121	s. ii a.C.
Π2	P. Berol. 7503 + 7804	s. i p.C.
Π3	P. Brit. Mus. 484E	s. i
Π4	P. Oxy. 15.1807	s. ii
Π5	P. Köln. 185	s. ii
Π6	P. Vindob. G.40603	s. ii–iii
Π7	P. Brit. Mus. 273B	s. iv
Π8	P. Vindob. G.29776	s. iv

Versio Latina

L	*Aratus Latinus*	s. viii

Codices

A	Parisinus gr. 2403	s. xiii–xiv
C	Casanatensis 356	s. xiii–xiv
D	Parisinus gr. 2841	s. xiii
E	Edinburgensis Adv. MS 18.7.15	s. xiii
H	Vaticanus gr. 1307	s. xi
K	Charecovensis Univ. 369 (olim Mosquensis)	s. xiv
M	Marcianus 476	s. xi
N	Vaticanus gr. 199	s. xiii–xiv
P	Palatinus gr. 40	s. xiv
Q	Salmanticensis M 233	s. xv
S	Scorialensis Σ iii 3	s. xv
T	Estensis α T 9 14	s. xv
V	Vaticanus gr. 1910	s. xiii–xiv
Y	Vaticanus gr. 1371	s. xv–xvi

Breuiata

A^ac	ante correctionem
A^pc	post correctionem
A^sl	supra lineam

A^mg	in margine
A^γρ	uaria lectio
add.	addidit
codd.	consensus codicum adhibitorum
coni.	coniecit, coniecerat
del.	deleuit
edd.	editores
fort.	fortasse
l	lemma
om.	omisit, omiserunt
rell.	reliqui
rest.	restituit
sch.	scholion Marcianum
sch. (S)	scholion Scorialense
uid.	uidetur
≃	similis

Coniecturas fecerunt

Arnaud, G. d' (v. 327), *Lectionum Graecarum libri duo* (Hagae 1790)

Bergk, Th. (vv. 966, 1001), *Philologus* 16 (1860) 603–4

Frieseman, H. (v. 99), *Collectanea Critica* (1786)

Kaibel, G. (vv. 124, 966, 1002, 1076, 1119), *Göttingische gelehrte Anzeiger* 1 (1893) 946–60

Lobeck, C. A. (966, 1001), Ῥηματικόν (1846); ad *Aiac.*³ (1866)

Ludwig, W. (vv. 752, 950), *Hermes* 91 (1963) 443–4, 434–6

Rehm, A. (1146), 'Parapegma', *RE* 18.4 (1949) 1299

Schmidt, M. (vv. 33, 648), *Philologus* 9 (1854) 397, 551

Schneider, J. G. (vv. 906, 982, 1076, 1108), *Griechisch–deutsches Wörterbuch* (Lipsiae 1819)

Schrader, J. (v. 610), *Observationum Liber* (1761)

Spitzner, J. (vv. 685–6) *De Versu Graecorum Heroico* (Lipsiae 1816)

Turnebus, A. (v. 640), *Adversariorum Libri XXX* (1604)

Wilamowitz (vv. 376, 859, 1001) ap. Maass

ΦΑΙΝΟΜΕΝΑ

Ἐκ Διὸς ἀρχώμεσθα, τὸν οὐδέποτ᾽ ἄνδρες ἐῶμεν
ἄρρητον. μεσταὶ δὲ Διὸς πᾶσαι μὲν ἀγυιαί,
πᾶσαι δ᾽ ἀνθρώπων ἀγοραί, μεστὴ δὲ θάλασσα
καὶ λιμένες· πάντη δὲ Διὸς κεχρήμεθα πάντες.
5 τοῦ γὰρ καὶ γένος εἰμέν· ὁ δ᾽ ἤπιος ἀνθρώποισι
δεξιὰ σημαίνει, λαοὺς δ᾽ ἐπὶ ἔργον ἐγείρει
μιμνήσκων βιότοιο, λέγει δ᾽ ὅτε βῶλος ἀρίστη
βουσί τε καὶ μακέλῃσι, λέγει δ᾽ ὅτε δεξιαὶ ὧραι
καὶ φυτὰ γυρῶσαι καὶ σπέρματα πάντα βαλέσθαι.
10 αὐτὸς γὰρ τά γε σήματ᾽ ἐν οὐρανῷ ἐστήριξεν
ἄστρα διακρίνας, ἐσκέψατο δ᾽ εἰς ἐνιαυτὸν
ἀστέρας οἵ κε μάλιστα τετυγμένα σημαίνοιεν
ἀνδράσιν ὡράων, ὄφρ᾽ ἔμπεδα πάντα φύωνται.
τῷ μιν ἀεὶ πρῶτόν τε καὶ ὕστατον ἱλάσκονται.
15 χαῖρε, πάτερ, μέγα θαῦμα, μέγ᾽ ἀνθρώποισιν ὄνειαρ,
αὐτὸς καὶ προτέρη γενεή. χαίροιτε δὲ Μοῦσαι,
μειλίχιαι μάλα πᾶσαι· ἐμοί γε μὲν ἀστέρας εἰπεῖν
ᾗ θέμις εὐχομένῳ τεκμήρατε πᾶσαν ἀοιδήν.
οἱ μὲν ὁμῶς πολέες τε καὶ ἄλλυδις ἄλλοι ἐόντες
20 οὐρανῷ ἕλκονται πάντ᾽ ἤματα συνεχὲς αἰεί·
αὐτὰρ ὅ γ᾽ οὐδ᾽ ὀλίγον μετανίσσεται, ἀλλὰ μάλ᾽ αὕτως

1–6 + 10–15 Clem. *Strom.* 5.14   1–9 Aristobulus ap. Euseb. *PE*
13.12.6; Theophilus Antioch. *ad Autolycum* 2.8 Grant; Stob. 1.1.3   1–3
Apostolius 6.95   1–2 (τὸν... ἄρρητον) sch. (BG) Germ. pp. 57, 110
Br.   1 Anon. περὶ ἐξηγήσεως p. 34 Martin *SAV*; (... ἀρχώμεσθα)
Theoc. 17.1; Strat. *AP* 12.1.1; Hdn ii.910, 25L; Macr. *Sat.* 1.18.15; sch. Pi.
N. 5.46; sch. A.R. 1.1–4a; Vita II p. 12 Martin   2–3 (μεσταὶ... ἀγοραί) Luc. *Icar.* 24, *Prom.* 14; sch. (BLV) Θ 250 p. 229b Bekker   2–4
(μεσταὶ... λιμένες) sch. Pi. *P.* 4.344a   3–4 (μεστὴ... λιμένες) Luc.
Epigr. 41.5–6   5 (... εἰμέν) *Act. Ap.* 17.28; Clem. Al. *Strom.* 1.19   6–
7 (-βιότοιο) ≃ Clem. Al. *Protr.* 11   6 Plu. 722D   8–10 Ach. p. 29
Maass   8–9 (λέγει ...) *Et. Flor.*, Miller *Mélanges* p. 80 s.v. γυρῶσαι
9 (... γυρῶσαι) *Et.M.* 243, 57   10–13 Orion, *Anthol.* 5.14 Meineke   10–12 Aetius, *Plac.* 2.19 Diels; Ach. p. 29; Stob. 1.24.4   11–

VISIBLE SIGNS

Let us begin with Zeus, whom we men never leave unspoken. Filled with Zeus are all highways and all meeting-places of people, filled are the sea and harbours; in all circumstances we are all dependent on Zeus. [5] For we are also his children, and he benignly gives helpful signs to men, and rouses people to work, reminding them of their livelihood, tells when the soil is best for oxen and mattocks, and tells when the seasons are right both for planting trees and for sowing every kind of seed. [10] For it was Zeus himself who fixed the signs in the sky, making them into distinct constellations, and organised stars for the year to give the most clearly defined signs of the seasonal round to men, so that everything may grow without fail. That is why men always pay homage to him first and last. [15] Hail, Father, great wonder, great boon to men, yourself and the earlier race! And hail, Muses, all most gracious! In answer to my prayer to tell of the stars in so far as I may, guide all my singing.

The numerous stars, scattered in different directions, [20] sweep all alike across the sky every day continuously for ever. The axis, however, does not move even slightly

12 (ἐσκέψατο ...) sch. p. 376 Martin   12 Cyrillus *An. Par.* iv.192, 12 Cr.   13–15 (ὄφρ' ...) Clem. Al. *Protr.* 7   19–23 Hippolytus, *Haer.* 4.46.6   19 Anon. περὶ ἐξηγήσεως p. 33 Martin   21–3 Ach. p. 61; Jo. Diac. in Hes. *Th.* 746ff., p. 485 Gaisford

5 εἰμέν ΜΕ: ἐσμέν S Act. Apost. Theophil. Clem. Aristobul. Stob.   7 ἀρίστη ΜΕ: ἀρίστου S: ἀροστή Asclepiades in sch. Ach.ᵞᵖ   10 τά γε ΜΕ Stob.: τά τε S: τάδε Aᵖᶜ Aetius Ach. Orion (*haec* L)   12 ἀστέρας codd.: ἀστέρες Cyrill.   σημαίνοιεν codd.: σημαίνουσιν Stob. Cyrill.   13 φύωνται MES: γένωνται D   15 θαῦμα MES: χάρμα Aᵖᶜ (*gaudium* L)   17 πᾶσαι ΜΕˢˡ (*omnes* L): πᾶσιν Ε: om. S   18 ἦ ΜΕ: εἰ S   19 ἐόντες codd.: ἰόντες grammatici multi in sch.   21 μετανίσσεται ΜΕˢˡS: -νείσεται Ε

ἄξων αἰὲν ἄρηρεν, ἔχει δ᾽ ἀτάλαντον ἁπάντη
μεσσηγὺς γαῖαν, περὶ δ᾽ οὐρανὸν αὐτὸν ἀγινεῖ.
καί μιν πειραίνουσι δύω πόλοι ἀμφοτέρωθεν·
25 ἀλλ᾽ ὁ μὲν οὐκ ἐπίοπτος, ὁ δ᾽ ἀντίος ἐκ βορέαο
ὑψόθεν ὠκεανοῖο. δύω δέ μιν ἀμφὶς ἔχουσαι
Ἄρκτοι ἅμα τροχόωσι· τὸ δὴ καλέονται Ἅμαξαι.
αἱ δ᾽ ἤτοι κεφαλὰς μὲν ἐπ᾽ ἰξύας αἰὲν ἔχουσιν
ἀλλήλων, αἰεὶ δὲ κατωμάδιαι φορέονται,
30 ἔμπαλιν εἰς ὤμους τετραμμέναι. εἰ ἐτεὸν δή,
Κρήτηθεν κεῖναί γε Διὸς μεγάλου ἰότητι
οὐρανὸν εἰσανέβησαν, ὅ μιν τότε κουρίζοντα
Λύκτῳ ἐν εὐώδει, ὄρεος σχεδὸν Ἰδαίοιο,
ἄντρῳ ἔνι κατέθεντο καὶ ἔτρεφον εἰς ἐνιαυτόν,
35 Δικταῖοι Κούρητες ὅτε Κρόνον ἐψεύδοντο.
καὶ τὴν μὲν Κυνόσουραν ἐπίκλησιν καλέουσι,
τὴν δ᾽ ἑτέρην Ἑλίκην. Ἑλίκῃ γε μὲν ἄνδρες Ἀχαιοὶ
εἰν ἁλὶ τεκμαίρονται ἵνα χρὴ νῆας ἀγινεῖν,
τῇ δ᾽ ἄρα Φοίνικες πίσυνοι περόωσι θάλασσαν.
40 ἀλλ᾽ ἡ μὲν καθαρὴ καὶ ἐπιφράσσασθαι ἑτοίμη,
πολλὴ φαινομένη Ἑλίκη πρώτης ἀπὸ νυκτός·
ἡ δ᾽ ἑτέρη ὀλίγη μέν, ἀτὰρ ναύτῃσιν ἀρείων·
μειοτέρη γὰρ πᾶσα περιστρέφεται στροφάλιγγι·
τῇ καὶ Σιδόνιοι ἰθύντατα ναυτίλλονται.
45 τὰς δὲ δι᾽ ἀμφοτέρας οἵη ποταμοῖο ἀπορρὼξ
εἰλεῖται μέγα θαῦμα Δράκων, περί τ᾽ ἀμφί τ᾽ ἐαγὼς

22–3 (... γαῖαν) Anon. 1 p. 90 Maass   23 (περὶ ...) Hdn ii.291, 1;
Et.M. 10, 18   24–7 (... τροχόωσι) Ach. pp. 61–2   24–5 (... ἐπίοπτος)
A.D. Synt. 1.157   26 (ὑψόθεν ὠκεανοῖο) sch. (BL) ε 6 p. 144b Bekker
27 (τὸ ...) sch. (T) Σ 488b; sch. (B) Σ 488 p. 507b Bekker   29–30
(αἰεὶ ... τετραμμέναι) Ach. p. 73   30–1 (εἰ ...) Ach. p. 83   33
(ὄρεος ...) Str. 10.4.12; Et.M. 276, 14   35 Anon. Ambros. An. Var. Gr.
p. 225 Studemund   36 Hdn i.263, 32; ii.920, 13   37–8 (Ἑλίκη ...
τεκμαίρονται, om. Ἀχαιοὶ) sch. (L) Γ 190 p. 106a Bekker; Et.M. 332, 16
43 sch. (T) Σ 488b, sch. (B) Σ 488 p. 507b Bekker   46 (... Δράκων)
Hippol. Haer 5.16.15   46 (ἀμφί τ᾽ ἐαγὼς) Hi. 1.4.3

from its place, but just stays for ever fixed, holds the earth in the centre evenly balanced, and rotates the sky itself. Two poles terminate it at the two ends; [25] but one is not visible, while the opposite one in the north is high above the horizon. On either side of it two Bears wheel in unison, and so they are called the Wagons. They keep their heads for ever pointing to each other's loins, and for ever they move with shoulders leading, [30] aligned towards the shoulders, but in opposite directions. If the tale is true, these Bears ascended to the sky from Crete by the will of great Zeus, because when he was a child then in fragrant Lyctus near Mount Ida, they deposited him in a cave and tended him for the year, [35] while the Curetes of Dicte kept Cronus deceived. Now one of the Bears men call Cynosura by name, the other Helice. Helice is the one by which Greek men at sea judge the course to steer their ships, while Phoenicians cross the sea relying on the other. [40] Now the one is clear and easy to identify, Helice, being visible in all its grandeur as soon as night begins; the other is slight, yet a better guide to sailors, for it revolves entirely in a smaller circle: so by it the Sidonians sail the straightest course.

[45] Between the two Bears, in the likeness of a river, winds a great wonder, the Dragon, writhing around and

23 οὐρανὸν αὐτὸν MᵃᶜEᵃᶜ: -ὸς -ὸν MᵖᶜEᵖᶜS Hdn Ach.: -ὸν -ὸς Hippol.: -ὸς -ὸς Jo. Diac.: -ὸς αὐτὸν mathematici in sch.   24 ἀμφοτέρωθεν codd.: ἀμφὶς ἐόντες Ach.   26 ὠκεανοῖο MᵞᵖES: ἐκ βορέαο M   ἔχουσαι ME (habentes L): ἔχουσιν S Ach.   27 ἅμα τροχόωσι E: ἁματροχόωσι M: ἅμα τροχόωσαι S   ἅμαξαι MEᵃᶜ S: ἅμ- Eᵖᶜ   28 δ' ἤτοι M: δή τοι ES   31 μεγάλου ἰότητι MES: μεγάλοιο ἕκητι Mᵞᵖ Ach.   32 τότε MS: ποτὲ E   33 Λύκτῳ Grotius: Δίκτῳ codd.: Δίκτη Buhle: λίκνῳ Voss: δικτάμῳ (deleto ἐν) M. Schmidt   Ἰδαίοιο codd. Strabo EM: Αἰγείοιο nonnulli in sch.: Αἰγαίοιο Stephanus   34 uersum om. et inter lineas add. E   ἔνι κατέθεντο Voss: ἐγκατέθεντο ME: ἐγκατέθητο S: τ' ἐγκατέθεντο Reeve   35 ἐψεύδοντο MESˢˡ: ἐψεύσαντο S   36 καὶ Mᵞᵖ: οἳ MES Hdn   39 πίσυνοι om. et s.l. add. E   42 et 44 om. S   43 μειοτέρη ME: προτέρη S   46 περὶ ME sch.: ὑπὸ S

μυρίος· αἱ δ᾽ ἄρα οἱ σπείρης ἑκάτερθε φέρονται
Ἄρκτοι, κυανέου πεφυλαγμέναι ὠκεανοῖο.
αὐτὰρ ὅ γ᾽ ἄλλην μὲν νεάτῃ ἐπιτείνεται οὐρῇ,
50 ἄλλην δὲ σπείρῃ περιτέμνεται. ἡ μέν οἱ ἄκρη
οὐρὴ πὰρ κεφαλὴν Ἑλίκης ἀποπαύεται Ἄρκτου,
σπείρῃ δ᾽ ἐν Κυνόσουρα κάρη ἔχει· ἡ δὲ κατ᾽ αὐτὴν
εἰλεῖται κεφαλὴν καί οἱ ποδὸς ἔρχεται ἄχρις,
ἐκ δ᾽ αὖτις παλίνορσος ἀνατρέχει. οὐ μὲν ἐκείνη
55 οἰόθεν οὐδ᾽ οἷος κεφαλῇ ἐπιλάμπεται ἀστήρ,
ἀλλὰ δύο κροτάφοις, δύο δ᾽ ὄμμασιν, εἷς δ᾽ ὑπένερθεν
ἐσχατιὴν ἐπέχει γένυος δεινοῖο πελώρου.
λοξὸν δ᾽ ἐστὶ κάρη, νεύοντι δὲ πάμπαν ἔοικεν
ἄκρην εἰς Ἑλίκης οὐρήν· μάλα δ᾽ ἐστὶ κατ᾽ ἰθὺ
60 καὶ στόμα καὶ κροτάφοιο τὰ δεξιὰ νειάτῳ οὐρῇ.
κείνη που κεφαλὴ τῇ νίσσεται, ἧχί περ ἄκραι
μίσγονται δύσιές τε καὶ ἀντολαὶ ἀλλήλῃσι.
τῆς δ᾽ ἀγχοῦ μογέοντι κυλίνδεται ἀνδρὶ ἐοικὸς
εἴδωλον. τὸ μὲν οὔτις ἐπίσταται ἀμφαδὸν εἰπεῖν,
65 οὐδ᾽ ὅτινι κρέμαται κεῖνος πόνῳ, ἀλλά μιν αὔτως
ἐν γόνασιν καλέουσι· τὸ δ᾽ αὖτ᾽ ἐν γούνασι κάμνον
ὀκλάζοντι ἔοικεν· ἀπ᾽ ἀμφοτέρων δέ οἱ ὤμων
χεῖρες ἀείρονται, τάνυταί γε μὲν ἄλλυδις ἄλλη
ὅσσον ἐπ᾽ ὀργυιήν· μέσσῳ δ᾽ ἐφύπερθε καρήνῳ
70 δεξιτεροῦ ποδὸς ἄκρον ἔχει σκολιοῖο Δράκοντος.

---

47 (σπείρης ἑκάτερθε) Hi. 1.4.3   48 [Plu.] *Vit. Hom.* 2.160 Bernardakis
49–54 (... ἀνατρέχει) Hi. 1.2.4   52–3 Hi. 1.5.7; (... κεφαλήν) 1.4.2
56–7 S.E. *Math.* 5.98 Bury   58–60 Hi. 1.4.4   61–2 Hi. 1.4.7; Hyg.
4.3.3; Ach. pp. 52, 71; sch. (HQ) κ 86; (ἧχι ...) Posid. fr. 49 E–K; Str.
2.3.8; Hippol. *Haer.* 4.47.3; Ach. p. 71 (om. ἄκραι), p. 52; Eust. in
κ 86   61 (... νίσσεται) sch. p. 304 Martin   69–70 (μέσσῳ ...) Hi.
1.2.6, 1.4.9   69 (μέσσῳ ...) Att. p. 6 Maass   70 Hippol. 4.47.5,
5.16.16

---

47 φέρονται M^γρ Hi.: φύονται MES   49 ἄλλην codd. Hi.: ἄλλης
Martin   ἐπιτείνεται S Hi.: ἐπιτέλλεται M^γρ sch.: ἀποτείνεται M:

about at enormous length; on either side of its coil the
Bears move, keeping clear of the dark-blue ocean. It
reaches over one of them with the tip of its tail, [50] and
intercepts the other with its coil. The tip of its tail ends
level with the head of the Bear Helice, and Cynosura
keeps her head within its coil. The coil winds past her very
head, goes as far as her foot, then turns back again and
runs upwards. In the Dragon's head there is not just a
single star shining by itself, [56] but two on the temples
and two on the eyes, while one below them occupies the
jaw-point of the awesome monster. Its head is slanted
and looks altogether as if it is inclined towards the tip of
Helice's tail: the mouth and the right temple are in a very
straight line with the tip of the tail. [61] The head of the
Dragon passes through the point where the end of settings
and the start of risings blend with each other.

Near it there circles a figure like a man toiling. No one
is able to say definitely [65] what it is or on what task the
man is intent, but they just call him the man on his knees;
again, labouring on its knees, the figure looks like a man
crouching. From both his shoulders arms are raised and
extend in different directions to a full stretch. He has the
tip of his right foot above the mid-point of the tortuous
Dragon's head.

ἀποτέμνεται H: ὑποτέμνεται E   50 περιτέμνεται M^pc ES: -λαμβά-
νεται M^ac   54 αὖτις ME^slS: αὐτῆς E   ἐκείνη codd.: ἐκείνῳ Maass
55 ἐπιλάμπεται MES: ἐπιτέλλεται M^yp   56 κροτάφοις codd.: κροτάφους S.E.   ὄμμασιν codd.: ὄμματα S.E.   59 μάλα ES: μάλιστα M   60 οὐρῇ codd.: οὐρῆς Voss   61 νίσσεται MS: νίσεται D:
νείσσεται E Hi.: νείσεται Hyg.: νήχεται E^yp   62 ἀλλήλῃσι ME Hi.:
-αισι S: -οισι D: ἠελίοιο Ach. ter   63 τῆς δ' MES: τῇ δ' A: τῆς δ'
Maass   ἀγχοῦ Buhle: αὐτοῦ codd.   65 οὐδ' ὅτινι M: οὐδέ τινι
ES: οὐδὲ τίνι Voss   πόνῳ MS: πόνος E   66 ἐν γόνασιν codd.:
Ἐγγόνασιν Bekker   67 ἀπ' M^ac?ES: ἐπ' M^pcM^yp   69 ἐπ' MES: ἐς
A   ὀργυιήν codd.: ὄργυιαν Voss   μέσσῳ ME: -ου A^pc Att.: μέσῳ
S   καρήνῳ ME: -ου A^pc Att.: -α S

αὐτοῦ κἀκεῖνος Στέφανος, τὸν ἀγαυὸν ἔθηκε
σῆμ' ἔμεναι Διόνυσος ἀποιχομένης Ἀριάδνης,
νώτῳ ὕπο στρέφεται κεκμηότος εἰδώλοιο.
νώτῳ μὲν Στέφανος πελάει, κεφαλῇ γε μὲν ἄκρῃ
75 σκέπτεο πὰρ κεφαλὴν Ὀφιούχεον, ἐκ δ' ἄρ' ἐκείνης
αὐτὸν ἐπιφράσσαιο φαεινόμενον Ὀφιοῦχον,
τοῖοί οἱ κεφαλῇ ὑποκείμενοι ἀγλαοὶ ὦμοι
εἴδονται· κεῖνοί γε καὶ ἂν διχόμηνι σελήνῃ
εἰσωποὶ τελέθοιεν. ἀτὰρ χέρες οὐ μάλα ἶσαι·
80 λεπτὴ γὰρ καὶ τῇ καὶ τῇ ἐπιδέδρομεν αἴγλη·
ἀλλ' ἔμπης κἀκεῖναι ἐπόψιαι· οὐ γὰρ ἐλαφραί.
ἀμφότεραι δ' Ὄφιος πεπονήαται, ὅς ῥά τε μέσσον
δινεύει Ὀφιοῦχον. ὁ δ' ἐμμενὲς εὖ ἐπαρηρὼς
ποσσὶν ἐπιθλίβει μέγα θηρίον ἀμφοτέροισι
85 Σκορπίον, ὀφθαλμῷ τε καὶ ἐν θώρηκι βεβηκὼς
ὀρθός. ἀτὰρ οἱ Ὄφις γε δύω στρέφεται μετὰ χερσί,
δεξιτερῇ ὀλίγος, σκαιῇ γε μὲν ὑψόθι πολλός.
καὶ δή οἱ Στεφάνῳ παρακέκλιται ἄκρα γένεια,
νειόθι δὲ σπείρης μεγάλας ἐπιμαίεο Χηλάς·
90 ἀλλ' αἱ μὲν φαέων ἐπιδευέες, οὐδὲν ἀγαυαί.
ἐξόπιθεν δ' Ἑλίκης φέρεται ἐλάοντι ἐοικὼς
Ἀρκτοφύλαξ, τόν ῥ' ἄνδρες ἐπικλείουσι Βοώτην,
οὕνεχ' ἁμαξαίης ἐπαφώμενος εἴδεται Ἄρκτου.
καὶ μάλα πᾶς ἀρίδηλος· ὑπὸ ζώνῃ δέ οἱ αὐτὸς
95 ἐξ ἄλλων Ἀρκτοῦρος ἐλίσσεται ἀμφαδὸν ἀστήρ.
ἀμφοτέροισι δὲ ποσσὶν ὕπο σκέπτοιο Βοώτεω

71–2 sch. A.R. 3.997–1004a; Alex. Aphr. in Mete. 362b10, p. 104, 17 H.
74–5 (... Ὀφιούχεον) Hi. 1.2.7, 1.4.11   77–9 (... τελέθοιεν) Hi. 1.5.21
79–80 (ἀτὰρ ...) Hi. 1.4.16   82 (... πεπονήαται) Hi. 1.4.17
85–6 (... ὀρθός) paraphr. Hi. 1.4.5   90 Att. p. 7; Hi. 1.4.18   91–2
(... Ἀρκτοφύλαξ) Hi. 1.2.5   96–7 (... Παρθένον) Hi. 1.2.5

---

71 ἀγαυὸν M^γρ sch. sch. A.R.: ἀγαυὸς MES sch. Alex. Aphr.   73
ὕπο στρέφεται scripsi: ὑποστρέφεται codd.   κεκμηότος MES:
κεκμηκότος C   79 εἰσωποὶ MS: ἰσωποὶ E   χέρες E: χεῖρες MS
μάλα ἶσαι ES: μάλ' ἶσαι M: μάλ' εἶσαι Hi.^B: μάλ' εἶσαι Buhle: μάλ'

[71] There too the famous Crown, which Dionysus established to be an illustrious memorial to the departed Ariadne, circles close to the back of the labouring figure.

The Crown is close to his back, but beside the top of his head observe the head of Ophiuchus, and from that you can identify the whole of Ophiuchus as clearly visible, [77] so bright are the brilliant shoulders that appear lying below his head: even in the light of the full moon these can be visible. But his hands are not equally bright; [80] for faint is the light that runs along this side and that; nevertheless even these are visible, for they are not dim. Both hands struggle to hold the Serpent that writhes round Ophiuchus' waist. He constantly, with a good firm stance, tramples with both his feet the great monster [85] Scorpion, standing upright on its eye and its breast. But the Serpent writhes in his two hands, a short section in his right, while large and high it rises in the left.

Now the point of the Serpent's jaw lies close to the Crown, but under its coil you can look for the great Claws, [90] though these are lack-lustre and not at all brilliant.

Behind Helice there comes, like a man driving, Arctophylax, whom men call Bootes, because he is seen to be just touching the Wagon-Bear. All of him is very conspicuous; below his belt circles Arcturus itself, a star distinct from the rest.

[96] Beneath the two feet of Bootes you can observe the

ἀῖσαι Hi.ᴬ   80 λεπτὴ γὰρ codd. Hi.: λεπτοτέρη Maass   καὶ τῇ καὶ τῇ D: τῇ καὶ τῇ MᵖᶜES Hi.ᴮ: καὶ τῇ Mᵃᶜ Hi.ᴬ   ἐπιδέδρομεν MES Hi.: ἐξεπιδέδρομεν T   81 ἐλαφραί MEʸᵖ: ἀμαυραί MˢˡE: ἀμυδραί K   82 ὄφιος MS: ὄφεος E   πεπονήαται ES: πεπονείαται M Hi.   τε μέσσον MEʸᵖ: τε μέσον S: μάλιστα E (del. fort. Planudes)   85 ὀφθαλμῷ codd. sch.: ὀφθαλμοῖς Maass   90 ἐπιδευέες codd. Hi.: ἐπιμεμφέες Att.   οὐδὲν ME: οὐ μὲν S   93 οὕνεχ' ἁμαξαίης MEᵃᶜ: οὕνεκ' ἀμ- Eᵖᶜ   94 ὑπὸ codd.: ἐπὶ Voss   96 ὑπο σκέπτοιο Maass: ὑποσκέπτοιο ME Hi.: ὑποσκέπτεο S: ὑποσκέψαιο Tˢˡ: ὕπο σκέψαιο Voss   βοώτεω MEᵃᶜ²S Hi.: βοώτου Eᵖᶜ

Παρθένον, ἥ ῥ' ἐν χειρὶ φέρει Στάχυν αἰγλήεντα.
εἴτ' οὖν Ἀστραίου κείνη γένος, ὅν ῥά τέ φασιν
ἄστρων ἀρχαῖον πατέρ' ἔμμεναι, εἴτε τευ ἄλλου,
100 εὔκηλος φορέοιτο. λόγος γε μὲν ἐντρέχει ἄλλος
ἀνθρώποις, ὡς δῆθεν ἐπιχθονίη πάρος ἦεν,
ἤρχετο δ' ἀνθρώπων κατεναντίη, οὐδέ ποτ' ἀνδρῶν
οὐδέ ποτ' ἀρχαίων ἠνήνατο φῦλα γυναικῶν,
ἀλλ' ἀναμὶξ ἐκάθητο καὶ ἀθανάτη περ ἐοῦσα.
105 καί ἑ Δίκην καλέεσκον· ἀγειρομένη δὲ γέροντας
ἠέ που εἰν ἀγορῇ ἢ εὐρυχόρῳ ἐν ἀγυιῇ,
δημοτέρας ἤειδεν ἐπισπέρχουσα θέμιστας.
οὔπω λευγαλέου τότε νείκεος ἠπίσταντο
οὐδὲ διακρίσιος περιμεμφέος οὐδὲ κυδοιμοῦ,
110 αὔτως δ' ἔζωον· χαλεπὴ δ' ἀπέκειτο θάλασσα,
καὶ βίον οὔπω νῆες ἀπόπροθεν ἠγίνεσκον,
ἀλλὰ βόες καὶ ἄροτρα καὶ αὐτὴ πότνια λαῶν
μυρία πάντα παρεῖχε Δίκη, δώτειρα δικαίων.
τόφρ' ἦν ὄφρ' ἔτι γαῖα γένος χρύσειον ἔφερβεν.
115 ἀργυρέῳ δ' ὀλίγη τε καὶ οὐκέτι πάμπαν ἑτοίμη
ὡμίλει, ποθέουσα παλαιῶν ἤθεα λαῶν.
ἀλλ' ἔμπης ἔτι κεῖνο κατ' ἀργύρεον γένος ἦεν,
ἤρχετο δ' ἐξ ὀρέων ὑποδείελος ἠχηέντων
μουνάξ, οὐδέ τεῳ ἐπεμίσγετο μειλιχίοισιν,
120 ἀλλ' ὁπότ' ἀνθρώπων μεγάλας πλήσαιτο κολώνας,
ἠπείλει δήπειτα καθαπτομένη κακότητος,
οὐδ' ἔτ' ἔφη εἰσωπὸς ἐλεύσεσθαι καλέουσιν·
"οἵην χρύσειοι πατέρες γενεὴν ἐλίποντο
χειροτέρην· ὑμεῖς δὲ κακώτερα τεξείεσθε.

98–9 (... ἔμμεναι) Ach. pp. 29, 85   100 (εὔκηλος φορέοιτο) A.D. *Adv.*
p. 148, 10 Schn.   108–13 Stob. 1.15.10   110 (χαλεπὴ...) Tz. in
Hes. *Op.* 163 Gaisford   114–15 Tz. *Ch.* 10.303   124 (ὑμεῖς...) Hes-
iodo perperam attrib. sch. Th. 3.67.2

---

97 χειρὶ Ε^γρS sch. (*manu* L): χερσὶ ΜΕ   99 ἀρχαῖον Μ Ach.^M:
ἀρχαίων ES Ach.: ἀρχαῖοι Frieseman 161   101 ἀνθρώποις Α: -ους
MES: -ων Μ^sl   102 κατεναντίη ΜΕ: κατ' ἐναντίον S   104 uersum

Maiden, who carries in her hand the radiant Spica. Whether she is the daughter of Astraeus, who, they say, was the original father of the stars, or of some other, [100] may her way be peaceful! There is, however, another tale current among men, that once she actually lived on earth, and came face to face with men, and did not ever spurn the tribes of ancient men and women, but sat in their midst although she was immortal. [105] And they called her Justice: gathering together the elders, either in the market-place or on the broad highway, she urged them in prophetic tones to judgements for the good of the people. At that time they still had no knowledge of painful strife or quarrelsome conflict or noise of battle, [110] but lived just as they were; the dangerous sea was far from their thoughts, and as yet no ships brought them livelihood from afar, but oxen and ploughs and Justice herself, queen of the people and giver of civilised life, provided all their countless needs. That was as long as the earth still nurtured the Golden Age. [115] But with the Silver she associated little, and now not at all willingly, as she longed for the ways of the earlier folk. But nevertheless she was still with this Silver Age too. She would emerge from the sounding mountains towards evening all alone, and not engage anyone in friendly conversation. [120] But filling the broad hillsides with people, she would then speak menacingly, rebuking them for their wickedness, and say she would never more come face to face with them, even if they called her: 'What an inferior generation your golden

---

om. et in mg. suppl. M   107 ἐπισπέρχουσα ΜΕ: ἐπισπεύδουσα S   109 περιμεμφέος ΜΕS sch. Stob.: πολυμεμφέος Μʸᵖ sch.   110 ἀπέκειτο codd.: ἐπέκειτο Tzetzes   111 ἀπόπροθεν ΜᵃᶜΕS: ἀπόπροθι Μᵖᶜ   115 ἑτοίμη ΜΕʸᵖS: ὁμοίη Ε Tzetzes   119 οὐδέ τεῳ ΜΕ: οὐδέ τῳ S: οὐδ' ἑτέρῳ Αᵖᶜ   121 δήπειτα Maass: δ' ἤπειτα ΜΕS: δή 'πειτα Voss: δὴ ἔπειτα Bekker   122 εἰσωπὸς ΜS: ἰσωπὸς Ε   καλέουσιν ΜΕS: χατέουσιν Αᵖᶜ   124 τεξείεσθε ΜΕ: τ' ἐξείεσθε S: τέκν' εἴσεσθε Voss: τῆς τέξεσθε Buttmann: τέκνα τεκεῖσθε Kaibel 950

125 καὶ δή που πόλεμοι, καὶ δὴ καὶ ἀνάρσιον αἷμα
ἔσσεται ἀνθρώποισι, κακῶν δ᾽ ἐπικείσεται ἄλγος."
ὡς εἰποῦσ᾽ ὀρέων ἐπεμαίετο, τοὺς δ᾽ ἄρα λαοὺς
εἰς αὐτὴν ἔτι πάντας ἐλίμπανε παπταίνοντας.
ἀλλ᾽ ὅτε δὴ κἀκεῖνοι ἐτέθνασαν, οἱ δ᾽ ἐγένοντο
130 χαλκείη γενεὴ προτέρων ὀλοώτεροι ἄνδρες,
οἳ πρῶτοι κακοεργὸν ἐχαλκεύσαντο μάχαιραν
εἰνοδίην, πρῶτοι δὲ βοῶν ἐπάσαντ᾽ ἀροτήρων,
καὶ τότε μισήσασα Δίκη κείνων γένος ἀνδρῶν
ἔπταθ᾽ ὑπουρανίη, ταύτην δ᾽ ἄρα νάσσατο χώρην,
135 ἧχί περ ἐννυχίη ἔτι φαίνεται ἀνθρώποισι
Παρθένος ἐγγὺς ἐοῦσα πολυσκέπτοιο Βοώτεω.
   τῆς ὑπὲρ ἀμφοτέρων ὤμων εἰλίσσεται ἀστὴρ
[δεξιτερῇ πτέρυγι· Προτρυγητὴρ δ᾽ αὖτε καλεῖται·]
τόσσος μὲν μεγέθει, τοίη δ᾽ ἐγκείμενος αἴγλῃ,
140 οἷος καὶ μεγάλης οὐρὴν ὕπο φαίνεται Ἄρκτου.
δεινὴ γὰρ κείνη, δεινοὶ δέ οἱ ἐγγύθεν εἰσὶν
ἀστέρες· οὐκ ἂν τούς γε ἰδὼν ἔτι τεκμήραιο,
οἷός οἱ πρὸ ποδῶν φέρεται καλός τε μέγας τε
εἷς μὲν ὑπωμαίων, εἷς δ᾽ ἰξυόθεν κατιόντων,
145 ἄλλος δ᾽ οὐραίοις ὑπὸ γούνασιν· ἀλλ᾽ ἄρα πάντες
ἁπλόοι ἄλλοθεν ἄλλος ἀνωνυμίη φορέονται.
   κρατὶ δέ οἱ Δίδυμοι, μέσσῃ δ᾽ ὕπο Καρκίνος ἐστί,
ποσσὶ δ᾽ ὀπισθοτέροισι Λέων ὕπο καλὰ φαείνει.

---

125 sch. A. *Pr.* 191a   130–2 Stob. 1.9.2   131 (κακοεργὸν ...) Lucill.
AP 11.136.1   131–2 Plu. 998a; Max. Tyr. 24.1   143–5 (... γούνασιν) Hi. 1.2.9   143–4 Hi. 1.5.5   147–8 Hi. 1.2.9, 1.5.1   148
sch. Call. fr. 110.65–8   149–51 Hi. 2.1.18; sch. (D) E 385 p. 160a
Bekker

---

125 καὶ δὴ καὶ ME^{sl}S: καὶ δή που E: καὶ δὴ H   ἀνάρσιον codd.:
ἀνάρθμιον sch. A. *Pr.*   126 ἔσσεται ME: ἔσεται S: ἔσσετ᾽ ἐν K:
εἴσετ᾽ ἐν V   κακὸν ME: κακὸν M^{sl}: κακοῦ S: κακοῖς T: τινων A^{pc}
ἐπικείσεται MES: οὐκ ἔσσεται M^{sl}   ἄλγος ME: ἀλκή M^{sl}   128
ἔτι πάντας ME: ἔτι πάνπαν M^{sl}: ἐπιπάνπαν A^{pc}: ἔτι πάμπαν
S   129 ἐτέθνασαν ME: ἐτέθνεσαν S   131 κακοεργὸν codd.:

fathers have left! And you are likely to beget a still more evil progeny. [125] There will surely be wars, yes, and unnatural bloodshed among men, and suffering from their troubles will come upon them.' So saying she made for the mountains, and left the people all staring after her. But when these men also had died and there were born [130] the Bronze Age men, more destructive than their predecessors, who were the first to forge the criminal sword for murder on the highways, and the first to taste the flesh of ploughing oxen, then Justice, conceiving a hatred for the generation of these men, flew up to the sky and took up her abode in that place, [135] where she is still visible to men by night as the Maiden near conspicuous Bootes.

Above her two shoulders there circles a star [on her right wing: it is called again the Vintager], of similar magnitude and inset with a brightness equal to [140] that of the star which can be seen beneath the tail of the Great Bear. Impressive is the Bear, and impressive are the stars that she has nearby: once you have sighted them, you do not need any other guide, such are the stars that in beauty and magnitude move before her feet, one in front of the forelegs, one before the legs that descend from her loins, [145] and another under the hind knees. But all of them, individually in different positions, go on their way without a name.

Beneath the Bear's head are the Twins, beneath her belly the Crab, and under her hind legs the Lion shines

---

χαλκοεργὸν Stob.   133 καὶ codd.: δὴ Maass   134 ἔπταθ' ὑπουρανίη MS (sub caelo L): ἔπτατ' ἐπουρανίη E   ἄρα νάσσατο ME: ἄρ' ἐνάσσατο A: ἄρ ἐνάσσατο S   136 βοώτεω MS: βοώτου E   138 uersum om. L: del. Voss   140 οἷος ME: om. S   μεγάλης MˢⁱE: μεγάλην MS   ὗπο φ- E coni. Maass: ὑποφ- MS   142 ἔτι τεκμήραιο Voss: ἐπιτεκμήραιο MS: ἐπὶ τεκμήραιο E   143 οἷός MES sch. Hi. 1.5.5: τοῖος A Hi. 1.2.9   145 ἄλλος δ' codd.: οἱ δ' ἄρα M. Schmidt   146 ἄλλος ES: δ' ἄλλος M   147 ὗπο E coni. Maass: ὑπὸ M: ὗπο S   148 ὗπο Maass: ὑπὸ E: ὗπο MS

ΦΑΙΝΟΜΕΝΑ

ἔνθα μὲν ἠελίοιο θερείταταί εἰσι κέλευθοι,
150 αἱ δέ που ἀσταχύων κενεαὶ φαίνονται ἄρουραι
ἠελίου τὰ πρῶτα συνερχομένοιο Λέοντι.
τῆμος καὶ κελάδοντες ἐτησίαι εὐρέϊ πόντῳ
ἀθρόοι ἐμπίπτουσιν, ὁ δὲ πλόος οὐκέτι κώπαις
ὥριος. εὐρεῖαί μοι ἀρέσκοιεν τότε νῆες,
155 εἰς ἄνεμον δὲ τὰ πηδὰ κυβερνητῆρες ἔχοιεν.
εἰ δέ τοι Ἡνίοχόν τε καὶ ἀστέρας Ἡνιόχοιο
σκέπτεσθαι δοκέοι καί τοι φάτις ἤλυθεν Αἰγὸς
αὐτῆς ἠδ᾽ Ἐρίφων, οἵ τ᾽ εἰν ἀλὶ πορφυρούσῃ
πολλάκις ἐσκέψαντο κεδαιομένους ἀνθρώπους,
160 αὐτὸν μέν μιν ἅπαντα μέγαν Διδύμων ἐπὶ λαιὰ
κεκλιμένον δήεις· Ἑλίκης δέ οἱ ἄκρα κάρηνα
ἀντία δινεύει. σκαιῷ δ᾽ ἐπελήλαται ὤμῳ
Αἲξ ἱερή, τὴν μέν τε λόγος Διὶ μαζὸν ἐπισχεῖν·
Ὠλενίην δέ μιν Αἶγα Διὸς καλέουσ᾽ ὑποφῆται.
165 ἀλλ᾽ ἡ μὲν πολλή τε καὶ ἀγλαή· οἱ δέ οἱ αὐτοῦ
λεπτὰ φαείνονται Ἔριφοι καρπὸν κάτα χειρός.
πὰρ ποσὶ δ᾽ Ἡνιόχου κεραὸν πεπτηότα Ταῦρον
μαίεσθαι. τὰ δέ οἱ μάλ᾽ ἐοικότα σήματα κεῖται,
τοίη οἱ κεφαλὴ διακέκριται· οὐδέ τις ἄλλῳ
170 σήματι τεκμήραιτο κάρη βοός, οἷά μιν αὐτοὶ
ἀστέρες ἀμφοτέρωθεν ἑλισσόμενοι τυπόωσι.
καὶ λίην κείνων ὄνομ᾽ εἴρεται, οὐδέ τοι αὔτως
νήκουστοι Ὑάδες, ταὶ μέν ῥ᾽ ἐπὶ παντὶ μετώπῳ
Ταύρου βεβλέαται· λαιοῦ δὲ κεράατος ἄκρον
175 καὶ πόδα δεξιτερὸν παρακειμένου Ἡνιόχοιο
εἷς ἀστὴρ ἐπέχει, συνεληλάμενοι δὲ φέρονται.
ἀλλ᾽ αἰεὶ Ταῦρος προφερέστερος Ἡνιόχοιο

149 Et.M. 447, 8; Zonar. Lex. p. 1031 Tittmann   151–3 (... ἐμπίπτουσιν) sch. A.R. 2.498   151 Plu. 366A   155 (... πηδὰ) Str. 8.5.3
161–2 (Ἑλίκης ... δινεύει) Hi. 1.2.10   163–4 Str. 8.7.5   174–6
(λαιοῦ ... ἐπέχει) Hi. 1.2.10, 1.10.4   177–8 Hi. 1.5.14

150 φαίνονται MS: φορέονται E   151 ἠελίου ... λέοντι codd.: ἠελίῳ

brightly. This is where the sun's track is hottest, [150] and the fields are seen bereft of their corn-ears when the sun first comes into conjunction with the Lion. This is the time when the whistling etesian winds sweep strongly across the broad sea, and it is no longer seasonable for ships to be under oars. Then let broad-beamed ships be my pleasure, [155] and let helmsmen hold their steering-oars into the wind.

If you are minded to observe the Charioteer and the Charioteer's stars, and rumour has reached you of the Goat herself and the Kids, who have often looked down on men being tossed upon the heaving sea, [160] you will find the Charioteer lying large to the left of the Twins, while opposite Helice circles his head at that extremity. Fastened to his left shoulder is the sacred Goat, who is said to have tendered her breast to Zeus: the interpreters of Zeus call her the Olenian Goat. [165] Now she is large and brilliant, but her Kids there on the Charioteer's wrist shine faintly.

Near the feet of the Charioteer look for the horned Bull crouching. This constellation is very recognisable, so clearly defined is its head: one needs no other [170] sign to identify the ox's head, so well do the stars themselves model both sides of it as they go round. Their name is also very popular: the Hyades are not just nameless. They are set out all along the Bull's face; the point of its left horn [175] and the right foot of the adjacent Charioteer are occupied by a single star, and they are pinned together as they go. But the Bull is always ahead of the Charioteer in sinking

---

... λέοντος nonnulli in sch.   155 τὰ codd. sch. Strabo: τε Maass   157 δοκέοι MS^{sl}: δοκέει ES (uidetur L)   158 ἠδ' codd.: ἢ Kaibel 951   πορφυρούσῃ ΜΕ: πορφυρεούσῃ S   159 κεδαιομένους ΜΕS: κεραιομένους Ε^{γρ}S^{γρ} sch.^{γρ} 163 ἐπισχεῖν codd.: ὑποσχεῖν Strabonis Eton. et Par.   166 κάτα Voss: κατὰ codd.   170 αὐτοὶ ΜΕ: αὐτὸν S   172 ὄνομ' ES: οὔνομ' Μ   174 ταύρου ΜΕ^{sl}S: ταύρῳ Ε   175 παρακειμένου Hi. 1.10.4: -κείμενον codd. Hi. 1.2.10

εἰς ἑτέρην καταβῆναι, ὁμηλυσίῃ περ ἀνελθών.
    οὐδ᾽ ἄρα Κηφῆος μογερὸν γένος Ἰασίδαο
180 αὔτως ἄρρητον κατακείσεται, ἀλλ᾽ ἄρα καὶ τῶν
οὐρανὸν εἰς ὄνομ᾽ ἦλθεν, ἐπεὶ Διὸς ἐγγύθεν ἦσαν.
αὐτὸς μὲν κατόπισθεν ἐὼν Κυνοσουρίδος Ἄρκτου
Κηφεὺς ἀμφοτέρας χεῖρας τανύοντι ἔοικεν·
ἴση οἱ στάθμη νεάτης ἀποτείνεται οὐρῆς
185 ἐς πόδας ἀμφοτέρους, ὅσση ποδὸς ἐς πόδα τείνει.
αὐτὰρ ἀπὸ ζώνης ὀλίγον κε μεταβλέψειας
πρώτης ἱέμενος καμπῆς μεγάλοιο Δράκοντος.
    τοῦ δ᾽ ἄρα δαιμονίη προκυλίνδεται οὐ μάλα πολλῇ
νυκτὶ φαεινομένη παμμήνιδι Κασσιέπεια·
190 οὐ γάρ μιν πολλοὶ καὶ ἐπημοιβοὶ γανόωσιν
ἀστέρες, οἵ μιν πᾶσαν ἐπιρρήδην στιχόωσιν.
οἵη δὲ κληῖδι θύρην ἔντοσθ᾽ ἀραρυῖαν
δικλίδα πεπλήγοντες ἀνακρούουσιν ὀχῆας,
τοῖοί οἱ μουνὰξ ὑποκείμενοι ἰνδάλλονται
195 ἀστέρες. ἡ δ᾽ αὔτως ὀλίγων ἀποτείνεται ὤμων
ὀργυιήν· φαίης κεν ἀνιάζειν ἐπὶ παιδί.
    αὐτοῦ γὰρ κἀκεῖνο κυλίνδεται αἰνὸν ἄγαλμα
Ἀνδρομέδης ὑπὸ μητρὶ κεκασμένον. οὔ σε μάλ᾽ οἴω
νύκτα περισκέψεσθαι, ἵν᾽ αὐτίκα μᾶλλον ἴδηαι·
200 τοίη οἱ κεφαλή, τοῖοι δέ οἱ ἀμφοτέρωθεν
ὦμοι καὶ πόδες ἀκρότατοι καὶ ζώματα πάντα.
ἀλλ᾽ ἔμπης κἀκεῖθι διωλενίη τετάνυσται,
δεσμὰ δέ οἱ κεῖται καὶ ἐν οὐρανῷ· αἱ δ᾽ ἀνέχονται
αὐτοῦ πεπταμέναι πάντ᾽ ἤματα χεῖρες ἐκείνῃ.

---

179 Hippol. 4.48.14   184–7 Hi. 1.2.12   184–5 Hi. 1.5.19   188–
90 (οὐ μάλα ...) Hi. 1.5.21   188–9 Hi. 1.2.14   188 (... προκυλίνδεται) Hi. 1.5.20   197–8 (... κεκασμένον) Hi. 1.2.14   198–201 (οὔ
σε ...) Hi. 1.5.22

---

179 μογερὸν MES: ἱερὸν V   180 κατακείσεται codd.: -κείαται
Maass   182 ἐὼν MES: ἰὼν V   183 ἔοικεν Martin: ἐοικὼς codd.
184 οὐρῆς MEHi. 1.1.12: Ἄρκτου M^{γρ}S Hi. 1.5.19 (Arcturi L)   185 ἐς

to the horizon, though it rises simultaneously.

Nor will the suffering family of Cepheus, son of Iasius,
[180] be just left unmentioned: their name also has reached
the sky, for they were akin to Zeus. Behind the Bear Cynosura Cepheus himself is like a man stretching out both his
arms. The line that extends from the tip of her tail to each
of his feet equals the distance from foot to foot. [186] And
you have only to look a little way past his belt if you are
searching for the first coil of the great Dragon.

In front of him revolves the tragic Cassiepeia, not very
large, but visible on the night of a full moon; [190] only a
few zigzagging stars adorn her, giving her all over a distinct outline. Like to a key with which men attacking a
double door barred on the inside knock back the bolts,
[194] such is the appearance of the individual stars that
together comprise her. She extends outstretched arms just
from her small shoulders: you would say she was grieving
over her daughter.

There too revolves that awesome figure of Andromeda,
well defined beneath her mother. I do not think you will
have to look all round the night sky in order to sight her
very quickly, [200] so clear are her head, the shoulders on
either side, the feet at her extremity, and all her girdle.
Even there, however, she is extended with outstretched
arms, and bonds are laid on her even in the sky; those
arms of hers are raised and out-spread there all the time.

prius MS: εἰς E   187 πρώτης EˢˡS Hi.ᴮ: πρώτην ME   καμπῆς
EˢˡS Hi.: καμπὴν ME   μεγάλοιο MES (magni L): σκολιοῖο Q
Hi.   190 οὐ MEᵖᶜS: ἦ Eᵃᶜ   191 πᾶσαν ME: πάμπαν S: πάντες A
192–6 om. L   192 οἴη Grotius: οἵην codd.   193 δικλίδα πεπλήγοντες EʸᵖS: δικλίδ' ἐπιπλήσσοντες ME   ὀχῆας Voss: ὀχῆες codd.
194 τοῖοι MᵖᶜES: τοῖον Mᵃᶜ   195 αὕτως S: αὐτῶν ME   ὀλίγων
M: -ον MʸᵖE?(littera erasa)S   ἀποτείνεται ME: ἀνατείνεται EˢˡS
196 ὀργυιὴν ES: ὀργυήν M: ὄργυιαν P coni. Voss   198 κεκασμένον
codd. Hi.: κεκομμένον sch.ʸᵖ   199 περισκέψεσθαι Martin: -σκέ-
ψασθαι codd.   204 ἐκείνη Voss: ἐκεῖναι codd.

205 ἀλλ' ἄρα οἱ καὶ κρατὶ πέλωρ ἐπελήλαται Ἵππος
γαστέρι νειαίρῃ, ξυνὸς δ' ἐπιλάμπεται ἀστὴρ
τοῦ μὲν ἐπ' ὀμφαλίῳ, τῆς δ' ἐσχατόωντι καρήνῳ.
οἱ δ' ἄρ' ἔτι τρεῖς ἄλλοι ἐπὶ πλευράς τε καὶ ὤμους
Ἵππου δεικανόωσι διασταδὸν ἶσα πέλεθρα,
210 καλοὶ καὶ μεγάλοι. κεφαλὴ δέ οἱ οὐδὲν ὁμοίη,
οὐδ' αὐχὴν δολιχός περ ἐών· ἀτὰρ ἔσχατος ἀστὴρ
αἰθομένης γένυος καί κε προτέροις ἐρίσειε
τέτρασιν, οἵ μιν ἔχουσι περίσκεπτοι μάλ' ἐόντες.
οὐδ' ὅ γε τετράπος ἐστίν· ἀπ' ὀμφαλίοιο γὰρ ἄκρου
215 μεσσόθεν ἡμιτελὴς περιτέλλεται ἱερὸς Ἵππος.
κεῖνον δὴ καί φασι καθ' ὑψηλοῦ Ἑλικῶνος
καλὸν ὕδωρ ἀγαγεῖν εὐαλδέος Ἵππου κρήνης.
οὐ γάρ πω Ἑλικὼν ἄκρος κατελείβετο πηγαῖς,
ἀλλ' Ἵππος μιν ἔτυψε, τὸ δ' ἀθρόον αὐτόθεν ὕδωρ
220 ἐξέχυτο πληγῇ προτέρου ποδός· οἱ δὲ νομῆες
πρῶτοι κεῖνο ποτὸν διεφήμισαν Ἵππου κρήνην.
ἀλλὰ τὸ μὲν πέτρης ἀπολείβεται, οὐδέ ποτ' αὐτὸ
Θεσπιέων ἀνδρῶν ἑκὰς ὄψεαι· αὐτὰρ ὅ γ' Ἵππος
ἐν Διὸς εἰλεῖται καί τοι πάρα θηήσασθαι.
225 αὐτοῦ καὶ Κριοῖο θοώταταί εἰσι κέλευθοι,
ὅς ῥά τε καὶ μήκιστα διωκόμενος περὶ κύκλα
οὐδὲν ἀφαυρότερον τροχάει Κυνοσουρίδος Ἄρκτου.
αὐτὸς μὲν νωθὴς καὶ ἀνάστερος οἷα σελήνη
σκέψασθαι, ζώνῃ δ' ἂν ὅμως ἐπιτεκμήραιο
230 Ἀνδρομέδης· ὀλίγον γὰρ ὑπ' αὐτὴν ἐστήρικται.
μεσσόθι δὲ τρίβει μέγαν οὐρανόν, ἧχί περ ἄκραι
Χηλαὶ καὶ ζώνη περιτέλλεται Ὠρίωνος.

206–7 (ξυνὸς ...) Hi. 1.2.14   215 (ἡμιτελής) Tauro perperam attrib.
sch. Nic. *Ther.* 123   223–4 (αὐτὰρ ... εἰλεῖται) sch. (B) Germ. p. 56
Br.   224 (... εἰλεῖται) sch. (T) Φ 444a; Epimer. Hom. 5 *An. Ox.* i.169
Cr.   225–7 Phlp. *in Mete.* A 3 p. 41, A 8 p. 112 H.   225 Hi. 1.6.6;
Heliodori comm. in D.T. p. 99 Hilgard; A.D. *Adv.* 176.21 Schn.;
(... Κριοῖο) ibid. 207.10   226–7 sch. (T) Σ 488b; sch. (B) Σ 488 p.

[205] Now the monster Horse is actually pinned to her head by its lower belly: there shines a star that is common to its navel and the head at her extremity. The three other stars mark off lines of equal length upon the flanks and shoulders of the Horse; [210] they are beautiful and bright. Its head is not at all comparable, nor its neck, though it is long. But the end star on its shining mouth could well rival the former four, which outline it so very conspicuously. But it is no quadruped; at its navel edge [215] the sacred Horse is halved in the middle as it goes round. This was the Horse, they say, that from the heights of Helicon produced the good water of fertilising Hippocrene. The summit of Helicon was not then flowing with streams, but the Horse struck it, and from that very spot a flood of water [220] gushed out at the stroke of its forefoot; the shepherds were the first to call that draught the Horse's Spring. So the water wells out of a rock, and you can see it never far from the men of Thespiae; but the Horse revolves in the realm of Zeus and you may view it there.

[225] There too are the paths of the Ram, the swiftest because it speeds round the longest circle and yet does not lag behind the Bear Cynosura as it runs. The Ram itself is faint and starless, as if observed by moonlight, but you can still identify it from the girdle of Andromeda: for it is set a little way below her. [231] It traverses the great sky centrally, where the tips of the Claws and Orion's belt revolve.

507b Bekker   228–30 Hi. 1.6.6   229–30 (ζώνη. . .) Hi. 1.2.14
231–2 Hi. 1.6.11

---

209 πέλεθρα MES: κέλευθα Μ^{γρ}   212 κε S: κεν ΜΕ   217 ἵππου
κρήνης codd.: Ἱπποκρήνης Voss   218 τω ΜΕ^{ρc}S: που Ε^{ac}   221
ἵππου κρήνην codd.: Ἱπποκρήνην Bekker   222 ἀπολείβεται MES:
ἀπομαίεται Μ^{γρ}   223 ὃ γ' Buttmann: ὁ codd.   224 ἐν διὸς ES:
ἔνδιος M Diodorus in sch.   229 ὅμως M^{sl} Hi.: ὁμῶς MES

ἔστι δέ τοι καὶ ἔτ' ἄλλο τετυγμένον ἐγγύθι σῆμα
νειόθεν Ἀνδρομέδης· τὸ δ' ἐπὶ τρισὶν ἐστάθμηται
235 Δελτωτὸν πλευρῆσιν, ἰσαιομένησιν ἐοικός
ἀμφοτέραις· ἡ δ' οὔτι τόση, μάλα δ' ἐστὶν ἑτοίμη
εὑρέσθαι· περὶ γὰρ λοιπῶν εὐάστερός ἐστι.
τῶν ὀλίγον Κριοῦ νοτιώτεροι ἀστέρες εἰσίν.
οἱ δ' ἄρ' ἔτι προτέρω, ἔτι δ' ἐν προμολῇσι νότοιο
240 Ἰχθύες· ἀλλ' αἰεὶ ἕτερος προφερέστερος ἄλλου
καὶ μᾶλλον βορέαο νέον κατιόντος ἀκούει.
ἀμφοτέρων δέ σφεων ἀποτείνεται ἠΰτε δεσμὰ
οὐραίων ἑκάτερθεν ἐπισχερὼ εἰς ἓν ἰόντα.
καὶ τὰ μὲν εἰς ἀστὴρ ἐπέχει καλός τε μέγας τε,
245 ὅν ῥά τε καὶ Σύνδεσμον ὑπουράνιον καλέουσιν.
Ἀνδρομέδης δέ τοι ὦμος ἀριστερὸς Ἰχθύος ἔστω
σῆμα βορειοτέρου· μάλα γάρ νύ οἱ ἐγγύθεν ἐστίν.
ἀμφότεροι δὲ πόδες γαμβροῦ ἐπισημαίνοιεν
Περσέος, οἵ ῥά οἱ αἰὲν ἐπωμάδιοι φορέονται.
250 αὐτὰρ ὅ γ' ἐν βορέω φέρεται περιμήκετος ἄλλων.
καί οἱ δεξιτερὴ μὲν ἐπὶ κλισμὸν τετάνυσται
πενθερίου δίφροιο· τὰ δ' ἐν ποσὶν οἷα διώκων
ἴχνια μηκύνει κεκονιμένος ἐν Διὶ πατρί.
ἄγχι δέ οἱ σκαιῆς ἐπιγουνίδος ἤλιθα πᾶσαι
255 Πληϊάδες φορέονται· ὁ δ' οὐ μάλα πολλὸς ἁπάσας
χῶρος ἔχει, καὶ δ' αὐταὶ ἐπισκέψασθαι ἀφαυραί.
ἑπτάποροι δὴ ταί γε μετ' ἀνθρώπους ὑδέονται,
ἓξ οἷαί περ ἐοῦσαι ἐπόψιαι ὀφθαλμοῖσιν.
οὐ μέν πως ἀπόλωλεν ἀπευθὴς ἐκ Διὸς ἀστήρ,

---

233 + 235–8 Hi. 1.6.6   239–40 (... Ἰχθύες) Hi. 1.6.8   245 (Σύνδεσμον ὑπούραιον) Hyg. 3.29   246–7 Hi. 1.2.14   248–9 Hi. 1.2.15
251–2 (... δίφροιο) Hi. 1.2.15, 1.4.11   253 (κεκονιμένος) Hyg. 3.11.2
bis   254–5 Hi. 1.2.15; (... φορέονται) 1.4.11, 1.6.12   257–61 Ath. 11
492B–C   257–8 sch. Pi. N. 2.17a   258 + 261–3 (ἑπτὰ ...) Tz. in Lyc.
p. 102 Scheer   258 (... ἐπόψιαι) Hi. 1.6.14

---

233 ἔτ' S Hi.: om. ME   234 ἐστάθμηται ES: ἐστάλμαται M: ἐστήρικται Mᵞᵖ   236 ἀμφοτέραις E Hi.ᴮ: ἀμφοτέρης MS: ἀμφοτέρησ' D

There is yet another constellation formed near by beneath Andromeda: [235] the Triangle is measured out on three sides, recognisably isosceles; the third side is shorter, but it is very easy to find, for it is well starred compared to the other two. Its stars are a little to the south of those of the Ram.

Still farther ahead and more in the approaches to the south [240] are the Fishes; but one is always more prominent than the other and hears more the fresh onset of the north wind. From both of them stretch, as it were, chains from the tail-parts, coming together in an unbroken line on both sides. One beautiful bright star occupies this position, [245] and they call it the celestial Knot. Let Andromeda's left shoulder be your guide to the more northerly Fish, for it is very close to it.

The two feet of Andromeda will be pointers to her suitor Perseus, as they move for ever above his shoulders. [250] He runs taller than other figures in the north. His right hand is stretched out towards his bride's mother's chairseat, and as if on some immediate pursuit he takes long strides as he runs in the realm of his father Zeus.

Near his left knee all in a cluster [255] the Pleiades move. The space that holds them all is not great, and they are individually faint to observe. Seven in number they are in the lore of men, although there are only six apparent to the eye. No star at all has been lost from our ken in Zeus

---

237 λοιπῶν scripsi: πολέων codd. Hi. (*urbium* L): τ' ἀλλέων Voss
239 προμολῇσι MS sch. (S) sch. (MD) 240: προβολῇσι E sch. (AV) 240
Hi.   243 οὐραίων codd.: οὐράων Maass   ἰόντα Voss: ἰόντων
codd.   245 ὑπουράνιον Hyg.: ὑπούραιον M^{mg}S: ὑπούραῖον (sic)
M: ὑπουραῖον E   248 ἐπισημαίνοιεν codd.: ἐπιδινεύονται Hi.^B
249 περσέος E: -έως M Hi.^A: -ῆος Hi.^B: -ες S   253 κεκονιμένος MES:
κεκονημένος C: κεκονισμένος Hyg.   254 ἐπιγουνίδος codd. Hi.:
ὑπογουνίδος Diodorus in sch.   257 μετ' ἀνθρώπους MES sch.: μετ'
ἀνθρώποις C Ath.: ἐν ἀνθρώποις V: ἐπ' ἀνθρώποισι A: κατ' ἀνθρώπους sch. Pi.

ΦΑΙΝΟΜΕΝΑ

260 ἐξ οὗ καὶ γενεῆθεν ἀκούομεν, ἀλλὰ μάλ' αὕτως
εἴρεται. ἑπτὰ δὲ κεῖναι ἐπιρρήδην καλέονται
Ἀλκυόνη Μερόπη τε Κελαινώ τ' Ἠλέκτρη τε
καὶ Στερόπη καὶ Τηϋγέτη καὶ πότνια Μαῖα.
αἱ μὲν ὁμῶς ὀλίγαι καὶ ἀφεγγέες, ἀλλ' ὀνομασταὶ
265 ἦρι καὶ ἑσπέριαι, Ζεὺς δ' αἴτιος, εἰλίσσονται,
ὅ σφισι καὶ θέρεος καὶ χείματος ἀρχομένοιο
σημαίνειν ἐπένευσεν ἐπερχομένου τ' ἀρότοιο.
    καὶ χέλυς ἐστ' ὀλίγη· τὴν δ' ἄρ' ἔτι καὶ παρὰ λίκνῳ
Ἑρμείης ἐτόρησε, Λύρην δέ μιν εἶπε λέγεσθαι.
270 κὰδ δ' ἔθετο προπάροιθεν ἀπευθέος εἰδώλοιο
οὐρανὸν εἰσαγαγών. τὸ δ' ἐπὶ σκελέεσσι πέτηλον
γούνατί οἱ σκαιῷ πελάει, κεφαλῇ γε μὲν ἄκρη
ἀντιπέρην Ὄρνιθος ἑλίσσεται· ἡ δὲ μεσηγὺ
ὀρνιθέης κεφαλῆς καὶ γούνατος ἐστήρικται.
275 ἤτοι γὰρ καὶ Ζηνὶ παρατρέχει αἰόλος Ὄρνις,
ἄλλοθεν ἠερόεις, τὰ δέ οἱ ἔπι τετρήχυνται
ἀστράσιν οὔτι λίην μεγάλοις, ἀτὰρ οὐ μὲν ἀφαυροῖς.
αὐτὰρ ὅ γ' εὐδιόωντι ποτὴν ὄρνιθι ἐοικὼς
οὔριος εἰς ἑτέρην φέρεται, κατὰ δεξιὰ χειρὸς
280 Κηφείης ταρσοῖο τὰ δεξιὰ πείρατα τείνων·
λαιῇ δὲ πτέρυγι σκαρθμὸς παρακέκλιται Ἵππου.
    τὸν δὲ μετασκαίροντα δύ' Ἰχθύες ἀμφινέμονται
Ἵππον. πὰρ δ' ἄρα οἱ κεφαλῇ χεὶρ Ὑδροχόοιο
δεξιτερὴ τάνυται· ὁ δ' ὀπίστερος Αἰγοκερῆος
285 τέλλεται. αὐτὰρ ὅ γε πρότερος καὶ νειόθι μᾶλλον

---

261 (ἑπτὰ ...) Hi. 1.6.14; Eust. in τ 71   264–7 Ath. 11 490A   268–
9 (τὴν...) Hippol. 4.48.2   270–2 (... πελάει) Hi. 1.4.12   270 Hi. 1.5.20
272 (... πελάει) Hi. 1.4.11   276–7 Hi. 1.6.15   279–81 (κατὰ ...) Hi.
1.2.16, 1.10.7   279–80 (κατὰ ...) Hi. 1.4.11   281 (σκαρθμὸς) sch.
Theoc. 4.19

---

261 δὲ κεῖναι MS: δ' ἐκεῖναι E Hi. Ath. Tz.   264 ὁμῶς MES: ὁμοῦ K:
ὅμως P coni. Voss   266 ὅ σφισι P: ὃ σφισι V: ὅς σφισι ME: ὅς φησι S
267 ἐπένευσεν Ath.: ἐκέλευσεν codd.   268 χέλυς ἐστ' scripsi: χέλυς ἦτ'

[260] since our oral tradition began, but this is just what is said. Those seven are called by name Alcyone, Merope, Celaeno and Electra, Sterope, Taygete and honoured Maia. All alike they are small and faint, but they are famous [265] in their movements at morning and evening, and Zeus is the cause, in that he authorised them to mark the beginnings of summer and winter and the onset of ploughing time.

The Tortoise too is small; when Hermes was actually still in his cradle, he hollowed out the shell and bade it be called a Lyre. [270] He set it down in front of the unknown figure, when he had brought it to the sky. The figure, as he crouches, comes near it with his left knee, while the Bird's head at one extremity circles opposite it: the Lyre is set fast between the Bird's head and the knee.

[275] Yes, there is even a dappled Bird accompanying Zeus, hazy in some parts, while other parts on it bristle with stars, not very bright, though still not dim. Just like a bird in fair-weather flight, it glides on the breeze towards the horizon, stretching its right wing-tip in the direction of Cepheus' right hand, [281] while close to its left wing lies the prancing Horse.

The two Fishes range about the Horse as it prances among them. Beside the Horse's head the right hand of the Water-pourer stretches out: he rises after Capricorn. Capricorn lies ahead and lower down, where the powerful

MES: χέλυς ἠδ' Voss: δὲ χέλυς Buttmann: χέλυς ἦν Kaibel 951   τὴν δ' codd.: τήνδ' Voss   ἄρ' Bekker: ἄρ MS: ἄρ' E   269 ἑρμείης E: ἑρμήεις M: ἑρμείας S   271 εἰσαγαγών codd.: εἰς ἀγαγών Maass 276 ἄλλοθεν scripsi: ἀλλ' ὁ μὲν codd. Hi.: ἄλλα μὲν Martin   ἔπι τετρήχυνται Voss: ἐπιτετρήχυνται codd. Hi.^A: ἐπιτετρήχαται (ην paenult. suprascr.) Hi.^B: πτερὰ τετρήχυνται K: ἐπὶ τετρήχυνται Martin 280 κηφείης M^pcE: κηφήεις M^ac: κηφῆος S   πείρατα τείνων MES: πείρατα φαίνων Hi. ter: σήματα φαίνων A   281 πτέρυγι M^slE^slS Hi.: om. ME   282 μετασκαίροντα codd.: μετασκαίροντε Maass: μετὰ σκαίροντα Martin   284 τάνυται ES: τετάνυσται M: τετάνυσθ' Ald.

κέκλιται Αἰγόκερως, ἵνα ἷς τρέπετ' ἠελίοιο.
μὴ κείνῳ ἐνὶ μηνὶ περικλύζοιο θαλάσσῃ
πεπταμένῳ πελάγει κεχρημένος. οὔτε κεν ἠοῖ
πολλὴν πειρήνειας, ἐπεὶ ταχινώταταί εἰσιν,
290 οὔτ' ἄν τοι νυκτὸς πεφοβημένῳ ἐγγύθεν ἠὼς
ἔλθοι καὶ μάλα πολλὰ βοωμένῳ. οἱ δ' ἀλεγεινοὶ
τῆμος ἐπιρρήσσουσι νότοι, ὁπότ' Αἰγοκερῆι
συμφέρετ' ἠέλιος· τότε δὲ κρύος ἐκ Διός ἐστι
ναύτῃ μαλκιόωντι κακώτερον. ἀλλὰ καὶ ἔμπης
295 ἤδη πάντ' ἐνιαυτὸν ὑπὸ στείρῃσι θάλασσα
πορφύρει· ἴκελοι δὲ κολυμβίσιν αἰθυίῃσι
πολλάκις ἐκ νηῶν πέλαγος περιπαπταίνοντες
ἥμεθ', ἐπ' αἰγιαλοὺς τετραμμένοι· οἱ δ' ἔτι πόρσω
κλύζονται, ὀλίγον δὲ διὰ ξύλον Ἄϊδ' ἐρύκει.
300 καὶ δ' ἄν ἔτι προτέρῳ γε θαλάσσῃ πολλὰ πεπονθώς,
τόξον ὅτ' ἤέλιος καίει καὶ ῥύτορα τόξου,
ἑσπέριος κατάγοιο πεποιθὼς οὐκέτι νυκτί.
σῆμα δέ τοι κείνης ὥρης καὶ μηνὸς ἐκείνου
Σκορπίος ἀντέλλων εἴη πυμάτης ἐπὶ νυκτός.
305 ἤτοι γὰρ μέγα τόξον ἀνέλκεται ἐγγύθι κέντρου
Τοξευτής· ὀλίγον δὲ παροίτερος ἵσταται αὐτοῦ
Σκορπίος ἀντέλλων, ὁ δ' ἀνέρχεται αὐτίκα μᾶλλον.
τῆμος καὶ κεφαλὴ Κυνοσουρίδος ἀκρόθι νυκτὸς
ὕψι μάλα τροχάει, ὁ δὲ δύεται ἠῶθι πρὸ
310 ἀθρόος Ὠρίων, Κηφεὺς δ' ἀπὸ χειρὸς ἐπ' ἰξύν.
ἔστι δέ τις προτέρῳ βεβλημένος ἄλλος Ὀϊστός,

---

287 Longin. 26.1   292–9 Stob. 1.17.4   299 (ὀλίγον ...) Longin.
10.6; [Plu.] *Vit. Hom.* 2.160 Bernardakis; (ὀλίγον ... ξύλον) sch. (T) Ο
628; sch. (ABL) Ο 628 p. 422a Bekker   303–10 Hi. 1.7.1

---

286 ἷς τρέπετ' ἠελίοιο Grotius: τρέπετ' ἠελίοιο Μ primitus S: τρέπετ'
ἠελίοιο ἷς Μ postea: τρέπετ' ἠελίου ἷς Ε: τε τρέπετ' ἠελίου ἷς Α
287 θαλάσσῃ ΜΕ Longin.: θαλάσσης S   291 ἔλθοι ΕS: ἔλθοις Μ
βοωμένῳ codd.: βοωμένη Maass   293 συμφέρετ' codd.: ἐμφέρετ' Stob.
τότε δὲ ΜΕ: τότε δὴ S: τὸ δέ τοι V   294 μαλκιόωντι codd.: μαλ-

sun turns back. [287] In that month I hope you will not be surged about by the sea through taking to open waters. Neither by day can you make much headway, for the days pass most swiftly then, [290] nor in your terror by night will the dawn come soon, however much you cry out. It is then that the dread southerlies strike, when the sun meets up with Capricorn; then the icy cold from Zeus is more cruel to the freezing sailor. But for that matter [295] the sea surges under the stem all the year long; and we, like diving shearwaters, often sit gazing round the ocean from our ships, turning our eyes towards the beaches; but the surf there is still far off, and only a little timber keeps death away.

[300] After much suffering at sea even in the previous month, when the sun inflames the bow and the Drawer of the bow, you should put ashore in the evening and not continue to trust the night. A sign of that season and that month will be the rising of the Scorpion at the end of night. [305] The Archer actually draws his great bow near the sting; the rising Scorpion stands a little ahead of him, and he then rises shortly after. At that time the head of Cynosura runs very high up at the end of night, and just before dawn Orion sets entirely, and Cepheus from hand to waist.

[311] Ahead of the Archer is another Arrow lying all by

κίοντι Stob.   κακώτερον codd.: κακώτατον Stob.   296 κολυμβίσιν codd.: κολυμβάσιν Stob.   297 πολλάκις S: πολλάκι δ' ME
περιπαπταίνοντες ME Stob.: παραπαπτ- S   298 δ' ἔτι E l (M)
Stob.^{SA} ut uid.: δέ τι MS Stob.^{M}: δέ τοι A   πόρσω ME: πρόσσω S:
πόρρω Stob.   299 ἐρύκει MES Stob.: ἐρύκοι A   300 ἔτι M^{sl}S
(adhuc L): ἐπὶ ME   301 καίει E: καίῃ MS   ῥύτορα ES: ῥύτηρα M:
ῥυτῆρα A   304 ἐπὶ M Hi.: ἔτι E^{γρ}S: ἀπὸ E   305 μέγα MES
Hi.^{LVmg}: μετὰ Hi.^{AB} (post L)   306 παροίτερος M^{sl}ES Hi.: -ον M
307 ἀνέρχεται ME Hi.: ἀνέλκεται S   308 καὶ M^{sl}ES: om. M   311
τις S l (M): τοι ME

αὐτὸς ἄτερ τόξου· ὁ δέ οἱ παραπέπταται Ὄρνις
ἀσσότερον βορέω. σχεδόθεν δέ οἱ ἄλλος ἄηται
οὐ τόσσος μεγέθει, χαλεπός γε μὲν ἐξ ἁλὸς ἐλθὼν
315 νυκτὸς ἀπερχομένης· καί μιν καλέουσιν Ἀητόν.
Δελφὶς δ' οὐ μάλα πολλὸς ἐπιτρέχει Αἰγοκερῆι,
μεσσόθεν ἠερόεις· τὰ δέ οἱ περὶ τέσσαρα κεῖται
γλήνεα, παρβολάδην δύο πὰρ δύο πεπτηῶτα.
καὶ τὰ μὲν οὖν βορέω καὶ ἀλήσιος ἠελίοιο
320 μεσσηγὺς κέχυται· τὰ δὲ νειόθι τέλλεται ἄλλα
πολλὰ μεταξὺ νότοιο καὶ ἠελίοιο κελεύθου.
λοξὸς μὲν Ταύροιο τομῇ ὑποκέκλιται αὐτὸς
Ὠρίων. μὴ κεῖνον ὅτις καθαρῇ ἐπὶ νυκτὶ
ὑψοῦ πεπτηῶτα παρέρχεται ἄλλα πεποίθοι
325 οὐρανὸν εἰσανιδὼν προφερέστερα θηήσασθαι.
τοῖός οἱ καὶ φρουρὸς ἀειρομένῳ ὑπὸ νώτῳ
φαίνεται ἀμφοτέροισι Κύων ἐπὶ ποσσὶ βεβηκώς,
ποικίλος, ἀλλ' οὐ πάντα πεφασμένος, ἀλλὰ κατ' αὐτὴν
γαστέρα κυάνεος περιτέλλεται· ἡ δέ οἱ ἄκρη
330 ἀστέρι βέβληται δεινῷ γένυς, ὅς ῥα μάλιστα
ὀξέα σειριάει· καί μιν καλέουσ' ἄνθρωποι
Σείριον. οὐκέτι κεῖνον ἅμ' ἠελίῳ ἀνιόντα
φυταλιαὶ ψεύδονται ἀναλδέα φυλλιόωσαι·
ῥεῖα γὰρ οὖν ἔκρινε διὰ στίχας ὀξὺς ἀΐξας,
335 καὶ τὰ μὲν ἔρρωσεν, τῶν δὲ φλόον ὤλεσε πάντα.
κείνου καὶ κατιόντος ἀκούομεν· οἱ δὲ δὴ ἄλλοι
σῆμ' ἔμεναι μελέεσσιν ἐλαφρότεροι περίκεινται.
ποσσὶν δ' Ὠρίωνος ὑπ' ἀμφοτέροισι Λαγωὸς
ἐμμενὲς ἤματα πάντα διώκεται· αὐτὰρ ὅ γ' αἰεὶ

319–20 Anon. περί ἐξηγήσεως p. 33 Martin; (... κέχυται) Ach. p. 53
322–3 (... Ὠρίων) sch. Pi. N. 2.17   331–2 (... Σείριον) Tz. in Lyc. p. 148
331 (... σειριάει) Theon Smyrn. p. 202 T. H. Martin; sch. Pi. O. 8.111

---

312 αὐτὸς MES: γυμνὸς V   παραπέπταται MES: παρακέκλιται V
313 ἀσσότερον MES: -ος Q coni. Martin   314 ἐλθὼν Grotius: ἐλθεῖν
codd.   315 ἀπερχομένης MES sch.: ἐπερχομένης A   ἀητόν ME:

itself without a bow. The Bird is outstretched beside it, nearer to the north. Close to it another bird is wafted, inferior in size, but stormy when it rises from the sea at the departure of night; and men call it the Eagle.

[316] The very slight Dolphin runs just above Capricorn, dark in the centre, but four jewels outline it, two lying parallel to two.

Now these are the stars that are broadcast between the north and the sun's wandering path. But many others rise below this, between the south and the track of the sun.

[322] Aslant from the cut-off figure of the Bull lies Orion himself. Anyone whose glance misses him when he is positioned high up on a clear night may be sure he can never sight anything better to identify when he gazes up at the sky.

[326] Such is also his guardian Dog, seen standing on its two legs below the soaring back of Orion, variegated, not bright overall, but dark in the region of the belly as it moves round; but the tip of its [330] jaw is inset with a formidable star, that blazes most intensely: and so men call it the Scorcher. When Sirius rises with the sun, trees can no longer outwit it by feebly putting forth leaves. For with its keen shafts it easily pierces their ranks, [335] and strengthens some, but destroys all the growth of others. We also hear of it at its setting. The other stars lying round about Sirius define the legs more faintly.

Under the two feet of Orion the Hare is hunted constantly all the time: Sirius moves for ever behind it as if in

---

ἀετόν S: Ἀίητόν Voss   317 περὶ MES: παρὰ A: ἐπὶ Q   320 νειόθι τέλλεται codd.: νειόθεν ἄρχεται Ach.: νειόθεν ἔρχεται Voss   323 ὅτις ME: ὅστις S   ἐπὶ S: ἐν M: ἐνὶ E: ὑπὸ Q   324 ἄλλα ME: ἀλλὰ S   325 θηήσασθαι codd.: θηήσεσθαι Maass   326 οἱ MEᵃᶜS: τοι Eᵖᶜ   327 ἐπὶ Arnaud 2.155–6 ex sch. (super L): ὑπὸ codd.   328 ἀλλ' οὐ MES: οὐ μὲν V   330 δεινῷ Ceporinus: δεινὴ codd.   ὅς ῥα MEᵖᶜS: ὅρ ῥα Eᵃᶜ   332 ἀνιόντα E: ἀνιόντι MS   338 ποσσὶν Eᵖᶜ: ποσσὶ MEᵃᶜS

340 Σείριος ἐξόπιθεν φέρεται μετιόντι ἐοικώς,
καί οἱ ἐπαντέλλει καί μιν κατιόντα δοκεύει.

ἡ δὲ Κυνὸς μεγάλοιο κατ' οὐρὴν ἕλκεται Ἀργώ
πρυμνόθεν· οὐ γὰρ τῇ γε κατὰ χρέος εἰσὶ κέλευθοι,
ἀλλ' ὄπιθεν φέρεται τετραμμένη, οἷα καὶ αὐταὶ
345 νῆες, ὅτ' ἤδη ναῦται ἐπιστρέψωσι κορώνην
ὅρμον ἐσερχόμενοι· τὴν δ' αὐτίκα πᾶς ἀνακόπτει
νῆα, παλιρροθίη δὲ καθάπτεται ἠπείροιο·
ὣς ἥ γε πρύμνηθεν Ἰησονὶς ἕλκεται Ἀργώ.
καὶ τὰ μὲν ἠερίη καὶ ἀνάστερος ἄχρι παρ' αὐτὸν
350 ἱστὸν ἀπὸ πρώρης φέρεται, τὰ δὲ πᾶσα φαεινή·
καί οἱ πηδάλιον κεχαλασμένον ἐστήρικται
ποσσὶν ὑπ' οὐραίοισι Κυνὸς προπάροιθεν ἰόντος.

τὴν δὲ καὶ οὐκ ὀλίγον περ ἀπόπροθι πεπτηυῖαν
Ἀνδρομέδην μέγα Κῆτος ἐπερχόμενον κατεπείγει.
355 ἡ μὲν γὰρ Θρήϊκος ὑπὸ πνοιῇ βορέαο
κεκλιμένη φέρεται, τὸ δέ οἱ νότος ἐχθρὸν ἀγινεῖ
Κῆτος, ὑπὸ Κριῷ τε καὶ Ἰχθύσιν ἀμφοτέροισι,
βαιὸν ὑπὲρ Ποταμοῦ βεβλημένον ἀστερόεντος.
οἷον γὰρ κἀκεῖνο θεῶν ὑπὸ ποσσὶ φορεῖται
360 λείψανον Ἠριδανοῖο πολυκλαύτου ποταμοῖο.
καὶ τὸ μὲν Ὠρίωνος ὑπὸ σκαιὸν πόδα τείνει.
δεσμοὶ δ' οὐραῖοι, τοῖς Ἰχθύες ἄκροι ἔχονται,
ἄμφω συμφορέονται ἀπ' οὐραίων κατιόντες,
Κητείης δ' ὄπιθεν λοφιῆς ἐπιμὶξ φορέονται
365 εἰς ἓν ἐλαυνόμενοι, ἑνὶ δ' ἀστέρι πειραίνονται,
Κήτεος ὃς κείνου πρώτῃ ἐπίκειται ἀκάνθῃ.

οἱ δ' ὀλίγῳ μέτρῳ ὀλίγη δ' ἐγκείμενοι αἴγλῃ
μεσσόθι πηδαλίου καὶ Κήτεος εἰλίσσονται,
γλαυκοῦ πεπτηῶτες ὑπὸ πλευρῇσι Λαγωοῦ,

---

335 Plu. 683F   349–50 Hi. 1.8.1   358 Hi. 1.8.5; (... Ποταμοῦ)
sch. (A) B 380a   360 (... Ἠριδανοῖο) Eust. in D.P. p. 141 Bernhardy   367–85 Att. pp. 13–14, Hi. 1.8.8   367–9 Hi. 1.8.2

---

340 μετιόντι ES l (M): μητιόωντι M   341 κατιόντα ME: ἐπιόντα

pursuit, [341] rises after it and watches it as it sets.

Close to the great Dog's tail is Argo towed stern first. Its course is not that of a ship proceeding on its normal business, but its movement is backward-turned, like that of real [345] ships when the sailors have already turned the stern about on entering harbour: all the crew quickly back water, and the ship surging astern makes fast to the land. So this Argo of Jason is towed stern first. Dark and starless from the prow as far as the actual mast she goes, but the rest is all bright. [351] The steering-oar is detached and set fast under the Dog's hind legs as it runs ahead.

Although she lies no small distance away, Andromeda is threatened by the approach of the great Sea-monster. [355] For in her course she lies exposed to the blast of the north wind from Thrace, while the southerly brings against her the hostile Monster, below the Ram and the two Fishes, and positioned a little above the starry River. For under the gods' feet that too moves as a separate group, [360] a remnant of Eridanus, river of much weeping. It extends below the left foot of Orion. The tail-chains, by which the extremities of the Fishes are held, both come together as they descend from the tail-parts, and behind the Monster's back-fin move jointly [365] as they converge, and terminate in a single star that lies close to the top of the Monster's spine.

Other stars covering a small area, and inset with slight brilliance, circle between Argo's steering-oar and the Monster, lying below the flanks of the grey Hare, [370]

ΕΥΡS   δοκεύει ΜΥΡΕΥΡS: διώκει ΜΕ (*sectatur* L)   344 αὐταὶ codd. (*haec* L): ἄλλαι Voss ex sch.   345 ἐπιστρέψωσι ΜΕS: ἀποσ-τρέψωσι ΜΥΡ: ἐπιτρέψωσι Η: ἐπιστέψωσι Richter ad V. G. 1.304   349 ἄχρι ΜΕ Ηi.: οἷα S   350 πᾶσα ΜΕS Ηi.: πάντα Α   φαεινή ΜS Ηi.ᴮ: φαείνει Ε Ηi.ᴬ   354 ἐπερχόμενον ΜΕ: ἐπερχομένην S: ἐπειγόμενον Α   359 οἷον Μ: οἷον Ε: τοῖον S   360 πολυκλαύ-του ΜΕ: -κλαύστου S   362 ἄκροι ΜΕ: ἀμφὶς S   363 οὐραίων codd.: οὐράων Maass   366 ἐπίκειται ΕS: ἐπίκεινται Μ

370 νώνυμοι· οὐ γὰρ τοί γε τετυγμένου εἰδώλοιο
βεβλέαται μελέεσσιν ἐοικότες, οἷά τε πολλὰ
ἐξείης στιχόωντα παρέρχεται αὐτὰ κέλευθα
ἀνομένων ἐτέων, τά τις ἀνδρῶν οὐκέτ' ἐόντων
ἐφράσατ' ἠδ' ἐνόησεν ἅπαντ' ὀνομαστὶ καλέσσαι
375 ἤλιθα μορφώσας· οὐ γάρ κ' ἐδυνήσατο πάντων
οἰόθι κεκριμένων ὄνομ' εἰπεῖν οὐδὲ δαῆναι.
πολλοὶ γὰρ πάντη, πολέων δ' ἐπὶ ἶσα πέλονται
μέτρα τε καὶ χροιή, πάντες γε μὲν ἀμφιέλικτοι·
τῷ καὶ ὁμηγερέας οἱ ἐείσατο ποιήσασθαι
380 ἀστέρας, ὄφρ' ἐπιτὰξ ἄλλῳ παρακείμενος ἄλλος
εἴδεα σημαίνοιεν· ἄφαρ δ' ὀνομάστ' ἐγένοντο
ἄστρα, καὶ οὐκέτι νῦν ὑπὸ θαύματι τέλλεται ἀστήρ·
ἀλλ' οἱ μὲν καθαροῖς ἐναρηρότες εἰδώλοισι
φαίνονται, τὰ δ' ἔνερθε διωκομένοιο Λαγωοῦ
385 πάντα μάλ' ἠερόεντα καὶ οὐκ ὀνομαστὰ φέρονται.
νειόθι δ' Αἰγοκερῆος ὑπὸ πνοιῇσι νότοιο
Ἰχθῦς, ἐς Κήτεος τετραμμένος αἰωρεῖται
οἷος ἀπὸ προτέρων, Νότιον δέ ἑ κικλήσκουσιν.
ἄλλοι δὲ σποράδην ὑποκείμενοι Ὑδροχοῆϊ
390 Κήτεος αἰθερίοιο καὶ Ἰχθύος ἠερέθονται
μέσσοι νωχελέες καὶ ἀνώνυμοι· ἐγγύθι δέ σφεων,
δεξιτερῆς ἀπὸ χειρὸς ἀγαυοῦ Ὑδροχόοιο
οἵη τίς τ' ὀλίγη χύσις ὕδατος ἔνθα καὶ ἔνθα
σκιδναμένου, χαροποὶ καὶ ἀναλδέες εἰλίσσονται.
395 ἐν δέ σφιν δύο μᾶλλον ἐειδόμενοι φορέονται
ἀστέρες, οὔτε τι πολλὸν ἀπήοροι οὔτε μάλ' ἐγγύς,

---

380 (ἐπιτὰξ) Hellad. *Chrest.* ap. Phot. *Bibl.* 532a36ʙ   389–91 (...
μέσσοι) Phlp. *in Mete.* Α 8 p. 112, 34 H.   389 Alex. Aphr. *in Mete.*
346a20, p. 42, 24 H.

---

371 βεβλέαται ΜΕ: βέβληνται S Att. Hi.   373 ἀνομένων S Att. Hi.:
ἀνυμένων ΜΕ   374 ἠδ' MES sch. Att.: οὐδ' H Hi.   375 κ' ἐδυνήσατο Voss: γ' ἐδυνήσατο Hi.ᴮ: κε δυνήσατο MES Hi.ᴬ   376 εἰπεῖν
codd.: εἰπέμεν Wilamowitz ex M. Schmidt, *Annal. Philol.* (1855) 224
377 δ' ἐπὶ E Hi.: ἐπὶ Μ: δέ τοι S   379 ὁμηγερέας MES: -γυρέας Eˢˡ

without a name; they are not cast in any resemblance to the body of a well-defined figure, like the many that pass in regular ranks along the same paths as the years complete themselves, the constellations that one of the men who are no more devised and contrived to call all by names, [375] grouping them in compact shapes: he could not, of course, have named or identified all the stars taken individually, because there are so many all over the sky, and many alike in magnitude and colour, while all have a circling movement; therefore he decided to make the stars into groups, so that different stars arranged together in order [381] could represent figures; and thereupon the named constellations were created, and no star-rising now takes us by surprise; so the other stars that shine appear fixed in clear-cut figures, but those beneath the hunted Hare [385] are all very hazy and nameless in their courses.

Below Capricorn and exposed to the winds of the south hovers the Fish, turned to face the Monster, distinct from the former two: they call it the Southern Fish.

Other stars lying scattered below the Water-pourer [390] hang in the sky between the celestial Monster and the Fish, but they are faint and nameless. Close to them, like a light spray of water being sprinkled this way and that from the right hand of the illustrious Water-pourer, some pale and feeble stars go round. [395] Among them go two rather brighter stars, not so very far apart nor yet very close, one

---

οἱ S Hi.: κεν E: om. M   381 ὀνομάστ᾽ ἐγένοντο scripsi: ὀνομαστὰ γένοντο MS Hi.: ὀνομ- γένοιντο A: ὀνομ- γένοιτο E   382 ὑπὸ codd. Hi.ᴬ: ἐν Hi.ᴮ: ἐνὶ Voss   τέλλεται codd.: λάμπεται Att.   385 ἠερόεντα ES Hi.ᴮ: ἠρόεντα A Hi.ᴬ: ἠερόωντα M   φέρονται MESᵖᶜ Hi.: φύωνται Sᵃᶜ: πέλονται A   387 αἰωρεῖται A 1 (M): αἰώρηται S: ἠώρηται ME   388 οἷος ME: οἶος S   390 κήτεος MES: ἰχθύος V αἰθερίοιο ME: αἰθερίου S   ἰχθύος MES: κήτεος V   391 μέσσοι ME: μεσσόθι S   σφεων V: σφέων S: σφῶν ME   393 οἵη A: οἴη MES   394 σκιδναμένου MᵖᶜS: κιδναμένου MᵃᶜE   395 ἐειδόμενοι MES: ἀειδ- Mˢˡ: ἐρειδ- D   396 οὔτε τι ES: οὔτε τοι M   οὔτε μάλ᾽ A: οὐδὲ μάλ᾽ MES

εἷς μὲν ὑπ᾽ ἀμφοτέροισι ποσὶν καλός τε μέγας τε
Ὑδροχόου, ὁ δὲ κυανέου ὑπὸ Κήτεος οὐρῇ.
τοὺς πάντας καλέουσιν Ὕδωρ. ὀλίγοι γε μὲν ἄλλοι
400 νειόθι Τοξευτῆρος ὑπὸ προτέροισι πόδεσσι
δινωτοὶ κύκλῳ περιηγέες εἰλίσσονται.
   αὐτὰρ ὑπ᾽ αἰθομένῳ κέντρῳ τέραος μεγάλοιο
Σκορπίου ἄγχι νότοιο Θυτήριον αἰωρεῖται.
τοῦ δ᾽ ἤτοι ὀλίγον μὲν ἐπὶ χρόνον ὑψόθ᾽ ἐόντος
405 πεύσεαι· ἀντιπέρην γὰρ ἀείρεται Ἀρκτούροιο.
καὶ τῷ μὲν μάλα πάγχυ μετήοροί εἰσι κέλευθοι
Ἀρκτούρῳ, τὸ δὲ θᾶσσον ὑφ᾽ ἑσπερίην ἅλα νεῖται.
ἀλλ᾽ ἄρα καὶ περὶ κεῖνο Θυτήριον ἀρχαίη Νύξ,
ἀνθρώπων κλαίουσα πόνον, χειμῶνος ἔθηκεν
410 εἰναλίου μέγα σῆμα· κεδαιόμεναι γὰρ ἐκείνη
νῆες ἀπὸ φρενός εἰσι, τὰ δ᾽ ἄλλοθεν ἄλλα πιφαύσκει
σήματ᾽, ἐποικτείρουσα πολυρροθίους ἀνθρώπους.
τῷ μή μοι πελάγει νεφέων εἰλυμένον ἄλλων
εὔχεο μεσσόθι κεῖνο φανήμεναι οὐρανῷ ἄστρον,
415 αὐτὸ μὲν ἀνέφελόν τε καὶ ἀγλαόν, ὕψι δὲ μᾶλλον
κυμαίνοντι νέφει πεπιεσμένον, οἷά τε πολλὰ
θλίβετ᾽ ἀναστέλλοντος ὀπωρινοῦ βορέαο.
πολλάκι γὰρ καὶ τοῦτο νότῳ ἔπι σῆμα τιτύσκει
Νὺξ αὐτή, μογεροῖσι χαριζομένη ναύτῃσιν.
420 οἱ δ᾽ εἰ μέν κε πίθωνται ἐναίσιμα σημαινούσῃ,
αἶψα δὲ κοῦφά τε πάντα καὶ ἄρτια ποιήσωνται,
αὐτίκ᾽ ἐλαφρότερος πέλεται πόνος· εἰ δέ κε νηῒ
ὑψόθεν ἐμπλήξῃ δεινὴ ἀνέμοιο θύελλα
αὔτως ἀπρόφατος, τὰ δὲ λαίφεα πάντα ταράξῃ,
425 ἄλλοτε μὲν καὶ πάμπαν ὑπόβρυχα ναυτίλλονται,

402–7 Hi. 1.8.14   402–3 Hi. 1.8.23

---

399 γε ES: om. M   400 ὑπὸ MES: ἐπὶ V   401 δινωτοὶ E: δεινω-
τοὶ MS: ἄγνωτοι Grotius   403 αἰωρεῖται MES: ἠώρηται Q:
αἰώρηται Hi.ᴬ bis   404 τοῦ δ᾽ ἤτοι ΜΕ: τοῦ δή τοι S   406 τῷ
codd.: τοῦ Hi.   πάγχυ ΜΕ: πολλὰ S .407 ἀρκτούρῳ codd.:

beautiful and bright star beneath the two feet of the Water-
pourer, the other below the dark Monster's tail. Men call
them collectively the Water. But a few others [400] below
the Archer, under his forefeet, are curved in a ring as they
go circling round.

Now below the blazing sting of the great monster Scorpion, close to the south hovers the Altar. [404] This constellation you will observe only for a short time above the
horizon, for its period of visibility is the opposite of Arcturus'. In fact the paths of Arcturus come fully overhead,
whereas the Altar goes quickly under the western sea. Yet
even round that Altar ancient Night, [409] sad for the suffering of men, has set an important sign of storm at sea;
for ships in distress are not to her liking, and she displays
different signs in different ways in her pity for storm-tossed
men. So pray, I beg you, that at sea this constellation be
not visible in mid-sky overarched by clouds everywhere
else, [415] cloudless itself and brilliant, but higher up op-
pressed by billowing clouds, as they are often packed when
an autumn northerly piles them up. For Night herself frequently contrives this sign also for a southerly, showing
favour to sailors in distress. [420] And if they give heed to
her timely signal, and promptly make everything ready
and shipshape, in due course their trouble is easier; but if
a terrible squall of wind falls upon the ship from on high
quite unexpectedly, and disorders all of the canvas, [425]
sometimes they sail on entirely submerged, sometimes, if

-οὔρου Hi. (*Arcturi* L)   411 ἀπὸ E: ἄπο MS   πιφαύσκει MES:
πιφάσκει A: ἐπιφάσκει C   412 πολυρροθίους MEˢˡ: παλιρρ- E:
περιρρ- S   413 εἰλυμένον M: εἰλυμένων MˢˡEᵃᶜ: εἰλυμένος Eᵖᶜ coni.
Scaliger ad Man. 5.340: εἰλυμμένον S: εἰλυμένῳ sch.ʸᵖ   ἄλλων codd.:
ἄλλῳ Grotius: ἄλλως Scaliger: ἀχλυῖ Buttmann   414 φανήμεναι E:
φαήμεναι MS   415 ἀνέφελον M: ἀννέφελον ES   417 βορέαο MES:
ἀνέμοιο A (*uentum* L)   418 ἔπι 1 (K) Stephanus: ἐπὶ codd.   421 δὲ
V coni. Voss: τε MES   423 ἐμπλήξῃ ME: ἐμπλήξει S   424 ταράξῃ
MES: ταράξει D: τινάξῃ A: τινάξει V

ἄλλοτε δ᾽, αἴ κε Διὸς παρανισσομένοιο τύχωσιν
εὐχόμενοι, βορέω δὲ πάρ᾽ ἀστράψῃ ἀνέμοιο,
πολλὰ μάλ᾽ ὀτλήσαντες ὅμως πάλιν ἐσκέψαντο
ἀλλήλους ἐπὶ νηΐ. νότον δ᾽ ἐπὶ σήματι τούτῳ
430 δείδιθι, μέχρι Βορῆος ἀπαστράψαντος ἴδηαι.
    εἰ δέ κεν ἑσπερίης μὲν ἁλὸς Κενταύρου ἀπείη
ὦμος ὅσον προτέρης, ὀλίγη δέ μιν εἰλύοι ἀχλὺς
αὐτόν, ἀτὰρ μετόπισθεν ἐοικότα σήματα τεύχοι
Νὺξ ἐπὶ παμφανόωντι Θυτηρίῳ, οὔ σε μάλα χρὴ
435 ἐς νότον ἀλλ᾽ εὔροιο περισκοπέειν ἀνέμοιο.
δήεις δ᾽ ἄστρον ἐκεῖνο δύω ὑποκείμενον ἄλλοις·
τοῦ γάρ τοι τὰ μὲν ἀνδρὶ ἐοικότα νείοθι κεῖται
Σκορπίου, ἱππούραια δ᾽ ὑπὸ σφίσι Χηλαὶ ἔχουσιν.
αὐτὰρ ὁ δεξιτερὴν αἰεὶ τανύοντι ἔοικεν
440 ἀντία δινωτοῖο Θυτηρίου, ἐν δέ οἱ ἀπρὶξ
ἄλλο μάλ᾽ ἐσφήκωται ἐληλάμενον διὰ χειρὸς
Θηρίον· ὣς γάρ μιν πρότεροι ἐπεφημίξαντο.
    ἀλλ᾽ ἔτι γάρ τι καὶ ἄλλο περαιόθεν ἕλκεται ἄστρον·
Ὕδρην μιν καλέουσι. τὸ δὲ ζώοντι ἐοικὸς
445 ἠνεκὲς εἰλεῖται, καί οἱ κεφαλὴ ὑπὸ μέσσον
Καρκίνον ἱκνεῖται, σπείρη δ᾽ ὑπὸ σῶμα Λέοντος,
οὐρὴ δὲ κρέμαται ὑπὲρ αὐτοῦ Κενταύροιο.
μέσσῃ δὲ σπείρῃ Κρητήρ, πυμάτῃ δ᾽ ἐπίκειται
εἴδωλον Κόρακος σπείρην κόπτοντι ἐοικός.
450 ναὶ μὴν καὶ Προκύων Διδύμοις ὕπο καλὰ φαείνει.
    ταῦτά κε θηήσαιο παρερχομένων ἐνιαυτῶν
ἑξείης παλίνωρα· τὰ γὰρ καὶ πάντα μάλ᾽ αὔτως

431–8 Hi. 1.8.18   439–40 (... Θυτηρίου) Hi. 1.8.23

---

426 παρανισσομένοιο MS: -νεισομένοιο E   427 βορέω MES:
βορέου A   δὲ MES: δ᾽ ἷς C   πάρ᾽ ἀστράψῃ Martin: παραστράψῃ H: παραστράψει S: παραστρέψῃ M: παραστρέψειε V: παρα-
τρέψῃ E   ἀνέμοιο MS: ἀνέμου ἷς A: ἷς ἀνέμοιο E   428 μάλ᾽ ὀτλήσαντες MES: μάλα τλήσαντες A   ὅμως ME: ὁμῶς S   429 ἐπὶ νηΐ
S: ἐπὶ νῆα ME   430 ἀπαστράψαντος MES: ἀποστρέψαντος A: ἄπ᾽
ἀστράψαντος Maass   431 κεν codd.: τοι Hi.[B]: τοί κεν Hi.[A]   432

---

they find Zeus coming to help them as they pray, and there is lightning in the north, in spite of their many travails they do look again upon each other on board ship. With this sign fear a southerly, until you see Boreas flashing lightning.

[431] If the Centaur's shoulder should be as far from the western horizon as from the eastern, and a slight haze shroud the constellation, while behind it Night is fashioning recognisable signs on the radiant Altar, you must certainly be on the lookout not for a southerly but for an easterly wind. [436] You will find this constellation lying below two others: part of it, resembling a man, lies beneath the Scorpion, and the Claws have the horse's hindpart under them. He looks as if he is always stretching his right hand [440] towards the rounded Altar, and fast in his hand is tightly gripped another constellation, the Beast; for so our predecessors named it.

But yet another constellation sweeps across the horizon: they call it the Hydra. Like a living thing [445] it winds at great length, its head comes below the middle of the Crab, its coil under the Lion's body, and its tail hangs over the Centaur himself. On its middle coil lies the Bowl, and on the last one the figure of a Raven that looks like one pecking the coil. [450] Yes, and there too Procyon shines brightly beneath the Twins.

These you can see as the years pass returning in succession; for these figures of the passing night are all well fixed

---

ὦμος codd. sch. Hi.: ὦμοι Maass   433 τεύχοι ME: τεύχει S: τεῦχε Hi.ᴬ: φαίνοι Hi.ᴮ   435 περισκοπέειν S Hi.: -σκοπεύειν ME   436 ἄλλοις MES: ἄστροις A   437 τοῦ γάρ τοι MES Hi.ᴬ: τοῦ δ' ἤτοι V Hi.ᴮ.   438 χηλαὶ MES: χείλε' Mᵞᵖ   ἔχουσιν MES: ἄγουσιν V Hi. 440 δινωτοῖο E: δεινωτοῖο MS   441 ἄλλο μάλ' ME: ἄλλο μὲν S 442 ἐπεφημίξαντο MES: διεφημίξαντο V   443 τι καὶ Martin: τε καὶ S: καὶ ME: καὶ ἔτ' V: καλὸν Maass   445 ἠνεκὲς ES: ἠνεμὲς M   450 ὑπο E: ὑπο MS: ὑπὸ D   452 παλίνωρα codd.: παλίνορσα Grotius

οὐρανῷ εὖ ἐνάρηρεν ἀγάλματα νυκτὸς ἰούσης.
οἱ δ᾽ ἐπιμὶξ ἄλλοι πέντ᾽ ἀστέρες οὐδὲν ὁμοῖοι
455 πάντοθεν εἰδώλων δυοκαίδεκα δινεύονται.
οὐκ ἂν ἔτ᾽ εἰς ἄλλους ὁρόων ἐπιτεκμήραιο
κείνων ἧχι κέονται, ἐπεὶ πάντες μετανάσται.
μακροὶ δέ σφεων εἰσὶν ἑλισσομένων ἐνιαυτοί,
μακρὰ δὲ σήματα κεῖται ἀπόπροθεν εἰς ἓν ἰόντων.
460 οὐδ᾽ ἔτι θαρσαλέος κείνων ἐγώ· ἄρκιος εἴην
ἀπλανέων τά τε κύκλα τά τ᾽ αἰθέρι σήματ᾽ ἐνισπεῖν.
ἤτοι μὲν τά γε κεῖται ἀλίγκια δινωτοῖσι
τέσσαρα, τῶν κε μάλιστα ποθὴ ὄφελός τε γένοιτο
μέτρα περισκοπέοντι κατανομένων ἐνιαυτῶν.
465 σήματα δ᾽ εὖ μάλα πᾶσιν ἐπιρρήδην περίκειται
πολλά τε καὶ σχεδόθεν πάντη συνεεργμένα πάντα·
αὐτοὶ δ᾽ ἀπλατέες καὶ ἀρηρότες ἀλλήλοισι
πάντες, ἀτὰρ μέτρῳ γε δύω δυσὶν ἀντιφέρονται.
εἴ ποτέ τοι νυκτὸς καθαρῆς, ὅτε πάντας ἀγαυοὺς
470 ἀστέρας ἀνθρώποις ἐπιδείκνυται οὐρανίη Νύξ,
οὐδέ τις ἀδρανέων φέρεται νεόμηνι σελήνη,
ἀλλὰ τά γε κνέφαος διαφαίνεται ὀξέα πάντα·
εἴ ποτέ τοι τημόσδε περὶ φρένας ἵκετο θαῦμα
σκεψαμένῳ πάντη κεκεασμένον εὑρέι κύκλῳ
475 οὐρανόν, ἢ καί τίς τοι ἐπιστὰς ἄλλος ἔδειξε
κεῖνο περιγληνὲς τροχαλόν (Γάλα μιν καλέουσι)·
τῷ δή τοι χροιὴν μὲν ἀλίγκιος οὐκέτι κύκλος
δινεῖται, τὰ δὲ μέτρα τόσοι πισύρων περ ἐόντων

---

453 Ath. 11 489E   454–5 Ach. p. 42   460–1 (... αἰθέρι) Ach. p. 42;
(ἄρκιος ...) Anon. 1 p. 93 Maass   467–8 Hi. 1.9.1   467 (... ἀπλατέες) Att. p. 16 Maass   468 (δύω ...) Choerob. in Theod. p. 398, 14
Hilgard   471 Hdn i.413, 18; ii.216, 5   476 Ach. p. 55; Phlp. in Mete.
A 1 p. 6, 7 H.   477–9 Hi. 1.9.14

---

453 εὖ ἐνάρηρεν codd.: αἰὲν ἄρηρεν Ath.   455 πάντοθεν codd.:
ἔμπαλιν Ach.   457 κείνων S: κείνους ME   458 ἐνιαυτοί MES:
ἐνιαυτῶν A   460 οὐδ᾽ ἔτι Ach.: οὐδέ τι MES: οὐκέτι A   θαρσαλέος ES: θαρσαλέως M Ach.   464 κατανομένων MS: κατανυμένων

in the sky just as they are.

But there are five other stars among them, but quite unlike them, [455] that circulate all the way through the
twelve figures of the zodiac. You cannot in this case identify where these lie by looking at other stars, for they all
change their positions. The years of their orbits are long,
and at long intervals are their configurations when they
come from afar into conjunction. [460] I am not at all
confident in dealing with them: I hope I may be adequate
in expounding the circles of the fixed stars and their guide-
constellations in the sky.

There are indeed these four circles set like wheels, for
which there will be particular desire and need if you are
studying the measurements of the self-fulfilling years. [465]
Many guide-stars lie along them all, to mark them, all
bound closely together all the way; the circles themselves
are without breadth and fastened all to each other, but in
size two are matched with two.

If ever on a clear night, when all the brilliant [470] stars
are displayed to men by celestial Night, and at new moon
none in its course is dimmed, but all shine sharply in the
darkness – if ever at such a time a wondering has come
into your mind [474] when you observed the sky split all
the way round by a broad circle, or someone else standing
beside you has pointed out to you that star-emblazoned
wheel (men call it the Milk), no other circle that rings the
sky is like it in colour, but two of the four are equal to it in

---

V: κατανυομένων A: ἀνυομένων E   465 περίκειται MS: ἐπίκειται E
466 συνεεργμένα MES: συνεερμένα N coni. Buttmann   467 δ'
ἀπλατέες Hi.: δὲ πλατέες Att.: δ' ἀπλανέες MES (sine errore L)   469
ὅτε ES: ὅτι M   471 νεόμηνι MES sch.ʸᵖ: διχόμηνι A sch. Hdn
(bipertita luna L)   472 γε κνέφαος ME: γ' ἐκ νέφεος A: γ' ἐκ νεφέων S
474 κεκεασμένον M: κεκασμένον S: κεκαασμένον E   475 ἢ ME: εἰ S
ἐπιστὰς V: ὑποστὰς MES (subsistens L)   476 περιγληνὲς ME: περιγ-
ληφὲς S: περίγληνον Ach.   477 τῷ δή τοι MES Hi.ᴮ: τῷ δ' ἤτοι
V Hi.ᴬ: τῷδ' ἤτοι Voss

οἱ δύο, τοὶ δέ σφεων μέγα μείονες εἰλίσσονται.
480 τῶν ὁ μὲν ἐγγύθεν ἐστὶ κατερχομένου βορέαο.
ἐν δέ οἱ ἀμφότεραι κεφαλαὶ Διδύμων φορέονται,
ἐν δὲ τὰ γούνατα κεῖται ἀρηρότος Ἡνιόχοιο,
λαιὴ δὲ κνήμη καὶ ἀριστερὸς ὦμος ἐπ' αὐτῷ
Περσέος, Ἀνδρομέδης δὲ μέσην ἀγκῶνος ὕπερθε
485 δεξιτερὴν ἐπέχει· τὸ μέν οἱ θέναρ ὑψόθι κεῖται
ἀσσότερον βορέαο, νότῳ δ' ἐπικέκλιται ἀγκών.
ὁπλαὶ δ' Ἵππειοι καὶ ὑπαύχενον Ὀρνίθειον
ἄκρη σὺν κεφαλῇ καλοί τ' Ὀφιούχεοι ὦμοι
αὐτὸν δινεύονται ἐληλάμενοι περὶ κύκλον.
490 ἡ δ' ὀλίγον φέρεται νοτιωτέρη οὐδ' ἐπιβάλλει
Παρθένος, ἀλλὰ Λέων καὶ Καρκίνος. οἱ μὲν ἄρ' ἄμφω
ἐξείης κέαται βεβολημένοι, αὐτὰρ ὁ κύκλος
τὸν μὲν ὑπὸ στῆθος καὶ γαστέρα μέχρι παρ' αἰδῶ
τέμνει, τὸν δὲ διηνεκέως ὑπένερθε χελείου
495 Καρκίνον, ἧχι μάλιστα διχαιόμενόν κε νοήσαις
ὀρθόν, ἵν' ὀφθαλμοὶ κύκλου ἑκάτερθεν ἴοιεν.
τοῦ μὲν ὅσον τε μάλιστα δι' ὀκτὼ μετρηθέντος,
πέντε μὲν ἔνδια στρέφεται καθ' ὑπέρτερα γαίης,
τὰ τρία δ' ἐν περάτῃ· θέρεος δέ οἱ ἐν τροπαί εἰσιν.
500 ἀλλ' ὁ μὲν ἐν βορέῳ περὶ Καρκίνον ἐστήρικται.
ἄλλος δ' ἀντιόωντι νότῳ μέσον Αἰγοκερῆα
τέμνει καὶ πόδας Ὑδροχόου καὶ Κήτεος οὐρήν·
ἐν δέ οἵ ἐστι Λαγωός, ἀτὰρ Κυνὸς οὐ μάλα πολλὴν
αἴνυται, ἀλλ' ὁπόσην ἐπέχει ποσίν· ἐν δέ οἱ Ἀργὼ
505 καὶ μέγα Κενταύροιο μετάφρενον, ἐν δὲ τὸ κέντρον

480–2 Hi. 1.10.1   481–8 Hi. 1.2.19   483–4 (... Περσέος) Hi. 1.10.5
484–5 (Ἀνδρομέδης ... ἐπέχει) Hi. 1.10.6   487–8 (... κεφαλῇ) Hi.
1.10.7   488–9 (καλοί ...) Hi. 1.10.9   490–6 Hi. 1.10.10   497–9
Gem. 5.24; [Procl.] *Sph.* 4; (om. ὅσον et μάλιστα) Anon. 1 p. 94 Maass;
(... περάτῃ) Hi. 1.3.5, 1.9.10   498–9 Ach. p. 56   501–6 Hi. 1.2.21,
1.10.16

---

479 μέγα μείονες M^{γρ}E Hi.^B: μέγ' ἀμείνονες MS   481–96 his uersi-

size, while the others as they turn are much smaller.

[480] One of the latter is close to the onset of the north wind. On it move the two heads of the Twins, on it lie the knees of the steadfast Charioteer, and after him the left leg and left shoulder of Perseus. It occupies the middle of Andromeda's right arm above the elbow; her palm lies above it, [486] nearer the north, her elbow inclines to the south. The Horse's hoofs, the Bird's neck with the head at one extremity, and the bright shoulders of Ophiuchus revolve riding round the actual circle. [490] The Maiden goes a little farther south and does not touch it, but the Lion and the Crab do. These two lie in position one after the other, and the circle cuts the Lion below the breast and belly as far as the genitals, the Crab all the way below the shell, where you can most clearly observe it being divided [496] straight through at the point where the eyes go on either side of the circle. If the circle is measured approximately in eight parts, five revolve in the sky above the earth, and the other three below the horizon. The summer solstices are on it. [500] This circle is fixed in the north on the latitude of the Crab.

Another circle in the opposing south cuts the middle of Capricorn, the Water-pourer's feet, and the Monster's tail. The Hare is on it, but it does not take up much of the Dog, only the space the Dog occupies with its feet. On it are the Argo [505] and the Centaur's great back, on it is

bus in E elutis (481–6) ac deletis (487–96) nouos in margine supposuit Planudes   482 τὰ M Hi. bis Πι: τε A: τι S   483 αὐτῷ codd.: αὐτοῦ Hi. bis   484 περσέος S Πι: περσέως M Hi. bis   489 αὐτὸν MES: αὐτοῦ sch.   490 φέρεται ME Πι: φαίνεται S   491 ἄρ’ ES: ἄρ M: ἄμ’ V Hi.   492 βεβολη*μένοι* MES[sl]: βεβλημένοι S Hi. 495 νοήσαις S: νοήσεις ME: νοήσῃς H   496 ἴοιεν ME: ἴομεν S 498 ἔνδια στρέφεται MES: ἐνδιαστρέφεται A   καθ’ ὑπέρτερα ME: καθ’ ὑπέρτατα S: καὶ ὑπέρτατα M[γρ]   501–6 his uersibus in E deletis nouos in margine supposuit Planudes   501 ἀντιόωντι codd.: ἀντιόωντα nonnulli in sch.   505 τὸ ME Hi. 1.10.16, Hi.[A] 1.2.21: τε S: οἱ Hi.[B] 1.2.21

Σκορπίου, ἐν καὶ τόξον ἀγαυοῦ Τοξευτῆρος.
τὸν πύματον καθαροῖο παρερχόμενος βορέαο
ἐς νότον ἠέλιος φέρεται, τρέπεταί γε μὲν αὐτοῦ
χειμέριος· καί οἱ τρία μὲν περιτέλλεται ὑψοῦ
510 τῶν ὀκτώ, τὰ δὲ πέντε κατώρυχα δινεύονται.
μεσσόθι δ' ἀμφοτέρων, ὅσσος πολιοῖο Γάλακτος,
γαῖαν ὑποστρέφεται κύκλος διχόωντι ἐοικώς·
ἐν δέ οἱ ἤματα νυξὶν ἰσαίεται ἀμφοτέρῃσι
φθίνοντος θέρεος, τοτὲ δ' εἴαρος ἱσταμένοιο.
515 σῆμα δέ οἱ Κριὸς Ταύροιό τε γούνατα κεῖται,
Κριὸς μὲν κατὰ μῆκος ἐληλάμενος διὰ κύκλου,
Ταύρου δὲ σκελέων ὅσση περιφαίνεται ὀκλάς.
ἐν δέ τέ οἱ ζώνη εὐφεγγέος Ὠρίωνος
καμπή τ' αἰθομένης Ὕδρης, ἐνί οἱ καὶ ἐλαφρὸς
520 Κρητήρ, ἐν δὲ Κόραξ, ἐνὶ δ' ἀστέρες οὐ μάλα πολλοὶ
Χηλάων, ἐν τῷ δ' Ὀφιούχεα γοῦνα φορεῖται.
οὐ μὴν Αἰητοῦ ἀπαμείρεται, ἀλλά οἱ ἐγγὺς
Ζηνὸς ἀητεῖται μέγας ἄγγελος· ἡ δὲ κατ' αὐτὸν
Ἱππείη κεφαλὴ καὶ ὑπαύχενον εἰλίσσονται.
525 τοὺς μὲν παρβολάδην ὀρθοὺς περιβάλλεται ἄξων
μεσσόθι πάντας ἔχων· ὁ δὲ τέτρατος ἐσφήκωται
λοξὸς ἐν ἀμφοτέροις, οἵ μίν ῥ' ἑκάτερθεν ἔχουσιν
ἀντιπέρην τροπικοί, μέσσος δέ ἑ μεσσόθι τέμνει.
οὔ κεν Ἀθηναίης χειρῶν δεδιδαγμένος ἀνὴρ
530 ἄλλῃ κολλήσαιτο κυλινδόμενα τροχάλεια
τοῖά τε καὶ τόσα πάντα περὶ σφαιρηδὸν ἑλίσσων,
ὡς τά γ' ἐναιθέρια πλαγίῳ συναρηρότα κύκλῳ

513–14 Hi. 1.9.9   515–17 Hi. 1.10.18   518–20 (... Κόραξ) Hi.
1.10.19   520–1 (ἐνὶ ...) Hi. 1.10.19   522–4 Hi. 1.10.21   529–30
(... κολλήσαιτο) Anon. 1 p. 94

506 ἀγαυοῦ MES Hi. 1.10.16: ἐλαφροῦ Μγρ sch. Hi. 1.2.21 (leuioris L)
507 παρερχόμενος MES: -όμενον A: κατερχόμενος Μsl: διερχόμενος
D   512 ὑποστρέφεται MES: ἐπιστρέφεται V: ὕπο στρέφεται Maass
διχόωντι C: διχάοντι MES   515–24 his uersibus in E deletis nouos

the Scorpion's sting, on it the bow of the brilliant Archer. This is the last circle that the sun comes to as it passes southward from the clear north wind, and there is its winter solstice. Three of its eight parts go round above the horizon, the other five circle underground.

[511] Between these two, as large as the circle of white Milk, a circle like one bisected curves below the earth. On it the days are equal to the nights on two occasions, at the waning of summer and again at the beginning of spring. [515] As a guide the Ram and the knees of the Bull lie on it, the Ram as drawn lengthwise along the circle, but of the Bull only the widely visible bend of the legs. On it is the belt of the radiant Orion and the coil of the blazing Hydra, on it too are the faint [520] Bowl, on it the Raven, on it the not very numerous stars of the Claws, and on it the knees of Ophiuchus ride. It is certainly not bereft of the Eagle: it has the great messenger of Zeus flying near by; and along it the Horse's head and neck move round.

[525] The axis holding them all at the centre rotates these parallel circles at right angles to itself; but the fourth is gripped obliquely between the two tropics, which hold it on opposite sides, while the middle one cuts it in the middle. In no other way would a man trained in the crafts-manship of Athene weld together revolving wheels [531] in such a pattern and of such a size, rounding off the whole like a sphere, than the system of celestial circles, which,

---

in margine supposuit Planudes   515 οἱ codd.: τοι Hi.   517 ὀκλάς
Hi.: ὀκλάξ ΜΕ: ὀκλάξ S   518 εὐφεγγέος MES: ἐΰφεγγέος A
521 γοῦνα φορεῖται MES: γούνατα κεῖται V Hi. (*genibus iacent* L)
522 ἀπαμείρεται ΜΕ Hi.: ἀπομείρεται Α: ἀπαμείβεται S   οἱ ΜΕ:
μάλ᾽ S   523 ἀητεῖται MS: ἀεὶ κεῖται E   αὐτὸν ES Hi.: αὐτοὺς M
524 ὑπαύχενον MS: ἱππαύχενον E   525 περιβάλλεται S: περιτέλλεται ΜΕ   529 οὔ κεν ES l (M): οὐκ ἐν M   δεδιδαγμένος codd.:
δεδαημένος Anon. 1   530 κολλήσαιτο codd.: κοσμήσειεν Anon. 1
531 περὶ σφαιρηδὸν Ε: περισφαιρηδὸν MS   532 ὡς ΜΕ: ὣς S
ἐναιθέρια ES: ἐν αἰθέρια Α: ἐν αἰθέρι (erasa in fine littera) M

ἐξ ἠοῦς ἐπὶ νύκτα διώκεται ἤματα πάντα.
καὶ τὰ μὲν ἀντέλλει τε καὶ αὐτίκα νειόθι δύνει
535 πάντα παραβλήδην, μία δέ σφεων ἐστὶν ἑκάστου
ἑξείης ἑκάτερθε κατηλυσίη ἄνοδός τε.
αὐτὰρ ὅ γ᾽ ὠκεανοῦ τόσσον παραμείβεται ὕδωρ,
ὅσσον ἀπ᾽ Αἰγοκερῆος ἀνερχομένοιο μάλιστα
Καρκίνον εἰς ἀνιόντα κυλίνδεται, ὅσσον ἀπάντη
540 ἀντέλλων ἐπέχει, τόσσον γε μὲν ἀλλόθι δύνων.
ὅσσον δ᾽ ὀφθαλμοῖο βολῆς ἀποτείνεται αὐγή,
ἑξάκις ἂν τόσση μιν ὑποδράμοι· αὐτὰρ ἑκάστη
ἴση μετρηθεῖσα δύω περιτέμνεται ἄστρα.
ζωϊδίων δέ ἑ κύκλον ἐπίκλησιν καλέουσι.
545 τῷ ἔνι Καρκίνος ἐστί, Λέων δ᾽ ἐπὶ τῷ, καὶ ὑπ᾽ αὐτὸν
Παρθένος, αἱ δ᾽ ἐπί οἱ Χηλαὶ καὶ Σκορπίος αὐτός,
Τοξευτής τε καὶ Αἰγόκερως, ἐπὶ δ᾽ Αἰγοκερῆι
Ὑδροχόος· δύο δ᾽ αὐτῷ ἔπ᾽ Ἰχθύες ἀστερόωνται,
τοὺς δὲ μέτα Κριός, Ταῦρός δ᾽ ἐπὶ τῷ Δίδυμοί τε.
550 ἐν τοῖς ἥλιος φέρεται δυοκαίδεκα πᾶσι
πάντ᾽ ἐνιαυτὸν ἄγων, καί οἱ περὶ τοῦτον ἰόντι
κύκλον ἀέξονται πᾶσαι ἐπικάρπιοι ὧραι.
τοῦ δ᾽ ὅσσον κοίλοιο κατ᾽ ὠκεανοῖο δύηται,
τόσσον ὑπὲρ γαίης φέρεται, πάσῃ δ᾽ ἐπὶ νυκτὶ
555 ἓξ αἰεὶ δύνουσι δυωδεκάδες κύκλοιο,
τόσσαι δ᾽ ἀντέλλουσι. τόσον δ᾽ ἐπὶ μῆκος ἑκάστη
νὺξ αἰεὶ τετάνυσται, ὅσον τέ περ ἥμισυ κύκλου
ἀρχομένης ἀπὸ νυκτὸς ἀείρεται ὑψόθι γαίης.

534–9 (... κυλίνδεται) Hi. 2.1.17   537–40 Gem. 7.7   537–9 (...
ἀνιόντα) Ach. p. 52 bis   541–3 Hi. 1.9.11; S.E. Math. 1.304; Cleom.
2.1.82; paraphr. Sporus in sch. p. 320 Martin   542–4 (αὐτὰρ ...)
sch. E. Ph. 1   544 Hdn ii.516; Et.M. 413, 15   545–9 Plu. Plac. 1.6
553–8 Hi. 1.9.11   554–8 (πάσῃ ...) Gem. 7.13   555 Ach. p. 54

---

534 αὐτίκα MES: ἀντία M^γρ   536 κατηλυσίη MS: κατήλυσις ἠδ᾽
E: κατηλυσίη τ᾽ Voss   537 ὠκεανοῦ τόσσον MES Ach. bis: ὠκεανοῖο τόσον C Hi. Gem.   538 ἀνερχομένοιο E^slS: ἐρχομένοιο ME
541 ἀποτείναται Hi. Cleom.: ἀποτέμναται codd. Sporus in sch.: ἀπο-

united by the oblique circle, speed from dawn to nightfall all the time. Three of the circles rise and anon sink down [535] all parallel, and each of them has one point of setting and of rising successively on either side. But the fourth moves along as much of the water of ocean as rolls from about Capricorn's rising to the rising of the Crab, the arc of its settings on the other side equalling the whole arc covered by its risings. [541] Six times the length of the beam from an observer's eye-glance would subtend this circle, and each sixth measured equal intercepts two constellations. Men call it by name the circle of the Zodiac. [545] On it is the Crab, and next the Lion, and under that the Maiden, after her the Claws and the Scorpion itself, the Archer and Capricorn, and after Capricorn the Water-pourer; after him the two Fishes are starred, after them the Ram, the Bull after that and the Twins [550]. Through all these twelve signs goes the sun as it brings the whole year to pass, and as it goes round this circle, all the fruitful seasons increase. The arc that moves above the earth equals the arc that is sunk beneath the gulf of ocean, and every night [555] six twelfths of the circle always set and the same number rise. Every night always extends in length corresponding to the semicircle that rises above the earth from the beginning of night.

λάμπεται S.E.   542 τόσση μιν M^γρES S.E.: τόσσ' ἡμῖν M Hi.^B
Cleom.   ὑποδράμοι MS Hi. Sporus S.E. Cleomedis codd. duo: ὑπ-
εκδράμοι E: ὑποδράμῃ A Cleomedis codd. rell.]μη Π6   543 περιτέμνεται ME^sl Hi. sch. E. *Ph.*: περιτέλλεται E S.E. Cleom.]ελλεται Π6:
περιγίνεται S   544 ζωϊδίων Q sch. E. *Ph.*: ζωΐδιον MES   545 τῷ
MES: τῷ δ' V Plut.   δ' ἐπὶ V Π6 Plut.: ἐπὶ ME: τ' ἐπὶ S   καὶ ὑπ'
αὐτὸν ES: καὶ ὑπ' αὐτοῦ M: μετὰ δ' αὐτὸν Plut.   546 αἱ δ' codd.:
ἡδ' Plut.   548 αὐτῷ ἔπ' Voss: αὐτῷ A: αὐτὸν ἔπ' E: αὐτὸν ἐπ' M
Plut.: αὐτὸν ὑπ' S   ἀστερόωνται codd.: αστεροω[Π6: ἀστερόεντες
Plut.   549 δ' ἐπὶ ME: τ' ἐπὶ S   553 κοίλοιο ME: κύκλοιο S
555 δυωδεκάδες Q Hi. Gem. Ach.: δυωδεκάδος MES   557 τετάνυσται MES: τετάνυται Hi.^A: τάνυται C Hi.^B   ὅσον M^sl: τόσον M:
ὅσσον S: τόσσον E Hi.

οὔ κεν ἀπόβλητον δεδοκημένῳ ἤματος εἴη
560 μοιράων σκέπτεσθαι ὅτ᾽ ἀντέλλησιν ἑκάστη·
αἰεὶ γὰρ τάων γε μιῇ συνανέρχεται αὐτὸς
ἠέλιος. τὰς δ᾽ ἄν κε περισκέψαιο μάλιστα
εἰς αὐτὰς ὁρόων· ἀτὰρ εἰ νεφέεσσι μέλαιναι
γίνοιντ᾽ ἢ ὄρεος κεκρυμμέναι ἀντέλλοιεν,
565 σήματ᾽ ἐπερχομένῃσιν ἀρηρότα ποιήσασθαι.
αὐτὸς δ᾽ ἂν μάλα τοι κεράων ἑκάτερθε διδοίη
ὠκεανός, τά τε πολλὰ περιστέφεται ἑοῖ αὐτῷ,
νειόθεν ὁππῆμος κείνων φορέῃσιν ἑκάστην.
οὔ οἱ ἀφαυρότατοι, ὅτε Καρκίνος ἀντέλλησιν,
570 ἀστέρες ἀμφοτέρωθεν ἑλισσόμενοι περίκεινται,
τοὶ μὲν δύνοντες, τοὶ δ᾽ ἐξ ἑτέρης ἀνιόντες.
δύνει μὲν Στέφανος, δύνει δὲ κατὰ ῥάχιν Ἰχθῦς·
ἥμισυ μέν κεν ἴδοιο μετήορον, ἥμισυ δ᾽ ἤδη
ἐσχατιαὶ βάλλουσι κατερχομένου Στεφάνοιο.
575 αὐτὰρ ὅ γ᾽ ἐξόπιθεν τετραμμένος ἄλλα μὲν οὔπω
γαστέρι νειαίρῃ, τὰ δ᾽ ὑπέρτερα νυκτὶ φορεῖται.
τὸν δὲ καὶ εἰς ὤμους κατάγει μογερὸν Ὀφιοῦχον
Καρκίνος ἐκ γονάτων, κατάγει δ᾽ Ὄφιν αὐχένος ἐγγύς.
οὐδ᾽ ἂν ἔτ᾽ Ἀρκτοφύλαξ εἴη πολὺς ἀμφοτέρωθεν,
580 μείων ἡμάτιος, τὸ δ᾽ ἐπὶ πλέον ἔννυχος ἤδη.
τέτρασι γὰρ μοίραις ἄμυδις κατιόντα Βοώτην
ὠκεανὸς δέχεται· ὁ δ᾽ ἐπὴν φάεος κορέσηται,
βουλυτῷ ἐπέχει πλεῖον δίχα νυκτὸς ἰούσης,
ἦμος ὅτ᾽ ἠελίοιο κατερχομένοιο δύηται.
585 κεῖναί οἱ καὶ νύκτες ἐπ᾽ ὀψὲ δύοντι λέγονται.
ὣς οἱ μὲν δύνουσιν, ὁ δ᾽ ἀντίος οὐδὲν ἀεικής,
ἀλλ᾽ εὖ μὲν ζώνῃ εὖ δ᾽ ἀμφοτέροισι φαεινὸς

559–68 Hi. 2.1.2   575–6 Hi. 2.2.16   577–8 Ach. p. 73   579–82
(... δέχεται) Hi. 2.2.12   581–2 (... δέχεται) sch. (EHPQV) ε 272
582–3 (ὁ δ᾽ ...) Hi. 2.2.17   585 (ὀψὲ ...) Hdn ii.932, 19

559 δεδοκημένῳ MES: δεδοκημένον A Hi.ᴬ: δεδόκειμεν Hi.ᴮ   560
ἀντέλλησιν ἑκάστη codd.: -λλωσιν -ται Hi. (oriuntur uniuersa L)   564

It can be well worth while, if you are watching for daybreak, [560] to observe when each twelfth of the Zodiac
rises, for the sun itself always rises with one of them. It will
be best if you can identify them by looking at the actual
constellations; but if they are darkened by clouds or obscured by a mountain when they rise, [565] you must find
for yourself reliable pointers to their rising. The ocean itself can give you on both its horns the many constellations
with which it garlands itself, whenever it brings up each
twelfth of the Zodiac from below.

Not the faintest, when the Crab rises, [570] are the circling stars that lie round the ocean to east and west, some
setting, some rising from the other horizon. Setting is the
Crown, and setting the Fish as far as its spine; half of the
setting Crown you can see in the sky, while half is already
cast down by the world's edge. [575] The backward-turned
figure, in the parts up to the lower belly, is not yet set, but
the upper parts move in darkness. The Crab also brings
down the toiling Ophiuchus from knees to shoulders, and
brings down the Serpent close to the neck. No more will
Bootes bulk large above and below the horizon, the lesser
part being above, and the greater already in darkness. It
takes four signs of the Zodiac together for the ocean to
receive Bootes' setting. When he is sated with daylight, he
occupies more than half of the passing night in the loosing
of his oxen, in the season when he begins setting as the sun
goes down. [585] These nights are named after his late
setting. So these constellations set, while opposite them no
meagre one, but brilliant with his belt and two shoulders,

γίνοιντ' V Hi.: γίνοντ' MES   565 ἐπερχομένῃσιν A Hi.^{B}: -μένοισιν
MES Hi.^{A} 567 περιστέφεται Buttmann: περιστρέφεται codd. Hi.
(circumuertitur L)   573 ἴδοιο ES: ἴδηαι M   575 ὅ γ' ἐξόπιθεν codd.
Hi.: ὁ Γνὺξ ὄπιθεν Voss: Γνὺξ ὄπιθεν Maass   ἄλλα MES: ἀλλὰ C:
ἀλλ' ὁ Hi.^{A} 581 ἄμυδις ES Hi. sch. ε 272: ἤδη MS^{sl} 585 οἱ V:
τοι MES   ἐπ' ὀψὲ ES: ἐποψὲ M

ὤμοις Ὠρίων, ξίφεός γε μὲν ἶφι πεποιθώς,
πάντα φέρων Ποταμόν, κέραος παρατείνεται ἄλλου.
590 ἐρχομένῳ δὲ Λέοντι τὰ μὲν κατὰ πάντα φέρονται
Καρκίνῳ ὄσσ' ἐδύοντο, καὶ Αἰετός. αὐτὰρ ὅ γε γνὺξ
ἥμενος ἄλλα μὲν ἤδη, ἀτὰρ γόνυ καὶ πόδα λαιὸν
οὔπω κυμαίνοντος ὑποστρέφει ὠκεανοῖο.
ἀντέλλει δ' Ὕδρης κεφαλὴ χαροπός τε Λαγωὸς
595 καὶ Προκύων πρότεροί τε πόδες Κυνὸς αἰθομένοιο.
οὐ μέν θην ὀλίγους γαίης ὑπὸ νείατα βάλλει
Παρθένος ἀντέλλουσα. Λύρη τότε Κυλληναίη
καὶ Δελφὶς δύνουσι καὶ εὐποίητος Ὀϊστός.
σὺν τοῖς Ὄρνιθος πρῶτα πτερὰ μέσφα παρ' αὐτὴν
600 οὐρὴν καὶ Ποταμοῖο παρηορίαι σκιόωνται·
δύνει δ' Ἱππείη κεφαλή, δύνει δὲ καὶ αὐχήν.
ἀντέλλει δ' Ὕδρη μὲν ἐπὶ πλέον ἄχρι παρ' αὐτὸν
Κρητῆρα, φθάμενος δὲ Κύων πόδας αἴνυται ἄλλους,
ἕλκων ἐξόπιθεν πρύμναν πολυτειρέος Ἀργοῦς·
605 ἡ δὲ θέει γαίης ἱστὸν διχόωσα κατ' αὐτόν,
Παρθένος ἦμος ἅπασα περαιόθεν ἄρτι γένηται.
οὐδ' ἂν ἐπερχόμεναι Χηλαί, καὶ λεπτὰ φάουσαι,
ἄφραστοι παρίοιεν, ἐπεὶ μέγα σῆμα Βοώτης
ἀθρόος ἀντέλλει βεβολημένος Ἀρκτούροιο.
610 Ἀργὼ δ' εὖ μάλα πᾶσα μετήορος ἵσταται ἤδη·
ἀλλ' Ὕδρη, κέχυται γὰρ ἐν οὐρανῷ ἤλιθα πολλή,
οὐρῆς ἂν δεύοιτο. μόνην δ' ἐπὶ Χηλαὶ ἄγουσι
614 δεξιτερὴν κνήμην αὐτῆς ἐπιγουνίδος ἄχρις
615 αἰεὶ γνύξ, αἰεὶ δὲ Λύρη παραπεπτηῶτος,
ὅντινα τοῦτον ἄϊστον ὑπουρανίων εἰδώλων

591–3 (αὐτὰρ ...) Hi. 1.4.14   594–5 Ach. p. 73   596–7 (ἀντέλλουσα ...) Hi. 2.1.25   597–606 (Λύρη ...) Hi. 2.2.36   603–6 (φθάμενος ...) Hi. 2.1.25   605–6 paraphr. Att. p. 20   607–10 Att. p. 20
607–9 Hi. 1.4.19–20, 2.2.18   612 (μόνην ...) + 614 Hi. 1.4.13
616–18 (... θηεύμεθα) Ach. p. 74   618–22 (τοῦ ... φορέουσιν) Hi.
2.2.44

---

595 πρότεροι ΜΕ: πότεροι S   597 κυλληναίη ΕS: κυληναίη Μ Hi.

Orion, trusting in the might of his sword, extends along the other horizon, bringing with him all of the River.

[590] At the Lion's coming the constellations that were setting with the Crab now go down completely, and so does the Eagle. The crouching figure is already partly set, but his left hand and foot are not yet curving under the billowing ocean. Rising are the Hydra's head, the glassy-eyed Hare, [595] Procyon, and the forefeet of the blazing Dog.

Not a few constellations does the rising Maiden send below the earth's extremity. Hermes' Lyre and the Dolphin are setting then, and the well-shaped Arrow. With these the Bird from its westernmost wing-tip to its actual [600] tail and the farthest reach of the River are in shadow; down goes the Horse's head, and down goes also its neck. Still more of the Hydra rises, as far as the Bowl itself, while the Dog, rising before it, brings up its other feet, towing behind it the stern of the many-starred Argo; [605] the latter runs across the earth, bisected right at the mast, as soon as the Maiden appears completely over the horizon.

Nor can the coming of the Claws, although their light is faint, be unwittingly missed, since the great constellation Bootes rises complete, distinguished by Arcturus. [610] The whole of Argo is by now standing above the horizon; but the Hydra, being spread across the sky at great length, will lack its tail. The Claws bring up only the right leg as far as the actual knee [615] of the ever-kneeling, ever-crouching beside the Lyre, mysterious one, whoever he is,

---

599 μέσφα codd.: μέχρι Hi.   603 φθάμενος codd. Hi. sch.: φθαμένοις Voss   605 γαίης codd. Hi.: γαίη Voss   606 ἄρτι γένηται codd. Hi.: ἀντιφέρηται Hi.ᴬ 2.1.25   609 βεβολημένος codd. Att. Hi.ᴮ bis sch.: βεβλημένος Hi.ᴬ bis   610 εὖ Att.: οὐ MES: αὖ J. Schrader, *Observ. Lib.* 51   ἵσταται V Att. (*adsistens* L): ἔσσεται MES: ἔσσυται Voss   612 μόνην MES Hi.: μόνον T   613 δεινὸν ἐφεστηῶτ' ὀφιούχεα· τοῦ μὲν ἔπειτα addidit Planudes in imo margine E: om. MES Hi.   615 παραπεπτηῶτος ΜΕ: -ῶτα Eˢ¹S   616 ὑπουρανίων MS: ἐπουρανίων E

ΦΑΙΝΟΜΕΝΑ

ἀμφότερον δύνοντα καὶ ἐξ ἑτέρης ἀνιόντα
πολλάκις αὐτονυχεὶ θηεύμεθα. τοῦ μὲν ἄρ' οἴη
κνήμη σὺν Χηλῇσι φαείνεται ἀμφοτέρῃσιν,
620 αὐτὸς δ' ἐς κεφαλὴν ἔτι που τετραμμένος ἄλλῃ
Σκορπίον ἀντέλλοντα μένει καὶ ῥύτορα τόξου·
οἱ γάρ μιν φορέουσιν, ὁ μὲν μέσον ἄλλα τε πάντα,
χεῖρα δέ οἱ σκαιὴν κεφαλήν θ' ἅμα τόξον ἀγινεῖ.
ἀλλ' ὁ μὲν ὣς τρίχα πάντα καταμελεϊστὶ φορεῖται,
625 ἥμισυ δὲ Στεφάνοιο καὶ αὐτὴν ἔσχατον οὐρὴν
Κενταύρου φορέουσιν ἀνερχόμεναι ἔτι Χηλαί.
τῆμος ἀποιχομένην κεφαλὴν μέτα δύεται Ἵππος,
καὶ προτέρου Ὄρνιθος ἐφέλκεται ἔσχατος οὐρή.
δύνει δ' Ἀνδρομέδης κεφαλή· τὸ δέ οἱ μέγα δεῖμα
630 Κήτεος ἠερόεις ἐπάγει νότος, ἀντία δ' αὐτὸς
Κηφεὺς ἐκ βορέω μεγάλῃ ἀνὰ χειρὶ κελεύει.
καὶ τὸ μὲν ἐς λοφιὴν τετραμμένον ἄχρι παρ' αὐτὴν
δύνει, ἀτὰρ Κηφεὺς κεφαλῇ καὶ χειρὶ καὶ ὤμῳ.
καμπαὶ δ' ἂν Ποταμοῖο καὶ αὐτίκ' ἐπερχομένοιο
635 Σκορπίου ἐμπίπτοιεν ἐΰρρόου ὠκεανοῖο,
ὃς καὶ ἐπερχόμενος φοβέει μέγαν Ὠρίωνα.
Ἄρτεμις ἱλήκοι· προτέρων λόγος, οἵ μιν ἔφαντο
ἑλκῆσαι πέπλοιο, Χίῳ ὅτε θηρία πάντα
καρτερὸς Ὠρίων στιβαρῇ ἐπέκοπτε κορύνῃ,
640 θήρης ἀρνύμενος κείνῳ χάριν Οἰνοπίωνι.
ἡ δέ οἱ ἐξ αὐτῆς ἐπετείλατο θηρίον ἄλλο,
νήσου ἀναρρήξασα μέσας ἑκάτερθε κολώνας,
σκορπίον, ὅς ῥά μιν οὖτα καὶ ἔκτανε πολλὸν ἐόντα

625–26 Ach. p. 73   632–3 Ach. p. 73

618 αὐτονυχεὶ MES^ac: -χὶ S^pc   621 ῥύτορα ΜΕ^pcS: ῥήτορα Ε^ac
τόξου codd.: τόξων Hi.   623 κεφαλήν θ' Ε^sl: κεφαλῇ θ' MES: κεφαλῇ Α   624 καταμελεϊστὶ Μ: καταμμ- Ε^sl: κατὰ μελ- S   627
μέτα δύεται Ε coni. Grotius: μεταδύεται Μ: μετὰ δύεται S   629
δεῖμα ΜΕ^pc: δεῖγμα S   631 ἐκ S: ἐν ΜΕ   χειρὶ codd.: χερσὶ Voss
κελεύει S: κελεύων ΜΕ   632 ἄχρι παρ' αὐτὴν codd.: ἄχρις

118

among the celestial figures, whom we often observe both setting and then rising from the other horizon all on the same night. Only his leg is visible at the rising of the two Claws, [620] but the figure himself, turned upside down in the other direction, still awaits the rising of the Scorpion and the drawer of the bow. These bring him up, the former the waist and all the rest, while the bow brings the left hand and the head. Thus he comes up all piecemeal in three parts, [625] but half the Crown and the very tip of the Centaur's tail are produced by the Claws while they are still rising. At this time the Horse sets after its departed head, and the tail-tip of the Bird that has gone before trails down after it. [629] Andromeda's head sets; the cloudy south brings against her the great menace of the Monster, but Cepheus himself, confronting it in the north, waves it back with his mighty hand. So the Monster, moving in the direction of its back-fin, sets as far as that, while Cepheus sets with head and hand and shoulder.

The windings of the River will plunge into the fair stream of ocean as soon as the Scorpion arrives, [636] which also puts great Orion to flight at its coming. May Artemis be gracious! It is a tale of the ancients, who said that stalwart Orion seized her by her robe, when in Chios he was smiting all the wild creatures with his stout club, [640] striving to secure a hunting gift for Oenopion there. But she immediately summoned up against him another creature, breaking open the centre of the island's hills to left and to right, a scorpion that stung and killed him for

---

ἀπ' οὐρῆς Voss   633 χειρὶ codd.: χερσὶ Voss   ὤμῳ codd. Ach.ᴹ: ὤμοις Ach.ⱽ   634 αὐτίκ' ἐπερχομένοιο codd.: αὐτίκα ἐρχομένοιο Voss   638 ἑλκῆσαι M: ἑλκῦσαι E: ἑλκύσαι S   640 θήρης codd.: θοίνης Turnebus *Advers. Lib.* 150b   ἀρνύμενος codd.: αἰνύμενος sch.ʸᵖ κείνῳ codd.: κλεινῷ Heyne ad Apollod. 54   641 ἐξ αὐτῆς codd.: ἐξαυτῆς Matthiae   ἐπετείλατο sch.ʸᵖ: ἐπεστείλατο V: ἐπετείνατο MES 642 κολώνας codd.:]αις Π2: Κολώνας Maass

πλειότερος προφανείς, ἐπεὶ Ἄρτεμιν ἤκαχεν αὐτήν.
645 τοὔνεκα δὴ καί φασι περαιόθεν ἐρχομένοιο
Σκορπίου Ὠρίωνα περὶ χθονὸς ἔσχατα φεύγειν.
οὐδὲ μὲν Ἀνδρομέδης καὶ Κήτεος ὅσσ᾽ ἐλέλειπτο
κείνου ἔτ᾽ ἀντέλλοντος ἀπευθέες, ἀλλ᾽ ἄρα καὶ τοὶ
πανσυδίῃ φεύγουσιν. ὁ δὲ ζώνῃ τότε Κηφεὺς
650 γαῖαν ἐπιξύει, τὰ μὲν εἰς κεφαλὴν μάλα πάντα
βάπτων ὠκεανοῖο· τὰ δ᾽ οὐ θέμις, ἀλλὰ τά γ᾽ αὐταὶ
Ἄρκτοι κωλύουσι, πόδας καὶ γοῦνα καὶ ἰξύν.
ἡ δὲ καὶ αὐτὴ παιδὸς ἐπείγεται εἰδώλοιο
δειλὴ Κασσιέπεια· τὰ δ᾽ οὐκέτι οἱ κατὰ κόσμον
655 φαίνεται ἐκ δίφροιο, πόδες καὶ γούναθ᾽ ὕπερθεν,
ἀλλ᾽ ἤ γ᾽ εἰς κεφαλὴν ἴση δύετ᾽ ἀρνευτῆρι
μειρομένη καμάτων, ἐπεὶ οὐκ ἄρ᾽ ἔμελλεν ἐκείνη
Δωρίδι καὶ Πανόπῃ μεγάλων ἄτερ ἰσώσασθαι.
ἡ μὲν ἄρ᾽ εἰς ἑτέρην φέρεται. τὰ δὲ νειόθεν ἄλλα
660 οὐρανὸς ἀντιφέρει, Στεφάνοιό τε δεύτερα κύκλα
Ὕδρης τ᾽ ἐσχατιήν, φορέει τ᾽ ἐπὶ Κενταύροιο
σῶμά τε καὶ κεφαλὴν καὶ Θηρίον, ὅ ῥ᾽ ἐνὶ χειρὶ
δεξιτερῇ Κένταυρος ἔχει. τοὶ δ᾽ αὖθι μένουσι
τόξον ἐπερχόμενον πρότεροι πόδες ἱπποτάφηρος.
665 τόξῳ καὶ σπείρῃ Ὄφιος καὶ σῶμ᾽ Ὀφιούχου
ἀντέλλει ἐπιόντι· καρήατα δ᾽ αὐτὸς ἀγινεῖ
Σκορπίος ἀντέλλων, ἀνάγει δ᾽ αὐτὰς Ὀφιούχου
χεῖρας καὶ προτέρην Ὄφιος πολυτειρέος ἀγήν.
    τοῦ γε μὲν ἐν γόνασιν, περὶ γὰρ τετραμμένος αἰεὶ
670 ἀντέλλει, τότε μὲν περάτης ἐξέρχεται ἄλλα,

649–52 (ὁ δὲ ...) Ach. p. 72   650–2 Hi. 1.7.19   664 (πρότεροι ...)
Eust. in γ 68

---

645 ἐρχομένοιο EˢˡS (superueniente L): ἀρχομένοιο ME   648 ἔτ᾽ P (quoque
L): δ᾽ MES   ἀπευθέες codd.: ἀπευθέος Voss: ἀπευθέα M. Schmidt
651 ἀλλὰ τά γ᾽ MES Ach.ᴹ: ἀλλὰ τά τ᾽ Hi.ᴬ: ἀλλ᾽ ἄστατος Hi.ᴮ:
ἀλλ᾽ ἀτὰρ Ach.ⱽ   αὐταὶ codd. Π2: αὐτὰ Hi.ᴮ Ach.ᴹ: αὐτοὶ Ach.ⱽ
655 γούναθ᾽ ME: χεῖρες EʸᵖS (manus L)   657 μειρομένη codd.: αἱρο-

all his size, emerging even more massive, because he had outraged Artemis herself. [645] That is why they say that when the Scorpion comes over the horizon, Orion flees round the earth's boundary. Also the remaining stars of Andromeda and the Monster are not ignored while the Scorpion is still rising: they too disappear completely. At that time Cepheus with his belt [650] grazes the earth, while he dips all his head parts in the ocean; the rest he may not (the Bears themselves prevent them), his feet and legs and loins. Also sorrowful Cassiepeia herself hurries after the image of her daughter; but the part of her seen in the chair, feet and knees uppermost, is no longer comely: [656] she goes down head first like a tumbler, having her own share of trouble, for she had no hope of being a rival to Doris and Panope without severe penalty. So she moves towards one horizon. But the sky opposite brings up others from below, the second curve of the Crown [661] and the tail end of the Hydra, brings too the Centaur's body and head, and the Beast that the Centaur holds in his right hand. The forefeet of the rider-beast wait where they are for the rising of the bow. [665] The coil of the Serpent and the body of Ophiuchus rise at the coming of the bow; the rising Scorpion itself brings their heads, and upraises the actual hands of Ophiuchus and the foremost section of the richly-starred Serpent.

As for the figure on his knees, since he always rises upside down, the other parts then emerge from the horizon,

---

μένη Maass   καμάτων Reeve: γονάτων codd. sch. (a femoribus et genibus L)   659 νειόθεν ἄλλα EᵞᵖS (nuper ad altera L): νειόθι μᾶλλον ME   661 φορέει τ' S: φορέοι τ' M: φορέοντ' E   ἐπὶ codd.: ἔπι Voss 662 ὅ ῥ' ἐνὶ E: ὅρ' ἐν M: ὅρρ' ἐνὶ EˢˡS   664 ἱπποτάφηρος scripsi: ἱππότα φηρός ESˢˡ (equi sepultoris L): ἱππόφηρος M: ἱππότα θηρός Mˢˡ (uide Martin SAV p. 355) S: ἱπποταφηρός K: ἱπποτόφηρος Grotius 667 αὐτὰς ME sch.: αὐτὸς S   668 ἀγήν MᵖᶜEᵖᶜ: αὐγήν MᵃᶜS 670 ἄλλα MS: ἁλὸς E

γυῖά τε καὶ ζώνη καὶ στήθεα πάντα καὶ ὦμος
δεξιτερῇ σὺν χειρί· κάρη δ' ἑτέρης μετὰ χειρὸς
τόξῳ ἀνέρχονται καὶ Τοξότῃ ἀντέλλοντι.
σὺν τοῖς Ἑρμαίη τε Λύρη καὶ στήθεος ἄχρις
675 Κηφεὺς ἠῴου παρελαύνεται ὠκεανοῖο,
ἦμος καὶ μεγάλοιο Κυνὸς πᾶσαι ἀμαρυγαὶ
δύνουσιν, καὶ πάντα κατέρχεται Ὠρίωνος,
πάντα γε μὴν ἀτέλεστα διωκομένοιο Λαγωοῦ.
ἀλλ' οὐχ Ἡνιόχῳ Ἔριφοι οὐδ' Ὠλενίη Αἴξ
680 εὐθὺς ἀπέρχονται· τὰ δέ οἱ μεγάλην ἀνὰ χεῖρα
λάμπονται, καί οἱ μελέων διακέκριται ἄλλων
κινῆσαι χειμῶνας ὅτ' ἠελίῳ συνίωσιν·
ἀλλὰ τὰ μέν, κεφαλήν τε καὶ ἄλλην χεῖρα καὶ ἰξύν,
Αἰγόκερως ἀνιὼν κατάγει, τὰ δὲ νείατα πάντα
685 αὐτῷ Τοξευτῆρι κατέρχεται. οὐδ' ἔτι Περσεύς,
οὐδ' ἔτι ἄκρα κόρυμβα μένει πολυτείρεος Ἀργοῦς·
ἀλλ' ἤτοι Περσεὺς μὲν ἄτερ γουνός τε ποδός τε
δεξιτεροῦ δύεται, πρύμνης δ' ὅσον ἐς περιαγήν.
αὐτὴ δ' Αἰγοκερῆι κατέρχεται ἀντέλλοντι,
690 ἦμος καὶ Προκύων δύεται, τὰ δ' ἀνέρχεται ἄλλα,
Ὄρνις τ' Αἰητός τε τά τε πτερόεντος Ὀϊστοῦ
τείρεα καὶ νοτίοιο Θυτηρίου ἱερὸς ἕδρη.
Ἵππος δ' Ὑδροχόοιο μέσον περιτελλομένοιο
ποσσί τε καὶ κεφαλῇ ἀνελίσσεται. ἀντία δ' Ἵππου
695 ἐξ οὐρῆς Κένταυρον ἐφέλκεται ἀστερίη Νύξ,
ἀλλ' οὔ οἱ δύναται κεφαλὴν οὐδ' εὐρέας ὤμους
αὐτῷ σὺν θώρηκι χαδεῖν· ἀλλ' αἴθοπος Ὕδρης
αὐχενίην κατάγει σπείρην καὶ πάντα μέτωπα.
ἡ δὲ καὶ ἐξόπιθεν πολλὴ μένει· ἀλλ' ἄρα καὶ τὴν
700 αὐτῷ Κενταύρῳ, ὁπότ' Ἰχθύες ἀντέλλωσιν,

672–3 (κάρη ... ἀνέρχονται) Hi. 2.2.58   693–5 Ach. p. 73   693–4
(... ἀνελίσσεται) Hi. 2.3.6   693 Att. p. 21

---

671 γυῖα ΜΕᵃᶜʸᴾS: γοῦνα Εᴾᶜ   ὦμος ΜΕ: ὦμοι ΕʸᴾS (humeri L)
673 ἀνέρχονται codd.: ἀνέλκονται Hi.   680 δέ codd.: τε Maass

[671] the legs, the belt, all the breast, and the shoulder with the right hand; but the head with the other hand come up at the rising of the bow and the Archer. At the same time as these Hermes' Lyre and Cepheus as far as the breast ride up from the eastern ocean, [676] when all the brilliance of the great Dog is also setting, and down goes the whole of Orion and all of the unendingly pursued Hare. But in the Charioteer the Kids and the Olenian Goat do not [680] immediately depart: along his great arm they still shine, and are distinguished from his other limbs in the raising of storms when they come together with the sun; but some parts of the Charioteer, the head, the other arm and the waist, are sent down by Capricorn's rising, whereas all the lower half [685] actually sets with the Archer. Neither Perseus nor the stern of richly-starred Argo still remains: Perseus indeed sets except for his right knee and foot, and the stern of Argo as far as the curvature. The latter goes down completely at the rising of Capricorn, [690] when Procyon also sets, and other constellations rise, the Bird, the Eagle, the stars of the winged Arrow, and the holy seat of the Altar in the south.

When the waist of the Water-pourer rises, the Horse with feet and head comes coursing up. Opposite the Horse [695] starry Night draws the Centaur down tail first, but cannot yet find room for his head and broad shoulders together with the actual breastplate; but she does bring down the fiery Hydra's neck coil and all its head stars.

Much of the Hydra remains behind; but this too, [700] along with the Centaur itself, Night annexes completely

---

685–6 οὐδ' ἔτι bis Spitzner 151 (*iam non . . . neque adhuc* L): οὐδέ τι codd. 688 δ' M: θ' S: om. E   περιαγήν MES: -αυγήν D]αυγην Π2   691 τ' αἰητός H: θ' αἰητός MS: τ' ἠδ' ἀετός E   692 νοτίοιο Q: νοτίου MES   693 μέσον Hi. sch.(S): νέον codd. Att. Ach.   695 ἀστερίη MS: οὐρανίη E: ἑσπερίη Ach. (*uespere* L)   696 οὐδ' ME: ἠδ' S   ὤμους codd.:]μοις Π2   698 μέτωπα codd. Π2: πρόσωπα Maass   699 ἀλλ' ἄρα codd.: αλ[ ]α (alio α huic suprascripto) Π2   700 ὁπότ' codd.: οπου Π2

ΦΑΙΝΟΜΕΝΑ

ἀθρόον ἐμφέρεται. ὁ δ' ἐπ' Ἰχθύσιν ἔρχεται Ἰχθῦς
αὐτῷ κυανέῳ ὑποκείμενος Αἰγοκερῆι,
οὐ μὲν ἅδην, ὀλίγον δὲ δυωδεκάδ' ἀμμένει ἄλλην.
οὕτω καὶ μογεραὶ χεῖρες καὶ γοῦνα καὶ ὦμοι
705 Ἀνδρομέδης δίχα πάντα, τὰ μὲν πάρος, ἄλλα δ' ὀπίσσω,
τείνεται, ὠκεανοῖο νέον ὁπότε προγένωνται
Ἰχθύες ἀμφότεροι· τὰ μέν οἱ κατὰ δεξιὰ χειρὸς
αὐτοὶ ἐφέλκονται, τὰ δ' ἀριστερὰ νειόθεν ἕλκει
Κριὸς ἀνερχόμενος. τοῦ καὶ περιτελλομένοιο
710 ἑσπερόθεν κεν ἴδοιο Θυτήριον, αὐτὰρ ἐν ἄλλη
Περσέος ἀντέλλοντος ὅσον κεφαλήν τε καὶ ὤμους.
αὐτὴ δὲ ζώνη καί κ' ἀμφήριστα πέλοιτο
ἢ Κριῷ λήγοντι φαείνεται ἢ ἐπὶ Ταύρῳ,
σὺν τῷ πανσυδίῃ ἀνελίσσεται. οὐδ' ὅ γε Ταύρου
715 λείπεται ἀντέλλοντος, ἐπεὶ μάλα οἱ συναρηρὼς
Ἡνίοχος φέρεται· μοίρη γε μὲν οὐκ ἐπὶ ταύτῃ
ἀθρόος ἀντέλλει, Δίδυμοι δέ μιν οὖλον ἄγουσιν.
ἀλλ' Ἔριφοι λαιοῦ τε θέναρ ποδὸς Αἰγὶ σὺν αὐτῇ
Ταύρῳ συμφορέονται, ὅτε λοφιή τε καὶ οὐρὴ
720 Κήτεος αἰθερίοιο περαιόθεν ἀντέλλωσι.
δύνει δ' Ἀρκτοφύλαξ ἤδη πρώτη τότε μοίρη
τάων, αἳ πίσυρές μιν ἄτερ χειρὸς κατάγουσι
λαιῆς· ἡ δ' αὐτοῦ μεγάλη ὑπὸ τέλλεται Ἄρκτῳ.
ἀμφότεροι δὲ πόδες καταδυομένου Ὀφιούχου
725 μέσφ' αὐτῶν γονάτων Διδύμοις ἔπι σῆμα τετύχθω

704–9 (... ἀνερχόμενος) Hi. 2.1.24   708–13 Hi. 2.3.18   712–14
(ἀνελίσσεται) Hi. 2.3.21   712 (πέλοιτο) Att. p. 24, Hi. 2.3.32   713
Att. p. 22   718–19 (... συμφορέονται) Hi. 1.5.15   721–2 Hi. 2.2.12

---

701 ἰχθῦς ΜΕ: ἰχθύς S   703 οὐ codd.: οι Π2   δυωδεκάδ' ἀμμένει
ΜΕˢˡ: δ- ανυμενει Π2: δ- ἐμμένει Α: δυωδεκάδα μένει ES   ἄλλην
codd.:]λκην Π2   708 ἐφέλκονται MES Hi.: αφ[ ]λκονται Π2
709 ἀνερχόμενος codd. Hi. 2.1.24 Π2: ἀνελκόμενος Hi. 2.3.18   τοῦ
καὶ codd. Hi. bis: και μη Π2   711 περσέος MESᴾᶜ]ος Π2: περσέως
Sᵃᶜ   712 ζώνηι codd. Att. Hi.: ζωνηι Π2   κ' codd. Hi.ᴬ: om. Hi.ᴮ
Π2   πέλοιτο codd. Hi. Π2: πέλονται Att. nonnulli in Hi. 2.3.32:

124

when the Fishes rise. With the Fishes comes the Fish that
lies beneath dark Capricorn itself, not entirely, but a small
part waits for the next sign. So too the tragic arms and
knees and shoulders [705] of Andromeda extend all divided,
one side ahead, the other behind, when the two Fishes are
just emerging from the ocean; the stars on her right hand
the Fishes themselves draw up, but those on the left the
rising Ram brings up. When it rises you can also [710] see
the Altar in the west, and on the other horizon only just
the head and shoulders of Perseus rising.

But it may be questioned whether the belt itself is visible
at the end of the Ram's rising or with the Bull, [714] during
whose rising he emerges entirely. One constellation that is
not left behind when the Bull rises is the Charioteer, who
comes closely attached to it; yet he does not wholly rise
with this sign, but the Twins bring him up completely.
However the Kids and the sole of his left foot with the Goat
herself accompany the Bull, at the time when the back-fin
and tail [720] of the celestial Monster rise over the horizon. Bootes is by this time already setting with the first of
the four signs that bring him down, all but his left hand:
this circles there below the Great Bear.

Let the two legs of Ophiuchus setting [725] as far as the
actual knees be a sure signal for the Twins rising from the

γένοιτο Hi. 2.3.18   713 λήγοντι codd. Hi. Π2 sch.: ἀνιόντι Att.:
λήγουσα coni. Hi. 2.3.20   714 πανσυδίη M: πανσυδίην S: πασ-
συδίην E: πασσυδίη Att.   717 δέ μιν οὖλον MS: γέ μεν [sic] οὖλον
E: γε μεν ουροι Π2   721 ἤδη codd. Hi. Π2: τότε δή Voss   τότε
codd.: ἐπὶ Hi. Voss: δε τε Π2   722 πίσυρες ES Hi.: πίσσυρες M:
]σαρες Π2   μιν Hi.B: μὲν codd. Hi.A   723 αὐτοῦ MES:]του Π2:
αὐτῷ K (ei L)   μεγάλη MS: -ης E: -ας Π2   ὑπὸ τέλλεται scripsi:
ὑποτέλλεται ES: ὑπερτέλλεται M: ἐπιτέλλεται C:]πιτελλετ[Π2:
ὑποτείνεται Martin   ἄρκτῳ MS: ἄρκτου E:]υ[Π2: ἄρκτος T   724
δὲ Q coni. Morel: τε MES   725 διδύμοις MS: om. et s.l. add. E   ἔπι
Bekker: ἐπὶ codd.: επι Π2   τετύχθω codd.:]υκτω Π2: τετύχθων
Voss

ἐξ ἑτέρης ἀνιοῦσι. τότ' οὐκέτι Κήτεος οὐδὲν
ἕλκεται ἀμφοτέρωθεν, ὅλον δέ μιν ὄψεαι ἤδη.
ἤδη καὶ Ποταμοῦ πρώτην ἁλὸς ἐξανιοῦσαν
καμπὴν ἐν καθαρῷ πελάγει σκέψαιτό κε ναύτης,
730   αὐτὸν ἐπ' Ὠρίωνα μένων, εἴ οἱ ποθι σῆμα
ἢ νυκτὸς μέτρον ἠὲ πλόου ἀγγείλειε·
πάντη γὰρ τά γε πολλὰ θεοὶ ἄνδρεσσι λέγουσιν.
οὐχ ὁράᾳς; ὀλίγη μὲν ὅταν κεράεσσι σελήνη
ἑσπερόθεν φαίνηται, ἀεξομένοιο διδάσκει
735   μηνός· ὅτε πρώτη ἀποκίδναται αὐτόθεν αὐγή,
ὅσσον ἐπισκιάειν, ἐπὶ τέτρατον ἦμαρ ἰοῦσα·
ὀκτὼ δ' ἐν διχάσιν, διχόμηνα δὲ παντὶ προσώπῳ.
αἰεὶ δ' ἄλλοθεν ἄλλα παρακλίνουσα μέτωπα
εἴρει ὁποσταίη μηνὸς περιτέλλεται ἠώς.
740   ἄκρα γε μὴν νυκτῶν κεῖναι δυοκαίδεκα μοῖραι
ἄρκιαι ἐξειπεῖν. τὰ δέ που μέγαν εἰς ἐνιαυτόν,
ὥρη μέν τ' ἀρόσαι νειούς, ὥρη δὲ φυτεῦσαι,
ἐκ Διὸς ἤδη πάντα πεφασμένα πάντοθι κεῖται.
καὶ μέν τις καὶ νηΐ πολυκλύστου χειμῶνος
745   ἐφράσατ' ἢ δεινοῦ μεμνημένος Ἀρκτούροιο
ἠέ τεων ἄλλων, οἵ τ' ὠκεανοῦ ἀρύονται
ἀστέρες ἀμφιλύκης, οἵ τε πρώτης ἔτι νυκτός.
ἤτοι γὰρ τοὺς πάντας ἀμείβεται εἰς ἐνιαυτὸν
ἠέλιος μέγαν ὄγμον ἐλαύνων, ἄλλοτε δ' ἄλλῳ
750   ἐμπλήσσει, τοτὲ μέν τ' ἀνιών, τοτὲ δ' αὐτίκα δύνων,

733-9 Gem. 8.13   738 Ach. p. 50   745 sch. A.R. 2.1098-9a

---

727 δέ codd.: γε Π2   728 πρώτην A: πρώτης MES   731 μέτρον
MES: μέτρων D   733 ὅταν ES:]ταν Π2: ὅτ' ἂν M   κεράεσσι
codd.: κεράεσσα Gem.   734 διδάσκει codd. Gem.:]σκη Π2   735
ὅτε ES Gem.: ὅταν A: ὅτι M   πρώτη M Π2: πρώτην C: πρῶτον
EᵃᶜS: πρῶτον δ' Eᵖᶜ   ἀποκίδναται MES Gem.: ἐπικίδναται D Π2
αὐτόθεν codd.: αυτ[Π2: ἔνδοθεν Gem.   736 ὅσσον ME Gem.: ὅσον S:
οισσον Π2   ἐπισκιάειν codd.: -άει Π2 Gem.: -άει δ' Wilamowitz:
ὑποσκιάειν Voss   ἰοῦσα ME: ἰοῦσαν D: ἰούσῃ S: [ ]γ[ ]υσα Π2:
ἄγουσα coni. Buttmann   737 διχάσιν H: διχᾶσιν M: δίχασιν D:

opposite horizon. At that time no part of the Monster is any longer crossing either horizon: you can now see it complete. Now too a sailor on a clear night at sea can observe the first bend of the River emerging from the sea, [730] as he waits for Orion himself, to see if a sign will at some point predict for him the length of either the night or the voyage; for everywhere the gods give these many predictions to men.

Don't you see? When the moon with slender horns is sighted in the west, she declares a waxing [735] month; when the first light shed from her is enough to cast a shadow, she says she is entering on the fourth day; eight days she indicates at half-moon, mid-month when she is with full face. As she continually changes her aspect with different phases, she tells which day of the month is taking its course.

[740] For declaring the endings of nights those twelve signs of the Zodiac are certainly reliable. But as for the times of the great year, the time to plough fallow land, the time to plant trees, these are already all available as revealed by Zeus. Also many a man aboard ship has noticed signs of a surging storm by paying heed to either dread Arcturus [746] or some other stars that are drawn from the ocean at morning twilight and when it is still early night. In fact the sun overtakes them all throughout the year as he drives his great swathe, and impinges on different stars at different times, now at his rising and now again at his

---

διχασιν Π2: διχάσι S Gem.: διχάσει Ε   738 παρακλίνουσα codd. Gem.: παρακλεινουσα Π2: παρεκκλίνουσα Ach.   μέτωπα codd. Π2 Gem.: πρόσωπα Ach. sch.   739 ὁποσταίη codd. Gem.: υποσταιη Π2   740 μὴν codd. Π2: μὲν Voss   δυοκαίδεκα ES Π2: δυώδεκα M 741 δέ που codd.: γε που Π2   742 νειούς codd.: νειουθ Π2   744 πολυκλύστου Ε Π2: -τοιο MS   745 ἐφράσατ' ἢ δεινοῦ codd. Π2: φράζεσθαι δ' αἰνοῦ sch. A.R.   746 ἠέ τεων Ε: ἢ ἐτέων MS   747 ἀστέρες codd.:]ερος Π2   τε codd.: δε Π2   749 ὄγμον ΕΥᵖS Π2 Π7: οἶμον ΜΕ   750 ἐμπλήσσει D Π2 Π7: ἐμπλήσει MES: ἐμπελάσει Ceporinus: ἐμπελάει Stephanus

ἄλλος δ᾽ ἀλλοίην ἀστὴρ ἐπιδέρκεται ἠῶ.
γινώσκεις τάδε καὶ σύ, τὰ γὰρ συναείδεται ἤδη
ἐννεακαίδεκα κύκλα φαεινοῦ ἠελίοιο,
ὅσσα τ᾽ ἀπὸ ζώνης εἰς ἔσχατον Ὠρίωνα
755 νὺξ ἐπιδινεῖται Κύνα τε θρασὺν Ὠρίωνος,
οἵ τε Ποσειδάωνος ὁρώμενοι ἢ Διὸς αὐτοῦ
ἀστέρες ἀνθρώποισι τετυγμένα σημαίνουσι.
τῷ κείνων πεπόνησο. μέλοι δέ τοι, εἴ ποτε νηῒ
πιστεύεις, εὑρεῖν ὅσα που κεχρημένα κεῖται
760 σήματα χειμερίοις ἀνέμοις ἢ λαίλαπι πόντου.
μόχθος μέν τ᾽ ὀλίγος, τὸ δὲ μυρίον αὐτίκ᾽ ὄνειαρ
γίνετ᾽ ἐπιφροσύνης αἰεὶ πεφυλαγμένῳ ἀνδρί.
αὐτὸς μὲν τὰ πρῶτα σαώτερος, εὖ δὲ καὶ ἄλλον
παρειπὼν ὤνησεν, ὅτ᾽ ἐγγύθεν ὦρορε χειμών.
765 πολλάκι γὰρ καί τίς τε γαληναίη ὑπὸ νυκτὶ
νῆα περιστέλλει πεφοβημένος ἦρι θαλάσσης·
ἄλλοτε δὲ τρίτον ἦμαρ ἐπιτρέχει, ἄλλοτε πέμπτον,
ἄλλοτε δ᾽ ἀπρόφατον κακὸν ἵκετο. πάντα γὰρ οὔπω
ἐκ Διὸς ἄνθρωποι γινώσκομεν, ἀλλ᾽ ἔτι πολλὰ
770 κέκρυπται, τῶν αἴ κε θέλῃ καὶ ἐς αὐτίκα δώσει
Ζεύς· ὁ γὰρ οὖν γενεὴν ἀνδρῶν ἀναφανδὸν ὀφέλλει
πάντοθεν εἰδόμενος, πάντη δ᾽ ὅ γε σήματα φαίνων.
ἄλλα δέ τοι ἐρέει ἤ που διχόωσα σελήνη
πληθύος ἀμφοτέρωθεν ἢ αὐτίκα πεπληθυῖα,
775 ἄλλα δ᾽ ἀνερχόμενος, τοτὲ δ᾽ ἄκρη νυκτὶ κελεύων
ἥλιος. τὰ δέ τοι καὶ ἀπ᾽ ἄλλων ἔσσεται ἄλλα
σήματα καὶ περὶ νυκτὶ καὶ ἤματι ποιήσασθαι.

752–5 (τὰ γὰρ ...) Anon. περὶ ἐξηγήσεως p. 34 Martin;
(συναείδεται ...) Ach. p. 48   773 (διχόωσα σελήνη) Anon. περὶ
ποσότητος An. Ox. ii.325 Cr.; Et.M. 516, 9

---

752 τάδε ΜΕ: τὰ S   τὰ MS: om. et s.l. add. Ε   συναείδεται
codd.: συναγείρεται Ach.: συναείρεται Ludwig 444   758 τῷ Π2
(τωι): τῶ codd.   μέλοι ΜΕ sch.: μέλει S   759 κεχρημένα ΜΕS:
κεκριμένα C: κεκρυμμένα Voss   763 τὰ πρῶτα S: πρῶτα ΜΕ   ἄλλον
Ceporinus: ἄλλῳ MES (cum alio L): ἄλλων Aac   764 παρειπὼν

setting, [751] and so different stars look down on different kinds of day. You too know all these (for by now the nineteen cycles of the shining sun are all celebrated together), all the constellations that night revolves from the belt to Orion again at the end of the year and Orion's fierce Dog, [756] and the stars which, when sighted in Poseidon's realm or in that of Zeus himself, give clearly defined signs to men.

Therefore take pains to learn them. And if ever you entrust yourself to a ship, be concerned to find out all the signs that are provided anywhere of stormy winds or a hurricane at sea. [761] The effort is slight, but enormous is later the benefit of being observant to the man who is always on his guard: in the first place he is safer himself, and also he can help another with his advice when a storm is rising near by. [765] For often a man on a calm night secures his ship in fear of the sea at dawn: sometimes the trouble sweeps over the third day, sometimes the fifth, and sometimes arrives unexpectedly. For we men do not yet have knowledge of everything from Zeus, but much still [770] is hidden, whereof Zeus, if he wishes, will give us signs anon; he certainly does benefit the human race openly, showing himself on every side, and everywhere displaying his signs. Some things the moon will tell you, for example, when halved on either side of full, or again when she is full, [775] and other things the sun will tell you when rising and again in warnings at the beginning of night. And there will be other signs for you to make your own from other sources concerning night and day.

codd.: παρρε[Π2   ὥρορε ES: ὄρωρε M   765 τίς τε ES: τε M: τίς κε Martin   766 περιστέλλει codd.: -λλοι Martin   ἤρι codd.: ἤρα West ad Th. 852   767 δὲ S: δὴ A: μὲν ME   770 κε θέλῃ καὶ MS: κ' ἐθέλῃ καὶ D coni. Martin: κε θέλησιν E   ἐς αὐτίκα MS: ἐσαυτίκα E   771 οὖν M: om. ES   774 πληθύος Voss: πλήθουσ' codd.   775 τοτὲ ME: τότε S   κελεύων codd.: κελεύει Maass (iubet L)   776 τοι S: που ME   777 ἤματι ES: ἤματα M

σκέπτεο δὲ πρῶτον κεράων ἑκάτερθε σελήνην.
ἄλλοτε γάρ τ' ἄλλη μιν ἐπιγράφει ἕσπερος αἴγλη,
780 ἄλλοτε δ' ἀλλοῖαι μορφαὶ κερόωσι σελήνην
εὐθὺς ἀεξομένην, αἱ μὲν τρίτη, αἱ δὲ τετάρτη·
τάων καὶ περὶ μηνὸς ἐφεσταότος κε πύθοιο.
λεπτὴ μὲν καθαρή τε περὶ τρίτον ἦμαρ ἐοῦσα
εὔδιός κ' εἴη, λεπτὴ δὲ καὶ εὖ μάλ' ἐρευθὴς
785 πνευματίη, παχίων δὲ καὶ ἀμβλείῃσι κεραίαις
τέτρατον ἐκ τριτάτοιο φόως ἀμενηνὸν ἔχουσα
ἢ νότῳ ἄμβλυνται ἢ ὕδατος ἐγγὺς ἐόντος.
εἰ δέ κ' ἀπ' ἀμφοτέρων κεράων τρίτον ἦμαρ ἄγουσα
μήτ' ἐπινευστάζῃ μήθ' ὑπτιόωσα φαείνη,
790 ἀλλ' ὀρθαὶ ἑκάτερθε περιγνάμπτωσι κεραῖαι,
ἑσπέριοί κ' ἄνεμοι κείνην μετὰ νύκτα φέροιντο.
εἰ δ' αὔτως ὀρθὴ καὶ τέτρατον ἦμαρ ἀγινεῖ,
ἦ τ' ἂν χειμῶνος συναγειρομένοιο διδάσκοι·
εἰ δέ κέ οἱ κεράων τὸ μετήορον εὖ ἐπινεύη,
795 δειδέχθαι βορέω· ὅτε δ' ὑπτιάησι, νότοιο.
αὐτὰρ ἐπὴν τριτόωσαν ὅλος περὶ κύκλος ἑλίσσῃ
πάντη ἐρευθόμενος, μάλα κεν τότε χείμερος εἴη·
μείζονι δ' ἂν χειμῶνι πυρώτερα φοινίσσοιτο.
σκέπτεο δ' ἐς πληθύν τε καὶ ἀμφότερον διχόωσαν,
800 ἠμὲν ἀεξομένην ἠδ' ἐς κέρας αὖθις ἰοῦσαν.
καὶ οἱ ἐπὶ χροιῇ τεκμαίρεο μηνὸς ἑκάστου·
πάντη γὰρ καθαρῇ κε μάλ' εὔδια τεκμήραιο,
πάντα δ' ἐρευθομένῃ δοκέειν ἀνέμοιο κελεύθους,

778–817 Stob. 1.26.6   794–7 + 805–10 Gal. ix.909 Kühn

---

778 πρῶτον codd.: πρώτη Stob.: πρώτην Voss   781 ἀεξομένην MS
Stob.: -ης E   783 ἐοῦσα MES: ἔχουσα C: ἰοῦσα N Stob.ᶠᴾ   784 εὖ
ME: οὐ S Stob. (non L)   786–7 om. E   787 post 788 M   ἢ codd.
Π2 Stob.: ἠὲ anon. in mg. ed. Oxon. 1672   νότῳ codd. Stob.: νότου
Martin   ἄμβλυνται Mair: ἀμβλύνεται M Stob.: ἀμβλύεται S: ἀμβ-
λύνετ' anon. in Oxon.: ἀμβλύνει Dorville ad Charit. p. 386: ἀμβλύνοιτ'
ἂν Voss   788 εἰ δέ κ' ME: ἢ δέ τ' S   ἀπ' MES Stob.: ἐπ' A
789 μήτ' ἐπινευστάζῃ K: μήτε τι νευστάζῃ M Stob.: -ζοι E: -ζει S

Observe first the moon at her two horns. Different evenings paint her with different light, [780] and different shapes at different times horn the moon as soon as she is waxing, some on the third day, some on the fourth; from these you can learn about the month that has just begun. If slender and clear about the third day, she will bode fair weather; if slender and very red, wind; if the crescent is thickish, with blunted horns, [785] having a feeble fourth-day light after the third day, either it is blurred by a southerly or because rain is in the offing. But if, when she brings the third day, the moon does not lean forward from the line of the two horn-tips, or shine inclining backwards, [790] but instead the curve of the two horns is upright, westerly winds will blow after that night. But if she brings in the fourth day also similarly upright, she will certainly give warning of a gathering storm; if the upper one of the horns should lean well forward, [795] expect a northerly; when it inclines backward, a southerly. But when the whole disc curves round her on the third day, reddening all over, then she will certainly be a stormy sign; a fierier redness will mean a severer storm.

Observe the moon at the full and at the two halves, [800] both when newly waxing and when coming again to a crescent. And judge from her colour the weather for each month: if she is clear all over, you can deduce fair weather, if red all over, expect wind on the way, if dark in

---

φαείνη Voss: φαείνοι codd. Stob.   790 περιγνάμπτωσι ES: -γνάπτωσι M Stob.: -γνάμπτουσαι A: -γνάμπτουσα Voss   791 κ' codd.: γ' Stob.   792 ἀγινεῖ MES Stob.: ἀγινοῖ N: ἀγινῆ Voss   793 ἤ τ' E: ἤ τ' M: ἤ τ' S   διδάσκοι Morel: διδάσκει codd. Stob.   794 εἰ δέ codd. Stob. Gal.: ηνδε Π2   ἐπινεύη Voss: ἐπινεύοι MES Gal.: ἐπινεύει Stob.   796 τριτόωσαν ME Gal. Stob.: τριτόεσσαν S   ὅλος codd.: ὅλην Gal.: ὅλον Stob.   ἐλίσση M Gal.: ἐλίσσοι ES: ἐλίσσει Stob.   798 ἄν S Stob.F: αὖ ME Stob.P   800 ἡμὲν H: ἡ μὲν MES: ἤ μὲν C: ἤμεν Stob.   801 χροιῇ Epc S Stob.: χροιὴν MEac   ἑκάστου codd.: ἕκαστα Voss   802 γὰρ codd.: μὲν Stob.   803 κελεύθους codd.: κέλευθον Stob.F: κέλευθος Stob.P

ἄλλοθι δ᾽ ἄλλο μελαινομένη δοκέειν ὑετοῖο.
805 σήματα δ᾽ οὔ τοι πᾶσιν ἐπ᾽ ἤμασι πάντα τέτυκται·
ἀλλ᾽ ὅσα μὲν τριτάτῃ τε τεταρταίῃ τε πέλονται
μέσφα διχαιομένης, διχάδος γε μὲν ἄχρις ἐπ᾽ αὐτὴν
σημαίνει διχόμηνον, ἀτὰρ πάλιν ἐκ διχομήνου
ἐς διχάδα φθιμένην· ἔχεται δέ οἱ αὐτίκα τετρὰς
810 μηνὸς ἀποιχομένου, τῇ δὲ τριτάτῃ ἐπιόντος.
εἰ δέ κέ μιν περὶ πᾶσαν ἀλωαὶ κυκλώσωνται
ἢ τρεῖς ἠὲ δύω περικείμεναι ἠὲ μί᾽ οἴη,
τῇ μὲν ἰῇ ἀνέμοιο γαληναίης τε δοκεύειν,
ῥηγνυμένῃ ἀνέμοιο, μαραινομένῃ δὲ γαλήνης·
815 ταὶ δύο δ᾽ ἂν χειμῶνι περιτροχάοιντο σελήνην,
μείζονα δ᾽ ἂν χειμῶνα φέροι τριέλικτος ἀλωή,
καὶ μᾶλλον μελανεῦσα, καὶ εἰ ῥηγνύατο μᾶλλον.
καὶ τὰ μὲν οὖν ἐπὶ μηνὶ σεληναίης κε πύθοιο.
ἠελίοιο δέ τοι μελέτω ἑκάτερθεν ἰόντος·
820 ἠελίῳ καὶ μᾶλλον ἐοικότα σήματα κεῖται,
ἀμφότερον δύνοντι καὶ ἐκ περάτης ἀνιόντι.
μή οἱ ποικίλλοιτο νέον βάλλοντος ἀρούρας
κύκλος, ὅτ᾽ εὐδίου κεχρημένος ἤματος εἴης,
μηδέ τι σῆμα φέροι, φαίνοιτο δὲ λιτὸς ἀπάντῃ.
825 εἰ δ᾽ αὔτως καθαρόν μιν ἔχει βουλύσιος ὥρη,
δύνει δ᾽ ἀνέφελος μαλακὴν ὑποδείελος αἴγλην,
καί κεν ἐπερχομένης ἠοῦς ἔθ᾽ ὑπεύδιος εἴη·
ἀλλ᾽ οὐχ ὁππότε κοῖλος ἐειδόμενος περιτέλλῃ,
οὐδ᾽ ὁπότ᾽ ἀκτίνων αἱ μὲν νότον αἱ δὲ βορῆα
830 σχιζόμεναι βάλλωσι, τὰ δ᾽ αὖ πέρι μέσσα φαείνῃ,

822–91 Stob. 1.25.9

---

804 ὑετοῖο ΜΕ^{γρ}S:]ετοοι[Π7: ἀνέμοιο Ε   805 οὔ τοι Voss (sic L):
οὐτὰρ Μ: οὔτ᾽ ἂρ ES: οὔτ᾽ ἄρα Gal.: οὐ μάλα Stob.   806 τε prius E
Gal. Stob.: om. MS   πέλονται MES Stob.: πέληται D Gal.   807
διχαιομένης ΜΕ Gal.: διχεομένης S: διχαζομένης Α Stob.   808 διχομήνου MES Stob.:]ου Π7: -μήνης Τ Gal.   809 ἔχεται Μ Gal.: δέχεται
ES Stob.: ἔπεται Diggle   δέ οἱ MES Gal.: δέ μιν Κ: μὲν Stob.   810
ἀποιχομένου MES Gal. Stob.:]οιχ[Π8: ἀπερχομένου Α   τῇ δὲ S

patches, look out for rain. [805] But the signs are not all established for you for all the days of the month: those that occur on the third and fourth days are valid up to the half-moon, those at the half foretell right up to mid-month, and after mid-month again to the waning half-moon; next after this is the fourth day [810] from the end of the month, and after that the third of the following month. If haloes encircle the moon entirely, either three or two surrounding it, or only one, from the one expect wind or calm, wind if it breaks, calm if it is fading; [815] the two running round the moon denote a storm, a triple halo will bring a greater storm, more so if it is dark, still more so if broken. So these are the signs for the month that you can learn from the moon.

Pay attention to the sun when its course is in the east or the west: [820] even more reliable signs are established in the sun, both when setting and when rising over the horizon. May his disc not be mottled when first he strikes the earth, whenever you are in need of a fine day, and may he not bear any mark, but be seen pure all over! [825] And if the time for unyoking the oxen similarly finds him clear, and he sinks his soft light unclouded at dusk, then he will still be in fair weather at the ensuing dawn; but not so, when in his circling course he has a hollow look, nor when some of his diverging rays strike the south and some the north, while the centre is very bright: [831] then he is

---

Gal.: ἡ δὲ M Stob.: ἠδὲ E   ἐπιόντος Voss: ἀπιόντος codd. Gal. Stob.
811 κυκλώσωνται A Π7 Stob.: -σονται MES   815 ταὶ ES Stob.: τῶ
M: τῶ C   σελήνην S Π7 Stob.: σελήνη ME   817 ῥηγνύατο codd.
Stob.: ῥηγνῦτ' ἔτι Voss   822 ἀρούρας S Stob.: ἀρούραις ME
825 ἔχει S: ἔχοι ME Stob. (habuerit L)   βουλύσιος ES: βουλήσιος M
Stob.   826 δύνει ES: δύνοι M Stob.   ἀνέφελος S: ἀννέφελος ME
μαλακὴν ... αἴγλην codd. Stob.: -κῆ ... -λη Martin   ὑποδείελος MS
Stob.: ὑποδείελον A: ὑπὸ δείελος E: ὕπο δείελος Voss   827 εἴη codd.
Stob.: εἴης Voss   828 περιτέλλη M: -τέλλει ES: -τέλλοι H Stob.
830 αὖ codd. Stob.ᶠ: ἂν Stob.ᴾ   πέρι scripsi: περὶ codd. Stob.
φαείνῃ ME Stob.: φαείνει S: φαείνοι C

ἀλλά που ἢ ὑετοῖο διέρχεται ἢ ἀνέμοιο.

σκέπτεο δ᾽, εἴ κέ τοι αὐγαὶ ὑπείκωσ᾽ ἠελίοιο,
αὐτὸν ἐς ἠέλιον, τοῦ γὰρ σκοπιαὶ καὶ ἄρισται,
εἴ τί που ἢ οἱ ἔρευθος ἐπιτρέχει, οἷά τε πολλὰ
835 ἑλκομένων νεφέων ἐρυθαίνεται ἄλλοθεν ἄλλα,
ἢ εἴ που μελανεῖ· καί τοι τὰ μὲν ὕδατος ἔστω
σήματα μέλλοντος, τὰ δ᾽ ἐρευθέα πάντ᾽ ἀνέμοιο.
εἴ γε μὲν ἀμφοτέροις ἄμυδις κεχρωσμένος εἴη,
καί κεν ὕδωρ φορέοι καὶ ὑπηνέμιος τανύοιτο.
840 εἰ δέ οἱ ἢ ἀνιόντος ἢ αὐτίκα δυομένοιο
ἀκτῖνες συνίωσι καὶ ἀμφ᾽ ἑνὶ πεπλήθωσιν,
ἤ ποτε καὶ νεφέων πεπιεσμένος ἢ ὅ γ᾽ ἐς ἠῶ
ἔρχηται παρὰ νυκτὸς ἢ ἐξ ἠοῦς ἐπὶ νύκτα,
ὕδατί κεν κατιόντι παρατρέχοι ἤματα κεῖνα.
845 μηδ᾽, ὅτε οἱ ὀλίγη νεφέλη πάρος ἀντέλλησι,
τὴν δὲ μέτ᾽ ἀκτίνων κεχρημένος αὐτὸς ἀερθῇ,
ἀμνηστεῖν ὑετοῖο. πολὺς δ᾽ ὅτε οἱ πέρι κύκλος
οἷον τηκομένῳ ἐναλίγκιος εὐρύνηται
πρῶτον ἀνερχομένοιο, καὶ ἂψ ἐπὶ μεῖον ἴῃσιν,
850 εὔδιός κε φέροιτο, καὶ εἴ ποτε χείματος ὥρῃ
ὠχρήσαι κατιών. ἀτὰρ ὕδατος ἡμερινοῖο
γινομένου, κατόπισθε περὶ νέφεα σκοπέεσθαι
κὰδ δὴ δυομένου τετραμμένος ἠελίοιο.
ἢν μὲν ὑποσκιάῃσι μελαινομένη εἰκυῖα
855 ἠέλιον νεφέλη, ταὶ δ᾽ ἀμφί μιν ἔνθα καὶ ἔνθα
ἀκτῖνες μεσσηγὺς ἑλισσόμεναι διχόωνται,
ἦ τ᾽ ἂν ἔτ᾽ εἰς ἠῶ σκέπαος κεχρημένος εἴης.
εἰ δ᾽ ὁ μὲν ἀνέφελος βάπτῃ ῥόου ἑσπερίοιο,
ταὶ δὲ κατερχομένου νεφέλαι καὶ οἰχομένοιο

---

831 διέρχεται ME Stob.: παρέρχεται S   832 ὑπείκωσ᾽ ME Stob.:
ὑπείκουσ᾽ S: ὑπεῖεν ἂν T coni. Grotius   833 σκοπιαὶ καὶ MES:
σκοπιαί εἰσιν A Stob.: σκοπιαί εἰσιν Buttmann   834 που ἢ οἱ P: που
εἴ οἱ S: που ἢ καὶ A: οἷ που ἢ ME: που καὶ Stob.: οἱ ἢ που Voss
836 μελανεῖ A: μελάνει MES Stob.   τοι S Stob.: σοι ME   837
ἐρευθέα E: εὐρεθέα Stob.: ἐρεύθεα MS   838 ἀμφοτέροις ME: ἀμφοτέρων S Stob.   κεχρωσμένος Mˢ¹E Stob.: κεχρημένος MS   840 οἱ
MES: τοι A Stob.   δυομένοιο codd.: δυσομένοιο Voss   842 ὅ γ᾽

passing perhaps through either rain or wind.

Study, if his beams should allow you, the sun himself (for looking directly at him is best), to see if either a blush runs across him, as often [835] he reddens here and there when clouds are trailing over him, or if there is any dark patch: let the latter be your sign for oncoming rain, and red spots always for wind. If he should be tinged with both red and black together, then he will both bring rain and continue his course in wind. [840] If at his rising or later setting his rays are concentrated and packed round one point, or if overarched with clouds he passes either to dawn from nightfall or from dawn to night, he is likely to run through these days in pouring rain. [845] Do not, when a light cloud rises first, and he himself comes up after it deficient in light, fail to expect rain. But when a thick belt of cloud around him starts broadening out as if it were melting when the sun first rises, and then goes smaller again, [850] his passage is likely to be in fair weather, and so too if ever in the winter season he goes pale at his setting. But if there has been rain during the day, carefully observe the clouds after it, facing in the direction of the setting sun. [854] If a cloud that looks like darkening shades the sun, and his rays on either side of him diverge this way and that as they move between, then you will certainly still be in need of shelter until dawn. But if he plunges cloudless into the western water, and the clouds standing near him are red while he is setting and after he is gone, there is no

---

A: ὅτ᾽ MES: ὅς γ᾽ Stob.   844 παρατρέχοι M Stob.: παρατρέχει ES   846 μέτ᾽ E coni. Voss: μετ᾽ MS Stob.   κεχρημένος ES Stob. (*utitur* L): κεχρωσμένος M   847 πέρι κύκλος Voss: περὶ κύκλος E Stob.: περίκυκλος MS   851 ἡμερινοῖο S sch. Stob.: ἡμερίοιο ME   853 κὰδ δὴ Voss: καὶ δὴ codd. Stob.   856 ἐλισσόμεναι MES: -ομένην A Stob.   διχόωνται MES: διχόωσιν A: διχόωντα Stob.   858 ἀνέφελος A Stob.P: ἀννέφελος MES Stob.F   βάπτη Voss: βάπτοι MES Stob.: βάπτει N   ἑσπερίοιο MEpcS: ὠκεανοῖο Eac   859 καὶ codd.: ταί τ᾽ Wilamowitz: κατά τ᾽ Reeve   οἰχομένοιο MES: ἀποιχο- Kyp: ἔτ᾽ οἰχο- Stob.: ἐπερχο- A

860 πλησίαι ἑστήκωσιν ἐρευθέες, οὔ σε μάλα χρὴ
αὔριον οὐδ᾽ ἐπὶ νυκτὶ περιτρομέειν ὑετοῖο,
ἀλλ᾽ ὁπότ᾽ ἠελίοιο μαραινομένῃσιν ὁμοῖαι
ἐξαπίνης ἀκτῖνες ἀπ᾽ οὐρανόθεν τανύωνται,
οἷον ἀμαλδύνονται ὅτε σκιάῃσι κατ᾽ ἰθὺ
865 ἱσταμένη γαίης τε καὶ ἠελίοιο σελήνη.
οὐδ᾽, ὅτε οἱ ἐπέχοντι φανήμεναι ἠῶθι πρὸ
φαίνωνται νεφέλαι ὑπερευθέες ἄλλοθεν ἄλλαι,
ἄρραντοι γίνονται ἐπ᾽ ἤματι κείνῳ ἄρουραι.
μηδ᾽ αὔτως, ἔτ᾽ ἐόντι πέρην ὁπότε προταθεῖσαι
870 ἀκτῖνες φαίνωνται ἐπίσκιοι ἠῶθι πρό,
ὕδατος ἢ ἀνέμοιο κατοισομένου λελαθέσθαι·
ἀλλ᾽ εἰ μὲν κεῖναι μᾶλλον κνέφαος φορέοιντο
ἀκτῖνες, μᾶλλόν κεν ἐφ᾽ ὕδατι σημαίνοιεν·
εἰ δ᾽ ὀλίγος τανύοιτο περὶ δνόφος ἀκτίνεσσιν,
875 οἷόν που μαλακαὶ νεφέλαι φορέουσι μάλιστα,
ἤ τ᾽ ἂν ἐπερχομένοιο περιδνοφέοιντ᾽ ἀνέμοιο.
οὐδὲ μὲν ἡελίου σχεδόθεν μελανεῦσαι ἁλωαὶ
εὔδιοι· ἀσσότεραι δὲ καὶ ἀστεμφὲς μελανεῦσαι
μᾶλλον χειμέριαι, δύο δ᾽ ἂν χαλεπώτεραι εἶεν.
880 σκέπτεο δ᾽ ἢ ἀνιόντος ἢ αὐτίκα δυομένοιο
εἴ πού οἱ νεφέων τὰ παρήλια κικλήσκονται
ἢ νότου ἠὲ βορῆος ἐρεύθεται ἢ ἑκάτερθε,
μηδ᾽ οὕτω σκοπιὴν ταύτην ἀμενηνὰ φυλάσσειν.
οὐ γάρ, ὅτ᾽ ἀμφοτέρωθεν ὁμοῦ περὶ μέσσον ἔχωσιν
885 ἠέλιον κεῖναι νεφέλαι σχεδὸν ὠκεανοῖο,
γίνεται ἀμβολίη Διόθεν χειμῶνος ἰόντος·
εἴ γε μὲν ἐκ βορέαο μί᾽ οἴη φοινίσσοιτο,

864–65 (κατ᾽ ἰθὺ ... ἠελίοιο) Ach. p. 47

---

860 πλησίαι MS Stob.: πλησίον E   ἐρευθέες codd. Stob.: υπερευθ[
Π2   863 τανύωνται Μᵖᶜ: τανύονται ΜᵃᶜES Stob.   864 ἀμαλδύνονται Α Π2 1 sch.: -δύνηται MES: -δύνωνται Stob.   865 ἱσταμένη
codd. Ach.ⱽ: -μένης Ach.ᴹ Stob.   σελήνη codd.: σελήνης

need at all for you [861] to be afraid of rain tomorrow or even during the night, but there is when the sun's rays suddenly lengthen in the sky and look as if they are dying away, just as they weaken when the moon shades them, when it stands directly between earth and sun. [866] Nor, when reddish clouds appear here and there, when the sun delays his appearance before dawn, do the fields go un-watered on that day. And similarly, when the sun is still below the horizon, and the rays reaching out before him seem shadowy before dawn, [871] do not overlook the coming onset of rain or wind; if these rays should come more in darkness, they are more likely to be a sign of rain; if only a slight murkiness spreads over the rays, [875] such as soft mists can very often bring, then they really will be enveloped in the gloom of an oncoming wind. Nor do dark haloes close to the sun portend fair weather: the closer they are and the more unwaveringly dark, the stormier their forecast, and two will mean an even greater storm.

[880] Observe, when the sun is rising or later setting, whether those clouds of his that are called parhelia are red to the south or the north or on both sides, and do not just keep up the observation carelessly. For when on both sides at once these clouds flank the sun between them close to the horizon, [886] there is no putting off the storm that is coming from Zeus; but if only one on the north side

---

Stob.   866 φανήμεναι A Stob. φ[α]νημ[Π2: φαήμεναι ME: φαείμε-
ναι S   867 φαίνωνται M: φαίνονται ES Stob.   870 φαίνωνται Π2
ut uid. coni. Voss: φαίνονται codd. Stob.   872 φορέοιντο MES
Stob.: φορέονται A   875 μαλακαὶ E Stob.: μάλα καὶ M (magis et L):
καὶ μαλακαὶ S   877 ἠελίου MEᴾᶜS: ἠελίοιο Eᵃᶜ   878 ἀστεμφὲς
ME: ἀστεμφέες S Stob.   879 χαλεπώτεραι MEˢˡS Stob.: -ταται E
(pessimae L)   εἶεν EᴾᶜS Stob.: εἰσι MEᵃᶜ   880 σκέπτεο ES Stob.:
σκέπταιο M   δ' om. S   883 οὕτω codd. Stob. (ita L): αὕτως
Buttmann   φυλάσσειν MES Stob.: φυλάσσου A   884 ὅτ' ME
Stob.: ἔτ' A: om. S   ἔχωσιν MS Stob.: ἔχουσιν E   885 κεῖναι ME
Stob.: κἀκεῖναι S   886 ἰόντος MES: ἐόντος A Stob.

ἐκ βορέω πνοιάς κε φέροι, νοτίη δὲ νότοιο,
ἢ καί που ῥαθάμιγγες ἐπιτροχόωσ᾽ ὑετοῖο.
890 ἑσπερίοις καὶ μᾶλλον ἐπίτρεπε σήμασι τούτοις·
ἑσπερόθεν γὰρ ὁμῶς σημαίνετον ἐμμενὲς αἰεί.
σκέπτεο καὶ Φάτνην· ἡ μέν τ᾽ ὀλίγῃ εἰκυῖα
ἀχλύϊ βορραίη ὑπὸ Καρκίνῳ ἡγηλάζει.
ἀμφὶ δέ μιν δύο λεπτὰ φαεινόμενοι φορέονται
895 ἀστέρες, οὔτε τι πολλὸν ἀπήοροι οὔτε μάλ᾽ ἐγγύς,
ἀλλ᾽ ὅσσον τε μάλιστα πυγούσιον οἰήσασθαι·
εἷς μὲν πὰρ βορέαο, νότῳ δ᾽ ἔπι ἔρχεται ἄλλος.
καὶ τοὶ μὲν καλέονται Ὄνοι, μέσση δέ τε Φάτνη.
εἰ δὲ καὶ ἐξαπίνης πάντη Διὸς εὐδιόωντος
900 γίνετ᾽ ἄφαντος ὅλη, τοὶ δ᾽ ἀμφοτέρωθεν ἰόντες
ἀστέρες ἀλλήλων αὐτοσχεδὸν ἰνδάλλονται,
οὐκ ὀλίγῳ χειμῶνι τότε κλύζονται ἄρουραι.
εἰ δὲ μελαίνηται, τοὶ δ᾽ αὐτίκ᾽ ἐοικότες ὦσιν
ἀστέρες ἀμφότεροι, περί χ᾽ ὕδατι σημαίνοιεν.
905 εἰ δ᾽ ὁ μὲν ἐκ βορέω Φάτνης ἀμενηνὰ φαείνοι
λεπτὸν ἐπαχλύων, νότιος δ᾽ Ὄνος ἀγλαὸς εἴη,
δειδέχθαι ἀνέμοιο νότου· βορέω δὲ μάλα χρὴ
ἔμπαλιν ἀχλυόεντι φαεινομένῳ τε δοκεύειν.
σῆμα δέ τοι ἀνέμοιο καὶ οἰδαίνουσα θάλασσα
910 γινέσθω καὶ μακρὸν ἔπ᾽ αἰγιαλοὶ βοόωντες,
ἀκταί τ᾽ εἰνάλιοι ὁπότ᾽ εὔδιοι ἠχήεσσαι
γίνωνται, κορυφαί τε βοώμεναι οὔρεος ἄκραι.
καὶ δ᾽ ἂν ἐπὶ ξηρὴν ὅτ᾽ ἐρῳδιὸς οὐ κατὰ κόσμον
ἐξ ἁλὸς ἔρχηται φωνῇ περιπολλὰ λεληκώς,

---

888 δὲ MS Stob.: τε E   889 ἢ καί που MES Stob.: ἢ καί που A: εἰ
καί που Tˢˡ: ἢ εἴ που legisse Φ coni. Martin ex *aut si alicubi* L   890
ἐπίτρεπε σήμασι τούτοις MʸᴾE: ἐπίτρεχε σήμασι τούτοις MS: ἐπίτρε-
πες ἤμασι (ἤματιᴾ) τούτοις Stob.: ἀληθέα τεκμήραιο edd. ante Buttmann   891 σημαίνετον ME Stob.: σημαίνεται S   893 ἡγηλάζει H
sch.: ἡγηλάζει ME: ἠγιλάζει S   896 ὅσσον C: ὅσον MS: ὅσσος E
μάλιστα ME: μᾶλλον S   οἰήσασθαι MES: οἰήσεσθαι A: οἰίσασθαι
Maass: ὠίσασθαι Martin   897 νότῳ codd.: Νότον Voss   ἔπι ἔρχεται Zannoni: ἐπιέρχεται MES: ἐπικέκλιται A Π4ᵐᵍ (*uocantur* L): ἐπι-

should be glowing, it will bring blasts from the north, and if the south one, southerlies; or possibly a shower of rain is sweeping across. [890] Pay heed to these signs especially in the west, for in the west both parhelia alike are always reliable signs.

Observe also the Manger: like a slight haze in the north it leads the year in company with the Crab. On either side of it move two faintly shining [895] stars, not at all far apart and not very close, but as far as the approximate estimate of an ell; one comes on the north side, the other on the south. Now these are called the Asses, and between them is the Manger. If suddenly, when the sky is clear all over, [900] it disappears completely, and the stars that go on either side appear close to each other, then the fields are drenched with no mean storm. If the Manger should darken and the two stars be at the same time recognisable, they will be giving a sign of rain. [905] If the one to the north of the Manger shines faintly, being slightly hazy, and the southern Ass is bright, expect wind from the south; and wind from the north you must certainly look for if the hazy and the bright stars are the other way round.

[909] Let a sign of wind be also a swelling sea and beaches roaring a long way off, sea-coasts reverberating in fair weather, and a mountain's summit-peak sounding. Also when a heron in irregular flight comes in from the sea to dry land uttering many a scream, [915] it will be moving

---

δέρκεται Voss   899 εἰ δὲ καὶ scripsi: ἤ τε καὶ codd.: ἤδ' εἴ γ' Voss: ἤτε κεῖ Martin   εὐδιόωντος Α: εὐδιάοντος MES   900 ἰόντες codd.: ἐόντες Maass   904 περί χ' MS: πέρι χ' Ε: περὶ δ' Α: ἐπί χ' Maass   905 φαείνοι ΜΕ: φαείνει S   906 ἐπαχλύων Schneider Lex. s.v.: ἐπαχλυόων codd.   908 ἀχλυόεντι MS: ἀχλυόωντι Ε   909 σῆμα δέ τοι S: σήματα δ' ἔτ' M: σήματα δέ τ' Ε   910 ἔπ' Martin: ἐπ' M: ἐπ- ES   911 εἰνάλιοι codd.: εἰνάλιαι Buttmann   912 γίνωνται M: γίνονται S: γίγνονται Ε   914 περιπολλὰ M: περὶ πολλὰ Ε: περίαλλα S

915 κινυμένου κε θάλασσαν ὕπερ φορέοιτ' ἀνέμοιο.
καί ποτε καὶ κέπφοι, ὁπότ' εὔδιοι ποτέωνται,
ἀντία μελλόντων ἀνέμων εἰληδὰ φέρονται.
πολλάκι δ' ἀγριάδες νῆσσαι ἢ εἰναλίδιναι
αἴθυιαι χερσαῖα τινάσσονται πτερύγεσσιν,
920 ἢ νεφέλη ὄρεος μηκύνεται ἐν κορυφῇσιν.
ἤδη καὶ πάπποι, λευκῆς γήρειον ἀκάνθης,
σῆμ' ἐγένοντ' ἀνέμου, κωφῆς ἁλὸς ὁππότε πολλοὶ
ἄκρον ἐπιπλώωσι, τὰ μὲν πάρος, ἄλλα δ' ὀπίσσω.
καὶ θέρεος βρονταί τε καὶ ἀστραπαὶ ἔνθεν ἴωσιν,
925 ἔνθεν ἐπερχομένοιο περισκοπέειν ἀνέμοιο.
καὶ διὰ νύκτα μέλαιναν ὅτ' ἀστέρες ἀΐσσωσι
ταρφέα, τοὶ δ' ὄπιθεν ῥυμοὶ ἐπιλευκαίνωνται,
δειδέχθαι κείνοις αὐτὴν ὁδὸν ἐρχομένοιο
πνεύματος· εἰ δέ κεν ἄλλοι ἐναντίοι ἀΐσσωσιν,
930 ἄλλοι δ' ἐξ ἄλλων μερέων, τότε δὴ πεφύλαξο
παντοίων ἀνέμων, οἵ τ' ἄκριτοί εἰσι μάλιστα,
ἄκριτα δὲ πνείουσιν ἐπ' ἀνδράσι τεκμήρασθαι.
    αὐτὰρ ὅτ' ἐξ εὔροιο καὶ ἐκ νότου ἀστράπτησιν,
ἄλλοτε δ' ἐκ ζεφύροιο καὶ ἄλλοτε πὰρ βορέαο,
935 δὴ τότε τις πελάγει ἐνὶ δείδιε ναυτίλος ἀνήρ,
μή μιν τῇ μὲν ἔχῃ πέλαγος τῇ δ' ἐκ Διὸς ὕδωρ·
ὕδατι γὰρ τοσσαίδε περὶ στεροπαὶ φορέονται.
πολλάκι δ' ἐρχομένων ὑετῶν νέφεα προπάροιθεν
οἷα μάλιστα πόκοισιν ἐοικότα ἰνδάλλονται,
940 ἢ διδύμη ἔζωσε διὰ μέγαν οὐρανὸν ἶρις,
ἢ καί πού τις ἅλωα μελαινομένην ἔχει ἀστήρ.

---

916 (κέπφοι) sch. Ar. *Pac.* 1067   921 (λευκῆς ...) Eust. in Ε 408
926–31 Phlp. *in Mete.* A 7 p. 100, 7Η

---

915 κινυμένου MS: κιννυ- Ε: κινου- A   ὕπερ Bekker: ὑπερ- codd.
916 ποτέωνται Ceporinus: ποτέονται codd.   917 εἰληδὰ M: εἰληδὰ
ES   918 εἰναλίδιναι C: εἰναλιδίναι A: εἰναλιδῖναι ES: εἰν ἁλὶ δῖναι
M: εἰναλιδῦναι M^{yp} sch.   919 τινάσσονται codd. Π4^{pc} Π5^{pc}: τινάσ-
σωνται Π4^{ac} Π5^{ac}   921 πάπποι codd.: παμποι Π4 Π5   923 ἐπι-

before a wind that is stirring over the sea. And sometimes too when petrels fly in fair weather, they move in flocks to face oncoming winds. Often wild ducks or sea-diving gulls beat with their wings on the land, [920] or a cloud lengthens on the tops of a mountain. Before now the fluffy down of the white thistle's old age has been a sign of wind, when it floats abundantly on the surface of the mute sea, some of it drifting ahead, some behind. Also in summer the direction of thunder and lightning [925] is the direction from which to expect the onset of wind. And during black night, when shooting stars are frequent, and the trails behind them are bright, expect a wind coming on the same course as these stars; and if others shoot in the opposite direction, [930] and others again in different directions, then beware of winds from all quarters, in which case they are especially indecisive, and their blasts make it difficult for men to judge the weather.

Now when there is lightning in the east and south, and sometimes in the west and sometimes in the north, [935] it is then that some mariner at sea is afraid that he may be caught by the sea on the one hand and rain from Zeus on the other: for with rain so many lightning flashes come from all around. Often before the coming rains there appear clouds that look very like fleeces, [940] or a double rainbow girdles the great sky, or again perhaps some star has a darkening halo.

πλώωσι Κ Π4 Π5: ἐπιπλόωσι Μ: ἐπιπλείωσι ΕS   924 ἔνθεν MS:
ἔνθα Ε: ἔνθ' Voss   ἴωσιν codd.: ἐπίωσιν Voss: ἔωσιν Maass   927
τοὶ δ' codd. Π4 Π5: τοῖς δ' Phlp.: τοῖς Maass   ἐπιλευκαίνωνται
Voss]ῳνται Π5sl: -ονται Phlp.: επι[λευκα]νθ[ω]σιν Π5: επ[ιλευ]κα[
Π2: επι[Π4: ὑπολευκαίνονται codd.   929 εἰ δέ κεν Α Phlp.: ἢν δέ
κεν ΜΕS Π4 Π5: ἢν δὲ καὶ Bekker ex sch.   ἐναντίοι ΜΕ: ἐναντίον S   930 ἄλλοι δ' ΜΕ Π4pc Π5pc (alteri autem L): ἄλλοις S Π4ac
Π5ac   τότε δὴ codd. Phlp.: τοτε δ Π4: τοτε δαυ Π2   πεφύλαξο S
Phlp.: πεφύλαξαι ΜΕ   935 ἔνι δείδιε Ε: ἐνὶ δείδιε S: ἐνιδείδιε Μ
936 ἔχῃ ΜΕS: ἔχοι Α   937 περὶ στεροπαὶ Ε: περιστεροπαὶ MS:
πέρι στεροπαὶ Martin   940 μέγαν ΜΕS: μμ- Εsl

πολλάκι λιμναῖαι ἢ εἰνάλιαι ὄρνιθες
ἄπληστον κλύζονται ἐνιέμεναι ὑδάτεσσιν,
ἢ λίμνην πέρι δηθὰ χελιδόνες ἀΐσσονται
945 γαστέρι τύπτουσαι αὔτως εἰλυμένον ὕδωρ,
ἢ μάλα δείλαιαι γενεαί, ὑδροισιν ὄνειαρ,
αὐτόθεν ἐξ ὕδατος πατέρες βοόωσι γυρίνων,
ἢ τρύζει ὀρθρινὸν ἐρημαίη ὀλολυγών,
ἤ που καὶ λακέρυζα παρ' ἠϊόνι προὐχούσῃ
950 κύματος ἐρχομένου χέρσῳ ὑπέτυψε κορώνη,
ἤ που καὶ ποταμοῖο ἐβάψατο μέχρι παρ' ἄκρους
ὤμους ἐκ κεφαλῆς, ἢ καὶ μάλα πᾶσα κολυμβᾷ,
ἢ πολλὴ στρέφεται παρ' ὕδωρ παχέα κρώζουσα.
   καὶ βόες ἤδη τοι πάρος ὕδατος ἐνδίοιο
955 οὐρανὸν εἰσανιδόντες ἀπ' αἰθέρος ὀσφρήσαντο·
καὶ κοίλης μύρμηκες ὀχῆς ἐξ ὤεα πάντα
θᾶσσον ἀνηνέγκαντο· καὶ ἀθρόοι ὦφθεν ἴουλοι
τείχε' ἀνέρποντες, καὶ πλαζόμενοι σκώληκες
κεῖνοι, τοὺς καλέουσι μελαίνης ἔντερα γαίης.
960 καὶ τιθαὶ ὄρνιθες, ταὶ ἀλέκτορος ἐξεγένοντο,
εὖ ἐφθειρίσσαντο καὶ ἔκρωξαν μάλα φωνῇ,
οἷόν τε σταλάον ψοφέει ἐπὶ ὕδατι ὕδωρ.
   δή ποτε καὶ γενεαὶ κοράκων καὶ φῦλα κολοιῶν
ὕδατος ἐρχομένοιο Διὸς πάρα σῆμ' ἐγένοντο,
965 φαινόμενοι ἀγεληδὰ καὶ ἰρήκεσσιν ὁμοῖον
φθεγξάμενοι. καί που κόρακες δίους †σταλαγμοὺς†
φωνῇ ἐμιμήσαντο σὺν ὕδατος ἐρχομένοιο,

946–7 Plut. 912c   947 (πατέρες ...) Et. Flor. p. 79 s.v. γύρινοι
956–7 (... ἀνηνέγκαντο) Plu. 967F   963–4 sch. Nic. Ther. 406

---

942 ἢ codd.: ἠδ' Voss   943 ἄπληστον ME: ἄπλητον S   ἐνιέμεναι
ME^{sl}S: ἀνιέμεναι E   944 πέρι δηθὰ ES: περὶ δηθὰ A: περιδηθὰ
M   945 αὔτως MES: αὖτως Martin   εἰλυμένον MS: εἰλυμένον E:
εἰλουμένον Y^{sl}: εἰλεύμενον Voss: εἰλεύμενον Martin   946 μάλα δείλαιαι Plut.: μαλα δ[Π3: μᾶλλον δειλαὶ codd.   947 ἐξ ὕδατος codd.:
ἐκ λίμνης Plut.   βοόωσι M: βοάωσι E: βοῶσι S   948 τρύζει S:
τρύζῃ ME Π3   950 κύματος Π3: χείματος codd.   χέρσῳ ME:

Often lake-birds or sea-birds splash themselves insatiably by diving into the water, or swallows go darting round a lake for a long time, [945] striking with their bellies the water enclosed as it is, or these very pitiful generations, a boon to water-snakes, the fathers of tadpoles croak from the water itself, or a solitary tree-frog croaks its dawn-song, or perhaps a chattering crow along a projecting shore-line [950] dips its head into an oncoming wave on the shore, or perhaps immerses itself in a river from its head to the top of its shoulders, or even plunges in completely, or walks restlessly to and fro at the water's edge croaking hoarsely.

Now also before rain from heaven cattle, [955] gazing up at the sky, sniff the air; and ants quickly bring up all their eggs from their hole; and there are seen millipedes in swarms climbing up walls, and those worms that men call the black earth's entrails crawling about. [960] And domestic fowls, the progeny of the cock, busily pick off their lice and cackle loudly, with a sound like rain-drops drumming one after the other. Sometimes too families of ravens and tribes of jackdaws are a sign of rain coming from Zeus, [965] when they appear in flocks and screeching like hawks. Ravens too can imitate the heavenly drops with their cry, when rain is coming at the time, or sometimes,

---

χέρση S: χερσαῖ' Maass: χέρσονδ' Ludwig 435   ὑπέτυψε ME^{sl}S: ἐπέτυψε E   952 post 955 M recte S Π3 inter lineas rest. E   953 πολλή S Π3: πολλά ME   955 ὀσφρήσαντο M: ὠσφρήσαντο ES 956 ἐξ ὦεα Maass: ἐξ ὦεα Plut.: ἐξώεα MES: ἐξ ἑα (ἤϊα Leopardi) nonnulli in Plut.   958 τείχε' Koechly: τείχη MES   960 ταὶ A (quae L): τοὶ MES   961 ἐφθειρίσσαντο Morel: -ίσαντο S: -ήσαντο ME ἔκρωξαν MES: ἔκραξαν C   μάλα ME: μεγάλη S (maxima L)   962 τε ME: ὅτε S (quando L)   ψοφέει S: ψοφάει ME   964 πάρα codd.: περὶ sch. Nic.   965 ἰρήκεσσιν A: ἱρήκεσσιν MES   ὅμοιον MES: ὁμοῖα A (similia L): ὁμοῖοι A^{sl} 966 δίους MS: δίους γε E: δίοιο Grotius: δίας Bergk: Ζῆνα Voss: Διὸς οἷα Kaibel 959   σταλαγμοὺς codd.: σταλαγμοῦ Grotius: πέμφιγας Bergk: σταλόωντα Voss (σταλάοντα Lobeck Rhem. 175): σταλημοὺς Koechly: ῥαθάμιγγας Diggle

ἤ ποτε καὶ κρώξαντε βαρείῃ δισσάκι φωνῇ
μακρὸν ἐπιρροιζεῦσι τιναξάμενοι πτερὰ πυκνά.
970 καὶ νῆσσαι οἰκουροὶ ὑπωρόφιοί τε κολοιοὶ
ἐρχόμενοι κατὰ γεῖσα τινάσσονται πτερύγεσσιν,
ἢ ἐπὶ κῦμα διώκει ἐρωδιὸς ὀξὺ λεληκώς.
τῶν τοι μηδὲν ἀπόβλητον πεφυλαγμένῳ ὕδωρ
γινέσθω, μηδ' εἴ κεν ἐπὶ πλέον ἠὲ πάροιθεν
975 δάκνωσιν μυῖαι καὶ ἐφ' αἵματος ἱμείρωνται,
ἢ λύχνοιο μύκητες ἀγείρωνται περὶ μύξαν
νύκτα κατὰ νοτίην· μηδ' ἢν ὑπὸ χείματος ὥρην
λύχνων ἄλλοτε μέν τε φάος κατὰ κόσμον ὀρώρῃ,
ἄλλοτε δ' ἀΐσσωσιν ἄπο φλόγες ἠΰτε κοῦφαι
980 πομφόλυγες, μηδ' εἴ κεν ἐπ' αὐτόφι μαρμαίρωσιν
ἀκτῖνες, μηδ' ἢν θέρεος μέγα πεπταμένοιο
νησαῖοι ὄρνιθες ἐπασσύτεροι φορέωνται.
μηδὲ σύ γ' ἢ χύτρης ἠὲ τρίποδος πυριβήτεω,
σπινθῆρες ὅτ' ἔωσι πέρι πλέονες, λελαθέσθαι,
985 μηδὲ κατὰ σποδιὴν ὁπότ' ἄνθρακος αἰθομένοιο
λάμπηται πέρι σήματ' ἐοικότα κεγχρείοισιν,
ἀλλ' ἐπὶ καὶ τὰ δόκευε περισκοπέων ὑετοῖο.
εἴ γε μὲν ἠερόεσσα παρὲξ ὄρεος μεγάλοιο
πυθμένα τείνηται νεφέλη, ἄκραι δὲ κολῶναι
990 φαίνωνται καθαραί, μάλα κεν τόθ' ὑπεύδιος εἴης.
εὔδιός κ' εἴης καὶ ὅτε πλατέος παρὰ πόντου
φαίνηται χθαμαλὴ νεφέλη, μηδ' ὑψόθι κύρῃ,
ἀλλ' αὐτοῦ πλαταμῶνι παραθλίβηται ὁμοίη.
σκέπτεο δ' εὔδιος μὲν ἐὼν ἐπὶ χείματι μᾶλλον,
995 εἰς δὲ γαληναίην χειμωνόθεν. εὖ δὲ μάλα χρὴ

976-7 (... νοτίην) sch. Ar. V. 262b   976 Hdn 1.61, 13; ii.94, 31;
ii.679, 13; sch. (A) O 302b; Et.M. 594, 14

---

969 ante 962 S   τιναξάμενοι MES: τινασσόμενοι C   971 γεῖσα
MS: γεῖσσα E   974 γινέσθω MS: γιγνέσθω E   975 ἱμείρωνται S:
ἱμείρονται ME   976 ἀγείρωνται Morel: ἀγείρονται codd. Hdn
sch. O 302 Et.M. s.v. μύκης: ἐγείρονται A sch. Ar. V. (erecte L)   μύξαν

croaking twice in a low tone, they make a loud rustling by flapping their close-feathered wings. [970] Also domestic ducks and jackdaws that live under the roof beat with their wings as they come in under the eaves, or the heron speeds out to sea with shrill cries.

Let none of these warnings be neglected if you are on your guard against rain, not if flies bite more than usual and lust after blood, [976] not if snuff collects round the wick of a lamp on a humid night, nor if during the winter season sometimes the flame of a lamp rises steadily, and sometimes sparks fly off it like airy [980] bubbles, nor if there are flickering rays on the lamp itself, nor if, when the summer sky is widely clear, island birds are on the move flock after flock. And do not you overlook a pot or a tripod that stands over a fire when more sparks than usual envelop it, [985] nor when in the ashes of burning charcoal there are spots glowing all over like millet seeds, but watch for these signs too, if you are on the look-out for rain.

But if a faint mist stretches along the base of a high mountain, and the summit peaks [990] are seen clear, then you are very likely to have good weather. Good weather you will also have when a low cloud is seen at sea level, not high up, but compressed right there like a ledge of rock. When in fair weather look out all the more for storm, [995] and for calm when it is stormy. You should observe

---

codd. Hdn sch. Ar. V.: μύξας Et.M.M: μοῖραν sch. (A) O 302   977 νοτίην sch. Ar. V. (austrum L): σκοτίην codd.   ἦν A l (KA): om. MES 978 ὁρώρη E: ὀρώρηες M: ὀρώρει S   979 ἄπο K: ἀπὸ E: ἀπο MS 980 ἐπ' αὐτόφι E: -φιν M: ἀπόπροθι S   μαρμαίρωσιν A: -ουσιν C: -ονται Mʸᵖ: μαραίνονται ME: -ωνται S   981 ἦν ME: εἰ S   982 νησαῖοι Schneider Lex.: νησσαῖοι codd.   φορέωνται MEᴾᶜ: φορέονται EᵃᶜS   983 πυριβήτεω ESᴾᶜ: -βήτοιο Mᴾᶜ: περιβήταιο Mᵃᶜ: -βήτεω Sᵃᶜ   984 πέρι M: περί E: περι- S   986 πέρι Bekker: περὶ codd. 987 περισκοπέων MES: -σκεπέων A: -σκοπεύων C   988 παρὲξ ME: πάρεξ A: παρ' ἐξ S   990 φαίνωνται A: φαίνονται MES   991 εἴης ES: εἴεις M   παρὰ MES: περὶ A   992 μηδ' MES: μήθ' A κύρη M: κυρῆ ES   993 παραθλίβηται ME: -θλίβεται S: πάντα θλίβηται A   995 εἰς MES: εἰ A

ἐς Φάτνην ὁράαν, τὴν Καρκίνος ἀμφιελίσσει,
πρῶτα καθαιρομένην πάσης ὑπένερθεν ὁμίχλης·
κείνη γὰρ φθίνοντι καθαίρεται ἐν χειμῶνι.
καὶ φλόγες ἡσύχιαι λύχνων καὶ νυκτερίη γλαύξ
1000 ἥσυχον ἀείδουσα μαραινομένου χειμῶνος
γινέσθω τοι σῆμα, καὶ ἥσυχα ποικίλλουσα
ὥρη ἐν ἑσπερίη κραυγὴν πολύφωνα κορώνη,
καὶ κόρακες μοῦνοι μὲν ἐρημαῖον βοόωντες
δισσάκις, αὐτὰρ ἔπειτα μετ' ἀθρόα κεκλήγοντες,
1005 πλειότεροι δ' ἀγεληδόν, ἐπὴν κοίτοιο μέδωνται,
φωνῆς ἔμπλειοι· χαίρειν κέ τις οἰήσαιτο,
οἷα τὰ μὲν βοόωσι λιγαινομένοισιν ὁμοῖα,
πολλὰ δὲ δενδρείοιο περὶ φλόον, ἄλλοτ' ἐπ' αὐτοῦ,
ἧχί τε κείουσιν καὶ ὑπότροποι ἀπτερύονται.
1010 καὶ δ' ἄν που γέρανοι μαλακῆς προπάροιθε γαλήνης
ἀσφαλέως τανύσαιεν ἕνα δρόμον ἤλιθα πᾶσαι,
οὐδὲ παλιρρόθιοί κεν ὑπεύδιοι φορέοιντο.
ἧμος δ' ἀστερόθεν καθαρὸν φάος ἀμβλύνηται,
οὐδέ ποθεν νεφέλαι πεπιεσμέναι ἀντιόωσιν,
1015 οὐδέ ποθεν ζόφος ἄλλος ὑποτρέχῃ οὐδὲ σελήνη,
ἀλλὰ τά γ' ἐξαπίνης αὔτως ἀμενηνὰ φέρωνται,
μηκέτι τοι τόδε σῆμα γαληναίης ἐπικείσθω,
ἀλλ' ἐπὶ χεῖμα δόκευε· καὶ ὁππότε ταὶ μὲν ἔωσιν
αὐτῇ ἐνὶ χώρῃ νεφέλαι, ταὶ δ' ἄλλαι ἐπ' αὐταῖς,
1020 ταὶ μὲν ἀμειβόμεναι ταὶ δ' ἐξόπιθεν, φορέωνται.
καὶ χῆνες κλαγγηδὸν ἐπειγόμεναι βρωμοῖο
χειμῶνος μέγα σῆμα, καὶ ἐννεάγηρα κορώνη

1022 (χειμῶνος) Suda iv.800 s.v. χειμὼν ὀρνιθίας

---

996 ἀμφιελίσσει ES: -σσῃ M   999 ἡσύχιαι MES: -ιοι Aˢˡ   1001
ἥσυχα codd. sch.: ἡνίκα Stephanus: ἦν λίγα Lobeck ad *Aiac.*³ 246: ἦχ'
ὅτε Voss: εἰ συχνὰ Bergk *Philol.* 16, 603: εἰ τρίχα Wilamowitz   1002
ἐν MES: om. T: ὅθ' Kaibel 959   κραυγὴν Maass *Aratea* 278: κρώξῃ
MES: κρώζῃ A: κρώζει P: κρώζων Grotius: κρωγμὸν Buttmann
1003 ἐρημαῖον Martin: ἐρημαῖοι codd.   1004 μετ' ἀθρόα M: μετ-
αθρόα A: μετὰ θρόα S: μετ' ἀθρόου E: μέγ' ἀθρόα Buttmann   κεκλή-

very carefully the Manger, which the Crab carries round
in its circular course, as soon as it clears itself of all the
cloud below it; for it clears when a storm is dying away.
Also let the steady flames of lamps and the night owl
[1000] gently hooting be for you the sign of a fading
storm, likewise the imitative crow gently modulating its cry
at eventide, and solitary ravens giving a lone cry twice,
and then after that an uninterrupted succession of cries,
[1005] and large numbers of them in flocks, in full voice
when they are thinking of roosting; one can imagine that
they feel happy, seeing how they utter these cries like
clarion calls, and often do so round the foliage of a tree,
sometimes actually on it, where they come to roost and
flap their wings at their home-coming. [1010] Also perhaps
cranes before a gentle calm will all together set one un-
swerving course, and fly in fair weather without turning
back.

When the bright light of the stars is dimmed, and yet no
serried clouds at all occlude them, [1015] and no other
darkness interferes with them, and no moonlight either,
but they just suddenly go faint in their course, let that not
now impress you as a sign of calm, but expect a storm; expect it too when some clouds stay in the same place, while
others advance upon them, either passing them or lagging
behind. [1021] Geese too, when hurrying noisily to their
feeding-grounds, are an important sign of storm, likewise

γοντες S: κεκληγότες M: κεκληγῶτες E   1005 πλειότεροι A: πλειότερον MES   μέδωνται ME: μέδονται S   1006 κε E: καὶ MS
οἰήσαιτο Voss: ὠίσσοιτο ME: ὠίσσαιτο A^{sl}: ὠίσαιτο P: οἰίσσοιτο C:
ὀίσοιτο S: οἰίσσαιτο Maass   1008 περὶ φλόον E^{sl}S: καταφλόον M:
κατὰ φλόου E   1009 ἀπτερύονται E: ἀπτερρύονται M: αὖτ’ ἐρύον-
ται S: αὖ πτερύωνται P   1012 ὑπεύδιοι S: ἐπεύδιοι ME   1013
ἀστερόθεν ME: οὐρανόθεν S   1014 οὐδέ ποθεν A: οὐδ’ ὄπιθεν M:
οὐδ’ ὄπιθεν E: οὐδ’ ὄπισθεν S   1015 ὑποτρέχῃ T^{pc}: -τρέχει MS:
-τρέχοι E   1016 φέρωνται ME: φέρονται S   1017 τοι E^{sl} S: om. M
1018 μὲν ἔωσιν ME: μενέωσιν A: μὲν ἐῶσιν S: γε μένωσιν Buttmann
1019 ἐνὶ H: ἐν MES   ἐπ’ S: ὑπ’ ME sch.   1020 φορέωνται M:
φερέονται E: φορέονται S   1021 ἐπειγόμεναι ME: -νοι S

νύκτερον ἀείδουσα, καὶ ὀψὲ βοῶντε κολοιοί,
καὶ σπίνος ἠῷα σπίζων, καὶ ὄρνεα πάντα
1025 ἐκ πελάγους φεύγοντα, καὶ ὀρχίλος ἢ καὶ ἐριθεὺς
δύνων ἐς κοίλας ὀχεάς, καὶ φῦλα κολοιῶν
ἐκ νομοῦ ἐρχόμενα τραφεροῦ ἐπὶ ὄψιον αὖλιν.
οὐδ' ἂν ἔτι ξουθαὶ μεγάλου χειμῶνος ἰόντος
πρόσσω ποιήσαιντο νομὸν κηροῖο μέλισσαι,
1030 ἀλλ' αὐτοῦ μέλιτός τε καὶ ἔργων εἰλίσσονται·
οὐδ' ὑψοῦ γεράνων μακραὶ στίχες αὐτὰ κέλευθα
τείνονται, στροφάδες δὲ παλιμπετὲς ἀπονέονται.
μηδ', ὅτε νηνεμίη κεν ἀράχνια λεπτὰ φέρηται,
καὶ φλόγες αἰθύσσωσι μαραινόμεναι λύχνοιο,
1035 ἢ πῦρ αὔηται σπουδῇ καὶ ὑπεύδια λύχνα,
πιστεύειν χειμῶνι. τί τοι λέγω ὅσσα πέλονται
σήματ' ἐπ' ἀνθρώπους; δὴ γὰρ καὶ ἀεικέϊ τέφρῃ
αὐτοῦ πηγνυμένη νιφετοῦ ἐπιτεκμήραιο,
καὶ λύχνῳ χιόνος, κέγχροις ὅτ' ἐοικότα πάντη
1040 κύκλῳ σήματ' ἔχῃ πυριλαμπέος ἐγγύθι μύξης,
ἄνθρακι δὲ ζώοντι χαλάζης, ὁππότε λαμπρὸς
αὐτὸς ἐείδηται, μέσσῳ δέ οἱ ἦΰτε λεπτὴ
φαίνηται νεφέλη πυρὸς ἔνδοθεν αἰθομένοιο.
πρῖνοι δ' αὖ καρποῖο καταχθέες οὐδὲ μέλαιναι
1045 σχῖνοι ἀπείρητοι, πάντη δέ τε πολλὸς ἀλωεὺς
αἰεὶ παπταίνει, μή οἱ θέρος ἐκ χερὸς ἔρρῃ.
πρῖνοι μὲν θαμινῆς ἀκύλου κατὰ μέτρον ἔχουσαι
χειμῶνός κε λέγοιεν ἐπὶ πλέον ἰσχύσοντος·
μὴ μὲν ἄδην ἔκπαγλα περιβρίθοιεν ἀπάντη,
1050 τηλοτέρω δ' αὐχμοῖο συνασταχύοιεν ἄρουραι.
τριπλόα δὲ σχῖνος κυέει, τρισσαὶ δέ οἱ αὖξαι

1024 Hdn i.176, 17; ii.945, 19

1025 πελάγους codd.: πελάγευς Voss   1027 ἐπὶ ὄψιον Μ^ac: ἐπιό-
ψιον Μ^pcΕ: ἐπίοψον S: ἐπὶ ὄψιν Α   1028 ἔτι ξουθαὶ Voss: ἐπὶ
ξουθαὶ Ε: ἐπιξουθαὶ MS   1033 κεν Ε: ἔν Μ: om. S   φέρηται
MS: φέρωνται Ε: φέρονται Α   1034 αἰθύσσωσι Μ: αἰθύσσουσι ES

the nine-lives-old crow cawing at night, and jackdaws chattering late, and the chaffinch chirping at dawn, and all kinds of birds [1025] flying in from the sea, and a wren or a robin diving into a deep hole, and tribes of jackdaws coming from their landward pastures to roost in the evening. Also when a severe storm is coming, the buzzing bees will no longer go foraging for wax, [1030] but busy themselves at home with their honey and honey-combs; and up above long lines of cranes do not maintain a steady course, but wheeling round return back home. And do not, when in calm weather light cobwebs are adrift, and the flames of a lamp flicker feebly, [1035] or fire and lamps in fair weather are kindled with difficulty, rely on weather that will be stormy. Why list all the signs that are available to men? For example, even in dirty ashes that become clogged where they lie you can detect a warning of snow-showers, [1039] and again of snow from a lamp, when spots like millet seeds envelop it all in a circle close to the burning wick, and in live charcoal there are signs of hail, when the coal itself is seen to be bright, while a kind of faint haze appears in its centre inside the burning fire.

[1044] On the other hand evergreen oaks with their burden of fruit and the dark mastich are not untried, and the crofter is always busily watching everywhere, lest the summer slip from his grasp. Evergreen oaks moderately well endowed with closely set mast will tell of a winter likely to be more severe than usual: hope that they will not be very excessively overladen all over, [1050] and that the fields at the same time will produce crops quite remote

---

μαραινόμεναι M: μελαιν- ES (nigris L)   1035 αὖηται ES: αὕηται l (m) bis sch.: αὔνηται M   σπουδῇ Buttmann (uix L): σποδιῇ codd. 1038 νιφετοῦ T: νιφετῷ MES   1040 ἔχῃ M: ἔχει ES   1044 αὖ A: οὐ MES   1045 ἀλωεὺς A: ἀλ- MES   1046 θέρος ES: θέρεος M ἔρρῃ MES: ἔρροι T   1048 ἰσχύσοντος MES: ἰσχύσαντος A 1049 μὴ μὲν ES: μή μιν M: μὴ μεῦ A: μηδὲν C

γίνονται καρποῖο, φέρει δέ τε σήμαθ᾽ ἑκάστη
ἑξείης ἀρότῳ. καὶ γάρ τ᾽ ἀροτήσιον ὥρην
τριπλόα μείρονται, μέσσην καὶ ἐπ᾽ ἀμφότερ᾽ ἄκρας·
1055 πρῶτος μὲν πρώτην ἄροσιν, μέσσος δέ τε μέσσην
καρπὸς ἀπαγγέλλει, πυμάτην γε μὲν ἔσχατος ἄλλων.
ὅντινα γὰρ κάλλιστα λοχαίη σχῖνος ἄρηται,
κείνῳ κ᾽ ἐξ ἄλλων ἄροσις πολυλήϊος εἴη,
τῷ δέ γ᾽ ἀφαυροτάτῳ ὀλίγη, μέσσῳ δέ τε μέσση.
1060 αὔτως δ᾽ ἀνθέρικος τριχθὰ σκίλλης ὑπερανθεῖ
σήματ᾽ ἐπιφράσσασθαι ὁμοίου ἀμητοῖο·
ὅσσα δ᾽ ἐπὶ σχίνου ἀροτὴρ ἐφράσσατο καρπῷ,
τόσσα καὶ ἐν σκίλλης τεκμαίρεται ἄνθεϊ λευκῷ.
αὐτὰρ ὅτε σφῆκες μετοπωρινὸν ἤλιθα πολλοὶ
1065 πάντη βεβρίθωσι, καὶ ἑσπερίων προπάροιθε
Πληϊάδων εἴποι τις ἐπερχόμενον χειμῶνα,
οἷος ἐπὶ σφήκεσσιν ἑλίσσεται αὐτίκα δῖνος.
θήλειαι δὲ σύες, θήλεια δὲ μῆλα καὶ αἶγες
ὁππότ᾽ ἀναστρωφῶσιν ὀχῆς, τὰ δέ γ᾽ ἄρσεσι πάντα
1070 δεξάμεναι πάλιν αὖτις ἀναβλήδην ὀχέωνται,
αὔτως κε σφήκεσσι μέγαν χειμῶνα λέγοιεν.
ὀψὲ δὲ μισγομένων αἰγῶν μήλων τε συῶν τε
χαίρει ἄνολβος ἀνήρ, ὅ οἱ οὐ μάλα θαλπιόωντι
εὔδιον φαίνουσι βιβαιόμεναι ἐνιαυτόν.
1075 χαίρει καὶ γεράνων ἀγέλαις ὡραῖος ἀροτρεὺς
ὥριον ἐρχομέναις, ὁ δ᾽ ἀώριος αὐτίκα μᾶλλον.
αὔτως γὰρ χειμῶνες ἐπέρχονται γεράνοισι,

1057 (λοχαίη σχῖνος) *Et. Flor.* 208 s.v. λόχαιον

1054 ἄκρας Ceporinus: ἄκρα MES: ἄκραι C   1056 ἀπαγγέλλει
MES: ἐπαγγέλλει Α   1057 γὰρ MS: καὶ Ε   1058 κ᾽ Voss: γ᾽ codd.
1059 δέ γ᾽ M: δέ τ᾽ ES   ἀφαυροτάτῳ ES: -τέρῳ M   1060 αὔτως
ES: οὔτως M   ὑπερανθεῖ ΜΕ: -αρθῇ A: -ανθείη S   1061 ὁμοίου
Voss: ὁμοῖον ΜΕᵖᶜS: ὁμοίοον Εᵃᶜ   1062 ἐπὶ MES (*per* L): ἐνὶ A
ἐφράσσατο M: ἐπεφράσσατο Ε: ἐπιφράσατο S   1063 τόσσα καὶ ἐν
MES: τόσσα δὲ καὶ A: τοσσάδε καὶ Voss: τόσσα δὲ καὶ Mair: τοσ-

from drought. The mastich buds three times, its growths of
fruit are three in number, and each growth brings signs in
succession for ploughing. In fact men divide the ploughing
season into three stages, the middle one and the two extremes: [1055] the first fruiting signals the first ploughing,
the middle one the middle, and the last of all the latest.
For according to the best crop that the prolific mastich
achieves, so the ploughing will have its richest harvest of
all, according to the weakest, a poor one, and according to
the medium, a medium. [1060] Similarly the stalk of the
squill has three rich flowerings, for observing the signs of a
corresponding harvest: all the signs that the farmer observed in the fruit of the mastich he identifies also in the
white flower of the squill.

Now when wasps in autumn swarms [1065] are massing
everywhere, even before the setting of the Pleiades, one
can tell the onset of winter, such is the whirling that suddenly eddies in the wasps. And when sows and ewes and
she-goats return to mating, and after receiving all this from
the males, mate all over again repeatedly, [1071] they will
foretell a long winter, just like the wasps. But when the
mating of goats and sows and ewes is late, the poor man is
glad, because he does not keep very warm, and the mating
of the beasts indicates a mild season. [1075] The punctual
farmer is also glad to see flocks of cranes arriving on time,
the unpunctual when they come rather later. For the

σάδε κεν Martin   τεκμαίρεται codd.: τεκμαίροιτ' Martin   1064
πολλοὶ MES^{sl}: πολλὰ S   1066 ἐπερχόμενον χειμῶνα MES: -ομένου
-ῶνος A^{sl}   1069 ἀναστρωφῶσιν ES: -στροφῶσιν M: -στραφῶσιν A
τὰ δέ γ' ME: τάδε γ' S: ταὶ δ' Martin   ἄρσεσι MES: ἄρσενα A
(masculos L)   1070 ὀχέωνται M: ὀχέονται ES   1071 αὕτως M: αὐτὰρ
S^{ac}: αὐτῷ ES^{pc}: οὕτω C   κε Voss: καὶ codd.   1073 θαλπιόωντι
M: θάλπονται E^{ac}S: κεν θάλπονται E^{pc}   1074 φαίνουσι M: φαίνωσι ES
βιβαιόμεναι MS: βιαιόμεναι E: βιβαζόμεναι Grotius   1076 ἀώριος
codd.: ἀώροις Schneider Lex.: ἀώριον Kaibel 960   μᾶλλον ES: μάλα
M   1077 αὕτως MES: οὕτως C   χειμῶνες M: χειμῶνος ES

πρώϊα μὲν καὶ μᾶλλον ὁμιλαδὸν ἐρχομένῃσι
πρώιον· αὐτὰρ ὅτ' ὀψὲ καὶ οὐκ ἀγεληδὰ φανεῖσαι
1080 πλειότερον φορέονται ἐπὶ χρόνον οὐδ' ἅμα πολλαί,
ἀμβολίη χειμῶνος ὀφέλλεται ὕστερα ἔργα.
εἰ δὲ βόες καὶ μῆλα μετὰ βρίθουσαν ὀπώρην
γαῖαν ὀρύσσωσιν, κεφαλὰς δ' ἀνέμοιο βορῆος
ἀντία τείνωσιν, μάλα κεν τότε χείμερον αὐταὶ
1085 Πληϊάδες χειμῶνα κατερχόμεναι φορέοιεν.
μηδὲ λίην ὀρύχοιεν, ἐπεὶ μέγας οὐ κατὰ κόσμον
γίνεται οὔτε φυτοῖς χειμὼν φίλος οὔτ' ἀρότοισιν·
ἀλλὰ χιὼν εἴη πολλὴ μεγάλαις ἐν ἀρούραις
μήπω κεκριμένη μηδὲ βλωθρῇ ἐπὶ ποίῃ,
1090 ὄφρα τις εὐεστοῖ χαίρῃ ποτιδέγμενος ἀνήρ.
οἱ δ' εἶεν καθύπερθεν ἐοικότες ἀστέρες αἰεί,
μηδ' εἷς μηδὲ δύω μηδὲ πλέονες κομόωντες·
πολλοὶ γὰρ κομόωσιν ἐπ' αὐχμηρῷ ἐνιαυτῷ.
οὐδὲ μὲν ὀρνίθων ἀγέλαις ἠπειρόθεν ἀνήρ,
1095 ἐκ νήσων ὅτε πολλαὶ ἐπιπλήσσωσιν ἀρούραις
ἐρχομένου θέρεος, χαίρει· περιδείδιε δ' αἰνῶς
ἀμητῷ, μή οἱ κενεὸς καὶ ἀχύρμιος ἔλθῃ,
αὐχμῷ ἀνιηθείς. χαίρει δέ που αἰπόλος ἀνὴρ
αὐταῖς ὀρνίθεσσιν, ἐπὴν κατὰ μέτρον ἴωσιν,
1100 ἐλπόμενος μετέπειτα πολυγλαγέος ἐνιαυτοῦ.
οὕτω γὰρ μογεροὶ καὶ ἀλήμονες ἄλλοθεν ἄλλοι
ζώομεν ἄνθρωποι· τὰ δὲ πὰρ ποσὶ πάντες ἑτοῖμοι
σήματ' ἐπιγνῶναι καὶ ἐς αὐτίκα ποιήσασθαι.
ἀρνάσι μὲν χειμῶνας ἐτεκμήραντο νομῆες,
1105 ἐς νομὸν ὁππότε μᾶλλον ἐπειγόμενοι τροχόωσιν,

1091–3 Phlp. *in Mete.* A 7 p. 100, 1 H.

1078 ἐρχομένῃσι M: -ένοισι ES   1079 πρώϊον codd.: πρώϊος Voss:
πρώϊοι Maass   1080 πλειότερον M: -ότεραι ES sch.   φορέονται
M: προτέρων τε ES   οὐδ' ἅμα πολλαί A sch.: οὐ μάλα πολλῇ
MES: οὐ μάλα πολλαί Δ   1084 αὐταὶ M: αὗται ES   1086 μηδὲ
Ceporinus: μὴ δὲ MES: εἰ δ' A   1087 ἀρότοισιν S: ἀρότῃσιν

coming of winters corresponds to that of the cranes, early
when they come early and more in companies; but when
they appear late and not in flocks, [1080] and take a longer
time, not in large numbers together, the late farm-work
benefits from the winter's delay. If cattle and sheep dig the
ground after fruit-laden autumn, and strain their heads
against a north wind, then the Pleiades themselves at their
setting will bring on a very stormy winter. [1086] It is to be
hoped they will not dig too much, since, if they do, the
winter is excessively long, and friendly to neither trees nor
crops; but on the broad corn-fields may heavy snow lie
over the young shoots before they are separately distinguishable and tall, [1090] so that a watchful man may
enjoy prosperity. It is to be hoped that the stars above will
always be recognisable, and that there will not be one or
two or more comets: for many comets mean a dry year.

The mainland farmer does not like flocks of birds,
[1095] when from the islands in large numbers they invade
his cornlands at the coming of summer: he is terribly
alarmed for his harvest, in case it turns out empty ears and
chaff, distressed by drought. But the goatherd is rather
pleased with the same birds, when they come in moderate
numbers, [1100] because he expects thereafter a year of
plentiful milk. So it is that we suffering restless mortals
make a living in different ways; but all are only too ready
to recognise signs that are right beside us, and to adopt
them for the moment.

Shepherds foretell storms from sheep [1105] when they

ME   1088 ἐν A sch. (KA): ἐπ' MES sch. (MS)   1089 ἐπὶ MES:
περὶ A   1091 οἱ δ' M: μὴ δ' ES Phlp.   1092 μηδ' Voss: μήθ' codd.
Phlp.   μηδὲ Maass: μήτε codd. Phlp.: μηδὲ S: μὴ δὲ ME: μήτε Phlp.
1095 ἐπιπλήσσωσιν M: ἐπὶ πλήσσωσιν C: ἐπιπλήσωσιν ES   1096
ἐρχομένου ES: -έναις M   περιδείδιε ES: -δείδιαι M   1099 αὐταῖς
M: ταύταις ES: ἐν ταῖς A   1101 οὕτω M: οὕτως ES   ἀλήμονες
ES: ἀλήμενες M   1103 ἐς αὐτίκα MS: ἐσαυτίκα E   1104 ἐτεκμήραντο ES: ἐπιτεκμήραντο M

ἄλλοι δ' ἐξ ἀγέλης κριοί, ἄλλοι δὲ καὶ ἀμνοὶ
εἰνόδιοι παίζωσιν ἐρειδόμενοι κεράεσσιν·
ἢ ὁπότ' ἄλλοθεν ἄλλοι ἀναπλήσσωσι πόδεσσι,
τέτρασιν οἱ κοῦφοι, κεραοί γε μὲν ἀμφοτέροισιν·
1110 ἢ καὶ ὅτ' ἐξ ἀγέλης ἀεκούσια κινήσωσι
δείελον εἰσελάοντες ὅμως, τὰ δὲ πάντοθι ποίης
δάκνωσιν πυκινῇσι κελευόμενα λιθάκεσσιν.
ἐκ δὲ βοῶν ἐπύθοντ' ἀρόται καὶ βουκόλοι ἄνδρες
κινυμένου χειμῶνος· ἐπεί, βόες ὁππότε χηλὰς
1115 γλώσσῃ ὑπωμαίοιο ποδὸς περιλιχμήσωνται,
ἢ κοίτῳ πλευρὰς ἐπὶ δεξιτερὰς τανύσωνται,
ἀμβολίην ἀρότοιο γέρων ἐπιέλπετ' ἀροτρεύς.
οὐδ', ὅτε μυκηθμοῖο περίπλειοι ἀγέρωνται
ἐρχόμεναι σταθμόνδε βόες βουλύσιον ὥρην,
1120 σκυθραὶ λειμῶνος πόριες καὶ βουβοσίοιο
αὐτίκα τεκμαίρονται ἀχείμεροι ἐμπλήσεσθαι.
οὐδ' αἶγες πρίνοιο περισπεύδουσαι ἀκάνθαις
εὔδιοι, οὐδὲ σύες φορυτῷ ἔπι μαργαίνουσαι.
καὶ λύκος ὁππότε μακρὰ μονόλυκος ὠρύηται,
1125 ἢ ὅτ' ἀροτρήων ὀλίγον πεφυλαγμένος ἀνδρῶν
ἔργα κατέρχηται, σκέπαος χατέοντι ἐοικὼς
ἐγγύθεν ἀνθρώπων, ἵνα οἱ λέχος αὐτόθεν εἴη,
τρὶς περιτελλομένης ἠοῦς χειμῶνα δοκεύειν.
οὕτω καὶ προτέροις ἐπὶ σήμασι τεκμήραιο
1130 ἐσσομένων ἀνέμων ἢ χείματος ἢ ὑετοῖο
αὐτὴν ἢ μετὰ τὴν ἢ καὶ τριτάτην ἔτ' ἐς ἠῶ.

1123 (σύες ...) Democr. fr. 147   1124 (μονόλυκος) Eust. in ζ 133

1106 ἄλλοι ... ἄλλοι codd. (alii L): ἄλλη ... ἄλλη Voss   1108 ἀναπλήσσωσι A (percutientes L): -πλήσωσι MES: -πλίσσωσι Schneider Lex.
1110 κινήσωσι MES: κινήσουσι C   1111 ὅμως H: ὁμῶς MES   ποίης
MS: ποίου E   1112 πυκινῇσι S: πυκνῇσι M: πυκινοῖσι E   κελευόμενα MS: -όμεναι E   1114 κινυμένου M: κιννυ- ES: κινου- A
1115 περιλιχμήσωνται Mᵖᶜ: -σονται Mᵃᶜ ES   1116 δεξιτερὰς M:
-τερᾶς A: -τερὰ S: δεξιὰ E   τανύσωνται M: τανύσονται ES
1118 οὐδ' MES (neque L): ἠδ' A: οἱ δ' Voss   ἀγέρωνται MS: ἀγέ-

run to pasture more hastily than usual, and some of the
flock, now rams, now lambs, frolic on the way, butting
each other with their horns; or when here and there they
kick up their legs, the nimble ones with four, the horned
with two; [1110] or when the men move them from the
flock, driving them home in the late afternoon despite
their reluctance, and they keep nibbling the grass all the
way, though urged on by showers of stones. Ploughmen
and herdsmen learn from cattle that a storm is brewing;
for when cattle with their tongues lick round the hooves of
their forefeet, [1116] or stretch themselves on their right
flanks when resting, the veteran ploughman expects a post-
ponement of ploughing. Also, when cows herd together
with continuous lowing, homeward bound at unyoking
time, [1120] the dispirited calves sense that sooner or later
they will be feeding on the meadow-pastures in stormy
weather. And it is no sign of good weather when goats are
busy about the prickly evergreen oak, or sows go frantic
with the blown straw. Also when a lone wolf howls loud,
[1125] or when, little wary of farming men, it comes down
to the farm-lands, as if in need of shelter close to men, to
make a lair right there, then expect a storm within the
cycle of three days. So too by prior signs you can estimate
[1130] that there will be winds or storm or rain the same
day or the one after it or even on the third morning. For

ρονται E   1119 ἐρχόμεναι MS: -όμενοι E coni. Voss   βόες codd.:
βοῶν Maass: βόας Kaibel 946   βουλύσιον ὥρην codd.: βουλυσίῳ
ὥρῃ Martin   1120 post σκυθραὶ lacunam coni. Buttmann   λειμῶνος MES: χειμῶνος A (hiemis L): δ' ἄλλωνται Voss   καὶ codd.:
κατὰ Voss   1121 ἐμπλήσεσθαι ES (satiari L): -ασθαι C: ἐμπλήσσεσθαι
M   1123 ἔπι μαργαίνουσαι Voss: ἐπιμαργ- codd.   1124 μονόλυκος
S: μονόλλυκος M: μονώλυκος E   1125 ὅτ' codd.: ὅ γ' Buttmann
ἀροτρήων MEᵃᶜS: ἀροτήρων Eᵖᶜ   1126 σκέπαος ES: σκέπας M
1127 λέχος MES: λόχος Mᵞᵖ nonnulli in sch.   1128 δοκεύειν ES:
δοκεύει M   1129 καὶ MES: κε C   1130 ἐσσομένων M: ἐσπομένων
E: ἐπομένων S   1131 μετὰ τὴν ES: μετ' αὐτὴν M

ἀλλὰ γὰρ οὐδὲ μύες, τετριγότες εἴ ποτε μᾶλλον
εὔδιοι ἐσκίρτησαν ἐοικότα ὀρχηθμοῖσιν,
ἄσκεπτοι ἐγένοντο παλαιοτέροις ἀνθρώποις,
1135 οὐδὲ κύνες· καὶ γάρ τε κύων ὠρύξατο ποσσὶν
ἀμφοτέροις χειμῶνος ἐπερχομένοιο δοκεύων,
καὶ κεῖνοι χειμῶνα μύες τότε μαντεύονται.
καὶ μὴν ἐξ ὕδατος καὶ καρκίνος οἴχετο χέρσον,
χειμῶνος μέλλοντος ἐπαΐσσεσθαι ὁδοῖο.
1140 καὶ μύες ἡμέριοι ποσσὶ στιβάδα στρωφῶντες
κοίτης ἱμείρονται, ὅτ' ὄμβρου σήματα φαίνει.
τῶν μηδὲν κατόνοσσο. καλὸν δ' ἐπὶ σήματι σῆμα
σκέπτεσθαι, μᾶλλον δὲ δυοῖν εἰς ταὐτὸν ἰόντων
ἐλπωρὴ τελέθοι, τριτάτῳ δέ κε θαρσήσειας.
1145 αἰεὶ δ' ἂν παριόντος ἀριθμοίης ἐνιαυτοῦ
σήματα, συμβάλλων εἴ που καὶ ἐπ' ἀστέρι τοίη
ἠὼς ἀντέλλοντι φαείνεται ἢ κατιόντι,
ὁπποίην καὶ σῆμα λέγοι. μάλα δ' ἄρκιον εἴη
φράζεσθαι φθίνοντος ἐφισταμένοιό τε μηνὸς
1150 τετράδας ἀμφοτέρας· αἱ γάρ τ' ἄμυδις συνιόντων
μηνῶν πείρατ' ἔχουσιν, ὅτε σφαλερώτερος αἰθὴρ
ὀκτὼ νυξὶ πέλει, χήτει χαροποῖο σελήνης.
τῶν ἄμυδις πάντων ἐσκεμμένος εἰς ἐνιαυτὸν
οὐδέποτε σχεδίως κεν ἐπ' αἰθέρι τεκμήραιο.

1132 ποτε M: ποθι ES   1133 ἐοικότα Maass: ἐοικότες codd.   1134
παλαιοτέροις ES: -τάτοις M   1135 ὠρύξατο codd. sch. (*effodit* L):
ὠρέξατο l nonnulli in sch.   1137 post 1141 ES: om. P   καὶ κεῖνοι
M: κἀκεῖνοι ES   1138–41 om. C: seclusit Martin   1138 οἴχετο M:
οἴχεταιο E: οἴχεται S: ᾤχετο A   χέρσον ES: χέρσῳ M   1140 μύες
codd.: σύες R. F. Thomas *HSCPh* 90, 91–2   1141 φαίνει E: φαίνοι
MS: φαίνῃ Martin   1142 κατόνοσσο Υ: κατόνησο MES: κατόκνη-
ησο Τ   1143 δυοῖν ES: δυεῖν M   1144 τελέθοι MES: τελέθει
P   1146 σήματα codd.: ἤματα Rehm *RE* 18.4.1299   1147 φαείνεται
A: κατέρχεται MES   1148 ὁπποίην Voss: ὁπποῖον ME: ὁποῖον S
καὶ A: κε M: τε ES   σῆμα λέγοι MS: λέγοι σῆμα E   1149 ἐφισταμένοιο M: ἐπερχομ- ES   1151 σφαλερώτερος M: -ώτατος ES

that matter even mice, squeaking more than usual in good weather and capering as if they were dancing, did not go unobserved by earlier men, [1135] nor did dogs: for a dog digs with its two paws when it expects the onset of a storm, and the aforesaid mice are also storm-prophets at such a time. Why, even a crab comes out of the water on to land when a storm is about to launch itself on its course. [1140] Also mice in the daytime, tossing straw with their paws, have a desire to rest when it shows signs of rain.

Do not despise any of these warnings. It is a good idea to observe one sign after another, and if two agree, it is more hopeful, while with a third you can be confident. [1145] You should count the signs all the time through the passing year, checking whether, at the rising or setting of a star, such a day appears as the sign foretells. It can be especially reliable [1149] to observe both the fourth last day of the waning month and the fourth of that just begun: these contain the boundaries of the months' convergence, when the sky on eight nights is more fallible, for want of the yellow moon. If you have watched for these signs all together for the year, you will never make an uninformed judgement on the evidence of the sky.

COMMENTARY

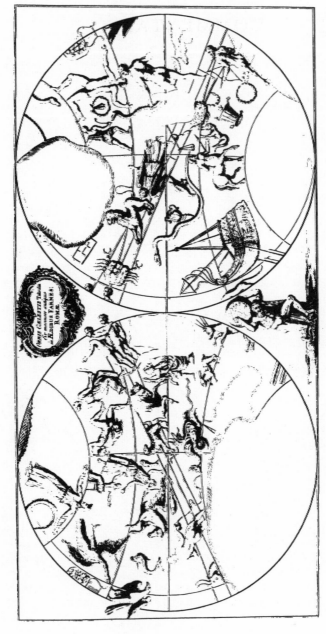

Fig. 1 A projection of the second-century Farnese Atlas globe by Foulkes Stich in Bentley's edition of Manilius (London 1739), showing figures of the Greek constellations, celestial circles and zodiac belt.

ΦΑΙΝΟΜΕΝΑ Most of the manuscripts that provide a heading to the text give Ἀράτου φαινόμενα, but others have Ἀράτου Σολέως φαινόμενα or τὰ φαινόμενα Ἀράτου ποιητοῦ. The commonest conclusion to the text is τέλος τῶν φαινομένων Ἀράτου, but there is a variant with τῶν φαινομένων καὶ διοσημειῶν (see note on 733–757). Hipparchus confirms the title for one of Eudoxus' books in τὸ μὲν οὖν ἐν αὐτῶν ἐπιγράφεται Ἔνοπτρον, τὸ δὲ ἕτερον Φαινόμενα (1.2.2), and for A. in τῇ γὰρ Εὐδόξου συντάξει κατακολουθήσας τὰ Φαινόμενα γέγραφεν (1.1.8).

The association of this participle with astronomy appears to begin with Plato, who in his later years, with remarkable insight, suggested that the observed movements of the planets are more apparent than real (*Lg.* 822a), and is said to have encouraged research with the aim of discovering a simple planetary hypothesis that could account for the complexity of the observed movements: τίνων ὑποτεθεισῶν ὁμαλῶν καὶ τεταγμένων κινήσεων διασωθῇ τὰ περὶ τὰς κινήσεις τῶν πλανωμένων φαινόμενα (Sosigenes ap. Simp. *in Cael.* 488 Heiberg; see Vlastos 60). Aristotle also uses τὰ φαινόμενα for the observed movements of the planets (*Cael.* 293a25–30, 293b27). But Eudoxus is the first to have extended the scope of the term to include the observed positions and movements of the fixed stars, perhaps with the intention of constructing an accurate frame of reference against which the vagaries of the planets could be plotted. In adopting the same title for his poem A. has extended the range of τὰ φαινόμενα still further, to include aerial and terrestrial signs observed in the prediction of weather changes: cf. φαίνεσθαι of birds (965), clouds (867, 992), mountain-tops (990).

1–18 PROEM

A. begins with a short proem, which owes its form to the traditions of Hesiodic epic and its content to the contemporary themes of Stoicism. The main section is a hymn to Zeus, the divinity that pervades the whole cosmos and is the source of all forms of life. He is in this sense our father, and acts like a father in helping men to cope with the struggle for existence, especially in agriculture. To this end he has established the constellations in the sky to serve as a guide to the seasons throughout the year, and that is why Zeus is so widely worshipped (1–14). The conclusion is a salutation, first to Zeus, and secondly to the Muses, whose favour the poet requests for his poem (15–18).

The proem contains several elements that look back to Hesiod and some of the *Homeric Hymns*: the god with whom the poet proposes to begin, the following relative clause, the praise of the god's attributes, and the invocation. There are also many verbal echoes, which will be noted as they occur. But the subject-matter of the proem is new. There is no reference to the old myths at all. Instead we have the Stoic concept of Zeus as the πνεῦμα that pervades the cosmos, the source of all life, an intelligence that reveals its divine πρόνοια in making the universe intelligible and favourable. This hymn has much in common with the contemporary Hymn to Zeus by Cleanthes.

The proem is full of poetic artistries that are appropriate to the hymnic style, though they are also characteristic of A.'s composition in other parts of the *Phaenomena*. Such are anaphora (2–3, 7–8, 15–16), other repetitions (e.g. Διός 1–4, and words in the invocation that recall the themes of the hymn), chiasmus (2–3), balanced phrases (9), internal rhyme (2, 6, 9).

See Pasquali 113–22, Wilamowitz *HD* 2.262–5, Schwabl 336–42, West on Hes. *Th.* 1–115 and *Op.* 1–10, James 34–8.

1 ἐκ Διὸς ἀρχώμεσθα A. begins with Zeus because his whole poem illustrates the presence of Zeus as sky and weather god and the providence of Zeus in providing the signs that are helpful to mortals. References to Zeus are frequent and occur in a variety of contexts: the pervading life force 1, 2, 4; the benefactor 5, 10, 15, 743, 769, 771; the sky 224, 253, 259, 756; the creator of the constellations 11, 265; the source of weather 293, 426, 886, 899, 936, 964; the mythological god 31, 163–4, 181. The invocation of Zeus, which follows the hymn, is therefore relevant to the whole poem. On Zeus as the sky cf. *SVF* 1.169 (Zeno), 2.1076–7 (Chrysippus); Macr. *Sat.* 1.18.15, *Somn.* 1.17.14.

This opening phrase echoes Hes. *Th.* 1 Μουσάων Ἑλικωνιάδων ἀρχώμεθ' ἀείδειν and 36 Μουσάων ἀρχώμεθα. Other varieties of this formula are to be found in the *Homeric Hymns*: ἄρχομ' ἀείδειν (2.1, 11.1, 16.1, 22.1, 26.1, 28.1), σεῦ δ' ἐγὼ ἀρξάμενος (5.293, 9.9), Μουσάων ἄρχωμαι (25.1), ἄρχεο Μοῦσα (31.1). So Demodocus in θ 499 θεοῦ ἄρχετο, and Nestor to Agamemnon in Ι 97 ἔν σοι μὲν λήξω, σέο δ' ἄρξομαι. Imitations are also found in non-epic poets, e.g. Theogn. 1–2 οὔποτε σεῖο λήσομαι ἀρχόμενος οὐδ' ἀποπαυόμενος, Ion, *Eleg.* fr. 27.6 ἐκ Διὸς ἀρχόμενοι, Alcm. fr. 29 ἀείσομαι ἐκ Διὸς ἀρχομένα, Pi. *N.* 2.3 ἄρχονται Διὸς ἐκ προοιμίου, 5.25 Διὸς ἀρχόμεναι, Ar. *V.* 846 Ἑστίας ἀρχόμενοι (cf. Diggle on E. *Phaethon* 249–50).

Among the contemporaries of A. Apollonius opens his epic with a new variant, ἀρχόμενος σέο Φοῖβε. But Theocritus begins his 17th idyll with the same phrase as A., and there has been much debate about which poet was the imitator, or whether both poets produced independently the same variation of an old theme. Gow's comment on Theoc. 17.1 ends by leaving the question undecided. But there are some grounds for thinking that in this case A. was the originator and Theocritus the imitator. (1) Later writers ascribe the phrase to A., e.g. sch. Theoc. Ἀρατείᾳ κέχρηται εἰσβολῇ, Strat. *AP* 12.1.1 ἐκ Διὸς ἀρχώμεσθα, καθὼς εἴρηκεν Ἄρατος, Cic. *Rep.* 1.36 *imitemur ergo Aratum, qui magnis de rebus dicere exordiens a Ioue incipiendum putat*, Quint. *Inst.* 10.1.46 *ut Aratus ab Ioue incipiendum putat*, Macr. *Somn.* 1.17.14 *hinc illud est 'ab Ioue principium ...', quod de Arato poetae alii mutuati sunt*. (2) Zeus is significant for the whole of the *Phaenomena*, whereas Theocritus brings in Zeus merely to give the poem a frame and make possible a flattering comparison with Ptolemy. (3) Theocritus completes his line differently, with καὶ ἐς Δία λήγετε, Μοῖσαι. It is characteristic of the imitator to vary his borrowing with a new turn of some kind, and in this case the metrically convenient change to the 2nd person introduces an awkwardness that Gow's translation overlooks. (4) In 7.53 and 22.21–2 Theocritus has clearly taken his astronomical details from A. (see notes on 158 and 1065, 889 and 996), and it is reasonable to suppose that he is paying him a compliment also in 17.1. Vahlen, *Opuscula Academica* 1 (1907) 303ff., Fantuzzi, *Materiali e Discussioni* 5 (1980) 163ff., Pendergraft, *QUCC* 53 (1986) 49ff.

Cicero translates *ab Ioue Musarum primordia* (fr. 1), Virgil imitates with *ab Ioue principium* (*E.* 3.60), cleverly producing variation in each word, and there are later echoes of the phrase in Ov. *Met.* 10.148, *Fast.* 5.111, Calp. Sic. 4.82, V. Max. 1 pr. 17, Stat. *Sil.* 1. pr. 19.

ἄνδρες Maass (*Aratea* 319–20) infers from the opening words and the supposed triple salutation in 15–17 that the poet is here addressing friends at a symposium: cf. Ach. *Comm.* (Maass *Comm.* 81, 26–9) πρέπει δὲ καὶ ποιηταῖς μάλιστα αὕτη ἡ ἀρχή, ἐπεὶ καὶ ἐν τοῖς συμποσίοις τρεῖς κρατῆρας ἐκίρνων, καὶ τὸν μὲν πρῶτον Διὸς Ὀλυμπίου, τὸν δὲ δεύτερον Διοσκούρων καὶ ἡρώων, τὸν δὲ τρίτον Διὸς Σωτῆρος. Maass therefore construes ἄνδρες as vocative. Erren (*PAS* 15) rejects the idea of a real symposium speech, but allows that the language is suggestive of such an occasion. There is however nothing in the poet's language to justify this assumption, it has no relevance to the theme of the poem, and the salutation in 15–17 is formally a double one, not triple: see note on 16. A. is using ἄνδρες in the sense of men as opposed to gods (a common Homeric use, e.g. A 544), as again in 13 ἀνδράσιν. Note A.'s variation in the words he uses to express this simple meaning: ἄνθρωποι (3, 5), πάντες (4), λαοί (6), and the unexpressed subject of ἱλάσκονται (14).

ἐῶμεν In view of the negative οὐ- there is of course no question of taking this verb as subjunctive, as some translators have done, e.g. Lamb, Schott.

2 ἄρρητον Once in Homer (ξ 466) and once in Hesiod (*Op.* 4), in each case positively and in the simple sense 'unspoken'. A. has it twice, here and in 180, both times with a negative. Here he means that we continually glorify Zeus, and presumably he is thinking of both religious ceremonies and everyday language with expressions like νὴ Δία. As Martin comments, A. is to some extent saying the opposite of Hesiod, who asserts that it is the will of Zeus that makes men ῥητοί τ' ἄρρητοί τε. Sch. Germ. 57, 110 (Martin *SAV* 47–8) give another explanation: *quoniam nihil aliud est uox quam percussus aer, uidetur conuenienter dixisse, auctoritatemque rei praestat 'plenas Ioue uias' referens et 'omnis hominum conuentus'. nihil eorum quae in terra sint sine aere est.* But it is more likely that A. means the spoken appreciation of Zeus, as summed up in line 14.

For this negative idiom cf. Pl. *Lg.* 793b οὔτε ἄρρητα ἐᾶν, Plut. 973c μηδὲν ἄρρητον ἀπολιπεῖν. The positive appears in Manetho 6(3).737 ἄρρητον ἐάσω. Here the phrase seems curiously contrived, as if designed to lead up to the word ἄρρητον, emphatically placed at the beginning of the next line and followed by a strong sense pause. The reason could be merely to draw attention to the passage in Hesiod; but it may be that the poet is indulging in a pun on his own name, which in Greek usually has a long first syllable, and occurs with η in the second syllable in Call. *E.* 27.4 and Leon. *AP* 9.25.1 = *HE* 2573. Cf. Nestor's son Ἄρητος (γ 414), the form of whose name A. may have cultivated for himself as appropriate for a poet in the epic tradition. If it is right to see a deliberate acrostic in 783–7, a mere pun here is not impossible. It would serve as a sort of signature at the outset of the poem, modestly positioned in the second line after Zeus in the first. Cf. the punning on names in *AP* 5.115 = *GP* 3196ff. (Phld.), 11.218 = *HE* 1371ff. (Crat.), 12.165 = *HE* 4520ff. (Mel.), and the pun on Eudoxus ascribed to Antigonus in the Aratean *Vita* 1 (Martin *SAV* 8). The conceit of the poet's signature is otherwise illustrated by the acrostics in Nic. *Ther.* 345ff. and *Alex.* 266ff. See my note in *CQ* 31 (1981) 355, P. Bing, *HSCP* 93 (1990) 281–5. (I have since learned that the suggestion of a pun here was made earlier by W. Levitan in *Glyph* 5 (1979) 68 n. 18.)

μεσταὶ δὲ Διός The Stoic Zeus is identified with the πνεῦμα, a compound of air and fire, which is the active principle permeating the whole spherical cosmos, giving it unity and life. It is conceived on the analogy of the vitality that pervades the whole of the living body. Cf. Clem. Al. *Protr.* 7 Ἄρατος μὲν οὖν διὰ πάντων τὴν δύναμιν τοῦ θεοῦ διήκειν νοεῖ. See e.g. Halm, *Origins of Stoic Cosmology* (1977) 163ff., Lapidge, *The Stoics*, ed. Rist (1978) 168ff., Long, *Hellenistic Philosophy*, 2nd edn (1986) 155ff. A. restricts his description to the world of land and sea that human beings inhabit and use, because he is primarily concerned

with the benefits Zeus gives to men. Cf. E. *Hipp.* 447–50 of Aphrodite.
He recalls and corrects the Hesiodic outlook of *Op.* 101 πλείη μὲν γὰρ
γαῖα κακῶν, πλείη δὲ θάλασσα. The anaphora of μεσταὶ ... μεστὴ
and πᾶσαι ... πᾶσαι followed by πάντη ... πάντες is characteristic of
the hymnic style, and the variation of endings is particularly Hellenistic.
See also Traina, *Maia* 8 (1956) 39ff., Bossi, *Museum Criticum* 13–14 (1978–
79) 323ff.

The fame of this passage is well illustrated by later quotations (see
Testimonia) and semi-quotations, e.g. Luc. *Epigr.* 41.5–6 (*AP* 11.400) καὶ
γὰρ σοῦ μεσταὶ μὲν ὁδοί, μεστὴ δὲ θάλασσα καὶ λιμένες, *Nigr.* 16 μεσταὶ
γὰρ αὐτοῖς τῶν φιλτάτων πᾶσαι μὲν ἀγυιαί, πᾶσαι δὲ ἀγοραί, Aris-
tid. *Jov.* 7 πάντα δὲ πανταχοῦ Διὸς μεστά, *Sarap.* 55 μεσταὶ δὲ ἀγοραί,
φασί, καὶ λιμένες καὶ τὰ εὐρύχωρα τῶν πόλεων.

ἀγυιαί   The word is Homeric, and A.'s use of it in a context of
earth and sky recalls the sunset formula δύσετό τ' ἠέλιος σκιόωντό τε
πᾶσαι ἀγυιαί (β 388). Here A. uses the word with reference to roads
along which men travel, by way of making a contrast with ἀγοραί, the
places where men meet for a purpose. This antithesis is balanced by a
corresponding one between θάλασσα, the open sea where ships go on
voyages, and λιμένες, where they come to rest close to the cities of men.
The epithet ἀγοραῖος traditionally belongs to Zeus (e.g. A. *Eum.* 973,
Hdt. 5.46.2), but ἀγυιεύς is always Apollo's, and while there is a Ζεὺς
λιμένιος mentioned by Pausanias (2.34.112), θάλασσα is always Poseidon's province. The Stoic Zeus has now supplanted the older gods,
and the cosmos is now monotheistic. This idea is well summed up in
line 4.

3 πᾶσαι ... ἀγοραί   The rhyming sequence of 2 is continued here.
It is appropriate to the hymnic style of the proem, but elsewhere
avoided by A., unless used for special effects: cf. 911–12. Note the chiasmus μεσταὶ ... πᾶσαι ... πᾶσαι ... μεστή.

4 πάντη   -η is explained as an old instrumental ending (Schwyzer
1.201, 550; Barrett on E. *Hipp.* 563; Palmer 283); cf. λάθρη, κρυφῆ, πῆ,
ἧχι (61). The common alternative with -ῃ, a fem. dat. sg. ending, is
suited to noun and pronoun stems (σπουδῇ, ἄλλῃ): see LSJ and K–B
2.305–6. Here there is no way of determining which form A. used, but
at least πάντη throughout, ἀπάντη (22 al.) and ἧχι (61 al.) follow the
tradition of scribes and editors. Cf. Call. *H.* 2.70 Pfeiffer, A.R. 2.302
Fränkel. In 14 I have preferred τῷ.

κεχρήμεθα   This verb expresses both need and use, the former sense
normally c. gen., the latter c. dat. Here a combination of both seems to
be required, namely that we are entirely dependent on Zeus, the life-
giving force. Sch. Germ. *ratione etiam 'omnes cuius [Iouis* Breysig] *usum*

desideramus', nam cuncti mortales ostendunt usum suspirio, sed per quae [*quem* Breysig] *uiuimus aere indigent*, Cleanthes 15–16. There is also a Homeric echo here, of γ 48 πάντες δὲ θεῶν χατέουσ' ἄνθρωποι, and perhaps of Hes. *Op.* 634 βίου κεχρημένος ἐσθλοῦ.

5 τοῦ γὰρ καὶ γένος εἰμέν A. now casts his Stoicism in the form of the old mythologies: since we derive our life from Zeus, we may be described as his children. This is an important step in the argument of the proem, because it leads on to the concept of Zeus as also a father, and therefore a kindly influence: καί brings out this new point.

The phrase is famous because it is quoted by St Paul (who was also a Cilician) in his sermon to the Athenians (Acts 17.28): ὡς καί τινες τῶν καθ' ὑμᾶς ποιητῶν εἰρήκασιν· τοῦ γὰρ καὶ γένος ἐσμέν. The other poet implied by the plural is probably Cleanthes, whose *Hymn to Zeus* 4 ἐκ σοῦ γὰρ γένος ἐσμέν (γενόμεσθα Meineke) may well be A.'s source here. On Cleanthes' text see James 30–1, Hopkinson *HA* 28.

At the same time A. recalls Homeric ἐκ γὰρ ἐμεῦ γένος ἐσσί (Ε 896), ἐκ θεόφιν γένος ἦεν (Ψ 347), and Hes. *Th.* 96 ἐκ δὲ Διὸς βασιλῆες. Cf. A.R. 3.920 ἐξ αὐτοῖο Διὸς γένος.

εἰμέν Ionic–Epic. The Attic–Koine ἐσμέν of S and early editors was probably due to the influence of the *N.T.*

ἤπιος This epithet is characteristic of a father, recalling β 47 πατὴρ δ' ὡς ἤπιος ἦεν. A. can therefore defer the title πατήρ until his salutation in 15. In Hes. *Th.* 407 Phoebe bore Leto to be ἤπιον ἀνθρώποισι καὶ ἀθανάτοισι θεοῖσι. Hesiod's Zeus is a hard god, who makes life difficult (*Op.* 42, 47–9, 57), in spite of being πατὴρ ἀνδρῶν τε θεῶν τε (59). In this respect A. is again correcting Hesiod and bringing Zeus up to date. At the same time, as Solmsen (127) has pointed out, the idea of providential gods can also be traced back to Hesiod, e.g. *Op.* 398 ἔργα τά τ' ἀνθρώποισι θεοὶ διετεκμήραντο, and even a benevolent Zeus (*Op.* 279ff. ἀνθρώποισι δ' ἔδωκε δίκην κτλ.). Cf. E. *Ba.* 861 of Dionysus, δεινότατος, ἀνθρώποισι δ' ἠπιώτατος. For Christian approval see Theophil. Antioch. 2.8.

ἀνθρώποισι The double-spondee ending with this word is Homeric, e.g. Δ 320 ἀλλ' οὔ πως ἅμα πάντα θεοὶ δόσαν ἀνθρώποισιν, a line which A. may possibly be recalling, since both the metrical pattern and the subject-matter are similar. On the *spondeiazon* see Introd. p. 35.

6 δεξιά The adj. is suggestive of the traditional Zeus giving a favourable omen on the right (e.g. Ν 821). But here the word means not so much 'favourable' as 'helpful': many of the signs are warnings of bad weather, but men are enabled by them to take suitable precautions. The repetition in line 8, however, does have the normal sense. Cf. Ι 236 ἐνδέξια σήματα φαίνων, Call. *H.* 1.69.

λαούς Usually of the common people as opposed to their leaders (e.g. γ 214), here *vis-à-vis* Zeus; cf. 112, 116.

ἐπὶ ἔργον ἐγείρει A. recalls Hes. *Op.* 20 of Eris ἥ τε καὶ ἀπάλαμόν περ ὁμῶς ἐπὶ ἔργον ἐγείρει, and implies a contrast between the older competitive rivalry and the more kindly incentives of the Stoic Zeus. Virgil shows an awareness of the line in *G.* 1.121ff. Plutarch has an adapted quotation in 722D (Ζεὺς) κινεῖ πάντα πράγματα, δεξιὰ σημαίνων λαοὺς δ' ἐπὶ ἔργον ἐγείρων. Cf. Clem. Al. *Protr.* 11 (Χριστὸς) ὁ τοῦ θεοῦ γεωργός, δεξιὰ σημαίνων λαοὺς δ' ἐπὶ ἔργον ἀγαθὸν ἐγείρων, μιμνήσκων βιότοιο ἀληθινοῦ. For the similar idea of dawn stirring men to work see Diggle on E. *Phaethon* p. 95.

7 μιμνήσκων βιότοιο The active verb c. gen. usually refers to the past, especially to suffering (e.g. γ 103), perhaps only here of future action to be done. βίοτος only here in A., as βίος with the same meaning in 111. The metrical position is the same in Ξ 122 ἀφνειὸν βιότοιο, and Hes. *Op.* 499 χρηίζων βιότοιο.

λέγει This everyday verb, used as a variation of the technical σημαίνει, makes the message from Zeus seem more personal, and :he anaphora in 8 emphasises the effect. This predictive sense of λέγω is rare, and may owe something to its use with oracles' responses (e.g. Hdt. 8.136.1). Cf. 732, 1048, 1071, 1148. In this poem there is an obvious need to find a wide range of variations for the verb σημαίνω.

βῶλος Properly a hard clod of earth, but used here for soil more generally, perhaps because it suggests the hard work of cultivation. It is also a Homeric *hapax*, σ 374 εἴκοι δ' ὑπὸ βῶλος ἀρότρῳ, and A. is consciously hinting at the Homeric passage, which has the same context of tilling the soil. Ludwig (*Hermes* 443) notes the similarities in verb position, caesura, word division and sound in the two half-lines. At the same time A. varies the sense of ἀρότρῳ with βουσί τε καὶ μακέλῃσι.

8 μακέλῃσι Tools for digging or breaking up or moving earth. Homer has the form μάκελλα (Φ 259), used in the construction of an irrigation channel, but it is Hesiod's μακέλη (*Op.* 470) that is adopted by later hexameter poets. A. possibly has in mind the scene described by Hesiod of a slave following the plough (*Op.* 470–1) ἔχων μακέλην πόνον ὀρνίθεσσι τιθείη | σπέρμα κατακρύπτων. A.R. 4.1533 has μακέλῃσιν in the same *sedes*, but in a grave-digging scene. Cf. Theoc. 16.32, D.P. 1115.

δεξιαὶ ὧραι δεξιαί is almost superfluous, since ὧρα by itself can mean the 'right time', but the repetition after δεξιά (6) serves to underline the favour of Zeus and is appropriate to the hymnic style of the proem. ὧραι are times of year (cf. 13, 552, and the more usual sg. in 303, 742, 1053), and the signs are provided by Zeus in the risings and settings of the constellations: see note on 265. ὥρη c. inf. is Homeric, e.g. φ 428 (also aorist). A. seems to recall Hes. *Op.* 781 φυτὰ δ᾽ ἐνθ-ρέψασθαι ἀρίστη (a day of the month), but for variation uses ἀρίστη with a dative (7–8). A. does not use ὥρη c. gen. of action, as Hes. *Op.* 460, 575, but c. adj. 552, 825, 1053, 1119, See note on 742.

9 γυρῶσαι Lit. to put a plant in a round hole (from γῦρος 'circle'). *Et.M.* 243 Ἄρατος "καὶ φυτὰ γυρῶσαι". σημαίνει τὸ φιαλῶσαι καὶ περιφράξαι, ἢ βόθρον ὀρύξαι, ἐν ᾧ τὰ φυτὰ κατατίθενται. Cf. *Gp.* 5.20.1 γυρώσομεν δέ, τουτέστι περισκάψομεν, διετεῖς ἤδη γενομένας, εἰς βάθος δύο ποδῶν, πλάτος δὲ τριῶν. A. uses the verb for planting generally as opposed to raising from seed. The more usual verb is φυτεῦσαι (742).

πάντα 'all kinds of'; cf. 1024; also E 60 δαίδαλα πάντα, Hes. *Op.* 116 ἐσθλὰ δὲ πάντα. Here the word implies a programme for the whole year.

βαλέσθαι Cf. X. *Oec.* 17.10 ἐμβαλὼν τὸ σπέρμα τῇ γῇ. Max. 467 imitates with πάντα φέρει κλυτὰ ἔργα φυτευέμεν ἠδὲ βαλέσθαι, and 499 ἐν νείοισι βάλοιο σπέρματα.

This line concludes a series (5–9), in which sense breaks occur at varying positions in the lines.

10 αὐτός The pronoun brings out the greatness of Zeus, and thereby enhances his benevolence; cf. 16. D.P. 1170ff. has several echoes of these lines: αὐτοὶ γὰρ καὶ πρῶτα θεμείλια τορνώσαντο | ... αὐτοὶ δ᾽ ἔμπεδα πάντα βίῳ διετεκμήραντο, | ἄστρα διακρίναντες. Cf. Orph. fr. 247.29 αὐτὸς δὴ μέγαν αὖθις ἐπ᾽ οὐρανὸν ἐστήρικται, *Orac. Sibyll.* 3.27 Rzach αὐτὸς δ᾽ ἐστήριξε τύπον μορφῆς μερόπων τε, V. *G.* 1.353 *ipse pater statuit quid menstrua luna moneret.*

τά γε σήματ᾽ The variant τε makes no sense, and τάδε is both too specific and less well attested, whereas γε provides just enough emphasis to make clear the reference back to the idea in σημαίνει (6).

ἐν οὐρανῷ ἐστήριξεν The verb suggests technically the fixed stars and emotionally the certainty of the signs from Zeus. A. repeats it, also at line-ends, at 230, 274, 351, 500, recalling perhaps Δ 443, of Eris, οὐρανῷ ἐστήριξε κάρη, and Hes. *Th.* 779, of the house of Styx, κίοσιν ἀργυρέοισι πρὸς οὐρανὸν ἐστήρικται. Cf. *h.Hom.* 4.11, Emped. 27.2, Nic. *Ther.* 20.

The hymn ends with *spondeiazontes* in alternate lines (10, 12, 14), and it is possible that this is an artifice designed to give an added solemnity to the conclusion. A. has such clusters elsewhere in the poem: 32, 33, 35; 229, 230, 232; 419, 420, 421; 754, 755, 757; 926, 927, 929.

11 ἄστρα διακρίνας A. contrasts ἄστρα as constellations with ἀσ-τέρες as individual stars: see also 380, 382, where A. has a different version of the origin of the constellations. The divine myth is appropriate to the hymn (and there is an echo of it in 265), but a poem with an essentially scientific theme may reasonably celebrate human invention also. For ἄστρον as an individual constellation see 414, 436, 443. The imitation in D.P. 1173 is cited on 10 αὐτός.

ἐσκέψατο A. normally uses this verb of looking at or looking for with interest or concern, e.g. of the Kids pitying men at sea (159), the men themselves in a storm (428), men observing stars (157, 560) or weather signs (1143). Here too the overtones of concern are present, but the sense is rather that of looking ahead and organising a calendar for the year. This line is recalled in the summing-up injunction at the very end of the poem (1153).

εἰς ἐνιαυτόν The year plays an important role in the poem, because of the annual cycle of star movements and weather changes. It receives special treatment in 740–57, but cf. also 295, 451, 464, 551, 1145, 1153.

12 ἀστέρας The key stars, which by their risings and settings mark the progress of the year. They are identified by their positions in constellations, and it was for the identification of these that the constellations were originally designated; cf. 747, 757. Cyril's conjecture ἀστέρες (from 756–7) required the consequential changes to οἵ τε and σημαίνουσιν. Maass adopted it without the latter changes, but punctuating after ἐσκέψατο δ', thus making the οἵ κε clause dependent on that verb. This produces a very unnatural run of words, quite out of keeping with the otherwise polished and lucid style of the rest of the hymn. Emendation is needless; σκέπτομαι c. acc. can mean 'look out for' in the sense of providing for the future: cf. Pl. R. 342a τέχνης τῆς τὸ σύμφερον εἰς αὐτὰ ταῦτα σκεψομένης τε καὶ ἐκποριούσης, D. 24.158 λόγους σχολὴν ἄγοντ' ἐσκέφθαι.

οἵ κε μάλιστα Cf. ὅς τε μάλιστα in Homeric star contexts, E 5, ν 93.

τετυγμένα Frequent in Homer of good craftsmanship, e.g. κ 210 τετυγμένα δώματα Κίρκης (same sedes). When A. uses this participle to describe a constellation, he must mean by 'well-constructed' that its shape is clearly defined and therefore easily recognisable (233, 370). When he uses it of signs, he must mean that the signs are clearly recognisable and therefore may be taken as reliable. Cf. 725 τετύχθω and 805 τέτυκται, where the implications are similar.

12–13 τετυγμένα σημαίνοιεν ... ὡράων The differences of opinion in the interpretation of these words have been summarised by Martin, but his solution is not entirely satisfactory. There are two basic problems: the precise syntactical relationship of the words, and the precise meaning of ὡράων. The latter is generally translated as 'seasons', but this term is not appropriate. The context is the farmer's calendar for the whole year, and the day-to-day star signs that mark its progress.

Therefore ὡράων repeats the sense of ὧραι (8) and means the times of the year. As to the syntax, Martin takes the genitive to be dependent on σημαίνοιεν, as in 266–7, where the genitives express the times of year and the work to be done. He also compares 756–7, but there the genitives are the sea (horizon) and sky, where the stars are to be observed, not the times or the weather that the stars predict. There, as here, the verb is accompanied by τετυγμένα (= τετυγμένα σήματα), a normal internal acc. There A. leaves it to be understood that what the stars indicate are times of year, but here he expresses this in ὡράων, and the genitive may be most simply explained as an attributive genitive depending on 'the nominal idea which belongs to the verb' (Goodwin GG 229). Then μάλιστα with τετυγμένα makes the point that the signs from the stars are particularly reliable, compared with the more terrestrial weather signs, of which we still have only an imperfect understanding (768ff.).

13 ἔμπεδα πάντα φύωνται This phrase is a medley of Homeric imitation, recalling such lines as β 227 ἔμπεδα πάντα φυλάσσειν, ι 109 ἀνήροτα πάντα φύονται, and perhaps even ψ 206 ἔμπεδα πέφραδ' Ὀδυσσεύς, with its context of the sure sign given to Penelope. The plural verb with n.pl. subject is not uncommon in Homer, especially when there could be some emphasis on the sense of multiplicity in the subject (Chantraine 2.17–18), as in ι 109 just cited. Cf. 381, 385, 510, 590f., 939, 1036. Clem. Al. Strom. 5.14 ascribes to Sophocles οὐδὲ θεοῖς αὐθαίρετα πάντα πέλονται (TrGF Adesp. 621). Orph. Arg. 307 imitates in ὄφρ' ἔμπεδα πάντα φυλασσόμενοι πεπίθοιντο.

Here A. mentions only agriculture as the activity that benefits from the star signs, and reserves navigation for special attention in his introduction to the weather signs (758–72).

14 τῷ This adv. probably had the instrumental form τῶ in Homer, but later came to be thought of as a dative, e.g. in S. OT 510, Pl. Tht. 179d. For the Hellenistic poets editorial practice varies, and Fränkel in A.R. reads τῶ, while Pfeiffer in Callimachus and Gow in Theocritus read τῷ. Since Aldus only Mair has printed the Homeric form in A. See Schwyzer 2.579, Chantraine 1.248–9, Palmer 284, McLennan on Call. H. 1.58. A. repeats the adv. in 379, 413, 758, always at the beginning of a line: cf. B 250, 254, al. In 758 Π 2 (saec. i) reads τωι.

πρῶτόν τε καὶ ὕστατον This traditional formula means, in effect, 'from beginning to end'; cf. sch. διὰ παντὸς χρόνου καθ' ἑκάστην ὥραν. A. is primarily imitating Hes. Th. 34 σφᾶς δ' αὐτὰς πρῶτόν τε καὶ ὕστατον αἰὲν ἀείδειν, where the phrase occupies the same sedes, and the context is similar. The same phrase occurs in h.Hom. 21.4, and a variation in 29.5 πρώτη πυμάτη τε. Theognis in a more fulsome address to Apollo (1–4) adds a middle term πρῶτόν τε καὶ ὕστατον ἔν τε μέσ-

οισιν, but for Hestia retains the traditional πρώτη καὶ πυμάτη (1146).
West on Hes. *Th.* 34 collects similar phrasing from different contexts.
With this line A. rounds off with a kind of ring composition, returning
to the theme of the first line.

ἱλάσκονται Traditionally used of paying homage to a god in the
hope of making him ἵλαος. A. follows the practice of Homer and Hesiod
in using this form of the verb at the end of a line, e.g. Λ 386, 472, Z
380, *Th.* 91, 417, *Op.* 338. Cf. *h.Hom.* 2.292. Here the *spondeiazon* gives an
impressively solemn conclusion to the first part of the hymn.

15–18 INVOCATION OF ZEUS AND THE MUSES

Hesiod ends the proem of the *Theogony* with a salutation of the Muses,
appealing for their inspiration and outlining the theme of his proposed
song. Cf. χαῖρε, χαίρετε at the end of most of the *Homeric Hymns*, and
also in 3.14, 166. A. follows this hymnic convention, but before invoking
the Muses and asking for their support, he first invokes Zeus with phrases
that sum up the effect of 1–14. He thus establishes a contrast to Hesiod,
who only incidentally mentions the praise of Zeus as one activity of the
Muses (*Th.* 36–7).

15 πάτερ An ancient title (West ad Hes. *Th.* 36 Διὶ πατρί); cf. Δ 235
πατὴρ Ζεύς, Α 503 Ζεῦ πάτερ. A. gives it a new meaning as an attribute
of the Stoic god, having already prepared the way for it in line 5; cf.
Cleanth. 34 πάτερ, Call. *H.* 1.94 χαῖρε, πάτερ. On the father analogy
see T. R. Stevenson, *CQ* 42 (1992) 429–30.

μέγα θαῦμα The variant χάρμα appears as a correction in A, and is
clearly the reading underlying the *magnum gaudium* of L. It probably
came in from Ω 706 χαίρετ’, ἐπεὶ μέγα χάρμα πόλει τ’ ἦν (of Hector).
Primarily θαῦμα is used of something seen (θεάομαι), e.g. θαῦμα ἰδέσθαι (Ε 725, etc.). A. has it of the visual effect of stars in 46, 473, and
perhaps here too there is a suggestion of the visual effect of Zeus, the
sky-god, and his signs. However, the reference is sometimes extended to
senses other than sight, e.g. Hes. *Th.* 834 θαύματ’ ἀκοῦσαι, S. *Tr.* 673
θαῦμ’ ἀνέλπιστον μαθεῖν. The phrase μέγα θαῦμα is Homeric, recalling
τ 36 ὦ πάτερ, ἦ μέγα θαῦμα (on sensing a divine presence); cf. Ν 99,
h.Hom. 3.156, also in same *sedes*, and Melanipp. 762.1 *PMG* ὦ πάτερ,
θαῦμα βροτῶν. In later poets cf. A.R. 1.943, Mosch. *Eur.* 38, Orph. *L.*
187, 574, [Opp.] *C.*. 3.430, *H.* 4.270, Nonn. *D.* 4.436, Q.S. 1.299.

μέγ’ ἀνθρώποισιν ὄνειαρ A. recalls Hes. *Op.* 822 (of the lucky days)
ἐπιχθονίοις μέγ’ ὄνειαρ. Cf. *Th.* 871 (of the winds) θνητοῖς μέγ’ ὄνειαρ,
h.Hom. 2.269 (of Demeter) θνητοῖσί τ’ ὄνειαρ, Theoc. 13.34 μέγα στιβά-
δεσσιν ὄνειαρ.

16 αὐτὸς καὶ προτέρη γενεή A. is clearly echoing Hes. *Op.* 160 ἡμίθεοι, προτέρη γενεή κατ' ἀπείρονα γαῖαν, and may also have in mind Ψ 790 οὗτος δὲ προτέρης γενεῆς προτέρων τ' ἀνθρώπων (Antilochus referring to Odysseus). But both ancient and modern critics have found it difficult to decide who is or are referred to as προτέρη γενεή here, and several different interpretations have been put forward.

Sch. (M) record five in the following order: (1) Zeus, (2) the Titans, (3) elder brothers of Zeus, (4) earlier astronomers, (5) the heroic age. Sch. (S) also contribute (6) the ancestors of Zeus, (7) the golden age.

To turn to the moderns, (1) is adopted by Voss ('selbst auch erster Geschlechtsursprung'), who refers to line 5, and quotes Orph. *H.* 13.7 γέννα, φυὴ μείωσι, ... γενάρχα. So Schott, 'ja, unser Ursprung du!' Cf. Froevig, *SO* 15–16 (1936) 47, who notes that in Greek the idea of all men being descended from Zeus is purely Stoic. The more recent majority, however, have favoured (5). Maass *Aratea* 317 takes the reference to be the same as in Hesiod, and connects this triple salutation with the old tradition of a triple invocation at symposia, to the Olympians, the heroes, and Zeus Soter. Wilamowitz *HD* 2.264 associates the gods of the heroic age with the Stoic gods underlying the monotheistic cosmos. Martin follows Wilamowitz, arguing that the Hesiodic line provides the identification. Luck, *AJPh* 97 (1976) 218, dwells on the mythical figures associated with the stars in the *Phaenomena*, and quotes Cat. 64.384ff. as showing the influence of A. Pasquali (117–20) agrees with (4), adding the philosophers and astronomer-poets, the source of much of A.'s material. This view is elaborated by Effe, *Rh.M.* 113 (1970) 171, and partially accepted by Erren.

The diversity of those interpretations which are based on the assumption that we have here a triple invocation, and some rather far-fetched attempts to find a relevance appropriate to A.'s proem, suggest that the basic hypothesis is unsatisfactory. Only two salutations seem to be implied by χαῖρε and χαίροιτε. The first, to Zeus, sums up the preceding hymn, the second, to the Muses, introduces the rest of the poem and its main theme. No other invocation is needed, and no other name in the poem is significant enough to qualify for inclusion as a third member.

In *CQ* 31 (1981) 355–7 I therefore supported the first interpretation, taking προτέρη γενεή to mean 'yourself also our progenitor', and seeing in this a reference back to γένος (5), of us as children of Zeus. I had, however, overlooked the significance of αὐτὸς καί as a Homeric idiom, used to add another noun closely identified with the person referred to in αὐτός, e.g. I 301 αὐτὸς καὶ τοῦ δῶρα, with reference to Agamemnon, N 331 and Π 279 αὐτὸν καὶ θεράποντα, with reference to Idomeneus and Patroclus respectively. More relevant to the present passage are *h.Hom.* 2.493 αὐτὴ καὶ κούρη and 13.2 αὐτὴν καὶ κούρην, both in invocations of Demeter. In each case Persephone is not separately invoked, but coupled with Demeter in the one salutation. Cf. A.'s variation in 158 αὐτῆς ἠδ' Ἐρίφων, a closely related group. In view of these instances προτέρη γενεή should denote a group to which Zeus belongs, and with which he is closely associated. But as there is no other god so particularly related to Zeus, the reference must be to the whole company of the immortals, the race of gods as opposed to the human race (I owe this interpretation to Professor Reeve). In 771 A. calls the latter γενεὴν ἀνδρῶν, a phrase which looks back to Z 149, with Homer's comparison of human biology to that of trees. From the Stoic point of view as presented in the *Phaenomena* there are only the two races, the divine and the human, and A. here may be seen to have updated Hesiod by eliminating the ἡμίθεοι of *Op.* 160 and promoting Hesiod's phrase to the divine level.

χαίροιτε A new variation for the traditional imperative. The deferential optative suggests the tone of a suppliant; cf. 100 εὔκηλος φορέοιτο, 637 Ἄρτεμις ἰλήκοι. For the 2nd pers. cf. δ 193 πίθοιό μοι.

17 μειλίχιαι An adj. most chacteristically used to describe speech, e.g. M 267, ζ 148, θ 172. Here it is an apt epithet for the Muses, whose winsomeness is perceived in the words spoken by their poets; cf. 119.

μάλα πᾶσαι μάλα is often used by A. to emphasise an adj., especially πᾶς (cf. 94, 610, 650, 805, 952), and πολλός (188, 255, 291, 316, etc.). It nearly always precedes (for exceptions see 213, 428), and therefore is more likely intended to go with πᾶσαι than with μειλίχιαι. Cf. *h.Hom.* 3.189 Μοῦσαι μέν θ' ἅμα πᾶσαι ἀμειβόμεναι ὀπὶ καλῇ. The variant πᾶσιν may have come from sch. (M) μειλίχιαι αἱ Μοῦσαι ὅτι πρὸς πάντας καὶ καθόλου εὐμενεῖς. The Muses, of course, do not favour everybody.

ἐμοί γε μέν A. introduces himself with the strong form of the pronoun, instead of the traditional μοι of B 484, α 1, Hes. *Th.* 114. He is following the lead given by Hes. *Op.* 10 and *h.Hom.* 3.546 with ἐγώ. Cf. 460 ἐγώ. Further emphasis is to be seen in γε μέν, which should probably be taken as an instance of the rare progressive use (Denniston 387); cf. Hes. *Sc.* 5, Thgn. 1215, and also in A. 100, 378, 399, 508, 588, 988. See also Buttmann, Excursus 1.

ἀστέρας εἰπεῖν A very brief statement of theme, comparable with Hes. *Op.* 10 Πέρσῃ ἐτήτυμα μυθησαίμην, in contrast to *Th.* 105–13. A.'s words, in fact, introduce only the first part of the poem, to 757, which rounds off the theme with the language of the proem. A new theme is then stated in 759–60.

18 ᾗ θέμις An early epic formula, used by Hesiod at the beginning of a line in *Op.* 137 ᾗ θέμις ἀνθρώποισι κατ' ἤθεα (for the nominative

pronoun attracted to the gender of θέμις, see West on *Th.* 396, Kirk on
B 73); cf. I 33, 134, *h.Hom.* 3.541, and later A.R. 4.1129, Lyc. 369. In all
these cases the phrase refers back to the preceding verb as something
that it is proper to do in accordance with established custom. Here it
cannot be said that ἀστέρας εἰπεῖν is such a custom, and the adverbial ᾗ
is therefore required, meaning 'in the proper manner'; cf. A.R. 1.692.
There is, however, an ambiguity noted by sch. (Vat. 191) τὸ θέμις ἀμφί-
βολον. ἤτοι γὰρ τῷ προτέρῳ συναπτέον ἢ τῷ ἑξῆς, ἤτοι ἀστέρας
εἰπεῖν ὡς προσῆκον τεκμήρατε, ἢ εὐχομένῳ ὡς προσῆκον παρέχετε
εἰπεῖν. Hopkinson has put forward a third possibility, that the phrase
could qualify τεκμήρατε (sc. 'I am not praying to be told things which
are οὐ θέμις') (*HA* 140). In view of the traditional use of this phrase, I
think it must be taken as referring to ἀστέρας εἰπεῖν, and the proper
manner of doing this is to use the epic verse of Homer and Hesiod, who
introduced the stars into Greek poetry.

εὐχομένῳ C. inf., of praying or wishing that one may be able to do
something; cf. B 401 εὐχόμενος θάνατόν τε φυγεῖν, Pi. *P.* 4.293 εὔχε-
ται,... οἶκον ἰδεῖν, Emped. 131.3.

τεκμήρατε An unusual choice of verb; hence the baffled sch. καὶ εἰς
τέλος ἀγάγετε· τὸ γὰρ τέκμωρ τέλος. ἄλλοι δὲ δείξατε. The active
use of this verb is rare and post-homeric, meaning 'to show by a sign';
cf. A. *Pr.* 605–6 τέκμηρον ὅ τι μ' ἐπαμμένει | παθεῖν, Nic. *Ther.* 679–80
of the plant ἥ θ' Ὑπεριονίδαο παλινστρέπτοιο κελεύθους | τεκμαίρει.
Here the Muses are asked, as it were, to give signs to the poet as to
what he should write, and the aorist means that they are invited to begin now, that is, with the next line. It is probably no coincidence that
the verb is one that A. uses very frequently in the rest of the poem, in
the middle voice, of men observing and interpreting signs. Q.S. 12.308
varies with πᾶσάν μοι ἐνὶ φρεσὶ θήκατ' ἀοιδήν.

19–453 THE CONSTELLATIONS

The first main section of the poem is devoted principally to a detailed
description of the constellations. It is ostensibly a guide to the identification of those, and therewith to the identification of individual bright
stars, whose positions are defined by distinct parts of the figures described. The ultimate object is to be able to tell the time of the year by
watching for the successive risings or settings of stars as set out in the
calendars, the parapegmata published on stone in many Greek cities.

The constellations are arranged in two main areas, the northern (19–
318) and the southern (322–450), with a brief transitional passage between them and a similarly brief conclusion after the latter. The north-

ern area includes all the Zodiac, and is thus much larger than the southern, which lacks not only the more southerly constellations of the Zodiac, but also the stars nearer to the south pole and invisible to Mediterranean observers. Within each area the constellations are arranged in groups, each starting with a conspicuous constellation or with a reference to a constellation already described. The northern area has six groups. The first is the circumpolar group of the Bears and Dragon, and the other five are in sectors radiating out from this central region. The second starts from the Dragon, the third and fourth from the Great Bear, the fifth from the Little Bear, and the sixth from the kneeling figure, the first constellation to be described in group 2. The southern area lacks a central point of reference, but the first of its three groups is based on Orion, the second takes the Sea-monster as starting-point, and the third is centred on the Altar.

A. has followed the arrangement used by Eudoxus in his *Phaenomena*, according to Hipparchus: καὶ γὰρ Εὔδοξος ὡς καὶ Ἄρατος πρῶτον ἀναγράφει τὰ βορειότερα ἄστρα τοῦ ζῳδιακοῦ, ἔπειθ' οὕτως τὰ νοτιώτερα (1.2.17). For the descriptions of the constellations A. also follows the example of Eudoxus. Hipparchus makes a point of proving this by quoting parallel passages, and does so because the dependence of A. on Eudoxus has apparently been doubted by many: ὅτι μὲν οὖν τῇ Εὐδόξου περὶ τῶν φαινομένων ἀναγραφῇ κατηκολούθηκεν ὁ Ἄρατος, μάθοι μὲν ἄν τις διὰ πλειόνων παρατιθεὶς τοῖς ποιήμασιν αὐτοῦ περὶ ἑκάστου τῶν λεγομένων τὰς παρὰ τῷ Εὐδόξῳ λέξεις. οὐκ ἄχρηστον δὲ καὶ νῦν δι' ὀλίγων ὑπομνῆσαι διὰ τὸ διστάζεσθαι τοῦτο παρὰ τοῖς πολλοῖς (1.2.1).

A comparison of such parallel passages reveals the technique by which A. transformed his model into verse, sometimes following him closely, more usually with much variation and poetic artistry, sometimes adding mythical and other material, occasionally even correcting Eudoxus. The *Phaenomena* is often described as a mere versification of Eudoxus, but it is rather a work of much originality and poetic craftsmanship, as will be illustrated from time to time in the ensuing commentary.

19–62 CIRCUMPOLAR GROUP: THE POLE, THE BEARS, THE DRAGON

19–26 *The axis and the poles*

The sky rotates round a fixed axis, which passes through the centre of the earth, and terminates at the celestial poles, the south pole, which is invisible, and the north pole, which is visible.

19 οἱ μέν   The demonstrative article, much used by A. (25, 28, 36, 39, 44, al.), takes up ἀστέρας (17), and thus links the introduction with the first main section of the poem. The stars are here introduced as numerous, scattered all over the sky, partaking of its rotatory movement, and continuously in motion. They are also all alike (ὁμῶς), and the reference is therefore to the fixed stars only. At long range comes the contrast of the planets, οἱ δ' . . . οὐδὲν ὁμοῖοι (454).

πολέες   Homeric form (B 417, al.), used only here by A., who elsewhere has πολλοί (190, al.). The adj. is something of an understatement for the vast number of the stars, but the fact is later emphasised by πολλά (371) and the anaphora πολλοί . . . πολέων (377). This is one of the factors that create a problem for anyone trying to identify the important ones.

ἄλλυδις ἄλλοι   The Homeric usage is only with sg. pron. and verbs of motion, e.g. Λ 486 Τρῶες δὲ διέτρεσαν ἄλλυδις ἄλλος, which is perhaps intended to suggest individuals scattering; cf. ε 71, A.R. 2.980, 4.1293. A. has adapted the phrase to the description of a static pattern of scattered stars, varying the pronoun to a pl.; cf. A.R. 4.513. But in view of 68 with sg. pron. in another static pattern, the change to pl. here is probably not significant.

ἐόντες   The variant ἰόντες is probably a corruption due to the normal use of the phrase with verbs of motion. In this case the stars are not moving in different directions.

20 οὐρανῷ ἕλκονται   The sch. give two interpretations of the dative, the purely instrumental ὑπὸ τοῦ οὐρανοῦ ἕλκονται and the sociative συμπεριφέρονται τῷ οὐρανῷ. A. uses ἕλκεσθαι frequently of the regular westward movement of stars (342, 348, 443, 727), but with no suggestion that the sky is carrying them round; cf. 835 of cloud movement. He even develops the conceit of one constellation pulling another up over the horizon (604 ἕλκων, 708 ἕλκει). Cf. E. *Ion* 1149. The verb here should therefore not be taken too literally: it is one of many variations, such as φορέονται (29), φέρονται (47), εἰλεῖται (46), ἐλίσσεται (95). There is however some support for the sociative dative in Cicero's *cum caelo . . . feruntur* (fr. 3), and it is adopted by Voss ('mit dem Himmel') and Martin ('avec le ciel'). But the sociative use would be comparable with M 207 πέτετο πνοιῇς ἀνέμοιο, ι 82 φερόμην ὀλοοῖς ἀνέμοισι, and would imply that the stars are somehow influenced by the sky's rotation. A third possibility is to take the dative as locative, as Mair does ('are drawn across the heavens'), and Erren ('werden . . . am Himmel hingezogen'). The locative, however, requires a verb of rest, e.g. 414 φανήμεναι οὐρανῷ ἄστρον, or at least action in one place, such as Λ 523–4 ἐνθάδ' ὁμιλέομεν Δαναοῖσιν | ἐσχατιῇ πολέμοιο. Cf. S. *El.* 174. The movement will therefore have to be seen as not 'across the sky' but 'in the sky', as in 94 ὑπὸ ζώνῃ ... ἑλίσσεται simply marks the position of Arcturus in Bootes, and does not mean that it actually rotates beneath the belt stars; cf. 250 ἐν βορέῳ φέρεται, 521 ἐν τῷ δ' [the equator] ... φορεῖται.

πάντ' ἤματα συνεχὲς αἰεί The triple reiteration of the same sense is intended to emphasise the eternity of the celestial movements. It recalls ι 74 ἔνθα δύω νύκτας δύο τ' ἤματα συνεχὲς αἰεί. Cf. 339, 891. The long first syllable in συνεχές is common in epic: cf. M 26 and sch. (A), A.R. 2.738, Call. *H.* 2.60, Theoc. 20.12, Nic. *Alex.* 304, Q.S. 14.601. Schwyzer (1.288) compares lengthening before ν in ἔννεπε, ἐννεσίη.

21 ὅ γ' This anticipatory use of the demonstrative article, introducing a new noun several words later or even in the next line, is Homeric (A 409, B 402, Λ 488–9, ο 54–5). A. makes frequent use of this technique, especially in introducing new constellations (e.g. 239, 282, 342, 353). An unusual instance is 714ff., where the name of the constellation appears two lines later in a subordinate clause.

μετανίσσεται A Homeric verb from a similar context of celestial movement, ἦμος δ' ἠέλιος μετενίσετο βουλυτόνδε (Π 779, ι 58), a line that A. recalls again 583, 825 and 1119. Cf. A.R. 4.628, Opp. *C.* 1.499. In fact Hipparchus' discovery of precession of the equinoxes led to the realisation that the earth's axis does have a slow movement of its own through the polar stars (Dicks *EGA* 15–16, 163).

αὔτως A. makes frequent use of this adv., in a sense often corresponding to English 'just'. It frequently stresses one element in a contrast, or in a positive–negative antithesis, e.g. (*a*) 'not A but just B' (21, 65, 110, 260, 1016); (*b*) 'not just A, but B' (180); (*c*) 'A and not just B' (172); (*d*) 'just', without contrast (195, 424, 452, 945). In other passages the basic sense of 'same' is significant, and the adverb means (*e*) 'just as before' (792), (*f*) 'likewise' (825, 869, 1060), and (*g*) c. dat. 'like' (1071, 1077).

For A. the manuscripts throughout attest αὔτως, for Homer both αὔτως and αὔτως, but the former is the natural adv. from αὐτός. The aspirated form may have come in with Attic, probably on the analogy of οὔτως. αὔτως in A. sometimes corresponds to αὔτως in Homer, e.g. (*a*) ξ 151, (*d*) Γ 220, ζ 143, (*e*) Λ 133, but otherwise A. seems to have evolved a usage of his own. A.R. and Theocritus largely follow the Homeric practice, and editors print αὔτως: see Mooney on 1.692. So Jebb (on *OT* 931) for the few instances in Sophocles. For a full discussion see K–G 1.654–5; also Chantraine 2.158, Mazon, *Introduction à l'Iliade* (1959) 135; on the accent A.D. 174.1 Schneider.

22 ἄξων First occurrence in the sense of axis of the cosmos. Cf.

Gem. 4.1 ἄξων καλεῖται ἡ διάμετρος τοῦ κόσμου, περὶ ἥν στρέφεται ὁ κόσμος. There is no reference to the axis in the meagre fragments of Eudoxus, but Plato (*Ti.* 40c) and Aristotle (*Cael.* 293b32, 296a27) use πόλος in this sense.

ἄρηρεν   Intrans. perf. of ἀραρίσκω. Cf. 453 ἐνάρηρεν. The part. is commoner (383, 467, 482, 565), as in Homer. Man. 2(1).9, of the fixed stars, δι' αἰθέρος αἰὲν ἄρηρεν.

ἀτάλαντον ἀπάντη   A. has taken the phrase from Emped. fr. 17.19, where Strife is said to be equal to each of the elements: so Guthrie *HGP* 2.154. In Homer too ἀτάλαντος is only figurative, e.g. B 627 ἀτάλαντος Ἄρηϊ, N 795 ἀτάλαντοι ἀέλλῃ (both in same *sedes*). A. uses the phrase more literally, having in mind perhaps also Hes. *Th.* 524 ἴσον ἀπάντῃ and Parm. fr. 8.44, of the sphere, ἰσοπαλὲς πάντῃ. The axis, being a diameter, has the spherical earth evenly balanced all round it. P. R. Hardie, *CQ* 33 (1983) 223 n. 17, suggests the possibility of an etymological pun on the name Atlas.

ἀπάντη   See note on 4 πάντη.

23 μεσσηγύς   Basically used with reference to an area or point between two places, which are either specified (e.g. 320, E 769) or understood from the context (e.g. 856, Ψ 521). Here the scholia give some muddled explanations, suggesting that it refers to the position of the axis through the centre of the earth: ἴσην γὰρ αὐτὴν ἐξ ἑκατέρου μέρους ποιεῖ αὐτὸς μέσος ὤν (Martin *SAV* 67). So Voss, Zannoni, Martin ('la terre qu'il traverse en son centre'). But this suits neither the verb ἔχει nor the sense of μεσσηγύς implying a point between two places. If the axis is said to hold the earth μεσσηγύς, the position must be the centre of the cosmos, i.e. between the north and south celestial poles. Thus Mair 'in the midst it holds the earth', and similarly Erren. This is perhaps a slight extension of the normal usage, but still less innovative than [Theoc.] 25.237 ἤματος ἦν τὸ μεσηγύ. The line thus has a certain balance, with the earth at the centre and the sky revolving round it, a neat summing-up of the classical Greek cosmos. For a recent discussion of the pre-Aristotelian cosmos see D. Fehling, *Rh.M.* 128 (1985) 195–231.

The scholion quoted above adds καὶ εἰς δύο αὐτὴν διαιρῶν. This is explained more fully in another (68), to the effect that the earth at the centre divides the cosmos into two hemispheres (on which see Erren's note). This curiosity has no relevance to the present passage.

An imitation appears in *AP* 1.99.1 μεσσηγὺς γαίης τε καὶ οὐρανοῦ ἵσταται ἀνήρ.

οὐρανὸν αὐτὸν   Five variants are attested from antiquity. (1) οὐρανὸν αὐτὸν· sch. (MAS) περιάγει, φησίν, ὁ ἄξων τὸν οὐρανόν. οὐχ οὕτως δὲ ἔχει. ὁ γὰρ οὐρανὸς ἀφ' ἑαυτοῦ στρέφεται. ὥσπερ δὲ λέγομεν ὅτι ὁ χρόνος πάντα φέρει, καὶ τοὺς ὁδοιπόρους ἡ ὁδός, οὕτω καὶ ὁ ἄξων τὸν οὐρανόν. Cf. 525–6, of the celestial circles, τοὺς μὲν παρβολάδην ὀρθοὺς περιβάλλεται ἄξων μεσσόθι πάντας ἔχων. Var. At. fr. 14.1 Morel *uidit et aetherio mundum torquerier axe.* See P. R. Hardie (cited on 22) 223–4 on Atlas as a personification of the world-axis. This makes good sense, and is adopted by Voss, Buttmann, Bekker, Mair and Zannoni. The emphatic αὐτόν contrasts the grandeur of the sky with the slenderness of the axis. This reading has the advantages of keeping the same subject for the three verbs, and ἀγινεῖ transitive. Cf. Germ. 21 (*axis*) *orbem agit.* (2) οὐρανὸς αὐτόν· sch. (MQDΔVA) περὶ δὲ τὸν ἄξονα αὐτὸν πάντα τὰ ἄστρα ὁ οὐρανὸς ἀγινεῖ ... καὶ περιφέρει. This is the reading of editors before Bekker, and is supported by Lasserre (41), who takes the verb as intrans. But ἀγινέω is elsewhere always trans., e.g. 38, 356, 623, 666, 792. (3) οὐρανὸς αὐτόν· sch. ἀλλ' οἱ μαθηματικοὶ τὸ αὐτὸν δασύνουσιν, ἵν' ἦ ἑαυτόν. ὁ δὲ λόγος· περὶ δὲ τὸν ἄξονα ἄγει καὶ στρέφει ὁ οὐρανὸς ἑαυτόν. This is an obvious corruption, a clumsy way of expressing what would normally be done by the middle voice. Clem. Al. *Strom.* 5.8.48 ἡ τοῦ κόσμου κατὰ τὸν ποιητὴν Ἄρατον περιφορά gives no clue to his reading. (4) οὐρανὸν αὐτός· not attested by manuscripts, but adopted by Martin and Erren, and approved by Keydell (*Gnomon* 30, 584) and Chantraine (*R.Ph.* 31,298). This has essentially the same meaning as (3), but is preferred by Martin because αὐτός marks the importance of the axis in being the pivot for the sky's movement. This seems a rather exaggerated emphasis, since the axis does not really turn the sky. (5) οὐρανὸς αὐτός is adopted by Maass, but this, like (2), requires the verb to be taken intransitively.

ἀγινεῖ Lengthened epic form of ἄγω, e.g. ξ 105. Brunck (1780) on A.R. 1.613, Chantraine 1.353.

24 πειραίνουσι Rare poetic form of περαίνω, again in 365 of where star-chains end; cf. χ 175, 192. A. also uses the verb of completing a length of voyage (289); cf. μ 37. See Ronconi 257–9, and Martin's note.

πόλοι πόλος is connected with πολέω, and so primarily associated with movement. (1) It describes the region where the stars move, the sky, e.g. E. *Ion* 1154 Ἄρκτος στρέφουσ' οὐραῖα χρυσήρη πόλῳ, *Or.* 1685 λαμπρῶν ἄστρων πόλον, and where birds fly, Ar. *Av.* 179 ὀρνίθων πόλος. (2) Plato then uses it for the axis of the cosmos, *Ti.* 40c τὸν διὰ παντὸς πόλον τεταμένον. (3) Eudoxus is the first to use it of the pole, fr. 11 ἔστι δέ τις ἀστὴρ μένων ἀεὶ κατὰ τὸν αὐτὸν τόπον· οὗτος δὲ ὁ ἀστὴρ πόλος ἐστὶ τοῦ κόσμου. Eudoxus may have been perpetuating a very old tradition dating back to c. 2750 BC, when the bright star α Draconis was close to that position. The pole moves slowly in a cycle of

c. 26,000 years, and in classical antiquity there was no star at the north pole. See Dicks *EGA* 15. Hipparchus (1.4.1) corrects Eudoxus, referring to Pytheas as his authority: ἐπὶ γὰρ τοῦ πόλου οὐδὲ εἷς ἀστὴρ κεῖται, ἀλλὰ κενός ἐστι τόπος, ᾧ παράκεινται τρεῖς ἀστέρες, μεθ' ὧν τὸ σημεῖον τὸ κατὰ τὸν πόλον τετράγωνον ἔγγιστα σχῆμα περιέχει, καθάπερ καὶ Πυθέας φησὶν ὁ Μασσαλιώτης. A. may have heard of Pytheas' discovery (perhaps c. 300 BC), since he does not repeat the error of Eudoxus. On the pole-star see Heath 8 n. 2.

ἀμφοτέρωθεν Cf. φ 408 in similar sense, E 726 in same *sedes*.

25 ὁ μὲν οὐκ ἐπίοπτος The existence of a south celestial pole was a necessary inference from the discovery of the spherical cosmos. Eudoxus refers to it as τὸν ἀφανῆ πόλον (fr. 77), likewise Arist. *Cael.* 285b21 and Attalus ap. Hi. 1.8.15, whereas Hipparchus himself here and elsewhere refers to distances ἀπὸ τοῦ νοτίου πόλου. Cf. Gem. 4.2 νότιος δὲ ὁ διὰ παντὸς ἀόρατος ὡς πρὸς τὸν ἡμέτερον ὁρίζοντα. The passage in *Cael.* 285b is interesting for the idea it puts forward that the south pole must be the top of the cosmos, but Aristotle seems to have given up this theory later, and there is no indication that A. has it in mind here. He mentions the south pole first so that he can pass directly from the north pole to the Bears. The adj. ἐπίοπτος appears first here.

ἀντίος The north pole, at the opposite end of the cosmic axis. Eudoxus (fr. 76) calls it ὁ πόλος ὁ ἀεὶ φανερὸς τοῦ κόσμου, Att. ap. Hi. 1.8.15 simply τὸν φανερὸν πόλον, Hipparchus normally ὁ βόρειος πόλος (1.4.1). Cf. Gem. 4.2 βόρειος μὲν ὁ διὰ παντὸς φαινόμενος ὡς πρὸς τὴν ἡμετέραν οἴκησιν.

ἐκ βορέαο The prep., here denoting the position of the pole, suggests the direction from which the sight of it comes to the observer; cf. 887, 905, 933, also Theoc. 22.40 ἐκ βυθοῦ (with Gow's note). Similar is the use of ἑκάτερθε(ν) 47, 496, 527, 536, 642, 882, and ἑσπερόθεν 734.

26 ὑψόθεν The prepositional use c. gen. is not Homeric, but cf. Pi. *O.* 3.12 γλεφάρων ... ὑψόθεν, A.R. 2.806 Ἀχερουσίδος ὑψόθεν ἄκρης. Cf. 423 abs., as in Homer.

ὠκεανοῖο Sch. (MA) ὠκεανὸν λέγει ὁ Ἄρατος τὸν ὁρίζοντα. Sch. (Q) πρότερος δὲ Ὅμηρος ὠκεανὸν τὸν ὁρίζοντα προσηγόρευσε λέγων ἐπὶ μὲν τῆς ἀνατολῆς "Ἠὼς μὲν κροκόπεπλος ἀπ' Ὠκεανοῖο ῥοάων ὤρνυθ'" [Τ 1-2], ἐπὶ δὲ τῆς δύσεως "ἐν δ' ἔπεσ' Ὠκεανῷ λαμπρὸν φάος ἠελίοιο" [Θ 485]. Cf. Η 422, Σ 489.

26-44   The Bears

The pole is enclosed by two Bears, also called Wagons, which keep the same position relative to each other all the time as they move round it shoulders first. Legend says they were translated to the sky by Zeus in recognition of their care for him in his infancy. Their names are Cynosura and Helice. Greek sailors steer by the latter, which is very conspicuous, Phoenicians by the former, which is slight, but closer to the pole.

26 ἀμφὶς ἔχουσαι An apparent imitation of α 54 ἀμφὶς ἔχουσι. But that is said of the pillars of Atlas keeping earth and sky apart. Here A. is describing the position of the Bears on opposite sides of the pole, a different use of ἀμφίς, well illustrated by γ 486 ἀμφὶς ἔχοντες, of two horses on either side of their yoke. A. is giving the observer an important clue to the identification of the Bears, since their relative position remains the same all the time. The adv. therefore goes strictly with ἔχουσαι, not with τροχόωσι, as Martin's translation suggests. A. gives first the position of the constellations and then their movement. The variants ἔχουσιν and τροχόωσαι derive from Achilles, but the latter is metrically impossible.

27 Ἄρκτοι A. starts his catalogue of the northern constellations with the Bears, because the Great Bear is self-evident as a bright and well-defined group of stars. It is one of the earliest recorded constellations, and one of the few named in Homer, who has the same line once in each epic (Σ 487, ε 273) Ἄρκτόν θ᾽, ἣν καὶ Ἄμαξαν ἐπίκλησιν καλέουσιν. The constellation consisted then of the seven bright stars only, as Hipparchus says (1.5.6), καθόλου τε οἱ ἀρχαῖοι πάντες τὴν Ἄρκτον ἐκ τῶν ἑπτὰ μόνων ἀστέρων διετύπουν. Cf. Str. 1.1.21 τοὺς ἑπτὰ τῆς μεγάλης ἄρκτου ἀστέρας. Later, as the seven stars seemed to allow for body and tail only, many adjacent stars were brought in to provide head and legs, and so the modern Ursa Major is a much larger constellation. In fact the conspicuous seven do not suggest such an animal at all: cf. S.E. *Math.* 5.98 τί γὰρ ὅμοιον ἔχουσιν ἄρκτῳ οἱ ἑπτὰ ἀστέρες, διεστῶτες ἀπ᾽ ἀλλήλων; The same is true of the fainter and smaller Little Bear, which took its name from the Great Bear, because it also has seven stars forming a similar pattern. For the plural cf. 48, 652, and for the Little Bear see note on 36.

The origin of the name Ἄρκτος therefore requires some explanation, and Szemerényi has plausibly suggested (*Trends and Tasks in Comparative Philology*, 1961, 19) that it is a corruption of a Near Eastern word for 'wagon', such as Akkadian *eriqqu*, or a Phoenician equivalent. This would have been borrowed in the form r̥ku or r̥ko and become ἄρκος and then ἄρκτος. Cf. Eustath. 1156.17 ἡ δὲ ἄρκτος ὅτι μετὰ τοῦ τ̄ λέγεται, δηλοῖ ὁ γράψας οὕτως· ἄρκτον, οὐχὶ ἄρκον. τὸν μέντοι ἄνεμον ἄνευ τοῦ τ̄ ἀπαρκίαν ... πνοὴν ἄρκιον. Since the Bear was used primarily in navigation, as a guide to north, and had been at an earlier date closer to the pole, the name could well have come to the Greeks from the Phoenicians. The form ἄρκος may have been responsible for the Arcadian myth of Callisto, daughter of Lycaon, identified with the Bear in the sky: Hes. fr. 163, sch. Arat. 27, sch. Germ. 58, 64, *Catast.* 1, Hyg. 2.1.

The standard Greek name for the Great Bear is ἡ Μεγάλη Ἄρκτος (Eud. fr. 15; Hi. 1.4.2; Gem. 3.8) or Ἄρκτος Μεγάλη (Ptol. *Alm.* 7.5). The old Latin name was *Septentriones* (Pl. *Am.* 273, Cic. fr. 5) or *Septentrio* (Vitr. 9.4.1), but other poets use *Arctus* (Ov. *Fast.* 3.793, Man. 1.275), *Helice* (Ov. *M.* 8.207), *Callisto* (Cat. 66.66), *plaustrum* (Prop. 3.5.35), *temo* (Enn. *scen.* 216), *ursa* (Ov. *F.* 2.153), and the standard name is now Ursa Major. *RE* 2.1172, 7.2859, Roscher VI 873, Allen 419.

ἅμα τροχόωσι A. recalls ο 451 ἅμα τροχόωντα θύραζε. This homely scene, a child running with his nurse, makes an amusing contrast to the cosmic movement of the stars. Cf. ἁματροχιάς in Ψ 422 and Call. fr. 383.10. ἅμαξα is derived from ἅμα and ἄξων, the axle of wagon-wheels, but A. ingeniously suggests that here it refers to the axis of the sky. Cf. the etymologies in 315, 331.

τροχόωσι Epic diectasis is particularly common in -άω verbs, and may have originated in these. A likely explanation is that the uncontracted form, e.g. -άουσι, was first contracted to -ῶσι, then expanded again to fill the same number of *morae* as the original form had, but with the vowel assimilated to the stem vowel, -όωσι. Cf. Μ 312 εἰσορόωσι. For a full discussion see Chantraine 1.75ff.; also Lobeck *Rhem.* 171ff., Palmer 95, Kirk on Β 198. In this inflexion A. also has ἀντιόωσιν (1014), βοόωσι (947), γανόωσι (190), δεικανόωσι (209), ἐπιτροχόωσ' (889), κερόωσι (780), κομόωσιν (1093), στιχόωσιν (191), but most frequent use of diectasis in participial forms: -όων (456, 906), -όωντα (372), -όωντος (899), -όωντι (278, 294, 434, 501, 512, 1073), -όωντες (1003, 1092), -όωσα (605, 789), -όωσαν (796, 799), -όωσαι (333); see also -όωνται (600, 856), and the variations ἐπιπλώωσι (923), ὁράᾳς (733), ὁράαν (996).

τὸ δή Acc. in adverbial sense, strengthened by δή, 'therefore'; cf., in same *sedes*, Γ 176 τὸ καὶ κλαίουσα τέτηκα, θ 332 τὸ καὶ μοιχάγρι' ὀφέλλει.

Ἄμαξαι See note on 27 Ἄρκτοι. Originally this was a name for the Great Bear only, but A. now applies it, with Ἄρκτοι, to the Little Bear also. Callimachus then uses it of the Little Bear by itself in fr. 191.54 τῆς Ἀμάξης ἐλέγετο σταθμήσασθαι τοὺς ἀστερίσκους, making his reference clear with the diminutive noun for 'stars'.

28 αἱ δ' ἤτοι The variant δή τοι is less likely here, because there is no call for such emphasis, and A. on the whole is sparing with his use of δή. The new sentence requires the simple connective, as again in 404, 477. Cf. Η 451 τοῦ δ' ἤτοι, and Hes. *Th.* 142 οἱ δ' ἤτοι (with West's note), *Op.* 333 τῷ δ' ἤτοι; Denniston 553.

κεφαλὰς ... ἰξύας The parts of bodies and other objects referred to in the constellations represent particular stars. Hipparchus identifies the head of the Great Bear according to Eudoxus and A.: ἡ μὲν γὰρ κεφαλὴ τῆς Μεγάλης Ἄρκτου κατὰ τοὺς προειρημένους ἄνδρας ἐστὶν ὁ βορειότερος ἀστὴρ τῶν δύο τῶν ἡγουμένων ἐν τῷ πλινθίῳ (1.5.2), 'the more northerly of the two leading (i.e. westerly) stars in the quadrilateral', the star now known as α Ursae Majoris. The corresponding star in the Little Bear is β Ursae Minoris. The loin-star is described by Hipparchus as ὁ ἐπὶ τῆς ὀσφύος τῆς Μεγάλης Ἄρκτου λαμπρός (3.1.5), and identified by Manitius as δ Ursae Majoris, the point at which the tail joins the body; the corresponding star is ζ Ursae Minoris.

ἐπ' ἰξύας αἰὲν ἔχουσιν   As the Bears move round the pole, each keeps its head aligned in the direction of the other's loins. This sense of ἐπί is usual with verbs of motion, e.g. Μ 239 εἴτ' ἐπὶ δεξί' ἴωσι, γ 171 (νεοίμεθα) νήσου ἔπι Ψυρίης, αὐτὴν ἐπ' ἀριστέρ' ἔχοντες. A. imitates the latter phrase, leaving the movement to be understood. Q.S. in his turn imitates A. in 4.74 ὅτε δὴ κεφαλὰς μὲν ἐπ' ἀντολίην ἔχον ἄρκτοι, so revealing his ignorance of astronomy, since the Bears' heads inevitably point in opposite directions all the time.

29 κατωμάδιαι φορέονται   The adj. occurs once in Homer, of a discus 'thrown from shoulder height', δίσκου οὖρα κατωμαδίοιο (Ψ 431). The corresponding adv. occurs twice, of a driver wielding his whip, μάστιγι κατωμαδὸν ἤλασεν ἵππους (Ο 352), μάστι δ' αἰὲν ἔλαυνε κατωμαδόν (Ψ 500). In the Hellenistic poets the meaning is 'hanging from the shoulder', e.g. Call. H. 6.44 κατωμαδίαν δ' ἔχε κλᾷδα, fr. 597 δέρμα κατωμάδιον, fr. 24.10 κα]τωμαδίης οὐλάδ[ος, Mosch. fr. 4.2 πήρην δ' εἶχε κατωμαδίην, AP 9.13B.3 = GP 961 κατωμάδιον βάρος. Cf. A.R. 2.679 ἰοδόκη τετάνυστο κατωμαδόν.

Here the context of the adj. is different from any of these, and the precise meaning is not immediately clear. The scholia are irrelevantly concerned with rising and setting, but give hints of an explanation in ἐπὶ τὰς κεφαλάς and τὰ ἐμπρόσθια. Germ. 30–1 also indicates a setting movement in *pronas rapit orbis in ipsos | declinis umeros*. Among modern translators some are unclear, e.g. Voss 'um die Schultern' and Mair 'shoulder-wise', while Erren's 'rücklings' goes unexplained. Only Martin discusses the problem, and at length. He points out that in A. φορεῖσθαι is often little more than a synonym for κεῖσθαι or even εἶναι, when it is the relative position of a star or constellation that is being described (e.g. 249, 255, 359, 521, 576), and suggests that the adj. here should refer to the position of the shoulders of the two Bears relative to each other. He translates 'elles évoluent toujours dos à dos'. Le Boeuffle, following Martin, translates Germanicus similarly with 'épaules contre épaules'. This, however, gives a meaning to κατωμάδιος

which it is difficult to relate to its other known uses, and also it is doubtful whether the idea of reciprocity in 28 is meant to be continued into 29.

It may be helpful in the first place to identify the shoulders of
the Bears. Many constellation figures have shoulder-stars, e.g. 67 the
Kneeler, 77 Ophiuchus, and some, including these two, are confirmed
by Hipparchus (2.2.8, 1.4.6). But Hipparchus has no shoulder-stars for
the Bears, and indeed there is no star of any brightness available for
that position, since the two leading stars in each Bear already represent
the head and forelegs. It seems that A. has chosen this adj. for the sake
of giving a new context to a Homeric *hapax*, and if he has a particular
star in mind, he must have combined head and shoulders in the same
one. This assumption is supported by ὑπωμαίων (144) for the forelegs
of the Great Bear (cf. 1115). Now the head stars in both Bears are the
most north-westerly of their respective stars, and so lead their constellations in their circuits of the north pole. I suggest that what A. means
is that each Bear's movement is 'from the shoulder', and that the sense
of movement in φορέονται is in this case significant, as it is in νίσσεται
(61) and φέρεται (279, 340).

30 ἔμπαλιν εἰς ὤμους τετραμμέναι The translators do not make
satisfactory sense of this phrase: Voss 'rückwärts gegen die Schulter
gekehrt', Mair 'turned alternate on their shoulders', Erren 'sich gegen-
seitig die Schulter zukehrend'. Martin takes it as clarifying κατωμάδιαι,
'tournées épaules contre épaules dans deux sens opposés'. The Bears do
lie in opposite directions, but εἰς ὤμους hardly suggests the meaning
'shoulder to shoulder'. The words need to be examined more precisely
in the light of A.'s usage.

τετραμμένος in A. always means facing or pointing in a certain direction: men facing towards the shore (298) or the sun (853), constellations
pointing backwards (344, 575), and with εἰς a figure aligned with respect
to another constellation or to one of its own parts. Cf. 387, 620 and
632. In the case of the Bears the line of each constellation runs from
the tail to the head and shoulders. But since the Bears are always on
opposite sides of the pole, their alignments point in opposite directions
(ἔμπαλιν: cf. 908) from the point of view of the observer. A. does not
repeat the sense of 29, but adds a note on the relative alignment of the
Bears.

εἰ ἐτεὸν δή This introduces the first of a series of myths that afford
relief from the technical material, and sometimes also remind the
reader of the Stoic proem by returning to the theme of Zeus. They are
also suggestive of the mythical element in Hesiodic poetry, and are thus
not digressions, but essential features of the genre. The introductory
phrase is Homeric, and particularly suited to a genealogical context:

1 529 εἰ ἐτεόν γε σός εἰμι, π 300 εἰ ἐτεόν γ' ἐμός ἐσσι. In A.R. 1.154 εἰ
ἐτεόν γε πέλει κλέος, on the legend of Lynceus' eyesight, the phrase
affects a kind of detached scepticism, though the precise tone is difficult
to determine: see T. C. W. Stinton, *PCPS* n.s. 22 (1976) 63. On the
theme of truth and untruth in poetry, derived from Hesiod (*Th.* 7–8),
see S. Goldhill, *PCPS* n.s. 32 (1986) 26ff.
Here the special stressing of ἐτεόν with δή (cf. N 375), followed immediately by an emphatically placed Κρήτηθεν, suggests that A. is hinting at Epimenides' notorious Κρῆτες ἀεὶ ψευσταί (fr. 1), quoted in Call.
H. 1.8. It would be a humorous touch characteristic of Hellenistic
writers' attitude to the old myths. And since the first hymn is believed to
be early, perhaps c. 280 BC (Hopkinson *HA* 121), it is possible that A. is
subtly alluding to Callimachus here. Dr Hopkinson has pointed out to
me that A. has 'echoes' of the same hymn also in other lines in this passage, e.g. 32 κουρίζοντα, 33 ὄρεος σχεδὸν Ἰδαίοιο, and perhaps 35 Δικταῖοι Κούρητες . . . ἐψεύδοντο.

31 Κρήτηθεν Cf. Γ 233. This myth of the infancy of Zeus in Crete
appears first in Hes. *Th.* 477–84: the sending of Rhea to Lyctus, Zeus
being received by Gaia, and the hiding of the infant in a cave. The
story may have come originally from Epimenides, ὁ τὰ Κρητικὰ γε-
γραφώς (sch. QS 72). Cf. the Ariadne myth (71–2).

κεῖναί γε The association of the Bears with the infant Zeus appears
here for the first time. The old star-myth relates, naturally, to the very
conspicuous Great Bear only, and it is the Arcadian Callisto who is immortalised in the sky. On the other hand the traditional nurse of the
infant Zeus is the goat Amaltheia, whom A. identifies with the goat-star
Capella in 163. Here A. appears to have combined the essentials of
both these traditions in order to provide a new myth that would include
the two celestial Bears. His version seems not to have become well
known. Sch. (MS) on 27 recount at length the Callisto story, and only
sch. (Q) adds briefly Ἄρατος δέ φησι τὴν Κυνόσουραν καὶ Ἑλίκην ἐν
Κρήτῃ οὔσας γενέσθαι τρόφους τοῦ Διός, καὶ διὰ τοῦτο τῆς οὐρανοῦ
μνήμης ἀξιωθῆναι. Similarly Hyginus under *Arctus Minor* adds (2.2.1)
nonnulli etiam Helicen et Cynosuram nymphas esse Iouis nutrices dicunt [cf.
Germ. 39 *hinc Iouis altrices Helice Cynosuraque fulgent*]; . . . *et utrasque Arctos
appellatas esse.* And *Catast.* 2 gives a garbled version of these, Ἄρατος δὲ
αὐτὴν καλεῖ Ἑλίκην, ἐκ Κρήτης οὖσαν, γενέσθαι δὲ Διὸς τρόφον, . . .

Διὸς μεγάλου Appropriate as cult title of Cretan Zeus (Cook, *Zeus*,
2.344–5), here recalling Hes. *Th.* 465 Διὸς μεγάλου διὰ βουλάς. Elsewhere as stock epithet, cf. A. *Supp.* 1052, Pi. *O.* 7.34.

ἰότητι A Homeric word, mostly dat., especially of gods (T 9, al.);
here a variation of Hesiod's διὰ βουλάς. On etymology and usage see

Leumann 127ff. The *sedes* here is not Homeric, but cf. A.R. 4.360 ἀναιδήτῳ ἰότητι.

32 οὐρανὸν εἰσανέβησαν The idea of ascending into the sky belongs primarily to heavenly bodies rising, e.g. H 422–3, of the sun, ἐξ ... ὠκεανοῖο | οὐρανὸν εἰσανιών, Mimn. 12.4, of Dawn, ὠκεανὸν προλιποῦσ᾽ οὐρανὸν εἰσανέβη. A. is echoing the early poets and giving the phrase the new context of a catasterism. There is a quaintness in the use of this very direct verb without any suggestion of how the ascent was made; cf. *AP* 7.587.2, to a dead philosopher, οὐρανὸν εἰσανέβης. A.R. is, in a way, more Homeric in 1.1100, of Zeus, ὅτ᾽ ἐξ ὀρέων μέγαν οὐρανὸν εἰσαναβαίνῃ, and in 2.938 of Artemis. But Homer uses this verb only of terrestrial ascents, and A. is here partly recalling Z 74 = P 320 Ἴλιον εἰσανέβησαν.

ὅ Acc. n. as causal conj. is found in Homer, e.g. I 534 χωσαμένη ὅ οἱ οὔτι θαλύσια ... Οἰνεὺς ῥέξ᾽. Cf. 1073; Chantraine 2.288.

κουρίζοντα Once in Homer, χ 185 (σάκος) ὃ κουρίζων φορέεσκε, and once in Hesiod, in a rare transitive sense (*Th.* 347). A.'s use of the part. to describe the infant Zeus may be compared with A.R. 3.134 ἄντρῳ ἐν Ἰδαίῳ ἔτι νήπια κουρίζοντι, and Call. *H.* 1.54 σεο κουρίζοντος, also 4.324 κουρίζοντι (Apollo), 3.5 κουρίζουσα (Artemis). Cf. Q.S. 4.432, Colluth. 242. Callimachus may have been the model here, since the theme is particularly appropriate in the *Hymn to Zeus*, and not at all necessary in A.R. and A.: see note on 30 εἰ ἐτεὸν δή. The case variation in the three poets seems deliberate, and is characteristic of imitation technique. The artistry of these five lines on the Zeus myth is enhanced by the three σπονδειάζοντες, which add a certain grandeur.

33 Λύκτῳ The transmitted reading is clearly Δίκτῳ, and both scholia and modern editors explain it as a by-form of the name of Mt Dicte, either masculine or neuter. But such a form is otherwise unknown, and it is difficult to see why A. should have used it. Martin therefore favours Δίκτη, and indeed the Dictaean tradition became well established: cf. Call. *H.* 1.4, V. *G.* 4.152. But then it is curious that such a familiar name should have been corrupted to an unfamiliar one. Strabo (10.4.12) like most readers, assumed that A. was referring to Mt Dicte, though he does not quote the first half of the line: καὶ γὰρ ἡ Δίκτη πλησίον, οὐχ, ὡς Ἄρατος, ὄρεος σχεδὸν Ἰδαίοιο· καὶ γὰρ χιλίους ἡ Δίκτη τῆς Ἴδης ἀπέχει, πρὸς ἀνίσχοντα ἥλιον ἀπ᾽ αὐτῆς κειμένη.

A quite different solution was proposed by Zenodotus of Mallia (in sch.): sch. δίκτον ἤκουσε τὸ καλούμενον δίκταμνον, καὶ διὰ τοῦτο καὶ εὐῶδες τοῦτο εἰρῆσθαι. He also notes that dittany was used in making childbirth easier; cf. Euphor. fr. 111 Powell, of Eileithyia, στεψαμένη θαλεροῖσι συνήντετο δικτάμνοισι. This explanation was adopted by Maass, but there is no other record of a noun δίκτον, and besides the context seems to require a place name between the general reference to Crete (31) and the cave (34). Grotius' conjecture Λύκτῳ is much more convincing, as it looks back to the Hesiodic origin of the myth in *Th.* 477 of Rhea pregnant with Zeus: πέμψαν δ' ἐς Λύκτον, Κρήτης ἐς πίονα δῆμον, and 481-2 ἔνθα μιν ἶκτο φέρουσα θοὴν διὰ νύκτα μέλαιναν, | πρώτην ἐς Λύκτον. The name is relatively unfamiliar, though it is mentioned twice in Homer (Β 647, Ρ 611), and it is very close to Δίκτον. Cf. Harrison 182. The geographical problem, however, remains, since Lyctus is in the region of Mt Dicte and a long way from Ida. The answer must lie in the poetic tradition, which tends to confuse these two names in their association with the birth of Zeus. Thus Call. *H.* 1.4 Δικταῖον is followed by Ἰδαίοισιν ἐν οὔρεσι (6), and in the same hymn Δικταῖαι Μέλιαι (47) by Ἰδαίοις ἐν ὄρεσσι (51). Cf. A.R. 1.509 Δικταῖον ναίεσκεν ὑπὸ σπέος, 3.134 ἄντρῳ ἐν Ἰδαίῳ.

εὐώδει A. is recalling *h.Hom.* 26.6 ἄντρῳ ἐν εὐώδει, of the child Dionysus. Aristides gives an adapted quotation in *Iov.* 2 οὐ Κρήτης ἐν εὐώδεσιν ἄντροις τραφείς. K. Schwenk (*Philologus* 17, 1861, 451) notes that fragrance is often associated with gods, e.g. Ο 153, of Zeus, ἀμφὶ δέ μιν θυόεν νέφος ἐστεφάνωτο, *h.Hom.* 2.277 of Demeter, 4.231 and 237 of Hermes, 7.36 of Dionysus. Cf. Theogn. 9, Aesch. *Pr.* 115, E. *Hipp.* 1391, A.R. 4.430, Mosch. 2.91, V. *A.* 1.403, Ov. *Fast.* 5.376. See N. J. Richardson, *Homeric Hymn to Demeter* (1974), 252.

σχεδὸν Ἰδαίοιο Sch. (S) ἔνιοι μὲν γράφουσι "σχεδὸν Αἰγείοιο", παρ' Ἡσιόδου λαβόντες, φάσκοντος τραφῆναι τὸν Δία Αἰγαίῳ ἐν ὄρει πεπυκασμένῳ ὑλήεντι (*Th.* 484). This variant arose out of the problem of Dicte: see preceding note. σχεδόν c. gen. is Homeric, e.g. ε 288 Φαιήκων γαίης σχεδόν.

34 ἄντρῳ For attempts to identify the Hesiodic cave of Zeus near Lyctus see West on *Th.* 477.

ἄντρῳ ἔνι κατέθεντο Voss's emendation eliminates the hiatus after a long vowel without metrical stress; cf. 1002 ὥρη ἐν ἑσπερίῃ. The verb occurs in Homer in the same *sedes*, ν 71-2 τά γ' ἐν νηΐ γλαφυρῇ ... δεξάμενοι κατέθεντο. Cf. sch. ἄντρον ἐν ᾧ κατέθεντο. Professor Reeve has suggested ἄντρῳ τ' ἐγκατέθεντο as a possible alternative.

εἰς ἐνιαυτόν I.e. till the end of his first year; see note on 11 and Harrison 193.

35 Δικταῖοι Κούρητες The various legends involving the Curetes are fully discussed by Strabo (10.3.1-13). They are associated with many different places, but in the story of the birth of Zeus they are Cretan:

10.3.19 ἐν δὲ τοῖς Κρητικοῖς λόγοις οἱ Κούρητες Διὸς τροφεῖς λέγονται καὶ φύλακες, εἰς Κρήτην μεταπεμφθέντες ὑπὸ τῆς Ῥέας. Cf. Opp. *C.* 11 Ῥείη κόλποις ἐνικάτθετο Κρήτης. Sometimes Ida is specified, e.g. A.R. 2.1234 Ζεὺς ἔτι Κουρήτεσσι μετετρέφετ᾽ Ἰδαίοισιν, D.S. 5.70.2 δοῦναι λάθρᾳ τοῖς Κούρησιν ἐκθρέψαι τοῖς κατοικοῦσι πλησίον ὄρους τῆς Ἴδης, Ov. *Fast.* 4.207; less often Dicte (Apollodor. *Bibl.* 1.1.6), sometimes both (Call. *H.* 1.47, 51). It is clear that Dicte and Ida are used freely as names meaning simply 'Crete', and here Δικταῖοι means essentially 'Cretan'. Cf. Lucr. 2.633–4 *Dictaeos referunt Curetas qui Iouis illum* | *uagitum in Creta quondam occultasse feruntur*, V. *A.* 3.131 *Curetum adlabimur oris*, and Nonnus' imitation in *D.* 28.276 Δικταῖοι Κορύβαντες. In Homer κούρητες are young warriors (Τ 193, 248), and the connection with κοῦρος is brought out in A.'s word-play with κουρίζοντα (32), like that of Callimachus in *H.* 1.52 and 54.

Κρόνον ἐψεύδοντο The legend of the Curetes performing a war-dance and beating their shields to prevent Cronus hearing the infant's cries is given by Call. *H.* 1.52–4. Apollodor. *Bibl.* 1.1.7 adds that τοῖς δόρασι τὰς ἀσπίδας συνέκρουον. Cf. Lucr. 2.633–9, Ov. *Fast.* 4.207–10. The descriptive imperfect is preferable to the variant ἐψεύσαντο, which may have come from Call. *H.* 1.7.

36 Κυνόσουραν Dog's Tail is an apt name for this little star group, and must have been the original Greek name before it became the Μικρὰ Ἄρκτος of Eudoxus (fr. 15) and later astronomers. A. also has the variation Κυνοσουρίδος Ἄρκτου (182, 227). In Latin *Cynosura* is usual: Cic. fr. 6, Vitr. 9.4.6, Ov. *Fast.* 3.107, Germ. 39, Man. 1.299, Luc. 3.219, V.Fl. 1.17, Avien. 122. Cic. *Luc.* 66 introduces a figurative use with *meas cogitationes dirigo, non ad illam paruulam Cynosuram* etc.: cf. Eng. 'Cynosure'. Κυνόσουρα was later added to the number of the nymphs who tended Zeus in Crete: *Catast.* 2 Ἀγλαοσθένης δὲ ἐν τοῖς Ναξικοῖς φησι τροφὸν γενέσθαι τοῦ Διὸς Κυνόσουραν. Cf. Hyg. 2.2.1, sch. (S) 39.

ἐπίκλησιν καλέουσι A Homeric phrase, which recalls the astronomical lines Σ 487, ε 273, Χ 29. Cf. Hes. *Th.* 207 ἐπίκλησιν καλέεσκε.

37 Ἑλίκην This name for the Great Bear is presumably derived from its conspicuously wheeling movement round the pole. It appears first here, and is naturally the preferred name in poetry (37, 41, 59, 91, 161). For variation A. combines it with Ἄρκτος in 51, resorts to the technical, but clumsy, Μεγάλη Ἄρκτος twice (140, 723), and invents the epithet ἀμαξαίη in 93. A.R. in 3.745 recalls the Homeric scene in ε 272, but replaces Homer's Ἄρκτος with A.'s Ἑλίκη, and twice follows A. in combining the two names (2.360, 3.1195). The Latin poets make much use of *Helice*, e.g. Cic. fr. 6, Ov. *Met.* 8.207, Germ. 39, Man. 1.296, Sen. *HO* 1539, Mart. 4.3.6, Avien. 122.

Note the elaborate artistry of these nine lines contrasting the two Bears (36–44). First we have a four-line chiasmus, with variation of cases, and repetition of one name but not the other, Κυνόσουραν ... Ἑλίκην, Ἑλίκη ... τῇ, and including the antithesis of Ἀχαιοί ... Φοίνικες (36–9); then the parallelism of the two couplets with ἡ μὲν ... ἡ δ᾽, and contrast of brightness and size (40–3); and finally the single line that concludes the passage, both providing a variation of 39 and bringing us back to the theme of the first line, Κυνόσουρα (44).

Ἑλίκη γε μὲν ἄνδρες Ἀχαιοί A. is presumably thinking of Odysseus sailing east and using the Bear as a guide to north: τὴν γὰρ δή μιν ἄνωγε Καλυψώ, δῖα θεάων, | ποντοπορευέμεναι ἐπ᾽ ἀριστερὰ χειρὸς ἔχοντα (ε 276–7). In later writers ἄρκτος has become a technical term, e.g. Hdt. 1.148 πρὸς ἄρκτον τετραμμένος.

38 εἰν ἁλί Homeric εἰν ἁλὶ κεῖται at the end of a line (η 244, ι 25) is imitated in h.Hom. 3.38, Call. H. 4.3. A. gives the phrase a new position and a new context. Cf. 158.

τεκμαίρονται This verb, because of the nature of the subject-matter, occurs several times in this poem, here c. dat. of the sign from which one derives information: cf. 170, 802, 1063, and, with the dative reinforced by ἐπί, 801, 1129, 1154. A.R. imitates in 1.108 πλόον ἠελίῳ τε καὶ ἀστέρι τεκμήρασθαι. Cf. Call. H. 1.85, 2.35 (in different contexts).

ἵνα Relative adv. of place, indicating the direction in which to sail. It is rare with verbs of motion, but cf. δ 821 ἵν᾽ οἴχεται of Telemachus, who has sailed to an unknown destination. At the same time ἵνα χρή in this *sedes* has a quaint reminiscence of ζ 27 ἵνα χρὴ καλὰ μὲν αὐτὴν ἕννυσθαι, a reference to Nausicaa's wedding.

νῆας ἀγινεῖν After a brief reference to the sea in 2–3 A. now introduces the theme of seafaring, which plays an important role throughout the poem. Note the variations of the phrase in περόωσι θάλασσαν (39) and ναυτίλλονται (44). On ἀγινεῖν see 23.

39 Φοίνικες Because of the slow shift of the pole relative to the fixed stars (see note on 21), the Great Bear gradually moved away from it over the centuries from c. 2000 BC, and the Little Bear came closer. See R. Thiel's diagram in *And There Was Light* (1958) 16. By the eighth century the head star (β Ursae Minoris) was fairly close, and with γ would have made an easy guide to the pole. It is therefore not surprising that the Phoenicians in the course of their far-flung trading voyages should have used these stars instead of the Great Bear. This tradition about the Phoenicians is first attested here, and Call. fr. 191.53–5 supports it, though at the same time giving credit to Thales for delineating the constellation for the Greeks: Θάλητος, ὅς τ᾽ ἦν ἄλλα δεξιὸς γνώμην | καὶ τῆς Ἀμάξης ἐλέγετο σταθμήσασθαι | τοὺς ἀστερίσκους, ἢ πλέουσι Φοίνικες. Cf. Str. 1.1.6 οὐδὲ γὰρ εἰκὸς ἦν πω τὴν ἑτέραν ἠστροθετῆσθαι, ἀλλ᾽ ἀφ᾽ οὗ οἱ Φοίνικες ἐσημειώσαντο καὶ ἐχρῶντο πρὸς τὸν πλοῦν, παρελθεῖν καὶ εἰς τοὺς Ἕλληνας τὴν διάταξιν ταύτην. A.'s striking antithesis became a favourite with Latin poets, e.g. Ov. *Epist.* 17.149 *nec sequor aut Helicen aut qua Tyros utitur Arcton, Fast.* 3.107–8. *Arctos, quarum Cynosura petatur | Sidoniis, Helicen Graia carina notet, Tr.* 4.3.1, Man. 1.298–302, Luc. 3.218–19, Sil. 3.665, V.Fl. 1.17–18.

πίσυνοι Λ 9 ἠνορέῃ πίσυνοι, same *sedes*. Note the alliteration in this line.

περόωσι θάλασσαν ζ 272, of Phaeacian seafaring.

40 καθαρή Not 'bright', as Mair translates, but 'clear' in the sense of being clearly defined; cf. 383, of the constellation figures. This epithet begins an unusual series of four descriptive words characterising the Great Bear. The succession of η sounds enhances the effect.

ἐπιφράσσασθαι ἑτοίμη This use of the verb in the sense of 'recognise' is Homeric, e.g. σ 94 ἵνα μή μιν ἐπιφρασσαίατ᾽ Ἀχαιοί. Cf. 76 of another constellation, and 1061 of weather signs. For ἑτοίμη 'easy' c. inf. cf. 236–7. A similar use occurs in Homer of a plan that is not easy to carry out, Ι 425 οὔ σφισιν ἥδε γ᾽ ἑτοίμη, | ἣν νῦν ἐφράσσαντο.

41 πολλή In star descriptions A. uses πολλός and πολλή to denote size (cf. 87, 165, 188, 255, 316, 611, 699), but not brightness, as is suggested by Zannoni's 'splendendo d'intensa luce' and Martin's 'si elle brille de tout son éclat'. Even in the case of the bright star Capella (165) A. makes a distinction between its apparent size (πολλή) and its brightness (ἀγλαή). Here the brightness of the Bear is expressed in the remainder of the line: see the following note.

φαινομένη Translators regularly construe with πολλή, e.g. Mair 'appearing large', Erren 'sie gross erscheint'; so Zannoni and Martin, quoted in preceding note, who also take φαινομένη to mean 'shining', a sense that this passive verb never bears. It is, of course, pointless to say that the Great Bear appears large at nightfall: it appears equally large all night. A. uses φαίνεσθαι frequently, which is not surprising in a poem entitled Φαινόμενα, always of things being seen or sighted, and sometimes in the more specialized sense of stars being visible (e.g. 135). The point here is that the Great Bear is visible as soon as the sky begins to get dark: sch. εὐθέως γὰρ δύναντος ἡλίου φαίνεται. It is a measure of the constellation's brightness. In the same way the brightest stars can be defined as those that are visible at full moon. So Cassiepeia is νυκτὶ φαεινομένη παμμηνίδι (189), and the shoulder stars of Ophiuchus καὶ ἂν διχόμηνι σελήνῃ | εἰσωποὶ τελέθοιεν (78–9). Here then φαινομένη means εἰσωπός, and should be construed with πρώτης ἀπὸ νυκτός. A.

has thus assigned to the Bear four distinct characteristics: a clearly designed pattern, ease of identification, size and brightness.

For hiatus after -η bearing metrical stress cf. (2nd foot) 42, 813, 880, 920, 940; (3rd foot) 41, 77, 106, 135, 518, 587, 694; (4th foot) 52, 80, 322, 423, 463, 989; (5th foot) 323, 427, 713, 765, 842, 882, 892, 948; (6th foot) 679.

42 ὀλίγη With reference to size only, as πολλή (41). The Little Bear is also much fainter than the Great Bear, but it does have three brightish stars. The Pleiades, on the other hand, are both a small group and all faint, and A. therefore adds ἀφεγγέες to ὀλίγαι (264).

ἀρείων In Homer especially of strong heroes, e.g., in same *sedes*, B 707 (Protesilaus), but also of things, Δ 407 τεῖχος ἄρειον. Cf. Hes. *Op.* 207, of the hawk, πολλὸν ἀρείων. Later it can mean simply 'better' (cf. ἄριστος), A. *Th.* 305 γαίας πέδον τᾶσδ' ἄρειον. Here the Homeric sense of strength suggests greater reliability.

43 μειοτέρη ... στροφάλιγγι In A.'s day the seven stars of the Little Bear revolved round the pole at distances varying from c. 8° (head star β) to about 13° (end-of-tail star α, the present pole star). The curve in the line of stars enhances the impression of a rotating figure, hence the addition of πᾶσα to the description. The seven stars of the Great Bear revolved at distances from c. 19° (head star α) to c. 30° (end-of-tail star η). The smaller circle of the former therefore shows clearly that it is the closer to the pole. Cic. fr. 7.5 *cursu interiore breui conuertitur orbe*; Man. 1.299 *angusto Cynosura breuis torquetur in orbe* imitates also the structure of A.'s line, which, by being enclosed between adj. and noun, seems to suggest the circling movement of the stars. Cf. D.P. 584, of the midnight sun at Thule, λοξοτέρη γὰρ τῆμος ἐπιστρέφεται στροφάλιγγι.

μειοτέρη A late form of μείων, probably on the analogy of Homeric πλειότερος (cf. 644). It occurs first here and in A.R. 2.368, both times in same *sedes*, as also πλειότερος in both Homer and A.

περιστρέφεται στροφάλιγγι A striking example of *figura etymologica*. The verb suggests the technical language of Arist. *Cael.* 273a2 ὁ χρόνος ἐν ᾧ περιεστράφη (ὁ οὐρανός) and Euc. *Phaen.* pr. (p. 8, 29 Menge) κόσμου περιστροφῆς χρόνος. The noun is Homeric, in a context of swirling dust (Π 775), and A.R. 3.759 uses it of water, ὠκείῃ στροφάλιγγι. Cf. Q.S. 3.64, of a whirlwind.

44 Σιδόνιοι Sch. (Q) καθολικῶς δὲ Σιδωνίους τοὺς Φοίνικάς φησιν ἀπὸ μιᾶς πόλεως τῆς Σιδῶνος. The tradition refers to Phoenicians generally (cf. 39, Call. fr. 191.54, Luc. 3.220), but the poets vary the name with *Poeni* (Man. 1.301), *Sidonii* (Ov. *Fast.* 3.108), *Tyrii* (V.Fl. 1.17).

This line is a complete variation of 39, ingeniously maintaining the same word-order: τῇ καὶ corresponds to τῇ δ᾽ ἄρα, Σιδόνιοι to Φοίνικες, ἰθύντατα adv. to πίσυνοι adj., and ναυτίλλονται to the phrase περόωσι θάλασσαν.

ἰθύντατα Once in Homer, in a moral sense, Σ 508 δίκην ἰθύντατα εἴποι, here literal, of the straightest course.

ναυτίλλονται Homeric verb, e.g., in same *sedes*, ξ 246 ναυτίλλεσθαι. Cf. A.R. 1.236 ναυτίλλεσθαι, 918 ναυτίλλοιντο, 4.299 ναυτίλλοντο.

45–62 *The Dragon*

Between the Bears winds the Dragon, approaching the head of the greater with the tip of its tail, and enclosing the lesser's head in its coil. Five stars mark its own head, which points towards the tip of Helice's tail and grazes the horizon when due north.

Once the Bears have been identified, it is not difficult to pick out the Dragon, though it is not as conspicuous as A.'s description suggests. Its brightest star (α) was very close to the pole c. 3000 BC, and legends of the Dragon dominating the universe may well derive from that period. It probably came to the Greeks from the Babylonians. The sch. variously identify with the snakes killed by Cadmus and Apollo, and the snake that guarded the golden apples of the Hesperides.

The name Δράκων appears first in A., but he may have taken it from Epimenides, in view of sch. 46 φέρεται δὲ περὶ τοῦ Δράκοντος Κρητικὸς μῦθος· ἐπιόντος ποτὲ τοῦ Κρόνου, ὁ Ζεὺς εὐλαβηθεὶς ἑαυτὸν μὲν εἰς δράκοντα μετεμόρφωσε. Eudoxus called it ὁ διὰ τῶν Ἄρκτων Ὄφις (fr. 33) and simply ὁ Ὄφις (fr. 15), Hipparchus Δράκων (1.2.3). It seems likely that, when the other Serpent was introduced, it was called Ὄφις (82), and the adjacent figure Ὀφιοῦχος, and Δράκων then became fixed as the name of the circumpolar constellation. In Latin it is variously called *Draco* (Cic. fr. 8.2, Vitr. 9.4.6, Man. 1.627, Germ. 58, Avien. 140), *Anguis* (V. *G.* 1.205, 244, Sen. *Thy.* 871, Man. 1.306), and even *Serpens* (Vitr. 9.4.6, Germ. 49, Hyg. 2.3.1). *RE* 5.1647–8, Roscher VI 881ff., Allen 202ff.

45 οἵη ποταμοῖο ἀπορρώξ Sch. (M) ἐν τούτῳ δὲ Ἡσιόδου ζηλωτὴς φαίνεται· οὗτος γὰρ ποταμὸν εἴκασε δράκοντι εἰπών [fr. 70.23] "καί τε δι᾽ Ἐρχομενοῦ ἠπειγμένος εἶσι δράκων ὥς", οὗτος δὲ τοὐναντίον δράκοντα ποταμῷ ἀπείκασεν. Strabo (9.3.16) quotes the line with εἰλιγμένος. Cf. Sen. *Thy.* 871 *fluminis instar lubricus Anguis*. A. adds the simile to Eudoxus' bare statement (fr. 15) μεταξὺ δὲ τῶν Ἄρκτων ἐστὶν ἡ τοῦ Ὄφεως οὐρά.

ἀπορρώξ as noun means literally 'a piece broken off', hence the basic sense of a 'portion' in Nic. *Ther.* 518 ἀπορρὼξ δραχμαίη. Here sch.

quote as A.'s Homeric model Στυγὸς ὕδατός ἐστιν ἀπορρώξ from κ
514 (of Cocytus) and B 755 (of Titaressus), adding in explanation ἀπόρ-
ροια καὶ ἀπόσπασμα. These rivers have their source in the water of
Styx, as Lucan says of the latter (6.378), *hunc fama est Stygiis manare pal-
udibus amnem*. But 'outflow' or 'offshoot' is not a suitable meaning here,
and various other explanations have been put forward. (*a*) Influenced
perhaps by Cicero's *rapido cum gurgite* (fr. 8.1) and Germ. 48 *abrupti fluminis*, Ceporinus' Latin version gives *qualis fluuii decursus*, and hence Voss
'dem entstürzenden Bache vergleichbar', and Erren 'wie ein Wasser-
fall'. This interpretation may be due to the influence of the adjectival
use of ἀπορρώξ meaning 'steep', but here the point of the simile lies in
the winding of the river, and that is rarely compatible with a torrent. (*b*)
Maass goes back to the basic sense of a 'portion' with 'tamquam desecta
amnis portiuncula' (*Aratea* 271), and Mair's 'the branch of a river' is
similar. But there seems to be little point in so delimiting the expression, when 'winding like a river' is all the meaning that is required.
(*c*) Martin finds A.'s Homeric source rather in ι 359, where Odysseus'
wine is called ἀμβροσίης καὶ νέκταρός ἐστιν ἀπορρώξ, and translates
'pareil au flot d'une rivière'. Although 'flot' adds nothing to the simile,
and is in any case hardly valid as a translation of ἀπορρώξ, I think
Martin is right in looking back to this line of the *Odyssey* for an explanation of A.'s usage. There the word is used figuratively, i.e. the wine
tastes like ambrosia and nectar. So in Ar. *Lys.* 811 Timon the mis-
anthrope is called Ἐρινύων ἀπορρώξ, and the metaphor becomes comparable with Eng. 'a chip of the old block'. Cf. *AP* 7.571.3 (Leont.) προτέρων μελέων ὀλίγη τις ἀπορρώξ. Here A. is strengthening his simile
with a bold metaphor, meaning that the Dragon's winding is in the very
likeness of a river. Cf. Hes. fr. 293 ποταμῷ ῥείοντι ἐοικώς, quoted by
Servius on V. *G.* 1.245 *in morem fluminis*, and Germ. 48 *fluminis instar*, repeated in Sen. *Thy.* 871; also Q.S. 1.304 πέτρη Σιπύλοιό τ' ἀπορρώξ.
For the short vowel in hiatus cf. 686, 951, 962, 1133.

46 εἰλεῖται Here and again in 53 this verb has a double sense. In
the first place it suggests the continuous circling motion that all stars
share (cf. 224), but at the same time it describes the sinuous pattern of
the constellation figure (cf. 445).

μέγα θαῦμα Surprisingly repeated so soon after the use of the
phrase in 15. It certainly brings out the visual significance of the noun,
and perhaps is meant to suggest the traditional awesomeness of the
Dragon's position dominating the universe.

θαῦμα Δράκων Correption before δρ-, as again in 70, 187; cf. Λ 39,
Μ 202. Contrast 1011 ἕνα δρόμον. See Spitzner 101.

περί τ' ἀμφί τ' Cf. Ρ 760 (in same *sedes*), *h.Hom.* 2.276, Hes. *Th.*

848, fr. 150.28, Call. fr. 260.13, *H.* 4.300, A.R. 2.1208, 3.633, and Latin imitations in V. *G.* 1.245 *circum perque duas*, Man. 1.305 *has inter fusus circumque amplexus utramque.* The double bend of the Dragon is suggested by the doubling of the adv.

ἐαγώς Pf. act. in intrans. sense, 'bending'. Cf. Hdt. 1.184, of the Euphrates, περὶ καμπὰς πολλὰς ἀγνύμενος. For the form cf. ἔαγε in Hes. *Op.* 534, and Sapph. 31.9 (text uncertain). The dialect is Attic, but may be also Aeolic; see R. Hiersche, *Glotta* 44 (1966) 1–5, and West, *Th.*, p. 82.

47 μυρίος The sg. with reference to size is usually figurative, as in 761 with ὄνειαρ, and Σ 88 πένθος ἐνὶ φρεσὶ μυρίον. Here it expresses the surprisingly great length of the Dragon, as you follow it from head to tail. It is a hyperbole, designed to make the constellation seem very impressive. Cf. Diosc. *AP* 9.568.1 = *HE* 1677 μυρίος ἀρθείς, Νεῖλε. There is perhaps an echo of A. in the language of A.R. 1.843–4 ἄλλοθεν ἄλλαι μυρίαι εἰλίσσοντο, of the young women escorting Hypsipyle.

οἱ A. makes very frequent use of this dative of the old demonstrative pronoun οὗ. It is a weak pronoun, enclitic, and often referring back to a noun outside its own clause, sometimes in deliberate contrast with it. Here οἱ refers to the Dragon, and is equivalent to a possessive pronoun, 'its': cf. 77, 86, 88, 94, al. The usage is Homeric, e.g. α 300 ὅ οἱ πατέρα κλυτὸν ἔκτα, where οἱ is Orestes, and the subject of ἔκτα Aegisthus. Cf. S. *Tr.* 650 ἅ δέ οἱ φίλα δάμαρ, with Jebb's note. K–G 1.565ff.

σπείρης ἑκάτερθε The Bears actually lie on either side of the Dragon's tail, not the coil, as Hipparchus notes (1.4.3): ἰδίᾳ δὲ ὁ Ἄρατος ἐπὶ τοῦ Δράκοντος ἀγνοεῖ, πρῶτον μὲν τῷ φάσκειν σπείρης ἑκάτερθε φέρεσθαι τὰς Ἄρκτους· τῆς γὰρ οὐρᾶς ἑκατέρωθέν εἰσι, καὶ οὐ τῆς σπείρας. ἀντεστραμμένων γὰρ αὐτῶν καὶ ὡσανεὶ παραλλήλως κειμένων ἡ οὐρὰ τοῦ Δράκοντος μεταξὺ αὐτῶν διὰ μήκους παρατέταται· ἡ δὲ σπείρα τὴν μὲν Μικρὰν Ἄρκτον περιλαμβάνει, τῆς δὲ Μεγάλης πολὺ κεχώρισται. A. is apparently not following Eudoxus here (fr. 15, cited on 45), and may simply have regarded the tail as part of the coil.

φέρονται The prevailing φύονται of the manuscripts could only mean 'grow', and does not make sense here. Hipparchus' paraphrase with φέρεσθαι (1.4.3) implies φέρονται, which A. uses in giving star positions, to remind the reader that they are continually moving; cf. 176, 385.

48 κυανέου Cf. E. *IT* 7 κυανέαν ἅλα. In Homer this adj. usually means 'dark', and is not an epithet of the sea, but A. may be recalling μ 243, of the sea-bed ψάμμῳ κυανέη (same *sedes*); cf. Λ 39 κύανεος ἐλέλικτο δράκων.

πεφυλαγμέναι ὠκεανοῖο   A. adds a further detail to the lore of the Bears, which he had not included in 26ff. There he was concerned with the relative positions of the Bears and the pole, here with the fact that the Bears never set, for which his source was not Eudoxus but Homer: Ἄρκτον ... ἥ τ' αὐτοῦ στρέφεται καί τ' Ὠρίωνα δοκεύει, | οἴη δ' ἄμμορός ἐστι λοετρῶν Ὠκεανοῖο (Σ 487–9, ε 273–5). Cf. Eustathius on the latter passage: οὐχ ἧττον δὲ καὶ ἐν τοῖς Ἀράτου. A.'s imitation preserves Homer's last word, but creates variations with the plural Ἄρκτοι, and the change from adj. to a more imaginative participle. Cf. S. *Tr.* 130 ἄρκτου στροφάδες κέλευθοι. Virgil imitates A. more than Homer in *G.* 1.246 *Arctos Oceani metuentes aequore tingi.* Cf. Sen. *Thy.* 867 *monstraque nunquam perfusa mari,* Nonn. *D.* 25.136–7 δρόμον Ἄρκτου | ἄβροχον Ὠκεανοῖο καὶ οὐ ψαύοντα θαλάσσης, 43.186–7 Ὠκεανῷ δὲ | λούετο διψὰς Ἅμαξα. Here I translate 'ocean' for the sake of the Homeric reminiscence. πεφυλαγμέναι c. gen. of separation, as 930 πεφύλαξο: cf. 766 πεφοβημένος.

49 ἄλλην μὲν νεάτῃ ἐπιτείνεται οὐρῇ   Eudoxus puts the relative positions more clearly (fr. 15): ἡ τοῦ Ὄφεως οὐρὰ τὸν ἄκρον ἀστέρα ὑπὲρ τῆς κεφαλῆς ἔχουσα τῆς Μεγάλης Ἄρκτου, i.e. λ Draconis lies to the north of α Ursae Majoris. Of the many variants for the verb only ἐπιτείνεται makes sense, whereas ἀποτείνεται can be explained as coming in from 184, ἐπιτέλλεται from its common use as a star rising, and the -τέμνεται compounds from the influence of the following line. Voss, Mair, and Martin take ἐπιτείνεται to mean 'stretches towards', and Martin in consequence reads ἄλλης as a more appropriate case for expressing direction towards. But it is more likely that ἐπι- here means 'over', in view of Eudoxus' ὑπὲρ τῆς κεφαλῆς. So Erren 'streckt sich über'. Cf. 51 πὰρ κεφαλήν.

50 ἄλλην δέ   The Little Bear.

σπείρῃ περιτέμνεται   The verb is Homeric, but of cattle-rustling (λ 402, ω 112). A. uses it again of stars, as a geometrical term (543). Here the curve of the Dragon's coil seems to cut off Cynosura from Helice. Cf. D.P. 354, of the Tiber, ὃς ἱμερτὴν ἀποτέμνεται ἄνδιχα Ῥώμην. The reading of M περιλαμβάνεται comes from Hi. 1.5.7 τὴν κεφαλὴν αὐτῆς καὶ τοὺς πόδας περιλαμβανομένους ὑπὸ τῆς σπείρας τοῦ Δράκοντος.

50–54   Eudoxus (fr. 15) takes the length of the Dragon in three sections: (1) the tail between the Bears, with its end-star over the Great Bear's head (see on 45 and 49); (2) the main coil, round the Little Bear, καμπὴν δὲ ἔχει παρὰ τὴν κεφαλὴν τῆς Μικρᾶς Ἄρκτου καὶ παρατέταται ὑπὸ τοὺς πόδας· (3) a second bend, ending in the head stars, ἑτέραν δὲ καμπὴν ἐνταῦθα ποιησάμενος πάλιν ἀνανεύων ἔμπροσθεν τὴν κεφαλήν. A. also disposes his material in three sections, but with much overlapping: (1) the tail and main coil (49–50), (2) the tail and main coil again, with additional details (50–2), (3) the coil and the backward bend (52–4). A.'s version seems designed to make the most of the antitheses in the situation, but his out-of-order details, the changes of subject, and the difficulty of identifying some of the pronouns deny the passage the clarity that normally goes with this genre of poetry.

50–51 ἡ μέν οἱ ἄκρη οὐρή Repetition of ὅ γ' ... μὲν νεάτη ... οὐρῇ (49), with variation of cases and adj. οἱ refers to the Dragon: cf. 47.

κεφαλήν See note on 28.

ἀποπαύεται Homeric only in sense of 'cease from', e.g. Θ 473; only here of a line terminating, like πειραίνονται (365).

52 σπείρη δ' ἐν Rare position of ἐν, unless an adj. follows; cf. μ 103 τῷ δ' ἐν. See 545 τῷ ἔνι.

κάρη Epic acc. sg., e.g. Χ 74 πολιόν τε κάρη. Cf. 170, and nom. 58, 672. A. also has κρατί (147, 205), καρήατα (666). Hi. 1.4.2 identifies the head star as τῶν ἐν τῷ πλινθίῳ ... ὁ μὲν βορειότερος, i.e. the modern β Ursae Minoris. For the hiatus see note on 41.

ἡ δέ Sc. σπείρη τοῦ Δράκοντος.

52–53 κατ' αὐτὴν εἰλεῖται κεφαλήν With the change of subject A. now (as if demonstrating to an observer) traces the line of the Dragon stars from tail to head, thus repeating the information just given, but from a different angle. In κατ' αὐτήν the prep. marks a point in the curve which lies, as it were, abreast of the Bear's head, and the mildly emphatic αὐτήν implies that this is quite a bright star and should be easily recognised. The curve may be said to begin just about this point. On εἰλεῖται see note on 46, although in this line the movement is mainly in the tracing of the figure, as is shown by the following ἔρχεται. κεφαλήν is a variation of κάρη (52).

53 οἱ ποδὸς ἔρχεται ἄχρις Hi. 1.4.2 also identifies the star γ Ursae Minoris as the forelegs, the figure being seen, as it were, in silhouette: ὁ δὲ νοτιώτερος ἐπὶ τῶν ἐμπροσθίων ποδῶν. The hind legs will then be the fainter star η, and Eudoxus correctly describes the line of the Dragon at this point as running parallel to and south of these two stars: παρατέταται ὑπὸ τοὺς πόδας (fr. 15).

The sg. ποδός is strange, but A. must mean the hind legs, since the curve goes at least as far as that position, and he may have had in mind that the two legs are represented by a single star. On the other hand Eudoxus has τοὺς πόδας, and though the Latin verse translations omit this difficult clause, Vitr. 9.4.6 follows A. in saying that the Dragon (*Serpens*) *circum Cynosurae caput iniecta est fluxu porrectaque proxime eius pedes.*

And *Aratus Latinus* has *ad pedes ueniat*. There is therefore a case for considering πόδας here, the acc. without prep. depending on ἔρχεται (cf. A 322 ἔρχεσθον κλισίην), and ἄχρις adv. after the noun, as in P 599 γράψεν δέ οἱ ὀστέον ἄχρις, the phrasing of which A. may in fact be recalling here. But the expression then becomes clumsier, the meaning of ἄχρις in Homer is uncertain (see B. Mader, *Lfrg. E.*), and A. uses ἄχρις elsewhere only c. gen. or c. prep. (614, 674; 349, 602, 632, 807). It is better to see ποδός as a typical variation of sg. for pl., and explain it with the supralinear gloss in Q, τοῦ ὀπισθίου.

54 ἐκ δ᾽ αὖτις cf. Π 654 ἐξαῦτις, in same *sedes*. The context requires the sense 'back again' rather than 'immediately' as in 641 ἐξ αὐτῆς.

παλίνορσος A. ingeniously recalls the famous snake simile in Γ 33 δράκοντα ἰδὼν παλίνορσος ἀπέστη (the only instance in Homer). Empedocles has the word in the same *sedes* as A., in fr. 35.1 παλίνορσος ἐλεύσομαι, fr. 100.23 (αἷμα) παλίνορσον ἀπαΐξειε. Among later occurrences are A.R. 1.416, Call. fr. 344, Opp. *H.* 3.351 παλίνορσος ἀνέδραμεν (perhaps an echo of A.), *C.* 4.376, Nonn. *D.* 14.17, Colluth. 339, 352. LSJ derive -ορσος from ὅρρος, others from ὄρνυμι: see Kirk on Γ 33. The former seems the more likely, in view of Ar. *Ach.* 1179 τὸ σφυρὸν παλίνορρον ἐξεκόκκισεν, and the fact that the word always has a strong sense of going back, but not necessarily a rapid motion. The latter, if required, is added by the accompanying verb.

ἀνατρέχει This lively verb recalls the sense and rhythm of Λ 354 ἀπέλεθρον ἀνέδραμε. It is purely descriptive of the figure, and has nothing to do with star movement. The coil runs through the stars α ι η ζ to δ, where the figure turns sharply back to connect with the head stars at ξ.

ἐκείνη Sch. τῇ σπείρᾳ, without further comment. But the head can hardly be said to belong to the coil, hence Maass's ἐκείνῳ, adopted by Martin. It is true that in A. κεῖνος and ἐκεῖνος nearly always refer back, but here the nearest masc. reference is ὅ γ᾽ (49), and it may be better to take the pron. with the more immediate κεφαλῇ, as in 61; cf. 197 κάκεῖνο ... ἄγαλμα. The impressive head of the Dragon, with five stars to denote it, may then be seen as being in contrast with Cynosura's head (53), which is only a single star. See also the following note.

55 οἰόθεν οὐδ᾽ οἷος In the positive Homeric form οἰόθεν οἷος (Η 39, 226; cf. A.R. 2.28, 4.1198) the two words reinforce each other, 'by himself alone'. A. has put this in a negative form, with the double negative for emphasis, 'not by itself or alone', i.e. not a single star by itself. The whole sequence from οὐ to κεφαλῇ is an unbroken phrase, and should not be interrupted with a comma after οἰόθεν, as in Voss and Martin.

LSJ are misleading in noting οἰόθεν here as 'without οἶος'. The alternation of ου and οι gives an unusual sound effect. Leumann 258ff.

ἐπιλάμπεται Once in Homer, but act., P 650 ἥλιος δ' ἐπέλαμψε: so *h.Hom.* 4.141, of the moon. The passive is Hellenistic, here and 206, also A.R. 2.920, all c. dat.

56 δύο κροτάφοις δύο δ' ὄμμασιν S.E. *Math.* 5.98 Mau δράκοντος κεφαλῇ οἱ πέντε, ἐφ' ὧν φησιν ὁ Ἄρατος· ἀλλὰ δύο κροτάφους δύο δ' ὄμματα. Maass accepts the acc., construing with ἐπέχει. But it is more natural to take the dat. with ἐπιλάμπεται, since the run of words suggests οὐδ' οἶος ... ἀλλὰ δύο. See also M. Marcovich, *Philologus* 107 (1963) 314. The temples are γ and ξ Draconis, the eyes β and ν, the jawpoint μ. See further on 62.

ὑπένερθεν The position in the figure, which is naturally thought of as below the eyes, not the astronomical position of the star, which is west of the other head-stars.

57 ἐσχατιὴν ... γένυος In Homer the farthest part of an area is ἐσχατιή, e.g. πολέμοιο (Λ 524). This star is not only the farthest point in the jaw, but also the end of the whole line of stars that delineate the constellation, and A. may be suggesting this with his choice of word. It is a faint star, and Hipparchus calls it ἡ γλῶσσα (1.4.4), ὁ ἐν ἄκρῳ τῷ στόματι (1.4.8), and ὁ ἐν τῷ χάσματι (3.2.5). In Ptolemy it is the first star in Draco, being the farthest west, and is named ὁ ἐπὶ τῆς γλώσσης (*Alm.* 7.5.3).

ἐπέχει Almost a technical term in A. for a star occupying a certain position; cf. 176, 244, 485, 504, 540, 583.

δεινοῖο πελώρου The awesomeness of the Dragon is enhanced by the echoes of Ε 741 Γοργείη κεφαλή (cf. λ 634), Hes. *Th.* 856, of Typhoeus, κεφαλὰς δεινοῖο πελώρου, also 825 δεινοῖο δράκοντος, *Sc.* 223–4 κάρη δεινοῖο πελώρου | Γοργοῦς.

58 λοξόν Instead of continuing the line south-west from the end of the great coil at δ, the head stars go off at an angle towards the west.

νεύοντι The angle of the head makes it appear to be bending forward; cf. 789, 794, of the moon's inclination.

59 κατ' ἰθύ One obvious, and probably ancient, method of determining star positions is to note three that lie on a straight line; cf. Hi. 3.5.22 of two small stars in Taurus ἐπ' εὐθείας ἄκρῳ τῷ δεξιῷ κέρατι πρὸς ἀνατολὰς κειμένων. The method is of some help in identifying A.'s stars, and in this case the two that point towards η Ursae Majoris must be γ and μ Draconis. For κατ' ἰθύ c. dat. Hp. *Off.* 3 καθημένῳ μὲν πόδες ἐς τὴν ἄνω ἴξιν κατ' ἰθὺ γούνασι, Arist. *Mete.* 363b26 κατὰ διάμετρον αὐτῷ κεῖται, Euc. *Elem.* 1.14 ἐπ' εὐθείας ἔσονται ἀλλήλαις, Hi. 3.5.22 (cited above) and 1.4.4 (see following note).

60 κροτάφοιο τὰ δεξιά Hipparchus finds fault with A. here: οὐ γὰρ ὁ δεξιὸς κρόταφος, ἀλλ' ὁ ἀριστερὸς ἐπ' εὐθείας ἐστὶ τῇ γλώσσῃ τοῦ Ὄφεως καὶ τῇ ἄκρᾳ οὐρᾷ τῆς Μεγάλης Ἄρκτου (1.4.4). He rejects the explanation of Attalus that A. imagined the head to be turned to face outside the cosmos, and goes on to lay down the rule that the constellation figures are designed to be viewed as facing the earth, except when drawn in profile: ἅπαντα γὰρ τὰ ἄστρα ἠστέρισται πρὸς τὴν ἡμετέραν θεωρίαν καὶ ὡς ἂν πρὸς ἡμᾶς ἐστραμμένα, εἰ μή τι κατάγραφον αὐτῶν ἐστί (1.4.5). A. must certainly have meant γ Draconis, since the other temple (ξ) is too far out of line to be an alternative. Cf. 70. It appears there was no corresponding passage in Eudoxus, since Hipparchus makes no reference to him at this point.

νειάτῳ οὐρῇ The adj. does not appear elsewhere with two terminations. A. alone has the same usage in the similar phrase ἔσχατος οὐρή (625, 628). All three instances seem deliberate, and there is no need to emend with Voss. The adj. usually means 'lowest' or 'outermost', but here A. uses it as a variation for ἄκρος. The phrasing may recall η 127 νείατον ὄρχον.

61 που The particle marks an approximation; cf. Hdt. 1.181 μεσοῦντι δέ κου τῆς ἀναβάσιος. Denniston 492.

νίσσεται A Homeric verb, for which both single and double σ are attested. The favoured etymology is from a reduplicated present stem *νι-νσ-: Monro HG 39, Schwyzer 1.690, West on Th. 71. Chantraine (1.440) finds this phonetically difficult, and prefers to explain the form as desiderative. It seems likely that both spellings were current in the Hellenistic period. For A. here, also 21, 426, the transmitted reading is certainly νίσσεται. Cf. A.R. 2.824, 1030, 4.628. See also Martin's note on the possible confusion of νέω 'go' and νέω 'swim'. The ingenious variant νήχεται is explained by Petavius, Uran. 3.5.124B 'hoc est, in summo aequore fluitare'. It comes from sch. 62 ἡ κεφαλὴ ἡ τοῦ Δράκοντος κατὰ τοῦτο τὸ μέρος νήχεται καὶ κολυμβᾷ.

ἧχι Instr. -η; see note on 4 πάντη. The adv. is Homeric, and often in this position, e.g. Γ 326, ζ 94. A. repeats with some variation of position in 135, 231, 457, 495, 1009. Cf. Call. H. 1.10, 2.91, 4.49, al. D.P. 258 imitates with ἧχί περ ἄκραι, 176 ἄκρη.

61–62 ἄκραι μίσγονται δύσιές τε καὶ ἀντολαί The western and eastern horizons are thought of as arcs along which different stars have their setting and rising points, which vary according to the latitude of the observer. The extremities of these two arcs merge at due north, where a star at that distance from the pole may be seen to set and then rise, just grazing the horizon. Stars farther north are circumpolar and do not set at all. Hipparchus gives the polar distances of the three most southerly stars of the Dragon: the jaw-tip (μ) $34\frac{3}{5}°$, the southerly eye (β) $35°$, and the southerly temple (γ) $37°$. Now the arctic circle for the latitude of Athens (ὁ ἀεὶ φανερὸς κύκλος ἐν τοῖς περὶ Ἀθήνας τόποις) also has a polar distance of about $37°$. Therefore the Dragon's head lies entirely within that circle, with only the left temple actually lying on it (1.4.8). Hipparchus thus agrees with Eudoxus (but without quoting him) and A., who say that the Dragon's head just grazes the horizon, and disagrees with Attalus, who makes it set for a short time (1.4.7). Cf. Cleom. 1.5.22 καὶ ἂν ... πρὸς ἄρκτον ἰὼν εἰς τὸ Ἑλληνικὸν τῆς γῆς ἀφίκηται κλίμα, πρὸς ὃ καὶ τὰ Φαινόμενα τῷ Ἀράτῳ πεποίηται, ἐφάψεται αὐτῷ τοῦ ὁρίζοντος ἡ τοῦ δράκοντος κεφαλὴ καὶ οἱ τῆς ἑλίκης πόδες, Mart. Cap. 8.827 *Draconis caput, quod iam notaueram, usque ad finitoris circulum peruenire.*

This concept of extreme setting and rising points for stars probably originated in the ancient practice of noting the most northerly and southerly points of sunset and sunrise on the horizon as a means of determining the two solstices: see, e.g., Dicks *EGA* 16. Crates may have had this tradition in mind when he compared κ 86 ἐγγὺς γὰρ νυκτός τε καὶ ἤματός εἰσι κέλευθοι, a tale of the far north. According to sch. Arat., however, he allowed a period of four hours between sunset and sunrise, according to Gem. 6.11 only one hour. These solar parallels may explain how the sch. came to confuse the issue with references to the meridian considered as a dividing line between the rising and the setting sun. Cf. Posid. fr. 49, 350–4. Strabo (2.3.8) is equally unhelpful when he explains δύσιες and ἀντολαί in A. as west and east. The misunderstanding may point to the cause of the corruption in Ach. *Isag.* 35 (Maass *Comm.* 71), where ἠελίοιο is substituted for ἀλλήλῃσι.

63–90 DRAGON'S HEAD GROUP: THE KNEELER, THE CROWN, THE SERPENT-HOLDER AND SERPENT, THE SCORPION, THE CLAWS

63–70 The Kneeler

Close to the Dragon's head is a figure like a man labouring at some task, with knees bent, known simply as the one on his knees. Both arms are raised and outstretched, and his right foot is over the Dragon's head.

The namelessness of this constellation suggests that it is not of Greek origin, but probably from the Near East. Van der Waerden (*EW* 2.68) identifies it with Babylonian UR.KU 'Dog'. Greek astronomers called it simply ὁ ἐν γόνασι (var. γούνασι): Eudox. fr. 17, Hi. 1.2.6, Gem. 3.8, Ptol. *Alm.* 7.5.7. A. uses the allusive τοῦ ἐν γόνασιν (669) and without

COMMENTARY: 63-64

art. (66), sim. ὁ γνὺξ | ἥμενος (591–2) and αἰεὶ γνύξ (615), also εἴδωλον
with an epithet such as κεκμηός (73), ἀπευθές (270). Later writers identified the figure with various monster-slayers and other heroes, e.g. sch.
69 listing Heracles, Prometheus, Theseus, Tantalus, Thamyras, Ixion.
In Latin the constellation appears as *Engonasin* (Cic. fr. 12, Man. 5.646),
Ingeniculatus (Vitr. 9.4.5), *Nixus* (Cic. fr. 33.45), *nisus in genibus* (Vitr. 9.4.4),
nixa genu species (Man. 5.645), and finally *Hercules* (Hyg. 2.6.1) became
standardised as the modern name. Allen 238, Boll–Gundel in Roscher
vi 896ff., Rehm in *RE* 5.2563.

63 τῆς δ' ἀγχοῦ A. is taking the Dragon's head as the starting-
point from which to find Engonasin, and the pronoun therefore refers
back to κεφαλή (61); cf. 45, 137, 188, 282, all with similar reference to
preceding lines. But the traditional αὐτοῦ, 'there', does not make sense
with τῆς, though frequent enough by itself in similar transitions, at the
beginning of the line, e.g. 71, 197, 225. Maass therefore read τῇ as adv.
reinforcing αὐτοῦ, and this has been accepted by Mair, 'right there',
and Martin 'dans la même région'. But the adverbs would then seem to
refer specifically to the position just described on the arctic circle, as if
it were also the position of Engonasin. The sense required is clearly
given by sch. ἀντὶ τοῦ συνεγγύς, and more precisely πλησίον δὲ τῆς
κεφαλῆς. Moreover Eudoxus wrote (fr. 17) παρὰ δὲ τὴν κεφαλήν, and
the Latin translators seem to imply that they understood the sense as
'near': Germ. 65 *haut procul*, Avien. 170–1 *oculosque in proxima mundi | de-
clines*. Buhle's ἀγχοῦ is therefore very plausible, and was adopted by
Voss. It is palaeographically close to αὐτοῦ, goes well with the gen. τῆς,
and gives the precise sense required. A. does not use ἀγχοῦ elsewhere,
but he does have ἄγχι c. gen. in similar contexts (254, 403). The use of
ἀγχοῦ c. gen. is also Homeric (ω 709, ζ 5).

μογέοντι ... ἀνδρὶ ἐοικός Cf. Homeric ἐοικώς with ἀνδρί (Ε 604, κ
278) and with part. act. (Ο 586, λ 608); see also 91, 183, 278, 340, 444,
449, 512, 1126. The kneeling position suggests straining hard at some
great labour, hence also κάμνον (66), κεκμηότος (73). Cf. A.R. 1.739 μογέοντι ἐοικώς, Theoc. 1.41 κάμνοντι τὸ καρτερὸν ἀνδρὶ ἐοικώς.

κυλίνδεται Sch. οὐχ οὕτω δὲ αὐτὸ κυλίνδεται, ἀλλὰ συγκατα-
φερομένῳ τῷ οὐρανῷ συμφέρεται. Sometimes A. chooses a verb of
motion that also suits the figure being described, e.g. εἰλεῖται (46), but
there is no double sense here. Cf. 197, 539, and, of an artificial model,
530.

64 εἴδωλον Again of this constellation 73, 270; and of others 370,
383, 449, 653. A.R. 3.1004, of Ariadne's crown, πάννυχος οὐρανίοις
ἐνελίσσεται εἰδώλοισιν, recalls especially 383.

τὸ μὲν οὔτις ἐπίσταται Q.S. 12.33 τόν γ' οὔτις ἐπίσταται.

201

ἀμφαδόν Cf. adj. in ἀμφαδὰ ἔργα (τ 391, A.R. 3.615). In Homer the adv. means 'openly' (Apollon. *Lex.*, p. 27 Bekker φανερῶς), and is used with verbs of action and speech, e.g. α 296 ἠὲ δόλῳ ἢ ἀμφαδόν. A. gives the adv. a different slant, 'definitely', 'with certainty'; cf. 95, describing the conspicuousness of Arcturus. A.R. 4.1511 reverts to the Homeric sense with εἴ μοι θέμις ἀμφαδὸν εἰπεῖν. Q.S. 14.54 ἀμφαδὸν εἰσοράασθαι. A. also has ἀναφανδόν (771).

εἰπεῖν In old sense of 'name'; cf. A 90 ἦν Ἀγαμέμνονα εἴπῃς.

65 ὅτινι Epic ὅτις (323; α 47) declines only in the second part of the compound. Homer has acc. ὅτινα (θ 204, ο 395), dat. ὅτεῳ (β 114), and Delph. dat. ὅτινι appears in *IG* 2².1126.25. Similar is the Attic use of gen. ὅτου and dat. ὅτῳ (Th. 1.23.5, 1.36.1). Here the only variant that suits metre and sense is ὅτινι (if we allow that οὐδὲ τίνι is a scholarly correction), and there is no reason to reject it. Chantraine 1.280, Schwyzer 1.617.

κρέμαται κεῖνος πόνῳ The v.l. πόνος is supported by sch. (Q) οὐδὲ ᾧτινι ὁ τοσοῦτος ἐπήρτηται πόνος, and sch. (S) οὐδέ τινι ἐκεῖνος ὁ πόνος ἐπίκειται. But the trouble is not impending: it is there all the time. Besides, this interpretation merely repeats the first question, who the figure is. πόνος is a corruption influenced by κεῖνος. The second question is what he is labouring at, and this is how the Latin translations understand it: Germ. 66 *non illi nomen, non magni causa laboris*, Avien. 174 *cuius latuit quoque causa laboris*.

The sense of κρέμαται has also been in dispute. LSJ take it as equivalent to ὀκλάζει, presumably on the basis of sch.(S) ὀκλάζει ἐκ τοῦ καμάτου. This is to understand πόνῳ as 'exhaustion', whereas it is much more likely to mean a task that the figure is labouring at, as seen eternally in action in the sky. Martin suggests 'pour quel travail il est suspendu au ciel', referring to the same verb in 447. But in 447 κρέμαται describes the position of the Hydra's tail hanging over the Centaur. Here Martin's meaning goes awkwardly with a dat. of purpose. Ceporinus' Latin version, *cui incumbat ille labori*, gives the sense required by the context, and by the poet's imaginative style, and most modern translators agree with it, e.g. Mair 'on what task he is bent'. Admittedly there appears to be no exact parallel for this use of κρέμασθαι c. dat., but cf., in a different figurative sense, Pi. *O.* 6.74-5 μῶμος ἐξ ἄλλων κρέμαται φθονεόντων | τοῖς.

αὔτως 'Just' the allusive phrase, not a real name. See note on 21.

66 ἐν γόνασιν Without article, like αἰεὶ γνύξ (615); both phrases receive some emphasis from their position in enjambment. See note on 63-70.

τὸ δ' αὖτ' The neut. takes up εἴδωλον (64). There is thus an alternation of neut. and masc., perhaps intended to contrast the star group with the personality imposed on it. The antithesis in τὸ μὲν (64) ... τὸ δ' is between our ignorance of the name and our clear perception of the form: we do not know what it is, but on the other hand (αὖτε), and this is the important thing, we can describe the figure in detail.

κάμνον Not in the sense of fatigue (Erren 'ermattet'), but of hard work: cf. ξ 65 ὅς οἱ πολλὰ κάμῃσι, θεὸς δ' ἐπὶ ἔργον ἀέξῃ.

67 ὀκλάζοντι A crouching or squatting posture with knees bent. Homer has only μετοκλάζει (N 281), of a coward crouching and shifting from leg to leg. In S. *OC* 196 ὀκλάσας describes a sitting position, in X. *An.* 6.1.10 ὤκλαζε a movement in the Persian (or Cossack) dance ὄκλασμα. Sch. (Q) 69 give a late interpretation of this figure as Heracles sagging under the weight of the sky: τὸν οὐρανὸν αὐτὸς ἀντεβάστασε καὶ πρὸς τὸ βάρος ὤκλασεν. For A.'s meaning see note on 65 κρέμαται. Cf. 517 ὀκλάς, A.R. 3.122 ὀκλαδόν, Nonn. *D.* 30.48 γούνατι ... ὀκλάζοντι. See metrical note on 416 κυμαίνοντι.

ὤμων The stars β and δ Herculis are the right and left shoulders respectively. Nonn. *D.* 1.317 ἐπ' ἀμφοτέρων δέ οἱ ὤμων. Here ἀπ' is preferable with ἀείρονται. Cf. Hes. *Th.* 671 χεῖρες ἀπ' ὤμων ἀΐσσοντο.

68 χεῖρες ἀείρονται The right arm and hand are probably the stars γ ω Herculis, the left arm and hand μ ξ ο. Since Eudoxus puts the right hand on the Tropic of Cancer (fr. 66), though A. actually omits this detail in his corresponding passage at 488–9, this star must be ω Herculis, not γ Serpentis, as Manitius supposed (*Hi.* p. 368). The Farnese globe shows the arm bent and the hand on the Tropic. In Renaissance star-maps the right hand also holds a club, added after the identification of the figure with Hercules had become standardised.

τάνυται Once in Homer P 393 τάνυται δέ τε πᾶσα διαπρό, of an oxhide being stretched, otherwise here and 284. The stem is athematic (in place of τανύεται); cf. αἴνυται (504, 603), ἀρνύμενος (640). Chantraine 302, Schwyzer 1.696, Shipp 146–7.

69 ὀργυιήν A. is recalling ι 325 ὅσον τ' ὄργυιαν ἐγὼν ἀπέκοψα, κ 167 πεῖσμα δ' ὅσον τ' ὄργυιαν ἐϋστρεφές· cf. Ψ 327 ὅσον τ' ὄργυι' ὑπὲρ αἴης. But Homeric ὄργυια is proparoxytone with final α short. Voss, who restored the Homeric form here and in 196, with no more comment than 'dem Freunde des Altedlen geben wir ὄργυιαν zurück', has been followed by Maass, Martin and Erren. But Eustathius (ad ι 325) comments that this noun later became oxytone, and Hdn Gr. 2.613 notes that the change of accent went with a change in the length of the final -α. Hence Attic ὀργυιά in X. *Mem.* 2.3.19, sch. Arat. 69, and Hsch. The Ionic form is then ὀργυιή, as in Hp. *Morb.* 4.7 (546, 20) μεταρθέντα δ' ὁκόσον ὀργυιήν, of wild plants. The manuscripts are virtually unanimous here and in 196 (Pal. gr. 40 has ὀργυιάν at 196, but this is copied and corrected in Vat. 1371). A. means that the arms are extended at full stretch, as in measuring a fathom of rope; he is not using the term as a measure of angular distance.

μέσσῳ δ' ἐφύπερθε καρήνῳ Eudox. fr. 17 ὑπὲρ τῆς κεφαλῆς τὸν δεξιὸν πόδα ἔχων. The Dragon's head is thought of as being the top of that figure (cf. 54 ἀνατρέχει), so that the foot which lies just beyond it is seen as being above it. There may be also the suggestion that when the Dragon's head is at its highest altitude, the Kneeler's foot to the south of it will be higher in the sky. In Homer ἐφύπερθε is always adv. (same *sedes* Ι 213, ω 645, δ 150, ι 383). The prepositional use would normally be c. gen., as in A.R. 2.393 (cf. ὕπερθε 484), and Hipparchus reports that Attalus so altered A.'s text παρὰ τὸ βούλημα τοῦ ποιητοῦ, whereas the dative ἐν πᾶσι τοῖς βιβλίοις γράφεται (1.4.9). The dative may be meant to bring out the force of the prefix ἐφ-, and the sense of being right on top of the Dragon's head: the star in question is indeed very close to it.

70 δεξιτεροῦ ποδός Hipparchus finds fault with both Eudoxus (fr. 17) and A. for making this the right foot: παρ' ἑκατέρῳ γὰρ αὐτῶν ἠγνόηται· τὸν γὰρ ἀριστερὸν ἔχει πόδα ὁ ἐν γόνασιν ἐπὶ τῆς κεφαλῆς τοῦ Δράκοντος, καὶ οὐ τὸν δεξιόν (1.2.6). Elsewhere he refers to the error as a mere oversight: παρεωρακέναι μοι δοκοῦσιν ..., ἀλλ' οὐ διημαρτηκέναι (1.4.9). The conspicuously angled line of stars η σ τ φ χ Herculis, which may have originally suggested the idea of a kneeling figure, must be the right leg, if the figure is to be conceived as facing the earth (see note on 60). The bent left leg is then represented by the stars π θ ι Herculis, and the last, the foot, lies close to the centre of the Dragon's head, whereas the right leg is well to the west of it. Germanicus takes note of Hipparchus' criticism and translates *Serpentis capiti figit uestigia laeua* (69); cf. Hyg. 6.1. But Avien. 192 remains faithful to his model.

σκολιοῖο A.R. 4.1541 δράκων σκολιὴν εἰλιγμένος ἔρχεται οἶμον. Greg. Naz. *Carm.* 4.101 σκολιοῖο δράκοντος.

71–73 The Crown

Ariadne's Crown is at the kneeling figure's back. This is a small and not very bright constellation, but its well-defined curve of stars (θ β α γ δ ε Coronae) is easily recognised. As a constellation it was known to Pherecydes (sch. λ 320), and its morning rising appeared in Euctemon's parapegma (Gem. *Cal.* Libra 7). To distinguish it from the later Southern Crown Ptolemy calls it Στέφανος βόρειος (7.5.6). In Latin it is *Corona* (Cic. fr. 13, Germ. 71, Man. 1.319, V. *G.* 1.222, Ov. *AA* 1.558), and now

Corona Borealis. The association of the Crown with Ariadne may have originated with Epimenides (fr. 25), but it is first specifically mentioned here and in A.R. 3.1003 ἀστερόεις στέφανος, τόν τε κλείουσ' Ἀριάδνης. Cf. Call. fr. 110 (Cat. 66).59–60, Man. 5.253 *clara Ariadnaeae quondam monumenta coronae, Anecd. Bas.* (Maass *Aratea* 384) *simili modo et de Corona Ariadnes. hanc enim per Dionysum quasi exornatam in carmine suo et ille Coronam manifeste, quod fabulationem primus reddidit, Catast.* 5, Tert. *Scorp.* 10.4 *facilius Aratus Persea et Cephea et Erigonam et Ariadnam inter sidera deliniabit,* Hyg. 2.5.1. Roscher VI 892ff., Allen 174ff.

71 αὐτοῦ A transitional adv., indicating that the Crown is in the same part of the sky: its position is defined more precisely in 73.

κἀκεῖνος This crasis is not Homeric (see Chantraine 1.85). It is attested by all MSS here, but not by M in 1137; cf. Call. frr. 257, 274.1, and Fraenkel on A.R. 1.83.

ἀγαυόν The manuscripts support ἀγαυός, which certainly makes good sense with Dionysus: in Homer it is used of gods and heroes. But here it seems somewhat otiose, whereas with the Crown the epithet makes a point in bringing out the importance of these stars as both legend and constellation. The stars themselves are not particularly bright (one of 2nd mag., one of 3rd, four of 4th), but the epithet conveys a sense of distinction, not just brightness: A. uses it again of stars in 90, 392, 469, 506. The Latin translators, though not normally reliable evidence for the Greek text, take the epithet with the Crown: Cicero with typical hyperbole, *eximio posita est fulgore Corona* (fr. 13), Germ. 71 *clara Ariadnaeo sacrata est igne Corona.* Cf. Ov. *Epist.* 17.151 *claramque Coronam,* Man. 1.319 *claro uolat orbe Corona,* sch. ἐὰν δὲ "ἀγαυόν" ᾖ, τὸν ἐπίσημον (σημαίνει δὲ καὶ τὸν ἔνδοξον), ὅτι τὸν τῆς ἐρωμένης στέφανον ἀγαυὸν ἐποίησεν ἐν οὐρανῷ, τουτέστι λαμπρόν.

72 σῆμ' ἔμεναι Word-play on two meanings of σῆμα, 'memorial' (e.g. Β 814) and 'constellation'. Man. 1.323 *Cnosia desertae fulgent monumenta puellae.*

Διόνυσος ... Ἀριάδνης A. does not enlarge on the romantic myth of Dionysus and Ariadne, presumably because he does not regard it as being relevant to his main purpose. Sch. 71 τὸν κίσσινον στέφανον ὃν ἐφόρει μετὰ θάνατον τῆς Ἀριάδνης. Nonnus imitates this line in *D.* 48.971 Στέφανον περίκυκλον ἀποιχομένης Ἀριάδνης. Alex. Aphr. *in Mete.* 362b10 (on the earth's habitable zone) ὁ στέφανος ὁ ἐν τοῖς ἄστροις, ὃν λέγουσι τῆς Ἀριάδνης ὄντα ὑπὸ Διονύσου κατατερισθῆναι (ὁ γοῦν Ἄρατος οὕτως περὶ αὐτοῦ λέγει "αὐτοῦ ... Ἀριάδνης"). The Crown passed overhead for observers in Greek latitudes.

73 νώτῳ ὕπο στρέφεται Hi. 1.2.7 τὸν δὲ Στέφανον ὁ μὲν Εὔδοξός φησιν ὑπὸ τὸν νῶτον τοῦ ἐν γούνασι κεῖσθαι (fr. 18). The back star must be ζ Herculis, more strictly the right flank (Hi. 2.2.8); but this line may explain why the figure on the Farnese Atlas globe has his back turned to the observer. Since the Crown lies near the middle and to the west of the figure, ὑπό means not literally 'below' nor astronomically 'to the south of', but 'close to', as a small object dominated by the proximity of a tall one, e.g. B 866 ὑπὸ Τμώλῳ γεγαῶτας. Editors have preserved the compound verb of the manuscripts, but the prefix here does not qualify the verb, as it does in 512, 593, or in the normal sense of 'turn back', 'return'; the Crown does not 'revolve beneath' (LSJ) the kneeling figure's back; ὕπο gives its relative position, στρέφεται its circular movement, and the two pieces of information are quite distinct. Cf. 96 ποσσὶν ὕπο, 450 Διδύμοις ὕπο.

κεκμηότος Rare form of epic part., Λ 802 κεκμηότας in same *sedes*.

74–87 The Serpent-holder and the Serpent
This large and complex star-group contains two intertwined constellations, which are always listed separately in Greek star catalogues. The origin is unknown: perhaps the basic group was the snake, and the holder added to it by the Greeks. The name Ὀφιοῦχος is constant from Eudoxus (fr. 19) to Ptolemy (*Alm.* 7.5.13), likewise Ὄφις, but to avoid confusion with other star-snakes it is sometimes called ὁ ἐχόμενος Ὄφις (Eudox. fr. 66), ὁ Ὄφις ὃν ἔχει Ὀφιοῦχος (Hi. 2.2.2), Ὄφις Ὀφιούχου (Ptol. *Alm.* 7.5.14). In Latin the names are *Ophiuchus* (Cic. fr. 14), the standard title from antiquity to the present, with the variations *Anguitenens* (Man. 5.389), *Anguifer* (Col. 11.2.49), *Serpentarius* (*Catast.* 6), *Anguis* (Cic. fr. 15), *Serpens* (Germ. 86), which is now the standard name. At a later date Ophiuchus was identified with Asclepius (sch., and Hyg. 2.14.5), because of his association with the serpent. Roscher VI 920ff., Allen 297ff., 374ff.

74 νώτῳ ... πελάει The anaphora of the noun, supplemented by a verb which repeats the sense of ὕπο, makes an unusual kind of transition. Its purpose is to take us back to the Kneeler, after the brief sidestep to incorporate the Crown, so that we can now proceed from the Kneeler in a different direction to identify the next constellation. πελάω, a poetic form of πελάζω, appears first in *h.Hom.* 744 γῇ πελάαν. A. uses it again (272) in a similar context. Cf. [Opp.] *C.* 1.515.

κεφαλῇ ... ἄκρη The head of the kneeling figure. Since this is represented by only one star (α Herculis), ἄκρη must be meant to describe it as being at the southern extremity of the constellation. The dat. depends on πάρ, awkwardly separated by the verb; cf. Ω 254 Ἕκτορος ὠφέλετ' ἀντὶ ... πεφάσθαι (K–G 1.532–3), Eudox. fr. 19 πλησίον δ' ἐστὶ τῆς τούτου κεφαλῆς ἡ τοῦ Ὀφιούχου κεφαλή. Cf. W. Hübner, *Rh. M.* 133 (1992) 264–74.

75 κεφαλὴν Ὀφιούχεον The star α Ophiuchi. These two figures lie upside down relative to each other, so that their heads are almost side by side. That of Ophiuchus is the brighter (2nd mag.), and therefore makes a good starting-point for the identification of the rest of the constellation. This is probably why A. refers to it with the emphatic ἐκείνης at the end of the line. The adj. occurs only in A. (also 488, 521), and is probably the poet's own invention.

76 αὐτόν The rest of the constellation; cf. 433.

ἐπιφράσσαιο The sense includes both noticing and recognising; cf. 40 with note, and the simple verb in 374, 745. The potential opt. without κεν is occasional in Homer, e.g. γ 231 ῥεῖα θεός γ᾽ ἐθέλων καὶ τηλόθεν ἄνδρα σαώσαι. Cf. 96, 248, 1144, Call. fr. 57.1 αὐτὸς ἐπιφράσσαιτο, *H.* 5.103 τὸ μὲν οὐ παλινάγρετον αὖθι γένοιτο, Theoc. 2.33–4 τὸν ἐν Ἅιδα | κινήσαις ἀδάμαντα. Chantraine 2.217, K–G 1.225–6.

φαεινόμενον A. lengthens -ον at a caesura again in 577, 706; cf. A 85 θεοπρόπιον ὅ τι οἶσθα. Spitzner 61. On the meaning of φαίνομαι in A. see note on 41. Most translators take the participle here to mean 'bright', e.g. Mair 'starlit', Voss and Erren 'leuchtenden', Martin 'reconnaissable à son éclat', but what A. means is that you will recognize it as clearly visible: so Zannoni. Ophiuchus is not a brilliant constellation, and A. picks out only the head and shoulders as reasonably bright. The four-word line seems to add a touch of grandeur to the impression A. gives of Ophiuchus, which extends into the southern hemisphere as far as the Scorpion (85).

77 ἀγλαοὶ ὦμοι The right shoulder has two stars close together, β γ Ophiuchi, the left shoulder is κ. These three are all 3rd-mag. stars, and therefore not as brilliant as A.'s description would suggest. Hipparchus notes that they are less bright than the principal stars of Cassiepeia (1.5.21).

78 εἴδονται Of visibility; cf. Θ 599 πάντα δὲ εἴδεται ἄστρα.

διχόμηνι σελήνη Hi. 1.4.16 τοὺς γὰρ ἐν τοῖς ὤμοις τοῦ Ὀφιούχου φήσας λαμπροὺς εἶναι, ὥστε καὶ ἐν πανσελήνῳ ἂν θεωρεῖσθαι, 1.5.21 τῶν ἐν τοῖς ὤμοις τοῦ Ὀφιούχου, οὕς φησι καὶ ἐν τῇ πανσελήνῳ ἐκφανεῖς εἶναι. Cf. Hi. 1.6.10, on the Ram, οὔτε λαμπροὺς ἀστέρας ἔχοντα, δυναμένους ἂν καὶ ἐν σελήνη λαμπρῶς θεωρεῖσθαι. Full moon was traditionally a convenient time for determining the brightest stars, and it seems likely that the later grading of stars into six magnitudes was related to their visibility at different lunar phases. Cf. 189 παμμήνιδι, 228 σελήνη alone, and the opposite situation in 471 νεόμηνι. Man. 1.469–70 *medio cum luna implebitur orbe,* | *certa nitent mundo tum lumina.* A.R. 1.1231–2 imitates this technical language in a diffferent context, διχόμηνις ἀπ' αἰθέρος αὐγάζουσα | βάλλε σεληναίη: cf. 4.167.

79 εἰσωποί Once in Homer, Ο 653 εἰσωποὶ δ' ἐγένοντο νεῶν, where the meaning seems to be active, 'facing', though the precise point of it in the context is disputed. So A.R. 2.751. A. uses it in the passive sense, 'visible', here and in 122.

τελέθοιεν Frequent in Homer in sense of 'be', e.g. Μ 347 ζαχρηεῖς τελέθουσι, in same *sedes*.

χέρες The right hand is ν Ophiuchi, the left δ ε, and all three stars are shared with the Serpent; cf. Hi. 1.4.17 οἱ ἐν ταῖς χερσὶ τοῦ 'Οφιούχου ἀστέρες κοινοί εἰσι καὶ τοῦ "Οφεως, confirming 82. All are 3rd-mag. stars.

μάλα ἴσαι Homeric εἶσαι at end of line (ε 175, ζ 271) is preferred by Buhle, Voss, Martin and Erren, with the support of a group of Hipparchus manuscripts. But those of A. attest ἴσαι, the only form used by A. elsewhere. Cf. 377 ἐπὶ ἴσα. It is the reading of most other editors, from Aldus to Maass and Mair.

80 λεπτῇ γὰρ καὶ τῇ καὶ τῇ The reading of M and S λεπτή γὰρ τῇ καὶ τῇ leaves the line one syllable short. Scribal conjecture filled the gap by adding either ἐξ- to ἐπιδέδρομεν or καί before the first τῇ. The first is read by editors before Voss, but it is difficult to see the point of the additional prefix, which also leaves the line without an acceptable caesura. Voss preferred the second, which seems to be supported by sch. καὶ τῇ ἀριστερᾷ γὰρ χειρὶ καὶ τῇ ἄλλῃ, ἤγουν τῇ δεξιᾷ. This reading was adopted by Bekker and Mair. Maass filled the gap with λεπτοτέρη, on the strength of the continuation of the sch., λεπτοτέρα καὶ ἀμυδροτέρα ὡς πρὸς σύγκρισιν τῶν ὤμων ἐπίκειται λαμπηδών. This has been accepted by Martin and Erren. I have followed Voss, on the ground that λεπτή is attested by all manuscripts and is a better antithesis to ἀγλαοί than the comparative.

ἐπιδέδρομεν αἴγλη A. is recalling ζ 45 λευκὴ δ' ἐπιδέδρομεν αἴγλη, and is imitated in turn by by A.R. 2.670–1 λεπτὸν δ' ἐπιδέδρομε νυκτὶ | φέγγος and Opp. *C.* 3.37 ὀλίγη δ' ἐπιδέδρομεν αἴγλη. For the hiatus τῇ ἐπιδ. see note on 41.

81 ἐπόψιαι A. means that they are only relatively faint, and so still quite visible. In fact the hand stars are of the same magnitude as the shoulder stars, the only distinction being that β in the right shoulder and δ in the left hand are slightly brighter than the other four. Cf. Hi. 1.4.16–17 δοκεῖ δέ μοι καὶ περὶ τῶν ἐν ταῖς χερσὶ τοῦ 'Οφιούχου ἀστέρων κατὰ τὸ μέγεθος αὐτῶν ἀγνοεῖν ... οἱ δ' ἐν τῷ "Οφει ἀστέρες, ὃν ἔχει ὁ Ὀφιοῦχος, οὐ λειπόμενοί εἰσι τῇ λαμπρότητι τῶν ἐν τοῖς ὤμοις. The hand stars are part of the Serpent. A. has ἐπόψιαι again in 258, of the Pleiades. Cf. *h.Hom.* 3.496. The fem. pl. both here and at 258 could have been due to the influence of the preceding fem. pl.; but cf. 911, 918, 942, also 625, 628.

ἐλαφραί Elsewhere of stars 337, 519, but only in A. The variant ἀμαυραί comes from the gloss in M.

82 Ὄφιος See note on 74–87. In modern maps and catalogues the Serpent is sometimes divided into two parts, *Serpens caput* and *Serpens cauda* (*sic*), one on either side of Ophiuchus. For the Ionic gen. cf. Hes. *Th.* 322, Nonn. *D.* 25.144 Ὀφιοῦχος Ὄφιν δινωτὸν ἀείρων.

πεπονήαται Ion. 3rd pl., normally πεπονέαται (Hdt. 2.63); cf. βεβλέαται (174, 371), κέαται (492). In epic the vowel is sometimes lengthened, e.g. Β 90 πεποτήαται, Λ 657 βεβλήαται, Φ 206 πεφοβήατο. Antim. fr. 39 πεπονήατο, A.R. 2.263 πεπονήατο. The form in -είαται properly belongs to stems in -ει, e.g. κείαται (ω 527), and the variant here is probably a corruption due to confusion of vowel sounds. Chantraine 1.477, Spitzner 151.

The verb is chosen to suggest hands struggling to hold the serpent in their grasp; cf. Ο 447 πεπόνητο καθ᾽ ἵππους. The gen. is of that with which the action is occupied; cf. 758 κείνων πεπόνησο, 1030 μέλιτός τε καὶ ἔργων εἰλίσσονται.

83 δινεύει A lively verb, describing position but suggesting movement. There seems to be some verbal echo of Δ 541 δινεύοι κατὰ μέσσον, of a man in battle. Cf. 162, also pass. 455, 489, 510.

ἐμμενές Elsewhere with αἰεί, as in Κ 361 and ι 386. The adverb brings out the permanance of the constellations. Cf. 339, 891.

ἐπαρηρώς Intrans. perf. part. only here. In Homer the verb has the sense of fastening securely in building, whether trans., as in Ξ 167 θύρας σταθμοῖσιν ἔπηρσε, or intrans., Μ 456 μία δὲ κληῒς ἐπαρήρει. Cf. *h.Hom.* 4.50. Mair and LSJ construe with ποσσίν, but ποσσὶν ... ἀμφοτέροισι is a phrase designed to go with ἐπιθλίβει, and the part. is better taken absolutely: cf. 482 ἀρηρότος.

84 ποσσίν The right foot is the 3rd-mag. star θ Ophiuchi, the left the faint stars ψ ω ρ, which in Ptolemy are end of leg and foot (*Alm.* 7.5.13). Hipparchus corrects A. here, noting that only the left leg comes close to the Scorpion, whereas the right leg is bent back: τῇ δὲ ἀριστερᾷ μόνον κνήμῃ βέβηκεν ἀποτεταμένη, μεταξὺ κειμένη τοῦ τε μετώπου καὶ τοῦ στήθους τοῦ Σκορπίου· τὸ δὲ δεξιὸν σκέλος ἔχει συνεσταλμένον (1.4.15).

ἐπιθλίβει First attested here, but not noted in LSJ. The size of the figure suggests that heavy pressure is being put on the Scorpion.

85 Σκορπίον Emphatically introduced at the beginning of the line after the build-up of μέγα θηρίον. This must have been one of the earliest constellations to be named, being a well-defined group with many bright stars in it, and easily identified with the creature it is named after. Latin writers call it *Scorpio* (Vitr. 9.3.3), *Scorpios* (Hor. *Carm.* 2.17.17), *Scorpius* (V. *G.* 1.35), and *Nepa* (Man. 2.32), and the standard modern name is Scorpius (Scorpio only in astrology). Considering the brilliance of the Scorpion, it is interesting that A. introduces it here so briefly and without any elaboration. This is because it is so conspicuous and familiar that the observer does not need the assistance of any other stars as a guide to it. It could be said rather that it is the Scorpion that helps us to identify the feet of Ophiuchus. A. has reserved a special passage for the Scorpion later (634–68), where its rising is relevant to the myth of Artemis and Orion. It is also mentioned in 304–7, 402–3, 438, 505–6, 546 and 621. The Scorpion was (and still is) entirely south of the equator, and mostly also south of the ecliptic.

ὀφθαλμῷ The reading of the MSS is supported by sch. τῷ μὲν ἀριστερῷ ποδὶ ἐπὶ τοῦ ὀφθαλμοῦ βαίνων, τῷ δὲ δεξιῷ ἐπὶ τοῦ θώρακος, and ὁ γὰρ εἷς ποῦς κεῖται μεταξὺ τοῦ ὀφθαλμοῦ καὶ τοῦ θώρακος. But Hipparchus, without quoting the actual verses, comments: ὁ Ἄρατος ὀρθόν φησι κεῖσθαι αὐτὸν τῇ θέσει βεβηκότα ἔν τε τοῖς ὀφθαλμοῖς τοῦ Σκορπίου καὶ τῷ στήθει (1.4.15). Hence Cic. fr. 15.5, Avien. 240, and *Arat. Lat. oculos*. Hipparchus does not elsewhere refer to an eye star in the Scorpion, but calls the three bright leading stars (β δ π) the forehead, e.g. 3.5.8 ὁ μέσος τῶν ἐν τῷ μετώπῳ τοῦ Σκορπίου τριῶν λαμπρῶν ἀστέρων: cf. Ptol. 8.1.29. A. is presumably thinking of a single star, β or δ Scorpii, and it could equally well represent one eye or both eyes. Hipparchus may simply be interpreting A.'s sg. as pl. Cf. 560.

ἐν is to be taken with both ὀφθαλμῷ and θώρηκι: cf. 713. The ἀπὸ κοινοῦ construction has a limited use in Homer, but cf. μ 27 ἢ ἁλὸς ἢ ἐπὶ γῆς. For examples with ἐν cf. Alcm. *PMG* 98 θοίναις δὲ καὶ ἐν θιάσοισιν, S. *OT* 1205 τίς ἄταις ἀγρίαις, τίς ἐν πόνοις, Ar. *Ach.* 533 μήτε γῇ μήτ' ἐν ἀγορᾷ, *Eq.* 567, 610, Nic. *Ther.* 640 πετάλοισι καὶ ἐν καλύκεσσι. See K–G 1.550, Kiefner 27–9. For other types see 103 ἀρχαίων, 842 ὁ γ'.

θώρηκι The three stars σ α τ Scorpii, the middle one of which is the 1st-mag. star Antares (Hi. 3.3.6 ὁ μέσος τῶν ἐν τῷ στήθει καὶ λαμπρότατος). Hipparchus points out that the right foot of Ophiuchus cannot be represented as standing on the breast of the Scorpion (see note on 84), and quotes Eudoxus with approval: τὸν γὰρ δεξιὸν πόδα αὐτοῦ ὑπὲρ τὸ σῶμα κεῖσθαί φησι τοῦ Σκορπίου, ὡς καὶ ἔχει τῇ ἀληθείᾳ, καὶ οὐκ ἐπὶ τοῦ στήθους (1.4.15). For the same reason he also finds fault with A.'s ὀρθός as a description of Ophiuchus' stance.

βεβηκώς Perhaps a hint of Archil. 114.4 ἀσφαλέως βεβηκὼς ποσσί.

86 Ὄφις See note on 74–87.

στρέφεται The verb suggests both the circling movement, as in 498, 512, and the apparently writhing form of the Serpent figure; cf. 83 δινεύει.

μετὰ χερσί A Homeric phrase, of holding something that lies between the hands: Λ 184 ἔχε δ' ἀστεροπὴν μετὰ χερσίν (same *sedes*), Λ 4, Ε 344.

87 δεξιτερῇ . . . σκαιῇ Cf. σκαιῇ δεξιτερῇ δ' (Α 501, Hes. *Th.* 179). In Homer only of hands, in A. also of other parts of the body: 70, 175, 614, 688; 162, 254, 272, 361.

ὀλίγος . . . πολλός See notes on 41 and 42. The right hand (ν Ophiuchi) holds the Serpent's tail, a short line of 3rd- and 4th-mag. stars (ζ η θ Serpentis). The head section is a longer line with more stars, including one of 2nd mag., rising northward from the left hand (δ ε Ophiuchi). The brightest are μ ε α δ β γ κ ι Serpentis, the last four forming a well-defined head. Q.S. 12.313 οὐρεῖ τ' οὔτε λίην χθαμαλῷ οὔθ' ὑψόθι πολλῷ.

88–90 The Claws
Originally a part of the Scorpion, the Claws were detached to form a separate constellation when the Zodiac of twelve signs was created. The name Χηλαί remained in use from Eudoxus (fr. 71) to Hipparchus (3.3.4), but an alternative name Ζυγόν makes its first appearance in Hi. 3.1.5 (*l. susp.* Manitius), and this is the name mostly used by Geminus, e.g. in his list of the Zodiac (1.2); cf. Manetho 2.136–7 Χηλαί θ', ἃς καὶ δὴ μετεφήμισαν ἀνέρες ἱροὶ | καὶ Ζυγὸν ἐκλήισσαν. Ptolemy used both names, the former especially for the constellation (*Alm.* 8.1.1), the latter for the astrological sign (*Tetr.* 2.3.33). The idea of the Balance may have been prompted by the proximity of Virgo, identified with the goddess of Justice, but it is later associated with the equinox, which holds the year in balance: V. *G.* 1.208 *Libra die somnique pares ubi fecerit horas*; cf. Man. 1.267. *Libra* appears also in Hor. *Carm.* 2.17.17, Ov. *Fast.* 4.386, Vitr. 9.3.2, Hyg. 1.7.1, Avien. 59, and is now the standard name. *Chelae* is affected by Cic. fr. 33.3, V. *G.* 1.33, Germ. 89, Luc. 1.659, Avien. 250. *Iugum* is rare, e.g. Cic. *Div.* 2.98, and Man. 1.611 has *iuga Chelarum*.

88 καὶ δή As if said by instructor to pupil, pointing out something new and interesting; cf. Ar. *Pax* 178 καὶ δὴ καθορῶ τὴν οἰκίαν τὴν τοῦ Διός. Denniston 249.

211

οἱ I.e. the Serpent's; see note on 47.

παρακέκλιται Of adjacent position; cf. Call. *H.* 4.72 ὅλη Πελοπηὶς ὅση παρακέκλιται Ἰσθμῷ.

ἄκρα γένεια The most northerly star of the Serpent's head (ι Serpentis). A. identifies the group of β γ κ ι, which form the head, by referring to a constellation already introduced (the Crown), then draws the observer's eye back to the Serpent's coil (μ), in order to pass from there to the next constellation, the Claws.

89 νειόθι C. gen., as in Φ 317 νειόθι λίμνης. Cf. 386, 400, 437, of other astronomical positions.

σπείρης The coil is not obvious, but may be thought of as a curve running from δ Ophiuchi through μ to ε and α Serpentis.

ἐπιμαίεο Homeric verb, c. acc. 'grasp', e.g. in same *sedes* λ 531 ἐπεμαίετο κώπην. The imper. here recalls ε 344 ἐπιμαίεο νόστου. For the figurative use cf. A.R. 3.816 νόῳ ἐπεμαίεθ' ἕκαστα. A. uses the verb again, but c. gen., in 127.

90 φαέων Cf. Hes. fr. 252.4 φαέεσσι σελήνης, Call. *H.* 3.182 φάεα of daylight.

ἐπιδευέες Hi. 1.4.18 quotes this line with ἐπιδευέες and goes on to cite Attalus with ἐπιμεμφέες: φησὶ δὲ ὁ Ἄτταλος μὴ διὰ τὸ μικροὺς εἶναι τοὺς ἐν ταῖς Χηλαῖς ἀστέρας λέγειν τὸν Ἄρατον φαέων ἐπιμεμφέας αὐτὰς εἶναι, ἀλλὰ διὰ τὸ τέσσαρας μόνον εἶναι τοὺς πάντας ... οὐ δοκεῖ δέ μοι διὰ τοῦτο λέγειν αὐτὰς φαέων ἐπιμεμφέας καὶ μηδὲν ἀγαυάς, ἀλλ' ὡς ἂν μὴ λαμπράς.

The two variants were therefore in existence before Hipparchus, but the textual tradition of A. attests only ἐπιδευέες. Voss was the first editor to prefer 'das poetische ἐπιμεμφέες', and he has been followed by Maass, Martin and Erren. Voss relates the adj. to Homeric ἐπιμέμφεσθαί τινος, comparing περιμεμφής (109), and he explains ἐπιδευέες as a gloss. But it is difficult to reconcile the sense of ἐπιμεμφής with the context here. Voss takes it as active, and translates 'wegen der Lichter jedoch sehr klagen sie', though 'light' has to be understood as 'lack of light'. Martin's 'dépourvues de tout éclat' gives the sense required by the context, but it is hardly a translation of the Greek. Erren understands the adj. rather in the passive sense of 'nicht einwandfrei'. The editors who adopt this reading thus disagree about what it means. In Nic. fr. 74.15 and *AP* 6.260.3 (Gem.) the meaning is 'to be spurned'. It seems unlikely that A. would describe any sign set in the sky by Zeus as either 'complaining' or 'blameworthy'. The comparable περιμεμφής (109) is an epithet of war, and very appropriate in that context. It is not easy to account for the appearance of ἐπιμεμφέες so early in the tradition, but it might conceivably have arisen from a dittography of μὲν φαέων. At all events there is no justification for rejecting the united testimony of the manuscripts, supported by Hipparchus. It has the right sense for the context, and gives a characteristic echo of Homeric lines, e.g. φ 185, 253 βίης ἐπιδευέες. Cf. A.R. 1.866 γάμων ἐπιδευέες.

As we learn from Hi. 1.4.18, Attalus thought that A. called the Claws lack-lustre because they consisted of only four stars. Hipparchus maintains that it is not lack of numbers but lack of brightness that is relevant, aptly comparing 607 Χηλαὶ καὶ λεπτὰ φάουσαι. The four stars are β Librae (2nd mag.), α and σ (3rd), γ (4th). It is therefore not a distinguished constellation.

ἀγαυαί See note on 71.

91–146 BEAR'S TAIL GROUP: BOOTES, THE MAIDEN, AND NAMELESS STARS NEAR THE BEAR

91–95 Bootes

Behind the Bear is Arctophylax or Bootes, a conspicuous constellation containing the bright star Arcturus.

Bootes originated in the association of the bright star Arcturus with the seven stars of the Great Bear when these were known as the Wagon (see note on 27 Ἄρκτοι). The constellation itself may have been already known to the Babylonians, whose star šu.pa has been identified with Arcturus (Waerden EW 2.67). Thus Bootes represents the original name, while Arcturus and Arctophylax are consequential to the change to the Greek Ἄρκτος. The constellation is not an obvious group, but is devised as a human figure so that individual stars can be identified by reference to parts of the body. This figure is curiously devised around Arcturus, which is not a part of the body, and actually listed separately by Ptolemy as ὁ ὑπ' αὐτὸν ἀμόρφωτος (Alm. 7.5.5). Bootes first appears in ε 272 (see note on 585), as important for navigation; Hesiod refers to Arcturus as a calendar star (Op. 566, 610 and fr. 292). Eudoxus calls the constellation Arctophylax (fr. 24), A. both Arctophylax (92, 579, 721) and Bootes (92, 96, 136, 581, 608), Hipparchus Arctophylax when commenting directly on A. (2.2.2), elsewhere Bootes (1.2.5), Geminus (3.8) and Ptolemy (7.5.5) only Arctophylax. The later tendency to give mythical names to constellation figures gave Bootes such names as Arcas, son of Callisto; Icarus, father of Erigone; and Philomelus, son of Ceres (Hyg. 2.4). In Latin both Bootes and Arctophylax appear in Cic. fr. 16.1, Germ. 91, 139, Man. 1.316, but the former is the commoner and is the standard modern name. There are also such variations as Custos (Vitr. 9.4.1), Custos Vrsae (Ov. Fast. 2.153), Icarus (Prop. 2.33.24, Ov. Met. 10.450). Allen 92ff., Hähler in RE 3.717, Roscher VI 886ff.

91 ἐξόπιθεν δ' Ἑλίκης A. introduces the new section with the point of departure for the recognition of the constellations. This is one of the passages quoted by Hipparchus to prove that A. has used Eudoxus as his source (1.2.5). Eudoxus wrote ὄπισθεν δὲ τῆς Μεγάλης Ἄρκτου ἐστὶν ὁ Ἀρκτοφύλαξ (fr. 24). The brief passage also illustrates A.'s technique of combining close imitation with variation and poetic amplification.

ἐξόπιθεν as prep. c. gen. is post-Homeric, e.g. Ar. *Ach.* 868 ἐξόπισθέ μου.

ἐλάοντι From the left shoulder (γ Bootis) a line of stars runs northward to represent the left arm (λ) and hand (θ ι κ), as if raised above the end of the wagon-shaft (η Ursae Majoris).

92 Ἀρκτοφύλαξ See note on 91–95.

ἐπικλείουσι Once in Homer, in same *sedes*, but in the sense of 'praise': α 351 ἐπικλείουσ' ἄνθρωποι. Here the meaning is equivalent to ἐπίκλησιν καλέουσι (36, 544). Cf. A.R. 2.1156 ἐμὲ δ' αὐτὸν ἐπικλείοιτέ κεν Ἄργον.

93 οὕνεχ' Perhaps modelled on H 138ff. τὸν ἐπίκλησιν κορυνήτην | ἄνδρες κίκλησκον ... | οὕνεκ' ἄρ' ... κορύνῃ ῥήγνυσκε φάλαγγας.

ἀμαξαίης A new formation, probably on the analogy of Homeric ἀναγκαίη as noun (Z 85), as Ronconi suggests (197); cf. 813 γαληναίης, 818 σεληναίης. It is not an adj., as LSJ define it, but a substantive, as Martin notes: the two names are ingeniously joined together, as if hyphenated; cf. 182 Κυνοσουρίδος Ἄρκτου. Here the first name is doubly significant: it distinguishes the Great Bear from the Little, and it explains the name Bootes. Nonnus imitates in *D.* 47.252 ἀμαξαίης ἐπαφώμενον Ἀρκάδος Ἄρκτου.

ἐπαφώμενος The simple verb ἀφάω is Homeric (Z 322), as is ἀμφαφάω (δ 277), and may be derived from ἀφή in sense of 'touch'; but see Chantraine 1.355. The compound suggests a light touch (cf. Mosch. 2.50–1 ἐπαφώμενος ἠρέμα χερσὶ | πόρτιος), and was perhaps chosen by A. because Bootes' hand stars lie just a little above the end-star of the Wagon (η Ursae Majoris). Cf. *AP* 5.222.1 (Agath.) κιθάρης ἐπαφήσατο.

εἴδεται In Homeric *sedes* of A 228 εἴδεται εἶναι, but with sense of B 280 εἰδομένη κήρυκι. A.'s use with dependent part. seems to be an innovation.

94 πᾶς ἀρίδηλος Apart from Arcturus, Bootes is not a distinctive constellation: it has one star of 2nd mag. (ε the belt), and four of 3rd (β the head, γ δ shoulders, η left leg), and as a whole it does not make an obvious figure. A. is probably transferring the brilliance of Arcturus to the constellation as a whole.

ὑπὸ ζώνῃ The belt is ε Bootis, which Hipparchus calls ὁ ἐν τῇ ζώνῃ λαμπρός (3.2.1), τῶν ἐν τῇ ζώνῃ λαμπρότατος (3.3.7). The sch. give the name Arcturus to this star: ἕνα δὲ ἔχει ἐν μέσῃ τῇ ζώνῃ, ὅστις διὰ τὴν ὑπερβολὴν τῆς λαμπρότητος ἰδίως καὶ αὐτὸς λέγεται Ἀρκτοῦρος. On the strength of this and sch. A.R. 2.1099, which describes Arcturus as ἐπὶ τῆς ζώνης, Voss reads ἐπὶ. The scholia may have misunderstood Hipparchus; but there can be no doubt that ὑπό, in both senses of 'below' with reference to the figure and 'to the south of', accurately describes the position of Arcturus.

95 ἐξ ἄλλων Ἀρκτοῦρος On Arcturus see especially notes on 91–95 and 585. Here the 1st-mag. star is being distinguished from the rest of the constellation, because it is by far the brightest. The phrase ἐξ ἄλλων means essentially ἐκ πάντων. Cf. Σ 432, where ἐκ μέν μ' ἀλλάων repeats the sense of 431 ἐμοὶ ἐκ πασέων, also 1058, and 1056 ἔσχατος ἄλλων. The force of ἄλλων is to emphasise the distinction.

ἑλίσσεται This verb, also in the form εἱλίσσεται (137), refers to the daily rotation of stars, though its function is simply to mark relative position; cf. 273. Here there is no double meaning, as with εἱλεῖται in 46 and 53.

ἀμφαδόν Cf. 64. Here the meaning is that the star can be clearly observed and identified.

96–136 The Maiden
Below Bootes is the Maiden carrying an ear of corn, daughter of Astraeus or some other. One tradition makes her an immortal, who once lived among men and was called Justice. That was the Golden Age, unmarred by war or seafaring, but self-sufficient with agriculture. In the Silver Age she was still on earth, but only to rebuke men for their increasing wickedness. When the Bronze Age came, with war and eating the flesh of oxen, she withdrew to the sky, where she may still be seen.

The description of the Maiden is limited to giving its position and naming its brightest star, Spica. It is a rather elongated and not very obvious star-group, lying along the line of the ecliptic. Spica is a 1st-mag. star, but the next in brightness are five of 3rd mag. The constellation was presumably formed around Spica, and its association with corn suggests that it originated in the observation of the morning rising of Spica as a sign of harvest time, the most important date in the calendar. This star has been identified with the Babylonian star AB.SIN, which also meant an ear of corn (Waerden *EW* 2.71). The origin of the name Παρθένος probably lies in an earth-goddess cult, as that of Demeter and Kore, and it remains the same from Eudoxus (fr. 25) to Ptolemy (7.5.27). In Latin the name became standardised as *Virgo*, but an alternative is *Erigone*, daughter of Icarus (or Icarius): V. *G.* 1.33,

Man. 2.31–2, Avien. 962, Hyg. 2.4.4. Tert. *Scorp.* 10.4 *facilius Aratus Persea et Cephea et Erigonam et Ariadnam inter sidera deliniabit.* [Sen.] *HO* 69 and Luc. 9.535 have derived from Arat. 98 the name *Astraea.* Allen 460ff., Gundel in *RE* 18.4.1936–57, Roscher vi 959ff.

A. devotes the rest of this extended passage to a mythical excursus based on the identification of the Maiden with the goddess of Justice. This theme looks back to Hesiod's Δίκη (*Op.* 220–62), and also to his myth of the Ages (109–55). A. does not follow Hesiod into the Heroic and Iron Ages, because his need goes only as far as the ascent of Justice into the sky. It also suits his purpose to stop at this point and correct Hesiod's pessimistic ending by making Justice still watch over men. Placed at this juncture, the passage also brings some poetic relief after the detailed technicalities required by the description of the preceding constellations. See Solmsen 124–8, Wilamowitz *HD* 2.265ff., Schwabl 343ff.

96 ποσσίν The stars ζ (right) and η (left) Bootis.

ὕπο σκέπτοιο The manuscripts of A. and Hi. 1.2.5 support ὑπο-σκέπτοιο, but, while this could be taken with Παρθένον in the sense of 'look up at' (cf. ὑποβλέπω), the dat. ποσσίν requires the preposition. So Eudox. fr. 25 ὑπὸ δὲ τοὺς πόδας ἡ Παρθένος ἐστίν, and sch. ὑπὸ δὲ τοῖς ἀμφοτέροις ποσὶ τοῦ Βοώτου ἐστὶν ἡ Παρθένος. For ὕπο cf. 73, 140, 147, 148, 450.

Βοώτεω This line is echoed in 136, and the two thus make a framework for the passage, linking it with the context both before and after it. There is also a chiasmus in the arrangement of the two names, so as to lead the reader from Βοώτης to Παρθένος, and then back from Παρθένος to Βοώτης.

The Ion. gen. sg. is Homeric, e.g. ξ 459 συβώτεω, with synizesis, perhaps for original -αο (Chantraine 1.69–70). A. also has βορέω (250, 313, etc.) from Ξ 395.

97 Παρθένον The new constellation is introduced in enjambment, as in 27, 66, 85, 92, etc.

The choice of name probably reflects that of Kore for Persephone (cf. E. *Hel.* 1342 περὶ παρθένῳ Δηοῖ θυμωσαμένᾳ), but its association with justice also suggests Hes. *Op.* 256 ἡ δέ τε παρθένος ἐστὶ Δίκη, Διὸς ἐκγεγαυῖα. Cf. A. *Th.* 662 ἡ Διὸς παῖς παρθένος Δίκη. It is a title of respect also given to Athena and Artemis.

ἐν χειρὶ φέρει Στάχυν The 1st-mag. star α Virginis or Spica occupies the position of the left hand in the figure of the Maiden. The variant χερσί can hardly be right, since the right-hand side of the figure is quite a distance from the left, and A. is usually precise in relating stars to parts of a figure. The sg. is supported by lemma and sch. οὐ διεσάφησε ποίᾳ χειρὶ ..., θεωρεῖται δὲ ἐν τῇ ἀριστερᾷ, and by *manu* in Germ. 97, Avien. 286 and *Arat. Lat.* Hipparchus refers to the star as ὁ Στάχυς, without naming a hand, but Geminus defines it as ὁ ἐν ἄκρᾳ τῇ ἀριστερᾷ χειρὶ τῆς Παρθένου κείμενος (3.6), and similarly Ptolemy (7.5.27). Cf. Manetho 2.134–5 στάχυάς τ᾽ ἐν χειρὶ φέρουσα | Παρθένος, Nonn. *D.* 41.228 στάχυν ἀστερόεντα, *Sphaera* 10 ἔχουσα ... χειρὶ Δήμητρος Στάχυν.

αἰγλήεντα Homeric adj., in phrase αἰγλήεντος Ὀλύμπου (Λ 532, υ 103), and at end of line in *h.Hom.* 32.9 αἰγλήεντας. Cf. Max. *Cat.* 192 Καρκίνῳ αἰγλήεντι, Triph. 515 οὐρανῷ αἰγλήεντι.

98 εἴτ᾽ οὖν Ἀστραίου The name comes from Hes. *Th.* 378–82 Ἀστραίῳ δ᾽ Ἠὼς ἀνέμους τέκε ... | ἄστρα τε λαμπετόωντα, τά τ᾽ οὐρανὸς ἐστεφάνωται. West on *Th.* 376 suggests that the name was invented to provide a father for the stars. With εἴτ᾽ ... εἴτε ... ἄλλος Α. is following a Hellenistic interest in mythical origins of gods, especially where there are conflicting versions. As a hymnic theme this looks back to *h.Hom.* 1.1ff., on Dionysus, οἱ μὲν γὰρ Δρακάνῳ σ᾽, οἱ δ᾽ Ἰκάρῳ ἠνεμοέσσῃ φάσ᾽ κτλ., where five versions are first dismissed before the poet gives the 'correct' one. Here the theme is treated more critically, and with several amusing touches: the idea of Astraeus being father of a constellation, the sly reference to Hesiod in φασιν, and to Zeus in τευ ἄλλου. There is also no suggestion that the myth which follows is a true version, but merely λόγος ἄλλος. The tone is similar in Antag. fr. 1.1ff. ἐν δοιῇ μοι θυμός, ἐπεὶ γένος ἀμφίσβητον, | ἤ σε θεῶν τὸν πρῶτον ἀειγενέων, Ἔρος, εἴπω, κτλ., and in Call. *H.* 1.5ff. ἐν δοιῇ μάλα θυμός, ἐπεὶ γένος ἀμφήριστον. | Ζεῦ, σὲ μὲν Ἰδαίοισιν ἐν οὔρεσί φασι γενέσθαι, | Ζεῦ, σὲ δ᾽ ἐν Ἀρκαδίῃ· πότεροι, πάτερ, ἐψεύσαντο; See Hopkinson *HA* 122, 140, Hutchinson *HP* 65–6.

γένος Of a single offspring, cf. Φ 186 φῆσθα σὺ μὲν ποταμοῦ γένος ἔμμεναι.

ὅν ῥά τέ φασιν Cf. P 674, in same *sedes*.

99 ἀρχαῖον ἀρχαῖος is used of persons as original members of a family or city (e.g. Call. *H.* 5.60 ἀρχαίων Θεσπιέων) or as characters in heroic or earlier times (e.g. Call. *E.* 59.1 ὠρχαῖος Ὀρέστας). Here there is more point in taking the epithet with the father, as a character from the *Theogony*, than with the stars, and ἀστραίων would be a natural corruption after ἄστρων. Martin finds the former 'dépourvu de sens', and adopts Frieseman's ἀρχαῖοι (*Collect. Crit.* 161). But the reference in φασιν is to Hesiod, and A. uses ἀρχαῖος elsewhere of the mythical ages only (103, 408). Men of historical times, who created our folk-lore, are πρότεροι (442, 637) and παλαιότεροι (1134).

εἴτε τευ ἄλλου Presumably Zeus, if A. is thinking of Δίκη as daughter of Zeus and Themis (Hes. *Th.* 902), in which case the god of the old myths has nothing to do with the Stoic god. The phrase is imitated in Opp. *H.* 1.291 οὔτε τευ ἄλλου, and 3.513 ἠέ τευ ἄλλου.

100 εὔκηλος φορέοιτο A Hellenistic affectation, suggesting some boldness on the part of the poet in telling a story, usually about a goddess, which she might find offensive. See note on 637 Ἄρτεμις ἱλήκοι. Here the assumed offence would lie in the querying of her ancestry. The sch. gloss with ἥσυχος, and also with εὐμενὴς φέροιτο ἐν οὐρανῷ. In early epic εὔκηλος means 'without fear', e.g. Hes. *Op.* 671 εὔκηλος τότε νῆα . . . ἑλκέμεν ἐς πόντον, but in Hellenistic poets it usually means 'quiet', 'peaceful', e.g. Theoc. 2.166 εὐκάλοιο κατ' ἄντυγα Νυκτός. Here too the idea of a calm night for seafaring would be appropriate, but A. is probably extending this meaning to that of 'favourable', so anticipating the later image of Justice in the sky (135). There is a quaintness in the combining of εὔκηλος, suggesting a personified goddess, with φορέοιτο, which describes the circling movement of the stars.

ἄλλος . . . λόγος A. introduces his myth of the Ages with a reminiscence of Hesiod's introduction to the same, ἕτερόν τοι ἐγὼ λόγον ἐκκορυφώσω (*Op.* 106). Cf. Xenoph. fr. 7.1 ἄλλον ἔπειμι λόγον, Stesich. fr. 192.1 οὐκ ἔστ' ἔτυμος λόγος οὗτος.

ἐντρέχει Once in Homer, but literally of legs in armour (T 385); only here of a story being current.

101 δῆθεν With the force of a strong δή, often ironical, implying that what is said is untrue, but here rather an amused affectation of incredulity; cf. Call. fr. 260.23 ὡς δῆθεν ὑφ' Ἡφαίστῳ τέκεν Αἶα. F. W. Thomas (*CQ* 8, 1958, 441ff.) suggests that δῆθεν has the force of inverted commas, but while this would be true of E. *Ion* 831 Ἴων, ἰόντι δῆθεν ὅτι συνήντετο, the sense here is better represented by an exclamation mark. In earlier usage the particle regularly comes immediately after the words it qualifies, but later it sometimes precedes, e.g. E. *Or.* 1320 ὡς δῆθεν οὐκ εἰδυῖα τἀξειργασμένα, and Call. fr. 260.23.

ἐπιχθονίη Homeric adj., usually an epithet of mortals, e.g. A 266, in same *sedes*, ἐπιχθονίων τράφεν ἀνδρῶν, here predicative in sense of ἐπὶ χθονί (A 88). A. is perhaps following the lead of Hesiod, who uses it of δαίμονες, who are φύλακες θνητῶν ἀνθρώπων (*Op.* 122–3).

A.'s description of the Golden Age begins here, though it is not named until 114. Then follows a balancing passage of fourteen lines on the Silver Age, and the whole episode is rounded off with a shorter piece on the Bronze Age (129–36). The overall pattern suggests that of strophe – antistrophe – epode.

102 κατεναντίη The adj. is found only here, from adv. κατεναντίον in Homer and Hesiod, e.g. Φ 567, *Sc.* 73. Sch. καὶ θεὸς οὖσα, φησί, κατ' αὐτοὺς ἐφοίτα εἰς τὸ φανερὸν τοῖς ἀνθρώποις, διὰ τὸ εἶναι αὐτοὺς δικαίους. The theme of gods consorting with mortals is a part of the Golden Age tradition, and A. seems to be recalling the old days in Phaeacia, η 201–2 αἰεὶ γὰρ τὸ πάρος γε θεοὶ φαίνονται ἐναργεῖς | ἡμῖν. Cf. Cat. 64.384ff. *praesentes namque ante domos inuisere castas | heroum et sese mortali ostendere coetu | caelicolae ... solebant*, V. E. 4.15–16 *diuisque uidebit | permixtos heroas et ipse uidebitur illis.*

102–103 οὐδέ ποτ' ... οὐδέ ποτ' After bucolic diaeresis β 203, κ 464, Hes. *Op.* 176, 228; at beginning of line Α 155, Ε 789, Hes. *Th.* 221, 796. I have not found another instance of the double use.

103 ἀρχαίων See 85 ἔν. For adjj. used ἀπὸ κοινοῦ cf. Theoc. 10.35 σχῆμα δ' ἐγὼ καὶ καινὰς ἐπ' ἀμφοτέροισιν ἀμύκλας, Kiefner 37–8.

ἠνήνατο Double augment, as in Η 185 ἀπηνήναντο. Cf. Hermesian. 7.97 πάσας δ' ἠνήνατο λέσχας.

φῦλα γυναικῶν A phrase from Ι 130 and Hes. *Th.* 591; cf. *Sc.* 4 and fr. 1.1 γυναικῶν φῦλον (see West on *Th.* 1019ff.). Both 102 and 103 have internal monosyllabic rhyme; the former could be accidental, but the latter, with adj. and noun, seems deliberate. Cf. 118, 1125, and with contrasting words 144, 750 (all in -ων). So Α 152, 339, Hes. *Op.* 481, 489.

104 ἀναμὶξ ἐκάθητο Sch. παρὰ τὸ ἡσιόδειον· ξυναὶ γὰρ τότε δαῖτες ἔσαν, ξυνοὶ δὲ θόωκοι (fr. 1.6). The verb here suggests law courts in session: Ar. *Nub.* 208 δικαστὰς οὐχ ὁρῶ καθημένους, Th. 5.85 ὑμεῖς οἱ καθήμενοι. There is a Pythagorean element in the concept of justice being essential to the worlds of both gods and men: Iamblich. *VP* 46 τοὺς γὰρ ἀνθρώπους εἰδότας ὅτι τόπος ἅπας προσδεῖται δικαιοσύνης μυθοποιεῖν τὴν αὐτὴν τάξιν παρά τε τῷ Διὶ τὴν Θέμιν καὶ παρὰ τῷ Πλούτωνι τὴν Δίκην καὶ κατὰ τὰς πόλεις τὸν νόμον. J. Carcopino, *Virgile et le mystère de la IVe églogue* (1943) 26. The adv. ἀναμίξ appears elsewhere only in prose (Hdt. 1.103, Th. 3.107.4).

105 Δίκην Dike in Hes. *Th.* 902 is daughter of Zeus and Themis, sister of Eunomia and Eirene. She, whether personified or not, is the main theme of *Op.* 213–85, as being superior to Hubris as a guide to human behaviour. She is often maltreated by corrupt men, but when her advice is followed, she brings prosperity and peace to communities. She is also respected by Zeus, to whom she reports the wickedness of men. On the relation of Dike to Themis see Harrison 516ff.

καλέεσκον Cf. Ζ 402 τόν ῥ' Ἕκτωρ καλέεσκε Σκαμάνδριον.

ἀγειρομένη The middle represents Dike as president of her own senate. Cf. Jason in A.R. 4.1334–5 ἑταίρους | εἰς ἓν ἀγειράμενος μυθήσομαι.

106 εὐρυχόρῳ ἐν ἀγυιῇ The adj. primarily refers to broad dancing-places, e.g. Β 498 εὐρύχορον Μυκαλησσόν, Ι 478 Ἑλλάδος εὐρυχόροιο.

Later poets seem to have connected it with χῶρος rather than χορός: hence εὐρυχόρους ἀγυιάς (Pi. *P.* 8.55, E. *Ba.* 87), D. 21.52 orac. 3 εὐρυχόρους κατ' ἀγυιάς. Wilamowitz *HD* 2.268 notes that the adj. here is not purely ornamental: it is only in wide roads that meetings can be held. There may also be an echo here of Hes. *Op.* 197 χθονὸς εὐρυοδείης. The balancing of ἀγορῆ and ἀγυιῇ, enhanced by the internal rhyme, recalls the Proem (2–3), and so brings out the relevance of this episode to the general theme of the poem. The double hiatus, before and after ἤ, is unusually harsh, but it does not seem to have any special significance.

107 δημοτέρας A Hellenistic adj., referring to the people as opposed to their rulers; the suffix brings out this sense of contrast: cf. δεξιτερῆ (87). Thus A.R. 1.783 δημότεραι ... γυναῖκες, the women of the town as opposed to Hypsipyle, 3.606 ἔργα πιφαύσκετο δημοτέροισιν, Aeetes to his people, Call. fr. 228.71–2 δαμοτέρων ... τῶν μεγάλων, Pers. *AP* 9.334.2–3 μεγάλων ... δημοτέρων. Here the elders are urged to make judgements for the good of the people: sch. πραείας καὶ οὐ τυραννικάς, also δημωφελεῖς.

ἤειδεν The verb suggests the charm and antiquity of a goddess's speech in an ancient epic; the tense brings out the constant reiteration of her message.

ἐπισπέρχουσα Sch. ἐπισπουδάζουσα διδάσκουσα, whence the variant in S. The verb is Homeric, literally in Ψ 430 κέντρῳ ἐπισπέρχων, in χ 451 of Odysseus giving orders. Cf. Th. 4.12.1 ὁ μὲν τούς τε ἄλλους τοιαῦτα ἐπέσπερχε, Opp. *H.* 5.641 ἐπισπέρχουσά τε μύθοις.

θέμιστας Judgements given by men in authority after hearing conflicting claims in disputes. In Homeric society this authority comes from Zeus, who awards them σκῆπτρόν τ' ἠδὲ θέμιστας (Ι 99); thus they are δικασπόλοι, οἵ τε θέμιστας | πρὸς Διὸς εἰρύαται (Α 238–9). Hence the anger of Zeus with men οἳ βίῃ εἰν ἀγορῇ σκολιὰς κρίνωσι θέμιστας (Π 387). The theme is developed by Hesiod, in *Th.* 85–6, on the βασιλεύς who is favoured by the Muses, so that πάντες ἐς αὐτὸν ὁρῶσι διακρίνοντα θέμιστας | ἰθείῃσι δίκῃσιν. In *Op.* 9 he announces it as a major topic for the poem, δίκῃ δ' ἴθυνε θέμιστας, and in 221 refers to men who are δωροφάγοι, σκολιῆς δὲ δίκης κρίνωσι θέμιστας. See West on the relevant passages in Hesiod. The importance of this topic for A.'s picture of the world under a benevolent Zeus is emphasised by this impressive four-word line which concludes the sentence.

108 λευγαλέου τότε νείκεος A reference to Ν 97 πολέμοιο μεθήσετε λευγαλέοιο. The absence of war is one of the traditional characteristics of the Golden Age. Hesiod does not specify this in his account (*Op.* 109–26), but implies it in the phrase κακῶν ἔκτοσθεν ἁπάντων (115). It is similarly implied in V. *E.* 4.17, while Ovid follows A. more positively in *Met.* 1.97ff. *nondum praecipites cingebant oppida fossae* etc. Hesiod brings in the activities of Ares first in the Bronze Age (145–6). Here A. is also recalling Emped. fr. 128.1ff., a passage on the primitive age of innocence, before the cosmic cycle began to fall into disorder: οὐδέ τις ἦν κείνοισιν Ἄρης θεὸς οὐδὲ Κυδοιμός | οὐδὲ Ζεὺς βασιλεὺς οὐδὲ Κρόνος οὐδὲ Ποσειδῶν, | ἀλλὰ Κύπρις βασίλεια. He may also have had in mind fr. 109.3 νείκεϊ λυγρῷ.

ἠπίσταντο C. gen., as with verbs meaning 'become aware of', so here 'had no experience of' (cf. Th. 1.141.3 χρονίων πολέμων καὶ διαποντίων ἄπειροι). For ἐπίσταμαι cf. Φ 406 φόρμιγγος ἐπιστάμενος, Hdt. 3.103 μὴ ἐπιστέαται αὐτῆς. K–G 1.361–2.

The spondaic beginning and ending of this line produce a certain solemnity that suits the sense.

109 διακρίσιος A disagreement that leads to quarrels and fighting, when there is no arbiter to settle it with a wise judgement. The choice of word seems deliberate as a contrast to Hesiod's judge διακρίνοντα θέμιστας (*Th.* 85).

περιμεμφέος Only here, but supported by the manuscripts, and probably to be regarded as the *lectio difficilior*. The variant πολυμεμφέος appears elsewhere only in Nonnus (*D.* 4.35, al.), and there is no obvious reason for preferring it here. A. makes much use of περι- in the sense of 'very': περιμήκετος (250), περιτρομέειν (861), περιπολλά (914), περιδείδιε (1096), περίπλειοι (1118). Compounds of -μεμφής can be either active (Nonn. *D.* 4.35 πολυμεμφέα φώνην) or passive (Nic. fr. 74.14–15 οὐδὲ Φάσηλις | ... ἐπιμεμφής). The former sense is given here by sch. τῆς ἀδίκου διαχωρίσεως τῆς ἐχούσης μέμψεις καὶ ψόγους καὶ ἀμφισβητήσεις. Tr. 'quarrelsome conflict'.

κυδοιμοῦ An evocative word from epic, describing the noise and confusion of battle, as in Κ 524–5 ἄσπετος ὦρτο κυδοιμὸς | θυνόντων ἄμυδις. A. recalls Emped. 128.1 οὐδέ τις ἦν κείνοισιν Ἄρης θεὸς οὐδὲ Κυδοιμός.

110 αὔτως δ' ἔζωον This seems to recall Hes. *Op.* 112 ὥστε θεοὶ δ' ἔζωον ἀκηδέα θυμὸν ἔχοντες. αὔτως: i.e. 'without trying to be richer or more powerful' (cf. 21).

ἀπέκειτο θάλασσα The second feature of the Golden Age is the absence of seafaring, because all the necessities of life could be procured at home. As with war, Hesiod makes no specific reference to the sea in his account of the Golden Age, and only introduces it in the Heroic Age, when the Greeks sailed to Troy (164–5). He returns to the theme in 236–7 οὐδ' ἐπὶ νηῶν | νίσονται, καρπὸν δὲ φέρει ζείδωρος ἄρουρα, a passage that A. also has in mind here. Virgil follows A. in *E.* 4.38–9 *cedet et ipse mari uector, nec nautica pinus | mutabit merces.* Cf. Tib. 1.3.37

nondum caeruleas pinus contempserat undas, Ov. *Met.* 1.94–5 *nondum ... in liquidas pinus descenderat undas.* Hence the Latin poets' theme of seafaring as a crime, e.g. Lucr. 5.1006 *improba nauigii ratio tum caeca iacebat*, V. *E.* 4.31ff. *priscae uestigia fraudis, | quae temptare Thetim ratibus ... iubeant*, Hor. *Carm.* 1.3.21–4 *nequiquam deus abscidit | prudens Oceano dissociabili | terras, si tamen impiae | non tangenda rates transiliunt uada*, Prop. 1.17.13–14 *a pereat quicumque ratis et uela parauit | primus et inuito gurgite fecit iter.*

ἀπέκειτο means that the sea was not so much out of sight as out of reckoning: men had not yet considered crossing the sea. Cf. Pi. *N.* 11.46 προμαθείας δ' ἀπόκεινται ῥοαί, Philostr. *VA* 8.21 ῥητορικὴ μὲν γὰρ ἀπέκειτο ἀμελουμένη. Philostr. *VA* 6.2 quotes Hes. *Op.* 151 with ἀπέκειτο for οὐκ ἔσκε, which must be a memory-quotation influenced by A.

111 βίον Hes. *Op.* 31 ᾧτινι μὴ βίος ἔνδον ἐπηετανὸς κατάκειται. The word is also a reminder of the Proem, 6 βιότοιο.

ἀπόπροθεν Cf. 459, Q.S. 7.391 νηὸς ἀπόπροθι πολλὸν ἰούσης.

ἠγίνεσκον Iterative forms in -σκον do not normally take an augment, e.g. ρ 294 (Chantraine 1.482). A. may have been influenced by Σ 493 ἠγίνεον.

112 βόες καὶ ἄροτρα A. deliberately disagrees with Hesiod in allowing agriculture to be one of the activities of the Golden Age. In *Op.* 117–18, καρπὸν δ' ἔφερε ζείδωρος ἄρουρα | αὐτομάτη πολλόν τε καὶ ἄφθονον, Hesiod implies that there was no need for men to cultivate the soil. So V. *E.* 4.40–1. But the Stoics thought of the arts as being all as old as man: Norden, *Jahrbücher für classische Philologie*, Suppl. 19 (1893) 425–6, H. Herter, *Maia* 4 (1963) 477, E. Bréhier, *Chrysippe et l'ancien Stoïcisme* (1951) 146. Solmsen (127) sees this innovation as A.'s 'boldest and final integration of Hesiodic motifs and at the same time his most eloquent act of homage'. A.'s words in fact recall the section on ploughing in *Op.* 405–57. Hesiod's curse on ἔργα βοῶν (*Op.* 46) has no place in A.'s philosophy. With βόες καὶ ἄροτρα we are reminded of βουσί τε καὶ μακέλῃσι (8), and thus another link with the Proem is provided.

Wilamowitz (*HD* 2.269) would understand after βόες καὶ ἄροτρα some such verb as ἐπόριζον, and take only Δίκη with παρεῖχε, but the run of the words is against this, and παρεῖχε can be understood as agreeing with its nearest subject.

πότνια λαῶν A conflation of πότνια θηρῶν (Φ 470) and ποιμένα λαῶν (Β 243). πότνια Μαῖα (263) corresponds more to Homeric usage, e.g. Α 551.

113 μυρία πάντα Hes. *Op.* 116–17, of the Golden Age, ἐσθλὰ δὲ πάντα | τοῖσιν ἔην. A. exaggerates the benefits, with μυρία expressing the number (cf. Α 2 μυρί' Ἀχαιοῖς ἄλγε') and πάντα variety (cf. Ε 60 δαίδαλα πάντα).

COMMENTARY: 114–117

δώτειρα δικαίων An adaptation of δωτῆρες ἐάων (θ 325, Hes. *Th.* 46, 111, 633), δῶτορ ἐάων (θ 335, *h.Hom.* 18.12, 29.8). δικαίων looks back to δημοτέρας θέμιστας (107), the n. pl. referring to just decisions in response to all individual claims. Cf. D. 21.67 τῶν ἴσων καὶ τῶν δικαίων ἕκαστος ἡγεῖται ἑαυτῷ μετεῖναι ἐν δημοκρατίᾳ. The triple alliteration of δ follows a triple alliteration of π, making an effective conclusion to the six-line description of life in the Golden Age.

114 τόφρ' ἦν Mair understands Dike as subj., expanding ἦν to mean 'she had her dwelling on earth'. This is also unsatisfactory because it implies that she was there only for the duration of the Golden Age. It is simpler to take ἦν as impers. Cf. l 551 τόφρα δὲ Κουρήτεσσι κακῶς ἦν. For τόφρα followed by ὄφρα cf. δ 289.

γένος χρύσειον Hes. *Op.* 109 χρύσεον μὲν πρώτιστα γένος μερόπων ἀνθρώπων. Gold is regarded as the most precious of metals, and especially associated with the gods, literally in Δ 2–3 χρυσέῳ ἐν δαπέδῳ ... χρυσέοις δεπάεσσι, figuratively in Γ 64 μή μοι δῶρ' ἐρατὰ πρόφερε χρυσέης Ἀφροδίτης. In later writers gold can be a symbol of moral goodness and integrity: Pl. *Phaedr.* 235e φίλτατος εἶ καὶ ὡς ἀληθῶς χρυσοῦς, Call. fr. 75.31 ἤλεκτρον χρυσῷ φημί σε μειξέμεναι.

ἔφερβεν *h.Hom.* 30.1–2 Γαῖαν | ... ἣ φέρβει ἐπὶ χθονὶ πάνθ' ὁπόσ' ἐστίν.

115 ἀργυρέῳ Hes. *Op.* 127–8 δεύτερον αὖτε γένος πολὺ χειρότερον μετόπισθεν | ἀργύρεον. Hesiod's Silver Age is characterised by a softening in the upbringing of children, so that they become aggressive towards each other and neglectful of religious duties (127–39). A. is entirely concerned with the partial withdrawal of Dike and the increasing wickedness of men, but he does not give specific examples of their wickedness. A. introduces his account of the Silver Age with the key word, in a kind of chiasmus after χρύσειον at the end of the preceding passage.

ὀλίγη A rare adverbial use, but cf. 953 πολλή, 1045 πολλός.

ἑτοίμη Cf. *Th.* 1.80.4 οὔτε ἑτοίμως. The variant ὁμοίη may have come from sch. 107 μεταστάντων δὲ ἐκείνων οὐκέτι ὁμοίως συνῆν αὐτοῖς, or, as Maass suggests, from π 182 καί τοι χρὼς οὐκέθ' ὁμοῖος.

116 ὡμίλει C. dat., as β 21 μνηστῆρσιν ὁμιλεῖ. For the theme of a restricted epiphany see Williams on Call. *H.* 2.9 ὡπόλλων οὐ παντὶ φαείνεται.

παλαιῶν The word looks back to 103 ἀρχαίων, of the Golden Age. Manetho 2(1).135 Παρθένος ἀνθρώπων γενεὴν ποθέουσα παλαιῶν.

ἤθεα λαῶν Hes. *Op.* 222, of Dike, ἣ δ' ἕπεται κλαίουσα πόλιν καὶ ἤθεα λαῶν.

117 κεῖνο κατ' ἀργύρεον γένος ἦεν Sch. καὶ κατ' ἐκεῖνο ἦν τοῖς

223

ἀνθρώποις, ἤγουν κατὰ τὸ ἀργυροῦν γένος. Some difficulty has been felt with the use of simple ἦεν without any qualification such as ἐπιχθονίη in 102. Mair expands in translating 'in that Silver Age was she still upon the earth'. Maass emends sch. ἦν to συνῆν. Wilamowitz *HD* 2.269 notes that ἦν cannot mean παρῆν, and also finds it unsatisfactory to take κεῖνο with κατ' ἀργύρεον γένος. He therefore proposes to understand κεῖνο as subj. of ἦν and as referring back to the situation just described. Martin agrees and translates 'la coutume, au siècle d'argent, se maintenait'. Similarly Erren. This seems to require of ἦν an equally expanded sense. It also interrupts the continuity of Dike as subject from 115 to 128. Moreover the use of κεῖνο agreeing with ἀργύρεον γένος and referring back to ἀργυρέῳ (115) is very characteristic of A.: cf. 197 κἀκεῖνο agreeing with αἰνὸν ἄγαλμα and referring back to παιδί (196). The only problem then is the precise meaning of κατά c. acc. It is not temporal, as Mair and Martin translate; the point is rather that Dike was among the silver generation of men. Cf. Hes. *Op.* 160, of the heroic race, κατ' ἀπείρονα γαῖαν, and local uses in Α 229 κατὰ στρατὸν εὐρὺν Ἀχαιῶν, Ε 84 κατὰ κρατερὴν ὑσμίνην, Ζ 56 κατὰ οἶκον, α 344 καθ' Ἑλλάδα καὶ μέσον Ἄργος. It is also to be noted that the sch. paraphrase ἔτι with καί, that is, its sense is not temporal, but additional: in spite of her affection for the golden, Dike was with the silver generation too.

118 ἤρχετο The impf. is rare in the simple verb, perhaps because of the need to avoid confusion with the impf. of ἄρχομαι. A. uses it also in 102, in both cases in the sense of repeated action.

ἐξ ὀρέων The partial withdrawal of Dike to the mountains is a new development of the myth. The mountains represent the natural primitive world, inhabited by nymphs and other spirits of nature, and as yet uncorrupted by men. Cf. Hes. *Th.* 129–30 γείνατο δ' οὔρεα μακρά, θεᾶν χαρίεντας ἐναύλους | Νυμφέων, αἳ ναίουσιν ἀν' οὔρεα βησσήεντα, ζ 123 νυμφάων, αἳ ἔχουσ' ὀρέων αἰπεινὰ κάρηνα. See also note on 135.

ὑποδείελος Only here and 826, where sunset makes clear the time of day intended. In Φ 111 δείλη similarly means dusk, as opposed to dawn and midday: ἔσσεται ἢ ἠὼς ἢ δείλη ἢ μέσον ἦμαρ. Hes. *Op.* 810, 821 ἐπὶ δείελα. [Theoc.] 25.223 gives an earlier hour with προδείελος. A. also has adv. δείελον (1111).

ἠχηέντων The double spondee suggests a certain grandeur, as of palaces thronged with people: δώματα ἠχήεντα (δ 72, *h.Hom.* 2.104), δόμοι ἠχήεντες (Hes. *Th.* 767); also of nature, *h.Hom.* 14.5 οὔρεά τ' ἠχήεντα, Q.S. 2.1 ὀρέων ὑπὲρ ἠχηέντων. A. also has ἠχήεσσαι (911) of beaches.

119 μουνάξ As the following words explain, she keeps her distance from the people. The adv. is Homeric, of solo dancing (θ 371) and single-handed fighting (λ 417), both in same *sedes*. A. also has it twice, the second time of stars (194), and in a different *sedes*. The rhythm of an initial spondee in enjambment followed by a sense pause is unusual, but cf. 283, 494, 520, 723.

οὐδέ τεῳ Π 227 οὐδέ τεῳ σπένδεσκε θεῶν.

ἐπεμίσγετο Of friendly intercourse in ζ 241 Φαιήκεσσ' ὅδ' ἀνὴρ ἐπιμίσγεται ἀντιθέοισι (cf. 205), Hes. *Th.* 802 οὐδέ ποτ' ἐς βουλὴν ἐπιμίσγεται οὐδ' ἐπὶ δαῖτας, A.R. 3.658 οὐδέ τί πω πάσαις ἐπιμίσγεται ἀμφιπόλοισιν. In these examples conversation is only implied, here it is specifically stated.

μειλιχίοισιν Sc. ἔπεσσι, as in Κ 542 ἔπεσσί τε μειλιχίοισι. Cf. Δ 256 προσηύδα μειλιχίοισιν, Ζ 214, A.R. 3.31 ἀμείβετο μειλιχίοισιν. But Orph. *Arg.* 1147 μύθοισι προσηύδα μειλιχίοισι.

120 ὁπότ' ... **κολώνας** Professor Reeve has pointed out that here a surprising action not previously mentioned is introduced in a subordinate temporal clause; in English a participle may be so used, but not a subordinate clause. Cf. ἐπεάν in Hdt. 4.2.1, 62.3, 67.1, 2, 69.1, 71.4, 72.2, 5, 172.2; ὅκως ibid. 4.130.

πλήσαιτο The word suggests the time of day between dawn and noon known as πληθούσης ἀγορᾶς (X. *Mem.* 1.1.10; cf. *An.* 2.1.7, Hdt. 4.181, etc.).

κολώνας Broad hills or rocks in cities, where people would assemble for meetings, such as the Pnyx and Areopagus in Athens. The word occurs twice in Homer, αἰπεῖα κολώνη, of a rock outside Troy (Β 811), and the acropolis of Thryoessa (Λ 711), in both cases at the end of a line. In 989 the word is used of high mountains.

121 δἤπειτα Frequent in Homer, mostly after a verb, and in this *sedes* (e.g. Ο 163, Υ 338, α 290, θ 378, λ 121); Hes. *Th.* 405, 562, *Op.* 292. Cf. Call. *H.* 4.160, 6.87, fr. 488, A.R. 3.770, 4.70. MSS of A. mostly read δ' ἤπειτα, West (*Th.* p. 100) reports the same for Hesiod (but δἤπειτα for Homer), and Hopkinson the same for Callimachus (*H.* 6.87). Editors of Homer prefer the synizesis δὴ ἔπειτα, but the crasis is closer to the MSS, and West favours it for Hesiod, likewise Pfeiffer and Fränkel for the Alexandrians, Maass and Zannoni for A.

καθαπτομένη In Homer also this verb is usually participial, but mostly of addressing in a friendly or neutral manner. An angry context is σ 415 ἀντιβίοις ἐπέεσσι καθαπτόμενος. Cf. Hes. *Op.* 332 χαλεποῖσι καθαπτόμενος ἐπέεσσι. A. gives the meaning a new slant c. gen., expressing an accusation.

κακότητος Γ 366 τείσασθαι Ἀλέξανδρον κακότητος. In Hes. *Op.* 287 κακότης is contrasted with ἀρετή.

122 εἰσωπός Cf. 79. The word is a reminder of the star context of this whole passage, and looks forward to φαίνεται (135).

καλέουσιν The variant χατέουσιν is preferred by Voss as a more effective word. But καλέουσιν has strong support, and is equally effective, 'even if they invite her'. Cf. Germ. 128 *per uota uocatis, Arat. Lat.* (from misreading as κλαίουσιν) *fletus.*

123–126 This is the only passage of direct speech in the poem, and it is presumably modelled on the five-line speech in Hes. *Op.* 54–8, where Zeus angrily threatens Prometheus. Both speeches predict trouble for future generations. In 207–9 the speech of the hawk voices similar threats to the nightingale, but direct speech is characteristic of the αἶνος, whereas it did not become a feature of didactic poetry. Elsewhere in the *Works and Days* there are only two half-lines (453–4) and one single line (503). Here A. has digressed from his technical subject-matter, and one may compare the longer speech of Nature in Lucr. 3.933ff. It is significant that Virgil has no direct speech in the *Georgics* until he comes to the Aristaeus episode in 4.321ff., where the conventions of epic become appropriate. Serv. *G.* 2.474 *hoc Aratus dicit, iustitiam primo et in urbibus, postea tantum in agris fuisse, ubi eam inducit loquentem, an abscedat a terris.* The increasing decline in the three generations is picked out in the adjj. χρύσειοι ... χειροτέρην ... κακώτερα, with triple variation of gender. The most notable imitation of this passage is Hor. *Carm.* 3.6.46ff. *aetas parentum peior auis tulit | nos nequiores mox daturos | progeniem uitiosiorem.* The basic theme is already in β 276–7.

124 χειροτέρην A reminiscence of Hes. *Op.* 127 γένος πολὺ χειρότερον, introducing the Silver Age.

τεξείεσθε An apparently desiderative form, only here. Voss rejected it without argument, Kaibel 950 as unacceptable for both sense and form, Wilamowitz *HD* 2.269–70 as a misguided archaism. Of the emendations the most attractive is Kaibel's τέκνα τεκεῖσθε from *h.Hom.* 5.127, adopted by Martin and Erren. Nevertheless the manuscript evidence is strong, and it is difficult to believe that anyone other than the poet would have invented the transmitted verb. A. is very innovative with language throughout the poem. The difficulty has arisen from taking the verb as desiderative: the sense is wrong and the middle is unparalleled. It must therefore be regarded as a future, as Veitch explains it, comparing it with θερείομαι in Nic. *Ther.* 124 and *Alex.* 567, a new poetic form of θέρομαι. Schwyzer 1.789, Defradas 275.

125 καὶ δή που An 'extremely rare' combination, according to Denniston (268). Here it introduces the surprisingly violent consequences of κακότης. There may also be a dramatic touch, appropriate to a speech, as in Call. *H.* 2.3 καὶ δή που τὰ θύρετρα καλῷ ποδὶ

Φοῖβος ἀράσσει. The following καὶ δὴ καὶ adds a more horrifying crime.

ἀνάρσιον αἷμα   A *callida iunctura*, the adj. normally suggesting enemies, the noun kinsmen. The adj. is Homeric, e.g. ω 365 δυσμενέες καὶ ἀνάρσιοι. Cf. A. *Ag.* 511, Theoc. 17.101. αἷμα 'bloodshed' is frequent in tragedy, e.g. A. *Supp.* 449 ὅπως δ᾽ ὅμαιμον αἷμα μὴ γενήσεται. Sch. A. *Pr.* 191a quotes this line with ἀνάρθμιον: cf. π 427, Η 302. Wilamowitz, *Hermes* 25 (1890) 167, Martin, *SAV*, p. xxvi, 13.

126   This line recalls Hes. *Op.* 200–1, after the departure of Aidos and Nemesis from the earth, τὰ δὲ λείψεται ἄλγεα λυγρὰ | θνητοῖς ἀνθρώποισι, κακοῦ δ᾽ οὐκ ἔσσεται ἀλκή. Ludwig (441) notes A.'s imitation and variation here, with ἀνθρώποισι in the same *sedes*, κακόν and ἄλγος reflecting ἄλγεα and κακοῦ, and ἔσσεται in a different clause and *sedes*. Cf. also *Th.* 876 κακοῦ δ᾽ οὐ γίνεται ἀλκή.

κακῶν   The variants are κακοῦ, κακόν, κακοῖς. The last has minimal support, and can be explained as an attempt to provide an indirect object for the verb. A dat. sg. was proposed by Voss, to give the meaning 'der Unthat folgt das Nachweh', but there is no parallel for such a use of ἐπίκειμαι. Martin, however, accepts κακῷ, but translates 'sur la faute s'appesantira la peine': this gives a very unlikely sense to τὸ κακόν, which is normally used of trouble suffered (see below). The variant κακόν (adj.) is read by Maass and Mair, but it seems rather pointless with ἄλγος (when is an ἄλγος not κακόν?), and it is probably better to regard it as a corruption influenced by the neuter noun. This leaves κακοῦ and κακῶν, both referring to the trouble prophesied by Dike, and these are best suited to the context. The sg. takes up Hesiod's κακοῦ in *Op.* 201, and was the reading of editors before Voss. It could, however, be a corruption due to the influence of the Hesiodic line, the latter part of which has actually replaced the original text in some MSS. On the whole κακῶν (read by Zannoni) seems preferable. It belongs to the M tradition, and the pl. refers more clearly to the troubles envisaged in 125. τὰ κακά is regularly used of the external troubles that beset men: cf. ξ 289 πολλὰ κάκ᾽ ἀνθρώποισιν ἑώργει, Β 304 κακὰ Πριάμῳ καὶ Τρῶσι φέρουσαι, and especially Hes. *Op.* 91 of primitive men living νόσφιν ἄτερ τε κακῶν, 179 μεμείξεται ἐσθλὰ κακοῖσιν, 265 οἷ αὐτῷ κακὰ τεύχει ἀνὴρ ἄλλῳ κακὰ τεύχων. Then ἄλγος is the suffering that comes from these troubles; cf. E. *Supp.* 807 τὰ κύντατ᾽ ἄλγη κακῶν, S. *Ph.* 734 ἄλγος ἴσχεις τῆς παρεστώσης νόσου.

ἐπικείσεται   Ζ 458 κρατερὴ δ᾽ ἐπικείσετ᾽ ἀνάγκη.

127 ὀρέων ἐπεμαίετο   The passage on the Silver Age is rounded off by a piece of ring composition, with Dike returning to the mountains whence she came (118).

For the verb cf. μ 220 σκοπέλου ἐπιμαίεο (same *sedes*); in different context and *sedes*, 89.

λαούς Cf. 6; here the people as opposed to Dike. The word appears in the same *sedes* in γ 214 ἦ σέ γε λαοί.

128 πάντας The variant πάμπαν ('completely'), the reading of editors before Voss, hardly makes sense with παπταίνω.

ἐλίμπανε A rare verb, not in epic; but Sappho has in fr. 94.2 κατελίμπανεν, 5 ἀπυλιμπάνω.

παπταίνοντας The word suggests a wistful sadness, as again in περιπαπταίνοντες (297); cf. A.R. 1.1171, of Heracles and his lost oar. In Homer the feeling is often that of fear, e.g. χ 380, Π 283; cf. A.R. 2.608, of the Argonauts at the Symplegades. The alliteration is very marked here, as in 297.

129–136 The Bronze Age is marked by the onset of war, as predicted in 125, and by the eating of the flesh of cattle. Hesiod's Bronze Age (*Op.* 143–55) was also guilty of introducing war, and its only other characteristic was that men did not eat grain.

The structural pattern of these eight lines has been in dispute since Wilamowitz (*HD* 2.270), taking καί (133) in its copulative sense, made οἱ πρῶτοι κτλ. a main clause, and let the sentence run on to a semicolon at ὑπουρανίη. Martin followed, but with a change of structure, printing οἳ δ' ἐγένοντο κτλ. as the first main clause and ending that sentence at ἀροτήρων. Erren seems to have combined the translations of both. None of these versions is satisfactory, because all overlook A.'s Homeric model with apodotic καί, e.g. Α 493–4 ἀλλ' ὅτε δή ῥ' ἐκ τοῖο δυωδεκάτη γένετ' ἠώς, | καὶ τότε δὴ πρὸς Ὄλυμπον ἴσαν θεοί and Χ 208–9 ἀλλ' ὅτε δὴ τὸ τέταρτον ἐπὶ κρούνους ἀφίκοντο, | καὶ τότε δὴ χρύσεια πατὴρ ἐτίταινε τάλαντα. Cf. Α 477–8, γ 130ff.; Denniston 308. The whole passage of eight lines should in fact be regarded as one sentence, designed in two balanced halves of four lines each, introduced by ἀλλ' ὅτε and καὶ τότε respectively. The first half has a pair of temporal and a pair of relative clauses, all describing the Bronze Age; the second contains a double main clause, balanced by an adverbial clause and a participial phrase, and deals with Dike's return to the sky. So Mair. See Ferrari 77ff., Defradas 275, Hattink 28. The long sentence is a feature of A.'s poetry: cf. 367ff., 469ff.

129 ἐτέθνασαν μ 393 βόες δ' ἀποτέθνασαν ἤδη. Hesiod ends the Silver Age similarly with αὐτὰρ ἐπεὶ καὶ τοῦτο γένος κατὰ γαῖα κάλυψε (*Op.* 140).

οἱ δ' The demonstrative article pointing to ἄνδρες at the end of the next line: see note on 21.

130 χαλκείη γενεή Hes. *Op.* 143–4 γένος μερόπων ἀνθρώπων |

χάλκειον. The artistry of putting in apposition words of different number and gender is taken further by Virgil, e.g. *A.* 6.580–1 *hic genus antiquum Terrae, Titania pubes,* | *flumine deiecti.*

ὀλοώτεροι Γ 365, Ψ 439 ὀλοώτερος ἄλλος, in same *sedes*.

131 κακοεργόν Once in Homer, σ 53–4 ἀλλά με γαστὴρ | ὀτρύνει κακοεργός; Theoc. 15.47 οὐδεὶς κακοεργός, [Opp.] *C.* 2.442 κακοεργέ. Lucillius parodies amusingly in *AP* 11.136.1 οὐχ οὕτω κακοεργὸν ἐχαλκεύσαντο μάχαιραν.

ἐχαλκεύσαντο A. recalls Hephaestus in Σ 400 χάλκευον δαίδαλα πολλά, and S. *Aj.* 1034 Ἐρινὺς τοῦτ' ἐχάλκευσε ξίφος. Cf. Call. fr. 115.17, Cat. 66.49–50 *qui principio sub terra quaerere uenas* | *institit ac ferri stringere duritiem,* Tib. 1.10.1 *quis fuit, horrendos primus qui protulit enses?*

μάχαιραν Γ 271 ἐρυσσάμενος χείρεσσι μάχαιραν. The dagger is probably chosen because the name suggests μάχη.

132 εἰνοδίην Once in Homer, Π 259–60 σφήκεσσιν ἐοικότες ἐξεχέοντο | εἰνοδίοις; Antip. *AP* 9.3.1 = *GP* 668 εἰνοδίην καρύην. Here the word suggests brigandage, a kind of lawlessness that often went unpunished, as Wilamowitz notes.

βοῶν ἐπάσαντ' ἀροτήρων A. refers to oxen specifically as animals used for ploughing (cf. Hes. *Op.* 405 βοῦν τ' ἀροτῆρα), because agriculture is an essential feature of his Golden Age: cf. 112, and the link with the section on weather signs in 1113, 1119. Sch. οἱ ἀρχαῖοι ἐφυλάττοντο τοὺς ἐργάτας βοῦς καθιερεύειν. τοῦτο δὲ καὶ Ὅμηρος οἶδε [γ 382–3, Ζ 93–4, Λ 729]. ἀσεβὲς γὰρ ἦν τὸν ἀρότην βοῦν φαγεῖν ... φασὶ δὲ καὶ τοὺς ἑταίρους τοῦ Ὀδυσσέως τοιούτους βοῦς κατεδηδοκέναι, ὠργίσθαι δὲ τὸν Ἥλιον, ἐπεὶ οἱ ἀροτῆρες βοῦς τοῦ ὁρᾶν ἡμᾶς τὸν ἥλιόν εἰσιν αἴτιοι, τροφῆς ὄντες ποριστικοί. Cf. Emped. fr. 128.8 ταύρων τ' ἀκρήτοισι φόνοις οὐ δεύετο βωμός, V. *G.* 2.536–7 *ante etiam sceptrum Dictaei regis et ante* | *impia quam caesis gens est epulata iuuencis,* and Servius *Arati est hoc, qui dicit quod maiores bouem comesse nefas putabant,* Greg. Naz. *Carm.* 3.485 βοὸς κταμένου ἀροτῆρος.

This abstention must have arisen from the purely practical reason that ploughing oxen were too precious to be wasted in eating, but later tradition linked it with the total vegetarianism of Orphics and Pythagoreans, e.g. E. *Hipp.* 952 δι' ἀψύχου βορᾶς, Pl. *Lg.* 782c ἀκούομεν ἐν ἄλλοις ὅτι οὐδὲ βοὸς ἐτόλμων [Stallbaum: ἐτολμῶμεν codd.] γεύεσθαι ... σαρκῶν δ' ἀπείχοντο ὡς οὐχ ὅσιον ὂν ἐσθίειν ... Ὀρφικοί τινες λεγόμενοι βίοι ... This rule of abstention from all kinds of flesh was based on the belief that all forms of life were akin, and the eating of meat was therefore a sort of cannibalism. Plutarch, however, in commending Pythagoras' doctrine, quotes 131–2 from A., adding οὕτω τοι καὶ οἱ τυραννοῦντες ἄρχουσι μιαιφονίας (998A). Aristoxenus, however

229

(fr. 7 *FHG* 2.273), says that πάντα μὲν τὰ ἄλλα συγχωρεῖν αὐτὸν ἐσθίειν ἔμψυχα, μόνον δ' ἀπέχεσθαι βοὸς ἀροτῆρος καὶ κριοῦ.

ἐπάσαντ' Aor. of πατέομαι. Α 464 σπλάγχνα πάσαντο, c. gen. ι 87 σίτοιό τ' ἐπάσσαμεθ' ἠδὲ ποτῆτος.

ἀροτήρων Adj., as Hes. *Op.* 405; subst. in 1062.

133 καὶ τότε Apodotic; see note on 129–136. Cf. Call. *H.* 6. 113–14 ἀλλ' ὄκα ... καὶ τόχ'. A. is probably also recalling Hes. *Op.* 197, where καὶ τότε δὴ πρὸς Ὄλυμπον begins a new sentence on the departure of Aidos and Nemesis from the earth.

134 ἔπταθ' Athematic aor., as in N 587 ἀπὸ δ' ἔπτατο πικρὸς ὀϊστός. The flight of Dike here may have been the origin of the wings which were added to the constellation figure by the time of Hipparchus: 2.5.6 ὁ ἐν ἄκρᾳ τῇ ἀριστερᾷ πτέρυγι τῆς Παρθένου (β Virginis).

ὑπουρανίη With adverbial force, a development of Homeric ὑπ-ουράνιον κλέος (Κ 212, ι 264), which probably means 'fame that reaches to the sky': cf. Θ 192 κλέος οὐρανὸν ἵκει, τ 108. So Ρ 675 ὑπουρανίων πετεηνῶν of birds (like the eagle) that fly up to the sky. In 616 ὑπουρανίων εἰδώλων A. is thinking of the constellations as attached to the under-surface of the sky, as opposed to ἐπουράνιοι of the gods who live above the sky (Ζ 129, al.). The variant in A. is due to the influence of the latter usage. Avien. 350 *subuecta per auras*.

νάσσατο Aor. med. of ναίω, c. acc., as Β 629 Δουλίχιόνδ' ἀπενάσσατο, 'went back to settle in'. A.R. 4.274–5 μυρία δ' ἄστη | νάσσατ' ἐποιχόμενος; but Hes. *Op.* 639 νάσσατο δ' ἄγχ' Ἑλικῶνος ὀϊζυρῇ ἐνὶ κώμῃ. A.R. uses the same form in the same metrical position as A., but with transitive sense, in 1.1356 νάσσατο παῖδας, 4.567 νάσσατο κούρην. The v.l. ἄρ' ἐνάσσατο (preferred by Voss) would involve a breach of Hermann's Bridge. The corruption was probably due to the influence of preceding ἔπταθ'.

The departure of Dike to the sky is modelled on that of Aidos and Nemesis in Hes. *Op.* 197–201. Ovid imitates in *Met.* 1.149–50 *Virgo caede madentes | ultima caelestum terras Astraea reliquit.*

χώρην Cf. χῶρος (256) of sky-space occupied by stars.

135 ἦχί περ Cf. 61. Here the force of περ is limitative (Denniston 483): though Dike has left the earth, she is at least still visible in the sky.

ἐννυχίη Cf. Hes. *Th.* 10 ἐννύχιαι, of the Muses hymning Zeus. West notes that gods prefer to walk on earth at night, when mortals are seldom abroad: *Op.* 730 μακάρων τοι νύκτες ἔασιν. There is a kind of progression in the visibility of Dike to men, first in broad daylight (102 by implication), then at dusk (118), finally at night. This is linked to her changes of location, in cities (106), in the mountains (127), in the sky (134). Schwabl 347.

ἔτι φαίνεται   A. concludes the episode of Dike on a hopeful note, in deliberate contrast to Hesiod's account of the departure of Aidos and Nemesis, προλιπόντ' ἀνθρώπους (*Op.* 199).

136 Παρθένος ... Βοώτεω   The episode ends with the framework corresponding to 96–7, and a return to the catalogue of constellations.

πολυσκέπτοιο   Not 'far-seen' (LSJ and Mair), but seen over a wide area, i.e. 'conspicuous', like περίσκεπτοι (213). For most of the ancients the fixed stars were all equidistant from the earth. The adj. occurs only here, and is designed rather quaintly to echo the opt. σκέπτοιο (96).

137–146 Some nameless stars
As an appendix to the section on the Maiden some bright stars are noted, which lie between the Maiden and the Great Bear, but are not part of any constellation figure, and are therefore nameless. The original figures could not incorporate all the stars that were later mapped, and Hipparchus made the figures obsolete by devising a system of co-ordinates, whereby all star positions could be determined. But the tradition of the figures was too strong, and even Ptolemy lists separately the stars that he calls ἀμόρφωτοι. Other nameless groups are noted by A. in 370–1, 385, and 391. The stars here are conveniently placed for A. to lead the reader back from the Maiden to the Bear, which is the point of reference for the identification of the next group of constellations.

137 ἀμφοτέρων ὤμων   The stars γ δ Virginis, respectively the left or southern shoulder (Hi. 3.2.9, 12) and the right or northern (Hi. 3.4.12, 3.5.5). Both are 3rd-mag. stars. The bright star 'above' them, i.e. to the north, must be ε Virginis, also of 3rd mag.

εἰλίσσεται   A frequent variation for the circular movement of stars: cf. 265, 368, 394, 401, 479, 524.

138   This line is in all the older MSS, but is deleted or bracketed by all editors since Voss, except Zannoni. There are good reasons for treating it as an interpolation. In 490 A. describes the Maiden as lying south of the tropic of Cancer, and not touching it. This means that ε Virginis, which was then some degrees north of the tropic, was not a part of the constellation figure. The wings must therefore have been added later, at least by the time of Hipparchus, who includes β and η Virginis as points on the left wing (2.5.6, 3.4.11), and ε simply as Προτρυγητήρ (2.5.5), without reference to its position on the figure. In A.'s time there were several unattached bright stars, and that is why the position of each is given as lying in a certain direction from a constellation, not as a part of it. If A. had meant to describe this as a wing star, he would not also have given its position with respect to the shoulders.

The line is also suspect on other grounds. (1) The sch. do not quote any part of it as a lemma. On 137 they describe the star as τοῦ ἀστέρος τοῦ ἐπικειμένου ἐν τῷ δεξιῷ ὤμῳ τῆς Παρθένου, ὅστις σφόδρα ἐστὶ λαμπρὸς καὶ καλεῖται Προτρυγητήρ, but make no reference to a wing. (2) The line is not translated in Germanicus or Avienius or Aratus Latinus. (3) The sentence 137–40 reads well if τόσσος is in apposition to ἀστήρ. (4) There is no obvious point in αὖτε. The interpolation must have entered the tradition at quite an early date, presumably from a marginal gloss: cf. sch. cited above, and Hyg. 3.24 *in utrisque pennis binae, quarum una stella quae est in dextra penna ad humerum defixa* Προτρυγητήρ *uocatur. Catast.* 9 ὁ δ᾽ ἐν τῇ δεξιᾷ πτέρυγι μεταξὺ τοῦ τε ὤμου καὶ τοῦ ἄκρου τῆς πτέρυγος Προτρυγητὴρ καλεῖται, Vitr. 9.4.1 *supra umerum dextrum lucidissima stella nititur, quam nostri prouindemiatorem, Graeci protrugeten uocant.* The name of this star is explained by its MR in early September: sch. πρὸ γὰρ τῆς τοῦ τρυγητοῦ ὥρας ὀλίγον προανατέλλει. In Latin it is *Vindemitor* (Ov. *Fast.* 3.407, Plin. *Nat.* 18.309), *Vindemiator* (Col. 11.2.24), and in modern catalogues *Vindemiatrix*.

139 τόσσος μὲν μεγέθει, τοίη δ᾽ ... αἴγλη Cf. 367 ὀλίγῳ μέτρῳ, ὀλίγη δ᾽ ... αἴγλη. A. appears to distinguish between the size and the brightness of stars, but it is not clear what the essence of the distinction is. In naked-eye astronomy size and brightness often mean the same thing. Attalus offers a solution in paraphrasing with τὰ μεγέθη καὶ τὰ χρώματα (Hi. 1.8.10), but αἴγλη is nowhere suggestive of colour, and where colour is intended, A. uses χροιή (378, 477, 801). Hipparchus actually paraphrases αἴγλη in 367 with μεγέθει (1.8.12). It seems therefore that A. regarded the amount of sky-space occupied as a different characteristic of a star from its brightness. Hipparchus certainly makes no such distinction, and it may have been he who initiated the use of μέγεθος as a technical term for the 'magnitude' of a star, e.g. in 1.4.16, of certain stars in Ophiuchus.

It follows that τοίη after τόσσος is simply a variation, as in Theoc. 7.90–1, 24.72.

ἐγκείμενος Cf. 367. A. uses κεῖσθαι frequently of star positions, meaning little more than εἶναι (168, al.). Here the star is literally 'set in the sky'.

140 ὕπο φαίνεται Maass's correction, anticipated by Planudes. A. has ὑπό c. acc. of star positions also in 230, 361, 445, 446. The compound verb is unlikely to have been used c. acc. This star is probably α Canum Venaticorum, sometimes known as Cor Caroli. It too is of 3rd mag., and lies due south of ε Ursae Majoris, in an area otherwise devoid of bright stars.

141 δεινή Elsewhere used by A. of the Dragon (57), Sirius (330), a squall (423), and Arcturus (745). The word often suggests some sort of danger, e.g. Sirius for heat, Arcturus for storms, but there is nothing ominous about the Bear, and A. merely means that it is an impressive sight. Cf. θ 22 δεινός τ' αἰδοῖός τε, of Odysseus transformed. A. exaggerates the impressiveness of the other stars, which are all of 3rd mag. **ἐγγύθεν εἰσίν** ζ 279 οὗ τινες ἐγγύθεν εἰσίν. Cf. 181, 247, 480.

142 οὐκ ἂν τούς γε ἰδὼν ἔτι τεκμήραιο Sch. refer τούς γε to the Great Bear, and report that some even suggest Cynosura. But these are already fully introduced in 27ff., and we now move on to the three unallocated stars, the δεινοὶ ἀστέρες of 141–2. For the rest, the general sense must be that, once you have sighted them below the Bear, you do not need any other guide to their identification. To provide this meaning the transmitted reading ἐπιτεκμήραιο by itself is taken by some editors to be sufficient, e.g. Martin 'il n'y a vraiment plus d'autre repère à chercher'. But in the other instances of this verb (229, 456, 932, 1038) the prefix lacks this accumulative force (LSJ c4). In 456 it is used with ἔτ' εἰς ἄλλους ὁρόων, and in 169–70 the simple verb with ἄλλῳ σήματι gives the same meaning as is required here. For ἔτι in the sense of taking a further (and in this case unnecessary) step see R. D. Dawe on S. *OT* 115. Similar to the present line is Pi. *O.* 1.5–6 μηκέθ' ἀλίου σκόπει | ἄλλο θαλπνότερον ἐν ἁμέρᾳ φαεννὸν ἄστρον. Cf. also 456 and 460.

143 οἷος Sch. οὐκ εἰκασμοῦ, ἀλλὰ θαύματος: cf. 170, 1007, 1067. The exclamatory clause has causal force, e.g. in Homer ω 629–30 θαύμαζ' Ἀχιλῆα, | ὅσσος ἔην οἷός τε, Z 166, Ο 286–7, Ε 757–8; in tragedy A. *Pr.* 908–9, E. *Hipp.* 878–9, *HF* 816–17; in prose Hdt. 1.31 ἐμακάριζον ... οἵων τέκνων ἐκύρησε, Th. 2.41.3, X. *Cyr.* 7.3.14, Pl. *Symp.* 209d. See K–G 2.370–1, Barrett on E. *Hipp.* 877–80. The v.l. τοῖος is *lectio facilior*, perhaps influenced by 169.

πρὸ ποδῶν The feet of the Bear are β and γ Ursae Majoris, and πρό is appropriate in both senses: in front with respect to the figure, and west with respect to its movement.

καλός τε μέγας τε Homeric phrase, e.g. Φ 108 of Achilles, ζ 276 of Odysseus. Cf. 244, 397, also of stars.

143–145 Hi. 1.2.9 quotes these lines to illustrate A.'s dependence on Eudoxus: πρὸ δὲ τῶν ἐμπροσθίων ποδῶν τῆς Ἄρκτου ἀστήρ ἐστι λαμπρός, λαμπρότερος δὲ ὑπὸ τὰ ὀπίσθια γόνατα, καὶ ἄλλος ὑπὸ τοὺς ὀπισθίους πόδας (fr. 28). The identification of these three stars is not easy. Hi. 1.5.5 makes it clear that Eudoxus identified the forefeet with β Ursae Majoris: ὅτι δὲ ἐπὶ τῶν ἐμπροσθίων ποδῶν κεῖται ὁ νοτιώτερος τῶν ἡγουμένων ἐν τῷ πλινθίῳ [the quadrilateral formed by the stars α β γ δ], φανερὸν ποιεῖ ὁ μὲν Εὔδοξος. We therefore have to look for a bright star to the west of β, and the obvious one is θ. Hi. 1.5.6 confirms this: τοῦ γὰρ νοτιωτέρου τῶν ἡγουμένων ἐν τῷ πλινθίῳ εἷς μόνος προηγεῖται λαμπρὸς ἀστήρ, ὁ νῦν ἐν τοῖς ἐμπροσθίοις σκέλεσι δεικνύμενος. It is at this point that Hipparchus adds his note about the ancients' figure of the Bear comprising only the seven stars (see note on 27), and in this context the ancients clearly include Eudoxus. Moreover both Eudoxus and A. indicate single stars, and A. says they are near the Bear. I would therefore prefer to identify them as θ ψ χ: θ and ψ are 3rd-mag. stars, χ only 4th-, but still bright enough to be recognised in the clear sky of ancient Greece.

144 ὑπωμαίων First here, perhaps on the analogy of οὐραῖος (145); cf. 1115.

ἰξυόθεν Only here, but cf. [Opp.] *C.* 2.6 ἰξυόφιν. The word points back to 28 ἰξύας, the loins star (δ), from which the hind legs (γ) are said to descend. A. puts this nameless star to the west of γ, whereas Eudoxus puts it to the south; it is about south-west, if the star is ψ.

145 οὐραίοις ὑπὸ γούνασιν A variation of phrase for 'hind legs'. The star χ Ursae Majoris is due south of γ. The adj. is Homeric (Ψ 520), and [Theoc.] 25.268–9 has πόδας οὐραίους, of Heracles' lion.

ἀλλ' ἄρα Often used to mark an antithesis, especially after a negative, as in 180, 648; cf Z 418, δ 718. M. Schmidt (551–2) sees no antithesis here, and interprets in the light of Germanicus' version, which departs from A. entirely and refers to the other stars in the extended figure of the Bear: *namque alii, quibus expletur ceruixque caputque,* | *uatibus ignoti priscis sine honore feruntur* (145–6). We need not, however, suppose that Germanicus misunderstood A.: it is characteristic of him to bring A. up to date, as it were. Avienius remains faithful to his model: *non tamen his species, non sunt cognomina certa* (365). The point is that, although these stars are close to the Bear, and identifiable from it, nevertheless they are not a part of it, and cannot be referred to as such. The force of ἄρα is to strengthen ἀλλά, in this case after a positive statement, as in 408, 699; cf. Τ 96, in same *sedes*.

146 ἁπλόοι Single stars listed individually, not as parts of a constellation. Sch. note that the name Ἡλακάτη was given to them by some astronomers, perhaps because they are grouped together here. Also Κόνων δὲ ὁ μαθηματικὸς Πτολεμαίῳ χαριζόμενος Βερονίκης πλόκαμον ἐξ αὐτῶν κατηστέρισε. But the stars of Coma Berenices are both too faint and too far from the Bear to be identified with these.

ἄλλοθεν ἄλλος Β 75, in same *sedes*. Elsewhere (e.g. 411, 867, 1101) A. uses the phrase with pl. pron.: here the sg. emphasises the separateness of the four stars.

ἀνωνυμίη Only here, probably formed on the analogy of ἐπωνυμία. A. varies with ἀνώνυμοι (391), νώνυμοι (370), οὐκ ὀνομαστά (385).

147–178 BEAR'S BODY GROUP: THE TWINS, THE CRAB, THE LION, THE CHARIOTEER AND THE BULL

147–148 A. now takes the stars α β γ of the Bear as starting-points for identifying the next three constellations westward along the Zodiac. Again he follows Eudoxus (fr. 28) closely: ὑπὸ δὲ τὴν κεφαλὴν τῆς Μεγάλης Ἄρκτου οἱ Δίδυμοι κεῖνται, κατὰ μέσον δὲ ὁ Καρκίνος, ὑπὸ δὲ τοὺς ὀπισθίους πόδας ὁ Λέων.

Hipparchus in a lengthy argument (1.5.1–13) criticises both A. and Eudoxus for saying that the Twins and Crab are below the Great Bear: the Bear's head (α) and forelegs (β), which mark the western limit of the Bear, lie approximately on the meridian of the 3rd degree of the Lion. Thus only the Lion may be said to lie below the Bear; the Crab and Twins are farther west: τούτων δ᾽ οὕτως ἐχόντων, πῶς ἐστι δυνατὸν ὑπὸ τὴν Ἄρκτον τούς τε Διδύμους καὶ τὸν Καρκίνον κεῖσθαι, εἴπερ ἥ τε κεφαλὴ καὶ οἱ ἐμπρόσθιοι πόδες αὐτῆς κατὰ τὴν γ᾽ τοῦ Λέοντος κεῖνται μοῖραν; δεῖ οὖν ὑπὸ μὲν τὴν Ἄρκτον τὸν Λέοντα μόνον τετάχθαι (8–9). Hipparchus, however, is interpreting ὑπό strictly in the sense of 'due south of', and is also measuring the Lion in relation to the 30° of the zodiacal sign. Eudoxus and A. are clearly using it with a much wider reference, ranging from south to south-west. Hipparchus in fact admits that Attalus and all the other commentators find no fault with A. here (1.5.1).

147 κρατί Sc. τῆς Μεγάλης Ἄρκτου, the star α Ursae Majoris. The Twins lay approximately south-west of it.

Δίδυμοι This constellation seems to have evolved from the two bright stars α and β Geminorum, which make an obvious pair in the sky. They were known to the Babylonians (Waerden *EW* 2.64, 67), and appear early in Greece in an inscription from Thera (*IG* 12.359). They were variously identified with Apollo and Heracles, Amphion and Zethus, Triptolemus and Iasion, but most of all with Castor and Pollux, now their standard names. In A. the two stars represent the heads of Castor and Pollux respectively (481). Call. *H.* 5.24–5 refers to them as Λακεδαιμόνιοι ἀστέρες. In Latin the constellation is *Gemini* (Cic. fr. 22.1, Germ. 148, Ov. *Fast.* 5.694, Man. 1.265, Hyg. 2.22, Avien. 369).

μέσση Perhaps best represented by the star β Ursae Majoris; the Crab lay to the south-south-west of it.

Καρκίνος The Crab is a small and rather faint constellation. Its name may have come from Egypt, and Boll–Gundel (Roscher VI 952) suggest the scarab as a possible origin. On the other hand its most notable feature, the nebula Praesepe, which the Greeks called Φάτνη, has been identified with the Babylonian NANGAR (Waerden *EW* 2.64). On its usefulness as a weather sign, depending on whether it was visible or not, see 892ff. The Crab also became important when the summer solstice moved into it, and the tropic of Cancer then marked the most northerly point of the ecliptic (500). Hähler in *RE* 3.1459–60, Allen 107ff., Roscher VI 951ff.

148 ὀπισθοτέροισι Only here, a variation of ὀπίστερος (284) and Eudoxus' ὀπίσθιος. Maass compares Hsch. ὀπισθότατος and Hes. *Th.* 921 λοισθότατος.

Λέων The Lion is a prominent constellation, easily recognised by the sickle shape and 1st-mag. star Regulus. Since Africa is the home of lions, it may have originated in Egypt, especially in the era when it contained the summer solstice, and its MR heralded the flooding of the Nile. But it also corresponds to the Babylonian UR.GU.LA, which means either 'hound' or 'lion', and Regulus is LUGAL, meaning 'king' (Waerden *EW* 2.64, 67). The Greeks may therefore have taken their Lion directly from the Babylonians.

In A. the Lion marks the hottest time of the year (149–51); it lies on the tropic of Cancer (491) and also on the ecliptic (545). The extent of the constellation is marked out by references to its body (446), as a guide to the coil of the Hydra, and to its breast, belly and genitals (493), as defining the line (α θ β) of the summer tropic. Hi. 2.1.10 also refers to A. (but not in this poem) as θεωρῶν τὴν κεφαλὴν τοῦ Λέοντος ἀνατέλλουσαν, the head being presumably the top of the sickle curve, the stars ε μ ζ. Regulus (α Leonis) is often referred to as ὁ ἐν τῇ καρδίᾳ τοῦ Λέοντος λαμπρός (Hi. 2.5.7), and sometimes called Καρδία Λέοντος (Gem. 3.5). So Hor. *Carm.* 3.29.19 *stella uesani Leonis* (see *CR* 63, 1949, 8–9), Col. 11.2 *Leonis in pectore clara stella*, Plin. *Nat.* 18.271 *regia in pectore Leonis stella*. In view of the heraldic association of the lion with kings, it came to be called Βασιλίσκος (first in Gem. 3.5); sch. ὁ Λέων ἔχει ἐπὶ τῆς καρδίας ἀστέρα λαμπρὸν Βασιλίσκον λεγόμενον, ὃν οἱ Χαλδαῖοι νομίζουσιν ἄρχειν τῶν οὐρανίων. The modern Regulus appears first in Copernicus. Gundel in *RE* 12.1973ff., Roscher VI 954ff., Allen 252ff.

ὕπο Anastrophe with separation from preceding subst. is more characteristic of tragedy and Plato, e.g. S. *Ant.* 70 ἐμοῦ γ᾽ ἂν ἡδέως δρῴης μέτα, *Tr.* 370 ὃ τοῦδε τυγχάνω μαθὼν πάρα, E. *El.* 1026 ἔκτεινε πολλῶν μίαν ὕπερ, Pl. *Ap.* 19c ὧν ἐγὼ οὐδὲν οὔτε μέγα οὔτε μικρὸν πέρι ἐπαΐω. See K–B 1.333, Schwyzer 2.427.

καλὰ φαείνει Repeated in 450. Max. 442 καλὰ φαείνοι.

149 ἔνθα μέν μέν emphatic, as in δ 87 ἔνθα μὲν οὔτε ἄναξ. In view of 151 this refers to the Lion only. Although the actual solstice was in the Crab, the hottest time of the year was about a month later, when the sun was in the Lion. Hor. *Carm.* 3.29.19–20 *stella uesani Leonis | sole dies referente siccos, Epist.* 1.10.16–17 *momenta Leonis, | cum semel accepit solem furibundus acutum,* Ov. *AA* 1.68 *cum sol Herculei terga Leonis adit,* Mart. 9.90.12 *feruens iuba saeuiet Leonis.*

θερείταται A novel superlative, imitated in Nic. *Ther.* 469 (of midday) ὅτ' ἠελίοιο θερειτάτη ἵσταται ἀκτίς, Nonn. *D.* 2.545 φάος αἰτίζουσα θερείτατον. A. means 'hottest', not 'very hot' (LSJ).

εἰσι κέλευθοι Repeated in 225, 343, 406. The line-ending is Homeric, Κ 66, κ 86; cf. Parm. fr. 1.11, A.R. 1.500. Here κέλευθοι describes the sun's track along the ecliptic, the plural suggesting repetition year after year.

150 ἀσταχύων Homeric form with prothetic α, *hapax* in Β 148 ἐπί τ' ἠμύει ἀσταχύεσσιν, also *h.Hom.* 2.454 ἀσταχύεσσιν, 456 ἀσταχύων (same *sedes* as in A.); later in Antim. fr. 82, and Call, *H.* 4.284, 6.20, fr. 75.46. Here the fields are bereft of corn-ears because they have just been harvested: sch. αἱ γὰρ προτρυγήσεις διὰ τοῦ ἡλίου τὸ κατ' ἀρχὰς συνερχομένου τῷ Λέοντι. Cf. Germ. 153 *densas laetus segetes bene condet arator,* Avien. 399 *flauos tondentur semina crines.* Other sch. suggest a reference to the rape of Persephone in κενεαὶ ἄρουραι, but that is a winter myth. The point of the allusion to crops here is to relate this constellation to a central theme of the poem and its Hesiodic model. There are other echoes of the gen. pl. in anon. *AP* 9.21.6 = *FGE* 1331, Asclep. *AP* 12.36.4 = *HE* 1029. Cf. συνασταχύοιεν (1050).

κενεαί Contrast 1097, with reference to drought.

151 τὰ πρῶτα Adv., in same *sedes* as the familiar ἐξ οὗ δὴ τὰ πρῶτα διαστήτην (Α 6); similarly Call. *H.* 2.58, 64, 4.22, 149. Cf. 763.

συνερχομένοιο Λέοντι Hipparchus (2.1.18) quotes these three lines as supporting evidence for his view that A. puts solstitial and equinoctial points at the beginning of the relevant constellations, whereas Eudoxus puts them in the middle: περὶ γὰρ τὴν τοῦ Κυνὸς ἀνατολὴν καὶ τὰ καύματα μάλιστα γίνεται· αὕτη δὲ γίνεται μετὰ τριάκοντα ἔγγιστα ἡμέρας ἀπὸ τῆς θερινῆς τροπῆς. μετὰ τοσαύτας ἄρα ἡμέρας ἔγγιστα κατ' αὐτὸν ὁ ἥλιος ἐν τῇ ἀρχῇ τοῦ Λέοντος γίνεται. ἐν ταύτῃ τῇ τροπῇ τοίνυν τὴν ἀρχὴν ἐπέχει τοῦ Καρκίνου. See also on 538. Sch. τινὲς δὲ τολμῶσι γράφειν "ἠελίῳ ... Λέοντος" ἀπαιδεύτως. οὐ γὰρ τὰ ζῴδια συνέρχονται, ἀλλ' ὁ ἥλιος ἕκαστον ἐπιπορεύεται. The fixed stars are regarded as a constant frame of reference, with respect to which the sun's position is always changing. Plu. 366a cites line 151 as an indication of the time when the Nile is in full flood.

152 τῆμος A Hesiodic touch, recalling *Op.* 585, on high summer, τῆμος πιότατί τ' αἶγες. This brief passage on summer (149–55) contrasts with the longer and more graphic digression on winter (287–99), though both are associated with their respective solstices.

κελάδοντες Especially of rushing water (e.g. Σ 576), but of wind in β 421 Ζέφυρον κελάδοντ' ἐπὶ οἴνοπα πόντον, a line clearly recalled by A. here.

ἐτησίαι 'Annual' northerly winds experienced in the eastern Mediterranean, useful for Greek ships coming home from Black Sea ports (Cic. *ND* 2.131), but a hindrance to shipping from Alexandria (Caes. *BC* 3.107). Sch. note that the etesians actually commence while the sun is still in Cancer, and this is confirmed by Eudoxus in Gem. *Cal.* Canc. 27 (= 22 July): Κύων ἑῷος ἐπιτέλλει· καὶ τὰς ἑπομένας ἡμέρας νε′ ἐτησίαι πνέουσιν· αἱ δὲ πέντε πρόδρομοι καλοῦνται. The sun, however, entered Leo on the 27th, and sch. (Q) say ἄρχεσθαι τοὺς ἐτησίας πνεῖν ἔτι ὄντος ἡλίου ἐν τῷ Καρκίνῳ, σφοδροτέρους δὲ γίνεσθαι ὅτε ἐν τῷ Λέοντι. See also Hdt. 6.140, Arist. *Mete.* 361b35, Sen. *NQ* 5.10, Gell. 2.22, L. Casson, *Ancient Mariners* (1960) 115.

There are different views on how long the etesians may be expected to prevail, till Leo 17 (12 Aug.) according to Euctemon, till Virgo 5 (31 Aug.) according to Callippus. The latter date allows 40 days, which agrees with A.R. 2.525–6 γαῖαν ἐπιψύχουσιν ἐτήσιαι ἐκ Διὸς αὖραι | ἤματα τεσσαράκοντα, and with the v.l. in Plin. *Nat.* 2.124. Eudoxus (loc. cit.) gives them 55 days, sch. Arat. (Q) 60: πνέουσι δὲ μέχρι Ἄρκτου ἐπιτολῆς ὡς ἐπὶ πλῆθος ἑξήκοντα ἡμερῶν. For Ἄρκτου read Ἀρκτούρου: the Bear does not set and rise, whereas the MR of Arcturus according to Eudoxus was Virgo 19 (= 14 Sept.). These two names are often confused.

εὐρέϊ πόντῳ Homeric phrase, e.g. δ 498. The dat. after a compound in ἐν is also Homeric, e.g. δ 508 τρύφος ἔμπεσε πόντῳ.

153 ἀθρόοι A vivid adj., suggesting a horde of advancing troops, as in Β 439–40 ἀθρόοι ὧδε κατὰ στρατὸν εὐρὺν Ἀχαιῶν | ἴομεν. Arist. *Mete.* 367a31 uses the adv. of wind moving in a mass: μὴ διασπώμενον γὰρ τὸ μὲν ἔξω τὸ δ' ἐντός, ἀλλ' ἀθρόως φερόμενον ἀναγκαῖον ἰσχύειν μᾶλλον.

πλόος It is curious that this noun occurs only once in Homer, γ 169 δολιχὸν πλόον ὁρμαίνοντας. Cf. 731.

154 ὥριος Poetic form of ὡραῖος; cf. 1 131, Hes. *Op.* 543, Nonn. *D.* 3.19 πλόος ὥριος ἦεν. A. makes play with both forms in 1075–6.

εὐρεῖαί μοι The idea of a broad ship for safety derives from Hes. *Op.* 643 νῆ' ὀλίγην αἰνεῖν, μεγάλη δ' ἐνὶ φορτία θέσθαι. Cf. Pers. 5.141–2 *nihil obstat quin trabe uasta | Aegaeum rapias.*

The sudden introduction of the first person gives the warning a greater emphasis, as does the second person in 287. Here and in 413 the subtle μοι is enough to suggest the poet's personal concern for the suffering of others, and with the plural verb (298, 769) he expresses more positively a sense of involvement; cf. 198 οἴω. The tone is different from that of Hesiod's personal complaint in *Op.* 174–5, and reflects the new age. Cf. Servius on Virgil's imitations of *A.* in *G.* 1.456 *gratiosiorem sensum fecit interposita suae personae commemoratione*, and 2.475 *suam autem personam pro quocumque ponit*.

155 τὰ πηδά The steering oars, one on each side of the stern, which are held into the wind when the ship is running before it. Homer has the sg. as a rowing oar (η 328), and πηδάλιον as a steering oar, πηδάλιον μετὰ χερσὶ θεούσης νηὸς ἔχοντα (γ 281). Str. 8.5.3 κατ' ἀποκοπὴν ... τὰ πηδὰ τὰ πηδάλια Ἄρατός φησι. Maass read τε for τά in view of frequent Homeric use of δέ τε, and is followed by Martin. But τά is confirmed by Strabo and sch., and means 'their' oars (Defradas 275). See note on 482, and cf. other uses with nouns (424, 461, 478, 505, 691, 837, 1102). Bernhardy (305) notes Homer's use of the article for emphasis, especially deictic, e.g. Σ 485 τὰ τείρεα, 486 τό τε σθένος. See also Leumann 12 n.

κυβερνητῆρες θ 557 in same *sedes*.

156–166 The Charioteer

This constellation, with the Goat and Kids, is on the left side of the Twins and opposite the Great Bear's head. The Goat is on his left shoulder, the Kids are on his wrist.

The Charioteer, with its 1st-mag. star Capella, seems to have a Babylonian origin, but how it acquired its name is not at all clear. Waerden *EW* 2.71 has identified it with Babylonian GAM ('bent sword' or similar meaning). As known to the Greeks its brightest stars form a recognisable pentagon that lies partly in the Milky Way, and this pattern would have allowed a typical figure with head, shoulders and legs. But S. Lombardo, *AW* 2 (1979) 107ff., suggests a reorientation of the figure to a silhouette with arms outstretched in front. The traditional figure, however, is head δ, shoulders α β, hands η θ, feet ι, and β Tauri. The Greek constellation is a composite one, since its brightest star, the Goat, derives its name from a different source. An adjacent group of fainter stars then came to be known as the Kids, a name that Hyginus (2.13.3) ascribes to Cleostratus. The Goat and Kids are prominent in Greek calendars, usually associated with stormy weather at their ER in September (see 158–9).

The figure was sometimes identified as Erichthonius (*Catast.* 13), or

Orsilochus or Myrtilus (Hyg. 2.13.2). In Nonn. *D.* 38.424 it is Phaethon. In Latin writers the name is either *Heniochus* (Man. 1.362) or *Auriga* (Germ. 157), now the standard name. Rehm in *RE* 8.28off., Roscher VI 915ff., Allen 83ff.

156 ἀστέρας Ἡνιόχοιο The apparent duplication is probably meant to distinguish between the overall figure and the Goat and Kids group within it. Cf. 301 τόξον ... τόξου, and Δ 47 καὶ Πρίαμος καὶ λαὸς ἐϋμμελίω Πριάμοιο.

157 δοκέοι δοκέει is a likely corruption in view of the following indicatives.

φάτις What people say; cf. ζ 29 φάτις ἀνθρώπους ἀναβαίνει, E. *Hipp.* 129–30 μοι | πρῶτα φάτις ἦλθε δεσποίνας.

ἤλυθεν The variation of mood suits the change of tense, and brings out the greater probability of the Goat and Kids being known, because of their appearance in the parapegmata.

Αἰγός The origin of the name is unknown, but it is an obvious one for a pastoral people to give to the conspicuous star group formed by the 1st-mag. Capella (α Aurigae) and the three 3rd- and 4th-mag. stars ε ζ η. Adapted to the figure of the Charioteer, ε has become the left elbow (Hi. 3.3.2) and ζ η the Kids on the left hand: 2.2.57 τὴν δὲ Αἶγά φησι καὶ τοὺς Ἐρίφους, ὧν ἐστὶν ἡ μὲν ἐπὶ τοῦ ἀριστεροῦ ὤμου, οἱ δ' ἐν τῇ ἀριστερᾷ χειρί, 2.3.33 τοῦ Ἡνιόχου τὴν ἀριστερὰν χεῖρα, ἐν ᾗ οἱ Ἔριφοι κεῖνται. As a weather sign the Goat's most important date was its ER on 15 Sept., an event marked by χειμὼν κατὰ θάλασσαν (Gem. *Cal.* Virgo 20). Hence Hor. *Carm.* 3.7.6 *insana Caprae sidera*, Ov. *Met.* 3.594 *sidus pluuiale Capellae, Fast.* 5.113 *signum pluuiale.* The Goat also became identified with the mythical Amalthea (see 163).

158 ἠδ' Ἐρίφων ἠδέ is appropriate, since the Goat and Kids are essentially a group; indeed it is the presence of the latter that distinguishes the former from other bright stars.

The Kids also became famous as a weather sign, because their ER on 28 Sept. was marked by the onset of rough weather: Gem. *Cal.* Libra 3 Εὐκτήμονι Ἔριφοι ἐπιτέλλουσιν ἑσπέριοι· χειμαίνει. A. makes a point of referring again to this weather sign in 679–82. These two passages are the likely source of other poets' use of the Kids as synonymous with storms at sea: Theoc. 7.53–4 χὤταν ἐφ' ἑσπερίοις Ἐρίφοις νότος ὑγρὰ διώκῃ | κύματα, V. *A.* 9.668 *pluuialibus Haedis*, Hor. *Carm.* 3.1.28 *impetus aut orientis Haedi*, Ov. *Tr.* 1.11.13 *nimbosis dubius iactabar ab Haedis.* Poets, regardless of the astronomy, sometimes make this event a setting, if a setting is more appropriate to the context, e.g. Call. *E.* 18.5–6 φεῦγε θαλάσσῃ | συμμίσγειν Ἐρίφων, ναυτίλε, δυομένων. The Kids also may be thought of as abandoning the sea in rough weather. So, of deaths at sea, *AP.* 7.502.4, 640.1, 11.336.2. Cf. Ov. *Met.* 14.711 *freto surgente cadentibus Haedis.* Sch. explain with reference to the MS of the Kids in December: ἡ γὰρ ἑῴα δύσις τῶν Ἐρίφων χειμῶνα φέρει ἡλίου Τοξότην διανύοντος. But the calendars do not see fit to mention this, presumably because storms are regarded as the normal weather in winter, and ships are rarely at sea then.

εἰν ἁλί Cf. 38.

πορφυρούσῃ Sch. μελαινομένῃ. Cf. 296 πορφύρει in similar context. The poetic source is Ξ 16 ὅτε πορφύρῃ πέλαγος μέγα κύματι κωφῷ. Cf. A.R. 1.935 πορφύροντα διήνυσαν Ἑλλήσποντον.

159 ἐσκέψαντο The animate verb implies some concern for suffering mortals, and suits the Stoic notion of cosmic sympathy. Being in the sky the stars are an extension of Zeus. Cf. 408–12, Night's pity for storm-tossed ships.

κεδαιομένους Sch. ἀντὶ τοῦ φθειρομένους. γράφεται "κεραιομένους" ἀντὶ τοῦ κεραϊζομένους. The verb κεδαίω is a late epic form of κεδάννυμι. Cf. A.R. 2.626 μελεϊστὶ κεδαιόμενος θανέεσθαι, Nic. *Ther.* 425 κεδαιομένη φέρετ' ὀδμή. The line-ending has a metrical echo of Ψ 788 παλαιοτέρους ἀνθρώπους and Hes. *Th.* 231 ἐπιχθονίους ἀ.

160 αὐτόν Sc. Ἡνίοχον. Cf. 76. 160, 433.

ἐπὶ λαιά The left hand of the western twin (θ Geminorum) points directly to the Charioteer a short distance to the west. This is a much simpler guide than that of Eudoxus, who describes the figure as λοξὸς ὢν ὑπὲρ τοὺς πόδας τῶν Διδύμων (fr. 29), which involves taking a longer line north-west across the ecliptic. Vitr. 9.4.2, however, follows Eudoxus.

161 δήεις Homeric verb, only in present form, with future meaning, e.g. N 260, η 49. A. resumes the second person from 156–7, as an instructor giving detailed pointers to a learner. The sch. commend the realism of κεκλιμένον: οὐ γάρ ἐστιν ἔξορθος, ἀλλ' ὥσπερ ἐπινεύων καὶ πρὸς τὸ ἐλαύνειν ἐπειγόμενος.

ἄκρα κάρηνα Eudoxus fr. 29 κατέναντι δὲ τῆς κεφαλῆς τῆς Μεγάλης Ἄρκτου ὁ Ἡνίοχος ἔχει τοὺς ὤμους. In view of this, most translators (e.g. Voss, Mair, Zannoni) have understood A. to mean that the Bear's head lies opposite the Charioteer, and οἱ goes with ἀντία δινεύει. This seems to be the sense intended by Cic. fr. 25.2 *aduersum caput huic Helice truculenta tuetur,* and Germ. 164 *Maiorisque Vrsae contra delabitur ora.* On the other hand, sch. ἡ κεφαλὴ αὐτοῦ means that the head of the Charioteer is opposite the Bear, and this appears to be the meaning of Avien. 413 *Helices caput inclinatur ab ore.* On the possible ambiguities see J. Soubiran, Cic. p. 201, Avien. p. 200: he takes the traditional view of A.'s meaning. Erren translates as the Bear's head, but in his list of stars in *PAS* 320 gives Auriga's head (δ) as the star in 161. There are good reasons for thinking that the latter identification is right, and that A. deliberately varied Eudoxus' material in this detail as well as in 160–1. He is proceeding logically with his guide to the stars: first the constellation as a whole is identified from the Twins, then the head star can be recognised by reference to the Bear, the left shoulder is defined by Capella, and the hand stars below it identify the Kids. The language itself requires this interpretation: position is denoted by ἀντία c. gen. (cf. 440, 694, 917, 1084, Φ 481, o 377), whereas c. dat. it implies hostility (Pi. *P.* 4.285, Hdt. 7.236.3). Since only position is being indicated here, Ἑλίκης must go with ἀντία, κάρηνα with οἱ (cf. 47). See Martin's translation.

ἄκρα describes the position of the head star at one extremity of the figure, lying well to the north of the shoulders. Cf. 207 ἐσχατόωντι καρήνῳ. The poetic pl. is no doubt influenced by the fact that the noun is always in a plural context in Homer, e.g. Ι 407 ἵππων ξανθὰ κάρηνα. It appears with sg. name in E. fr. 537.2 κάρηνα ... Μελανίππου.

162 δινεύει Cf. 83; but here of the circular movement only.

ἐπελήλαται The shoulder and the Goat are one and the same star, with names derived from different traditions; cf. 205, 441, and 176 συνεληλάμενοι. This meaning derives from Homeric ἐλαύνω of beating out metal, e.g. Μ 295–6 καλὴν χαλκείην ἐξήλατον, ἣν ἄρα χαλκεὺς | ἤλασεν. Hence the compound verb in Ν 804 of Hector's shield, with beaten bronze fastened on top of the layers of hide, πολλὸς δ' ἐπελήλατο χαλκός. The choice of verb may also be a reminder that these are fixed stars. Erren translates 'geschmiedet', and suggests that A. may be thinking of goldsmiths' work.

163 ἱερή As often in Homer of men or things that manifest the power of gods, e.g. Ρ 464 of Automedon ἱερῷ ἐνὶ δίφρῳ. Cf. 215, 692.

λόγος Perhaps Epimenides; cf. D–K fr. 21.

Διὶ μαζὸν ἐπισχεῖν Hyg. 2.13.4 *Musaeus autem dicit Iouem nutritum a Themide et Amalthea nympha, ... Amaltheam autem habuisse capram quamdam ut in deliciis, quae Iouem dicitur aluisse.* Strabo associates the name with the town of Aegion: 8.7.5 ἱστοροῦσι δ' ἐνταῦθα τὸν Δία ὑπ' αἰγὸς ἀνατραφῆναι, καθάπερ φησὶ καὶ Ἄρατος. Cf. Eust. ad Β 574, *Catast.* 13 Μουσαῖος γάρ φησι Δία γεννώμενον ἐγχειρισθῆναι ὑπὸ Ῥέας Θέμιδι, Θέμιν δὲ Ἀμαλθείᾳ δοῦναι τὸ βρέφος, τὴν δὲ ἔχουσαν αἶγα ὑποθεῖναι, τὴν δ' ἐκθρέψαι Δία. Like the myth of the nursing Bears in Crete, this is a reminder of the importance of Zeus in the poem. A. may have taken this detail from Call. *H.* 1.48–9 σὺ δ' ἐθήσαο πίονα μαζὸν | αἰγὸς Ἀμαλθείης. Cf. Call. fr. anon. 89 (O. Schneider 2.722) κεῖθι δέ οἱ πρώτη μαζὸν ἐπέσχ᾽ Ἐρίφῃ, sch. τὴν δὲ Αἶγα Νίκανδρος [fr. 114] Ἀμάλθειαν καὶ Διὸς τροφόν, Ov. *Fast.* 5.120–1 *ubere, quod nutrix posset habere Iouis.* | *lac dabat illa deo*, Man. 1.366 *nobilis et mundi nutrito rege Capella.* The variant ὑποσχεῖν is preferred by Voss on the strength of E. *Ion* 1372 μαστὸν οὐχ ὑπέσχεν and Q.S. 6.140 ὑποσχομένη. But in *Ion* Dobree reads οὐκ ἐπέσχεν: cf. Χ 83 μαζὸν ἐπέσχον, E. *Andr.* 225.

On the myth of Amaltheia in general see Stoll in Roscher 1 262–6.

164 Ὠλενίην Sch. (M) ὠλενίη δὲ λέγεται διὰ τὸ ἐπὶ τῆς ὠλένης τοῦ Ἡνιόχου. ἤ, ὡς ἄλλοι, Ὠλένου θυγάτηρ. (S) τινὲς δὲ Ὠλένου θυγατέρα. ἢ διὰ τὸ εἶναι ἐπὶ τῆς ὠλένης τοῦ Ἡνιόχου. ἢ ἐξ Ὠλένης [Ὠλένου Martin] πόλεως. Hyginus (2.13.3) reports one derivation, *Olenum quemdam fuisse nomine, Vulcani filium; ex hoc duas nymphas Aega et Helicen natas, quae Iouis fuerunt nutrices.* He also mentions an eponymous city in Elis. Strabo (8.7.5), after citing 164, adds δηλῶν τὸν τόπον, διότι πλησίον Ὠλένη. Homer names an Ὤλενος (Β 639) in Aetolia, Hesiod (fr. 12) in Achaea; both mention a πέτρη Ὠλενίη (Β 617, fr. 13) in Elis. There appears to be no evidence for the true derivation of this name, or for A.'s source. But it is quite probable, as Martin suggests, that A. introduced it here because of its supposed derivation from ὠλένη: cf. his etymology of Ἅμαξαι in 27. There is an echo of this line in Nonn. *D.* 1.450–1 ἢ σχεδὸν Ἡνιόχηος, ὃς Ὠλενίην ἐν Ὀλύμπῳ | ... Αἶγα τιταίνει, also 23. 314 Αἶγα Διὸς τροφόν. Cf. Ov. *Ep.* 17.188 *Oleniumque pecus*, *Met.* 3.594, *Fast.* 5.113 *Oleniae ... Capellae*, Man. 5.130 *Olenie seruans praegressos tollitur Haedos*, Sen. *Med.* 313 *Oleniae sidera Caprae.*

ὑποφῆται Once in Homer, Π 235, of the Selloi, the interpreters of the will of Zeus at Dodona. The word is used of those who speak under the inspiration of another: see Gow on Theoc. 16.29 Μουσάων δὲ μάλιστα τίειν ἱεροὺς ὑποφήτας. Cf. 17. 115, 22.116, A.R. 1.1311 Νηρῆος θείοιο πολυφράδμων ὑποφήτης.

165 πολλή τε καὶ ἀγλαή See note on 41. Hi. 3.3.3 ὁ ἐπὶ τοῦ ἀριστεροῦ ὤμου λαμπρός.

οἱ δέ οἱ An unusual piece of word-play. A. makes much use of this idiom, but elsewhere with different forms of the article. The dat. refers to the Goat, 'her Kids'.

166 λεπτὰ φαείνονται Cf. 607, 894. The stars ζ η are of 4th and 3rd mag. respectively.

καρπὸν κάτα χειρός καρπὸν κάτα is added to distinguish the hand from the arm; cf. Ω 671–2 ἐπὶ καρπῷ χεῖρα γέροντος | ἔλλαβε, ω 398 κύσε χεῖρ᾽ ἐπὶ καρπῷ, E. *Ion* 1009 κἀπὶ καρπῷ ... χερὸς φέρω. Another way of making this distinction is ἄκρην οὔτασε χεῖρα (Ε 336); *Sphaera* 24 καρπὸν κατ᾽ ἄκρας χειρός.

167–178 The Bull

The Bull's head has a distinct outline, the group known as the Hyades. Its left horn is the same star as the Charioteer's right foot. The Bull rises with, but sets before, the Charioteer.

The nucleus of this constellation is the conspicuous V-shaped group α θ γ δ ε Tauri, of which α is the 1st-mag. star Aldebaran. This group alone as the Bull appears to have a Babylonian source in GUD.AN.NA ('heavenly bull'), which corresponds to the Greek constellation (Waerden *EW* 68). It was seen as a bull's head, perhaps with Aldebaran as the eye, and was important in Old Babylonian times as marking the sun's position at the vernal equinox (Allen 378). This tradition of leading the year survives in V. *G.* 1.217–18 *candidus auratis aperit cum cornibus annum | Taurus.* But the original Greek name for this star-group was Ὑάδες (173), which appears first in Σ 486, among the stars on Achilles' shield, then Hes. *Op.* 615 and fr. 291 (with names for the five stars as nymphs). In the parapegma of Euctemon (fl. 430 BC) it is the Hyades that are named for risings and settings (Gem. *Cal.* Scorp. 27, al.), whereas Ταῦρος appears first in Eudoxus (fr. 29). The Bull must, however, have been established by the late fifth century, when the Greek zodiac was finalised (Dicks *EGA* 87). The figure was extended to take in the Charioteer's right foot as its left horn (174), and three adjacent stars to represent the bent fore-legs (515–17); behind the head and forelegs the figure is simply cut off (322). Later the ancient Pleiades were incorporated in the constellation, but A. still lists them separately (254–67).

The Bull came to be identified with the various mythological bulls associated with Europa, Pasiphae and Theseus, and seen as the image of Io (sch. 167, *Catast.* 14, Hyg. 2.21.1). Ovid eruditely refers to one of the Hyades in *Fast.* 6.712 *stabis Agenorei fronte uidenda bouis.* Gundel in *RE* 5A. 53ff., Roscher VI 938ff., Allen 378ff.

167 πὰρ ποσί Cf. N 617, Ξ 411 in same *sedes*. The stars are ι Aurigae and β Tauri.

κεραόν Cf. Γ 24 in same *sedes*. The juxtaposition of Ἡνιόχου and κεραόν anticipates 174–6.

πεπτηότα This epic form appears to serve as pf. part. of both πίπτω in the sense of 'lying', and πτήσσω of 'crouching'. See K–G 2.524, 528, Chantraine 1.428, Monro *HG* 29, Veitch 479, 501. In Homer the latter meaning applies in ξ 354 of Odysseus hiding in a thicket, ξ 474 of men in ambush, χ 362 of Medon hiding, Β 312 of nestlings cowering; the former in Φ 503 of arrows lying around, χ 384 of dead bodies, ν 98 of adjacent headlands. In A. the sense 'crouching' suits the figure of the Bull here, in view of sch. ὥσπερ γὰρ ὀκλάσας ἐστίν, and 517 ὀκλάς. The same is appropriate to the Kneeler in 615. Elsewhere in

A., in descriptions of star positions, 'lying' is all that is required: 318 Dolphin, 324 Orion, 353 Andromeda, 369 nameless stars. Martin on 324, following Maass, Index 'extensum', derives the part. from πίτνω = πετάννυμι, with the sense 'étendu'; see also Mair on this line, and Ceporinus '*expansum*'. But this is hardly suited to the compact figure of the Bull, and not at all to the tiny Dolphin (318). All the instances in A. will in fact admit the simple sense 'lying', but, as 'crouching' is particularly appropriate to the figures of the Bull and the Kneeler, the latter meaning may also be implied. The part. can therefore serve the dual purpose of noting the position and describing an obvious characteristic of the figure, in the manner of εἰλεῖται (46), δινεύει (83), etc.

168 μαίεσθαι Inf. as imper. This inf. occurs once in Homer (ξ 356), in the same *sedes*, but not as imper.

ἐοικότα I.e. looking like a bull's head, and so 'recognisable'; sch. οἱ γὰρ ἀστέρες αὐτοῦ βούκρανον ἀληθῶς διαγράφουσι, καὶ διὰ τοῦτό εἰσι γνώριμοι. Cf. 433, 820, and A.R. 1.1141 in a different context. The sense may have been influenced by Hes. *Op.* 235 τίκτουσιν δὲ γυναῖκες ἐοικότα τέκνα γονεῦσι. See Edwards 137.

169 τοίη οἱ κεφαλή For the Bull's head see note on 167–178. τοίη has causal force, like οἵη in 143, but the exclamatory clause is not appropriate here: it naturally depends on a personal verb.

διακέκριται Cf. 11, 681, of distinct star groups. There may be some reminiscence of θ 195 καί κ' ἀλαός τοι, ξεῖνε, διακρίνειε τὸ σῆμα. A. makes a point of stressing the recognisability of constellations wherever possible.

οὐδέ τις ἄλλῳ κτλ. Cf. 142, 456.

170 κάρη Cf. 52, 58, 672.

οἷα Adv., expressing indirect exclamation; see note on 143.

171 ἀμφοτέρωθεν The five stars outline the head on both sides.

ἐλισσόμενοι See note on 95 ἐλίσσεται.

τυπόωσι Primarily of stamping an impression, thence fig. of modelling, drawing, moulding; cf. Mel. *AP* 12.56.2 = *HE* 4573 Πραξιτέλης Κύπριδος παῖδα τυπωσάμενος.

172 λίην 'very much', as again in 277, 1086. Cf. Α 553 καὶ λίην σε πάρος γ' οὔτ' εἴρομαι. The Hyades are well known, and this is emphasised by the repetition of the sense in a negative form.

εἴρεται Pass. only here and 261 of the Pleiades. Homer has act. and med., e.g. λ 137 νημερτέα εἴρω, 542 εἴροντο δὲ κήδε' ἑκάστη.

αὔτως See note on 21.

173 νήκουστοι Pass. only here, 'unheard' meaning 'unknown'; act. in Emped. 137.3 νήκουστος ὁμοκλέων.

Ὑάδες See note on 167–178. The five stars (169) are given names in

Hes. fr. 291 νύμφαι Χαρίτεσσιν ὁμοῖαι, | Φαισύλη ἠδὲ Κορωνὶς εὐστέφανός τε Κλέεια | Φαιώ θ' ἱμερόεσσα καὶ Εὐδώρη τανύπεπλος, | ἃς Ὑάδας καλέουσιν ἐπὶ χθονὶ φῦλ' ἀνθρώπων. The sch. also say that Thales referred to two stars, E. *Phaethon* (fr. 780N = fr. inc. sed. 2 Diggle) three, Achaeus (fr. 46N = *TrGF* F 46) four, Musaeus (18) five, Hippias and Pherecydes (*FGrH* 6 F 9, 3 F 90) seven, probably to match them with the Pleiades: sch. (S) 174 τὰ δὲ ὀνόματα τούτων εἰσὶ ταῦτα· Ἀμβροσία, Φαισύλη, Κλειτή, Εὐδώρα, Βρομεία, Κισσηίς. Because they are in Homer and Hesiod, they are mentioned in E. *Ion* 1156 and *El.* 468.

The Hyades were prominent in Greek calendars, especially at their MS in late November: Gem. *Cal.* Scorp. 27 Εὐκτήμονι Ὑάδες δύονται· καὶ ἔτι ὔει. 29 Εὐδόξῳ Ὑάδες δύνουσι· καὶ χειμαίνει σφόδρα. Greek tradition therefore usually derived the name from ὔειν: sch. 171 οἱ δὲ ὅτι δυόμεναι αἴτιαι ὑετοῦ γίνονται. Hence V. *A.* 1.744, 3.516 *pluuiasque Hyadas*, Hor. *Carm.* 1.3.14 *tristis Hyadas*, Ov. *Fast.* 5.166 *nauita quas Hyadas Graius ab imbre uocat*, Sen. *Med.* 311–12 *pluuias* | *Hyadas*. But constellations were always named after figures, so that particular stars could be identified from their parts, and the derivation from ὗς is therefore much more likely. The formation that suggested a bull's head could also suggest a pig's, and the group would have been known as the Pig or Sow. The sg. is perhaps to be read in the Milesian parapegma (Gundel in *RE* 8.2.2615). Cf. Ptol. *Tetr.* 2.12.3 κατὰ τὴν Ὑάδα, and Stat. *Silv.* 1.6.21 *tantis Hyas inserena nimbis*. The Latin name supports the derivation from ὗς: Cic. *ND* 2.111 *nostri imperite Suculas, quasi a subus essent non ab imbribus nominatae*. The plural would have developed from the fact that there are several stars in the group: cf. 254–67 on the Pleiades.

παντὶ μετώπῳ The five stars, strictly speaking, outline the front of the Bull's head. Hi. 2.6.6 refers to the star ε as τῶν ἐπὶ τοῦ ἀριστεροῦ μετώπου ὁ βορειότερος, and to γ at the point of the V as ὁ ἐν τῷ ῥύγχει (3.4.8).

174 βεβλέαται Lit. 'have been thrown', and used by A. as one of his many variations for the sense of 'lie' in referring to positions of stars; cf. 371, also 311 βεβλημένος, 330 βέβληται, 492 κέαται βεβολημένοι. The Homeric form is βεβλήαται (Λ 657, λ 194), but in Ionic the η is shortened to ε, e.g. Hdt. 6.24 περιεβεβλέατο, Hp. *Cord.* 1.2 περιεβλέαται (3rd pers. sg.).

174–176 The star β Tauri does double duty as the left horn-tip of the Bull and the right foot of the Charioteer (see note on 167–178). Eudox. fr. 29 describes the latter as ἔχων τὸν δεξιὸν πόδα κοινὸν τῷ ἐν ἄκρῳ τῷ ἀριστερῷ κέρατι τοῦ Ταύρου. A.'s version is a good illustration of his variation technique in expansion, arrangement, vocabulary, syntax and word-form.

174 κεράατος An expansion of κέρᾱτος (Hermipp. 43), perhaps coined by A. on the analogy of καρήατος (Ψ 44), an expansion of κάρητος (ζ 230). Q.S. imitates in 6.225, 238. Cf. κεράατα in Nic. *Ther.* 291, [Opp.] *C.* 2.494, Nonn. *D.* 11.80. The neglect of Hermann's Bridge is mitigated by word-end in the fourth princeps (West *GM* 155); cf. 186, 572, 784.

176 ἐπέχει See note on 57.

συνεληλάμενοι Sch. τῷ τόνῳ ὡς "οὐτάμενοι". ὑφαιρεθέντος γὰρ τοῦ σ ἀναβιβάζεται ὁ τόνος. ὁ δὲ νοῦς· συνηρμοσμένοι. On the metaphor see note on 162 ἐπελήλαται.

177–178 The Bull rises simultaneously with the Charioteer, but sets before it. In Greek latitudes, since the axis of the celestial sphere is inclined obliquely to the horizon, the more northerly of the stars that rise and set describe greater arcs above the horizon than the more southerly; therefore of two stars that rise simultaneously the more southerly, with its smaller arc from east to west, will reach its setting point sooner than the more northerly. Autolycus of Pitane (flor. c. 320 BC) expressed this in the form of a theorem (*De sphaera* 9): ἐὰν ἐν σφαίρᾳ μέγιστος κύκλος λοξὸς ὢν πρὸς τὸν ἄξονα ὁρίζῃ τό τε φανερὸν τῆς σφαίρας καὶ τὸ ἀφανές, τῶν ἅμα ἀνατελλόντων σημείων τὰ πρὸς τῷ φανερῷ πόλῳ ὕστερον δύνει, τῶν δὲ ἅμα δυνόντων τὰ πρὸς τῷ φανερῷ πόλῳ πρότερον ἀνατέλλει. Cf. Gem. 14.4 συμβαίνει μὴ πάντα τὰ ἅμα ἀνατέλλοντα καὶ ἅμα δύνειν, ἀλλὰ τῶν ἅμα ἀνατελλόντων ἀεὶ τὰ πρὸς μεσημβρίαν μᾶλλον αὐτῶν κείμενα πρότερον δύνειν διὰ τὸ ἐλάττονα τμήματα ὑπὲρ γῆς φέρεσθαι, 14.8 μνημονεύει δὲ καὶ τούτων ἐπὶ ποσὸν Ἄρατος λέγων οὕτως [177–8]. ἐν γὰρ τούτοις φησὶ τὸν Ταῦρον ἅμα τῷ Ἡνιόχῳ ἀνατείλαντα πρότερον δύνειν. γίνεται δὲ τοῦτο παρὰ τὴν τῶν τμημάτων ὑπεροχήν, ὧν ὑπὲρ γῆς φέρονται καὶ ὑπὸ γῆν οἱ ἁπλανεῖς ἀστέρες.

Hipparchus also cites 177–8, to point out that only the feet of the Charioteer rise simultaneously with the Bull, the rest with the Fishes and the Ram (1.5.14). After a reference to the same error in 718–19, he finds A. at fault also in making the Bull set first: parts near the feet of the Charioteer actually set before the Bull, and the right foot simultaneously with Taurus 27° (17). Hipparchus, however, is here referring to the 30° arc of the ecliptic, which is the 'sign' of the zodiac and does not entirely correspond to the constellation. A. is certainly thinking of the constellations, and it would have suited his purpose if only parts of the two could be seen rising together, and at least the Hyades set before the Charioteer. Hipparchus remarks that Attalus found no fault with A. here (18). But he makes no mention of Eudoxus, which suggests that this is A.'s own addition to the subject-matter.

177 προφερέστερος C. inf., as in K 352–3 βοῶν προφερέσteραί εἰσιν | ἑλκέμεναι, though with different sense.

178 εἰς ἑτέρην The western horizon, as again 279, 659; cf. 571, 617, 726 ἐξ ἑτέρης of the eastern. The fem. may be derived from its use with χείρ understood, e.g. γ 441.

ὀμηλυσίη I.e. simultaneously with the Charioteer. The word occurs only here, but cf. 536 κατηλυσίη, also A.R. 4.886, h.Hom. 2.228, 4.37 ἐπηλυσίη, Agath. AP 9.665.4 συνηλυσίη.

179–267 CYNOSURA GROUP: CEPHEUS, CASSIEPEIA, ANDROMEDA, THE HORSE, THE RAM, THE TRIANGLE, THE FISHES, PERSEUS, THE PLEIADES

179–187 Cepheus

The family of Cepheus is also in the sky. He is behind Cynosura, and his feet form a triangle with her tail, while his belt is near the Dragon.

The origin of the constellation Cepheus is unknown: the name appears first in Eudox. fr. 33, and there seems to be no corresponding name in Babylonian texts. It is significant that Cepheus is linked with Cassiepeia, Andromeda and Perseus, all in the same region of the sky. Voss therefore plausibly suggested (p. 34) that these are Greek constellations formed about the end of the fifth century and derived from the tragic legend involving those characters, perhaps under the influence of the *Andromeda* plays of Sophocles and Euripides. Such an origin may be implied by *Catast.* 15 ἦν δέ, ὡς Εὐριπίδης φησίν, Αἰθιόπων βασιλεύς, Ἀνδρομέδας δὲ πατήρ· τὴν δ' αὐτοῦ θυγατέρα δοκεῖ προθεῖναι τῷ κήτει βοράν, ἣν Περσεὺς ὁ Διὸς διέσωσε, δι' ἣν καὶ αὐτὸς ἐν τοῖς ἄστροις ἐτέθη. 36 ἱστορεῖ δὲ ταῦτα Σοφοκλῆς ὁ τῶν τραγῳδιῶν ποιητὴς ἐν τῇ Ἀνδρομέδα. Cf. Hyg. 2.9. These romantic dramas certainly were popular in Athens, as is attested by the references in Aristophanes and the frequent portrayal of scenes from them on Attic vases. These four constellations were conveniently close to the Horse, which came to be identified with Pegasus (see note on 205), and a place was found for the Sea-monster, which A. associates with Cepheus and Andromeda in 629–31.

Cepheus is not an obvious group, but its pattern of mainly 3rd-mag. stars allows for the convenient features of head (ζ), shoulders (α ι), belt (β) and feet (γ κ). It is far enough north to be half-circumpolar (649–52), and the figure is orientated with the feet towards the pole. It does not appear in the Greek calendars, but its ER is included in some versions of the Julian: Hor. *Carm.* 3.29.17–18 *iam clarus occultum Andromedae pater | ostendit ignem* (a rare reference for the special interest of Maecenas), Col. 11.2.51 *Cepheus uespere exoritur, tempestatem significat.* Tümpel in *RE* 2.1109ff., Roscher VI 884ff., Allen 155ff.

179 Κηφῆος In Hdt. 7.61.3 Cepheus, son of Belus and father of Andromeda, became grandfather of Perses, the eponymous hero of the Persians; cf. 150. In illustrations, therefore, the constellation figure is usually represented in oriental garb, and *Arat. Lat.* translates *Cepheus Medorum genus.* Euripides, however, makes him an Ethiopian king (*Catast.* 15).

μογερόν An adj. characteristic of tragedy, e.g. A. *Pr.* 565 of Io, S. *El.* 93 of the house of Atreus, E. *Tr.* 783, 790 of Andromache and Hector. A. does seem to have the theatre in mind here. Cf. A.R. 3.853.

Ἰασίδαο A reminiscence of λ 283 Ἀμφίονος Ἰασίδαο, an entirely different legend. There are two traditions about the ancestry of Cepheus, and the link between them may be the name Belus. In the Herodotean version (see above) Cepheus is son of the Persian Belus; here he is a descendant of Iasus, king of Argos, through Io and the Egyptian Belus (Apollod. *Bibl.* 2.1.3, Paus. 2.16.1). The sch. are confused: see Martin *SAV* 171. It is clear from 181 that A. has chosen the version that makes Cepheus a descendant of Io, as a reminder of the importance of Zeus in this poem.

180 αὔτως ἄρρητον Cf. 21, 172–3, also 2 ἄρρητον after neg.

κατακείσεται Lit. of lying hid, P 677 θάμνῳ ὑπ' ἀμφικόμῳ κατακείμενος, here fig. of remaining obscure. The fut. means that these relatively new constellations will soon become famous because of this poem. Maass needlessly emends to κατακείαται on the strength of ω 527 (which is in any case pl.).

181 οὐρανὸν εἰς ὄνομ' ἦλθεν For the position of εἰς cf. ο 541 Πύλον εἰς. A. humorously combines the literal and figurative meanings of οὐρανός and ὄνομα.

ἐπεὶ Διὸς ἐγγύθεν ἦσαν A reminiscence of η 205 ἐπεί σφισιν ἐγγύθεν εἰμέν, Σ 133 ἐπεὶ φόνος ἐγγύθεν αὐτῷ. For ἐγγύθεν c. gen. cf. 480, 1127; also Λ 723.

182 Eudox. fr. 33 ὑπὸ δὲ τὴν οὐρὰν τῆς Μικρᾶς Ἄρκτου. A. follows with variation. The starting-point for the identification of this group is the Little Bear, and the whole of Cepheus is correctly described by Eudoxus as being below, i.e. to the south of, its tail. But A.'s κατόπισθεν is also valid, being relative to the figure of the Bear.

Κυνοσουρίδος First here, and 227, 308. A. combines the two names with their distinct origins. Manetho imitates in 2.(1).24 καὶ κεφαλῆς ἀγχοῦ βαιῆς Κυνοσουρίδος Ἄρκτου. Ov. *Tr.* 5.3.7 *suppositum stellis Cynosuridos Vrsae*, Germ. 189 *tangit Cynosurida caudam.*

183 ἀμφοτέρας χεῖρας τανύοντι Not in Eudoxus. A. has in fact exaggerated the effect of outstretched arms. To the west of the right shoulder (α) the stars η and θ represent a short bent arm (279, 310, 631, 633), while east of the left shoulder (ι) there is only a line of very faint stars to serve as an arm. Hi. 1.11.16 refers to a left arm, which is probably the left shoulder star. Because of this line the Farnese globe shows Cepheus with long, outstretched arms.

ἔοικεν Martin's correction of ἐοικώς seems necessary. The sentence already has one part., and it is unlikely that A. should have added another with ἐστί understood. Cf. 439. The corruption would have come from the more frequent use of the part. (91, 278, 340, 512, 1126).

184 ἴση οἱ στάθμη Eudox. fr. 33 τοὺς πόδας ὁ Κηφεὺς ἔχει πρὸς ἄκραν τὴν οὐρὰν τρίγωνον ἰσόπλευρον ποιοῦντας. A. rewrites, but agrees with Eudoxus in saying that the star at the tip of the Bear's tail (now Polaris) makes an equilateral triangle with the two feet of Cepheus (γ κ). This is good enough as a rough guide, but Hipparchus (1.5.19) finds fault with all his predecessors (ἀγνοοῦσι πάντες): ἡ γὰρ μεταξὺ τῶν ποδῶν ἐλάσσων ἐστὶν ἐκατέρας τῶν λοιπῶν, ὥστε ἰσοσκελὲς τρίγωνον γίνεσθαι, καὶ μὴ ἰσόπλευρον.

ἴση A. has Epic ῑ also in 79, 377, 543, 656, 658; Attic ῐ in 235, 513. See W. Wyatt on the quantity of ι before σ (192).

στάθμη A carpenter's rule or a straight line drawn by means of it. Thus Odysseus, lining up the planks for his raft, ἐπὶ στάθμην ἴθυνεν (ε 245), and similarly the axes in φ 121.

οὐρῆς Cf. 49 νεάτη ἐπιτείνεται οὐρῇ. The variant Ἄρκτου is less appropriate with the adj. Germ. 189 *caudam*, Avien. 446 *extrema ... Vrsa*. The corruption would have come from either a gloss or the end of 182.

185 ὅσση ποδὸς ἐς πόδα τείνει An ingenious and lucid version of Eudoxus' geometry, with some word-play on the three inflexions of πούς in one line. Cleverness in versifying mathematical material is a feature of A.'s style: cf. 497-8, 537-43.

186 ζώνης Eudox. fr. 33 τὸ δὲ μέσον αὐτοῦ πρὸς τῇ καμπῇ τοῦ διὰ τῶν Ἄρκτων Ὄφεως. A. has called Cepheus' central star (β) the belt; Hi. (3.3.12) refers to it as ὁ ἐν τῷ σώματι λαμπρός. It is a 3rd-mag. star.

μεταβλέψειας The prefix suggests the observer following the outline of Cepheus northward towards the Little Bear and then changing his line of vision westwards to the Dragon. Cf. A.R. 1.725-6, of Jason's brilliant cloak, τῆς μὲν ῥηίτερόν κεν ἐς ἠέλιον ἀνιόντα | ὅσσε βάλοις ἢ κεῖνο μεταβλέψειας ἔρευθος. For breach of Hermann's Bridge with pentasyllabic ending cf. Κ 317, Ψ 760, α 241, δ 684, σ 140, χ 291. See note on 174 and Ludwich 137.

187 πρώτης ἱέμενος καμπῆς Sch. take ἱέμενος with ἀπὸ ζώνης and βλέψειας (omitting μετα-) with acc. καμπήν. But the position of ἱέμενος between adj. and noun shows that it is intended to go with that phrase, and the Homeric use c. gen. gives an appropriate sense: cf. κ 529 ἱέμενος ποταμοῖο ῥοάων, Λ 168 ἱέμενοι πόλιος. This bend is the first from the head, where the line of stars from the other direction παλίνορσος ἀνατρέχει (54).

μεγάλοιο The epithet recalls μέγα θαῦμα (46) and μυρίος (47). The variant σκολίοιο makes equally good sense in the context of this line, but it is attested only by Hipparchus, who could have been influenced by 70 in quoting this line from memory. Germanicus, with *sinuosi* (192), follows Hipparchus, as he does elsewhere, even to the extent of correcting A.'s astronomy: e.g. his version of 184–5 pointedly makes the triangle isosceles (188–91). Avienius follows Germanicus with *flexi* (449), though he is faithful to A. in the matter of the triangle. Modern editors are divided between μεγάλοιο (Bekker, Mair, Zannoni) and σκολιοῖο (Voss, Maass, Martin, Erren), but Maass *Aratea* 79 remains uncertain. Hipparchus is not always reliable with poetic epithets that are not astronomically significant (cf. 506), and in this case it is better to follow the manuscripts' reading. It is in any case more characteristic of A. to vary his epithets, e.g. of the Hare, 369 γλαυκοῦ, 594 χαροπός; 390 Κήτεος αἰθερίοιο, 398 κυανέου.

188–196 Cassiepeia

Cassiepeia is a small constellation with bright stars in the form of a key. The arms are outstretched as if in sorrow.

This circumpolar constellation is conspicuous in the north because of its five bright stars set in the form of a wide-angled **W**. Without β it corresponds to the Babylonian LU.LIM, perhaps 'stag' (Waerden *EW* 71). With the addition of a few fainter stars the Greek constellation is seen as a female figure in silhouette, seated on a chair, as the Farnese globe clearly shows. *Catast.* 16 ἐσχημάτισται ἐγγὺς ἐπὶ δίφρου καθημένη. A. makes no reference to the chair in this passage, but brings it in later in 251–2. Here he is concentrating on the tragic figure of Cassiepeia herself. In 192–3 he compares this figure to an ancient key, and it is possible that this star-group was at one time known as the Key: see note on 192.

In Latin the central Greek vowel is sometimes retained, as *Cassiepia* (Cic. fr. 30, Vitr. 9.4.2, Germ. 193, Man. 1.354), otherwise *Cassiope*, perhaps influenced by the Corcyrean town of that name (Ov. *Met.* 4.738, Man. 5.504), and *Cassiopea* (Virg. *Cat.* 9.28). The standard name is now Cassiopeia. Allen 142ff., Roscher VI 908ff., Bubbe in *RE* 10.2.2322ff.

188 τοῦ Eudox. fr. 34 τοῦ μὲν Κηφέως ἔμπροσθέν ἐστιν ἡ Κασσιέπεια. The προ- in προκυλίνδεται therefore refers to the way the figures are orientated towards each other, not to their celestial movement. Cassiepeia actually lies to the east of Cepheus, and so follows him round the pole.

δαιμονίη An epithet suited to the tragic house of Cepheus: cf. 179 μογερόν, 197 αἰνόν, 654 δειλή. With reference to misfortune it is rarely used of persons, but rather of circumstances, e.g. Lys. 6.32 ὑπὸ δαιμονίου τινὸς ἀγόμενος ἀνάγκης, Pl. *Hp. Maj.* 304c δαιμονία τις τύχη.

προκυλίνδεται Once in Homer, of the sea, οὐδ' ἄρα τε προκυλίνδεται οὐδετέρωσε (Ξ 18). But here προ- corresponds to Eudoxus' ἔμπροσθεν and κυλίνδεται to ἐστιν.

οὐ μάλα πολλή Sch. καὶ γὰρ μικρὸν ἐπέχει τοῦ οὐρανοῦ τόπον. See note on 41. Some translators, e.g. Voss and Martin, have taken πολλή to refer to brightness, which makes nonsense of the following line. This error is due to Hipparchus' criticism (1.5.21), which implies that he understood οὐ μάλα πολλή to mean 'not very bright', since he points out that most of Cassiepeia's stars are brighter than the shoulder stars of Ophiuchus, which A. has described as being visible at full moon (77–9), and almost brighter than all but two stars in Andromeda (cf. 198–201). Hipparchus' misunderstanding shows that A.'s use of πολλή could be ambiguous even to Greek readers. Erren rightly translates 'gar nicht gross'. Cassiepeia is indeed a small constellation with bright stars.

189 νυκτὶ φαεινομένη παμμηνίδι See notes on 41 φαινομένη and 78 διχόμηνι σελήνη. Cassiepeia has three stars of 2nd mag. and three of 3rd, and its position well to the north of the moon's track makes it that much more visible.

190 οὐ γάρ μιν πολλοί A. is indulging in some word-play with this phrase after οὐ μάλα πολλή (188), contrasting the different meanings of sg. and pl. The verbal artifice may have contributed to the confusion discussed above on 188. Since A. is describing only the figure of Cassiepeia herself, without the chair, he may be referring to just the four bright stars α γ δ ε. There is also a Homeric echo here; see the following note.

ἐπημοιβοί This rare adj. occurs twice in Homer, and A. imitates both passages here. In ξ 513 οὐ γὰρ πολλαὶ χλαῖναι ἐπημοιβοί τε χιτῶνες the reference is to a change of clothing, and A. recalls the language but not the sense. Of Μ 455–6 δικλίδας ὑψηλάς· δοιοὶ δ' ἔντοσθεν ὀχῆες | εἶχον ἐπημοιβοί, μία δὲ κληῒς ἐπαρήρει the context too is recalled in 190–3. Cf. Parm. 1.14 κληῒδας ἀμοιβούς. The bolts are ἐπημοιβοί in the sense that they overlap each other, but how the adj. is meant to apply to the stars of Cassiepeia is not immediately obvious. Mair and Martin translate simply with 'alternate stars' and 'd'un éclat alterné'. Erren translates 'nicht reichlich und zum Wechseln', explaining the sense as drawn from the *Odyssey* passage and applied to the queen as clothed in stars. This seems to me both pointless and far-fetched. The context requires a specific detail in the formation of the star-group, and I suggest that this is to be seen in the zig-zag pattern of the stars that represent the queen herself (i.e. without the chair), namely the line formed by α γ δ ε. See also my note on 192. Nic. *Ther.* 365 uses the adj. in another context, of swellings that occur in different places one after the other.

γανόωσιν Τ 359 κόρυθες λαμπρὸν γανόωσαι. Cf. 27 τροχόωσι, with note on diectasis. Here the verb is transitive.

191 ἐπιρρήδην Primarily of explicit speech, e.g. A.R. 2.640 ἐπιρρήδην μετέειπεν. Cf. 261 of names. Here the sense is transferred to that of a clear visual outline.

στιχόωσιν The stars give the figure a clear outline. The act. is trans. only here (LSJ wrongly 'stand in rows'), intrans. in 372, also A.R. 1.30, Mosch. 2.142; cf. Ο 635 ὁμοστιχάει. The rhyming couplet is a mark of the Hesiodic style; cf. 266–7, 364–5, 888–9, 1115–16, *Op.* 383–4, 471–2, 672–3, 689–90. It marks a balance or a contrast, and may sometimes suggest popular verses illustrating star or weather lore.

192–193 οἵη δὲ κληῖδι ... ἀνακρούουσιν ὀχῆας The reading of the MSS, with οἵην and ὀχῆες, would mean that the constellation is compared to a door, and that the bolts knock back the door. But the Homeric language of the simile recalls scenes in which the bolts are knocked back by a key, and it is to a key that A. compares Cassiepeia. The most relevant passage is φ 47–50 ἐν δὲ κληῖδ' ἧκε, θυρέων δ' ἀπέκοπτεν ὀχῆας | ἄντα τιτυσκομένη ... τόσ' ἔβραχε καλὰ θύρετρα | πληγέντα κληῖδι, πετάσθησαν δέ οἱ ὦκα. Penelope inserts her key through a hole in the door, and with it knocks back the bolts that are holding the two wings of the door closed on the inside. We also know from φ 6 that she is carrying a κληῖδ' εὐκαμπέα, and the key that best suits this description is the so-called temple-key (H. Diels, *Parmenides Lehrgedicht*, Berlin 1897, Anhang 'Über altgriechische Thüren und Schlösser', pp. 123–7). Diels gives several illustrations of such keys from Greek art, e.g. from three Hermitage vases, no. 1734 (fig. 6), no. 349 (fig. 7), no. 452 (fig. 8). See also Diels, *Antike Technik*, 3rd edn (1920), pp. 46–8. This key is a long rod with two bends in it; the shorter end is the handle, the longer operates the bolts on the inside of the door. Cf. Μ 454–6 (cited on 190), Ζ 89, ω 455.

The temple-key, of course, does not suggest the familiar W-shape of the constellation, but if we take only the stars that represent Cassiepeia herself (and this is the group that corresponds to the Babylonian LU.LIM:

Fig. 2 Maiden carrying a temple-key; after H. Diels, *Parmenides Lehrgedicht* (Berlin 1897) fig. 7.

see note on 188–196), the resemblance to the temple-key is clear, as A. Schott was the first to point out in his note on 189–90 (p. 61). The head star (ζ) could be included, to extend the γ α line, but it is much fainter and not exactly in line. For other illustrations of archaic keys see E. Kunze and H. Schleif, *Olympische Forschungen*, Band I (Berlin 1944), p. 166, Taf. 72b, C. Waldstein, *The Argive Heraeum*, II (Boston 1905), Taf. 133, no. 2722.

θύρην ἔντοσθ' ἀραρυῖαν δικλίδα Μ 454–5 πύλας ... στιβαρῶς ἀραρυίας | δικλίδας ... ἔντοσθεν ὀχῆες, β 344–5 σανίδες πυκινῶς ἀραρυῖαι | δικλίδες, ρ 267–8 θύραι δ' εὐερκέες εἰσὶ | δικλίδες. Cf. A.R. 1.786–7 θύρας ... δικλίδας. A.R. also has δικλίδες as subst. (3.236), likewise Theoc. 14.42 sg. δικλίδος.

193 δικλίδα πεπλήγοντες The two variants give exactly the same sense, and have equal authority in the MSS. All editors except Maass read ἐπιπλήσσοντες, a verb that occurs once in Homer, Κ 500 τόξῳ ἐπιπλήσσων, of Odysseus lashing his horses. Otherwise it is normally used of verbal attack, but in 1095 A. has it uniquely intrans. of birds invading the cornlands. On the other hand, πεπλήγων is a variant given by sch. (B) for πεπληγώς in Β 264, and G. Giangrande has shown that Hellenistic poets sometimes made a point of imitating Homeric variants (see e.g. *Scripta Minora Alexandrina* I, 1980, 35ff.). The part. is used by Callimachus in *H.* 1.53 of the Curetes τεύχεα πεπλήγοντες, and Nonnus borrows the phrase for the Corybantes (*D.* 28.327). A. seems to have much in common with this early hymn (see note on 32 κουρίζοντα), and a borrowing of this unusual part. in the same *sedes* would be credible.

The Homeric sch. gloss the part. in B 264 with πλήσσων, and a similar gloss here would account for the variant reading. This epic use of a perf. part. with a present inflexion has an Aeolic origin (Chantraine 1.430): cf. 1004 κεκλήγοντες.

ἀνακρούουσιν ὀχῆας A variation of Homeric ἀνέκοπτεν ὀχῆας (φ 47). Cf. Aen. Tact. 18.6 ἀνακρουσθεῖσα βάλανος, Theoc. 24.49 ἀνακόψατ' ὀχῆας, Q.S. 8.377 ἐπειρύσσαντες ὀχῆας. The subj. is 'men' understood, as in 36 καλέουσιν. ὀχῆες is a corruption intended to provide a subject.

194 μουνάξ Cf. 119. Here each bright star in the group contributes its individual brilliance; so θ 371, of two dancers, μουνάξ ὀρχήσασθαι, λ 417 of fighters μουνάξ κτεινομένων.

ὑποκείμενοι The stars are the underlying material of which the figure of Cassiepeia consists.

ἰνδάλλονται Repeated in 901, 939. The verb is Homeric, but only sg. A.R. 3.812 has ἰνδάλλοντο in same *sedes*, likewise [Opp.] *C.* 3.458, Q.S. 6.479 ἰνδάλλονται.

195 ὀλίγων ἀποτείνεται ὤμων The only star in a position to represent the shoulders is the bright star α, and therefore ὀλίγων cannot mean 'faint', as Mair and Martin understand it. A. never uses ὀλίγος with reference to brightness (see note on 42). The shoulders are 'small' because the figure is small (188) and they are denoted by only one star. The arms may then be thought of as stretching to β on her right side and θ on her left.

196 ὀργυιήν For the form see note on 69. The word simply means her outstretched arms, and sch. suggest ἐσχημάτισται ὥσπερ στερνοκοπουμένη.

φαίης κεν A variation of the simile formulae Γ 220, O 697; A.R. 4.997 φαίης κεν ἑοῖς περὶ παισὶ γάνυσθαι. Cf. Theoc. 1.42, Opp. *H.* 5.553, [Opp.] *C.* 2.87, 516, 3.318. Also οὐδέ κε φαίης (Γ 392, Δ 429, P 366, γ 124).

ἀνιάζειν With ῑ, as sometimes in Homer, e.g. χ 87 θυμῷ ἀνιάζων. A.R. 4.1347 μοι ἀνιάζοντι, Call. fr. 260.68 ἀνιάζουσι δὲ πυκνοί.

ἐπὶ παιδί In causal sense; cf. Theoc. 13.48–9 ἔρως ἀπαλὰς φρένας ἐξεφόβησεν | Ἀργείῳ ἐπὶ παιδί. The last word points forward to the next constellation.

197–204 Andromeda

Andromeda is below her mother, and is easily recognised by the stars that mark her head, shoulders, feet and belt. Her arms remain chained for ever in the sky.

This too is a Greek constellation, probably devised about the end of the fifth century. It is recognisable by the line of bright stars (α δ β γ), which straddle three of the old Babylonian constellations: see Waerden *EW* 66, fig. 7. The Andromeda legend is briefly referred to in Hes. fr. 135.6 and Sapph. fr. 133. It became widely known through the plays of Sophocles and Euripides. *Catast.* 17, Hyg. 2.11; Allen 31ff., Roscher vi 931ff.

197 αὐτοῦ γάρ   The particle neatly links the mourning mother with the suffering daughter.

κυλίνδεται   Cf. 63, 188, 539. all in same *sedes* as Λ 307, 347, β 163.

αἰνόν   Cf. 179 μογερόν, 188 δαιμονίη. A. has transferred the familiar meaning of αἰνός 'dread', as in μόρος αἰνός (Σ 465), to the tragic spectacle of the victim herself. It makes a kind of oxymoron with ἄγαλμα, which is normally a pleasing object (cf. ἀγάλλομαι, and 453 ἀγάλματα).

198 ὑπὸ μητρί   Most of Andromeda lies due south of Cassiepeia, and A. is therefore more accurate than Eudoxus in fr. 34 ταύτης δὲ ἔμπροσθεν ἡ Ἀνδρομέδα, with reference to the supposed orientation of the figures. Eudoxus then gives further technical information about Andromeda's position, but A. omits it all at this point. and instead develops his own theme of Andromeda as a tragic figure. He does, however, use much of Eudoxus' material later, in 205–7 and 246–7.

κεκασμένον   The verb is καίνυμαι 'excel', with pf. part. 'excelling in', e.g. Δ 339 δόλοισι κεκασμένε, Hes. *Th.* 929 παλάμῃσι κεκασμένον. From this the meaning changes to 'well equipped with', e.g. Pi. *O.* 1.27 ἐλέφαντι φαίδιμον ὦμον κεκαδμένον, and simply 'well-equipped', A. *Eum.* 766 εὖ κεκασμένον δόρυ. Here the sense is 'well equipped with stars', ὡς πρὸς σύγκρισιν τῆς μητρός (sch.). The choice of word presumably indicates some excellence in the design of the figure. Since κεκασμένον is well attested and makes good sense, we may dismiss κεκομμένον (the mourning mother beating her breast), and Voss's unattested archaic τετασμένον.

οὔ σε μάλ' ὀΐω   A Homeric formula with variations: Α 170 οὐδέ σ' ὀΐω, Ε 252 οὐδέ σε πείσεμεν οἴω, *h.Hom.* 4.156 νῦν σε μάλ' ὀΐω. On the first person see note on 154; here the didactic poet shows his personal interest in his subject-matter.

199 περισκέψεσθαι   A. means that Andromeda is so easy to recognise that you do not have to search the night sky for long to identify her. Mair's 'wait for a night' is mistakenly based on sch. οὐδαμῶς δέ σε ὑπολαμβάνω νύκτα ἐπιτηρῆσαι ἀσέληνον. The aor. inf. of the sch. appears to support the transmitted reading here, but after οἴω that tense is used only with reference to the past: cf. Α 588, γ 27–8. The regular use after οἴω 'expect' is the fut. inf.: cf. Α 289 οὐ πείσεσθαι ὀΐω, and the references given in the preceding note. It seems necessary therefore to adopt Martin's emendation.

ἵν' αὐτίκα μᾶλλον ἴδηαι Martin explains 'pour ne trouver la constellation qu'au bout d'un certain temps', but this, as Keydell (584) points out, is to take ἵνα as consecutive; it is also a clumsy way of saying that you can find Andromeda very quickly. Buttmann in Excursus II of his edition gives *statim* as the meaning of αὐτίκα here, but Martin maintains that it never means 'immediately' (except perhaps in 422), but marks a lapse of time or a succession or an opposition. A. certainly uses αὐτίκα in a subtle variety of temporal senses, and the precise shade of meaning is not always clear. In 903 it probably has the basic sense of 'at the same time', but elsewhere a shorter or longer time is implied. Here A. means a relatively short time (cf. 307, 346, 634, 809), in 1067 'suddenly', in 422 a relatively longer time (cf. 761, 1076, 1121, and ἐς αὐτίκα in 770, 1103); in a novel use of the adverb the lapse of time also brings out an antithesis (534, 750, 774, 840, 886). In these cases the event so marked always comes later than the preceding event, and it is misleading to suggest, as Buttmann does, that αὐτίκα is sometimes purely adversative. Here the addition of μᾶλλον has the force of 'more quickly than you might expect' (cf. 307), whereas in 1076 it suggests that the time is later in the season than usual.

ἴδηαι Homeric form, always at line-ends, e.g. Γ 130 ἵνα θέσκελα ἔργα ἴδηαι, ζ 311 ἵνα νόστιμον ἦμαρ ἴδηαι; also after ὄφρα (Ε 221), ὅθι (Ν 229), αἴ κεν (Ρ 652), πρίν (Σ 135), ἐπήν (σ 269). A. ignores the digamma here and in 430, also in 573, 710 ἴδοιο, but not in 142 ἰδών.

200 κεφαλή The 2nd-mag. star α Andromedae, which was originally one of the four stars forming the great square: see 206.

201 ὦμοι Since A. is picking out the brightest stars only, he is probably thinking of the 3rd-mag. star δ, which Eudoxus (fr. 34) refers to as the left shoulder, lying above the more northerly of the Fishes.

πόδες Not mentioned in the fragments of Eudoxus, but A. must mean the 2nd-mag. star γ, which Hipparchus (2.6.13) calls the left foot. The epithet ἀκρότατοι refers not to the extremity of the feet, but to their position at one end of the constellation; cf. 74, 161, 207.

ζώματα πάντα Eudox. fr. 34 τὴν δὲ ζώνην ὑπὲρ τοῦ Κριοῦ, πλὴν τὸ Τρίγωνον, ὅ ἐστι μεταξύ. A.'s variation here suggests that he has in mind not only the 2nd-mag. star β, but also the fainter two (μ ν) which make up the belt. Cf. Hi. 1.6.5 τῶν ἐν τῇ ζώνῃ τῆς Ἀνδρομέδας ἀστέρων. For ζῶμα as a woman's girdle cf. S. *El.* 452, Pers. *AP* 6.272.1 = *HE* 2863.

202 κἀκεῖθι I.e. in the sky. ἐκεῖθι occurs once in Homer (ρ 10); for crasis in A. cf. 71, 129.

διωλενίη Sch. ἐκτεταμένας χεῖρας ἔχουσα. The adj. occurs only here and Antip. *AP* 7.711.3 = *HE* 550 διωλένιον φλόγα, of people holding up torches in both hands.

τετάνυσται   Perhaps a verbal echo of 1 116 in same *sedes*.

203 δεσμά   A. probably imagines the hand stars as also representing the bonds. Hipparchus (1.10.6) gives three stars for the right hand (1 κ λ), and (2.6.2) only one star for the left, but ζ η would be appropriate here. Nonn. *D.* 25.130 δεσμὸν ἔχω καὶ ἐν ἀστράσιν, 47.450 δεσμοὺς Ἀνδρομέδῃ καὶ ἐν ἀστράσιν ὤπασε Περσεύς.

204 πεπταμέναι ... χεῖρες   The same two words are associated in the entirely different context of Φ 531 πεπταμένας ἐν χερσὶ πύλας ἔχετ'. A. uses the same part. of sea and sky in 288, 981.

πάντ' ἤματα   Cf. 20, 339, 533, a recurring reminder of celestial eternity.

ἐκείνη   ἐκεῖναι seems pleonastic after αἱ and αὐτοῦ, whereas ἐκείνη brings the reader's attention back to the suffering Andromeda, thus giving a nearer point of reference for οἱ in 205. Corruption to agreement with χεῖρες would be natural.

205–224 The Horse

Andromeda's head is pinned to the navel of the Horse by a common star, and with it three other bright stars form a square. Its head and shoulders are marked by fainter stars, except for the one on the mouth. The Horse is not a quadruped, but is cut off at the navel. It is said to have created on Helicon the spring Hippocrene with a kick of its forefoot. The water still flows from the rock near Thespiae, while the Horse is visible in the sky.

The basis of this constellation is a large and very obvious square formed by four bright stars, which the Babylonians knew as ικυ, a square piece of land. See A. Ungnad, *ZDMG* 77 (1923) 81ff., Waerden *EW* 66–7 and fig. 7. It seems probable that some form of this name suggested to the Greeks their word for 'horse': cf. Myc. *iqo*, Lat. *equos* (Palmer 227). The Greek constellation is thus the result of an attempt to create the outline of a horse out of the available stars: cf. the likely derivation of the Ἄρκτοι (27).

In Greek astronomy the name is always Ἵππος. It appears first in Euctemon's parapegma (Gem. *Cal.* Leo 17), then in Eudox. fr. 66. In Latin it is normally *Equus* (Cic. fr. 32.1, Germ. 209, Man. 1.348, etc.). But since A. identified this Horse with the one that created the spring Hippocrene (216ff.), it eventually came to be called Pegasus (Germ. 222, *Catast.* 18, Hyg. 2.18.1, Nonn. *D.* 38.401), and this is the standard modern name.

There are no wings on A.'s figure of the Horse, nor among the stars referred to by Hipparchus. Hence *Catast.* 18 διὰ τὸ μὴ ἔχειν πτέρυγας, ἀπίθανον δοκεῖ τισι ποιεῖν τὸν λόγον. The mythical tradition of a winged Pegasus goes back to Hes. *Th.* 284 χὼ μὲν ἀποπτάμενος προλιπὼν χθόνα and Pi. *I.* 7.44–5 πτερόεις | ἔρριψε Πάγασος | δεσπόταν. Cf. Asclep. Tragil. fr. 12 τὰ γὰρ νῶτα, ὡς ἔφημεν, πτερωτὰ εἶχεν ὁ ἵππος (but probably rather the Alexandrian Asclep. Myrl.: Müller, *FHG* 3.299, 303). By the time of the Farnese globe the constellation certainly has wings, and Ptolemy (7.5.19) includes some references to a wing. Cf. the late development of a winged Maiden (note on 134). So Ov. *Fast.* 3.454 *pro pede penna fuit*, Germ. 222–3 *Pegasus aethere summo | uelocis agitat pennas*, Man. 5.24 *quaque uolat stellatus Equus*, Hyg. 2.18.1 *Equus autem subuolasse et inter sidera ab Ioue constitutus existimatur*. A. has apparently introduced the Pegasus myth because of its association with Zeus (224).

205 κρατί The 2nd-mag. star α Andromedae.

πέλωρ In Homer of Hephaestus (Σ 410), Cyclops (ι 428), Scylla (μ 87), all in same *sedes*.

ἐπελήλαται See note on 162.

206 γαστέρι νειαίρῃ Ε 539, 616, Ρ 519 νειαίρῃ δ' ἐν γαστρί, Π 465 νείαιραν κατὰ γαστέρα. Eudox. fr. 34 τὸν δ' ἐν τῇ κεφαλῇ ἀστέρα κοινὸν ἔχει τῷ τῆς κοιλίας τοῦ Ἵππου. A. expands to express the same sense in two different ways, with chiasmus and variation: κρατὶ ... γαστέρι ... ὀμφαλίῳ ... καρήνῳ. He places the essential theme, ξυνὸς ἀστήρ, between the two cola of the chiasmus. Cf. 576, Max. 257 νειαίρης γαστρὸς λύσις, *Sphaera* 35–6 Ἵππῳ συνάπτουσ' Ἀνδρομέδα τὸν κρᾶτ' ἔχει, | τὸν αὐτὸν Ἵππου γαστρὶ κοινὸν ἀστέρα.

ξυνός Twice in Homer (Π 262, Σ 309), only here in A. Neither poet has κοινός. Hesiod uses both (fr. 1.6, *Op.* 723).

ἐπιλάμπεται ἀστήρ Cf. 55.

207 ὀμφαλίῳ Dim. form, first here and 214, but not implying the diminutive sense. The form is convenient in dactylic verse: cf. Nic. *Alex.* 596, *AP* 7.506.8 (Leon.). Here the word serves as a variation of γαστέρι (206) and Eudoxus' κοιλίας.

ἐσχατόωντι Homeric verb formed from adj. ἔσχατος, found only in part. with diectasis and at end of line: Κ 206 εἴ τινά που δηΐων ἕλοι ἐσχατόωντα, of one straying near the boundary of the camp. Cf. Β 508, 616 (Chantraine 1.359). Here it describes the position of Andromeda's head at one extremity of the constellation, as πόδες ἀκρότατοι (201) at the other, not as LSJ 'sinciput'. Cf. Call. *H.* 4.174 ἐφ' ἑσπέρου ἐσχατόωντος, Theoc. 7.77 Καύκασον ἐσχατόωντα.

208 τρεῖς ἄλλοι The 2nd-mag. stars α β and 3rd-mag. γ Pegasi. Of these α represents the shoulders, β the forequarters, γ the hinder part of the back. Here πλευράς must be intended to include both β and γ: a line joining them would go diagonally across the Horse's flank.

209 δεικανόωσι Cf. Theoc. 24.57, of the infant Heracles, ἑρπετὰ δεικανάασκεν. In Homer the verb is only med. and describes a gesture of welcome, e.g. Ο 86 δεικανόωντο δέπασσιν.

διασταδόν First here and A.R. 2.67, 4.942, all in same *sedes*. So Homeric ἀνασταδόν (Ι 671, Ψ 469).

πέλεθρα Homeric form of πλέθρον (normally 100 feet), describing the length of Ares in his fall (Φ 407), and similarly of Tityos (λ 577). Thus a length of heroic proportions is implied. A.'s use of a term often employed in land measurement suggests some awareness of the Babylonian original (see note on 205–224).

210 κεφαλή The 3rd-mag. star θ Pegasi.

211 αὐχὴν δολιχός The line of the neck runs south-west from α (shoulder) through ξ ζ to θ (head), beyond which the line of the head turns north-west to the 2nd-mag. star ε (mouth).

212 αἰθομένης Of brightness only, as in 519 (Hydra); there are overtones of destructiveness in 402 (Scorpion's sting) and 595 (Dog).

γέννος The mouth star (see note on 211); cf. 57 of the Dragon, 330 of the Dog. Hipparchus calls it ὁ ἐν τῷ ῥύγχει (2.5.16), ὁ ἐν τῷ στόματι (2.6.11).

κε προτέροις Lengthening of syllables with final short vowels before initial πρ- is almost invariable in A.: -α 151, 763, 938; -ε 285, 348, 706, 735, 747, 778, 869; -ι 239, 300, 309, 866, 870, 949; -ο 270, 350, 388, 400. The only exception is 737 παντὶ προσώπῳ. One other lengthening of κε probably occurs in 1071 before σφήκεσσι, otherwise κεν is used only before vowels and single consonants. Voss preferred κε as 'Dichtersprache'.

ἐρίσειε A reminiscence of the well-known line Γ 223 οὐκ ἂν ἔπειτ' Ὀδυσῆΐ γ' ἐρίσσειε βροτὸς ἄλλος (cf. ο 321).

213 τέτρασιν Cf. 205-9.

περίσκεπτοι Homeric only in the phrase περισκέπτῳ ἐνὶ χώρῳ (α 426, κ 211, 253, ξ 6), in same *sedes*.

214 τετράπος Poetic form of τετράπους, presumably on the analogy of Homeric τρίπος (Χ 164); cf. Hes. *Sc.* 312.

ἄκρου An unusual position for a navel, here at one extremity of a constellation, where the figure coincides with Andromeda's head (cf. 207).

215 μεσσόθεν ἡμιτελής An imitation of Parm. fr. 8.44 μεσσόθεν ἰσοπαλές, of the sphere. For the adv. cf. A.R. 1.1168 μεσσόθεν ἆξεν ἐρετμόν. The adj. appears once in Homer, Β 701 δόμος ἡμιτελής of Protesilaus' house; cf. Nonn. *D.* 8.30, 9.2, 14.267.

Geminus (3.8) lists among the constellations a Προτομὴ Ἵππου καθ' Ἵππαρχον. The name does not occur in the *Commentary*, but must have been written by Hipparchus as a description of the half-figure of the Horse, like A.'s Ταύροιο τομῇ (322) of the same feature in the figure of the Bull. Even Ptolemy designates it as a separate tiny constellation of four faint stars, still immortalised in the modern Equuleus.

περιτέλλεται This verb describes the observed movement from east to west above the horizon of stars (232, 329), of a celestial circle as marked out by stars (509), of constellations after rising (693, 709), of the sun after sunrise (739, 828, 1128). In Homer it is used only of time, B 551, Θ 404, λ 295; cf. h.Hom. 2.445.

ἱερός ῑ as in 692 and other similar phrases in hexameter endings, e.g. Θ 66 ἱερὸν ἦμαρ, Π 407 ἱερὸν ἰχθύν, Hes. Op. 597, 805 ἱερὸν ἀκτήν, Call. E. 9.1 ἱερὸν ὕπνον, fr. 803 ἱερὸς ὄρνις, D.P. 298 ἐπιτέλλεται ἱερὸς Ἴστρος. See LSJ fin., Wyatt 155. Here the epithet points forward to the supernatural creation of the spring (219) and the association with Zeus (224). The myth serves to illustrate the benefits given by gods to men.

216 φασι The vague source-reference is traditional, as is the metrical position of the verb: cf. 645, B 783 ὅθι φασὶ Τυφωέος ἔμμεναι εὐνάς, Hes. Th. 306 τῇ δὲ Τυφάονά φασι μιγήμεναι. In 98 (end of line) A. clearly hints at Hesiod, but here only parts of the Pegasus legend are Hesiodic: the birth from Medusa's blood, the naming from where it was born, Ὠκεανοῦ παρὰ πηγάς, the flight up to the sky, and present life of service to Zeus (Th. 280–6). Pegasus is elsewhere associated with Bellerophon (Th. 325, fr. 43a.84, Pi. I. 7.44ff., E. fr. 306N). The association of Pegasus with Helicon and Hippocrene may have been A.'s own invention, inspired by Hes. Th. 5–7, in which case φασι is unusually subtle. Cf. Catast. 18 Ἄρατος μὲν οὖν φησι τὸν ἐπὶ τοῦ Ἑλικῶνος εἶναι ποιήσαντα κρήνην τῇ ὁπλῇ, ἀφ' οὗ καλεῖσθαι Ἵππου κρήνην.

ὑψηλοῦ A variation of Hesiod's ὄρος μέγα (Th. 2) and ἀκροτάτῳ (7). Cf. 218.

217 εὐαλδέος First here, in act. sense of making things grow; cf. Ψ 599 ληΐου ἀλδήσκοντος, the growing crop.

Ἵππου κρήνης Voss prints as one word, on the ground that εὐαλδέος would otherwise have to be taken with ἵππου. Not necessarily. A. is particularly concerned with the derivation of the name, and the MSS accent as two words (cf. Hes. Th. 6). Callimachus separates the words in H. 5.71 ἵππω ἐπὶ κράνᾳ. The ending with two disyllabic spondees is rare and therefore emphatic; cf. τ 342 Ἠῶ δῖαν, Θ 565 Ἠῶ μίμνον. Ludwich 42.

The site of Hippocrene is described by Pausanias (9.31.3), and has been identified with the modern Kryopegadi, c. 3½ km above the valley of the Muses, just below the summit of Mt Zagaras (P. W. Wallace, GRBS 15 (1974) 5ff.). J. G. Frazer, Pausanias' Description of Greece (1913), 5.158, comments: 'The coldness and clearness of the water of this perennial spring are famous in the neighbourhood, especially among the herdsmen, who love to fill their skin-bottles at it.'

218 κατελείβετο Once in Homer, Σ 109 μέλιτος καταλειβομένοιο. A. imitates Hes. *Th.* 786, of Styx, ἐκ πέτρης καταλείβεται. Cf. Theoc. 7.136–7 ἱερὸν ὕδωρ | Νυμφᾶν ἐξ ἄντροιο κατειβόμενον.

πηγαῖς Pl., as in Homer, of running water: Υ 9 πηγὰς ποταμῶν, Hes. *Th.* 282 Ὠκεανοῦ παρὰ πηγάς. A. has probably chosen this word here because it suggests Hesiod and the naming of Pegasus.

219 ἔτυψε With the feet, Ψ 764 ἴχνια τύπτε πόδεσσι. A. uses the verb again of swallows just skimming the water (945). A.R. 4.1446 λὰξ ποδὶ τύψεν ἔνερθε, τὸ δ' ἀθρόον ἔβλυσεν ὕδωρ.

ἀθρόον Cf. 153; here the word suggests a copious and steady stream.

αὐτόθεν Emphasising the very spot that received the kick; cf. 735, 947, 1127. The adv. is Homeric, e.g. Τ 77, of Agamemnon speaking, αὐτόθεν ἐξ ἕδρης, οὐδ' ἐν μέσσοισιν ἀναστάς.

ὕδωρ With ῡ, as in Homer at end of line, e.g. γ 300, here in noticeable contrast to the normal short vowel in 217; cf. 537, 936, 945, 962, 973. So ὕδατος 393, 787, 836, 851, 871, 964, 967 (ε 475); ὕδατι 844, 873, 904, 937, 962 (χ 439). Cf. Call. *H.* 6.28, A.R. 4.1446, Theoc. 7.136. Chantraine 1.104, Wyatt 231.

220 ἐξέχυτο Epic aor. med. in passive sense; cf. τ 470 τὸ δ' ἐπὶ χθονὸς ἐξέχυθ' ὕδωρ. Chantraine 1.382.

προτέρου ποδός The forefoot is perhaps specified because it is the foreleg that is fitted into the star group, and this detail in the myth would help in providing an αἴτιον for the constellation. The alliteration of π is very marked in this line and the next.

The miracle is often referred to by other writers: Call. fr. 2.1 ποιμένι μῆλα νέμοντι παρ' ἴχνιον ὀξέος ἵππου, Nic. fr. 54 Schn. ὁ Πήγασος τῇ ὁπλῇ τὴν κορυφὴν πατάξας, Honest. *AP* 9.225.1–2 = *GP* 2414–15 Ἀσωπὶς κρήνη καὶ Πηγασὶς ὕδατ' ἀδελφά | ἵππου καὶ ποταμοῦ δῶρα ποδορραγέα, Str. 8.379 Πήγασον ... τὸν δ' αὐτόν φασι καὶ τὴν Ἵππου κρήνην ἀναβαλεῖν ἐν τῷ Ἑλικῶνι πλήξαντα τῷ ὄνυχι τὴν ὑποῦσαν πέτραν, *Catast.* 18 (cited on 216), Ov. *Met.* 5.257ff. *fama noui fontis ... quem praepetis ungula rupit* | ... *factas pedis ictibus undas*, *Fast.* 5.8 *grata Medusaei signa tenetis equi*, *Pont.* 4.8.80 *ungula Gorgonei quam caua fecit equi.*

νομῆες The word provides a link with the section on weather signs, where it appears (1104) in the same *sedes*; cf. Ρ 65, ρ 214, 246.

221 διεφήμισαν First here, otherwise mainly in prose; cf. 442 ἐπεφημίξαντο. Hes. *Op.* 764 has φημίξουσι with play on φήμη, of spreading a report, Call. fr. 75.14 φημίζομεν and 58 ἐφήμισαν of naming, as here. So D.P. 50 Ὑρκανίην ἕτεροι διεφημίξαντο.

Ἵππου κρήνην See note on 217. The repetition of the name highlights the ring-composition of this short mythical episode, with its chiastic pattern of themes: (*a*) the place, Helicon (216); (*b*) the name and the water (217–18); (*c*) the horse's kick (219–20); (*b*) the name and the water (221–2); (*a*) the place, Thespiae (223). Cf. 367–85.

222 ἀπολείβεται Once in Homer, in same *sedes*, η 107 ἀπολείβεται ὑγρὸν ἔλαιον. The verb corresponds to κατελείβετο (218), with significant change of tense.

οὐδέ ποτ' αὐτό A reminiscence of Hes. *Th.* 759 οὐδέ ποτ' αὐτούς, also in a context of seeing and the sky. Voss's τοι (cf. 172), adopted by Martin, is unnecessary, and even unlikely so close to τοι in 224. A. is making a humorous contrast between the visibility of the spring (ὄψεαι) and that of the Horse (θηήσασθαι).

223 Θεσπιέων ἀνδρῶν Thespiae lay at the foot of Mt Helicon on the east side, near modern Erimokastro and Kaskaveli (*D. Kl. Pauly* 5.754). The earlier name Thespeia is mentioned once in Homer (B 498). It had a minor cult of the Muses (cf. ρ 385 θέσπιν ἀοιδόν), linking it with the Hesiodic tradition (Str. 9.2.25, Paus. 9.26.4, 27.4). In Call. *H.* 5.60 Θεσπιέων is gen. of Θεσπιαί, here of Θεσπιεύς. Cf. A.R. 1.106, Orph. *Arg.* 123, Nonn. *D.* 4.336.

ἑκάς Ν 262–3 οὐ γὰρ ὀΐω | ἀνδρῶν δυσμενέων ἑκάς.

ὄψεαι Epic form, again in 727; cf. Δ 353, Ι 359, ω 511, Call. *H.* 5.89.

αὐτὰρ ὅ γ' Ἵππος The transmitted reading ὁ Ἵππος is not impossible, since A. allows hiatus after a short vowel in this position in 962 ὕδατι ὕδωρ. But it is more likely that here he is imitating the Homeric formula αὐτὰρ ὅ γ' ἥρως (Ε 308, 327, Θ 268, Κ 154, Λ 483, al.). This reading, proposed by Buttmann, and approved by Kaibel in his review of Maass (951), has been adopted by Martin citing Par. 2726. A. uses αὐτὰρ ὅ γε in this position also in 339 and 591, at the beginning of the line in 21, 49, 250, 278, 537 and 575, elsewhere in 258.

224 ἐν Διὸς εἰλεῖται An imitation with variation of Hes. *Th.* 285 Ζηνὸς δ' ἐν δώμασι ναίει, of Pegasus. The elliptical use of ἐν is as early as Homer, e.g. η 132 ἐν Ἀλκινόοιο.

θηήσασθαι Epic form of Ionic aor. θεήσασθαι; cf. ε 74 θηήσαιτο. With the end of the episode A. returns to his didactic purpose, the need to observe the stars; cf. 135 of Dike, 325 of Orion.

225–232 The Ram
The Ram moves round the largest circle, but keeps up with Cynosura. Its stars are faint, but you can identify it from the belt of Andromeda above it. Its path is on the celestial equator, like the Claws and Orion's belt.

This is basically a small group of three stars (α β γ) forming a wide angle, which may have suggested a ram's horn. In Hipparchus these three are the head (1.6.7), and other stars are brought in to make forelegs, back and tail. A. makes no reference to any part of the Ram's body, and he may have been thinking purely of this group of three. The constellation has a Babylonian origin, corresponding to LU. HUN. GA, a 'hired worker' (Waerden *EW* 68), and was said to have been introduced to the Greeks by Cleostratus (Plin. *Nat.* 2.31). The Ram was important because it was on the ecliptic as well as the equator, and therefore associated with the spring equinox: cf. Ov. *Met.* 10.164–5 *quotiensque repellit | uer hiemem Piscique Aries succedit aquoso*. In Latin it is normally *Aries* (now the standard name), but there are poetic variants, such as *Corniger* (Man. 5.39), *Laniger* (Germ. 240), and it is sometimes identified with the ram that carried Phrixus and Helle, e.g. Ov. *Fast.* 3.852, of the sun at the equinox, *hic here Phrixeae uellera pressit ouis, Catast.* 19, Hyg. 2.20. Gundel in *RE* 11.1869ff., Roscher VI 934ff., Allen 75ff.

225 θοώταται The Ram lies on the celestial equator (cf. 515), and since this is a great circle, the stars on it move faster round the pole than those that lie on smaller circles. Hyg. 4.3.1 *hunc autem Aratus omnium siderum celerrimum esse demonstrat, etiam minore Arcto, quae breui spatio uertitur, praestare.*

226 μήκιστα The longest track is the greatest circle. The adj. is Homeric, but in sense of 'tallest' (λ 309). The technical term for a 'great circle' is μέγιστος κύκλος (Euc. *Phaen.* 2).

διωκόμενος Purely of speed, without the sense of pursuit; cf. 533, 972. In 339, 384, 678 the suggestion of pursuit is appropriate to the Hare.

κύκλα The heterocl. pl. is used in Homer only of wheels, e.g. Σ 375. In this poem the noun is much in demand, and A. probably uses this form for the sake of variation: cf. 461, 660, 753. The pl. suggests the Ram's repeated circuits.

227 ἀφαυρότερον As adv. only here. The Ram does not take any longer to complete its circuit of the pole. The Little Bear is chosen for comparison because it is closest to the pole and therefore on the smallest circle. A. uses this adj. mostly of faint stars (256, 277, 569).

τροχάει Cf. 27, 309, also of star movements.

Κυνοσουρίδος Ἄρκτου Cf. 182.

228 νωθής Once in Homer, Λ 559, of a donkey. The adj. seems particularly suited to an animal (cf. Pl. *Ap.* 30e), and A. has probably chosen it for the Ram for this reason, with an appropriate shift of meaning. The word is connected with ὠθέω (Frisk 2.330–1, Wyatt 55).

νωθὴς καὶ ἀνάστερος οἷα σελήνη Attalus (ap. Hi. 1.6.10) makes a distinction between the two adjj., taking the first with reference to the outline of the figure (οὔτε ἀκριβῶς διατετυπωμένον), and this is probably right, since A. is not in the habit of using doublets with the same meaning, and αὐτός points to the figure as a whole. On the faintness of the Ram Hipparchus comments (1.6.5): ὁ Ἄρατος ἀγνοεῖν μοι δοκεῖ, λέγων αὐτὸν ἀφανῆ γίνεσθαι ἐν τῇ πανσελήνῳ διὰ τὴν μικρότητα τῶν ἀστέρων, δεῖν δὲ σημειοῦσθαι τὴν θέσιν αὐτοῦ ἐκ τῶν ἐν τῇ ζώνῃ τῆς Ἀνδρομέδας ἀστέρων. He points out that the three head stars of the Ram are actually brighter than those in Andromeda's belt (1.6.7). In fact the former have two of 2nd mag. and one of 4th, the latter one of 2nd mag. and two of 4th. On the other hand Andromeda as a whole is much more conspicuous, and this may have been what Hipparchus had in mind. With ἀνάστερος A. certainly exaggerates, considering the brightness of α and β, though it could be said that these two are not enough to make the figure of the Ram recognisable; cf. 349. For the measurement of magnitude by reference to moonlight see notes on 78 and 189.

229 ζώνη Cf. 201 ζώματα. The three stars β μ ν Andromedae are in an almost straight line that points to the head of the Ram. Hipparchus (1.6.7) objects that there is no need to look to Andromeda for a guide.

230 ὑπ' αὐτήν Actually to the south-east, beyond the Triangle.

ἐστήρικται See note on 10 ἐστήριξεν. In different contexts, but also at end of line, Call. *H.* 2.23, A.R. 4.816.

231 μεσσόθι On the celestial equator. This is an approximation, as the three brighter stars were some degrees north of the equator in A.'s time. The fuller description of the equator also begins with μεσσόθι (511).

τρίβει The metaphor of a well-worn track (τρίβος) is appropriate to the continuous movement of a star on the same circle round the sky. Cf. Antiphil. *AP* 9.34.1–2 = *GP* 979–80 of a ship τρίψασαν ἀμετρήτοιο θαλάσσης | κύματα.

ἠχί περ ἄκραι Cf. 61.

232 Χηλαὶ καὶ ζώνη Hipparchus (1.6.10) criticises Attalus for thinking that A. is referring to the equator as another guide to the position of the Ram. His purpose here is to define the line of the equator by reference to familiar stars, the Claws (already introduced in 89) and Orion's belt (familiar to all without introduction). See the fuller description of the equator (511–24), which includes the Ram (516), Orion's belt (518) and the Claws (520–1).

περιτέλλεται Cf. 215.

233–238 The Triangle
Below Andromeda lies Deltoton, like an isosceles triangle, small, but with many stars. The Ram is to the south of it.

This is a very small constellation of three stars forming a thin triangle (α β γ), two of 3rd and one of 4th mag., but distinct enough to be recognisable. It is not in itself a Babylonian constellation, its stars forming part of APIN, the 'plough' (Waerden *EW* 66–7, fig. 7). In Eudox. fr. 34, Hi. 1.6.5, Ptol. 7.5.21 it is called Τρίγωνον, but Gem. 3.8 and *Catast.* follow A. with Δελτωτόν, the latter associating it with the name Διός (20); cf. Hyg. 2.19. The standard Latin name is *Triangulum*, but Germ. 235 and Man. 1.353 have *Deltoton*. This constellation is not on the Farnese globe. Wagner in *RE* 4.2702, Roscher VI 933–4, Allen 414ff.

233 ἐγγύθι Abs., as in H 341, Hes. *Op.* 288; c. gen. 305, 391, 1040, Hes. *Op.* 343, Theoc. 21.8; all in same *sedes*.

234 νειόθεν Once in Homer, K 10, in same *sedes*; cf. A.R. 1.1197. The Triangle is close to and due south of γ Andromedae (see 201).

ἐπὶ τρισὶν ἐστάθμηται Lit. of measuring with a rule (184 στάθμη); cf. E. *Ion* 1137 πλέθρου σταθμήσας μῆκος εἰς εὐγωνίαν. The use of ἐπί is unusual, defining the form in which the figure consists.

235 Δελτωτόν Prop. adj. with verbal suffix, 'provided with'; cf. πτερωτός, σκιωτός. Sch. ἀπὸ Διὸς τὸ πρῶτον τοῦ ὀνόματος δι' Ἑρμοῦ τεθέντος. φασὶ δὲ καὶ τὴν τῆς Αἰγύπτου θέσιν εἶναι ἐκ τοῦ ἐν ἄστροις τριγώνου.

ἰσαιομένησιν Cf. 513 ἰσαίεται, Nic. *Alex.* 399, fr. 74.56. The polysyllabic part. as a variation of the simple adj. makes possible a four-word line, which suggests that there is something impressive about this delta in the sky.

ἐοικός Cf. 168 ἐοικότα, of a group of stars that is 'recognisable' as the figure it is supposed to represent. Here A. means that the three stars are recognisable as an isosceles triangle, the proper form of a Δ. See Martin on this absolute use of ἐοικός, which is peculiar to A.

236 ἀμφοτέραις The transmitted reading is -ης or -ησ'; but the former, rare enough in Homer (Chantraine 1.202), is not found elsewhere in A., nor is there an example of elision at a caesura with a sense pause. On the other hand -αις occurs 11 times elsewhere in A. (as against -ησι 16 times), in particular at a caesura in 581, 1075, 1088, 1094, and is likely to be the original reading here, corrupted by the influence of the preceding double -ησιν. The variation is Aratean: cf. 785 ἀμβλείῃσι κεραίαις.

As to the meaning, ἀμφοτέραις does not mean, as Martin suggests, 'two' of the three, but 'the two' that are obviously relevant in the context, the equal sides. So in 513 'the two' nights are the equinoctial, in 327 'the two' legs are the hind legs, in 1109 and 1136 the forelegs.

ἡ δ' οὔτι τόση The third side, actually very short. Sch. τῶν γὰρ τεσσάρων ἀστέρων τοῦ τριγώνου οἱ γ' ἐπὶ τῆς βάσεως: the stars are β δ γ (but δ is only 5th-mag. and very close to γ).

ἑτοίμη   C. inf.; cf. 40.

237 περί   Homeric use in sense of superiority, e.g. Δ 375 περὶ δ᾽ ἄλλων φασὶ γενέσθαι, and with predicative adj., as here, Α 417–18 ὀϊζυρὸς περὶ πάντων | ἔπλεο. Cf. A.R. 1.830 περὶ γὰρ βαθυλήϊος ἄλλων, [Theoc.] 25.119 ἀφνειὸν μήλοις περὶ πάντων ἔμμεναι, and Call. *H.* 5.58 with Bulloch's note on the accentuation.

λοιπῶν   As Voss pointed out, the traditional πολέων does not make sense. The subject is the short side, and it is being compared, not with some indefinite 'many' (Mair) or 'beaucoup de constellations' (Martin), but with the other two sides; sch. ἡ κάτω τοῦ Δελτωτοῦ γραμμὴ εὐκατάληπτός ἐστι· περισσῶς γὰρ τῶν προκειμένων ἀστέρων ἐστὶν ἔκλαμπρος. Voss's solution τ᾽ ἀλλέων has been ignored by his successors, no doubt because it involves the addition of τ᾽, and the rare ἀλλέων: Homer has three instances of ἀλλάων (Σ 432, τ 326, ω 418), but the regular gen. pl. fem. is ἄλλων (K–B 1.379). τ᾽ ἄλλων would be possible, though unlikely to be corrupted; perhaps προτέρων (cf. 212 προτέροις referring to previously mentioned stars), which might seem to be supported by sch. προκειμένων, though unlikely so close to προτέρω (239). Another possibility is λοιπῶν, which appears in sch. (A) as an addition to the text of sch. (M) ἡ κάτω τοῦ Δελτωτοῦ γραμμὴ κατὰ τὸ μέγεθος τῶν λοιπῶν πλευρῶν, and twice in the unpublished sch. (E) τὸ δελτωτὸν τριγωνόν ἐστιν ἰσοσκελές, τὴν ὑποτείνουσαν βραχυτέραν τῶν λοιπῶν ἔχον ... οἱ γ᾽ ἐπὶ τῆς βάσεώς εἰσι καθεξῆς κείμενοι βραχύτερον μέντοι διάστημα τῶν λοιπῶν πλευρῶν ἔχοντες. Cf. 647 ὅσσ᾽ ἐλέλειπτο, and Hi. 2.2.51 δύνειν μὲν τά τε λοιπὰ μέρη τοῦ Ποταμοῦ καὶ τὰ λοιπὰ μέρη τῆς Ἀνδρομέδας καὶ τοῦ Κήτους.

εὐάστερος   The sense of the prefix is probably 'well provided' (cf. εὔδενδρος, εὔπυργος, εὔφυλλος), so that the short line is easily identified. At the same time the adj. may have overtones of propitiousness, in view of the association of Δ with Zeus (see note on 235). The word occurs first here, then only in Orph. *H.* 9.3, of the moon.

238 τῶν   The stars of the Triangle.

Κριοῦ νοτιώτεροι   Hipparchus (1.6.5,7) objects that there is no need to use the Triangle as a guide to the Ram, since the latter is marginally brighter. But A.'s intention is rather to mark the position of the Triangle between Andromeda and the Ram. Cf. Eudox. fr. 34 τὴν δὲ ζώνην ὑπὲρ τοῦ Κριοῦ, πλὴν τὸ Τρίγωνον, ὅ ἐστι μεταξύ.

239–247 The Fishes
To the west and south are the Fishes, one more northerly than the other. Their tails are joined by chains, which meet in a bright star called the Knot. Andromeda's left shoulder is close to the more northerly Fish.

This is a large but not very bright zodiacal constellation extending to the east and south of the Horse. It seems to have a Babylonian origin in the two constellations šɪᴍ.ᴍᴀḤ ('great swallow'), part of which has become the south-westerly Fish, and *Anunitu* ('sky-dweller'), part of which corresponds to the north-easterly Fish. See Waerden *EW* 66–7, fig. 7. This origin is supported by sch. 242 τοῦτον τοίνυν τὸν βορειότερον Ἰχθὺν χελιδόνος ἔχειν τὴν κεφαλήν φασιν. ὃν Χαλδαῖοι καλοῦσι χελιδονίαν Ἰχθύν. On the other hand A. Bouché-Leclerc (*L'astrologie grecque*, Paris 1899, 148) proposes an Egyptian origin, and W. Gundel thinks this more probable. In mythology the Fishes are rescuers of Venus and Cupid from the Euphrates (Ov. *Fast.* 2.461ff., Hyg. 2.30), and of the Syrian goddess Derceto from the lake at Bambyce (*Catast.* 38, Avien. 541–2), sch. Δερκετὼ τὴν Ἀφροδίτης θυγατέρα ἐμπεσοῦσαν εἰς θάλασσαν ἔσωσαν. Latin *Pisces*, but poets sometimes use the sg. (Cic. fr. 33.19, V. *G.* 4.234, Ov. *Met.* 10.165). W. Gundel in *RE* 20.1775ff., Roscher VI 978ff., Allen 336ff.

239 προτέρω I.e. to the west, the direction of the sky's movement. Hipparchus (1.5.20) corrects those who think that A. uses πρότερα of stars lying to the east, and refers to this line to show that the sense is the opposite. He explains προτέρω with reference to the Ram, rightly, since the Fishes lie more south than west of the Triangle. A. has here a verbal echo of Homer's εἰ δέ κ' ἔτι προτέρω (Ψ 526, ε 417). Max. 28 ἤ τ' ἂν ἔτι προτέρω.

ἔτι δ' ἐν προμολῇσι νότοιο The variant προβολῇσι is the reading of editors before Matthiae. It is adopted, with some hesitation, by Maass (*Aratea* 85), who explains it as referring to 'uim uenti proicientem', recalling ε 331 Νότος Βορέη προβάλεσκε φέρεσθαι. Maass decides in the end to follow Hipparchus as 'antiquissimum testem'. But Hipparchus is not always a reliable witness to readings that are not astronomically significant (e.g. 280 τείνων); and προβολή is not used of movement in the sense of 'thrusting forward', but of static positions, as of weapons or land 'projecting'. Here A. is describing a position well to the south, and προμολῇσι makes good sense: cf. the similar figurative use in Call. *H.* 3.99 ἐπὶ προμολῆς ὄρεος, Damag. *AP* 7.9.1 = *HE* 1379 παρὰ προμολῇσιν Ὀλύμπου. If A. has in mind a boundary between north and south, this would be the ecliptic, and the Fishes lie mostly just to the north of it, with a part of the chains crossing over into the southern sky.

The second ἔτι carries over the comparative context of the first, and Voss's ἐπί is unnecessary. Hipparchus (1.6.8) finds fault with A. for suggesting that the whole constellation lies south of the Ram: he goes on to prove his point by comparing the polar distances of key stars in both constellations. Hipparchus is right, of course, but A.'s words can be understood as implying that one half of the constellation lies to the west of the Ram and the other half to the south of it.

240 προφερέστερος ἄλλου In Homer προφερέστερος means 'superior' in some stated or implied respect, e.g. jumping (θ 128), archery (θ 221), strength (φ 134), ploughing (Κ 352). In Hesiod the superlative denotes the most important of a group (*Th.* 79, 361). A. describes the stars of Orion as προφερέστερα θηήσασθαι (325), which implies a superiority in brightness, and perhaps also distinctness of form, and the Bull is προφερέστερος Ἡνιόχοιο (177) specifically in respect of its earlier setting.

The last example is presumably responsible for Cicero's interpretation, *quorum alter paulo praelabitur ante* (fr. 33.12). So Martin, 'plus vite que l'autre'. But this can only be true of the more southerly Fish, whereas line 241 shows that A. is concerned with the more northerly one. Erren is aware of this, but still translates 'dem anderen voraus', and assumes that A. has confused the two Fishes. Such a glaring error would, however, be unusual for A., and Hipparchus has no criticism of this line. Sch. had in fact already corrected Cicero's error, offering a different explanation: οὐχὶ τὸ πρότερος ἐλθὼν ἐπὶ τὴν δύσιν, ὡς ὁ Ταῦρος (177) ... ἀλλὰ τὸ κρεῖττον, ὑπὸ λαμπροτέρων ἀστέρων διατυπούμενος. This is hardly true: the northerly Fish does have the brightest star in the constellation, but it is only 3rd-mag., otherwise both Fishes are equally faint.

A more likely meaning is that given by Avien. 548–9 *quorum alius rigida consurgit in aera forma | celsior.* One Fish is more prominent to observers in Mediterranean latitudes because it is farther north, and line 241 thus specifies the respect in which its superiority lies. So Mair, 'one is higher than the other'. A. seems to be making some deliberate play with wind directions in these three lines.

241 βορέαο νέον κατιόντος The verb is a technical term for a wind suddenly springing up at sea, e.g. Thuc. 2.25.4 ἀνέμου δὲ κατιόντος μεγάλου (is it purely a coincidence that A.'s choice of word recalls an episode that took place near a promontory called Ἰχθῦς?); cf. 2.84.3, 6.2.4. Contrast Η 63–4 Ζεφύροιο ... | ὀρνυμένοιο νέον. The Greeks used wind names for compass directions (see Böker, 'Windrosen', *RE* 8A. 2325ff.), and A. brings this out again in 355, 386. Cf. Ov. *Fast.* 3.400ff. *conditus e geminis Piscibus alter erit. | nam duo sunt: austris hic est, aquilonibus ille | proximus; a uento nomen uterque tenet.*

ἀκούει Cf. 336, with different sense, κατιόντος ἀκούομεν.

242 σφεων Non-reflexive, monosyllabic and enclitic, as in Homer, e.g. Σ 311, in same *sedes*. Chantraine 1.267.

ἠύτε δεσμά Homeric formula, regularly at end of line, e.g. Α 359; cf. 979, 1042. A. uses the n.pl. here and 203 (cf. *h.Hom.* 4.157), and varies with m.pl. in 362. Opp. *H.* 1.535 ἠύτε δεσμῷ. The chains are two lines of faint stars, also called Λίνοι (Gem. 3.7) or τὸ λίνον (*Catast.* 21); Vitr. 9.5.3 *tenuis fusio stellarum, quae graece uocitantur harpedonae.*

243 οὐραίων Properly an adj. (cf. 145, 352, 362), but difficult to explain as such here. Martin takes it as qualifying ἀμφοτέρων, with an adv. force 'à l'endroit de leur queue', but this is very strained and unconvincing. As Voss points out, the n.pl. is used as subst. meaning the 'tail parts', e.g. Hp. *Vict.* 3.79, Men. *Kol.* fr. 7, Luc. *VH* 2.1, all of fish. In E. *Ion* 1154 οὐραῖα must refer to the actual tail, or perhaps 'tail stars' (Jerram), of the Bear, and here Voss and Mair translate simply as 'tails'. Maass simplifies the problem by reading οὐράων ... ἰόντων, comparing sch. (M) 244 εἰς συναφὴν παραγινομένων τῶν οὐρῶν, but it is the chains, not the tails, that converge in one star (see note on ἰόντα).

A. repeats οὐραίων as subst. in 363, and it is likely that he does mean the 'tail-end' of each Fish, not the tail, because the faint star-groups forming the Fishes do not provide the outline of a tail, and only one star in each case may be said to mark the point where the Fish ends and the chain begins (Erren *PAS* 321). On the Farnese globe the northerly Fish has no tail at all, the more southerly a mere vestige. Geminus seems to be paraphrasing A. when he writes οἱ δὲ ἀπὸ τῶν οὐραίων μερῶν τῶν Ἰχθύων (3.7); cf. sch. (M) 242 ἀμφοτέρων δὲ ἐκ τῶν οὐραίων δεσμός τις ἀποτείνεται. The Latin versions, of course, have *e caudis* (Cic. fr. 33.14), *cauda* (Ger. 244), *caudas* (Avien. 553), but they are not reliable guides to A.'s meaning.

ἐπισχερώ A Homeric adv., e.g., in same *sedes*, of nymphs, Σ 68 ἀκτὴν εἰσανέβαινον ἐπισχερώ, here of an unbroken line of stars. Cf. A.R. 1.330, 528, al., Theoc. 14.69, Pi. *I.* 6.22 ἐν σχερῷ.

ἰόντα As is clear from 262-3 and the constellation figure, it is the chains that converge; cf. Cic. fr. 33.16, Germ. 245, Avien. 554. The corruption to gen. could have been due to the influence of οὐραίων, or perhaps to the citing of 459 εἰς ἓν ἰόντων. Maass reads ἰόντων *pro* ἰουσῶν, comparing Θ 455, Hes. *Op.* 199; but these are duals, not plurals.

244 εἷς ἀστὴρ ἐπέχει The 4th-mag. star α Piscium. For the verb see note on 57; cf. Hi. 1.11.20 of the same star's position, measured in degrees of the ecliptic: ὁ γὰρ Σύνδεσμος τῶν Ἰχθύων ... ἐπέχει Κριοῦ μοίρας γ′ δ″.

καλός τε μέγας τε The brightness of important stars tends to be exaggerated by A. The same phrase is used of θ Ursae Majoris, a 3rd-mag. star (143).

245 ὅν ῥά τε καί The cluster of particles draws attention to the interesting name.

Σύνδεσμον First attested in Callippus' calendar (Gem. *Cal.* Aries 1), for MR on Spring equinox. Cf. Hi. 1.11.20, Gem. 3.8, Ptol. *Alm.* 8.1.33. In Latin it is *Nodus* (Cic. fr. 33.17, Germ. 246, Avien. 556).

ὑπουράνιον This reading is attested only by Hyg. 3.29 *Aratus graece* σύνδεσμον ὑπουράνιον, *Cicero nodum caelestem dicit* (fr. 33.17); cf. Avien. 556 *caelestem memorat quem sollers Graecia nodum.* The MSS read, with varying accentuation, ὑπούραιον, ὑπουραῖον and ὑπούραῖον. Maass adopts the first of these, comparing 362 δεσμοὶ οὐραῖοι, and Mair translates 'the Knot of Tails', but this is unsatisfactory, since it is the chains that are attached to the tails, whereas the Knot unites the chains. Hipparchus calls this star ὁ σύνδεσμος τῶν Ἰχθύων (1.11.20, 3.1.1b) and τῶν λίνων (2.6.1b, 3.3.9). not τῶν οὐρῶν. Also the prefix ὑπ- is hard to explain: the Knot is south of the more northerly Fish's tail, but west of that of the more southerly Fish. These problems of the confusion of accents and the meaning of this adj. are solved if the latter is seen as a corruption due to the presence of οὐραίων in 243. But ὑπουράνιον makes good sense, and has a parallel in 616 ὑπουρανίων εἰδώλων, the prefix expressing the idea that the stars are attached to the under-surface of the sky: see note on 134 ὑπουρανίη.

Hyg. 3.29 goes on to explain that the Knot lies at the point where its meridian meets the equator, and can therefore be thought of as the Knot of the celestial sphere (see Le Boeuffle p. 197, n. 15). This was the point of the vernal equinox, which Hipparchus chose as the starting-point for his measurement of the ecliptic. Hyginus' lore is therefore post-Aratean, and cannot have been a part of A.'s meaning.

246 ὦμος ἀριστερός The star δ Andromedae (cf. 201). A. gives further directions for locating the Fishes, taking a detail from Eudox. fr. 34 ἡ Ἀνδρομέδα, τὸν μὲν ἀριστερὸν ὦμον ἔχουσα τῶν Ἰχθύων ὑπὲρ τοῦ πρὸς βορρᾶν.

248–253 Perseus

Andromeda's feet are a guide to the shoulders of Perseus, and his right hand points towards Cassiepeia's chair.

Perseus is a Greek constellation, corresponding in part with Babylonian šu.gi, 'old man' (Waerden *EW* 67). The flying hero was an obviously suitable figure for a constellation. It has several bright stars, two of 2nd mag., five of 3rd. The figure is orientated along a north-west to south-east line, so that suitable stars can represent head (τ), shoulders (γ θ), right hand (η), belt (α), left leg (ε ξ ζ), right leg (μ). The left hand is normally portrayed as carrying the Gorgon's head, the bright variable star β or Algol, but this detail is not mentioned by A., nor is it in the fragments of Eudoxus. Rathman in *RE* 19.992ff., Roscher VI 913ff., Allen 329ff.

248–255 Hi. 1.2.15 quotes most of these lines, in order to illustrate A.'s dependence on Eudoxus (fr. 35): παρὰ δὲ τοὺς πόδας τῆς Ἀνδρομέδας ὁ Περσεὺς ἔχει τοὺς ὤμους, τὴν δεξιὰν χεῖρα πρὸς τὴν Κασσιέπειαν ἀποτείνων, τὸ δὲ ἀριστερὸν γόνυ πρὸς τὰς Πλειάδας.

248 πόδες The bright star γ Andromedae represents the left foot (cf. 201), the right is probably a faint cluster close to Perseus' left shoulder (θ).

γαμβροῦ Essentially a relation by marriage. In N 428 the term is used of Alcathous as son-in-law of Anchises, in 464 as brother-in-law of Aeneas. Here, where Andromeda is represented as for ever in chains, Perseus is for ever a suitor, or perhaps bridegroom-to-be; cf. Pi. *P.* 9.116 ἄντινα σχήσοι τις ἡρώων, ὅσοι γαμβροί σφιν ἦλθον.

ἐπισημαίνοιεν C. gen. 'will be a guide to'; cf. 12–13.

249 Περσέος Editors since Voss have preferred the Ionic gen., as in Β 406 Τυδέος, Γ 37 Ἀτρέος, Hdt. 7.150.2 Περσέος.

ἐπωμάδιοι First here and Theoc. 29.29 πτέρυγας ... ἐπωμαδίαις, later *AP* 9.11.3, *A.Pl.* 4.108.2, Nonn. *D.* 15.53, 150. Cf. 29 κατωμάδιαι. A. pictures Andromeda as standing on the shoulders of Perseus, though actually only one foot comes close to one shoulder. Eudoxus is a little more realistic with παρὰ τοὺς πόδας.

250 ἐν βορέω Elliptical use, as 224 ἐν Διός, repeated in 500. Chantraine (2.104–5) suggests that this usage may have originated in an association of ἐν and εἰς with partitive genitives (cf. ἐμποδών).

περιμήκετος ἄλλων The adj. occurs twice in Homer, Ξ 287 of a giant pine that reaches the sky, and ζ 103 of Mt Taygetus. The addition of the comparative gen. reflects the sense of superiority in περι- (cf. 237), and is probably influenced by the Homeric use with superlatives, e.g. Α 505 ὠκυμορώτατος ἄλλων. The epithet here suggests the heroic stature of Perseus in romantic drama, but the length of the constellation figure, while matching that of Andromeda, is less than that of Ophiuchus.

251 δεξιτερή The star η Persei. The characteristic ἅρπη does not appear in A.'s figure of Perseus, but is first attested in Hi. 2.5.15 ὁ ἐν τῇ ἅρπῃ νεφελοειδής (the double cluster H.VI 33 and 34).

κλισμόν Θ 436 ἐπὶ κλισμοῖσι καθῖζον. Cassiepeia's chair is not mentioned at all in 188–96, where A. is concerned solely with the dramatic figure of the queen herself. He has instead reserved it for inclusion in his description of Perseus. The Latin translators render κλισμὸν δίφροιο with one word (Cic. fr. 33.23 *sedes*, Germ. 252 and Avien. 565 *solium*), and most moderns do the same, but a pointless pleonasm is not in A.'s manner, and it is more likely that κλισμόν (usually a 'couch') is intended to mean the 'seat' of the chair. Erren translates 'zur Lehne', but it is rather to the seat of the chair (the line κ δ) that Perseus' hand is seen to be pointing, and it is perhaps significant that the seat of the chair is shown clearly on the Farnese globe.

τετάνυσται See note on 202.

252 πενθερίου The adj. first attested here. Call. *H.* 3.149 πενθερή, of Heracles' wife's mother. A. means the mother of his bride-to-be; cf. 248 γαμβροῦ. A. makes much play with the family connections of this μογερὸν γένος (179).

δίφροιο Normally a stool without back or arms. Ath. 5 192E ranks it as the meanest of Homeric seats (see Neil on Ar. *Eq.* 1164), and in Pl. *R.* 328c it is still a stool with a cushion on it. But it has status as a Homeric word, and combined with Homeric κλισμός enhances the figure in the sky. A. seems to make a point of avoiding the common θρόνος.

τὰ δ' ἐν ποσίν Lit. of what lies immediately before one, fig. of what requires immediate attention: cf. Pi. *P.* 8.32 τὸ δ' ἐν ποσί μοι τράχον (his composition), E. *Alc.* 739 τοὐν ποσὶν γὰρ οἰστέον κακόν. Voss and Erren are mistaken in translating 'mit den Füssen', Mair and Martin needlessly literal with 'that which lies before his feet' and 'quelque chose à ses pieds'. Perseus is engaged in the pursuit of the Monster that threatens Andromeda.

253 ἴχνια μηκύνει A transfer of meaning from footprints to moving feet; cf. Cat. 64.341 *praeuertet celeris uestigia ceruae.* A long line of bright stars marks the figure's left leg (ν ε ξ ζ), but the right is shorter, fainter and bent at the knee (δ μ and faint stars to the south). Cf. 687–8. A.'s words suggest the long strides of a man running.

κεκονιμένος Once in Homer, Φ 541–2 κεκονιμένοι ἐκ πεδίοιο | φεῦγον; cf. κονίοντες πεδίοιο (Ν 820, Ψ 372, 449, θ 122). Sch. καὶ γὰρ νεφελοειδεῖς εἰσι περὶ τοὺς πόδας αὐτοῦ συστροφαὶ καὶ κονιορτώδεις, ἅτε τοῦ Γαλαξίου κύκλου γειτνιῶντος. Perseus does lie in the Milky Way, and A. may well have had this in mind when he envisaged a runner covered with dust: cf. 511 πολιοῖο Γάλακτος. This explanation was evidently not known to the Latin translators: Cic. fr. 33.25 *puluerulentus uti de terra elapsus repente,* Avien. 567 *puluerulenta quasi cano procul aere.* Cf. Hyg. 3.11.2 *cum uellet Aratus eum currentem obscure significare, usus Aeoliorum consuetudine, eum* κεκονισμένον *dixit. Aeolii enim, cum uolunt aliquem decurrere significare,* ἀποκόνισσε *dicunt.* For the form of the part. cf. Hes. *Op.* 481, Ar. *Ec.* 291, Theoc. 1.30 (with Gow's note).

Διὶ πατρί Three levels of religious lore are combined in this phrase: the sky itself as a god, as in ὗε δ' ἄρα Ζεύς (Μ 25); the Homeric father-god (μ 63 Διὶ πατρί); and the Stoic god as father of all life (cf. 5, 15).

254–267 The Pleiades
This is a small and faint group near Perseus, traditionally of seven stars, though only six are visible. They are particularly famous at morning and evening appearances for marking the beginnings of seasons: see my fuller note on 265.

This cluster is one of the oldest of star-groups, because it is easy to recognise, even without reference to adjacent constellations. It is one of the Babylonian 36 stars, named MUL.MUL (Waerden *EW* 64, 66, 71). In Greek it appears first on the Shield of Achilles (Σ 486), and Odysseus observes it on his westerly course (ε 272). Hesiod brings out its importance in the farmer's calendar, especially at its MR in early summer (*Op.* 383, 572) and at its MS in early winter (384, 615), the latter being also significant for seafarers (619–20). Thereafter it is part of the standard star-lore of Greek and Latin poets, first as a notable constellation, e.g. Alcm. 1.60, [Sapph.] *PMG* fr. adesp. 976, A. fr. 312–13 Radt, Pi. *N.* 2.11, E. *IA* 7–8, *Ion* 1152, *Or.* 1005, *Phaethon* 66, 171 Diggle; later as a seasonal sign, e.g. Arat. 1066, 1085, Theoc. 13.25, *Ep.* [25.5], A.R. 3.225–6, Alex. Aet. *CA* 18.5. The Latin poets follow the Homeric tradition in Pl. *Am.* 275, V. *G.* 1.137–8, Prop. 3.5.36, Ov. *Fast.* 3.105, Sen. *Med.* 96, V.Fl. 2.67, 5.46; more frequently, and often allusively, they follow the Hesiodic tradition of weather signs, e.g. V. *G.* 1.221, 225, 4.232–3, Hor. *Carm.* 4.14.21–2, Prop. 1.8.10, 2.16.51, Ov. *Fast.* 5.599–600, *Pont.* 1.8.28, Luc. 8.852, Stat. *Th.* 4.120, *Silv.* 3.2.76, V.Fl. 1.647, 2.357, 406, 4.269, 5.305, 415.

The Pleiades were for long an unattached group, and A. lists it here because it is close to Perseus (cf. Eudox. fr. 35). Hipparchus mentions it only with reference to adjacent stars, but not as part of any constellation. Gem. 3.3. associates it with the Bull's back, Nic. *Ther.* 122–3 with the Bull's tail, as do Vitr. 9.3.1 and Plin. *Nat.* 2.110. Finally Ptol. *Alm.* 7.5.23 adds four of the Pleiades to the stars of Taurus, and the cluster is now accepted as part of that constellation.

The name of the cluster varies in both form and number, and there has been disagreement since antiquity about the original meaning of the word. The epic form Πληϊάδες occurs in the lines quoted above from Homer, Hesiod, *PMG* fr. adesp. 976, A. and A.R., the Attic Πλειάδες in E. *Phaethon*, Eudoxus, Attalus (Hi. 1.6.12), Hipparchus when discussing these and A. (1.6.12, 14), and Geminus in six out of seven references. The Latin form of this, *Pleiades*, eventually became the standard name. It appears with Homeric scansion in V. *G.* 1.138, Hor. *Carm.* 4.14.21, Prop. 2.16.51, 3.5.36, Germ. 256, Sen. *Med.* 96, V.Fl. 5.46, Avien. 568, and with trisyllabic scansion in Ov. *Fast.* 3.105. The sg. Πλειάς is equally common, e.g. in E. *Ion* 1152, *Or.* 1005 (Πελ- Eust.), *IA* 8, [Theoc.] *Ep.* 25.5–6, but especially in technical prose, e.g. Hp. *Epid.* 1.1 (Πληϊάδα), Arist. *HA* 553b31, *D.S.* 1, 7, Hi. 2.5.15, 2.6.6 al., where he is setting out his own work on star positions, Gem. *Cal.* Taur. 13, *Catast.* 23, Ptol. *Alm.* 7.5.23. In Latin *Pleas* appears in V. *G.* 4.233, *Pleias* (trisyll.) in Ov. *Pont.* 1.8.28, and the normal form later is *Plias*, e.g. Luc. 8.852, Stat. *Silv.* 3.2.76, V.Fl. 1.647. V.Fl. 2.67 has *Pleione*, mother of the Pleiades (Ath. 11 490D). Another early form of the name is Πελειάδες. It appears first in Hes. fr. 288, 289, 290, then in Alcm. 1.60 (Πεληάδες), Simon. fr. 555.5, A. fr. 312.4, Pi. *N.* 2.11, Lamprocl. fr. 736, Theoc. 13.25, Moero 1.9 (Powell); and Πέλειαι is attested (Ath. 11 491C) for Simmias (Powell 7) and Posidippus.

The derivations suggested in antiquity are listed in sch. 254–5: Ἄτλαντος δὲ καὶ Πληιόνης γενεαλογοῦνται Πλειάδες, παρ' ὃ καὶ λέγονται· ἢ ἐπεὶ πλείοσίν εἰσι χρειώδεις, τοῖς τε πλέουσι καὶ γεωργοῦσι· ἢ ὅτι εἰς πελείας μετεμορφώθησαν τὸν Ὠρίωνα φεύγουσαι· ἢ ἀπὸ τοῦ πολεῖν ἐκ περιόδου καὶ συμπληροῦν τὸν ἐνιαυτόν· ἀπὸ τούτων γὰρ κατ' ἐξοχὴν πλείων ἐκλήθη ὁ ἐνιαυτός. Cf. sch. Hes. *Op.* 382 and sch. Σ 486 (quoted by Martin *SAV* 202 and 552ff.). The derivation from πλεῖν was the most favoured in antiquity, because of the association with weather, but this is not how constellations were named. The only authentic-looking origin is πελειάδες, and Hes. *Op.* 619–20 Πληϊάδες σθένος ὄβριμον Ὠρίωνος | φεύγουσαι preserves the primary star-myth; Proclus in Hes. *Op.* 382 (Gaisford 245) ἀπὸ τοῦ εἰς πελείας μεταμορφωθῆναι ἐκ τοῦ φεύγειν τὸν Ὠρίωνα ὡς τοξότην. The form Πελειάδες is more frequent in earlier writers than later, but it is never forgotten, and Ath. 11 489ff. quotes a long (though misguided) discussion by Asclepiades Myrleanus. The shortening of the name to 'Pleiades' probably reflects popular usage, and the Homeric influence would have standardised it. The variation to the sg. may have been adopted by the astronomers because the stars form one small group, and all the constellations except the Twins and the Fishes have sg. names. The Latin name *Vergiliae* is standard among Roman writers, and only poets use the forms of the Greek name. Virgil also has *Atlantides* and *Maia* (*G.* 1.221, 225). Gundel in *RE* 21.2486ff., Roscher VI 942ff., Allen 391ff.

254 οἱ Perseus'; see note on 47. A. transfers the last phrase of Eudoxus' description of Perseus (cited on 248–255) to his introduction of the Pleiades, with characteristic variation.

σκαιῆς ἐπιγουνίδος The star ε Persei. Hipparchus (1.4.11) commends A. for making clear which knee is meant, but finds fault with him for describing this star as close to the Pleiades, and with Attalus even more for suggesting that A.'s ἄγχι should be taken to mean not ἐγγύς but ἐγγυτάτω (1.6.12–13). He points out that the stars marking the left foot (ζ ο) and leg (ξ) are much closer. A. has misconstrued Eudoxus' ἀποτείνων πρός: Perseus' leg certainly stretches towards the Pleiades. A. uses Homeric ἐπιγουνίς (ρ 225, σ 74) as a variation for γόνυ, but it properly means 'thigh': cf. Theoc. 26.34, A.R. 3.875. Sch. Διόδωρος [sc. Alexandrinus mathematicus: see Martin HT 30–1] μὲν "ὑπογουνίδος" γράφει, ὅπως ἡ κνήμη σημαίνοιτο. Μηνόφαντος δὲ ἐπιγουνίδα τὴν κνήμην, διὰ τὸ εἶναι ἐπ' αὐτῆς τὸ γόνυ. δύναιτο δ' ἂν καὶ ἀπὸ μέρους ὅλον τὸ σκέλος ἀκούεσθαι. These are all attempts to 'correct' the error noted by Hipparchus by shifting the reference to a position farther down the leg.

ἤλιθα Sch. ἀθρόως. Cf. 375, 611, 1011, 1064. In Homer always with πολλή, e.g. Λ 677 of captured herds, ε 483 of leaves. Here the adv. brings out the compactness of the star cluster. Cf. A.R. 3.342, 4.117, 1265.

255 οὐ μάλα πολλός The visible cluster occupies only a little more space than the moon. The phrase is usually positive in Homer (e.g. α 1), but A. makes much use of the neg.: 168, 316, 503, 520. The addition of ἀπάσας after πᾶσαι immediately above intensifies the contrast between the large number of stars and the small space.

256 χῶρος The sense of a measured space in the sky is probably derived from the Homeric use with reference to the ground, Γ 344 δια-μετρητῷ ἐνὶ χώρῳ.

καὶ δ' αὐταί Cf. Ι 709 καὶ δ' αὐτός in same, φ 110 καὶ δ' αὐτοί in different *sedes*. The combination of καί and δέ adds something that is distinct from what precedes (Denniston 199). The individual stars (αὐ-ταί) are difficult to make out, compared with the conspicuousness of the cluster as a whole. Cf. 300, 1010.

257 ἑπτάποροι The Pleiades are traditionally seven in number. The number seven had a certain mystical quality in antiquity, probably because it was the number of the planets (i.e. the visible five and the sun and moon); it is also the number of the bright stars in the Great Bear and Orion. For other contexts see D. Fehling, *Die Quellenangaben bei Herodot* (Berlin 1971) 160–1. The adj. appears first in *h.Hom.* 8.7, of the planets, ἑπταπόροις ἐνὶ τείρεσιν, where -πόροις has more point, because of the different planetary orbits and periods. It is first used of the Pleiades in E. *IA* 7–8 τῆς ἑπταπόρου | Πλειάδος, *Or.* 1005 ἑπταπόρου τε δραμήματα Πλειάδος, *Rh.* 529–30 ἑπτάποροι | Πλειάδες αἰθέριαι. Cf. *Phaethon* 171 Diggle ἑπτὰ Πλειάδων ἔχων δρόμον, Nonn. *D.* 2.17 Πλειάδος ἑπταπόροιο, 8.76 ἑπταπόρου, 38.380 ἑπτάστερος ἠχώ, *Catast.* 23 ἑπτάστερος καλεῖται.

μετ' ἀνθρώπους Where the verb does not express movement μετά is sometimes used in the sense of 'among', e.g. Β 143 πᾶσι μετὰ πληθύν, χ 352 ἀεισόμενος μετὰ δαῖτας. Chantraine 2.118.

ὑδέονται A Hellenistic verb, but see Pfeiffer on Call. frr. 371 and 372. Cf. A.R. 2.528 τὰ μὲν ὣς ὑδέονται, 4.264–5 πρόσθε σεληναίης ὑδέονται | ζώειν; act. in Call. H. 1.76 ὑδείομεν, frr. 371, 372 ὑδέοιμι, ὑδέουσιν, Nic. Alex. 47 ὑδεῦσι. Perh. cogn. with αὐδή (Frisk). Hsch. ὑδεῖν· ὑμνεῖν, ᾄδειν, λέγειν.

258 ἒξ οἷαι Hipparchus disagrees (1.6.14): ψευδῶς δὲ λέγεται ὑπὸ τοῦ Ἀράτου καὶ τὸ τὰς Πλειάδας ἒξ μόνον ἀστέρας περιέχειν ... λανθάνει δὲ αὐτόν· τῷ γὰρ ἀτενίσαντι ἐν αἰθρίῳ καὶ ἀσελήνῳ νυκτὶ φαίνονται ἀστέρες ἑπτὰ ἐν αὐτῇ περιεχόμενοι. He cannot understand how Attalus overlooked this error. A major difficulty in counting the Pleiades is that of separating points of light that are set so close together, but people with good eyesight have been able to distinguish seven or even more stars in this cluster (Allen 410). Ov. Phaen. fr. 1 (Morel) Pliades ante genus septem radiare feruntur, | sed tamen apparet sub opaca septima nube, Fast. 4.170 quae septem dici, sex tamen esse solent, Hyg. 2.21.3 hae numero septem dicuntur, sed nemo amplius sex potest uidere, Ath. 11 492B ἒξ δὲ τὰς πάσας γενέσθαι Πλειάδας, ἐπείπερ ὁρῶνται τοσαῦται, λέγονται δὲ ἑπτά, καθάπερ καὶ Ἄρατός φησιν, Phlp. in Mete. 345a οἶμαι δὲ καὶ τὸ ἑπταπόρου δρόμημα Πλειάδος διὰ τοὺς ἑπτὰ πλανωμένους εἰρῆσθαι· αἱ γὰρ λεγόμεναι Πλειάδες ἒξ εἰσι καὶ μόναι, καθάπερ Ἄρατος εἴρηκε, καὶ τοῦτο τοῖς εἰς αὐτὰ ἀποβλέπουσι φαίνεται, Tz. in Hes. Op. 383 ἐν τῇ μέσῃ δὲ τοῦ Ταύρου, ἤγουν ἐν τῇ ζώνῃ, κεῖνται αἱ Πλειάδες αἱ ἒξ, αἵτινες λέγονται καὶ κοινῶς ἐξάστερον.

ἐπόψιαι See note on 81.

259 ἀπευθής Pass., as again in 270, 648; once in Homer in this sense: γ 88–9 κείνου δ' αὖ καὶ ὄλεθρον ἀπευθέα θῆκε Κρονίων. | οὐ γάρ τις δύναται σάφα εἰπέμεν ὁππόθ' ὄλωλεν. Sch. τοῦτο χαριεντιζόμενος ἐπὶ τῇ μυθολογίᾳ ὅτι ἑπτά εἰσι. The tone of amused detachment on the subject of ancient lore is typical of A. and other Hellenistic poets: see note on 30 εἰ ἐτεὸν δή, Hutchinson HP 44–5 on Callimachus. So Ovid makes play with the notion of a lost Pleiad, Merope hiding for shame at marrying a mortal, or Electra for grief over the sack of Troy (Fast. 4.171–8). Cf. Hyg. 2.21.3, Q.S. 13.551–3 φασὶ καὶ αὐτὴν Ἠλέκτρην βαθύπεπλον ἐὸν δέμας ἀμφικαλύψαι ἀχλύϊ καὶ νεφέεσσιν ἀποιχομένην χόρου ἄλλων. A. himself has this myth in his Ἐπικήδειον πρὸς Θεόπροπον (SH 103). Cicero heavy-handedly amplifies with sed frustra, temere a uulgo, ratione sine ulla | septem dicier (fr. 33.32–3). See M. P. O. Morford, CPh 62 (1967) 112ff.

ἐκ Διός Cf. 253 ἐν Διὶ πατρί.

260 γενεῆθεν ἀκούομεν Adv. only here and, in a more restricted sense, AP 7.445.3 ἄγραυλοι γενεῆθεν ὀρειτύποι. A. may be recalling the tradition as expressed by Ar. Cael. 270b13 ἐν ἅπαντι γὰρ τῷ παρ-

ἐληλυθότι χρόνῳ κατὰ τὴν παραδεδομένην ἀλλήλοις μνήμην οὐθὲν φαίνεται μεταβεβληκὸς οὔτε καθ' ὅλον τὸν ἔσχατον οὐρανὸν οὔτε κατὰ μόριον αὐτοῦ τῶν οἰκείων οὐθέν. Hence the sensation when Hipparchus *nouam stellam in aeuo suo genitam deprehendit* (Plin. *Nat.* 2.95).

αὔτως I.e. they are just known as being seven in number, and there is no need to look for any further explanation. Cf. 21.

261 δὲ κεῖναι Buhle adopted δ' ἐκεῖναι from K and has been followed uncritically by subsequent editors.

ἐπιρρήδην See note on 191.

262–263 Without explicitly referring to the myth, A. takes the names from the tradition of the Pleiades as daughters of Atlas, e.g. Hes. *Op.* 383 Πληϊάδων Ἀτλαγενέων, Simon. *PMG* 555.3ff. ἔτικτε δ' Ἄτλας ἑπτὰ ἰοπλοκάμων φιλᾶν θυγατρῶν τάνδ' ἔξοχον εἶδος ὅσαι καλέονται Πελειάδες οὐράνιαι, A. fr. 312 αἱ δ' ἐπτ' Ἄτλαντος παῖδες ὠνομασμέναι ... ἄπτεροι Πελειάδες. Sch. Pi. *N.* 2.17 quote three lines from an early poem, commonly attributed to Hesiod (fr. 169): Τηϋγέτη τ' ἐρόεσσα καὶ Ἠλέκτρη κυανῶπις | Ἀλκυόνη τε καὶ Ἀστερόπη δῖη τε Κελαινὼ | Μαῖά τε καὶ Μερόπη, τὰς γείνατο φαίδιμος Ἄτλας. Sch. Σ 486 give a similar list from Hellanicus fr. 19a J: τὰς μὲν ἑπτὰ θεοῖς συνελθεῖν, Ταϋγέτην Διί, ὧν γενέσθαι Λακεδαίμονα, Μαῖαν Διί, ἀφ' ὧν Ἑρμῆς, Ἠλέκτραν Διί, ὧν Δάρδανος, Ἀλκυόνην Ποσειδῶνι, ὧν Ὑριεύς, Στερόπην Ἄρει, ὧν Οἰνόμαος, Κελαινὼ Ποσειδῶνι καὶ αὐτὴν συγγενέσθαι, ὧν Λύκος, Μερόπην δὲ Σισύφῳ θνητῷ ὄντι, ὧν Γλαῦκος· διὸ καὶ ἀμαυρὰν εἶναι. Cf. *Catast.* 23, Ov. *Fast.* 5.83ff. A. has condensed the three Hesiodic lines into two, altering the order, omitting the epithets and the Atlas clause, but adding an epithet to Maia. Note the pattern of triple τε and triple καί.

263 Στερόπη The form of the name in Hellanicus (see preceding note) and *Catast.* 23. So Avien. 581 *et Sterope*, but Germ. 263 follows the Hesiodic tradition with Asterope, and the MSS for Cic. fr. 33.36 are divided: metre allows either.

πότνια Cf. 112. Here A. follows *h.Hom.* 4.19, 183 of Maia, perhaps deliberately because she is mother of Hermes, inventor of the lyre, the next constellation to be described (269).

264 ὁμῶς After dealing with the number and names of the Pleiades, A. resumes the theme of 256 that all alike are faint stars, and goes on to contrast their faintness with their fame.

ὀλίγαι Strictly of the size of the individual stars, but the choice of word seems to reflect οὐ μάλα πολλός (255) of the size of the cluster as a whole. Cf. 42, 195.

ἀφεγγέες 'Faint', compared with most star-groups; cf. E. *Ph.* 543

νυκτός τ' ἀφεγγὲς βλέφαρον, if, as I think likely, E. means the moon as the pale eye of night compared with the sun as the bright eye of day.

ὀνομασταί Sch. ἀντὶ τοῦ ὀνομασταί εἰσι καὶ ἐπίδοξοι διὰ τὸ καὶ τὴν ἀνατολὴν αὐτῶν καὶ τὴν δύσιν πρὸς ἀναγκαῖον εἶναι τοῖς ἀνθρώποις. Cf. Theogn. 23 πάντας δὲ κατ' ἀνθρώπους ὀνομαστός. Elsewhere in A. the adj. means 'named' (381, 385).

265 ἦρι καὶ ἑσπέριαι Cf. similar combination of adv. and adj. in Call. *H.* 1.87 ἑσπέριος κεῖνός γε τελεῖ τά κεν ἦρι νοήσῃ. These are the morning and evening phenomena known as risings and settings, which marked the progress of the year in the ancient lore of farmers and sailors. The fixed stars rise and set about four minutes earlier each day, relative to the sun. Once a year, therefore, in the course of this apparent westward movement, each star or constellation overtakes the sun, and for some time before and after this conjunction it is too close to the sun to be visible. In the time of Eudoxus the period of invisibility of the Pleiades lasted about forty days (cf. Hes. *Op.* 385-6 αἳ δή τοι νύκτας τε καὶ ἤματα τεσσαράκοντα | κεκρύφαται), from the beginning of April to about mid-May. Their last visible setting, after sunset, before they were too close to the sun to be seen, was known as the Evening Setting (ES), and their reappearance in the east some forty days later, when they were far enough ahead of the sun to be seen rising for the first time before sunrise, was the Morning Rising (MR). Two other phenomena were also used to mark specific days in the calendar, about midway between the MR and the next ES. When the Pleiades had advanced far enough ahead of the sun to be visible almost all night, there came a day when they were seen rising for the last time just after sunset, and this was called the Evening Rising (ER). A little later came the day when they were seen to set just before sunrise, and this was the Morning Setting (MS). For a full and lucid account of risings and settings see A. L. Peck in his Loeb edition of Aristotle, *HA* vol. 2 (1970), Appendix A and Graph B.

Geminus records from the calendar of Eudoxus: Aries 10 (= 1 Apr.) Πλειάδες ἀκρόνυχοι δύνουσι . . .· ὑετὸς γίνεται (ES); Taur. 22 (= 14 May) Πλειάδες ἐπιτέλλουσι· καὶ ἐπισημαίνει (MR); Libra 8 (=3 Oct.) Πλειάδες ἐπιτέλλουσιν (ER); Scorp. 19 (= 13 Nov.) Πλειάδες ἑῶαι δύνουσι . . .· καὶ χειμάζει (MS). The importance of the Pleiades lay in the fact that their risings and settings spanned most of the farming and seafaring year; in particular the beginning of the latter and the ending of both were marked by their MR in May and MS in November, and it is these two dates that A. has in mind here (cf. 266, 1066, 1085). They are the relevant dates for Hesiod: *Op.* 383-4 Πληϊάδων Ἀτλαγενέων ἐπιτελλομενάων | ἄρχεσθ' ἀμήτου, ἀρότοιο δὲ δυσομενάων (MR and MS), 572 of the snail

Πληϊάδας φεύγων (MR), 614–16 of ploughing ἐπὴν δὴ | Πληϊάδες θ' Ύά-
δες τε τό τε σθένος 'Ωρίωνος | δύνωσιν (MS), and 619–20 of gales at sea
εὖτ' ἂν Πληϊάδες σθένος ὄβριμον 'Ωρίωνος φεύγουσαι | πίπτωσιν ἐς
ἠεροειδέα πόντον (MS). Cf. A. *Ag.* 5–6 τοὺς φέροντας χεῖμα καὶ θέρος
βροτοῖς | λαμπροὺς δυνάστας, Theoc. 13.25 ἆμος δ' ἀντέλλοντι Πε-
λειάδες, Autom. *AP* 7.534.5–6 δύσιν δ' ὑπὸ Πλειάδος αὐτὴν | πον-
τοπορῶν αὐτῇ Πλειάδι συγκατέδυς.

Ζεὺς δ' αἴτιος A reminder and illustration of 10–13. The interlaced
pattern of ὀνομασταὶ ἦρι καὶ ἑσπέριαι εἱλίσσονται and Ζεὺς δ' αἴτιος,
ὅ σφισι κτλ. emphasises the importance of both Zeus and the Pleiades.
This is a new variety of hyperbaton in that it involves three clauses instead of the usual two, as e.g. in S. *OT* 1251, Call. fr. 178.9–10, Theoc.
16.16.

266 ὅ σφισι The art. as rel. pron. is derived from its use as
demonstr., but is rare in the nom.; cf. A 388 ἠπείλησεν μῦθον, ὁ δὴ
τετελεσμένος ἐστί, H 365ff. τοῖσι δ' ἀνέστη | Δαρδανίδης Πρίαμος ... |
ὁ σφιν εὔφρονέων ἀγορήσατο. Here it has an explanatory force, as in
Π 835 Τρωσὶ φιλοπτολέμοισι μεταπρέπω, ὅ σφιν ἀμύνω. The art. is
preferred as *lectio difficilior*, supported by the single σ in S. The sense is
confirmed by sch. ὅστις αὐταῖς κτλ. Chantraine 2.166.

θέρεος καὶ χείματος These two terms are sometimes used in such a
way as to cover the whole year, the warm, good-weather season, and the
cold, bad-weather season. So in Alcinous' garden (η 117–18) τάων οὔ-
ποτε καρπὸς ἀπόλλυται οὐδ' ἀπολείπει | χείματος οὐδὲ θέρευς, ἐπετή-
σιος, and in Hes. *Op.* 640 Ἄσκρη, χεῖμα κακῆ, θέρει ἀργαλέη, οὐδέ
ποτ' ἐσθλῇ. These periods are to some extent elastic, depending on the
weather from year to year (cf. 1077–81), but are precise enough in practice. For the same reason Thucydides organises his record of the war ὡς
ἕκαστα ἐγίγνετο κατὰ θέρος καὶ χειμῶνα (2.1), the periods when
military and naval operations were more frequent and less frequent
respectively. The Pleiades thus became the conventional dividers of
the year: e.g. *D.S.* 6 διχοτομεῖ δὲ τὸν μὲν ἐνιαυτὸν Πλειάς τε δυομένη
καὶ ἀνατέλλουσα· ἀπὸ γὰρ δύσεως μέχρι ἀνατολῆς τὸ ἥμισυ τοῦ
ἐνιαυτοῦ ἐστιν. So Virgil, with characteristic invention, *Taygete simul os
terris ostendit honestum | Pleas et Oceani spretos pede reppulit amnis, | aut eadem
sidus fugiens ubi Piscis aquosi | tristior hibernas caelo descendit in undas* (*G.*
4.232–5).

267 ἐπένευσεν Attested only by Athenaeus, but apparently confirmed by Avien. 611 *conuolui caelo summae pater adnuit aethrae.* Cicero and
Germanicus ignore this reference to Zeus. The verb is traditional for
Zeus expressing his will, e.g. A 528 ἐπ' ὀφρύσι νεῦσε Κρονίων. It is also
used as a command, c. dat. et inf. I 620–1 Πατρόκλῳ ὅ γ' ἐπ' ὀφρύσι

νεῦσε σιωπῇ | Φοίνικι στορέσαι πυκινὸν λέχος. The reading of the MSS can be explained as an obvious gloss.

ἀρότοιο A reminiscence of Hes. *Op.* 384 and 616, where the Pleiades' setting is a signal for ploughing. Winter and ploughing are associated also in *Op.* 450–1 of the cry of cranes, ἥ τ' ἀρότοιό τε σῆμα φέρει καὶ χείματος ὥρην | δεικνύει. Voss's emendation is an attempt to bring the line more into harmony with *Op.* 384, but there is no justification for this. The rhyming couplet that closes this section is reminiscent of Hesiod's style in *Op.* 383–4. It may be suggestive of popular jingles associated with weather; cf. 190–1. It may not be deliberate in 1 481–2.

268–318 KNEELER GROUP: THE LYRE, THE BIRD, THE WATER-POURER, CAPRICORN, THE ARCHER, THE ARROW, THE EAGLE, THE DOLPHIN

A. now takes the observer back across the pole to pick up the familiar Kneeler (Engonasin), and with that constellation as a guide proceeds to identify the remainder of the northern constellations.

268–274 The Lyre

The Lyre was invented by Hermes in his cradle, and placed in the sky in front of the unnamed figure, whose left knee comes close to it. It lies between that and the head of the Bird.

The Lyre is a small constellation, probably devised for the identification of its one bright star, the 1st-mag. α Lyrae, now known as Vega. Its importance was calendarial: Gem. *Cal.* gives for Euctemon its MS Leo 17 (12 Aug.), MR Scorp. 10 (4 Nov.), ES Aquar. 3 (24 Jan.), ER Taur. 4 (26 Apr.). Λύρα is the earliest use of the name attested in Greek. It has been identified with the Babylonian UZA 'goat' (Waerden *EW* 67), but W. Gundel has suggested the Greek choice of name may have been inspired by that of the Egyptian constellation *Sit* 'tortoise' (Roscher VI 905).

The standard name for the constellation is Λύρα, but in the calendars and Ptol. *Alm.* 7.5.8 it also means Vega, which Hipparchus calls ὁ ἐν τῇ Λύρᾳ λαμπρός (1.6.15). Variations are few: Nonn. *D.* 1.257 φόρμιγξ, and late uses of κιθάρα, κιθάριον (Boll, *Sphaera* 104). In Latin *Lyra* is standard, but Cicero uses *Fides* (fr. 33.42), and Varro claims *quod Graeci Lyram uocant, Fidem nostri* (*R.* 2.5.12). Columella has the forms *Fidis* (11.2.40) and *Fidicula* (11.2.4), the latter being repeated in Plin. *Nat.* 18.222. Only Avien. 618 adopts A.'s χέλυς (268) as a name, *Chelys*. Gundel in *RE* 13.2489ff., Roscher VI, 904ff., Allen 280.

268 καὶ χέλυς ἐστ' ὀλίγη Following 264, this introduces another small constellation. χέλυς is probably intended to be a description of its form, not its name, which is given in 269, and repeated in 597, 615, 674. Cf. Man. 5.324–5 *surgente Lyra testudinis enatat undis | forma.* The υ is long in early epic (*h.Hom.* 4.24, 33, 153), but short later, in E. *Alc.* 447 (lyr.), Call. *H.* 2.16, Antip. *AP* 6.118.4 = *HE* 499, Opp. *H.* 5.404.

The reading of MSS and sch. (ἤτ', ἤ τ') is unsatisfactory. It could presumably mean '(there is) also a tortoise, which is small', but this is too clumsy. Mair's 'Yonder, too, is the tiny Tortoise' gives the pronoun a deictic force, which is hardly possible, and in any case premature, since the position of the Lyre is a long way from the Pleiades, and is not defined until 270. Voss's ἤδ' would require a preceding reference, as in α 185 νηῦς δέ μοι ἤδ' ἔστηκεν, though Martin adopts it as a deictic pronoun. Kaibel's ἤν refers to the time when the lyre was invented, but A. is describing the present sky at this point, and only moves to the past in the next line. Here ἐστ' is appropriate, as I proposed in *CQ* 31 (1981) 360: while A. tends to prefer more interesting verbs, he nevertheless uses ἐστί eight times in the first half of the poem. Corruption could have come from misreading εc as Η, a common early form of η (F. H. Sandbach in a letter to me from C. O. Brink, March 1985).

ἄρ' The particle draws attention to an interesting myth, and the transmitted ἄρ gives the right meaning. But ἄρα is occasionally used in this sense (Denniston 44 1.(1)), and there are close parallels for the present context in Archil. fr. 185.5 West τῷ δ' ἄρ' ἀλώπηξ κερδαλῆ συνήντετο (cf. 174.2), Call. fr. 194.101–2 τὴν δ' ἄρ' ὑποδρὰξ οἶα ταῦρος ἡ δάφνη | ἔβλεψε.

παρὰ λίκνω I.e. he was just out of his cradle. A. recalls *h.Hom.* 4.21–2 οὐκέτι δηρὸν ἔκειτο μένων ἱερῷ ἐνὶ λίκνω, | ἀλλ' ὁ γ' ἀναΐξας, and 63–4 καὶ τὴν μὲν κατέθηκε φέρων ἱερῷ ἐνὶ λίκνω | φόρμιγγα γλαφυρήν.

269 Ἑρμείης Ionic form, as in Hes. *Op.* 68, fr. 66.4. So Call. *H.* 3.69, 143, 4.272, Nic. *Alex.* 561. A.R. uses the Homeric form Ἑρμείας, except that in 4.1137 all MSS have Ἑρμείης. The *h.Hom.* 4 has Ἑρμῆς throughout, but 19 has both the Homeric (1, 40) and the Ionic (28). The Aratean MSS are divided, and modern editors prefer the Ionic form.

The myth of Hermes' invention of the lyre is told in *h.Hom.* 4.24–51. He finds a tortoise at the cave entrance (24–6), takes it inside (40), gouges out the flesh (42), attaches a frame of reeds (47–8), stretches oxhide round it (49), and adds two side pieces and a cross-bar (50) and seven strings of sheep-gut (51). He then invents a plectrum to play it with (53). Hermes is designated the inventor of the lyre by Nic. *Alex.* 560–1, Bion fr. 7.8, Apollod. 3.10.2, Paus. 8.17.5; cf. Hor. *Carm.* 1.10.6. Call. *H.* 4.253 makes Apollo create the seven-stringed lyre.

The introduction of the Hermes myth is not without some significance for the *Phaenomena*. Hermes is not only a son of Zeus, but also son of Maia, just named as one of the Pleiades, with the honorific epithet πότνια (263). There is another link with the Pleiades, which is probably a later invention, since A. himself gives no hint of it, that the choice of seven strings was influenced by the number of the Pleiades: Hyg. 2.7.2 *septem chordas instituisse ex Atlantidum numero*, Avien. 626 *carmina Pleiadum numero deduxerat*. Hermes had a planet assigned to him too, though this may not be meaningful for A.'s purpose. In Stoic lore he was sometimes equated with Zeus as the rational element in the cosmos: cf. Sen. *Ben.* 4.8 *Mercurium, quia ratio penes illum est numerusque et ordo et scientia.* The third-century Stoic Herillus of Carthage wrote a book entitled *Hermes* (D.L. 7.165). At the same time Hermes as inventor of the lyre is a patron of literature, and this line may recall the invocation of the Muses in 16–18.

ἐτόρησε   In Homer this verb means 'pierce', e.g. Λ 236 οὐδ' ἔτορε ζωστῆρα, Ε 337–8 δόρυ χροὸς ἀντετόρησεν | ἀμβροσίου διὰ πέπλου. Mair and Martin therefore refer it here to the piercing of holes for the strings. But A.'s choice of this verb seems intended rather to recall *h.Hom.* 4.42 αἰῶν' ἐξετόρησεν ὀρεσκῴοιο χελώνης, of Hermes cutting or gouging out the flesh: see Allen and Sykes ad loc. Cf. Apollod. 3.10.2 (χελώνην) ἐκκαθάρας. In the Homeric hymn the strings are the last items to be added, and there is no explanation of how they were attached. LSJ explain τορέω = τορνεύω here, as in *AP* 9.162.3 = *FGE* 1342, but there is no suggestion that Hermes' work on the shell involves any carving.

Λύρην   The Homeric terms for this stringed instrument are φόρμιγξ (Α 603) and κίθαρις (α 153). In *h.Hom.* 4 it is the finished instrument that is called φόρμιγξ (64), but when Hermes first plays it to Apollo, the phrase is λύρῃ δ' ἐρατὸν κιθαρίζων (423); cf. Call. *H.* 2.33 ἥ τε λύρη as an attribute of Apollo. For the smaller instrument in private use λύρα became the standard word, κιθάρα for the elaborated form, as used in public performances.

εἶπε   C. inf., in sense of commanding, as in ο 76–7, χ 262–3.

270 κὰδ δ' ἔθετο   Homeric apocope breaking a succession of short syllables; cf. δ 344 κὰδ δ' ἔβαλε. But metrical considerations do not always apply, as in 853 κὰδ δὴ δυομένου, which must be seen as a variation of 724 καταδυομένοιο. See Chantraine 1.87. The influence of the Homeric apocope has led the poet to write a quaint imitation of the sound of the whole line κὰδ δ' ἔβαλε προπάροιθε νεὸς κυανοπρῴροιο (Ι 482), though the two contexts have nothing in common.

προπάροιθεν   Hipparchus (1.5.20) claims that this is wrong because the Lyre lies to the east of the Kneeler. As elsewhere (e.g. 188) he un-

COMMENTARY: 271–274

derstands 'before' as meaning 'to the west', the direction of the sky's movement. But A. is thinking of the direction in which the figure of the Kneeler is supposed to be facing, and that is eastwards. The Alexandrian Anacreon (ap. Hyg. 1.6.2) is not specific on this point, and differs from A. also in his identification of the figure: ἀγχοῦ δ' Αἰγείδεω Θησέος ἐστὶ λύρη (CA p. 130).

ἀπευθέος εἰδώλοιο A reference back to 64 εἴδωλον and οὔ τις ἐπίσταται.

271 οὐρανὸν εἰσαγαγών It is more natural to take this as the compound verb than to separate εἰς as preposition after its noun, as in 539. Cf. 32, 325, 955, and H 423 οὐρανὸν εἰσανιών, Π 232 οὐρανὸν εἰσανιδών.

πέτηλον Sch. ἢ τὸ ἀναπεπταμένον ἢ τὸ πεπτηκός. The latter is confirmed by 615 Λύρη παραπεπτηῶτος, and the sense required is that of 'crouching' (66–7); cf. 167 πεπτηότα, of the Bull. The adj. is formed from the root πετ- (cf. πίπτω), and occurs only here in this sense. LSJ follow the first explanation of sch., but that is not appropriate to the figure described.

272 γούνατί οἱ σκαιῷ The star θ Herculis. Hipparchus quotes this phrase in 1.4.11 and 12 to illustrate A.'s correct use of the terms 'left' and 'right' in descriptions of figures. The pron. οἱ is the Lyre, as is also ἡ in 273.

κεφαλή γε μὲν ἄκρη The Bird's head is β Cygni, and it is called ἄκρη because it lies at one extremity of the constellation: cf. 74, 201. Perhaps because there is so little to be said about the Lyre, A. expands his description of its position into a chiasmus of three lines, with case variations in 274. The passage also assists the transition from one constellation to the next.

273 ἀντιπέρην β Cygni is 'opposite' in the sense that it lies on the other side of the Lyre from θ Herculis. Cf. 405, 528; A.R. 2.177.

Ὄρνιθος With κεφαλή, but misleadingly placed after ἀντιπέρην, which is used c. gen. in 405. A.'s chiastic patterning sometimes mars his normal clarity of exposition: cf. 413–16.

274 ὀρνιθέης Only here, allowing a trisyllabic form of ὀρνίθειος.

275–281 The Bird
This Bird has a partly faint, partly ruffled appearance, like a bird in flight. One wing extends towards Cepheus, the other towards the Horse.

This constellation has the form of a large cross lying along the line of the Milky Way. Four bright stars (β η γ α) in an almost straight line from south-west to north-east denote the head, neck, centre and tail respectively, while stars at either side mark the right (δ ι κ) and left (ε ζ) wings. The Babylonians devised a different figure out of these stars and part of Cepheus (Waerden *EW* 68), and the Bird was therefore taken from some other source or invented by the Greeks. The regular Greek name, from Eudox. fr. 39 to Ptol. *Alm.* 7.5.9, is Ὄρνις, but when it comes to be identified with the swan in mythology, the alternative Κύκνος appears: *Catast.* 25, and Hyg. 2.8.1 *Olor. hunc Cygnum Graeci appellant.* Sch. τοῦτον τὸν Ὄρνιν οἱ μὲν λέγουσι κύκνον ὄντα κατασтερισθῆναι μὲν εἰς τιμὴν τοῦ Ἀπόλλωνος ἅτε μουσικὸν ὄντα [hence in another scholion οὐκ ἀπεικὸς δέ, ὡς μουσικὸν ὄντα, τὸν Ὄρνιν πλησίον εἶναι τῆς Λύρας]· οἱ δέ, ὡς Ζεὺς εἰκασθεὶς ὡμίλησε Λήδα· κατὰ δὲ τοὺς πλείστους, Νεμέσει. The Latin names are *Ales* (Cic. fr. 33.47, Avien. 633), *Volucris* (Cic. 471, Vitr. 9.4.3), *Auis* (Germ. 275), *Cycnus* (Man. 1.337, Avien. 636), *Cygnus*, which is the standard modern name (Germ. 466). On the spelling of *cycnus/cygnus* see Housman, *Juvenalis Saturae* xxii. Gundel s.v. Kuknos in *RE* 11.2442ff., Roscher vi 906ff., Allen 192ff.

275 ἤτοι γάρ Humorously confirming, after an apparently casual mention of it in 273, that there is actually a Bird in the sky! Cf. 305, and more seriously 748. On ἤτοι = ἦ τοι see Denniston 553–4.

Ζηνὶ παρατρέχει Again Zeus is primarily the sky (cf. 253, 259), but recalls the Homeric god, and is also a reminder of the omnipresent Stoic god. The form Ζηνί with παρα- seems intended as an echo of Δ 1 θεοὶ πὰρ Ζηνὶ καθήμενοι (= H 443). The verb suggests the role of an attendant accompanying the sky-Zeus in his westward movement; cf. 844 παρατρέχοι of the sun accompanying a rain-storm. The choice of τρέχω, however, while appropriate for the Bears (27), is rather less suited to the flying bird.

αἰόλος Sch. ἐπεὶ τὰ μέν εἰσιν αὐτοῦ ἀνάστερα, τὰ δὲ ἠστέρωται. The sense of variegated colouring is not Homeric, but is common in later poets, e.g. A. *Th.* 494 αἰόλην πυρὸς κάσιν, of fiery smoke, S. *Tr.* 94 αἰόλα νύξ, the varied brightness and darkness of the night sky, Call. *H.* 3.91 ἕνα δ᾽ αἰόλον, of a dog's colouring. Here the sense is explained by 276–7. Cf. 328 ποικίλος.

276 ἄλλοθεν ἠερόεις ἠερόεις, prop. 'misty' (cf. 630, 988), here means 'faint' (cf. 317, 385, and 349 ἠερίη). In 317 and 349 the adj. contrasts one part of a constellation with another part, but here the transmitted reading ἀλλ᾽ ὁ μέν contrasts the whole, as faint, with parts that are quite bright, and this does not make sense. Two translators, however, make the constellation partly faint and partly bright: Cic. fr. 33.49–50 *altera pars huic obscura est et luminis expers, | altera nec paruis nec claris lucibus ardet,* Germ. 279ff. *multa uidebis | stellarum uacua in Cygno, multa ignea rursus | aut medii fulgoris erunt.* But Avien. 637–8 seems to give the transmitted text in *non claro lucidus astro, | sed tamen os flagrans et guttura longa coruscans.*

Martin emends to ἄλλα μέν on the analogy of 575–6, but this puts μέν in a phrase attached to Ὄρνις and δέ in a clause with a different subject and verb. A. elsewhere observes the normal usage of placing these particles in parallel word-groups. I therefore read ἄλλοθεν on the analogy of 317 μεσσόθεν ἠερόεις, τὰ δέ οἱ ... The Bird could never be described as a faint constellation (see note on 275–281), but there are certainly some very dim areas between the bright stars.

τὰ δέ οἱ ἔπι τετρήχυνται   Ionic form of τραχύνω, with 3rd sg. ending, as in Arist. *Pr.* 901b11 τετράχυνται γὰρ ὁ φάρυγξ αὐτοῖς. Cf. 787 ἄμβλυνται. The point of the metaphor is not immediately clear, and sch. offer two explanations: ἤτοι ὅτι πολλοὶ ἀστέρες τὰς ἁπλώσεις τῶν πτερῶν ἀποτελοῦσι, διὸ τετράχυνται, ἢ ὅτι τοῦ πτεροῦ ἐπιψαύει ὁ Γαλαξίας κύκλος, διὸ ὥσπερ τραχὺ ἀποτελεῖ, ὅπερ καὶ ἐπὶ τοῦ Περσέως ἐλέγομεν (253 κεκονιμένος). Another scholion also mentions wings (τὰ δὲ πτερὰ αὐτοῦ τετράχυνται), but it is not clear why extended wings should be seen as 'rough'. The line of the Bird's wings is well marked, but they are not particularly rich in stars. Similarly the Milky Way gives a good explanation of κεκονιμένος, but it does not suggest a rough or ruffled expanse of feathers. In any case A. has nothing to say about wings at this point, and the variant πτερά for ἐπί probably came from the sch. The contrast here is between the almost starless parts and those that have many stars. The latter, then, must refer not to the wings but to the northern or tail end of the figure, which is very rich in stars, including the brightest of all, the 1st-mag. Deneb. There is, however, no way of associating τραχύς with brightness, and the point of the metaphor is that this area of the constellation is 'bristling' with stars, as if all these points of light were raised above the general surface of the sky.

The compound verb of the MSS is unsatisfactory, because the prefix and the verb have different functions (cf. 73), ἐπί denoting the position of the stars in the figure, the verb describing the stars' appearance. οἱ ἔπι gives the required sense; for enclitic governed by prep. cf. 546 ἐπί οἱ, 847 οἱ πέρι. Martin takes ἐπί as adv., but it is not clear what position in the constellation is being indicated by 'above'; certainly not the upper side of the bird, as Erren seems to imply with 'seine Oberseite', in view of the convention that all constellation figures are envisaged as facing the earth (Hi. 1.4.9).

277 οὔτι λίην μεγάλοις   Hipparchus disagrees (1.6.15): καὶ γὰρ πολλοὺς καὶ λαμπροὺς ἀστέρας ἔχει ὁ Ὄρνις, τὸν δὲ ἐν τῇ οὐρᾷ καὶ σφόδρα λαμπρόν, ἔγγιστά τε ἴσον τῷ ἐν τῇ Λύρᾳ λαμπρῷ. Hipparchus is right: Deneb is mag. 0.03, Vega 1.26. Since he does not include Eudoxus in his criticism here, this line is presumably A.'s own addition to his source material.

278 εὐδιόωντι Epic part., primarily of sky or sea, e.g. 899 Διὸς εὐδιόωντος, A.R. 2.371 κόλπῳ ἐν εὐδιόωντι, Opp. *C.* εὐδιόωσα ... θάλασσα; also in A.R. of a bird εὐδιόων πτερύγεσσιν (2.935), and of men εὐδιόωντες (2.903), enjoying fair weather.

ποτήν Adv. acc.; cf. ε 337 αἰθυίη δ᾽ εἰκυῖα ποτῇ [v.l. ποτήν], *h.Hom.* 4.544 ποτῆσι [v.l. πτερύγεσσι] τελήέντων οἰωνῶν.

279 οὔριος Rare in epic, mostly in drama, of ship or wind.

ἑτέρην The western horizon; cf. 178.

κατὰ δεξιὰ χειρός A metrically convenient variation of κατὰ δεξιὰν χεῖρα; cf. 60, 707. The prototype is ε 277, *h.Hom.* 4.153 ἐπ᾽ ἀριστερὰ χειρός, thereafter S. fr. 598 Radt χειρὸς ἐς τὰ δεξιά, [Theoc.] 25.18 ἐπὶ δεξιὰ χειρός, *CA* Epimetra 2.2 ὅταν κατὰ δεξιὰ χειρὸς ἀστράπτῃ, A.R. 2.1266 ἐπ᾽ ἀριστερὰ χειρῶν. The right hand is η θ Cephei: cf. 183.

In 1.2.16 Hipparchus quotes Eudoxus to show how closely A. sometimes paraphrases him: παρὰ δὲ τὴν δεξιὰν χεῖρα τοῦ Κηφέως ἡ δεξιὰ πτέρυξ ἐστὶ τοῦ ῎Ορνιθος, παρὰ δὲ τὴν ἀριστερὰν πτέρυγα οἱ πόδες τοῦ ῎Ιππου (fr. 39). A.'s variation technique is illustrated here in almost every word: κατά for παρά, δεξιά for τὴν δεξιάν, χειρός for χεῖρα, Κηφείης for τοῦ Κηφέως, ταρσοῖο for πτέρυξ, τὰ δεξιὰ πείρατα for ἡ δεξιά, τείνων for ἐστί, λαιῇ for τὴν ἀριστεράν, πτέρυγι for πτέρυγα, σκαρθμός for οἱ πόδες, παρακέκλιται for εἰσί understood; but for the last word the same noun is in the same case, ῎Ιππου. In 1.4.11 Hipparchus again quotes 279–80, to illustrate A.'s use of right and left in the constellation figures.

280 Κηφείης Adj. only here, presumably A.'s own coinage, with Attic termination, as ῾Ιππείη (524), Κητείης (364).

ταρσοῖο Primarily a wicker crate (ι 219), then more frequently the flat of the foot (Λ 377), or a bank of oars (Hdt. 8.12.1); as 'wing' first here and A.R. 2.934.

πείρατα τείνων The tip of the right wing is κ Cygni. Although Hipparchus reads φαίνων consistently in 1.2.16, 4.11, and 10.7, this could be a quotation from memory, and as the word has no astronomical significance, it is not to be preferred to the united testimony of the MSS. τείνων has more point, since the wing is extended in the direction of Cepheus, and it is also more alliterative. Cf. 433 τεύχοι. The v.l. σήματα φαίνων here attests a similar confusion with 1141.

281 λαιῇ δὲ πτέρυγι The line of stars ε ζ μ Cygni.

σκαρθμός An imaginative paraphrase of Eudoxus' πόδες, probably represented by the stars π Pegasi and μ Cygni. The two lines of stars that extend westwards from the forequarters of the Horse (β) do suggest a prancing position. Sch. Theoc. 4.19 σκαίρει· ἔνθεν καὶ σκαρθμὸς ὁ πούς παρ᾽ Ἀράτῳ. Cf. A.R. 3.1260 σκαρθμῷ ἐπιχρεμέθων, of a war-horse,

Nic. *Ther.* 139 σκαρθμοὺς ἐλάφων. In B 814 the adj. πολυσκάρθμοιο means 'dancing'.

καρακέκλιται Cf. Call. *H.* 4.72 of land ὅση παρακέκλιται Ἰσθμῷ.

282–299 *The Water-pourer and Capricorn*

A. now makes a transition via the Horse and the Fishes to the part of the Zodiac that lies in the southern sky, the constellations through which the sun then passed in winter. He takes the opportunity to enlarge on the theme of the dangers of seafaring and the suffering of men in their ships.

The Water-pourer is a Babylonian constellation associated with the rainy season, perhaps from the time it contained the winter solstice (c. 4000–2000 BC). It corresponds to the Babylonian GU.LA 'waterman' (Waerden *EW* 64), and forms part of the area of sky that A. calls the Water (399) and the Babylonians called the Sea. The nucleus of the constellation is a small Υ-shaped group (γ ζ η π) resembling an inverted cup, from which a stream of faint stars appears to pour out. The outline of a figure is attached to this, with α and β as the shoulders, δ and ι as the feet, and ε as the left hand, while the stars of the cup also serve as the right hand. A. gives only a brief introduction to the Water-pourer here, reserving further description for 391–9, the stream of water, and other references at 502, 548 and 693.

The standard Greek name is Ὑδροχόος (*Sphaera* 154 has Ὑδρηχόος), but A. has a dative Ὑδροχόηι (389), which suggests a nom. Ὑδροχοεύς, and Cat. 66.94 *Hydrochoi* after *proximus* is most likely a dat., implying perhaps Ὑδροχοεῖ in Call. fr. 110 (though Pfeiffer thinks this unlikely). Elsewhere in Latin the standard name is *Aquarius* (as it still is), e.g. Cic. fr. 33.56, V. *G.* 3.304, Hor. *S.* 1.1.36, Man. 1.272, Germ. 285, Avien. 648. At some stage the figure came to be identified with Ganymede (*Catast.* 26, Hyg. 2.29), hence Ov. *Fast.* 2.145 *puer Idaeus*, Man. 4.709 *Iuuenis*. Another alternative is *Vrna*, as in Man. 2.561, Sen. *Thy.* 865, Luc. 9.537. Roscher VI 974ff., Allen 45ff.

In the Babylonian sky the Goat-horned, Capricorn, was a kind of goat-fish, SUḪUR.MAŠ (Waerden *EW* 68), perhaps not altogether equivalent to the Greek constellation. The nucleus seems to have been the short, but quite conspicuous, angled line of the stars α ν β, which suggest the shape of a horn (Hi. 3.2.6, 3.3.7 refers to them as the horns). In A. all eleven references are to the constellation as a whole. Its sole importance lies in the fact that it contained the sun at the winter solstice, and the southern tropic is therefore named after it. The traditional goat-figure has a fish's tail because it is associated with the rainy season and is in the part of the sky that A. calls the Water (399).

The name appears first in Eudox. fr. 73 τὰ μέσα τοῦ Αἰγόκερω, and

Αἰγόκερως is thereafter the standard name in Greek. But in *Catast.* 27 it is described as ὅμοιος τῷ Αἰγίπανι, and connected with the legend of the goat that suckled Zeus in Crete (Epimen. fr. 44); cf. Hyg. 2.28. In Latin *Aegoceros* is sometimes used (Germ. 286, Sen. *Thy.* 864), with gen. *Aegocerotis* (Lucr. 5.615) and acc. *Aegoceron* (Luc. 10.213), but the normal name is *Capricornus* (Cic. fr. 33.59, Hor. *Carm.* 2.17.20, Prop. 4.1.86, Germ. 289, Avien. 649). *Caper* is a variation in Man. 2.179. Roscher VI 971ff., Allen 135ff., Haebler in *RE* 3.1550.

282 μετασκαίροντα The part. picks up the σκαρθμός of the Horse and Maass was mistaken in altering it to a dual agreeing with the Fishes. Martin and Erren take μετά as prep., meaning that the Fishes are 'behind' the Horse, but it seems more natural to retain the compound verb and see the two prefixes as in a way reciprocal, the Fishes ranging on either side of the Horse, which prances among them. This compound appears only here, but there is a similarity in *h.Hom.* 3.197 μεταμέλπεται (which occurs only there) of Artemis dancing and singing with the other goddesses. Cf. Nonn. *D.* 5.183 οἷα περισκαίροντα, of fishes wrought in gold.

ἀμφινέμονται C. acc., as in Σ 186 ἀθανάτων, οἳ Ὄλυμπον ἀγάννιφον ἀμφινέμονται. There is a sense of horizontal movement in this verb, which balances the more lively vertical movement of the Horse.

283 χεὶρ Ὑδροχόοιο The most northerly star in the Water-pourer, π Aquarii, is quite close to the most southerly in the Horse, θ Pegasi.

284 τάνυται Cf. 68. For -ται as long syllable in hiatus at caesura cf. 582 δέχεται. The v.l. τετάνυσται comes from 202 and 251, where it suits the end of a line, but A. avoids elision at the main caesura; in other positions he elides τρέπεται (286), συμφέρεται (293), θλίβεται (417), δύεται (656), γίνεται (900). Here the present tense receives some support from Avien. 647 *se dextera tendit.*

ὀπίστερος A new comp., formed from adv. ὄπισθε, on the analogy of Homeric sup. ὀπίστατος (Θ 342, Λ 178) in same *sedes.* Nonn. *D.* 7.189 ὀπίστερον ὤθεεν ὕδωρ. Cf. παροίτερος (306, Ψ 459) from πάρος, ὑπέρτερα (498, Λ 290) from ὑπέρ. Chantraine 1.258. Aquarius is east of Capricorn in the Zodiac, and therefore rises and sets after it.

285 τέλλεται Primarily of coming into being, τέλλομαι being cogn. with πέλομαι (LSJ). The transition to the sense of 'rising' may have come through the use of the verb of dawn appearing, e.g. A.R. 1.1360 ἠοῦς τελλομένης. On the other hand ἐπιτέλλομαι appears early in this sense (Hes. *Op.* 383, 567; *h.Hom.* 4.371), and A.'s use of the simple verb may be a variation of the compound; cf. 320, 382.

It is curious that rising is replaced by setting in Cic. fr. 33.57 *serius haec obitus terrai uisit Equi uis,* and Germ. 286–7 *quo prior Aegoceros semper properare uidetur* | *Oceano mersus sopitas condere flammas.* Soubiran therefore suggests that these translators must have read ἕλκεται in A. But ἕλκεται can describe a rising just as well as a setting, e.g. 443 περαιόθεν ἕλκεται ἄστρον. The translators are merely playing variations on A. (the first to rise is naturally also the first to set). Germanicus also puts Capricorn before in place of Aquarius after, while Cicero actually makes a mistake in confusing Aquarius with the Horse. These lines illustrate the unreliability of the Latin versions as evidence for the text of the Greek.

πρότερος καὶ νειόθι μᾶλλον I.e. farther west and south; cf. 239, 320.

286 κέκλιται Merely a variation of κεῖται or even ἐστί.

Αἰγόκερως Adj. of Attic 2nd decl. with recessive accent; cf. δίκερως, ὑψίκερως, χρυσόκερως. Hdn 1.245L; K–B 1.321.

ἵνα ἲς τρέπετ' ἠελίοιο The part of the ecliptic that contains the (winter) solstice. The MSS offer four versions of this clause, but only one is metrically satisfactory, that of A, ἵνα τε τρέπετ' ἠελίου ἲς, which Voss adopts, comparing μ 175–6 μεγάλη ἲς | Ἠελίου, and Q.S. 1.356 ὅτ' Αἰγοκερῆι συνέρχεται ἠελίου ἲς. But, as Martin notes, in Homer ἲς always precedes the substantive in the genitive, e.g. Φ 356 ἲς ποταμοῖο, β 409 ἲς Τηλεμάχοιο. Moreover, since A is a descendant of M, its reading must be a correction designed to conform to the metre, and not an ancient variant. The genuine textual tradition is ἵνα τρέπετ' ἠελίοιο, and since M has ἲς added at the end of the line by a different hand, the simplest and most satisfactory solution is that of Grotius, accepted by Maass and Martin. For the elision cf. δύετ' ἀρνευτῆρι (656).

287–299 This fine passage on the dangers of seafaring in winter has much rhetorical colouring in sound effects and verbal patterns, a sensitive personal touch in the use of 2nd pers. sg. and 1st pers. pl. pronouns, and a certain pathos in the final picture of seamen in distress. It is balanced by a similar but longer passage (413–35) set among the southern stars.

287 μὴ κείνῳ ἐνὶ μηνί The passage opens dramatically with an earnest warning, reinforced by the alliteration of μή and μηνί. A. is probably referring to the actual month called Poseideon in the calendars of Athens, Delos and Miletus (Bickerman 20). Sch. (T) Ο 192 Ἀττικοὶ τὸν περὶ χειμερίους τροπὰς μῆνα Ποσειδεῶνα καλοῦσιν, Anacr. *PMG* 362 μεὶς μὲν δὴ Ποσιδηίων ἕστηκεν †νεφέλη δ' ὕδωρ ⟨   ⟩ βαρὺ δ' ἄγριοι χειμῶνες κατάγουσι.† Cf. Eust. *Il.* 1012.

περικλύζοιο θαλάσσῃ An imitation of the sound of the Homeric formula πολυφλοίσβοιο θαλάσσης (Α 34, Hes. *Op.* 648), which with its sibilants suggests the noise of stormy waters. For the ingenious echoing of gen. sg. ending with 2nd pers. opt. cf. 96 ὕπο σκέπτοιο and 136 πολυσκέπτοιο. There are no such sound effects in Virgil's smoother imitation, *G.* 1.456–7 *non illa quisquam me nocte per altum | ire neque a terra moneat conuellere funem.*

Longin. 26.1 quotes this line (along with O 697–8) to illustrate the effect of a change of person in making the hearer feel involved in the action: ἐναγώνιος δ᾽ ὁμοίως καὶ ἡ τῶν προσώπων ἀντιμετάθεσις καὶ πολλάκις ἐν μέσοις τοῖς κινδύνοις ποιοῦσα τὸν ἀκροατὴν δοκεῖν στρέφεσθαι. In Th. 6.3.2 περικλυζομένη is used of Ortygia when it was an island; here A. has given the verb a new context, that of a ship in the open sea. Cf. Q.S. 14.373 νῆες δὲ περικλύζοντο θαλάσσῃ, 512 νῆσοί τ᾽ ἤπειροί τε π. θ.

θαλάσσης is favoured by Buttmann, who compares Homeric usage, e.g. in Z 508 λούεσθαι ποταμοῖο, and similar uses in A., e.g. 564, 605, 609. But these genitives have a different meaning. It could, however, be said that the gen. here has the advantage of breaking the series of datives before and after. Still the instr. dat. seems the more natural case, and the gen. probably came in under the influence of the Homeric formula.

288 πεπταμένῳ The open sea, out of sight of land, where sailing is most dangerous; cf. 981 of a cloudless summer sky, after ζ 44–5 αἴθρη | πέπταται ἀνέφελος. The alliteration of π in 288–9 is very striking.

κεχρημένος C. dat. in sense of 'using', cf. 759; c. gen. 'needing' 4, 823, 846, 857.

ἠοῖ This extension of meaning to include the whole day probably originates in the use of 'dawn' in the counting of days, e.g. A 193 δυωδεκάτη γένετ᾽ ἠώς. Cf. 739, 1128, Theoc. 12.1 τρίτη σὺν νυκτὶ καὶ ἠοῖ. This is the first disadvantage of the winter, that the days are short; the second is the southerly gales (291–3); the third is the cold temperature (293–4).

289 πολλήν Sch. πολλὴν θάλασσαν. But strictly the noun to be understood is probably ὁδόν, which can be used of a voyage, e.g. β 285. For the omission of ὁδός cf. X. *An.* 6.3.16 πολλὴ μὲν γάρ, ἔφη, εἰς Ἡράκλειαν πάλιν ἀπιέναι, πολλὴ δὲ εἰς Χρυσόπολιν διελθεῖν.

πειρήνειας Cf. 24, 365. This poetic form appears also in *h.Hom.* 4.48, Pi. *I.* 8.26.

ταχινώταται Sch. αἱ ἡμέραι δηλονότι, presumably to be understood from ἠοῖ. An addition to sch. suggests a reminiscence of Hes. *Op.* 560 μακραὶ γὰρ ἐπίρροθοι εὐφρόναι εἰσίν: see Martin *SAV* p. 222. ταχινός is a late form (Call. *H.* 1.56, Theoc. 2.7, A.R. 2.1044).

290 οὔτ᾽ ἄν τοι ... ἠώς Variation of οὔτε κεν ἠοῖ (288).

νυκτός Not dependent on πεφοβημένῳ, as Martin translates, but adverbial, balancing ἠοῖ. It is not so much the night that the seamen are afraid of, but the sea (cf. 766). So Voss, Mair, Erren: see also West on

Hes. *Th.* 852. Germ. 291 *terrores auget nox atra marinos.* The long nights are in contrast to the shortness of the days.

πεφοβημένῳ Without dependent gen. also in Κ 510, Ο 4, Φ 606, A.R. 2.176.

291 βοωμένῳ The middle is appropriate to the sense of calling for help; cf. α 378, β 143 θεοὺς ἐπιβώσομαι, Theoc. 17.60 Εἰλείθυιαν ἐβώσατο. There is no justification for βοωμένη (pass.): it is certainly not supported, as Maass implies, by Cic. fr. 33.65–6 *non sese uestris aurora querelis | ocius ostendet,* nor necessarily by Germ. 292 *multum clamatos frustra speculaberis ortus,* which can be seen as a translator's variation (see Martin). The internal rhyming of the participles, if so intended, perhaps underlines the constant terror.

ἀλεγεινοί Epic form: cf. Ε 658, Σ 248, Call. *H.* 4.239. Q.S. 7.458 imitates with οἱ δ' ἀλεγεινοί (the seamen).

292 ἐπιρρήσσουσι νότοι Southerlies are characteristic of winter weather in the Mediterranean. They are often strong winds and pile up high seas along the northern coasts, especially when funnelled through the many straits between promontories and islands. Cf. Hor. *Carm.* 2.17.19–20 *tyrannus | Hesperiae Capricornus undae,* and 1.3.14ff. *rabiem Noti, | quo non arbiter Hadriae | maior,* probably reminiscences of this passage.

The verb is an epic form of ἐπιρράσσω, used of a hail-storm in S. *OC* 1503. Cf. Ω 454, 456 of forcibly shutting the bolt of a door, Max. 112 ἐπιρρήσσουσα χιτῶνας.

293 συμφέρετ' ἠέλιος A. elsewhere uses συνέρχεσθαι (151) and συνιέναι (682) of sun and stars coming into conjunction; the technical term for the noun is σύνοδος, e.g. Arist. *Mete.* 343b30 of planets and stars, Gem. 8.1 of sun and moon. Q.S. imitates in 1.356 ὅτ' Αἰγοκερῆι συνέρχεται ἡελίου ἷς, 2.533–4 ἐς Αἰγοκερῆα κιόντος | ἡελίου, 7.300–1 τῆμος ὅτ' Αἰγοκερῆι συνέρχεται ἠερόεντι | ἠέλιος. For the elision cf. 286, 762, 900, A.R. 3.514, 1026, 4.783, Theoc. 11.4, 28.6. See Spitzner 174.

κρύος ἐκ Διός Cf. Ε 91, Hes. *Op.* 626 Διὸς ὄμβρος. Here the cruelty of the primitive sky-god comes into conflict with the Stoic image of a kindly Zeus; but the powers of the latter are of course limited to giving warnings of trouble. It is difficult to judge whether A. is deliberately drawing attention to this interesting contrast; certainly κρύος is a deliberate change from the traditional association of Zeus with rain.

294 μαλκιόωντι Epic part. (μαλκιάω), only here, but conjectured by Crates for μυλιόωντες in Hes. *Op.* 530, presumably on the basis of this line: see West's note. The normal verb is μαλκίω with long ι: hence the v.l. in Stob.; cf. Cobet 130ff. There is no reason to suspect the MSS, since A. has other ἅπαξ λεγόμενα, e.g. 333 φυλλιόωσαι, 796 τριτόωσαν.

ἀλλὰ καὶ ἔμπης 'Nevertheless (it is not only at midwinter that the sea is dangerous, but) ...' A. here makes a transition to the general theme of the cruel sea.

295 ἤδη = German 'schon', perhaps best rendered in English by 'actually'. Cf. υ 90 οὐκ ἐφάμην ὄναρ ἔμμεναι, ἀλλ' ὕπαρ ἤδη.

ὑπὸ στείρῃσι θάλασσα στεῖρα is the forward part of the keel continued into the stem. Cf. A 481–2, β 427–8 ἀμφὶ δὲ κῦμα | στείρῃ πορφύρεον μεγάλ' ἴαχε νηὸς ἰούσης, but with a fair wind. Here the alliteration of sibilants suggests the sound of crashing waves (cf. 287).

296 πορφύρει Cf. 158 ἁλὶ πορφυρούσῃ. Antip. Sid. AP 10.2.1–2 = HE 438–9 οὐδὲ θάλασσα | πορφύρει τρομερῇ φριξὶ χαρασσομένη.

ἴκελοι ξ 308–9 οἱ δὲ κορώνησιν ἴκελοι περὶ νῆα μέλαιναν | κύμασιν ἐμφορέοντο. This adj. usually comes after its dependent dat., as also in Λ 467, Hes. Sc. 198, Pi. P. 2.77; but Ar. Av. 575 ἰκέλην εἶναι τρήρωνι πελείῃ.

κολυμβίσιν αἰθυίῃσι κολυμβίς is elsewhere a noun, the name of a water-bird, and only here an adj.; A. may have been influenced by the combination of the two names in Arist. HA 487a23 αἴθυια καὶ κολιμβίς. αἴθυια has not been precisely identified, but is thought to be most probably a shearwater (Thompson 27ff., Pollard 73, Peck on Arist. HA 542b20). The poetic simile looks back to ε 337 αἰθυίῃ δ' εἰκυῖα ποτῇ ἀνεδύσετο λίμνης, of Leucothea emerging, and again disappearing (353). So A.R. 4.966 ἀλίγκιαι αἰθυίῃσι, of nymphs diving. In 919 αἴθυια reappears as a weather sign, but here A. has made it a symbol of the restless and endangered sailor. Cf. Call. E. 58.4 αἰθυίῃ δ' ἴσα θαλασσοπορεῖ, fr. 178.33–4 ἐμὸς αἰὼν | αἰθυίης μᾶλλον ἐσῳκίσατο, 327 †αἰθυίης ὑπὸ πτερύγεσσιν ἔλυσαν πείσματα νηός.† In Call. H. 4.12, of Delos, the bird suggests a desolate coast, αἰθυίης καὶ μᾶλλον ἐπίδρομος ἠέπερ ἵπποις. Cf. anon. AP 6.23.2 = FGE 1103 εὐστιβὲς αἰθυίαις ἰχθυβόλοισι λέπας, Archias, AP 10.8.2 = GP 3759 (text uncertain). In Euphor. fr. 130 Pow. = 131.48 v.Gr. τῆς οὐδ' αἴθυιαι οὐδὲ κρυεροὶ καύηκες the context is fragmentary. In AP 7 the bird is associated with death at sea: Glaucus 285.3–4 = HE 1817–18 ὤλετο γὰρ σὺν νηί, τὰ δ' ὀστέα ποῦ ποτ' ἐκείνου | πύθεται αἰθυίαις γνωστὰ μόναις ἐνέπειν, Leon. Tar. 295.2 = HE 2075 τὸν αἰθυίης πλείονα νηξάμενον, Marc. Arg. 374.3–4 = GP 1395–6 ἀλλά με δαίμων | ἄπνουν αἰθυίαις θῆκεν ὁμορρόθιον. Hence Suda on Call. fr. 327 αἱ γὰρ αἴθυιαι ὅταν δύνωσι, κάκιστος οἰωνὸς ὑπάρχει τοῖς πλέουσι. τὴν δὲ αἰτίαν λέγουσιν, ὅτι γαλήνης οὔσης οὐ τολμᾷ προϊέναι φοβουμένη τὰ θαλάσσια ζῷα, χειμῶνα δὲ προορωμένη προέρχεται, τῶν ἄλλων ζώων ἐν ταῖς καταδύσεσιν ὄντων.

297 περιπαπταίνοντες Only here and Mosch. 4.108–9 περὶ δ' ὄμμασιν ἔνθα καὶ ἔνθα | πάπταινεν. The simple verb is frequent in

Homer, e.g. χ 380 πάντοσε παπταίνοντε, φόνον ποτιδεγμένω αἰεί, where the context of danger is comparable. Cf. A.R. 1.631 πάπταινον ἐπὶ πλατὺν ὄμμασι πόντον, 2.608 ἠέρα παπταίνοντες ὁμοῦ πέλαγός τε θαλάσσης. Again the alliteration of π is very striking (cf. 288–9), and is perhaps intended to emphasise the sense of terror. A. has hexasyllabic endings also in 442, 615, 1038, 1115.

298 ἥμεθ' With this sudden introduction of the 1st pers. the poet identifies himself with suffering humanity. It is one of the few personal touches in the poem: cf. 154, 413, 769, also with reference to the dangers of the sea.

αἰγιαλούς The association of this word with stormy seas goes back to the simile in Δ 422ff. ὡς δ' ὅτ' ἐν αἰγιαλῷ πολυηχέϊ κῦμα θαλάσσης | ὄρνυτ' ἐπασσύτερον Ζεφύρου ὕπο κινήσαντος· | πόντῳ μέν τε πρῶτα κορύσσεται, αὐτὰρ ἔπειτα | χέρσῳ ῥηγνύμενον μεγάλα βρέμει. In fact αἰγιαλός may be connected with αἰγίς 'hurricane' (LSJ, Frisk 1.31, 32).

πόρσω Later form of Homeric πρόσω and πρόσσω, e.g. Ρ 598 πρόσω τετραμμένος αἰεί, Λ 572 ὅρμενα πρόσσω. A. may have had in mind Pi. P. 3.22 ὅστις αἰσχύνων ἐπιχώρια παπταίνει τὰ πόρσω.

299 κλύζονται In Homer the pass. is used rather with the sea as subj., e.g. Ξ 392 ἐκλύσθη δὲ θάλασσα ποτὶ κλισίας τε νέας τε. But cf. A.R. 1.521 εὔδιοι ἐκλύζοντο τινασσομένης ἁλὸς ἀκταί. See 902, of fields drenched by rain, and 943 med., of birds diving.

ὀλίγον δὲ διὰ ξύλον Ἄϊδ' ἐρύκει A. concludes his purple passage with a kind of epigram. There is a reminiscence here of the storm simile in Ο 627–8 τρομέουσι δέ τε φρένα ναῦται | δειδιότες· τυτθὸν γὰρ ὑπὲκ θανάτοιο φέρονται. Longin. 10.6 compares the two passages: ἐπεχείρησε καὶ ὁ Ἄρατος τὸ αὐτὸ τοῦτο μετενεγκεῖν, "ὀλίγον ... ἐρύκει". πλὴν μικρὸν αὐτὸ καὶ γλαφυρὸν ἐποίησεν ἀντὶ φοβεροῦ· ἔτι δὲ παρώρισε τὸν κίνδυνον, εἰπὼν "ξύλον ἄϊδ' ἀπείργει". οὐκοῦν ἀπείργει. He naturally gives his preference to Homer for vividness and sense of impending disaster. But A.'s epigram is a model of λεπτότης, and is imitated by Juvenal in 12.58–9 *digitis a morte remotus | quattuor aut septem, si sit latissima, taedae*, and 14.288–9 *nauem mercibus implet | ad summum latus et tabula distinguitur unda*. With ὀλίγον A. means the meagre thickness of the ship's timbers, echoing Κ 161 ὀλίγος δ' ἔτι χῶρος ἐρύκει, where it is a narrow strip of ground that keeps the enemy off. Cf. Stat. *Silv.* 3.2.70 *fugimus exigua clausi trabe*, of human folly in leaving the land, Q.S. 7.297 ναῦται γὰρ ἀεὶ σχεδόν εἰσιν ὀλέθρου, 8.418 τυτθὴ δὲ βίη μέγα πῆμ' ἀπερύκει.

ξύλον The Homeric term for ship's timbers is νήϊα δοῦρα (ι 498), δούρατα μακρά (ε 162). But cf. Hes. *Op.* 808 νήϊά τε ξύλα πολλά, Th. 7.25.2 ξύλα ναυπηγήσιμα.

Ἄϊδ' Post-Homeric for 'death', e.g. Pi. *P.* 5.96 λαχόντες ἀΐδαν, A. *Ag.* 667 Ἄιδην πόντιον πεφευγότες, A.R. 4.1510 Ἄϊδα γίγνεται οἶμος.

300–310 *The Archer*

Even when the sun is in the Archer avoid seafaring by night. The MR of the Scorpion is a useful sign, as it rises before him, while the Little Bear is high in the sky, and Orion and Cepheus are setting.

The nucleus of this constellation is undoubtedly the group of bright stars suggesting the outline of a bow (λ δ ε) and arrow (ζ δ γ), but at an early stage adjacent stars were brought in to designate the figure of a man wielding the bow and arrow. The Archer was a Babylonian constellation, PA.BIL.SAG, a god of war and hunting (Waerden *EW* 71), and its introduction into Greece was attributed by Pliny (*Nat.* 2.31) to Cleostratus. It was usually figured as a centaur, perhaps to accommodate the line of faint stars including θ and ι as hind legs parallel to the more obvious α and β as forelegs. This is clearly the figure envisaged by A. in προτέροισι πόδεσσι (400), and by Hipparchus in 3.1.7 ὁ ἐν τοῖς ὀπισθίοις ποσὶ λαμπρός and 3.4.6 ὁ ἐν τῷ ἐμπροσθίῳ ποδί. An alternative made the Archer a biped, with horse's feet and satyr-like tail (*Catast.* 28), a figure that avoided confusion with the constellation Centaur. The Archer was sometimes identified with the centaur Chiron, sometimes with Crotus, son of Pan and Eupheme (Hyg. 2.27).

The standard Greek name was Τοξότης (673), but A. varies it, partly for metrical convenience, with Τοξευτής (306, 547), Τοξευτήρ (400), ῥύτορα τόξου (301) and τόξον alone (623, 665). In Latin the standard name is *Sagittarius* (Cic. fr. 33.297, Man. 1.691), but there are numerous variations, *Sagittipotens* (Cic. 73, Q. Cic. 11), *Arquitenens* (Cic. 182, Man. 2, 187, Avien. 684), *Arcus* (Cic. 78), *Sagittifer* (Germ. 392), *Sagittiger* (Avien. 842), *Chiron* (Luc. 6.393), *Crotus* (Col. 10.57), and even *Centaurus* (Man. 2.463 in a Zodiac context). Gundel in *RE* 11.2028–9 s.v. Krotus, Rehm in *RE* 1A.1746ff., Roscher VI 967ff., Allen 351ff.

300 ἔτι προτέρῳ Sch. ἀπὸ κοινοῦ τὸ μηνί. Although μηνί occurs thirteen lines earlier, the whole passage (287–99) is a description of what that month is like at sea, and A. now adds that the preceding month is also dangerous. The adv. προτέρω, read by Maass, is certainly possible, in view of Call. *H.* 3.72 σὺ δὲ προτέρω περ, ἔτι τριέτηρος ἐοῦσα, but otherwise it is used only of place, as by A. of star positions (239, 311). Here the adj. referring to the month is more likely, since that is specifically defined in 301, and it was so understood in antiquity: see sch. and Cic. fr. 33.72–3 *atque etiam supero ... mense.*

Similarly both ἐπί and ἔτι are possible. ἐπί c. dat. of time is Homeric, e.g. Θ 529 ἐπὶ νυκτί, Ν 234 ἐπ' ἤματι τῷδε. Cf. ξ 105, Hes. *Op.* 102. But these instances all point to a particular day or night; cf. 554 πάσῃ δ' ἐπὶ νυκτί. In 818 ἐπὶ μηνί has a sense of purpose. Here the warning applies to any time during the whole month, and this would normally be expressed by either ἐν or the simple dat. The scholia paraphrase with both ἐν τῷ προτέρῳ μηνί and τῷ προτέρῳ μηνί, and in 287 the prep. is ἐνί. On the other hand ἔτι is used with reference to preceding time, e.g. Th. 8.45.1 ἐν δὲ τούτῳ καὶ ἔτι πρότερον ... τάδε ἐπράσσετο, Pl. Sph. 242d ἀπὸ Ξενοφάνους τε καὶ ἔτι πρόσθεν ἀρξάμενον. And since ἔτι is better attested in the lemmata and supported by Arat. Lat., I agree with Martin's reading here.

πολλὰ πεπονθώς ν 6 μάλα πολλὰ πέπονθας, ρ 284 κακὰ πολλὰ πέπονθα.

301 τόξον The most distinctive part of the constellation: see note on 300–310. Hipparchus refers to it in 3.1.7 and 3.3.8 to identify particular stars in that part.

ὅτ' ἥέλιος καίει From 25 Nov. to 23 Dec., according to Gem. Cal. As with Capricorn, A. introduces the Archer solely for its seasonal significance, because weather signs are one of his basic themes.

ῥύτορα τόξου A variation for the metrically awkward Τοξότης; cf. 621. The noun is from ἐρύω 'draw', as in Ο 463–4 νευρὴν ἐν ἀμύμονι τόξῳ | ῥῆξ' ἐπὶ τῷ ἐρύοντι. The Homeric form is ῥυτήρ, e.g. φ 173 ῥυτῆρα βιοῦ τ' ἔμεναι καὶ ὀϊστῶν; cf. Alcm. PMG 170 Ἄρταμι ῥύτειρα τόξων, but Ar. Th. 108–9 ῥύτορα τόξων | Φοῖβον. The line has a kind of chiastic pattern; cf. 156. Q.S. imitates in 7.301–2 ἥέλιος μετόπισθε βαλὼν ῥυτῆρα βελέμνων | Τοξευτήν.

302 ἑσπέριος Cf. ο 505 ἑσπέριος δ' εἰς ἄστυ ... κάτειμι.

κατάγοιο With ἄν (300) the apodosis takes the form of a mild command or recommendation; cf. 1145. It is characteristic of ἄν to be placed early in the sentence; it cannot be construed with πεπονθώς, because a part. with ἄν never represents a protasis (Goodwin MT 71).

303 κείνης ὥρης καὶ μηνὸς ἐκείνου The season of the year is emphasised by the chiasmus, and also by the fact that the two phrases are practically synonymous. A more elaborate chiasmus follows in 304–7: Σκορπίος ἀντέλλων ... τόξον ... Τοξευτής ... Σκορπίος ἀντέλλων.

304 Σκορπίος ἀντέλλων The poets usually refer to a rising without indicating whether it is morning or evening (e.g. Hes. Op. 383). Here A. gives the full information, and even adds further clues in 308–10, because he is thinking of the endangered seaman actually observing the sky. When the Scorpion is seen rising just before dawn, this means that the Archer (the next constellation in the Zodiac) is now occupied by the sun. Hipparchus in 1.7.1–13 quotes and discusses this passage, especially 308–10, together with the comments of Attalus.

πυμάτης ἐπὶ νυκτός Sch. ἐπὶ τῆς ἐσχάτης νυκτός, ἤγουν ἐπὶ ὄρθρου. In Homer and classical authors ἐπί c. gen. is used of a period of time within which a circumstance is placed, e.g. Β 797 ἐπ' εἰρήνης, and even the later usage, as in Luc. Pisc. 31 ἐπὶ τοῦ βίου 'in their lives', is of circumstances, not time. The alternative ἔτι is therefore favoured by Voss, and it seems at first sight to have some support from Hi. 1.7.8 ἔτι τῆς νυκτὸς ἐνεστηκυίας and ἔτι νυκτὸς οὔσης (9). But there Hipparchus is refuting an error of Attalus in confusing the Scorpion's rising with that of the Archer in 308ff., and he is making the point that while the sun is in the Archer, the latter's rising can obviously not be seen because by then the dawn is too bright, but the Scorpion's earlier rising is visible, because there is still enough darkness then to allow stars to be seen. On 304, however, his MSS read ἐπί, and he paraphrases the line with σημεῖον ἔστω Σκορπίος ἀνατέλλων ληγούσης τῆς νυκτός (1.7.8). In fact ἔτι does not really make sense. There may be some point in saying 'while it is still dark', but not 'while the darkness is still at its end'. A.'s use of ἐπί may be unusual, but it is accepted by Hipparchus as meaning 'at' with reference to a point of time, and he aptly compares ἀκρόθι νυκτός (308) and ἠῶθι πρό (309). Nor are the Latin translators misled: there is no hint of ἔτι in iam prope praecipitante ... nocte (Cic. fr. 33.76), nocte suprema (Germ. 310), tempore noctis adultae (Avien. 680).

305 ἤτοι γάρ Strongly confirmatory, as in 275, 748.

μέγα τόξον The epithet gives the figure a somewhat heroic character, recalling Menelaus in Δ 124 μέγα τόξον ἔτεινε, but it is also appropriate to the bow in the sky, which is relatively large and conspicuous. In the MSS of Hipparchus μετά is certainly corrupt, since the figure of the Archer rises with his bow, not after it.

ἀνέλκεται A play on the two meanings of the verb: the constellation 'brings up' the stars, the archer 'draws back' his bow; cf. Λ 375 τόξου πῆχυν ἄνελκε.

κέντρου The stars λ υ Scorpii, both bright and very close together. The sting is mentioned first in Euctemon's calendar Gem. Cal. Sagitt. 10 (= 4 Dec.) τοῦ Σκορπίου τὸ κέντρον ἐπιτέλλει, then in Eudox. fr. 73 as lying on the winter tropic; cf. 505-6.

306 Τοξευτής A Homeric hapax, Ψ 850; cf. Call. fr. 70.2, D.P. 751.

παροίτερος Comparative adj. formed from adv. πάροιθε; cf. 284 ὀπίστερος. The adj. appears in same sedes in Ψ 459, 480, of chariots racing, and A.R. 4.982, of geographical position.

ἵσταται Properly describing position, but here associated with rising; cf. v.l. in 610, also Mosch. 2.2 νυκτὸς ὅτε τρίτατον λάχος ἵσταται, ἐγγύθι δ' ἠώς.

307 ὁ δ' ἀνέρχεται αὐτίκα μᾶλλον This is added as the converse of the preceding clause, and it serves the purpose of bringing us back to the rising of the Archer. It also throws some light on A.'s use of αὐτίκα (see note on 199), since the lapse of time denoted by αὐτίκα μᾶλλον here is exactly the same as that implied by ὀλίγον παροίτερος in 306.

308 τῆμος The time is when the Scorpion is completely above the horizon and the rising of the Archer is about to begin. In case the horizon is obscured at the time (cf. 563–4), A. gives three other constellations that may be visible in other parts of the sky at the same time: the Little Bear on the upper meridian, Orion setting in the west, and half of Cepheus disappearing below the northern horizon; cf. 646, 649–51. Hipparchus (1.7.2–4) quotes Attalus as saying that A. is wrong about Cepheus and right about the other two phenomena, when in fact the contrary is true, that A. is right about Cepheus and wrong about the other two.

κεφαλὴ Κυνοσουρίδος The star β Ursae Minoris (see 28).

ἀκρόθι Only here, and obviously referring to the end of night, whereas in 775 ἄκρῃ νυκτί, of sunset, denotes the beginning of night. In 740 I understand ἄκρα νυκτῶν as meaning the successive night-endings throughout the year.

309 ὕψι μάλα τροχάει Hipparchus (1.7.12) gives this the precise meaning of 'culminates', i.e. crosses the meridian, which happens later when the Water-pourer is rising: ὅταν ἄρα ἡ κεφαλὴ τῆς Μικρᾶς Ἄρκτου μεσουρανῇ, ἢ ὅπερ ἐστὶ ταὐτόν, ὕψι μάλα τροχάει, τότε οὐχ ὁ Σκορπίος ἄρχεται ἀνατέλλειν, ἀλλὰ τοῦ Ὑδροχόου πλεῖον ἢ τὸ ἥμισυ ἀνατέταλκε μέρος. But A. is not using technical language here, and means simply 'well up in the sky'. This would have been reasonably in accord with the phenomena, though admittedly a rather imprecise sign.

ἠῶθι πρό Also 866, 870. Chantraine (1.246) explains this Homeric formula in Λ 50 by taking ἠῶθι as adv. with locative suffix and πρό as a reinforcing adv., the phrase thus meaning 'at daybreak'; but at ε 469 and ζ 36 he allows the possibility of the meaning 'before dawn', with ἠῶθι being felt as dependent on πρό. Here the meaning is certainly 'before dawn', as Hipparchus makes clear (1.7.9): πρὸ τῆς ἠοῦς, καὶ οὐ, μὰ Δία, τοῦ ἡλίου ἀνατέλλοντος.

310 ἀθρόος Ὠρίων Hipparchus (1.7.13) comments that οὐδ᾽ ὁ Ὠρίων ὅλος δύνει τοῦ Σκορπίου ἀρχομένου ἀνατέλλειν, ὡς ὅ τε Ἄρατος λέγει καὶ ὁ Ἄτταλος αὐτῷ συναποφαίνεται, ἀλλὰ μᾶλλον τοῦ Τοξότου. But it may be argued against Hipparchus that Σκορπίος ἀντέλλων in A. means not the beginning of the Scorpion's rising, but the whole period of it; and further, that H. is using his system of signs measuring 30° each along the ecliptic, whereas A. means the constellations, which have to be identified visually by the observer. Now the Scorpion is a very large constellation, and it overlaps the 'signs' from Scorp. 3° to Sagitt. 9° (Hi. 3.3.5), so that when Orion's setting is complete, the *sign* of the Archer is beginning to rise, but the *constellation* of the Scorpion is still completing its rising. A. no doubt has in mind here the myth of Orion fleeing from the Scorpion, which he celebrates in 634–46.

Κηφεὺς δ' ἀπὸ χειρὸς ἐπ' ἰξύν Hipparchus (1.7.16–18) supports A. here against Attalus, who maintained that the southerly half of Cepheus was rising, not setting, at this time. His error lay in his assumption that A. was describing the situation during the rising of the Archer; but A. is helping the observer to anticipate the Archer's appearance, and the rising constellation is therefore the Scorpion. Cf. A.'s account of Cepheus setting while the Claws rise (633), set while the Scorpion rises (649–52), and rising while the Archer rises (674–5). Half of Cepheus is circumpolar, so that the figure sets from the waist upwards, the belt just grazing the horizon due north. The right hand is η θ, the waist β Cephei.

311–315 *The Arrow, the Eagle and the Dolphin*

To conclude his survey of the northern sky, A. groups together three small constellations that lie to the south of the Bird.

The Arrow is a tiny constellation of four stars, the brightest being of 3rd mag.; two represent the notched or feathered end (α β), one the centre (δ), one the point (γ). It has no connection with the Babylonian KAK.SI.DI ('arrow'), which was a part of our Canis Major, including Sirius (Waerden *EW* 69). Manitius credits it to Euctemon in Gem. *Cal.* Taur. 30, but this line could be a dittography, and Aujac wisely omits it. Its first appearance, then, is in Eudox. fr. 77. The standard name is Ὀϊστός, but in *Catast.* 29 it is Τόξον. The standard Latin name is *Sagitta* (Cic. fr. 33.84, Man. 5.24, Germ. 315, Avien. 689), with a variation *Telum* in Germ. 690. Roscher VI 923–4, Allen 349ff.

311 τις Better attested than τοι, to the extent that it is given by the lemma of sch. (M), while τοι can be explained by the influence of 233. For τις with following ἄλλος cf. 475. Cf. γ 293 ἔστι δέ τις, introducing a description.

προτέρω The Arrow is actually on the same meridian as part of the Archer, and even some degrees east of his bow. But it also lies more than 40° north of the latter, and so rose earlier in Greek latitudes. It is therefore προτέρω in time, but not farther west, as in 239.

βεβλημένος The part. denotes the position of the stars, as again in 358; cf. βεβολημένοι (492), βεβλέαται (174, 371). But here the word is chosen also to suggest that the Arrow has been shot into its place in the sky.

312 αὐτός Sch. ἀντὶ τοῦ μόνος, quoting Θ 99 Τυδεΐδης δ' αὐτός περ ἐών. Cf. 94–5 αὐτὸς | ἐξ ἄλλων Ἀρκτοῦρος, Ar. *Ach.* 504 αὐτοὶ γάρ ἐσμεν, Theoc. 5.85 αὐτὸς ἀμέλγεις; Gow on 2.89.

παραπέπταται "Ορνις The Bird is outstretched both lengthwise from tail to head and crosswise from wing-tip to wing-tip. It is some distance north of the Arrow, but is an obvious starting-point in looking for this inconspicuous group. D.P. 98 imitates with παραπέπταται ἄσπετος ἰσθμός. It is possible that A. chose this verb because the sound of it is suggestive of flying, especially in forms of πέταμαι.

313 ἀσσότερον A double comparative form (Chantraine 1.258), variation of Homeric ἀσσοτέρω adv. in ρ 572 παραὶ πυρί and τ 506 varied with gen. πυρός. Martin prints ἀσσότερος on the strength of ἀσσότεραι in 878. But there the adj. is one of a pair of adjj. with εἰσί understood, whereas here the adv. is more appropriate with the verb describing position, as again in 486 with κεῖται.

σχεδόθεν δέ οἱ Π 800 σχεδόθεν δέ οἱ ἦεν ὄλεθρος, β 267 σχεδόθεν δέ οἱ ἦλθεν Ἀθήνη. A. also uses this adv. c. gen. in 877 and abs. in 466.

ἄλλος ἄηται The phrase is designed to balance the ending of 311, and the verb is chosen for the sake of the word-play with Ἀητός (315); cf. 523 ἀητεῖται. The act. is used of winds blowing, e.g. Hes. *Op.* 516 δι' αἶγα ἄησι, the pass. of being beaten by or carried on the wind, e.g. ζ 131 ὑόμενος καὶ ἀήμενος. Here the picture of the bird riding the wind currents is just what the form of the basic three stars suggests. A.R. 2.81 has a verbal echo of this phrase ἐπ' ἄλλῳ ἄλλος ἄηται (δοῦπος).

These two constellations are allotted two and a half lines each, and the names balance each other at the ends of the first and last lines.

The Eagle has been identified with the Babylonian constellation Amušen 'eagle' (Waerden *EW* 67). Its nucleus must have been the conspicuous group of three stars forming a slightly bent line, which suggests the outline of a bird in flight (now γ α β Aquilae). The Greek constellation came to be expanded to include several outlying stars in a very forced figure of an eagle standing with wings half-folded (as on the Farnese globe), but A. may be thinking essentially of the central three, since he makes no reference to any individual star. The Eagle appears in the calendars as early as Democritus, who notes its MR (Gem. *Cal.* Sagitt. 16 = 10 Dec.), while Euctemon gives both risings and both settings. In E. *Rh.* 531 μέσα δ' Αἰετὸς οὐρανοῦ ποτᾶται it signals the coming of dawn. It is interesting that A. does not introduce the Eagle here as the bird of Zeus, but reserves this title for 523, where its central position on the equator is mentioned.

The standard Greek name is Ἀετός, but A. uses the variations Ἀητός (315, with shortened α), Αἰητός (522, 691), Αἰετός (591). The Latin name is *Aquila*, but the poets also use *Iouis ales* (Cic. fr. 33.294, Man. 1.343,

Germ. 316, Avien. 1105) and *Iouis armiger* (Germ. 317, Avien. 694). Roscher VI 924ff., Allen 55ff.

314 τόσσος μεγέθει Cf. 139.

χαλεπός Of stormy weather, as again in 879. A. alludes to the MR as in Democritus' parapegma for 10 Dec. (see note on 313): Ἀετὸς ἐπιτέλλει ἅμα ἡλίῳ· καὶ ἐπισημαίνειν φιλεῖ βροντῇ καὶ ἀστραπῇ καὶ ὕδατι ἢ ἀνέμῳ ἢ ἀμφότερα ὡς ἐπὶ τὰ πολλά. Sch. διὸ εἶπε τοῖς πλέουσι "χαλεπός", διὰ τὸ τότε κρύος.

ἐλθών The part. is required by the sense, and is supported by sch. τὴν ἑῴαν ἐπιτολὴν ποιούμενος, and again χαλεπὸς οὗτος καὶ δεινὸς ἀνατείλας.

315 ἀπερχομένης The occasion is the morning (see 314); the v.l. may have been due to the influence of ἐπερχομέμης ἠοῦς (827) and the greater frequency of this part. in A., rather than confusion with the ER in May. For the use of this verb of time cf. Pl. *Lg.* 954d ἀπελθόντος ἐνιαυτοῦ.

Ἀητόν The α is shortened for the sake of the supposed derivation of the name from ἄημι (see 313). Cf. other poetic derivations in 27, 164.

316–18 *The Dolphin*

This is another tiny constellation, but it is curiously recognisable by its compact shape of five stars, none brighter than 3rd mag., forming a quadrilateral with one side extended. Its origin is unknown, but it is presumably Greek, in view of the frequency of the dolphin in Greek art and literature. It appears first in Euctemon's parapegma (Gem. *Cal.* Capr. 2 = 25 Dec., MR). The name is normally Δελφίς, but in *Catast.* 31 it is Δελφίν. In Latin it is *Delphinus*, but with the variations *Delphin* (Ov. *Fast.* 1.457, Germ. 321) and *Delphis* (Avien. 700). Roscher VI 926–7, Allen 198ff.

316 πολλός Of size, not brightness; cf. 41.

ἐπιτρέχει ἐπι- 'over' (cf. 49 ἐπιτείνεται), since the verb describes the position of the Dolphin to the north of Capricorn. But -τρέχει also represents the circling movement of the stars, and at the same time suggests the speed of the real dolphin; cf. 27 τροχόωσι. A. uses ἐπιτρέχει differently in 767 and 834.

317 μεσσόθεν ἠερόεις There are no stars in the space between the four about to be mentioned; this allows the star pattern to stand out distinctly, despite the smallness of the group. Cf. 276.

περὶ ... κεῖται In *tmesi*; cf. 337, 465, 570.

318 γλήνεα Once in Homer, of ornaments ω 192 (θάλαμον) ὃς γλήνεα πολλὰ κεχάνδει, and similarly in A.R. 4.427–8 of a robe πολέσιν μετά ... γλήνεσιν. The word is probably connected with γλήνη 'eyeball', hence Nic. *Ther.* 227-8 ἐνωπῆς | γλήνεα of a viper's eyes. A. is thinking of the stars as adornments of the night sky; cf. 453 ἀγάλματα. So Max. 11-12 ὀπωρίνοις ἐνὶ γλήνεσιν αὐγάζοιτο | Χηλάων.

παρβολάδην A. is describing a parallelogram, the little figure roughly outlined by the four stars, a useful guide to the recognition of the group. In 525 the adv. is mathematically exact when used of the parallel circles; cf. 535 παραβλήδην. A.R. 4.936 gives the adv. a new context, of dolphins swimming abreast of the ship, and it seems likely that he is deliberately recalling A.'s constellation.

πεπτηῶτα See note on 167 πεπτηότα.

319-321 TRANSITION TO THE SOUTHERN CONSTELLATIONS

This short piece of framework is elegantly patterned. The two hemispheres are allocated $1\frac{1}{2}$ lines each, and introduced by the antithesis τὰ μὲν ... τὰ δέ. There is a balancing of the north and the ecliptic in the first line with the south and the ecliptic in the third, and the same two lines present a chiasmus with their endings ἀλήσιος ἠελίοιο ... ἠελίοιο κελεύθου. There is also a metrical symmetry in that both lines have the sequence D D D D D S. These lines are balanced by 451-3 at the end of the section on stars.

319 βορέω In this context the north pole, but νότοιο in 321 means the southern limit of stars visible to observers in Greece.

ἀλήσιος Only here, a variation of ἄλη 'wandering' (e.g. κ 464). Here the word means the ecliptic, and is a reminder of the fact that the sun is one of the Greek 'planets' because it moves across the background of the fixed stars.

320 κέχυται Another variation for verbs expressing the position of stars; cf. 611.

τέλλεται See note on 285. Voss (adapting Achilles) reads νειόθεν ἔρχεται, because A. is describing only those stars that are visible in Greece. But τέλλεται implies that they appear above the horizon, and νειόθι indicates their position farther south.

321 ἠελίοιο κελεύθου Cf. 149, 321. A. follows Eudoxus in choosing the ecliptic as the dividing line between north and south instead of the equator: cf. Hi. 1.2.17 Εὔδοξος ὡς καὶ Ἄρατος πρῶτον ἀναγράφει τὰ βορειότερα ἄστρα τοῦ ζῳδιακοῦ, ἔπειθ' οὕτως τὰ νοτιώτερα. And since some of the southern zodiacal constellations extend well south of the ecliptic, this produces a very unbalanced arrangement of the material, so that the northern sky takes up 300 lines, and the southern only 129. Hipparchus lists the Zodiac as a third group.

322–450 THE SOUTHERN CONSTELLATIONS, ARRANGED IN THREE GROUPS, BASED SUCCESSIVELY ON ORION, THE SEA-MONSTER, AND THE ALTAR

322–352 Orion group: Orion, the Dog, the Hare and Argo

322–325 Orion

This is one of the obvious star-groups, and is easily likened to a human figure, with shoulders (α γ), feet (β κ) and belt (δ ε ζ). It has been identified with the Babylonian SIBA.ZI.AN.NA 'true shepherd of the sky' (Waerden *EW* 67–8), and is one of the earliest of Greek constellations, appearing with the Pleiades, the Hyades, and the Bear on the Shield of Achilles (Σ 486); cf. ε 274. Later poets, following Homer, sometimes use Orion simply as a prominent feature of the night sky (E. *Cyc.* 213, *Ion* 1153, A.R. 3.745, V. *A.* 3.517). But a different role for Orion is introduced by Hesiod, that is as a seasonal guide at its MR in June–July (*Op.* 598), morning culmination in September (609), and MS in November (615). Thereafter its normal reference in the poets is seasonal, e.g. Theoc. 7.54, V. *A.* 1.535, Hor. *Carm.* 1.28.21, Prop. 2.16.51. Cf. Eudox. in Gem. *Cal.* Scorp. 19 (= 13 Nov.) Ὠρίων ἄρχεται δύνειν· καὶ χειμάζει, Arist. *Mete.* 361b31 ἄκριτος δὲ καὶ χαλεπὸς ὁ Ὠρίων εἶναι δοκεῖ, καὶ δύνων καὶ ἐπιτέλλων, διὰ τὸ ἐν μεταβολῇ ὥρας συμβαίνειν τὴν δύσιν καὶ τὴν ἀνατολήν, θέρους ἢ χειμῶνος, *Pr.* 941b31 χαλεπὸς δή λέγεται καὶ δύνων καὶ ἀνατέλλων ὁ Ὠρίων διὰ τὴν ἀοριστίαν τῆς ὥρας.

How this constellation came to be named after the Boeotian hunter is not known, but the connection must lie in the theme of hunting. This idea may have originated in the fact that Orion follows the Pleiades (see note on 254–267), and Hes. *Op.* 619–20 brings out the notion of pursuit and flight. This may explain why the Bear in Homer keeps a watchful eye on Orion. The hero Orion, however, is described in Homer as a hunter of wild beasts with a club as a weapon, still engaged in this pursuit in Hades: Ὠρίωνα πελώριον εἰσενόησα | θῆρας ὁμοῦ εἰλεῦντα ... | χερσὶν ἔχων ῥόπαλον παγχάλκεον (λ 572–5). The celestial Orion was then accommodated to the myth and provided with a Dog (326–37), a Hare to hunt (338–41), and for weapon a sword (588), later also a club (Hi. 1.7.15). The grandeur of the constellation matches the stature of the hero (Homer's πελώριον, Pi. *I.* 4.53 φύσιν Ὠαριωνείαν, Euphor. 104 πελώριον Ὠρίωνα). The hero's ability to walk on the sea (*Catast.* 32 = Hes. fr. 148a δοθῆναι δὲ αὐτῷ δωρεὰν ὥστε ἐπὶ τῶν κυμάτων πορεύεσθαι καθάπερ ἐπὶ τῆς γῆς) must have originated in the sight of the constellation rising upright on the eastern horizon; cf. V. *A.* 10.763–5. The death of Orion from a scorpion's sting is a genuine astral myth (636–43).

The regular form of the name is 'Ωρίων with ι long, but 'Ωαρίων with ι short appears in E. *Hec.* 1102, Corinna *PMG.* 654 iii.38, Call. *H.* 3.265, and presumably also in fr. 110.94. The Latin poets sometimes shorten the initial *O*, e.g. V. *A.* 1.535, 4.52, 10.763, Hor. *Epod.* 15.7, Prop. 2.16.51; and more rarely the central *o*, e.g. Ov. *Fast.* 5.493, *Met.* 8.207. An alternative Latin name is *Iugulae* (Pl. *Am.* 275) or *Iugula* (Var. *L.* 7.50), which may originally have referred to a part of the constellation, probably the belt: see Goold on Man. 5.175.

A. goes back to the Bull for guidance in locating Orion, but this is a formality, since Orion is too conspicuous and well known to need a sign-post. Other details are reserved for other contexts, the belt on the equator (232, 518), the feet above the Hare (338), the left foot above the River (361), the MS (309–10), the setting of belt, shoulders and sword (587–8), the complete setting (677), the importance of Orion as a weather sign (730) and as a point of reference for measuring the whole round of the sky (754–5); in addition there is a more extended passage on the myth of Orion and the Scorpion (636–46).

322 λοξός I.e. south-east.

τομῇ The figure of the Bull consists of only a foremost half, being cut off at the stars ξ ο on its western limit. A. does not mean that Orion is south-east of the cut-off: its position is too far east to be so described. The scholia note this, and explain that τομή is the dividing line between the Bull and the Twins. But Ταύροιο τομή can hardly mean this. It must mean the actual figure of the Bull, cut off as it is, as προτομή Ἵππου (Gem. 3.8) must have meant the half-figure of the Horse (cf. 215). There is a verbal echo in Pall. *AP* 9.5.3 δένδροιο τομῇ.

ὑποκέκλιται Once in Homer (ε 463 ὑπεκλίνθη), but in a different context; for star positions cf. 286 κέκλιται, 88, 281 παρακέκλιται, 486 ἐπικέκλιται.

αὐτός The pronoun lends a certain distinction to the name of an important constellation figure, which is also enhanced by the enjambment; cf. 630, 666.

323 μὴ κεῖνον Cf. 287 μὴ κείνῳ also with following opt., a lively way of drawing attention to something of special interest. The 3rd pers. is rather less effective than the 2nd.

καθαρῇ ἐπὶ νυκτί Editors after Voss have read ἐνί here, but this is attested only in MSS derived from M, and is a correction of M's ἐν. ἐπί is therefore more likely to be the earlier reading, and is also more in keeping with A.'s use of it c. dat. of time: 585 ἐπ' ὀψὲ δύοντι, 713 ἐπὶ Ταύρῳ, 716 μοίρῃ ἐπὶ ταύτῃ, 805 πᾶσιν ἐπ' ἤμασι, 818 ἐπὶ μηνί, 868 ἐπ' ἤματι. Cf. Hes. *Op.* 102 νοῦσοι δ' ἀνθρώποισιν ἐφ' ἡμέρῃ, αἱ δ' ἐπὶ νυκτί, and A.R. 1.934 ἐπὶ νυκτί ... νηὸς ἰούσης. There is some distinction between the two prepositions, in that ἐνί is purely temporal (287 ἐνὶ μηνί), whereas ἐπί tends to give rather the circumstances in which the action takes place, which is certainly the case in this instance. The reading ἐν may have come from sch. 325 ἐν καθαρᾷ καὶ ἀσελήνῳ νυκτί.

324 ὑψοῦ πεπτηῶτα Sch. 325 ἀντὶ τοῦ μεσουρανοῦντα. A. is not thinking of Orion being precisely on the meridian, only well up in the sky; cf. 309 ὕψι. For πεπτηῶτα cf. 318 and note on 167.

ἄλλα Editors before Voss, reading ἀλλά, printed a comma after παρέρχεται, and so were obliged to translate μή as *non* and ὅτις as *quisquam* (Ceporinus). Voss restored ἄλλα and sense to the passage, but his retained comma (also in the texts of Zannoni, Martin and Erren) is misleading. A. means that anyone who misses Orion cannot expect to find a better constellation to identify. Cf. Cic. fr. 33.104–6 *quem qui suspiciens in caelum nocte serena | late dispersum non uiderit, haud ita uero | cetera se speret cognoscere signa potesse.* Cf. 142 and Pi. *O.* 1.5–6.

325 οὐρανὸν εἰσανιδών ω 307, in same *sedes*.

προφερέστερα Cf. 240. Here the point of the superiority lies in the brightness and clear form of Orion.

θηήσασθαι The aor. inf. (with no temporal reference) is supported by sch. 323 μηκέτι προσδοκάτω ... ἄλλα ἄστρα λαμπρότερα ἰδεῖν, 325 μὴ νομίσῃ ἄλλα αὐτοῦ λαμπρότερα θεάσασθαι. In Homer cf. π 71–2 οὔ πω χερσὶ πέποιθα | ἄνδρ' ἀπαμύνασθαι. Q.S. imitates in 10.380 ἐλπομένη καὶ ἔτ' ἄλλα κακώτερα θηήσασθαι.

Buttmann in his Excursus III argues for a lacuna after 325 with some reference to the prominent features of Orion, such as his belt, sword and shoulders, as on Andromeda τοίη οἱ κεφαλή (200), and on Ophiuchus τοῖοί οἱ ... ὦμοι (77). In the case of Orion the expected τοῖος goes on to introduce the Dog, and Buttmann explains the omission of some lines by haplography. Germanicus in fact amplifies his version with *tale caput magnique umeri, sic balteus ardet, | sic uagina ensis, pernici sic pede lucet* (331–2), before continuing with *talis ei custos* etc. The argument is plausible, and the καί before φροῦρος might seem to give it some support. But there is no such additional material in the scholia or Cicero's version (102–6) or *Arat. Lat.* Orion needs no lengthy introduction, since he can easily be identified without it, and A. has reserved the interesting details for other parts of the poem (see note on 322–325 fin.). Cf. note on the brief introduction of the Scorpion (85). See also Maass, *Hermes* 19 (1884) 120, and Martin's note.

326–337 The Dog

Behind Orion is his guard Dog, dim about the belly, but with a brilliant star at its jaw, called Sirius. Its heliacal rising brings heat that either strengthens or destroys plants, and its setting is also well known. Fainter stars represent its legs.

Sirius was known to the Babylonians as KAK.SI.DI or *gag.si.sa* 'arrow', but they had no constellation corresponding to the Greek Dog (Waerden *EW* 67–9, 71–2, fig. 9). The Dog was primarily a name for Sirius, which follows the hunter across the sky, as is shown by the earliest reference to it in X 26–9 παμφαίνονθ᾽ ὥς τ᾽ ἀστέρ᾽ ἐπεσσύμενον πεδίοιο, | ὅς ῥά τ᾽ ὀπώρης εἶσιν, ἀρίζηλοι δέ οἱ αὐγαὶ | φαίνονται πολλοῖσι μετ᾽ ἀστράσι νυκτὸς ἀμολγῷ· | ὅν τε κύν᾽ Ὡρίωνος ἐπίκλησιν καλέουσι. The Dog-star was important because of its MR at the hottest time of the year, and it is called Κύων in all the parapegmata. In Eup. 147 πρὸ τοῦ Κυνός refers to its MR in July, in S. fr. 432.11 Radt Κυνὸς ψυχρὰν δύσιν its MS in November. Call. fr. 75.35 gives it the dog-name Μαῖρα. The constellation was formed with adjacent stars, and is first mentioned in Eudox. fr. 73 τοῦ Κυνός οἱ πόδες and fr. 82 τοῦ Κυνὸς τὰ ἐμπρόσθια. A. refers to the stars that mark the jaw (330), the forefeet (504, 595), the hind feet (327, 352, 603), and the tail (342).

The Latin name is normally *Canis*, but *Canicula* appears in Var. *R.* 1.28.2, Hor. *Carm.* 1.17.17, 3.13.9, *S.* 2.5.39, Ov. *AA* 2.231, Pers. 3.5. For Sirius see note on 332. For the constellation see *Catast.* 33, Hyg. 2.35, Roscher VI 995ff., Allen 117ff.

326 τοῖος Martin compares 200 τοίη οἱ κεφαλή, and takes the sense to be that the brightness of the Dog is another reason for the observer's not missing Orion. This is unlikely, since Orion has just been introduced as the most conspicuous of the constellations and recognisable in itself as soon as sighted. A. means rather that the Dog is also immediately recognisable, because it contains the brightest of the fixed stars. For τοῖος abs. cf. Δ 289 τοῖος πᾶσιν θυμὸς ἐνὶ στήθεσσι γένοιτο, i.e. similar to the courage of the Aiantes. We are now passing on to the next constellation, and τοῖος makes a convenient transition.

φρουρός Not elsewhere known as Orion's watch-dog, but *Catast.* 33 recalls another myth, ὅτι ἐστὶν ὁ δοθεὶς Εὐρώπῃ φύλαξ.

ἀειρομένῳ ὑπὸ νώτῳ The Dog lies to the south-east of Orion, and is noticeably below and behind him when Orion is upright in the east. Here ἀείρεσθαι is not used in the sense of rising, but of moving across the sky; cf. 405, 558, E. *Alc.* 450 ἀειρομένας παννύχου σελάνας (sch. μετεωριζομένης πλησιφαοῦς τῆς σελήνης).

327 ἐπὶ ποσσί ὑπὸ ποσσί does not make sense: it cannot refer to Orion's feet, since it is the Hare that lies under them (338), and in any case it clashes with ὑπὸ νώτῳ. The traditional picture is of the Dog standing on its hind legs (the star ζ), with its forelegs (β) above them, and the aptness of ἐπί is confirmed by sch. ἤτοι τοῖς ὀπισθίοις· ἐπ᾽

αὐτῶν γὰρ βεβηκώς ἐστιν. The corruption to ὑπό could have come from the preceding line. For ἀμφότεροι of the two implied by the context, where more than two are involved, cf. 236, 513, 1109, 1136.

328 ποικίλος Sch. ποικιλίαν ἀστέρων ἐστὶν ἰδεῖν ὅταν ἄστρον τι ἔχῃ καὶ ἀμυδροὺς καὶ λαμπροὺς ἀστέρας παραλλήλους ... τὸ δὲ παραλλήλους εἴπομεν ὅτι οὐ δεῖ εἶναι ὁμοῦ μόνους λαμπρούς, οὔτε τὸ ἀνάπαλιν, ἀλλὰ δεῖ κρᾶσιν εἶναί τινα. Similarly the Bird is called αἰόλος (275) because it is a mixture of bright areas and dim areas. Cf. ποικίλλοιτο (822) of the sun's disc with dark patches on it, and ποικίλλουσα (1001) of the crow's varied note. The scholia give an alternative explanation of ποικίλος as referring to the colourful brilliance of Sirius, but here it is the constellation as a whole that A. is describing.

πεφασμένος Once in Homer (Ξ 127), but as pf. part. pass. of φημί, here of φαίνω; cf. Sol. 13.71 πλούτου δ' οὐδὲν τέρμα πεφασμένον ἀνδράσι κεῖται. A. uses it again in 743. The strong bucolic diaeresis is common in A., but its occurrence in three successive lines is unusual: this does not appear to have any particular significance here.

328–9 κατ' αὐτὴν γαστέρα κυάνεος The part of the figure where the belly should be is not marked by any stars. The use of κατά in the sense of 'at' is similar to its use in geometry, e.g. Euc. 1.10 ἡ Α Β εὐθεῖα δίχα τέτμηται κατὰ τὸ Δ σημεῖον. κυάνεος is equivalent to ἠερόεις (276, 317).

περιτέλλεται Cf. 215, 232, 509.

330 βέβληται A development of the Homeric sense of being hit with a weapon, as in Θ 514 βλήμενος ἢ ἰῷ ἢ ἔγχεϊ. The constellation is, as it were, implanted with this bright star; cf. 609 βεβολημένος Ἀρκτούροιο. A. uses this pf. pass. more frequently of stars in their positions: 174, 311, 358, 371, 492.

δεινῷ The transmitted δεινή has some support from Germ. 333 *ore timendo*, but there are good reasons for preferring to take the epithet with ἀστέρι. It is the star that is dangerous, and is so described in the following lines: cf. Χ 30 κακὸν δέ τε σῆμα τέτυκται. From a stylistic point of view the allocation of two adjj. to one noun is unusual for A., whereas the distribution of epithets gives a stylish chiasmus, of the type much favoured by Latin poets, e.g. V. *G.* 1.218 *auerso cedens Canis occidit astro*. The corruption can be easily explained by the attraction of γένυς. Tzetzes in Hes. *Op.* 415 ἀστήρ ἐστι κείμενος ὑπὸ τὸ γένειον τοῦ κυνός, ὥς φησιν Ἄρατος.

331 ὀξέα Adv., as again in 472; perhaps influenced by Homeric ὀξέα κεκληγώς (Ρ 88).

σειριάει First here in sense of scorching, to show the derivation of Σείριος. Nonnus imitates in *D.* 5.269 πυρὶ σειριάοντα κατεύνασεν ἀστέρα Μαίρης. Otherwise the verb is a medical term for one suffering from heat-stroke (σειρίασις).

332 Σείριον This name for the Dog-star is not in Homer, who refers to it in Ε 5 ἀστέρ᾽ ὀπωρινῷ and Χ 29 κύν᾽ Ὡρίωνος, but appears first in Hesiod (*Op.* 417, 587, 609, *Sc.* 153, 397), and thereafter is almost confined to the poets. It is not used in the parapegmata, nor by Hipparchus or Geminus or even Ptolemy, who includes the names of some other bright stars. In early poets it is sometimes an adj., e.g. Hes. *Op.* 417 Σείριος ἀστήρ (cf. Q.S. 8.30–1), Alcm. *PMG* 1.62–3 σήριον | ἄστρον, A. *Ag.* 967 σειρίου κυνός (cf. S. fr. 803 Radt, [Opp.] *C.* 3.322), Lyc. 397 ἀκτὶς Σειρία. Cf. V. *A.* 10.273 *Sirius ardor.* In E. *IA* 7, as in Alcman's simile, Sirius is named as a bright star. But elsewhere, because of its MR at the hottest time of the year, it denotes burning heat, especially the parching effect on crops, with the consequent sense of destruction: Hes. *Op.* 587 κεφαλὴν καὶ γούνατα Σείριος ἄζει (cf. *Sc.* 397, 153), Archil. fr. 107 West Σείριος καταυανεῖ (Hsch. refers unconvincingly to the sun), A. *Ag.* 967, E. *Hec.* 1102–3 Σείριος ἔνθα πυρὸς φλογέας ἀφίησιν | ὄσσων αὐγάς, A.R. 2.516–17 ἔφλεγε νήσους | Σείριος, 3.957–9 Σείριος ... μήλοισι δ᾽ ἐν ἄσπετον ἧκεν ὀιζύν. A. elaborates this theme in 332–5. Cf. Q.S. 8.31 Σείριος, ὅς τε βροτοῖσι φέρει πολυκηδέα νοῦσον. *Catast.* 33 notes a wider use of the word: τοὺς δὲ τοιούτους ἀστέρας οἱ ἀστρολόγοι σειρίους καλοῦσι διὰ τὴν τῆς φλογὸς κίνησιν, but gives no example. It is an unlikely use on the part of astronomers, but Ibycus (*PMG* 280) appears to apply σείρια to all the brightest stars, though presumably not to all stars, as Theon Smyrn. (p. 146 Hiller) says: πάντας τοὺς ἀστέρας οἱ ποιηταὶ σειρίους καλοῦσιν. For a figurative use beyond the astral context see Tim. *PMG* 791.179ff. σείριαί τε νᾶες Ἑλλανίδες, αἳ κατὰ μὲν ἧλικ᾽ ὠλέσαθ᾽ ἥβαν νέων πολυάνδρων. The derivation of σείριος is uncertain (see Frisk 2.688). Gundel, *RE* 3A.314–51.

The Latin poets normally use Sirius in contexts of heat, drought and disease, e.g. V. *G.* 4.425 *rapidus torrens sitientis Sirius Indos, A.* 3.141 *sterilis exurere Sirius agros,* 10.274 *sitim morbosque ferens,* Tib. 1.7.21 *arentes cum findit Sirius agros,* V.Fl. 1.683 *Calabri populator Sirius arui.*

ἅμ᾽ ἠελίῳ ἀνιόντα This might be thought to refer to the 'true' MR, when Sirius rises simultaneously with the sun and is therefore still invisible. But A. almost certainly means the visible rising ahead of the sun, which is the traditional phenomenon, especially in Egypt: cf. Gem. *Cal.* Canc. 23 (= 18 July) Δωσιθέῳ ἐν Αἰγύπτῳ Κύων ἐκφανὴς γίνεται, 30 Καλλίππῳ ... Κύων ἀνατέλλων φανερὸς γίνεται. The phrase makes play with Homeric ἅμ᾽ ἠελίῳ ἀνιόντι (Σ 136, ψ 362).

333 φυταλιαί With particular reference to orchards and vineyards (Ζ 195), especially in Hellenistic poets, e.g. Call. *H.* 5.26 (see Bulloch's note), A.R. 3.1400 (a four-word line), Leon. Tar. *AP* 6.44.2 = *HE* 2542, Anon. *AP* 7.714.6 = *HE* 3885. Cf. Nonn. *D.* 41.48. The four-word line seems intended to be impressive, enhanced by the alliteration of φ λ δ. The poets preserve the folk-lore of Sirius being the cause of the heat, as Geminus observes (17.26): πάντες μὲν γὰρ ὑπολαμβάνουσιν ἰδίαν δύναμιν ἔχειν τὸν ἀστέρα καὶ παραίτιον γίνεσθαι τῆς τῶν καυμάτων ἐπιτάσεως ἅμα συνεπιτέλλοντα τῷ ἡλίῳ. τοῦτο δ' οὐκ ἔστιν οὕτως ἔχον. We need not, however, assume that A. was unaware of the true explanation.

ψεύδονται Usually of verbal deception, e.g. A. *Ag.* 1208; here the trees try to elude the power of Sirius by sheltering behind a barrage of leaves. Cf. 35.

ἀναλδέα φυλλιόωσαι The point of ἀναλδέα is that the leafage is not strong or dense enough to keep out the heat, not that the trees are unfruitful (LSJ). A. uses the adj. again in 394 of faint stars. The part., with epic diectasis, occurs only here, a coinage to balance φυταλιαί.

334 ῥεῖα The power to do everything with ease was ascribed only to gods; cf. Γ 381 ῥεῖα μάλ' ὥς τε θεός, of Aphrodite, more frequently of Zeus (Ο 490, Hes. *Op.* 6-7, 379), elsewhere of Hermes (*h.Hom.* 4.417), Hecate (Hes. *Th.* 442-3), Apollo (Call. *H.* 2.50). Closer to the present passage is Hes. *Th.* 254, of the nymph Cymodoce's power to calm waves and winds. The divine overtones of this adv. enhance the impression given of Sirius as a celestial force. See West on Hes. *Op.* 5ff. But A. may be also recalling Β 475 ῥεῖα διακρίνωσιν, of goatherds separating their herds.

ἔκρινε διά Anastrophic tmesis; cf. 940, 979, 984, 986, and in Homer Ρ 91 λίπω κάτα, 1 17 φυγὼν ὕπο, 534 ὀλέσας ἄπο. The gnomic aor. here runs parallel with the pres. ψεύδονται. The primary meaning of κρίνω, 'sift', is extended to express the idea of penetrating the camouflage of the leaves.

ὀξὺς ἀΐξας The alliteration of sibilants, especially the double ξ, brings out the sense of intensity in the heat; cf. 331, and Archil. 107, of Sirius, ὀξὺς ἐλλάμπων. The α in ἀΐσσω is normally long, as in 926, 929, 944; cf. Ε 81 φασγάνῳ ἀΐξας. But Homer shortens it at the end of a line in Φ 126 ὑπαΐξει; see Wyatt 180.

335 ἔρρωσεν Rarely act. (cf. Plu. *Pomp.* 76 ῥῶσαι), only here of plant life.

φλόον Blossom or fruit, as in 1008. The line is quoted by Plu. *Quaest. Conviv.* 683F on φλοίειν as used by the poets in the sense of 'flourish': τὴν χλωρότητα καὶ τὸ ἄνθος τῶν καρπῶν φλόον προσαγορεύειν.

336 κατιόντος ἀκούομεν Either the ES at the end of April or the MS at the beginning of December. We know about these phenomena from the parapegmata, e.g. Gem. *Cal.* Taur. 4 (= 26 Apr.) Εὐδόξῳ Κύων ἀκρόνυχος δύνει, Sagitt. 12 (= 6 Dec.) Εὐδόξῳ Κύων ἑῷος δύνει.

οἱ δὲ δὴ ἄλλοι Cf. α 26. The other stars are there simply to form an outline suggesting the figure of a dog.

337 σῆμ' ἔμεναι Cf. 72, the inf. expressing purpose as in Φ 405 (λίθον) τόν ῥ' ἄνδρες πρότεροι θέσαν ἔμμεναι οὖρον ἀρούρης.

μελέεσσιν Especially the stars β (forelegs), ζ (hind legs), and δ ε η (the centre of the body).

ἐλαφρότεροι They are less bright than Sirius, but not at all faint, since β δ η are 2nd-mag. stars, ε ζ 3rd.

338–341 The Hare
Below Orion the Hare is incessantly pursued and watched by Sirius.

The Hare appears to be a Greek constellation in origin, devised to suit the hunting context of Orion and the Dog. It is mentioned first in Eudox. fr. 73 as being on the winter tropic. It is a small constellation, designed to fit the available stars in such a way that it faces west, as if running ahead of the Dog. The centre of the body is marked by the stars α β Leporis, the forelegs by ε, and the hind legs by γ δ. The name is always in the epic form Λαγωός, in Latin always *Lepus*. Gundel, *RE* 12.458ff., Roscher VI 993ff., Allen 264ff.

338 ποσσίν The Hare lies immediately south of β and κ Orionis.

339 ἐμμενὲς ἤματα πάντα A. recalls the simile in K 361 λαγωὸν ἐπείγετον ἐμμενὲς αἰεί and 364 διώκετον ἐμμενὲς αἰεί. For the accumulation of synonyms cf. 20, 891.

340 ἐξόπιθεν The adv. suits both the astronomical position of Sirius to the east of the Hare and the orientation of the two figures, both facing west. Cf. 91.

μετιόντι In Homer of following in support (Z 341), here of hostile pursuit. Man. 5.233 *praegressum quaerit Leporem comprendere cursu*, Nonn. *D.* 47.253 Κύνα ... καταΐσσοντα Λαγωοῦ (of Procyon), sch. (MK) οὐ καλῶς προσέθηκεν, ἐπειδὴ τὰ ὕστερον ἀνατέλλοντα πρότερα δύνει τῶν βορειοτάτων, μάλιστα τὰ πρὸς τὸν νότον κείμενα. The comment is pedantic: it is the star Sirius, not the whole Dog, that rose and set after the Hare.

341 ἐπαντέλλει Lit. of one star rising after another; cf. sch. ὁ Τοξότης ἐπανατέλλων τῇ Λύρᾳ. But fig. in E. *HF* 1053 of murder rising up to denounce the murderer. Here the literal sense prevails, but there are overtones of hostility from the context. In Strato, *AP* 12.178.2 οἷος ἐπαντέλλων ἀστράσιν ἥλιος the comparison is the significant point; in E. *Ph.* 105 the sense is literal.

δοκεύει   The v.l. διώκει merely repeats διώκεται (339), from which it presumably came into the tradition, whereas δοκεύει has Homeric overtones. It recalls the simile in Θ 338–40, of the dog hunting a boar or lion, ending in ἑλισσόμενόν τε δοκεύει, and the star scene in Σ 488; cf. Ψ 325. The rhyming verbs at caesura and end bring out the balance of rising and setting; cf. 534.

342–352 Argo

Argo behind the Dog moves backwards, like a ship entering harbour, when the crew turn her about and beach her. Argo is starless from prow to mast, but otherwise bright, and the steering-oar is below the Dog's hind legs.

Argo is the largest of the southern constellations, and was not entirely visible from Greece. It was seen complete, however, from Alexandria, and its inspiration may well have been Egyptian, since there is no evidence for a Babylonian origin. The Greeks, looking south, saw it on a sea horizon in the direction of Egypt. The Egyptians had several ships in their sky, but the most likely source is the ship of Osiris, which was near Orion and the Dog (see Boll *Sphaera* 169ff.): cf. Plu. 359E τὸ πλοῖον, ὃ καλοῦσιν Ἕλληνες Ἀργώ, τῆς Ὀσίριδος νεὼς εἴδωλον ἐπὶ τιμῇ κατηστερισμένον οὐ μακρὰν φέρεσθαι τοῦ Ὠρίωνος καὶ τοῦ Κυνός. The Greek name is first attested in Eudox. fr. 73, and is regular in Greek authors. Hipparchus twice refers to the constellation as τὸ πλοῖον (1.8.1, 3.1.14), but these are contexts in which he has already called it Argo. The ship-figure has no forward part (cf. the incomplete Bull and Horse). Eudoxus refers to the stern and mast (fr. 73), the steering-oar and ship's bottom (fr. 74); A. mentions the mast (350), stern (604), prow (350), steering-oar (351) and stern-ornament (686). For the bright star Canopus see note on 351. The Latin poets also use *Argo*, but have several variations, e.g. *Nauis* (Cic. fr. 33.390), *Carina* (Germ. 374), *Puppis* (id. 489), *Ratis* (Man. 1.623). In modern star-maps Argo is normally subdivided into three separate constellations, called Carina, Puppis and Vela. Roscher VI 1005ff., Allen 64ff.

342 κατ' οὐρήν   κατά is suggestive of close pursuit; cf. Hdt. 9.89.3 ὁ στρατὸς αὐτοῦ οὗτος κατὰ πόδας ἐμεῦ ἐλαύνων, S. *Aj.* 32 κατ' ἴχνος ᾄσσω. The Dog's tail is represented by η Canis Majoris, and the line of fainter stars denoting the after part of the ship's keel comes very close to it, following it westwards.

ἕλκεται   Cf. 20, 443, 727 of stars, 835 of cloud movement. Here the idea of a ship being towed is also suggested, as in 604 ἕλκων describes the Dog pulling Argo up over the horizon. This line begins a short piece

311

of ring-composition concluding with the same words ἕλκεται Ἀργώ (348). The sequence of themes is: backward motion – ship entering harbour – backward motion.

343 πρυμνόθεν A rare form, also in A.R. 4.911 in same *sedes*, of a wave rising astern. In 348 A. varies with the Homeric *hapax* πρύμνηθεν (Ο 716).

κατὰ χρέος Of a ship sailing on its normal business, therefore prow first. The sense here may have developed from the Homeric use in λ 479 ἦλθον Τειρεσίαο κατὰ χρέος, which combines the idea of Odysseus' business in the west and that of consultation, as foreshadowed in κ 492 χρησομένους. Cf. A.R. 4.530 on Phoebus giving two tripods to Jason περόωντι κατὰ χρέος.

344 ὄπιθεν φέρεται τετραμμένη The stern stars of Argo are at its western limit, and the figure therefore seems to move backwards; cf. 575 of the Kneeler. The orientation of other constellations is described with τετραμμένος also in 30, 387, 620, 632.

αὐταί Real ships, as opposed to the imaginary figure in the sky. Cf. Α 4 αὐτούς, the visible bodies as opposed to the departed ψυχαί, λ 602 αὐτός the real Heracles with the gods, as opposed to his ghost in Hades. Sch. ὥσπερ καὶ αἱ ἄλλαι νῆες and Cic. fr. 33.128 *non aliae naues* do not justify the reading of ἄλλαι here against the united testimony of the MSS.

345 νῆες, ὅτ' ἤδη Cf. A.R. 3.914 Ἄργος, ὅτ' ἤδη.

ἐπιστρέψωσι κορώνην The manoeuvre is that of turning the ship under oars until the stern is pointing towards the place where the ship is to be beached. Cf. Th. 2.90.4 ἄφνω ἐπιστρέψαντες τὰς ναῦς μετωπη-δὸν ἔπλεον, of altering course through 90° to change the formation of a fleet from line ahead to line abreast; so ἐπιστροφή in 2.90.5 and 91.1. Here κορώνη is strictly the curved ornament that terminates the stern-post: sch. αὐτὸ τὸ τῆς πρύμνης ἀκροστόλιον. Virgil imitates this line in G. 1.303–4 *ceu pressae cum iam portum tetigere carinae, | puppibus et laeti nautae imposuere coronas*, with a punning variation at the end. We need not assume either that Virgil misunderstood A. or that A.'s meaning is correctly represented by Virgil, as Richter supposed when he proposed ἐπιστέψωσι here (*Georgica*, 1957). For illustrations of akrostolia see J. S. Morrison and R. T. Williams, *Greek Oared Ships* (1968), plates 13 and 14. Cf. 686 ἄκρα κόρυμβα.

346 ὅρμον ἐσερχόμενοι Cf. Α 435 τὴν δ' εἰς ὅρμον προέρεσσαν ἐρετμοῖς. ὅρμος is a position within a protected bay or harbour, where a ship can safely lie, whether beached or moored or at anchor.

αὐτίκα See note on 199.

346–347 ἀνακόπτει νῆα A variation of the more usual ἀνακρούειν

COMMENTARY: 347–350

or ἀνακρούεσθαι, e.g. A.R. 4.1650 νῆα περιδδείσαντες ἀνακρούεσκον ἐρετμοῖς, Hdt. 8.84.1 πρύμναν ἀνεκρούοντο. The scholia interpret as a braking movement, as if the ship were still moving forward: ἀνωθεῖ εἰς τὸ ἐναντίον καὶ ἀνακρούει, ἵνα μὴ ὁρμῇ χρησαμένη ἡ ναῦς ἀθρόως ἐμπέσῃ τῇ γῇ. But here the crew have turned the ship about and now back water to bring the stern on to the land.

347 παλιρροθίη A Homeric adj., recalling especially 1 485 (νῆα) ἤπειρόνδε παλιρρόθιον φέρε κῦμα; also more naturally of the backdraw of a wave in ε 430. Cf. 1012, of cranes flying back to land, and a figurative use in Luc. *AP* 9.367.12 οὐλομένης πενίης κῦμα παλιρρόθιον.

ἠπείροιο The double spondee at the end of the line, coming after the four dactyls, may suggest movement being halted, but cf. 1 235 κεῖθ' ἁλὶ κεκλιμένη ἐριβώλακος ἠπείροιο.

348 πρύμνηθεν See note on 343 πρυμνόθεν.

Ἰησονίς Normally a patronymic form (cf. Κεκροπίς), here used as possessive adj.; cf. A.R. 1.411 πόλιν . . . Αἰσωνίδα, 2.299 Κρήτης Μινωίδος. The more usual fem. adj. is Ἰησονίη, as in A.R. 1.960, 988, 1148; cf. Avien. 756 *Iasoniam . . . Argo*, 808 *Puppis Iasoniae*.

349 τὰ μὲν ἠερίη The forward part of the ship is not represented by any stars, and is usually omitted in diagrams, e.g. on the Farnese globe. Hipparchus (1.8.1) says A. is mistaken in calling the part from the prow to the mast starless (ἀναστέριστον), because there are in fact two bright stars at the cut-off (ἐν τῇ ἀποτομῇ τοῦ πλοίου), the more northerly one on the deck, the more southerly on the keel, and both of these lie well to the east of the mast. These two are perhaps ψ and φ Velorum, both of 3rd mag. They may not have been included in the constellation as visualised by Eudoxus. A. uses ἠερίη as a variation of ἠερόεις (276, 317, 385). Cf. A.R. 1.580, 4.1239 of land dimly sighted.

ἀνάστερος First attested 228 and here. Hi. 1.7.21, 8.1 has ἀναστέριστος in this sense, *Catast.* 22 ἄναστρος.

ἄχρι παρ' Again in 602, 632, but perhaps not elsewhere; ἄχρις ἐπ' (807) is more usual. The curious v.l. in S may be due to the influence of οἷα καὶ αὐταί (344).

350 ἱστὸν ἀπὸ πρώρης The stars representing the mast were probably the three now designated as γ α β Pyxidis (Hi. 3.1.1b, 3.3.4, Ptol. *Alm.* 8.1.40): γ is the top, α β the centre, and the line continues southward to the level of the deck, though there is no star to mark that point. The prow is purely notional (see 349).

τὰ δὲ πᾶσα φαεινή The part of the ship from mast to stern, which forms the constellation. It lies in the Milky Way and has many bright individual stars.

351 πηδάλιον Sch. ἐπ' ἄκρου δὲ τοῦ πηδαλίου κεῖται μέγας

313

ἀστὴρ ἐπώνυμος τοῦ Κανώβου τοῦ κυβερνήτου Μενελάου. οὐ μνημονεύει δὲ τοῦ ἀστέρος ὁ Ἄρατος. οὐδὲ γὰρ τοὺς περὶ τὴν Ἑλλάδα τόπ-
ους οὐδὲ τοὺς ἔτι βορειοτέρους ἐπέχει, ἀλλ' ἔστιν ἀφανὴς ὑπὸ γῆν
φερόμενος. φαίνεται δὲ πρῶτον ἀπὸ Ῥόδου τοῖς ἐπ' Αἴγυπτον πλέουσι.
We do not have the corresponding passage of Eudoxus here, but in fr.
74 on the ἀφανὴς κύκλος, on and within which stars are too far south to
be visible, he includes among the stars that mark this circle τῆς Ἀργοῦς
τὸ ἔδαφος καὶ τὸ πηδάλιον, and separately at the end of the list ὁ δὲ ἐξ
Αἰγύπτου ὁρώμενος ἀστήρ ἐστιν ἐν αὐτῷ. Hipparchus (1.11.7-8) dis-
agreed with Eudoxus on the invisibility of Canopus, pointing out that
it could be observed from the latitude of Rhodes, and he therefore
extended the steering-oar to include it. So Gem. 3.15, Ptol. *Alm.* 8.1.40.
But for A. we must take the more northerly τ Puppis as the original end
of the oar.

κεχαλασμένον Sch. παρηωρημένον. While not in use the steering-
oar hangs loosely down the ship's side; cf. Germ. 355 *demisso.*

352 οὐραίοισι Cf. 145, 245, 362.

προπάροιθεν The oar is not positioned in front of the figure of the
Dog, but lies well below it, i.e. to the south, and the point of the adv. is
that it sets before the Dog. Contrast 270.

353-401 Sea-monster group: the Sea-monster, the River, the origin of
the constellations, the Southern Fish, the Water

353-366 The Sea-monster and the River
Andromeda is threatened by the Monster in the far south. It lies below
the Ram and Fishes and above the River, which starts under Orion's
foot. The Fishes' Knot is close to its back-fin.

The Sea-monster is a large and shapeless constellation extending
from about the equator in a south-westerly direction. Its brightest stars
provide a head group (α γ δ), a body group (ζ θ η τ) and a tail (ι and
perhaps β: but see note on 398). It may have an origin in Babylonian
monster-lore, but there is no clear identification of it with any of the
oriental constellations: Gundel, *RE* 11.365. Its association with the
Andromeda myth is certainly Greek (cf. *Catast.* 36), as A. makes clear
by the way he introduces it here and refers to it again in 629-33. It
appears first in Eudox. fr. 73 as Κῆτος, and this is the standard name
in Greek.

Latin writers use a variety of names: *Pistrix* (Cic. fr. 33.140), *Pistris*
(Avien. 809), *Pristis* (Germ. 356), *Belua* (Germ. 362) and *Cetus* (Vitr. 9.5.3),
which is also the modern name.

353 οὐκ ὀλίγον περ ἀπόπροθι Ψ 832, δ 811 μάλα πολλὸν ἀπόπροθι. The reference to Andromeda serves a double purpose, recalling the dramatic role of the monster in the legend, and technically instructing the observer, who has identified Argo, to turn now to a different part of the sky to find the next constellation. Its position is then more precisely defined in 357-8 and 362-6.

πεπτηυῖαν Recalling Andromeda's πεπτάμεναι χεῖρες (204). See also note on 167.

354 μέγα Κῆτος ε 421 ἠέ τί μοι καὶ κῆτος ἐπισσεύῃ μέγα δαίμων. Q.S. 6.290 μέγα κῆτος recalls A. For varieties of κῆτος see Ael. *NA* 9.49.

ἐπερχόμενον The Sea-monster rises after Andromeda, and the prefix therefore suits both the celestial phenomena and the hostile approach in the legend (cf. Homer's ἐπισσεύῃ).

κατεπείγει Ψ 623 ἤδη γὰρ χαλεπὸν κατὰ γῆρας ἐπείγει. The verb is otherwise used mainly in prose.

355 Θρήϊκος Epic form, with ι short in Homer (Β 595, Δ 533), long here and A.R. 1.24, Call. *H.* 3.114 (but short in 4.63 Θρήϊκος Αἵμου). The Thracian wind, Θρασκίας, is described by Aristotle (*Mete.* 363b) as blowing from a point between the Argestes (the direction of midsummer sunset) and Aparctias (due north), i.e. somewhere between NW and NNW. Here as an adj. it defines more precisely the noun Boreas, which can be used generally for any northerly wind.

πνοιῇ Cf. 386, also Manetho 2.(1).23 ἐπὶ κρυεροῦ πνοιῇσιν.

356 κεκλιμένη Cf. 161.

νότος In Arist. *Mete.* 363b the wind from due south, but here it represents a southerly direction more generally.

357 Κριῷ τε καὶ Ἰχθύσιν The position is now given with respect to two constellations already identified (225, 240). The Sea-monster's head is SE of the Ram, its body to the south of the Fishes.

358 βαιόν Mostly in drama, e.g. S. *Ph.* 20 βαιὸν δ' ἔνερθεν. Homer has only the Ionic form. e.g. ι 462 ἐλθόντες δ' ἠβαιόν, Β 380 οὐδ' ἠβαιόν, where sch. (ABT) note παρὰ μέντοι τοῖς νεωτέροις δισσὴ ἡ χρῆσις, quoting A. here and Call. fr. 625 ἠβαιήν. Imitations of A. appear in [Opp.] *C.* 1.176 βαιὸν ὑπὲρ δειρῆφι and Q.S. 2.464 βαιὸν ὑπὲρ κνημῖδος, 10.149 βαιὸν ὑπὲρ σάκεος.

ὑπὲρ Ποταμοῦ In such contexts ὑπέρ normally means 'to the north of' (137, 447), but here only the head of the Sea-monster lies farther north than the River, and even then more north-west than north. However, Hipparchus (1.8.5) quotes this line with approval, and also the words of Eudoxus (fr. 52) ὑπὸ δὲ τὸ Κῆτος ὁ Ποταμὸς κεῖται. Since the River has not been mentioned before, A. intends this more as an introduction to the River than a further definition of the Sea-monster.

The River is a very long line of not very bright stars, winding west from Orion's foot, then curving round to run east, then west again and south. Hi. 1.8.4. Its most southerly star visible in Greece was probably θ: now it ends farther south in the bright star Achernar. The River appears to be a Greek constellation, since there is no clear evidence of a river in this part of the sky in either Babylonian or Egyptian lore.

Ποταμός is the standard name in the astronomers, attested first in Eudox. fr. 73 τοῦ Ποταμοῦ ἡ καμπή on the winter tropic. It came to be variously identified: see sch. (S) ≈ Catast. 37 καλεῖται κατὰ μὲν τὸν Ἄρα-τον Ἠριδανός· οὐδεμίαν δὲ ἀπόδειξιν φέρει περὶ αὐτοῦ. ἕτεροι δέ φασι δικαιότατα αὐτὸν εἶναι Νεῖλον· μόνος γὰρ οὗτος ἀπὸ μεσημβρίας τὰς ἀρχὰς ἔχει. Hes. Th. 338 is a likely source for A.'s choice of name, but there may have been another in the Hesiodic account of the Phaethon legend (fr. 311), in view of sch. Strozz. in Germanici Aratea (Breysig 174): Hesiodus autem dicit inter astra collocatum propter Phaethonta ... in Eridanum fluuium, qui et Padus, cecidisse. This legendary river was usually located by the Greeks in the north-west (cf. Hdt. 3.115), and variously identified with the Rhone, the Rhine, and most of all the Po. In Latin Eridanus is the commonest name (Cic. fr. 33.145), but variations are Amnis (Germ. 362), Flumen (Cic. 152); Man. 1.440 Flumina combines this river with the stream flowing from Aquarius' jar. The modern name is Eridanus. Escher, RE 6.446–7., Roscher VI 989ff., Boll Sphaera 134ff., Allen 215ff., Diggle Phaethon, index p. 238 s.v. Eridanus.

βεβλημένον Cf. 311, 492.

ἀστερόεντος Δ 44 ἀστερόεντι in same sedes.

359 οἶον The v.l. οἷον, if comparative, has nothing to refer back to, and, if exclamatory (sch. θαυμαστικῶς, as in 143), does not make sense with γάρ, which is there to explain what this River is that has just been named for the first time. Buttmann's explanation of οἶον, 'quo augetur notio uocis λείψανον', is accepted by Martin, who translates 'un simple débris'. But this is not the sense of οἶος, which means 'alone', 'by itself', 'separate': cf. 388 οἶος ἀπὸ προτέρων, 376 οἰόθι κεκριμένων, and with numerals 258, 812, 887. Here the point is that the River is a separate constellation.

θεῶν ὑπὸ ποσσί The creation myth represented the sky as a floor for the gods to dwell on: Hes. Th. 128 ὄφρ' εἴη μακάρεσσι θεοῖς ἕδος ἀσφα-λὲς αἰεί. The conceit of the gods standing or walking on the sky appears first here and presumably in Call. fr. 110.69 (Cat. 66.69 me nocte premunt uestigia diuom). Cf. V. E. 5.57 sub pedibusque uidet nubes et sidera Daphnis.

360 λείψανον Ἠριδανοῖο On the identification of the Eridanus see note on 358 ὑπὲρ Ποταμοῦ. The remnant of the river is presumably what was left after being scorched by the solar chariot driven by Phaethon; cf. Nonn. *D.* 38.429 καὶ ποταμὸς πυρίκαυτος ἀνήλυθεν εἰς πόλον ἄστρων, and Ovid's catalogue of burnt-up rivers in *Met.* 2.241ff.

Ἠριδανοῖο ... ποταμοῖο The internal dissyllabic rhyme gives an emphasis to the name (see Kirk on Γ 133). A. follows especially Π 174 Σπερχειοῖο διιπετέος ποταμοῖο, δ 477, 581 Αἰγύπτοιο διιπετέος ποταμοῖο (cf. Σ 607, μ 1), also Hes. *Th.* 242, 959 Ὠκεανοῖο τελήεντος ποταμοῖο. Cf. Antim. fr. 53.7 ποταμοῖο παρὰ ῥόον Αἰσήποιο, A.R. 3.877 Ἀμνισοῖο λοεσσαμένη ποταμοῖο, also 1.217, 2.904, 4.516. Nicander makes play with this Homeric feature in his signature lines *Ther.* 957, *Alex.* 629. A. has other rhyming lines: in -οιο 435, 634, 693, 831, 876, 925; -οντα 617, -οντι 821, 1147, -οντες 571; -ῃσι 619.

πολυκλαύτου Sch. εἶπεν ὅτι αἱ Ἡλιάδες παρὰ ταῖς τοῦ Ἠριδανοῦ ὄχθαις ὀδυρόμεναι τὸν ἀδελφὸν εἰς αἰγείρους μετεβάλοντο, ὅπου αὐτῶν καὶ τὸ δάκρυον ἤλεκτρον ποιεῖ. Cf. Q.S. 5.268 of the Heliades μυρόμεναι μεγάλοιο παρὰ ῥόον Ἠριδανοῖο. The form -κλαυτος is generally better attested than -κλαυστος: Archil. 94.3, Hom. *Epigr.* 3.5, A. *Ag.* 1526, E. *Ion* 869, Emp. 62.1. For the sense here cf. Mosch. 3.73 of Arethusa μύρασθαι καλὸν υἷα πολυκλαύτοισι ῥεέθροις. For the Heliades see Diggle *Phaethon*, note on 358.

361 ὑπὸ σκαιὸν πόδα The River begins with λ Eridani very close to β Orionis, and its first reach is to the west, but the rest of the constellation runs through declinations south of Orion's foot.

362 δεσμοὶ δ᾿ οὐραῖοι After a brief digression on the River, A. returns to the Sea-monster and locates it with reference to stars on its other side. On the Fishes' chains see 242–5. The sole reason for referring to them again here is that the Knot in which they meet is close to the back-fin of the Monster. There was no need to repeat so much of the information given in the earlier passage, and A. seems to be simply indulging in a display of variation technique, e.g. δεσμοί for δεσμά, οὐραῖοι for οὐραίων, ἄμφω for ἀμφοτέρων, συμφορέονται for εἰς ἓν ἰόντα, ἀπ᾿ οὐραίων for ὑπούραιον.

ἄκροι The v.l. ἀμφίς hardly makes sense, and is probably an intrusion from 26 or from θ 340 δεσμοὶ μὲν τρὶς τόσσοι ἀπείρονες ἀμφὶς ἔχοιεν.

363 οὐραίων Cf. 243. Maass cites Cic. fr. 33.151 *caudarum a parte locata* as an argument for reading οὐράων, but the phrase is even better evidence for οὐραίων in the sense of 'tail parts'.

There are no scholia on 361–3, but all the Latin translations include these lines.

364 Κητείης Adj. formed on the analogy of Homeric ἱππείη (Κ 568), ταυρείην (Κ 258). A. also has Ἱππείη (554), Κηφείης (280). Cf. Mosch. 2.119 κητείοις νώτοισιν, Opp. *H.* 5.670 κητείη τε βίη.

317

ὄπιθεν   C. gen., as P 468 στῆ δ' ὄπιθεν δίφροιο.

λοφιῆς   Once in Homer (τ 446), of a boar's bristling back, here the back-fin; cf. D.S. 3.41, of a dolphin. There is no particular star available to represent this feature, and none is so designated in Ptolemy's catalogue. But there is a wedge-shaped group of very faint stars reaching from γ δ Ceti to just below α Piscium (the Knot), which would fit the description of Hipparchus in 1.11.20: ὁ γὰρ Σύνδεσμος τῶν Ἰχθύων, ὃς κεῖται κατὰ τὴν κεφαλὴν τοῦ Κήτους ἐπὶ τῆς λοφιᾶς αὐτοῦ. Erren suggests a group of stars north of the head (PAS 323), but not close enough to the Knot to be suitable. The back-fin is in fact a useful dividing point between the head and the rest of the body, when A. describes the constellation as rising and setting in two sections under successive signs of the Zodiac (632, 719); cf. Hi. 2.2.46, 49, 2.3.33, 35.

ἐπιμίξ   In Homer usually of the confusion of battle, e.g. Ξ 60 ἐπιμίξ κτείνονται, here simply of coming together.

365 εἰς ἕν   Cf. E. Andr. 1172, Or. 1640.

ἑνὶ δ' ἀστέρι   An echo of εἷς ἀστήρ (244), with variation of case. The star is α Piscium.

πειραίνονται   In same sense as the act. in 24. The spondaic ending recalls χ 175 = 192 with πειρήναντε.

366 πρώτη ... ἀκάνθη   The top of the spine as a variation for λοφιή. Cf. ἄκανθα of fish, Ar. V. 969; of snakes, Theoc. 24.32; of dragon, A.R. 4.150, also Nonn. D. 1.189 (constellation).

367-385 The origin of the constellations
This is one of the two digressions with which A. relieves his description of the southern sky, the second being 408-30. The present passage begins and ends with the unnamed stars below the Hare, and this theme provides a framework that fits the digression into the context. Cf. the setting of the Dike passage, 96-136. Inside the frame A. has woven a chiastic pattern of themes in what is essentially one long sentence: (a) the stars beneath the Hare are nameless (367-70), (b) because they do not make a figure like the regular constellations (370-3), (c) which were formed by someone into groups of stars and named (373-5), (d) because it was impossible to identify stars individually, since they all look alike (375-8); (c) so he decided to arrange the stars in groups (379-81), (b) and thus we have the familiar constellations (381-2), (a) whereas the stars beneath the Hare are nameless (383-5). The chiastic pattern, well known from Cat. 64 and 68A, and from the Aristaeus episode in V. G. 4.457-522, thus appears to have a Hellenistic origin. See L. P. Wilkinson, *The Georgics of Virgil* (1969), 327-8.

The poetic artistry was apparently not understood by the ancient commentators. Attalus ap. Hi. 1.8.9–10 (fr. 17 Maass) found the passage repetitive and confusing. He thus supposed that A.'s purpose was merely to explain that these stars were nameless because they did not form an obvious group. Hipparchus disagrees, to the extent of thinking that the original namer never meant to include all the stars in constellations.

For discussions of this passage see Martin's long note on 370–85, M. Erren in *Hermes* 86 (1958) 240–3 and *PAS* 145–51, my note in *Antichthon* 1 (1967) 12–15, M. L. Pendergraft, *Eranos* 88 (1990) 99–106.

367–370 The syntax of these lines is a little strange. We expect A. to be saying that 'the stars which circle between the Steering-oar and the Monster, etc., are nameless', the main clause thus ending emphatically with the new theme. This is how the lines are translated by Ceporinus and Zannoni. But this requires the rel. οἵ, whereas it is characteristic of A. to use the demonstrative art. to introduce a new topic, e.g. 19, 239, and there is no doubt that this is what A. means here. The loose structure is unusual, but νώνυμοι has its emphasis by coming last and at the beginning of a line. Cf. the similar passage 389–91.

367 μέτρῳ The area of sky covered by this group of stars: sch. ἔν τε ὀλίγῳ χωρίῳ.

ἐγκείμενοι Cf. 139.

368 μεσσόθι πηδαλίου καὶ Κήτεος Hi. 1.8.2–3 ἐν δὲ τούτοις παρεωρακέναι μοι δοκεῖ (οὕτως γὰρ δεῖ λέγειν), ὑπολαβὼν μεταξὺ τοῦ πηδαλίου καὶ τοῦ Κήτους κεῖσθαι τοὺς ἀνωνύμους ἀστέρας. δεῖ γὰρ αὐτοὺς μεταξὺ τοῦ Ποταμοῦ καὶ τοῦ πηδαλίου κεῖσθαι. Since the stars in question lie south of the Hare, they have the steering-oar to the east and the River to the west, as Eudoxus says (fr. 52): μεταξὺ δὲ τοῦ Ποταμοῦ καὶ τοῦ πηδαλίου τῆς Ἀργοῦς, ὑπὸ τὸν Λαγωόν, τόπος ἐστὶν οὐ πολύς, ἀμαυροὺς ἀστέρας ἔχων. Hipparchus rightly criticises A. for this error. The stars may be those that are now the constellation Columba.

369 γλαυκοῦ This colour adj. is used more characteristically of the sea (Π 34, Ar. *Ran.* 665, A.R. 1.182), the olive (S. *OC* 701, Nic. *Ther.* 680), eyes (γλαυκῶπις). See Leumann 149 on its origin in γλαυκῶπις = 'owleyed', later taken to be formed from an adj. γλαυκός; hence the uncertainty about its meaning. Maxwell-Stuart describes the basic colour as a 'pale milky blue' (1.120). He rejects Erren's 'nachtblauen' here (82), but does not offer an alternative. The adj. seems chosen to suggest the lack-lustre appearance of the stars and also the natural colour of the animal, perhaps 'grey'.

πεπτηῶτες Cf. 167.

Λαγωοῦ Cf. 338–41.

370 νώνυμοι Twice in Homer (ν 239, ξ 182), in the sense of 'unknown', otherwise νώνυμνος. A. may have here an echo of Hes. *Op.* 154 νώνυμνοι, similarly in enjambment.

τετυγμένου Cf. 12, 233, 757. The idea of craftsmanship is probably implied here, since these are man-made figures. Ronconi, however, thought otherwise (pp. 194–6).

371 βεβλέαται Little more than a synonym of εἰσί; cf. 174.

372 ἐξείης στιχόωντα A. is stressing the regularity of the successive risings and settings that mark the passage of the year, an idea that is further strengthened by αὐτὰ κέλευθα. στιχόωντα recalls Homeric ἐστιχόωντο, especially of troops (B 92) and ships (B 516). Cf. A.R. 1.30 ἐξείης στιχόωσιν of rows of beeches.

αὐτὰ κέλευθα Μ 225 ἐλευσόμεθ᾽ αὐτὰ κέλευθα. Cf. 1031. For αὐτός = ὁ αὐτός cf. κ 263 αὐτὴν ὁδόν (also A.R. 1.199), φ 366 αὐτῇ ἐνὶ χώρῃ, Thgn. 334 αὐτὸς ἔτι.

373 ἀνομένων Pass. of a period coming to an end, e.g. Κ 251 μάλα γὰρ νὺξ ἄνεται, ἐγγύθι δ᾽ ἠώς, Hdt. 7.20.1 πέμπτῳ δὲ ἔτεϊ ἀνομένῳ. Cf. 464, and A.R. 2.494 νέον ἤματος ἀνομένοιο.

τις ἀνδρῶν οὐκέτ᾽ ἐόντων The concept of a single εὑρέτης for any human institution is common in ancient thought. Prometheus in A. *Pr.* 457–8 claims ἀντολὰς ἐγὼ | ἄστρων ἔδειξα τάς τε δυσκρίτους δύσεις: sch. τούτων τὴν εὕρεσιν καὶ Παλαμήδη προσῆψεν. Palamedes in S. fr. 432.3 Radt οὐράνιά τε σήματα. Usually the supposed originator is anonymous: cf. Pl. *Cra.* 388D τίς παραδίδωσιν ἡμῖν τὰ ὀνόματα οἷς χρώμεθα; and the following discussion. The poets make wider use of the theme, e.g. E. *Hipp.* 408–9 ἥτις πρὸς ἄνδρας ἤρξατ᾽ αἰσχύνειν λέχη | πρώτη θυραίους, Ar. *Lys.* 946 κάκιστ᾽ ἀπόλοιθ᾽ ὁ πρῶτος ἑψήσας μύρον, Call. fr. 110.48–50. The theme is even commoner in the Latin poets, e.g. Pl. *Men.* 451–2, Aquil. *com.* 1.1–2, Lucr. 5.1041–2, Hor. *Carm.* 1.3.10ff., Prop. 1.17.13–14, 2.6.27–8, 4.3.19–20, Tib. 1.4.59, 1.10.1. See A. Kleingünther, Πρῶτος εὑρέτης. *Untersuchungen zur Geschichte einer Fragestellung, Philologus* Suppl. 26.1 (1933), esp. 78–80.

374 ἐφράσατ᾽ ἠδ᾽ ἐνόησεν ἐφράσατο here must mean 'devised', not merely 'angemerkt' (Voss) or 'noted' (Mair). The sense is made clear when the theme recurs in 379–81, the point being that the εὑρέτης created the constellations in addition to naming them. Cf. Leon. *AP* 9.25.2, of Aratus, δηναιοὺς ἀστέρας ἐφράσατο, Man. 1.109, of *ratio, attribuitque suas formas, sua nomina signis*, S.E. *Math.* 5.97 εἰκὸς γὰρ τοὺς παλαιοὺς τὰ τοιαῦτα τῶν ὀνομάτων τίθεσθαι κατὰ ψιλὴν τὴν τοῦ χαρακτῆρος ἐμφέρειαν, τάχα δὲ οὐδὲ κατ᾽ αὐτὴν ἀλλ᾽ εὐσήμου χάριν διδασκαλίας.

The v.l. οὐδ᾽ is as early at least as Hipparchus, and may have been responsible for his misunderstanding of the passage. Attalus correctly paraphrases ὁ πρῶτος διατάξας τὰ ἄστρα καὶ ... ὄνομα περιθείς (fr. 17: see note on 367–385), also sch. ἐσκέψατο καὶ διενοήθη. The context requires ἠδ᾽: see the above summary (on 367–385). The correct reading seems to carry a verbal echo of θ 94 Ἀλκίνοος δέ μιν οἶος ἐπεφράσατ᾽ ἠδ᾽ ἐνόησεν, the incorrect of E 665 τὸ μὲν οὔ τις ἐπεφράσατ᾽ οὐδ᾽ ἐνόησε, which may have been the source of the corruption.

ὀνομαστί Mainly prose, e.g. Hdt. 6.79.1.

375 ἤλιθα Cf. 254. The sense here is 'compactly': sch. ἀθρόα καὶ ὁμοῦ μορφῶσαι.

κ᾽ ἐδυνήσατο κε δυνήσατο is not ruled out on metrical grounds, since A. elsewhere allows a trochaic break in the fourth foot after an enclitic, e.g. 186, and frequently even after δέ (e.g. 174, 572, 784). But the use of the augment is regular in A.: see the verbs in the narrative passages 32–5, 71, 102, 102–34, 269–70, 637–44. Cf. Ξ 423 ἀλλ᾽ οὔ τις ἐδυνήσατο.

376 οἰόθι κεκριμένων This refers to the brighter stars taken individually. These are so alike that they are difficult to identify except by their position relative to adjacent stars, and this is indeed the reason why many of the original constellations were devised.

εἰπεῖν A. occasionally allows a spondaic word in the fourth foot: 112 αὐτή, 373 ἀνδρῶν, 625 αὐτήν, 683 ἄλλην, 775 ἄκρη, 887 οἴη, 1030 ἔργων, and with preceding preposition, which may mitigate the effect, 230, 342, 447, 497, 776. There is therefore no need for emendation.

δαῆναι Aor. inf. *δάω 'learn'; cf. δ 493 ἴδμεναι οὐδὲ δαῆναι ἐμὸν νόον.

377 πολέων δ᾽ The sense supports δ᾽, since two problems make the identification difficult, the great number of the stars, and the fact that so many look alike. Att. fr. 17M πολλῶν γὰρ ὑπαρχόντων ἀστέρων καὶ ἐνίων τὰ μεγέθη καὶ τὰ χρώματα ὅμοια ἐχόντων. Alliteration of π is very marked in this line.

ἐπὶ ἶσα M 436, O 413 ἐπὶ ἶσα μάχη τέτατο.

πέλονται With n.pl. subject; see note on 13.

378 χροιή Epic form, once in Homer (Ξ 164); cf. 477, 801.

ἀμφιέλικτοι First here, of the stars' circular movement; cf. Nonn. D. 4.365 ταχὺς ἀμφιέλικτος (δράκων).

379 ὁμηγερέας A Homeric word, of the Greek army A 57 ὁμηγερέες τ᾽ ἐγένοντο, and of the gods O 84 ὁμηγερέεσσι.

οἱ ἐείσατο An extension of the Homeric impersonal use, e.g. η 343 τῷ δ᾽ ἀσπαστὸν ἐείσατο κοιμηθῆναι. Cf. Lat. uisum est.

380 ἐπιτάξ Not as LSJ 'in a row', but 'in an orderly pattern'; in a different sense Call. fr. 178.9 'by previous arrangement'. Hellad. Chrest.

ap. Phot. *Bibl.* 532a, VIII Henry (Budé 1978), ἐπιτάξ *apud Callimachum et Aratum.*

381 ἄφαρ β 95 ἄφαρ δ' ἡμῖν μετέειπε.

ἐγένοντο Editors from Aldus to Voss read γένοιντο, but it is not satisfactory to make this verb also depend on ὄφρα. ἄφαρ δ' introduces the next stage, and an indicative is required, coupled by καί with τέλλεται. Subsequent editors read γένοντο, but in view of A.'s regular practice in the use of the augment (see note on 375), it seems better to print ἐγένοντο here, as in 129, 922, 964, 1134. On the pl. verb with n.pl. subject see 13, 377, 385, al.

382 ὑπὸ θαύματι τέλλεται Sch. 379 οὐκέτι ἐν θαύματι ἀνατέλλει ἀστήρ. There is no need to emend ὑπό, since sch. ἐν is merely a prose version of the poet's ὑπό, as is ἀνατέλλει for τέλλεται. A. here returns to the theme of regularity, as in 371: we now recognise the regularity of the stars, because we can identify them from the constellations, and no star-rising takes us by surprise. On τέλλεται with reference to rising, see note on 285.

383 ἐναρηρότες The verb is appropriate to a man-made design; cf. ε 236 εὖ ἐναρηρός, and φ 45 *in tmesi.* This line is perhaps recalled in A.R. 3.1004 οὐρανίοις ἐνελίσσεται εἰδώλοισιν.

384–385 The concluding lines of the passage bring us back to the beginning and so renew the link with the context. The conclusion of the chiastic pattern is marked by much variation, ἔνερθε . . . Λαγωοῦ of ὑπὸ πλευρῆσι Λαγωοῦ (369), μάλ' ἠερόεντα of ὀλίγη . . . αἴγλη (367), οὐκ ὀνομαστὰ φέρονται of εἰλίσσονται . . . νώνυμοι (368–70). There is a similarity in A.R. 3.801 λωβήεντα καὶ οὐκ ὀνομαστὰ τελέσσαι.

386–388 The Southern Fish
A. gives only the position, orientation and name of this constellation here, the same again at 701–2, and a reference to its back in 572. Its origin may be the Babylonian KUA 'fish' (Waerden *EW* 68); its first appearance in Greek is in Eudox. fr. 76 ἥ τε οὐρὰ τοῦ Νοτίου Ἰχθύος. Hipparchus also refers to the bright star in its mouth, which must be the 1st-mag. star Fomalhaut, but A. notes this as an unattached star (397), and his plan of this constellation therefore does not quite correspond to that of Hipparchus and the modern Piscis Austrinus. The standard Greek name is Νότιος Ἰχθύς, otherwise simply Ἰχθύς or ὁ μέγας καλούμενος Ἰχθύς (*Catast.* 38). In Latin *Piscis* is common, otherwise *Australis Piscis* (Cic. fr. 33.167), *Piscis Austrinus* (Vitr. 9.5.3), *Notius Piscis* (Man. 1.438), with such variations as *Piscem quem dicimus Austri* (Cic. 171), *geminis diuersus Piscibus unus* (Germ. 379), *Austri . . . incola Piscis* (Avien. 1081). Roscher VI 1019–20.

386 νειόθι δ' Αἰγοκερῆος Actually south-east of Capricorn. **ὑπὸ πνοιῇσι νότοιο** Cf. 355, with note on the custom of naming directions after winds. The use of ὑπό c. dat. recalls δ 402 πνοιῇ ὕπο Ζεφύροιο, of the conditions under which Proteus emerges from the sea. From the point of view of the Greeks the Fish lies in the latitudes from which their south wind comes.

387 Ἰχθῦς On the accent see Hdn 2.615, 22L πάντα τὰ εἰς ῦς περισπώμενα ὑπὲρ μίαν συλλαβὴν ὄντα ὑποκοριστικά ἐστιν ... χωρὶς ... τοῦ ὀσφῦς, ὀφρῦς, ἰχθῦς. **ἐς Κῆτος τετραμμένος** A. gives the position with reference to a constellation already described. The Water from the jar of the Waterpourer is actually closer (sch. 386 ὃν κάπτειν λέγουσιν ὕδωρ ἀπὸ τῆς τοῦ Ὑδροχόου ἐκχύσεως), but the latter has not yet been introduced. A line with a sole dactyl in the fourth foot is rare in Homer, e.g. Θ 472 (Ludwich 27). Cf. 731, 1006. **αἰωρεῖται** Sch. ἤτοι ἁπλῶς φέρεται, ἢ τὸ κυριώτερος, ἐπειδήπερ ἐπὶ νότον ἐστὶν ἄνω αἰωρουμένη καὶ μετεωριζομένην ἔχει τὴν ὄψιν ὡς ἐπὶ τὸ Κῆτος. The word is perhaps chosen to suggest the constellation hovering low over the southern horizon. Cf. 403 of the Altar, which is even farther south.

388 οἶος The single Fish in the south is thus distinguished from the two Fishes in the north (239ff.). **κικλήσκουσιν** δ 355 Φάρον δέ ἑ κικλήσκουσι. Cf. Β 813 and Hes. *Op.* 818 also in same *sedes.*

389–401 The Water

This is an area of faint stars that do not combine to make a recognisable figure. They lie south-east of the Water-pourer, between the Seamonster and the Southern Fish, and they include a cascade of stars running down from the Water-pourer's hand and two bright individual stars. There is a smaller group below the Archer.

The Water is not a distinct enough group to be useful for identifying particular stars, and so it never became a regular constellation. Hipparchus makes mention of τοῦ ἐν τῷ Ὑδροχόῳ ὕδατος (2.6.3), and Ptolemy τῶν ἐπὶ τῆς ῥύσεως τοῦ ὕδατος (8.1.32), but Geminus lists it as a separate constellation (3.13). Cic. fr. 33.179 and Avien. 841 follow A. in calling the group *Aqua*, but Germanicus omits the name (387–8).

389 σποράδην Alex. Aphr. *in Mete.* p. 42, 19 Hayduck πλήρης γὰρ ὁ τόπος φαίνεται ὢν μεγίστων τε καὶ λαμπροτάτων ἄστρων "καὶ ἔτι τῶν σποράδων καλουμένων" [346a20]. εἴη δ' ἂν ἄστρα μὲν ... ὢν καὶ Ἄρατος μνημονεύει, σποράδας δὲ τοὺς καθ' αὑτοὺς ὄντας, περὶ ὧν καὶ Ἄρατος οὕτως μνημονεύει λέγων [389].

Ὑδροχοῆι A variant form (see note on 282–299), also in Nonn. *D.* 23.315.

390 Κήτεος αἰθερίοιο Repeated in 720.

ἠερέθονται The choice of this verb for a swarm of faint stars may have been suggested by Φ 12, of locusts, ὅθ' ὑπὸ ῥιπῆς πυρὸς ἀκρίδες ἠερέθονται. The sense is similar to that of αἰωρεῖται (387, 403), both verbs being related to ἀείρω.

391 νωχελέες Prop. 'sluggish', hence 'weak' in E. *Or.* 800 πλευρὰ νωχελῆ νόσῳ, only here of stars. Cf. νωχελίη, a Homeric *hapax*, of the gods' weakness (T 411).

392 δεξιτερῆς ἀπὸ χειρός The stars γ ζ η π Aquarii, which also represent the cup: see note on 282–299.

ἀγαυοῦ Cf. 71, 90, 469, also of stars.

393 χύσις ὕδατος A simile for the band of faint stars that runs south-west and then south-east from the cup. In Hipparchus and Ptolemy ὕδωρ is the specific name for these stars, *Catast.* 26 is allusive with ἔκχυσιν πολλὴν ποιεῖται ὑγροῦ. In ε 483, 487 and τ 443 χύσις is used of a pile of leaves. Imitations of A. appear in A.R. 4.1416 πετραίην χύσιν ὕδατος, Mus. 327 χύσις ὕδατος, Nonn. *D.* 38.318 χύσιν ἄστρων.

ἔνθα καὶ ἔνθα A Homeric phrase (β 213, al.). Sch. διὰ τὰς καμπὰς τῶν ἐκχεομένων ὑδάτων. Cf. 855, of the sun's rays.

394 σκιδναμένου Both σκίδναμαι and κίδναμαι are Homeric, but the latter is used only of dawn spreading over land (Θ 1) or sea (Ψ 227), whereas the former is used of water in η 129–30 δύω κρῆναι ἡ μέν τ' ἀνὰ κῆπον ἅπαντα | σκίδναται, and is therefore more likely to have been A.'s choice here, especially at the beginning of a line. This form also enhances the alliterative effect of the sibilants in these two lines, which may be thought of as suggesting the sound of falling water. Contrast 735 ἀποκίδναται, of moonlight.

χαροποί This adj. has a range of meanings (Hsch. περιχαρής, γλαυκός, ξανθός, φοβερός), and the sense in particular cases is often unclear. It is used most characteristically as an epithet of eyes, especially of animals' eyes, e.g. λ 611 χαροποί τε λέοντες, the sole Homeric example, and similarly Hes. *Th.* 321, *Sc.* 177. Cf. *h.Hom.* 4.194 χαροποί τε κύνες, S. *Ph.* 1146 χαροπῶν τ' ἔθνη θηρῶν, Ar. *Pax* 1065 χαροποῖσι πιθήκοις. X. *Cyn.* 3.3.2–3 lists this quality as a defect in dogs, Arist. *HA* 492a3 and *GA* 779b14 as a colour which is distinguished from γλαυκός. When used later of human eyes the work seems to suggest a bright gleam, e.g. Theoc. 12.35 χαροπὸν Γανυμήδεα, 20.25 ὄμματά μοι γλαυκᾶς χαροπώτερα πολλὸν Ἀθάνας, Asclep. *AP* 5.153.3–4 χαροπαὶ Κλεόφωντος ... γλυκεροῦ βλέμματος ἀστεροπαί. Here the adj. is coupled with ἀναλδέες, and the stars in this group are certainly all faint, so that χαροποί can hardly suggest any degree of brightness. It must therefore describe a colour, and something like 'greyish' would not be inappropriate. Though these stars are faint, they are numerous, and could be seen as having a kind of pale luminosity, rather like the Pleiades. A. uses the adj. similarly of the Hare (594), but also of the moon (1152), where it presumably describes a subdued brightness. Here A. may have chosen an adj. that would suit both the stars and the water they are likened to: cf. Orph. fr. 245.21 χαροποῖο θαλάσσης, Mel. *AP* 12.53.4 = *HE* 4331 εἰς χαροπὸν δερκομέναν πέλαγος, Maced. *AP* 9.275.2 = *GP* 2547 χαροποῖς κύμασιν. See Gow on Theoc. 12.35. Maxwell-Stuart (2.92) takes the basic colour to be 'a pale off-yellow'.

395 ἐειδόμενοι Prop. 'appearing', as in 828, here as adj. 'bright'; cf. 1042 ἐείδηται with λαμπρός.

396 οὔτε τι α 202 οὔτε τι μάντις ἐὼν οὔτ' οἰωνῶν σάφα εἰδώς. Cf. 460.

ἀπήοροι Only here in epic; lit. 'hovering afar' (ἀείρω), here 'apart'. Pi. *P.* 8.86 c. gen. ἐχθρῶν ἀπάοροι. This line is repeated without variation in 895. For the sense cf. 1117 οὔτε σχεδὸν οὔτ' ἀποτηλοῦ.

397 εἷς μέν This must be α Piscis Austrini, now known as Fomalhaut: see note on 386–388. It lies due south of δ Aquarii, the right foot of that figure, and south-east of the left (1).

398 ὁ δέ The only available bright star seems to be β Ceti, which is actually one of the two tail stars of the Monster in Hi. 2.2.49 τῶν γὰρ ἐν τῇ οὐρᾷ αὐτοῦ δύο λαμπρῶν ὁ μὲν νοτιώτερος. A. may have taken only the more northerly of the two (ι Ceti) as the tail star, which would suit the sense of 502, since ι was then closer to the southern tropic than β. So Eudox. fr. 73 τοῦ Κήτους ἡ οὐρά.

κυανέου The dark colour (cf. 329) suggests both the lack of bright stars in this constellation and the colour of the imagined marine creature.

399 Ὕδωρ See note on 389–401.

400 νειόθι Τοξευτῆρος A. now shifts to a different part of the sky, two zodiacal constellations farther west. Sch. identify this nameless group as the curved line of stars that later became a separate constellation with its own name and mythological associations: εἰσὶ δὲ καὶ ἄλλοι ὁμοίως ἀφανέστεροι ἐν κύκλου περιγραφῇ οὓς τῶν νεωτέρων τινὲς Οὐρανίσκον καλοῦσιν, οἱ δὲ Νότιον Στέφανον, εἶναι δὲ αὐτὸν οἱ μὲν Προμηθέως, οἱ δὲ Ἰξίονος τροχόν. These stars (now γ α β δ Coronae Austrinae) lie to the south of the body of the Archer, but close on the west side of the forelegs, if the latter include the stars α β. Germanicus clarifies the position with *est et sine honore Corona | ante Sagittiferi paulum*

325

pernicia crura (391–2). If the identification is correct, A. must be using ὑπό c. dat. in the sense of 'close to', as of a small object dominated by a larger, e.g. ξ 533 πέτρη ὑπο γλαφυρῇ εὖδον, Β 866 ὑπὸ Τμώλῳ γεγαῶτες. It appears so on the Farnese globe.

Hipparchus makes no reference to this group, nor do the meagre fragments of Eudoxus, nor *Catast.*, Vitruvius, Manilius. But Gem. 3.13 lists it as a separate constellation, Νότιος Στέφανος, ὑπὸ δέ τινων Οὐρανίσκος προσαγορευόμενος, and Ptolemy Στέφανος Νότιος, his penultimate constellation. Hyg. 3.26 fin. calls it *Corona Centauri*. Gundel, *RE* 3A.2359ff.

401 δινωτοί The adj. suggests the work of a craftsman, as in τ 56 (κλισίην) δινωτὴν ἐλέφαντι καὶ ἀργύρῳ. Cf. 440, 462. It may have been this description that led to the forming of the new constellation Corona. Grotius' ἄγνωτοι (ΑΓ *e* ΔΙ), adopted by Martin, is based on Cic. fr. 33.182 *obscurae sine nomine cedunt* and Germ. 391 *sine honore*. But the Latin translations are often too free to be reliable evidence for a conjectural reading in the Greek text. *Sphaera* 54 δινωτὸς ἄστρων κύκλος ἀμφέλισσεται.

περιηγέες Emped. fr. 28 σφαῖρος κυκλοτερὴς μονίη περιηγέϊ γαίων. A.R. 3.138 imitates A. with διπλόαι ἀψῖδες περιηγέες εἰλίσσονται. Cf. Call. *H.* 2.59, 4.198, fr. 342, Opp. *C.* 1.189, *H.* 1.216, 3.81.

402–450 Altar group: the Altar, the Centaur, the Beast,
the Hydra, the Bowl, the Raven, Procyon

402–30 The Altar

The Altar, below the Scorpion, is the converse of Arcturus in the north. It was put there by Night to help sailors: it is a sign of storm when seen overarched by clouds, and sailors should then trim their ship and prepare for a southerly, until they see lightning in the north.

A. begins this group with the Altar because he can lead into it from the familiar and very conspicuous Scorpion. It was a small group near the extreme southern limit of the visible sky, with no star brighter than 3rd mag., and probably hard to identify without the Scorpion's tail as a guide. A. makes no reference to any particular part of it, but the curved line of the stars θ α ε Arae could have been seen as representing the top, and β γ ζ the base. This would correspond to the upright figure on the Farnese globe. Hipparchus and Ptolemy, however, give the figure a different orientation.

The origin of this constellation is unknown. It has not been identified clearly with any Babylonian group, and an Egyptian source has been thought more likely: see Gundel *RE* 6A.757–8 and Roscher VI 1017. In

Greek it is attested first in Eudox. fr. 74 as Θυμιατήριον, one of the constellations that mark the limit of visibility (ὁ ἀφανὴς κύκλος), and this is the standard name in Hipparchus (1.8.14, al.), Geminus (3.13), and Ptolemy (*Alm.* 8.1.46). For metrical reasons A. uses Θυτήριον. Later names are Βωμός (*Sphaera* 49, Maass p. 158) and Νέκταρ (*Catast.* 39). The standard Latin name is *Ara*, but Germ. 394 has *Turibulum*, going back to Θυμιατήριον.

402 αἰθομένῳ κέντρῳ Cf. 305, where the sting is a guide to the Archer. Here the Altar is due south of the whole curve of the Scorpion below the sting. The epithet suits the brilliance of these stars, two of which are 2nd-mag., and it may also suggest the effect of a real scorpion's sting: sch. αἰθόμενον δὲ αὐτό φησι τὸ κέντρον ὡς πρὸς τὰ τοῦ Σκορπίου δήγματα. ἔνιοι γὰρ σφόδρα διάπυρον ἔχουσι τοῦ κέντρου τὸ τύμμα.

403 ἄγχι νότοιο The Altar is so far south that it seems close to the pole, though sch. exaggerate with καὶ τοῦ νοτίου πόλου ἐπιψαῦον.

Θυτήριον The only earlier use of this noun is as 'sacrificial victim' in E. *IT* 243. It appears later in Q.S. 4.553ff. as a storm sign in imitation of this passage: ὅτ' εὐρέα πόντον ὀρίνει | λαίλαπι καὶ ῥιπῇσι, Θυτήριον εὖτ' ἀλεγεινόν | ἀντέλλῃ ναύτῃσι φέρον πολύδακρον ὀϊζύν. Sch. (M) θυτήριόν ἐστι λιβανώτιδι ὅμοιον: it is as a censer that it is represented on the Farnese globe. It was at some time linked with mythology as the altar on which the gods swore their oath against Cronus (sch. S and *Catast.* 39), and against the Titans (sch. M and Hyg. 2.39).

αἰωρεῖται See note on 387.

404 ὑψόθ' ἐόντος Merely above the horizon (cf. 558 ὑψόθι γαίης), but in this case not high above it. The words seem chosen to echo Κ 16 ὑψόθ' ἐόντι of Zeus and Ρ 676 ὑψόθ' ἐόντα of an eagle, and the case here is no doubt a conscious variation.

405 πεύσεαι Of becoming aware of something by observation, a shade of meaning not given by LSJ. This form occurs once in Homer (Σ 19), in the same metrical position, but with the normal meaning of hearing a message.

ἀντιπέρην γὰρ ἀείρεται Ἀρκτούροιο A. appears to be saying that the Altar moves across the sky (cf. 326) opposite Arcturus, and it is not immediately clear what he means. The earliest interpretation is that of Attalus, who took the sense to be that the Altar bears the same relation to the south pole as Arcturus does to the north: περὶ δὲ τοῦ Θυμιατηρίου ποιούμενος τὸν λόγον φησὶν αὐτὸ κεῖσθαι πρὸς τὸν ἀφανῆ πόλον οὕτως ἔχον, ὡς ἀστὴρ ὁ καλούμενος Ἀρκτοῦρος πρὸς τὸν φανερὸν πόλον. διό φησι τοῦ Θυμιατηρίου τὴν ὑπὲρ γῆς φορὰν βραχεῖαν εἶναι, τοῦ δὲ Ἀρκτούρου πολλήν (fr. 18 Maass). His second sentence certainly expresses what A. says, but Attalus does not explain how it follows from the first. Hipparchus agrees with Attalus' first sentence, but explains it with reference to polar distances: ὅσον ἀπέχει ὁ Ἀρκτοῦρος ἀπὸ τοῦ ἀεὶ φανεροῦ πόλου (1.8.14). He then goes on (16) to refute both A. and Attalus by showing that the Altar and Arcturus are far from being equidistant from their respective poles: in fact Arcturus is 59° from the north pole and the central star in the Altar 46° from the south pole. Mair and Martin accept this explanation, together with the implication of an error on the part of A. So also Schott in his note on 405–6 (p. 64). Ovenden (94) estimates that this would be right for 2300 BC!

The Latin translators transmit a simplified interpretation, that the Altar in the far south lies opposite Arcturus in the far north: Cic. fr. 33.186 *nam procul Arcturo aduersa est de parte locata*, Germ. 394 *Turibulum uicinum Austris sacro igne uidebis*, Avien. 849–54 in a more laboured version. J. Soubiran, in his note on Cicero's line (p. 210), understands the sense of the Greek as 'il se lève en opposition avec Arcture', but notes that Arcturus would already have been on the meridian when the Altar was rising; cf. Erren *PAS* 66–7. There could admittedly be a kind of opposition between the two, when the Altar is low in the south-east and Arcturus still high in the north-west.

But it is more satisfactory to interpret this line with reference to the two following lines, as Attalus did, the point of the contrast being the comparative length of the two arcs above the horizon: Arcturus describes a very large arc, the Altar a very small one (406–7; cf. 404 ὀλίγον . . . ἐπὶ χρόνον). This certainly depends to some extent on their polar distances, but more essentially on the latitude of the observer. Erren (*PAS* 66) calculates that for an observer at 37° N the Altar would have been above the horizon for about $4\frac{1}{2}$ hours and Arcturus below it for the same length of time. They were therefore respectively below and above the horizon for about $19\frac{1}{2}$ hours. It is in this respect, then, that the Altar is the opposite of Arcturus, and A. is not at all in error: what he particularly has in mind is the comparative periods of visibility, since these are directly observable. Cf. 406–7. ἀείρεται thus refers to the movement across the sky (cf. 326, 558), not to the moment of rising, as understood by Mair and Erren. My note in *CQ* 31 (1981) 360–1 is here expanded and to some extent corrected. The confused passage in Avien. 849–54 proves to be right for the Altar in 853–4 *breuis olli semita caeli | occasusque celer*. Q.S. 13.482 ἀντιπέρηθε δυσαέος Ἀρκτούροιο echoes 405.

406 πάγχυ Ionic form of πάνυ, frequent in Homer, e.g. Ξ 143, ρ 217 with μάλα in same *sedes*. The emphatic adverbs bring out the fact that Arcturus passed right overhead.

μετήοροι Twice in Homer (Θ 26, Ψ 369). A. uses it again of stars above the horizon in 573, 610, and of the upper horn of the crescent moon in 794.

407 Ἀρκτούρῳ There is no need to adopt, with Maass and Martin, τοῦ Ἀρκτούρου from Hi. 1.8.14, which was probably a misquotation influenced by Attalus' paraphrase (quoted on 405). The dative is confirmed by sch. καὶ τῷ μὲν Ἀρκτούρῳ σφόδρα μετέωροι καὶ μεγάλαι εἰσὶν αἱ περιφοραί. A. probably chose the dat. as a case variation after the preceding gen.

θᾶσσον As often, with a sense of immediacy rather than a simple comparison: cf. Β 440 ἴομεν, ὄφρα κε θᾶσσον ἐγείρομεν ὀξὺν Ἄρηα. The Altar's visible arc is not just shorter but very short compared with that of Arcturus.

ὑφ' ἑσπερίην ἅλα νεῖται Cf. Ψ 51 νέεσθαι ὑπὸ ζόφον ἠερόεντα.

408 ἀλλ' ἄρα καί In this run of particles ἄρα draws attention to an interesting phenomenon, while the other two contrast its importance with the stars' very brief appearance. The transition to the extended passage on stormy weather at sea depends on the fact that the Altar is a winter constellation. At 692 it is listed as rising simultaneously with the rising of Capricorn, and at 710 it sets as the Ram rises. It is therefore visible at night during the latter part of the winter, and can be used as a weather sign because it is seen almost due south, the direction from which the prevailing wind blows in winter.

ἀρχαίη Νύξ Here Night, as the night sky, is synonymous with Zeus as the power that gives men helpful signs out of sympathy for their suffering; cf. the Goat and Kids in 159. The epithet ἀρχαίη looks back to Hesiod, who in *Th.* 123 names Erebus and Night as the prime divinities created out of Chaos. Hesiod's epithets for Night are μέλαινα (20, 123), δνοφερή (107), ἐρεβεννή (213), ὀλοή (224, 757), ἐρεμνή (744, 758). A. improves on this gloomy image of Night by making the goddess sympathetic, just as he reforms the Hesiodic Zeus: see note on 5 ἤπιος. Personified Night recurs in 419, 434, 470.

In Homer νύξ occurs at the end of a line preceded by ἀμφιλύκη (Η 433), ἀμβροσίη (δ 429, 574, η 283), οὐρανόθεν (ι 69, μ 315), and the unusual παροίχωκεν δὲ πλέων (Κ 252). A. is close to the Homeric model in 470 and 695, but here the spondaic fifth foot gives a certain solemnity to the line; cf. Δ 182 εὐρεῖα χθών. Hes. *Th.* 726 ἀμφὶ δέ μιν νύξ, Theoc. 2.60 ἇς ἔτι καὶ νύξ.

410 εἰναλίου ε 67 εἰνάλιαι in same *sedes*.

κεδαιόμεναι Cf. 159 in similar context, also A.R. 2.626. Sch. variously ἀποφθειρόμεναι, χειματόμεναι, σκεδαννύμεναι, σκορπιζόμεναι.

ἐκείνῃ Sc. τῇ Νυκτί.

411 ἀπὸ φρενός A variation of Homeric ἀπὸ θυμοῦ denoting displeasure, e.g. A 562–3 πρῆξαι δ' ἔμπης οὔ τι δυνήσεαι, ἀλλ' ἀπὸ θυμοῦ | μᾶλλον ἐμοὶ ἔσεαι. Sch. οὐκ ἀρέσκουσιν αὐτῇ, ἀποθύμιαί εἰσιν. The v.l. ἄπο derives from the usage of some grammarians when the sense is 'far from'. Sch. D.T. 271, 16 Hilgard καὶ ἡ ἀπό, ὅταν γένηται ἄπο, ἐπίρρημα σημαίνει, οἷον ἄπο πτολέμοιο μένοντα· σημαίνει γὰρ ἐνταῦθα τὸ ἄποθεν (Σ 64). Aristarchus, however, read ἀπό. K–B 1.333.

πιφαύσκει Frequent in Homer, especially of revealing in words, e.g. μ 165 τὰ ἕκαστα λέγων ἑτάροισι πίφαυσκον, ψ 202 οὕτω τοι τόδε σῆμα πιφαύσκομαι. Sch. πανταχόθεν πολλὰ τεκμήρια ἐπιδείκνυται. Cf. Emped. 17.15 πιφαύσκων πείρατα μύθων.

412 πολυρροθίους First attested here, probably modelled on Homeric παλιρρόθιος (ε 430, ι 485), of waves. A. has transferred the sense to men caught in the roaring waves, but Q.S. 7.395 πολυρροθίοιο θαλάσσης reverts to the Homeric use. The four-word line makes an effective conclusion to this long sentence on Night.

413 τῷ μή μοι The warning is stressed by the negative at the beginning of the sentence, as in 287. Here again the 1st pers. pron. adds a note of personal concern that is in keeping with the cosmic sympathy of the context: see note on 154.

νεφέων εἰλυμένον ἄλλων The MSS tradition essentially supports this reading, and the sense of 413–14 is explained by sch. (M): μὴ δή, φησίν, ἐν πελάγει μέσῳ ὤν, τῶν πλησίον τοῦ Θυτηρίου καὶ ἀνωτέρων ἄλλων ἀστέρων ὑπὸ νεφῶν κεκαλυμμένων, εὔχου αὐτὸ ἐν μέσῳ οὐρανοῦ ἀνέφελον καὶ εὐσύνοπτον ἰδεῖν, and again, μὴ οὖν, φησίν, ἐν μέσῳ πελάγει ὤν, εὔχου ἰδεῖν τὰ μὲν ἀνωτέρω αὐτοῦ ἄστρα κεκαλυμμένα νέφεσιν, αὐτὸ δὲ ἀνέφελον. Cf. sch. (D) τουτέστιν ἐκ νεφῶν ἄλλων εἰλυμένον τὸ Θυτήριον. The weather conditions, then, are such that the Altar is seen low in the south and clear, while the sky above it is heavily clouded. Thus εἰλυμένον, lit. 'wrapped round', will mean that the constellation has an arch of clouds enclosing it. The same verb is used in 432 of a slight haze covering a star, but the different meaning here is confirmed by 415, which shows that the constellation itself is visible. The unusual instr. gen. is a feature of A.'s syntax, e.g. 564 ὄρεος κεκρυμμέναι, 842 νεφέων πεπιεσμένος. The main problem is the interpretation of ἄλλων.

A variant εἰλυμένῳ is given by sch. (M): ἔνιοι δὲ τὸ εἰλυμένον εἰλυμένῳ γράφουσι, καὶ συνάπτουσιν αὐτὸ τῷ πελάγει, ἵν' ᾖ οὕτως· ὅπως μὴ ἐγκεκλεισμένος ᾖς τῷ πελάγει. So Buttmann's εἰλυμένος ἀχλύϊ of the seaman. This is a confused explanation: it takes the participle first with the sea and then with the person, and both of these are impossible, since it is in the sky that the clouds are located. Martin has adopted the dative, together with Grotius' ἄλλῳ, and construed both words with οὐρανῷ, translating 'au milieu d'un ciel enveloppé de nuages partout ailleurs'. So Erren, 'bei sonst von Wolken verhülltem Himmel'. This gives the right kind of sense, but it involves two changes to the traditional text, and imposes on 413 an excess of datives, as well as the awkwardness of having to construe two of them with another in the next line.

We must revert, then, to the original text, taking εἰλυμένον, in the sense of 'overarched', with ἄστρον, and ἄλλων with νεφέων, which is what the run of the words would suggest; any interpretation that involves detaching ἄλλων from νεφέων is certainly very implausible. The problem of ἄλλων can be better resolved by understanding it in its pleonastic sense. It is not, however, superfluous: it is intended to contrast the clouds everywhere else with the visible constellation. Cf. Δ 81 ὧδε δέ τις εἴπεσκεν ἰδὼν ἐς πλησίον ἄλλον, and especially S. OT 6–7 ἀγὼ δικαιῶν μὴ παρ' ἀγγέλων, τέκνα, | ἄλλων ἀκούειν αὐτὸς ὧδ' ἐλήλυθα, where ἄλλων stresses the contrast between hearsay and first-hand information.

This interpretation is confirmed by the pattern of 413–16, in which A. makes artistic play with the antithesis between the visibility of the Altar and the mass of clouds above and on either side of it. The arrangement is in the form of a chiasmus, in which νεφέων εἰλυμένον (413) is answered by νέφει πεπιεσμένον (416), and φανήμεναι (414) by ἀνέφελόν τε καὶ ἀγλαόν (415). Thus the verbal pattern (banked clouds – Altar clear – Altar clear – banked clouds) is designed to illustrate the actual scene that the poet is describing. See my article in *CQ* 31 (1981) 361–2.

The Latin poets do not attempt to introduce this chiastic figure, but they give the essential meaning of the Altar being clear in an otherwise cloudy sky: Cic. fr. 33.192ff. *nam cum fulgentem cernes sine nubibus atris | Aram sub media caeli regione locatam, | a summa parte obscura caligine tectam . . . ,* Germ. 402–3 *si sordebunt cetera caeli | nubibus obductis, illo splendente . . . ,* Avien. 857ff. *ne tibi, cum denso conducitur aere caelum, | inter nimbiferas nubes spectabilis exstet | Ara poli.*

414 μεσσόθι Mair construes with ἄλλων, translating 'amidst the others' (cf. 368, 511 c. gen.). But this does not make sense in the context, since the Altar is the only constellation visible; ἄλλων should go with νεφέων (see preceding note). It is better to take μεσσόθι with οὐρανῷ (sch. ἐν μέσῳ οὐρανοῦ), with the specific sense of 'on the meridian', which is roughly the position of the Altar under the conditions here described. Cf. 231 with μέγαν οὐρανόν, with reference to the equator.

φανήμεναι The context requires the sense of 'being sighted', not of 'shining brightly', and so φανήμεναι is to be preferred to φαήμεναι. Cf. I 240 ἄρᾶται δὲ τάχιστα φανήμεναι Ἠῶ δῖαν.

415 ἀνέφελον Once in Homer, ζ 45 πέπταται ἀνέφελος, a famous passage describing the αἴθρη where the gods live. Cf. 826, 858, Call. fr. 238.18, Q.S. 9.5. For lengthening before ν cf. 852 περὶ νέφεα: Chantraine 1.177, Wyatt 82.

416 κυμαίνοντι An imaginative metaphor that suggests clouds being piled up by the wind like waves on a beach. The rarity of this word-type in this position draws attention to the metaphor; cf. 67 ὀκλάζοντι, the only other instance in A. The Homeric model is ὀτρύνοντι, which occurs only in Δ 414. Altogether I have noted 47 instances (34 different words) in the *Iliad*, and 40 instances (24 different words) in the *Odyssey*. See O'Neill 146, Table 21.

νέφει πεπιεσμένον Cf. 842, of the sun, νεφέων πεπιεσμένος.

417 θλίβετ' The effect of air pressure; cf. Pl. *Ti.* 91a τῷ πνεύματι θλιφθέν. For the elision see note on 293.

ἀναστέλλοντος Apparently a technical term for wind piling up clouds; sch. φιλεῖ γὰρ προαναστέλλειν ὁ πνεῖν μέλλων ἄνεμος τὰ ὑπερκείμενα νέφη καὶ πυκνοῦν. Cf. Arist. *Pr.* 943a35 οἱ ἄνεμοι ἀναστέλλουσι τὰ νέφη.

ὀπωρινοῦ With ι long, as always in Homer; also in Hes. *Op.* 677, but not 674. Cf. 948 ὀρθρινόν.

βορέαο This is the reading of almost all MSS and of all editions before Voss, who adopted the v.l. ἀνέμοιο, because it is the south wind, not the north, that packs the clouds above the Altar. Voss refers to Hes. *Op.* 674–7 on the first onset of stormy weather at the end of summer: ὀπωρινὸν ὄμβρον | καὶ χειμῶν' ἐπιόντα Νότοιό τε δεινὰς ἀήτας, | ὅς τ' ὤρινε θάλασσαν ὁμαρτήσας Διὸς ὄμβρῳ | πολλῷ ὀπωρινῷ, χαλεπὸν δέ τε πόντον ἔθηκεν. The variant appears to be supported by the sch. ὁ πνεῖν μέλλων ἄνεμος, and by Avien. 861 *uento*. On the other hand οἷά τε introduces a comparison, and this can just as well refer to a similar phenomenon of banked-up clouds caused by other winds at other seasons. Now the Altar is a winter constellation (see on 408), and the southerly is the prevailing wind in winter. But the comparative clause refers to autumn weather, and a northerly is perfectly appropriate in this season: Φ 346–7 ὡς δ' ὅτ' ὀπωρινὸς Βορέης νεοαρδέ' ἀλωὴν | αἶψ' ἀγξηράνῃ, ε 328–9. ὡς δ' ὅτ' ὀπωρινὸς Βορέης φορέῃσιν ἀκάνθας | ἂμ πεδίον, the latter in a passage describing strong winds at sea. A.'s choice of a north wind here may therefore be a conscious literary reminiscence, especially as the storm in *Od.* 5 is very much in the background throughout this extended passage. Boreas is also associated with driving clouds in Ψ 213 νέφεα κλονέοντε πάροιθεν and Hes. *Op.* 553 πυκνὰ Θρηικίου Βορέω νέφεα κλονέοντος. Moreover, καί in 418 ('also for a southerly') makes sense if the preceding reference has been to a northerly: it is conveniently ignored in Avien. 864. The v.l. ἀνέμοιο can be explained as having come from the sch., and there is no good reason for rejecting the transmitted reading. Cf. Q.S. 8.91 ἐπιόντος ὀπωρινοῦ βορέαο.

418 νότῳ ἔπι Cf. ἐπί in 725, 873, 994, 1093.

τιτύσκει Epic verb, here in sense of τεύχω. It occurs only here in A., and may have been suggested by Φ 342 Ἥφαιστος δὲ τιτύσκετο θεσπιδαὲς πῦρ, which is in the same context as ὀπωρινὸς Βορέης, cited on 417. The active is post-Homeric, being first attested in B. 5.49 νίκαν Ἱέρωνι φιλοξείνῳ τιτύσκων.

419 μογεροῖσι χαριζομένη ναύτῃσιν A reiteration of ἀνθρώπων κλαίουσα πόνον (409) and ἐποικτείρουσα πολυρροθίους ἀνθρώπους (412), the central theme of this passage.

420–429 A. now shifts the focus of his attention from the sympathy of the cosmic powers to the miseries of human life at sea, even allowing for the helpfulness of the former. This unusually long sentence (cf. 129–36, 367–85, 469–79) is worked out in two contrasting conditions, with the main emphasis given to the second and its consequences. The first consists of two clauses of one line each, with the apodosis expressed in less than a line. The second also has two clauses, which together fill just over two lines, but the apodosis takes up four and a half lines describing the miserable plight of men at sea. The distribution of sense pauses at different metrical points lends variety and a certain momentum to the sentence.

420 ἐναίσιμα A Homeric adj. from αἶσα, combining the senses of 'timely' and 'right', e.g. of omens, Β 353 ἀστράπτων ἐπιδέξι', ἐναίσιμα σήματα φαίνων, β 159 ὄρνιθας γνῶναι καὶ ἐναίσιμα μυθήσασθαι.

421 αἶψα δέ δέ is necessary, as Voss notes, to connect the two clauses, as again in 424; the transmitted τε was probably due to the influence of the following τε.

κουφά τε πάντα καὶ ἄρτια Sch. λέγει δὲ κοῦφα πρὸς τὸ ἐγχαλάσαι τοῖς τοῦ ἁρμένου ποσὶ καὶ μὴ φιλονεικεῖν ἐναντίοις τοῖς πνεύμασιν. The situation is that the sheets (ropes attached to the lower corners of the sail) are taut in order to let the breeze fill the sail, but if the wind is too violent, there is excessive strain on the sail and the sheets have to be eased. Cf. E. *Or.* 706–7 καὶ ναῦς γὰρ ἐνταθεῖσα πρὸς βίαν ποδὶ | ἔβαψεν, ἔστη δ' αὖθις, ἢν χαλᾷ πόδα, S. *Ant.* 715–17 αὕτως δὲ ναὸς ὅστις ἐγκρατῆ πόδα | τείνας ὑπείκει μηδέν, ὑπτίοις κάτω | στρέψας τὸ λοιπὸν σέλμασιν ναυτίλλεται, a figurative warning to Creon to relax and not endanger the state. The technical sense of κοῦφος here is paralleled only in Theoc. 13.52 κουφότερ', ὦ παῖδες, ποιεῖσθ' ὅπλα· πλευστικὸς οὖρος. See Gow's note and sch. εὔλυτα καὶ εὐτρεπῆ ποιεῖτε τὰ ἱστία. There the action required is to get the ship's rigging ready for sailing, here it is a question of getting it ready for a squall. Voss comments 'κοῦφα ποιεῖσθαι τὰ ὅπλα heisst in des Seemanns Sprache, die Geräthe, das Takelwerk ordnen zur Fahrt; denn κοῦφος ist leicht, flink, lauffertig'. In this passage it may also suggest the idea of easing off the tautness of sheets and sail. The context here does not admit of taking κοῦφα in the sense of lightening the ship by jettisoning cargo, as Mair seems to imply in 'quickly lighten their craft', and Martin in 'ils diminuent leur charge'; so Erren in his note on this line. On receiving a gale warning sailors did not immediately throw everything overboard.

ἄρτια expresses a certain orderliness, e.g. Sol. 4.32 Εὐνομίη δ' εὔκοσμα καὶ ἄρτια πάντ' ἀποφαίνει. Here it supplements the sense of readiness in this nautical use of κοῦφα. The easing of tension is also suggested by the runs of dactyls in this line and the next, where alliteration of π is also noticeable.

422 ἐλαφρότερος ... πόνος Cf. Max. 563 ἤ τ' ἂν κουφότερός τε πόνος.

423 ἐμπλήξῃ Χ 469 ἔρκει ἐνιπλήξωσι, of birds. A. uses the verb more imaginatively in 750, of the sun overtaking stars in its annual course.

δεινὴ ἀνέμοιο θύελλα Reminiscent of the storm in ε 317 δεινὴ μισγομένων ἀνέμων ἐλθοῦσα θύελλα, and of Helen's wish in Ζ 346 οἴχεσθαι προφέρουσα κακὴ ἀνέμοιο θύελλα. Cf. Μ 253, κ 54, μ 288, 409. In A.R. 1.1203 ὑψόθεν ἐμπλήξασα θοὴ ἀνέμοιο κατάιξ the variation with the rare κατάιξ suggests that the latter poet is the imitator. Q.S. 13.396 θοαὶ βορέαο θύελλαι.

424 ἀπρόφατος First attested here and 768. Cf. A.R. 2.268, and the adv. in 1.1201, both in the context of a storm simile.

λαίφεα πάντα Not Homeric in this sense, but A. may have had in mind the storm theme in Alc. 326.7–8 λαῖφος δὲ πὰν ζάδηλον ἤδη | καὶ λακίδες μεγάλαι κατ' αὖτο. Cf. h.Hom. 3.406 οὐδ' ἔλυον λαῖφος. Since Greek ships normally carried one large square sail, the pl. may be regarded as poetic, perhaps on the analogy of Homeric ἱστία (ι 70), though it might also suggest the several parts of the sail. Then πάντα will refer to the sail as a whole; cf. A.R. 2.1253 λαίφεα πάντ' ἐτίναξε, Call. H. 4.319 τὰ λαίφη. So λαίφεα in later poets: Antip. AP 10.2.7 = HE 444, Orph. Arg. 765, Q.S. 5.85, [Opp.] C. 2.232, Marc. Arg. AP 10.4.2 = GP 1452, Paul. Sil. AP 10.15.5.

425–426 ἄλλοτε μὲν ... ἄλλοτε δ' Cf. ε 331–2 of winds at sea.

ὑπόβρυχα Once in Homer, ε 319 τὸν δ' ἄρ' ὑπόβρυχα θῆκε πολὺν χρόνον. Cf. *h.Hom.* 33.11–12 τὴν δ' ἄνεμός τε μέγας καὶ κῦμα θαλάσσης | θῆκαν ὑποβρυχίην. In describing the ship as submerged A. may also have in mind the simile in Ο 624–8, especially ἡ δέ τε πᾶσα | ἄχνη ὑπεκρύφθη. Cf. Opp. *H.* 1.145 ὑπόβρυχα μιμνάζουσι, 5.594 δύνοντες ὑπόβρυχα, and Q.S. 13.485 πολλαὶ ὑπόβρυχα νῆες ἀμαλδύνοντ' ἐνὶ πόντῳ, at the rising of the Altar.

426 αἴ κε Aeolic and Homeric, e.g. Δ 353 αἴ κέν τοι τὰ μεμήλῃ. Cf. 770.

παρανισσομένοιο Elsewhere of passing by (*h.Hom.* 3.430, A.R. 2.1030), only here of coming near in order to help.

427 βορέω δὲ πάρ' ἀστράψῃ ἀνέμοιο Confusion in the MSS (see Martin's schema in *HT* 287) allows for two lines of interpretation: (1) a change of wind to the north (-στρέψῃ, -τρέψῃ), (2) lightning in the north (-αστράψῃ). The first is that of sch. τοῦ βορέου ἡ δύναμις ἐναντίῳ τῷ νότῳ πνεύσασα διασκορπίσῃ τὰ νέφη καὶ αἴθραν ποιήσῃ. Boreas is traditionally a clearing wind: cf. ε 296 Βορέης αἰθρηγενέτης, and *D.S.* 53 ὅταν βορέας νεφέλας πολλὰς κινῇ ἐκπνέων μέγας, εὐδίαν σημαίνει. This is the situation implied in Cicero's very free version: *sin grauis inciderit uehementi flamine uentus* (fr. 33.198). Germanicus omits this line, but translates 430 with *quam pars effulserit orbis, | quae Borean caelum spectantibus indicet ortum* (412–13). One difficulty with the Greek text is that the subject of the transitive verb is not clear. It could perhaps be Zeus, but it seems that the v.l. ἀνέμου ἴς was introduced (probably from Hes. *Op.* 518) for the purpose of providing one. Other difficulties are which transitive verb should be preferred, and how to interpret the genitive depending on it. The early editors read παρατρέψῃ ἀνέμοιο, but their standard translation, *etiam uis Boreae superauerit uenti* (Ceporinus, 1523) hardly matched the Greek, nor did it when Buhle adopted ἀνέμου ἴς. Maass, reading παραστρέψῃ, takes the verb intransitively, with ἀνέμου ἴς as subject, but this only shows up the difficulty of making sense of this text.

On the other hand the reference to lightning suits both the language and the context: ἀστράψῃ is impersonal and intransitive, the gen. can depend on παρά, and the sense is repeated in 430. Avien. 871 *si Boreae stringat rutili coma fulguris auras* supports this interpretation. Moreover lightning in the north is a standard weather sign, as in *D.S.* 33 ἐὰν νότου πνέοντος βορράθεν ἀστράπτῃ, παύεται. And since *D.S.* represents A.'s source for much of the material in 778–1141, it is likely to have played the same part here too. In this context Βορέω ἀνέμοιο means not the wind but the direction, as in Hdt. 2.101 τὰ πρὸς βορέην ἄνεμον τετραμμένα προπύλαια. Cf. 355, 386. There remains only the minor problem of the compound verb, which is not attested elsewhere and does not have an obvious meaning. Martin's πάρ' ἀστράψῃ offers a simple solution, and is almost certainly right.

428 ὀτλήσαντες Cogn. with τλῆναι, the o- prefixed for rhythmical reasons (Frisk 2.440). This verb is Hellenistic, e.g. Call. fr. 303 κενεὸν πόνον ὀτλήσοντες, A.R. 3.769, 4.1227, Paul. Sil. AP 5.226.7, Max. 336 ὀτλήσας μάλα πολλά. Here the participle expresses the leading idea in the clause, as in S. El. 551 γνώμην δικαίαν σχοῦσα τοὺς πέλας ψέγε. Here ὅμως is to be taken with the part.

ἐσκέψαντο An imaginative way of indicating survival by describing the men's relief in seeing each other alive again.

430 δείδιθι Epic imper., twice in Homer (E 827, Ξ 342).

ἀπαστράψαντος The compound verb is attested first here, then in later writers, e.g. J. AJ 3.217 τοσαύτη γὰρ ἀπήστραπτεν ἀπ' αὐτῶν αὐγή, of flashing stones on a priest's robes, Luc. Gall. 7 οἵαν τὴν αὐγὴν ἀπαστράπτον, of dazzling gold, [Opp.] C. 1.220 ἀπαστράπτει πολὺς αἰθήρ, of sunset, 3.479 ἀπαστράπτουσιν ὀπωπαί. In all these the sense is of flashing or reflected light, but here, in view of 427, the phenomenon must be lightning. It is not clear which sense, clearing sky or lightning, is intended by the scholion ἕως ἂν ἀπαστράψαντος αὐτοῦ τοῦ βορέου αἰσθήσῃ, but at least A. must mean flashing lightning, with Boreas, as often Zeus, taking the place of the impersonal subject. So Mair, Martin, Erren. Maass preserves the simple verb by reading βορῆος ἀπ', but this introduces a breach of Hermann's Bridge.

The partit. gen. with verbs of perception is unusual after ἰδεῖν, but cf. Ar. Ra. 815 ἡνίκ' ἂν ὀξύλαλον παρίδῃ [v.l. περ ἴδῃ] θήγοντος ὀδόντα, X. Mem. 1.1.11 οὔτε πράττοντος εἶδεν οὔτε λέγοντος ἤκουσεν, Pl. R. 558a οὔπω εἶδες ἐν τοιαύτῃ πολιτείᾳ ἀνθρώπων καταψηφισθέντων θανάτου ...; See K-G 1.361. Since all four instances involve a participle, it seems that the gen. with ἰδεῖν is used only of observing something happening.

431-442 The Centaur and the Beast
If the Centaur is hazy as well as the Altar, expect an easterly wind. The human part lies below the Scorpion, the equine part below the Claws, and the right hand points in the direction of the Altar. He holds the Beast firmly in his hand.

The Centaur is a large and shapeless constellation, imagined as a centaur by Greeks who observed it standing on their southern horizon. It has been identified with the Babylonian EN.TE.NA.MAŠ.LUM (Waerden EW 67). The standard Greek name is Κένταυρος (Eudox. fr. 73, Hi. 1.8.18, Gem. 3.13, Ptol. Alm. 8.1.44), but sometimes Χείρων (Hermippus in sch. Arat. 436, Catast. 40). The Latin name is Centaurus, but occasionally *Chiron* (Germ. 421, Ov. *Fast.* 5.379, Luc. 9.536, and implied in Man. 5.353ff.), or *Pholos* (Hyg. 2.38.2). A. refers to several particular stars in the Centaur: head (662, 696), shoulders (432, 696), breast (696), right hand (439, 663), tail (625), forelegs (664). There is no mention of the thyrsus held in the left hand, as in Hi. 2.5.14, 3.5.6, and in later descriptions, but not on the Farnese globe. The brightest stars (α β), representing the forelegs, and the modern Crux, the hind legs, would have been very close to the limit of visibility for observers in Athens. Roscher VI 1012ff., Allen 148ff.

431 εἰ δέ κεν ... ἀπείη Suggesting a rather unlikely possibility, 'if it should happen that ...', as occasionally in Homer, e.g. Α 60 εἴ κεν θάνατόν γε φύγοιμεν, Ι 445–6 εἴ κέν μοι ὑποσταίη θεὸς αὐτὸς | γῆρας ἀποξύσας θήσειν νέον ἡβώοντα. See Chantraine 2.277–8. This is the only instance in A., but there is no reason to reject the MSS testimony in favour of Hipparchus' τοι, as do Maass and Martin.

ἁλός The horizon, a variation of the usual ὠκεανός (26, al.); cf. 314, 407, 728.

432 ὦμος Hipparchus (1.8.19) objects that A. does not specify which shoulder he means, pointing out that the two shoulders represent two different stars, and also that these are some distance apart in longitude, so that they do not culminate at the same time. The left shoulder is ι Centauri, the right θ, and they are about $11\frac{1}{2}°$ apart. The latter, however, is the brighter star (2nd mag. as against 3rd), and it may be that A. means the right shoulder. Cicero solves the problem by translating *umeros* (fr. 33.203), Maass by reading ὦμοι.

προτέρης The eastern horizon, elsewhere ἑτέρης (571, 617, 726). When A. describes the star as equidistant from both horizons, he is not thinking of a point precisely on the meridian, but of an approximate position somewhere near its highest altitude.

εἰλύοι ἀχλύς Sch. τὴν ἐκ τῶν νεφῶν ἀορασίαν. Here the stars are obscured, whereas in 413 they are enclosed by clouds. Schott suggests fine sand as a cause, since the predicted wind is easterly.

433 αὐτόν The Centaur as a whole; cf. 76.

ἐοικότα σήματα There have been four different interpretations of this phrase, each with a different picture of the relative appearance of the two constellations. (1) The Centaur is hazy, but thereafter becomes clear, with overarching clouds, like the Altar in 413–16. This view depends on Hi. 1.8.20 κἂν ἐπιγένηται τὰ ὅμοια σημεῖα τοῖς ἐπὶ τοῦ Θυτηρίου, and is accepted by Martin: 'Comme pour l'Autel, les nuées s'accumulent autour du Centaure, mais non sur la constellation elle-même.' This requires ἐοικότα to mean 'similar to', and Hipparchus' text provided τοῖς to that end, but there is no such dative in A., and without it this meaning is not possible. Besides, the Altar-type phenomenon should predict a southerly, not an easterly wind. (2) The Centaur is hazy, and thereafter (or behind it) the Altar is clear as in 413–16. Thus sch. (M) 431 μετὰ δὲ ταῦτα ἐπὶ τῷ Θυτηρίῳ τὰ προειρημένα σημεῖα ἀποτελοίη ἡ νύξ, and sch. (S) 432 τὸ δὲ Θυτήριον ἐκ τοῦ ὄπισθεν μέρους ἀναλογοῦν τοῖς προειρημένοις σημείοις. Here ἐοικότα is taken as referring back to the passage on the Altar, but the word by itself cannot convey this meaning. (3) Both the Centaur and the Altar are hazy: sch. (M) 431 τὰ δὲ ἐπὶ τῷ Θυτηρίῳ σημεῖα ὅμοια ᾖ. This is the sense approved by Voss, Mair and Erren, but παμφανόωντι surely implies that the Altar is visible. (4) The Centaur is hazy, but the Altar is clearly recognisable: sch. (K) Martin p. 278, line 27 τουτέστι φανερὰ καὶ γνώριμα. This is a peculiarly Aratean idiom, e.g. 168 ἐοικότα σήματα of the obvious configuration of stars in the Bull, 820 of weather signs from the sun, 903–4 ἐοικότες ... ἀστέρες of the two Asses, 1091 of the constellations being recognisable in a clear sky. This is the only interpretation that makes sense of the Greek: ἀτάρ in A. usually introduces a contrast (42, 79, 211, al.), here the clear stars as against the hazy, μετόπισθεν is right for the Altar's position, as it rises after the Centaur, and παμφανόωντι marks it as completely visible. The confusion has arisen from neglect of A.'s idiosyncratic use of ἐοικότα.

τεύχοι The more imaginative verb, attested by the MSS and supported by sch. ἀποτελοίη, is to be preferred to the more conventional φαίνοι of some Hipparchan MSS. The corruption may have been due to the influence of 772 and 1141.

434 παμφανόωντι Cf. ν 29 ἥλιον ... παμφανόωντα, Σ 206 δαῖε φλόγα παμφανόωσαν. Here it recalls 415 ἀγλαόν, and implies that the constellation is clearly visible (see on 433). Cf. Q.S. 7.346 ἀστέρι παμφανόωντι, Orph. *Arg.* 781 ἀστέρα παμφανόωντα.

435 περισκοπέειν ἀνέμοιο Gen. with verb meaning 'look for'; cf. 925, 987, also 559 δεδοκημένος, 795 δειδέχθαι, 813 δοκεύειν, 880 σκέπτεο. See Erren *PAS* 301ff. on A.'s extensive use of the gen. For the internal rhyme see note on 360.

436 δήεις Cf. 161, and ζ 291 δήεις ἀγλαὸν ἄλσος in same *sedes*.

δύω This form as dat. reflects Homeric indecl. usage, e.g. Ν 407 δύω κανόνεσσ' ἀραρυῖαν.

ὑποκείμενον A. gives directions for finding the Centaur by saying that it lies south of the Scorpion and the Claws. Hipparchus (1.8.21–2) objects that it is in fact almost wholly south of the Maiden, except that the right shoulder and hand and the forelegs of the horse extend under the Claws. He goes on to prove this by citing the longitude (in degrees of the ecliptic) of some individual stars, and he is quite right, if ὑπο- is taken to mean due south. But A. may mean simply that it lies farther south, in this case immediately south-west of the Scorpion and Claws, which are the closest constellations to the Centaur, and an obvious guide for the observer to follow. Cf. 702, where the direction is south-east. Hipparchus also notes that Attalus overlooks this 'error', assuming that A. is correct.

438 ἱππούραια The hind half of the horse, not merely the 'horse-tail' (LSJ), since it is contrasted with the human half, which forms the front. The word occurs only here and Hi. 1.8.22. The reading ἄγουσιν in Hipparchus' MSS comes from 612, where it describes a rising.

439 δεξιτερήν The star η Centauri. A line (θ η) from the right shoulder to the right hand points directly south-east to the Altar, which is chosen as a guide here because it has already been identified. This also allows the position of the Beast to be precisely located between Centaur and Altar.

440 δινωτοῖο Cf. 401, 462.

ἀπρίξ From intensive α- with root of πρίω (Frisk 1.126, Pearson on S. fr. 354.3), prop. of nails biting into what is held. Cf. S. *Aj.* 310 κόμην ἀπρὶξ ὄνυξι συλλαβὼν χερί, Pl. *Tht.* 155e ἀπρὶξ τοῖν χεροῖν λαβέσθαι, Theoc. 15.68 ἀπρὶξ ἔχευ, Εὐνόα, ἁμῶν, 24.55 θῆρε δύω χείρεσσιν ἀπρὶξ ἀπαλαῖσιν ἔχοντα.

441 ἐσφήκωται Once in Homer, of hair clasped, P 52 ἐσφήκωντο. Cf. 526, and Nic. *Ther.* 289 ἐσφήκωται in same *sedes* as here.

ἐληλάμενον Cf. 162, 176, 489, 516.

442 Θηρίον The Beast is a compact constellation, with stars of 3rd mag., but none brighter. Its origin is unknown, probably earlier than Eudoxus, in view of A.'s reference to πρότεροι (442). The name Θηρίον is standard in Greek (Eudox. fr. 73, Hi. 2.2.53, Gem. 3.13, Ptol. *Alm.* 8.1.45, *Catast.* 40). Cic. fr. 33.211–12 *quadrupes qua uasta tenetur,* | *quam nemo certo donauit nomine Graium* means that they did not specify what kind of beast. Latin names include *Fera* (Cic. 453), *Bestia* (Vitr. 9.5.1), *Hostia* (Hyg. 3.37.2). The modern name Lupus is of uncertain origin, perhaps from the Lycaon myth in Ov. *Met.* 1.237. Roscher vi 1016–17, Allen 278–9.

ἐπεφημίξαντο Cf. 221 διεφήμισαν, probable source of the v.l. The aor. and fut. in -ξ- are characteristic of Doric (Giangrande, *Hermes* 98, 1970, 275); cf. Pi. *O.* 6.56 κατεφάμιξεν. In epic, Hes. *Op.* 764 φημίξουσι, Euphor. 57 Powell φημίξαντο, D.P. 50 διεφημίξαντο, Nonn. *D.* 14.74 ἐφημίξαντο.

443–450 The Hydra, the Bowl, the Raven and Procyon
The Hydra winds like a living thing, with its head below the Crab, its coil below the Lion, and its tail over the Centaur. The other three constellations are closely associated with it.

The Hydra is a long series of stars, running roughly parallel to the ecliptic from about 10° N to 20° S. It has one bright star of 2nd mag., six of 3rd, and the great majority are fainter. A. does not refer to any particular star, but only to parts of the constellation: the head (445, 594), the neck coil (698), the main coil (446, 448, 519), the last coil (448) and the tail (447, 661). It appears to have originated in the Babylonian mᴜš 'serpent', which included the star β Cancri (Waerden *EW* 67-8, fig. 8). In A. it is always Ὕδρη, but elsewhere Ὕδρος (Eudox. fr. 77, Hi. 3.1.1b, Gem. 3.13, Ptol. *Alm.* 8.1.41, *Catast.* 41). In Latin it is *Hydra* (also the modern name), but varied with *Hydros* (Germ. 426) and *Anguis* (Vitr. 9.5.1, Ov. *Fast.* 2.243, Man. 1.415). Gundel *RE* 18.653ff., Roscher vi 1008-9, Allen 246ff.

443 τι καὶ ἄλλο Maass's conjecture is unlikely, since καλός in A. normally has long α, the only exception being 1142. For τις with ἄλλος cf. 99, 475, 746, Q.S. 12.487 ἐλπομένη τι καὶ ἄλλο κακώτερον. See West, *Th.* 87, on how easily τι καί could become τε καί.

περαιόθεν Sch. νῦν περαίην τὴν ἀνατολὴν λέγει, citing Ψ 243 νύκτα μὲν ἐν περάτῃ δολιχὴν σχέθεν. A. has περαιόθεν with reference to the eastern horizon also in 606, 645, 720. An alternative explanation is given by sch. (ΜΚ) ἢ ἐκ τῶν πέραν καὶ πόρρω τοῦ Κενταύρου. This does make sense, in that the observer, having identified the Beast, must then look beyond the Centaur to find the Hydra. However, ἕλκεται is suited to the idea of movement over the horizon, as in 604, 708, 727. What A. really means is that the Hydra is another of the visible constellations.

445 ἠνεκές From verbal stem ἐνεκ-, of carrying on without interruption; cf. Emped. 17.35, 135.2 (ἠνεκέως), Call. fr. 26.8. A. has also διηνεκέως (494), from Homeric adj. διηνεκής (Η 321, ν 195). For the great length of the Hydra see note on 443-450.

εἰλεῖται Cf. 46 of the Dragon, similarly with double sense.

κεφαλή A group of stars (δ ε ζ η σ) close to the Crab.

μέσσον Not very significant, since the Crab is so small, but it may be an echo of Eudox. fr. 66 τὰ μέσα τοῦ Καρκίνου.

446 σπείρη The great bend formed by the stars λ ν ξ β Hydrae; the line of the curve may also be thought of as taking in α β Crateris and ending at β Corvi (cf. 448 ἐπίκειται). The extent of the bend matches that of the Lion due north of it.

447 οὐρή The stars γ π Hydrae, which lie due north of the Centaur's shoulders.

Κενταύροιο Cf. 661 and A.R. 4.812, in the same *sedes*.

448-9 The Bowl and the Raven. These are small constellations, usually represented as actually standing on the Hydra (cf. ἐπίκειται).

The Bowl appears not to have been known to the Babylonians, since two of its stars (α β) were included in their MUŠ (Waerden *EW*, fig. 8). It was probably invented by the Greeks, presumably before Eudoxus, though the name does not occur in any of his extant fragments. Κρητήρ in A. (cf. Ψ 741), it is always Κρατήρ in prose, e.g. Hi. 3.1.2, Gem. 3.13, Ptol. *Alm.* 8.1.42, *Catast.* 41. The regular Latin name is *Crater* (also modern), with the variations *Creterra* (Cic. fr. 33.219) and *Cratera* (Hyg. 2.40.3). Gundel, *RE* 11.1612, Roscher vi 1010, Allen 182ff.

The Raven descends from the Babylonian constellation UGA 'raven' (Waerden *EW* 67–8 and fig. 8). It has one star of 2nd and three of 3rd mag., and its shape is easy to identify. Its name is invariably Κόραξ in Greek (Eudox. fr. 108, Hi. 1.10.19, Gem. 3.13, Ptol. *Alm.* 8.1.43, and *Catast.* 41). *Coruus* is the regular Latin name, the modern name still Corvus. Haebler, *RE* 4.1665–6, Roscher vi 1011, Allen 179ff.

448 μέσση δὲ σπείρη It is possible to take this as the middle one of three bends (cf. 1055–6 of the three harvests), the other two being the neck bend (698) and the slight curve of the tail: cf. the illustration on the Farnese globe. In *Catast.* 41 the stars are actually listed according to five bends. But σπείρη in 446 must be the great central bend, and positions related to the middle and end of it are recognisably suited to the Bowl and the Raven. Ovid gives a different slant to the adj. in *Fast.* 2.243–4 *continuata loco tria sidera, Coruus et Anguis | et medius Crater inter utrumque iacet.*

ἐπίκειται Hyg. 2.40.1 *Hydra. in qua Coruus insidere et Crater positus existimatur.* So on the Farnese globe the Bowl and the Raven are both shown standing on the Hydra's coil. But where a star is shared by two constellations, A. makes a point of saying so (e.g. 176, 206), otherwise the constellations are assumed to be distinct. Thus in 366 πρώτη ἐπίκειται ἀκάνθη the Knot star comes close to the back-fin, but does not overlap with it: cf. Th. 4.53.2 of an offshore island. So *Catast.* 41 ἱκανὸν ἀπέχων ἀπὸ τῆς καμπῆς ὁ Κρατὴρ κεῖται.

449 κόπτοντι The beak is represented by the star α Corvi, which comes close to the line of the Hydra's curve. The verb is used in Homer of a snake striking (M 204); for birds pecking cf. Arist. *HA* 609b5. Note the effective alliteration of κ; cf. X 33, ρ 521, σ 335.

450 Procyon. A. completes his guide to the southern stars by passing from the Hydra's head to Procyon a short distance to the west. This is primarily the 1st-mag. star that still bears the name, identified with the Babylonian AL.LUL (Waerden *EW* 67). The name brings out its importance as the forerunner of Sirius, so important in the ancient calendar: see on 326–337. The Greeks made it into a constellation by adding the star β with its close companion γ (Hi. 3.1.13 ὁ ἡγούμενος καὶ διπλοῦς). The Greek name is always Προκύων for both star and constellation (Eudox. fr. 82, Hi. 3.1.13, Gem. 3.13, Ptol. *Alm.* 8.1.39, *Catast.* 42). In Latin *Procyon* is known especially for its MR at the hottest time of the year. Cicero therefore amplifies A.'s Προκύων (595) with *Procyon qui sese feruidus infert | ante Canem* (fr. 33.377-8.), and Horace follows with *iam Procyon furit (Carm.* 3.29.18). So Pliny *(Nat.* 18.268) *Procyon matutino aestuosus, quod sidus apud Romanos non habet nomen, nisi Caniculam hanc uolumus intellegi.* But *Canicula* was already a name for Sirius (see on 326-337). An alternative had, however, been offered by Vitr. 9.5.2 *Geminos autem minusculus Canis sequitur contra Anguis caput; maior item sequitur minorem.* Today the constellation is Canis Minor. Böker, *RE* 23.613ff., Roscher VI 1002ff., Allen 131ff.

ναὶ μὴν καί A lively progression, which seems to introduce the final constellation with a modest flourish. Cf. D.P. 1011, Nic. *Ther.* 51, 896, Mel. *AP* 4.1.47 = *HE* 3972, *AP* 12.63.3 = *HE* 4486, Opp. *H.* 1.404, 3.482, 5.392. καὶ μὴν καί (Mair without comment) appears to be rare and only in prose authors (Denniston 352).

Διδύμοις ὕπο Strictly due south of the two bright stars Castor and Pollux.

καλὰ φαείνει Cf. 148.

451-453
A. concludes the whole section on the constellations with a short passage that matches the transition from north to south (319-21) in length and sense pause, as also in the dactylic final line. The passage brings out especially the regularity and reliability of the night sky.

451 θηήσαιο Cf. ρ 315 αἶψά κε θηήσαιο. The Homeric reminiscence here is continued in the rest of the line, which recalls α 16 περιπλομένων ἐνιαυτῶν.

ἐνιαυτῶν See note on 11 εἰς ἐνιαυτόν. The pl. draws attention to the recurrence of the annual star cycle and the importance of being able to rely on it for predictions of weather. Originally ἐνιαυτός meant the completion of a year cycle: see C. J. Emlyn-Jones, *Glotta* 45 (1967) 156ff., R. S. P. Beekes, *Glotta* 47 (1969) 138ff.

452 παλίνωρα Only here (if Hsch. παλινώρους· ἄκοντας is corrupt). Sch. 454 πάλιν τὰς ὥρας ἄγοντα ἢ πάλιν κατὰ τὰς ὥρας ἀνατέλλοντα καὶ δύνοντα. Grotius' παλίνορσα is not suitable, since that means that the direction of the movement is reversed: see note on 54. The stars return by continuing on the same circular track. The point here is that their return is predictable, whereas that of the planets is not.

453 οὐρανῷ εὖ ἐνάρηρεν A reminder of the opening lines of this section, οὐρανῷ ἕλκονται (20) of the stars, and αἰὲν ἄρηρεν (22) of the axis. The latter is the source of the misquotation in Ath. 11 489E, where the stars are likened to studs, with a reference to Λ 633.

ἀγάλματα The figures that the constellations represent; cf. 197, of Andromeda. They are not put in the sky primarily to be 'ornaments' (Mair), 'parures' (Martin), 'Schmuckstücke' (Erren), but for the more practical purpose of being recognisable, and so giving warning of seasonal and weather changes. ἀγάλματα is the subject, with its anticipatory article in the preceding line (cf. 21), and the point of the sentence is that they are fixed and therefore reliable. Manilius elaborates on this point in 1.474ff. Cf. Ferrari, *SIFC* 17 (1940) 77ff.

454-461 THE PLANETS

For the sake of completeness A. adds a note on the five visible planets, which came to be called Ἑρμοῦ, Ἀφροδίτης, Ἄρεως, Διός, and Κρόνου ἀστέρες (Pl. *Epin.* 987b-c, Ach. *Isag.* 17 Maass p. 43). The problem of explaining their erratic movements was the chief concern of astronomers from Eudoxus onwards, and therefore a subject of general interest. But they have nothing to contribute to A.'s purpose, since they are of no practical use for measuring time or telling the seasons. The two remaining 'planets' of the Greeks, the sun and the moon, do, however, play an important part in weather-forecasting, and they are prominent in the final section of the poem, especially 778-891. See Erren *PAS* 154-8.

454 ἐπιμίξ Cf. 364, but here the mingling may be said to cause some confusion. Cf. Λ 525 after οἱ δὲ δὴ ἄλλοι, Ψ 242 after τοὶ δ᾿ ἄλλοι.

οὐδὲν ὁμοῖοι Though the planets look like the fixed stars, by A.'s time they were seen to be different on several counts: they were at different distances from the earth, but all nearer the earth than the fixed stars; they showed complex movements, sometimes even retrograde; they moved eastwards through the Zodiac in different periods; they showed variations in speed and magnitude; and Aristotle said they did not twinkle like the fixed stars (*Cael.* 290a19).

455 πάντοθεν ... δινεύονται A. is describing the slow eastward movement of the planets through the Zodiac, which Mercury and Venus complete in one year, Mars in about $2\frac{1}{2}$, Jupiter in about 12, Saturn in about 30. See Gem. 1.24-9. He may also have in mind the retrograde motions, which Plato perhaps hinted at in *Ti.* 40c ἐπανακυκλήσεις καὶ προχωρήσεις, and which Eudoxus tried to account for in his geometrical model, as expounded by Arist. *Met.* 12.8. The verb δινεύονται then expresses the basic circular motion through the Zodiac, modified by retrogradation and variation of speed. Cf. π 63 of the wanderings of

Odysseus, φησὶ δὲ πολλὰ βροτῶν ἐπὶ ἄστεα δινηθῆναι. The adv. πάντοθεν here has the sense of πάντοσε, as in P 680, of Menelaus' eyes,
πάντοσε δινείσθην πολέων κατὰ ἔθνος ἑταίρων. The movement is not
'on every side of' (Mair) the Zodiac constellations, but all the way
through them. The gen. defines the area within which both the adv.
and the verb apply. The v.l. in Ach. p. 42 could have come from a gloss
describing the planetary movements as 'backward', i.e. 'eastward', as
opposed to the westward motion of the fixed stars; cf. sch. 454 on the
sun and moon οὗτοι γὰρ οἱ δύο τὸ ἀνάπαλιν πορεύονται.

δυοκαίδεκα In same *sedes* as Z 93, K 560, θ 59, π 251. In 550, 740 the
metrical position is the same as B 557, Υ 225, ξ 13, σ 293, τ 578.

456 εἰς ἄλλους ὁρόων Cf. υ 373 ἐς ἀλλήλους ὁρόωντες. The fixed
stars are unreliable as guides to the planets.

457 κείνων A. uses (ἐπι)τεκμαίρεσθαι c. gen. of finding evidence
for something uncertain or unknown (801, 1038, 1129); c. acc. of direct
recognition (170). Planetary positions are in the former category.

κέονται With pres. ending in -ο-, as in Χ 510, π 232. See Chantraine
1.476. A. also has the more usual κέαται (492).

μετανάσται Homeric *hapax* (Ι 648), in derisive sense of 'vagrant'.
The planets move continually from one constellation to the next in the
Zodiac. Cf. Nonn. *D.* 38.385 ἐμὸς μετανάστιος ἀστήρ (Hermes).

458 μακροὶ ... ἐνιαυτοί The periods of the planetary orbits round
the Zodiac to the point at which the reckoning of each began. A. is
thinking particularly of Mars, Jupiter and Saturn, whose periods are
longer than the solar year: see on 455. As these are all different, and
none is a multiple of the solar year, they are of no practical use for the
measurement of time. A. does not actually make this point, but perhaps
leaves it to be implied. For the measurement of longer periods he cites
only the Metonic cycle at 752-3. The concept of planetary 'years' comes
from Plato, who in his creation myth imagines the planetary periods as
having been created for the express purpose of measuring time: ἐξ οὖν
λόγου καὶ διανοίας θεοῦ τοιαύτης πρὸς χρόνου γένεσιν, ἵνα γεννηθῇ
χρόνος, ἥλιος καὶ σελήνη καὶ πέντε ἄλλα ἄστρα, ἐπίκλην ἔχοντα
πλανητά, εἰς διορισμὸν καὶ φυλακὴν ἀριθμῶν χρόνου γέγονεν (*Ti.*
38c). The v.l. may be reflected in Opp. *H.* 2.686 and Q.S. 2.506 ἑλισσομένων ἐνιαυτῶν.

459 μακρὰ δὲ σήματα ... ἀπόπροθεν εἰς ἓν ἰόντων The reference
in this line is to the so called Great Year, the period from the time when
all the planets are in conjunction to the next recurrence of the same
phenomenon. Sch. σφόδρα πολὺς ὁ χρόνος καὶ μεγάλα τὰ τεκμήρια
ἀπόπροθεν καὶ ἐκ τοῦ διεστηκέναι αὐτοὺς κατὰ τὴν περιφορὰν συ-
νερχομένων καὶ εἰς ταὐτὸ συνιόντων. αἰνίττεται δὲ εἰς τὸ εἰρημένον

ὑπὸ τῶν φυσικῶν καὶ φιλοσόφων καὶ μαθηματικῶν, ὧν καὶ δοκιμώ-
τερος ὁ Πλάτων. τότε γὰρ εἶπον μέγαν ἐνιαυτόν, ὅτε συνέρχονται
οἱ ζ' οὗτοι ἀστέρες ἐν ἑνὶ ζῳδίῳ ὑπὸ τὴν αὐτὴν μοῖραν. The Platonic
reference is to *Ti.* 39d ἔστιν δ' ὅμως οὐδὲν ἧττον κατανοῆσαι δυνατὸν
ὡς ὅ γε τέλεος ἀριθμὸς χρόνου τὸν τέλεον ἐνιαυτὸν πληροῖ τότε, ὅταν
ἁπασῶν τῶν ὀκτὼ περιόδων τὰ πρὸς ἄλληλα συμπερανθέντα τάχη
σχῇ κεφαλὴν τῷ τοῦ ταὐτοῦ καὶ ὁμοίως ἰόντος ἀναμετρηθέντα κύκλῳ.
The seven planets include the sun and moon, and Plato's eighth
period is that of the sphere of the fixed stars. For the further development of the Great Year, and attempts to calculate a length for it, see L.
Zimmermann, *MH* 30 (1973) 179ff., D. E. Hahn, *Origins of Stoic Cosmology*
(1977) 185–6, 196, B. L. Van der Waerden, *AHES* 18 (1978) 359–84.

μακρά is clearly meant to balance μακροί, but the figure is awkwardly
contrived, since with σήματα it cannot mean 'long'. Sch. μεγάλα is not
helpful. A. must mean that successive occurrences of the conjunction of
the planets are a long time distant from each other. Martin prefers to
take μακρά as adv., complementing ἀπόπροθεν, but the word pattern
shows it to be intended as an adj. The sense of σήματα also is not immediately evident. Martin explains it as 'les points de repère fournis par
les étoiles fixes', presumably the constellation in which they are seen.
But the phenomenon could occur in any constellation, and it is perhaps
more likely that the word describes the configuration of the planets
themselves in the same constellation, which would certainly present a
striking 'sign' of the end of one era and the beginning of the next.
A.R. 1.39 has an interesting imitation, of the arrival of two of the
Argonauts, ἄμφω συμφορέονται, ἀπόπροθεν εἰς ἓν ἰόντες. The fact that
the first half of the line comes from 363 makes it probable that Apollonius is the imitator.

460 οὐδ' ἔτι θαρσαλέος κείνων A. affects some diffidence when it
comes to describing the movements of the planets. This is an early form
of *recusatio*, as Ludwig has pointed out (*Hermes* 91, 1963, 439). A. is
credited with having written a work on the planets: Ach. 15 Maass
p. 42 ἐν δὲ τῷ ἐπιγραφομένῳ αὐτοῦ Κανόνι [see *SH* 90] τὸν περὶ αὐτῶν
ποιούμενος λόγον ἁρμονίᾳ τινὶ καὶ συμφωνίᾳ μουσικῇ τὰς κινήσεις
αὐτῶν λέγει γεγονέναι. Though the problem of explaining planetary
movements was still unsolved, it would not have been difficult to give
an account of the observed data and the nature of the apparent irregularities. Achilles explains: παραιτεῖται δὲ διὰ πολλὰς αἰτίας, πρῶτον
ὅτι φαινόμενα ἠθέλησε καὶ πᾶσι σύμφωνα δεῖξαι ἄστρα, οὗτοι δὲ
πολλὴν διαφωνίαν ἔχουσι καὶ οὐδὲ πᾶσίν εἰσι φανεροί (15). But A.'s
real reason for not giving an account of the planets was that they were
irrelevant to his purpose in this poem: see on 454–461. It is worth

noting that A. ignores the growing cult of astrology, which Eudoxus had positively rejected (Cic. *Div.* 2.87). The coyness of A.'s *recusatio* here seems to be reflected in Virgil's doubts about his ability to write a philosophical poem (*G.* 2.483–4).

οὐδέ τι is not appropriate, since A. has shown that he understands the basic characteristics of the observed planets. οὐδ' ἔτι means that he does not feel qualified to go further in explaining them; see note on 142.

The gen. κείνων is probably best explained by taking θαρσαλέος as implying also the sense of ἔμπειρος, ἐπιστήμων, etc. (K–G 1.369–70); cf. the unusual σοφὸς κακῶν in A. *Suppl.* 453. Maass compares it with adjj. of desire (*Aratea* 52), but this does not match the required sense.

ἐγώ The nom. is an emphatic assertion of the poet's personality, and A. uses it only here, where its force is modified by being attached to an apparently modest disclaimer. Hesiod is bolder in *Op.* 10, 106, 286, with strong contrast to τύνη and σύ. Cf. *h.Hom.* 3.546.

ἄρκιος εἴην Cf. 1148 in same *sedes*, echoing Κ 304 ἄρκιος ἔσται and Hes. *Op.* 501, 577 ἄρκιος εἴη. So [Theoc.] 25.190. In 741 ἄρκιαι A. follows the Homeric sense of 'certain' or 'reliable', e.g. Β 393. Here the meaning 'competent', of a person, is Hellenistic; cf. A.R. 2.799, Call. *H.* 6.34, fr. 236.2. Hyg. 4.8.2 *Aratum ipsum negare se difficiles earum cursus interpretari posse*, Quint. 10.1.55 *sufficit tamen operi cui se parem credidit.*

461 ἀπλανέων Of stars first in Plato, *Ti.* 40b ὅσ' ἀπλανῆ τῶν ἄστρων, thereafter the standard technical term, replacing Aristotle's τοὺς ἀστέρας τοὺς ἐνδεδεμένους (*Cael.* 290a19), sometimes as subst., e.g. Arist. *Mete.* 343b9 τῶν ἀπλανῶν λαμβάνουσι κόμην τινές, but normally as adj. with ἀστέρες or ἄστρα (Autol. *Ort.* 1, Euc. *Phaen.* 1, Hi. 1.1.9, Gem. 7.1, etc.). So in the poets, Leon. *AP* 9.25.3 = *HE* 2575 ἀπλανέας τ' ἄμφω καὶ ἀλήμονας, Anon. *AP* 9.822.3 ἀπλανέες δ' ἑκάτερθε καὶ ἀντιθέοντες ἀλῆται, Nonn. *D.* 1.230, 498.

κύκλα The only pl. form used by A. (cf. 226, 660, 753). The n.pl. is Homeric, in contexts where Monro (p. 84) suggests it means a set of wheels, e.g. Ε 722, Σ 375, both instances of wheels provided by gods. Here too a set of wheels may be imagined, anticipating 462 δινωτοῖσι and 530 τροχάλεια. With these two transitional lines A. introduces his next subject, the celestial circles. For the heteroclite pl. cf. κέλευθα (372, 1031), used as a variation of the normal m.pl. (149, 225, 343, 406, 803).

τά τ' αἰθέρι σήματ' A reminiscence of Parm. fr. 10.1–2 εἴσῃ δ' αἰθερίαν τε φύσιν τά τ' ἐν αἰθέρι πάντα | σήματα. Here the loc. αἰθέρι is Homeric, e.g. Δ 166 αἰθέρι ναίων. σήματα refers particularly to the constellations marking the celestial circles; cf. 465.

ἐνισπεῖν Homeric aor. of ἐνέπω, with prefix ἐνι- (Chantraine 1.388); cf. δ 323 λυγρὸν ὄλεθρον ἐνισπεῖν. The form seems to be particularly associated with divine or prophetic words (e.g. B 80, Z 438, Λ 186, Ξ 470, Ω 388), and A. probably chose it as suitable for Muse-inspired poetry (cf. 18). He uses it only here, as a variation recalling the ending of the proem ἀστέρας εἰπεῖν (17).

462–757 THE MEASUREMENT OF TIME
Celestial circles (462–558), simultaneous risings and
settings (559–732), periods of time (733–7)

Now that the constellations have been identified, the next step is to show how to make use of them in order to measure the passage of time, and so to estimate the possibilities of favourable conditions for farming or sailing. The basis of this demonstration is the system of four circles which the mathematicians have drawn on the celestial sphere for the purpose of providing points of reference in defining the apparent position of the sun relative to the fixed stars at any time of the year. Three of the circles illustrate the observable north–south–north movement of the sun that goes with the change of seasons.

All three are drawn at right angles to the axis of the celestial sphere. Midway between the two poles lies the equator, so called because it makes the days and nights equal when the sun is on it; it is overhead at the terrestrial equator, which is named after it. Some 24° north is the northern or summer tropic, a circle on which lies the most northerly point reached by the sun at midsummer. As that point was in the constellation of the Crab in A.'s time, the corresponding terrestrial circle came to be called the tropic of Cancer. For the origin of the term 'tropic' see note on 499 τροπαί. Similarly the southern or winter tropic is a circle drawn 24° south of the equator, overhead at the earth's tropic of Capricorn.

Because of the earth's orbit round the sun, the sun's position as viewed from the earth appears to move slowly eastward, completing the circuit of the sky in one year. The rate of this apparent movement is about four minutes per day, or two hours per month, and the twelve constellations through which it moves form the belt known as the zodiac. The sun's precise track through the zodiac is called the 'ecliptic', because it is only when the moon is on the same track that eclipses can occur. See also note on 525–558. The ecliptic is represented geometrically by a great circle running round the globe at an angle of 24° to the equator (see note on 537). The two points where it crosses the equator mark the position of the sun at the equinoxes, and where it touches the two tropics, the solstices.

Finally A. notes briefly how all periods of time are marked by celestial phenomena: the month, day and night, the year and seasons, and the 19-year cycle.

In the first two of these three sections A. is still following Eudoxus, as we know from references and quotations in Hi. 1.10.14ff. and 2.1–3, and from such comments as ἔτι πρότερον Ἀράτου Εὔδοξος ἀναγέγραφεν, ᾧ καὶ νομίζομεν κατηκολουθηκέναι τὸν Ἄρατον (1.10.13) and καὶ ὁ Εὔδοξος δέ, ᾧ κατηκολούθηκεν ὁ Ἄρατος, τὸν αὐτὸν τρόπον ὑποτίθεται ἐν ταῖς Συνανατολαῖς τὰς ἀρχὰς τῶν ζῳδίων ἐπὶ τῆς ἀνατολῆς (2.1.26). But the last section is added by A. himself, to remind the reader once again of the benevolence of Zeus.

462–558 THE CELESTIAL CIRCLES

On 462–500 see Wilamowitz *HD* 2.270–4.

462–479 *Introduction*

Four circles are useful for the measurement of the year: the tropics, the equator, and the ecliptic. The last two may be compared in size with the Milky Way, both being great circles of the sphere, while the other two are smaller. It may well have been Eudoxus who introduced these circles into the geometry of the celestial sphere, though the equator and the ecliptic are implied in Plato's *Timaeus* myth as the circles of the Same and the Different (36c). All four are described by Autolycus (late fourth century) in his *De Sphaera quae mouetur* (cf. J.-P. Brunet, *AAC* 73–82) and by Euclid in his *Phaenomena* (cf. P. Chiron, *AAC* 83–9).

462 ἤτοι μέν Confirming that the κύκλα foreshadowed in 461 are now to be expounded in detail. Cf. Υ 435 ἀλλ' ἤτοι μὲν ταῦτα θεῶν ἐν γούνασι κεῖται.

ἀλίγκια Cf. θ 174 ἀλίγκιος ἀθανάτοισιν, with similar 6th foot, and A.R. 4.966 ἀλίγκιαι αἰθυίῃσιν with spondaic 5th.

δινωτοῖσι Elsewhere in A. an adj. (401, 440), here subst. 'turned wheels'. A. is perhaps echoing Parm. fr. 1.7–8 δοιοῖς γὰρ ἐπείγετο δινωτοῖσιν | κύκλοις ἀμφοτέρωθεν. Cf. 477–8 κύκλος δινεῖται, and 529–33. The point is that these are mathematical circles, and therefore perfect figures.

463 ποθὴ ὄφελός τε On the practical uses of astronomy for the measurement of time see Κ 251–3 ἀλλ' ἴομεν· μάλα γὰρ νὺξ ἄνεται, ἐγγύθι δ' ἠώς, | ἄστρα δὲ δὴ προβέβηκε, παρῴχωκεν δὲ πλέων νὺξ | τῶν δύο μοιράων, τριτάτη δ' ἔτι μοῖρα λέλειπται, and more recently X. *Mem.* 4.7.4 ἐκέλευε δὲ καὶ ἀστρολογίας ἐμπείρους γίγνεσθαι, καὶ ταύτης μέντοι μέχρι τοῦ νυκτός τε ὥραν καὶ μηνὸς καὶ ἐνιαυτοῦ δύνασθαι γιγνώσκειν, ἕνεκα πορείας τε καὶ πλοῦ καὶ φυλακῆς. Cf. 4.3.4, and J. Martin in *AAC* 91.

464 μέτρα The key-word that characterises this section of the poem; cf. 731.

περισκοπέοντι C. acc. of observing carefully; cf. 852 med.

κατανομένων See note on 373.

465 εὖ μάλα πᾶσιν Cf. *h.Hom.* 3.171, Theoc. 24.94, [25.19].

ἐπιρρήδην Sch. ὡς ἐξονομακλήδην. ἐπειδὴ οὗτοι [sc. κύκλοι] καθ' ἑαυτοὺς ἀόρατοί εἰσι καὶ οὐδὲ καταλαμβάνονται, διὰ τοῦτό φησιν ὅτι σημεῖα ἑκάστῳ ἐπιρρήδην καὶ δυνάμενα ληφθῆναι ἐκ τοῦ σύνεγγυς καὶ πανταχόθεν συνηγμένα. Cf. 191, 261.

466 συνεεργμένα The sense required by the context is that these guide-stars lie close to their circles all the way round, and this meaning is aptly suggested by συνεεργμένα. Mair translates 'closely penned together', sch. variously συνηρμοσμένα, συνηγμένα, συνημμένα, all of which give essentially the same meaning. Buttmann (anticipated by Vat. 199) proposed συνεερμένα (from συνείρω), claiming support from Cic. fr. 33.243 *uinctos inter se et nodis caelestibus aptos*, and is followed by Maass, Martin (who cites specifically *aptos*), and Erren. But this line of Cicero refers to the circles themselves and how they are connected to each other, and his version of 466 is his 241 *quae densis distincta licebit cernere signis*. In any case συνεερμένα only gives a variation of the same sense, and there is no reason to prefer it against the testimony of the MSS. Homer has συνέεργω of fastening together, e.g. rams (ι 427), mast and keel (μ 424), chiton with belt (ξ 72), and Plato uses συνέρξας of the god binding body and soul together (*Ti.* 34c).

467 ἀπλατέες The MSS tradition ἀπλανέες is not without sense, since the circles are fixed like the stars, and this meaning could be seen to be supported by ἐστήρικται (500) of the northern tropic. It is also implied by Avien. 934 *ipsae inconcussa retinentur sede per annos*. But αὐτοί is there to distinguish the notional circles from the visible stars that lie close to them, and is pointless with ἀπλανέες, which only makes them similar. The corruption is easily explained by the proximity of ἀπλανέων (461). In this instance, where the contested word is a technical term, the testimony of Hipparchus is compelling, and it is supported by sch. (MK), which, though the lemma is ἀπλανέες, define the adj. as νοητοί (M), νοητῶς (K), adding in explanation διὸ καὶ σημείων τινῶν ἐδεήθημεν κατὰ τὴν ἐπίγνωσιν τῶν τόπων αὐτῶν, οὐ δυναμένων τῇ ὄψει ληφθῆναι, καθάπερ ὁ γάλακτος τύπος ὃς καλεῖται γαλαξίας.

Hipparchus therefore reads ἀπλατέες, since a notional line has no breadth, but at the same time he records a variant αὐτοὶ δὲ πλατέες, and notes that Attalus prefers this reading (1.9.1). Attalus says that astronomers suppose these circles to have a certain breadth (πλατεῖς ὑπο-τίθενται), because the solstitial points do not always lie on the same circle: διὰ τὸ τὸν ἥλιον τὰς τροπὰς μὴ ἀεὶ ἐπὶ τοῦ αὐτοῦ κύκλου ποιεῖσθαι, ἀλλὰ ποτὲ μὲν νοτιώτερον, ποτὲ δὲ βορειότερον. Hipparchus adds that this was also the view of Eudoxus in his *Enoptron*: φαίνεται δὲ διαφορὰν τῶν κατὰ τὰς τροπὰς τόπων καὶ ὁ ἥλιος ποιούμενος, ἀδηλοτέραν δὲ πολλῷ καὶ παντελῶς ὀλίγην, i.e. compared with the moon (1.9.2). This early theory was probably influenced by the known variations in latitude of the moon and the planets, and perhaps confirmed by imprecise observations of the sun's position at the solstices in different years. Hipparchus goes on to argue that A. cannot have meant this, since his account of the circles elsewhere implies that he is thinking of a mathematical line without breadth (τοῖς μαθηματικοῖς ἀκολούθως ἀπλατεῖς αὐτοὺς νοεῖ ὑπάρχοντας), and cites in evidence 513–14 on the equator: οὐ γὰρ ἐπὶ μίαν μόνον ἡμέραν ἰσημερίαν ἂν ἦγεν ἔν τε τῷ ἔαρι καὶ τῷ φθινοπώρῳ, ἀλλὰ καὶ πλείονας, εἰ πλάτος εἶχε, similarly 497–9 on the northern tropic, and 541–3 and 553–8 on the ecliptic (1.9.9–11). A. may be consciously recalling Euclid's famous definition in *Elem.* 1.1 γραμμὴ δὲ μῆκος ἀπλατές. See Martin ad loc., Erren *PAS* 159.

ἀρηρότες ἀλλήλοισι The four circles are interconnected by means of the ecliptic, which crosses one and touches the other two; see 526–8.

468 δύω δυσὶν ἀντιφέρονται The equator and the ecliptic are equal in size, both being great circles; the two tropics are smaller, and equal to each other. Homer uses ἀντιφέρεσθαι of a fighter matched against another in strength (Φ 482, 488). Cf. Opp. *H.* 1.175 ἀνδράσιν ἀντιφέρονται.

469–479 The structure of this passage has been differently understood by editors, with consequent variation of punctuation. The first eight lines clearly contain two conditional clauses, but the apodosis is not so obvious, Voss, Mair and Martin have taken Γάλα μιν καλέουσι as the apodosis, while Maass puts a dash after τροχαλόν, thus suggesting an aposiopesis before the naming phrase. Either solution creates something of an anticlimax after the impressive build-up in the preceding lines, and Kaibel, in his review of Maass (*Götting. Gel. Anz.* 1, 1893, 944), calls it 'eine nahezu komische Wirkung'. The real apodosis, as has been pointed out by Kaibel (ibid.), Wilamowitz (*HD* 2.273), and Erren (*PAS* 160–3), lies in lines 477–9, and the obscurity is due to the fact that the main emphasis is on the second of the three clauses, while the other two are in a sense subordinate to it. The gist of what A. is saying here is: if you look at the sky on a clear night, and see or have pointed out to you that brilliant belt called the Milk, two of the circles are the same size as it. A. has thus introduced the Milky Way as a visible illustration of a celestial great circle, but at the same time he has taken the opportunity to bring out the impressive spectacle that it presents to the observer by elaborating this periodic sentence of eleven lines, with its two balanced subordinate clauses of four lines each, which culminate in the name of the phenomenon. The passage is therefore not a digression that interrupts A.'s ecphrasis of the four circles, as Ferrari has suggested (*SIFC* 17, 1940, 77–96), but plays an integral part in the ecphrasis itself.

As to punctuation, Kaibel suggested commas all the way until the final full stop, Wilamowitz put a dash at the end of 472 and semicolons before and after Γάλα μιν καλέουσι, Erren has a semicolon at the end of 476 and commas elsewhere. I have adopted Professor Reeve's suggestion that the structure of this long sentence is best shown by putting semicolons after each subordinate clause and brackets round Γάλα μιν καλέουσι.

470 Νύξ It is probably right to see a personification of Night here, as in 408, 419, 434, 695. The epithet οὐρανίη is appropriate to a goddess, e.g. Pi. fr. 10.1 Θέμιν οὐρανίαν.

471 ἀδρανέων A verbal form perhaps coined by A. from the adj. ἀδρανής, being attested only here and in the poet's imitators, Opp. *H.* 1.296 and Nonn. *D.* 32.280. Cf. ὀλιγοδρανέων (Ο 246).

νεόμηνι σελήνη Sch. τὸ δὲ διχόμηνι γράφεται καὶ νεόμηνι, τῇ νεωστὶ καὶ πρῶτον ἐκ συνόδου φαινομένη, ἐπειδὴ τότε ἐμφανῆ εἰσι τὰ ἄστρα μὴ καταυγαζόμενα ὑπὸ τοῦ σεληνιακοῦ φωτός. The variants are both ancient, and while the latter is the one that is explained by the sch. here, and elsewhere (ad 474) assumed to be correct, εἰ τοίνυν ἀσελήνου νυκτὸς οὔσης θελήσεις τὸν γαλαξίαν σκέψασθαι, the Latin translators obviously read the former: Cic. 247 *nec pleno stellas superauit lumine luna*, Avien. 938 *nec scindunt medium Phoebeia lumina mensem*, Arat. Lat. *bipertita luna* (p. 276, 11). The tradition of the MSS, however, almost wholly attests νεόμηνι, which was accepted by all editors until Voss adopted διχόμηνι and was followed by all subsequent editors. The argument for this reading is that it is the full moon that makes a star faint: e.g. Martin translates 'quand la pleine lune ne vient pas obscurcir leur éclat'. But it is pointless to require the full moon in this context, since the moon at any phase dims the stars to a greater or lesser extent, and what A. has in mind is the brilliance of the Milky Way on a moonless night. This is precisely the time designated by νεόμηνι σελήνη, when the moon is in conjunction with the sun, and so completely absent from the night sky. A.'s phrase in fact reflects the technical expression νουμηνία κατὰ σελήνην, which distinguishes the astronomical new moon from the calendaric new moon νουμηνία κατ' ἄρχοντα. Cf. Th. 2.28 νουμηνίᾳ κατὰ σελήνην. ὥσπερ καὶ μόνον δοκεῖ εἶναι γίγνεσθαι δυνατόν, ὁ ἥλιος ἐξέλιπε, and Gomme ad loc. The v.l. most probably came from 78, where the full moon is appropriate. On the other hand νεόμηνι occurs only here, and is on that account less likely to be corrupt.

472 κνέφαος Unqualified, as Homeric νυκτός (ν 278); cf. 872. Chantraine 2.59.

473 τημόσδε The suffix appears to have a purely emphatic force; cf. Call. *H.* 1.21, A.R. 2.957, Theoc. 10.49.

περὶ φρένας ἵκετο Cf. ι 362 περὶ φρένας ἥλυθεν οἶνος, Λ 89 περὶ φρένας ἵμερος αἱρεῖ, *h.Hom.* 3.461, Alcm. *PMG* 3.1, Q.S. 2.615, 4.208, 12.116, 14.80.

474 κεκεασμένον From κεάζω 'split'; cf. σ 309, of timber, νέον κεκεασμένα χαλκῷ. Sch. τὸν γαλαξίαν σκέψασθαι, ᾧ πᾶς διχοτομεῖται ὁ οὐρανός. This is a bold and original metaphor.

475 ἐπιστάς The MS tradition attests ὑποστάς, which is read by all editors before Buhle. But sch. 469 paraphrase with ἢ καὶ ἄλλος παρεστηκώς τις ἔδειξεν, and this sense is well suited to the context: cf. the recurring theme of pointing out stars to the learner, and the idea of helping others in 763–4. Ceporinus' edition of 1523 prints ὑποστάς with the translation *astans*, and similarly Zannoni with 'standoti da presso'. But there is no evidence that ὑφίστασθαι ever had this meaning, whereas ἐφίστασθαι c. dat. occurs in Homer in the sense of 'standing close to', e.g. Ν 133 ἐφέστασαν ἀλλήλοισιν, Λ 644 θύρησιν ἐφίστατο. Cf. the prose usage with ἐπί c. acc., Hdt. 3.77 ἐπιστᾶσι ἐπὶ τὰς πύλας, Pl. *Symp.* 212d ἐπιστῆναι ἐπὶ τὰς θύρας.

476 περιγληνές Only here. Cf. 318 γλήνεα, [Theoc.] 25.241 περιγληνώμενος ὄσσοις.

τροχαλόν Only here as subst. Cf. 530 τροχάλεια.

Γάλα The name is attested as early as Parm. fr. 11.2 γάλα τ' οὐράνιον, and established as simply τὸ γάλα by Aristotle, who devotes a chapter (*Mete.* A 8) to a discussion of earlier theories. He refutes the suggestions that the Milky Way was the path of a star that fell at the time of Phaethon or was once the path of the sun (Pythagoreans), that it is the light of stars within the earth's shadow and so not dimmed by the sun (Anaxagoras and Democritus), or a reflection of our vision towards the sun (unattributed). He himself explains it as due to the igniting of the outermost layer of the air by contact with the movement of the sky. Cf. Heath 247–8; Dicks 209. Aristotle notes that the Milky Way is a great circle, οὗτος δ' ὁ κύκλος ἐν ᾧ τὸ γάλα φαίνεται τοῖς ὁρῶσιν, ὅ τε μέγιστος ὢν τυγχάνει, and that it is full of bright stars, ἄστρων ὁ τόπος πλήρης ἐστὶν τῶν μεγίστων καὶ λαμπροτάτων (346a). This long tradition of Greek interest helps to explain why A. elaborates the

Milky Way theme, though its immediate relevance is that it provides a visible illustration of a celestial great circle.

Hipparchus refers to this passage as περὶ τοῦ γαλαξίου κύκλου (1.9.14), and Geminus calls it ὁ τοῦ γάλακτος κύκλος (5.69). The term γαλαξίας is later (D.S. 5.23, Luc. *V.H.* 1.16, *Catast.* 44), and Ptolemy uses ὁ γαλακτίας (*Alm.* 8.2); cf. Mart. Cap. 8.826 *galaxias*. Only Avien. 942 refers to it as *lac*. The normal Latin term is *lacteus* with *circulus* (Plin. *Nat.* 18.280, Hyg. 2.43) or *orbis* (Germ. 458, Man. 1.753), and poetic variations are *lactea* with *uia* (Ov. *Met.* 1.168–9) and *plaga* (Stat. *Silv.* 1.2.51).

477 τῷ δή τοι This introduces the main clause (see note on 469– 479); δ᾽ ἤτοι is unlikely, since A. does not use apodotic δέ elsewhere. Voss read τῷδ᾽ ἤτοι, but ὅδε is normally deictic in Homer (Monro 216), and A. does not use that pron. except in 752 τάδε and 1017 τόδε. For δή τοι with demonstr. pron. cf. Hes. *Th.* 1015, *Op.* 385.

χροιήν Once in Homer (Ξ 164). The colour is simply the whiteness of the stars; cf. Phlp. *in Mete.* A 1 τοῦ γαλαξίου, ὅς ἐστι τῷ χρώματι λευκός, διὸ καὶ οὕτως ὠνόμασται, ὡς καὶ Ἄρατος αὐτὸν ὀνομάζει.

ἀλίγκιος Cf. 462.

478 δινεῖται Primarily of the daily rotation, but suggestive also of the circular form of the Milky Way; cf. δινεύονται 489, 510, δινωτοῖσι 462.

πισύρων Aeolic form, occasionally used in epic, e.g. Ο 680, ε 70 (see J. B. Hainsworth's note); cf. 722, Call. *H.* 3.105, A.R. 2.1110, Nic. *Ther.* 182.

479 οἱ δύο The equator and the ecliptic, both great circles.

μέγα μείονες The two tropics are smaller circles than the equator. Hipparchus finds fault with A. for saying they are πολλῷ ἐλάσσονες: they are smaller by less than $\frac{1}{11}$ (1.9.15). The adverbial use of μέγα with an adj. is Homeric, e.g. Β 239 μέγ᾽ ἀμείνονα, 274 μέγ᾽ ἄριστον, Α 158 μέγ᾽ ἀναιδές, Π 46 μέγα νήπιος. Leumann (120) suggests that it developed from the use of the neut. adj. in μέγα φρονέων (e.g. Λ 296 of Hector). With μείονες it seems to be a humorous touch.

480–500 The northern tropic (tropic of Cancer)

A. shows how the line of this circle may be identified by noting the bright stars that lie on or close to it. Hipparchus, who calls this tropic ὁ θερινὸς τροπικός, quotes the corresponding text of Eudoxus and then A.'s lines as far as 488, remarking that A. writes ἀπὸ τῶν ἐσχάτων ἀρξάμενος (1.2.18–19). This is a major example of variation. Eudoxus starts with the Crab and moves eastward round the tropic to finish again with the Crab, whereas A. begins with the Twins and moves westward to end with the Crab. In 1.10.1–15 Hipparchus returns to the tropic, noting that A. has followed E. in most of the details, but has differed in a few cases (13–15). Hyg. 4.2.1 follows A.'s arrangement. Hipparchus disagrees with A.'s choice of some stars as guides to the tropic, but, writing some two centuries after E., he had the advantage of solstice records over a longer period and more accurate observations on his own part, and so was able to determine the position of the tropic with more precision; he made it approximately 24° N: ὁ μὲν γὰρ θερινὸς τροπικὸς τοῦ ἰσημερινοῦ βορειότερός ἐστι μοίραις ὡς ἔγγιστα κδ'. See note on 527 λοξός. For the Planudean text of 481–96 see Introd. pp. 56–7.

480 κατερχομένου βορέαο Cf. 241 βορέαο νέον κατιόντος.

481 ἐν δέ οἱ The anaphora of ἐν from here to 550 makes the catalogue of stars on the circles seem like a work of art, the model being the shield of Achilles in Σ 483–608.

κεφαλαὶ Διδύμων A. starts his list by keeping as close as possible to Eudox. fr. 66 αἱ κεφαλαὶ τῶν Διδύμων, thereby establishing the passage as technical and authentic. The stars are α and β Geminorum (cf. 147). Hi. 1.10.2 puts the latter at 30° north of the equator and the former at $33\frac{1}{2}°$. Allowing for the effect of precession, their positions are now about 28° and 32° N respectively.

482 τὰ γούνατα Most editors since Bekker have preferred the v.l. τε, because δέ τε is a common formula in enumerating passages, e.g. A 403, B 90, 210, Hes. *Op.* 311, 631. See Maass *Aratea* 100. But A. uses it only five times (518, 898, 1045, 1052, 1059), and only once in the present catalogue of stars that mark the circles. On the other hand τά is attested by the MSS and supported by Πι (s.ii a.C.). Martin (HT 210) regards the latter as providing an early date for the supposed corruption, but it is more reasonable to see it as confirming the correctness of the MSS. There is also a Homeric model for this line in Σ 485 ἐν δὲ τὰ τείρεα πάντα, which begins the third line in the Homeric ecphrasis and has the same metrical pattern as A.'s half-line. Cf. 155 τὰ πηδά, 424 τὰ δὲ λαίφεα, 505 τὸ κέντρον, 492 ὁ κύκλος, 220 οἱ δὲ νομῆες.

Here again A. is close to Eudox. fr. 66 τὰ γόνατα τοῦ Ἡνιόχου. Hipparchus says that the Charioteer has no stars at his knees (1.10.3): the stars nearest to the tropic are the feet, which are at 27° N (ι Aurigae) and $23\frac{1}{2}°$ (β Tauri). He thinks it unlikely that by γούνατα A. means those stars, since he has already referred to the latter as πόδα in 175. It is possible that the configuration of the Charioteer was somewhat different for Eudoxus, and that he designated ι as the knees and β as the feet.

ἀρηρότος Again in 565 of reliable signs. Here the epithet may be intended to suggest also the steadfast figure.

483 λαιὴ δὲ κνήμη καὶ ἀριστερὸς ὦμος Eudox. fr. 66 τοῦ Περσέως ὁ ἀριστερὸς ὦμος καὶ ἡ ἀριστερὰ κνήμη. Hipparchus again disagrees (1.10.5), noting that the central bright star in Perseus (α) is 16° north of the tropic, and the left shoulder (θ) even farther north, He does not refer to the left leg at this point, but mentions it elsewhere as ὁ ἐν τῇ ἀριστερᾷ κνήμῃ (1.6.13), probably ξ Persei, nearer the tropic, but still a few degrees north of it. On Perseus see 248–53. The stars do not make an obvious figure, and A.'s grouping may have been different from that of H.

484 Ἀνδρομέδης Eudox. fr. 66 ἡ δεξιὰ χεὶρ τῆς Ἀνδρομέδας καὶ τὸ μεταξὺ τῶν ποδῶν. A. departs from his source here, elaborating the first detail and ignoring the second. Here too H. comments (1.10.6) that A.'s stars are too far north of the tropic: the stars on the right shoulder are over 30° N, and the right hand is 32° N; the elbow must therefore be well to the north of the tropic. A. and H., however, may again be thinking of different stars. In 201 the shoulders seem to be represented by the bright star δ, the elbow may then be θ σ, and if the tropic cuts the arm half-way between the shoulder and the elbow, the position agrees very closely with the positions of the other stars so far noted.

ὕπερθε In relation to the figure, i.e. between the elbow and the shoulder; cf. 655. A. seems to be recalling Λ 252 κατὰ χεῖρα μέσην ἀγκῶνος ἔνερθε.

485 ἐπέχει The subject changes to the tropic, which here 'occupies' a position in the figure; cf. 57, 176, 244 of stars.

μέν οἱ A. ignores the digamma here and in 707, as Homer in ν 430 κάρψε μέν οἱ. Cf. Theoc. 15.112 and Gow ad loc.

θέναρ Once in Homer (E 339), also of the hand; cf. Paul. Sil. *AP* 5.248.6 οὐκέτι γὰρ μαζοῖς σὸν θέναρ ἐμπελάσει. In 718 A. uses it of the foot.

486 νότῳ Hi. 1.10.6 ὁ ἀγκὼν βορειότερός ἐστιν ἱκανῶς τοῦ τροπικοῦ, καὶ οὐ νοτιώτερος, ὡς Ἄρατός φησιν. But what A. is saying is that the elbow is south of the hand, not south of the tropic.

ἐπικέχλιται Once in Homer, ἐπικεκλιμένας σανίδας (M 121). Here the verb seems an apt choice for an elbow.

487 ὁπλαὶ δ' Ἵππειοι Eudox. fr. 66 οἱ τοῦ Ἵππου πόδες. Hipparchus' comment is (1.10.7) τίνας μὲν οὖν ἀστέρας ἐτίθει ἐπὶ ταῖς ὁπλαῖς, ἄδηλον. But he then refers back to 281, in which the Horses' feet are said to lie close to the Bird's left wing, and since the tip of the latter (ζ Cygni) is 23° N, A. would seem to be about right with the adjacent feet of the Horse. The likely stars are therefore π Pegasi and μ Cygni, the latter of which Manitius on Hi. 2.5.11 identifies as ὁ νοτιώτερος τῶν ἐμπροσθίων ποδῶν.

The adj. has elsewhere three terminations, e.g. δ 40, Theoc. 16.81,

but the MSS of both Hipparchus and A. attest -οι. On the Horse see
205–24.

ὑπαύχενον Ὀρνίθειον Eudox. fr. 66 ὁ αὐχὴν τοῦ Ὄρνιθος καὶ ἡ
ἀριστερὰ πτέρυξ. ὑπαύχενον occurs only here and 524. There is no
particular significance in the prefix, since the word is merely a variation
of Eudoxus' αὐχήν, and both writers refer to the same star, η Cygni:
see on 275–281.

488 ἄκρῃ σὺν κεφαλῇ The star β Cygni, which Hipparchus calls τὸ
ῥύγχος (1.10.8). It is a bright star, and this may be why A. has chosen it
instead of the fainter wing-tip star listed by Eudoxus. Hipparchus finds
both unsuitable, the former being 25° 20′ N, the latter 31°.

Ὀφιούχεοι ὦμοι Eudox. fr. 66 ἡ κεφαλὴ τοῦ Ὀφιούχου. A. has
again departed from Eudoxus, substituting the shoulders for the head,
perhaps because they are brighter (cf. 77). Hipparchus notes (1.10.9) that
A. is completely wrong here: the right shoulder (β) is about 7° N, actually nearer the equator than the tropic, while the left shoulder (κ) is
about 15° N. In 1.10.14 he adds that Eudoxus is more accurate with the
head star (α), but even that is some 7° south of the tropic.

489 δινεύονται Of the diurnal rotation; cf. 455, 510.

ἐληλάμενοι To be taken closely with αὐτὸν περὶ κύκλον, i.e. they
move round the actual line of the tropic; cf. 516. Manitius (Hi. 1.10.9)
and Erren understand the verb in the sense of ἐπελήλαται (162, 205) and
συνεληλάμενοι (176), translating 'fest gefüget' and 'geschmiedet' respectively. but without a prefix the verb is unlikely to have that meaning.
The sense of movement is more appropriate here, especially with περί;
sch. περιελαθέντες καὶ ἐγκείμενοι.

490 οὐδ᾽ ἐπιβάλλει Sch. καὶ οὐκ ἐπιψαύει αὐτοῦ (sc. τοῦ κύκλου).

491 Παρθένος Eudox. fr. 66 τῆς δὲ Παρθένου ⟨τὰ⟩ μικρὸν ἄνωθεν.
Hipparchus quotes 490–6 (1.10.10) and adds ταῦτά μοι δοκεῖ συμφώνως
τοῖς φαινομένοις εἰρηκέναι. A. leaves a large gap in the tropic after the
shoulders of Ophiuchus, where Eudoxus lists the right hand of Engonasin (probably γ Herculis) and the neck of the Serpent (β). He might
well have omitted the Maiden, which is entirely south of the tropic, but
this constellation is important in the scheme of things (see 96–136).

ἀλλὰ Λέων καὶ Καρκίνος Sch. κατὰ κοινοῦ τὸ ἐπιβάλλει· ἀλλ᾽ ὁ
Λέων καὶ ὁ Καρκίνος ἐπιψαύουσι τοῦ κύκλου.

μὲν ἄρ᾽ Referring back to a name just introduced; cf. E 45, Hes. Th.
289 τὸν μὲν ἄρ᾽. Maass and Martin prefer ἄμ᾽ in view of H 255, Ψ 686,
φ 188. But this conflicts with ἐξείης: the Lion and the Crab come one
after the other, not together. In non-technical details the text of Hipparchus does not carry special weight.

492 κέαται Cf. Λ 659, Π 24 κέαται βεβλημένοι, in same *sedes*. A. also has κέονται (457).

βεβολημένοι Better attested here and in 609, a characteristic variation after 311, 358 βεβλημένος, -ον. The v.l. shows the influence of the latter, and perhaps of Λ 659, Π 24. Voss introduced it because of the Homeric parallel, and is followed by most modern editors. But βεβολημένος is also a Homeric form, e.g. Ι 9, κ 247. Cf. Q.S. 7.537, 8.177, 10.276, al.

493 ὑπὸ στῆθος καὶ γαστέρα μέχρι παρ' αἰδῶ Eudox. fr. 66 τὰ διὰ τοῦ σώματος κατὰ μῆκος τοῦ Λέοντος. A. improves on E. by naming specific parts of the Lion's body, but it is not easy to identify these with particular stars. Hipparchus assigns two stars to the breast, α Leonis or Regulus, ὃν δή τινες ἐν τῇ καρδίᾳ τιθέασι, and η Leonis to the north of it. He makes the tropic pass between these two stars (1.10.10). Farther east he aligns it between θ in the thighs and ι in the legs, and he sums up by confirming ὅτι διὰ μήκους ὑπ' αὐτοῦ ὁ Λέων τέμνεται ὑπὸ τὸ στῆθος καὶ τὴν λαγόνα (1.10.11). If A. is thinking of specific stars representing breast, belly and genitals, these would have to be α θ β, which make an obvious line close to the line of the tropic; but he may be referring more loosely to the parts of the conventional figure. Hi. 2.5.6 identifies β Leonis with the tip of the tail. Homer has αἰδώς for αἰδοῖα in Β 262, where Kirk notes that the genitals are seldom mentioned in epic; cf. Χ 75, Q.S. 13.98.

494 διηνεκέως Cf. δ 836, η 241, μ 56. See note on 445 ἠνεκές.

ὑπένερθε χελείου Eudox. fr. 66 ἔστι δὲ ἐν τούτῳ τὰ μέσα τοῦ Καρκίνου. Hi. 1.10.12 confirms this, giving the precise positions of the four stars surrounding the nebula: see on 147 and 892–908. Here ὑπένερθε cannot mean 'south of', since the line goes through the centre of the Crab. A. is probably thinking of the tropic crossing in front of the Crab, as in an armillary sphere the circle might be attached to the inside of the Zodiac band; so observers on earth, looking up at the Crab, imagine the tropic as being nearer to them, and in that sense below the constellation. Cf. 997 of cloud below the Crab, also 542 ὑποδράμοι, 854 ὑποσκιάῃσι, 1015 ὑποτρέχῃ. χέλειον is a rare variation of χέλυς, normally a tortoise's shell: cf. 268, and Nic. *Alex.* 561.

495 διχαιόμενον Poetic form of διχάζω, only in A., here and 807.

496 ὀρθόν Of a straight line; cf. S. *Aj.* 1254 ὀρθὸς εἰς ὁδὸν πορεύεται, E. *Hel.* 1556 οὐκ ἤθελ' ὀρθὸς σανίδα προσβῆναι κάτα.

ἵν' Sch. interpret as consecutive, οὕτως ὀρθῶς καὶ θαυμαστῶς διχῆ αὐτὸν τέμνει, ὡς καὶ διὰ μέσων τῶν ὀφθαλμῶν εἶναι τὸν κύκλον. So Buhle 'recte ut oculi a circulo utrimque eant', and Martin 'coupé en deux d'une ligne si droite qu'il a un œil de chaque côté du cercle'. This is an unparalleled use of ἵνα. Wilamowitz takes it as final, but very much weakened in force (*HD* 274); but the context hardly admits this meaning. The only possible solution is to take ἵνα as introducing an adverbial clause of place, defining more precisely the position already indicated by ἧχι, i.e. where you can most clearly (μάλιστα) observe the tropic passing across the Crab, namely at the point where the eyes are on either side of it. The opt. reflects the mood of νοήσαις, and denotes what the observer can expect to see. Comparable uses of ἵνα are ρ 250 ἄξω τῆλ' Ἰθάκης, ἵνα μοι βίοτον πολὺν ἄλφοι ('to a place where'), and [Theoc.] 25.61 αὖλιν ἐφ' ἡμετέρην, ἵνα κεν τέτμοιμεν ἄνακτα (Gow 'for there'). See K–G 2.378, Schwyzer 2.672–3. Only Manitius so translates, 'grad' wo' (Hi. 1.10.10).

ὀφθαλμοί The stars γ δ Cancri, which are about 3° apart. Hi. 1.10.12 puts the former about $2\frac{1}{2}°$ north of the tropic, the latter almost on it.

ἴοιεν A. uses the verb of motion because of the stars' continuous westward movement, but its primary function is to denote their position; cf. 352. Hence sch. εἶναι.

497 τοῦ μέν Sc. κύκλου.

ὅσον τε μάλιστα A combination of two expressions, both of which can mean 'approximately'; e.g. κ 517 ὅσον τε πυγούσιον, Th. 3.92.6 σταδίους μάλιστα τεσσαράκοντα. Cf. 896.

δι' ὀκτὼ μετρηθέντος διά c. gen. expresses equal intervals into which a line is divided; cf. Th. 3.21.3 διὰ δέκα δὲ ἐπάλξεων πύργοι ἦσαν. The technical language is appropriate in a didactic poem, as again in 541–3 with μετρηθεῖσα. The verb occurs once in Homer, γ 179 μετρήσαντες.

498–499 πέντε... τὰ τρία A. is referring to an early method of determining terrestrial latitude. The northern tropic is a circle parallel to the celestial equator, and so, when observed from the earth's equator, it cuts the horizon at right angles and is bisected by it. As the observer moves north, the angle sharpens and more of the tropic is above the horizon than below it, until eventually (at about 67° N) the whole tropic is circumpolar. Between these two extremes the ratio of the segment above to the segment below the horizon indicates the latitude of the observer, and the method is a rough but useful one for Mediterranean latitudes. A. has taken the ratio 5 : 3 from Eudoxus' *Enoptron*, according to Hi. 1.2.22 καὶ γὰρ ὁ Εὔδοξος ἐν τῷ ἐπιγραφομένῳ Ἐνόπτρῳ τὸν τροπικὸν τέμνεσθαί φησιν οὕτως, ὥστε λόγον ἔχειν τὰ τμήματα πρὸς ἄλληλα τὸν αὐτὸν οἷον ἔχει τὰ ε' πρὸς τὰ γ'. Attalus agrees (fr. 21). Hi. 1.3.7 equates this ratio with that of the longest day to the shortest night, and with a latitude of 41° N, adding that this is wrong for central

Greece, but right for the Hellespont. Hi. 1.3.10 also records that Eudoxus ἐν τῷ ἑτέρῳ συντάγματι (which must be the *Phaenomena*) gives the ratio 12:7, and as this represents a latitude even farther north (Dicks *EGA* 154), it appears that A. has chosen the more accurate of the two ratios provided by his source. Even so, as Hipparchus complains, it is not exactly right for Athens, but such precision was not possible in the fourth century, and the ratio 5:3 is a conveniently simple one that is roughly valid for central Greece. See Hyg. 4.2.2, Dicks *EGA* 19–23, Erren *PAS* 193–7, Aujac *Str.* 163–4, Neugebauer *HAMA* 711.

498 ἔνδια In Homer this word denotes a time in the middle of the day, e.g. Λ 726 ἔνδιοι ἱκόμεσθ᾽, δ 450 ἔνδιος δ᾽ ὁ γέρων ἦλθ᾽ ἐξ ἁλός. So Theoc. 16.95, A.R. 4.1312, Call. fr. 238.15, 260.55. Hence Voss translates 'in den Hohen des Tages', Mair and LSJ 'in the daytime', Erren 'auf der Tagseite'. But this is not true. What A. means is that there are five eighths of the tropic above the horizon and three eighths below it at all times, day and night; cf. sch. τὰ μὲν πέντε μέρη ὑπέργεια καὶ ἐν ὕψει ⟨ἂν⟩ εὑρεθείη κινούμενα, τὰ δὲ λοιπὰ τρία ἐν δύσει καὶ ὑπὸ γῆν. Therefore ἔνδια here means 'in the sky', and the sense is confirmed by καθ᾽ ὑπέρτερα γαίης. Cf. 954 ἐνδίοιο. This may be what Martin means by 'dans la partie lumineuse du ciel', but his version is not clear. Thus A. has adopted a Homeric word, but with a different meaning.

στρέφεται Merely the regular westward movement of the sky.

499 ἐν περάτῃ The farthest point, hence the horizon. Cf. ψ 243 of Athene holding night still hovering on the western horizon. A. has the phrase in the same metrical position, but extends the meaning to 'below the horizon' (LSJ wrongly refer it to the southern hemisphere). For the west cf. Call. *H.* 4.169. In 670 and 821 περάτης denotes the eastern horizon; cf. A.R. 1.1281.

τροπαί The most ancient method of determining the solstices was to observe the most northerly and most southerly points on either horizon at which the sun set and rose, especially the sunsets, which are easier to observe. The plural is always used with reference to one solstice, presumably because it is a phenomenon that recurs at the same point every year. In ο 404 this is the most likely explanation of ὅθι τροπαὶ ἠελίοιο (Waltz; Stanford ad loc.). In Hesiod it is the seasonal dates that are indicated, the winter solstice in *Op.* 479, 564, the summer in 663. So Alcm. *PMG* 17.5 of midsummer. Here it is the position of the sun at the point where the ecliptic touches the tropic, from which the sun simply continues on its course through the Zodiac, and there is no observable turning. Cf. τρέπεται 286, 508. For ἐν following a pronoun cf. μ 103 τῷ δ᾽ ἐν ἐρινεός ἐστι.

500 ἐν βορέῳ Cf. 250.

ἐστήρικται A suitable verb for the fixed stars (cf. 230, 274, 351), and so also for the tropic, the position of which is defined by them.

501–510 The southern tropic (tropic of Capricorn)

Hipparchus, who calls it ὁ χειμερινὸς τροπικός, agrees with A.'s choice of stars except for the Scorpion's sting (1.10.16). He cites the corresponding passage of Eudoxus (fr. 73) in 1.2.20, which shows that this time A. has followed his model in working eastward round the circle. Cf. Hyg. 4.4. For the Planudean version of 501–6 see p. 57.

501 ἀντιόωντι Diectasis, as in α 25 ἀντιόων, Nic. *Ther.* 77 ἀντιόωντα. A. is using the participle in the sense of ἀντίος in 25; sch. ἐν τῷ νοτίῳ τῷ ἐξ ἐναντίας τοῦ βορέω, and ἐν τῷ νοτίῳ τῷ ἔχοντι ἐναντίαν θέσιν τοῦ βορρᾶ, and again (MA) νότιον ἔχων τὴν θέσιν, ἐναντίος ἐστὶ τῷ θερινῷ τροπικῷ. Maass favoured the v.l. rejected by sch. τινὲς δὲ ἔγραψαν "ἀντιόωντα νότῳ" ἀμαθῶς. Martin has refuted it at length. The southern tropic is on the opposite side of the equator, but not 'aux antipodes': the two circles are only about $47\frac{1}{2}°$ apart. Cf. 528.

μέσον Αἰγοκερῆα Eudox. τὰ μέσα τοῦ Αἰγόκερω. This constellation lacks bright stars (see on 285–299), and it is likely that no particular stars are denoted by μέσον and τὰ μέσα. This tropic is less precisely defined, the references being mostly to figures and their parts: it was too far south for easy star recognition.

502 πόδας Ὑδροχόου καὶ Κήτεος οὐρήν A. reproduces the chiasmus of Eudox. οἱ πόδες τοῦ Ὑδροχόου καὶ τοῦ Κήτους ἡ οὐρά, which shows that the latter had learnt from Plato some sense of style. For the Water-pourer see 282–5. The feet may be δ Aquarii, which Hi. 3.3.8 calls the right foot. The Monster's tail is probably ι Ceti, which Hi. 3.1.8 calls the more northerly of the two tail stars. See on 398.

503 Λαγωός Eudox. τοῦ Ποταμοῦ ἡ καμπή, καὶ ὁ Λαγωός. A. omits the River, perhaps because he has not yet introduced the great bend, a curving line of rather faint stars; the bends are mentioned in 634, 728. The Hare is so small that it is not necessary to refer to particular stars. A. does not mention any part of the Hare until 594 (the sides).

503–504 κυνὸς οὐ μάλα πολλὴν ... ποσίν Eudox. τοῦ Κυνὸς οἱ πόδες καὶ ἡ οὐρά. A. omits the tail star, though he has already mentioned it in 342, and amplifies the reference to the feet. Hi. 1.10.17 notes without comment the words of Eudoxus, and in fact the tropic would have passed between the forefeet (β) and the tail (η). Sch. explain οὐ μάλα πολλήν with reference to a portion of the body: ὀλίγην μερίδα ἐπέχει τοῦ σώματος τοῦ Κυνός, ἄχρι τῶν ἐμπροσθίων ποδῶν. It is perhaps more likely that A. would have understood χώρην: cf. 134 of the Maiden's place in the sky, and 255–6 of the Pleiades οὐ μάλα πολλὸς ἁπάσας χῶρος ἔχει. He may also have had in mind Ψ 520–1 οὐδέ τι πολλή | χώρη μεσσηγύς.

504 αἴνυται A Homeric verb, e.g. (literal) Λ 580 αἴνυτο τεύχε᾽ ἀπ᾽ ὤμων, (figurative) ξ 144 μ᾽ Ὀδυσσῆος πόθος αἴνυται. A. extends the sense to that of taking up space; cf. 603 with a further extension of meaning.

Ἀργώ Eudox. τῆς Ἀργοῦς ἡ πρύμνα καὶ ὁ ἱστός. A. omits the specific star references, leaving only the name of the constellation, which is too large to be of any practical use as a guide to the tropic. He has already referred to the stern (343) and the mast (350).

505 Κενταύροιο μετάφρενον Eudox. τοῦ Κενταύρου ὁ νῶτος καὶ τὰ στήθη. A. chooses a Homeric word, well defined in E 56–7 μετάφρενον οὔτασε δουρί | ὤμων μεσσηγύς, διὰ δὲ στήθεσφιν ἔλασσεν. Cf. sch. (ΚΑ) αἱ φρένες ἐν τῷ στήθει περίκεινται. μετάφρενον γὰρ τὸ μετὰ τὴν φρένα ἤγουν τὸ ὄπισθεν τῆς φρενός, τὸ δίμοιρον τῆς ῥάχεως. The line indicated runs through the upper part of the human body, just below the shoulders (θ 1).

τὸ κέντρον Eudox. τὸ Θηρίον καὶ τοῦ Σκορπίου τὸ κέντρον. A. omits the Beast, with good reason, since it lay entirely south of the tropic; cf. Hi. 1.10.17 πολλῷ γὰρ νοτιώτερόν ἐστι τὸ Θηρίον τοῦ χειμερινοῦ τροπικοῦ. It is possible that A. is deliberately correcting Eudoxus here; cf. note on 24 πόλοι.

Editorial tradition since Aldus has favoured τε here, but the support of M and the text of Hipparchus in both quotations gives τό rather more weight, and Zannoni has adopted it. Homeric use of δέ τε has not had much influence on A., who on the other hand does make frequent use of the def. art.: see notes on 155, 482. In this case it may indicate that the sting is already familiar from 305, 402. Hi. 1.10.16 objects that the sting stars (λ υ) are not an accurate guide to the tropic: οἱ μέντοι γε ἐν τῷ κέντρῳ τοῦ Σκορπίου νοτιώτεροί εἰσι τοῦ χειμερινοῦ τροπικοῦ πλέον ἢ μοίραις η΄. μᾶλλον οὖν τὰ μέσα τοῦ Σκορπίου ἐπὶ τοῦ χειμερινοῦ τροπικοῦ κεῖται κύκλου.

506 τόξον ἀγαυοῦ Τοξευτῆρος Eudox. εἶτα διὰ τοῦ Τοξότου πρὸς τὰ μέσα τοῦ Αἰγόκερω συνάπτει. The bow is the most identifiable part of the constellation (see 300–10), and sometimes represents the whole, but in this case it is the relevant part, since the tropic passed through the centre of it. A. thus defines the position more accurately than Eudoxus. He also omits as superfluous E.'s continuation of the circle to bring it back to Capricorn.

ἀγαυοῦ   Maass prints ἐλαφροῦ as the *lectio difficilior*: it is not visually justified, and ἀγαυοῦ would be a natural correction (*Aratea* 103). So Martin and Erren. There is some support in Max. 25 Τοξευτῆρος ἐλαφροῦ, and in *Arat. Lat. leuioris*. But it is difficult to believe that A. could have called the Archer ἐλαφρός, an adj. which he uses in 81 with the sense of being so faint as to be difficult to see. The Archer is in one of the brightest parts of the Milky Way: when we look at it we are looking towards the centre of our Galaxy (Norton 104–5), and it contains three stars of 2nd and seven of 3rd mag. Elsewhere the bow is μέγα (305), and the constellation dignified with αὐτός (685). Cf. Cic. fr. 33.181–2 *magni* | *Arquitenentis*, Germ. 491 *magnus micat Arcus*, fr. 4.157 *clara Sagittiferi tetigit cum lumina signi*. A. uses ἀγαυός of the Crown (71), the Water-pourer (392), stars generally on a moonless night (469), and negatively of the Claws (90). The v.l. is obviously an early corruption, and its source is probably the misquotation in Hi. 1.2.21. A marginal gloss in M attempts an explanation with καθὸ οἱ τοξόται ψιλοί εἰσιν.

507 τὸν πύματον   The tropic of Capricorn is the third and last circle that the sun comes to from the tropic of Cancer via the equator. By placing this phrase immediately after Τοξευτῆρος and before giving his description of the equator A. has introduced an element of confusion. Hence sch. τοῦ Τοξότου οὐκ ἔστι τι νοτιώτερον. τοῦτο οὖν ὅτι εἰς τὸν Τοξότην πύματον καὶ ἔσχατον φέρεται ὁ ἥλιος ὡς ἐπὶ τὸν νότον κατιών, καὶ λοιπὸν διερχόμενος ὡς ἐπὶ τὰ βόρεια ἀπὸ Αἰγοκέρωτος.

καθαροῖο   Sch. ὅτι αἰθρηγενέτης ὁ ἄνεμος.

παρερχόμενος   Apparently not attested elsewhere c. gen. The vv.ll. κατ- and δι- derive from the sch. quoted above on τὸν πύματον.

508 φέρεται   C. acc. τὸν πύματον, while ἐς νότον must be taken with παρερχόμενος.

τρέπεται   Variation of 499 οἱ ἐν τροπαί εἰσιν. Cf. 286.

γε μέν   Affirmative, bringing out the particular point of importance; cf. 17.

509 χειμέριος   Normally used in sense of 'stormy', as in 760, 879, also B 294, whereas χειμερινός is regularly used of winter. But cf. Hes. *Op.* 494 ὥρῃ χειμερίῃ, 564–5 μετὰ τροπὰς ἠελίοιο | χειμέρι' ἐκτελέσῃ Ζεὺς ἤματα.

509–10 τρία ... τὰ δὲ πέντε   The converse of 498–9 for observers in Greece. περιτέλλεται ὑψοῦ is a variation of στρέφεται καθ' ὑπέρτερα γαίης.

510 κατώρυχα   An original extension of the literal sense 'underground', as in A. *Pr.* 452 κατώρυχες δ' ἔναιον, and a variation of 499 ἐν περάτῃ.

511–524 The equator

The celestial equator is a great circle bisected by the horizon, and the equinoxes occur when the sun crosses it. A. lists the constellations and some particular stars that lie on it. Hipparchus in 1.10.22 reports the details in Eudoxus that are different or are omitted by A. (fr. 71), adding only a brief quotation in 2.1.20 (fr. 69). He gives his own criticisms in 1.10.18–21. Hyg. 4.3.2 follows A. closely.

511 ὅσσος πολιοῖο Γάλακτος I.e. a great circle; cf. 478–9. For πολιός 'white', not 'grey' (Mair), see West on Hes. *Op.* 477.

512 ὑποστρέφεται Cf. 593 ὑποστρέφει intrans. c. gen. Maass reads ὕπο στρέφεται, but the compound verb is more suitable here, since both parts of it relate to the earth, whereas in 73 only the prep. is relevant to νώτῳ.

διχόωντι The epic diectasis seems right here in view of διχόωσα (605, 773, 799), διχόωνται (856). The part. is used in 605, 773 and 779 of the half-ship Argo and the half-moon, so here of the circle that is apparently halved by the horizon. A. thus contrasts the equator with the tropics, which are divided by the horizon in the ratio of 5:3. Mair is mistaken in assuming the part. to be active, 'and with imaginary line bisects the sphere'. Erren translates accurately 'der einem halbierten gleicht'.

513 ἐν δέ οἱ ἤματα The expression is somewhat condensed: it is when the sun is on the equator that the days are equal to the nights.

ἀμφοτέρῃσι 'the two' (cf. 236), i.e. at both equinoxes, autumn and spring.

514 φθίνοντος θέρεος In non-technical language θέρος often denotes the warmer part of the year, associated with the growth and harvesting of crops, seafaring and campaigning, χεῖμα the colder part, when these activities are limited. Thus the two periods comprise the whole year: cf. ἢ 117–18 οὐδ᾽ ἀπολείπει | χείματος οὐδὲ θέρευς, Hes. *Op.* 640 Ἄσκρῃ, χεῖμα κακῇ, θέρει ἀργαλέῃ. See Gomme, *Historical Commentary on Thucydides* 3.703–10. Spring and autumn are then subdivisions of θέρος, but while spring is easily recognised as the beginning of the active year, autumn is harder to define as a season, being a term mainly associated with harvests: it is called variously ὀπώρα, μετόπωρον, φθινόπωρον. A. is not concerned with harvests here, but with an astronomical date in what might be seen as the third subdivision of θέρος, and it may be with this in mind that he has taken over φθίνοντος from its lunar usage, first of the waning moon, e.g. ξ 162 τοῦ μὲν φθίνοντος μηνός, τοῦ δ᾽ ἱσταμένοιο, and later of the last ten days of the calendaric month, e.g. Th. 5.54.3 τετράδι φθίνοντος. Cf. 1149 of the month, 998 of winter. Hi. 1.9.9 paraphrases with ἔν τε τῷ ἔαρι καὶ τῷ φθινοπώρῳ. Stylistically A. follows the antithesis of the Homeric line, with the additional figure of a chiasmus.

τοτὲ δ' Without a preceding τοτὲ μέν. Cf. 775, and Λ 62–3 ἐκ νεφέων ἀναφαίνεται οὔλιος ἀστὴρ | παμφαίνων, τοτὲ δ' αὖτις ἔδυ νέφεα. Cf. Denniston 166 (ii).

εἴαρος ἰσταμένοιο Cf. Hes. *Op.* 569 ἔαρος νέον ἰσταμένοιο, Nonn. *D.* 38.345 ἤματος ἰσταμένοιο.

515 σῆμα δέ οἱ The v.l. τοι illustrates the occasional unreliability of Hipparchus' text. Here it is influenced by 303, 909, and the frequent use of the 2nd pers. pron. in the poem. In this line οἱ depends on κεῖται (cf. 168). For Planudes' version of 515–24 see p. 57.

Ταύροιό τε γούνατα The only legs in the Bull are the forelegs: see 167–78. The relevant star is perhaps μ Tauri.

516 Κριὸς μὲν κατὰ μῆκος Eudox. τά τε τοῦ Κριοῦ μέσα (fr. 69). A. means that the figure lies lengthwise along the equator, but Hipparchus (1.10.18) comments that only the hind legs of the Ram lie on the equator, the rest of the constellation being wholly north of it. For A. the Ram may have consisted solely of the three head stars: see on 225–32.

517 σκελέων ὅσση ... ὀκλάς Sch. ὁπόση ἐστὶ κλάσις καὶ καμπὴ τῶν σκελῶν. A. is giving a more precise description of γούνατα (315), for which the only available stars are the angled formation λ μ ν southwest of the Hyades (see on 167–178). Thus ὅσση represents the limited extent of the group. But ὅσση presupposes a nom. fem. sg. substantive following, as sch. indicate, and Maass adopted ὀκλάς from MSS of Hi. 1.10.18. This noun is not attested elsewhere, but Frisk (2.373) envisages it as a possible basis for ὀκλάζω. A. is similarly the only source for διχάς (737, 807, 809), associated with διχάζω, and other fem. nouns in -άς with corresponding verbs in -άζω are γυμνάς, νομάς, σκιάς, φοιτάς. The reading ὀκλάξ may have been due to the influence of A.R. 3.1308, of Jason bringing the bull down on its knees, τὸν δ' ἐν χθονὶ κάββαλεν ὀκλάξ, which was perhaps intended as an echo of A. with variation. Cf. Luc. 3.254–5 *nisi poplite lapso | ultima curuati procederet ungula Tauri.*

περιφαίνεται Being on the celestial equator, the Bull can be seen from almost everywhere. Cf. Ν 179 ὄρεος κορυφῇ ἔκαθεν περιφαινομένοιο.

518 ζώνη Hi. 1.10.19 ἡ μὲν οὖν τοῦ Ὠρίωνος ζώνη κεῖται ἐπὶ τοῦ ἰσημερινοῦ. Cf. 232, 587, 754; the stars are δ ε ζ Orionis.

εὐφεγγέος Maass prints εὐφεγγέος but this is unlikely, since Homer uses the disyllabic form of this prefix when the second syllable is long, e.g. Α 17 ἐυκνήμιδες, θ 392 φᾶρος ἐυπλυνές. The only sure instance in A. is 635 ἐυρρόου. Cf. Call. fr. 75.73 ἐυπλοκάμων, *H.* 3.190 ἐύσκοπον.

519 καμπὴ δ' αἰθομένης Ὕδρης Hi. 1.10.19 ἡ δὲ σπεῖρα τοῦ Δράκοντος. The use of Δράκων for Ὕδρος is strange (see note on 443–450). For this and other reasons, relating to the positions of the constellations in the time of Hipparchus, Manitius (p. 297, n. 12) suspects that this four-line comment is a later addition. αἰθομένης is perhaps chosen to suggest the fearfulness of this monster: the stars of the Hydra are not particularly bright. Cf. 212, 402, 595.

520 Κρητήρ . . . Κόραξ See note on 448–449.

521 Χηλάων Eudox. fr. 69 τὰ (μέσα) τῶν Χηλῶν. The Scorpion's Claws are now Libra (see 89–90). Hi. 1.10.20 says that only the bright star in the northern claw (β Librae) is near the equator, the rest well to the south of it.

Ὀφιούχεα γοῦνα φορεῖται For Ophiuchus see 74–87, the adj. 75, 488. With the rare epic pl. A. recalls Z 511 γοῦνα φέρει, and he repeats the noun in 652, 704. The v.l. γούνατα κεῖται has come in from 515. Hi. 1.10.20 puts the knees (ζ η) 3½° and more than 10° respectively south of the equator. Cf. Phoenix 2.13 (CA p. 233) εἰς τὰ γοῦνα.

522 Αἰητοῦ See on 313–315; this variation of the normal epic form appears again in 691.

ἀπαμείρεται Cf. Hes. Th. 801 θεῶν ἀπαμείρεται αἰὲν ἐόντων with West's note, A.R. 3.785 ζώης ἀπαμείρεται, Nonn. D. 29.160, also v.l. in ρ 322 ap. Pl. Lg. 777a. The v.l. here (ἀπομείρεται) would mean the opposite, that the equator does not 'take up a part of' the Eagle; cf. Hes. Op. 578. This reading is implied by sch. τοῦ μὲν Ἀετοῦ οὐκ ἀπολαμβάνει τι, ἀλλὰ μόνον ἐγγὺς αὐτοῦ ἐστιν ὁ τοῦ Διὸς ἄγγελος Ἀετός, and is preferred by Voss, Buttmann and Erren, by the last on the ground that it fits the reconstruction of the Aratean sphere. But A. is professing to list the stars that are actually on the equator, and his meaning must be that the equator is not without a share of the Eagle. Eudoxus is more precise with τοῦ τ' Ἀετοῦ τὴν ἀριστερὰν πτέρυγα (fr. 71), and Hi. 1.10.21 confirms that A. is not in error: συνεγγίζει δὲ καὶ ταῦτα τῇ ἀληθείᾳ. See also Martin ad loc.

οἱ ἐγγύς The v.l. μάλ' is probably a reminiscence of 396 and 895. A. elsewhere uses ἐγγύς either c. gen. (136, 578) or abs. (396, 787, 895). Here ἐγγύς should probably be taken in the latter sense and οἱ as ethic dat.; cf. Λ 339–40 οὐδέ οἱ ἵπποι | ἐγγὺς ἔσαν.

523 Ζηνὸς . . . ἄγγελος Ω 292, 296. Cf. A. Supp. 212 Ζηνὸς ὄρνιν, S. Ant. 1040 Ζηνὸς ἀετοί, E. Ion 158–9 Ζηνὸς | κῆρυξ.

ἀητεῖται Only here, perhaps coined by A. for the play on Αἰητός: cf. 313 ἄηται with Ἀητόν.

κατ' αὐτόν The v.l. αὐτούς could only refer to the preceding constellations, which lie at intervals all round the circle, whereas κατά implies a certain proximity. Mair translates 'facing the Eagle', but αὐτόν is more likely to be the tropic like οἱ and τῷ above.

524 Ἱππείη κεφαλὴ καὶ ὑπαύχενον The stars are ε θ Pegasi (head) and ζ ξ (neck); cf. 601. But Eudox. fr. 71 τοῦ δὲ Ἵππου καὶ τὴν ὀσφύν refers to γ Pegasi. Hi. 1.10.23 comments that this star is more than $3\frac{1}{2}°$ north of the equator, and so A. appears to have corrected Eudoxus in this instance. The adj. is Homeric, e.g. K 568 φάτνη ἐφ᾽ ἱππείῃ. Cf. 487, 601. For ὑπαύχενον cf. 487.

525–558 The ecliptic

Before listing the constellations that lie on the ecliptic, A. explains how this circle combines with the other three to make a perfectly designed system, and how the points where the ecliptic cuts the horizon on each side move along a wide arc between one solstice and the next. If a hexagon with each side equal to the radius of this circle is inscribed within it, each side will subtend two constellations. These twelve constellations form the Zodiac, and the sun passes through them in the course of a year. In the course of a night six of them rise and six set. See Aujac *Zodiaque* 6–27; H. Gundel, 'Zodiakos', *RE* 10A. 462ff.

525 Cf. 318; sch. ὡσανεὶ παραβλητικῶς καὶ παραλλήλως κειμένους. The four circles are otherwise described in 467–8, and now three are for the first time characterised as being parallel.

ὀρθούς The geometrical sense of 'at right angles'; cf. Euc. *Phaen.* 2 ἐν μιᾷ κόσμου περιφορᾷ ὁ μὲν διὰ τῶν πόλων τῆς σφαίρας κύκλος δὶς ἔσται ὀρθὸς πρὸς τὸν ὁρίζοντα. These three circles are here contrasted with the ecliptic, which is λοξός (527).

περιβάλλεται The axis is thought of as rotating the circles round itself; cf. 23 περὶ δ᾽ οὐρανὸν αὐτὸν ἀγινεῖ. The v.l. may be due to the influence of περιτέλλεται in 509 and elsewhere (215, 232, 329, 739).

526 μεσσόθι πάντας ἔχων Cf. 22–3 ἔχει δ᾽ ἀτάλαντον ἁπάντη μεσσηγὺς γαῖαν.

ἐσφήκωται Sch. τὸ δὲ ἐσφήκωται ἀντὶ τοῦ συνέχεται, an imaginative metaphor for the way the ecliptic seems tightly held in place by the two tropics. The word suggests a physical model, such as an armillary sphere, with the zodiacal band fixed inside the framework of the other circles; cf. Pl. *Ti.* 36c, Gem. 5.45–8. Aujac *Zodiaque* 11 'Aratos ... fait une allusion non déguisée à la représentation de ces cercles dans la sphère armillaire.' The construction of a model seems also to be implied by the comparison in 529–31. Primarily the word describes something gripped so tightly that it is pinched in like a wasp's waist, e.g. P 52 ἐσφήκωντο of hair in a clasp, Nic. *Ther.* 289 ἐσφήκωται of a snake's narrow neck. Here, however, there is no such shape, and only the tight grip is meant; cf. 441. Perhaps this sense has been influenced by that of σφίγγω, as in Emp. 38.4 Τιτὰν ἠδ' αἰθὴρ σφίγγων περὶ κύκλον ἅπαντα, Pl. *Ti.* 58a ἡ τοῦ παντὸς περίοδος ... σφίγγει πάντα καὶ κενὴν χώραν οὐδεμίαν ἐᾷ λείπεσθαι.

527 λοξός The plane of the ecliptic circle, which passes through the centre of the celestial sphere, is inclined to the equator, and the angle of inclination is known as the obliquity of the ecliptic. The credit for discovering it is given by Eudemus to Oenopides (DK 1.41.7) in the later fifth century, and thereafter the ecliptic was regularly referred to as λοξός, e.g. Arist. *Met.* 1071a ὁ ἥλιος καὶ ὁ λοξὸς κύκλος, Autol. *Sph.* 11 ἐν σφαίρᾳ μέγιστος κύκλος λοξὸς ὢν πρὸς τὸν ἄξονα, Cleanth. *SVF* 1.123 καθ' ἕλικας κινεῖται· λοξαὶ γάρ εἰσι καὶ αὗται. Cf. Gem. 5.51, V. *G.* 1.239 *obliquus*, Prop. 4.1.82, Man. 3.319, Mart. Cap. 8.808. The angle of inclination, which also represents the angular distance of each tropic from the equator, is estimated to have been c. 23° 43′ in the time of Hipparchus, who for practical purposes rounds it off at about 24°: ὁ μὲν γὰρ θερινὸς τροπικὸς τοῦ ἰσημερινοῦ βορειότερός ἐστι μοίραις ὡς ἔγγιστα κδ′. See Dicks *GFH* 90, *EGA* 17, 19, 88, 157, Neugebauer *HAMA* 43.

528 ἀντιπέρην The tropics are opposite each other on either side of the equator; cf. 501 ἀντιόωντι.

μέσσος δέ ἑ μεσσόθι τέμνει A. calls the equator μέσσος for the sake of the contrast with the tropics and also for the word-play with μεσσόθι; cf. 1055, 1059. The contrasting positions of equator and tropics are also marked by the antithesis of μεσσόθι and ἑκάτερθεν. Some scholars have taken the meaning to be that the equator cuts the ecliptic 'in two', e.g. Mair 'bisects it', Martin 'le coupe en deux moitiés égales', Erren 'schneidet ihn in der Mitte', though the last is somewhat ambiguous, like the Greek. But A. uses μεσσόθι frequently, never in a context of dividing in two, but always of a central position: cf. 231, 414, 526, and c. gen. 'between' 368, 511. So Hes. *Op.* 369. Moreover, while it is true that the equator does cut the ecliptic in two, that fact is not relevant in this context, which is all about the relative positions of the circles. Cic. fr. 33.300 translates correctly with *media de parte*, and marks the contrast with *partibus extremis* (299). Germ. 517 *secat medium* and Avien. 1018 *medium medius secat* are both ambiguous.

529 Ἀθηναίης χειρῶν δεδιδαγμένος Some sch. seem to take this literally as referring to a pupil of Athene, e.g. (M) αὐτῆς τῆς Ἀθηνᾶς ὁ μαθητής, (MS) ἀπὸ τῆς Ἀθηνᾶς ἀνὴρ ζωγράφος λαβὼν τορνευτὴν σφαῖραν. But χεῖρες Ἀθηνᾶς is a Hellenistic metaphor for perfection in the arts and crafts: cf. Herod. 6.65-6 τῆς Ἀθηναίης | αὐτῆς ὁρῆν τὰς χεῖρας οὐχὶ Κέρδωνος (a cobbler), Rufin. *AP* 5.70.3 = Page 26.3 χεῖρας

Ἀθήνης, of a woman, Q.S. 12.83 δέδαεν δέ μιν ἔργον Ἀθήνη, of Epeius and the wooden horse. Here the craftsman, as Martin says, would be a wheelwright. Elsewhere χεῖρες alone can mean artistry, e.g. ο 126, Theoc. *Ep.* 8.5, Herod. 4.72. The gen. is Homeric, e.g. Π 811 διδασκόμενος πολέμοιο, ε 250 εὖ εἰδὼς τεκτοσυνάων.

530 ἄλλη Some sch. (not 'tous les scholiastes', as Martin says) paraphrase with οὕτω, and so make the passage mean that no craftsman could make such a system of wheels as there is in the sky: e.g. M^mg οὐκ ἂν οὕτω τέκτων καλῶς ἁρμόσειε τροχοὺς ὥσπερ οἱ ἐν τῷ αἰθέρι καλῶς κεκόλληνται. Hence Cic. 302–5 *ut nemo, cui sancta manu doctissima Pallas | sollertem ipsa dedit fabricae rationibus artem, | tam tornare cate contortos possiet orbis | quam sunt in caelo diuino numine flexi.* Cf. Germ. 518–19, Avien. 1018ff. But this is not the sense of ἄλλη, which means 'in any other way': cf. A.R. 3.818–19 οὐδ᾽ ἔτι βουλὰς | ἄλλη δοιάζεσκεν. What A. means is that the perfect craftsman could not create such a system of revolving wheels in any other way than the celestial system. So sch. (MΔΑ) οὐκ ἂν ὑπὸ τῶν χειρῶν τῆς Ἀθηνᾶς δεδιδαγμένος τις ἀνὴρ ἄλλως κολλήσειε κυλιομένους τοὺς κύκλους ὡς αὐτοὶ ἐν τῷ αἰθέρι ... For ὡς = 'than' cf. Pl. *R.* 526c ἃ γε μείζω πόνον παρέχει ... οὐκ ἂν ῥᾳδίως οὐδὲ πολλὰ ἂν εὕροις ὡς τοῦτο. Martin prints ἐλίσσων· followed by ὡς in 532. This gives essentially the same sense, but it breaks up what is more effective as one long sentence, which is a characteristic of A.'s style in passages that are intended to be impressive: cf. 129–36, 413–17, 469–79.

κολλήσαιτο The choice of word suggests Plato's divine craftsman in *Ti.* 75d (τὰ νεῦρα) ὁ θεὸς ἐπ᾽ ἐσχάτην τὴν κεφαλὴν περιστήσας κύκλῳ περὶ τὸν τράχηλον ἐκόλλησεν, and the god fitting together the circles of the Same and the Different in 36c συνάψας αὐταῖς τε καὶ ἀλλήλαις. A. seems to have an actual model in mind here, perhaps an armillary sphere (cf. 494), or the sphere with an illustration of the Milky Way on it, alluded to by Aristotle in *Mete.* 346a fin.: θεωρείσθω δ᾽ ὅ τε κύκλος καὶ τὰ ἐν αὐτῷ ἄστρα ἐκ τῆς ὑπογραφῆς. τοὺς δὲ σποράδας καλουμένους οὕτω μὲν εἰς τὴν σφαῖραν οὐκ ἔσται τάξαι διὰ τὸ μηδεμίαν διὰ τέλους ἔχειν φανερὰν ἕκαστον θέσιν, εἰς δὲ τὸν οὐρανὸν ἀναβλέπουσίν ἐστι δῆλον. Cf. Pl. *Lg.* 898a, of one kind of celestial movement, τῶν ἐντόρνων οὖσαν μίμημά τι κύκλων. On the assimilation of the sky to a human artefact see also P. R. Hardie, *JHS* 105 (1985) 17 n. 43, and M. L. West, *The Orphic Poems* (1983) 33 n. 99.

τροχάλεια Only here; cf. 476 τροχαλόν. They are rings or circular bands, not (as LSJ) a globe or sphere, though they could be thought of as composing an armillary sphere.

531 τοῖά τε καὶ τόσα The arrangement and the great size of the circles, matching those in the sky. Erren 'soviele', but there are only four in the system.

περὶ σφαιρηδὸν ἑλίσσων   A verbal echo of N 204 σφαιρηδὸν ἑλιξάμενος, of Ajax throwing a severed head into the mêlée, and later imitated in Nonn. *D.* 38.248 σφαιρηδὸν ἑλίσσων. Most translators take the phrase to describe the rotating movement, e.g. Mair 'wheeling them all around', Martin 'les animerait tous du même mouvement autour d'un pivot'. But this is not satisfactory, since that movement is circular, and besides the circular motion has already been allowed for in κυλινδόμενα (530). The more likely explanation is that A. is describing an armillary sphere; cf. 494, 526, 530. See also Schott & Böker, p. 111 'Arat beschreibt in seinen vv. 525 bis 540 eine Armillarsphäre und nicht das System der sphärengeometrischen Kreise auf der Kugel', and Erren *PAS* 172ff. This is the only interpretation that suits the sense of σφαιρηδόν. But it requires also a different meaning for περὶ ... ἑλίσσων, and there is a clue to what this must be in 796 ὅλος περὶ κύκλος ἑλίσσῃ, of the phenomenon of earthshine, when the whole disc rounds off the circle of the crescent moon. Here the craftsman is said to be rounding off the ensemble of circles to make the form of a sphere. So Erren 'alle zur Kugelgestalt umeinanderwindend'. This meaning requires the verb περιελίσσων, and therefore rules out the v.l. περισφαιρηδόν, which is not attested anywhere else.

532 ὡς   See note on 530 ἄλλῃ; K–G 2.304, A5.

πλαγίῳ   A variation of the technical term λοξός. Cf. Pl. *Ti.* 38e–39a κατὰ δὴ τὴν θατέρου φορὰν πλαγίαν οὖσαν.

συναρηρότα   The whole system is fastened together by the ecliptic. Cf. 715, A.R. 1.497, 2.1112, Q.S. 14.529.

533 διώκεται   Of mere speed, not pursuit; cf. 226, and ν 162 ῥίμφα διωκομένη, of a ship. The movement from dawn to night means strictly from east to west.

ἤματα πάντα   Cf. 20, 204, 339, and Hes. *Th.* 305 ἀγήραος ἤματα πάντα, Max. 117 κεχολώσεται ἤματα πάντα.

534 τὰ μέν   The equator and the tropics, which, being at right angles to the axis, cut the east and west horizons always at the same points for observers at the same latitude.

ἀντέλλει   The circles are imagined as rising and setting, because the stars that mark them are rising and setting. There is a marked sense of contrast in αὐτίκα here, but the temporal meaning still underlies it: see note on 199. For the internal rhyme cf. 341.

νειόθι   Elsewhere of position (89, 285, 320, 386, 400, 437), here of motion; cf. A.R. 1.63 ἐδύσετο νειόθι γαίης.

535 παραβλήδην   Once in Homer, Δ 6, fig. with ἀγορεύων, here a variation of παρβολάδην (318, 525); cf. Manetho 2.(1).34, also of circles, ἀλλήλοις δὲ παραβλήδην στρωφώμενοι αἰεί.

μία The one point on each horizon where each circle crosses it; cf. 534.

536 ἐξείης The successive risings and settings of the stars on each circle; cf. 372, 452, 492.

κατηλυσίη Only here and A.R. 4.886 κατηλυσίη ζεφύροιο. Cf. ὁμηλυσίη (178), ἐπηλυσίη (h.Hom. 2.228, 4.37). The stem is ἐλυθ- (cf. ἔρχομαι). κατηλυσίη τ' is read by Voss and subsequent editors except Maass, and this has some support from sch. καὶ ἐκ δύσεως καὶ ἐξ ἀνατολῆς. Cf. Q.S. 6.484 καταιβασίαι τ' ἄνοδοί τε. But the MSS tradition attests the hiatus, which A. uses freely, e.g. in 631, 694, 714, 840, 880. κατήλυσις ἡδ' is an emendation, perhaps by Planudes; cf. anon. AP 10.3.1 = FGE 1468 εἰς Ἀΐδην ἰθεῖα κατήλυσις.

537 ὅ γ' The ecliptic.

ὠκεανοῦ τόσσον This reading has the support of the MSS, and there is no obvious reason for preferring the v.l., as do Maass, Martin and Erren. A. has ὠκεανοῦ again in 746. It may be significant that A. nowhere else combines τόσον with ὅσον or τόσσον with ὅσον (cf. 539–40, 540–1, 553–4, 556–7), although both Homer and Hesiod sometimes do, e.g. Γ 12, Ρ 410, Op. 679–80; cf. Call. H. 1.64, 2.42.

537–539 The point at which the ecliptic meets the horizon oscillates along the arc between its farthest south, where it touches the tropic of Capricorn, and its farthest north, where it touches the tropic of Cancer. Hi. 2.1.16 τὸν δὲ ζῳδιακὸν ἐν τῇ τοιαύτῃ περιφερείᾳ τοῦ ὁρίζοντος τὰς ἀνατολὰς καὶ δύσεις ποιεῖσθαι, ἡλίκην παραχωρεῖ ἐν αὐτῷ ἀπὸ τῆς τοῦ Αἰγόκερω ἀνατολῆς ἕως τῆς τοῦ Καρκίνου ἀνατολῆς.

538 Αἰγοκερῆος ἀνερχομένοιο Hi. 2.1.17 argues from this that A. puts the solstitial points at the beginning of each of these constellations, though this does not seem to be necessarily implied by the term 'rising'. But in 151 the addition of τὰ πρῶτα makes the argument clearer. See Neugebauer HAMA 596.

μάλιστα Denoting a close approximation when used of numbers or measurements; cf. 497, 896, Th. 1.93.5 ἥμισυ μάλιστα ἐτελέσθη, Hi. 2.3.17 συνανατέλλει μέσῳ μάλιστα τῷ Αἰγόκερῳ.

539–540 ὅσσον ... ἐπέχει, τόσσον ... δύνων The arc of the western horizon along which sunset points oscillate is equal to the arc of the eastern horizon just described, i.e. between the tropics of Capricorn and Cancer. Note that ἐπέχει is also to be understood with τόσσον. Line 540 is designed to begin and end symbolically with a rising and a setting. The sense of cosmic balance is also brought out by the elaborate chiasmus of τόσσον ... ὅσσον ... ὅσσον ... τόσσον in 537–40. This sequence is followed by a similar pattern in ὅσσον ... τόσση (541–2), the reiteration being suggestive of the geometric style appropriate to a scientific passage.

ἄλλοθι I.e. along the western horizon; cf. ἄλλος of the opposite horizon in 589, 710.

541–543 This sentence suggests a geometric proposition, the essence of which would be: if a regular hexagon, with each side equal to the radius of the ecliptic circle, is inscribed within the ecliptic, each side will subtend two constellations. This mathematical preamble to the Zodiac implies that the division into twelve constellations derives from the very nature of things. Sch. ἑξάγωνόν ἐστι τοῦτο τὸ σχῆμα καὶ φυσικώτατον. καὶ γὰρ αἱ μέλισσαι, φύσει ζῶσαι καὶ οὐ λόγῳ, τὰς κατατρήσεις τῶν κηρίων ἑξαγώγους ποιοῦσι, Arist. *Cael.* 306b ἐν μὲν γὰρ τοῖς ἐπιπέδοις τρία σχήματα δοκεῖ συμπληροῦν τὸν τόπον, τρίγωνον καὶ τετράγωνον καὶ ἑξάγωνον, Euc. *Elem.* 4.15 εἰς τὸν δοθέντα κύκλον ἑξάγωνον ἰσόπλευρόν τε καὶ ἰσαγώνιον ἐγγράψαι, with the corollary ὅτι ἡ τοῦ ἑξαγώνου πλευρὰ ἴση ἐστὶ τῇ ἐκ τοῦ κέντρου τοῦ κύκλου. Cf. Sporus in sch. (MAS), also Man. 1.539–60.

541 ὀφθαλμοῖο βολῆς Cf. δ 150 ὀφθαλμῶν τε βολαί. The eye of the observer is a concept used by Aristarchus of Samos, a contemporary of A., in representing the earth as the centre of the cosmos: *Sizes and Distances*, prop. 8 ὅταν ὁ ἥλιος ἐκλείπῃ ὅλος, τότε ὁ αὐτὸς κῶνος περιλαμβάνει τόν τε ἥλιον καὶ τὴν σελήνην, τὴν κορυφὴν ἔχων πρὸς τῇ ἡμετέρᾳ ὄψει. The true centre of the cosmos is, of course, the centre of the earth, but Aristarchus chose to regard the earth's radius as insignificant, compared with the distance of the sky, and so for mathematical purposes assumed the observer's eye to be the centre; cf. hypothesis 2 τὴν γῆν σημείου τε καὶ κέντρου λόγον ἔχειν πρὸς τὴν τῆς σελήνης σφαῖραν. This mathematical convenience was discarded by Hipparchus, when he realised that parallax had to be taken into account, and he actually used the latter to calculate the distance of the moon from the earth (Ptol. *Alm.* 5.11). Here A. draws on sources later than Eudoxus, ἀκολούθως τοῖς μαθηματικοῖς (Hi. 1.9.13 in another but similar context).

ἀποτείνεται αὐγή Vision is thought of as a beam emanating from the eyes and going direct to the object observed. Cf. S. *Aj.* 69–70 ὀμμάτων ἀποστρόφους | αὐγὰς ἀπείρξω σὴν πρόσοψιν εἰσιδεῖν. Pl. *Ti.* 45c gives a similar account of τὸ τῆς ὄψεως ῥεῦμα, in daylight ἐκπῖπτον ὁμοῖον πρὸς ὁμοῖον ..., ὅπηπερ ἂν ἀντερείδῃ τὸ προσπῖπτον ἔνδοθεν πρὸς ὃ τῶν ἔξω συνέπεσεν. This theory of vision was found convenient for mathematical calculations, and Solmsen notes that 'throughout Euclid's optical theorems our vision is conceived as a ray whose direction is from our eye to the object' (*Aristotle's System of the Physical World*, 1960,

p. 419). Euc. *Opt.* 1 ὑποκείσθω οὖν τὰς ἀπὸ τοῦ ὄμματος ὄψεις κατ᾽ εὐθείας γραμμὰς φέρεσθαι. S.E. *Math.* 1.304 ἡ ἀπὸ τῆς ἡμῶν ὄψεως πρὸς τὴν ἀνατολὴν ἐκβαλλομένη εὐθεῖα. Cf. sch. (MΔKUA) ἐκβαλλομένας ἀπὸ τῆς ὄψεως ἐπὶ τὸν οὐρανὸν εὐθείας. (ἄλλως) ὅσον ἡ ὁρατικὴ ὄψις, τουτέστιν ἀκτὶς ἡ ἀφ᾽ ἡμῶν ἀφιεμένη, ἐπέχει μέχρι τῆς τοῦ ἀνωτάτω οὐρανοῦ ἐπιφανείας.

With the transmitted reading ἀποτέμνεται the line could be taken to mean 'the length of the beam from the eye as cut off (by the ecliptic)', but this is not how the scholia just quoted explain it. Sporus ap. sch. (MAS) interprets as ὅσον δὲ τῆς ἀπὸ τοῦ ὀφθαλμοῦ βολῆς (τῆς ἀκτῖνος) ἀποτέμνεται καὶ ἀφαιρεῖται ἡ αὐγὴ τοῦ αἰθέρος. Cf. Avien. 1038–40 *si quis | dirigat obtutus agilis procul, hosque locorum | defessos longo spatio tener amputet aer.* But αὐγὴ τοῦ αἰθέρος could mean only the sun (cf. 832) or the moon (cf. 735), whereas here we are concerned with the stars along the line of the ecliptic. It seems likely therefore that ἀποτέμνεται is an early corruption, perhaps influenced by περιτέμνεται in the same position two lines below. The required meaning is given by ἀποτείνεται, which is read by most editors since Buttmann. Cf. 184, 195, 242, of distances in the sky.

542 ἑξάκις ἂν τόσση μιν ὑποδράμοι Sch. (MA) ἐν παντὶ κύκλῳ ἡ ἐκ κέντρου πρὸς τὴν περιφέρειαν πίπτουσα εὐθεῖα ἑξάκις ὑποτείνει τὴν ὅλην περιφέρειαν. Sch. (S) has inserted in the middle of the scholion on 550 a diagram of the ecliptic circle, with inscribed hexagon, and the sun on its course round it. See note on 541–543. Hi. 1.9.12 ἥ τε γὰρ βολὴ τοῦ ὀφθαλμοῦ εὐθεῖά ἐστι καὶ αὕτη ἑξάκι καταμετρεῖ τὸν μέγιστον καὶ ἁπλατῆ κύκλον. Man. 1.553–6 *qua per inane meant oculi quaque ire recusant, | binis aequandum est signis; sex tanta rotundae | efficiunt orbem zonae, qua signa feruntur | bis sex aequali spatio texentia caelum.*

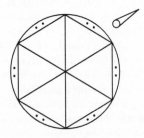

Fig. 3 The ecliptic circle, with inscribed hexagon, and the sun on its course; after J. Martin, *Scholia in Aratum Vetera* (Stuttgart 1974) p. 332.

ὑποδράμοι A poetic equivalent of the mathematical ὑποτείνω, 'subtend'. The prefix implies that the hexagon is drawn inside the circle, and therefore is beneath the sky.

ἑκάστη Sc. αὐγή, i.e. each side of the hexagon, which is equal in length to the ray from the eye to the ecliptic.

543 περιτέμνεται Cf. 50. Here the chord formed by each side of the hexagon intercepts, or subtends, one sixth of the ecliptic.

ἄστρα Cf. 11. The constellations of the Zodiac vary greatly in size, but A. here treats each pair as an exact sixth of the whole circle. He was presumably following the mathematicians, for whose calculations this assumption would obviously have been convenient. A. thus foreshadows the practice of Hipparchus, who divided the ecliptic into twelve equal arcs of 30° each, naming them after the respective constellations, but referring to them as δωδεκατημόρια (as opposed to ζώδια); cf. 2.1.8 οὔτε τοῖς δωδεκατημορίοις ἴσα ἐστὶ τὰ φαινόμενα ζώδια, οὔτ' ἐν τοῖς ἰδίοις κεῖται τόποις ἅπαντα, ἀλλὰ τινὰ μὲν αὐτῶν ἐλάσσονά ἐστι τοῦ δωδεκατημορίου, τινὰ δὲ πολλῷ μείζονα, καθάπερ εὐθέως ὁ μὲν Καρκίνος οὐδὲ τὸ τρίτον μέρος ἐπέχει τοῦ δωδεκατημορίου, ἡ δὲ Παρθένος καὶ τοῦ Λέοντος καὶ τῶν Χηλῶν ἐπιλαμβάνει, τῶν δὲ Ἰχθύων ὁ νοτιώτερος ὅλος σχεδὸν ἐν τῷ τοῦ Ὑδροχόου κεῖται δωδεκατημορίῳ, Cleom. 2.1.82 δύο δὲ δωδεκατημορίων τὸ ἀπὸ τῆς γῆς πρὸς αὐτόν [sc. τὸν ἥλιον] ἐστι διάστημα, ὡς καὶ Ἄρατος ἐπὶ τοῦ ζῳδιακοῦ φησι λέγων οὕτως [541-3]. ἄστρα δὲ ἄρτι κέκληκε τὰ δύο δωδεκατημόρια τοῦ ζῳδιακοῦ.

544 ζωϊδίων The MSS and sch. attest ζωΐδιον, but there is no evidence for this adj., though Lobeck *Proll.* 356 compares μοιρίδιος, νυμφίδιος, etc. Here ἐπίκλησιν καλέουσι (cf. 36) implies that A. is referring to an already established designation, and ζωϊδίων is therefore an appropriate reading: cf. Arist. *Mete.* 343a24 οἱ γὰρ πλανώμενοι πάντες ἐν τῷ κύκλῳ ὑπολείπονται τῷ τῶν ζῳδίων, Autol. *Ort. et Occas.* 1.4 τὰ ἐπὶ τοῦ τῶν ζῳδίων κύκλου ἄστρα, Euc. *Phaen.* 7 ὁ τῶν ζῳδίων κύκλος. The other term in use at this time is ὁ ζῳδιακὸς κύκλος or simply ὁ ζῳδιακός (Autol. *Ort. et Occas.* 1.4, Euc. *Phaen.* 6), and A. might have used it here, as later Nonn. *D.* 6.68 ζῳδιακὸν περὶ κύκλον. But ζωϊδίων is more suitable, because this line introduces a list of the actual constellations that mark the ecliptic, without any reference to particular stars, as in the case of the other circles. Hipparchus has not recorded which term Eudoxus used, but he himself prefers ὁ ζῳδιακός with or without κύκλος (1.6.4, 1.2.17), or the more precise ὁ διὰ μέσων τῶν ζῳδίων with or without κύκλος (1.9.3, 12). Ach. *Isag.* 23 notes the less common terms ἡλιακός and ἐκλειπτικός, the latter so called because it is only when the moon is also on this circle that eclipses can occur. See also 527 λοξός. Cic. 317-18 claims to have invented an appropriate Latin term: *zodiacum hunc Graeci uocitant, nostrique Latini [Latine ?]* | *orbem signiferum perhibebunt nomine uero.* And *signifer orbis* was duly adopted in Lucr. 5.691, Germ. 526, varied with greater precision to *signifer circulus* in Vitr. 6.1.1, and reduced to *signifer* alone in Avien. 1034.

545–549 The twelve constellations are now set out very compactly in five lines, in the style of traditional verses designed for memorising. Cf. the twelve-line version of Man. 1.263–74 and Sen. *Thy.* 850–66. This is the only one of the four circles for which such a need would be obvious. It is likely that the origin of the Greek Zodiac lay partly in Babylonian astronomy, but there is no conclusive evidence as to whether the oblique path of the ecliptic was known to the Babylonians before the Greeks became aware of it: see Van der Waerden, 'History of the Zodiac', *AO* 16 (1952–3) 216–30, Neugebauer *HAMA* 593, Dicks *EGA* 172–3. What is clear is that the Greek Zodiac must have been formalised in Greece by the last third of the fifth century, since Meton and Euctemon used it in their parapegmata. Its whole purpose was the solar calendar, as A. points out in 550–2, thus underlining its importance for the main theme of his poem. It provides the basic framework for the whole of the next section, the simultaneous risings and settings (559–732).

545 Καρκίνος Cf. 147. A. begins with the Crab, where the ecliptic touches the summer tropic (495), the sun's position at the summer solstice; cf. Hyg. 4.5 *Aratus non, ut reliqui astrologi, ab Ariete duodecim signa demonstrat, hoc est uere incipiente, sed a Cancro, hoc est ipsa aestate.* The Athenian new year traditionally began with the first new moon after the summer solstice (Pl. *Lg.* 767c ἐπειδὰν μέλλῃ νέος ἐνιαυτὸς μετὰ θερινὰς τροπὰς τῷ ἐπιόντι μηνὶ γίγνεσθαι), though the regularity of this practice is questioned by Bickerman (37). The later custom of reckoning the Zodiac from the Ram derives from Hipparchus' equating of the vernal equinox with the first point of Aries.

Λέων δ' In listing the constellations that mark the celestial circles A. for the most part sets them out in distinct phrases with δέ or καί as the connecting particle, using τε only where two names are grouped together in the same phrase, e.g. 488, 519, 547, 549. Here Λέων ἐπὶ τῷ is added in a separate phrase after τῷ ἔνι Καρκίνος, and the connective should therefore be δέ. There is no asyndeton anywhere else in these catalogues.

ὑπ' αὐτόν The v.l. μετά is the obvious prep., but it has involved a rephrasing of the end of the line, and therefore suggests a corruption. The unexpected ὑπό means 'to the south of', since the ecliptic now tends rapidly southward. For ὑπό c. acc. of position without motion cf. 140, 230, 361, 493. A. frequently uses this prep. c. dat., but never c. gen.

546 Παρθένος Cf. 97, 491.

Χηλαὶ καὶ Σκορπίος These are coupled together because they originally formed one constellation; cf. 98. But the impressive sight of the Scorpion is brought out by the addition of αὐτός; cf. 666.

547 Τοξευτής τε καὶ Αἰγόκερως These are probably grouped together because they are associated with midwinter and danger to seafarers; cf. 285–310.

548 Ὑδροχόος Cf. 282–5.

αὐτῷ ἔπ' Since the Fishes lie farther north, ὕπ' (as in 545) is not appropriate. With ἔπ' the dat. is required. Although ἐπί occurs five times in these five lines, variation is provided by the anastrophe.

ἀστερόωνται There is no need to depart from the text of the MSS and papyrus in favour of the v.l., as do Voss, Maass, Martin and Erren, likewise LSJ 'f.l. for ἀστερόεντες'. The latter is a prosaic attempt to construe all the constellation names with ἐστί (545). A. is simply introducing a second main verb to give variety to the catalogue; cf. the change of construction in 501–6, and the series of verbs in 481–96. Nonnus imitates with Ἰχθύας ἀστερόεντας (D. 6.244, 23.302, 38.369). For diectasis in pass. cf. N 675 δηϊόωντο.

549 Κριός, Ταῦρος δ' ἐπὶ τῷ Δίδυμοί τε Cf. 225–32, 167–78, 147. The compactness of this line is imitated by Orac. Sibyll. 13.70 Rzach Κριὸς Ταῦρος Δίδυμοί τε, Manetho 2.(1).133 Κριὸς καὶ Ταῦρος, Δίδυμοι δ' ἐπὶ τῷδε.

551 ἐνιαυτὸν ἄγων Of the regular seasons. Cf. A.R. 4.1286 ἠὲ καὶ ἠέλιος μέσῳ ἤματι νύκτ' ἐπάγησιν, Theoc. 16.71 οὔπω μῆνας ἄγων ἔκαμ' οὐρανὸς οὐδ' ἐνιαυτούς, 25.86 δείελον ἦμαρ ἄγων, Q.S. 2.503–4 θεσπέσιον περὶ κύκλον, ὃν ἠελίῳ ἀκάμαντι | Ζεὺς πόρεν εἰς ἐνιαυτὸν ἐὺν δρόμον.

552 ἐπικάρπιοι ὧραι The phrase recalls the providence of Zeus (13), and looks forward to 1044–63.

553 τοῦ δ' ὅσσον I.e. one half of the ecliptic, which is at any given time bisected by the horizon; see further on 555.

κοίλοιο The adj. is appropriate to the ocean, because the sun seems to sink into it, but not to the horizon, which is a mathematical line without depth.

δύηται Subj. without ἄν in a general relative clause is Homeric, e.g. μ 191 ἴδμεν δ' ὅσσα γένηται, σ 136–7 τοῖος γὰρ νόος ἐστὶν ... | οἷον ἐπ' ἦμαρ ἄγησι πατήρ. Here δύηται refers to the whole period beneath the horizon, not just the actual setting. Chantraine 245–6.

555 ἐξ αἰεὶ δύνουσι δυωδεκάδες The technical term for a 'sign' of the Zodiac, meaning a 30° arc of the ecliptic, is δωδεκατημόριον. It appears first as a twelfth part of the ecliptic, without reference to constellations, in Autol. *Ort. et Occas.* 2.1 τοῦ ζῳδιακοῦ ἐν δωδεκατημόριον ἐν ᾧ ἐστιν ὁ ἥλιος. See note on 543 ἄστρα. A. is saying here that, since the horizon bisects the ecliptic (cf. 553), six of the signs set every night and six rise. Suppose, for example, that the sun is in Cancer, then at sunset Cancer is on the western horizon, and the sign diametrically opposite, Capricorn, will therefore be on the eastern horizon; at the following sunrise the sun and Cancer are now on the eastern horizon, and Capricorn is on the western. This is true for any night, whatever its length; cf. Man. 3.241-2 *in quocumque dies deducitur astro,* | *sex habeat supra terras, sex signa sub illis.* Because the ecliptic is oblique to the equator, the angle it makes with the horizon is changing continually as the sky goes round, and the time each sign takes to rise varies accordingly. Cf. Euc. *Phaen.* prop. 9, Gem. 7.12-17. The *Anaphoricus* of Hypsicles calculates the length of time that each sign of the Zodiac takes to rise for observers in Alexandria: see Neugebauer's Introduction to the edition by De Falco and Krause (Göttingen 1966). A., however, makes no reference to this aspect of the astronomy, presumably because he is observing the constellations, not the mathematical signs. The same is true of Polybius' practical hints for generals, who have to be able to tell the time of night by the stars (9.15.7-8). See Erren *PAS* 177-80, 316, Neugebauer *HAMA* 40, 712ff., Aujac *Zodiaque* 19-24.

556-568 τόσον δ' ἐπὶ μῆκος κτλ. The length of any night is equal to the time it takes for six successive Zodiac constellations to rise. This amplifies 553-6, but in such a way as to focus attention on the basic theme of the next section of the poem, how to estimate the time of night, or, more especially, how long it will be before dawn comes; see 559-68.

557 νὺξ αἰεὶ τετάνυσται λ 19 ἐπὶ νὺξ ὀλοὴ τέταται.

558 ὑψόθι γαίης C. gen. only here in A., elsewhere adv. (87, 404, 485, 992). Cf. A.R. 4.848 ἠελίου ὅτ' ἄνεισι περαίης ὑψόθι γαίης, where the subject-matter suggests that A.R. is the imitator. Cf. Opp. *C.* 1.537.

559-732 SIMULTANEOUS RISINGS AND SETTINGS

559-568 Introduction

To estimate how long it will be till day comes, observe the rising of each Zodiac constellation before the one that the sun is in. If a Zodiac constellation is obscured, make use of the other constellations that ring the horizon at the same time. The purpose of the following lines (569-732) is to provide just such information. A. takes the Zodiac constellations in the order of 545-9, and gives under each heading the other constellations or parts of constellations that are either rising or setting at the same time as the Zodiac constellation is rising.

The ancient commentators understood the purpose of these observations as being to tell the hour of the night. Thus Attalus ap. Hi. 2.1.5 πειρᾶται ὑποδεικνύειν, πῶς ἄν τις διὰ τῶν ἄστρων δύναιτο τὴν ὥραν τῆς νυκτὸς ἐπιγινώσκειν. He goes on to explain that if you know what degree of what sign of the Zodiac the sun is in at setting, you know that the diametrically opposite degree of sign is rising at the beginning of night; and since six signs rise during each night, you can calculate at any time how much of the night has passed and how much is left ἕως τῆς τοῦ ἡλίου ἀνατολῆς (6).

Hi. 2.1.2–3 gives the same interpretation as Attalus, implies that Attalus agrees with A., and proceeds to argue that both are in error: (1) different signs take different lengths of time to rise; (2) if you go by the constellations, these are all of different sizes and do not correspond to the respective signs; (3) some constellations are only partly on the ecliptic and partly north or south of it. It is therefore impossible ἀκριβῶς ἢ ὡς ἔγγιστα τὴν τῆς νυκτὸς ὥραν ἐπιγνῶναι εἰς τὸ πρὸς τῇ ἀνατολῇ ζῴδιον ἀναβλέψαντας (2.1.13).

The same preoccupation with hours appears in sch. (MΔUA) μαθήσεται μετὰ πόσας ὥρας ἔσται ἡ ἡμέρα. But A. in fact makes no mention of hours either here or anywhere else, and when he uses ὥρη of the time of day, he means the less precise timing of everyday life: βουλύσιος ὥρη (825, 1119), ὥρη ἐν ἑσπερίῃ (1002). For his purpose it is sufficient to measure the passage of night by noting the successive risings of the six constellations (cf. 555–6), and it does not matter that their sizes and rising times are unequal, since the sole concern of the observer is to estimate when dawn will come.

559 οὖ κεν ἀπόβλητον B 361 οὔ τοι ἀπόβλητον ἔπος ἔσσεται, ὅττι κεν εἴπω, and pl., but also in same *sedes*, Γ 65. A. also has the word twice, varying the position in 973.

δεδοκημένῳ Epic part., once in Homer, usually assigned to δέχομαι (LSJ, Chantraine 1.435), but also to δοκάω (Autenrieth) and δοκέω (Veitch). Its meaning is fairly constant, combining the senses of 'waiting' and 'watching'. Thus O 730, of Ajax under attack, ἔνθ' ἄρ' ὅ γ' ἑστήκει δεδοκημένος (Eustath. ad loc. κυνηγετικὴ κυρίως λέξις, ὅτε ζῷον ἐπιὸν δέχονταί τινες. Leaf compares Δ 107 δεδεγμένος), Hes. *Sc.* 214 ἧστο ἀνὴρ ἁλιεὺς δ.; c. gen. here and A.R. 4.900 αἰεὶ δ' εὐόρμου δεδοκημέναι, of the Sirens; c. acc. Nic. *Ther.* 122 Πληιάδων φασίας δ., Opp. *C.* 1.518 ὑπνώοντα πέλας δ., Nonn. *D.* 30.88 ὑσμίνην δ. All examples fill the same metrical position.

560 μοιράων A. uses μοῖρα for a twelfth of the Zodiac in this section of the poem (581, 716, 721, 740). Though he is clearly thinking of the visible constellations, this word suggests that equal parts are meant, and this is confirmed by the term δυωδεκάδα in 703. A. may have been influenced in his choice of word by the Homeric use in Κ 252-3 πα-ροίχηκεν δὲ πλέων νύξ | τῶν δύο μοιράων, τριτάτη δ' ἔτι μοῖρα λέ-λειπται. In Hipparchus (1.7.11, al.) μοῖρα has become the technical term for a degree of a sign. In reading -ωσιν ἕκασται here he seems to stress the night-long succession of rising signs.

561 μιῇ συνανέρχεται A. takes no account of the position of the sun within the constellation, because he is not concerned with calculating a precise time of night.

562 τὰς δ' ἄν κε An imitation of ι 334 οἱ δ' ἔλαχον τοὺς ἄν κε καὶ ἤθελον αὐτὸς ἑλέσθαι, a line from a very familiar episode. The combination of ἄν and κε(ν) is occasional in Homer, e.g. also in Ν 127, and, separated by μέν, Λ 187, 202, ε 361, ζ 259. Attempts have been made to eliminate these by emendation (Monro 331, Chantraine 2.345), but at least some of them must have been in A.'s text of Homer.

563 εἰς αὐτάς I.e. observing them directly, as opposed to inferring their presence from the observation of other constellations.

564 ὄρεος Instr. gen.; cf. 413 νεφέων εἰλυμένον, 842 νεφέων πεπιεσ-μένος.

565 ἐπερχομένῃσιν The fem. is maintained throughout from μοιρ-άων ... ἑκάστη (560) to ἑκάστην (568). Clues to the rising of Zodiac constellations must be looked for in the positions of those that are visible.

ἀρηρότα Cf. 482; here the point is that the signs must be reliable.

ποιήσασθαι Inf. as imper., giving general directions or advice, following upon the circumstances outlined in the conditional clause; cf. Η 77-9 εἰ μέν κεν ἐμὲ κεῖνος ἕλῃ ... | τεύχεα συλήσας φερέτω ... | σῶμα δὲ οἴκαδ' ἐμὸν δόμεναι πάλιν. The usage is frequent in the section on weather signs, e.g. 795, 813, 883, 907. For the sense of 'getting for oneself' see also 777; cf. β 125-6 μέγα μὲν κλέος αὐτῇ | ποιεῖτ(αι), Hes. Op. 407 ἄρμενα ποιήσασθαι.

566 κεράων The eastern and western arcs of the horizon; cf. 589 of the eastern arc. In Hes. Th. 789 and A.R. 4.282 κέρας is a branch of Ocean's stream.

διδοίη The opt. expresses the hope that at least some part of the horizon will be clear.

567 περιστέφεται Mair retains the reading of the MSS, and translates 'the many constellations that wheel about him'. But relative to the horizon the constellations move up or down, not in circles. A. is thinking rather of the many constellations that ring the horizon on a clear night. Sch. (ΜΔΚUΑ) ὁ ὠκεανὸς ἐξ ἀμφοτέρων τῶν κεράτων παρέχει τεκμήρια δι' ἄστρων, ἅπερ, ἕκαστον ἐκ τούτων, πολλὰ ἐπιστεφανοῦται ἑαυτῷ καὶ περίκειται, ὅταν ἑκάστην μοῖραν ἕκαστον ἄστρον ἀναφέρηται. A. is probably recalling Σ 485 τὰ τείρεα πάντα, τά τ' οὐρανὸς ἐστεφάνωται, and Hes. *Th.* 382. (T. Worthen, *Glotta* 66, 1988, 1–19, explains as the horizon-sky encircling the stars like a diadem.) A. also recalls ε 303–4 οἵοισιν νεφέεσσι περιστέφει οὐρανὸν εὐρὺν | Ζεύς. Cf. Q.S. 8.52 περιστέφει οὐρανὸν ὄρφνη. Martin takes τά τε (= σήματα) as subject, as in sch. But ὠκεανός is subject of διδοίη and φορέησιν, and naturally goes as subject with ἑοῖ αὐτῷ. Maass punctuates after περιστέφεται, thus taking ἑοῖ αὐτῷ rather awkwardly with φορέησιν.

568 ὀππῆμος Only here, epic form on analogy of ὁππότε (828, 922, al.), ὅππη (Μ 48, ι 457). Schwyzer 2.650.

κείνων The Zodiac constellations, to which the others (τά τε πολλά) are guides.

569–589 *Rising of the Crab*

Before discussing in detail the συνανατολάς τε καὶ ἀντικαταδύσεις as expounded by A. and Eudoxus (2.2.1), Hipparchus makes two general statements about his method. One is (2.1.14) that he will treat the signs of the Zodiac as exact twelfths of the ecliptic (δωδεκατημόρια τοῦ ζῳδιακοῦ κύκλου) and not as the visible constellations (τὰ ἠστερισμένα); he therefore gives his own calculations of star positions by reference to degrees, or even fractions of degrees, of the 30° arcs of the ecliptic that constitute the mathematical signs. A. is certainly thinking of the visible constellations (cf. 563 εἰς αὐτὰς ὁρόων, 573 ἥμισυ μέν κεν ἴδοιο μετήορον, etc.), which vary in size and in their contact with the actual ecliptic circle, but for this purpose he is treating them as twelfths (555 δυωδεκάδες κύκλοιο), presumably because it suits his poetic purpose to present the cosmos as a perfectly designed structure (529–33). It is likely that Eudoxus also meant the constellations, and assumed, for mathematical convenience, that each occupied a twelfth of the circle, but it is improbable that he used a system of 30° arcs, which is not attested before the second century BC (Dicks, *JHS* 86, 1966, 27–8; *EGA* 157). The other statement of Hipparchus is (2.1.23, 26) that he will assume that, when A. and Eudoxus introduce the rising of a sign, it is the beginning of the rising that is meant, and the other constellations named are in the positions in which they are visible on the eastern or western horizon at that moment. This means that the latter have arrived at these positions during the rising of the preceding sign of the Zodiac.

569 οἱ Sc. ὠκεανῷ.

570 ἀμφοτέρωθεν On both the eastern and western horizons; cf. 566.

571 ἐξ ἑτέρης ἀνιόντες For ἑτέρη of the eastern horizon cf. 617,

726; of the western 178, 279, 659. The internal rhyme brings out the balanced antithesis of the sense; cf. 617, 821, and note on 360.

572–589 Hi. 2.2.4 reports Eudoxus as listing these constellations (with the exception of the River) in a slightly different order, taking the northern group first, and not saying whether they are rising or setting; he gives the visible parts as they are seen at the moment when the Crab begins to rise: φησὶ τὸν ἐν γόνασιν ὅλον εἶναι φανερόν, τοῦ δὲ Στεφάνου τὸ ἥμισυ, καὶ τὴν τοῦ Ἀρκτοφύλακος κεφαλήν, καὶ τὴν τοῦ Ὀφιούχου κεφαλήν, καὶ τὴν οὐρὰν τοῦ ἐχομένου Ὄφεως, τῶν δὲ πρὸς νότον τὸν Ὠρίωνα ὅλον, καὶ τοῦ Νοτίου Ἰχθύος τὸ πρὸς τὴν κεφαλήν (fr. 81). Hipparchus comments that the simultaneous risings recorded by both Eudoxus and A. are more correct for the division of the ecliptic assumed by A. than for that assumed by E. (2.2.6). Hyg. 4.12.4 follows A., but with much brevity.

572 δύνει μὲν Στέφανος Hi. 2.2.5 comments that A. is approximately right, since the Crown begins setting when Gemini 23° is rising, and is wholly set when Cancer 3½° is rising. The Crown is a small constellation (see note on 71), and Eudoxus shows a sense of precision in listing it as half-set. A. chooses to expand this half-and-half position of the Crown into two further lines, but they are awkwardly placed after the interposed reference to the Fish. The resultant double antithesis seems very contrived, especially as the Crown and the Fish are both setting and do not offer any real contrast. Mart. Cap. 8.841 *oriente Cancro occidunt Corona Ariadnes et Austrini Piscis pars dimidia.*

ῥάχιν Once in Homer, Ι 208, of a boar; elsewhere also of animals, only here of a fish.

Ἰχθῦς The Southern Fish, as identified by Hi. 2.2.2 in his paraphrase of this passage: τοῦ δὲ Νοτίου Ἰχθύος τὸ ἕως τῆς ῥάχεως. The sg. alone is sufficient to distinguish this constellations from the northern Fishes: cf. 387, 390, 701. A. has transferred it here from its final position in Eudoxus, because it is one of the setting constellations.

573 μετήορον A variation of ὑψόθι γαίης (558). In this case the stars are only just above the horizon; cf. 406, 610.

574 ἐσχατιαί In Homer freq. of land, but only sg., e.g. ξ 104 ἐσχατιῇ βόσκοντ'. Cf. Hdt. 3.106 αἱ δ' ἐσχατιαί κως τῆς οἰκεομένης, of the far east, Call. *H.* 4.139 ἐσχατιαὶ Πίνδοιο, Theodorid. *AP* 7.738.1 = *HE* 3554 ἐσχατιαὶ Σαλαμῖνος. A. means the western horizon: sch. ἐσχατιὰς δὲ τὰς δύσεις φησίν, ἐπεὶ καὶ προτέρην (432) τὴν ἀνατολὴν λέγει.

βάλλουσι From sense of 'let fall' or 'throw down', e.g. Α 314 εἰς ἅλα λύματα βάλλον, ι 137 εὐνὰς βαλέειν. Cf. 596.

575 ὅ γ' ἐξόπιθεν Identified by Hi. 2.2.2 τοῦ δὲ ἐν γόνασι τὰ ὑπὲρ τὴν γαστέρα, and again 2.2.16 ἐπὶ τοῦ ἐν γόνασι, before citing 575–6.

Cf. Eudoxus' list (note on 572–589). Since this constellation has no personal name, it is always referred to allusively (64–6, 73, 270–1, 591–2, 615–16, 669), and in this line the reference was often misunderstood. Hence sch. ὁ δὲ Νότιος Ἰχθὺς εἰς τοὐπίσω τραπείς, adding, in view of the difficulty of explaining the details with reference to the Fish, διό τινες ἐπὶ τὸν ἐν γόνασι τοῦτο μετενηνόχασι. τὰ γὰρ ὑπέρτερα αὐτοῦ ἐπὶ κεφαλὴν ἤδη δέδυκεν. Cic. 355–6 and Avien. 1084–7 take the line as referring to the Fish, Germ. 591–2 omits everything between the Fish and Ophiuchus, *Arat. Lat. ipsa quoque a retro conuersa* attaches the phrase to the Crown. At least the Latin translators prove, as Martin notes, that they did not read γνύξ in their Greek texts, and this makes the emendations of Voss and Maass so much less convincing.

ἐξόπιθεν means 'behind' always in Homer (Δ 298, Π 611, Ρ 521, 527), and elsewhere in A. (91, 340, 604, 699, 1020); so ὄπιθεν in 364, 927, but 'backwards' in 344. Traglia 250–8 has suggested another possible sense, 'upside down', since the figure does have this orientation at both rising and setting, the head star being the most southerly of all. But there is no evidence that the adv. ever has this meaning, and it seems an unlikely extension of the normal usage. Traglia sees 'behind' (sc. the Crown) as another possibility, and Martin actually combines both these meanings in 'l'homme qui est derrière, renversé'. This does not consort well with τετραμμένος, which A. always uses in the sense of 'turned in a certain direction' (30, 298, 344, 387, 620, 632, 853). The only feasible meaning is therefore 'backwards', and this is how it is understood by Mair, Schott, Zannoni, Erren, and Borgogno in *SIFC* 44 (1972) 138–43, though Mair in a footnote gives as an alternative 'reversed, i.e. standing upon his head'. The figure of the Kneeler is rightly described as 'backward-turned', since his back is to the west, the direction of the sky's movement. A close parallel is 344 ὄπιθεν φέρεται τετραμμένη, of Argo, and the Kneeler himself is similarly described at his rising, 669 περὶ γὰρ τετραμμένος αἰεί.

ἄλλα μέν Acc. of reference, contrasting with τὰ δ᾽ ὑπέρτερα (Martin); cf. 592. Hi. 2.2.8 corrects A. here, claiming that only the head, right shoulder and right arm are set.

576 γαστέρι νειαίρῃ Ε 539, 616, Ρ 519 νειαίρῃ δ᾽ ἐν γαστρί. The reference is probably to the stars ε ζ, later called the belt (671). Cf. 206, of the Horse.

ὑπέρτερα 'Upper' is relative to the figure, actually the more southerly part.

νυκτί I.e. below the horizon; cf. 580 ἔννυχος.

577 μογερόν With lengthening *in arsi*, as in 76 φαεινόμενον Ὀφιοῦχον. The epithet here refers to the effort involved in controlling the ser-

381

pent. Hi. 2.2.9 finds both Eudoxus and A. correct in giving the head (α Ophiuchi) and shoulders (β γ ι κ) as the stars that have set. The horizon would have cut Ophiuchus obliquely from the left knee to the right shoulder.

578 αὐχένος ἐγγύς Hi. 2.2.10 says that more than the head of the Serpent has set; he agrees with Eudoxus that only the tail is still visible.

579 ἀμφοτέρωθεν Above and below the horizon, as A. explains in 580; cf. Hi. 2.2.15 εὐλόγως αὐτός φησι μηκέτι πολὺ αὐτοῦ καὶ ὑπὲρ γῆν καὶ ὑπὸ γῆν ὑπὸ τοῦ ὁρίζοντος ἀπολαμβάνεσθαι. Cf. 727.

580 ἡμάτιος ... ἔννυχος Hi. 2.2.15 τὸ μὲν γὰρ ἡμάτιον σημαίνει τὸ ὑπὲρ γῆν τοῦ κόσμου, τὸ δὲ ἔννυχον τὸ ὑπὸ γῆν. Sch. ἡμάτιος δὲ ὑπέργειος, ἔννυχος ὑπόγειος. Both words are Homeric, the former used most notably of Penelope in β 104 ἡματίη μὲν ὑφαίνεσκεν μέγαν ἱστόν, the latter once only (Λ 716).

581 τέτρασι γὰρ μοίραις Bootes takes a long time to set, because its most northerly stars approach the horizon at a very acute angle, and some are in fact circumpolar. Hi. 2.2.11 notes that for both Eudoxus and A. the four rising signs of the Zodiac are the Ram, the Bull, the Twins and the Crab. Thus Eudox. fr. 113 ὅταν ὁ Κριὸς ἀνατέλλῃ, τῶν μὲν πρὸς ἄρκτους τοῦ Ἀρκτοφύλακος οἱ πόδες δύνουσι, and fr. 82 ὅταν δ' ὁ Καρκίνος ἀνατέλλῃ, ... δύνει δὲ τῶν μὲν πρὸς ἄρκτους ἡ τοῦ Ἀρκτοφύλακος κεφαλή. Similarly A. in 721–2 implies that by the time the Bull rises the setting of Bootes has already begun during the rising of the Ram, and here he implies that the setting of Bootes is completed during the rising of the Crab, since none of it is left visible when the Lion rises. The implication is confirmed by Attalus fr. 24 Maass τοῦ ποιητοῦ σαφῶς λέγοντος, ὅτι ὅλος μὲν δεδυκὼς γίνεται Λέοντος πρὸς ἀνατολὰς ὄντος. Hipparchus affirms that both Eudoxus and A. are wrong (2.2.14): οὔτε δὲ τέσσαρσι ζῳδίοις ὁ Ἀρκτοφύλαξ ἀντικαταδύνει, ὡς οὗτοί φασιν, ἀλλὰ δυσὶ μόνον καὶ ἔλασσον ἢ ἡμίσει: its setting actually begins with the rising of Taurus 6° and ends with that of Cancer 18½°, except for the left hand and elbow (which are circumpolar). Q.S. follows the poetic tradition in 10.341 τέτρασι γὰρ μοίρῃσι βροτῶν διαμείβεται αἰών. Cf. sch. (E) ad ε 272.

ἄμυδις Homeric adv., usually coupling two nouns or verbs together (e.g. ε 467, μ 415), here emphasising the long time taken up by the four successive risings; cf. 838, 1150, 1153. The reading is supported by sch. τέτρασι ζῳδίοις ὁμοῦ. The v.l. is meaningless here, and can be explained as a repetition of ἤδη at the end of 580.

582 ὠκεανὸς δέχεται Argent. AP 5.16.2 = GP 1302 ἀστέρες οὓς κόλποις Ὠκεανὸς δέχεται.

κορέσηται A witty personification; sch. χαριέντως εἶπεν ... ὅτι τοσοῦτον χρόνον ἀναλίσκει φαινόμενος.

583 βουλυτῷ Aptly chosen to go with the name Bootes; sch. (MΔUA) ad νυκτὸς ἰούσης: ἐν τῷ βουλυτῷ, τουτέστιν ἐν τῇ δύσει, μένει πλέον τοῦ ἡμίσεος τῆς νυκτός. As a time of day the word means late afternoon: Π 779 ἦμος δ' ἠέλιος μετενίσετο βουλυτόνδε, Ar. *Av.* 1499–1500 σμικρόν τι μετὰ μεσημβρίαν ... βουλυτὸς ἢ περαιτέρω; cf. A.R. 3.1342, Q.S. 7.621. A. also has βουλύσιος ὥρη (825, 1119). Apollon. *Lex.* βουλυτός· ἡ δειλινή, ἡ ὀψία. On Greek terminology for times of day see F. Franciosi, *AA* 29 (1981) 139ff.

δίχα νυκτός Imitation of μ 312 ἦμος δὲ τρίχα νυκτὸς ἔην, the night there being divided into three watches. Hsch. τὸ μεσονύκτιον.

584 ἦμος ὅτ' The pleonasm appears to be Hellenistic, e.g. A.R. 4.267, 452, 1310, Orph. *A.* 120; elsewhere A. uses ἦμος alone (606, 676, 690, 1013). The pure subj. gives a general reference, since the phenomenon occurs annually: cf. δ 400 ἦμος δ' ἠέλιος μέσον οὐρανὸν ἀμφιβεβήκῃ, the only Homeric example with ἦμος. Monro *HG* 265, Chantraine 2.254.

In 579–82 A. has been explaining how long Bootes takes to set in the course of each diurnal rotation, whether the setting occurs during day or night. Now he turns to the particular time of year when Bootes' setting takes place, and is visible, just after sunset, and lasts from then until past midnight. To make this sequence of thought clear it is necessary to punctuate with a full stop after δέχεται, as in the editions of Aldus and Ceporinus, rather than the colon used by subsequent editors. Then ἐπήν means 'on the nights when', and ἦμος ὅτ' means 'in the season when'.

585 οἱ While the v.l. τοι is a very suitable particle, as drawing the reader's attention to an interesting piece of folk-lore (cf. 172), the pron. seems necessary to supplement the part. δύοντι. It is the late-setting of Bootes that is in question.

ὀψὲ δύοντι Hi. 2.2.17 ὅταν γὰρ ταῖς Χηλαῖς ἄρχηται συγκαταδύνειν τοῦ ἡλίου ἐν αὐταῖς ὄντος, ἐν ᾧ καταδύνει καιρῷ αἱ νύκτες ἐπ' Ἀρκτούρῳ λέγονται. Bootes always begins to set when the Claws are setting, but when this happens at the time of year when the sun is in the Claws (Libra), the setting occurs late in the day, and that is why these evenings are named after Bootes (or its bright star Arcturus). The time of year indicated would have been about the end of October, and therefore the sight of Arcturus lingering late in the north-west on successive evenings was a conspicuous warning of the onset of wintry weather. Cf. Gem. *Cal.* Scorp. 5 (= 30 Oct.) Εὐκτήμονι Ἀρκτοῦρος ἑσπέριος δύεται· καὶ ἄνεμοι μεγάλοι πνέουσιν, Scorp. 8 (= 2 Nov.) Εὐδόξῳ Ἀρκτοῦρος ἀκρόνυχος δύνει· καὶ ἐπισημαίνει· καὶ ἄνεμος πνεῖ, Antip. *AP* 11.37.1–2 = *GP* 615–16 ἤδη τοι φθινόπωρον, Ἐπίκλεες, ἐκ δὲ Βοώτου | ζώνης Ἀρκτούρου λαμπρὸν ὄρωρε σέλας, Mus. 213 ὀψεδύοντα Βοώτην.

383

A. is here quoting from ε 272, of Odysseus at sea, Πληιάδας τ' ἐσορῶντι καὶ ὀψὲ δύοντα Βοώτην, where (pace Stanford) Bootes may well mean Arcturus, as LSJ suggest: cf. sch. (PQ) Βοώτην ἀστέρα λέγει. The understanding of the line, however, has been confused by an ancient explanation that Bootes' setting takes so long because it sets vertically, and 'late-setting' developed into 'slow-setting' as a permanent epithet of the constellation: sch. (E) τὸν Βοώτην, ὅτι πολυχρόνιον ποιεῖται τὴν κατάδυσιν οὕτω πεπτηκότα τῇ θέσει ὥστε ὀρθὸν καταφέρεσθαι. Hence sch. Arat. 585 Ὅμηρος "ὀψὲ δύοντα Βοώτην", ἀντὶ τοῦ βραδέως δυόμενον, and the standard epithets of Bootes in the Latin poets, tardus (Cat. 66.67, Prop. 2.33.24, Ov. Met. 2.177, Sen. Med. 315), and piger (Ov. Fast. 3.405, Mart. 8.21.3, Juv. 5.23, Claud. Rapt. Pros. 2.190). But ὀψέ never means 'slowly', and in this phrase must have its common meaning 'late in the day': cf. Φ 232 δείελος ὀψὲ δύων, Th. 4.106.3 ταύτῃ τῇ ἡμέρᾳ ὀψὲ κατέπλεον. It is possible that the Homeric phrase also is a conscious allusion to the time of year, and in that case it may have been intended as a weather warning, since the great storm raised by Poseidon follows hard upon it. Cf. Χ 26–30 of Sirius as a seasonal sign.

586 ἀντίος On the eastern horizon, therefore rising.

οὐδὲν ἀεικής An echo of Ω 594 οὔ μοι ἀεικέα δῶκεν ἄποινα. The phrase has a certain dramatic effect in anticipating Orion two lines below. No contrast is intended with Bootes, which is elsewhere characterised as πολυσκέπτοιο (136) and μέγα σῆμα (608).

587 ζώνῃ Cf. 232, 518, 754.

588 ὤμοις The stars α γ Orionis, of 1st and 2nd mag. respectively.

ξίφεος The line of faint stars below the belt, containing the now famous nebula.

ἶφι An imitation of the Homeric instrumental use, as with ἀνάσσεις (Α 38), μάχεσθαι (Β 720), but with the variation of verb requiring to be understood as dative. The only Homeric instance of the latter is Β 363 ὡς φρήτρη φρήτρηφιν ἀρήγῃ (see Kirk's note). A. ignores the digamma, as Homer in Β 720, Δ 287. Cf. 980 αὐτόφι.

589 Ποταμόν See note on 358. The River does not appear in Eudoxus' list in fr. 81, cited on 572–589.

κέραος Cf. 566.

590–595 Rising of the Lion
Stars setting during the rising of the Crab are now set, likewise the Eagle and most of the Kneeler; risen are the Hydra's head, the Hare, Procyon, and the Dog's forefeet. Hi. 2.2.31 summarises, and reports (32) τῷ δὲ Ἀράτῳ ὁμοίως καὶ ὁ Εὔδοξος ἀποφαίνεται (Eud. fr. 84). He corrects some details in their accounts of the Kneeler, the Hare, and the Dog (33–5). Hyg. 4.12.5.

590 ἐρχομένῳ Hi. 2.2.31 τοῦ δὲ Λέοντος ἀρχομένου ἀνατέλλειν.

591 Αἰετός The Eagle, being very small, has both begun and completed its setting while the Crab is rising. Cf. 313–15.

γνύξ Homeric adv., only with ἐριπών, e.g. Ε 309; cf. A.R. 2.96, 3.1310. Here it is a variation of ἐν γούνασι (66), not to be understood as a name, as Mair and Zannoni print it (Γνύξ), since the full phrase is ὁ γνὺξ ἥμενος. This is another allusive reference to the constellation that has no proper name: cf. 575, 615. Traglia 256.

592 γόνυ καὶ πόδα λαιόν The stars θ and ι Herculis. Hi. 2.2.33 comments that the right knee (τ) is also still above the horizon at the time the Lion's rising begins.

593 ὑποστρέφει A. varies his cases with this verb, 512 c. acc., here c. gen. The intrans. use is rare, but cf. Μ 71, though in a different sense. A. follows his three dactylic lines of 8, 9, 9 words respectively with a more spondaic four-word line for contrast.

594 Ὕδρης κεφαλή Cf. 445.

χαροπός See note on 394. The Hare's brightest stars are one of 2nd mag. and four of 3rd. The epithet therefore suits the subdued brightness of the constellation, but it may also suggest the eyes of the real animal. **Λαγωός** Hi. 2.2.34 ὁ δὲ Λαγωὸς οὐ μόνον τῷ Καρκίνῳ συνανατέλλει, ὡς ὁ Ἄρατος ὑπολαμβάνει, ἀλλὰ καὶ τοῖς Διδύμοις. This means that, if the Hare is already up when the rising of the Lion begins, it must have been rising during the rising period of the Crab. It is a very small constellation, and does not take long to rise, but Hipparchus puts the beginning of its rising back to the very end of the preceding sign's rising, sc. Gemini 27°. It will therefore be well above the horizon by the time the Lion begins to rise.

595 Προκύων An even smaller constellation; cf. 450.

πρότεροί τε πόδες Κυνός The bright star β Canis Majoris; cf. 327, 504. Hi. 2.2.35 ὁ δὲ Κύων ὅλος τῷ Καρκίνῳ συνανατέλλει πλὴν τοῦ ἐν τῇ οὐρᾷ, καὶ οὐχ, ὡς ὁ Ἄρατός ⟨φησιν⟩, οἱ ἐμπρόσθιοι μόνον αὐτοῦ πόδες συνανατέλλουσι τῷ Καρκίνῳ. Here again Hipparchus is thinking of the constellation rising with the preceding sign, and so visible by the time the Lion begins to rise.

596–606 Rising of the Maiden
Setting are the Lyre, the Dolphin, the Arrow, and parts of the Bird, the River and the Horse; risen are parts of the Hydra, the Dog and Argo. Hi. 2.2.36 τῷ δὲ Ἀράτῳ τὰ αὐτὰ καὶ ὁ Εὔδοξος λέγει. καὶ μάλιστά γε ἐκ τούτων φανερός ἐστιν ὁ Ἄρατος ὡσανεὶ παραγράφων τὰ ὑπὸ τοῦ Εὐδόξου εἰρημένα. Hipparchus adds that they are correct in all cases except the Arrow (37) and the River (38). Hyg. 4.12.6.

596 θην Denniston (288) gives this rare particle a force rather weaker than δή, and finds it almost confined to Homer and Sicilian poetry. A. has it only here, after οὐ μέν, as twice in Homer, Θ 448 οὐ μέν θην κάματόν γε μάχῃ ἔνι κυδιανείρῃ, ε 211 οὐ μέν θην κείνης γε χερείων εὔχομαι εἶναι.

νείατα Homeric, in similar context, Θ 478–9 οὐδ' εἴ κε τὰ νείατα πείραθ' ἵκηαι | γαίης καὶ πόντοιο.

597 Λύρη See note on 268–274.

Κυλληναίη Because invented by Hermes (cf. 269). This form of the adj. is a variant of Κυλλήνιος (*h.Hom.* 4.304, al.), and occurs only here; it is not given by LSJ.

598 Δελφίς See note on 316–318.

εὐποίητος Cf. γ 434 εὐποίητόν τε πυράγρην. A. has varied slightly the Homeric position of the adj.; cf. A.R. 3.871 εὐποίητον ἱμάσθλην.

Ὀϊστός See note on 311–315. Hi. 2.2.37 makes the setting of the Arrow begin with the rising of Cancer $26\frac{1}{2}°$ and end with Leo $1\frac{1}{2}°$.

599 πρῶτα πτερά The first part of the wings to set is the tip of the left wing, ζ Cygni; cf. 281. Cf. the similar effect of A.R. 4.771 κουφά πτερά at the bucolic diaeresis.

μέσφα παρ' Cf. Call. *H.* 4.47 μέσφ' ἐς. μέσφα occurs once in Homer, of time, Θ 508 μέσφ' ἠοῦς ἠριγενείης, otherwise it is mainly Hellenistic. A. uses it again c. gen. in 725, 807. See Schwyzer 2.550.

600 οὐρήν The bright star α Cygni or Deneb.

Ποταμοῖο παρηορίαι For the River see 358. Homer has παρηορίαι twice for side-traces attaching an outrunning horse to the regular pair: Θ 87 ἵπποιο παρηορίας, Π 152 ἐν δὲ παρηορίῃσιν. A. has the phrase in the same metrical position as the former. He uses παρηορίαι to denote the farthest stretch of the River: sch. τοῦ Ἠριδανοῦ τὰ ἄκρα ἄρχεται σκιάζεσθαι. The point of the metaphor seems to be that the long northerly line of stars, which runs westward from Orion, and then bends back towards the east, is thought of as the main figure, so that the final section running south-west occupies a position that suggests side-traces attached to a chariot and pair. Hi. 2.2.38 comments that οἱ περὶ τὸν Εὔδοξον wrongly make the River begin its setting with the Lion's rising, but the most south-westerly star, which is also the brightest, sets with the rising of Virgo 7°. This would be θ Eridani, the first to set of the stars visible from Greece.

σκιόωνται Homeric form, only in the formulaic line δύσετό τ' ἠέλιος σκιόωντό τε πᾶσαι ἀγυιαί (β 388, γ 487, al.), a line already echoed by A. in 2. Cf. 864 σκιάῃσι, A.R. 1.451 αἱ δὲ νέον σκοπέλοισιν ὕπο σκιόωνται ἄρουραι. Here the verb is not meant literally, but as an extension of the language available to express the sense of disappearing below the horizon.

601 Ἱππείη κεφαλή ... αὐχήν Cf. 210–11, 524.

602 Ὕδρη See 443–50. The Hydra's head has already risen with the Lion (594), now more of it rises, more again with the Claws (611), and the tail finally with the Scorpion (661).

603 Κρητῆρα Cf. 448–9, where the Bowl is described as resting on the Hydra's central bend. A. imitates the lengthening before φθ in Ψ 779 ὡς ἦλθε φθάμενος, σ 204 αἰῶνα φθινύθω.

φθάμενος Homeric middle, e.g. Ε 119 ὅς μ' ἔβαλε φθάμενος, Ψ 779, Hes. *Op.* 554 τὸν [sc. Βορέην] φθάμενος ἔργον τελέσας. The sch. give a garbled explanation, referring to the prior rising of the Dog's forelegs (cf. 595): ὁ δὲ Σείριος τοὺς ὀπισθίους πόδας ἀναιρεῖται, φθασάντων τῶν ἐμπροσθίων. διὸ εἶπε "φθάμενος", ὅτι τοὺς ὀπισθίους φθάνει πόδας ἀνατέλλων. Voss therefore read φθαμένοις, and was followed by Maass. Martin notes that we have here two separate scholia, both attesting the lemma φθάμενος. He finds φθαμένοις impossible to construe, and understands the Hydra as object of φθάμενος. It would be more accurate to refer back immediately to the Bowl, which dominates the central part of the Hydra. Thus A. may be seen to be indulging in a humorous reminiscence of Ψ 778–9 κρητῆρ' ... φθάμενος, from one of the amusing moments in the *Iliad*.

αἴνυται Cf. 504; here the verb is used of bringing above the horizon.

ἄλλους = ἑτέρους; cf. 49, 50, 240, 589, 897. These are the hind legs, since the forelegs are already up.

604 ἕλκων Cf. Θ 486 ἕλκον νύκτα μέλαιναν ἐπὶ ζείδωρον ἄρουραν.

πολυτειρέος Again of Argo (686) and of the Serpent (668); cf. τείρεα (692 and Σ 485). For Argo see 342–52.

605 ἡ δὲ θέει γαίης For the verb cf. Α 483 ἡ δ' ἔθεεν κατὰ κῦμα, of Odysseus' ship, Autom. *AP* 10.23.4 = *GP* 1526 μέσσα θέει πελάγη, Orph. *Arg.* 632 προχοὰς ἤμειψε θέουσα, of the ship *Argo*. γαίης is local gen., of the space over which the motion takes place, probably derived from the partitive use (Chantraine 2.58–9, K–G 1.384–5; see also on 635); cf. Δ 244 πολέος πεδίοιο θέουσαι, Ψ 521 πολέος πεδίοιο θέοντος, Ω 264 ἵνα πρήσσωμεν ὁδοῖο. Sch. require ὑπέρ to be understood, and paraphrase ὑπέργειος φέρεται. Voss argues that, since Argo is not fully up until the next sign (610), the sense required here is that it is still rising: he therefore reads γαίη, 'zu dem Erdrand läuft sie'. But it is the purpose of this catalogue to give the stars that are already visible when each sign begins to rise, and the gen. thus makes good sense. Hi. 2.2.39 τῆς δὲ Ἀργοῦς φησι τὴν πρύμναν μόνον συνανατέλλειν τῷ Λέοντι.

ἱστὸν διχόωσα κατ' αὐτόν Hi. 2.2.40–4 records that Attalus misunderstood this, supposing it to mean that Argo now rises only as far as half-way up the mast. Hipparchus explains that the participial phrase describes the figure of the constellation as ἡμίσεια οὖσα ἕως τοῦ ἱστοῦ (2.2.44), and A. implies this in 349–50. The dividing line is not horizontal, but vertical, like the cut-off in the figures of the Horse (215 ἡμιτελής) and the Bull (322 τομῇ). Sch. ὁ γὰρ ἱστὸς ἐπ' ἄκρου ἐστὶ διχοτομήματος, ἐπειδὴ ἡμίτομός ἐστιν.

606 ἧμος ... ἄρτι 'As soon as'; cf. Theoc. 2.103–4 ὡς ἐνόησα | ἄρτι θύρας ὑπὲρ οὐδὸν ἀμειβόμενον.

περαιόθεν Cf. 443, 645, 720, in same *sedes*, also with reference to the horizon; A.R. 4.71 of a voice from the other side of a river.

607–633 Rising of the Claws

Risen wholly or partly are Bootes, Argo, Hydra, the Kneeler (which requires the period of three signs to complete its rising), the Crown and Centaur; setting wholly or partly are the Horse, the Bird, Andromeda, the Monster and Cepheus. Hi. 2.2.45–50 paraphrases A. and has criticisms to make in respect of the Centaur, Andromeda, the Monster and Cepheus. Hyg. 4.12.7.

607 λεπτὰ φάουσαι Cf. 90 φαέων ἐπιδευέες, οὐδὲν ἀγαυαί. The verb φάω appears once in Homer, ξ 502 φάε δὲ χρυσόθρονος Ἠώς.

608 ἄφραστοι Cf. *h.Hom.* 4.353, with similar sense and same metrical position. Martin misleads in translating 'on ne saurait laisser passer sans mention'. It is the brightness of Arcturus that ensures that the rising of the Claws will not be missed.

609 ἀθρόος Cf. 310, 717 of constellations. Here the choice of word may be intended to bring out the sense of Bootes rising quickly, all within the rising time of one Zodiac sign, in contrast to its long drawn out setting (581). Hi. 2.5.1 ἀνατέλλει δὲ ὅλος ὁ Βοώτης ἐν ὥραις ἰσημεριναῖς δυσὶν ὡς ἔγγιστα, two equinoctial hours being the rising time of one sign.

βεβολημένος For the form cf. 492, for the sense 330 ἀστέρι βέβληται of the Dog, another constellation that is particularly marked by its brightest star. Cf. Mus. 196 βεβολημένος ὀξέι κέντρῳ. Sch. καταλαμπόμενος τῷ Ἀρκτούρῳ and LSJ s.v. βολέω 'dominated by' give a comment on, rather than a translation of, this participle.

610 εὖ It is clear from 605 that Argo has risen by the time the Maiden's rising begins. Hi. 2.2.42 ὅλην φησὶ τὴν Ἀργὼ ἀνατεταλκέναι. Sch. first explain ἡ δὲ Ἀργὼ μετέωρος ἤδη πᾶσα· μέρη γὰρ αὐτῆς συνανατέλλει Λέοντι, ὥστε ὁμοῦ ταῖς Χηλαῖς τὴν πᾶσαν ἀνατεταλκέναι, but then add γραπτέον δὲ "οὐ μάλα πᾶσα", ἐπειδὴ οὐχ ὅλη κατηστέρισται, καθὼς εἴπομεν, ἀλλ' ἡμίτομος. The source of οὐ in MSS is presumably a gloss to this effect. There is no need for Schrader's αὖ, adopted by Voss, since εὖ μάλα makes good sense and the phrase is characteristic of A. (cf. 465). The Latin translators have no negative here, and *Arat. Lat. tranquilla* suggests that εὖ μάλα was read as an adj. with prefix εὐ-.

ἵσταται The tense of the reading ἔσσεται in some MSS is inappropriate, since the context seems rather to require a present or perfect: see Hi. 2.2.42 and sch. in the preceding note. The requirement is better served by ἵσταται (first printed by Bekker), with the meaning 'stands': cf. 306, 865, and K 173 ἐπὶ ξυροῦ ἵσταται ἀκμῆς. As ἵσταται is attested as early as Attalus (fr. 25) and accepted by Hipparchus, who quotes him (2.2.42), it has considerable authority. The presence of ἔσσεται can be explained as being part of the corruption that introduced οὐ for εὖ (see preceding note). Voss's ἔσσυται (cf. A.R. 4.595 ἔσσυτο of Argo surging ahead) is ingenious, but the speed implied is too violent a movement for the regular westward course of the stars.

611 κέχυται The Hydra is a long and winding line of stars; cf. 393–4 χύσις ὕδατος ... σκιδναμένου. In 320 the same verb describes a much wider scattering of stars.

ἤλιθα πολλή A Homeric phrase, recalling especially ι 330 κέχυτο μεγάλ᾽ ἤλιθα πολλά, ε 483 φύλλων γὰρ ἔην χύσις ἤλιθα πολλή. Cf. 1064, and 254 with πᾶσαι.

612 οὐρῆς Hi. 2.2.45 τοῦ δὲ Ὕδρου τὰ πρὸς τὴν οὐρὰν μόνον ὑπὸ γῆς εἶναι. The part of the Hydra now risen is the curve between the Bowl, which rose with the Maiden (602–3), and the tail, which will rise with the Scorpion (661).

613 This line has been recognised as an interpolation since Buhle. The Greek is faulty, it interrupts the grammatical sequence μόνην ... κνήμην, it is not included in the lines cited in Hi. 1.4.13, and there is no hint of it in any of the Latin versions or in the scholia. The line appears first in E, added in the lower margin of fol. 103ʳ by Planudes, to whom Martin has already attributed it. Hipparchus makes no reference to Ophiuchus in his paraphrase of this passage (2.2.45), but in 2.2.55 he finds fault with A. in 666–8 for not knowing that the westernmost stars in Ophiuchus have actually risen with the Claws: ὁ δὲ Ἄρατος ἀγνοεῖ ἐν τοῖς περὶ τὸν Ὀφιοῦχον· ἡ γὰρ ἀριστερὰ χεὶρ αὐτοῦ μόνον ταῖς Χηλαῖς συνανατέλλει. The interpolation seems to be a clumsily composed attempt to correct this error. Hence μόνον in T.

614 δεξιτερὴν κνήμην Hi. 2.2.45 ἀνατεταλκέναι δὲ τοῦ ἐν γόνασι τὴν δεξιὰν κνήμην μόνον ἕως τοῦ γόνατος. The relevant stars are χ φ τ Herculis.

ἐπιγουνίδος See note on 254. Cf. A.R. 3.875 ἐπιγουνίδος ἄχρις, Nonn. *D.* 5.239, Paul. Sil. *AP* 5.255.9 ἐπιγουνίδος ἄχρι.

615 γνύξ The adv. without article is used here as the equivalent of a participle in the genitive, as is clear from the parallel παραπεπτηῶτος: sch. τοῦ ἀεὶ ἐν γόνασιν ὄντος καὶ πλησίον τῆς Λύρας ὀκλάζοντος. It should not be understood as the name of the constellation, as by Mair and Zannoni; cf. 591.

Λύρη παραπεπτηῶτος Cf. 272 γούνατί οἱ σκαιῷ πελάει. For the sense of 'crouching' cf. 167 πεπτηότα. Mention of the Lyre here may imply that it too can be included among the rising constellations, though Hi. 2.2.45 does not refer to it. It would have been a useful addition in view of its very bright star Vega.

616 ὄντινα τοῦτον A. has taken these words from Λ 611–12 Νέστορ' ἔρειο | ὄντινα τοῦτον ἄγει βεβλημένον ἐκ πολέμοιο, where the context similarly involves an unidentified figure, but the grammatical construction is different. There the combination of deictic οὖτος with the interrogative pronoun is a succinct way of saying τίς οὖτός ἐστιν ὃν ἄγει; Other examples of οὖτος attracted into the interrogative clause are υ 377 οἷον μέν τινα τοῦτον ἔχεις ἐπίμαστον ἀλήτην, h.Hom. 4.261 τίνα τοῦτον ἀπηνέα μῦθον ἔειπας; Cf. S. Ant. 7, OC 388, Pl. Phd. 61c, and with ὅδε, Γ 192, ζ 276, 1 348: see Diggle Studies 42. A. has given this early usage a new turn by employing it with indefinite ὅστις, an idiom that is perhaps anticipated in θ 28 ξεῖνος ὅδ', οὐκ οἶδ' ὅς τις, ἀλώμενος ἵκετ' ἐμὸν δῶ. It seems, however, to be mainly a prose use, e.g. Hdt. 1.86 καταγινεῖν θεῶν ὅτεῳ δή, Th. 8.87.6 ἥτινι δὴ γνώμη ὁ Τισσαφέρνης ἀφικνεῖται, Pl. Hp. Ma. 282d ἄλλος δημιουργὸς ἀφ' ἧστινος τέχνης. A.R. 4.746 in turn imitates A. with ὄντινα τοῦτον ἄϊστον ἀνεύραο πατρὸς ἄνευθεν, in a similar context of an unidentified man.

ἄϊστον In Homer of disappearing into obscurity, never to be heard of again, e.g. α 242 οἴχετ' ἄϊστος, ἄπυστος, 235 κεῖνον μὲν ἄϊστον ἐποίησαν, Ξ 258 καί κε μ' ἄϊστον ἀπ' αἰθέρος ἔμβαλε πόντῳ. Here it is equivalent to ἀπευθής (270) of the same figure. Cf. A.R. 4.746, cited in the preceding note, Q.S. 13.557 κεύθεται αἰὲν ἄϊστος.

ὑπουρανίων Cf. 134. There is perhaps a verbal echo of Ρ 675 ὑπουρανίων πετεηνῶν. A.R. 3.1004 may be recalling A. with οὐρανίοις ... εἰδώλοισιν, the latter being a characteristic Aratean word for constellations.

617 ἀμφότερον Adv., as frequently in Homer in same sedes, e.g. Γ 179; cf. Call. H. 6.35, 79, [Theoc.] 25.69, A.R. 3.987, 4.1652. The internal rhyme accentuates the balance of the line; cf. 571, 821.

ἐξ ἑτέρης Cf. 571, 726.

618 αὐτονυχεί Once in Homer, Θ 197 αὐτονυχὶ νηῶν ἐπιβησέμεν ὠκειάων. The form in -εί is better attested for A., and the v.l. in -ί can

COMMENTARY: 619–621

be explained as influenced by the Homeric text. A.R. 4.1130 follows the latter in both form and position.

Sch. ὁ δὲ ἐν γόνασι τῶν ἀμφιφανῶν ἄστρων ἐστίν, ὃν συμβέβηκε διὰ τῆς αὐτῆς νυκτὸς θεωρεῖσθαι ἀνατέλλοντα καὶ δύνοντα. The two participles here have been wrongly interchanged, the point being that this constellation is far enough north for its setting to be observed soon after sunset and its rising shortly before the following dawn. The scholion then notes that it lies between the arctic circle and the summer tropic, and refers to 498–9 for the ratio of 5:3 for the lengths of day and night when the sun is on the tropics. The Kneeler did in fact extend from about 20°N (the head star) to about 50°N, where the left foot comes close to the Dragon's head (69–70), which just grazes the horizon (61–2). The scholion then rightly identifies the time of year for this phenomenon as midwinter, but mistakenly gives the first and ninth hours of the day, instead of the night, as the times of the setting and rising. The most northerly stars in the constellation would naturally be set for quite a short time, but A. is concerned with the constellation as a whole, and the most southerly star would have risen some nine hours after its setting. It would have been possible to make this double observation only for a few weeks around the winter solstice, when the Kneeler was near conjunction with the sun and the nights sufficiently long (Erren PAS 188). Geminus 14.11 puts Arcturus in the same category: ὅθεν καί τινα τῶν ἄστρων ἀμφιφανῆ καλεῖται, καθάπερ καὶ ὁ Ἀρκτοῦρος. μετὰ γὰρ τὴν τοῦ ἡλίου δύσιν πλεονάκις θεωρεῖται δύνων τε ἐν τῇ αὐτῇ νυκτὶ καὶ προανατέλλων τοῦ ἡλίου φαίνεται. Since the period available in any one year is so limited, πλεονάκις here and πολλάκις in A. probably refer to observations made over many years.

θηεύμεθα Epic form, especially of observing something impressive, e.g. ι 218 ἐλθόντες δ' εἰς ἄντρον ἐθηεύμεσθα ἕκαστα, Ψ 728 θηεῦντό τε θάμβησάν τε, Η 444, β 13, Call. fr. 115.15. See H. J. Mette, Glotta 39 (1961) 49–50.

619 κνήμη The right leg (cf. 614).

ἀμφοτέρῃσιν The adj. seems otiose, unless it is meant to give a verbal antithesis to οἴη.

620 τετραμμένος Besides moving backwards (575) the Kneeler is also upside-down, the head star (α Herculis) being farthest south; cf. 669–70.

ἄλλη I.e. below the horizon.

621 Σκορπίον ... ῥύτορα τόξου Hi. 2.2.45 τὸ δὲ λοιπὸν αὐτοῦ σῶμα πλὴν τῆς ἀριστερᾶς χειρὸς ⟨καὶ τῆς κεφαλῆς⟩ ὑπὲρ γῆν εἶναι τοῦ Σκορπίου πρὸς τῇ ἀνατολῇ ὄντος· τὴν δὲ ἀριστερὰν χεῖρα καὶ

391

τὴν κεφαλὴν μετέωρον φαίνεσθαι τοῦ Τοξότου ἀνατέλλοντος. For ῥύτορα τόξου cf. 301. A. here anticipates 669–73.

622 μέσον ἄλλα τε πάντα The waist is represented by the stars ε ζ
Herculis, and ἄλλα πάντα means the rest of the central part of the
figure, viz. the thighs (η π) and the shoulders (β δ). For ἄλλα τε πάντα
in same *sedes* cf. M 285, Ψ 483, A.R. 1.1209, 4.888, Triph. 688, Q.S.
12.5.

623 χεῖρα δέ οἱ σκαιήν The group μ ξ ο Herculis.

κεφαλήν θ' ἅμα The MSS are divided between κεφαλῇ θ' ἅμα and
κεφαλῇ ἅμα. The former does not make sense, but the latter is supported
by sch. 620 ἡ δὲ ἀριστερὰ χεὶρ ἅμα τῇ κεφαλῇ, and is read by Voss,
Martin and Erren. On the other hand, if A. wrote κεφαλῇ ἅμα, it is difficult to explain the intrusion of the senseless θ'. However, if A. wrote
κεφαλήν θ' ἅμα, the corruption to the dat. can be explained by the
presence of ἅμα, and the removal of θ' can be seen as a later attempt to
restore sense to the line. There are also good positive reasons for reading κεφαλήν θ' ἅμα: Hi. 2.2.45 paraphrases with τὴν δὲ ἀριστερὰν χεῖρα
καὶ τὴν κεφαλήν, Avien. 1147 translates with *laeuam et caput* (Cic. and
Germ. ignore this line), and there could be an echo of Hes. *Th.* 677
χειρῶν τε βίης θ' ἅμα ἔργον ἔφαινον, where θ' ἅμα has the same *sedes* as
here. This is the reading of Bekker, Maass, Mair and Zannoni.

τόξον See 300–10. Here and at 664–5 the bow stands for the whole
constellation, since it is the Zodiac sign that is intended.

624 καταμελεϊστί Only here and Manetho 6.4, with lengthening
before μ, as in σ 339 διὰ μελεϊστὶ τάμησαν (same *sedes*), ι 291 (different
sedes). Pi. *O.* 1.49 has κατὰ μέλη without the lengthening. The only other
instance in A. is διὰ μέγαν (940), also in same position. The adv. here
must be a compound, since κατά *in tmesi* would denote a setting constellation. A. maintains the unity of this constellation by dealing with
the rising of the whole figure at this point, though he does come back to
it later at 669–73.

625 ἥμισυ δὲ Στεφάνοιο Hi. 2.2.46 ἀνατέλλειν δέ φησιν ἅμα ταῖς
Χηλαῖς καὶ τὸ ἥμισυ τοῦ Στεφάνου. The second half of the Crown
comes up at 660. The division of so small a constellation into two reflects the scientific precision of Eudoxus.

ἔσχατον οὐρήν ἔσχατος with two terminations recurs in 628 but
does not appear to be attested in any other author. It allows the fem. to
be used in hexameters, and A. is following Homeric and Hesiodic models
at the end of a line, such as δ 442 ὀλοώτατος ὀδμή, Τ 88 ἄγριον ἄτην,
Op. 466 ἱερὸν ἀκτήν: cf. 628, 692 ἱερὸς ἕδρα, and Kastner 22–5. Hi.
2.2.46 paraphrases with τὴν οὐράν, but A. seems to make a point of
specifying the end star π, probably the farthest south visible to an ob-

COMMENTARY: 627–631

server in Greece. Ptolemy's catalogue has no tail star, but the Farnese globe gives the Centaur a long tail hanging down close to the hind legs. Hi. 2.2.47 recognises the tail star, but makes the comment that it is not the tail and hindquarters generally that rise first, but the left shoulder, which is much farther north.

627 δύεται Ἵππος The head and neck of the Horse have already set with the rising of the Maiden (601), and now the rest of it sets. Hi. 2.2.46 δύνειν δὲ πάλιν τό τε σῶμα τοῦ Ἵππου ὅλον.

628 προτέρου Ὄρνιθος The more westerly part of the Bird, from left wing-tip to tail, which has already set (599–600).

ἐφέλκεται The verb is suited to a bird in flight, the tail trailing after the front part. Cf. 695, and N 597 τὸ δ᾿ ἐφέλκετο μείλινον ἔγχος.

ἔσχατος οὐρή Cf. 625. Hi. 2.2.46 καὶ τὴν οὐρὰν τοῦ Ὄρνιθος. There is no significant star to mark the tip of the tail other than the bright α Cygni, and ἔσχατος may mean simply that it is the last star to set. A. ignores the whole eastern half of the Bird, whereas Hi. 2.6.7 notes that the last star to set is the right wing-tip.

629 Ἀνδρομέδης κεφαλή α Andromedae, the star shared with the Horse (200, 206–7). Hi. 2.2.46 καὶ τὴν κεφαλὴν τῆς Ἀνδρομέδας, followed by the comment (48) τῆς δὲ Ἀνδρομέδας οὐ μόνον ἡ κεφαλὴ δέδυκε τῶν Χηλῶν πρὸς τῇ ἀνατολῇ οὐσῶν, ἀλλὰ καὶ αἱ χεῖρες ἀμφότεραι. A. makes all the rest of Andromeda set with the Scorpion's rising (647–9).

δεῖμα Once in Homer, meaning 'fear', E 682 of Hector δεῖμα φέρων Δαναοῖσι. The use as an object of fear is later, e.g. S. Ph. 927, Philoctetes to Neoptolemus, ὦ πῦρ σὺ καὶ πᾶν δεῖμα, E. HF 700, of monsters killed by Heracles, δείματα θηρῶν.

630, 632–3 Κήτεος ... δύνει At 2.2.46 Hipparchus correctly reports A. as saying that τοῦ Κήτους τὸ ἀπὸ τῆς οὐρᾶς ἕως τῆς λοφιᾶς sets with the rising of the Claws. But at 2.2.49 his text claims that both Eudoxus and A. make the Monster set with the rising of the Maiden: τὸ δὲ Κῆτος οὐ τῇ Παρθένῳ ἄρχεται ἀντικαταδύνειν, ὡς οὗτοί φασιν, κτλ. The discrepancy suggests some later interference with the text (cf. Manitius, n. 19, p. 299, on a suspected similar corruption in 2.2.58), or possibly a confusion of the symbols used for the signs of the Zodiac.

630 ἠερόεις The southerly was notorious for bringing clouds; cf. 416–18, 787, and the same adj. with νεφέλῃ (988–9).

ἐπάγει νότος Cf. 354–8, esp. τὸ δέ οἱ νότος ἐχθρὸν ἀγινεῖ Κῆτος.

631 Κηφεύς See 179–87.

ἀνὰ χειρὶ κελεύει Sch. 629 ὁ δὲ Κηφεὺς ὥσπερ ἀποσοβῶν τὸ Κῆτος φαίνεται, 630 ἐκτείνει γὰρ τὴν χεῖρα ὥσπερ παρακελευόμενος τῇ παιδὶ ἐκκλίνειν τὸ κῆτος. The gesture of Cepheus has thus been interpreted

393

as being directed towards either the Monster or Andromeda. In the first case he is driving the Monster back, which suits both the prefix (LSJ omit ἀνακελεύω) and an early sense of κελεύω, 'urge' or 'drive', as in ω 326 ἵπποι, τοὺς ὁ γέρων ἐφέπων μάστιγι κέλευε. Lines 630–3 are all about the Monster and Cepheus, and ἀντία brings out the opposition between them; thus Cic. 415 *hanc* [sc. *Pistricem*] *contra Cepheus non cessat tendere palmas.* The scene makes a typical astral myth, explaining why the Monster does not come farther north than about 40° above the horizon before turning away and setting. Cf. the similar myth of Orion fleeing before the Scorpion (645–6). The second explanation expresses a warning sign (cf. 775), and is supported by Avien. 1161–2 *uaga bracchia Cepheus | exserit et saeuam pelagi monet adfore pestem.* This is adopted by Martin, 'apercevant au loin venir Cetus, avertit Andromède d'un signe de la main'. He quotes as parallel A.R. 1.555, where Chiron with a wave of a hand wishes the Argonauts a safe return, πολλὰ βαρείῃ χειρὶ κελεύων. This certainly seems to be an imitation of A., but it is adapted to a different context, and there is no ἀνά. Moreover, as far as the myth is concerned, Andromeda is chained, as Voss pointed out, and cannot escape.

It is not clear which arm is meant here. Both are referred to in 183, and the right arm in 279; neither arm is conspicuous, but the right is better defined than the left. Voss read χερσί on the strength of Cic. 415, 417 *palmas*, Avien. 1161 *bracchia*, 1165 *ulnas*, and Hyg. 4.12.7 *cum manibus et humeris.* But these plurals no doubt reflect the later tradition of widely outstretched arms, as seen on the Farnese globe, whereas Hi. 2.2.46 paraphrases 633 with χεῖρα.

Editors to Voss have read κελεύων, since Bekker κελεύει. The indic. is required to balance ἐπάγει, and is supported by Cic. 415 *non cessat,* Avien. 1162 *monet,* and *Arat. Lat. iubet.* The participle can be explained as having come from 775, or a gloss quoting A.R 1.555.

632 ἐς λοφιὴν τετραμμένον The back-fin (cf. 364, 719) sets before the head, and so the movement is in the direction of the fin. This is what τετραμμένος means: see note on 30. The tail stars of the Monster have already set (Hi. 2.2.49), although A. does not include this under the preceding signs. Martin is mistaken when he says that the Monster 'se couche la tête la première'. The head is the most northerly part of the constellation, and is among the last to set: cf. Hi. 3.2.8 πρῶτος μὲν ἀστὴρ δύνειν ἄρχεται ὁ νοτιώτερος τῶν ἐν τῇ οὐρᾷ.

ἄχρι παρ' αὐτήν Sc. λοφιήν. Voss infers from Hi. 2.2.46 τὸ ἀπὸ τῆς οὐρᾶς ἕως τῆς λοφιᾶς that Hipparchus must have read ἄχρις ἀπ' οὐρῆς here. But A. leaves it to be understood that the setting begins with the tail stars, and notes only how far it proceeds during this sign's rising.

633 κεφαλῇ καὶ χειρὶ καὶ ὤμῳ Hi. 2.2.46 τοῦ δὲ Κηφέως κεφαλήν τε καὶ χεῖρα καὶ ὤμους (sc. δύνειν), and later (50) τοῦ δὲ Κηφέως ἡ κεφαλὴ μόνον δύνει· οἱ δὲ ὦμοι αὐτοῦ ἐν τῷ ἀεὶ φανερῷ τμήματι κεῖνται, καθάπερ προειρήκαμεν. The reference is to 1.7.20 ἐν γὰρ τοῖς περὶ τὴν Ἑλλάδα τόποις οὐχ οἷον ἕως τῆς ζώνης δύνει ὁ Κηφεύς, ἀλλ' οὐδὲ ἕως τῶν ὤμων. οἱ γὰρ ἐν τῇ κεφαλῇ αὐτοῦ κείμενοι ἀστέρες μόνον δύνουσιν· οἱ δὲ ὦμοι ἐν τῷ ἀεὶ φανερῷ τμήματι φέρονται, οὔτε δύνοντες οὔτε ἀνατέλλοντες. There follow precise calculations of the polar distances of these stars. A. is however consistent in 649-51, where the horizon cuts the upside-down figure of Cepheus at the belt. On χειρί see note on 631.

The MSS give ὤμῳ, which is supported by the Mediceus of Achilles. But Hipparchus has the pl. in both paraphrase and comments (see above), so too the Vaticanus of Achilles and Cic. 417 *humeris*, Hyg. 4.12.7 and *Arat. Lat. humeri*. Earlier editors, also Bekker, Mair and Zannoni, read ὤμῳ, Voss, Maass, Martin and Erren ὤμοις. Both make sense, but if the latter is right, it is difficult to explain the prevalence of the former in the MSS. If, however, the sg. is right, the pl. can be seen as a lapse on the part of Hipparchus, used to thinking in terms of both shoulders, and also to reading the pl. in other passages referring to the shoulders of figures, esp. at the end of a line (67, 77, 195, 488, 696), and most especially as the last term of two or three (208, 704, 711). A. does not elsewhere mention the shoulders of Cepheus, and he may have meant here the right shoulder (α), which is a 1st-mag. star, and is associated with the right arm or hand of 631. See also note on 650.

634-668 *Rising of the Scorpion*

Setting are the River, the rest of Andromeda and the Monster, part of Cepheus, and Cassiepeia; risen are parts of the Crown, the Hydra, the Centaur, and the Beast, also parts of the Serpent and Ophiuchus. This passage is relieved by a lively account of the Orion and Scorpion myth (637-46), which is ignored by Hipparchus in his paraphrase (2.2.51-3) and by Hyg. 4.12.8.

634 καμπαί All of the winding River that lies north of the final reach, which set with the Maiden's rising (600). Hi. 2.2.51 τοῦ δὲ Σκορπίου ἀρχομένου ἀνατέλλειν ὁ Ἄρατός φησι δύνειν μὲν τά τε λοιπὰ μέρη τοῦ Ποταμοῦ.

αὐτίκ' ἐπερχομένοιο Cf. β 367 οἱ δέ τοι αὐτίκ' ἰόντι κακὰ φράσσονται ὀπίσσω, ρ 327 (Ἄργον) αὐτίκ' ἰδόντ' Ὀδυσῆα. The meaning 'as soon as' seems to confirm Hipparchus' view that A. is giving the constellations visible at the beginning of each sign's rising (2.1.23). V. Loebe (5) notes the breach of Hermann's Bridge (West *GM* 37-8), comparing 585, 1023, and Homeric precedent in ε 272; cf. also 186, 657, and especially 903. See O'Neill 140, table 5. Voss's emendation αὐτίκα ἐρχομένοιο, approved by Maass, gives a rare hiatus (cf. 45, 951, 962, 1133), and is not to be preferred to the transmitted reading. The recurrence of the same verb two lines farther on is no cause for suspicion. A. is not too sensitive about repetition, especially where there is a variation of ending. For the internal rhyme cf. 360, 435, etc.

635 Σκορπίου See 85. The myth is naturally reserved for this place in the poem, because it depends directly on the simultaneous setting of Orion with the rising of the Scorpion. At the same time it helps to relieve the technical monotony of this whole section.

ἐμπίπτοιεν Cf. 153 c. dat., of the onset of the etesian winds and their effect on the surface of the sea. In δ 508 ἔμπεσε πόντῳ is of a rock falling into the sea, and in Θ 485 ἐν δ᾽ ἔπεσ᾽ Ὠκεανῷ the sun is thought of as doing the same. Here the stars are sinking rather into the region below the horizon, and the gen. describes the space within which the motion applies; see on 605. Monro (143) notes that this use of the gen. in Homer is almost confined to set phrases, and found only with the gen. in -οιο.

εὐρρόου Twice in Homer, of rivers, in same *sedes*: Η 329 εὔρροον ἀμφὶ Σκάμανδρον, Φ 130 ποταμός περ ἐΰρροος. Cf. Q.S. 4.11, 6.289, 8.488. See note on 518 εὐφεγγέος.

636 φοβέει In Homeric sense of 'put to flight', e.g. of Zeus, ὅς τε καὶ ἄλκιμον ἄνδρα φοβεῖ (Π 689, Ρ 177); cf. Ο 230, Φ 267.

Ὠρίωνα For Orion in general see 322-5; for Orion's setting see 310 and the comment of Hipparchus (1.7.13-15) that his setting is not complete until the rising of the Archer.

The myth of Orion and the Scorpion is first recorded here, but as a προτέρων λόγος (637), and it is possible that its origin lay in the more ancient star-lore of Egypt or the Near East, Both constellations are large, bright, and easily recognisable, so that the setting of the one while the other rises is one of the more obvious astral phenomena. When the Greeks came to identify the celestial hero-figure with Orion, they introduced an alternative version of his death. In the original myth Orion is killed by Artemis in Delos with an arrow (ε 121-4), either because he challenged her to a throw of the discus, or because he raped the Hyperborean maid Opis (Apollodor. 1.4.3), or because he attempted to rape Artemis herself (Hyg. *Fab.* 14.11). In the new version of A. a scorpion is sent by Artemis to kill Orion because he had laid hands on her, while he was ridding Chios of its wild beasts (638-9). This version is reflected in Hom. sch. (AD) Σ 486 συγκυνηγετῶν δὲ οὗτος Ἀρτέμιδι ἐπεχείρησεν αὐτὴν βιάσασθαι· ὀργισθεῖσα δὲ ἡ θεὸς ἀνέδωκεν ἐκ τῆς γῆς σκορπίον, ὃς αὐτὸν πλήξας κατὰ τὸν ἀστράγαλον ἀπέκτεινε. Ζεὺς δὲ συμπαθήσας κατηστέρισεν αὐτόν. διὸ τοῦ Σκορπίου ἀνατέλλοντος ὁ Ὠρίων δύνει. ἡ ἱστορία παρὰ Εὐφορίωνι (*CA* 101). From this developed the story that the scorpion was sent by Artemis because of his assault on her (Nic. *Ther.* 13–20), or because he had threatened to kill all the earth's wild animals (*Catast.* 32), and an alternative version that it was sent by the goddess Earth for the latter reason (*Catast.* 32, Hyg. *Astr.* 2.26 and 34.2). On scorpion myths in general see S. Eitrem, *SO* 7 (1928) 53–82. With Orion, Gundel, *RE* 3A.599–600, Roscher VI 986–8, Kerényi 203–4.

637 Ἄρτεμις ἱλήκοι φ 364–5 εἴ κεν Ἀπόλλων | ἡμῖν ἱλήκῃσι, the only instance of this verb in Homer (but cf. γ 380, π 184 ἵληθι); *h.Hom.* 3.165 ἱλήκοι μὲν Ἀπόλλων Ἀρτέμιδι ξύν. A.R. 2.708 quotes Orpheus invoking Apollo with ἱλήκοις. But here A. is affecting a certain coyness, as if apologising in advance for telling an embarrassing tale about Artemis, and hoping to mitigate the offence by presenting it as a time-honoured story; cf. 100 εὔκηλος φορέοιτο. This new twist to an old convention is imitated by A.R. 4.984–5 ἵλατε Μοῦσαι, | οὐκ ἐθέλων ἐνέπω προτέρων ἔπος, when he mentions the sickle with which Cronus castrated his father. Cf. D.P. 447 ἀλλ' ὁ μὲν ἱλήκοι, of Apollo, Hld. *AP* 9.485.10, Nonn. *D.* 10.314, Agath. *AP* 5.299.10 ἱλήκοις, Opp. *C.* 1.78 ἱλήκοιτε. Ovid amusingly takes off this Hellenistic topos in *Fast.* 5.532 *pudor est ulteriora loqui.* See Stinton 66ff.

προτέρων λόγος Cf. E. *Hel.* 513 λόγος γάρ ἐστιν οὐκ ἐμός, σοφῶν δ' ἔπος, fr. 484 (Melanippe) κοὐκ ἐμὸς ὁ μῦθος, ἀλλ' ἐμῆς μητρὸς πάρα, A.R. 4.985 προτέρων ἔπος, Call. *H.* 5.56 μῦθος δ' οὐκ ἐμός, ἀλλ' ἑτέρων (see Bulloch's note and Stinton 66ff.), Pl. *Symp.* 177a οὐ γὰρ ἐμὸς ὁ μῦθος, ἀλλὰ Φαίδρου τοῦδε. A. appeals to the authority of ancient lore in a variety of ways, e.g. 98, 164, 216, 260, 373, 442, 645.

ἔφαντο Epic middle form, at end of line, as in M 106 οὐδ' ἔτ' ἔφαντο, δ 638 οὐ γὰρ ἔφαντο, ν 211 ἦ τέ μ' ἔφαντο.

638 ἑλκῆσαι πέπλοιο The rare epic form of the verb gives a heroic colouring to the narrative, recalling the offence of Tityus in λ 580 Λητὼ γὰρ ἕλκησε. The position and case of the noun may suggest a different heroic context, the rescue of Aeneas by Aphrodite in E 315 πρόσθε δέ οἱ πέπλοιο φαεινοῦ πτύγμ' ἐκάλυψεν. Nic. *Ther.* 16 χερσὶ θεῆς ἐδράξατο πέπλων. Cf. Mus. 118 θαρσαλέη παλάμῃ πολυδαίδαλον εἶλκε χιτῶνα. On the peplos see Bieber, *Griechische Kleidung* (1928) 11ff., Bulloch on Call. *H.* 5.70. For the gen. cf. Λ 258 ἕλκε ποδός; K–G 1.348 Anm. 5, Chantraine 2.53.

Χίῳ Sch. αὕτη ἡ Χίος εἶχε πλεῖστα ἑρπετά, ὡς καὶ διὰ τὸ πολύθηρον αὐτὴν εἶναι ὀφιοῦσσαν καλεῖσθαι. πρὸς χάριν τοίνυν Οἰνοπίωνος ἦλθεν ἀπὸ Βοιωτίας ὁ Ὡρίων, ἄριστος ὢν κυνηγός, ὅπως καθάρῃ τὴν νῆσον. ἔχων δὲ σὺν αὐτῷ τὴν Ἄρτεμιν κυνηγοῦσαν ἀκόσμως ἐβιάζετο. ἡ δὲ κολώνην τῆς νήσου ἐποίησε διαρραγῆναι, καὶ ἀναδοθῆναι τὸν σκορπίον, ὑφ᾽ οὗ πληγεὶς ἀπώλετο. The legend of Orion and the scorpion seems to have been set in Chios because of Orion's association with Oenopion. Nonn. *D.* 4.338ff. connects it with Boeotia.

θηρία πάντα The version of sch. limits Orion's prey to the reptiles, but A. must mean all the wild animals (cf. 640). In *Catast.* 32 Orion is said to have threatened ὡς πᾶν θηρίον ἀνελεῖν τῶν ἐπὶ τῆς γῆς γιγνομένων. Cf. Hyg. 2.26 *dixisse etiam Dianae et Latonae se omnia quae ex terra oriantur interficere ualere.* Hence Q.S. 5.404 Αἴας δ᾽ ἀκαμάτῳ ἐναλίγκιος Ὡρίωνι, a new simile for Ajax slaughtering the sheep.

639 στιβαρῇ In epic mainly of heroes' limbs and weapons, e.g. Ε 745–6 ἔγχος | βριθὺ μέγα στιβαρόν, Nic. *Ther.* 17 στιβαροῖο κατὰ σφυρὸν ἤλασεν ἴχνευς, of Orion.

ἐπέκοπτε Once in Homer, of felling a sacrificial animal, γ 443 βοῦν ἐπικόψων.

κορύνη In one Homeric passage, with short υ, Η 141 σιδηρείη κορύνη ῥήγνυσκε φάλαγγας (the noun repeated in 143); the owner of the club is called κορυνήτης (138). The υ is short also in Theoc. 7.19, 43, but long in E. *Supp.* 715 (Theseus' club), [Theoc.] 25.63 (Heracles'), Nic. *Alex.* 409.

640 θήρης Cicero's *epulas* (425) merely points to the consequences of the hunt, and is not a valid argument for θοίνης.

ἀρνύμενος With the same conative force and metrical position as Α 159 τιμὴν ἀρνύμενοι Μενελάῳ. Cf. α 5.

κείνῳ χάριν Οἰνοπίωνι Oenopion, son of Dionysus and Ariadne, came from Crete to Chios, where he founded a city and established vines (D.S. 5.79.1). There are conflicting versions of his association with Orion. According to one Orion attempted to rape the king's daughter Merope, and was thereupon blinded and banished by Oenopion (Apollod. 1.4.3, *Catast.* 32, Hyg. 2.34.2, sch. Nic. *Ther.* 15). In the other he was a close friend of Oenopion and showed his devotion by hunting down the wild animals in the island: Hyg. 2.34.2 *nonnulli autem aiunt Oriona cum Oenopione prope nimia coniunctum amicitia uixisse, et quod ei uoluerit suum studium in uenando probare, Dianae quoque pollicitum quae supra diximus.* The first version is ascribed to Hesiod (fr. 148a). Sch. (S) give a brief reference to the later Anacreon, ὡς Ἀνακρέων φησίν, "ὅτι μή, Οἰνοπίων ..." (*PMG* 505e). Apart from the mere fact that Anacreon is quoted in this context, there is nothing here to allow any judgement about whether he was one of A.'s sources for the second version of the legend.

Since relations between Orion and Oenopion are friendly, χάριν must have the concrete sense of a gift secured by means of the hunting; cf. Germ. 652 *pacatamque Chion dono dabat*, Avien. 1183 *audax ut facinus donum daret*.

It does not help to translate κείνῳ as simply 'jenen' (Erren), or 'that king' (Mair), or to ignore it (Martin). It is possible, with Voss, to take it as meaning 'the famous', but Oenopion is a relatively obscure hero; for this reason κλεινῷ is unlikely. Maass is more convincing with *ei qui illic regnabat*. A. regularly uses κεῖνος with reference to an immediately preceding noun (e.g. 31, 98), but he can also refer it to a context, and so give it a kind of adverbial sense. In 585 κεῖναι νύκτες looks back to 583 and means 'the nights at that time of year'; so here κείνῳ Οἰνοπίωνι looks back to Χίῳ, and means 'for Oenopion there'.

641 ἐξ αὐτῆς Sc. τῆς ὁδοῦ (LSJ), ὥρας (Voss), τῆς Χίου (sch.). Professor Diggle has suggested τῆς νήσου. Cf. Cratin. fr. 34K, Aen. Tact. 22.29, Polyb. 2.7.7. Editors since Matthiae have printed ἐξαυτῆς, but the single word appears first in P. Lond. 893.6 (AD 40), then several times in *NT*, e.g. Mark 6.25. See W. F. Arndt and W. F. Gingrich, *Greek Lexicon of the New Testament* (Cambridge 1957). For ellipse of a fem. noun cf. πολλήν (289, 503), εἰς ἑτέρην (178, 279, 659), ἐξ ἑτέρης (571, 617, 726).

ἐπετείλατο Sch. ἐπετείνατο· γράφεται καὶ ἐπετείλατο. ὁ δὲ λόγος· ἡ δὲ Ἄρτεμις ἐξ αὐτῆς τῆς Χίου ἐπετείλατο ἀναδοθῆναι, τουτέστιν ἐποίησε. The main tradition ἐπετείνατο does not offer an appropriate meaning, but Ceporinus' *immisit* gives what the context requires, and editors since Voss have preferred the variant. This has ancient authority, and *surgens* in *Arat. Lat.* points to the same verb in its commonest Aratean sense. Here A. is perhaps recalling α 327, of the troubled return of the Greeks, ὃν ἐκ Τροίης ἐπετείλατο Παλλὰς Ἀθήνη: the same form of the verb in the same position, and in the same context of revenge. Cf. A.R. 3.264–5 στυγερὰς ἐπετέλλετ' [ἐπετείλατ' codd.] ἀνίας | ἡμετέρῃ κραδίῃ, with similar meaning, and 2.1096, with different meaning but same form and position, ἐπετείλατο τήνδε κέλευθον.

642 ἀναρρήξασα A. makes the scene more frightening by recalling the alarm of Aidoneus in Υ 62–3 μή οἱ ὕπερθε | γαῖαν ἀναρρήξειε Ποσειδάων ἐνοσίχθων. The verb is particularly suited to the description of earthquakes, e.g. [Arist.] *De mundo* 400a25 σεισμοί τε γὰρ ἤδη βίαιοι πολλὰ μέρη τῆς γῆς ἀνέρρηξαν. In imitation of A. cf. Q.S. 11.23–4 ἀναρρήξασα χέρεσσι | τρηχὺ πέδον Λυκίης, 14.581 ῥήξας γαῖαν ἔνερθεν ἐπιπροέηκε κολώνην.

μέσας ἑκάτερθε κολώνας The sense of ἑκάτερθε so closely combined with μέσας κολώνας is not immediately obvious, and some translators have played it down, e.g. Voss 'da von einander sie riss', Erren 'mitten entzwei sprengend'. Martin explains the adv. as proleptic: 'la terre des collines fendue par le milieu est rejetée à droite et à gauche'. A., however, uses this adv. frequently, and always in contexts which show clearly two opposing points of reference: Fishes (243), tropics (527), horizons (536, 566, 819), horns (778, 790), north and south (882). Here the only opposition can be the directions to right and left of Artemis and Orion, who are hunting in these hills. Mair's 'the surrounding hills' seems to have this sense in mind. Here κολώνας must mean the higher hills of the island, not inhabited slopes, as in 100, and as suggested by *Catast.* 7 τοῦτον, φασίν, ἐποίησεν Ἄρτεμις ἀναδοθῆναι ⟨ἐκ⟩ τῆς Κολώνης τῆς Χίου νήσου.

643 σκορπίον The delayed entry of the scorpion and its position at the beginning of the line give the effect of suspense and surprise, which matches the episode itself. A. has this word in this position ten times out of eleven.

οὖτα Epic aor. with short α, 19 times in Homer, e.g. Ε 858 τῇ ῥά μιν οὖτα τυχών.

πολλόν Of impressive size; cf. 41 πολλή.

644 πλειότερος Comp. of πλεῖος, epic form of πλέως, once in Homer, λ 359 πλειοτέρῃ σὺν χειρί, of Odysseus laden with gifts. A. seems to use this form as if it were an extended form of πλείων (cf. 43 μειοτέρῃ), since here it is antithetical to πολλόν, while in 1005 it is used of greater numbers, and in 1080 of longer time. Such a usage is implied by *Et.M.* 675.19 τὸ παρὰ Καλλιμάχῳ "πλειοτέρη" οὐ παρὰ τὸ πλείων πεποίηται ἀλλὰ παρὰ τὸ πλεῖος. Ronconi (198), assuming the sense of 'fuller', suggested that A. could be thinking of the constellation 'with all its stars', but this is the scorpion before its elevation to the sky, and the point of the antithesis is purely a matter of size. In Call. fr. 757 πλειοτέρῃ φάρυγι and Nic. *Ther.* 119, of the thickness of a snake's body, the word is clearly from πλεῖος.

προφανείς An appropriate choice of word to denote a sudden and threatening appearance, as that of Odysseus in ω 160 ἐξαπίνης προφανέντ' (the participle in same *sedes*).

ἤκαχεν Reduplicated aor. of epic ἀχεύω, ἀχέω, used esp. of making people grieve by dying, e.g. Π 822 δούπησεν δὲ πεσών, μέγα δ' ἤκαχε λαὸν Ἀχαιῶν. The sense of harassing by robbery occurs in *h.Hom.* 4.286 ἀκαχήσεις μηλοβοτῆρας. Nonnus recalls the myth in *D.* 48.398 Ἄρτεμι ... τίς πάλιν Ὡρίων σε βιάζεται;

645 τοὔνεκα Frequently first word in Homer, e.g. Δ 477; with δή (but interrogative) Γ 405. The crasis is omitted by Bekker, Maass, Mair, but S and other MSS attest it; Chantraine (1.85) finds it impossible to eliminate it in Homer, and there seems to be no good reason for omitting it in A.

φασι   Clausen (162–3) notes that A. here endorses the antiquity of the myth as proclaimed by ἔφαντο (637), and also that Cicero similarly encloses his version of the passage between *Orion* (420) and *Orion* (435). Cf. D. P. Kubiak, *CJ* 77 (1981) 12ff.

ἐρχομένοιο   Cf. 590, 607, 709; ἀρχομένοιο does not in itself imply rising. The same corruption occurs at 590.

646 περὶ χθονὸς ἔσχατα φεύγειν   The choice of περὶ ἔσχατα suggests a race, with the horizon as one of the turning-points, and it seems likely that A. is recalling the great pursuit of Hector by Achilles in *Iliad* 22. In the simile of the chariot-race the horses run περὶ τέρματα (162), as the heroes themselves πόλιν πέρι (165); also the latter are contrasted in πρόσθε μὲν ἐσθλὸς ἔφευγε, δίωκε δέ μιν μέγ᾽ ἀμείνων (158), as Orion and the scorpion in 643–4. Even the rare ἀρνύμενος in 640, only here in A., might look back to Homer's ἀρνύσθην (160). There are also unexpressed similarities in the two pursuits. Orion and the Scorpion move round the earth for ever without one catching up with the other, as the men in Homer's dream simile (199–201). Nonn. *D.* 38.374 ἔτρεμεν Ὠρίων καὶ ἐν ἀστράσι.

647 ὅσσ᾽ ἐλέλειπτο   Hi. 2.2.51 τὰ λοιπὰ μέρη τῆς Ἀνδρομέδας καὶ τοῦ Κήτους. The head of Andromeda has already set (629), likewise the Monster up to its back-fin (632–3). The form ἐλέλειπτο occurs twice in Homer, and at the end of a line (Β 700, θ 475).

648 κείνου ἔτ᾽ ἀντέλλοντος   δ᾽ in the main tradition does not make sense; it may have come from a quotation of γ 88 κείνου δ᾽ αὖ καὶ ὄλεθρον ἀπευθέα θῆκε Κρονίων, intended to illustrate ἀπευθής, and survived because it appeared to balance μέν in 647. But ἔτι is appropriate, because the stars that are above the western horizon when the Scorpion starts to rise set during the remaining period of its rising. Cf. 626 ἀνερχόμεναι ἔτι Χηλαί.

ἀπευθέες   The construction is κατὰ σύνεσιν, and familiar enough in a variety of forms to present no difficulty here; cf. K–G 1.52ff., and in particular λ 14–15 Κιμμερίων ἀνδρῶν δῆμός τε πόλις τε, | ἠέρι καὶ νεφέλῃ κεκαλυμμένοι. The adj. agrees in sense with Andromeda and the Monster (see Martin), and is supported by the following τοί. There is no need for the emendation to n.pl., which is accepted by Maass.

The meaning of ἀπευθέες, however, is also in dispute. Elsewhere in A. it is passive in sense (259, 270), and it is so explained here by sch. (M) ἄπευστοι καὶ παρημελημένοι and sch. (S) οὐκ εἰσὶν ἀπευθεῖς καὶ ἀνήκουστοι. But modern editors have taken it in its active sense (cf. γ 184) and construed it with the preceding genitive: 'fail to mark his rise' (Mair), 'né resta ignara del sorgere di quello' (Zannoni), 'bleibt nicht mehr ohne Kunde von dessen Aufgang' (Erren). Martin therefore takes ἔτι with ἀπευθέες, 'ne reste pas non plus sans nouvelles de ce lever', an unlikely word-order. Voss eliminates it by reading ἐπαντέλλοντος, understanding A. to mean that these constellations are also fleeing before the might of the Scorpion. But the Scorpion myth ends at 646, and what A. means here is simply that the remaining stars of Andromeda and the Monster can also be observed setting while the Scorpion is still rising. Thus ἀπευθέες has its normal Aratean sense, and ἔτι is appropriate with ἀντέλλοντος (cf. 626). Buttmann's reconstruction of this passage has been given a suitable refutation by Martin, and there is no need to repeat it here.

649 πανσυδίη Epic form of prose πανσυδί (σεύω, σύδην), in Homer meaning 'with all speed', e.g. Β 12 with θωρῆξαι, Λ 709 with ἦλθον (Leumann 190). Later it means 'in force', Χ. *HG* 4.4.9 πασσυδία βοηθοῦντες, or 'completely', Ε. *Tro.* 797–8 πανσυδία | χωρεῖν ὀλέθρου διὰ παντός, Th. 8.1.1 πανσυδὶ διεφθάρθαι, A.R. 1.1162 πασσυδίη μογέοντας. Modern editors have taken it here in the first sense, e.g. Mair 'in full career', Martin 'sans tarder', Erren 'so schnell sie können'; so also Ronconi 143–4. This would be possible in a mythical passage, but Andromeda and the Monster are not fleeing in terror from the Scorpion: they have a myth of their own (629–31). In the real world the fixed stars do not change speed, and A. must mean that these constellations now set completely (cf. 647 ὅσσ᾽ ἐλέλειπτο); sch. σὺν παντὶ τῷ πλήθει, and (648) διόλου δεδύκασιν. Cf. 714 of Perseus rising completely, and Hi. 2.3.33 τὸν Περσέα ὅλον φαίνεσθαι ὑπὲρ γῆν.

650 γαῖαν ἐπιξύει The belt of Cepheus (β Cephei) just grazes the horizon when the constellation swings round to due north, while the head stars (δ ε ζ) and shoulders (α ι) set and soon rise again. Hi. 2.2.51 paraphrases with τοῦ Κηφέως τὰ ἀπὸ τῶν ὤμων μέχρι τῆς ζώνης. In 1.7.19 both A. and Attalus are criticised, because in Greek latitudes only the head stars of Cepheus set, while the shoulders and the rest are circumpolar. The right shoulder (α) is $35\frac{1}{2}°$ from the pole, the left shoulder (ι) is $34\frac{1}{4}°$, but the circle within which stars do not set is $37°$ from the pole, as seen from the latitude of Athens: the shoulder stars are therefore north of this circle and do not set. The Farnese globe follows Hipparchus, and shows only the head of Cepheus south of its arctic circle. A.'s error is perhaps due to actual observation of the stars when due north, with land intervening to obscure the true horizon. Cf. 61–2 on the Dragon's head.

Nonn. *D.* 38.355 imitates with κύκλον ἐπιξύων. The verb is otherwise found only in prose, e.g. Hp. *VC* 14 ἐπιξύειν χρὴ τῷ ξυστῆρι κατὰ βάθος καὶ κατὰ μῆκος, of scraping a scalp wound, Pl. *R.* 406a τυρὸν

COMMENTARY: 651–654

ἐπιξυσθέντα. Cf. Euc. *Phaen.* p. 2, 22–3 Menge οἱ ἐπὶ τοῦ ἀρκτικοῦ (ἀστέρες), οἳ καὶ φαίνονται ξύοντες τὸν ὁρίζοντα.

651 βάπτων ὠκεανοῖο Cf. 858, of the sun, βάπτῃ ῥόου ἑσπερίοιο. For the gen. cf. also 605, 635, Ε 6 λελουμένος ὠκεανοῖο, Hes. *Th.* 5–6. The intrans. verb occurs also in E. *Or.* 707 (ναῦς) ἔβαψεν.

τὰ δ' The rest of Cepheus, namely the feet, legs and loins (652).

οὐ θέμις Not a moral law, as in ξ 56 οὔ μοι θέμις ἔστ', but a physical or cosmic law, though perhaps carrying overtones of Stoic religious thought. Cf. 18.

652 Ἄρκτοι κωλύουσι Rather humorously the Bears are presented as guardians of the arctic circle, within which stars do not set. Eudoxus included τοὺς ἐπὶ τοῦ ἀρκτικοῦ κύκλου κειμένους ἀστέρας (fr. 64a) in his account of the celestial circles, and Hipparchus, who prefers to call it ὁ ἀεὶ φανερὸς κύκλος, puts it 37° from the pole. The arctic circle, however, unlike the others described by A., varies its position in accordance with the latitude of the observer, and there is a certain irony in the involvement of θέμις and the Bears as upholders of an unbreakable law.

πόδας καὶ γοῦνα καὶ ἰξύν The feet are represented by γ κ Cephei, but there are no other significant stars between these and the belt (β), and A. is probably looking at the figure of Cepheus as drawn on a star map. For γοῦνα cf. 521, 704; also Max. 427 γοῦνα θοώτερα καὶ πόδας ἴσχοι.

653 ἡ δὲ καὶ αὐτή A 520 ἡ δὲ καὶ αὔτως.

παιδός Andromeda; cf. 196.

ἐπείγεται εἰδώλοιο The gen. is Homeric, e.g. Τ 142 ἐπειγόμενός περ Ἄρηος, α 309 ὁδοῖο. Cf. 1021. Here the verb combines the eagerness of the mythological figure with the movement of the stars. Sch. misunderstand the gen.: λείπει ἡ "μετά", ἵν' ᾖ μετὰ τοῦ εἰδώλου.

654 δειλὴ Κασσιέπεια Cf. 188 δαιμονίη, 196 ἀνιάζειν ἐπὶ παιδί, Nonn. *D.* 25.135 δειλὴ Κασσιέπεια δι' αἰθέρος εἰς ἅλα δύνει.

τὰ δ' The anguish of the figure is expressed essentially in the head and outstretched arms (195–6), and τὰ δ' introduces the rest of the figure, the feet and knees specified in 655. Cf. 651–2.

οὐκέτι οἱ κατὰ κόσμον Another humorous touch (cf. 652). The head is the most southerly part of Cassiepeia, and the figure therefore swings round to the north-west in an upside-down position. A. may be recalling Zeus's threat to any god who intervenes in the war: Θ 12 πληγεὶς οὐ κατὰ κόσμον ἐλεύσεται Οὐλυμπόνδε. Cf. *h.Hom.* 4.255; Hyg. 2.10 *de hac Euripides et Sophocles et alii complures dixerunt ut gloriata sit se forma Nereidas praestare ... quae propter impietatem, uertente se mundo, resupinato capite ferri uidetur.*

403

655 δίφροιο Cf. 251–2.

πόδες καὶ γούναθ' Respectively ε and δ Cassiopeiae. The v.l. χεῖρες belongs to the wrong part of the figure; it comes from N 75 πόδες καὶ χεῖρες ὕπερθε (cf. E 122). Hi. 2.2.51 τὴν Κασσιέπειαν ὅλην πλὴν τὸ ἀπὸ τῶν ποδῶν ἕως τῶν γονάτων, Man. 1.686 *inuersae per sidera Cassiepiae.*

656 ἀρνευτῆρι This Homeric simile, adapted to suit the feminine subject, recalls particularly Π 742–3 ὁ δ' ἀρνευτῆρι ἐοικὼς | κάππεσ' ἀπ' εὐεργέος δίφρου. Cf. Μ 385, of a fall from a tower, μ 413 from a ship. ἀρνευτήρ is an acrobatic 'tumbler': sch. (M) ἐπὶ κεφαλὴν γὰρ δίκην κυβιστητῆρος δύεται. The word is derived from lambs butting with their heads down: sch. (S) ὅτι καὶ οἱ ἄρνες ἐν τῷ τρέχειν ἐπικέφαλα φέρονται. Cf. Eust. 910.37. So in Π 745–50 Patroclus taunts Cebriones for his prowess in tumbling, adding that he would make a good diver. Cf. Herod. 8.42. Here the word is usually translated 'diver' (Mair), 'plongeur' (Martin), 'palombaro' (Zannoni), 'Taucher' (Erren), and this is, of course, possible, especially if the figure is thought of as plunging into the ocean. But A. does not make this point, and tumbling is more suited to the movement of Cassiepeia, who curves over gradually into the inverted position, then rises again in the north-east to the upright position. The humorous possibilities of the tumbling movement, already exploited by Homer, are also hinted at here.

657 μειρομένη καμάτων The traditional text with γονάτων has been accepted by most editors, who take the participle as passive and the meaning as 'parted at' (Mair, Martin, Erren) or 'parted from' (Voss, LSJ). The explanation is that the body of the figure, when set, is separated by the horizon at or from the knees. But the sense assigned to the part. is the opposite of the natural meaning of μείρομαι (μοῖρα), 'receive a share of', as in I 616 ἴσον ἐμοὶ βασίλευε καὶ ἥμισυ μείρεο τιμῆς. A. uses the verb again in 1054 of distributing the harvest season over three stages. The negative sense is given by ἀπαμείρομαι (522 and Hes. *Th.* 801) or ἀπομείρομαι (Hes. *Op.* 578). West (*Th.* 801) calls μειρομένη γονάτων 'a very odd expression'. Maass emends to αἰρομένη, though his reading is not supported by his references to Cic. 443 *neque ex caelo depulsa decore* and Man. 1.686 *inuersae per sidera Cassiepiae,* but only by Avien. 1205–6 *solio uestigia ab alto | sustollit miseranda super.*

The phrase in fact presents other difficulties. It is not clear why A. should refer again to the knees here, after describing their position in 655; the horizon cuts the figure at the belt (649–50), not at the knees; and the following clause, explaining the offence for which Cassiepeia is being punished, does not seem to relate at all to the phrase with γονάτων. The difficulties are all resolved if μειρομένη is taken in its normal sense of 'having her share of', and γονάτων is replaced by a noun such as καμάτων. The corruption can be explained by the presence of γούναθ' two lines above, perhaps through a marginal gloss with γόνατα against that form. Cf. Cic. 446 *hanc illi tribuunt poenam Nereides almae*, Avien. 1208 *memor has poenas dolor exigit*.

οὐκ ἄρ' ἔμελλεν   Said of an event in the past that was destined not to be. A. is recalling the tragedy of Achilles in Σ 98–9 οὐκ ἄρ' ἔμελλον ἑταίρῳ | κτεινομένῳ ἐπαμῦναι. Cf. Call. *H.* 3.255.

658 Δωρίδι καὶ Πανόπῃ   Two of the fifty daughters of Nereus, selected from Σ 45 and Hes. *Th.* 250 Δωρὶς καὶ Πανόπη. The choice of rare names is characteristic of Hellenistic poets. A. has the names in the same part of the line, but varies the case. Sch. περὶ κάλλους ἐναντιωθῆναι ταῖς Νηρηΐσιν. *Catast.* 16 ταύτην ἱστορεῖ Σοφοκλῆς ... ἐν Ἀνδρομέδᾳ ἐρίσασαν περὶ κάλλους ταῖς Νηρηΐσιν εἰσελθεῖν εἰς τὸ σύμπτωμα, Hyg. 2.10.1 (quoted on 654).

μεγάλων ἄτερ   Sch. ἄνευ μεγάλων ζημιῶν καὶ τιμωριῶν. There is no difficulty in understanding the sense of punishment from the context, when the phrase is seen as an imitation of Δ 161 ἔκ τε καὶ ὀψὲ τελεῖ, σύν τε μεγάλῳ ἀπέτεισαν.

ἰσώσασθαι   Once in Homer, η 211–12 οὕς τινας ὑμεῖς ἴστε μάλιστ' ὀχέοντας ὀϊζὺν | ἀνθρώπων, τοῖσίν κεν ἐν ἄλγεσιν ἰσωσαίμην. A. is perhaps deliberately contrasting the arrogance of Cassiepeia with the modesty of Odysseus, who rejects the suggestion that he might be a god, and compares himself rather with the most unfortunate of mortals. In both instances the verb probably implies speech, 'to claim equality'.

659 εἰς ἑτέρην   Cf. 178, 279. The head and arms set on the northern horizon, but, of course, on the western side of due north.

νειόθεν ἄλλα   Sch. ὁ δὲ οὐρανός, φησί, κάτωθεν ἀπὸ τοῦ ὁρίζοντος ἄλλα ἄστρα ἀπὸ τῆς ἀνατολῆς φέρει. A. has completed the list of setting constellations, and now turns to those that rise with the Scorpion. The v.l. νειόθι μᾶλλον has its source in 285.

660 ἀντιφέρει   In Homer only middle and passive, and in sense of opposition, e.g. Α 589, Ε 701; see also note on 468. Arist. *Cael.* 291b2, of planetary movements, ἕκαστον γὰρ ἀντιφέρεται τῷ οὐρανῷ κατὰ τὸν αὐτοῦ κύκλον.

δεύτερα κύκλα   Hi. 2.2.52 ἀνατέλλειν δέ φησι τό τε λοιπὸν τοῦ Στεφάνου. The first half of the Crown rose with the Claws (625); κύκλα refers to the circular form of the constellation: cf. 401. Scaliger (on Man. 5.251) argued that this must be the Southern Crown, since the Northern Crown would have been near the meridian by this time. He seems to have a point, but Corona Australis was not invented until after Hipparchus. A. certainly means the northern Crown, and Hipparchus raises no objection.

405

661 ἐσχατιήν Hi. 2.2.52 τὴν οὐρὰν τοῦ Ὕδρου. Cf. 57 of the Dragon. This is all that is left of the Hydra after 612.

ἐπί Adv., not with anastrophe, as Voss, Bekker, Maass, Mair, Zannoni; see LSJ s.v. ἐπί, ε: cf. λ 84 ἦλθε δ᾽ ἐπὶ ψυχή.

662 σῶμά τε καὶ κεφαλήν Hi. 2.2.52 τοῦ Κενταύρου τὸ λοιπὸν σῶμα πλὴν τῶν ἐμπροσθίων ποδῶν. Only the end of the tail came up with the Claws (625); the forelegs rise later with the Archer (664). The head is three 4th-mag. stars (g i k), and by the body A. must mean the rest of this large constellation.

Θηρίον Hi. 2.2.52 ἀνατέλλειν δέ φησι καὶ τὸ Θηρίον, ὃ ἔχει ὁ Κένταυρος. Here A. differs from Eudoxus, who made the Beast rise with the Archer (fr. 94). For the Beast see 440–2.

ὅ ῥ᾽ With lengthening before ῥ; cf. χ 327 ὅ ῥ᾽ Ἀγέλαος ἀποπροέηκε.

663 δεξιτερῇ η Centauri (see 439).

αὖθι μένουσι Cf. Α 492, ε 208 αὖθι μένων.

664 τόξον See note on 623.

πρότεροι πόδες The bright stars α β Centauri.

ἱπποτάφηρος Sch. παρὰ τὸ ὁμηρικὸν ἦθος. τῷ γὰρ "ἱππότα" ἀντ᾽ εὐθείας ἐχρήσατο ὁ ποιητής, οὗτος δὲ ἀντὶ γενικῆς. This confirms the vowel α in the MSS, which would be difficult to explain if the original reading had been ἱπποτόφηρος, as proposed by Grotius and accepted by Voss as 'sprachrichtig'. On the other hand the gen. in -ᾰ is unparalleled, though Maass and Martin accept it. It is more likely that A. intended a novel compound, so that the word itself could suggest the combination of man and beast. Cf. Grotius 'tamquam tu equitem permixtum equo dicas'; but Lobeck (*Par.* 1.183) dismisses 'vocabulum vere centaureum et τερατοφυές'. There are several Homeric compounds with α as connecting vowel in nominal stems, e.g. κυνάμυια (Φ 394, 421), πυλαωρούς (Φ 530, Ω 681), θυραωρούς (Χ 69), ὀνομάκλυτος (Χ 51), ποδάνιπτρα (τ 504). Moreover the actual form ἱππότα was familiar in this metrical position as nom. with heroic names (Νέστωρ Β 336, Φυλεύς Β 628, Τυδεύς Ε 126, Οἰνεύς Ξ 117, Πηλεύς Π 33). The form φήρ is used by Homer for centaurs (Α 268, Β 743), and by Pindar with reference to Chiron (*P.* 3.4, 4.119). But it is otherwise rare, and the more familiar θηρός here is an easily explained corruption.

665 τόξῳ Repeated with case variation. By anticipating the next rising A. is able to deal with the whole of the Serpent and Ophiuchus in these four lines. The repetition, however, gives a seemingly unnecessary emphasis, and it may be that A. has deliberately chosen to blur the division between the sections, since he is writing a poem, not a technical treatise; cf. 679, 699–711. It is significant that Hipparchus holds over the details in this line to his paragraph on the rising of the Archer (2.2.56), and also that editors have a difficulty in deciding where to mark the beginning of a new paragraph: Maass and Mair indent at 665, I follow Bekker and Martin in preferring 669.

σπείρη Ὄφιος καὶ σῶμ' Ὀφιούχου   Hi. 2.2.56 τὸ σῶμα τοῦ 'Οφιούχου, καὶ τὴν οὐρὰν τοῦ Ὄφεως, ὃν ἔχει ὁ 'Οφιοῦχος. A. presumably means the central part of the figure of Ophiuchus and the central coil of the Serpent, which crosses it. Hipparchus apparently understands the coil as including the whole tail end of the Serpent.

666 καρήατα   The Serpent's head is the group β γ κ ι, the head of Ophiuchus the single bright star α. The pl. καρήατα is Homeric, e.g. in same *sedes* P 437 οὔδει ἐνισκίμψαντε καρήατα. Chantraine 1.231. Cf. Call. *H.* 2.60, 4.134, 236. Opp. *C.* 2.215, Nonn. *D.* 28.203, 241.

667 αὐτάς   The hands are thus marked as distinct from the σῶμα (665) for this purpose; see note on 79.

668 χεῖρας   Hi. 2.2.52 τοῦ 'Οφιούχου τὴν κεφαλὴν καὶ τὰς χεῖρας, ibid. 55 ὁ δὲ Ἄρατος ἀγνοεῖ ἐν τοῖς περὶ τὸν 'Οφιοῦχον· ἡ γὰρ ἀριστερὰ χεὶρ αὐτοῦ μόνον ταῖς Χηλαῖς συνανατέλλει, ἡ δὲ κεφαλὴ καὶ ἡ δεξιὰ χεὶρ τῷ Σκορπίῳ.

πολυτειρέος   See note on 604.

ἀγήν   The reading of all editors since Bekker, in place of the traditional αὐγήν, a more familiar word (cf. 541, 735, 832), but one which does not give the sense required by the context. The rare noun ἀγή (ἄγνυμι) means 'fragment' in A. *Pers.* 425 ἀγαῖσι κωπῶν, and E. *Supp.* 693 ἁρμάτων τ' ἀγαῖσι, but here sch. understand it as a 'bend': τὴν προτέραν περίκλασιν καὶ καμπὴν τοῦ Δράκοντος. Cf. Leont. *Sphaer. Arat.* 4 (p. 563 Maass) ἡ προτέρα καμπὴ τοῦ Ὄφεως, and Avien. 1220 *primam rutili spiram Serpentis.* Hence LSJ 'curve', Mair 'coil', Martin 'repli', Erren 'Beuge'. This interpretation may have been influenced by περιαγήν (668), or even by the words of Hipparchus, who expresses A.'s meaning accurately in 2.2.52 τοῦ Ὄφεως, ὃν ἔχει ὁ 'Οφιοῦχος, τὴν κεφαλὴν ἕως τῆς πρώτης σπείρας. This is the western part of the constellation, which runs from the head southwards to the star μ Serpentis, whence it bends eastwards across the body of Ophiuchus. A. must mean this first 'section' only, stopping short of the great bend, and this is more in keeping with the primary sense of the word. So Zannoni 'il primo frammento'. A.R. 1.554 πολιῇ δ' ἐπὶ κύματος ἀγῇ, of breaking surf, has the word in the same metrical position; cf. Numen. *SH* 584.5.

669–692 Rising of the Archer and Capricorn
Besides the parts of the Serpent and Ophiuchus already noted (665), there are risen when the Archer rises a part of the Kneeler, the Lyre and Cepheus; setting are the Dog, Orion and the Hare, and parts of the

Charioteer, Perseus and Argo. The remainder of the last three and Procyon set with the rising of Capricorn, while the Bird, the Eagle, the Arrow and the Altar have risen. Hi. 2.2.56–61 summarises, and comments on the Kneeler, Cepheus, Perseus and Argo. Hyg. 4.12.9–10.

669 τετραμμένος Cf. 620–1, where A. has anticipated the rising of the head star.

670 περάτης The eastern horizon, as in 821; contrast 499. Mus. III ἐκ περάτης δ' ἀνέτελλε.

ἄλλα Hi. 2.2.52 τοῦ ἐν γόνασι τὰ λοιπὰ πλὴν τῆς κεφαλῆς καὶ τῆς ἀριστερᾶς χειρός.

671 γυῖα ... ὦμος The right leg is η σ τ φ χ Herculis, the left leg π θ ι, the belt ε ζ; the breast is not represented by any particular star, but probably refers to the whole area between the belt and the shoulders, and the shoulder here is the right, β: the left will come with the head and left arm (672), and the v.l. ὦμοι may be excluded.

672 δεξιτερῇ σὺν χειρί Probably γ ω (see 68).

κάρη δ' ἑτέρης μετὰ χειρός The head is α, the left hand ο. It is here, in mid-sentence, that A. completes his transition to the stars that are risen when the Archer rises; cf. 665. The figure of the Kneeler thus overlaps the sections of the poem's subject-matter, as it does the signs of the Zodiac in the sky. Hi. 2.2.56 τοῦ δὲ Τοξότου μέλλοντος ἀνατέλλειν ὁ Ἄρατός φησι τὴν κεφαλὴν τοῦ ἐν γόνασι καὶ τὴν ἀριστερὰν χεῖρα ἀνατεταλκέναι. In Hi. 2.2.58 the text purports to find fault with A., saying (a) ἡ δὲ ἀριστερὰ χεὶρ τοῦ ἐν γόνασι ταῖς Χηλαῖς συνανατέλλει, καὶ οὐ τῷ Σκορπίῳ, and (b) that the left shoulder, which precedes the hand, rises with Scorp. 3°. The two statements are contradictory, as Manitius points out (p. 299, n. 19): since the shoulder precedes (i.e. is west of) the hand, the hand must rise with a later degree of the Scorpion, not with the preceding sign (Claws). In fact Hi. 2.5.3 identifies the left hand as the very last of the kneeling figure's stars to rise. The text of 2.2.58 seems therefore to have been tampered with (Manitius 'man fast zweifeln möchte, ob hier Worte des Hipparch vorliegen'), and the information given by A. may be taken as correct. The corruption may have originated in 2.2.55, where the constellation in question is Ophiuchus: ἡ γὰρ ἀριστερὰ χεὶρ αὐτοῦ μόνον ταῖς Χηλαῖς συνανατέλλει, ἡ δὲ κεφαλὴ καὶ ἡ δεξιὰ χεὶρ τῷ Σκορπίῳ.

673 ἀνέρχονται The v.l. no doubt comes from 305 τόξον ἀνέλκεται.

Τοξότῃ ἀντέλλοντι The normal word for 'archer' is used only here by A. On the other hand the spondeiazon with various forms of this verb is frequent: cf. 564, 569, 689, 700, 720. A.R. 1.776, of Hesperus, δόμων ὕπερ ἀντέλλοντα, is an obvious imitation.

COMMENTARY: 674–679

674 Ἑρμαίη τε Λύρη   The epithet recalls 269.

στήθεος ἄχρις   Hi. 2.2.56 καὶ τὴν Λύραν καὶ τοῦ Κηφέως τὰ ἀπὸ τῆς κεφαλῆς ἕως τοῦ στήθους. There is no particular star to represent the breast of Cepheus, and the reference must be to that part of the figure. Hi. 2.2.59 comments that only the head of Cepheus sets and rises, while the shoulders and breast are circumpolar (cf. 650); also that the most westerly of the head stars rises with Scorp. 28°, and the most southerly with Sagitt. 5½°, so that the head rises with both the Scorpion and the Archer. Hipparchus is referring to the signs, as usual, A. to the constellations.

675 ἠώου   Usually of morning, as in 1024, here of the eastern horizon; cf. A.R. 2.745.

παρελαύνεται   Med. as variation of Homeric act. intrans. of driving or sailing past, e.g. Ψ 638, μ 197, both c. acc. A. uses it c. gen., because the stars come up from the horizon after crossing it. LSJ give no example of the middle use.

676 μεγάλοιο Κυνός   Cf. 342. The constellation itself is small, but A. is thinking of its powerful star Sirius. The transition to the setting stars occurs here in mid-sentence. Hi. 2.2.57 δύνειν δέ φησι τόν τε Κύνα ὅλον καὶ τὸν Ὠρίωνα καὶ τὸν Λαγωόν.

ἀμαρυγαί   Esp. of flashing light, e.g. h.Hom. 4.45 ἀπ' ὀφθαλμῶν ἀμαρυγαί (in same sedes). Cf. Hes. Th. 827 ὑπ' ὀφρύσι πῦρ ἀμάρυσσεν. A.R. 2.42 follows A., in reference to the star Castor, φαεινομένου ἀμαρυγαί. Max. 152 Σεληναίης ἀμαρυγήν.

677 πάντα κατέρχεται Ὠρίωνος   Cf. Q.S. 7.304 ἄστρα κατερχομένοιο ποτὶ κνέφας Ὠρίωνος.

678 ἀτέλεστα   Adv., as ἀτέλεστον in π 111, of eating. Cf. Strat. AP 12.21.3 ἀτέλεστα λαλήσομεν. The adv. recalls 339 ἐμμενὲς ἤματα πάντα διώκεται, also a five-dactyl line.

679–685   The Charioteer is another constellation which overlaps the rising of two Zodiac constellations (cf. 672), but A. blurs the transition rather confusingly by putting the part from head to waist, which sets later with Capricorn's rising (680–4), before the part below the waist, which sets earlier with the Archer (684–5). The upper half of the figure sets later because it extends well into the north, and so lingers longer in the north-west sky before setting. Hi. 2.2.57 characteristically rearranges the subject-matter so that the earlier setting stars are listed first, along with the others that set with the Archer: δύνειν δέ φησι ... καὶ τοῦ Ἡνιόχου τὰ ἀπὸ τῶν ποδῶν ἕως τῆς ζώνης μέρη. Then follows τὴν δὲ Αἶγά φησι καὶ τοὺς Ἐρίφους, ὧν ἐστιν ἡ μὲν ἐπὶ τοῦ ἀριστεροῦ ὤμου, οἱ δ' ἐν τῇ ἀριστερᾷ χειρί, ἔτι δὲ τὴν κεφαλὴν καὶ τὴν δεξιὰν χεῖρα τῷ Τοξότῃ ἀντικαταδύνειν. The text of H. should surely

409

read Αἰγοκέρωτι instead of Τοξότῃ here, since H. is reporting what A. says (684), unless we are to assume that he has overlooked A.'s sudden transition to Capricorn. Equally strange is the phrase that follows, τὰ δὲ πρὸς τοὺς πόδας τῷ Σκορπίῳ, which looks like an interpolation, since H. has already included the lower half of the figure, and marked it as setting with the Archer.

679 Ἔριφοι οὐδ' Ὠλενίη Αἴξ See 156-8, 164.

680 μεγάλην ἀνὰ χεῖρα A variation of 166 καρπὸν κάτα χειρός.

681 λάμπονται In Homer mostly of flashing bronze, e.g. Π 71 (κόρυθος) λαμπομένης. The verb suits the bright Capella, but not the fainter Kids. It is essentially a poetic embellishment, to bring out the importance of these stars as weather signs.

διακέκριται Cf. 169, of the distinctive outline of the Bull. Here it denotes the distinctive role that the Goat and Kids play as weather signs at certain seasons.

682 κινῆσαι χειμῶνας, ὅτ' ἠελίῳ συνίωσιν It is reasonable to suppose that A. is referring to either the ES, the last occasion when the Goat and Kids are observable before conjunction, or the MR, when they are first observable after conjunction. Sch. consider only the latter of these two possibilities, but find that the MR of these stars is not at a stormy time of year. Cf. Gem. *Cal.* Taur. 9 (= 1 May).

The solution offered by sch. is that the reference is to the time of year when the sun is in the Archer, the key constellation in this passage. This sets the scene conveniently in winter, when the morning setting of Capella occurred, on Sagitt. 23 (= 17 Dec.) according to Eudoxus. This entry has, however, no weather note appended, and indeed special storm warnings are superfluous in winter. In any case A. specifically refers to 'storms' (pl.), not to the season of winter (sg.).

Erren (*PAS* 62-3) suggests that 'conjunction' here properly means the ES, and that A. is really thinking of the phenomenon of Capella lingering in the sky in all its brilliance for some time after the rest of the Charioteer has set. Into this scene he has then transferred from the parapegmata the weather warning appropriate to the MS of Capella, in a kind of *contaminatio*. There is nothing in these lines that gives any relevance to the idea of Capella's lingering brightness, like that of Arcturus in 581-5, but I agree with Erren in thinking that A. is confusing morning and evening phenomena.

When A. refers to 'conjunction', he means the MR, but the storm sign belongs to the ER in September, when the autumn gales begin to put an end to the summer weather. Gem. *Cal.* Virgo 20 (= 15 Sept.). Cf. 158 on the Kids' ER, 28 Sept., the only date on which they appear in the parapegmata as harbingers of storm. The confusion is characteristic of the poets, who tend to think mainly of risings and settings, and forget about whether the phenomenon is a morning or evening occurrence. Thus Hes. *Op.* 566-7 introduces the rising and setting of the Pleiades without indicating in either case whether morning or evening is meant.

Here A. makes a poetic conceit out of the popular notion that certain stars cause certain kinds of weather. Gem. 17.26-45 refutes at length this fallacy with particular reference to Sirius; see note on 333.

683 τὰ μέν The upper part of the Charioteer figure, then defined as the head (δ Aurigae), the right hand (θ), and the waist, by which A. probably means the area of the figure between the two hands, since there is no particular star to represent it. Hi. 2.2.57 names the belt as the upper limit of the lower half. For ἰξύς 'waist' cf. 310 of Cepheus.

684 Αἰγόκερως See 282-99.

νείατα The lower half of the figure, below the waist. The n.pl. occurs once in Homer, Θ 478, but there is no similarity in the context.

685 οὐδ' ἔτι The traditional οὐδέ τι can only mean that Perseus does not wait in any respect, and it is difficult to see what point there is in saying this, and why A. should emphasise it with anaphora, whereas ἔτι is appropriate with μένει. Cf. ἔτι with negative in 122, 456, 460, 579, 1028, and ἔτι in anaphora 239. There is support for it in sch. (despite the lemma) οὔτε ὁ Περσεὺς οὔτε τὸ ἀκροστόλιον τῆς Ἀργῴας πρύμνης ἔτι φαίνεται, and in Avien. 1246 *iam non alatus remoratur, Arat. Lat. iam non Perseus.* Voss is the only editor to read ἔτι here and in 686.

686 ἔτι ἄκρα F. Spitzner 151 requires ἔτι γ', but for short vowels in hiatus cf. 45, 951, 962, 1133.

ἄκρα κόρυμβα An echo of I 241 στεῦται γὰρ νηῶν ἀποκόψειν ἄκρα κόρυμβα, though there is no similarity in the context. The noun (heteroclite pl. of κόρυμβος) occurs only once in Homer. It is recalled, together with its context, in A. *Pers.* 410-11 κἀποθραύει πάντα Φοινίσσης νεὼς | κόρυμβ'. A.R. 2.601 ἀφλάστοιο παρέθρισαν ἄκρα κόρυμβα alludes to both the damaging of ships in Homer and the Argo of A. Cf. Manetho 2.(1).97-8 Ἀργοῦς | ... ἄκρα κόρυμβα, of the constellation, Nonn. *D.* 39.321, of a ship. Hipparchus in 2.2.57 understands the reference as being to the whole stern part of Argo (τῆς Ἀργοῦς τὴν πρύμναν), and in 2.2.61 says that its setting should have been put with the rising of the Scorpion, not the Archer. Elsewhere H. mentions one particular star as ὁ ἐν τῷ ἀκροστολίῳ τῆς Ἀργοῦς λαμπρός (2.5.5).

πολυτειρέος Ἀργοῦς Cf. 604.

687 ἤτοι Cf. 275, 305, 748.

γουνός τε ποδός τε The knee is a group of faint stars (five according to Hi. 3.5.20), the brightest of which is the 4th-mag. μ Persei; the right foot is even fainter, and may be represented by the star numbered 58R.

688 περιαγήν Sch. τῆς δὲ τοσοῦτον δέδυκεν ὅσον εἰς τὴν περίκλασιν καὶ καμπὴν τῆς πρύμνης. The noun occurs only here, the verb once in Homer, of the voice of Hector: Π 78 Τρωσὶ κελεύοντος περιάγνυται. Cf. Hes. *Sc.* 279, also of sound. A. uses the simple noun ἀγή in 668.

689 αὐτήν The Argo as a whole; Hi. 2.3.1 ἀντικαταδύνειν τήν τε Ἀργὼ ὅλην. In 2.2.61 Hipparchus comments that Argo actually begins setting half-way through the rising of the Claws.

690 Προκύων See note on 450.

τὰ δ' ἀνέρχεται ἄλλα Hi. 2.3.1 συνανατέλλειν δὲ τόν τε Ὄρνιθα καὶ τὸν Ἀετὸν καὶ τὸν Ὀϊστὸν καὶ τὸ Θυμιατήριον. For the Bird see 275–81, the Eagle 313–15, the Arrow 311–12, the Altar 402–30.

691 Ὄρνις Hi. 2.3.2–3 comments that Eudoxus and Aratus are wrong about the Bird's rising. Eudoxus says its right wing rises with the Scorpion, Aratus says with the Archer, but in fact it rises with the end of the Claws, and the star on the left wing-tip, the last to rise, comes up with the 22nd degree of the Archer. The reference to degrees shows that H. means the sign, not the constellation.

πτερόεντος Ὀϊστοῦ Cf. E 171 πτερόεντες ὀϊστοί in the same part of the line; the adj. is also used with ἰοῖ, ἰα (Π 773, Υ 68). Nonn. *D.* 7.132 and 16.9 repeat A.'s phrase.

692 τείρεα Once in Homer, of constellations, Σ 485 (already cited on 482 and 567). τείρεα is a metrically lengthened pl. of τέρας (cf. Τειρεσίας), and is cognate with ἀστήρ (**ster*). See A. Scherer, *Gestirnnamen bei den indogermanischen Völkern* (Heidelberg 1953) 30–1, Frisk 2.878, Wyatt 194–5. In Δ 76 a shooting star is ναύτῃσι τέρας, but there is nothing portentous about the use of the pl. here, which refers to a very small and faint constellation (see 311–15). A. does, however, use the adj. πολυτειρής of more impressive star-groups (604, 668, 686). In *h.Hom.* 8.7 αἰθέρος ἑπταπόροις ἐνὶ τείρεσιν the reference is to the planets. A.R. gives the word a more Homeric context in 3.1361–2 τὰ δ' ἀθρόα πάντα φαάνθη | τείρεα λαμπετόωντα, and 4.261 τείρεα πάντα τά τ' οὐρανῷ εἱλίσσονται. Antip. *AP* 9.541.3–4 (= *GP* 309–10) is more Aratean with τὸ μὲν ἡμῶν | τοὺς νοτίους, τὸ δ' ἔχει τείρεα τὰν βορέῃ, of two hemispherical cups. Max. 593, of Capricorn, κλυτὰ τείρεα.

ἱερὸς ἕδρη This fem. form is perhaps an imitation of Hes. *Op.* 597, 805 Δημήτερος ἱερὸν ἀκτήν, in the same metrical position; cf. the oracle in Hdt. 8.77 Ἀρτέμιδος χρυσαόρου ἱερὸν ἀκτήν. But A. has Αἲξ ἱερή (163) in a different part of the line. The epithet characterises primarily the Altar, as in Β 305 ἱεροὺς κατὰ βωμούς, and recalls the extended passage 408–535, where the Altar is said to have been established by the goddess Night for the benefit of suffering mortals. The association

412

of ἕδρα with gods is post-Homeric, e.g. Pi. *I.* 7.44 χαλκόπεδον θεῶν ἕδραν. Cf. 625, 628, and Kastner 25.

693–698 *Rising of the Water-pourer*

Part of the Horse has risen, parts of the Centaur and the Hydra set. Eudoxus gives also Cassiepeia and the Dolphin as rising (fr. 106). Germ. 691–2 adds the Dolphin and the Crown to the constellations that rise with Capricorn, Avien. 1260 the Dolphin only. Hyg. 4.12.11 is faithful to A. Hi. 2.3.4–10 comments on this section.

693 Ὑδροχόοιο See 282–99, and for the internal rhyme 360.

μέσον The reading of the MSS is unanimously νέον, but Hi. 2.3.6–9 quotes this line with μέσον and discusses the problem of text and interpretation. Critics, he says, find it difficult to understand why A., who elsewhere assumes that the signs of the Zodiac are just beginning to rise at the time when the phenomena he describes are visible, τὸν Ὑδροχόον μέσον ἀνατέλλειν ὑποτίθεται [implying that they take this to mean 'is at the mid-point of its rising']. τούτου δ' ἀπορουμένου ὁ Ἄτταλός φησιν ἁμάρτημα εἶναι, δεῖν δὲ γράφειν οὕτως· "Ἵππος δ' Ὑδροχόοιο νέον περιτελλομένοιο". This reading may have been suggested to Attalus by 706. The emendation seems to have become widely accepted, since Hipparchus goes on to say: λανθάνει δὲ τόν τε Ἄτταλον καὶ τοὺς ἄλλους τὸ βούλημα τοῦ ποιητοῦ, τάχα δὲ καὶ τὸ φαινόμενον. The figure of the Water-pourer, he explains, is orientated on a north–south line, with the head lying well to the north of the ecliptic and the feet well to the south of it, ἐν δὲ τῷ ζῳδιακῷ τὰ μέσα αὐτοῦ κεῖται. He therefore interprets μέσον as the mid-point of the figure: τοῦ Ὑδροχόου κατὰ μέσον τὸ σῶμα ἀνατέλλοντος ... καὶ οὐχὶ τὸ μέσον τοῦ ἐν τῷ δωδεκατημορίῳ μήκους, ὡς οἵ τε πολλοὶ καὶ ὁ Ἄτταλος ἐνδέχεται. He also reports that μέσον is the reading in all the copies he has consulted, and opposes any emendation: ἀναγκαῖον οὖν εἶναι δοκεῖ μοι μὴ μετατιθέναι τὸν στίχον, ὡς ὁ Ἄτταλος ὑποδεικνύει, ἐν πᾶσί γε δὴ τοῖς ἀντιγράφοις οὕτως αὐτοῦ γραφομένου.

The argument of Hipparchus is compelling. His text is supported by Gem. *Cal.* Aquar. 17 Ὑδροχόος μέσος ἀνατέλλει, and also by Cic. 472 *cum se medium caeli in regione locauit*, and Hyg. 4.12.11 *exoriens ad dimidiam partem corporis*. So sch. κατὰ μέσον τὸ σῶμα ἀνελθόντος. The adverbial use is rare, but cf. M 167 σφῆκες μέσον αἰόλοι.

694 ποσσί τε καὶ κεφαλῇ Hi. 2.3.4 τοῦ δὲ Ὑδροχόου ἀρχομένου ἀνατέλλειν φησὶ συνανατεταλκέναι τῷ Αἰγόκερῳ τοῦ Ἵππου τήν τε κεφαλὴν καὶ τοὺς πόδας. The Horse has only the forefeet (cf. 214, 220, 281, 487); the head is θ Pegasi (cf. 210).

ἀνελίσσεται Cf. 714. The meaning 'rise' is not given by LSJ.

695 ἐξ οὐρῆς Κένταυρον Hi. 2.3.4 δύνειν δὲ τὰ ὀπίσθια τοῦ Κενταύρου. For the tail cf. 625.

ἐφέλκεται Cf. 628. This is a morning setting, and Night is thought of as disappearing below the western horizon, drawing the last stars after it. The Centaur's movement is tail first: cf. 625–6 of its rising. This form of the verb is best known from π 294, τ 13 αὐτὸς γὰρ ἐφέλκεται ἄνδρα σίδηρος. Of Hesperus cf. E. *Ion* 1149.

ἀστερίη First attested here. Voss arbitrarily rejects as 'ein ungriechisches Wort', despite Nic. *Ther.* 725 ἀστέριον (a kind of spider) and D.P. 328 ἀστέριος καλὸς λίθος, and adopts ἑσπερίη from Ach. *Isag.* 36, citing also A.R. 2.42 ἑσπερίην διὰ νύκτα. Cicero translates *signipotens nox* (475). The quadrisyllabic epithet before the monosyllabic ending reflects Homeric ἀμφιλύκη (Η 433), ἀμβροσίη (δ 429), οὐρανόθεν (ε 294). Cf. 470; Q.S. 10.198 ἡελίῳ δύνοντι συνέρχεται ἑσπερίη νύξ.

696 κεφαλήν Cf. 662.

οὐδ' The v.l. ἠδ' probably originates in the paraphrase of the sch. on 694–701 ἡ μέντοι κεφαλὴ αὐτοῦ καὶ οἱ ὦμοι καὶ ὁ θώραξ οὐ δύνονται ἅμα τῷ Ὑδροχόῳ καταφέρεσθαι. It does not support ἠδ', as Voss claims, since in A.'s text the negative precedes the nouns. Another source may be Γ 227 κεφαλήν τε καὶ εὐρέας ὤμους.

εὐρέας ὤμους The epithet is purely literary, from Γ 210, 227, Π 360, Χ 488, all at line-ends; cf. *h.Hom.* 3.450, 4.217. For the relevant stars see note on 432.

697 θώρηκι Probably the star group μ ν φ Centauri, which Hipparchus describes as the most southerly part of the thyrsus, adding οἳ κεῖνται κατὰ μέσον πως τὸ στῆθος τοῦ Κενταύρου (3.5.6). It is likely that the figure according to Eudoxus and A. was simpler, and had not yet acquired a thyrsus held in the right hand.

χαδεῖν Aor. inf. χανδάνω. This rather humorous notion, that Night cannot yet find room below the horizon for the rest of the Centaur, is based on Ξ 33–4 οὐδὲ γὰρ οὐδ' εὐρύς περ ἐὼν ἐδυνήσατο πάσας | αἰγιαλὸς νῆας χαδέειν. Cf. Opp. *C.* 3.503 ὅσον χαδέειν τόσον ὄρνιν.

αἴθοπος A literary epithet; cf. 519 αἰθομένης. It recurs in Homer as a formulaic epithet of wine (e.g. Α 462) and bronze (e.g. Δ 495), once of smoke (κ 152). It has the same *sedes* here as in Homer.

698 αὐχενίην Hi. 2.3.4 τοῦ Ὕδρου τὸ ἀπὸ τῆς κεφαλῆς ἕως τῆς πρώτης σπείρας. This is the small bend in the line of stars θ ι α Hydrae, lying south-east of the head stars. The adj. occurs once in Homer, γ 449–50 πέλεκυς δ' ἀπέκοψε τένοντας | αὐχενίους.

μέτωπα A rare variation for the much used κεφαλή, and meaning all the head stars (cf. 445). The poetic pl. occurs once in Homer, of Artemis, ζ 107 πασάων δ' ὑπὲρ ἥ γε κάρη ἔχει ἠδὲ μέτωπα. Maass unnecessarily emends to πρόσωπα, on the strength of 737, where it describes the face of the full moon.

699-711 Rising of the Fishes and the Ram

Hydra and Centaur set completely, the Southern Fish and Andromeda have risen, the Altar sets and part of Perseus is in the east. The extended passage on Andromeda serves to blur the division between these two risings. Hi. 2.3.11-17 comments on the Fishes' rising, 18-32 on the Ram's; Hyg. 4.12.12 (Pisces), 12.1 (Aries).

699 πολλὴ μένει After 697-8 the tail end of the Hydra is still visible on the western horizon, as Eudoxus is reported as saying, τοῦ "Υδρου τὴν οὐρὰν ἔτι ὑπολείπεσθαι (Hi. 2.3.14). It is strange that Hipparchus represents A. as supposing that the Hydra sets completely during the rising of the Water-pourer (2.3.14), and (2.3.11) that, by the time the Fishes begin to rise, δεδυκέναι τά τε λοιπὰ τοῦ "Υδρου. The constellations listed as setting always start the period by being visible above the western horizon (cf. 566-8).

700 αὐτῷ Κενταύρῳ Dat. of accompaniment, with αὐτῷ for emphasis, since the Centaur is a large and impressive figure. Cf. I 541-2 χαμαὶ βάλε δένδρεα μακρὰ | αὐτῆσιν ῥίζῃσι καὶ αὐτοῖς ἄνθεσι μήλων. Hi. 2.3.15 comments that both Eudoxus and A. are wrong about the Centaur, since the forelegs are still above the horizon. But A. presumably means that the Centaur's setting is completed later during the period of the Fishes' rising.

Ἰχθύες See 239-47.

701 ἀθρόον Sc. τὴν "Υδρην. A. uses this adj. with two terminations also in 153. Eudoxus in the Enoptron has the Hydra setting only as far as the Raven (fr. 112a).

ἐμφέρεται Night (695) is still subject, though the sequence of thought is somewhat confused by the intervention of Hydra as fem. subject in 699. The middle, a rare use, means that Night gathers the Hydra into herself; cf. ο 378 καὶ φαγέμεν πιέμεν τε, ἔπειτα δὲ καί τι φέρεσθαι. The passive is Homeric (μ 419).

Ἰχθῦς The Southern Fish; cf. 386-8. Hi. 2.3.11 ἀνατεταλκέναι δὲ τὸν Νότιον Ἰχθὺν οὐχ ὅλον, ἀλλὰ παρὰ μικρόν. At 2.3.16 Hipparchus finds fault with both Eudoxus and A. for supposing that it rises almost entirely with the Water-pourer (i.e. if it is up by the time the Fishes start to rise, it must have risen during the preceding rising), whereas in fact most of it rises simultaneously with the Fishes. He illustrates with reference to particular stars on the tail and the mouth. On the accent see 387.

702 κυανέῳ Used elsewhere of dim areas of constellations, the belly of the Dog (329) and the Monster (398). Capricorn is similarly lacking in bright stars, and this is the only descriptive epithet that A. has given it.

ὑποκείμενος Αἰγοκερῆι A variation of 386 νειόθι Αἰγοκερῆος. A. adds this note on the position of the Fish in order to identify it clearly as the Southern Fish. Its position is actually south-east of Capricorn, and the prefix ὑπο- must therefore be taken to denote a position merely farther south, not due south; cf. 436.

703 ἄδην Perhaps a verbal echo of N 315 οἵ μιν ἄδην ἐλόωσι. The rough breathing in Homer is the reading of Aristarchus, and conforms to the probable derivation from root *sa (cf. Lat. satur, satis); see Monro on N 315, Fraenkel on A. Ag. 828, Chantraine 185. But the smooth breathing was also prevalent, and is attested here by all MSS and sch., though on 976 sch. (MKUA) quote Call. fr. 269 with ἄδην, sch. (ΔS) with ἄδην. Cf. Hes. fr. 239.2, A.R. 2.82. Chantraine notes the irregularities in the use of the breathings, and finds that in general the rough survives in words from Attic, Ionian and the Koine, the smooth in words that are originally Homeric, especially in the poets.

δυωδεκάδ' ἀμμένει This is the reading of all editors since Maass, before whom the v.l. δυωδεκάδα μένει was the standard text. With this μένει has the same sense as in 621 (cf. 663 μένουσι), and the lengthening before μ- is Homeric, e.g. before μαλακός, μέγαρον, μέγας, μελίη, μέλος, μόθος, although never before μένω. A. has it elsewhere in 624 καταμελεϊστί and 940 διὰ μέγαν. The change to ἀμμένει can be explained as the correction of a supposed metrical fault, and ἀμμένω is not, after all, an epic form. It belongs rather to lyric, both personal (Alc. PMG 346.1 τί τὰ λύχν' ὀμμένομεν;) and choral (S. El. 1389, 1397, Tr. 528, 648, E. Cyc. 514); but it is also found in dramatic iambics (S. Tr. 335, E. Andr. 444, Hec. 1281). A. does sometimes draw poetic material from the lyric poets (cf. 424 λαίφεα) and drama (cf. 668 ἀγήν), and here he seems to be echoing the language of S. Tr. 648 δυοκαιδεκάμηνον ἀμμένουσαι χρόνον, though there is no particular similarity in the context. The first-century AD papyrus also seems to support ἀμμένει. The compound here provides a variation on the single verb, which A. has already used in this form three times in the last hundred lines (621, 686, 699). For δυωδεκάς = δωδεκατημόριον see 555.

ἄλλην The next Zodiacal constellation, i.e. the Ram.

704 μογεραί Cf. 179 Κηφῆος μογερὸν γένος. The hands are particularly tragic because they are held by chains (202-4).

χεῖρες καὶ γοῦνα καὶ ὦμοι For hands, feet and shoulders see on 201 and 203. But here A. is thinking more of the right and left sides of the figure than of particular stars.

705 δίχα πάντα The figure is divided lengthwise by its centre-line, which rises parallel to the horizon. At the time when the Fishes begin to rise only the right side of Andromeda is above the horizon; cf. Hi. 2.3.11 τῆς Ἀνδρομέδας τὰ δεξιὰ μέρη κατὰ μῆκος. This means that the right half has risen during the rising of the Water-pourer, and the left will rise with the Fishes, as Hipparchus points out in 2.3.17. He finds both Eudoxus and A. to be in error, because each half in fact rises one sign earlier, i.e. with Capricorn and the Water-pourer respectively.

τὰ μὲν πάρος The right side is ahead, and so above the horizon; cf. 845, 923.

ὀπίσσω The normal Homeric position in the line (28 times out of 30 in the *Iliad*, 22 times in the *Odyssey*). There is perhaps a faint reminiscence of ξ 232 πολλὰ δ' ὀπίσσω. Cf. 923.

706 τείνεται The figure extends lengthwise along the line of the horizon; cf. 989 of a cloud.

νέον The adv. is Homeric, e.g. τ 400 παῖδα νέον γεγαῶτα. Closer to A.'s context is *h.Hom.* 4.371 ἠελίοιο νέον ἐπιτελλομένοιο, with similar lengthening of -ον. Hi. 2.1.24 quotes νέον ... Ἰχθύες in illustration of his argument that, when A. refers to the rising of a sign of the Zodiac, he means the beginning of its rising, and so here means ὅταν ἄρχωνται οἱ Ἰχθύες ἀνατέλλειν.

προγένωνται Once in Homer, of cattle coming into view, Σ 525 οἱ δὲ τάχα προγένοντο. Cf. A.R. 3.1292, [Theoc.] 25.134. Closer to A.'s use is Ti. Locr. 97a πᾶς δὲ ἐν μεγέθει ἀστὴρ ὑπὲρ τὸν ὁρίζοντα πρὸ ἀλίου προγενόμενος ἀμέραν ἀγγέλλει.

707 τὰ μέν οἱ A. ignores the digamma also in 50 ἡ μέν οἱ ἄκρη, 485 τὸ μέν οἱ θέναρ. Cf. ν 430 κάρψε μέν οἱ, A.R. 3.1205 τὸ μέν οἱ πάρος, Call. fr. 228.43 ἄρτι γάρ οἱ, Theoc. 15.112 πὰρ μέν οἱ ὥρια. Here Koechly's τά γε μέν, wrongly ascribed to Duebner by Maass, and adopted without ascription by Martin, is a needless emendation. See Maass *Aratea* 110–11, Pfeiffer on Call. fr. 2.3, Gow on Theoc. 15.112.

κατὰ δεξιὰ χειρός Cf. 279. The whole phrase is an amplification of τὰ μέν in 705; sch. τὰ μὲν οὖν δεξιὰ μέρη αὐτῆς.

708 ἐφέλκονται Here of a rising, in 628 and 695 of settings.

709 περιτελλομένοιο Cf. 232 and note. Here the case and metrical position recall *h.Hom.* 2.445 ἔτεος περιτελλομένοιο. Cf. 693.

710 ἑσπερόθεν Only in A. (also 734, 891), and always of the west. The Altar sets far south on the western horizon, and the short duration of its period of visibility (cf. 404–7) is well illustrated by the fact that it has risen with Capricorn only three signs earlier (692). Leontius, *Sphaer. Arat.* 4 Κριοῦ ἀνατέλλοντος τὸ Θυμιατήριον ὁρᾶται ἐπὶ δύσιν.

ἄλλη In sense of ἑτέρη (cf. 49, 50, 683), the eastern horizon.

711 ὅσον   Adv. with sense 'only'; cf. Ι 354 ἀλλ' ὅσον ἐς Σκαιάς τε πύλας καὶ φηγὸν ἵκανεν. K–G 2.412.

κεφαλήν τε καὶ ὤμους   The head star is τ, the shoulders (cf. 249) γ θ Persei. Hi. 2.3.22 quotes from Attalus: μέλλοντος μὲν τοῦ Κριοῦ ἀνατέλλειν ὁ Περσεὺς ὁμολογουμένως μέχρι τῶν ὤμων ἐκφανὴς γίνεται (fr. 28).

712–723   Rising of the Bull
Parts of Perseus, the Charioteer and the Monster have risen, part of Bootes sets; Hyg. 4.12.2. Hi. 2.3.18–32 discusses at length the meaning of 712–13.

712 ζώνη   The star α Persei, which Hipparchus calls ὁ ἐν μέσῳ τῷ σώματι λαμπρὸς ἱκανῶς ἀστήρ (2.3.13). The emphatic αὐτή distinguishes the belt from the stars just mentioned, because it involves a special problem about its time of rising.

ἀμφήριστα   Twice in Homer, in same *sedes*, ἀμφήριστον ἔθηκεν (Ψ 382, 527); elsewhere A.R. 3.627 νεῖκος πέλεν ἀμφήριστον, Call. *H.* 1.5 γένος ἀμφήριστον. Cf. Serapio, *CCAG* 1.100, of astrological predictions, ἐὰν δὲ ἀμφήριστοι εὑρεθῶσι, Hi. 2.3.30 ἀμφήριστόν φησιν εἶναι καὶ διστα ζόμενον.

The point of A.'s uncertainty here is raised by Hipparchus, who first quotes Attalus' explanation (2.3.22–3): since the head and shoulders of Perseus are visible by the time the Ram's rising begins, and his belt appears only a very short time thereafter, A. is in doubt whether he should include the belt with the stars visible at the Ram's rising or take it with the rest of Perseus as visible when the Bull begins to rise (Att. fr. 28). Hipparchus comments that Attalus is wrong in thinking that A. is so particular about such accuracy with regard to the belt of Perseus. The same problem would occur in the case of all constellations whose rising extends over two or more Zodiacal risings. Besides, the time of the belt's rising is not really in doubt, as Attalus assumes; it is already visible when the Ram's rising begins, and so in fact is the rest of Perseus, except the left foot and knee (24–6).

Hipparchus gives an entirely different explanation, namely that A.'s uncertainty is due to a discrepancy in the writings of Eudoxus. In the *Phaenomena* he says that the right side of Perseus rises with the rising of the Fishes (Voss wrongly suspects τοῖς Ἰχθύσι here), and so is visible at the beginning of the Ram's rising, but in his *Enoptron* he says that all but a small part of Perseus rises with the Fishes. Since the two books are almost always in agreement on such matters, A. is naturally in doubt about which of these two sources he should follow here (29–30). The explanation of Hipparchus makes good sense. In this highly technical section A. is obliged to follow his model more closely than he did in his earlier description of the constellations, the details of which he could check for himself from diagrams or from the night sky itself. He does not elsewhere question his source material in this section, and indeed his primary purpose is to illustrate the helpfulness of Zeus rather than to compose an astronomical textbook. See further on 713.

πέλοιτο Hi. 2.3.32 reports the existence of variants already in his time: διχῶς δὲ γραφομένου, ἐν μέν τισιν ἀντιγράφοις "καί κ' ἀμφήριστα πέλοιτο", ἐν δέ τισι "καί κ' ἀμφήριστα πέλονται", δεῖ γράφειν "πέλοιτο", καὶ οὐχ, ὡς ὁ Ἄτταλος, "πέλονται". τῷ γὰρ ἂν συνδέσμῳ τὸ "πέλοιτο" καταλλήλως λέγεται. Martin finds it strange that H. should write ἄν here, when he reads only κ' in the text, and suggests perhaps ἄν κ' (unthinkable here: see note on 562) for καί κ', though he does not press the conjecture in view of the papyrus reading. It was probably natural for H. to use the prose particle in his comment. He goes on to say that the plural verb is not necessary with ἀμφήριστα· σύνηθες γάρ ἐστι τὸ σχῆμα τοῦτο τῆς ἐκφοράς.

713 ἦ .... ἦ Homeric use with indirect question, e.g. B 299–300 ὄφρα δαῶμεν | ἦ ἐτεὸν Κάλχας μαντεύεται ἦε καὶ οὐκί, Π 436–8. Hdn. Gr. 2.24, 145, al. gives the accentuation ἦ, ἦε in the second place, but 'ἢ freq. in codd. of Homer and always in codd. of later writers' (Lentz). Here I have retained the ἦ of the MSS. See K–G 2.531.

λήγοντι Hi. 2.3.19–20 comments that this is probably an error, because when A. refers to a Zodiacal rising, he always means that it is the beginning of the constellation that is on the eastern horizon, not the middle or end of it. Attalus, he says, recognised the error and emended it: καὶ δεῖ τοι ἢ ὡς ἐκεῖνός φησι γράφεσθαι "ἢ Κριῷ ἀνιόντι φαείνεται ἢ ἐπὶ Ταύρῳ", ἢ νὴ Δία οὕτως, "ἢ Κριῷ λήγουσα φαείνεται", ὥστε τὸ "λήγουσα" ἐπὶ τὴν ζώνην ἀναφέρεσθαι (fr. 28). Cf. note on 569–589 and Hi. 2.1.13–6, citing 706 and 606 as referring to the first point of the Fishes and of the Maiden respectively at their rising. Similarly 567–8 may be taken to imply that A. lists the stars visible just above the horizon at the time when each Zodiacal constellation begins to rise. But in fact A. never says this specifically, and his method seems to be more flexible than the rigid convention imposed on him by Hipparchus. In 606 it is the whole of the Maiden that has just risen, and that means the end of the constellation's rising; in 626 the Claws are still rising, i.e. after the first point has appeared. It may therefore be more reasonable to assume that, when A. first introduces each rising, he is thinking of the first point of the constellation, but that elsewhere in some passages he also refers to later times within the relevant rising period.

Here there is no evidence of variants in the traditional text of A. at the time of Hipparchus, only of deliberate emendation designed to bring the line into conformity with the astronomical facts. But what we are concerned with is what A. actually wrote, and there is no reason to suppose that he did not mean what the text says, that the belt of Perseus is visible either towards the end of the Ram's rising or at the beginning of the Bull's. Martin argues similarly for the retention of λήγοντι. But he misunderstands Hipparchus in supposing that the question is whether the belt rises with the first degree of the Ram or with the first degree of the Bull, 'une distance de tout un signe!' The point is simply that if the belt is not visible by the time the Ram begins to rise, it will have to be listed with the stars that are visible when the Bull's rising begins.

714 πανσυδίη Cf. 649. Attalus (fr. 28) quotes this line with πασσυδίη.

ὅ γε Anticipating Ἡνίοχος two lines below; cf. 21.

715 λείπεται Sc. below the horizon.

συναρηρώς Cf. 532. The Charioteer lies to the north-east of the Bull, and so they rise simultaneously over the north-eastern horizon.

716 μοίρη A constellation of the Zodiac regarded as one twelfth of the whole circle; cf. 560, 581, 721, 740.

717 οὖλον Ionic form, twice in Homer, ρ 343 ἄρτον τ' οὖλον ἑλών, ω 118 μηνὶ δ' ἄρ' οὔλῳ. A. elsewhere uses ὅλος (727, 796, 900).

718 Ἔριφοι Cf. 158, 679, Hi. 2.3.33 τοῦ Ἡνιόχου τὴν ἀριστερὰν χεῖρα, ἐν ᾗ οἱ Ἔριφοι κεῖνται, καὶ τὸν ἀριστερὸν πόδα.

θέναρ More often of the hand, as in 485 and E 339, here of the foot; cf. Hp. *Mul.* 2.116 θέναρα τῶν ποδῶν, Call. fr. 24.1 ποδὸς θέναρ. The left foot is ι Aurigae.

Αἰγί Cf. 157, 679.

719 συμφορέονται This verb normally means 'bring together', as in 363, but here the prefix relates to Ταύρῳ, and the verb provides another variation for the sense of simultaneous rising; cf. 561 συνανέρχεται, 714 σὺν ... ἀνελίσσεται, 619 σὺν ... φαείνεται. This meaning is not given by LSJ.

ὅτε Lengthening of syllable with ictus before initial λ is frequent in Homer, e.g. ἰδὲ λόφον (Z 469, K 573), ὑπὸ λόφον (N 615), ποτὶ λόφον (λ 596), πεδία λωτοῦντα (M 283); cf. 1112. See West *GM* 15–16.

λοφιή τε καὶ οὐρή Cf. 364 and 398; Hi. 2.3.33 τοῦ Κήτους τὸ ἀπὸ τῆς οὐρᾶς ἕως τῆς λοφιᾶς.

Hi. 2.3.34–5 finds fault with both Eudoxus and A. with regard to both the Charioteer and the Monster. It is not only the left side of the former that rises with the Ram: the right shoulder rises with 22° of the Ram, and the more northerly head star even earlier, with the Fishes. The Monster begins to rise with the Fishes, and almost completes its rising with the Ram. Stars rising with the Ram are, of course, visible when the Bull's rising begins.

720 Κήτεος αἰθερίοιο Repeated from 390.

περαιόθεν Cf. 443, 606, 645.

721 Ἀρκτοφύλαξ The constellation Bootes (cf. 92, 579). Hi. 2.3.33 δεδυκέναι δέ φησι τοῦ Βοώτου τι μέρος, ibid. 36 ὅτι γε μὴν οὐδὲ ὁ Βοώτης τῷ Κριῷ ἄρχεται ἀντικαταφέρεσθαι, ὥς φασιν, ἀλλὰ τῷ Ταύρῳ, προειρήκαμεν ἀνωτέρω [2.2.28]. Stars rising with the Bull are visible when the Twins' rising begins; cf. note on 719.

ἤδη ... τότε Hi. 2.2.12 quotes this line with πρώτῃ ἐπὶ μοίρῃ, and is followed by Maass, who refers to 554 πάσῃ δ' ἐπὶ νυκτί. Voss reads τότε δή with ἐπί, referring to sch. 719 τότε δὴ καὶ ὁ Ἀρκτοφύλαξ ἄρχεται μετὰ τοῦ πρώτου ζῳδίου, but gives no reason for regarding the MSS text as unsatisfactory. The combination of ἤδη with τότε gives an emphatic 'already by that time', e.g. B 699 τότε δ' ἤδη ἔχεν κάτα γαῖα μέλαινα, Hes. *Op.* 588–9 ἀλλὰ τότ' ἤδη | εἴη πετραίη τε σκιή, A. *Pr.* 910–11 πατρὸς δ' ἀρὰ | Κρόνου τότ' ἤδη παντελῶς κρανθήσεται, *Il.* R. 417b θέοντες ἤδη τότε ἐγγύτατα ὀλέθρου. For other examples see J. Diggle, *GRBS* 14 (1973) 245 on E. *Supp.* 348. Hipparchus sometimes misquotes words that are not astronomically significant, and in this case he may have been influenced by 716.

πρώτη ... μοίρη The setting of Bootes was supposed to take as long as the rising of four successive signs of the Zodiac, namely the Bull, the Twins, the Crab and the Lion; see note on 581.

722 τάων Homeric, esp. in this position, e.g. β 119 τάων αἳ πάρος ἦσαν, Δ 46; cf. Call. fr. 43.54.

πίσυρες Cf. 478. For its use in this *sedes* cf. π 249 ἐκ δὲ Σάμης πίσυρές τε καὶ εἴκοσι (see Chantraine 114). Here the Aeolic form is also a variation after 581 τέτρασι.

ἄτερ χειρός Hi. 2.2.14 ὅλος δὲ δύνει πλὴν τῆς ἀριστερᾶς χειρὸς καὶ τοῦ ἀγκῶνος. The left hand (θ ι κ Bootis) is circumpolar and does not set: sch. (M) ἄδυτος γὰρ αὐτοῦ ἡ χείρ, ἐπειδὴ ἔνδον ἐστὶ τοῦ ἀρκτικοῦ, (S) ἡ μέντοι χεὶρ ἡ ἐντὸς ἀρκτικοῦ μόνη οὐ καταδύνει.

723 αὐτοῦ The MSS, misreported by Maass, overwhelmingly attest αὐτοῦ, and are supported by the papyrus. But editors since Morel (except Voss and Zannoni) have read αὐτῷ, explaining it with reference to Bootes, though Mair and Martin do not actually translate it. Erren 'die ist ihm unter der grossen Bärin ausgestreckt'. But αὐτῷ seems too emphatic for the sense that this interpretation requires. A. normally uses enclitic οἱ in such contexts, e.g. 329 ἡ δέ οἱ referring back to Κύων two lines above, but even the weak pronoun is not essential to the sense.

Voss explains αὐτοῦ by comparing Homer's ἥ τ' αὐτοῦ στρέφεται (Σ 488, ε 274) of the Bear, i.e. 'sie dreht sich in dem selbigen Raum an der grossen Bärin'. The reminiscence is apt in this context, and the hand is 'there' in the sense that it is always within the circle of visibility.

μεγάλη ὑπὸ τέλλεται Ἄρκτῳ MSS and papyrus all give -τέλλεται, but with different prefixes. ὑπερ- is unmetrical, and can be explained as a 'correction' of ὑπο-, because, when the figure of Bootes is seen in an upright position, his left hand is just above the end of the Bear's tail. The same reason accounts for the late v.l. μεγάλη ὑποτέλλεται ἄρκτος. ἐπι- looks like another attempt to correct ὑπο-, but ἐπιτέλλεται is used of a star rising (e.g. Hes. *Op.* 567), and is not appropriate here. Nor is ὑποτέλλεται, if it has to mean 'rises' (Mair): the verb occurs elsewhere only in A.R. 2.83 βρυχὴ δ' ἐπετέλλετ' ὀδόντων, of the noise arising from men boxing. Martin, taking the required sense to be that the hand reaches as far as the Great Bear, emends to ὑποτείνεται and adopts the v.l. μεγάλης Ἄρκτου as gen. of direction or point of contact. There appears to be no parallel for this verb in this sense, and it would be more satisfactory to find a suitable meaning for ὑπό with τέλλεται. Sch. give πλησίον ἐστὶ τῆς μεγάλης Ἄρκτου, and Bootes' hand is indeed very close to the end of the Bear's tail. I have considered taking ὑπό here in this sense, comparing the geographical use, e.g. Β 866 ὑπὸ Τμώλῳ γεγαῶτας, α 186 ὑπὸ Νηΐῳ, but this means being close to the foot of some high object, and the context here is different. Another possibility is 'behind', which would accurately describe the position of the hand relative to the Bear (cf. 91 ἐξόπιθεν δ' Ἑλίκης). But this usage is late, attested only in prose (see LSJ), and seems to imply being under the protection of something. It is more probable that A. is concerned here solely with the position of the hand at the time when the rest of Bootes has set. The hand is then close to the horizon at due north, while the body of the Bear is now well up in the northern sky. In this position the hand can reasonably be said to be moving below the Bear. The simple τέλλεται does not necessarily mean 'rises', but denotes movement across the sky; cf. 285, 320, 382, and see Keydell 584.

724–732 Rising of the Twins
Ophiuchus partly sets, the whole Monster and part of the River are visible. Hi. 2.3.37–8 τῶν δὲ Διδύμων ἀρχομένων ἀνατέλλειν ὁ Ἄρατος δύνειν μέν φησι τοὺς πόδας τοῦ Ὀφιούχου "μέσφ' αὐτῶν γονάτων", ἀνατέλλειν δὲ τὸ Κῆτος καὶ τοῦ Ποταμοῦ τὰ πρῶτα. ταῦτα δὲ συμφώνως τοῖς φαινομένοις ὑπ' αὐτῶν εἴρηται. Hyg. 4.12.3 adds Orion prematurely.

724 ἀμφότεροι δὲ πόδες Cf. 248. Here almost all MSS read τε, but this particle rarely connects sentences, and only then when the second is related in some sense to the first, e.g. ῥίγησέν τ' ἄρ' ἔπειτα (Λ 254), of Agamemnon's reaction to a wound. The usage occurs more in prose, especially in Thucydides, after whom Denniston (499) finds that it declines markedly. Here the sentences are not so related, since the second moves on to the next sign of the Zodiac. Throughout this section, when new signs are introduced with a new sentence, the connective is δέ (590, 634, 693, 699), unless the formula is negative, or the connective is omitted. Since the connective is not essential (cf. 665), τε could be thought of as having a habitual force (Denniston 521), but in that sense it is found only with relatives or other particles, and here the use would be unparalleled. Morel first prints δέ.

On the feet of Ophiuchus see 84.

725 μέσφ' Cf. 599, 807; here elided, as in Θ 508. Schwyzer 2.550. For the knees of Ophiuchus see 521.

Διδύμοις ἔπι Cf. 418 νότῳ ἔπι σῆμα τιτύσκει, 873 ἐφ' ὕδατι σημαίνοιεν. A. introduces the Twins in a different manner, as if illustrating the lesson given in 563-8.

τετύχθω Voss considered the sg. verb after πόδες to be 'eine unschickliche Figur' and emended to τετύχθων (from τετύχθωσαν) in view of sch. ἔστωσάν σοι τεκμήριον. But, as Martin points out, the verb is attracted to the number of the immediately preceding complement: cf. Pi. O. 11.4-6 ὕμνοι ὑστέρων ἀρχὰ λόγων τέλλεται. This is not the typical *schema Pindaricum*, in which the verb normally precedes the noun, e.g. E. Ba. 1350 δέδοκται ... τλήμονες φυγαί. Cf. Barrett on E. Hi. 1255 (Addenda p. 436). Here A. is recalling the context of Χ 30 κακὸν δέ τε σῆμα τέτυκται, of Sirius, and the language of φ 231 τόδε σῆμα τετύχθω.

726 ἐξ ἑτέρης Cf. 571, 617; the three instances show variation of the verb inflexion.

727 ἕλκεται ἀμφοτέρωθεν Either setting from above or rising from below the horizon; cf. 171, 200, 570, 884. A. here brings out the terrifying size of the Monster (cf. 354, 356, 629), in that it is seen complete only for a short time.

ὅλον After Homeric οὖλον (717) A. uses the Attic form here, 796, 900. So A.R. 2.680, 4.1166; Call. H. 2.2, 4.72, 6.34, but 2.76 οὖλον.

728 πρώτην The great southward bend from the end of the first westward line of stars (see note on 358), where Hi. 3.1.10 locates the first of the River's stars to rise.

ἁλὸς ἐξανιοῦσαν Cf. A.R. 4.759 Θέτιν ... ἁλὸς ἐξανιοῦσαν, 3.756-7. αἴγλη | ὕδατος ἐξανιοῦσα.

729 καθαρῷ Sch. ἐν καθαρῷ καὶ εὐδίῳ πελάγει, the second adj.

being apparently meant as an interpretation of the first. Perhaps the comment is influenced by the association of the same two words in 802, of the clear moon as a sign of good weather to come. A. uses καθαρός most frequently of the sky and the heavenly bodies, meaning 'cloudless', so that they can be clearly seen. Here too the context is that of stellar visibility, with particular reference to stars that are just above the horizon, and A. must mean simply a clear night at sea. I have not found any other instance of καθαρός as an epithet of the sea, and even this one is not cited by LSJ. Mair and Erren miss the point in translating 'on the open sea', 'auf hoher See'. The importance of men at sea being able to observe the constellations is stressed in the remainder of this sentence, as earlier in 562–5.

730 ἐπ' Ὠρίωνα μένων Grotius conjectured ἔτ' because ἐπιμένω in Homer does not mean 'wait for'. Voss pointed out that this sense does come later, but it is used only of events awaiting men, e.g. E. *Supp.* 624, Pl. *R.* 361d. It is more likely that A. is imitating the language of α 422 μένον δ' ἐπὶ ἕσπερον ἐλθεῖν, even though ἐπί goes with ἐλθεῖν, as is clear from 423 μέλας ἐπὶ ἕσπερος ἦλθε.

By anticipating the rising of Orion, A. brings us back full circle to link up with the rising of the Crab, when the upper half of Orion is visible in the east (587–9). Its brightness and easily recognisable form made it a natural choice as the point at which to mark the beginning and ending of the sky's rotation during the months when it was visible at some time of the night (July to April). Cf. 754–5.

εἴ οἴ ποθι Cf. A 128–9 αἴ κέ ποθι Ζεὺς | δῶσι, Ζ 526–7 with δώῃ. A. uses ποθι only here, recalling Homeric contexts in which men hope for the favour of Zeus.

731 μέτρον Lengthening with ictus at the caesura; cf. 706 νέον. Voss notes the Homeric colouring, and cites Δ 76 ἢ ναύτῃσι τέρας ἠὲ στρατῷ εὐρέϊ λαῶν. For time measurement cf. 464. Here it is not a question of 'l'heure de la nuit' (Martin), but of estimating the length of time since a previous observation or until a later observation; sch. τουτέστι τεκμαίρεται ἀπὸ τοῦ δεῖνος ἀστέρος ἀνατέλλοντος πόσον πλοῦν περαιώσει δύνοντος τοῦ σεσημειωμένου ἀστέρος. See note on 559–568.

ἠὲ πλόου Cf. Δ 76 ἠὲ στρατῷ, Ν 559 ἠὲ σχεδόν, φ 237 ἠὲ κτύπου, A.R. 1.308 ἠὲ Κλάρον, Nic. *Alex.* 362 ἠὲ πτερῷ. See Hilberg 74. Callimachus seems to have avoided the use of ἠέ in this position. It is surprising that πλόος occurs only once in Homer (γ 169), in same *sedes*.

ἀγγείλειε Cf. A.R. 4.1122 ἐναίσιμον ἀγγείλειεν.

732 θεοί A. concludes this section with a restatement of his Stoic message, recalling the language of the proem: πάντῃ (4), ἀνδράσιν (13), λέγει (7, 8). But θεοί is more Homeric than the Stoic Zeus, and brings out the contrast with men: cf. A 544 πατήρ ἀνδρῶν τε θεῶν τε, Κ 440–1 οὔ τι καταθνητοῖσιν ἔοικεν | ἀνδρεσσιν φορέειν, ἀλλ' ἀθανάτοισι θεοῖσιν.

733–757 THE MONTH AND THE YEAR

There is an old tradition that the weather signs begin here. The Berlin papyrus (Π2) marks the division with a marginal coronis, and some of the later MSS insert a new section heading, such as ἀρχή τῶν διοσημειῶν (E), ἀρχή τῆς διοσημείας (Par. suppl. gr. 652), while some even designate a new book, e.g. ἀρχή τοῦ γ' βιβλίου τοῦ καλουμένου διοσημεῖα (K), ἀράτου βιβλίον γ' τῶν φαινομένων τὸ καλούμενον διοσημίαι (Neapol. II F 48). Cf. sch. (MΔKUAS) 733 πληρώσας τὸν περὶ τῶν ὡρῶν διὰ τῆς τῶν ἄστρων καταλήψεως λόγον, ἔρχεται ἐπὶ ἄλλο βιβλίον σφόδρα βιωφελές, ὃ καλεῖται Διοσημεῖαι. On the other hand the earlier tradition of M and S shows no break in the text at this point. Curiously enough the earliest printed editions also have no break here (e.g. Ald., Ceporinus), whereas most later editors insert a new heading, e.g. Διοσημεῖα (Morel, Buhle, Bekker, Voss), Διοσημίαι (Mair), Προγνώσεις (Zannoni).

The transition to the weather signs, however, is not made until 758, and the insertion of a new heading at 733 is not justified by the subject-matter. The explanation must lie in the fact that the influential commentary of Hipparchus ends its references at this point (or, more strictly, at 729). Hipparchus was not concerned with the calendarial material in 733–57. But later readers presumably inferred that 732 marked the end of the astronomical section, and may have been further misled by the sudden introduction in 733 of the moon, which plays an important part in the weather signs from 773.

The origin of this error may be dated to the commentary of Boethus (second century BC), written in four books, the fourth being on weather signs, τὰς προγνώσεις (Gem. 17.48), but we do not know at which line the division was made: see Maass *Aratea* 152–8. Nor do we know where Cicero began his *Prognostica*, since the last extant line of his *Aratea* corresponds to *Phaen.* 700, and the first of his *Prognostica* to 864. Germanicus, however, ends his translation at *Phaen.* 731, which suggests that the division at 732 was current at least by the first century AD, as is indicated also by the Berlin papyrus. Avienius translates the whole poem and his MSS also indicate a major division after 732 (Soubiran p. 250 n. 10).

733–739 The successive phases of the moon mark the days of the month. Gem. 8.10–13, 9.11–16, V. *G.* 1.276. W. K. Pritchett, *BCH* 85 (1961) 27, quoting 733ff. in Mair's translation, says 'A. is a good witness for his own period, when a new religious movement involving the worship of the sun, moon and stars had spread over the ancient world.' The explanation is rather that A. has chosen the old natural lunar calendar as most suited to his poetic theme.

733 οὐχ ὁράᾳς; This abrupt and dramatic transition breaks the tedium of the long preceding section. The phrase is Homeric, and occurs in emotional contexts in speeches, e.g. Η 448, Ο 555, Φ 108, ρ 545, at the beginning of a line. In the last instance it is said by Penelope when drawing attention to the omen in Telemachus' sneeze. It may therefore be this line that A. is particularly recalling when he draws attention to the signs provided by the moon's phases. Cf. Call. *H.* 2.4 of a sign of the god's presence, Colluth. 340, Nonn. *D.* 7.30. The phrase is particularly apt here, since it was the sighting of the new moon that originally determined the beginning of the month. Latin poets imitate freely with *nonne uides* ... ? (Lucr. 2.196, al., V. *G.* 1.56, 3.103, 250, Hor. *S.* 1.4.109, *Carm.* 1.14.3, Ov. *Met.* 15.382, al., Avien. 1326 for this line).

κεράεσσι The two cusps of the lunar crescent, a meaning not given by LSJ; cf. 788, 794, 800, and κεραῖαι 785, 790. So *cornu* frequently, e.g. V. *G.* 1.428, *A.* 3.645.

734 ἑσπερόθεν Cf. 710, 891.

734–735 ἀεξομένοιο διδάσκει μηνός Gen. of what the person is taught, as in Π 811 διδασκόμενος πολέμοιο. Cf. 529 χειρῶν δεδιδαγμένος, 793 χειμῶνος συναγειρομένοιο διδάσκοι, 1048 with λέγω. The choice of word recalls Hes. *Op.* 772–3 μηνὸς | ἔξοχ᾽ ἀεξομένοιο, and it suits A.'s purpose to identify the calendar month closely with the moon. The regular verb is ἱσταμένου, e.g. ξ 162 τοῦ δ᾽ ἱσταμένοιο, Hdt. 6.106.3 ἱσταμένου τοῦ μηνός. The first sighting merely shows that the month has begun: the actual day could be the second or third. Sch. μῆνα κυρίως ἔλεγον οἱ Ἕλληνες τὸν χρόνον τὸν ἀπὸ τῆς σεληνιακῆς συνόδου.

735 ὅτε The v.l. ὅτι probably derives from the error of taking this as a clause depending on διδάσκει. With this clause, however, A. moves on to the first identifiable day, the fourth, when the crescent is bright enough to cast a shadow. See Martin on the interpretation of Maass and Wilamowitz with ὅτι and colon after αὐγή.

ἀποκίδναται A. is probably recalling Ψ 227 κίδναται ἠώς, Θ 1 ἐκίδνατο. Elsewhere the compound verb is used only of rivers: A.R. 4.133, D.P. 48.

αὐτόθεν Less emphatic than in 219, and probably chosen for the assonance with αὐγή.

αὐγή Of the moon also in *h.Hom.* 32.12 λαμπρόταται τ᾽ αὐγαὶ τότ᾽ ἀεξομένης τελέθουσιν.

736 ὅσσον ἐπισκιάειν Sch. (A) 735 ὅσον ἀμυδρὰν σκιὰν ἡμῶν τοῖς

426

σώμασι ποιεῖν, sch. 736 ὥστε καὶ σκιὰν δύνασθαι ποιεῖν. The infinitive expresses sufficiency; cf. X. *An.* 4.1.5 ἐλείπετο τῆς νυκτὸς ὅσον σκοταίους διελθεῖν τὸ πεδίον, Th. 1.2.2 νεμόμενοί τε τὰ αὐτῶν ἕκαστοι ὅσον ἀποζῆν. Maass and Wilamowitz read ἐπισκιάει (Π2 and Geminus) with the addition of δ', making 736 a complete sentence. This detaches the phrase from ἀποκίδναται αὐγή, without which ὅσσον hardly makes sense. Manitius in Gem. 8.13 translates 'Wirfft sie dann erst einen Schatten', but this does not seem to be a possible meaning for the Greek. For other discussions see Kaibel 956–7, Wilamowitz in *Berliner Klassikertexte* 5.1 (1907) 52–3, Keydell 583. Voss emended to ὑποσκιάειν, with the sense of casting a faint shadow, but there is no parallel for that meaning, and A. uses that compound of a cloud below the sun (854). For ἐπισκιάειν cf. [Opp.] *C.* 2.590, *Q.S.* 2.479.

ἰοῦσα Sch. γίνωσκε (ἀπὸ κοινοῦ) τεσσάρων οὖσαν ἡμερῶν τὴν σελήνην. It is probably better to understand σελήνη διδάσκει, construed with part., as occasionally with verbs of saying, e.g. E. *Tro.* 478 γυνὴ τεκοῦσα κομπάσειεν ἄν ποτε, *Or.* 1581 ἀρνῆ κατακτάς ...; Goodwin *MT* 361. Buttmann's suggestion ἄγουσα (i.e. *in tmesi*) is perhaps supported by the papyrus, but it does not suit the grammatical structure of 736–7, as Martin has shown.

737 ὀκτὼ δ' ἐν διχάσιν Sch. ὀκτὼ δὲ ἡμέρας ἄγει διχότομος οὖσα. The change from the ordinal to the cardinal number is a characteristic variation, and the half-line is a very condensed form of '(the moon indicates) eight (days when she is) at the half'. The brevity is an imitation of the calendaric style as used in the parapegmata, and by Hesiod in the 'Days': see esp. *Op.* 819–21. Kaibel, Maass and Wilamowitz take ὀκτώ and διχόμηνα as dependent on εἴρει (739), and punctuate with a comma after προσώπῳ. But it is more satisfactory, with Mair and Martin, to follow the traditional construction of grouping 735–7 together as noting specific days up to mid-month, and then concluding the passage with a general observation in the normal poetic style (738–9).

διχάσιν The noun διχάς recurs in 807 and 809, with case variation in the three instances, whereas the rare v.l., adopted by Voss, Maass and Mair, implies a noun δίχασις that is not elsewhere attested. Here the papyrus supports the MSS. The corruption may have come from writing the final ι as ει. The plural, to which Voss objected, means simply that this happens every month.

διχόμηνα δὲ παντὶ προσώπῳ A. is indulging in a slightly confusing word-play between the half-moon, which is the first quarter, and the half-month, which is full moon. He repeats this in 807–9. The apparent chiasmus in this line is purely verbal: in sense διχόμηνα balances ὀκτώ, and παντὶ προσώπῳ balances ἐν διχάσιν. Martin seems right in taking διχόμηνα as n.pl. adj. used as subst. (cf. sg. 808), thus balancing the pl. διχάσιν, but wrong in making it and ὀκτώ the subjects of their respective clauses: 'les huit jours (sont) dans la demi-lune, et le milieu du mois (a lieu) lorsqu'elle brille de toute sa face'. It is more satisfactory to understand the moon as subject throughout, from διδάσκει to εἴρει, i.e. '(she indicates) the half-month (when she is) with full face'. Voss may have understood διχόμηνα as acc. sg. of διχόμην, sc. σελήνην (cf. 78), since he translates 'Vollmond'. But the sense required is 'mid-month', the date indicated by the full moon. Cf. Ach. *Isag.* 21 (Maass p. 49) πεντεκαιδεκαταία γάρ ἐστιν, ὅτε πληροῦται.

738 ἄλλοθεν ἄλλα The different phases of the moon.

παρακλίνουσα The sense 'making slight changes' is unusual, but cf. Ar. *Pax* 981 παρακλίνασαι τῆς αὐλείας παρακύπτουσιν, of opening a door just enough to be able to peep out, and Pl. *Cra.* 400b ἂν μὲν καὶ σμικρόν τις παρακλίνῃ, of making the verbal change from σῶμα to σῆμα, also 410a σμικρόν τι παρακλίνοντες. There may be here a verbal reminiscence of Hes. *Op.* 262 ἄλλη παρκλίνωσι, though the sense there is quite different. Ach. *Isag.* 21 (Maass p. 50), quoting παρεκκλίνουσα πρόσωπα, explains the image as drawn from altering the inclination of a mirror, τὸ τοῦ κατόπτρου παράδειγμα αἰνιττόμενος.

μέτωπα The word denotes the frontal appearance of anything, here pl. because of the changing phases. The v.l. probably comes from the tradition of seeing a face in the markings on the moon, as in Plu. 920 Περὶ τοῦ ἐμφαινομένου προσώπου τῷ κύκλῳ τῆς σελήνης. Cf. S. fr. 871.6 πρόσωπα καλλύνουσα.

739 εἴρει See note on 172; for the active in prophetic sense cf. β 162, λ 137.

ὁποσταίη Only here. The suffix -αῖος was particularly productive in Ionic (Palmer 255). It developed a special use in the counting of days, first in Homer with πεμπταῖος (ξ 257) and Hesiod with δυωδεκαταῖος (*Op.* 751). Herodotus has δευτεραῖος (6.106), τριταῖος (6.120), τεταρταῖος (2.89), προτεραῖος (1.84), ὑστεραῖος (1.77), and Hippocrates adds ἑκταῖος, ἑβδομαῖος, ὀγδοαῖος, ἐναταῖος, ἑνδεκαταῖος, εἰκοσταῖος, τριακοσταῖος, τεσσαρακοσταῖος, ἑξηκοσταῖος, ὀγδοηκοσταῖος.

περιτέλλεται ἠώς See note on 232. For ἠώς meaning 'day' cf. 288, 1131, 1147, and with the same verb 1128.

740–757 The times of the year are indicated by the risings and settings of bright stars and by the course of the sun through the Zodiac: all this is familiar from the parapegmata (see note on 265). A. is not thinking of the broad division of the year into four seasons, which are determined by the solstices and equinoxes, nor of the 365 days of the year, which are determined by the sun, but of the dates that are significant for farm work (742) or for the likelihood of storms at sea (744).

740 ἄκρα It is not immediately clear what A. means by 'the extremities' of the nights, or what the connection is between 740-1 and 741-3. Voss understood ἄκρα as referring to both beginnings and ends of nights. But this is impossible: we can use the stars to predict the end of night (559-60, 730-1), but we cannot use them to predict when night will begin. Zannoni and Martin interpret with reference to the longest and shortest nights, i.e. at the two solstices. But we do not need all twelve signs of the Zodiac to determine these two dates, which in any case were traditionally judged either by observing the farthest north and south points on the horizon at which the sun rose and set, or by watching the length of a sundial's shadow. Erren refers ἄκρα to the actual points of sunrise and sunset on the horizons, viewed as the extremities of the night-arcs, with the implication that it is the north–south movement of these that marks out the four seasons. This could, of course, be equally well said of the day-arcs; but in any case it only incidentally involves the Zodiac, and besides there is nothing in this passage that suggests the four seasons are in question.

Line 740 refers back to 559-60. This is the point of κεῖναι, which is ignored by some translators, μοῖραι takes up μοιράων, and ἄκρα νυκτῶν is explained by δεδοκημένῳ ἤματος, as also by νυκτὸς μέτρον (731). The extremities are therefore the successive ends of the nights throughout the year; cf. 308 ἀκρόθι νυκτός. On the other hand in 775 ἄκρῃ νυκτί has the more usual reference to the beginning of night.

In this passage (740-51) A. is concerned with the use of the stars in determining the time of year. He has, however, already dealt at length with the stars, especially the Zodiac, in showing how the length of the night can be estimated (559-732), and now he makes the point that, while the stars can be useful in this limited way, they are also useful (perhaps even more useful) in determining dates throughout the whole year. The point is somewhat forced, and the sequence of thought unclear.

γε μήν The progressive use (Denniston 349), as in Hes. *Sc.* 139 χερσί γε μὴν σάκος εἷλε. Here γε retains its concessive force (see preceding paragraph). A. has a less emphatic example in 678. There is no need for Voss's emendation to the commoner γε μέν, which A. does not normally use in passing to a new topic: see note on 17.

μοῖραι See note on 560.

741 ἄρχιαι With the Homeric sense of 'sure', 'reliable', e.g. K 304 μισθὸς δέ οἱ ἄρκιος ἔσται, with neg. B 393. Cf. 1148.

τὰ δέ που The significant times of the year, first introduced in a general way, then illustrated by two particular examples. The qualifying particle suggests that the signs predicting these are rather less precise and reliable than the evidence for the time of night; cf. 759. A. uses που 16 times from here to the end of the poem, and only five times before this line.

μέγαν The adj. brings out the relative length of the year, in imitation of Hes. *Th.* 799 ἐπὴν νοῦσον τελέσει μέγαν εἰς ἐνιαυτόν (see West's note). Cf. 749 μέγαν ὄγμον ἐλαύνων, of the sun's course, anon. ap. Plu. 761E Ἀδμήτῳ πάρα θητεῦσαι μέγαν εἰς ἐνιαυτόν (*CA* p. 11), V. *A.* 3.284 *interea magnum sol circumuoluitur annum.* There is no question here of a reference to the so-called Great Year or a cycle of years; the latter appears briefly in 752–3.

742 ὥρη ... ὥρη A sense echo of the proem (7–9), and a verbal echo of λ 379 ὥρη μὲν πολέων μύθων, ὥρη δὲ καὶ ὕπνου. Cf. Dionys. *AP* 10.38 ὥρη ἐρᾶν, ὥρη δὲ γαμεῖν, ὥρη δὲ πεπαῦσθαι, V. *G.* 1.253 *messisque diem tempusque serendi,* Plu. 601A ὥραι σπόρων, ὥραι φυτειῶν.

νειούς Normally sg., as Κ 353 ἑλκέμεναι νειοῖο βαθείης πηκτὸν ἄρατρον, Hes. *Op.* 463 νειὸν δὲ σπείρειν.

φυτεῦσαι The combination of ploughing and planting reflects ι 108 οὔτε φυτεύουσιν χερσὶν φυτὸν οὔτ' ἀρόωσιν, and Hes. *Op.* 22 ἀρώμεναι ἠδὲ φυτεύειν. Cf. Ο 134 φυτεῦσαι in same *sedes*, but fig. sense.

743 ἐκ Διός A reminder of the opening line and the Stoic message of 10–13.

πάντα πεφασμένα πάντοθι Cf. 328 πάντα πεφασμένος in a different context. The emphasis on the ubiquity of Zeus's celestial signs recalls πάντη δὲ Διὸς κεχρήμεθα πάντες (4), with similar alliteration and πάντη varied with the rarer πάντοθι. The latter adv. is first attested here and 1111; cf. Mel. *AP* 4.1.48 = *HE* 3973 πάντοθι λαμπόμενον.

744 καὶ νηΐ This prepares the reader for the special attention paid to seafarers in the proem to the weather signs (758ff.). The position of the locative νηΐ, somewhat detached from the verb, is unusual; cf. Ν 390–1 τήν τ' οὔρεσι τέκτονες ἄνδρες | ἐξέταμον.

πολυκλύστου Homeric in the formulaic πολυκλύστῳ ἐνὶ πόντῳ (δ 354, ζ 204, τ 277, and Hes. *Th.* 189). A. has transferred the epithet to the storm and varied the case with a gen. This line is metrically rare, having one dactyl, and that in the third foot, and an epitrite word preceding a final trisyllable. It is the only instance in A.; Ludwich (152) gives 35 in the *Iliad* and 52 in the *Odyssey*, e.g. the recurring ὡς οὔτις μέμνηται Ὀδυσσῆος θείοιο (β 233, al.).

745 ἐφράσατ' C. gen. of observing a sign of something; c. acc. of direct observation, e.g. 1062, 1149, and with ἐπιφρ. 76, 1061. Theoc. 2.83–4 has ἐφρασάμαν c. gen in the latter sense. Bernhardy 177.

μεμνημένος The Homeric sense of 'paying heed to', as in ω 129–30. μεμνημένος οὔτε τι σίτου | οὔτ' εὐνῆς.

Ἀρκτούροιο A. is referring to the use of risings and settings for calendarial purposes: see note on 265. Before A. Arcturus was not normally associated with storms. Hesiod celebrated its MR as the time for harvesting the grapes (*Op.* 610–11; cf. Pl. *Lg.* 844e), and its ER as the end of winter (565–7). The MR was otherwise most noted in the calendar as marking the autumn equinox. Thus Hippocrates in his division of the seasons: θέρος δὲ ἀπὸ Πλειάδων μέχρι Ἀρκτούρου ἐπιτολῆς, φθινόπωρον δὲ ἀπὸ Ἀρκτούρου μέχρι Πλειάδων δύσιος (*Vict.* 3.68); cf. S. *OT* 1137 ἐξ ἦρος εἰς Ἀρκτοῦρον ἐκμήνους χρόνους, Th. 2.78.2 περὶ Ἀρκου ἐπιτολάς, Arist. *HA* 6.569 ἀρξάμενος ἀπ' Ἀρκτούρου μετοπωρινοῦ. This usage became so familiar that the name Arcturus without qualification could be used to denote this time of year, e.g. Hp. *Aer.* 10 ἐπὶ τῷ Ἀρκτούρῳ, *Epid.* 1.4 περὶ Ἀρκτούρου, 1.13 πρὸ Ἀρκτούρου. Since this date normally brought the end of good sailing weather, Euctemon's calendar noted against it χειμὼν κατὰ θάλασσαν (Gem. *Cal.* Virgo 10 and 20), and Democritus' σφοδροὶ καταχέονται ὄμβροι (fr. 14.5DK).

The MR, then, was probably the date that A. had in mind here. But he may also have considered the ES about the end of October, just before the onset of winter. Euctemon's note against this date is ἄνεμοι μεγάλοι πνέουσιν, and three days later Eudoxus has ἄνεμος πνεῖ (Gem. *Cal.* Scorp. 5 and 8). For this time of year cf. 585 and the Homeric storm in ε 291ff.

Here A. is only naming Arcturus as one example of a star that can be useful in predicting rough weather at sea. But it seems likely that it is this line that accounts for the tradition in later poets of associating Arcturus with storms. So A.R. 2.1098–9 Ζεὺς δ' ἀνέμου βορέαο μένος κίνησεν ἀῆναι, | ὕδατι σημαίνων διερὴν ὁδὸν Ἀρκτούροιο is a clear imitation of A., and the prediction is followed by the storm in 1102ff.; sch. 1098 quotes (inaccurately) this line. Cf. Alcaeus, *AP* 7.495.1 = *HE* 90 στυγνὸς ἐπ' Ἀρκτούρῳ πλόος, Perses ibid. 539.1–2 = *HE* 2895–6 κακὴν δύσιν ὑετίοιο | Ἀρκτούρου, and other lines in *AP* 7 associating Arcturus with drownings at sea: 295.5 = *HE* 2078, 392.1 = *GP* 2394, 503.4 = *HE* 2358. Hence the choice of Arcturus for the prologue to Plautus' *Rudens*, with the explanation *nam Arcturus signum sum omnium unum acerrimum:* | *uehemens sum exoriens, quom occido uehementior* (70–1), referring to both MR and ES. If A. is the source of this poetic conceit, it is unlikely that Arcturus appeared in the original comedy by Diphilus. Cf. V. *G.* 1.204 *Arcturi sidera* among signs of storm, Hor. *Carm.* 3.1.27–8 *saeuus Arcturi cadentis* | *impetus*, Ov. *Epist.* 17.187–8 *cum mihi luserit aequor* | *Plias et Arctophylax.*

It may seem surprising that A. has devoted so few lines to this important calendarial theme, which is so relevant to his purpose. His reasons may be (a) that Hesiod had already treated this subject in verse at some length, (b) that after so long a section on simultaneous risings and settings it would have been inartistic to introduce another extended passage on calendaric risings and settings, and (c) that he has brief references elsewhere to the other important weather stars, the Kids (158–9, 682), the Hyades (173), the Pleiades (265, 1065–6, 1085), and Sirius (332–6).

746 τεων Ionic form; cf. Hdt. 5.57.2, and interrog. ὦ 387, ζ 119.

ἀρύονται Prop. of drawing water, as in Hes. *Op.* 550 of the air ἀρυσσάμενος ποταμῶν ἀπὸ αἰεναόντων. From this context of moisture being drawn up from the sea A. has created an imaginative metaphor for stars slowly rising over a sea horizon.

747 ἀμφιλύκης Sc. νυκτός, once in Homer, of morning twilight, Η 433 οὔτ' ἄρ πω ἠώς, ἔτι δ' ἀμφιλύκη νύξ. A.R. 2.670–1 λεπτὸν δ' ἐπιδέδρομε νυκτὶ | φέγγος, ὅτ' ἀμφιλύκην μιν ἀνεγρόμενοι καλέουσιν.

ἔτι Better attested than ἐπί, and more relevant here with πρώτης than with πυμάτης in 304.

748 ἤτοι γάρ Cf. 305, of which, since it follows πυμάτης ἐπὶ νυκτός, this may be a verbal reminiscence. Here too the particles are strongly confirmatory. A. is explaining the seasonal risings of stars by the fact that the sun, in its eastward course along the ecliptic, overtakes them successively throughout the year.

ἀμείβεται With this verb, placed in the same metrical position, and combined with the part. ἐλαύνων, A. amusingly recalls the Homeric simile of the sure-footed acrobat leaping from horse to horse in Ο 683–4 ὁ δ' ἔμπεδον ἀσφαλὲς αἰεὶ | θρῴσκων ἄλλοτ' ἐπ' ἄλλον ἀμείβεται. The wonder of the sun's regular progress from bright star to bright star is thus imaginatively brought out by the heroic overtones of one word. The Homeric reference is then confirmed by ἄλλοτε δ' ἄλλῳ (749).

εἰς ἐνιαυτόν A theme from the proem (11), also restated in 741 and 1153.

749 ὄγμον Λ 68 ὄγμον ἐλαύνωσιν, of reapers cutting a swathe, Σ 546 στρέψασκον ἀν' ὄγμους, of ploughing furrows, *h.Hom.* 32.11 ὅ τε πλήθει μέγας ὄγμος, of the moon's course. The v.l. οἶμος is more obvious and less imaginative. Sch. ὄγμος κυρίως ἡ τάξις καλεῖται τῶν θεριζόντων, ὅπου ἀμῶνται, ἢ ὁ μεταξὺ δύο φυτειῶν τόπος ἀργός. ἐπειδὴ οὖν τὴν μέσην γραμμὴν τοῦ ζῳδιακοῦ ὁ ἥλιος πορεύεται, ἔχει δὲ ὁ κύκλος ἄλλας δύο ἑκατέρωθεν γραμμάς, διὰ τοῦτο εἶπεν ὄγμον τὸν τοῦ ἡλίου δρόμον. Cf. Call. fr. 335 ἤερος ὄγμοι, Theoc. 10.2 ὄγμον ἄγειν ὀρθόν, of reaping, Nic. *Ther.* 571 ὄγμον ἐλαύνων, of a hippopotamus in the grass.

750 ἐμπλήσσει Cf. 423 also c. dat., Homeric usage in the sense of 'come upon', 'fall into', e.g. M 72 τάφρῳ ἐνιπλήξωμεν ὀρυκτῇ (cf. O 344), Χ 469 ἕρκει ἐνιπλήξωσι. Cf. Pfeiffer on Call. fr. 75.37. The verb describes a movement that has a harmful effect, and here it makes a very bold metaphor: the effect of the sun 'impinging' on a star is to render it invisible for several weeks. Mair reads ἐμπλήσει, translating 'draws near', but this is not a possible sense for ἐμπίμπλημι. The conjectures ἐμπελάει and ἐμπελάσει are palaeographically weak, and in any case unnecessary.

τοτὲ μέν ... τοτὲ δ' Cf. ω 447–8 τοτὲ μὲν προπάροιθ' 'Οδυσῆος | φαίνετο θαρσύνων, τοτὲ δὲ μνηστῆρας ὀρίνων. A. uses the second term without the first in 514 and 775.

ἀνιών ... δύνων The participles are grammatically attached to ἐμπλήσει, but, strictly speaking, when the sun is overtaking a star, the immediate result is the star's ES only; the MR is denoted in the next line, with a new verb and a change of subject. The participial phrase thus plays an essentially parenthetical role, giving sunrise and sunset as the times when the star observations are made, but it is not so expressed grammatically. A. seems to be indulging in word-play with the different kinds of rising and setting at the cost of some confusion to the sense. A comma is therefore required after δύνων, rather than the traditional colon.

751 ἄλλος δ' ἀλλοίην Cf. 780, Hes. *Op.* 483 ἄλλοτε δ' ἀλλοῖος Ζηνὸς νόος, Pi. *I.* 4.5 ἄλλοτε δ' ἀλλοῖος οὖρος, Sem. 7.11 ὀργὴν δ' ἄλλοτ' ἀλλοίην ἔχει. Cf. Opp. *H.* 3.194. A. means that different stars have their MR at different times of the year. The phrase balances ἄλλοτε δ' ἄλλῳ (749).

ἐπιδέρκεται Hes. *Th.* 760 'Ἥλιος φαέθων ἐπιδέρκεται ἀκτίνεσσιν, and the same line with καταδέρκεται (but v.l. ἐπιδέρκεται) in λ 16. Cf. *Op.* 268 of Zeus's all-seeing eye. A. has here reversed the roles of star and dawn in *Op.* 610 'Αρκτοῦρον δὲ ἴδη ῥοδοδάκτυλος 'Ηώς.

752–757 The connection between these and the preceding lines has been somewhat obscured by the introduction of the 19-year cycle, the relevance of which is not immediately clear. Voss, Mair and Martin begin a new paragraph at 752, which would make sense if the poet's purpose had been to add a passage on that year-cycle to complete his exposition of the periods of time. But this is not satisfactory, because (*a*) the 19-year cycle is a reconciliation of the solar year with the lunar year (see note on 753), and so produces calendar years that are either shorter or (by intercalation) longer than the solar year, whereas the seasonal and meteorological phenomena, with which A. is primarily concerned, are related strictly to the solar year; (*b*) τάδε refers back to the annual pattern of risings and settings (744–51), and lines 754–7 also refer to the annual movement of the constellations and stars. Lines 752–7 should therefore be seen as a conclusion to the section on the year, and the clause 752–3 as a kind of parenthesis in it.

Why then did A. insert this brief reference to the 19-year cycle, if it was not strictly necessary for his purpose? I suspect that he wished to complete, for the sake of completeness, the tally of time-periods, in much the same way as he included a brief note on the planets (454–61) in order to complete the list of ἄστρα. In the present case, however, he was able to make the connection plausible, because the published copies of the cycle continued the established practice of giving astronomical and meteorological information against selected dates.

752 γινώσκεις Of knowing something from observation; cf. 769.

τάδε Referring back, as τόδε in 1017, but amplified by the clauses in 754–7.

σύ While the 2nd pers. is a regular feature of the didactic manner, the emphatic pronoun in the nom. case occurs elsewhere only in 983. The less emphatic dat. is commoner, e.g. 758, 773.

συναείδεται Sch. offer two explanations. The first is γίνωσκε ὅτι ἀναλογοῦντες ἀλλήλοις καὶ σύμφωνοι γίνονται οἱ τοῦ ἡλίου δρόμοι διὰ ιθ' ἐτῶν ἐπιθεωρούμενοι. Cf. the marginal gloss in Π8 συμφωνει. Martin accepts this meaning, but finds the sch. mistaken in saying that the years are in agreement with each other: the harmony of the cycle consists in reconciling the solar and lunar periods. He translates 'sont entrés dans l'accord désiré'. Ludwig (*Hermes* 444) agrees that the sch. are in error, but suggests that the translation would have to be expanded further to include 'mit den Kreisen des Mondes', and finds this too much to read into one word. But the sch. are not wrong. This couplet belongs to the section on the solar year only (see notes on 740–757 and 725–727), and the sch. mean that all the years are in agreement as far as risings and settings are concerned. Maass (*Aratea* 19) doubts whether συναείδεσθαι can be used for συναείδειν, and also makes the valid point that there is a lack of coherence between γινώσκεις and συναείδεται in this sense.

The second explanation of the sch. is καὶ αὐτὸς γινώσκεις· πάλαι γὰρ ἀείδεται καὶ φανερὰ τοῖς Ἕλλησι γέγονεν. This is accepted by Voss, with the comment 'συναείδεσθαι, in gemeinem Rufe sein, wie ein Lied oder Sprichwort: daher ἀοίδιμος, berühmt, ruchtbar'. So Mair 'celebrated by all', Zannoni 'corron sulle bocche di tutti'. Cf. Nonn. *D.* 13.463 ἀειδομένην Σαλαμῖνα, 24.49 -ου Διονύσου, 42.387 -ου ποταμοῖο. This makes good sense in the context, but Maass and Martin reject it, because it does not conform either to the normal use of συνάδω or to the composition of the verb itself. Ludwig agrees, and, while he has no objection to the v.l. συναγείρεται (apparently supported by *Arat. Lat. conueniunt*), except on the score that it is a *lectio facilior*, prefers to read συναείρεται, 'werden schon längst zusammengekoppelt', since the latter is a rare Homeric word, e.g. O 680 συναείρεται ἵππους, where the middle could have suggested the passive here in the same position. It is, however, not particularly relevant to the context to say that the 19-year cycle has simply been 'put together'; and besides, the tense of both these verbs is present, not perfect.

To go back, then, to συναείδεται: this verb is attested by all the manuscripts, the papyrus gloss συμφωνεῖ picks up the musical metaphor in it, and the idea of the cycle being by now familiar follows very aptly after γινώσκεις. The only real difficulty is the prefix συν-. Ludwig suggests that the verb would have to mean that the yearly cycles 'are sung [i.e. celebrated] by all', which is straining the sense of συν- too far, or that they are celebrated by being published on all the parapegmata, which he thinks is an improbable way of describing such a factual inscription. A better sense would be that these 'are all celebrated together' on the parapegmata. It is a bold figure of speech, but cf. 746 ἀρύονται, and 748 ἀμείβεται, both in this passage, and the meaning is exactly the right one for the context: people know all about risings and settings now, since these are so widely circulated in the parapegmata. The sch. also define the verb more simply as πρόκειται. See also the following note.

753 ἐννεακαίδεκα κύκλα The cycle of 19 years (κύκλα means the annual circuits of the sun through the Zodiac) was a calendarial system designed to reconcile the period of the lunar month with the period of the solar year. As the Athenian 12-month lunar year of 354 days fell short of the solar year by about 11 days, an attempt had already been made to make up the shortfall by intercalating a month every other year. When this proved unsatisfactory, an 8-year cycle was devised, with intercalary months in the 3rd, 5th and 8th years, but at the end of this cycle there was still a discrepancy of over two days. A more accurate 19-year cycle was then proposed, with seven intercalary months, making a total of 235 months or 6,940 days, which corresponded almost exactly to 19 solar years (Gem. 8.26–56). See also Bickerman 28–9, Neugebauer *HAMA* 354–7. The authorship of this cycle was usually credited to the Athenian Meton (fl. 430 BC), e.g. D.S. 12.36.1 ἐν δὲ ταῖς Ἀθήναις Μέτων Παυσανίου μὲν υἱός, δεδοξασμένος δὲ ἐν ἀστρολογίᾳ, ἐξέθηκε τὴν ὀνομαζομένην ἐννεακαιδεκαετηρίδα, τὴν ἀρχὴν ποιησάμενος ἀπὸ μηνὸς ἐν Ἀθήναις σκιροφοριῶνος τρισκαιδεκάτης. Cf. sch. Ar. *Av.* 997, *D.S.* 4, Ael. *VH* 10.7, Avien. 1370ff. Greek knowledge of this cycle may have come from Babylonian sources (Neugebauer *HAMA* 622–3), though the earliest record of its calendarial use is in the Babylonian calendar

c. 380 BC (Neugebauer *ESA* 140). There is no evidence that it was ever adopted by any Greek state for its civil calendar, but it was apparently published in parapegmata, with the traditional weather lore inserted against appropriate dates: D.S. 12.36.2 διὸ καί τινες αὐτὸν Μέτωνος ἐνιαυτὸν ὀνομάζουσι. δοκεῖ δὲ ὁ ἀνὴρ οὗτος ἐν τῇ προρρήσει καὶ προγραφῇ ταύτῃ θαυμαστῶς ἐπιτετευχέναι· τὰ γὰρ ἄστρα τήν τε κίνησιν καὶ τὰς ἐπισημασίας ποιεῖται συμφώνως τῇ γραφῇ· διὸ μέχρι τῶν καθ᾽ ἡμᾶς χρόνων οἱ πλεῖστοι τῶν Ἑλλήνων χρώμενοι τῇ ἐννεακαιδεκαετηρίδι οὐ διαψεύδονται τῆς ἀληθείας. Sch. Arat. οἱ μετ᾽ αὐτὸν [sc. Μέτωνα] ἀστρονόμοι πίνακας ἐν ταῖς πόλεσιν ἔθηκαν περὶ τῶν τοῦ ἡλίου περιφορῶν τῶν ἐννεακαιδεκαετηρίδων, ἀριθμήσαντες ὅτι καθ᾽ ἕκαστον ἐνιαυτὸν τοιόσδε ἔσται χειμών, καὶ τοιόνδε θέρος, καὶ τοιόνδε φθινόπωρον, καὶ τοιοίδε ἄνεμοι, καὶ ἄλλα πολλὰ πρὸς βιωφελεῖς χρείας τοῖς ἀνθρώποις. It is to this use of the Metonic cycle that A. alludes here. See also W. B. Dinsmoor, *The Archons of Athens in the Hellenistic Age* (1966) 309–59, G. J. Toomer, 'Meton', *Dictionary of Scientific Biography* 9 (1974) 337–40, Van der Waerden, *AHES* 29 (1984) 102ff.

754–755 After a brief reference to the 19-year cycle (see note on 752–757) A. continues with the constellations that mark the progress of the solar year. For observers of the sky he chooses as starting-point the MR of Orion's belt and as finishing-point the next occurrence of the same. Cf. sch. ὅσα, φησί, ἀπὸ τῆς ζώνης τοῦ Ὠρίωνος πάλιν εἰς αὐτὸν τὸν Ὠρίωνα ἡ νὺξ ἄστρα ἐπιφέρει. This is in keeping with A.'s own catalogue of zodiacal risings (569–732), which begins with the rising of the Crab and simultaneous risings that include Orion's belt (587–8); it ends with the rising of the Twins, when the next rising of Orion is anticipated (730). Hence the additional note in sch. ἤρξατο δὲ ἀπὸ Ὠρίωνος ὅτι ὑπόκειται Καρκίνῳ, καὶ ὅτι μάλιστα εἰς αὐτὸν οἱ πλέοντες ὁρῶσι.

Two minor problems originate in the scholia. One is the interpretation of ἔσχατον as the extremities (or feet) of Orion, and most editors have accepted this. But in this section A. is dealing solely with constellations, and not with the niceties of individual stars. The only possible sense of ἔσχατον here is adverbial, with reference to the reappearance of Orion 'at the end of the year'; cf. 74 ἄκρῃ, 207 ἐσχατόωντι. The other problem is the separation of the Dog's rising from that of Orion. Martin, who sees the Metonic cycle as the theme of 752–7, follows Ideler, *Handbuch der Chronologie* (1825–6) 327, in supposing that Orion's belt marks the beginning of that cycle, and the rising Orion's extremities and the Dog the end of it. But A's observer is not concerned with the precise measurement of the year. Orion and his Dog make a spectacular group that gives a rough and reliable sign of the end of one year and the beginning of the next. Cf. Man. 1.395–6 *hoc duce per totum decurrunt sidera mundum.* | *subsequitur rapido contenta Canicula cursu.*

755 ἐπιδινεῖται The middle occurs once in Homer, in the same position (υ 218), but fig., of turning over in the mind.

756–7 οἵ τε … ἀστέρες Parallel to ὅσσα τε (754), and depending on γινώσκεις. The arrangement of these two couplets is significant: familiarity with the constellations must come first, and from these it is then possible to identify the particular bright stars that provide the signs of the changing year. Cf. 10–12.

756 Ποσειδάωνος ὁρώμενοι ἢ Διὸς αὐτοῦ Sch. take the gen. as possessive, and explain εἰσὶ δὲ Ποσειδῶνος μὲν ἀστέρες οἱ τοὺς χειμῶνας καὶ τὰς εὐδίας δηλοῦντες, Διὸς δὲ τὰ πρὸς γεωργίαν εὔχρηστα μηνύοντες. Voss repeats this explanation without further comment, and Mair simply translates 'the stars of Poseidon, the stars of Zeus'. The distinction is unreal: signs from the rising and setting of stars are seasonal, and they are of interest to landsmen and seamen alike. Maass, recognising the difficulty, understands Poseidon and Zeus as the originators of weather changes: 'et quae stellae uices a Neptuno siue a Ioue ipso hominibus paratas indicant adspectae'. But he has to supply 'uices paratas' in order to make this construing of the Greek possible. In any case, while Zeus is frequently named as responsible for weather (265, 293, 426, 886, 899, 936, 964), Poseidon, who raises storms in the *Odyssey*, has no such place in A.'s scheme of things.

Martin takes the gen. with σημαίνουσι, as with σημαίνοιεν in 12–13: see his note on 12. Poseidon then represents the sea, as Zeus the sky, and A. means that these stars 'donnent aux hommes des signes invariables sur la mer, royaume de Poseidon, et sur le ciel même, royaume de Zeus'. But A. uses this gen. of what is specifically to be expected on particular days, e.g. ὡράων (13), θέρεος κτλ. (266–7), διχάδος (807), not in a general reference to weather conditions.

Erren puts forward a new interpretation, construing the gen. as locative with ὁρώμενοι (*PAS* 302–3). In his edition he translates 'in Poseidon geschaut oder in Zeus selbst', and he explains 'in Poseidon' as referring to stars observed on the horizon at rising or setting, while stars observed 'in Zeus' are those seen in the far north or culminating, as in the case of the Bears and the Altar respectively (p. 92). This is more promising. The gen. of 'place within which' is used elsewhere by A. of action within a certain area (e.g. 605 θέει γαίης), but also of a phenomenon observed in a certain direction (882 ἢ νότου ἠὲ βορῆος ἐρεύθεται). The gen. with ὁρώμενοι here may be seen as comparable with the latter instance. But Erren's explanation is not feasible. A. is concerned here with seasonal signs throughout the year, and these all come from risings and settings: circumpolar and culminating stars are therefore not relevant in this context. Erren is, however, probably right with Poseidon = ὠκεανός = the horizon, and I suggest that stars seen in Poseidon are stars that are setting, and stars seen in Zeus are stars that are rising. If this is right, it is a bold and original figure, in keeping with the heightened style of these lines from 744.

757 τετυγμένα σημαίνουσι The reliability of astronomical signs is opposed to the relative uncertainty of local weather signs (cf. 768–70), as set out in the final section of the poem. Line 757 is clearly designed to round off the astronomical part by closely echoing line 12 from the proem: ἀστέρας, οἵ κε μάλιστα τετυγμένα σημαίνοιεν.

758–1141 WEATHER SIGNS

So far A. has been demonstrating how general weather conditions are related to the time of year and to the annual movement of the constellations, which Zeus has set in the sky for this purpose. Now he passes to the forecasting of particular and local weather changes by observation of the appearance of sun, moon and stars, of clouds and winds, the behaviour of animal and bird life, and the growth of vegetation. Meteorology is still a part of astronomy, and this is an integral section of the *Phaenomena*, not a separate poem, as was for a long time supposed: see note on 733–757.

A popular tradition of weather lore must go back to the earliest centuries of settled agricultural communities and of seafaring peoples. In Greece the literary tradition appears to begin with Hesiod, who not only gives astronomical phenomena as a guide to seasonal changes, but also notes a few terrestrial signs: the cry of the migrating crane as a signal for ploughing and the onset of winter rains (*Op.* 448–51), the call of the cuckoo as a sign of rain at a time suitable for late ploughing (485–7), the associating of a north wind with cold weather, mist and rain (547–53), artichoke blossom and cicada song coinciding with the hottest spell in summer (582–4), and the first appearance of fig leaves at the top of the tree as a sign for the seafaring season to begin (680–1). The early parapegmata attested by Geminus include occasional notes on birds and vegetation: Eudoxus gives the appearance of the swallow on Pisc. 4, and of the kite on Pisc. 17, Callippus the same on Pisc. 2 and 30 respectively, Democritus notes the halcyon days on Pisc. 4, and leaf-fall on Scorp. 4.

The weather signs in the *Phaenomena* are closely related to those in the treatise ascribed to Theophrastus, entitled Περὶ σημείων ὑδάτων καὶ πνευμάτων καὶ χειμώνων καὶ εὐδιῶν, and commonly referred to as *De signis*. On the authorship and content of this work, and the probable source of A.'s weather signs, see Introduction pp. 21–3. A.'s arrangement of the material in this section seems complicated and rather confusing in contrast to the clear orderliness of most of the preceding two sections. The reason is that he has organised the subject-matter sometimes according to signs and sometimes according to weathers, with the result that similar signs appear in different places, e.g. the Manger in 892–908 and again in 995–8. This problem was also needlessly aggravated by the tradition of taking the section on weather signs as starting at 733, thus making the passage on the moon in 733–9 seem to conflict with 778–818.

Virgil's imitation in *G.* 1 (cf. Macr. *Sat.* 5.2.4 *quod in ipsis Georgicis tempestatis serenitatisque signa de Arati Phaenomenis traxerit*) has a more lucid arrangement, varied to suit his own poetic purpose: introduction (351–5), signs of bad weather (356–92), signs of fair weather (393–423), moon signs (424–37), sun signs (438–63). Plin. *Nat.* 18 follows A. more closely with introduction (340–1), sun signs (342–6), moon signs (347–50), star signs (351–3), inanimate nature (354–60), fish, birds, animals (361–4), other signs (365). Ptol. *Tetr.* 2.14 gives a list of celestial signs only, from sun (1–3), moon (4–6), fixed stars (7–8), comets, meteors, rainbows etc. (9–11). For other collections of weather signs see Aelian, *NA* 7.7–8, from birds and animals, *Geoponica* 1.2–4, from Aratus, Anon. Laurentianus (ed. Heeger), from various sources, esp. *Geoponica*, Luc. 5.540–56, the storm predictions of Amyclas.

758–777 INTRODUCTION

This 20-line passage is a kind of second proem, balancing and supplementing the 18-line proem at the beginning of the *Phaenomena*. In the first place there is encouragement to the reader to learn the signs and profit by the knowledge, so as to help both himself and others. Secondly the usefulness of weather lore is here applied to the sea, whereas in the earlier proem it concerns agriculture only. Thirdly the uncertainties of prediction are noted here, in contrast to the reliability of star signs (12), since Zeus, for all his forethought, has not yet revealed all. Nevertheless there is a great variety of signs available everywhere we look, from the moon, the sun, and many other day and night phenomena.

758 τῷ Cf. 14, 379, 413.

πεπόνησο Perf. med. imper., only here, but formed on the analogy of μέμνησο (A. *Ch.* 492, etc.), ἀλάλησο (γ 313). Cf. πεφύλαξο (930 and Hes. *Op.* 797), δέδεξο (Ε 228, al.). Here the form is perhaps intended to recall O 447 ὁ μὲν πεπόνητο καθ' ἵππους (Ronconi 201). The verb gives the sense of taking trouble to master something; cf. 82 πεπονήαται, also c. gen.

μέλοι The opt. is more suited than the indic. to the didactic context.

759 εὑρεῖν Sch. γίνωσκε καὶ μάνθανε.

κεχρημένα Perf. pass., a rare instance. Sch. ὅσα κεχρημένα καὶ ἀσφαλῶς εἰρημένα περὶ πλοῦ ἐστιν, a reference to reliable warnings. Voss suggested the sch. was thinking of χράειν, 'weissagen', but ruled this out because there was no parallel for this form of the perf. part. in this sense of the verb. He therefore read κεκρυμμένα (cf. ψ 110). But we cannot expect to find what is still hidden by Zeus, as A. makes clear in 769–70. The context is concerned with signs provided by Zeus, and this points to χράω with the normal form κεχρησμένα. But in Hdt. 4.164 some MSS read τὸν κεχρημένον θάνατον and in 7.141.1 τοῦ κακοῦ κεχρημένου, and it is quite possible that A. used κεχρημένα here. Hence Maass's cryptic note 'praedicta', with a reference to 743. But it is the weather that is predicted, not the signs. The passive of χράω, however, can be used also of things declared or appointed by a god: cf. E. Ion 792 τίς οὖν ἐχρήσθη; Here the signs are 'established' by Zeus, and κεχρημένα is an ingenious variation of πεφασμένα in 743. So Martin 'établis par la Providence pour prédire'.

760 λαίλαπι Homeric word in characteristic position. This line particularly recalls P 57 ἄνεμος σὺν λαίλαπι πολλῇ.

761 μόχθος For the sense of 'effort' cf. Hes. Sc. 305–6 ἀμφὶ δ' ἀέθλῳ | δῆριν ἔχον καὶ μόχθον. Virgil gives a new twist to the phrase in G. 4.6 in tenui labor.

μυρίον Cf. 47, of the length of the Dragon; here fig. of advantage, perhaps recalling o 452–3 ὁ δ' ὑμῖν μυρίον ὦνον | ἄλφοι. Elsewhere the sg. is more frequently used of troubles, e.g. πένθος (Σ 88), ἄχος (Υ 282), ἄχθος (S. Ph. 1168).

αὐτίκ' See note on 199.

ὄνειαρ Cf. 15, 946.

762 ἐπιφροσύνης The context of escaping danger at sea suggests that A. has in mind ε 437 εἰ μὴ ἐπιφροσύνην δῶκε γλαυκῶπις Ἀθήνη. ἐπιφροσύνη denotes a kind of shrewdness in observing a situation. In the Homeric passage it is an idea that Athene puts into Odysseus' head; here it is an expertise that one has to learn; in A.R. 4.1115 it is an idea that the quick-witted Arete thinks of herself. Homer also has the part. ἐπιφρονέουσα (τ 385) of the observant Eurycleia noticing the resemblance of the beggar to Odysseus.

πεφυλαγμένῳ Without dependent gen., as again in 973. This use appears once in Homer, Ψ 343 φρονέων πεφυλαγμένος εἶναι. Cf. Hermesian. *Leontion* 61 (*CA* p. 99) τὸν ἀεὶ πεφυλαγμένον ἄνδρα, Orph. *Arg.* 691 ὄφρ' ἂν πεφυλαγμένος εἴη, Max. 5 τῷ καὶ πεφυλαγμένος εἴης.

763 τὰ πρῶτα Adv., cf. 151.

σαώτερος Comp. once in Homer, same position, A 32; cf. [Theoc.] 25.59. Contrast the reason given by D.P. for learning geography (172–3): ἐκ τοῦ δ' ἂν γεραρός τε καὶ αἰδοιέστερος εἴης, | ἀνδρὶ παρ' ἀγνώσσοντι πιφαυσκόμενος τὰ ἕκαστα.

ἄλλον The dat. of the MSS may have come from sch. ἄλλῳ δὲ ἐκ δευτέρου παραινέσας, or possibly from -ειπών. παρεῖπον is used c. acc., e.g. A 555 μή σε παρείπῃ, A. *Pr.* 131 παρειποῦσα φρένας. Here the acc. suits both verbs, as in Z 337–8 νῦν δέ με παρειποῦσ' ἄλοχος ... | ὅρμησ' ἐς πόλεμον.

764 παρειπών With first syllable long, as in Z 62, 337, H 121, Λ 793, O 404. The last two instances also have the part. in enjambment.

ὦρορε Intrans perf. of ὄρνυμι, a variation of the normal ὄρωρε (cf. 978), occurring twice in Homer, N 78 μένος ὦρορε, θ 539 ὦρορε θεῖος ἀοιδός. This form is probably due to the influence of the aor. act. ὦρορε, which Homer has five times: Chantraine 1.397–8. A. may have produced here a verbal echo of one of these instances, τ 201 ὦρορε δαίμων.

765 τίς τε The particle has a generalising force, as in Homer, e.g. υ 45 καὶ μέν τίς τε χερείονι πείθεθ' ἑταίρῳ, Ι 632–3 καὶ μέν τίς τε κασιγνήτοιο φονῆος | ποινὴν ... ἐδέξατο. Denniston 533. Keydell (583) rejects Martin's reading τίς κε. A. has τίς τε in the same position and also preceded by καί.

γαληναίη Earliest example of this adj., though the suffix is particularly common in Ionic (Palmer 255); cf. 93 ἀμαξαίης. Satyr. *AP* 10.6.3 = *FGE* 331 γαληναίη δὲ θάλασσα, Philodem. ibid. 21.1 = *GP* 3246 Κύπρι γαληναίη, Nonn. *D.* 41.204 γαληναίῳ δὲ προσώπῳ, Opp. *H.* 1.460, 781, 3.447. A. uses the word later as subst. (813, 995, 1017).

ὑπὸ νυκτί Dat. of attendant circumstances (LSJ ὑπό B II 4); cf. A. *Ag.* 1030 ὑπὸ σκότῳ βρέμει. A.R. imitates with λυγαίῃ ὑπὸ νυκτί (3.323, 1361).

766 περιστέλλει The fig. sense is commonest in Herodotus, e.g. of protecting laws (2.147, 3.31), a political unit (1.98, 3.82; cf. A. *Eum.* 697), an army (9.60). The kind of protection required for a ship expecting a storm is to secure it by shortening sail and making fast all loose gear and cargo. Martin envisages the action required as running for harbour ('il arrive qu'on fasse rentrer son navire au port'). But this does not quite suit the basic meaning of περιστέλλω, and in any case A. has in mind a time-table of several days' sailing. A similar situation is described in 421.

πεφοβημένος Cf. 290; in Homer without gen. Κ 510, Ο 4, Φ 606.

ἦρι In Homer 'early', but associated with morning in τ 320 ἠῶθεν δὲ μάλ' ἦρι. West on Hes. *Th.* 852 suggests ἦρα here, on the ground that ἦρι θαλάσσης cannot mean 'the morning sea'. But in 265 A. attaches ἦρι rather loosely to ὀνομασταὶ ... εἰλίσσονται, where he means not that the Pleiades are famous in the morning, but that they are famous because of their morning risings and settings, and here he means that the sailor is afraid of a rough sea blowing up in the morning. It is the sea he is afraid of, not the morning: cf. 290.

767 ἄλλοτε δέ The reading of editors since Voss, since a contrast with ἦρι is required. Corruption to μέν was inevitable before the following ἄλλοτε δέ, especially in view of sch. ποτὲ μὲν μετὰ τρεῖς ἡμέρας ... ποτὲ δὲ μετὰ πέντε.

ἐπιτρέχει C. acc. the sense is normally of movement over an area, e.g. Ψ 433 τόσσον [i.e. the range of a discus] ἐπιδραμέτην, Hdt. 1.161 πεδίον πᾶν ἐπέδραμε, S. *Ant.* 589, of a swell running across the sea, ἔρεβος ὕφαλον ἐπιδράμῃ. The acc. of a period of time here is unparalleled, but A. has in mind not the onset of the storm, but its passage lasting a whole day. Contrast 316, 834 c. dat.

768 ἀπρόφατον Cf. 424.

769 ἐκ Διός A reminder of line 1. A. now qualifies his praise of the helpfulness of Zeus with a touch of realism, and the position of οὔπω at the end of the preceding line is particularly emphatic.

770 κέκρυπται A partial concession to Hesiod's κρύψαντες γὰρ ἔχουσι θεοὶ βίον ἀνθρώποισι (*Op.* 42).

αἴ κε θέλῃ Cf. 426 in similar context. Here A. recalls Θ 141–3 νῦν μὲν γὰρ τούτῳ Κρονίδης Ζεὺς κῦδος ὀπάζει | σήμερον· ὕστερον αὖτε καὶ ἡμῖν, αἴ κ' ἐθέλῃσι, | δώσει. There is also perhaps a hint of Hes. *Op.* 267–8 πάντα ἰδὼν Διὸς ὀφθαλμὸς καὶ πάντα νοήσας | καί νυ τάδ', αἴ κ' ἐθέλῃσ', ἐπιδέρκεται. In view of the Homeric alternative verb form Voss reads the same here, and has then to read εἰς in place of καὶ ἐς. But the variation is characteristic of A.'s Homeric borrowings. On [Theoc.] 25.53 θέλεις Gow approves the exclusion of the short form from Homer by Aristarchus and Zenodotus. Cf. A.R. 2.960 θέλον, Call. frr. 75.28 θέλῃς, 227.7 θέλει.

ἐς αὐτίκα The MSS favour two words here and in 1103, but editors since Morel (except Voss) have printed one. In Ar. *Pax* 366–7 εἰς τίν' ἡμέραν; εἰς αὐτίκα μάλ', two words seem to be required, and εἰς is similarly used with other adverbs, e.g. Θ 538 ἠελίου ἀνιόντος ἐς αὔριον, μ 126 ἐς ὕστερον ὁρμηθῆναι, υ 199–200 γένοιτό τοι ἔς περ ὀπίσσω | ὄλβος. See LSJ εἰς ΙΙ fin., K–G 1.539.

771 γὰρ οὖν A reassuring note after δώσει. See Denniston 445–6.

COMMENTARY: 772–775

γενεὴν ἀνδρῶν A reminiscence of Z 149 ἀνδρῶν γενεή.

ἀναφανδόν Once in Homer, Π 178 ὅς ῥ' ἀναφανδὸν ὄπυιε, but cf. λ 455 κρύβδην, μηδ' ἀναφανδά. Cf. 64, 95 ἀμφαδόν.

ὀφέλλει Associated with Zeus in Υ 242 Ζεὺς δ' ἀρετὴν ἄνδρεσσιν ὀφέλλει τε μινύθει τε, and in same *sedes* in Ο 383 κύματ' ὀφέλλει. Cf. 1081 ὀφέλλεται.

772 πάντοθεν In sense of πάντη, e.g. 732; cf. ξ 270 περὶ γὰρ κακὰ πάντοθεν ἔστη. Contrast 455. The metrical position is the commonest in Homer, e.g. Ν 28.

εἰδόμενος 'Visible'; cf. 78, 93, and Θ 559 πάντα δὲ εἴδεται ἄστρα. In Homer the part. always means 'resembling'.

πάντη A reminder of the proem, line 4. The alliteration there is also imitated here.

σήματα φαίνων So of Zeus giving portents in Β 353, Δ 381, φ 413, Hes. fr. 141.25.

773 ἄλλα δέ τοι ἐρέει A purely verbal imitation of the Homeric formula ἄλλο δέ τοι ἐρέω (Α 297 etc.), without significance for the context. These five lines (773–7) conclude the introduction to the weather signs and mark the transition from the sky to the other parts of the cosmos.

ἤ που Enclitic που 'for example', illustrating the point by mentioning three of the moon's phases, and implying that other phases too can be used as weather signs. Cf. Ζ 438 ἤ πού τίς σφιν ἔνισπε θεοπροπίων ἐῢ εἰδώς.

διχόωσα Half-moon, i.e. the first and last quarters. Cf. 799 and the variations διχαιομένη (807), διχάς (807, 809). *Et.M.* quotes, but without reference to A., διχόωσι σελήνην (516, 9).

774 πληθύος Ionic form, gen. once in Homer, Ι 641 πληθύος ἐκ Δαναῶν, same *sedes*, but different sense. Sch. (S) τῆς πληροσελήνου. Cf. 799 πληθύν, and sch. πληθὺν δὲ λέγει τὴν πανσέληνον.

ἀμφοτέρωθεν C. gen., not in Homer, nor elsewhere in A. Cf. Χ. *HG* 5.2.6 ἀμφοτέρωθεν μὲν τῆς ὁδοῦ.

αὐτίκα 'At another time', like τοτὲ in 775.

πεπληθυῖα A variation of the Homeric *spondeiazon* σελήνην τε πλήθουσαν (Σ 484). Q.S. 1.347 νεκύεσσί τε πεπληθυῖα.

775 ἄκρῃ νυκτί In contrast to 308 ἀκρόθι νυκτός and 740 ἄκρα νυκτῶν, this clearly means the beginning of night; cf. Hes. *Op.* 567 ἀκροκνέφαιος, Arist. *Mete.* 367b26 ἀκρόνυχον, *D.S.* 2 ἀκρόνυχοι, Theoc. fr. 3.3 ἀκρόνυχος, Crinag. *AP* 7.633.1 = *GP* 1867 ἀκρέσπερος, and the modern term 'acronychal' for 'evening' risings.

κελεύων A guiding or warning sign; cf. the warning gesture of Cepheus in 631, and Nonn. *D.* 37.278 ἐλατῆρι κελεύων. Maass's emendation, adopted by Martin and Erren, is unnecessary: with ἄλλα δ' understand ἐρέει from 773. This sentence (773–6) combines a balanced structure (ἄλλα ... ἄλλα) with a chiasmus (moon – two examples – two examples – sun). Each pair of examples has two participles, and all four show variation of endings; there is also a variation of conjunction within the pairs (ἢ ... τοτὲ δ'). Another element in the pattern is the antithesis of σελήνη at the end of the first line and ἠέλιος at the beginning of the fourth.

776 τοι The v.l. in M perhaps shows the influence of 741 τὰ δέ που. The dat. pron. is more suited to ἔσσεται and also to ποιήσασθαι.

777 περί C. dat. expressing anxiety; cf. Κ 240 ἔδεισεν δὲ περὶ ξανθῷ Μενελάῳ, Theoc. 13.55 ταρασσόμενος περὶ παιδί.

ποιήσασθαι Of making or taking something for one's own advantage; cf. 379, 565, and especially 1103.

778–908 CELESTIAL SIGNS
(From the moon (778–818), the sun (819–891), and the Manger (892–908))

The signs now have a meteorological basis, and are derived from the local and day-to-day appearance of the heavenly bodies, though these are also combined with weather lore based on the phases of the moon.

778–818 Signs from the moon
This section is divided into two parts, from new moon to first quarter (778–98), and from first quarter to the end of the month (799–818). In the first part the third and fourth days are critical, and weather signs are provided by the shape, colour and inclination of the crescent. The second part again deals with the colour of the moon, also with key dates that give signs valid for several days, and haloes.

778 σκέπτεο Imper. once in Homer (Ρ 652); cf. 75, and, as here, introducing a new topic, 799, 832, 880, 892, 994.

πρῶτον Having announced the moon and the sun as his next themes (773–7), A. decides to deal with the moon first. Voss emended to πρώτην, citing 41, 735, 747, Avien. 1446 *Cynthia cum primum caelo noua cornua promit*, and sch. (S) ἀπὸ πρώτης αὐξήσεως σκόπει τὴν σελήνην. But this line merely introduces the lunar crescent; cf. sch. (M) περισκέπτου δὲ πρῶτον. The first sighting of it comes in 781.

κεράων ἑκάτερθε Repeated from 566, there of the two horizons, here the two horns of the lunar crescent; sch. σκόπει τὴν σελήνην ἐξ ἀμφοτέρων τῶν κεράτων. ἑκάτερθε c. gen., normally 'on either side of' (e.g. 47, 496), here means 'on both of'; cf. 243, 566.

779 ἐπιγράφει In Homer of a grazing mark made on the skin (Δ 139, Ν 553), here with a suggestion of painting; sch. ἐπιχρωτίζει.

ἕσπερος A. personifies evening only here, but night more frequently (408, 419, 434, 470). The evening crescent is of course that of the new moon.

αἴγλη Cf. 80, 139, 367 of stars, 826 of the sun; δ 45 of sun and moon.

780 ἄλλοτε δ' ἀλλοῖαι Cf. 751.

μορφαί Twice in Homer, but only sg. and meaning 'comeliness' of speech (θ 170, λ 367). Here the pl. of the moon's changing phases has a faint echo of Pl. *R.* 380d ἄλλοτε ἐν ἄλλαις ἰδέαις τοτὲ μὲν αὐτὸν γιγνόμενον, ἀλλάττοντα τὸ αὐτοῦ εἶδος εἰς πολλὰς μορφάς.

κερόωσι Only here and Plb. 18.24.9 τοῖς δ' εὐζώνοις κερᾶν, 'to flank' the phalanx, i.e. to give it a protective cover; cf. περικερᾶν (5.84.8), ὑπερκερᾶν (11.23.5). Here the changing phases 'crescent' the moon, i.e. give the moon its changing crescent shapes, a bold poetic innovation (*pace* Voss), which is matched by other imaginative uses of verbs, e.g. 748 ἀμείβεται, 750 ἐμπλήσσει, 752 συναείδεται, 779 ἐπιγράφει. For the diectasis see note on 27 τροχόωσι.

781 ἀεξομένην Cf. 734, 800. So *h.Hom.* 32.12 λαμπρόταταί τ' αὐγαὶ τότ' ἀεξομένης, Opp. *H.* 5.590 μήνης μὲν ἀεξομένης. Cf. Θ 66 of day, *h.Hom.* 2.455 of spring. Virgil amplifies with *luna reuertentis cum primum colligit ignis* (*G.* 1.427).

τρίτη The new moon does not normally become noticeable until its third day. Cf. *D.S.* 12 σημαίνει δ' ὅτι ἂν σημαίνῃ τριταῖος ὢν ὁ μείς. The *Geoponica* begins its Aratean signs here, τριταία καὶ τεταρταία οὖσα ἡ σελήνη (1.2.1).

782 τάων Cf. 722. These are signs from the colour and thickness of the crescent.

μηνὸς ἐφεσταότος Sch. δυνήσῃ μαθεῖν περὶ ὅλου τοῦ μηνὸς εἰ ὀμβρινὸς ἢ ἀνεμώδης ἢ αὐχμηρὸς ἢ νήνεμος ἔσται. Here A. seems to mean that the new moon's appearance can serve as a guide to the weather for the whole month. Cf. *D.S.* 12, cited on 781, and V. *G.* 1.434-5, with reference to the fourth day, *totus et ille dies et qui nascentur ab illo | exactum ad mensem.* Later (806-7) he qualifies this by saying that the third- and fourth-day signs apply particularly to the days up to half-moon. The gen. ἐφεσταότος occurs once in Homer, in the sense 'standing' (Ρ 609 δίφρῳ ἐφεσταότος); here it means the month that is just begun or established. Contrast the pres. ἐφισταμένοιο (1149) of the beginning of the month only.

783 λεπτή The slender new crescent when its outline is clear-cut. The adj. is emphasised by the anaphora in 784, and more strikingly by the acrostic in 783–7. On the latter see J.-M. Jacques, *REA* 62 (1960) 48–61, and E. Vogt, *A&A* 13 (1966) 80–95. This acrostic is primarily a Homeric imitation, with ΛΕΠΤΗ closely resembling ΛΕΥΚΗ in ω 1–5, where it is presumably unintentional, since the adj. λευκή has no significance for the context. See Eust. 1385, 29. In 80 also A. has λεπτή in an imitation of Homeric λευκή (ζ 45). After A. the acrostic was used by Nicander as a signature in *Ther.* 345–53 and (incompletely) in *Alex.* 266–74. See Gow's note on the former, Cic. *Div.* 2.111–12 on acrostics in Ennius and the Sibylline verses, E. Courtney *Philologus* 134 (1990) 3–13. W. Levitan, *Glyph* 5 (1979) 55–68 sees deliberate acrostics also in 803–6 and (misspelled) in 808–12, but I am not convinced that these are intentional and significant.

Here the acrostic has a secondary purpose, to highlight one of the key words in the poetic theory of Callimachus and his circle. Hutchinson (*HP* 215 n. 4) is doubtful about this significance, but the repetition of λεπτή and the fact that the acrostic covers this sentence exactly does suggest that it is deliberate, and therefore significant. It may, of course, be intended playfully, like εἰ ἐτεὸν δή in 30, where an allusion to Callimachus is also possible. Cf. Call. *E.* 27.3–4 λεπταὶ | ῥήσιες of A.'s poetic style (which may be a response to this passage), fr. 1.11 κατὰ λεπτόν, and 1.24 Μοῦσαν λεπταλέην. A. introduces λεπτή here as a deliberate addition to the context, where *D.S.* 51 has καὶ ὁ μεὶς ἐὰν τριταῖος ὢν λαμπρὸς ᾖ, εὐδιεινόν. It may be also significant that he does this with the first item in his detailed list of signs, and that his first sign is for fair weather, a category that *D.S.* leaves to the last. Jacques (55) suggests that A. intends a good omen for his poetry. Cf. *Gp.* 1.2.1 λεπτὴ καὶ καθαρὰ φαινομένη εὐδίαν δηλοῖ, Ptol. *Tetr.* 2.14.4 λεπτὴ μὲν γὰρ καὶ καθαρὰ φαινομένη καὶ μηδὲν ἔχουσα περὶ αὐτὴν εὐδιεινῆς καταστάσεώς ἐστι δηλωτική, *CCAG* 8.1.139, 18 τριταία λεπτὴ καὶ καθαρά. Anon. Laur. 6 as *Gp.*

καθαρή Another Callimachean term applied to poetry, e.g. *H.* 2.111 καθαρή τε καὶ ἀχράαντος. Virgil renders with *pura* (*G.* 1.433), Pliny with *puro nitore* (*Nat.* 18.347).

ἐοῦσα Voss finds this feeble before εἴη, and reads ἰοῦσα. A. is not too sensitive about such repetitions (cf. 181–2, 213–14, 236–7, 246–7, 990–1), but the same verb in part. and main verb is certainly unusual. See Diggle *Studies* 66–7 and 120 for some parallels. However, ἐοῦσα gives the right sense, and is supported by sch. εἰ μὲν λαμπρὸν εἴη τὸ φῶς, εὐδίας ἐστὶ σημαντικόν, and οὖσα λεπτή ... εὐδίας ἐστὶ σημαντική.

784 εὔδιος An extension of the normal sense to mean a sign of fair weather; cf. 878. Anon. *AP* 12.156.3–4 = *HE* 3740–1 καὶ ποτὲ μὲν φαίνεις πολὺν ὑετόν, ἄλλοτε δ' αὖτε | εὔδιος.

εὖ The v.l. οὐ is not possible, since the context requires a positive adj.; sch. (MUAS) σφόδρα ἐρευθής. Avien. 1457 *ignito suppinxerit ora rubore*.

ἐρευθής *D.S.* 12 ἐὰν μὲν ᾖ πυρώδης, πνευματώδη σημαίνει τὸν μῆνα. V. *G.* 1.430–1 *at si uirgineum suffuderit ore ruborem,* | *uentus erit,* Plin. *Nat.* 18.347 *si rubicunda, uentos,* Ptol. *Tetr.* 2.14.5 λεπτὴ δὲ καὶ ἐρυθρά ... ἀνέμων ἐστὶ σημαντική, *CCAG* 8.1.139, 19 τριταία λεπτὴ πυρρά, πνεύματα μέλλοντα δηλοῖ. The redness is caused by dust in the atmosphere, raised by a distant wind.

785 πνευματίη Only here. A. may have chosen this suffix on the analogy of ἡμάτιος (580). The regular adj. is πνευματικός, though for the sense of portending wind *D.S.* uses πνευματώδης (12, 31).

παχίων The primary comp. suffix with short ι, e.g. A 249 γλυκίων, in preference to Homeric πάσσων (e.g. ζ 230); see Palmer 280. The adj. is in antithesis to λεπτή, and may be seen similarly as a deliberate addition hinting at current poetic theory: cf. Call. fr. 1.23 τὸ μὲν θύος ὅττι πάχιστον, 398 Λύδη καὶ παχὺ γράμμα καὶ οὐ τορόν. A. seems to be making the point by filling out his description of this sign to almost three lines. *D.S.* 12 has only ἐὰν δὲ ζοφώδης, ὑδατώδη, Plin. *Nat.* 18.347 *cornua eius obtusa pluuiam,* but *Gp.* 1.3.1 follows A. in expanding to τριταία καὶ τεταρταία οὖσα ἡ σελήνη, ἀμβλείας ἔχουσα τὰς κεραίας καὶ ἀχλυώδεις ὄμβρον προσημαίνει. Anon. Laur. 6 as *Gp.*, but 4.3 αἱ κεραῖαι τῆς σελήνης παχεῖαι φανεῖσαι χειμῶνα πολὺν δηλοῦσιν. *CCAG* 8.1.139, 21 τριταία παχὺ κέρας ἔχουσα καὶ παχεῖα οὖσα ἢ νότον ἢ χειμῶνα σημαίνει, Ptol. *Tetr.* 2.14.5 μέλαινα δὲ ἢ χλωρὰ καὶ παχεῖα θεωρουμένη χειμώνων καὶ ὄμβρων ἐστὶ δηλωτική.

ἀμβλείῃσι κεραίαις The adj. makes an antithesis to καθαρή, and is the more effective for being rarely applied to light. Cf. the verb in 787 and 1013. A. uses the noun again in 790. Virgil omits the sign, but echoes this phrase negatively in *G.* 1.433 *neque obtunsis per caelum cornibus;* Nonn. *D.* 18.115 Σεληναίῃσι κεραίαις.

786 τέτρατον ἐκ τριτάτοιο Sch. ἐν τετάρτῃ ἡμέρᾳ οὐκ ἔδει εἶναι τὸ φῶς αὐτῆς ἀμενηνόν, ἀλλ' ἔδει καὶ σκίαν ἀποπέμπειν. The adjj. thus mean 'fourth day' and 'third day', i.e. with the sense of τεταρταῖος and τριταῖος. In 806 A. combines the two forms. This use of the ordinal numbers may perhaps derive from their substantival use, e.g. X. *An.* 4.8.21 τρίτη δὲ καὶ τετάρτῃ. The form τρίτατος, with superlative suffix, is Homeric: cf. A 252, B 565, and Chantraine 1.261.

φόως Homeric diectasis, rare in nouns, e.g. in same *sedes* Λ 2 ἵν' ἀθανάτοισι φόως φέροι ἠδὲ βροτοῖσι, Ψ 226 φόως ἐρέων ἐπὶ γαῖαν. Chantraine 1.81.

ἀμενηνόν In Homer of men and ghosts, e.g. Ε 887, κ 521. Cf. 1016 of starlight.

787 ἢ νότῳ ἄμβλυνται The MSS reading with ἀμβλύνεται makes sense, but the short υ is unparalleled. The v.l. in S implies ἀμβλύω, a verb not otherwise attested; in any case the sense requires the suffix -ύνω, 'make blunt'. Most edd. since Bekker have adopted the conjecture ἠὲ νότῳ ἀμβλύνετ', but, though A. does elsewhere elide verbs in -ται, this involves a double emendation. Dorville's pres. act. is an intrans. use unlikely in a verb in -ύνω. Voss argues that the context requires the opt. with ἄν, because most signs look to the future, but here the crescent is already blunted (785), and it is the southerly that is presaged, not the blunting. The best solution is Mair's ἄμβλυνται, which he prints without comment, a perf. pass. without reduplication or augment; cf. Π 481, κ 283 ἔρχαται, Hdt. 1.125 ἀρτέαται, 3.155 ἔργασται. See Chantraine 1.421, G. Curtius, *The Greek Verb* (London 1880) 371–3. Mair's translation 'her beams are blunted' suggests a pl. ending, but the subject is the moon, and the ending is the normal 3rd sg. for verbs in -ύνω: cf. Hom. *Epigr.* 12.4 ὥρη μὲν ἀπήμβλυνται, Herod. 10.4 αὐγὴ τῆς ζοῆς ἀπήμβλυνται. See also 276 τετρήχυνται and note. Corruption of this rare form was almost inevitable, aided by sch. ἢ γὰρ νότῳ ἀμβλύνεται. Martin's νότου is unnecessary: the high cloud from the south is already dimming the moon before the wind reaches the observer.

ὕδατος ἐγγὺς ἐόντος Imitated by Q.S. 1.68 σῆμ' ἀνέμοιο καὶ ὑετοῦ ἐγγὺς ἐόντος.

788 εἰ δέ κ' C. subj., a regular Homeric usage when the condition applies to a particular occasion, e.g. β 218 εἰ μέν κεν πατρὸς βίοτον καὶ νόστον ἀκούσω. See Monro *HG* 266. This use is naturally suited to weather signs; cf. 420, 422, 794, 811, 832, 974, 980. A. however also uses the pure subj. in similar conditions, e.g. 840, 850, 858, 903, 988, 1082. In Homer this usage occurs in general sayings or indefinite conditions, but A. does not show any distinction, and uses it purely for stylistic variety in a section of the poem which inevitably contains a great abundance of conditional clauses.

ἀπ' ἀμφοτέρων κεράων The literal translations of Voss, 'von beiden Gehörn', and similarly of Erren, do not make the meaning clear, while those of Mair, 'neither horn nods forward', and similarly of Martin are incorrect, since only the upper horn can be said to lean forward or backward (cf. 794–5). What A. means is that the line joining the two horn-tips is not leaning either forward or backward, the angle of inclination being measured from the upright position. The use of ἀπό is perhaps borrowed from geometry: cf. Euc. *Elem.* 1.47 τὸ ἀπὸ τῆς τὴν ὀρθὴν γωνίαν ὑποτεινούσης πλευρᾶς τετράγωνον, where the square is drawn from the hypotenuse as a base. The v.l. ἐπ' is probably an attempt to solve the problem of understanding ἀπ'. Sch. ἐὰν ... ἀμφο-

448

τέροις τοῖς κέρασι μήτε νευστάζῃ, *D.S.* 27 ἐὰν δὲ καὶ ὁ μεὶς βορείου ὄντος ὀρθὸς εἰστήκῃ, ζέφυροι εἰώθασιν ἐπιπνεῖν, Plin. *Nat.* 18.347 *cornua*
... *erecta et infesta uentos semper significant.* The inclination of the moon has,
of course, no meteorological significance: it depends on the angle that
the ecliptic makes with the horizon at the time and the latitude of the
observer. It is interesting that this sign does not appear in Ptolemy or
the *Geoponica*; but it lasted long in popular weather-lore, e.g. 'When the
moon lies on her back, then the sou'west wind will crack; when she rises
up and nods, then nor'easters dry the sods' (R. Inwards, *Weather Lore*,
Wakefield 1969, 93).

ἦμαρ ἄγουσα Since the Greek month began with the observation of
the new moon after sunset, the 24-hour day was reckoned as beginning
in the evening for calendarial purposes (Bickerman 13–14).

789 ἐπινευστάζῃ Only here, if correct. The simple verb is Homeric, of the head nodding as a sign (Υ 162, μ 194) or drooping in faintness (σ 240). Here the compound ('bend over') is apt, as in 794 ἐπινεύῃ,
corresponding to *D.S.* 27 ἐπικύπτῃ. Cf. Χ 314 κόρυθι δ' ἐπένευε φαεινῇ.
Sch. μήτε ἐπινεύῃ τοῖς κέρασι.

ὑπτιόωσα Only here and 795, ὑπτιάω being a poetic form of ὑπ-
τιάζω. Cf. ἀντιάω (501), διχάω (605), εὐδιάω (278), σκιάω (600).

φαείνῃ Voss was probably right in emending the opt. of the MSS
to the subj., since A. does not normally vary the mood of verbs coupled
within the same clause: cf. 838–9, 841, 872–3, 903, 975, 989–90, 1013–
16, 1033–5, 1082–4. Sch. ἐάν, φησί, τριταίαν ἄγουσα ἡμέραν μήτε ὑπ-
τιάζῃ μήτε ἐπινεύῃ.

790 ὀρθαὶ ἑκάτερθε The two horn-tips of the crescent in line are
perpendicular to the horizon; cf. 792. *D.S.* 27 ἐὰν δὲ καὶ ὁ μεὶς βορείου
ὄντος ὀρθὸς εἰστήκῃ.

περιγνάμπτωσι Once in Homer, but trans., of doubling a head-
land (ι 80 περιγνάμπτοντα Μάλειαν). Here the verb is in the same
metrical position, but intrans. Cf. the intrans. περικάμψαντες in Pl.
Euthyd. 291b. To retain the same subject, Voss emended to ὀρθὰς ...
περιγνάμπτουσα κεραίας. But the change of subject is merely a grammatical one, made for the sake of variation: κεραῖαι in effect means the
crescent moon. Q.S. imitates with ἥμισυ πεπληθυῖα περὶ γναμπτῇσι
κεραίης (1.149).

791 ἑσπέριοί κ' ἄνεμοι *D.S.* 27 ζέφυροι (see note on 788).

792 αὔτως See note on 21.

ἀγινεῖ Voss emended to subj. to conform with the other verbs in
789–94. But here there is no κε, and the variation is intentional. Cf.
825.

793 ἤ τ' Strongly affirmative; cf. 857 and 876, also in apodosis, and

449

with ἄν and opt. The apodotic use is Homeric, e.g. μ 137–8 τὰς εἰ μέν κ' ἀσινέας ἐάᾳς νόστου τε μέδηαι, | ἤ τ' ἄν ἔτ' εἰς Ἰθάκην κακά περ πάσχοντες ἵκοισθε. See Monro *HG* 304, Denniston 532.

χειμῶνος Cf. *D.S.* 38 τὸ σελήνιον ἐὰν ὀρθὸν ᾖ μέχρι τετράδος καὶ εἰ εὔκυκλον, χειμάσει μέχρι διχοτόμου, Plin. *Nat.* 18.347 *utraque erecta noctem uentosam*, Varro ap. Plin. ibid. 348 *si quarto die luna erit directa, magnam tempestatem in mari praesagiet.*

συναγειρομένοιο Perhaps an echo of ω 802 εὖ συναγειρόμενοι.

διδάσκοι The reading of edd. since Morel. A.'s use of ἄν is confined to main clauses with opt.

794 τὸ μετήορον Sch. κέρας φησὶν ὑψηλὸν τὸ βορειότερον, also μετέωρον δὲ κέρας τὸ βόρειον κέκληκεν, ὡς πρὸς τὴν ἡμετέραν φαντασίαν. Sch. Germ. p. 202B *Aratus autem dicit, si aquilonium cornu lunae est porrectius, aquilonem inminere; item si cornu australe sit erectius, notum inminere.*

ἐπινεύῃ Voss's correction is necessary, since εἴ κε, the equivalent of ἐάν, is used only with subj.; cf. 788–9, 795, 811. Sch. ἐὰν συννεύῃ and ἐὰν μὲν ἐπινεύῃ. The verb is Homeric, e.g. Χ 314 κόρυθι δ' ἐπένευε φαεινῇ. *D.S.* 27 ὅταν μὲν ἡ κεραία ⟨ἡ ἄνω⟩ τοῦ μηνὸς ἐπικύπτῃ, βόρειος ὁ μείς. West on Hes. *Op.* 534 ἐπὶ νῶτα ἔαγε notes ἐπί meaning 'forward at an angle'.

795 δειδέχθαι Perf. inf. as imper., this form only in A. (also 907, 928) and Max. 149. The sense assigns it to δέχομαι, the intensive reduplication probably shows the influence of Homeric δειδέχαται at the beginning of a line, e.g. η 72. See, however, Kirk's note on Δ 4 on the correct spelling of δειδέχατ' and other forms of δειδίσκομαι, also Chantraine 1.433–4, Wyatt 105. For the sense cf. 1090 ποτιδέγμενος. Homer uses the verb c. acc. (e.g. Δ 107 ἐκβαίνοντα δεδεγμένος), A. characteristically c. gen.: cf. 907–8 βορέω ... δοκεύειν.

ὑπτιάῃσι Cf. 789. *D.S.* 27 ὅταν δ' ἡ κάτωθεν, νότιος.

796 τριτόωσαν Only here, no other part of τριτάω attested. The part., with Homeric diectasis, is formed from the adj. τρίτος: cf. 434 παμφανόωντι, also 789 ὑπτιόωσα from ὕπτιος. Sch. τριταίαν οὖσαν.

ὅλος περὶ κύκλος ἑλίσσῃ The scholia understand κύκλος as a ring round the moon: (1) ὅλην τὴν μηνοειδῆ κύκλος περιλάβῃ πανταχόθεν φοινισσόμενος, (2) τριταίαν οὖσαν κύκλος περίσχῃ, (3) κύκλον τινὰ ἐρυθρὸν περὶ αὐτὴν ἔχουσαν. The second of these adds an explanation from cloud interference: ἐγκαταδυόμεναι γὰρ αἱ ἀκτῖνες τῆς σελήνης ὑγροῖς τοῖς νέφεσι, κωλύονται μὲν ἐξικνεῖσθαι μέχρις ἡμῶν διὰ τὴν παχύτητα τῶν νεφῶν, αὐτὸν δὲ τὸν κύκλον τὰ νέφη διαυγοῦσι καὶ ἀνθύνουσιν (ἀλδαίνουσι A). So Avien. 1484 *deae conuoluat circulus oras.* Modern editors follow the scholia and Avienius. Voss adopted the v.l. ὅλην (derived from sch. 1), but his successors retain ὅλος, translating 'a complete halo' (Mair), 'un cercle entier' (Martin), 'ein ganzer Kreis' (Erren). A., however, deals with lunar haloes later (811–17), giving them their technical name ἀλωαί, and it is unlikely that he would have anticipated that theme here, especially with the less specific word κύκλος.

The most natural meaning of κύκλος in the present context is the moon's disc, a usage already well established in both verse and prose, e.g. Emped. B43 σεληναίης κύκλον εὐρύν, E. *Ion* 1155 κύκλος δὲ πανσέληνος, Hdt. 6.106.3 οὐκ ἐξελεύσεσθαι ἔφασαν μὴ οὐ πλήρεος ἐόντος τοῦ κύκλου. In 823 A. uses κύκλος also of the sun's disc; cf. A. *Pers.* 504, *Pr.* 91, S. *Ant.* 416. When the lunar crescent is slender, the outline of the dark part is faintly visible, a well-known phenomenon called 'earth-shine'. This is what A. means here, and this is the point of ὅλος. There is no corresponding passage in *D.S.*, but *Gp.* 1.3.1 (= Anon. Laur. 6), with reference to the 3rd-day and 4th-day moon, clearly means the lunar disc in καὶ ἐρυθρὸς δὲ ὁ κύκλος αὐτῆς φαινόμενος ἢ πυρώδης χειμῶνα σημαίνει. See also Schott's translation 'die ganze Scheibe' and his explanatory note on 'Erdschein'. For περὶ ... ἐλίσσῃ see note on 531.

797 ἐρευθόμενος A variation of ἐρευθής (784), used again in 803. Cf. A.R. 1.778 καλὸν ἐρευθόμενος, in the same metrical position, but describing the evening star. The inappropriateness of the word for the brilliantly white planet Venus suggests that Apollonius is the imitator.

χείμερος Only here and in 1084, a variation of the usual form χειμέριος. The adj. agrees with κύκλος, i.e. the moon, as a sign of stormy weather. Cf. εὔδιος and πνευματίη (784–5).

798 χειμῶνι As a variation A. expresses the weather to come as the cause of the reddening; cf. 815. Variation and chiasmus are combined in 797–8, with χειμῶνι responding to χείμερος, and φοινίσσοιτο both balancing and varying ἐρευθόμενος.

πυρώτερα Comp. adv. attested only here; sch. give the normal form in ὅσῳ μᾶλλον πυρρότερος ὁ κύκλος θεωρεῖται. Frisk suggests (2.652) that *πῦρος must have been the original form of πυρρός. Kathleen Forbes (*Glotta* 36, 1958, 262) notes a rare instance of πυρός as a v.l. in A. *Pers.* 316, also in some proper names in inscriptions. K–B derive from πῦρ, gen. πυρός, like other comp. adjj. formed without positive directly from nouns; cf. θεώτερος (ν 111, Call. *H.* 2.93), ὁπλότερος (B 707), ὑετώτατος (Hdt. 2.25).

φοινίσσοιτο The association of this and related words with bloodshed is perhaps intended to give this portent of storm a particularly ominous character; cf. 887.

799 σκέπτεο Cf. 778. Here and in 832–3 A. varies the construction with ἐς, as in μ 247 σκεψάμενος δ' ἐς νῆα. In 995, however, ἐς has a different sense.

COMMENTARY: 800–803

πληθύν   Cf. 774.

ἀμφότερον διχόωσαν   The first and last quarters. Cf. the same part. in 773, and in other contexts 512, 605. For ἀμφότερον adv. cf. 617, 821. By introducing the key phases of the moon here, A. anticipates 805–10.

800 ἠμέν   Formed from affirmative ἤ with μέν, only in epic. Here it is correlative with ἠδ', characteristically coupling opposites, with an alternation implied (Monro *HG* 309). Cf. Ε 751 ἠμὲν ἀνακλῖναι πυκινὸν νέφος ἠδ' ἐπιθεῖναι (solar myth of the gates of the Horae), Hes. *Op.* 775 ἠμὲν ὅις πείκειν ἠδ' εὔφρονα καρπὸν ἀμᾶσθαι, a line that A. probably had in mind, since it concerns days of the month (*Op.* 772–3 μηνὸς . . . ἀεξομένοιο), and the correlatives are in the same *sedes*.

αὖθις   The sequential use, e.g. S. *OT* 1402–3 οἷ' ἔργα δράσας ὑμῖν εἶτα δεῦρ' ἰὼν | ὁποῖ' ἔπρασσον αὖθις. Cf. 808 πάλιν.

801 οἱ ἐπὶ χροιῇ   For οἱ as a possessive pronoun see note on 47; here 'its', i.e. the moon's. The prep. has the same force as in 429 and 1129, denoting the evidence upon which the estimate of the weather is made.

μηνὸς ἐκάστου   *D.S.* 8 ὡς δ' αὔτως ἔχει καὶ περὶ τὸν μῆνα ἕκαστον. The month is regarded as a weather-cycle based on the moon's phases, in the same way as the year is a cycle based on the sun's changing seasons. *D.S.* 5 explains: ἡ γὰρ σελήνη νυκτὸς οἷον ἥλιός ἐστι· διὸ καὶ αἱ σύνοδοι τῶν μηνῶν χειμέριοί εἰσιν, ὅτι ἀπολείπει τὸ φῶς τῆς σελήνης ἀπὸ τετράδος φθίνοντος μέχρι τετράδος ἱσταμένου. ὥσπερ οὖν ἡλίου ἀπόλειψις γίνεται κατὰ τὸν ὅμοιον τρόπον καὶ τῆς σελήνης ἔκλειψις. Voss's emendation ('die einzelnen Eigenschaften des Monats') ignores this piece of ancient weather-lore; likewise Erren's explanation 'jede Mondphase' (n. 72 and *PAS* 271).

802 καθαρῇ   A. now generalises for the whole month the sign already given for the third day only (783). Similarly 803 repeats 783–4, and 804 gives a variation of 787. Varro ap. Plin. *Nat.* 18.348 *si plenilunio per dimidium pura erit, dies serenos significabit; si rutila, uentos; nigrescens imbres*, Gp. 1.2.1 ἐὰν διχόμηνος οὖσα καθαρὰ φανῇ, εὐδίαν προμηνύει. ἐρυθροτέρα δὲ οὖσα ἄνεμον σημαίνει, similarly Anon. Laur. 6.

τεκμήραιο   Cf. 1129, 1154, Call. *H.* 2.35.

803 ἐρευθομένη   Cf. 797.

δοκέειν   Only here c. acc. and in 804 c. gen. in sense of 'expect', illustrating A.'s need of all possible variations of this meaning in this third of the poem. The use with fut. inf., e.g. Η 192 δοκέω νικησέμεν Ἕκτορα δῖον, may have been an influence. Cf. δειδέχθαι c. gen. (795, 907), δοκεύειν c. gen. (813, 908), c. acc. (1128).

ἀνέμοιο κελεύθους   A reminiscence of ε 383 τῶν ἄλλων ἀνέμων κατέδησε κελεύθους, where the direction of the winds is significant, as also in Ξ 17 λιγέων ἀνέμων λαιψηρὰ κέλευθα. Here there is no such significance (cf. sg. ἀνέμοιο in 813, 814, 831, 837 etc.), and the phrase is merely a poetic elaboration of ἄνεμον.

804 μελαινομένη The passive is Homeric, in Ε 354 μελαίνετο δὲ χρόα καλόν. A. uses the part. (also 854, 941; cf. 817) to vary the adj. This line has a fourth-foot caesura with none in the third; the other instances are 201, 263, 398, 494, 502, 547, 973. The incidence in Homer is about once in 100 lines (Maas 60).

δοκέειν A. repeats the inf. as imper. from 803, but varies its position and its dependent case.

805 οὔ τοι οὔτε is not in question, since there is no other negative, and οὐ μάλα is merely intended to make sense, not to restore the correct text. Buttmann and Martin read οὐτάρ (= *nec tamen ideo*), but this is not attested anywhere else, nor is τἄρ for τάρα, which is particularly suited to dramatic dialogue, often with the sense of 'in that case', in response to a surprising remark: see Denniston 555. Voss may be right in reading τοι, but he apparently understands it as particle, whereas it makes better sense as pronoun. A. uses it frequently so with σῆμα, σήματα, with some form of εἶναι or an equivalent verb; cf. 303, 776, 836, 909, 1001, 1017, 1036. οὔ τοι read as οὕτω may explain *sic* in *Arat. Lat.* The corruption was perhaps due to the influence of οὔτ' ἄρ in epic (δ 605, Emp. 17.30, etc.).

πᾶσιν ἐπ' ἤμασι The point seems to be that, since the month is regarded as a weather unit, it might have been expected that signs in the early part of the month would foretell the weather for the rest of it, but in fact the pattern can change at certain critical phases of the moon. The rather strained word-play of πᾶσιν ... πάντα tends to obscure the meaning of this line: hence the different attempts of sch. to explain it. The clearest is sch. (ΚΑ) τουτέστι τὸ σημεῖον τὸ γινόμενον ἀπὸ τῆς τρίτης ἢ τετάρτης ἡμέρας τῆς σελήνης, μὴ ἔλπιζε τοῦτο ἕως τὸ τέλος ἐκβῆναι. Cf. Gal. v.9, p. 909 Kühn, after quoting lines 805–10, οὐκ εἰς ἅπαντά φησι τὸν ἐξ ἀρχῆς χρόνον ἐξαρκεῖν τὰ σημεῖα τῆς πρώτης φάσεως, μεταβολὰς δέ τινας φέρειν τάς τε διχοτόμους καὶ πανσελήνους. ἅπασα δ' ὀξύρροπος μεταβολὴ κρίσις ὀνομάζεται. For ἐπί c. dat. 'for' cf., with same verb, Φ 585 πολλὰ τετεύξεται ἄλγε' ἐπ' αὐτῇ [sc. τῇ πόλει].

τέτυκται In A. always of σήματα, whether signs or constellations (12, 233, 370, 725, 757).

806–810 Critical dates for weather change during the month are noted in *D.S.* 8 as a system of half-periods: διχοτομοῦσι γὰρ αἵ τε πανσέληνοι καὶ αἱ ὀγδόαι καὶ αἱ τετράδες, ὥστε ἀπὸ νουμηνίας ὡς ἀπ' ἀρχῆς δεῖ σκοπεῖν. μεταβάλλει γὰρ ὡς ἐπὶ τὸ πολὺ ἐν τῇ τετράδι, ἐὰν δὲ μή, ἐν τῇ ὀγδόῃ, εἰ δὲ μή, πανσελήνῳ· ἀπὸ δὲ πανσελήνου εἰς ὀγδόην φθίνοντος, καὶ ἀπὸ ταύτης εἰς τετράδα, ἀπὸ δὲ τετράδος εἰς τὴν νουμηνίαν. This mathematical approach suggests Pythagorean influence, which is indeed noted by sch. with reference to the number seven in the lunar month.

πέλονται Pl. verb with n.pl. subj. is common in Homer, mostly when the subject is a noun with a real plural sense, but also especially in lines ending with πέλονται (Monro *HG* 161), e.g. Ν 632, to Zeus, σέο δ' ἐκ τάδε πάντα πέλονται, θ 160, σ 367, Emped. 21.7, 110.7, A.R. 3.813, [Opp.] *C.* 1.400, Opp. *H.* 1.702. Here the pl. suggests the number of different signs available.

807 μέσφα Cf. 599, 725.

διχαιομένης Cf. 495, of the Crab bisected by the tropic. Here the part. is a variation of διχάς (737, 807, 809) and διχόωσα (773, 799). The regular term for the half-moon is διχότομος σελήνη (Arist. *Pr.* 911b36, Aristarch. Hyp. 3, Gem. 9.8, Ptol. *Alm.* 5.2). The v.l. is a correction to the normal form of this verb, διχάζω.

διχάδος Attested only in A.; see also 737, 809. The gen. is a variation of the dat. in 806, ἄχρις ἐπ' c. acc. varies μέσφα c. gen., and there is a chiasmus with case variation in διχάδος ... διχόμηνον ... διχομήνου ... διχάδα (807–9).

γε μέν See note on 17.

ἄχρις ἐπ' Cf. A.R. 4.1403 ἄχρις ἐπ' ἄκνηστιν. A. also has ἄχρις c. gen. (53, 614, 674), as in Homer, and ἄχρι παρ' c. acc. (349, 602, 632).

808 σημαίνει Abs. 'give weather signs', as frequently ἐπισημαίνει in the parapegmata.

διχόμηνον For the word-play with διχάς cf. 737. διχόμηνος is an adj., sc. σελήνην here; cf. *h.Hom.* 32.11 ἑσπερίη διχόμηνος. A. has perhaps a deliberate *figura etymologica* running through the poem with this word and the related διχόμην: -ι (78), -α (737), -ον, -ου (808). In contrast to the chiasmus of 807, this line has two balanced halves, with the suggestion of an internal rhyme.

809 φθιμένην Aor. med. part., normally of the dead, e.g. Θ 359 χερσὶν ὑπ' Ἀργείων φθίμενος. Also of time gone, S. *Aj.* 141 τῆς νῦν φθιμένης νυκτός. Since the reference here is to the waning moon, the intended sense must be the present (cf. 1149 φθίνοντος); hence the v.l. φθινομένην.

ἔχεται The *lectio difficilior*, which also gives the better sense, the fourth last day being the next significant phase after half-moon. Corruption to δέχεται explains the further corruptions μιν and subsequently μέν. For ἔχεσθαι of time cf. Th. 6.3.2 τοῦ ἐχομένου ἔτους, which Dover calls 'an abnormal expression ...', possibly adopted from Antiochos'. This verb, in the sense of 'being close to', is normally construed c. gen.

454

(originally partitive with the meaning 'cling to'), but here the dat. is no doubt used as with verbs expressing proximity. Cf. Pl. *Gorg.* 494e τὰ ἐχόμενα τούτοις ἐφεξῆς ἅπαντα, though Dodds takes the dat. with ἐφεξῆς, and suggests as an alternative that the true reading may be ἑπόμενα. So here Professor Diggle ἕπεται.

αὐτίκα See note on 199; here the lapse of time is four days.

τετράς Cf. Hes. *Op.* 794, same *sedes*, also with run-on. But Hesiod's day is in the middle of the three ten-day divisions of the month, i.e. the 14th, whereas this is the fourth last; cf. 1150 of both fourths in a two-part division of the month. In *h.Hom.* 4.19 τετράδι τῇ προτέρῃ the month is also bipartite. In Ar. *Nub.* 1131 Strepsiades counts the days towards the end of the Athenian calendar month: πέμπτη, τετράς, τρίτη· μετὰ ταύτην δευτέρα.

810 ἀποιχομένου A rare instance with present sense, as a variation for φθίνοντος (1149). Elsewhere A. conforms to the normal perfect sense, of the departed Ariadne (72), of stars already set (627). The innovation here is similar to the use of φθιμένην (809).

τῇ δὲ τριτάτῃ ἐπιόντος The ἀπιόντος of the MSS, as Voss pointed out, is senseless in the context. The third last day certainly comes after the fourth, but A. is listing only the critical days for weather change, and the next is the third of the new month. The part. ἐπιών is commonly used of time following, e.g. Hdt. 3.85 τῆς ἐπιούσης ἡμέρας, Ar. *Eccl.* 105 τὴν ἐπιοῦσαν ἡμέραν. τῇ (sc. ἕχεται) looks back to τετράς. The v.l. ἡ δέ is due to the influence of τριτάτη, and ἠδέ is probably an attempt to link the fourth and third days together, as the third and fourth at the beginning of the month (781, 806). The third is significant in the latter case, because it usually marks the first sighting of the new moon, but there is no such importance attached to the last sighting of the old moon.

811 ἀλωαί Epic form, as E 499 ἱερὰς κατ' ἀλωάς, Hes. *Op.* 599 εὐτροχάλῳ ἐν ἀλωῇ, in the primary sense of 'threshing-floor'. Attic ἅλως, with various pl. forms, e.g. Arist. *Mete.* 374a15 αἱ ἅλως, 344b3 αἱ ἅλῳ, *D.S.* 31 αἱ ἅλωνες, Ach. 32 ἅλωες. Since this is his first mention of haloes, A. deals with the subject at some length, and what he has to say applies to all haloes, so that he is then brief in reference to haloes round the sun (877–9) and stars (941). Aristotle discusses haloes in *Mete.* Γ 3, explaining them on the basis of his optical theory (cf. 541), that our vision is reflected from smooth surfaces (373a35). In this case the reflection occurs 'when the air and vapour are condensed into cloud, if the condensation is uniform and its constituent particles small' (372b16, Lee's translation). Aristotle discusses haloes as weather signs (372b18–34), with the general introduction διὸ καὶ σημεῖον ἡ μὲν σύστασις ὕδατός ἐστιν, αἱ μέντοι διασπάσεις ἢ μαράνσεις, αὖται μὲν εὐδιῶν, αἱ δὲ διασπάσεις πνεύματος, and particular observations to follow. See Gilbert 600–4. The scholia give several versions of Aristotle's explanation, the most detailed being sch. (MAS, MA) ἡ τοίνυν ὄψις κατὰ τὴν ἔνστασιν τοῦ ἀέρος τραχέσι μὲν προσπεσοῦσα αὐτοῦ που καταπαύεται, μηκέτι λαμβάνουσα ἑτέρας φορᾶς ἀρχήν, λείοις δὲ καὶ ὁμαλοῖς προσφερομένη, οἷά ἐστι τὰ ἔσοπτρα καὶ τὰ ὕδατα, ἤτοι ἐνδοτέρω διαδύεται οἱονεὶ ἐγκατακλωμένη, ἤ, εἴπερ τοῦτο ἀδυνατεῖ ποιεῖν δι' ἀντιτυπίαν τῶν σωμάτων, ἀνακλᾶται ἐμφανίζουσα κατ' ἐκεῖνον τὸν τόπον τὰ ὁρώμενα ἀφ' οὗ καὶ τὴν ἀρχὴν τῆς ἀνακλάσεως ποιεῖται. The modern explanation is that haloes are caused by refraction of light passing through ice crystals in high clouds; see Greenler 24–6 and plates 2-1, 2-2.

κυκλώσωνται Subj. after εἴ κε, as in 788–9, 794. On the circular form of the halo see Arist. *Mete*. 373a3 πάντοθεν δὲ ὁμοίως ἀνακλωμένης ἀναγκαῖον κύκλον εἶναι ἢ κύκλου μέρος· ἀπὸ γὰρ τοῦ αὐτοῦ σημείου πρὸς τὸ αὐτὸ σημεῖον αἱ ἴσαι κλασθήσονται ἐπὶ κύκλου γραμμῆς ἀεί. Lee notes that Aristotle here assumes what he is setting out to prove. The verb is used of dancing in Call. *H*. 3.267 περὶ βωμὸν ἀπείπατο κυκλώσασθαι, with similar fifth-foot spondee.

812 ἢ τρεῖς ἠὲ δύω Neither Aristotle nor *D.S.* mentions multiple haloes, but *Gp*. 1.3.1 follows A. with ἐὰν δὲ περὶ πᾶσαν τὴν σελήνην ἅλωνες δύο ἢ τρεῖς ὦσι, μέγιστον χειμῶνα ἔσεσθαι δηλοῦσι, καὶ μάλιστα εἰ μελαινότεραι ὑπάρχουσι. Cf. Varro ap. Plin. *Nat*. 18.349 *si gemini orbes cinxerint, maiorem tempestatem, et magis, si tres erunt aut nigri, interrupti atque distracti*, Ptol. *Tetr*. 2.14.6 παρατηρητέον δὲ καὶ τὰς περὶ αὐτὴν γινομένας ἅλως. εἰ μὲν γὰρ μία εἴη καὶ αὐτὴ καθαρὰ καὶ ἠρέμα ὑπομαραινομένη, εὐδιεινὴν κατάστασιν σημαίνει, εἰ δὲ δύο ἢ καὶ τρεῖς εἶεν, χειμῶνας δηλοῦσιν, ὑπόκιρροι μὲν οὖσαι καὶ ὥσπερ ῥηγνύμεναι τοὺς διὰ σφοδρῶν ἀνέμων, ἀχλυώδεις δὲ καὶ παχεῖαι τοὺς διὰ νιφετῶν, ὕπωχροι δὲ ἢ μέλαιναι καὶ ῥηγνύμεναι τοὺς δι' ἀμφοτέρων, καὶ ὅσῳ ἂν πλείους ὦσι τοσούτῳ μείζονας, Anon. Laur. 6 = *Gp*. 1.3.1.

μί' οἴη A Homeric phrase, e.g. 1 207 ταμίη τε μί' οἴη, in same *sedes*. A. uses it again in 887, in a different position. Cf. also Σ 565.

813 τῇ μὲν ἰῇ Aeolic numeral ἴα = μία, but from a different stem, perhaps pronominal, and related to Latin *is*: see Schwyzer 1.588, Chantraine 1.259, Frisk 1.702, Palmer 60. Here it is a Homeric imitation, e.g. Π 173 τῆς μὲν ἰῆς στίχος, Ι 319 ἐν δὲ ἰῇ τιμῇ, both in same *sedes*, Λ 174 τῇ δέ τ' ἰῇ in mid-line.

ἀνέμοιο γαληναίης τε A. apparently follows Aristotle (*Mete*. 372b19, quoted on 811) in first introducing the two kinds of weather predicted and then giving the respective signs for each, although Aristotle gives the two signs first, and then specifies the weathers predicted. Also Aristotle's word-pattern is chiastic, whereas A. repeats the two weathers in the same order, even to the extent of placing ἀνέμοιο twice in exactly the same position. The effect of the rhyme is enhanced by the preceding μὲν ἰῇ and -μένη in 813 and 814. Hence the haplography in Π8. It is remarkable that the next two lines have a similar correspondence in δ' ἂν χειμῶνι and δ' ἂν χειμῶνα, and that these groups are followed by the similar sounds of περιτρ- and φέροι τρ- respectively, as Dr K. J. McKay has pointed out to me. The rhyming effect is perhaps an imitation of Hesiod's style: cf. *Op.* 379–80 ῥεῖα δέ κεν πλεόνεσσι ... πλείων μὲν πλεόνων, 751–2 παῖδα δυωδεκαταῖον ... μηδὲ δυωδεκάμηνον. Cf. A. J. Carney, *CPh.* 12 (1917) 235. For γαληναίη as subst. cf. 995, 1017, also Call. *E.* 5.5, A.R. 1.1156.

δοκεύειν 'Expect', c. gen. also 908, 1136; c. acc. 1128; c. ἐπί + acc. 1018.

814 ῥηγνυμένη ἀνέμοιο Arist. *Mete.* 372b26 ὅταν δὲ διασπασθῇ, πνεύματος σημεῖον· ἡ γὰρ διαίρεσις ὑπὸ πνεύματος γέγονεν ἤδη μὲν ὄντος, οὔπω δὲ παρόντος. σημεῖον δὲ τούτου διότι ἐντεῦθεν γίγνεται ὁ ἄνεμος, ὅθεν ἂν ἡ κυρία γίγνηται διάσπασις, *D.S.* 31 σημαίνουσι δὲ πνεῦμα ῥαγεῖσαι περὶ ἄμφω, καὶ ᾗ ἂν ῥαγῇ ταύτῃ πνεῦμα, Pap. Wessely fr. ii, col. i, 4–10 προσδεχου [ε]αν δυο γενομεναι ραγωσιν [χ]ειμωνα [εα]ν δε τρεις ετι μειζω [οσ]ωι δ αν θαττον ραγηι [τ]οσου-τωι θαττον χειμων [εσ]ται.

μαραινομένη δὲ γαλήνης Arist. *Mete.* 372b30 ἀπομαραινομένη δὲ εὐδίας· εἰ γὰρ μὴ ἔχει πως οὕτως ὁ ἀὴρ ὥστε κρατεῖν τοῦ ἐναπολαμβα-νομένου θερμοῦ μηδ' ἔρχεσθαι εἰς πύκνωσιν ὑδατώδη, δῆλον ὡς οὔπω ἡ ἀτμὶς ἀποκέκριται τῆς ἀναθυμιάσεως τῆς ξηρᾶς καὶ πυρώδους· τοῦτο δὲ εὐδίας αἴτιον, *D.S.* 51 ἅλως δὲ ἐὰν ὁμαλῶς παγῇ καὶ μαρα-νθῇ, εὐδίαν σημαίνει. The verb is used particularly of fire or light dying away, e.g. Ι 212 φλὸξ ἐμαράνθη, *h.Hom.* 4.140 ἀνθρακιὴν δ' ἐμάρανε. So A. of sunlight (862), lamplight (1034), and more unusually of a storm (1000).

815 ταὶ δύο Referring back to δύω in 812, and marking a contrast with τῇ μὲν ἰῇ in 813. The use of the article with contrasting numerals is Homeric, e.g. Ε 271–2 τοὺς μὲν τέσσαρας ... τὼ δὲ δύ'; see Monro *HG* 228. A. has the Homeric form of the article also in τάων (561, 722, 782).

περιτροχάοιντο Med. only here, act. in Call. *H.* 4.28 πολέες σε περιτροχόωσιν ἀοιδαί. The adj. occurs once in Homer, of a circular device, Ψ 455 περίτροχον ἠΰτε μήνη.

816 τριέλικτος An ingenious use of an adj. previously applied to a snake's coils in the oracle in Hdt. 6.77.2 δεινὸς ὄφις τριέλικτος. Cf.

Nonn. *D.* 13.372 τριέλικτον ἔχων ἴνδαλμα κεραίης, 38.175 τριέλικτον ἱμάσθλην. Here the sign of terrible weather is perhaps intended to suggest the portent in the oracle.

817 μᾶλλον I.e. it will bring an even greater storm.

μελανεῦσα Cf. 877, 878. In this storm context A. may be recalling Η 64 μελάνει δέ τε πόντος, where the verb is μελάνω, only there in Homer. This form of the part. is Ionic, as in ζ 157 εἰσοιχνεῦσαν, Hes. *Th.* 11 ὑμνεῦσαι, Thgn. 737 νοεῦντες, Call. *E.* 52.1 μελανεῦντα. The Homeric passage is also recalled in A.R. 4.1574, with the Ionic form, βένθος ἀκίνητον μελανεῖ. A. also has μελανεῖ in 836.

ῥηγνύατο Pres. opt. med., with the original suffix diphthong υι reduced to ῡ. There are a few other instances of this development, e.g. in -νυμι verbs the Homeric pl. δαινύατ' (σ 248), which may have been A.'s model here, the corresponding sg. δαινῦτο (ω 665), and Attic πηγνῦτο (Pl. *Phd.* 188a). See Chantraine 1.51, Palmer 215, 309.

The pl. ending -ατο (from -ντο), however, is not in accord with the sg. subject. Buttmann suggested that τριέλικτος ἁλωή may be thought of as equivalent to τρεῖς ἁλωαί, and Mair implies the same in translating 'if the rings are broken'. Voss had recourse to emendation, and his ἔτι is certainly appropriate; cf. sch. (ΜΚΑ) εἰ δὲ δύο, χειμῶνα προσδόκα, καὶ ἔτι μείζονα ἐὰν τρεῖς. But the textual tradition is unanimous, and the emendation is clumsy and spoils the smoothness of the chiasmus. The most satisfactory solution is to understand the verb as sg., esp. as it comes so closely after μελανεῦσα. This is clearly implied by sch. καὶ εἰ μειζόνως ἀπολύεται. So A. Meineke, *Analecta Alexandrina* (1843) 158, also Martin and Chantraine 1.51. Schwyzer 1.671, n. 2, explains: 'Das lebendige Gefühl für -αται, -ατο war so sehr verlorengegangen, dass die Alexandriner (Zenodot, Kallimachos) solche Formen als Singuläre nehmen.' Cf. K–B 2.78. The confusion of the Homeric -αται and -ατο plurals with the common singular endings is illustrated by Zenodotus' reading ἐπιστέαται in Π 243; cf. *h.Hom.* 3.20 νόμος βεβλήαται, Call. fr. 87 Δειπνιὰς ἔνθεν μιν δειδέχαται, 497 κούρη δὲ παρείατο, Euphor. fr. 160 Powell = 158 Van Gron. φλεγεθοίατο. It is hard to say whether A.R. 4.481 κείαται ὀστέα is intended to be sg. or pl. Among later authors cf. Luc. *Syr. D.* 20 κειμήλιον ... ἀπεκέατο, 27 ἀνακέαται ... ἡ αἰτίη. Ronconi 200–1 lists ῥηγνύατο here as an erroneous formation for 3rd pers. sg.

818 ἐπὶ μηνί For ἐπί expressing purpose cf. σ 44–5 γαστέρες ..., τὰς ἐπὶ δόρπῳ | κατθέμεθα.

σεληναίης Ionic form, as in Emped. 43, in same *sedes*, σεληναίης κύκλον εὐρύν. Cf. Praxill. *PMG* 747.2 σεληναίης τε πρόσωπον, Ar. *Nub.* 614 φῶς Σεληναίης καλόν, where Dover sees it as a grandiloquent name,

COMMENTARY: 819–820

Pl. *Cra.* 409b Σελαναίαν δέ γε καλοῦσιν, Theoc. 2.165 χαῖρε, Σελαναία, A.R. 1.500, a very Aratean line, ἄστρα, σεληναίης τε καὶ ἠελίοιο κέλευθοι (also 1.1232, 4.167, 264), Call. *E.* 5.2, Herod. 3.61, Aesop. *AP* 10.123.4 = *FGE* 435, Opp. *C.* 1.113, Luc. *Astr.* 3.

819–891 Signs from the sun
The arrangement of material here is not so clear-cut as in the preceding section, but, on the basis of A.'s use of σκέπτεο to introduce a new topic, a triple division is plausible, with the first and third parts balancing each other in length and enclosing a much longer and more varied catalogue, which is mainly concerned with warnings of impending rain. In *D.S.* these signs appear separately grouped under different weathers, whereas Virgil, Pliny and Ptolemy follow A. in allocating a special section to sun signs (*G.* 1.438–68, *Nat.* 18.342–6, *Tetr.* 2.14.1–3); in *Gp.* 1.2–3 they are listed briefly, but very fully in Anon. Laur. 1–3.

819–831 The sun is significant at rising and setting, when a clear disc portends good weather, a marked disc rain or wind.

819 ἠελίοιο The key word opens the new section. A. does not often use this technique, which belongs more to a prose treatise than to a poem; see note on 665.

μελέτω Cf. η 208 Ἀλκίνο᾽, ἄλλο τί τοι μελέτω, and also in same *sedes* ω 152, β 304, δ 415. The impers. use c. gen. is post-Homeric.

ἑκάτερθεν Cf. 536 of circles and 566 of constellations on the two horizons.

820 μᾶλλον ἐοικότα Cf. 168. *D.S.* 5 compares both sun and moon with all other weather signs: μάλιστα δὲ κυριώτατα τὰ ἀπὸ τοῦ ἡλίου καὶ τῆς σελήνης. Virgil gives pre-eminence to the sun in the climax to his weather-signs, but otherwise follows the sense and pattern of 819–21 very closely in *G.* 1.438–40 *sol quoque et exoriens et cum se condet in undas | signa dabit; solem certissima signa sequentur, | et quae mane refert et quae surgentibus astris.* A., however, is merely comparing the sun with the moon in reliability. Sch. attempt an explanation: διὰ τί τὰ τοῦ ἡλίου σημεῖα βεβαιότερά φησι τῆς σελήνης; ἐπειδὴ πολλὴν ἔχων ἰσχὺν πρὸς τὸ διαλύειν ταῖς ἀκτῖσι τὰ ὑποπίπτοντα παχέα, νικώμενος ὑπ᾽ αὐτῶν μείζονα τὸν χειμῶνα προαπαγγέλλει. Cf. Plu. fr. 13 Sandbach: αἱ τοῦ ἡλίου πρὸς τὸν ἀέρα διαφοραὶ κυριώτεραι τῶν τῆς σελήνης εἰσί· δυναστεύων γὰρ ἡμέρας σαφέστερα δείκνυσι τὰ τεκμήρια. δεύτερον δὲ ὅτι λαμπρότερός ἐστι, καὶ εἰ μὴ μεγάλη καὶ ἰσχυρὰ τοῦ ἀέρος εἴη μεταβολή, οὐκ ἂν κρατηθείη· τὰς γὰρ μικρὰς καὶ ἐλαφρὰς ἀναστέλλει καὶ σκεδάννυσιν. On the fragments of Plutarch that appear in the sch. Sandbach comments: 'Plutarch's concern seems to have been to find in each case a single natural cause that would account both for the

459

weather-sign and for the weather it was supposed to foretell. He was thus in the tradition of, but not necessarily dependent on, the Stoic Boethus.'

821 δύνοντι ... ἀνιόντι A variation of 617 with different case and περάτης for ἑτέρης: cf. 571. The rhyme emphasises not only the antithesis but also the choice of sunrise and sunset as the two significant times for observing weather signs. Cf. Ptol. *Tetr.* 2.14.1 τὸν μὲν οὖν ἥλιον τηρητέον πρὸς μὲν τὰς ἡμερησίους καταστάσεις ἀνατέλλοντα, πρὸς δὲ τὰς νυκτερινὰς δύνοντα. These times are repeatedly mentioned throughout this section of the poem.

περάτης Cf. 499, 670, and A.R. 1.1281 of dawn ἐκ περάτης ἀνιοῦσα, which may be a conscious imitation of this line. Q.S. 8.2, 28 varies with ἐκ περάτων.

822 μή οἱ ποικίλλοιτο Variation to a negative form of expression; cf. 287, 845–7, 866–8, 983–4. ποικίλλειν usually suggests attractive colours and artistic workmanship, e.g. Σ 590 ἐν δὲ χορὸν ποίκιλλε, but here the colours are blemishes on the otherwise bright orb of the sun. Cf. 328 ποικίλος of the bright and dim areas of a constellation, Ptol. *Tetr.* 2.14.2 ποικίλον δὲ τὸν κύκλον ἔχων, of the sun, *CCAG* 8.1.138, 32 ἥλιος ποικίλος ἀπὸ ἀνατολῶν χειμέριος. Virgil imitates positively in *G.* 1.441 *ubi nascentem maculis uariauerit ortum.*

νέον βάλλοντος ἀρούρας An echo of τ 433 νέον προσέβαλλεν ἀρούρας. Cf. ε 479 ἥλιος φαέθων ἀκτῖσιν ἔβαλλεν (θάμνους), E. *Supp.* 650–1 ἀκτὶς ἡλίου ... ἔβαλλε γαῖαν, *Phaeth.* 3 and Diggle's note, A.R. 4.885 ἄκρον ἔβαλλε φαεσφόρος οὐρανὸν ἠώς, and a verbal imitation in 1.737 νέον βάλλοντο δομαίους.

823 κύκλος Cf. 796 of the moon's disc.

κεχρημένος C. gen. of being in need; cf. 4, 846, 857, and Homeric instances in same *sedes*, Τ 262, α 13, ξ 155, υ 378, χ 50.

824 σῆμα Here purely a dark mark, amplifying ποικίλλοιτο (822) and contrasting with λιτός. Cf. Ψ 455 λευκὸν σῆμα, a white mark on a horse's forehead without any other significance apart from making the horse thereby recognisable. The choice of word is a little ambiguous in this context of multiple σήματα foretelling weather, but it corresponds to σημεῖον in *D.S.* 50 ἥλιος μὲν ἀνιὼν λαμπρὸς καὶ μὴ καυματίας καὶ μὴ ἔχων σημεῖον μηδὲν ἐν ἑαυτῷ εὐδίαν σημαίνει. The awkwardness of σῆμα together with the unusual λιτός for λαμπρός, and its position following instead of preceding, suggests a variation technique characteristic of A. when he is following a source passage. For A.'s technique see 91, 147–8, etc.

λιτός Properly 'simple and inexpensive', but used by Aristotle of the plain style in *Rhet.* 1416b25 ποικίλος καὶ οὐ λιτός, and A. may be consciously recalling Aristotle in choosing this word to point the contrast to ποικίλοιτο. The adj. λιτός will also suggest the contemporary cult of the pure and unembellished style (cf. λεπτή and καθαρή in 783), since Callimachus uses it several times, presumably with such overtones, e.g. *H.* 2.10 ὃς οὐκ ἴδε, λιτὸς ἐκεῖνος, 5.25–6 λιτὰ βαλοῖσα | χρίματα, frr. 110.77–8 πολλὰ πέπωκα | λιτά, 100.4 λιτὸν ἔθηκεν ἕδος. Virgil echoes with *lucidus orbis erit* (*G.* 1.459), Pliny has *purus oriens atque non feruens serenum diem nuntiat* (*Nat.* 18.342); cf. Ptol. *Tetr.* 2.14.2 καθαρὸς μὲν γὰρ καὶ ἀνεπισκότητος καὶ εὐσταθὴς καὶ ἀνέφελος ἀνατέλλων ἢ δύνων εὐδιεινῆς καταστάσεώς ἐστι δηλωτικός, *Gp.* 1.2.2 (=Anon. Laur. 3.1) καὶ ὁ ἥλιος καθαρὸς ἀνατέλλων εὐδίαν σημαίνει.

ἀπάντη Cf. 22, 539, 1049.

825 αὔτως 'Similarly', as in 869, 1060.

ἔχει The textual tradition is divided between ἔχει and ἔχοι, but in the next line solidly attests δύνει. It is reasonable to assume that both verbs should have the same mood, since there is no obvious difference of tone intended between the two. This seems to be A.'s regular practice wherever there are two or more verbs depending on a single εἰ, though the presence of variants in the MSS makes it impossible to be dogmatic. Here the indicative is the better attested form, and more likely to have been corrupted in view of the optative in the apodosis: the addition of οι over ει in C and K may be seen as illustrating the 'correction' taking place. The change of mood from protasis to apodosis provides a useful variation, and in any case makes good sense, because the sign observed is a fact, whereas the inference from it is a future possibility; cf. 792–3.

βουλύσιος Only here and 1119. The adj. is formed from the noun βούλυσις (attested only in Cic. *Att.* 15.27.3), but it has the ῡ of Homeric βουλυτόνδε (Π 779, ι 58) and of βουλυτός (sc. καιρός) in Ar. *Av.* 1500 and A.R. 3. 1342. The unyoking of the oxen is associated with sunset, as here, and also with respite from the day's labour and the prospect of dinner: hence Cicero's quip αὐτῇ βουλύσει *cenantibus nobis*.

826 δύνει For the mood see note on ἔχει (825). The causal sense is very rare, and occurs only here in A. Cf. Ar. *Ran.* 49 καὶ κατεδύσαμέν γε ναῦς, Call. *E.* 2.3 ἥλιον λέσχῃ κατεδύσαμεν. *D.S.* 50 restricts the application of this sign: καὶ δυόμενος ἥλιος χειμῶνος [in winter] εἰς καθαρὸν εὐδιεινός ... καὶ ἐὰν χειμάζοντος [in stormy weather] ἡ δύσις γένηται εἰς καθαρόν, εὐδιεινόν. Virgil imitates with maximum variation: *at si, cum referetque diem condetque relatum,* | *lucidus orbis erit, frustra terrebere nimbis* (*G.* 1.458–9), Pliny more briefly *si et occidit pridie serenus, tanto certior fides serenitatis* (18.342), Anon. Laur. 3.4 δυόμενος δὲ δίχα νεφῶν καθαρὸς καὶ εἰς τὴν ἐπιοῦσαν ἡμέραν εὐδίαν προκαταγγέλλει, *CCAG* 8.1.138, 32 καθαρὸς εἰσδύς, εὔδιος καὶ τὴν ἐξῆς. Cf. Arist. *Pr.* 941a1 διὰ τί αἱ μὲν

461

καθαραὶ δύσεις εὐδιεινὸν σημεῖον, αἱ δὲ τεταραγμέναι χειμερινόν; ἢ ὅτι χειμὼν γίνεται συνισταμένου καὶ πυκνουμένου τοῦ ἀέρος; ὅταν μὲν οὖν κρατῇ ὁ ἥλιος, διακρίνει καὶ αἰθράζει αὐτόν, ὅταν δὲ κρατῆται, ἐπινεφῆ ποιεῖ.

ἀνέφελος Cf. 415, 858.

μαλακήν Rarely of light (LSJ give no instance); comparable, however, among things not susceptible to touch, are 1010 μαλακῆς ... γαλήνης, and Theophr. *HP* 6.7.4 ὀσμῇ μαλακωτέρᾳ.

ὑποδείελος See note on 118. Voss, who at 118 had proposed ἐπιδείελος (presumably on the strength of Hes. *Op.* 810, 821 ἐπὶ δείελα), here prefers a tmesis. But in Homeric tmesis the preposition only rarely follows the verb, and, when it does, comes immediately after it, e.g. ι 17 φυγὼν ὕπο. A.R. 1.1160 has ὑπὸ δείελον in the same *sedes*. The force of the preposition and prefix is 'at' or 'about'. For this use of the temporal adj. cf. 302 ἑσπέριος, [Theoc.] 25.223 προδείελος.

827 καί Apodotic, as in λ 110–11 τὰς εἰ μέν κ' ἀσινέας ἐάᾳς νόστου τε μέδηαι, | καί κεν ἔτ' εἰς Ἰθάκην κακά περ πάσχοντες ἵκοισθε. Cf. 133 in a temporal clause.

ὑπεύδιος Again in 990, 1035, and, with ῑ, 1012. Voss objects that the sun cannot be said to be 'besonnt', and therefore reads εἴης (cf. 990), but the point is that the sun will rise in a cloudless sky. A.R. uses this adj. of places (1.584, 3.1202).

828 κοῖλος I.e. with dark centre, as if there were a hole in it. Cf. *D.S.* 26 καὶ ἐὰν κοῖλος φαίνηται ὁ ἥλιος, ἀνέμου ἢ ὕδατος τὸ σημεῖον, Ptol. *Tetr.* 2.14.2 ὡς ἐφ' ἑαυτὸν κοιλούμενος, V. *G.* 1.442 *conditus in nubem medioque refugerit orbe*.

ἐειδόμενος Cf. 395, also A.R. 3.968, 4.221, Nic. *Ther.* 149, 272, 273, Mosch. 2.158. On the optical illusion sch. κατά τινας καιροὺς ὁ ἥλιος ὁρᾶται κοῖλος. τούτου δὲ αἴτιον τὰ ἔμπροσθεν αὐτοῦ ἱστάμενα νέφη, μελαινόμενα διὰ τὴν πολλὴν πύκνωσιν. πέφυκε δὲ πάντα τὰ διὰ τῶν μελάνων ὁρώμενα κοιλότητος φαντασίαν παρέχειν. οὕτω γὰρ καὶ οἱ ζωγράφοι, ὅσα μὲν βούλονται προσεχῆ δεικνύναι, τῷ λευκῷ ἀπογράφονται, ὅσα δὲ κοῖλα καὶ ἐν βάθει, τῷ μέλανι. Cf. Plu. fr. 14 Sandbach.

περιτέλλῃ The subjunctive without ἄν or κεν is appropriate, as in Homer, for what may occur repeatedly or at any time, e.g. Α 163–4 ὁππότ' Ἀχαιοὶ | Τρώων ἐκπέρσωσ' εὖ ναιόμενον πτολίεθρον. See Monro *HG* 263–4, Chantraine 2.256. Throughout the catalogue of weather signs, in such ὅτε and ὁπ(π)ότε clauses, the MSS are frequently divided between subjunctive (M) and indicative (S) where the two forms are metrically equivalent, as here; cf. 830 (φαείν-), 863, 867, 870, 912, 993, 1020, 1034, 1040, 1070, 1115, 1116. But both M and S have the subj. in 830 (βάλλωσι), 884, 923, 926, 1065, 1107, 1108, 1112, 1118, and indic. in

870, 916, 927. Elsewhere only subjunctives are used: 795, 845–6, 848–9, 864, 914, 933, 984, 986, 992, 1018, 1042–3, 1110, 1124. There is therefore good reason to follow Voss with the subj. in all instances; see also notes on 870, 916, 927, 1141.

Since this verb denotes the circular movement of heavenly bodies, not just the rising (see note on 739), the reference here is presumably to either sunrise or sunset, the observation of signs being restricted to those two occasions.

829 αἱ μὲν νότον αἱ δὲ βορῆα D.S. 26 ἐὰν αἱ ἀκτῖνες αἱ μὲν πρὸς βορρᾶν αἱ δὲ πρὸς νότον σχίζωνται τούτου μέσου ὄντος κατ' ὄρθρον, κοινὸν ὕδατος καὶ ἀνέμου σημεῖόν ἐστιν, Plin. Nat. 18.343 si in exortu spargentur partim ad austrum partim ad aquilonem, pura circum eum serenitas sit licet, pluuiam tamen uentosque significabunt, Anon. Laur. 2.6 ἐὰν ἀνίσχοντος τοῦ ἡλίου ἀκτῖνες πρὸς βορὰν [sic] ἢ πρὸς νότον ἀποτείνωσι, τὰ δὲ περὶ τὸν ἥλιον καθαρὰ ᾖ, ὕδωρ καὶ ἄνεμον προσδέχεσθαι χρή. Cf. Nonn. D. 38.368, of the Fishes, ὁ μὲν νότον, ὃς δὲ βορῆα. The description of rays diverging only southwards and northwards suggests that there are clouds above the sun obscuring the light in that direction, and Virgil, always keenly observant of natural phenomena, has added this detail in his imitation, ubi sub lucem densa inter nubila sese | diuersi rumpent radii (G. 1.445–6). Cf. Plu. fr. 15 Sandbach ὥσπερ ὅταν βλέφαρον καταγαγόντες ἢ περιθλίψαντες τῷ λύχνῳ τὴν ὄψιν προσβάλλωμεν, οὐ φαίνεται συνεχὲς τὸ φῶς ἀλλὰ πλάγιαι καὶ σποράδες αἱ αὐγαί· οὕτως ὅταν ἀχλὺς ἢ νέφωσις ἀνώμαλος πρὸ τοῦ ἡλίου στᾶσα περιθλίψῃ καὶ σείσῃ τὸν τῆς ὄψεως κῶνον εἰς λεπτὰς ἀκτῖνας καὶ ῥαβδοειδεῖς, ὃ πάσχομεν αὐτοὶ τῇ αἰσθήσει, τοῦτο περὶ τὸν ἥλιον εἶναι δοκοῦμεν.

830 σχιζόμεναι βάλλωσι This typical variation of the source of D.S. 26 σχίζονται suggests that A. is the imitator here. Ptol. Tetr. 2.14.2 ἀκτῖνας ἐρυθρὰς ἀποπέμπων. The apparent divergence of rays could equally well be regarded as a convergence, and may be explained as parallel lines which appear to converge at a distance.

πέρι The tmesis of MSS and edd. does not give satisfactory sense ('shines all around'?), and most translators ignore the περί, e.g. Mair 'is bright', Martin 'rayonne', Erren 'erstrahlt'. The adv., with anastrophe, brings out the contrast (also marked by αὖ) between the very bright centre and the fainter rays. It is common in Homer, e.g. β 88 πέρι κέρδεα οἶδεν, θ 63 τὸν πέρι Μοῦσ' ἐφίλησε.

φαείνη For the mood see note on 828 περιτέλλη.

831 ὑετοῖο ... ἀνέμοιο For internal rhymes see note on 360. Here the rhyme concludes a short section, as in 435.

διέρχεται C. gen., as in Υ 100 χροὸς ἀνδρομέοιο διελθέμεν, 263 διελεύσεσθαι μεγαλήτορος Αἰνείαο. The weather the sun is now passing through is thought likely to reach the observer later. παρέρχεται does not give a suitable sense, and cannot be used c. gen.

832–879 The middle section contains miscellaneous signs, most of rain, which seems to be the unifying feature in these lines, but some also of wind and fine weather. The arrangement of the material avoids the logical pattern of a prose work, and so has a rambling character that suggests perhaps an oral tradition of popular lore. At the same time the signs are set out in groups, within which the details bear some association with each other: red and dark markings (832–9), rays concentrated or overclouded (840–4), light mist at sunrise, thick mist later thinning, pale winter sunset (845–51), after rain cloudy sunset, red sunset, rays suddenly dimming (851–65), red sunrise, pale sunrise (866–76), haloes (877–9).

832 σκέπτεο See note on 778.

αὐγαί Pl. as in Homer, e.g. λ 498 ὑπ' αὐγὰς ἠελίοιο, and subsequent poets, e.g. Parm. fr. 15 αἰεὶ παπταίνουσα πρὸς αὐγὰς ἠελίοιο.

ὑπείκωσ' For the mood see note on 788. A. is thinking primarily of the danger of being blinded by looking directly at the sun, but the personal character of the verb suggests overtones of sun-god myths, e.g. the blinding of Phineus (A.R. 2.184, [Opp.] C. 2.617ff.). For the meaning 'allow' cf. S. OC 1184 (following 1182 ἔασον) καὶ νῷν ὕπεικε τὸν κασίγνητον μολεῖν.

833 αὐτόν The actual disc of the sun as opposed to the adjacent sky and clouds.

σκοπιαὶ καὶ ἄρισται The whole manuscript tradition supports σκοπιαί, which is a Homeric word, mostly denoting look-out positions (e.g. ξ 261) or peaks (Θ 557), but also used to describe the act of watching in θ 302 Ἥλιος γάρ οἱ σκοπιὴν ἔχεν. A. may well have had this passage in mind and wittily reversed the role of the sun here. Buttmann's tentative conjecture (adopted by Maass, Martin and Erren) would spoil this effect, and is in any case needless. The emphatic καί is common in A. (cf. 782, 827), and has more point than the colourless εἰσιν.

834 εἴ τί που ἤ οἱ The significant variables in the tradition here are που, οἱ, καί, and since there is not room for all three, we have to determine which should be retained and in what position. που is attested by all MSS, occurs frequently in reference to weather signs (15 times from 758 to the end, elsewhere 6 times), and is balanced by εἴ που in 836. As an enclitic particle it tends to gravitate to an early position, since it brings an element of uncertainty to the whole sentence rather than to any particular word: cf. 836, 1146, Υ 453, υ 207, and Denniston 493. It should therefore be retained near the beginning of the clause. οἱ provides ἐπιτρέχει with an object, which, if not expressed, would have to be understood: cf. 316 c. dat. It is therefore appropriate, and, if retained, must be placed close to ἐπιτρέχει, since it goes with this verb, but not (in view of the change of subject) with μελανεῖ. καί is least well attested and makes no obvious point: it can therefore be discarded.

ἔρευθος Virgil, with much variation, *nam saepe uidemus | ipsius in uultu uarios errare colores* (*G.* 1.451–2). *Gp.* 1.3.2 καὶ ὁ ἥλιος δὲ ἐρυθρὸς ἀνατέλλων καὶ μελαινόμενος ὄμβρους δηλοῖ. Cf. the same signs in respect of the moon (803–4). The noun ἔρευθος is rare before A., and attested only in prose (Hp. *Epid.* 1.26.ε). This passage is cleverly recalled in A.R. 1.725–6, of Jason's cloak, τῆς μὲν ῥηίτερόν κεν ἐς ἠέλιον ἀνιόντα | ὄσσε βάλοις ἢ κεῖνο μεταβλέψειας ἔρευθος (see also on 186). Call. *H.* 5.27 also recalls A. with a subtle rephrasing, τὸ δ' ἔρευθος ἀνέδραμε.

οἷά τε πολλά Cf. λ 536, similarly with enjambment, also ε 422, θ 160 in mid-line.

835 ἑλκομένων This participle, in other cases, begins a line in Ε 665, Χ 65, 464, Ψ 715. A. uses the verb elsewhere of the natural movement of stars (see note on 20).

ἐρυθαίνεται Cf. Κ 484 ἐρυθαίνετο δ' αἵματι γαῖα, Φ 21 ὕδωρ.

ἄλλοθεν ἄλλα Cf. 411, 738 in different metrical positions.

836 μελανεῖ Cf. part. in 817, 877, 878. The v.l. appears in texts of Η 64 μελάνει δέ τε πόντος ὑπ' αὐτῆς, which A. seems to be recalling. Buttmann would read μελανεῖ there too, pointing out that, since the verb is formed from μέλας, -ανος, it should be μελανέω or μελαίνω. See Palmer 264. Cf. A.R. 4.1574 βένθος ἀκίνητον μελανεῖ.

τοι Pron. dat., as frequently in A., e.g. (also after καί) 157, 224.

τὰ μέν Referring back to the dark patch; cf. 244. A. reverses the order of the signs to give a chiastic structure to these four lines. Virgil more concisely *caeruleus pluuiam denuntiat, igneus Euros* (*G.* 1.453). *D.S.* 11 gives only the dark marks: καὶ ἐὰν ἀνίσχων μέλαν σημεῖον ἴσχῃ, ... ὑδατικόν. *CCAG* 8.1.138, 34 μελαινονεφὴς καὶ ἐρυθρὸς φαινόμενος ἢ γινόμενος, ὑετώδης. Cf. also *D.S.* 27 ἔστι δὲ σημεῖα ἐν ἡλίῳ καὶ σελήνῃ, τὰ μὲν μέλανα ὕδατος τὰ δ' ἐρυθρὰ πνεύματος.

837 τὰ δ' ἐρευθέα πάντ' ἀνέμοιο Pliny transfers these signs from the sun's disc to the adjacent clouds: *idem uentos cum ante exorientem eum nubes rubescunt; quod si et nigrae rubentibus interuenerint, et pluuias* (*Nat.* 18.342). Editors up to Voss read the adj. ἐρευθέα, editors since Bekker the noun ἐρεύθεα. The latter is seen as taking up ἔρευθος (834); but τι there means 'any degree of', not 'any variety of' redness, and 'rednesses' here seems strange, unless it is taken to mean redness whenever it is observed. The sense required by the context is 'red marks', and this is better served by the adj., as in *D.S.* 27 τὰ δ' ἐρυθρὰ πνεύματος, and sch. τὰ δ' ἐρυθρὰ ἀνέμου. A. never uses ἐρυθρός, but always ἐρευθής (cf. 784, 860, 867).

For τά with n.pl. adj. denoting a part of a constellation or of the sun cf. 684 τὰ δὲ νείατα πάντα, 708 τὰ δ᾽ ἀριστερά, 830 τὰ δ᾽ ... μέσσα. For the association of redness with wind cf. the lunar signs in 784 and 803. πάντα refers to all occurrences.

838 ἀμφοτέροις Sch. εἰ δέ, φησίν, ἀμφοτέροις τοῖς καταστήμασι, τῷ τε μέλανι καὶ τῷ πυρρῷ, ἅμα καὶ κατὰ τὸ αὐτὸ ἐμπεριέχεται ὁ ἥλιος. The gen. in S is a corruption to suit the v.l. κεχρημένος, as in 823, etc.

ἄμυδις Here of two concurrent phenomena, as in μ 415 Ζεὺς δ᾽ ἄμυδις βρόντησε καὶ ἔμβαλε νηΐ κεραυνόν. The meaning is similar in 1153, but slightly different in 581 and 1150.

κεχρωσμένος Primarily 'touched', hence 'tinged' with colour; cf. Arist. *Mete.* 375a6, of the rainbow, ἀνάγκη τρίχρων τε εἶναι αὐτὴν καὶ τούτοις τοῖς χρώμασι κεχρῶσθαι μόνοις. Since the noun χρῶμα has a particular association with complexion, the verb here seems well suited to markings on the face of the sun. κεχρημένος is a more familiar participle (288, 823, 846, 857), but does not give a suitable sense here (with either gen. or dat.). Mair translates 'draped', following sch. ἐμπεριέχεται, an unlikely extension of the verb's meaning.

839 καί κεν ὕδωρ φορέοι Cf. Z 457 καί κεν ὕδωρ φορέοις.

ὑπηνέμιος τανύοιτο The required sense is that the weather will be windy as well as rainy. The adj. is applied to the sun as πνευματίη (785) to the moon; cf. εὔδιος (850), ὑπεύδιος (827), χειμέριαι (879). The prefix denotes attendant circumstances, as the preposition in δ 402 πνοιῇ ὕπο Ζεφύροιο: cf. ὑπεύδιος. The verb is rarely used to express length of time, but cf. 557 with its hint of λ 19. Here the sense is that the sun will continue on its course under windy conditions. Mair's 'will strain beneath the wind' is a very forced interpretation of the words.

840 οἱ See note on 47; here the pron. is grammatically detached from the gen. abs.

δυομένοιο The phrase echoes α 24 οἱ μὲν δυσομένου Ὑπερίονος, οἱ δ᾽ ἀνιόντος, where δυσομένου is a thematic aorist, but was regarded by the ancients as an imperfect, and is used by Homer as a present participle. Voss reads δυσομένοιο here, but A. is not so slavish an imitator; cf. 724, 853, 880. With this verb A. has the υ long in 309, 627, 722, 853, 880, and short in 553, 584, 656, 688, 690. Cf. A.R. 1.924–5 ἡελίοιο | δυομένου, 3.225–6 δυομένῃσιν | θέρμετο Πληιάδεσσιν, Call. *E.* 18.6 Ἐρίφων ... δυομένων, 20.1–2 ἡελίου δὲ | δυομένου. See O. Schneider 1.418.

841 συνίωσι Cf. Pl. *Ti.* 49c, of air condensing, συνιόντα καὶ πυκνούμενον, Arist *Mete.* 342a19, of an exhalation, διὰ τὸ συνιέναι, 364b33 συνιόντων τῶν νεφῶν. Presumably the rays appear concentrated because the sun is seen through a gap in heavy clouds. *Gp.* 1.2.4 makes this a sign of good weather: καὶ ἀνατέλλοντι δὲ καὶ δυομένῳ εἰ συστελλόμεναι φαίνονται ἀκτῖνες καὶ νέφη πεπιεσμένα περὶ αὐτόν, εὐδίαν δηλοῖ. *CCAG* 8.1.138, 33 ἐπισπώμενος εἰς ἑαυτὸν τὰς ἀκτῖνας, χειμέριος.

πεπλήθωσιν The phenomenon gives the impression that all the sun's rays are fully packed into one small space. This unusual meaning may be an extension of πεπληθυῖα (774) of the full moon. Cf. Theoc. 22.38, of a spring, ὕδατι πεπληθυῖαν, Pherecr. fr. 29K πρὶν ἀγορὰν πεπληθέναι.

842 ἤ ποτε The triple ἤ in 842-3 is confusing, since the first connects the two conditional clauses, whereas the second and third connect the two time phrases. Voss's εἴ (supported by C), however, lacks the necessary conjunction, and it is better to retain ἤ (= ἤ εἰ) and ascribe the awkwardness to A.'s style; cf. 832-6, where the first εἰ introduces a conditional clause, the second and third indirect questions.

νεφέων Instrumental use of the gen. (cf. 413, 564), a variation on the dat. with the same participle in 416. Cf. *CCAG* 8.1.138, 35 ὑπὸ νεφῶν πεπιεσμένος.

ὅ γ' The change of subject from the rays to the sun itself requires the pronoun here. The corruption to ὅτε was due to a misunderstanding of the structure of this sentence. For the ἀπὸ κοινοῦ construction cf. Γ 409 εἰς ὅ κέ σ' ἢ ἄλοχον ποιήσεται ἢ ὅ γε δούλην, Χ 157, Hes. *Op.* 246 ἢ τῶν γε στρατὸν εὐρὺν ἀπώλεσεν ἢ ὅ γε τεῖχος. See Kiefner 33.

843 παρὰ νυκτός A rare extension of the use of παρά from place to time, perhaps influenced by Homeric uses with ἔρχομαι, e.g. Μ 225, Ν 744, and especially χ 197-8 ἠριγένεια παρ' Ὠκεανοῖο ῥοάων | ... ἐπερχομένη. Here νυκτός means 'nightfall'; cf. Χ. *Cyr.* 1.4.2 ἐκ νυκτός. Similarly, but more naturally, the reference in ἐπὶ νύκτα is to nightfall. Note the variation of prepositions: ἐς ... παρὰ ... ἐξ ... ἐπί. The use of ἐπί in this sense is not common, but cf. η 288 ἐπ' ἠῶ καὶ μέσον ἦμαρ. The phrase ἐς ἠῶ recalls λ 375.

844 παρατρέχοι Cf. 275. The sun in its movement round the earth is thought of as accompanying the rainfall during this period, a poetic variation of the basic meaning 'it is likely to rain'; cf. 831.

845 μηδ' A variation in negative form; cf. 822, 866ff., 869ff.

πάρος Not to be construed with οἱ, as Mair 'before him'. As prep. πάρος always takes a genitive, and is regularly placed immediately before or after it, e.g. 954 πάρος ὕδατος, Α 453 ἐμεῦ πάρος. It is therefore an adverb, and οἱ expresses a slightly more distant relationship: in relation to the sun (from the observer's point of view) the cloud rises first. *CCAG* 8.1.139, 1 προανατέλλοντα ἔχων νέφη ... ὑετὸν σημαίνει.

ἀντέλλησι Cf. 560, 569, and note on 828.

846 τὴν δὲ μέτ' Cf. 549.

κεχρημένος The reading of M does not make sense, and is due to the influence of κεχρωσμένος in 838. The confusion is further illustrated by sch. (MAS) 846, which actually relate to 840–4 (Martin *SAV* 418). The sense of this line is given by sch. (M) 845 εἶτα αὐτὸς ἐπιὼν φέρηται ὥσπερ ἐνδεὴς ἀκτίνων, and by Avien. 1600–1 *ipseque pone sequens radiorum luce carere | cernatur.* For κεχρημένος in the sense of 'lacking', rather than 'needing', cf. α 13 νόστου κεχρημένον ἠδὲ γυναικός.

ἀερθῇ Cf. τ 540 ὁ δ' ἐς αἰθέρα δῖαν ἀέρθη, of a dream. With the aorist denoting the moment of rising contrast the present of stars already visible (326, 405, 558).

847 ἀμνηστεῖν A rare verb, used mainly with a negative, as here, to reinforce the positive sense of remembering. Cf. S. *El.* 482 οὐ γάρ ποτ' ἀμναστεῖ γ' ὁ φύσας σ' Ἑλλάνων ἄναξ, Th. 1.20.3 νῦν ὄντα καὶ οὐ χρόνῳ ἀμνηστούμενα, 3.40.7.

πολὺς ... κύκλος The antithesis to ὀλίγη νεφέλη (845) identifies κύκλος as a ring of cloud or mist.

οἱ πέρι The reading περί was traditional before Voss. There is no verb available with which it could be connected *in tmesi*, as in 317, but it could be treated as an adverb, in the manner of Τ 362 γέλασσε δὲ πᾶσα περὶ χθών. It seems, however, more natural to take it as a preposition with anastrophe (cf. 276). The prepositional phrase goes closely with πολὺς ... κύκλος, and is somewhat detached from the gen. abs. ἀνερχομένοιο in 849; cf. 822, 840, 847.

848 οἷον Cf. 864 and 875 with main verbs. Here it seems pleonastic with ἐναλίγκιος, but is perhaps intended to draw attention to a rather bold metaphor not normally used of clouds, though familiar in other figurative senses, e.g. ε 396.

τηκομένῳ ἐναλίγκιος The adj. is common in Homer, but always with a noun, except for one instance with a pronoun (Χ 410). The use with a participle here is perhaps influenced by the frequent use of ἐοικώς in this way: cf. 91, 340, al.

εὐρύνηται Once in Homer, θ 260 καλὸν δ' εὔρυναν ἀγῶνα. Cf. Theoc. 13.31 αὔλακας εὐρύνοντι βόες, D.P. 92, of the Adriatic, κεῖθεν δ' εὐρυνθεῖσα τιταίνεται. The four-word line with spondaic ending seems to suggest the slow, spreading movement of the mist.

849 ἀνερχομένοιο Gen. abs., ἡλίου being easily understood from the context: see Goodwin *MT* 338. The participle is grammatically detached from the dat. οἱ (847), though looking back to it in sense.

ἄψ Only here in A., though frequent in Homer, e.g. in same *sedes* Κ 211 καὶ ἄψ εἰς ἡμέας ἔλθοι. Most Homeric instances come at the beginning of a line.

ἐπὶ μεῖον ἴησιν   Cf. S. *Ph.* 259 κἀπὶ μεῖζον ἔρχεται.

850 φέροιτο   A. gives no indication of the grammatical change of subject, but there is no real confusion, since the sun is the significant subject of the whole passage.

χείματος   Here specifically the season, as in 266 and 977; otherwise it means stormy or wintry weather at any time (994, 1018, 1130). χείματος ὥρη recurs in [Opp.] *C.* 3.308, 4.437, *H.* 4.532, Mus. 293, Q.S. 2.218, 13.311.

851 ὠχρήσῃ   Once in Homer, λ 529 ὠχρήσαντα χρόα κάλλιμον, as also the noun (Γ 35). *D.S.* 50 καὶ ἐὰν δύνων χειμῶνος ὠχρὸς ᾖ, εὐδίαν σημαίνει. Avien. 1611 *pallidus ora cadens promittit pura serena.*

ἡμερινοῖο   'During the day', whereas ἡμέριος means 'ephemeral'; cf. ὀπωρινός (417), ἐαρινός, θερινός, νυκτερινός, χειμερινός (but χειμέριος 509, ε 485, Hes. *Op.* 494).

One scholion refers ἡμερινοῖο to the following day, and Martin suggests that Avien. 1616–17 *quin nascente die uenturos conuenit imbres | noscere* shows the influence of this. So Mair 'for tomorrow's rain'. This interpretation, however, does not suit either the normal sense of ἡμερινός or the present γινομένου (which Avienius represents with a future), and I agree with Martin in referring these words to the present, and viewing this sentence as a long one, running on to 857: if it rains during the day, study the clouds at sunset, and if the sun is covered by a cloud and its rays diverge on either side, you will need shelter in the morning. Cf. Ceporinus *at pluuia diurna facta, postea nubes circumspicito* …

852 κατόπισθε   Voss takes with γινομένου, not, however, as Martin says, as preposition with genitive, but as adverb (in the manner of ἐστί and γίγνεται with adverbs), 'wann der Tagregen hinterwärts oder vorübergezogen ist'. This is an unparalleled meaning for κατόπισθε, and it is more natural to take it with the following verb: cf. ω 546 ὅρκια δ' αὖ κατόπισθε μετ' ἀμφοτέροισιν ἔθηκε. For its use as adv. of time cf. *h.Hom.* 4.407 θαυμαίνω κατόπισθε τὸ σὸν κράτος.

περὶ νέφεα σκοπέεσθαι   Cf. 464 περισκοπέοντι, also c. acc. in the sense of observing carefully. For lengthening before ν cf. Δ 274 ἅμα δὲ νέφος εἵπετο πεζῶν: Monro *HG* 344–5, Chantraine 1.176–7. Cf. 977 κατὰ νοτίην.

853 κὰδ δή   Cf. 270.

δυομένου   See note on 840.

τετραμμένος ἠελίοιο   Elsewhere with εἰς (30), ἐς (387, 620, 632), ἐπί (298) in the sense of 'turned towards'. The genitive would naturally suggest 'turned away from', as in Σ 138 πάλιν τράπεθ' υἱὸς ἑοῖο, but the context requires 'turned towards', and the scholia explain πρὸς δυόμενον τὸν ἥλιον ἀφορῶν. The genitive here may therefore be explained as defining the direction in which the observer is facing, as is regular with ἀντί, and sometimes with ἀντίος etc., e.g. ὁ δ' ἀντίος ἦλθεν ἄνακτος. In this case A. may have been more directly influenced by Hes. *Op.* 727 ἀντ' ἠελίου τετραμμένος. A. uses the genitive very freely in other contexts: see Erren *PAS* 301–3, though this instance is omitted from his list.

854 ὑποσκιάῃσι The verb occurs only here, if σκοπέλοισιν ὕπο is accepted in A.R. 1.451. The point of the prefix is that the cloud comes between us and the sun, and therefore is below the sun: cf. 542 ὑποδράμοι. *D.S.* 11 καὶ ἐὰν καταφερομένου τοῦ ἡλίου ὑφίστηται νέφος, ὑφ' οὗ ἐὰν σχίζωνται αἱ ἀκτῖνες, χειμερινὸν τὸ σημεῖον.

μελαινομένη Cf. 804, 941. The participle does not seem to have any verbal force: it is explained by sch. (MA) as μέλαινα νεφέλη. A black cloud is only apparently black: the observer is looking at that part of it which is away from the sun. It may be that this is the point of εἰκυῖα, but on the other hand A. uses ἐοικώς in 512 and 1126 in a slightly otiose fashion, and it is perhaps better to adopt the same explanation here. Cf. Q.S. 1.306 ἀχνυμένη εἰκυῖα.

855 ἔνθα καὶ ἔνθα There is no implication of movement here, as in 393 and β 213. The phenomenon is comparable with that described in 829–30; cf. sch. (MAS) ἑκατέρωθεν τοῦ νέφους σχίζονται.

856 μεσσηγύς I.e. between the sun and the cloud; but see the following note.

ἑλισσόμεναι This is the better attested reading, and it is supported by one of the scholia, αἱ δὲ ἀκτῖνες ἅπασαι κατὰ μέσον τὸν δίσκον ἑλισσόμεναι εἰς δύο μέρη τοῦ δίσκου διασχισθῶσι. This clearly construes the participle with μεσσηγύς, but gives an unparalleled meaning to the adverb, and fails to explain how the verb is to be interpreted. The sun's rays do not appear to bend. Indeed it is a basic assumption of Greek geometry that they are straight, as in Eratosthenes' famous calculation: cf. Cleom. 1.10.50 ὑποκείσθω ἡμῖν ... τὰς καταπεμπομένας ἀκτῖνας ἀπὸ διαφόρων μερῶν τοῦ ἡλίου ἐπὶ διάφορα τῆς γῆς μέρη παραλλήλους εἶναι· οὕτως γὰρ ἔχειν αὐτὰς οἱ γεωμέτραι ὑποτίθενται. It is therefore difficult to make sense of Voss's 'vom inneren Kern auskreisende Stralen', or Mair's 'beams that wheel between the sun and it'. Hence the v.l., which transfers the participle to the cloud. Kaibel explained this as 'the cloud rolled up in the middle', and Martin has adopted this reading and meaning, 'enroulée au milieu d'eux'; so Erren 'die sich in der Mitte wälzt'. This is not satisfactory: it is not the cloud that is in the middle, but the rays; and the cloud is not rolled round anything, or seen to be making any kind of circular motion. Moreover the corruption to ἑλισσομένην explains the further corruption διχόωσιν in some MSS. It is simpler to understand ἑλισσόμεναι in its usual Aratean sense, with reference to the slow western movement of the sky, as in 171, 570, etc. of stars. Thus μεσσηγύς and ἑλισσόμεναι are syntactically independent: the former describes the relative position of the rays, the latter their setting movement.

διχόωνται Cf. the active forms of this verb in 512, 605, 773, 799. A.R. 4.1616 μήνης ὡς κεράεσσιν ἐειδόμεναι διχόωντο is an imitation that combines the participle and passive verb of this line with the κεράεσσι σελήνη of 733.

857 ἤ τ᾽ Apodotic use; cf. 793, 876. This line particularly recalls μ 138, which begins with ἤ τ᾽ ἂν ἔτ᾽ εἰς Ἰθάκην and gives a warning of trouble.

σκέπαος κεχρημένος εἴης A lively variation, indicating rainy or stormy weather. The former is understood by sch. (MA) ἴσθι κατὰ τὴν ὑστεραίαν ἐσόμενον ὑετόν, the latter by sch. (MAS) χειμῶνα προσδέχου and sch. (MΔUAS) χειμὼν γὰρ ἔσται. Storm is predicted in *D.S.* 11 (cited on 854), though this is in the section devoted to rain signs, and a similar portent is noted in the first of the storm signs, ἥλιος δυόμενος εἰς μὴ καθαρόν (38). Since in 1126 the lone wolf σκέπαος χατέοντι ἐοικώς is a sign of coming storm, A. is probably thinking of stormy weather here too.

858 ἀνέφελος Cf. 415.

βάπτῃ The subjunctive seems necessary in view of ἑστήκωσιν (860). A. does not normally vary the mood in pairs of subordinate clauses (cf. 841, 903). In Homer the pure subjunctive in a conditional protasis with εἰ, when the principal verb implies a reference to the future, has an indefinite force, e.g. Μ 245 εἴ περ γάρ τ᾽ ἄλλοι γε περὶ κτεινώμεθα πάντες. In this case it denotes an event that could happen at any time; cf. 840–1, 850–1, 858–60, 903, 988–90, 1082–4. See Monro *HG* 266, and cf. note on 828 περιτέλλῃ after ὁππότε. βάπτω occurs once in Homer (ι 392), in a famous simile, in the same form and *sedes*.

ῥόου ἑσπερίοιο Gen. of the space within which the action takes place (see notes on 605, 635). For the use with βάπτω cf. 651, 951; perhaps developed on the analogy of Homeric gen. with λούομαι, as in Ε 6 λελουμένος Ὠκεανοῖο, Ζ 508, Hes. *Th.* 5–6; cf. K-G 1.357. The phrase may also recall λ 21 ῥόον Ὠκεανοῖο.

859 καὶ οἰχομένοιο There is no difficulty about the meaning of the traditional reading: the sun is presented as setting in two stages, above the horizon and below the horizon. But there are several variants to be considered and explained. (1) ἐπερχομένοιο can only refer to sunrise, and, as Voss has pointed out, it was introduced by someone who did not understand the passage, and expected a setting–rising antithesis, such as occurs in many lines of the poem; the participle chosen comes from 634. (2) ἀποιχομένοιο is Homeric, but normally implies a sense of distance or detachment, such as the absence of Odysseus in α 135 or the death of Ariadne in 72 above. It is the reading adopted by Voss, but it is not appropriate here, with the sun just below the horizon. (3) ἔτ᾽ οἰχομένοιο, if given the unusual meaning of 'still going', would add nothing to κατερχομένου, and as 'still gone' would not make any sense. Mair translates 'or still when he is gone', but this transfers the sense of ἔτι to ἑστήκωσιν, and makes its placing clumsy and confusing. Martin and Erren, who adopt this reading without comment, translate 'même après son coucher' and 'auch wenn sie schon fort ist'. This does not seem to be a possible meaning for ἔτι, which is used rather to give some emphasis to the addition of a further point. If an adverb is required, the appropriate one is ἤδη, as in sch. καταδύνοντός τε αὐτοῦ καὶ ἤδη δεδυκότος. (4) ταί τ᾽, the reading of Maass, is open to a similar objection: it seems to make a distinction between clouds near the sun before and clouds near it after sunset. They are, or course, the same clouds during both stages. All these variants have one factor in common: they allow καί to be scanned short in hiatus, as it regularly is in A. (99 times), and it is reasonable to assume that they were devised for this purpose. But there is one other example of καί long in hiatus, καὶ ὄρνεα πάντα (1024) also at the bucolic diaeresis. We have therefore no compelling reason for being dissatisfied with the transmitted reading.

860 πλησίαι Cf. Δ 21, ε 71, κ 93 in same *sedes*; there is also perhaps an echo of Λ 593.

ἑστήκωσιν Voss notes that this verb implies the absence of wind, as in E 522ff. ἀλλ᾽ ἔμενον νεφέλῃσιν ἐοικότες, ἅς τε Κρονίων | νηνεμίης ἔστησεν κτλ.

ἐρευθέες The familiar portent of 'a red sky at night'. Cf. Plin. *Nat.* 18.343 *si circa occidentem rubescunt nubes, serenitatem futuri diei spondent, Gp.* 1.2.5 (=Anon. Laur. 3.6) νέφη ἐρυθρότερα διεσπασμένα περὶ δυσμὰς ἀνομβρίαν δηλοῦσι. See R. M. Smith, *Weather and Climate* 4 (1984) 36: 'Water droplets transmit or reflect the full spectrum of visible light, so that white light entering a cloud of droplets emerges as white light also. Dust or other dry particles, on the other hand, reflect light selectively, depending on the size of the particles. Light from the violet end of the spectrum is scattered back towards the source, while the longer wavelengths from the red end of the spectrum continue on their path towards the observer. Thus a red sky at night implies dry air, despite daytime convection, and therefore, presumably, dry conditions again next day.'

οὔ σε μάλα χρή Cf. similar Homeric line-endings, νῦν σε μάλα χρή (Π 492, Χ 268), οὐδέ τί σε χρή (Η 109, α 296), etc.

861 ἐπὶ νυκτί Cf. 323, 554, 868.

περιτρομέειν Once in Homer, σ 77 σάρκες δὲ περιτρομέοντο μέλεσσιν, though in a different sense. Here the verb introduces another variation for verbs of expecting, with the usual dependent genitive.

862 ἀλλ' Sc. περιτρομέειν χρή.

μαραινομένῃσιν Cf. 814, of the lunar halo. For the participle with ὁμοῖος cf. 1007, as frequently with ἐοικώς (91 etc.).

863 ἐξαπίνης For metrical position cf. κ 557, ξ 29, 38, ω 160.

ἀπ' οὐρανόθεν Four times in Homer, all in same *sedes*: Θ 365, Φ 199, λ 18, μ 381, the last two with reference to sunset. Cf. Θ 19 ἐξ οὐρανόθεν.

τανύωνται Cf. Ptol. *Tetr.* 2.14.2 ὡσεὶ μακρὰς ἀκτῖνας ἀπομηκύνων. For the subjunctive see note on 828 περιτέλλῃ.

864 ἀμαλδύνονται Homeric in the sense of 'destroy', but only once in the passive, Η 463 τεῖχος ἀμαλδύνηται, the likely source of the reading in the majority of MSS. The indicative is supported by the papyrus and Cic. *Prog.* fr. 1 *stinguuntur radii*. The weaker meaning here may have been influenced by *h.Hom.* εἶδος ἀμαλδύνουσα, of Demeter in disguise, in the same metrical position as here. Cf. Theoc. 16.59, A.R. 1.834, 4.112, Q.S. 13.12 ἀμαλδύνονται ὀπωπαί.

σκιάῃσι The active appears once in Homer, Φ 232 δείελος ὀψὲ δύων, σκιάσῃ δ' ἐρίβωλον ἄρουραν. Cf. 600, 854, A.R. 1.604, Nic. *Ther.* 30.

κατ' ἰθύ The moon being in the direct line between earth and sun at a solar eclipse. Homer has πρὸς ἰθύ οἱ (Ξ 403) of facing directly towards, Plato κατὰ μὲν τὸ εὐθὺ ἑστάναι (*R.* 436e) of a top in the vertical position. The comparison with an eclipse originates in *D.S.* 13 καὶ ὅταν ἀνίσχοντος τοῦ ἡλίου αἱ αὐγαὶ οἷον ἐκλείποντος χρῶμα ἴσχωσιν. A.'s elaboration of the comparison suggests that he is taking the opportunity to describe an interesting phenomenon that is not otherwise relevant to his subject.

865 ἱσταμένη Cf. Β 172 of Athene, and ἵσταται of stars in 306, 610, Χ 318; Sen. *Nat.* 1.12.1 *cum uterque orbis sub eodem libramento stetit*.

γαίης τε καὶ ἠελίοιο The gen. may be explained as defining the direction intended by κατ' ἰθύ: cf. 853.

866 ἐπέχοντι φανήμεναι LSJ give no instance of infinitive after ἐπέχω in the sense of 'delay', but comparable is X. *Mem.* 3.6.10 περὶ πολέμου συμβουλεύειν τήν γε πρώτην ἐπισχήσομεν. As in 414 the context requires the sense of φανήμεναι rather than φαμέναι, recalling Ι 240 ἀρᾶται δὲ τάχιστα φανήμεναι Ἠῶ δῖαν, the only instance of this infinitive in Homer. The phrase, suggesting a reluctance to rise, is an amusing variation of ἠῶθι πρό (309, 870).

867 φαίνωνται Cf. 828 περιτέλλῃ. Sch. ὅταν ... πρὸ τοῦ ὄρθρου φανῶσι νεφέλαι.

473

ὑπερευθέες   Only here and Opp. *H.* 3.167. This is the first of the rain signs in *D.S.* 10: ἐναργέστατον μὲν οὖν τὸ ἑωθινόν, ὅταν πρὸ ἡλίου ἀνατολῆς φαίνηται ἐπιφοινίσσον σημεῖον· ἢ γὰρ αὐθημερινὸν ἐπισημαίνει ἢ τριῶν ἡμερῶν ὡς ἐπὶ τὸ πολύ. This is the familiar 'red sky in the morning' sign.

ἄλλοθεν ἄλλαι   A. contrives to vary the pronoun endings throughout the poem: ἄλλα (411, 738, 835), ἄλλοι (1101, 1108), ἄλλος (146). A.R. 1.843 νεήνιδες ἄλλοθεν ἄλλαι.

868 ἄρραντοι   Only here and Str. 11.7.5. For the double negative giving emphasis, and also allowing a variation in the manner of expressing a weather forecast, cf. 845–7.

ἐπ' ἤματι κείνῳ   Cf. N 234, Τ 110 ἐπ' ἤματι τῷδε. See W. J. Verdenius on Hes. *Op.* 43 ἐπ' ἤματι.

869 ἐόντι πέρην   Sc. ἡλίῳ, dative with possessive force, as οἱ in 866. The adv. is particularly associated with the sea in earlier poets, e.g. Β 626, ω 752 πέρην ἁλός, Hes. *Th.* 215, 274 πέρην κλυτοῦ Ὠκεανοῖο, Α. *Ag.* 1200 πόντου πέραν, Pi. *N.* 5.21 πέραν πόντοιο. Here πέρην implies ὠκεανοῖο, the horizon.

προταθεῖσαι   The prefix pictures the rays appearing above the horizon before the sun rises; sch. προπεμφθεῖσαι. *D.S.* 11 ἐὰν ἀκτῖνες ἀνίσχοντος ἀνατείνωσι πρὶν ἀνατεῖλαι, κοινὸν ὕδατος σημεῖον καὶ ἀνέμου.

870 φαίνωνται   Cf. 828 περιτέλλη. Here the MSS all have indicative, but the papyrus vowel is probably ω.

ἐπίσκιοι   Sch. (M) ἀμυδρότεραι, μαλακαί, αἱ μὴ σφόδρα πεπιλημέναι μηδὲ πάνυ ζοφώδεις. S. *OC* 1650–1 uses this adj. in an active sense, ὀμμάτων ἐπίσκιον | χεῖρ'. For the weather sign cf. *D.S.* 11 ἐὰν ἐκ νεφελῶν ἀνέχῃ, ὑδατικόν, *Gp.* 1.3.2 ἀνατέλλοντος δὲ τοῦ ἡλίου, ἂν παρὰ τὰς ἀκτῖνας σκοτεινὸν νέφος φανῇ, ὄμβρον δηλοῖ.

871 κατοισομένου   Once in Homer, Χ 425 οὔ μ' ἄχος ὀξὺ κατοίσεται Ἄϊδος εἴσω. Here the middle is intransitive, and only here used of the onset of weather.

λελαθέσθαι   Redupl. aor. med., also in Homer with negative, Τ 136 οὐ δυνάμην λελαθέσθ' Ἄτης, Δ 127 οὐδὲ σέθεν, Μενέλαε, θεοὶ μάκαρες λελάθοντο, Π 200 μή τίς μοι ἀπειλάων λελαθέσθω. Cf. 984, also with μηδέ, another variation for the recurring sense of 'expect'.

872 ἀλλ'   The progressive use (Denniston 21), in this case supplementing the preceding information with more specific details. It is misleading to punctuate with a full stop after λελαθέσθαι, as in all the editions. This is another of A.'s long sentences (cf. 129–36, 367–85, 420–9, 469–79), arranged in groups of 3 + 2 + 3 lines: clouded rays before dawn mean rain or wind, rain if the cloud is dark, wind if light.

κνέφαος   Cf. 472. In Homer the word is always in the context of nightfall, once in gen., σ 370 ἄχρι μάλα κνέφαος. This bold extension

474

of meaning to describe dark cloud is unparalleled. The local gen. gives the conditions in which the rays move; cf. 605 γαίης.

φορέοιντο The movement is as usual (e.g. 29, 146) that of the sky, and the verb is thus a lively substitute for εἶεν.

873 ἐφ' ὕδατι The weather that the sign points to; cf. 994, 1093.

874 περὶ ... ἀκτίνεσσιν The separation is unusual, but cf. E 566 περὶ γὰρ δίε ποιμένι λαῶν. For ἀκτίνεσσιν in this position cf. λ 16, Hes. *Th.* 760, A.R. 4.126.

δνόφος The noun is rare, e.g. Simon. *PMG* 543.12 κυανέῳ δνόφῳ ταθείς, A. *Ch.* 52 δνόφοι καλύπτουσι δόμους. The adj. δνοφερός, however, is Homeric (ν 269, ο 50 of night, l 15 of water). A. follows up with a verb in 876.

875 μαλακαί Cf. 826. Since A. in 939 calls clouds πόκοισιν ἐοικότα, he may be thinking here of γ 38 κώεσιν ἐν μαλακοῖσιν.

876 ἤ τ' ἄν Cf. 793, 857.

περιδνοφέοιντ' Only here, reinforcing the rare δνόφος in 874. The suffix -έω was very productive in the formation of verbs from noun stems (Palmer 265–6).

ἀνέμοιο For the internal rhyme cf. 360, 435, 634, 831, 925.

877 σχεδόθεν Rarely c. gen., but cf. τ 447 στῆ ῥ' αὐτῶν σχεδόθεν.

μελανεῦσαι Cf. 817. The repetition in 878 moves on to the end of the line, in keeping with the forward movement of the sense pauses.

ἀλωαί See note on 811. *D.S.* 22 καὶ ἅλως αἱ μέλαιναι ὑδατικὸν καὶ μᾶλλον αἱ δείλης. Cf. Plin. *Nat.* 18.346 *si circa occidentem candidus circulus erit, noctis leuem tempestatem,* ... *si ater circulus fuerit, ex qua regione is ruperit se, uentum magnum,* CCAG 8.1.139, 10 περὶ τὸν ἥλιον συνισταμένη ἡ ἅλως, ἐὰν ἱκανὸν ἀπέχουσα ἀπ' αὐτοῦ καὶ μελανίζουσα θεωρῆται, χειμῶνα προσημαίνει· ἐὰν δὲ σύνεγγυς ἡ ἅλως ὑπάρχῃ, μείζονα χειμῶνα σημαίνει.

878 εὔδιοι A. freely varies the quantity of the ι to suit the inflexion and the metrical position: in εὔδιοι it is short also in 911, 1123, 1133, but long in 916 and (ὑπεύδιοι) 1012; in εὔδιος (784, 850, 991, 994) it is long, but short in ὑπεύδιος (827, 990); in εὔδια (802) and ὑπεύδια (1035) it is short, in εὔδιον (1074) and εὐδίου (823) long. On the other hand ἔνδιος keeps the ι long (498, 954), as in Homer, e.g. Λ 726, δ 450.

ἀσσότεραι A new adj., formed from the adverbs ἀσσότερον (313, 486) and ἀσσοτέρω (ρ 572, τ 506). The normal halo has an angular radius of 22°, but smaller ones, closer to the sun, are sometimes seen, e.g. of 18° and 8° (Greenler 25–6, 61, plates 2-22, 2-23). A. may, however, be thinking of the much commoner phenomenon known as a corona, a diffraction pattern of coloured rings of only a few degrees' radius (id. 139ff., plates 6 - 1, 6 - 2).

ἀστεμφές Adv. from Homeric adj., e.g. Γ 219 ἀστεμφὲς ἔχεσκεν

(σκῆπτρον), meaning 'firm', 'unshaken'. The Homeric adv. is ἀστεμφέως, e.g. δ 459 ἀστεμφέως ἔχομεν τετληότι θυμῷ. Cf. Hes. *Th.* 748,
of Atlas holding up the sky. Here the precise point of the adv. is not
immediately clear. Some translators make it refer to the quality of the
colour, e.g. Schott 'recht tief geschwärzt', Erren 'steifer geschwärzt'. But
even in poetry a halo can hardly be described as black, let alone a deep
black. Mair and LSJ relate it to uniformity, 'dark without relief'. But in
view of the Homeric and Hesiodic uses I think it is the time factor that
is significant, i.e. the halo remains unwaveringly dark all the time it is
visible. This may be what Martin means by 'd'un noir tenace' and Voss
by 'in derberem Schwartze'. Cf. sch. ἀντὶ τοῦ σκληρῶς καὶ ἀμετα-
κινήτως, Avien. 1643 *cingula nescia solui*.

879 χειμέριαι Denoting what the sign portends; cf. 784 εὔδιος, 785
πνευματίη, etc.

δύο See note on 812. Pliny seems to have understood this passage as
referring to rings of cloud: *si nubes solem circumcludent, quanto minus luminis
relinquent tanto turbidior tempestas erit, si uero etiam duplex orbis fuerit, eo atrocior*
(*Nat.* 18.344).

χαλεπώτεραι Cf. 314 of the Eagle's rising as a sign of storm.

880–891 The third section of the weather signs from the sun, balancing the first in length, introduces a new phenomenon, parhelia,
bright spots on either side of the sun. These foretell stormy weather,
with winds from north or south, and are most reliable when observed at
sunset.

880 ἀνιόντος ... δυομένοιο Repeated from 840.

881 παρήλια Adj., as in sch. 880 τὰ παρήλια λεγόμενα νέφη,
Posid. fr. 121E–K παρήλιόν φησι νέφος, στρογγύλον παρὰ τὴν τοῦ
ἡλίου ἔκλαμψιν, ἐκ τοῦ ἡλίου λάμπον, and Ptol. *Tetr.* 2.14.2 τὰ καλούμενα παρήλια νέφη. Arist. *Mete.* 372a11 and *D.S.* 22 have παρήλιοι as
noun. Cf. Sen. *Nat.* 1.11.2 *Graeci parhelia appellant quia in propinquo fere a sole
uisuntur.* Parhelia, popularly known as mock suns, false suns, or sun dogs,
are bright spots seen at a distance of 22° on either side of the sun and at
the same altitude. Thus Aristotle: παρήλιοι δὲ καὶ ῥάβδοι γίγνονται ἐκ
πλαγίας αἰεὶ καὶ οὔτ᾽ ἄνωθεν οὔτε πρὸς τῆς γῆς οὔτ᾽ ἐξ ἐναντίας, οὐδὲ
δὴ νύκτωρ, ἀλλ᾽ ἀεὶ περὶ τὸν ἥλιον, ἔτι δὲ ἢ αἰρομένου ἢ καταφερ-
ομένου· τὰ πλεῖστα δὲ πρὸς δυσμάς· μεσουρανοῦντος δὲ σπάνιον εἴ τι
γέγονεν, οἷον ἐν Βοσπόρῳ ποτὲ συνέπεσε· δι᾽ ὅλης γὰρ τῆς ἡμέρας
συνανασχόντες δύο παρήλιοι διετέλεσαν μέχρι δυσμῶν. Aristotle goes
on to explain this phenomenon in accordance with his theory of
ἀνάκλασις, the reflection of our vision back from the object sighted (see
note on 811, and *Mete.* 373a35–b33). The modern explanation is that
they are caused by light refracted through ice crystals with horizontal
bases. 'With the sun low in the sky, these plate crystals would have the

proper orientation to refract light to the observer from the sides of the halo, but not from the top of the halo ... The better the orientation of the ice crystals, the smaller and brighter are the resulting spots on either side of the sun. In some cases they can be quite bright and of an apparent size comparable to that of the sun' (Greenler 27; see also plates 2‑3, 2‑4). See Posid. 2.466ff.

882 ἢ νότου ἠὲ βορῆος Locative use of gen.; cf. 756 Ποσειδάωνος ὁρώμενοι ἢ Διός, and note. *D.S.* 22 ἐὰν παρήλιοι δύο γένωνται καὶ ὁ μὲν νοτόθεν ὁ δὲ βορρᾶθεν, καὶ ἄλως ἅμα, ὕδωρ διὰ ταχέων σημαίνουσι, Ptol. *Tetr.* 2.14.3 ἐξ ἀμφοτέρων μερῶν παρήλια νέφη, *CCAG* 8.1.139, 7 ὅταν ἐπὶ τῶν βορείων μερῶν τὰ παρήλια θεωρηθῇ ἐρυθρά, βορρᾶν προσημαίνει· ὅταν δὲ ἐξ ἀμφοτέρων τῶν μερῶν μέσον τὸν ἥλιον περιέχῃ, ὄμβρον καὶ ἄνεμον προσημαίνει, Anon. Laur. 1.9–10 ἡλίου ἀνατέλλοντος ἐὰν νεφέλια πολλὰ πρὸς μεσημβρίαν ἐγείρωνται, χειμῶνα δηλοῦσιν, εἰ δὲ ἀπὸ νότου, ὑετόν. ἐὰν ἀμφοτέρωθεν τοῦ ἡλίου παρήλιοι φαίνωνται, ἰσχυρὰ πνεύματα δηλοῦσιν. Cf. Sen. *Nat.* 1.13.3 *pluuiarum autem et hi soles ... indicia sunt, utique si a parte austri constiterunt, unde maxime nubes ingrauescunt; cum utrimque solem cinxit talis effigies, tempestas, si Arato credimus, surgit.*

883 οὕτω The awkwardness of taking οὕτω closely with ἀμενηνά ('so fahrlässig', Voss) prompted Buttmann's tentative conjecture, adopted by Maass, Martin and Erren. Certainly αὕτως gives the right sense, but it produces an ugly cluster of consonants, which is not in A.'s manner. He uses αὕτως mainly at line-ends and before vowels, only occasionally before γ, δ and κ, never before σ. It is, however, possible to understand οὕτω with weakened force in much the same sense as αὕτως, e.g. Β 120 μὰψ οὕτω, and, more akin to the present passage, Pl. *Tht.* 142d οὔκουν οὕτω γε ἀπὸ στόματος, 'not just off-hand'.

σκοπιήν Cf. 833, and again θ 302. Here A. may also be recalling Δ 275 ὅτ' ἀπὸ σκοπιῆς εἶδεν νέφος αἰπόλος ἀνήρ, in view of the cloud-watching and the position of σκοπιῆς (though the sense is different).

ἀμενηνά Adv., as also in 905, adj. in 786, 1016. The metrical position in all cases is that of κ 521 νεκύων ἀμενηνὰ κάρηνα.

φυλάσσειν Infinitive as imperative. The v.l. comes from sch. (MA) ἀμενηνῶς καὶ ὡς ἔτυχε φυλάσσου (Martin 431, 22). Mair's 'make the observation' treats the acc. as cognate, but A. is thinking of the watch for signs being maintained over the whole period of sunset. Martin's 'garde-toi d'être imprécis' would require a middle verb and a different construction.

884 ὁμοῦ With ἀμφοτέρωθεν. Cf. μ 424 ἄμφω συνέεργον ὁμοῦ, 'both together'.

ἔχωσιν For the pure subj. see note on 828. The v.l., adopted by

Bekker, Maass, Mair and Zannoni, comes from the prose version of sch. ὅτε ἐξ ἑκατέρου μέρους ἔχουσι τὸν ἥλιον.

885 κεῖναι νεφέλαι The parhelia.

886 ἀμβολίη With negative, another way of expressing 'expect soon'. Cf. 1081, 1117, A.R. 4.396 ἀμβολίην διζήμεθα δηιότητος, Q.S. 1.431, Triph. 42, Nonn. D. 36.477. The commoner poetic form is ἀμβολή, prose ἀναβολή.

Διόθεν Cf. 293, 936 ἐκ Διός of weather. Διόθεν is Homeric, e.g., in same sedes, O 489, Ω 561; cf. Hes. Op. 765 ἐκ Διόθεν.

887 ἐκ βορέαο A variation of ν 110 πρὸς βορέαο, in same sedes; cf. 241, 486, 897.

μί᾽ οἴη Cf. 812.

φοινίσσοιτο Cf. 798.

888 ἐκ βορέω πνοιάς D.S. 29 παρήλιος ὁπόθεν ἂν ᾖ ὕδωρ ἢ ἄνεμον σημαίνει. Arist. Mete. 377b24 notes ὕδατος σημεῖον ὁ παρήλιος, adding ὁ δὲ νότιος τοῦ βορείου μᾶλλον, ὅτι μᾶλλον ὁ νότιος ἀὴρ εἰς ὕδωρ μεταβάλλει τοῦ πρὸς ἄρκτον. There is no reference to wind here. The association of two parhelia in the west with winds from north and south is, of course, false, and may be compared with a similar fallacy about the Asses in the Manger (905–8). There may be some influence here from the lore about lightning indicating the direction of coming wind (924–5).

νοτίη δὲ νότοιο An elegantly brief antithesis, with all but the essential words understood, also with variation, νοτίη balancing ἐκ βορέαο and νότοιο balancing ἐκ βορέω.

889 ἢ καί που The particles add another possibility, namely rain: sch. ἔσθ᾽ ὅτε δὲ καί. Cf. E. Ion 432 ἢ καί τι σιγῶσ᾽ ὧν σιωπᾶσθαι χρεών; Pl. Gorg. 505d ἐάσεις χαίρειν τοῦτον τὸν λόγον, ἢ καὶ ἄλλῳ τῳ διαλέξῃ. See Denniston 306.

ῥαθάμιγγες A rare Homeric word for drops of blood (Λ 536, Υ 501) and particles of dust thrown up by horses' hooves (Ψ 502), only in the phrase ῥαθάμιγγες ἔβαλλον. It occurs once in Hesiod, of drops from the castration of Uranus, Th. 183 ὅσσαι γὰρ ῥαθάμιγγες ἀπέσσυθεν αἱματόεσσαι. Cf. Call. H. 5.11, with Bulloch's note, Anon. AP 9.362.12, [Opp.] C. 2.558, Opp. H. 3.161, Q.S. 2.557, Mus. 262.

ἐπιτροχόωσ᾽ Description of a passing shower; cf. 767 ἐπιτρέχει of a storm at sea, A.R. 4.1266 ἐπιτροχάει of the sea.

890 καὶ μᾶλλον I.e. even more than when they are in the east.

ἐπίτρεπε σήμασι τούτοις The reading transmitted by the MSS, and that of all edd. since Buttmann. Earlier edd., except Aldus, who omits this line (presumably by haplography), read ἀληθέα τεκμήραιο, but I have not been able to discover any MS source for this. Buhle notes that it is not the reading of the three MSS on which he bases his text, Maass attributes it to 'codices recentes' without specifying which, and Martin ignores it. Arguments against it are that it anticipates the sense of 891, in which γάρ introduces an explanation, not a repetition; that ἀληθής may be used of an oracle's prophecy, but hardly of a weather sign, which does not have that degree of certainty (cf. 768–70); that μᾶλλον is not used to form a comp. adj. (Ceporinus 'magis certa', Voss 'wahrhaftere'). The corruption may have originated in a misunderstanding of ἑσπερίοις καὶ μᾶλλον, and may also have been influenced by sch. (Ald.) τά γε μὴν περὶ τὴν δύσιν τοῦ ἡλίου συνιστάμενα σημεῖα ἀληθῆ, or the alternative τὰ δὲ ἐν τῇ δύσει ἀληθῆ in sch. (MKA).

ἐπίτρεπε Sch. παραινεῖ μᾶλλον τοῖς πρὸς τῇ δύσει τεκμηρίοις προσέχειν τὸν νοῦν. Although ἐπιτρέπω is not elsewhere attested with τὸν νοῦν understood, this gives the right sense for the context, and A. may have derived it from ι 12–13 σοὶ δ' ἐμὰ κήδεα θυμὸς ἐπετράπετο στονόεντα | εἴρεσθ', and Alc. *PMG* 335 οὐ χρὴ κάκοισι θῦμον ἐπιτρέπην. A second scholion explains with reference to the legal use of ἐπιτρέπω, understanding τὴν τῶν σημείων κρίσιν. τοῦτο γὰρ τὸ ἐπιτρέπειν ἀττικῶς, τὸ αἱρεῖσθαί τινα διαιτητὴν διακρίνοντα [? -οῦντα Reeve] τὸ ἀμφισβητήσιμον. But the idea of submitting a problem to arbitration is hardly appropriate here, even figuratively. The point is that the observer should pay particular attention to the signs at sunset. The v.l. ἐπίτρεχε is probably due to the influence of ἐπιτροχόωσ' (889).

σήμασι τούτοις Cf. 429 σήματι τούτῳ, also referring back.

891 ἑσπερόθεν Cf. 710, 734. The anaphora stresses the importance of the west at sunset, and also marks the concluding couplet of the section.

ὁμῶς σημαίνετον Almost all editors have adopted the v.l. σημαίνεται, but it is not entirely satisfactory. It is difficult to see the point of the medio-passive form. Mair takes it as an impersonal passive, 'warnings are given', Erren as middle, 'zeigen sich nämlich die Zeichen'. Martin ignores this problem in his note, but his free translation seems to imply that he takes it as middle: 'ils conservent invariablement leur signification'.

There is, however, a simpler explanation: the subject of σημαίνετον is the two parhelia, as natural a pair as eyes or hands, and ὁμῶς has its normal meaning of 'both alike'; cf. ι 320 κάτθαν' ὁμῶς ὅ τ' ἀεργὸς ἀνὴρ ὅ τε πολλὰ ἐοργώς. The correctness of the dual here is further supported by the obvious imitation of Κ 361 ἐπείγετον ἐμμενὲς αἰεί, 364 διώκετον ἐμμενὲς αἰεί. Lines 890–1 thus refer solely to the two parhelia, and not to all the solar signs, as some editors have supposed, influenced perhaps by Virgil's reminiscence in *G.* 1.450–1.

ἐμμενὲς αἰεί   Cf. 339, and N 517 ἔχεν κότον ἐμμενὲς αἰεί. The doublet strengthens the sense of reliability.

892–908 Signs from the Manger

The Manger is a star cluster (now M 44), visible as a small hazy patch in the centre of the constellation Cancer. Earlier references to the Crab concern its position relative to other stars (147, 446), the northern tropic (491, 494–6, 500), the ecliptic (539, 545), risings and settings (569–87). Here the point is purely meteorological, the visibility of the cluster as a guide to the weather. See again 995–8. The Manger lies between two faint stars called the Asses. If the Manger suddenly becomes invisible and the Asses seem closer together, a storm is portended; if the Manger is merely dim, rain; if one Ass is dim and the other bright, wind from the direction of the latter. D.S. has the first sign (43) and the second (23), but not the third. Ptol. *Tetr.* 2.14.9 omits the Asses, combines the first and second signs as predicting rain, and gives it as a sign of wind if the Manger is bright and shimmering. Plin. *Nat.* 18.353 follows A., but more briefly. Avienius translates more fully (1651–69), and has also an earlier mention of the Manger (383–8), which is not in A.

892 Φάτνην   D.S. 23 ἐν τῷ Καρκίνῳ δύο ἀστέρες εἰσίν, οἱ καλούμενοι Ὄνοι, ὧν τὸ μεταξὺ τὸ νεφέλιον ἡ Φάτνη καλουμένη. This implies that the name had already been given to the cluster, perhaps by Eudoxus from popular star-lore. Hipparchus calls the cluster τὸ Νεφέλιον (1.10, al.), but the popular name is given in Gem. 3.4. οἱ δὲ ἐν τῷ Καρκίνῳ νεφελοειδεῖ συστροφῇ ἐοικότες καλοῦνται Φάτνη, and similarly in Ptol. *Alm.* 7.5 and *Tetr.* 2.14.9; cf. *Catast.* 11 ἡ ἐν αὐτῷ ὁρωμένη Φάτνη. See Roscher VI 953–4, Allen 112–13. Theocritus imitates A. with a weather sign, 22.21–2 ἐκ δ᾽ Ἄρκτοι τ᾽ ἐφάνησαν Ὄνων τ᾽ ἀνὰ μέσσον ἀμαυρὴ | Φάτνη, σημαίνουσα τὰ πρὸς πλόον εὔδια πάντα. Nonnus invents a rival Manger in the sky, which (*D.* 1.459) ἰσοφυὴς λάμψειεν Ὄνων παρὰ γείτονι Φάτνῃ, so imitating also Call. fr. 110.59–62. In Latin Cicero keeps the Greek *Phatne* (*Prog.* fr. 2) but the standard name is *Praesepe*: Plin. *Nat.* 18.353 *nubecula quam praesepia uocant*, Avien. 1651 *conuenit hic etiam paruum Praesepe notare.*

εἰκυῖα   Cf. 854, and Homeric ἐϊκυῖα in same position (δ 122, μ 79, al.).

893 ἀχλύϊ   Cf. 432 ἀχλύς and 908 ἀχλυόεντι, of stars dimmed by a haze. Here the word describes the naturally hazy appearance of the cluster, due to the inability of the naked eye to resolve it into separate stars. See references on 892, and Man. 4.530 *niger obscura Cancer cum nube.* In modern times it used to be referred to as the Crab Nebula, long after Galileo's telescope had shown it to be a star cluster; see E. S. Carlos, *Sidereal Messenger of Galileo* (1880, repr. 1960) 43–4.

βορραίη   A rare form of βόρειος, proposed by Porson in A. *Th.* 527 (but see Hutchinson ad loc.); cf. Phil. *AP* 9.561.2 = *GP* 3002 Βορραίου Σκυθίης. The Crab is the most northerly constellation in the Zodiac.

ὑπὸ Καρκίνῳ ἠγηλάζει   There are two problems here, the unusual use of ὑπό, and the relevance of ἠγηλάζει. The Manger is not in any sense beneath the Crab, but occupies a fairly central position in it. Mair's 'beneath Cancer' is therefore not satisfactory. Erren accepts it and compares 493–6, where the tropic is said to run ὑπένερθε χελείου, but that is a conceit which implies the drawing of a line on a star map. Zannoni translates 'nel Cancro', which makes sense, but needs some justification as a translation of ὑπό. There seems to be no precise parallel for it, but a comparable use is that which denotes accompanying circumstances, e.g. 765 γαληναίη ὑπὸ νυκτί. The point of this line is that A. is introducing the Manger for the first time, and, as with the constellations earlier, he gives the observer directions for finding it, viz. with or within the Crab. Cf. Schott 'mit dem Krebs'.

Maass, according to his Index Verborum, takes ὑπό *in tmesi* with ἠγηλάζει. Martin approves the tmesis, and explains that the Manger 'marche à l'avant du Cancer dans la direction du nord'. Erren rightly rejects this interpretation with 'Die Krippe geht nicht vor dem Krebs her, und sie geht nicht in nördlicher Richtung' (*PAS* 280). The compound verb can therefore be discarded, but there remains the question of determining in what sense the Manger may be said to occupy a leading position. The only way of associating the Manger with a leading position is to link it with the Crab as the sign that begins the Athenian year with the summer solstice (see note on 545). I agree therefore with Erren that the Manger 'führt nichts anderes an als den Tierkreis'. It is for this reason that A. begins both his list of Zodiac signs (545) and his catalogue of risings and settings (569) with the Crab, and he would have had that leading position very much in mind here. From the observer's point of view it is the Manger that identifies the Crab, and in this sense the Manger may be thought of as leading the Zodiac in company with the Crab.

894 λεπτὰ φαεινόμεναι   Cf. 166, 607. The two stars are γ and δ Cancri, both of 4th magnitude.

895 A. uncharacteristically repeats this whole line without variation from 396. It is indispensable here but not there.

896 ὅσσον τε μάλιστα πυγούσιον   The phrase occurs twice in Homer, of the length of a trench, λ 25 βόθρον ὄρυξ' ὅσσον τε πυγούσιον ἔνθα καὶ ἔνθα, and, with slight variation, κ 517. Here μάλιστα is added to denote an approximate measurement: cf. 497, 538. A. uses the Homeric adj. πυγούσιον as adv. expressing distance, parallel to πολλόν: cf. A.R. 1.379 πήχυιον προύχοντα. Sch. 893 διάστημα ὅσον πυγῶνός ἐστιν. πυγὼν δέ ἐστιν ὁ ἀπὸ τοῦ ὠλεκράνου μέχρι τοῦ μετακονδυλίου ἐπὶ τὸν μικρὸν δάκτυλον τῆς χειρὸς κεκαμμένον μέτρον. This is the short cubit (= 20 δάκτυλοι), as opposed to πῆχυς, which is measured to the finger-tip (= 24 δάκτυλοι). A. has chosen the Homeric word for its epic association, but it is πῆχυς and δάκτυλος that are used by astronomers in the measurement of celestial arcs. The usage originates in the primitive practice of holding out fingers or a hand at arm's length against the sky to measure distances between stars or the altitude of the sun above the horizon, and the terms later became standardised to denote specific angular distances. Thus Hi. 3.5.2 gives the distance between the stars ν and α Leonis as μικρῷ μεῖον ἢ πῆχυν, and 2.5.5 the distance of a star in Argo from the meridian as ὡς ἡμιπήχιον. Neugebauer (*HAMA* 591) suggests that H. was using the older Babylonian cubit (= 30 fingers = 2° 30'), and this may be also the measure represented by πυγούσιον here. Cf. Str. 2.1.18 μετεωρίζεσθαι τὸν ἥλιον ἐπὶ πήχεις ἐννέα. Hi. 1.10.12 gives the distance between the two stars in question as 2° 30', while Ptolemy makes it 2° 50' (*Alm.* 7.5). See Schott and Böker 68.

οἰήσασθαι Attested by the MSS and accepted by edd. before Maass, as also by Veitch, LSJ and Zannoni; see also Lobeck *Phryn.* 719. It is a rare Attic form, probably derived from the normal future οἰήσομαι. There is an epic aor. med. found only in the forms ὀίσατο (α 323) and ὀισάμενος (ι 339) in Homer, and later ὠισάμην (A.R. 1.291, Mosch. 2.8., etc.), and in 1006 the MSS of A. support a corresponding optative. The emendations of Maass and Martin are designed to bring the infin. here into conformity with their conjectures for the optative there. But all attempts to devise a form to suit this double-spondee ending have produced unparalleled and unlikely forms: lengthening of ο in ὀίσασθαι, οι followed by ι in οἰίσασθαι, and an apparent augment in ὠίσασθαι. It is more reasonable to suppose that A. chose the Attic form because of its suitability for this part of the line. See also note on 1006.

897 πὰρ βορέαο Cf. 934. The genitive has the sense of a locative, 'on the north side'.

νότῳ δ' ἔπι ἔρχεται ἐπιέρχεται is the better attested of the variants in the MSS, and was the standard reading of edd. before Voss. But the ι of ἐπι- is normally elided in composition, always before -έρχομαι, and there is also some difficulty in making sense of the compound verb with νότῳ: Ceporinus translates 'appropinquat'. Voss's Νότον δ' ἐπιδέρκεται is based on Avien. 1655 *alter spectat in austrum*, but this translation is too free to be reliable as evidence for the Greek text. Most editors since Bekker have therefore adopted the v.l. ἐπικέκλιται. This, however, can be explained as a gloss derived from 486 νότῳ δ' ἐπικέκλιται ἀγκών, a supposition which receives some support from the marginal note in Π4 (the line of the text itself being lost). Zannoni's emendation seems to solve all the problems: for νότῳ ἔπι cf. 418, for ἐπί in hiatus cf. 1027 ἐπὶ ὄψιον, and for ἔρχεται of the westward movement of stars cf. 843 ἔρχηται of the sun's similar movement. The simple verb is then naturally construed with both prepositional phrases, and the intricate chiasmus of the line brings out the symmetry of the Manger and Asses group.

898 Ὄνοι   See note on 892. Hi. 1.10.12 refers to them as τῶν ἀπ' ἀνατολῆς περὶ τὸ νεφέλιον κειμένων δύο ἀστέρων ὁ μὲν νοτιώτερος ... ὁ δὲ βορειότερος. Ptol. *Alm.* 7.5 adds the names: τῶν ἑπομένων τοῦ τετραπλεύρου β' καλουμένων δὲ Ὄνων. Cf. *Catast.* 11 καλοῦνται δέ τινες αὐτῶν ἀστέρες Ὄνοι, οὓς Διόνυσος ἀνήγαγεν εἰς τὰ ἄστρα, Hyg. 2.23.2 *sunt quidam qui Asini appellantur, a Libero in testa Cancri duabus stellis omnino figurati.* Pliny calls them *Aselli* (18.353), Avienius both *Asini* (385) and *Aselli* (1653). These two stars are also known as the eyes of the Crab; cf. 496. See Theoc. 22.21–2 and Nonn. *D.* 1.458–9, cited on 892.

μέσση δέ τε Φάτνη   This phrase adds nothing new, but serves the dual purpose of rounding off the introductory lines with a reference back to the beginning, and at the same time leading on to the meteorological significance of the Manger.

899 εἰ δέ   The text of the MSS (ἦτε, ἤ τε) ends this sentence at 901, and thus makes 902 a separate sentence. This seems to produce a general statement about the Manger, that it disappears whenever the sky is wholly clear. But, as Voss and Martin have pointed out, what the context requires is a conditional clause for the weather sign and an apodosis for the weather portended. The scholia give four versions of the passage. One follows the transmitted text, ἥτις Φάτνη καὶ παντελῶς οὔσης εὐδίας αἰφνιδίως ἀφανὴς γίνεται, but is then obliged to supply ὅτε δὲ τοῦτο γίνεται to make the connection with 902. The other scholia variously interpret the four lines as a conditional sentence: (1) ἐάν, φησίν, οἱ μὲν ἀστέρες ἐγγὺς ἀλλήλων φαίνωνται, ἀφανὴς δὲ ἡ Φάτνη, τηνικαῦτα βαρὺν χειμῶνα προσδέχου. (2) ἐὰν εὐδίας οὔσης ἴδῃς τὴν Φάτνην αἰφνιδίως γενομένην ἀφανῆ, ... μέγαν χειμῶνα προσδόκα. (3) ἂν τοίνυν ἐξαίφνης ἀφανὴς μὲν ἡ Φάτνη γενηθῇ, ... χειμῶνα ἔπομβρον δηλοῖ. Cf. *D.S.* 43 ἡ τοῦ Ὄνου Φάτνη εἰ συνίσταται καὶ ζοφερὰ γίνεται, χειμῶνα σημαίνει, Plin. *Nat.* 18.353 *haec cum caelo sereno apparere desiit, atrox hiems sequitur,* Ptol. *Tetr.* 2.14.9 ἐπὰν αἰθρίας οὔσης αἱ συστάσεις ἀμαυραὶ καὶ ὥσπερ ἀφανεῖς ἢ πεπαχυμέναι θεωρῶνται, φορᾶς ὑδάτων εἰσὶ δηλωτικαί, Avien. 1657–60 *Praesepe repente | si sese ex oculis procul auferat, ... | nequaquam tenues agitabunt stagna procellae.*
Line 899 therefore requires εἰ or some equivalent, but it is difficult to

find a place for it as long as ἤ is retained; the difficulty is well illustrated by the conjectures of Voss and Martin, which create an awkwardness that is unnecessary in simply introducing a conditional clause. Keydell (584) is also doubtful about the crasis κεἰ. The demonstrative article is however not essential here, since the end of 898 has established Φάτνη as the immediately preceding subject, and this can be carried over into 899 and 903. It is characteristic of the demonstrative article that it takes up a noun or pronoun that is not the subject of the preceding sentence; cf. 5, 214, 284, 420, 582, 699, 755, 1150. It seems simplest therefore to read εἰ δέ in A.'s normal manner: ει and η are often confused in the MSS (cf. 788, 834, 842). This produces a series of εἰ clauses (cf. 788–94), and variation is provided by the different moods of the three verbs.

Διός Strictly the sky, but the accompanying fair weather may suggest the benevolence of the Stoic god; cf. 426, 743.

εὐδιόωντος The form with Homeric diectasis is preferable: cf. 278 and A.R. 1.424, 2.371, 903.

900 ἄφαντος ὅλη This seems to be a deliberate pun on Υ 303 ἄφαντος ὅληται, which is concerned with the possible disappearance of Dardanus' family. The sense of ὅλη is otherwise hardly significant, since the Manger is so small that it is unlikely to be partially visible. For ἄφαντος cf. also Ζ 60, and Parm. 9.3 φάεος καὶ νυκτὸς ἀφάντου. The sudden disappearance of faint stars is due to the presence of high cirrus clouds preceding a low-pressure system; cf. 1013.

ἰόντες The verb of motion here, as elsewhere, merely reflects the westward movement of the stars, and there is no need to emend to ἐόντες.

901 αὐτοσχεδόν Homeric adv. of close combat, only here c. gen. There seems to be a verbal echo of Ο 708 δῇουν ἀλλήλους αὐτοσχεδόν, and a metrical echo of Η 273 αὐτοσχεδὸν οὐτάζοντο. The adv. occurs in the same *sedes* also in Ν 496, 526, Ο 386, Ρ 530, Χ 293. The disappearance of the Manger produces the optical illusion that the two stars are closer together.

ἰνδάλλονται Cf. 194, 939.

902 κλύζονται Cf. 299, 943, and 287 περικλύζοιο. Q.S. 2.350 imitates with περικλύζονται ἄρουραι.

903 μελαίνηται D.S. 23 τοῦτο [sc. τὸ νεφέλιον] ἐὰν ζοφῶδες γένηται, ὑδατικόν. For the pure subjunctive after εἰ cf. 858.

αὐτίχ' Here probably 'at the same time'; see note on 199.

ἐοικότες Sch. ἐοικότες αὐτοῖς. Cf. 168, 1091.

904 περί Maass emends to ἐπί on the strength of 873 and perhaps 1093. But there is no reason why A. should not have varied the ex-

pression with περί, which he uses after σήματα (777) in a comparable, if not exactly similar, sense.

905 φαείνοι The optative is clearly right, since it matches the mood of the parallel clause. Voss's φανείη ('weil der verbundene Saz είη hat') is hard to understand: a change to aorist would suggest that the star suddenly appears bright. It does, however, have some support from sch. ἐάν, φησίν, ὁ ἐκ βορείου μέρους τῆς Φάτνης ἀμαυρὸς φανῇ.

906 λεπτόν Cf. λεπτά (166, 607, 894).

ἐπαχλύων The diectasis of the MSS is not attested elsewhere in this verb. The commonest form of the verb is the aorist, after μ 406 ἤχλυσε: cf. A.R. 3.963, Nonn. *D.* 4.380, Q.S. 1.79, 598, 14.462 (ἐπάχλυσεν), all with long υ. The only other instance of the present participle is in A.R. 4.1480 ἢ ἴδεν ἢ ἐδόκησεν ἐπαχλύουσαν ἰδέσθαι, and this gives strong support to Schneider's emendation here, since the astronomical context makes it likely that a deliberate echo of A. is intended. The corruption may have been due to the influence of ἀχλυόεντι (908).

ἀγλαός Cf. 77, 165, 415 of bright stars.

907 δειδέχθαι Cf. 795.

μάλα χρή Cf. 434, 860, 995. Note also the chiasmus of νότου βορέω in the middle of the line.

908 ἔμπαλιν Cf. 30, of the Bears being aligned in opposite directions, Pl. *Tht.* 193c οἱ ἔμπαλιν ὑποδούμενοι, of putting shoes on the wrong way round. Here the expression is a condensed way of saying 'from the hazy and bright stars being the other way round', i.e. the southern being hazy and the northern bright. Cf. Pliny's equal but different style of brevity: *si uero alteram earum aquiloniam caligo abstulit, auster saeuit, si austrinam, aquilo* (*Nat.* 18.353). The clearing of the Manger as a sign of fair weather is noted at 996–8, and in Theoc. 22.21–2.

ἀχλυόεντι Cf. Mus. 3 γάμον ἀχλυόεντα.

δοκεύειν See note on 813.

909–1043 MISCELLANEOUS SIGNS OF WEATHER CONDITIONS

In the preceding section A. has found it convenient to organise his material according to the observed signs. But the sub-celestial signs are so numerous and varied that he now changes his procedure and classifies according to the predicted weather systems, using the four traditional categories: wind (909–32), rain (933–87), fair weather (988–1012), storm (1013–43). Cf. *D.S.* rain (10–25), wind (26–37), storm (38–49), fair weather (50–5); Virgil, *G.* 1 wind (356–69), rain (370–92), fair weather

(393–414); *Geoponica* 1 fair weather (2), storm and rain (3), severe storm (4). Pliny continues his system of classifying by signs (*Nat.* 18.354–65). A.'s arrangement of the material now seems less methodical, and designed rather with the object of bringing out the great abundance and variety of the signs available to those who have eyes to see them: cf. 1036–7, 1101–3. See also note on 758–1141.

909–932 *Signs of wind*

The section heading is clearly marked in σῆμα δέ τοι ἀνέμοιο, and the signs are to be observed in the sea (909–12), sea-birds (913–19), clouds (920), thistledown (921–3), thunder and lightning (924–5), meteors (926–32).

909 οἰδαίνουσα The form in -άνω is transitive in Homer, and used of emotion in Ι 554 (χόλος) οἰδάνει ἐν στήθεσσι νόον (cf. A.R. 1.478), and 646 οἰδάνεται κραδίη χόλῳ, but it is intransitive in Ar. *Pax* 1165 φάληχ' ὁρῶν οἰδάνοντ', like οἰδέω. So here the derived form in -αίνω, and in A.R. 3.383 (φρένες) νειόθεν οἰδαίνεσκον.

909–912 These four lines elaborate the brief note in *D.S.* 29 θάλασσα οἰδοῦσα καὶ ἀκταὶ βοῶσαι καὶ αἰγιαλὸς ἠχῶν ἀνεμώδης. The characteristic variation suggests that A. is the imitator: the rare οἰδαίνω for the normal οἰδέω, with reversal of the word order; the interchange of ἀκταί and αἰγιαλός, with the latter in the plural; the masc. pl. participle with diectasis for the normal fem. pl.; the fem. pl. adj. for the masc. sg. ἠχῶν; the additional sign from mountain-tops, perhaps from the source of *D.S.* 31. Jermyn (29) discusses the sound effects in this passage, comparing Cicero's version (*Prog.* fr. 3) and Virgil's striking imitation in *G.* 1.356–9 *continuo uentis surgentibus aut freta ponti | incipiunt agitata tumescere et aridus altis | montibus audiri fragor aut resonantia longe | litora misceri et nemorum increbrescere murmur.* Cf. Homer's sea simile in Ξ 16–19. Pliny (359) separates the shore signs, *litora ripaeque si resonabunt tranquillo, asperam tempestatem,* from those of the open sea, *saepe et silentio intumescit inflatumque altius solito iam intra se esse uentos fatetur.* *Gp.* 1.11.7 reverts to the brief essentials: ἄνεμον δὲ προμηνύει θάλασσα κυμαίνουσα καὶ ἐπὶ αἰγιαλοῖς μεγάλα ἠχοῦσα. Cf. Pap. Wessely fr. 3.ii. 2–4 [θαλασσα οι]δουσα ευδιας ουσης [και ακται ψο]φουσαι και ηχουσαι [ανεμους σ]ημαινουσι.

910 γινέσθω A didactic touch; cf. 974, 1001, ἔστω 246, 836.

μακρὸν ἔπ' There is general agreement that A. is describing a sound that is heard a long way off: sch. (M) ὅταν ἐπὶ πολὺ ἠχῶσιν οἱ αἰγιαλοί, Avien. 1672–3 *cum litora curua resultant | sponte procul,* Virgil's *resonantia longe,* Mair's 'far sounding', etc. The sound can also be called 'loud', e.g.

sch. (MΔUAS) μέγα κράζοντες, Zannoni 'muggiscono forte', but it is the distance that is highlighted in μακρόν: cf. Γ 81 μακρὸν ἄϋσεν, Pl. *Prt.* 329a μακρὸν ἠχεῖ. There remains the problem of the transmitted reading ἐπ'. It cannot be taken *in tmesi* with βοόωντες, since ἐπιβοάω does not give the required sense. It could be an adverb, with the sense 'also', but this seems weakly superfluous, and no translator gives this meaning. Maass suggests that ἔπ' is the reading implied by Avien. 1673, comparing ζ 117 αἱ δ' ἐπὶ μακρὸν ἄϋσαν. It is risky to take the Latin translation as evidence for so subtle a detail in the Greek text, but the reading suggested is nevertheless very satisfactory, and Martin rightly adopts it. For the anastrophe cf. ε 251 τόσσον ἔπ'.

βοόωντες Cf. 1003 and B 97. In the choice of this verb A. is recalling P 264–5 ἀμφὶ δέ τ' ἄκραι | ἠϊόνες βοόωσιν. The scholia cite less aptly B 210 and ε 402. For the diectasis see note on 27 τροχόωσι.

911 ἀκταί τ' εἰνάλιοι Whereas αἰγιαλοί are usually sandy beaches, suitable for mooring ships (cf. 298, and B 210, Δ 422, Ξ 34, χ 385), ἀκταί are often rocky coasts exposed to rough seas (e.g. B 395, M 284, Υ 50, ε 425). The epithet is perhaps intended to suggest the idea of jutting out into the open sea, as it is more normally used of men or creatures whose life is spent on or in the sea: cf. 942, ε 67, Theoc. 21.39. It is attested with two terminations in E. *Hel.* 526–7, but more frequently with three, e.g. ε 67 κορῶναι εἰνάλιαι, Alc. *AP* 7.1.3 = *HE* 64, Antip. *AP* 9.10.1 = *GP* 169, Antiphil. *AP* 9.14.8 = *GP* 972, Diodor. *AP* 9.60.1 = *GP* 2184. It is curious that all MSS here read εἰνάλιοι, whereas at 942 all read εἰνάλιαι. Buttmann's emendation here restores uniformity, but we cannot rule out the possibility that the variation is intentional. The phrase seems to recall E. *Hel.* 1130–1 Αἰγαίαις τ' ἐνάλοις δόλιον | ἀκταῖς ἀστέρα λάμψας, and Tim. *PMG* 791.97–9 ἐβρίθοντο δ' ἀϊόνες, | οἱ δ' ἐπ' ἀκταῖς ἐνάλοις | ἥμενοι. The case endings in 911 form a chiastic pattern, as in 458. A different but comparable variation of usage may be seen in the scansion of εὔδιοι, with ι short in this line and long in 916 in the same metrical position after ὁπότ'.

ἠχήεσσαι Cf. A 157 οὔρεά τε σκιόεντα θάλασσά τε ἠχήεσσα. The word occurs elsewhere in Homer only in δ 72 δώματα ἠχήεντα. Cf. Hes. *Th.* 767 δόμοι ἠχήεντες, Leon. *AP* 7.652.1 = *HE* 2040 ἠχήεσσα θάλασσα.

912 γίνωνται See note on 828 περιτέλλῃ.

κορυφαί Frequent in Homer of mountain-tops, and here recalling particularly M 282 ὑψηλῶν ὀρέων κορυφὰς καὶ πρώονας ἄκρους. Cf. *h.Hom.* 2.38 ἤχησαν δ' ὀρέων κορυφαί.

βοώμεναι Cf. 910 βοόωντες, P 264–5, Q.S. 1.322 βοόωσί τε πάντοθεν ἄκραι. For the middle part. cf. 291.

913–19 The birds listed here appear in the reverse order in *D.S.* 28: gulls, ducks, petrels, herons, with the addition of sparrows. Virgil has gulls, coots, herons (360–4), Pliny coots, gulls, ducks (362).

913 καὶ δ' Cf. 256, 300, 1010.

ἐπὶ ξηρήν Sc. γῆν. Cf. X. *Oec.* 19.7 ἐν τῇ ξηρᾷ ἂν βαθὺν ὀρύττοις βόθρον, A.R. 4.1378 ξηρὴν ὑποδύσεται, and the neuter as subst. in Th. 8.105.1 ἐξέωσάν τε ἐς τὸ ξηρὸν τὰς ναῦς, A.R. 3.322 ποτὶ ξερόν, Nic. *Ther.* 704 ἐπὶ ξερόν.

ἐρωδιός *D.S.* 28 ἐρωδιὸς ἀπὸ θαλάσσης πετόμενος καὶ βοῶν πνεύματος σημεῖόν ἐστι, V. *G.* 1.363–4 *notasque paludes | deserit atque altam supra uolat ardea nubem*, Luc. 5.553–4 *ausa uolare | ardea sublimis pinnae confisa natanti*. Cf. 972. Aristotle uses ἐρωδιός as a general term for the heron, and identifies three different species (*HA* 609b). It appears once in Homer, as a good omen sent by Athena (K 274); cf. Ael. *NA* 10.37. Clearch. ap. Athen. 8 332e includes it as one of the birds known as παρευδιασταί, and Plu. 405D among the prophetic birds. Cf. Hippon. fr. 16 West. Cic. *Prog.* fr. 3.7 and Avien. 1676 both use *fulix* in translating this line. See Thompson 102–3, Pollard 68, 113.

οὐ κατὰ κόσμον Cf. 654, 1086. A. means an unsteadiness or irregularity in the course of the bird's flight; sch. τῇ ἀτάκτῳ πτήσει. Contrast the steady onward flight of cranes as a sign of good weather (1011–12). Here A. adds a detail not given by *D.S.* The line-end position is Homeric, e.g. υ 181; cf. K 472.

914 ἐξ ἁλὸς ἔρχηται Perhaps a reminiscence of δ 448 φῶκαι δ' ἐξ ἁλὸς ἦλθον. Cf. Call. fr. 522 δύπται δ' ἐξ ἁλὸς ἐρχόμενοι ἔνδιοι [εὔδιοι Schn.] καύηκες. But Pfeiffer sees no reference to a weather sign.

περιπολλά Not otherwise attested, but cf. A.R. 2.437 περιπολλὸν εὐφρονέων. The prefix intensifies the adverb, as in περικαλλής, whereas adverbial πέρι tends to imply a comparison, which is not in the context here. The same objection applies to the v.l. περίαλλα, though Bekker adopts it; cf. Nic. *Ther.* 620 καναχοὶ περίαλλα.

λεληκώς Once in Homer, X 141 ὀξὺ λεληκώς, of a hawk. A. has the latter phrase in 972, of the heron. Cf. μ 85 δεινὸν λελακυῖα of Scylla, Hes. *Op.* 207, the hawk to the nightingale, τί λέληκας;

915 κινυμένου Cf. 1114, K 280, κ 556, all in same *sedes*.

θάλασσαν ὕπερ Sch. πνεῖν μέλλοντος ἀνέμου ὑπὲρ τὴν θάλασσαν.

φορέοιτ' ἀνέμοιο The weather predicted is expressed as the weather accompanying the heron's flight.; cf. 844, 876.

916 κέπφοι A sea-bird, but one that has proved difficult to identify precisely. It frequents the surf in search of its food: sch. (M) ὁ κέπφος ἐνάλιον ζῷόν ἐστιν, ἀφρῷ τε χαίρων καὶ τούτῳ τρεφόμενος. Cf. Arist. *HA* 593b, Nic. *Alex.* 166ff., Lyc. 836. It is light and slender, and is said to run across the surface of the water: Dion. *Av.* 2.10 ἐκ τῆς κουφότητος οἱ ἁλιεῖς ὀνομάζουσιν· τὸ γὰρ ὕδωρ ἄκρον τοῖς ποσὶν ἐπιτρέχει καὶ σημαίνει τοῖς ἁλιεῦσιν ἐπιτυχίαν. Cf. Hsch. s.v. Because it is lightweight and easily caught, it is proverbial for stupidity: Ar. *Pax* 1067 καὶ κέπφοι τρήρωνες ἀλωπεκιδεῦσι πέπεισθε, sch. 1067 εὐηθὲς ζῷον ὁ κέπφος, 1067b τοὺς ἐλαφροὺς ταῖς φρεσὶ κέπφους καλοῦμεν. Cf. Ar. *Pl.* 912, Call. fr. 191.6, Cic. *Att.* 13.40.2. It is particularly associated with wind, because of its habit of facing directly into a breeze: sch. (ΜΔΚUAS) ἐπειδὰν οὖν προαίσθηται ὀλίγου πνεύματος πνεῖν μέλλοντος, ἵπταται, οὐ φεύγων τὸν ἄνεμον, ἀλλ' αὐτοῦ τοῦ ἀνέμου ἀντιπρόσωπος, ἐπειδὴ τὸ σῶμα σφόδρα ἰσχνὸν ἔχει. Hence the weather sign: *D.S.* 28 οἱ κέπφοι εὐδίας οὔσης ὅποι ἂν πέτωνται ἄνεμον προσημαίνουσι. On the problem of identification see W. W. Fowler, *CR* 32 (1918) 66–8, D. W. Thompson, ibid. 95–6 and *Glossary* (1936) 137–8, Pollard 196 'storm petrel'. J. Warham, in a personal note, identifies the bird as 'a petrel (*Calonectris diomedea diomedea*)'. For illustrations see Zoltán Kádár, *Survivals of Greek Zoological Illuminations in Byzantine Manuscripts* (Budapest 1978), 83 and plates 126, 2a–b, 135, 37a–b, K. Weitzmann, *Late Antique and Early Christian Book Illumination* (London 1977), plate 20.

ποτέωνται Cf. 828 περιτέλλῃ. Indic. due to φέρονται below.

917 ἀντία C. gen., as frequently in Homer, e.g. ο 377 ἀντία δεσποίνης φάσθαι. Cf. 440, 694, 1084.

εἰληδά Adv., only here, equivalent to Homeric ἰλαδόν (Β 93, of men mustering like a swarm of bees). The noun ἴλη is used mostly of men, but of lions in E. *Alc.* 581. The form εἰλ-, if correct, reflects εἴλη = ἴλη (Frisk 1.722), and appears as a variant in Β 93, also in Hdt. 1.73, 172, 202; εἰληδόν is attested in Antiphil. *AP* 9.14.6 = *GP* 970, where it means 'by coiling round'. A. seems to have associated the suffix particularly with swarming, since he has also ἀγεληδά (965, 1079), ἀγεληδόν (1005; cf. Π 160), ὁμιλαδόν (1078; cf. Μ 3, Ο 277, -ηδόν Hes. *Sc.* 170). In 1021 κλαγγηδόν is used of a flock of birds, as also in Β 463.

918 ἀγριάδες Cf. A.R. 1.28 φηγοὶ δ' ἀγριάδες, Call. fr. 75.13 αἶγας ἐς ἀγριάδας.

νῆσσαι *D.S.* 28 αἴθυιαι καὶ νῆτται καὶ ἄγριαι καὶ τιθασσαὶ ὕδωρ μὲν σημαίνουσι δυόμεναι, πτερυγίζουσαι δὲ ἄνεμον. Cf. Ael. *NA* 7.7 νῆτται δὲ καὶ αἴθυιαι πτερυγίζουσαι πνεῦμα δηλοῦσιν ἰσχυρόν = *CCAG* 8.1.138, 16 = Anon. Laur. 11.35. For domestic ducks as signs of rain see 970, 942ff.

εἰναλίδιναι Only here, perhaps coined by A. Sch. τὰς δὲ αἰθυίας εἰναλιδίνας φησὶν ἐπεὶ δυνουσῶν αὐτῶν τῇ θαλάσσῃ ἐπιγίνεταί τις δῖνος, τουτέστι κυκλοτερὴς τοῦ ὕδατος φορά. I follow Voss, Mair and LSJ in using the recessive accent: cf. Arch. *AP* 6.16.4 εἰναλίφοιτα. The variant -δῖναι no doubt comes from the tradition of breaking up the adj. into three words. A. uses the three terminations, as in 942 εἰνάλιαι.

919 αἴθυιαι For the identification and literary associations of this bird see note on 296. For the weather sign cf. *D.S.* 28 and Ael. *NA* 7.7 cited in preceding note, also Suda s.v. αἴθυια· αἱ γὰρ αἴθυιαι ὅταν δύνωσι, κάκιστος οἰωνὸς τοῖς πλέουσι. V. *G.* 1.361–2 *cum medio celeres reuolant ex aequore mergi | clamoremque ferunt ad litora* varies αἴθυιαι with *mergi* and for the rest recalls the heron's cry in 914.

χερσαῖα N.pl. as adv. The adj. is commonly used of land birds and animals (e.g. Hdt. 7.119.2, 2.123), and here it brings out the unnatural behaviour of sea-birds sensing the approach of bad weather.

τινάσσονται πτερύγεσσιν Repeated in 971; cf. also 969, β 151 τιναξάσθην πτερὰ πυκνά, Opp. *C.* 2.437, Q.S. 5.437 τινασσόμενος πτερύγεσσιν.

920 νεφέλη κτλ. A close paraphrase of *D.S.* 34 πρὸς κορυφῆς ὄρους ὁπόθεν ἂν νεφέλη μηκύνηται, ταύτῃ ἄνεμος πνευσεῖται. Plin. *Nat.* 18.356 makes this a storm sign: *cum in cacuminibus montium nubes consistunt, hiemabit.* This familiar phenomenon occurs when rising air condenses on the summits and forms a cloud, which remains formed as the moving air passes through it.

ὄρεος ... κορυφῇσιν A reminiscence of Γ 10 εὖτ᾽ ὄρεος κορυφῇσι Νότος κατέχευεν ὀμίχλην. Cf. 912.

921 πάπποι Appropriately named; cf. Eust. on Ε 408 ὡς ἐξ ὁμοιότητος ἴσως τοῦ παρ᾽ ἡμῶν προγόνου γέροντος πάππου, καὶ τὸ ἀκάνθινον ἐν ξηρότητι πολίωμα, ὅπερ Ἄρατος "λευκῆς γήρειον ἀκάνθης" λέγει. For the weather sign cf. *D.S.* 37 ἐὰν ἐν τῇ θαλάττῃ πάπποι φέρωνται πολλοὶ οἱ γινόμενοι ἀπὸ τῶν ἀκανθῶν, ἄνεμον σημαίνουσιν ἔσεσθαι μέγαν. Sch. ἡ ἄκανθα ἡ καλουμένη κινάρα ἐπειδὰν ἐξανθήσῃ ἀλλοιοῦται, γήραμα δὲ αὐτῆς ἐστιν ὁ καλούμενος πάππος. ἐν δὲ τοῖς παραθαλαττίοις χωρίοις, ἐπειδὰν πνεύσῃ ἄνεμος, οἱ πάπποι κοῦφοι ὄντες καὶ εὔθρυπτοι, ὑπὸ ὀλίγου ἀνέμου ἀνατρεπόμενοι, ἐμπίπτουσι τῷ ὕδατι, καὶ ἐπιπλέοντες δῆλοί εἰσιν ὅτι ἀνέμου κατιόντος σημεῖόν εἰσιν, Hsch. πάππος· ἄκανθα· ὅταν γηράσῃ καὶ ἀποξηρανθῇ καὶ ὑπὸ ἀνέμων ἐκριπίζηται καὶ τόπον ἐκ τόπου μεταβάλλῃ. Cf. S. fr. 868 γραίας ἀκάνθης πάππος, Eub. fr. 107 πάππος ἀπ᾽ ἀκάνθης. Virgil varies the weather sign with other light material in *G.* 1.368–9 *saepe leuem paleam et frondes uolitare caducas | aut summa nantis in aqua conludere plumas.* Similarly Plin. *Nat.* 18.360 *lanugo populi aut spinae uolitans aquisque plumae innatantes*, and *Gp.* 1.11.7 καὶ ἄκανθαι καὶ ξηρὰ φύλλα ἐναντία ὑπὸ τῶν ἀνέμων εἰλούμενα.

γήρειον The downy seed as a product of the flower's old age; cf. preceding note, and Eust. on λ 520 ἀπὸ τοῦ γῆρος ἀκάνθης ἐξάνθημα παρὰ τῷ Ἀράτῳ γήρειον. Nicander imitates in two similes, *Ther.* 329 σκίδναται ὡς γήρεια καταψηχθέντος ἀκάνθης, *Alex.* 126 οἷά τε δὴ γήρεια νέον τεθρυμμένα κάκτου.

ἀκάνθης A general name for any prickly plant, but especially the thistle. Poetic references to flying thistledown look back to ε 328 ὡς δ᾽ ὅτ᾽ ὀπωρινὸς Βορέης φορέῃσιν ἀκάνθας, the sole occurrence of this word in Homer. Cf. Mel. *AP* 4.1.37 = *HE* 3962 σκολιότριχος ἄνθος ἀκάνθης, Rufin. *AP* 5.48.5 = 19.5 Page πλοκαμοῖσι διαστίλβουσιν ἄκανθαι. In Theophr. *HP*, Index, ἄκανθα ἡ λευκή is identified by Hort as an acacia (*Acacia albida*), but A. is presumably using the epithet as a general description of thistledown.

922 κωφῆς A low swell (cf. 909) with no sound of breakers; cf. *Et.M.* ἀψόφῳ καὶ μηδένα ἦχον ἀποτελοῦντι. A. recalls the simile in Ξ 16–19 ὡς δ᾽ ὅτε πορφύρῃ πέλαγος μέγα κύματι κωφῷ, | … πρίν τινα κεκριμένον καταβήμεναι ἐκ Διὸς οὖρον, where sch. BL ἀφώνῳ, μηδέπω παφλάζοντι. Cf. Rufin. *AP* 5.35.7 = 11.7 Page. Latin has *surdus* in this sense, e.g. Prop. 4.3.53 *omnia surda tacent*, and, of the sea, also *caecus*, e.g. Sis. *hist.* fr. 104P *caecosque fluctus in se prouoluere leniter occepit*.

923 ἐπιπλώωσι The papyri confirm the reading of K, rightly aorist after ἐγένοντο. The form is athematic, with sources in Homer, e.g. Z 291 ἐπιπλὼς εὐρέα πόντον, γ 15 ἐπέπλως. Cf. Hes. *Op.* 650 ἐπέπλων, A.R. 2.152 ἐπέπλωμεν. From the aorist a present in -ώω was formed (see Chantraine 1.365), e.g. ε 284 ἐπιπλώων, Theoc. 17.91 ἐπιπλώοντι, Call. *H.* 4.213 ἐπιπλώουσα ('floating'), Opp. *H.* 1.9 ἐπιπλώουσι, 81 πλώοντα, Colluth. 212 παραπλώων. For the sense of 'floating' cf. also Hdt. 3.23 ἐπ᾽ αὐτοῦ [sc. τοῦ ὕδατος] ἐπιπλέειν, Arist. *HA* 622b ἐπιπλεῖ γὰρ ἐπὶ τῆς θαλάττης, *Mete.* 384b ἐπὶ τῷ ὕδατι ἐπιπλεῖ.

τὰ μὲν πάρος ἄλλα δ᾽ ὀπίσσω Cf. 705, of Andromeda rising, first one half, then the other. The adverbs express time in both instances, as does πάρος elsewhere in A. (101, 845); cf. λ 483 οὔ τις ἀνὴρ προπάροιθε μακάρτατος οὔτ᾽ ἄρ᾽ ὀπίσσω. Voss understands them of direction, 'einiges vorwärts, und anderes zurück'. But the down is drifting in patches, and the observer sees first one, then another; cf. N 799, of successive waves, πρὸ μέν τ᾽ ἄλλ᾽, αὐτὰρ ἐπ᾽ ἄλλα.

924 θέρεος Temporal rather than possessive, in view of the parallel passages: *D.S.* 32 θέρους ὅθεν ἂν ἀστραπαὶ καὶ βρονταὶ γίνωνται, ἐντεῦθεν πνεύματα γίνεται ἰσχυρά, *Gp.* 1.3.3 βρονταὶ δὲ καὶ ἀστραπαὶ ὅθεν ἂν γίγνωνται, ἐκεῖθεν τὸν χειμῶνα δηλοῦσιν (= Anon. Laur. 9), 1.11.8 βρονταὶ καὶ ἀστραπαὶ θέρους ὅθεν φέρονται, ἐκεῖθεν ἄνεμον προσδόκα. Cf. Plin. *Nat.* 18.354 *cum aestate uehementius tonuit quam fulsit, uentos ex ea parte denuntiat*.

ἔνθεν Relative, as in ε 195 ὁ μὲν ἔνθα καθέζετ᾽ ἐπὶ θρόνου ἔνθεν ἀν-ἔστη. Cf. Cerc. 18.40 Powell φόρτος ἔνθεν ἦλθεν ἔνθ' ἦλθεν. A.'s word-play with the same adv. as demonstrative appears to be unique, but the verb of motion suits ἔνθεν rather than ἔνθα, which Voss prefers because of the Homeric usage.

ἴωσιν The transmitted reading is appropriate with ἔνθεν, and Maass is not justified in altering it merely on the strength of the verbs in 19, 933, and D.S. 32.

925 ἐπερχομένοιο For the internal rhyme see note on 360.

περισκοπέειν Cf. 435.

926 ἀστέρες ἀΐσσωσι Arist. Pr. 942b16 διὰ τί, ὅταν ἀστέρες διᾴττωσιν, ἀνέμου σημεῖον; D.S. 37 ὅθεν ἂν ἀστέρες διᾴττωσι πολλοί, ἄνεμον ἐντεῦθεν· ἐὰν δὲ πανταχόθεν ὁμοίως, πολλὰ πνεύματα σημαίνουσι. Cf. 13 ἀστέρες πολλοὶ διᾴττοντες ὕδατος ἢ πνεύματος καὶ ὅθεν ἂν διᾴττωσιν ἐντεῦθεν τὸ πνεῦμα ἢ τὸ ὕδωρ, Gp. 1.11.9 ἀστέρες διαπίπτοντες [? διᾴττοντες] ὅπου τρέπονται, ἐκεῖ χρὴ τὸ πνεῦμα προσδέχεσθαι, Anon. Laur. 8.6 ἀστέρες ὅθεν διατείνουσιν [? διᾴττουσιν], ἐντεῦθεν ἄνεμον σημαίνει, Ptol. Tetr. 2.14.10 αἱ δὲ διαδρομαὶ καὶ οἱ ἀκοντισμοὶ τῶν ἀστέρων εἰ μὲν ἀπὸ μιᾶς γίνοιντο γωνίας, τὸν ἀπ' ἐκείνης ἄνεμον δηλοῦσι κτλ. Cf. also Plin. Nat. 2.100 fieri uidentur et discursus stellarum, numquam temere ut non ex ea parte truces uenti cooriantur, 18.351 discurrere hae uidentur interdum, uentique protinus secuntur in quorum parte ita praesagiere.

The source of the poetic meteor theme, with both speed of flight and trail of sparks, is the simile of Athena's descent in Δ 75–7 οἷον δ' ἀστέρα ἧκε Κρόνου πάϊς ἀγκυλομήτεω, | ἢ ναύτῃσι τέρας ἠὲ στρατῷ εὐρέϊ λαῶν, | λαμπρόν· τοῦ δέ τε πολλοὶ ἀπὸ σπινθῆρες ἵενται. In Alcm. PMG 3.66–7 Astymeloisa is compared to τις αἰγλάεντος ἀστὴρ | ὠρανῶ διαιπετής. In Ar. Pax 838–9 Trygaeus is asked τίνες δ' ἄρ' εἰσ' οἱ διατρέχοντες ἀστέρες, | οἳ καόμενοι θέουσιν; Theocritus' novel simile of Hylas' fall (13.50–2) implies a meteorite: ὡς ὅτε πυρσὸς ἀπ' οὐρανοῦ ἤριπεν ἀστὴρ | ἀθρόος ἐν πόντῳ, ναύτας δέ τις εἶπεν ἑταίροις | "κουφότερ', ὦ παῖδες, ποιεῖσθ' ὅπλα· πλευστικὸς οὖρος"; cf. note on 421. Virgil expands A.'s two lines to three, bringing out the effect of a meteor trail, in G. 1.365–7 saepe etiam stellas uento impendente uidebis | praecipitis caelo labi, noctisque per umbram | flammarum longos a tergo albescere tractus. He returns to the meteor theme later, but only as a portent, in A. 2.693ff. Lucan (5.56off.) combines both the weather sign and the portent, as part of a wider cosmic disturbance: uentis, | ad quorum motus non solum lapsa per altum | aera dispersos traxere cadentia sulcos | sidera.

It was probably Homer's use of ἀΐσσω that determined the choice of this verb as a technical term for meteors (and hence the English translation of it as 'shooting stars'). Thus Pl. R. 621b ἄττοντας ὥσπερ ἀστέρας, *D.S.* 13 and 37 cited above. Aristotle varies his terminology with διαδρομαὶ τῶν ἀστέρων (*Mete.* 341a33; cf. Ptol. *Tetr.* 2.14.10, sch. Arat. Par. 2424), διαθέοντες ἀστέρες (*Mete.* 341b3), as well as οἱ δοκοῦντες ἀστέρες διᾴττειν (341b35). Eventually διᾴττοντες ἀστέρες seems to have become the standard term: cf. *De mundo* 395a (not *De caelo*, as in LSJ), D.L. 2.29, Aetius 3.2.9, sch. Par. 2424, and Gem. 17.47 in the form τῶν διαΐσσόντων ἀστέρων. Meteors, of course, being matter that enters the atmosphere from outside and ignites because of the friction, have nothing to do with weather conditions. But Aristotle's theory of dry exhalations rising from the earth itself (*Mete.* A 4) seems to have given support to the traditional lore; cf. sch. ὅτε (ὁ αἰθήρ) ξηρὰς ἀναθυμιά-σεις δέχεται ἀπὸ τῆς γῆς, ξηρὸς ὢν καὶ αὐτὸς καὶ πυρώδης, πυκνού-μενος ἀποπέμπει τινὰς ὥσπερ σπινθῆρας. But Seneca is sceptical: *argumentum tempestatis nautae putant, cum multae transuolant stellae (Nat.* 1.1.12).

927 ταρφέα Homeric adv. in Homeric position, recalling especially Χ 142 ταρφέ' ἐπαΐσσει, of the hawk attacking the dove; cf. Μ 47 and Ν 718, of men in battle, θ 379 of dancers. In Homer the word describes action repeated over and over again (cf. Leumann 166), here the sighting of several meteors in succession, as can happen when the earth in its orbit passes through a trail of particles left by a comet. A.'s meaning is probably 'in quick succession', an exaggeration for poetic effect.

τοὶ δ' The reading of papyri, MSS and most editors. The article is perfectly satisfactory here, picking out a second and striking feature of some meteors, in much the same way as it marks contrasts in 900 and 903; cf. ταί in 855, 859, 1019. Philoponus' τοῖς δ', adopted by Martin and Erren, has no known ancient authority, though it can be understood as a kind of possessive dative. A. elsewhere uses a genitive with ὄπιθεν and ἐξόπιθεν (364, 91). Maass emends in favour of the relative, comparing 930, where he reads ἄλλοις, but I see no advantage in this. Where the transmitted text is unanimous, makes good sense, and is characteristic of A.'s style, there is no justification for rejecting it.

ῥυμοί In Homer ῥυμός is the pole of a chariot (Ε 729, Ζ 40, Κ 505, Π 371, Ψ 393, Ω 271), and it is recorded (Suda) as a name for the line of three stars that form the pole of the constellation Ἅμαξα (cf. 27). It seems unlikely, however, that there is any connection between this latter use and the meteor trails here. The etymology of the word (see Frisk s.v. ἐρύω) associates it basically with the sense of pulling or drawing. Aelian uses it of a horse's rein (*NA* 10.48), and in ῥυμουλκέω it means a towing-rope. A.'s bold innovation here suggests a line drawn across the sky. The scholia equate it with ὁλκοί: cf. A.R. 3.141 ἀστὴρ ὣς φλεγέθοντα δι' ἠέρος ὁλκὸν ἵησιν, Nonn. *D.* 24.90 ὁμοίιος ἀστέρος ὁλκῷ, Luc. 5.562 *sulcos* (cited on 926).

ἐπιλευκαίνωνται There is an interesting divergence in the textual tradition here between ἐπι- in the papyri, backed by Philoponus, and ὑπο- in the MSS, with the support of the great majority of editors. The choice of the latter is at first sight attractive, in view of the occurrence of this verb once in Homer, E 502 αἱ δ' ὑπολευκαίνονται ἀχυρμιαί. There the prefix has its weakening force, with reference to the whitish colour of the chaff, and the same would be appropriate here, since any trail would be fainter than the nucleus of the meteor itself. But ἐπιλευκαίνω also has the sense of being whitish, where it occurs elsewhere, e.g. Theophr. *HP* 3.12.9 τὴν δὲ χρόαν ξανθὸν ἐπιλευκαίνοντα (cf. Arist. *PA* 676a32). Sch. explain simply with λευκανθίζοντας ἀστέρας and αὕτη ἡ πορεία λευκαίνεται. Cf. A.R. 1.545 μακραὶ δ' αἰὲν ἐλευκαίνοντο κέλευθοι, of *Argo*'s wake. The reading of the MSS can be explained as due to the Homeric influence, which may also explain why they have the indicative. For the pure subjunctive with ὅτε see note on 828, and the parallel verb ἀίσσωσι.

928 δειδέχθαι Cf. 795, 907.

αὐτὴν ὁδόν Cf. θ 107 ἄρχε δὲ τῷ αὐτὴν ὁδὸν ἥν περ οἱ ἄλλοι. Sch. 927 give the popular explanation of the connection between meteors and weather: οἱ διᾴττοντες ἀστέρες ὅθεν ἐκπηδῶσιν, ἐκεῖθεν τὸ πνεῦμα δεῖ προσδοκᾶν· ὠθεῖ γὰρ αὐτοὺς ἐκεῖθεν.

929 εἰ δέ κεν Despite the support for ἥν in papyri and MSS its combination with κεν is doubtful: in σ 318 ἥν περ γάρ κ' ἐθέλωσιν Monro would read εἰ (*HG* 331). Here εἰ would be more characteristic of A.'s usage, especially in this part of the poem (cf. 788, 794, 811, 832, 974, 980). For confusion of εἰ and ἥν in the MSS see also 794, 903. The v.l. καί is not in the MSS (it is wrongly attributed to A by Maass), and is in any case pointless; it comes from sch. ἐὰν δὲ καὶ ἄλλοι.

ἐναντίοι The reading of S and the editors before Voss comes from sch. (MUS) ἐναντίον τῶν προειρημένων ὁρμῶσι. This weather sign is essentially in two parts, meteors moving (*a*) in one direction, (*b*) in different directions: see *D.S.* 37, cited on 926. A. inserts here an intermediate category, if the explanation of the scholia is right, namely meteors moving in the opposite direction to (*a*). The addition is somewhat superfluous, since these meteors can be assumed to be included in (*b*), and it is possible to eliminate it by taking ἐναντίοι with the v.l. ἄλλοις in 930. But the latter reading involves other difficulties (see next note), and it is more satisfactory to accept the interpretation of the scholia, and assume that A. merely wished to expand his lines on the meteor theme, which occurs only here in the poem, for the interest of the topic itself.

930 ἄλλοι δ' ἄλλοις has antiquity on its side, and is read by editors before Voss, and then by Maass. It provides a convenient predicate for ἐναντίοι, which otherwise has to rely on one understood from 929 (see preceding note). But ἐναντίος always means strictly 'opposite', whereas the context here requires the sense of many different directions. Ceporinus' translation shows the awkwardness of combining these two irreconcilable meanings: 'sin autem aliae contrario ruant, aliis ex aliis partibus'. Maass attempts to solve the problem by punctuating after ἄλλοις, and taking ἐξ ἄλλων μερέων with the apodosis, but this is clumsy, since τότε δή is emphatic, and should begin the apodosis (cf. 935 δὴ τότε, 133 καὶ τότε). Besides, παντοίων also means 'from different directions', and is more effective as a description of the winds if it is seen to answer ἐξ ἄλλων μερέων as a description of the meteors. It is perhaps significant that the correction of Π5 is by the first hand (Kramer ad loc.): δ and σ can easily be confused. The run of the words makes ἄλλοι go naturally with ἐξ ἄλλων, and A.'s three categories of meteor movement are thus picked out by the three terms, chosen with characteristic variation, αὐτὴν ὁδόν, ἐναντίοι, ἐξ ἄλλων μερέων.

μερέων A usage derived from geometry, e.g. Euc. *Elem.* 1.28 τὰς ἐντὸς καὶ ἐπὶ τὰ αὐτὰ μέρη, 'the interior angles on the same side'.

πεφύλαξο Cf. 758 πεπόνησο, Hes. *Op.* 797 πεφύλαξο δὲ θυμῷ, orac. ap. Hdt. 7.148.3 πεφυλαγμένος ἦσο καὶ κεφαλὴν πεφύλαξο, Nonn. *D.* 1.337, al., Pallad. *AP* 11.323.3, Mus. 216, Triph. 278.

931 παντοίων ἀνέμων A. recalls the storm simile in B 396–7 τὸν δ' οὔ ποτε κύματα λείπει | παντοίων ἀνέμων, ὅτ' ἂν ἔνθ' ἢ ἔνθα γένωνται, and the storm scene in ε 292–3 πάσας δ' ὀρόθυνεν ἀέλλας | παντοίων ἀνέμων.

ἄκριτοι As in Homer of speech in which nothing decisive is said, e.g. θ 505 ἄκριτα πόλλ' ἀγόρευον, of the Trojans confronted by the wooden horse. Here the fact that the winds are παντοῖοι makes the significant wind-direction unclear and the ensuing weather correspondingly hard to predict. Cf. Arist. *Mete.* 361b31 ἄκριτος δὲ καὶ χαλεπὸς ὁ Ὠρίων εἶναι δοκεῖ, because the significant rising and setting dates of Orion occur at transitional periods between seasons, when the weather is naturally unpredictable.

932 ἐπ' ἀνδράσι τεκμήρασθαι The compound verb is used by A. of a specific recognition (229, 456) or prediction (1038). The tmesis with enclosed dative is not to be confused with τεκμαίρεσθαι ἐπί c. dat., which is used of judging from a sign (1129) or with respect to weather (1154). The point of this conclusion to the long sentence on meteors is to draw attention once again to the ignorance of men in contrast to the omniscience of Zeus (cf. 768ff.).

933-987 Signs of rain

This is the longest part of the section on weathers, as in *D.S.* (10–25), and may be subdivided into signs from the sky (933–41), mainly water-birds (942–53), land creatures and birds (954–72), mainly domestic life (973–87).

933 αὐτάρ A. marks his transition here with a contrast: meteors from all quarters mean wind, whereas lightning from all quarters means rain. The point of the transition is thus deliberately blurred, and the new theme does not emerge until the end of the sentence.

ἐξ εὔροιο καὶ ἐκ νότου ἀστράπτῃσιν *D.S.* 21 ἀστραπαὶ δὲ ἐάν γε πανταχόθεν γένωνται, ὕδατος ἂν ἦ ἀνέμου σημεῖον. *D.S.* goes on to associate particular directions with particular conditions (times and winds), and in every case the forecast is rain. A. abbreviates his source by simply spelling out the four directions in these two lines. Cf. V. *G.* 1.370–3 *at Boreae de parte trucis cum fulminat et cum | Eurique Zephyrique tonat domus, omnia plenis | rura natant fossis atque omnis nauita ponto | umida uela legit*, Plin. *Nat.* 18.354 *atrocissime autem [hiemabit] cum ex omnibus quattuor partibus caeli fulgurabit*, *Gp.* 1.3.3 ἐὰν δὲ ποτὲ μὲν ἐκ νότου, ποτὲ δὲ ἐκ βορέου ἦ εὔρου ἀστραπαὶ φέρωνται, προορατέον ὅτι ἐκεῖθεν μὲν ὄμβρος, ἔνθεν δὲ ἄνεμος ἐπενεχθήσεται.

935 δὴ τότε Introducing an apodosis, a variation of τότε δή (930). Cf. A 476, and especially Hes. *Op.* 621 δὴ τότε παντοίων ἀνέμων θυίουσιν ἀῆται. Denniston 224.

πελάγει ἔνι Cf. δ 555 Ἰθάκη ἔνι.

ναυτίλος ἀνήρ Cf. 1098 αἰπόλος ἀνήρ. For ναυτίλος as adj. cf. A. *Ag.* 1442, S. *Ph.* 220 (v.l.), E. fr. 846.2.

936 τῇ μὲν ... τῇ δ' Cf. 80 καὶ τῇ καὶ τῇ.

ἐκ Διὸς ὕδωρ Cf. Ξ 19 ἐκ Διὸς οὖρον, A.R. 2.1120–1 τὸ δὲ μυρίον ἐκ Διὸς ὕδωρ | λῆξεν ἅμ' ἠελίῳ. For the association of Zeus with weather see also 293, 426, 886, 899, 964. Here the contrast between the water from above and the water below is somewhat contrived, since the danger comes from the lightning rather than from the rain, and A. feels obliged to add a note to explain this. It is just possible that he has in mind the old Semitic myth of the separation of the waters above the sky from the waters below it: cf. Genesis 1.6–8, and the story in Hdt. 4.158 of the hole in the sky above Irasa.

937 ὕδατι The repetition from the end of the preceding line emphasises the new weather theme.

τοσσαίδε Homer has both τοσ- and τοσσ-, the latter e.g. in ε 100 τίς δ' ἂν ἑκὼν τοσσόνδε διαδράμοι ἁλμυρὸν ὕδωρ, in same *sedes* and similar context of the sea. The sense must be 'so many' (so Buhle and Erren), not 'such' (Mair) or 'si précipités' (Martin).

περὶ στεροπαὶ φορέονται If περί is taken *in tmesi* with φορέονται, the sense will be that the lightning moves round the observer, changing direction as it goes. So Voss, 'schwingen so viele Leuchtungen sich umher', and similarly Erren (Voss sees the lightning as personified, like the sun in 831). Maass seems to agree, since he lists περιφορέονται in his Index. The sense required by the context is, however, not that the lightning moves round in a circle, but rather that it is seen in all directions (cf. *D.S.* 21 πανταχόθεν) in the course of one occasion. It may therefore be better to take περί adverbially, as in Τ 362 γέλασσε δὲ πᾶσα περὶ χθών. Cf. also 46. Martin prints πέρι without explanation, presumably as preposition with ὕδατι (his rather free translation does not make this point clear). But a preposition after a noun normally follows it immediately, as in 944 λίμνην πέρι, and besides, in this case the dative does not require a preposition: cf. 798 χειμῶνι.

938 προπάροιθεν As prep. of time cf. 1010, 1065; in Homer usually of place, but cf. λ 482–3 σεῖο δ᾽, Ἀχιλλεῦ, | οὔ τις ἀνὴρ προπάροιθε μακάρτατος.

939 πόκοισιν ἐοικότα *D.S.* 13 καὶ ὅταν νεφέλαι πόκοις ἐρίων ὅμοιαι ὦσιν, ὕδωρ σημαίνει, V. *G.* 1.397, in a negative variation, *tenuia nec lanae per caelum uellera ferri*, Plin. *Nat.* 18.355 *si nubes ut uellera lanae spargentur multae ab oriente, aquam in triduum praesagient*, Ptol. *Tetr.* 2.14.11 καὶ τὰ νέφη πόκοις ἐρίων ὄντα παραπλήσια προδηλωτικὰ ἐνίοτε γίνεται χειμώνων, Anon. Laur. 8.4 ἐὰν δὲ ὥσπερ πόκοι ἐρίων νεφέλια ἐστῶσιν ἀφ᾽ ἡλίου ἀνατολῆς, ὕδωρ ἐντὸς τριῶν ἡμερῶν σημαίνει. The simile is preserved in the name 'cirrus' for high clouds such as those preceding a low-pressure system (cf. 900). The word πόκος appears once in Homer, Μ 451 πόκον ἄρσενος οἰός.

ἰνδάλλονται Cf. 194, 901. The plural verb brings out the plurality of the clouds, especially after πόκοισιν: see note on 13.

940 διδύμη ... ἶρις *D.S.* 22 ὅταν ἶρις γένηται, ἐπισημαίνει· ἐάν τε πολλαὶ ἴριδες γένωνται, σημαίνει ὕδωρ ἐπὶ πολύ, V. *G.* 1.380–1 *et bibit ingens | arcus* (cf. Sen. *Nat.* 1.8.8), Plin. *Nat.* 18.353 *arcus cum sunt duplices, pluuias nuntiant*, Gp. 1.3.5 ἶρις δὲ διπλῆ φανεῖσα ὄμβρους δηλοῖ, Anon. Laur. 9 ἶρις ἤγουν τόξον διπλοῦν φανὲν ἐν τῷ οὐρανῷ ὄμβρους δηλοῖ, Ptol. *Tetr.* 2.14.11 αἵ τε συνιστάμεναι κατὰ καιροὺς ἴριδες χειμῶνα μὲν ἐξ εὐδίας, εὐδίαν δὲ ἐκ χειμῶνος προσημαίνουσι. The lore of the rainbow as a weather sign is very ancient, and appears already in Homer, Ρ 547ff. ἠΰτε πορφυρέην ἶριν θνητοῖσι τανύσσῃ | Ζεὺς ἐξ οὐρανόθεν, τέρας ἔμμεναι ἢ πολέμοιο | ἢ καὶ χειμῶνος δυσθαλπέος. Cf. Λ 27–8. A fainter secondary rainbow is sometimes seen outside the primary, with the colours in reverse order. The primary bow has an angular radius of 42°, the secondary 51° (Greenler 1, 4, 5). Aristotle refers to the double rainbow in *Mete.* 375a30 διπλῆ δὲ καὶ ἀμαυροτέρα τοῖς χρώμασιν ἡ περιέχουσα, καὶ τῇ θέσει τὰς χρόας ἐξ ἐναντίας ἔχει κειμένας.

ἔζωσε διά Maass, Index s.v. διέζωσε. For this anastrophic form of tmesis see note on 334 ἔκρινε διά (K–G 1.531); cf. Call. *H.* 1.44. A comparable use of the verb is X. *Mem.* 3.5.25 μέση διέζωσται ὄρεσιν ἐρυμνοῖς.

διὰ μέγαν For lengthening before μ see note on 624 καταμελεϊστί and cf. θ 520 διὰ μεγάθυμον (in same *sedes*).

οὐρανὸν ἶρις Homer ignores the digamma in E 353 but not in Λ 199.

941 ἅλωα The Attic form, as a variation of the Ionic in 811, 816, 877.

μελαινομένην Cf. 804 of the moon, 817 of lunar and 877–8 of solar haloes.

ἀστήρ Sch. οἱ λαμπροὶ τῶν ἀστέρων, ὡς πῦρ εἰσὶ καὶ ἀμαρυγὰς ἔχουσι καὶ παρέχουσιν, ὥσπερ ἡ σελήνη καὶ ὁ ἥλιος ἐκ τῆς τοῦ ἀέρος παχύτητος καὶ αὐτοὶ ἅλωας ἔξωθεν ἑαυτῶν ἔχουσι. *D.S.* makes no mention of star haloes: the reference in 22, cited on 877, seems to apply only to the sun. Stars in this case will naturally include planets, and Pliny lists separately *circulus nubis circa sidera aliqua pluuiam* (*Nat.* 18.353) and *si stellarum errantium aliquam orbis incluserit, imbrem* (352). Ptolemy mentions both, but gives the portent an astrological slant: καὶ αἱ περὶ τοὺς ἀστέρας δὲ τούς τε πλανωμένους καὶ τοὺς λαμπροὺς τῶν ἀπλανῶν ἅλως συνιστάμεναι ἐπισημαίνουσι τὰ οἰκεῖα τοῖς τε χρώμασιν ἑαυτῶν καὶ ταῖς τῶν ἐπαπειλημμένων φύσεσι (*Tetr.* 2.14.7).

942–953 Signs of rain from creatures associated with water: water-birds in general (942–3), swallows (944–5), frogs (946–8), crows (949–53). A. makes a small selection from the sourse of *D.S.* 15–16 and 42. What they predict is not specified here, but we may assume that the theme of rain continues from where it is announced in 936 and repeated in 938. Throughout this section the recurrence of the word ὕδωρ in different cases, in other senses than 'rain', is striking.

942–3 λιμναῖαι ἢ εἰνάλιαι ... ἐνιέμεναι ὑδάτεσσιν Much expanded and varied compared with *D.S.* 15 ὄρνιθες λουόμενοι μὴ ἐν ὕδατι βιοῦντες ὕδωρ ἢ χειμῶνας σημαίνουσι. *Gp.* 1.3.4 follows A. with ἔτι δὲ καὶ αἱ ὄρνις αἱ λιμναῖαι καὶ αἱ θαλάττιαι ἐπὶ ὕδατος συνεχῶς λουόμεναι χειμῶνα δηλοῦσιν. Cf. Ael. *NA* 7.7 ὄρνιθες οἱ μὲν θαλάττιοι καὶ οἱ λιμναῖοι ἐς τὴν γῆν ἰόντες ὡς ἔσται χειμὼν πολὺς οὐκ ἀγνόουσιν (≈ Anon. Laur. 11.42). These two lines are expanded in a version by Varro Atac. fr. 22M *tum liceat pelagi uolucres tardaeque paludis | cernere inexpletas studio certare lauandi | et uelut insolitum pennis infundere rorem,* and thence developed further by Virgil in *G.* 1.383–7 *iam uarias pelagi uolucres et quae*

Asia circum | dulcibus in stagnis rimantur prata Caystri | certatim largos umeris in-fundere rores, | nunc caput obiectare fretis, nunc currere in undas | et studio incassum uideas gestire lauandi. Virgil has added a reminiscence of B 461, and it may be that A. also had this famous Homeric simile in mind.

942 ἢ εἰνάλιαι Voss reads ἠδ', partly to eliminate the hiatus and partly because of the connectives in Varro, Virgil and *Gp.* But A. frequently keeps ἤ long in hiatus, with or without ictus, e.g. 106, 564, 713, 880 *bis*, 972), and the text of a translator or imitator is not evidence for the text of A. against the testimony of the MSS. A. may be recalling α 162 ἤ εἰν ἁλὶ κῦμα κυλίνδει.

943 ἄπληστον N.sg. adj. as adv. only here (LSJ give only n.pl.). A. makes frequent use of such adverbs, e.g. ἀμφότερον (617, 799, 821), βαιόν (358), δείελον (1111), ἥσυχον (1000), μετοπωρινόν (1064), νέον (241, 706, 822), νύκτερον (1023). This is an effective four-word line, with alliteration of sibilants suggesting the sound of splashing water.

κλύζονται Middle only here; cf. passive in 299, 902.

ἐνιέμεναι Middle only here in this sense. A. may have in mind the Homeric active of launching a ship, ἐνήσομεν εὐρέι πόντῳ (β 295, μ 293).

ὑδάτεσσι A post-Homeric aeolicism (see K–B 1.418), on the analogy of, e.g., ὀππάτεσσι (Sapph. 31.11), ἀρμάτεσσ' (Sapph. and Alc. inc. auct. 21). Cf. A.R. 3.860 λοεσσαμένη ὑδάτεσσιν, Theoc. 16.11 γονάτεσσι, Call. fr. 278.3 στομάτεσσι, Q.S. 6.363 δοράτεσσι.

944 δηθά Homeric, e.g. α 49 (in same *sedes*), E 587, K 52.

χελιδόνες *D.S.* 15 χελιδόνες τῇ γαστρὶ τύπτουσαι τὰς λίμνας ὕδωρ σημαίνουσι, *Gp.* 1.3.8 (≏ Anon. Laur. 11.49) χελιδόνες λίμναις ἢ δεξαμεναῖς ἢ ποταμοῖς περιπετόμεναι μετὰ βοῆς ὄμβρον σημαίνουσι. Cf. Varr. Atac. fr. 22.4 *aut arguta lacus circumuolitauit hirundo*, repeated in V. *G.* 1.377, Plin. *Nat.* 18.363 *hirundo tam iuxta aquam uolitans ut pinna saepe percutiat.* On the swallow in general see Thompson 314ff.

ἀΐσσονται For the middle cf. Z 509–10 ἀμφὶ δὲ χαῖται | ὤμοις ἀΐσσονται. Homer also has the aorist middle in Χ 195.

945 αὔτως See note on 21. Martin prints αὕτως, and takes it with τύπτουσαι, 'frappant à peine'; so Erren, but reading αὕτως, 'nur so obenhin'. But αὔτως in A. always precedes the word it qualifies: see next note.

εἰλυμένον Sch. τὸ ἤδη ἐκ τοῦ ἀνέμου συστραφὲν καὶ ἤδη ἀρξάμενον κινεῖσθαι. There are two difficulties in this interpretation. One is that there is no suggestion of wind in the context, and indeed wind rarely appears as an element in the conditions that presage rain in Greek weather-lore. The other is that εἰλύω means either 'encircle' (413) or 'cover' (432), and does not provide the sense of movement understood by the scholia. The change to εἰλέω or εἴλεω, as read by Voss and Martin, does supply the movement, but with water it suggests a rather violent eddying (cf. A.R. 2.571 νῆα δ' ἔπειτα πέριξ εἶλει ῥόος, *Gp*. 1.11.7 ξηρὰ φύλλα ἐναντία ὑπὸ τῶν ἀνέμων εἰλούμενα), which is not appropriate to the condition of the lake here, when the swallows are flying so close to the surface. Voss, however, accepts the idea of a 'Regenwind' and translates 'das gekräuselte Wasser'. Martin on the other hand explains the disturbance of the water as the result of the swallows' touch, translating 'la surface de l'eau où se dessinent des cercles'. This seems an unlikely extension of the meaning 'revolve', which A. uses elsewhere in the form εἰλεῖται (46, 53, 224, 445).

Other editors retain εἰλυμένον, and have difficulty in finding a meaning that suits both the verb and the context. Mair translates 'rippling', perhaps having in mind S. *Ph*. 291 εἰλυόμην and 702 εἰλυόμενος, of Philoctetes' limping gait, but this does not suit the perfect passive participle. Ronconi (182–3) has suggested 'ruffled', on the analogy of Homeric ἐλυσθείς (ι 433). Maass glosses with 'tectum', without further explanation. If he means that the lake is covered by mist, there is nothing in the context to suggest it; indeed the birds would be unable to see the insects they are trying to catch on the surface. Mist over the water is more likely to foretell good weather, as in 991–2. There is, however, another possible interpretation. Most translators either ignore αὔτως or take it with τύπτουσαι (see preceding note). But since A. elsewhere places the adv. before the word it qualifies, it should probably be construed with εἰλυμένον. There is no other instance of its use with a participle, but it occurs frequently before adjectives, e.g. 172, 180, 195, 424, 792, 825, 1016. Here the reference may be to the fact that a lake, being enclosed as it is, forces the swallows to fly round and round it for long periods at a time (δηθά).

946 μάλα δείλαιαι As Martin notes, μᾶλλον is hard to justify (though Maass takes it with the verb, comparing 415, 1105, 1132), and the apparent text of Plutarch is probably right. It is supported by the papyrus, and by *Arat. Lat.*, who translates μάλα by *quidem* also in 316, whereas for μᾶλλον he gives *magis* (14 times) and *maxime* (3 times). The pathetic δείλαιος seems more suited to small creatures, in contrast to the tragic δειλή of Cassiepeia (654).

γενεαί Not 'tribes' (Mair), nor 'Geschlecht' (Voss, Erren), 'engeance' (Martin), but 'generations'. Their misery continues through successive generations, and the point is further stressed by the elaborate phrase πατέρες γυρίνων.

ὕδροισιν Once in Homer, B 723 ὀλοόφρονος ὕδρου, of Philoctetes' snake-bite. Cf. Arist. *HA* 487a, 508b, and Nic. *Ther*. 416 on the χέλυδρος hunting frogs.

ὄνειαρ   An amusing echo of 15 and 761, where the benefits are those conferred on men by Zeus.

947 ἐξ ὕδατος   The v.l. in Plutarch is characteristic of a quotation from memory.

πατέρες ... γυρίνων   See note on 946 γενεαί. The quaint periphrasis perhaps recalls Ar. *Ran.* 211 λιμναῖα κρηνῶν τέκνα, and is imitated in Nic. *Ther.* 620 γερύνων καναχοὶ περίαλλα τοκῆες and *Alex.* 563. The application of πατήρ to animals seems to be rare in Greek, but in Latin poets cf. V. *G.* 3.128, 138, of horses. For the weather sign cf. *D.S.* 15 βάτραχοι μᾶλλον ᾄδοντες σημαίνουσιν ὕδωρ, V. *G.* 1.378 *et ueterem in limo ranae cecinere querelam*, Plin. *Nat.* 18.361 *ranae quoque ultra solitum uocales*, Plu. 912c οἱ βάτραχοι προσδοκῶντες ὄμβρον ἐπιλαμπρύνουσι τὴν φωνὴν ὑπὸ χαρᾶς, 982e ἄλλοτε δὲ λαμπρύνουσι τὴν φωνήν, ὑετὸν προσδεχόμενοι· καὶ τοῦτο σημεῖον ἐν τοῖς βεβαιοτάτοις ἐστίν. Jermyn (35) comments that frogs croak during or after rain, not before it. For γυρῖνος cf. Pl. *Tht.* 161d οὐδὲν βελτίων βατράχου γυρίνου.

948 τρύζει   Despite the papyrus' support for M's reading the indicative is required, in keeping with all the other verbs in this long sentence.

ὀρθρινόν   Hellenistic variation of ὄρθριον, here with ῑ, as ὀρθρινά in A.R. fr. 5.1 (*CA* p. 5) and Antip. *AP* 6.160.1 = *HE* 182. Cf. 417 ὀπωρινοῦ.

ἐρημαίη   Also Hellenistic; cf. A.R. 2.672, 4.1298, Mosch. 3.21, Pomp. *AP* 9.28.1 = *GP* 3967, Q.S. 7.455, Nonn. *D.* 5.546.

ὀλολυγών   Sch. ἡ ὀλολυγὼν ὄρνεόν ἐστιν ὑπὸ τὴν τρυγόνα, τῇ ἐρημαίῃ φιληδοῦν ... ἄλλοι δὲ ζῷον ἔνυδρον ὅμοιον γῆς ἐντέρῳ, πολὺ μέντοι γε ἰσχνότερον. Cf. sch. Theoc. 7.139. This word could mean any creature that makes a loud cry (ὀλολύζειν), and can also mean the cry itself, especially the mating call of the male frog (Arist. *HA* 536a11, Plu. 982e, Ael. *NA* 9.13). Here A.'s line is close to *D.S.* 42 ὀλολυγὼν ᾄδουσα μόνη ἀκρωρίας χειμέριον, except that this comes from a long list of storm signs, which are taken from domestic life, and are used by A. later in the poem (959, 1035, 1037, 1039, 1135). *D.S.* 15, however, includes among signs of rain χλωρὸς βάτραχος ἐπὶ δένδρου ᾄδων, along with frogs croaking (cf. 947) and swallows skimming the water (cf. 944), and this suggests that A. has taken ὀλολυγών to be the tree-frog, and placed it immediately after the lines about frogs. Cf. Plin. *Nat.* 32.92 *rana parua arborem scandens atque ex ea uociferans*; in 11.172 he says the male frog is called *ololygon*. The verb τρύζει, though more suggestive of the turtle-dove (τρυγών), is not an inappropriate choice for a low-pitched croak: cf. Q.S. 14.36 περιτρύζουσι of pigs. *Gp.* 1.3.11 follows A. with ὀλολυγὼν τρύζουσα ἑωθινόν. In Theoc. 7.139-40 ἁ δ' ὀλολυγών | τηλόθεν ἐν πυκιναῖσι βάτων τρύζεσκεν ἀκάνθαις comes immediately after cicadas chattering in a forest scene, and Gow finds that 'the case for the tree-frog is strong' there as in A. See Gow's full note ad loc. But in Agath. *AP* 5.292.5–6 καὶ λιγυρὸν βομβεῦσιν ἀκανθίδες· ἡ δ' ὀλολυγὼν | τρύζει, a clear imitation of both poets, a bird may be meant; so perhaps in Eub. fr. 104 Hunter ὀλολυγόνος ἔρωτι κατατετηκώς, and Nicaenet. fr. 1.9–10 ὀλολυγόνος οἶτον ἔχουσα | Βυβλίς. Cicero translates with *acredula* (*Prog.* fr. 4.5), on the suggested meanings of which see Soubiran p. 232. Cf. Avien. 1703 *ululae* and Soubiran p. 277.

949–950 λακέρυζα ... κορώνη *D.S.* 16 κορώνη ἐπὶ πέτρας κορυσσομένη ἦν κῦμα κατακλύζει ὕδωρ σημαίνει· καὶ κολυμβῶσα πολλάκις καὶ περιπετομένη ὕδωρ σημαίνει. The epithet is Hesiodic: *Op.* 747 μή τοι ἐφεζομένη κρώξῃ λακέρυζα κορώνη, fr. 304.1 ἐννέα τοι ζώει γενεὰς λακέρυζα κορώνη. Cf. Stes. *PMG* 209.i.9 λακέρυζα κορώνα, Ar. *Av.* 609 οὐκ οἶσθ' ὅτι πέντ' ἀνδρῶν γενεὰς ζώει λακέρυζα κορώνη; A.R. 3.929 τῇ θαμὰ δὴ λακέρυζαι ἐπηυλίζοντο κορῶναι. A. breaks up the Hesiodic phrase, so that the epithet is made to anticipate the noun at the end of the next line. The verb λάσκω is often used of birds and animals: cf. 914 and 972 λεληκώς of the heron. Virgil imitates with *tum cornix plena pluuiam uocat improba uoce* (*G.* 1.388).

The crow is a land bird, but does frequent the sea-shore: Arist. *HA* 593b καὶ αἱ κορῶναι δὲ νέμονται ἁπτόμεναι τῶν ἐκπιπτόντων ζῴων. Thompson 172–3 lists this crow separately as an 'undetermined seabird', but it is likely that A. has in mind the same bird here as in 1002 and 1022. His epithets (λακέρυζα, πολύφωνα, ἐννεάγηρα) all describe the bird of Hes. fr. 304.

παρ' ἠϊόνι προὔχούσῃ Cf. ζ 138 ἐπ' ἠϊόνας προὔχούσας, ω 82 ἀκτῇ ἐπὶ προὔχούσῃ.

950 κύματος ... ὑπέτυψε Ludwig (*Hermes* 424–6) argues convincingly for the papyrus reading κύματος. The transmitted χείματος is unsatisfactory, because the whole sentence is a catalogue of signs that predict not storm but rain, all looking back to 938 ἐρχομένων ὑετῶν. Storm (χεῖμα, χειμών) is a different weather, distinct from ἄνεμος, ὑετός, εὐδία: see notes on 758–1141 and 909–1043. The crow's sign comes later (1022). Here the rain sign is confirmed by *D.S.* 16 and *V. G.* 1.388 (see note on 949–950), also Hor. *Carm.* 3.17.12–13 *aquae nisi fallit augur | annosa cornix*, Luc. 5.555–6 *caput spargens undis, uelut occupet imbrem, | instabili gressu metitur litora cornix*. Cf. *Gp.* 1.3.7 κορώνη ἐπ' αἰγιαλοῦ τὴν κεφαλὴν διαβρέχουσα ἢ πᾶσα νηχομένη καὶ νυκτὸς σφοδρότερον κρώζουσα ὄμβρους προμηνύει, Avien. 1704–6 *improba si cornix caput altis inserit undis | ..., plurimus abruptis fundetur nubibus imber*.

This weather-lore tradition (except for Virgil and Horace, but including Plin. *Nat.* 18.363 *cum terrestres uolucres contra aquam clangores dabunt perfundentque sese, sed maxime cornix*) also confirms the association of the bird with incoming waves. We would therefore expect A. to have something to say about the crow splashing in the waves, but such sense is impossible if ὑπέτυψε means 'struts' (LSJ) or 'stalks' (Mair). As Ludwig notes, however, this is the only example of the verb that LSJ put in this category. Otherwise it has the sense of 'pushing down' into water or anything else that gives, in order to bring something up, e.g. Hdt. 2.136 κόντῳ γὰρ ὑποτύπτοντες ἐς λίμνην, to bring up mud from the bottom; cf. 3.130, 6.119, Ar. *Av.* 1145. Here it would make sense to suppose that the bird dips its head into the wave, then brings it up and splashes the water over itself. See Ludwig *Hermes* 436. This is precisely the sense given by Cic. *Prog.* fr. 4.8–9 *fuscaque non numquam cursans per litora cornix | demersit caput et fluctum ceruice recepit.* Cf. sch. ὑπέτυψεν ἀντὶ τοῦ ὑπῆλθεν. The mistranslation was probably due to Virgil's *spatiatur* (*G.* 1.389).

χέρσῳ Ludwig's tentative preference for χερσόνδ' (*Hermes* 435 n. 4) is based on Φ 238, *h.Hom.* 3.28, Theoc. 16.61. But in all these passages the action starts in the river or sea, and the bodies or waves come out on to the bank or shore. Here the action is on the shore, and takes place when the wave arrives. Nothing is gained by Maass's adverbial χερσαῖ' (cf. 919): it gives the same meaning as χέρσῳ.

951 ποταμοῖο ἐβάψατο Cf. 651, 858. The significance lies in the fact that crows are land birds: cf. *D.S.* 15 ὄρνιθες λουόμενοι μὴ ἐν ὕδατι βιοῦντες ὕδωρ ἢ χειμῶνας σημαίνουσι. For the hiatus at the main caesura see West *GM* 156.

μέχρι παρ' ἄκρους Cf. 493 μέχρι παρ' αἰδῶ.

952 ὤμους Rarely used of birds, but cf. Plu. 983B, of the female halcyon carrying the male, τοῖς ὤμοις ἐκεῖνον ἀναθεμένη.

κολυμβᾷ Cf. *D.S.* 16, cited on 949–950.

953 πολλή The v.l. πολλά is supported by sch. πολλάκις. But there is more than mere repetition in the action of the crow here, and πολλή gives the additional suggestion of urgency or restlessness. Cf. the restless activity of the farmer in 1045–6 πολλὸς ἀλωεὺς αἰεὶ παπταίνει.

στρέφεται Of movement to and fro, perhaps deliberately recalling the Homeric simile of the animal at bay, M 41ff. ἔν τε κύνεσσι καὶ ἀνδράσι θηρευτῆσι | κάπριος ἠὲ λέων στρέφεται ... | ταρφέα τε στρέφεται στίχας ἀνδρῶν πειρητίζων. Cf. Cic. *Prog.* fr. 4.8 *cursans per litora cornix,* V. *G.* 1.389 *sola in sicca secum spatiatur harena,* Luc. 5.556 *instabili gressu metitur litora cornix.*

παχέα Rarely of sound, but chosen here perhaps to suggest the language of current poetic theory; cf. 785 παχίων. The opposite is commoner, e.g. Agath. *AP* 11.352.5, of a chord, λεπτὸν ὑποτρύζουσα. Here the word suggests a combination of loudness and coarseness. Avien. 1705 *gutture rauco.*

κρώζουσα Cf. Hes. *Op.* 747 (see on 949–950), Ar. *Av.* 2 and 24 κρώζει, Euphor. fr. 89P ὑετόμαντις ὅτε κρώξειε κορώνη. A. uses this verb again of ravens (968) and even hens (961).

954-972 Signs of rain from land creatures and land birds: cattle (954–5), ants (956–7), millipedes (957–8), worms (958–9), hens (960–2), ravens and jackdaws (963–9), ducks, jackdaws and herons (970–2). For this selection see *D.S.* 15, 22, 19, 42, 17, 16 and 18 respectively. The rain theme is restated in the first line.

954 βόες *D.S.* 15 ἐὰν δὲ [βοῦς] εἰς τὸν οὐρανὸν ἀνακύπτων ὀσφραίνηται, ὕδωρ σημαίνει, Cic. *Prog.* fr. 4.10–11 *mollipedesque boues, spectantes lumina caeli,* | *naribus umiferum duxere ex aere sucum,* Varro Atac. fr. 22.5–6 *et bos suspiciens caelum (mirabile uisu)* | *naribus aerium patulis decerpsit odorem,* V. *G.* 1.375–6 *bucula caelum* | *suspiciens patulis captauit naribus auras,* Plin. *Nat.* 18.364 *boues caelum olfactantes,* Ael. *NA* 7.8 βοῦς ἐὰν βοᾷ καὶ ὀσφραίνηται, ὕειν ἀνάγκη. *Gp.* 1.3.10 omits the detail of sniffing the air, and gives only βόες πρὸς μεσημβρίαν ὁρῶσαι. *CCAG* 8.1.137, 10 βοὸς βοῶντος καὶ τὴν γῆν ὀσφραινομένου ὕειν ἀνάγκη (sim. Anon. Laur. 11.11), Avien. 1707–8, following Virgil rather than A., *imber erit, latis cum bucula naribus auras* | *concipit.*

ἐνδίοιο Normally of time during the day, hence Voss 'vor tagausdauerndem Regen'. But cf. 498 of constellations above the horizon, and sch. here μεσημβρινοῦ ἢ τοῦ οὐρανίου. So Mair 'from the sky'; cf. 936 ἐκ Διὸς ὕδωρ, 964 Διὸς πάρα.

955 οὐρανὸν εἰσανιδόντες Cf. 325, and ω 307 οὐρανὸν εἰσανιδών.

ἀπ' αἰθέρος ὀσφρήσαντο ἀπ' should probably be taken in *tmesi* with the verb, thus distinguishing the more active meaning 'sniff at' from the normal sense of the simple verb 'catch the scent of'. Martin takes πάρος as adverb and construes ὀσφρήσαντο with ὕδατος ('pressentent la pluie d'après l'odeur de l'air'), but this seems perverse, when the run of the words so clearly suggests that ὕδατος goes with πάρος and αἰθέρος with ὀσφρήσαντο. The Latin versions cited on 954 certainly understand the lines in this way. The form of the verb without augment is preferable, since it is the one more likely to have been corrupted. Sch. give an Aristotelian explanation: ὅταν τοίνυν ἀναθυμιάσεών τινων ἐκ τῆς τοῦ ἀέρος ἀκρασίας αἴσθηται, ἀφορῶν ὡς ἐπὶ τὸν οὐρανὸν ὀσφρᾶται τῆς τοῦ ἀέρος παχύτητος πρὶν γενέσθαι τὸν ὄμβρον. For three consecutive spondeiazontes cf. 419–21; see Gow's note on Theoc. 13.42 for other examples, also D.P. 908–10, Opp. *H.* 3.371–3, Q.S. 3.673–5, 694–6; cf. West *GM* 178.

956 μύρμηκες *D.S.* 22 μύρμηκες ἐν κοίλῳ χωρίῳ ἐὰν τὰ ὠὰ ἐκφέρωσιν ἐκ τῆς μυρμηκιᾶς ἐπὶ τὸ ὑψηλὸν χωρίον, ὕδωρ σημαίνουσιν, ἐὰν δὲ καταφέρωσιν, εὐδίαν. Cf. Varro Atac. fr. 22.7 *nec tenuis formica* *cauis non euehit oua*, V. *G.* 1.379–80 *saepius et tectis penetralibus extulit oua* | *angustum formica terens iter*, Plin. *Nat.* 18.364 *formicae concursantes aut oua progerentes.* The ants are actually carrying out their pupas, not their eggs (Platt, *CQ* 5, 1911, 255, Jermyn 35).

ὀχῆς ἕξ Contracted gen. (attested only here) of ὀχεά, here a hole in the ground; cf. 1026, Nic. *Ther.* 139. For the anastrophe cf. Ε 865 καύματος ἔξ, Ξ 472 κακῶν ἔξ, and in same *sedes* Ω 705 μάχης ἔκ.

ὤεα An early poetic form, cf. Ibyc. *PMG* 285 γεγαῶτας ἐν ὠέῳ, Sem. 11 West χηνὸς ὤεον, Call. *E.* 5.10 ὤεον ἀλκυόνος, Nic. *Ther.* 192 ὄφιος κηριτρόφου ὤεα. Plu. 967F cites 956–7 and notes a variant reading: τὰς δὲ τῶν σπερμάτων διαθέσεις καὶ διαψύξεις ἐκτὸς ὑετοῦ ποιεῖται σημεῖον ὁ Ἄρατος· ἢ κοίλης ... ἀνηνέγκαντο· καί τινες οὐκ "ᾠά" γράφουσιν, ἀλλ' "ἤια" ὡς τοὺς ἀποκειμένους καρπούς, ὅταν εὐρῶτα συνάγοντας αἴσθωνται καὶ φοβηθῶσι φθορὰν καὶ σῆψιν, ἀναφερόντων.

957 θᾶσσον In positive sense; cf. Β 440 ἴομεν, ὄφρα κε θᾶσσον ἐγείρομεν ὀξὺν Ἄρηα.

ἀνηνέγκαντο For the context of saving precious things cf. Hdt. 3.148 ἀνενεικάμενος τὰ ἔχων ἐξεχώρησε.

ὤφθεν This aorist passive from root ὀπ- is post-Homeric, e.g. S. *Ant.* 709 ὤφθησαν. The 3rd pl. ending *-nt, Greek -ν is a feature of dialects other than Attic/Ionic, and in Homer presumably Aeolic in origin: e.g. Α 57 ἤγερθεν, Γ 209 ἔμιχθεν, Θ 557 ἔφανεν. Chantraine *MHG* 365.

ἴουλοι *D.S.* 19 καὶ ἴουλοι πολλοὶ πρὸς τοῖχον ἕρποντες ὑδατικόν. A. improves on the prosaic πολλοί with the more visual effect of ἀθρόοι ὤφθεν, and varies further with plural for singular noun and compound for simple participle. His followers have omitted this interesting sign, perhaps because of uncertainty as to the identification of these creatures. Sch. (MA) ὁ δὲ ἴουλός ἐστι σκώληξ μυρίοις ποσὶ χρώμενος, ὅμοιος ταῖς σκολοπένδραις, (MΔUAS) οἱ μὲν ὁμοίους εἶναι σκολοπένδραις, οἱ δὲ αὐτὰς τὰς σκολοπένδρας, ἄλλοι δὲ τὸν σκώληκα τὸν μυρίοις ποσὶ χρώμενον, Arist. *HA* 523b18 ἴουλος with σκολόπενδρα as examples of wingless insects, and in *PA* 682b τὸ τῶν ἰούλων γένος is given as an example of long polypods, Numen. ap. Ath. 7 305A = *SH* 584 καὶ δὲ σύ γε μνήσαιο δελείατος ὅττι παρ' ἄκρα | δήεις αἰγιαλοῖο γεώλοφα· οἱ μὲν ἴουλοι | κέκληνται, μέλανες, γαιηφάγοι, ἔντερα γαίης, Plin. *Nat.* 29.136 *millipeda ab aliis centipeda aut multipeda dicta animal est e uermibus terrae pilosum, multis pedibus arcuatim repens tactuque contrahens se; oniscon Graeci uocant, alii iulon.* The moderns identify ἴουλοι here variously as 'millipedes' (Hort on *D.S.*, Schott, Zannoni, Martin), 'centipedes' (Mair), 'woodlice' (LSJ, Erren; cf. *OLD* on *iulus*).

958 τείχε' Despite the textual tradition it is likely that A. would have used the Homeric plural, as with γλήνεα (318), εἴδεα (381), ἐρεύθεα (837), ἤθεα (116), λαίφεα (424), νέφεα (852, 938), στήθεα (671). Homer has one example of elision, Δ 308 τείχε' ἐπόρθεον. The elision here may have been partly responsible for the corruption. As evidence for the Hellenistic use of this plural see Call. *H.* 2.67, 4.25.

πλαζόμενοι Cf. γ 95, 106, π 64 in same *sedes*. There is a certain humour in the use of this epic verb, particularly associated with the wanderings of Odysseus (e.g. α 2, ν 204, π 64), to describe the humble earthworm.

σκώληκες Once in Homer, N 654–5 ὡς τε σκώληξ ἐπὶ γαίῃ | κεῖτο ταθείς, in the sense of earthworm, as here. Elsewhere σκώληξ seems to be used as a more general term for any worm-like creature, especially an insect grub: cf. Arist. *GA* 733a–b and *HA passim*. Hence the distinguishing phrase added in the next line. A. has taken this detail from a storm sign (of *D.S.* 42 cited in next note). Only Pliny follows A. with *item uermes terreni erumpentes* (*Nat.* 18.364) as a sign of a weather change.

959 ἔντερα γαίης A popular name already well established, e.g. Arist. *IA* 705a27 οἵ τε ὄφεις καὶ τὸ τῶν καμπῶν γένος καὶ πρὸς τούτοις ἃ καλοῦσι ἔντερα γῆς, 709a28 τὰ δὲ ἰλυσπάσει χρώμενα, καθάπερ τὰ καλούμενα γῆς ἔντερα καὶ βδέλλαι. In *GA* 762b26 τὰ δὲ καλούμενα γῆς ἔντερα σκώληκος ἔχει φύσιν, ἐν οἷς ἐγγίγνεται τὸ σῶμα τὸ τῶν ἐγχέλεων, and (also of eels) *HA* 570a16 γίγνονται ἐκ τῶν καλουμένων γῆς ἐντέρων, ἃ αὐτόματα συνίσταται ἐν τῷ πηλῷ, the reference is apparently to worm-casts. A. takes the phrase from the storm signs in *D.S.* 42 γῆς ἔντερα πολλὰ φαινόμενα χειμῶνα σημαίνει, and clearly understands it as meaning 'worms'; LSJ surprisingly adopt Hort's suggestion that it might mean 'worm-casts'. Following A. cf. Numen. ap. Ath. 7 305A (cited on 957 ἴουλοι) and Nic. *Ther.* 388, associating worms with rain, ἠὲ καὶ ἔντερα γῆς οἷα τρέφει ὄμβριος αἶα. A precursor of the phrase may be seen in Alcm. *PMG* 89.3 φῦλά τ' ἑρπέτ' ὅσα τρέφει μέλαινα γαῖα. On descriptive animal names see A. B. Cook, *CR* 8 (1894) 381–2, especially for examples in Hesiod, and Ingrid Waern, *The Kenning in Pre-Christian Greek Poetry* (Diss. 1951), who quotes γῆς ἔντερον (44) as found today in a Doric form in S. Italy, but not the above examples.

960 τιθαὶ ὄρνιθες *D.S.* 17 ὅλως δὲ ὄρνιθες καὶ ἀλεκτρυόνες φθειριζόμενοι ὑδατικὸν σημεῖον, καὶ ὅταν μιμῶνται ὕδωρ ὡς ὗον, Ael. *NA* 7.7 ἀλεκτρυόνες γε μὴν καὶ ὄρνιθες οἱ ἠθάδες πτερυσσόμενοι καὶ φρυαττόμενοι καὶ ὑποτρύζοντες χειμῶνα δηλοῦσιν, *Gp.* 1.3.8 καὶ αἱ κατοικίδιαι ὄρνις πυκνῶς κονιώμεναι καὶ κρώζουσαι, Plu. 129A ἄτοπον γάρ ἐστι κοράκων μὲν λαρυγγισμοῖς καὶ κλωσμοῖς ἀλεκτορίδων ... ἐπιμελῶς προσέχειν, σημεῖα ποιουμένους πνευμάτων καὶ ὄμβρων. The adj. τιθός occurs only here, but cf. Alph. *AP* 9.95.1 τιθὰς ὄρνις.

ἀλέκτορος An early form, e.g. *Batr.* 192, Pi. *O.* 12.14, Simon. *PMG* 583. See Fraenkel on A. *Ag.* 1671. On the domestic fowl generally see Thompson 33ff., Pollard 88–9. ἀλέκτωρ, originally a fighting cock, was probably named in jest from epic Ἀλέκτωρ (ἀλέξω): Frisk 1.68 s.v. ἀλεκτρύων.

961 ἐφθειρίσσαντο Homeric aorist form, e.g. Η 449 ἐτειχίσσαντο (Chantraine 1.409). *D.S.* notes this characteristic also in ravens (16) and hawks (17).

ἔκρωξαν A. uses this verb also of crows (953) and ravens (968), Aristophanes of cranes (*Av.* 710). The choice of verb here seems to indicate that the cackling of the hens is noticeably louder than usual. The addition of φωνῇ suggests a degree of articulateness in their prediction, as illustrated by the following simile.

962 οἷόν τε The v.l. in S may be due to the influence of Ξ 295 οἷον ὅτε.

στάλαον σταλάω is elsewhere transitive, e.g. A.R. 4.1064. The usual intransitive verb is στάζω, but cf. E. *Ph.* 1388 ἐστάλασσ' ἱδρώς. For the form of the neuter participle cf. Ρ 55 καλὸν τηλεθάον (in same *sedes*).

ψοφέει ἐπὶ ὕδατι ὕδωρ Most translators have followed sch. μίμησιν τῆς ποιᾶς αὐτῶν φωνῆς δίδωσιν, ὥσπερ ὕδωρ ἐπὶ ὕδατι καταστάζον. But 'the noise of water dripping upon water' (Mair) is too soft a sound to be described by ψοφέει, which denotes a sharper noise, such as creaking, rattling, knocking, and is equally unsuited to being compared with ἔκρωξαν, which is a loud, throaty cry. Martin rightly compares 1142–3 ἐπὶ σήματι σῆμα | σκέπτεσθαι, η 120 ὄγχνη ἐπ' ὄγχνη γηράσκει, μῆλον δ' ἐπὶ μήλῳ, Hes. *Op.* 644 μεῖζον δ' ἐπὶ κέρδεϊ κέρδος, S. *Ant.* 595 πήματα φθιτῶν ἐπὶ πήμασι πίπτοντ', and explains ἐπί here in the same successive sense, 'one after another'. Cf. also A. *Ch.* 403–4 ἄτην | ἑτέραν ἐπάγουσαν ἐπ' ἄτῃ, S. *OC* 544 δευτέραν ἔπαισας ἐπὶ νόσῳ νόσον, A.R. 2.473 ἐπ' ἤματι δ' ἦμαρ ὀρώρει.

The triple hiatus is unusual, and is perhaps designed to suggest the discontinuity in the sound of the raindrops. K–B 1.196 give only this example; see also West *GM* 156.

963 δή ποτε Homeric only in the sense of 'one day', e.g. ζ 162 Δήλῳ δή ποτε (ἐνόησα). So in Sapph. fr. 166P, beginning a clause, φαῖσι δή ποτα Λήδαν ... εὔρην ὤιον, and in Call. *H.* 5.70, beginning a sentence, δή ποκα γὰρ πέπλων λυσαμένα περόνας. Denniston (213) gives no example that either means 'sometimes' or begins a sentence. This use of the single ποτέ meaning 'sometimes' has perhaps developed out of the correlative use, e.g. Pl. *R.* 560a ποτὲ μὲν οἶμαι. Cf. 916 καί ποτε, 968 ἢ ποτε.

κοράκων ... κολοιῶν In 963–9 A. rearranges many of the details which are given in separate sentences in *D.S.* 16. He begins with the second last: ἐάν τε κόρακες ἐάν τε κολοιοὶ ἄνω πέτωνται καὶ ἱερακίζωσιν, ὕδωρ σημαίνουσι. Cf. *Gp.* 1.3.8, briefly, καὶ κόρακες καὶ κολοιοὶ ἀθρόως ἐπιφαινόμενοι καὶ κρώζοντες, and Ael. *NA* 7.7, more fully, κόραξ δὲ αὖ καὶ κορώνη καὶ κολοιὸς δείλης ὀψίας εἰ φθέγγοιντο, χειμῶνος ἔσεσθαί τινα ἐπιδημίαν διδάσκουσι. κολοιοὶ δὲ ἱερακίζοντες, ὡς ἐκεῖνος λέγει, καὶ πετόμενοι πῇ μὲν ἀνωτέρω πῇ δὲ κατωτέρω, κρυμὸν καὶ ὑετὸν δηλοῦσι (≃ *CCAG* 8.1.138, 7 ≃ Anon. Laur. 11.22). Nic. *Ther.* 406 κόραξ τ' ὀμβρήρεα κρώζων (sch. ὅτι χειμῶνα δηλοῦσιν οἱ κόρακες καὶ ὁ Ἄρατος μαρτυρεῖ). The raven is also a sign of fair weather (1003ff.). Lucretius cites crows and ravens as characteristic weather-birds in 5.1083–6 *et partim mutant cum tempestatibus una | raucisonos cantus, cornicum ut saecla uetusta | coruorumque greges ubi aquam dicuntur et imbris | poscere et interdum uentos aurasque uocare.* Hor. *Carm.* 3.27.10 *imbrium diuina auis imminentum.* See Thompson 159ff.; on the hereditary aspect cf. 946.

φῦλα κολοιῶν Repeated in 1026. Cf. 103 φῦλα γυναικῶν, which also has the internal rhyme; here the rhyme is supported by the parallel word-grouping. With κολοιῶν in this position A. may be recalling P 755 τῶν δ' ὥς τε ψαρῶν νέφος ἔρχεται ἠὲ κολοιῶν. Cf. Π 583. For the weather sign see *D.S.* 16, *Gp.* 1.3.8, Ael. *NA* 7.7, quoted in preceding note; cf. also Ov. *Am.* 2.6.34 *pluuiae graculus auctor aquae.* Pliny associates jackdaws rather with storm in *Nat.* 18.363 *graculi sero a pabulo recedentes hiemem.* For the jackdaw in general see Thompson 155–6, Pollard 27–8.

964 Διὸς πάρα Cf. 293, 426, 886, 899, 936. Here the syntactical ambiguity may be intentional: both the rain and the sign come from Zeus. The scholia give only the more obvious sense, τοῦ ἐκ Διὸς ἐρχομένου ὕδατος.

965 φαινόμενοι A. has in mind κόρακες and κολοιοί as essentially the subject, rather than γενεαί and φῦλα. Cf. λ 14–15 Κιμμερίων ἀνδρῶν δῆμός τε πόλις τε, | ἠέρι καὶ νεφέλῃ κεκαλυμμένοι. See K–G 1.53–4 *constructio* κατὰ σύνεσιν.

ἀγεληδά Only here and 1079, elsewhere ἀγεληδόν (1005), once in Homer (Π 160). Virgil develops this into a Roman image in *G.* 1.381–2 *agmine magno | coruorum increpuit densis exercitus alis.*

ἰρήκεσσιν Cf. *D.S.* 16 and Ael. *NA* 7.7, cited on 963. A. may be recalling O 237, Π 582 ἴρηκι ἐοικώς, and other hawk similes (e.g. N 62, 819, v 86). In Homer and Hesiod speed of flight is the hawk's main characteristic, but here A. interprets *D.S.* ἱερακίζωσιν with reference to the bird's cry. Thompson (114) calls ἱέραξ 'the generic term especially for the smaller hawks and falcons'. The epic-Ionic form is ἴρηξ (cf. also Hes. *Op.* 203, 212, Hdt. 2.65, 67; see Frisk 1.712, Chantraine 1.156). The reading ἰρήκεσσιν here is probably due to the influence of the Attic form.

ὁμοῖον Cf. [Theoc.] 8.37–8 αἵπερ ὁμοῖον | μουσίσδει Δάφνις ταῖσιν ἀηδονίσι. The v.l. ὁμοῖα seems to be used only in prose and followed by superlatives (Hdt. 3.8, 57, Th. 7.29.4).

966 φθεγξάμενοι Cf. κ 139, Λ 603, ξ 492, φ 192, all in same *sedes*. The aorist denotes the act of breaking silence. For φθέγγεσθαι of a bird's cry taken as a portent cf. X. *An.* 6.1.23 (eagle), *D.S.* 16 (raven), Plu. 405D (heron, wren, raven); also of dogs, A.R. 3.1217.

δίους Of impressive natural phenomena; cf. Π 365 αἰθέρος ἐκ δίης, Emp. 109.2 αἰθέρα δῖον, A. *Pr.* 88 ὦ δῖος αἰθήρ. Here the epithet would also suggest the association of rain with Zeus; cf. 936, 964.

σταλαγμούς *D.S.* 16 καὶ ἐάν τε εὐδίας ἐάν τε ὕδατος ὄντος μιμῆται τῇ φωνῇ οἷον σταλαγμούς, ὕδωρ σημαίνει. Various methods have been used in attempts to solve the metrical problem of the short syllable στα-. One is to introduce a preceding short syllable: hence the v.l. with γε and the conjectures of Grotius, Voss and Kaibel. This might be justified on the analogy of Homeric examples with σκ- and ζ- in metrically intractable words: see West *GM* 17, with Hellenistic instances before ζ-. But A. follows the normal practice of lengthening before στ-, and indeed seems to make a point of producing such effects: cf. especially τε στάλαον (962), also 295, 334, 493, 498, 625, 1140. It is unlikely that he would have made an exception in this case. Another method is to introduce a short syllable after στα-: Koechly's conjecture is in itself attractive, and makes the corruption easy to explain palaeographically. But there is no evidence for such a form as σταλαημοί: Hesychius records only σταληδόνες. I have considered the possibility of a diectasis, σταλααγμούς. This is relatively rare in nouns (Chantraine 1.81), but A. has an innovative example in κεράατος (174). However, there seems to be no satisfactory parallel. Bergk's πέμφιγας assumes an intrusive gloss, and therefore can only be *exempli gratia*. So also Professor Diggle's suggestion '? ῥαθάμιγγας'. But in fact the textual tradition is very strong, and is confirmed as early as *Arat. Lat. stilicidia*. It seems best, then, to follow Buttmann and accept σταλαγμούς with metrical lengthening of the first syllable. Lengthening before λ is common when the syllable bears an ictus and the λ is initial, e.g. 719, 1112, and 1124 (where the λ begins the second part of a compound), but neither of these conditions obtains here. However, there is the unusual Homeric example of ἁλόντε (E 487), where the lengthened α does not have the ictus, and there could possibly be some influence from epic καλός (the original καλϝος being long forgotten): A. has the first syllable long without ictus in the re-

curring καλός τε μέγας τε (143, 244, 397); he also has one example of
the Attic use with short α (1142) This line is one of several spondeiazontes with a spondee also in the fourth foot (230, 262, 447, 497, 506,
744, 811, 887, 1030). It may be that the succession of long syllables here
is designed to suggest the sound of heavy rain-drops, as if to illustrate
φωνῇ ἐμιμήσαντο (967); cf. the triple hiatus in 962.

967 φωνῇ The repetition in this section (961, 967, 968) is very
striking, and seems to suggest that the birds' cries are in a sense articu-
late, because they convey a meaning. Cf. 1006, where the same word is
part of a longer description of birds in a human-like situation.

σὺν ... ἐρχομένοιο The usual sense of meeting (e.g. 151) or being
in conflict (cf. Mair 'clashing rain') is not appropriate here. The context
requires the sense of simultaneity: cf. Κ 224 σύν τε δύ' ἐρχομένω, Ψ 879
σὺν δὲ πτερὰ πυκνὰ λίασθεν. The ravens' cry means that the rain is
already approaching; cf. Ceporinus 'simul pluuia ueniente'.

968 ἤ ποτε Cf. 963 δή ποτε.

κρώξαντε In Homer the dual can always be explained with reference to some kind of duality, either two individuals or two groups being
implied in the subject. But dual and plural are often mixed, e.g. Λ 621–
2 τοὶ δ' ἱδρῶ ἀπεψύχοντο χιτώνων, | στάντε ποτὶ πνοιήν, and some
Hellenistic grammarians thought that the dual could be used as plural
in Homer: cf. sch. (A) Ω 282, and Zenodotus' readings in Α 567, Γ 459,
Ζ 112, etc. In h.Hom. 3.486–7 ἀλλ' ἄγεθ' ... | ἱστία μὲν πρῶτον κάθε-
τον λύσαντε βοείας the duals do seem to be intended as plurals, and it
may be partly because of this line that later poets occasionally affect a
dual for a plural as a kind of archaism, especially in participles. A.R.
actually imitates it in 3.206 κατειλύσαντε βοείαις. Cf. 1.384, if βρί-
σαντε is correct. A. repeats this idiom in 1023, and ps.-Theocritus has
two likely instances, with present participles, in 25.72 and 137. See Gow
on 25.72, also West on Hes. *Op.* 186, K–G 1.72–4. But A. may be
recalling Pi. *O.* 2.86 μαθόντες δὲ λάβροι παγγλωσσίᾳ κόρακες ὣς
ἄκραντα γαρύετον. H. Lloyd-Jones, *Greek Epic Lyric and Tragedy* (1990)
88, explains that dual by referring to the 'known fact that crows are
often seen in pairs'; cf. G. W. Most, *CR* 36 (1986) 304–5.

βαρείη δισσάκι φωνῇ A realistic description of the raven's cry; see
Witherby et al., *Handbook of British Birds*, vol. 1 (1944) 8 'Usual flight note
a repeated deep "pruk, pruk".' A. may also have had in mind that a
low-pitched voice is often associated with danger or trouble; cf. ι 257
δεισάντων φθόγγον τε βαρύν, of the Cyclops, S. *Ph.* 208 βαρεῖα τηλό-
θεν αὐδά, of Philoctetes.

The form δισσάκι is Hellenistic, on the analogy of epic πολλάκι 418,
etc.); cf. Call. fr. 186.6, Antip. *AP* 6.223.3, Anon. *AP* 9.20.2 = *FGE* 1321.

For the cry see *D.S.* 16 κόραξ πολλὰς μεταβάλλειν εἰωθὼς φωνάς, τούτων ἐὰν ταχὺ δὶς φθέγξηται ... ὕδωρ σημαίνει. Virgil varies with *tum liquidas corui presso ter gutture uoces | aut quater ingeminant* (*G.* 1.410–11). Cf. Plin. *Nat.* 18.362 *coruique singultu quodam latrantes seque concutientes, si continuabunt, si uero carptim uocem resorbebunt, uentosum imbrem.*

969 μακρόν Cf. 910, but here it is the loudness that is particularly intended; cf. 1124 μακρά.

ἐπιρροιζεῦσι Ionic ῥοιζέω, ῥοῖζος and cognate ῥοιβδέω, ῥοῖβδος describe a loud, disturbing noise such as whistling (Κ 502), piping (1 315), hissing (Hes. *Th.* 835, A.R. 4.129), the whizz of an arrow (Π 361), the sucking and spouting of Charybdis (μ 104–6), and the whirring of wings (S. *Ant.* 1004 πτερῶν γὰρ ῥοῖβδος οὐκ ἄσημος ἦν). Here some take the verb as referring back to the birds' cry, e.g. Voss 'gelten sie ein langes Geschrill', LSJ 'croak so as to forebode rain', Martin 'ils jettent un long cri strident'. But the aorist κρώξαντε seems rather to separate the double cry from the wing movement, as two successive acts, whereas the following participle comes in more naturally as an explanation of the unusual verb. So Mair 'they raise a loud whirring', Zannoni 'fanno un grande strepito', Erren 'trommeln ... einen weitschallenden Wirbel'. The two lines are thus evenly balanced, κρώξαντε followed by an adverbial phrase (968), and ἐπιρροιζεῦσι by a participial phrase (969).

τιναξάμενοι πτερὰ πυκνά *D.S.* 16 καὶ ἐπιρροιζήσῃ καὶ τινάξῃ τὰ πτερά. Ael. *NA* 7.7 κόραξ δὲ ἐπιτρόχως φθεγγόμενος καὶ κρούων τὰς πτέρυγας καὶ κροτῶν αὐτάς, ὅτι χειμὼν ἔσται κατέγνω πρῶτος. *CCAG* 8.1.138, 5 κόραξ κροτῶν τὰς πτέρυγας καὶ ἐπιτρόχως φθεγγόμενος χειμῶνα δηλοῖ ≃ Anon. Laur. 11.23.

τιναξάμενοι A. closely echoes the portent of the two eagles in β 151 ἔνθ' ἐπιδινηθέντε τιναξάσθην πτερὰ πυκνά. (It is conceivable that the dual participle here had some influence on A.'s choice of the dual in 968.) The variant present participle is probably due to sch. τὰ πτερὰ αὐτῶν πάντα ἀντιτινασσόμενοι, and perhaps also to the influence of 971 τινάσσονται. There, however, the verb is descriptive and in accord with ἐρχόμενοι, whereas here the aorist brings out the suddenness of the movement: cf. φθεγξάμενοι (965) and A.R. 2.1035 τιναξάμενος πτέρυγας. On the other hand the two aorist participles may be seen as a coincident use, in accord with the leading verb ἐμιμήσαντο (see Barrett on E. *Hipp.* 289–92), though the intervention of ἐπιρροιζεῦσι makes this explanation less likely for τιναξάμενοι.

πτερὰ πυκνά A formulaic phrase, used in different contexts with different verbs: Λ 454 περὶ πτερὰ πυκνὰ βαλόντες, Ψ 879 σὺν δὲ πτερὰ πυκνὰ λίασθεν, ε 53 πυκινὰ πτερὰ δεύεται ἁλμῇ, and the model for the present line, β 151, cited in the preceding note. In Homer πυκνός, πυκινός, when used in a literal sense, means 'compact' or 'close together', so describing solid doors (Ξ 167), a thick cloak (ξ 521), dense bush (Σ 320), serried ranks (Δ 281), a shower of missiles (Δ 576), close-set teeth (μ 92). Thus πτερὰ πυκνά suggests a basic sense of 'close-set feathers', thence 'thick plumage' or 'close-feathered wings'. This is the meaning understood by e.g. LSJ, Paley and Monro on Ψ 879, Merry on ε 53, and T. E. Page on V. G. 1.382, where *densis* implies the same understanding of the original. In later authors πυκνός develops a time sense, of actions repeated in close succession, and is so used with nouns implying motion, e.g. E. *Tr.* 235–6 πυκνὰς ... ὁδοὺς | ἐλθόντα. More recently Homer's πτερὰ πυκνά has been interpreted in this way, e.g. Lattimore 'beating wings' (Ψ 879), and Sappho's imitation of β 151, πύκνα δίννευτες πτέρα (fr. 1.11), is translated by D. L. Page 'rapid wings', while LSJ give 'fast-beating' for πύκνα and suggest that this meaning is perhaps true also for Homer. Similarly here in A. πυκνά has commonly been understood as referring to the repeated beating of the wings ever since Ceporinus' 'alas frequentes': e.g. Voss 'mit häufigem Schwunge', Mair 'with frequent flapping', Martin 'précipitamment'.

As far as Homer is concerned this sense of πυκνός seems to me unlikely. Not only is it a later use, but it is also unsuited to all the Homeric instances. In A 454 the wings are covering the carrion, not flapping, in Ψ 879 the bird is dead, in ε 53 the bird is diving, and in β 151 'beating' makes the epithet otiose, since it duplicates the meaning of the verb. It is more reasonable to take πυκνά as a permanent epithet of wings, which is appropriate in all the Homeric instances. I do not see why the same should not be true also for Sappho, since her imitation is so close: the Homeric epithet, like μελαίνας in the preceding line (cf. B 699), adds a heroic dimension to the stanza. Cf. Emped. 82.1 ταὐτὰ τρίχες καὶ φύλλα καὶ οἰωνῶν πτερὰ πυκνά, S. *OC* 17 πυκνόπτεροι. In A. the imitation is also very close, and it seems best to retain the Homeric meaning here too, with all its heroic associations. The verb itself supplies all the movement required, and πτερὰ πυκνά is essentially the equivalent of its variation πτερύγεσσιν in 919 and 971. Cf. anon. *AP* 9.209.3 περὶ δὲ πτερὰ πυκνὰ βαλοῦσα, and anon. *AP* 12.67.3 = *HE* 3754 ποτὶ πτερὰ πυκνὰ τινάξας. A.R. also echoes the Homeric phrase, but with variation of both form and meaning, in 2.1088 πυκινὰ πτερὰ τοῖσιν ἐφίεσαν. His use of the epithet to mean 'a shower of' is still in the Homeric tradition.

970 νῆσσαι *D.S.* 18 καὶ ἡ νῆττα ἥμερος ἐὰν ὑπιοῦσα ὑπὸ τὰ γεῖσα ἀποπτερυγίζηται, ὕδωρ σημαίνει. Cf. 918. This line has a chiastic pattern.

οἰκουροί Properly of those in charge of a house (e.g. E. *Hec.* 1277), or contemptuously of a stay-at-home (A. *Ag.* 1225, Ar. *V.* 970), here a poetic variant for the technical κατοικίδιος (*Gp.* 1.3.8) of domestic animals: cf. τιθαί and the opposite ἀγριάδες νῆσσαι (918). The fact that the ducks actually come under the shelter of the roof makes the choice of word particularly appropriate.

ὑπωρόφιοι Once in Homer, I 640 ὑπωρόφιοι δέ τοί εἰμεν, where obligations of hospitality are implied. A. is being ironical if he has that passage in mind, but perhaps he is also thinking of Ar. *Ran.* 1313, where αἵ θ' ὑπωρόφιοι κατὰ γωνίας are spiders. Tzetzes *Chil.* 8.514ff. ὁ κολοιὸς δ' ὑπάρχει καθ' Ὅμηρον καὶ Ἄρατον, Βαβρίαν καὶ τοὺς ἄλλους ἡ μικροτέρα κορωνὶς ἡ παρ' ὀπαῖς ὀρόφων.

κολοιοί Cf. 963, 1023, 1026. The sequence of οι sounds in this line produces an unusual effect, including a kind of internal rhyme, though the adj. at the caesura does not go with the noun at the end.

971 γεῖσα A technical word, already introduced into poetry by Euripides (*Ph.* 1158, 1180, *Or.* 1570, 1620). Cf. Theaet. *AP* 10.16.5 ὑπὸ γεῖσα δόμους τεύξασα χελιδών. According to Steph. Byz. s. Μονόγισσα the word is Carian (see Firsk 1.293). Cf. *IG* 2.463.51, Demetr. *Eloc.* 108.

τινάσσονται πτερύγεσσιν Cf. 919. The phrase is a variation of that in 969, but the repetition of the theme is nevertheless very close, and may be intended to suggest the technical treatise; cf. *D.S.* 18 with ἀποπτερυγίζηται and ἀποπτερυγίζωνται in successive clauses. The phrase recalls the Homeric bird scenes in Β 462 ἀγαλλόμενα πτερύγεσσι and β 149 τιταινομένω πτερύγεσσιν.

972 ἐπὶ κῦμα A poetic variation for ἐπὶ θάλατταν (*D.S.* 18).

διώκει Of speeding with an aim in view, but without requiring a specific grammatical object to be understood; cf. 226 διωκόμενος, Ε 223 ἔνθα καὶ ἔνθα διωκέμεν.

ἐρῳδιός Cf. 913. For this weather sign cf. *D.S.* 18 ἐὰν (ἐρῳδιός) ἐπὶ θάλατταν πετόμενος βοᾷ, μᾶλλον ὕδατος σημεῖον ἢ πνεύματος, Ael. *NA* 7.7 πετόμενος δὲ ἐρῳδιὸς τῆς θαλάττης εὐθὺ ὕδωρ ἐξ οὐρανοῦ ῥαγήσεσθαι αἰνίττεται, *CCAG* 8.1.138, 1 ἐρῳδιὸς ... βοῶν καὶ ἐκ νεφῶν ἐπὶ θάλατταν ἱπτάμενος ὕδωρ ἐξ οὐρανοῦ σημαίνει (≈ Anon. Laur. 11.21).

ὀξὺ λεληκώς Cf. Χ 141, of the hawk; A. uses the same participle of the heron in 914.

973-987 Miscellaneous signs of rain, mainly domestic: flies biting (974-5), snuff on a lamp-wick (976-7), flames burning irregularly (977-81), island birds in flocks (981-2), sparks round a cooking-pot (983-4), white spots on burning charcoal (985-6). The details, with one exception (see on 982), are in *D.S.* 23, 14, 19, 25 respectively. The rain theme is given in the first and last lines.

973 τῶν Referring back, as in 480, 1142; cf. 45 τάς, 137 τῆς, 525 τούς, 545 τῷ.

μηδὲν ἀπόβλητον Cf. 559. Here A. varies with a different negative and a different participle. For the warning in form of double negative cf. 845-7, 866-8, etc.

πεφυλαγμένῳ C. acc., in the sense of being able to anticipate; cf. Theoc. 16.95 (τέττιξ) ποιμένας ἐνδίους πεφυλαγμένος. A. elsewhere uses this participle c. gen. (48, 1125), where the sense is rather that of avoiding, though πεφύλαξο c. gen. (930) is comparable with the present passage; cf. also 762. The participle here would seem to support *numquam prudentibus imber | obfuit* (as against *imprudentibus*) in Virgil's imitation (*G.* 1.373-4). The point being made by both poets is that, if you are forewarned of bad weather, you can take steps to avoid being harmed by it; see H. H. Huxley ad loc.

974 ἐπὶ πλέον Cf. 580, 602, 1048; otherwise the phrase appears mainly in prose, e.g. Th. 6.54.1. A. may be recalling, with a variation, α 322 μᾶλλον ἔτ' ἢ τὸ πάροιθεν.

975 δάκνωσιν μυῖαι *D.S.* 23 καὶ τὸ δημόσιον τὸ περὶ τὰς μυίας λεγόμενον ἀληθές· ὅταν γὰρ δάκνωσι σφόδρα, ὕδατος σημεῖον. *Gp.* 1.3.9 καὶ μυῖαι ἐπὶ πλέον δάκνωσαι = Anon. Laur. 11.48. The word μυῖα, cognate with *musca* and 'midge' (*OLD* s.v.), covers various kinds of fly, and is particularly prominent in Homeric similes. The biting variety is proverbial for its boldness: Ρ 570-2 μυίης θάρσος ἐνὶ στήθεσσιν ἐνῆκεν, | ἥ τε καὶ ἐργομένη μάλα περ χροὸς ἀνδρομέοιο | ἰσχανάᾳ δακέειν. Cf. Τ 31, also Π 641 of flies swarming round milk-pails, and the annoying house-fly in Δ 130.

ἐφ' ... ἱμείρωνται *In tmesi.* The middle use (in the simple verb) is Homeric, e.g. α 41 ἧς ἱμείρεται αἴης. For the subj. after εἴ κε see note on 788.

976 μύκητες *D.S.* 14 καὶ οἱ μύκητες, ἐὰν νότια ᾖ (τὰ ὕδατα), ὕδωρ σημαίνουσι. Cf. Ar. *V.* 262-3 ἔπεισι γοῦν τοῖσιν λύχνοις οὑτοιὶ μύκητες· | φιλεῖ δ', ὅταν τοῦτ' ᾖ, ποιεῖν ὑετὸν μάλιστα, sch. Ar. φασὶν ὅτι ὑετοῦ μέλλοντος γενέσθαι οἱ περὶ τὴν θρυαλλίδα τοῦ λύχνου σπινθῆρες ἀποπηδῶσιν, οὓς μύκητας νῦν λέγει, ὡς τοῦ λύχνου ἐναντιουμένου τῷ νοτερῷ ἀέρι, sch. Arat. τὸ πῦρ ὡμολόγηται ξηρᾶς οὐσίας, ὑγρὸς δὲ ἀὴρ πολλάκις ἐν χειμῶνι ἐμπίπτων τῷ πυρὶ ἀποτελεῖ τούτους τοὺς σπινθῆρας, Call. fr. 269 ὁππότε λύχνου δαιομένου πυρόεντες ἄδην ἐγένοντο μύκητες, V. *G.* 1.392 *putris concrescere fungos* (portending a storm), Plin. *Nat.* 18.357 *pluuiae etiam si in lucernis fungi.* The primary meaning of μύκης appears to be 'fungus', e.g. in Theophr. *HP* 1.1.11, Nic. *Alex.* 525; here it means the 'snuff' that gathers round a lamp-wick in damp air.

ἀγείρωνται Despite the MSS the subjunctive is required in conformity with the two preceding verbs.

μύξαν Primarily 'mucus' (e.g. Hes. *Sc.* 267), here the wick of a lamp. Cf. Call. *E.* 55.1–2 εἴκοσι μύξαις | πλούσιον ἁ Κριτίου λύχνον ἔθηκε θεῷ.

977 νοτίην The σκοτίην of the MSS could either mean 'moonless' or be poetically intensive, and both senses are pointless here. On the other hand νοτίην gives the meaning required by the context, and corresponds to *D.S.* 14 (cited on 976). The corruption was probably an attempt to provide a long syllable, and may have been influenced by E. *Hec.* 68 ὦ σκοτία νύξ (cf. *Alc.* 268–9). For metrical lengthening before ν cf. 852, also Λ 811 κατὰ δὲ νότιος ῥέεν, μ 427 ἦλθε δ' ἐπὶ Νότος.

ὑπὸ χείματος ὥρην The accusative is better attested than the dative, and makes good sense, 'in the course of the winter'; *D.S* 14 χειμῶνος. Cf. Χ 102 νύχθ' ὑπο τήνδ' ὀλοήν, Hdt. 9.51.4 ὑπὸ τὴν νύκτα ταύτην ἐδόκεε τοὺς ἡμίσεας ἀποστέλλειν. The phrase χείματος ὥρη serves to distinguish χεῖμα 'season' from χεῖμα 'storm'; cf. 850, A.R. 2.1086.

978 φάος A transfer of meaning from the light to the actual flame, perhaps recalling τ 34 χρύσεον λύχνον ἔχουσα φάος περικαλλὲς ἐποίει (the only instance of λύχνος in Homer).

κατὰ κόσμον Denoting regularity of movement; the phrase is commoner in A. with a negative (654, 913, 1086).

ὀρώρῃ Cf. γούνατ' ὀρώρῃ in same *sedes* (Ι 610, Λ 477, Χ 388, σ 133). There may be here a sound echo of θ 380 κόμπος ὀρώρει or *h.Hom.* 32.4 κόσμος ὄρωρεν. For the sense of rising cf. Θ 135 φλὸξ ὦρτο. A. also has the form ὦρορε (764). The subjunctive is required here, as with the other verbs in this long clause.

979 ἀΐσσωσιν ἄπο For the anastrophic tmesis see note on 334.

φλόγες Rare in plural, but so used e.g. by Aristotle of meteors in *Mete.* 341b2 αἵ τε φλόγες αἵ τε καιόμεναι φαίνονται περὶ τὸν οὐρανόν. Here the word provides a useful variant for σπινθῆρες (984). Cf. *D.S.* 14 καὶ ὅταν χειμῶνος τὴν φλόγα ⟨ὁ λύχνος⟩ ἀπωθῇ διαλιπὼν οἷον πομφόλυγας, ὕδατος σημεῖον, καὶ ἐὰν πηδῶσιν αἱ ἀκτῖνες ἐπ' αὐτόν, καὶ ἐὰν σπινθῆρες ἐπιγένωνται, *Gp.* 1.3.9 λύχνου φλόγες μελαινόμεναι, V. *G.* 1.391–2 *testa cum ardente uiderent* | *scintillare oleum*, Plin. *Nat.* 18.357 *si flexuose uolitet flamma*.

980 πομφόλυγες This onomatopoeic noun and its verb have other figurative uses in poetry, e.g. Pi. *P.* 4.121 ἐκ δ' ἄρ' αὐτοῦ πομφόλυξαν δάκρυα, Ar. *Ran.* 249 πομφολυγοπαφλάσμασιν. Cf. Plato's reference to bubbles in *Ti.* 66b καὶ τὰ μὲν τῆς καθαρᾶς [sc. νοτίδος] διαφανεῖς περιστῆναι κληθείσας ὄνομα πομφόλυγας, and *D.S.* 14 cited in the

515

preceding note. The simile relates to both the form and the movement of the sparks; cf. sch. ὅταν οὖν περὶ ἁπτομένῳ λύχνῳ μύκητες συνιστῶνται χειμῶνος ὥρᾳ, αἵ τε φλόγες τεταγμένως καὶ κατὰ φύσιν εἰς ὕψος αἴρωνται, ποτὲ δὲ πλαγιάζωνται, καὶ λεπταὶ πομφόλυγες περὶ αὐτὰς γίνωνται καὶ σπινθῆρες ἀπορρέωσι.

ἐπ' αὐτόφι A. uses the Homeric instrumental ending as dat. (cf. 558 ἶφι), here with locative sense; cf. Τ 255 πάντες ἐπ' αὐτόφιν ['on the spot'] ἧατο σιγῇ, Μ 302 παρ' αὐτόφι. Cf. *D.S.* 14 ἐπ' αὐτόν. On the v.l. ἀπόπροθι see next note.

μαρμαίρωσιν Frequent in Homer in present participle, especially of light reflected from metal, e.g. Μ 195 ἔντεα μαρμαίροντα. The unmetrical vv. ll. probably originated in a reference to 1034 φλόγες ... μαραινόμεναι λύχνοιο. Once established the corruption led to the further corruption of ἐπ' αὐτόφι to ἀπόπροθι, as more appropriate to the new sense of the line. It seems clear that the double corruption was already current in antiquity, since it is the reading implied in Avien. 1720 *langueat ultro*, and also in the explanation of sch. (ΜΚΑ) πάλιν δὲ τῆς παχύτητος καὶ ὑγρότητος ἐκνικώσης σφόδρα, διόλου ὁ λύχνος λάμπειν οὐ δύναται, ἀλλ' ἀκτῖνας ἀφίησι λεπτὰς καὶ ἐσκορπισμένας, καὶ ἔστιν ἰδεῖν πόρρωθεν ὀλίγον τοῦ λύχνου ἀποστάντας διηκούσας λεπτὰς ἀπ' αὐτοῦ ἀκτῖνας, διὰ τὸ μὴ δύνασθαι δι' ὅλου λάμπειν ἐκ τοῦ ὑποκειμένου ἀέρος. When the correct verb was restored in M, the middle voice was evidently taken over from the original reading; but μαρμαίρω occurs only in the active, and the active is attested in A.

981 μηδ' ἤν A variation after μηδ' εἴ κεν (980), as in 977 after 974. The v.l. εἰ is, however, not impossible, since A. does use it with a subjunctive elsewhere (840, 850, 858, 903, 988, 1082), though not after μηδ'.

θέρεος μέγα πεπταμένοιο I.e. when the summer sky is entirely cloudless; sch. εὐδίας οὔσης ἐν θερινῷ καταστήματι. A. is perhaps recalling ζ 44–5 μάλ' αἴθρη | πέπταται ἀνέφελος, and the whole phrase seems to echo the sound of α 276 πατρὸς μέγα δυναμένοιο. Cf. 204, 288, and Call. fr. 238.17.

982 νησαῖοι ὄρνιθες *D.S.* 17 καὶ θέρους ὅταν πολλοὶ ἀθρόοι φανῶσιν ὄρνιθες οἳ βιοτεύουσιν ἐν νήσῳ, ὕδωρ σημαίνουσιν. The corruption to νησσαῖοι is ancient: cf. sch. αἱ νῆσσαι and νήσσας τὰς ὄρνις. It was presumably due to the influence of νῆσσαι in 970. The birds here seem curiously out of place among these domestic weather signs. *D.S.* groups them between hawks and domestic cocks and hens. A. may be deliberately blurring the lines between the sub-divisions of his material; cf. 665.

ἐπασσύτεροι Homeric word, denoting quick or close succession, one after another. It is used of ranks of soldiers (Δ 427) compared to waves (Δ 423), deaths in battle (Α 383, Θ 277, Μ 194, Π 418), and relays of lookouts (π 366). Cf. Hes. *Th.* 716 of rocks being thrown. Here A. must mean 'flock after flock' of birds in quick succession, as Voss translates, 'Schaaren an Schaaren', not 'en groupes serrés' (Martin), 'in dichtem Gedränge' (Erren). It is not clear what Mair means by 'in crowding companies'. A.R. is more innovative in his use of this word in the singular (1.579, 2.472), Nicander gives it new contexts (*Ther.* 246, 717). The etymology of ἐπασσύτεροι is uncertain. Some relate it to σεύομαι (cf. ἀνάσσυτος, ἐπίσσυτος, πανσυδίη), postulating *ἐπ-αν-(σ)συ, some see it as a contamination of ἀσσοτέρω with ἀγχύτερος or ἐγγύτερος (see Frisk 1.532).

983 σύ γ' Cf. 752. Here the importance of even the humble cooking-pot is emphasised.

χύτρης *D.S.* 19 καὶ χύτρα σπινθηρίζουσα πᾶσα περίπλεως ὕδατος σημεῖον, *Gp.* 1.3.6 εἰ δὲ καὶ εἰς χύτραν ἢ χαλκεῖον σπινθῆρες γίγνοιντο ὄμβρους δηλοῦσι, Anon. Laur. 11.50 ὁμοίως καὶ σπινθῆρες γενόμενοι ἐν χύτρᾳ ἢ ἐν χαλκῷ σκεύει τὸ αὐτὸ σημαίνουσιν, Plin. *Nat.* 18.358 *cum in aeno pendente scintillae coaceruantur*, but as a sign of wind. The χύτρα is an earthenware cooking-pot with handles.

τρίποδος πυριβήτεω The reminiscence of Ψ 702 μέγαν τρίποδ' ἐμπυριβήτην gives an amusingly heroic tone to this ordinary domestic scene. Both the Homeric epithet and its derivative here occur only once. The original dative (ἐν πυρὶ βαίνω) is retained in the compound; cf. 1040 πυριλαμπέος, ν 564 πυρίκαυστος, ι 387 πυριήκεα.

984 σπινθῆρες Once only in Homer, of a meteor, Δ 77 τοῦ δέ τε πολλοὶ ἀπὸ σπινθῆρες ἵενται. For the metrical lengthening at 2nd-foot caesura cf. Ο 351 κύνες ἐρύουσι, κ 64 πῶς ἦλθες, Ὀδυσεῦ; See Chantraine 1.104.

ἕωσι πέρι On anastrophic tmesis see 334, with πέρι 986.

λελαθέσθαι Cf. 871.

985 μηδέ Sc. λελαθέσθαι.

σποδιήν Once in Homer, ε 488 δαλὸν σποδιῇ ἐνέκρυψε.

ἄνθρακος *D.S.* 25 φασὶ δέ τινες καὶ εἰ ἐν ἄνθραξι [Schn., ἀστράσι codd.] λαμπρὰ χάλαζα ἐπιφαίνηται, χάλαζαν προσημαίνειν ὡς τὰ πολλά· ἐὰν δὲ ὥσπερ κέγχροι μικροὶ λαμπροὶ πολλοί, ἀνέμου μὲν ὄντος εὐδίαν, μὴ ἀνέμου δὲ ὕδωρ ἢ ἄνεμον. Here A. selects one detail and elaborates on it. Homer has the special word for burning charcoal in Ι 213 ἀνθρακιὴν στορέσας.

αἰθομένοιο Frequent in Homer in this position, especially after πυρὸς (Θ 563 etc.).

986 πέρι Cf. 984. The spots appear here and there all over the hot ashes.

σῆματ' An extension of meaning, perhaps influenced by the mathematical use of σημεῖον for a point, e.g. Euc. *Phaen.* 1 γῆ δὲ ἡμετέρα ὄψις [ἔστω], ἡ πρὸς τῷ Δ σημείῳ. *D.S.* 25 (cited on 985) has no corresponding term, merely ὥσπερ κέγχροι.

κεγχρείοισιν Extended form modelled on the epic adjectival suffix -ειος for -εος (cf. 114, 123 χρύσειον, -ειοι, 1008 δενδρείοιο), but 1039 κέγχροις. Millet seeds, because of their small size and large number, provide a standard of comparison for anything that has a granulated appearance; cf. *D.S.* 14, 42, 54. See LSJ s.vv. κέγχρος, κεγχριαῖος, κεγχρίας, κεγχροειδής, κεγχρώδης, κεγχρώματα, κεγχρωτός.

987 δόκευε A. uses δοκεύω (1) of watching continuously, c. acc., 341; (2) of watching for signs, with ἐπί c. acc., here; (3) of expecting weather, c. gen., 813, 908, 1136; c. acc. 1128; with ἐπί c. acc., 1018.

περισκοπέων C. gen. of watching for expected weather, also 435, 925; c. acc. of carefully observing seasons (464), clouds (852).

988–1012 Signs of fair weather
This is the shortest of the sections on weathers, presumably because unexpected good weather does no harm, and it is mainly bad weather that needs to be predicted. So *D.S.* has only five sections on signs of fair weather (50–4), in contrast to the 16 on rain, 12 on wind, and 12 on storm. A. has, of course, already noted the fair-weather signs provided by the moon (783–4, 802) and the sun (822–7, 847–51, 858–61). There now remain signs from cloud formations (988–93), from the Manger (994–8), and from lamps, owls, crows, ravens and cranes (999–1012).

988 ἠερόεσσα To translate as 'misty' (Mair), 'vaporeux' (Martin), 'nebelige' (Erren) is to make this epithet seem otiose, whereas A. intends it to be meaningful by placing it so far in advance of its noun. The essential force of ἠερόεις is to convey a sense of poor visibility, or even invisibility. In Homer it describes the darkness of Tartarus, where it is difficult to see anything (e.g. Θ 13, λ 57; cf. Hes. *Th.* 682). Homeric gods make people invisible by shrouding them ἠέρι πολλῇ (e.g. Γ 381, where see Kirk's note); cf. E 186, and West on Hes. *Th.* 745. Of particular interest is E 770 ὅσσον δ' ἠεροειδὲς ἀνὴρ ἴδεν ὀφθαλμοῖσιν, where the adverb is explicitly related to human vision. A. uses ἠερόεις of parts of constellations that appear very faint or starless (276, 317, 385, 630; cf. ἠερίη 349), and here ἠερόεσσα νεφέλη must mean a faint mist, which is what the context requires. Cf. *D.S.* 51 αἱ κηλάδες [Hort; cf. 31] νεφέλαι χειμῶνος εὐδιειναί and Jermyn 51 'low-lying mist, after a night-rain (or a heavy dew-fall), is not a bad indication that fine weather has begun: evaporation has already started, and will continue as the sun rises'. Sch. λεπτομερής.

παρέξ   In the primary use of this compound preposition παρ- denotes extension along a line parallel to, ἐξ distance from. If the former sense is dominant, the following case is acc., if the latter, gen. In I 7 παρὲξ ἅλα φῦκος ἔχευεν = παρ' ἅλα φῦκος ἐξέχευεν (Leumann 96), the seaweed is close inshore, and it is the length of the line that is important; in 1 116 νῆσος ἔπειτα λαχεῖα παρὲκ λιμένος τετάνυσται there is no reference to the length of the island, but its distance offshore is οὔτε σχεδὸν οὔτ' ἀποτηλοῦ (117). Here the scholia (988) paraphrase with ταῖς ὑπωρείαις παρεκτείνηται, and again (989) with παρὰ πυθμένα καὶ πεδιάδα μεγάλου ὄρους τείνηται. Cf. Gp. 1.2.4 ἀερώδους νεφέλης ὄρει περιτεταμένης καθαρὰς τὰς ἄκρας ὑπερφαινομένης τοῦ ὄρους, εὐδίαν δηλοῖ, D.S. 51 ὅταν τὰ νέφη πρὸς τὴν θάλασσαν αὐτὴν παραζωννύῃ, εὐδιεινόν. Virgil selects only the clouds, at nebulae magis ima petunt campoque recumbunt (G. 1.401). All the evidence suggests that παρέξ is meant to be taken with πυθμένα, and Mair translates accordingly 'be stretched along the base of a high hill'. The traditional explanation is easily understood from the Greek, and gives the familiar picture of a long, low cloud or mist lying across the lower slopes of a mountain, while the top is perfectly clear. On the accent of παρέξ see Hdn 2.63, 5 Lentz.

989 πυθμένα   Cf. ν 122, 372 παρὰ πυθμέν' ἐλαίης, Hes. Th. 931–2 θαλάσσης | πυθμέν' ἔχων, Orph. A. 92 πυθμένα γαίης. A. has adapted the sense to mean the lower slopes of a mountain.

τείνηται   The passive of this verb is used by A. only to express the state of being extended, e.g. 706, 1032; cf. ἀποτείνεται 184, 195, 242, ἐπιτείνεται 49, παρατείνεται 589. It is therefore unlikely that motion is intended here, as Voss suggested (see on 988).

ἄκραι δὲ κολῶναι   D.S. 51 Ὄλυμπος δὲ καὶ Ἄθως καὶ ὅλως τὰ ὄρη τὰ σημαντικὰ ὅταν τὰς κορυφὰς καθαρὰς ἔχωσιν, εὐδίαν σημαίνει. Gp. 1.2.4, cited on 988 παρέξ. For κολῶναι cf. 120.

990 φαίνωνται   The subjunctive is required, in accord with τείνηται. Cf. 858, 903.

ὑπεύδιος εἴης   Cf. 827. The variation to optative in the main clause is repeated in chiasmus in the next line.

991 εὔδιός κ' εἴης   Cf. 784. This clause introduces the second half of an elaborate chiasmus of six lines (988–93), with some variations: ὅτε instead of εἰ, three subordinate clauses instead of two, φαίνηται balancing φαίνωνται, and εὔδιος with long ι following ὑπεύδιος with short ι (cf. 911 and 916).

πλατέος παρὰ πόντου   The alliteration with πόντος is Homeric; cf. Α 350, β 421, κ 195, Φ 59. D.S. 51, cited on 988 παρέξ, Gp. 1.2.4 καὶ ὑπὲρ θαλάσσης νεφέλη φαινομένη παύσασθαι χειμῶνα δηλοῖ. For the rare use of παρά c. gen. with the force of a locative cf. 897 πὰρ βορέαο. The usage is similar to that of πληθύος ἀμφοτέρωθεν (774). The phrase must mean 'at sea level', in view of the following μηδ' ὑψόθι. Cf. sch. ἐν ταπεινώσει σχεδὸν καὶ πλησίον τοῦ ὕδατος.

992 χθαμαλή Perhaps an echo of ι 25 αὐτὴ δὲ χθαμαλή (same case in same *sedes*), of Ithaca, in a very familiar line. If so, it is arguable that A. understood the adj. to mean 'low-lying' in that passage also.

ὑψόθι κύρη Here κύρω is not used in its normal epic sense, followed by a case (cf. A.R. 363 αἰθέρι κύρει), but as frequently κυρέω in tragedy with the sense of εἰμί (cf. S. *Aj.* ποῦ μοι γῆς κυρεῖ;). The cloud is simply not overhead, where clouds are normally seen. Cf. 404, of the Altar, ὑψόθ' ἐόντος (in that case 'above the horizon'). Sch. καὶ μὴ ἐν ὕψει ὑπάρχῃ.

993 πλαταμῶνι Sch. πλαταμὼν πέτρα ἐστὶν ὀλίγον ἐξέχουσα τῆς θαλάσσης, λεία τις καὶ ὁμαλὴ καὶ πλατεῖα. Also πλαταμὼν δέ ἐστιν ἡ ὀλίγον ὑπερκύπτουσα τῆς θαλάσσης ὁμαλὴ πέτρα καὶ ὕφαλος. Cf. *h.Hom.* 128 λείῳ ἐπὶ πλαταμῶνι, A.R. 1.365–6 λείῳ ἐπὶ πλαταμῶνι, τὸν οὐκ ἐπέβαλλε θάλασσα | κύμασι, χειμερίη δὲ πάλαι ἀποέκλυσεν ἅλμη, Nonn. *D.* 10.328 παρὰ πλαταμῶνι λιπόσκιον.

παραθλίβηται The earliest and only poetic instance of this verb. The prefix must mean that the cloud is compressed at the sides, so that it looks like a rock or reef projecting from the sea. A. may have been influenced here by the rare metaphor παραζωννύη in *D.S.* 51 (cited on 991).

994 σκέπτεο See note on 778.

ἐπὶ χείματι Cf. 873, 1093. Elsewhere this use of ἐπί c. dat. is rare, but see S. *Ph.* 151 φρουρεῖν ὄμμ' ἐπὶ σῷ μάλιστα καιρῷ.

995 εἰς For the use of εἰς/ἐς in the poets see LSJ, and, for the tragedians in particular, D. J. Mastronarde and J. M. Bremer, *The Textual Tradition of Euripides' Phoinissai* (1982) 175–7. In the text of A. there are 17 instances where both forms are metrically valid: in 12 of these the MSS clearly attest ἐς (185, 387, 435, 620, 632, 688, 799, 800, 809, 996, 1026, 1104), in one they are divided, but may be seen to imply support for ἐς (508), and in four they wholly attest εἰς (650, 656, 995, 1143). Voss, Mair and Martin read εἰς in 1143 only, Maass in 508, 656, 1143. As there is no way of knowing what A.'s practice was, it seems helpful to reflect in the text the evidence of the MSS, which may possibly be significant, and print εἰς in 650, 656, 995 and 1143, elsewhere ἐς.

γαληναίην Cf. 765 (adj.), 813 and 1017 (noun).

χειμωνόθεν Only here. This ablatival suffix usually has a local sense when used with nouns, e.g. Διόθεν (886), ἠπειρόθεν (1094), οὐρἀνόθεν (863), πρύμνηθεν (348), λειμωνόθεν (Ω 451); for a temporal sense cf. ἑσπερόθεν (710, 734, 891).

996 Φάτνην See note on 892. *D.S.* 51 καὶ ἡ τοῦ ὄνου Φάτνη ὅτε ἂν καθαρὰ καὶ λαμπρὰ φαίνηται, εὐδιεινόν. Cf. Theoc. 22.22 Φάτνη σημαίνουσα τὰ πρὸς πλόον εὔδια πάντα.

Καρκίνος Cf. 893.

ἀμφιελίσσει The Crab carries the Manger round in its circular course. The essential meaning of this is simply that the Manger is in the constellation of the Crab: cf. 893 ὑπὸ Καρκίνῳ, another way of indicating the Manger's position, and 273 ἑλίσσεται, similarly used of giving a star's relative position. For this compound cf. 378 ἀμφιελικτοί of all the fixed stars.

997 πρῶτα Suggesting the sense of 'as soon as'; cf. δ 414 ἐπὴν δὴ πρῶτα κατευνηθέντα ἴδησθε.

καθαιρομένην Cf. καθαρός 783, 802, 825, 1013. But the verb is not normally used so literally, and here it may carry overtones of its more familiar sense of purging or purifying, especially when repeated in the next line.

ὑπένερθεν The cloud is below in the sense that it is closer to the earth, and so hides the stars from our view; cf. 494.

ὀμίχλης A misty cloud, as in Γ 10 εὖτ᾽ ὄρεος κορυφῇσι Νότος κατέχευεν ὀμίχλην, Ρ 649 ἠέρα μὲν σκέδασεν καὶ ἀπῶσεν ὀμίχλην.

998 κείνη Sc. Φάτνη, in view of καθαιρομένη (Φάτνην).

φθίνοντι Cf. φθίνοντος θέρεος (514), μηνός (1149).

ἐν χειμῶνι Cf. Theoc. 11.58 with same spondaic fifth foot.

999 φλόγες ἥσύχιαι *D.S.* 54 λύχνος χειμῶνος καιόμενος ἡσυχαῖος εὐδίαν σημαίνει. This sign is the opposite of that in 977–80. The coupling of lamps and the night owl suggests the time of day known as περὶ λύχνων ἁφάς (Hdt. 7.215).

νυκτερίη γλαύξ *D.S.* 52 γλαὺξ ἡσυχαῖον φθεγγομένη ἐν χειμῶνι εὐδίαν προσημαίνει· καὶ νύκτωρ χειμῶνος ἡσυχαῖον ᾄδουσα, *Gp.* 1.2.6 γλαὺξ ᾄδουσα συνεχῶς ἐν νυκτί, *CCAG* 8.1.138, 3 ἐν χειμῶνι ᾄσασα γλαὺξ εὐδίαν σημαίνει. Anon. Laur. 11.19 combines the last two. Ael. *NA* 7.7 εἰ δὲ εἴη χειμέρια, ᾄσασα γλαὺξ εὐδίαν μαντεύεται καὶ ἡμέραν φαιδράν. Virgil amplifies with realistic detail in *G.* 1.402–3 *solis et occasum seruans de culmine summo | nequiquam seros exercet noctua cantus.* See Jermyn 51. Cf. Plin. *Nat.* 18.362 *sic et noctua in imbre garrula.* The bird is identified as the little owl (or little grey owl), *Athene noctua*: see Thompson 76–8, Pollard 39 and 113. On the owl's hooting cf. Ar. *Lys.* 760–1.

1000 ἥσυχον See note on 943 ἄπληστον. The sequence in these three lines of ἡσύχιαι, ἥσυχον, ἥσυχα, with case variation, suggests a connection between the manner of the sign and the weather predicted. The four-word line, with its even distribution of dactyls and spondees, also seems to contribute a sense of calmness.

μαραινομένου   Elsewhere used of fading light (814, 862, 1034).

1001–1002 ἥσυχα ... κορώνη   D.S. 53 καὶ κορώνη ἕωθεν εὐθὺς ἐὰν κράξῃ τρίς, εὐδίαν σημαίνει, καὶ ἑσπέρας χειμῶνος ἡσυχαῖον ᾄδουσα. A. has perhaps omitted the first part and amplified the second part of his source. The text of the MSS here is unsatisfactory, since it lacks the conjunction required to make sense of κρώξῃ (κρώζῃ, κράζῃ). The emendations proposed have therefore been designed either to supply an appropriate conjunction, in place of ἥσυχα (Stephanus, Lobeck, Voss, Bergk, Wilamowitz) or in place of ἐν (Kaibel), or to eliminate the final verb (Grotius, Buttmann, Maass). Mair and Zannoni have simply retained the transmitted text and supplied the conjunction in their translations, which is hardly a solution to the problem.

Since there is evidently a corruption somewhere in the text, the first step is to determine where it most probably lies. D.S. is too brief to be helpful, though it may be seen as supporting ἥσυχα with following participle. The scholia, however, provide four very useful paraphrases: (1) καὶ τὰς κορώνας δὲ ἠρέμα ποικίλη τῇ φωνῇ χρωμένας (ΜΔΚΑS 999), (2) καὶ κορώνη ἑσπέρας ποικίλον φθεγγομένη καὶ μεθ᾽ ἡσυχίας (Μ 999), (3) ποικίλλουσα τὴν φωνὴν αὐτῆς εἰς διαφορὰς φωνῶν καὶ πολύφωνα κρώζουσα (ΜΔΚUA 1001), (4) ὅταν καὶ ἡ κορώνη ποικίλη τῇ φωνῇ καὶ ἥσυχα κρώζῃ καὶ μὴ τραχέα (ΜΔΚΑ 1001). All these would seem to confirm the authenticity of ποικίλλουσα, all but (3) that of ἥσυχα. Both words are also attested by the lemma at 1001. On the other hand ὥρη ἐν ἑσπερίη is represented by only ἑσπέρας in (2) and D.S., κρώζῃ by κρώζουσα in (3) and κρώζῃ (with ὅταν) in (4), whereas πολύφωνα is confirmed by (4). The corruption therefore lies in the first half of 1002.

Kaibel's ὥρη ὅθ᾽ ἑσπερίη is a simple and attractive solution, and is adopted by Martin. There are, however, two considerations that tell against it. One is that ὥρη ἐν ἑσπερίη is clearly an echo of the Homeric formula ὥρη ἐν εἰαρινῇ at the beginning of lines (Β 471, Π 643, σ 367, etc.), and it would be desirable to retain ἐν if possible. But the phrase may be explained as a corruption attributable to the Homeric formula. Secondly, the sequence of participial phrases in 1000–4 is a technique that A. uses elsewhere as a variation from clauses, most notable in 1021–7, and the intrusion of a clause here is from that point of view awkward. A more satisfactory solution will therefore be reached if the finite verb can be eliminated. As ποικίλλω is normally transitive, a noun depending on it would be appropriate, as in sch. (3) ποικίλλουσα τὴν φωνήν. Maass prints Buttmann's κρωγμόν, but his own κραυγήν seems to me palaeographically better, and especially close to the v.l. κράζῃ. This noun is used mostly of human cries, but cf. sch. (MKA) 999 κραυγάζει of the owl. In any case A. elsewhere describes animal behaviour with words normally used of humans (see note on 967 φωνῇ). But if κρώξῃ came from Hes. *Op.* 747 κρώξῃ λακέρυζα κορώνη, there is no way of telling what word it replaced.

1001 ἥσυχα ποικίλλουσα Ael. *NA* 7.7 κορώνη δὲ ἐπὶ δείπνου ὑποφθεγγομένη ἡσυχῇ ἐς τὴν ὑστεραίαν εὐδίαν παρακαλεῖ (≃ Anon. Laur. 11.24), *Gp.* 1.2.6 καὶ κορώνη πρᾴεως ἐν ἡμέρᾳ κρώζουσα. For ἥσυχα as adverb cf. Theoc. 2.11 ποταείσομαι ἄσυχα. A. uses ποικίλλω in 822, more normally, of colour, here unusually of sound; cf. Pi. *O.* 6.87 ποικίλον ὕμνον, *N.* 4.14 ποικίλον κιθαρίζων, *O.* 4.3 ποικιλοφόρμιγγος ἀοιδᾶς. The verb occurs once in Homer, Σ 590 χορὸν ποίκιλλε.

1002 ὥρῃ ἐν ἑσπερίῃ See note on 1001–1002. Here ὥρη is a time of night, the period of ἑσπέρα, which was followed by μέσαι νύκτες (Pl. *R.* 621b) and then ἀμφιλύκη νύξ (Η 433). *CCAG* 8.1.138, 9 κορώνη ἐπὶ δείπνῳ φθεγγομένη καὶ ἡσυχῇ ἑστῶσα τῇ ὑστεραίᾳ εὐδίαν σημαίνει. Anon. Laur. 11.24 combines this with Ael. *NA* 7.7 (see preceding note).

κραυγήν See note on 1001–1002.

πολύφωνα Usually understood as adv. with κρώξῃ (κρώζῃ), but Ceporinus translates 'garrula cornix', and this meaning is necessary if κραυγήν is read. This feminine ending seems not uncharacteristic of A.: cf. 942 εἰνάλιαι, 1022 ἐννεάγηρα. The latter, with κορώνη, looks back to Hesiod's line-ending λακέρυζα κορώνη (*Op.* 747), and it is likely that here A. is adding another variant to the Hesiodic tradition. Cf. | 568 γαῖαν πολυφόρβην, *h.Hom.* 2.211 πολυπότνια Δηώ, Pi. *N.* 3.2 τὰν πολυξέναν. Aristotle in *PA* 660a34 τῶν δ' ὀρνίθων ἔνιοι πολύφωνοί is describing imitative birds, and so Plu. 937c θαυμαστόν τι χρῆμα πολυφώνου καὶ πολυφθόγγου κίττης. It is possible that A. here is classing the crow with similar birds that are noted for their imitations of human speech (raven, jay, etc.), and that the epithet is a characteristic one, like ἐννεάγηρα, not merely tautological after ποικίλλουσα.

1003 μοῦνοι μέν *D.S.* 52 καὶ κόραξ δὲ μόνος μὲν ἡσυχαῖον κράζων, καὶ ἐὰν τρὶς κράζῃ μετὰ τοῦτο πολλάκις κράξῃ, εὐδιεινός. There are two parts to this portent: one is the croaking of a solitary raven (1003–4), the other the croaking of a whole flock (1005–6). The latter is not in the text of *D.S.* (Hort indicates a lacuna), but A. introduces it with πλειότεροι. The first part is set out in two participial phrases, the second balances it with a single adjectival phrase enclosing a clause. This concludes the series of adjectival and participial phrases that go with γινέσθω τοι σῆμα (1001).

ἐρημαῖον The transmitted ἐρημαῖοι comes awkwardly after μοῦνοι without a copula. It does have the support of sch. (M) μόνοι καὶ καθ' ἕνα ἐν τῇ ἐρημίᾳ, and one could compare S. *Ant.* 887 ἄφετε μόνην ἔρημον and *Ph.* 470–1 μὴ λίπῃς μ' οὕτω μόνον, | ἔρημον. But the contexts in Sophocles are quite different, and there is no support from either *D.S.* or sch. (MΔUAS) κατὰ μόνας μὲν ἐπιεικῶς φθεγγόμενοι. Martin's ἐρημαῖον is more satisfactory and more Aratean: cf. 948 τρύζει ὀρθρινόν, 1023 νύκτερον ἀείδουσα. A. may be seen to have followed the adverbial form in *D.S.* 52 (ἡσυχαῖον) and varied the sense. His text in its turn has some support from the imitation in Q.S. 12.513 ἐννύχιοι ὄρνιθες ἐρημαῖον βοόωντες.

βοόωντες Cf. 910.

1004 δισσάκις A variation of *D.S.* 52 τρίς. Virgil extends the variation in *G.* 1.410–11 *tum liquidas corui presso ter gutture uoces | aut quater ingeminant.* Jermyn (52) suggests that both A. and Virgil are thinking of rooks. Cf. 968.

αὐτὰρ ἔπειτα μετ' ἀθρόα For αὐτὰρ ἔπειτα cf. A 51, Π 497. The combination gives equal force to the contrasting and the progressive senses of the conjunction (Denniston 55). Here the meaning runs on without a pause, since the whole portent consists of the single croaks and then the unbroken sequence of croaking. In most modern texts, however, the contrast has been disrupted by the introduction of μέγα in place of μετά, whether as μεγάθροος (Voss) or μέγ' ἀθρόα (Buttmann, followed by Maass and Martin), on the strength of sch. λαμπροτέρᾳ τῇ φωνῇ χρώμενοι. Loudness is not in question here. *D.S.* 52 has simply πολλάκις, and the contrast is not between soft (*D.S.* ἡσυχαῖον) and loud, but between single and unbroken. The transmitted text should therefore be retained, with μετ' construed as adverb. This use is common in the form μετὰ δέ (e.g. O 67, Ψ 133, Hdt. 1.19 and 128), but here αὐτάρ takes the place of δέ. A. is following closely *D.S.* μετὰ τοῦτο. So Mair, who translates 'with frequent rapid screams'. I think the essential meaning of ἀθρόα is rather 'all in one mass', i.e. 'uninterrupted'; cf. Erren 'ununterbrochenen Lärm', though his text reads μέγ' ἀθρόα. For ἀθρόος of uninterrupted sound cf. Pl. *R.* 344d ὥσπερ βαλανεὺς ἡμῶν καταντλήσας τῶν ὤτων ἀθρόον καὶ πολὺν τὸν λόγον.

κεκλήγοντες A. recalls the uninterrupted bird-cries of P 756 οὖλον κεκλήγοντες. Cf. M 125, Π 430, P 759. This perfect part. of κλάζω, inflected like a present, is an Aeolic form (cf. B 264 πεπλήγων, Call. *H.* 1.53 πεπλήγοντες) probably adopted in epic for metrical convenience. The variant κεκληγῶτες also appears as a variant in the text of Homer, most strongly in ξ 30. Here the Aeolic form is better attested. See Chantraine 1.430–1.

1005 πλειότεροι Cf. 644. Though this form is strictly a comparative of πλέως, A. is clearly using it as equivalent to πλέονες. Maass omits δ' and takes πλειότεροι with the preceding participle, but the meaning and structure of the sentence require the antithesis μοῦνοι μέν and πλειότεροι δ'. See on 1003. The well attested variant πλειότερον may have come from 1080. Cf. *Gp.* 1.2.6 (=Anon. Laur. 11.29) καὶ κόρακες πλείονες ἀγεληδὸν ὥσπερ χαίροντες καὶ κρώζοντες ἀνομβρίαν δηλοῦσιν.

ἀγεληδόν Cf. 965, and Leon. *AP* 9.24.3 = *HE* 2149.

κοίτοιο μέδωνται An imitation of κοίτου τε μέδηται at the end of a line, and γ 334 κοίτοιο μεδώμεθα. Here and in the following lines A. sees the birds in a human-like situation (cf. 967), and there may be an element of Stoic thought in this. But the theme was already familiar in the animal and bird fable, e.g. Hes. *Op.* 202ff., Archil. fr. 174 West, Aesop, and in comedy, especially Aristophanes' *Birds*. Virgil imitates and amplifies in *G.* 1.411–14 *et saepe cubilibus altis | nescio qua praeter solitum dulcedine laeti | inter se in foliis strepitant; iuuat imbribus actis | progeniem paruam dulcisque reuisere nidos.* See Wilkinson 121.

1006 ἔμπλειοι Epic form of ἔμπλεος. Cf. χ 3 (φαρέτρην) ἰῶν ἐμπλείην, in same *sedes*, also ξ 113 οἴνου ἐνίπλειον, Antim. fr. 24.2 ἔμπλειον μέλιτος. This imaginative use with φωνῆς is echoed in 1118 μυκηθμοῖο περίπλειοι.

οἰήσαιτο In contrast to 896, where the transmitted text favours οἰήσασθαι, the MSS here give various forms of the stem ὀισ-. This aorist middle appears in only two parts in Homer, ὀίσατο (α 323, ι 213, τ 390) and ὀισάμενος (ι 339, κ 232, 258, ο 443), and these recur in a few later instances, but with -σσ- better attested, ὀίσσατο (A.R. 3.456, 1189, 4.14) and ὀισσάμενος (A.R. 2.1135, 3.926, fr. 2.41 Powell, and Polyb. 3.94.4 quoting κ 232). On this aorist see Chantraine 1.371–2, 405, Frisk 2.366. The optative should be ὀίσαιτο or ὀίσσαιτο, but a double spondee is required, and, as in 896, the readings of Buttmann, Maass and Martin are unconvincing. Since both 896 and 1006 have the same problem of a spondaic ending, it seems reasonable to assume that A. would have used the same verb-form in both cases (cf. 802 τεκμήραιο, 932 τεκμήρασθαι). The simplest solution is therefore to bring line 1006 into conformity with 896, and read οἰήσαιτο with Voss and Zannoni.

The expression is a kind of simile, similar to 196 φαίης κεν ἀνιάζειν.

1007–1009 The syntax of this passage is not immediately clear. On the face of it there is a series of contrasting or balancing pairs: τὰ μὲν ... πολλὰ δέ, πολλὰ ... ἄλλοτε, περὶ φλόον ... ἐπ' αὐτοῦ, τε κείουσιν ... ἀπτερύονται. But πολλά has no verb corresponding to βοόωσι, and

525

there is also a certain awkwardness in the fact that πολλά participates in two of these pairs. A. appears to have sacrificed clarity for the sake of artistry, as he does occasionally elsewhere (e.g. 413–16, 469–79). Most attempts to make sense of these lines have involved taking ἀπτερύονται with πολλά, thus detaching it completely from the ἧχι clause. So Voss, who disrupts even more the natural run of words in 1009 by punctuating after both κείουσιν and ὑπότροποι, and translating 'und wie sie häufig um des Baums Gezweige, manchmal auf ihm selbst, bald wo sie zur Ruhe gehn, bald vom Auffluge zurückkehrend, wiederholt (αὖ) die Fittige schlagen (πτερύονται)'. This introduces an antithesis ('bald ... bald') and a participle ('zurückkehrend'), neither of which is expressed in or even suggested by the Greek. Buttmann similarly took ἀπτερύονται with πολλά, and simplified the syntax by omitting καί and reading κακκείοντες: 'e pastu ad cubile reduces circa arborem, et in illa ipsa considentes, alas concutiunt'. This complex emendation would be hard to justify at a point where the manuscripts show no significant disagreement.

Maass (*Aratea* 355) divides the flock of birds into two groups, one hiding in the tree's foliage, the other perching on its branches, and he refers ὑπότροποι ἀπτερύονται to the latter group, ἧχι κείουσι to the former. This makes the passage even more confusing, and, as Martin points out, there is nothing in the text of the manuscripts that gives the sense of two groups. Martin himself sees the problem as arising simply from the misunderstanding of καί, which he takes in the sense of 'encore': the birds normally flap their wings on taking off, but here they do it again on returning. There is nothing in the text that even suggests a reference to the birds' behaviour at another time, and it is too much to read into the simple καί.

All these interpretations are unsatisfactory in that they dismiss too easily the natural significance of τε ... καί, which makes ἀπτερύονται so clearly a part of the subordinate clause. This is in fact where it properly belongs, because the whole of the passage (1003–9) is concerned with the cawing of the ravens: βοόωντες ... κεκλήγοντες ... φωνῆς ἔμπλειοι ... βοόωσι. In 969 their wing-flapping is combined with their cawing as a sign of rain, but here their wing movement is a part of their roosting ritual, which A. has added to the material derived from the source of *D.S.* for the sake of its picturesque appeal. The verb to be construed with πολλά must therefore be found elsewhere, and it is most easily supplied by understanding βοόωσι from the preceding line. Mair and Erren imply this in their translations, but both in their translations (Erren also in his text) unaccountably punctuate after κείουσιν.

1007 οἴα Cf. 170 and note on 143 οἷος.

τὰ μέν   Referring back to the cries just described, when the birds are thinking of roosting; the following δέ is progressive.

βοόωσι   Cf. 947.

λιγαινομένοισιν   Once in Homer, but active, κήρυκες δὲ λίγαι-νον (Λ 685). Cf. A. Th. 874, of mourners, Mosch. 3.81, of a singer. The choice of verb continues A.'s representation of the birds as having human qualities. The middle voice perhaps signifies that the bird-calls are for their own benefit.

1008 δενδρείοιο   A new form derived from Homeric δένδρεον. Cf. κεγχρείοισιν (986). A. may have had in mind τ 520, of the nightingale, δενδρέων ἐν πετάλοισι καθεζομένη πυκινοῖσιν. Cf. δ 458 δένδρεον ὑψι-πέτηλον. Nic. Ther. 832 follows A. with δενδρείου.

περὶ φλόον   περί is preferable to κατά because it makes a clearer contrast to the following ἐπί. φλόος, a form of φλοιός, is properly the bark of a tree, hence sch. περὶ τὸν φλοῦν καὶ τὸ στέλεχος. Cf. Α 236–7 περὶ γάρ ῥά ἑ χαλκὸς ἔλεψε | φύλλα τε καὶ φλοιόν. But A. clearly uses the word here in the sense of 'foliage', as in 335, a meaning which re-lates the noun more directly to the verb φλέω, which expresses the idea of abundance.

1009 ἧχί τε κείουσιν   A. is recalling Α 606–7 οἱ μὲν κακκείοντες ἔβαν οἰκόνδε ἕκαστος, | ἧχι ἑκάστῳ δῶμα. The translators of A. and LSJ, following the scholia (κείουσιν ἀντὶ τοῦ κοιμῶνται), take the verb here to mean simply 'roost', 'sleep'. But in Homer this desiderative form of κεῖμαι always means 'go to bed', 'go to rest', and there is no reason why it should not be understood in the same sense here. The tree is the place where the birds go to roost and flap their wings at their home-coming.

ὑπότροποι   In Homer always in the same metrical position, and with the sense of coming safely home from danger, e.g. Ζ 501 of Hector ὑπότροπον ἐκ πολέμοιο, χ 35 of Odysseus ὑπότροπον οἴκαδ' ἱκέσθαι. Cf. A.R. 4.439 of Jason's home-coming. Here the word suggests in the birds' behaviour a human feeling of security and contentment. Apollon. Lex. ὑπότροπον· ὑποστρέφοντα καὶ ἀφιγμένον.

ἀπτερύονται   The scholia offer two explanations of this otherwise unattested verb: τὸ γὰρ ἀπτερύονται οἰονεὶ τὰ πτερὰ χαλάσαντες· ἢ τὸ ἀπτερύονται ἀντὶ τοῦ διασείουσι τὰς πτέρυγας ὑποστρέψαντες. The first sense goes well with κείουσιν, but it seems to imply that ἀ- is the negating prefix, as in ἄπτερος, and an extension of meaning from 'wingless' to 'resting the wings' is very improbable. The second meaning requires that the ἀ- be taken as copulative, as in ἀδελφός, ἄκοιτις, ἄλο-χος, ἅπας, etc., and the stem πτερυ- may be explained as a shortened form of πτερυσσ-, on the analogy of ἀφύω from ἀφύσσω. See K–B

527

1.186, Palmer 260, E. Fraenkel, *Glotta* 2 (1910) 29ff., Frisk 1.126 s.v. ἀπτ-
ερέως 'quickly'. The scholia compare Archilochus κηρύλος πέτρης ἐπὶ
προβλῆτος ἀπτερύσσετο (fr. 41 West), where, however, ἐπτερύσσετο is
plausibly suggested in LSJ s.v. πτερύσσομαι: loss of augment is rare in
iambic verse. Dr J. Warham informs me that there is much commotion
as rooks (and also starlings) come in to roost, and much changing of
places until each bird finds its regular roosting position. The flapping of
wings plays a conspicuous part on such occasions, and this may be what
A. is referring to here.

1010 γέρανοι *D.S.* 52 ὅταν γέρανοι πέτωνται καὶ μὴ ἀνακάμπτω-
σιν, εὐδίαν σημαίνει· οὐ γὰρ πέτονται πρὶν ἢ ἂν πετόμενοι καθαρὰ
ἴδωσι. Cf. Ael. *NA* 7.7 πετόμεναι δὲ ἄρα ἡσυχῇ αἱ αὐταὶ [sc. γέρανοι]
ὑπισχνοῦνται εὐημερίαν τινὰ καὶ εἰρήνην ἀέρος, Plin. *Nat.* 18.362
grues silentio per sublime uolantes serenitatem. For other weather signs from
cranes see 1031ff., 1075ff. On the ancient lore of cranes in general see
Thompson 68ff., on weather signs also Pollard 111.

μαλακῆς Cf. 826.

προπάροιθε Cf. 938, 1065 for time usage, and for metrical position
Ο 423 νεὸς προπάροιθε μελαίνης, Ζ 307, ρ 297.

1011 ἀσφαλέως 'Without swerving'; cf. Ν 141 of a torrent, ν 86 of
a ship.

τανύσαιεν ἕνα δρόμον The repetitive character of the words in this
line has a cumulative effect in stressing two important points, the un-
swerving direction of the birds' flight (ἀσφαλέως τανύσαιεν δρόμον),
and the unanimity of their decision to follow it (ἕνα ἤλιθα πᾶσαι).
τανύω is used here in the sense of simply setting a course, without any
reference to its length; cf. A.R. 4.1582–3 πλόος ... τετάνυσται. The
translation in LSJ, 'form one long flight', is misleading. Plutarch has an
interesting note on the flight of cranes: πέτονται γὰρ, ὅταν ᾖ πνεῦμα
πολὺ καὶ τραχὺς ἀήρ, οὔχ, ὥσπερ εὐδίας οὔσης, μετωπηδὸν ἢ κόλπῳ
μηνοειδοῦς περιφερείας, ἀλλ' εὐθὺς εἰς τρίγωνον συνάγουσαι σχίζουσι
τῇ κορυφῇ τὸ πνεῦμα περιρρέον, ὥστε μὴ διασπᾶσθαι τὴν τάξιν
(967Β–Ϲ).

ἤλιθα πᾶσαι Cf. 254. Cranes are feminine in the famous Homeric
simile, Γ 3ff., and so in later poets, Hes. *Op.* 448ff., Ar. *Av.* 710, Call. fr.
1.14.

1012 παλιρρόθιοι Cf. 347.

ὑπεύδιοι See note on 878 εὔδιοι.

1013–1043 Signs of stormy weather
The terms χεῖμα and χειμών can mean either the season of winter or
wintry weather, usually a combination of wind, rain and cold, at any

time of the year. Sometimes the season is specified by the addition of ὥρη, as in 850, 977, but sometimes the ambiguity can be confusing, e.g. *D.S.* 42 ἐὰν χειμῶνος ὄντος μύκαι μέλαιναι ἐπιγίνωνται, χειμῶνα σημαίνει.

Storm signs are to be observed (1) in the sky: stars (1013–18) and clouds (1018–20); (2) in the air: calls of geese, crows, jackdaws, chaffinches (1021–4), movements of sea-birds, wrens, robins, jackdaws (1024–6), bees (1027–30), and cranes (1031–2); (3) near the ground: cobwebs (1033), lamps (1034–6); additional note on signs of snow and hail (1036–43). The material is to be found mainly in *D.S.* 38–42.

1013 ἀστερόθεν Only here, formed on the analogy of οὐρανόθεν (863). The vowel from stems in -o became the regular connecting vowel in composition; cf. πατρόθεν (K 68). See Monro *HG* 117–18. The v.l. can be explained as having originated in 863.

A. bases this sign on the source of *D.S.* 43 ἡ τοῦ ὄνου Φάτνη εἰ συνίσταται καὶ ζοφερὰ γίγνεται, χειμῶνα σημαίνει, but as he has already used this source for 899–902, he now extends the application of the sign to the stars in general, and elaborates the theme in a chiastic pattern of positive and negative clauses. See Virgil's imitation of A. in *G.* 1.395–7, expressing the negative as a sign of good weather (Jermyn 49–50, Wilkinson 239): *nam neque tum stellis acies obtunsa uidetur,* | *nec fratris radiis obnoxia surgere luna,* | *tenuia nec lanae per caelum uellera ferri.* Virgil means that the stars are clear on a moonless and cloudless night, but his intricate pattern of negatives is not easy to follow, and he must surely have assumed that his readers would be familiar with the Aratean passage. Pliny (*Nat* 18.352) follows A., omitting the moon: *cum repente stellarum fulgor obscuratur et id neque nubilo nec caligine, pluuia aut graues denuntiantur tempestates.* Cf. Anon. Laur. 8.9 εἰ δὲ καὶ ἄστρα ἀμαυρὰ φανῶσι χειμῶνα δηλοῖ.

ἀμβλύνηται Cf. ἀμβλείῃσι (785) and ἄμβλυνται (787) of the moon.

1014 οὐδέ ποθεν An unusual combination. A. is stressing the point that the stars apparently become faint suddenly without any cause. For the real cause see note on 900.

πεπιεσμέναι Elsewhere A. uses this participle of stars (416) and sun (842) affected by clouds; here the clouds are just dense enough to make the stars faintly visible, not as sch. νεφέλαι πεπιλημέναι αἱ τὴν ἀορασίαν ποιοῦσαι.

ἀντιόωσιν Cf. 501 ἀντιόωντι. Here the verb expresses a kind of confrontation, as the clouds intervene between the observer and the stars. A. may have developed this use from the hostile encounter in Ζ 127 δυστήνων δέ τε παῖδες ἐμῷ μένει ἀντιόωσιν.

1015 ζόφος ἄλλος Sch. ἄλλης τινὸς ἀχλύος. In Homer ζόφος is usually the darkness of Hades, or of the far west, and is associated with mist in v 241 ζόφον ἠερόεντα. Cf. *D.S.* 12 ζοφώδης of the moon (cited on 785).

ὑποτρέχῃ From the observer's point of view the cloud or mist is below the stars; cf. 542 ὑποδράμοι, 854 ὑποσκιάῃσι, 997 ὑπένερθεν.

οὐδὲ σελήνη A. seems to intend ὑποτρέχῃ to be understood also with σελήνη. In that case it would refer to the moon's westward movement during the night hours, and it is below the stars because it is closer to the earth. The moon's dimming effect, however, is caused by its brightness, and there is a certain awkwardness in having to use the same verb with these two very different subjects. Virgil does better in giving the moon an appropriate verb of its own, *surgere*, which indicates that the moon is above the horizon. It is conceivable that some such verb as φαίνηται should be understood with σελήνη, but that is even more awkward, and I do not think it is what A. intended.

1016 τά γ' Sc. ἄστρα. This line completes the four-line chiasmus by returning to the sense of 1013, with the significant addition of ἐξαπίνης. The suddenness of the stars' loss of light is an essential part of the sign, as in 899.

αὔτως I.e. just spontaneously, without any obvious external cause. Cf. 21, 65, 110, 260.

ἀμενηνά Cf. 786, 905, also of light.

φέρωνται The plural verb indicates that the poet is thinking particularly of the plurality of the subject; cf. 806. For the verb itself, with its reference to the diurnal westward movement of the stars, cf. 47, 176, 385.

1017 ἐπικείσθω Sch. μηκέτι τοῦτο τὸ σημεῖον εὐδίας σοι ἔστω. This gives the basic sense of the line, but ἐπικείσθω is an unexpected choice of verb, and may have overtones that suggest more than just 'being there'. The combination of this verb with σῆμα is perhaps a reminiscence of Theogn. 19–20 σοφιζομένῳ μὲν ἐμοὶ σφρηγὶς ἐπικείσθω | τοῖσδ' ἔπεσιν, and, if so, the idea of a guarantee may be intended. Cf. Luc. *Epigr.* 20 Macleod (*AP* 10.42) ἀρρήτων ἐπέων γλώσσῃ σφραγὶς ἐπικείσθω.

1018 ἐπὶ ... δόκευε Cf. 987.

ταὶ μὲν ἔωσιν It appears from sch. ἐν τῷ αὐτῷ τόπῳ μένωσιν that the variant μενέωσιν is ancient. But it still requires emendation to make sense, and in any case ταὶ μέν is necessary to balance ταὶ δ'. ἔωσιν is a normal Homeric form, e.g. l 140, where also it comes at a line-end.

1019 αὐτῇ ἐνὶ χώρῃ The better attested reading with ἐν gives hiatus without ictus; cf. 34. See Gow on [Theoc.] 25.275, West *GM* 156.

ἄλλαι ἐπ' αὐταῖς *D.S.* 45 ὅταν ἐστώτων νεφῶν ἕτερα ἐπιφέρηται

530

τὰ δ' ἠρεμῆ, χειμέρια. The essentials are that some clouds are stationary while others overtake them. A. maintains the framework as in *D.S.* with ἄλλαι a variation of ἕτερα and ἐπ' ... φορέωνται a variation of ἐπιφέρηται. A., however, takes the opportunity to add a second ταὶ μὲν ... ταὶ δέ antithesis within the ταὶ δέ clause of the first, subdividing the moving clouds into those now passing the stationary clouds and those still approaching. Since the moving clouds are naturally at a lower level than the others, the scholia explain the situation in detail: ὅταν τῶν νεφελῶν αἱ μὲν ὑψηλότεραι ἐν τῷ αὐτῷ τόπῳ μένωσιν ἀκίνητοι, αἱ δ' ὑπ' αὐταῖς διαρριπίζωνται, αἱ μὲν προηγούμεναι, αἱ δὲ καταλαμβάνουσαι (ΜΔUAS). Sch. (MAS) give a similar but less lucid explanation. The variant ὑπ' αὐταῖς presumably came from the scholia. It is the reading of editors from Buttmann to Zannoni, and, though it is not untranslatable, as Martin suggests with reference to Mair's failure to translate it, it goes awkwardly with the following line: it is, in fact, a comment on A.'s meaning, not an essential part of it. Here again (cf. 1007–9) A. has achieved some verbal artistry at the expense of clarity.

1020 ἀμειβόμεναι Properly of changing places, hence of crossing a threshold in Hes. *Th.* 749 ἀμειβόμεναι μέγαν οὐδόν: cf. Ι 409 (ψυχή), κ 328 (φάρμακα) ἀμείψεται ἕρκος ὀδόντων. A. has extended this use to mean 'moving past' without any sense of crossing a dividing line; cf. E. *Or.* 979–80 ἕτερα δ' ἕτερος [ἕτερον West, prob. rightly] ἀμείβεται | πήματ' ἐν χρόνῳ μακρῷ.

ἐξόπιθεν Sc. ἐπιφερόμεναι, or some such participle, balancing ἀμειβόμεναι.

1021 χῆνες *D.S.* 39 χῆνες βοῶντες μᾶλλον ἢ περὶ σῖτον μαχόμενοι χειμέριον, *Gp.* 1.3.9 καὶ χῆνες μετὰ κλαγγῆς ἐπειγόμεναι πρὸς τροφήν (≈ Anon. Laur. 11.48), Plin. *Nat.* 18.363 *et anseres continuo clangore intempestiui.* A. clearly means wild geese, as in the Homeric similes Β 460 and Ο 692. Geese were, however, domesticated early in Greece, as is seen from ο 161ff. and τ 536ff. On geese in general see Thompson 325–30.

κλαγγηδόν Once in Homer, Β 463, in the famous simile of the Asian geese. Cf. Opp. *C.* 4.405, Q.S. 11.116.

ἐπειγόμεναι The gender of χῆνες is feminine in ο 161 and 174, masculine in τ 536 and 552, elsewhere in Homer indeterminate. Here the reading of M is confirmed by *Gp.* 1.3.9.

βρωμοῖο Only here, a variation of Homeric βρωμή (κ 460, μ 302). A.R. 3.1058 and Nic. *Alex.* 499 retain the Homeric form. For the genitive cf. 653 ἐπείγεται εἰδώλοιο.

1022 ἐννεάγηρα Only here, perhaps inspired by Homeric compounds such as ἐννεάχιλοι (Ε 860), ἐννεαβοίων (Ζ 236), ἐννεάπηχυ (Ω 270). Adjectives formed from γῆρας normally end in -γήραος, -γήρως, e.g. ἀγήρως, μακρογήρως, πολυγήραος, but πολύγηρος is attested, and the scholia here have πολύγηρα. For the feminine ending cf. 1002 πολύφωνα.

The tradition that the crow lives as long as nine human generations goes back to Hes. fr. 304.1–2 ἐννέα τοι ζώει γενεὰς λακέρυζα κορώνη | ἀνδρῶν ἡβώντων. The number of generations is modified in Ar. Av. 609 οὐκ οἶσθ' ὅτι πέντ' ἀνδρῶν γενεὰς ζώει λακέρυζα κορώνη, but otherwise the crow's longevity is not specified. Cf. Com. Anon. fr. 311b Meineke ὑπὲρ τὰς ἐλάφους βεβιωκὼς ἢ τὰς κορώνας, AP 11.361.7 (Autom.) βίον ζώοιτε κορώνης, 389.1 (Lucill.) εἰ μὲν ζῇς ἐλάφου τανάον χρόνον ἠὲ κορώνης, Babr. Fab. 46.9 μή πω κορώνην δευτέρην ἀναπλήσας, Opp. C. 3.117 πολύζωοί τε κορῶναι. Pliny recalls that Hesiod cornici nouem nostras adtribuit aetates (Nat. 7.153), and Cicero says Theophrastus found fault with Nature quod ceruis et cornicibus uitam diuturnam ... dedisset (Tusc. 3.69). Latin poets make much play with this theme, e.g. Lucr. 5.1084 cornicum ut saecla uetusta, Hor. C. 3.17.13 annosa cornix, Ov. Am. 2.6.35–6 cornix inuisa Mineruae, | illa quidem saeclis uix moritura nouem, Met. 7.274 nouem cornicis saecula passae, Mart. 10.67.5 iam cornicibus omnibus superstes, Juv. 10.247 exemplum uitae fuit a cornice secundae, Auson. Ecl. 5.3 hos nouies superat uiuendo garrula cornix, Avien. 1742 cornix longaeua.

See Thompson 169, Pollard 25, 27, 99, A. H. Sommerstein ad Ar. Av. (1987) 605–9, p. 237, P. Bing, The Well-Read Muse (1988) 43. The lines attributed to Hesiod (fr. 304) by Plutarch (415c–D) compare the crow with the stag, the raven and the phoenix in an ascending order of longevity. I have not discovered any explanation suggested for the origin of this ancient myth.

1023 νύκτερον See note on 943 ἄπληστον. Cf. Orph. Arg. 877 νύκτερον ὄρφνην, D.S. 39 καὶ κορώνη καὶ κόραξ καὶ κολοιὸς ὀψὲ ᾄδοντες χειμέριοι.

ἀείδουσα With α long, as in 1000. This occurs only once in Homer, ρ 519 ἀείδῃ, but cf. h.Hom. 12.1 Ἥρην ἀείδω, Theogn. 4 ἀείσω, A.R. 4.1399 ἐφίμερον ἀείδουσαι, Theoc. 24.77 ἀκρέσπερον ἀείδοισαι, Call. fr. 26.8 ἠνεκὲς ἀείδω.

ὀψὲ βοῶντε Sch. δυϊκῷ ἀριθμῷ ἐχρήσατο ἀντὶ πληθυντικοῦ. τοῦτο γὰρ ἔθος αὐτῷ. τοῦτο καὶ Ὅμηρος οἶδεν. Cf. 968 κρώξαντε. The run of words here recalls 585 and ε 272, but the imitation is not significant as far as the sense is concerned. Professor Reeve has plausibly suggested that ὀψὲ βοῶντε is a pun on Homer's ὀψὲ ... Βοώτην. The imitation certainly explains the breach of Hermann's Bridge: cf. Porter 48. For the sense cf. D.S. 39 ὀψὲ ᾄδοντες. Cf. Ael. NA 7.7 κόραξ δὲ αὖ καὶ κορώνη καὶ κολοιὸς δείλης ὀψίας εἰ φθέγγοιντο, χειμῶνος ἔσεσθαί τινα ἐπιδημίαν διδάσκουσι.

1024 σπίνος *D.S.* 39 σπίνος στρουθὸς σπίζων ἔωθεν χειμέριον. Cf. Ael. *NA* 4.60 σπίνοι δὲ ἄρα σοφώτεροι καὶ ἀνθρώπων τὸ μέλλον προεγνωκέναι. ἴσασι γοῦν καὶ χειμῶνα μέλλοντα, καὶ χιόνα ἐσομένην προμηθέστατα ἐφυλάξαντο. Thompson identifies this bird as probably the chaffinch, also called σπίγγος, σπίζα (267). Pollard translates 'chaffinch' here, but describes the bird under σπίζα (38). In modern Greek Pring gives σπίνος as a general term for 'finch'.

ἠῷα A neat variation of the more usual nominative in agreement with the subject (e.g. Hes. *Sc.* 396 ἠῷος χέεν αὐδήν), which here would have produced an ugly cluster of consonants.

ὄρνεα πάντα *D.S.* 40 καὶ ἐὰν ἐκ πελάγους ὄρνιθες φεύγωσι, χειμῶνα σημαίνουσι, Ael. *NA* 7.7 ὄρνιθες δὲ ἐκ τοῦ πελάγους ἐς τὴν γῆν σὺν ὁρμῇ πετόμενοι μαρτύρονται χειμῶνα (≏*CCAG* 8.1.138, 18 ≏ Anon. Laur. 11.37), *Gp.* 1.3.11 καὶ τὰ ὄρνεα εἰς τὰ πρὸς πέλαγος μέρη φεύγοντα χειμῶνα προδηλοῦσι. Homer has ὄρνεον only once (N 64), but it is not uncommon in later verse and prose. For πάντα cf. 9 σπέρματα πάντα.

1025 πελάγους Ionic -ευς is suggested by Voss and adopted by Maass. But Homer has only Ἐρέβευς, θάμβευς, θάρσευς, θέρευς (K–B 1.436), and there is no reason to suppose that A. would not have used the Attic form.

ὀρχίλος *D.S.* 39 ὄρχιλος εἰσιὼν καὶ εἰσδυόμενος εἰς ὀπάς. The noun is proparoxytone also in Arist. *HA* 609a12 γλαὺξ καὶ ὄρχιλος πολέμια. Schwyzer 1.484–5 compares ποικίλος, κωτίλος, ναυτίλος, τροχίλος, φρυγίλος. The bird is identified as the wren by Thompson (219) and Pollard (36). Frisk (2.433) suggests the name may be connected with ὀρχέομαι because of the bird's liveliness. For Aesop's fable of the wren as king see Plu. 806E–F.

ἐριθεύς *D.S.* 39 καὶ ἐριθεὺς ὡσαύτως. The robin is more commonly called ἐρίθακος: cf. Ael. *NA* 7.7 ἐρίθακος δὲ ἐς τὰ αὔλια καὶ τὰ οἰκούμενα παριὼν δῆλός ἐστι χειμῶνος ἐπιδημίαν ἀποδιδράσκων. Arist. *HA* 632b29 calls it a bird of winter. Sch. Ar. *V.* 927/8b quotes the proverb οὐ τρέφει μία λόχμη δύο ἐριθάκους. See Thompson 100–1, Pollard 113.

1026 ὀχεάς Cf. 956 ὀχῆς of the ant, Call. fr. 575 of a snake, Nic. *Ther.* 139 of a viper.

φῦλα κολοιῶν Repeated without variation from 963.

1027 ἐκ νομοῦ ἐρχόμενα The corresponding storm sign in *D.S.* 40 is κολοιοὶ ἐκ τοῦ νότου πετόμενοι, where Maass would read νομοῦ (p. xxvi); the southerly in Greece is certainly associated with wet weather, but not necessarily with storms. Here the land-birds are contrasted with the sea-birds flying from their food source, the sea. Virgil transfers this theme to a flock of rooks *e pastu decedens* (*G.* 1.381).

τραφεροῦ Traditionally translated 'dry' (Ceporinus, Voss, Mair, Zannoni), a meaning that goes back at least to Hsch. τραφερήν· ξηράν. But, as Martin points out, this is erroneous: it presumably derives from the Homeric phrase ἐπὶ τραφερήν τε καὶ ὑγρήν (Ξ 308, υ 98) and the assumption that the antithesis there is between 'dry' and 'wet'. So LSJ 'dry land' (sc. γῆ). In these passages, however, and in *h.Hom.* 2.43 σεύατο δ᾽ ὥς τ᾽ οἰωνὸς ἐπὶ τραφερήν τε καὶ ὑγρήν, the context is one of travelling (Hera, Oedipus, Demeter), and the contrast is not between dry and wet, but between land and sea. Probably ὁδόν should be understood with both adjectives: cf. Α 312 ἐπέπλεον ὑγρὰ κέλευθα, A.R. 2.544–5 κέλευθος | ὑγρή τε τραφερή τε, 4.280–1 ὁδοὶ καὶ πείρατ᾽ ἔασιν | ὑγρῆς τε τραφερῆς τε. The adjective appears to be derived from τρέφω in the sense of 'thicken' (see Frisk 2.926), and the basic meaning is 'firm', 'solid'. Cf. Apollon. *Lex.* τραφερήν· τὸ γὰρ θρέψαι πῆξαι, Hsch. τραφερόν· πηκτόν, τρόφιμον, λευκόν, ξηρόν, πεπηγμένον, Eustath. 987.61–2 παρὰ τὸ τρέφω, τὸ πήγνυμι, ἡ εὐπαγὴς καὶ στερρὰ καὶ διαστελλομένη οὕτω τῆς ὑγρᾶς. In Hellenistic and later poets τραφερός describes land as opposed to sea without any connotation of travelling, e.g. [Theoc.] 21.18 τραφερὰν [τρυφερὰν codd.] προσέναχε θάλασσα, Orph. *L.* 653 αἵματος ὠτειληθὲν ἐπὶ τραφερὴν ῥαθάμιγγες, Opp. *H.* 1.204 τραφερὴν δὲ μέγ᾽ ἐχθαίρουσιν ἄρουραν, 5.313 ἐπὶ τραφερὴν ἀνάγοντες, 334 ἤθεσιν ἐν τραφεροῖσι πολὺ πλέον ἠὲ νέεσσι (Mair 'in landward haunts'), anon. *AP* 9.672.1 εἰ τραφερῆς πάσης ἀλιτέρμονα κύκλον ὁδεύσῃς. These examples suggest that A. here means 'from their landward feeding-grounds', in contrast to ἐκ πελάγους of the sea-birds. Martin translates 'un gras pâturage', and Erren similarly 'aus nahrhafter Weide', but this interpretation is supported solely by [Theoc.] 21.44 τις τῶν τραφερῶν (ἰχθύων), 'one of the fat ones' (see Gow ad loc.). But this use is quite out of line with all the other examples of τραφερός, and is in itself curious in seeming to imply a distinct category of fish that are fat. Perhaps we ought to read τρυφερῶν here (reversing the situation in line 18), with reference to the class of fish that are regarded as delicacies.

ὄψιον Normally with three terminations, and used with nouns expressing a period of time, e.g. Hdt. 7.167 μέχρι δείλης ὀψίης; cf. Pi. *I.* 4.38, Th. 8.26.1. Here the adjective has an adverbial force, 'late in the day'.

αὖλιν Primarily a tent for the night (Ι 232), here a roosting place for birds, from χ 470 αὖλιν ἐσιέμεναι. Cf. *h.Hom.* 4.71, 5.168, of cattle; with ἐπί, cf. Call. *H.* 3.87–8.

1028 ἔτι The transmitted ἐπιξουθαί is not found elsewhere, and,

COMMENTARY: 1029

though the compound has a parallel in ἐπίξανθος, the standard epithet of bees is ξουθός (see next note). Voss's emendation goes well with the negative and following verb (cf. 579).

ξουθαί The uncertainty about the meaning of this word even in antiquity is illustrated by the long list of equivalents in Hesychius. It seems likely, however, that the viable options can be narrowed down to two, a brownish colour and a vibrant sound: see, for example, the discussions by Fraenkel on A. *Ag.* 1142 and Kannicht on E. *Hel.* 1111, who support the former meaning, and Gow on Theoc. 7.142 and Dale on E. *Hel.* 1111, who argue for the latter; see also M. Silk, *CQ* 73 (1983) 317–19 on obsolete words with no guaranteed meaning. This word is used mostly of birds and insects, and in many examples either meaning could be understood, but there are several in which the colour sense is unlikely, as when it is descriptive of wings (*h.Hom.* 33.13, B. 5.17, Mnas. *AP* 7.192.4 = *HE* 2650; cf. ξουθόπτερος of bees in E. *Her.* 487, fr. 467.4, Lyr. Adesp. 7.13 *CA* p. 185), or as an epithet of winds (Chaerem. fr. 1.7), or of sound (Tib. Ill. *AP* 9.373.4 = *FGE* 2071, Opp. *H.* 4.123). It may therefore be that the colour meaning is a late development due to the false equating of ξουθός with ξανθός, as suggested by L. Méridier, *Rev. Phil. Anc.* 36 (1913) 264–78; cf. P. Kretschmer, *Glotta* 7 (1916) 354. The sense of vibrant sound is certainly more suitable in the context of bird song (A. *Ag.* 1142, E. *Hel.* 1111, Ar. *Av.* 214, 676, 744, Theoc. *Ep.* 4.11, Lyr. Adesp. 7.1 *CA* p. 185, Opp. *H.* 4.123), especially as in most cases the bird is the nightingale. In the case of bees the buzzing is their most distinctive characteristic, and the word seems to have become a poetic epithet regardless of context, as when the immediate interest is the honey, e.g. S. fr. 398.5 ξουθῆς μελίσσης κηρόπλαστον ὄργανον, E. *IT* 165 ξουθᾶν τε πόνημα μελισσᾶν, 634–5 ἀνθεμόρρυτον γάνος | ξουθῆς μελίσσης, Antiph. fr. 52.7 ξουθῆς μελίσσης νάμασιν. When the passage is about bees in flight, the sound sense becomes particularly appropriate, e.g. [Pl.] *Epigr.* 32.6–7 (Bergk) ξουθαὶ δ᾽ ἐφύπερθε μέλισσαι | ... λαροῖς ἐπὶ χείλεσι βαῖνον, Theoc. 7.142 πωτῶντο ξουθαὶ περὶ πίδακας ἀμφὶ μέλισσαι, Nic. *AP* 9.564.1–2 = *HE* 2775–6 μέλισσα ξουθά, Zon. *AP* 9.226.1–2 = *GP* 3472 ξουθαὶ σιμβληίδες ἄκρα μέλισσαι | φέρβεσθ᾽. Such is A.'s use of the epithet here, and Martin rightly translates 'bourdonnantes', correcting Mair's traditional 'tawny'.

1029 πρόσσω Homeric form, perhaps recalling the wasp simile in Π 265 πρόσσω πᾶς πέτεται. The meaning 'at a distance' is later, e.g. E. *Ph.* 596 ἐγγύς, οὐ πρόσω βέβηκεν, D.S. 46 ὅταν μέλιτται μὴ ἀποπέτωνται μακρὰν ἀλλ᾽ αὐτοῦ ἐν τῇ εὐδίᾳ πέτωνται, χειμῶνα ἐσόμενον σημαίνει. Virgil expands the topic in *G.* 4.191–4 *nec uero a stabulis*

535

pluuia impendente recedunt | longius, aut credunt caelo aduentantibus Euris, | sed circum tutae sub moenibus urbis aquantur | excursusque breuis temptant. Pliny notes briefly (*Nat.* 18.364) *segniterque et contra industriam suam apes conditae.* **νομόν** C. gen. with verbal sense of 'foraging for'; cf. the figurative use in Υ 249 and Hes. *Op.* 403 ἐπέων νομός. **κηροῖο** A. follows Arist. *HA* 553b27 γίγνεται δὲ κηρίον μὲν ἐξ ἀνθέων. Cf. Varro, *RR* 3.16.24 *ex olea arbore ceram*, Col. 9.14.20 (*Celsus*) *ait ex floribus ceras fieri*, Plin. *Nat.* 11.14.34 *ex floribus constructo fauo.* The ancients were apparently unaware that the wax is a secretion of the bee itself (Royds 76). Cf. Jermyn 111–12 'The wax is produced in thin semi-transparent flakes from glands under the abdomen of the young worker bee. These flakes the bee chews until they are sufficiently plastic for use as building material.'

1030 αὐτοῦ Adv., as in *D.S.* 46 (cited on 1029 πρόσσω). The placing of it before μέλιτος produces a clumsy ambiguity.

ἔργων Cf. 1126 and the Homeric use of ἔργα for the product of men's work on the land, e.g. Μ 283 ἀνδρῶν πίονα ἔργα, Π 392 μινύθει δέ τε ἔργ' ἀνθρώπων. Here the reference must be to the honeycombs, since the honey is mentioned separately. Cf. Call. *H.* 1.50 ἔργα μελίσσης, prob. honey (Hopkinson), Nic. *Alex.* 445 ἔργα διαθρύψαιο μελίσσης (the full comb), 547 πίοσιν ἔργοις and 554 ἱερὰ ἔργα (the honey). In Theoc. 22.42 φίλα ἔργα is used of the flowers where the bees work.

εἱλίσσονται Of being busily occupied with something; cf. Σ 372 ἑλισσόμενον περὶ φύσας, Pl. *Tht.* 194b ἐν αὐτοῖς τούτοις στρέφεται καὶ ἑλίττεται. The genitive defines the occupation, and is characteristic of A.; cf. 82, 758.

1031 ὕψου In contrast to the bees, which work close to the ground. But cf. Arist. *HA* 614b19, of cranes, εἰς ὕψος πέτονται πρὸς τὸ καθορᾶν τὸ πόρρω, καὶ ἐὰν ἴδωσι νέφη καὶ χειμέρια, καταπτᾶσαι ἡσυχάζουσιν.

γεράνων *D.S.* 38 καὶ ἐὰν ὑποστραφῶσι πετόμενοι, χειμῶνα σημαίνουσι. Cf. V. *G.* 1.374–5 *aut illum (imbrem) surgentem uallibus imis | aëriae fugere grues*, A. 10.264–6 *quales sub nubibus atris | Strymoniae dant signa grues atque aethera tranant | cum sonitu, fugiuntque Notos clamore secundo*, Ael. *NA* 7.7 γέρανοι ἐκ τοῦ πελάγους ἐς τὴν γῆν πετόμεναι χειμῶνος ἀπειλὴν ἰσχυροῦ ὑποσημαίνουσι τῷ συνιέντι, ibid. 3.14 κυβερνήτης ἰδὼν ἐν πελάγει μέσῳ γεράνους ὑποστρεφούσας καὶ τὴν ἔμπαλιν πετομένας συνεῖδεν ἐναντίου προβολῇ πνεύματος ἐκείνας ἀποστῆναι τοῦ πρόσω, *CCAG* 8.1.137, 14 γέρανοι ἀπὸ πελάγους ἱπτάμενοι εἰς τὴν γῆν ἰσχυρὸν χειμῶνα δηλοῦσιν. Cf. the converse sign of fair weather in 1011–12.

στίχες Cf. 334 of trees, frequently in Homer of troops, e.g. Δ 330.

1031–1032 αὐτὰ κέλευθα τείνονται Cf. Μ 225 ἐλεύσαμεθ' αὐτὰ κέλευθα. The phrase here is a variation of 1011 τανύσαιεν ἕνα δρόμον, and both verbs express direction, not effort, as in Ψ 375 τάθη δρόμος. Cf. sch. ἐπ' εὐθείας ποιούμεναι τὴν πτῆσιν.

1032 στροφάδες With participial force, 'wheeling round' to set course in the opposite direction, not 'on their return' (LSJ) or 'en cercles' (Martin).

παλιμπετές Twice in Homer, in same *sedes*. A. is particularly recalling ε 27 μνηστῆρες δ' ἐν νηῒ παλιμπετὲς ἀπονέωνται, where the theme is also of returning home; cf. Call. *H.* 3.256, 4.294. For other contexts cf. Π 395, A.R. 2.1250, 3.285, 4.1315.

ἀπονέονται Frequent in Homer, usually of withdrawing or returning from danger to a place of safety, especially home, e.g. ω 330 ἄψορροι προτὶ Ἴλιον ἀπονέοντο, Π 252 σόον δ' ἀνένευσε μάχης ἒξ ἀπονέεσθαι, Ξ 46, β 195. For the metrical lengthening of initial α cf. Ε 763 ἀποδίωμαι, ω 7 ἀποπέσησιν, Β 337 ἀγοράασθε. See Hoekstra, *Mnem.* 31 (1978) 18–20.

1033 μηδ' Variation to a negative form of warning; cf. 845, 869, 983. Here the separation of the negative from its verb is extended to three lines, which suggests that A. is becoming bolder in his use of this technique.

νηνεμίη Cf. A.R. 3.970. Homer expresses the same adverbial sense with the genitive, Ε 523 νηνεμίης, and also uses the word adjectivally in γαλήνη | ἔπλετο νηνεμίη (ε 391–2, μ 168–9). For the negative prefix combined with α cf. νήκουστοι (173).

ἀράχνια *D.S.* 29 (from the section on winds) ἀράχνια πολλὰ φερόμενα πνεῦμα ἢ χειμῶνα σημαίνει. Cf. Arist. *Pr.* 947a33 διὰ τί τὰ ἀράχνια τὰ πολλὰ ὅταν φέρηται, πνεύματός ἐστι σημεῖα, *Gp.* 1.3.9 ἀράχνια μὴ ὄντος ἀνέμου καταφερόμενα, Anon. Laur. 11.7 ἀράχνια μὴ παρόντος ἀνέμου πίπτοντα χειμῶνα δηλοῦσιν, Plin. *Nat.* 11.84 *multa aranea imbrium signa sunt.* A. recalls θ 280 ἠΰτ' ἀράχνια λεπτά, τά γ' οὔ κέ τις οὐδὲ ἴδοιτο.

1034 φλόγες Cf. 979, 999.

αἰθύσσωσι Sch. φλόγες ἠρέμα παραφερόμεναι, 'gently moving sideways', i.e. the first flickering of the flame that may give warning of an approaching gale. This sense of short, rapid movement, derived from fire, is extended by the poets to a variety of other contexts: cf. Sapph. fr. 2.7 αἰθυσσομένων δὲ φύλλων, B. fr. 16.4 ἐλπὶς διαιθύσσει φρένας, Pi. *P.* 4.83 (πλόκαμοι) ἅπαν νῶτον καταίθυσσον, A.R. 2.1253 παραιθύξας πτερύγεσσιν, [Opp.] *C.* 2.162. See W. B. Stanford, *Ambiguity in Greek Literature* (1972) 132ff.

μαραινόμεναι Sch. ὅταν ἀμαυρὸν ᾖ τὸ περὶ τοὺς λύχνους φέγγος καὶ μὴ εἰς ὕψος ἀνάπτηται. The v.l. appears in *Gp.* 1.3.9 καὶ λύχνου φλόγες μελαινόμεναι, and probably came from 804 or 941; cf. Anon.

Laur. 11.34 μελαινόμεναι. But the flame becomes weak, not dark. The prediction is different in *D.S.* 42 λύχνος εὐδίας ἡσυχαῖος καιόμενος χειμῶνα σημαίνει, Plin. *Nat.* 18.357 *si flexuose uolitet flamma* (but as a sign of rain).

1035 αὔηται Once in Homer, ε 490 σπέρμα πυρὸς σώζων, ἵνα μή ποθεν ἄλλοθεν αὔῃ. The compound ἐναύω is commoner, e.g. X. *Mem.* 2.2.12, Call. fr. 193.25.

σπουδῇ The essence of the storm warning is that the fire is difficult to light: *D.S.* 42 ἐὰν πῦρ μὴ θέλῃ ἅπτεσθαι, χειμέριον, Plin. *Nat.* 18.357 *uentum nuntiant lumina cum ... uix accenduntur.* This sense is supported by sch. 1031 μόγις ἁπτόμενον πῦρ, 1034 πῦρ τε μόγις ἀναπτόμενον, 1035 ὅτε πῦρ ἐφάπτεται μετὰ κακοπαθείας καὶ βραδέως, with the added explanation ὅτι πολλοῦ ὄντος τοῦ περιέχοντος ὑγροῦ βράδιον τὸ πῦρ ὑφάπτεται. Cf. Plu. fr. 16 Sandbach τὰ καυστὰ βραδέως ἐξάπτεται παχυμεροῦς τοὺς πόρους ἐπιφράττοντος τοῦ ἀέρος· διόπερ οἱ τὰς δᾷδας ἅπτοντες προτρίβουσιν ἐν τῇ τέφρᾳ, ἵνα ἀποκρουσθῇ εἴ τι ἔνικμον, καὶ τὸ πῦρ τῆς ὕλης μᾶλλον ἅψηται. This use of σπουδῇ is Homeric, e.g. γ 297 σπουδῇ δ᾿ ἤλυξαν ὄλεθρον. Corruption to σποδιῇ in the context of fire was natural, and may have been aided by its occurrence in ε 488, two lines before αὔῃ.

ὑπεύδια Cf. 827, 990, 1012.

λύχνα *D.S.* 42 καὶ ἐὰν λύχνος ἅπτεσθαι μὴ ἐθέλῃ, χειμῶνα σημαί-νει.

1036 πιστεύειν χειμῶνι A curiously elliptical expression, not to trust the weather because it is likely to be stormy. For the negative infinitive as imperative cf. 847, 871, 984; it is also Homeric, e.g. ρ 278 μηδὲ σὺ δηθύνειν.

ὅσσα πέλονται A. breaks off with a reminder that everyday weather signs are very numerous (cf. 772), and that only a small selection is being presented here. The abundance of these signs is also brought out by the use of the plural verb; cf. 377, 806. *Q.S.* 12.5–6 ἀσ-τέρας ἄλλα τε πάντα | σήμαθ᾿ ὅσ᾿ ἀνθρώποισι θεῶν ἰότητι πέλονται.

1037 ἐπ᾿ ἀνθρώπους 'A la disposition des hommes' (Martin). The usage is Homeric, e.g. ω 94 πάντας ἐπ᾿ ἀνθρώπους κλέος ἔσσεται, Κ 212–13 μέγα κέν οἱ ὑπουράνιον κλέος εἴη | πάντας ἐπ᾿ ἀνθρώπους. A. has the phrase in the same *sedes*, reminding the reader that the signs are available to all, but that they have to be carefully studied; cf. 743, 759, 772.

δὴ γάρ Frequent in Homer, more emphatic than γὰρ δή (Denniston 243); cf. Ν 122 δὴ γὰρ μέγα νεῖκος ὄρωρεν, metrically matched here. What is being so strongly emphasised is the idea that the providence of Zeus can be seen even in such trivial domestic phenomena.

ἀεικέϊ τέφρῃ   *D.S.* 42 καὶ τέφρα πηγνυμένη νιφετόν. The adjective contrasts the meanness of the ash with the impressiveness of most of the other signs. Cf. ν 437 ἀεικέα πήρην of Odysseus disguised, ω 250 αὐχμεῖς τε κακῶς καὶ ἀεικέα ἔσσαι, Odysseus taunting Laertes, Σ 45 νεκταρέῳ δὲ χιτῶνι μέλαιν' ἀμφίζανε τέφρη. Cf. Call. *H.* 2.84 περιβόσκεται ἄνθρακα τέφρη, Nonn. *D.* 17.205 αἴθοπι τέφρῃ.

1038 αὐτοῦ   The ash hardens where it lies; cf. 1030. Plin. *Nat.* 18.358 *cum cinis in foco concrescit.*

πηγνυμένη   Taken over with case variation from the source of *D.S.* 42.

νιφετοῦ   The genitive is necessary, as with the parallel χιόνος (1039) and χαλάζης (1041); cf. 229–30, 456–7, 801, 1129–30. The dative of the MSS is probably due to the attraction of the neighbouring datives. In Homer νιφετός is falling snow, sometimes contrasted with χιών as fallen snow: cf. Κ 7 ἢ νιφετόν, ὅτε πέρ τε χιὼν ἐπάλυνεν ἀρούρας, δ 566 οὐ νιφετός, οὔτ' ἄρ χειμὼν πολὺς οὔτε ποτ' ὄμβρος. Α. uses χιών as a variation of νιφετός in 1039, but as fallen snow in 1088.

1039 κέγχροις   Cf. 986. *D.S.* 42 καὶ ἐὰν ὥσπερ κέγχροις πολλοῖς κατάπλεως ᾖ, χειμερίσει· καὶ ἐὰν κύκλῳ περὶ τὸ λαμπρὸν ὦσιν εὐδίας οὔσης, χιονικόν.

1040 ἔχῃ   The scholia, like the MSS, paraphrase variously with ἐὰν ... ἔχῃ (MKA), ὅταν ... ἔχῃ (M), ὅτε ... ἔχει (M). For the pure subjunctive after ὅτε see note on 878 περιτέλλῃ.

πυριλαμπέος   Cf. 986 λάμπηται πέρι in a similar context. [Opp.] *C.* 3.72 echoes with a figurative use, of a leopard's eyes, (κόραι) αἰθομέναις ἴκελαι, πυριλαμπέες.

μύξης   Cf. 976.

1041 ἄνθρακι   *D.S.* 25 (from the section on rain signs) φασὶ δέ τινες καὶ εἰ ἐν ἄνθραξι λαμπρὰ χάλαζα ἐπιφαίνηται, χάλαζαν προσημαίνειν ὡς τὰ πολλά. Cf. 985.

ζώοντι   Cf. E. *Ba.* 8 πυρὸς ἔτι ζῶσαν φλόγα.

χαλάζης   Cf. Κ 6 πολὺν ὄμβρον ἀθέσφατον ἠὲ χάλαζαν.

1042 αὐτός   The charcoal, i.e. on the outside.

ἐείδηται   With prothetic vowel, as in 395 ἐειδόμενοι, 828 ἐειδόμενος. Cf. ἐείδεται in [Theoc.] 25.58, Nic. *Ther.* 441. Homer has ἐεισάμενος (Β 22), but the present participle is the commonest form, e.g. Pi. *N.* 10.15, A.R. 3.968, 4.221, 1616, Nic. *Ther.* 149, 272, 273, Mosch. 2.158. Prothesis occurs in a number of words beginning with ϝ; see Palmer (222), who concludes that there is no simple explanation of this phenomenon. In 379 ἐείσατο and Ι 645 ἐείσαο the initial vowel can be regarded as an augment.

ἠΰτε   In characteristic Homeric position, e.g. Β 872. Cf. 242, 979, A.R. 1.269.

1043 νεφέλη A darker patch on the charcoal, a detail not given by
D.S. Cf. ὀμίχλη (997) of the Crab nebula, and ἠερόεις (276, 317, 385) of
dark patches among the stars.

ἔνδοθεν C. gen.; cf. Ζ 247 ἔνδοθεν αὐλῆς.

αἰθομένοιο Cf. Θ 563 σέλᾳ πυρὸς αἰθομένοιο, Ζ 182 πυρὸς μένος
αἰθομένοιο.

1044–1141 SEASONAL AND LOCAL SIGNS

These comprise seasons (1044–63), winter (1064–93), summer (1094–
1103), local signs from animals (1104–41). A. rounds off his catalogue
with a miscellany of weather signs particularly useful to and observable
by the farmer on his own land. The details are to be found in different
sections of D.S., ranging from 15 to 55. This method sometimes gives
the impression of an overlap with an earlier passage, but in fact the
signs are always different. A.'s purpose in the organisation of his material is to introduce as much variety as possible, to avoid the monotony
of a prose treatise.

1044–1063 Seasonal signs from vegetation
This is the only passage involving plants, the evergreen oak and mastich
(1044–59), and the squill (1060–3). The signs they give are naturally
local guides to the progress of the agricultural year, which may be different from the regular calendarial year based on the solstices and equinoxes or the risings and settings of stars. Cf. sch. 1044 ἄρχεται λοιπὸν
καὶ ἀπὸ δένδρων τεκμήρια ἡμῖν διδόναι περὶ χειμώνων καὶ καιρῶν
ἐπιτηδείων πρὸς γεωργίαν.

1044 πρῖνοι D.S. 45 οἱ πρῖνοι ἐὰν εὐκαρπῶσι, χειμῶνες πολλοὶ
σφόδρα γίνονται, 49 οἱ πρῖνοι ὅταν εὐκαρπῶσι σφόδρα, ὡς μὲν τὰ
πολλὰ χειμῶνα ἰσχυρὸν σημαίνουσιν. These trees are evergreen oaks,
but there is some difficulty in determining which species is meant. In A.
it is traditionally taken to be the holm oak (cf. Avien. 1780 *ilex* and
modern translators), whereas in D.S. it is identified by Hort as the
kermes oak. For a comparative description see Russell Meiggs, *Trees and
Timber in the Ancient Mediterranean World* (1982) 45. Cf. Polunin & Ever.
52, 54, 189, 199, Polunin & Hux. 55–6, plate 2. The latter note that the
holm oak is often mistaken for the kermes oak, and certainly in the poets
πρῖνος seems to be used for either or both of these trees. Both are distinguished from the deciduous δρῦς (Call. fr. 194.65), and both produce
a small type of acorn known as ἄκυλος (1047, Amphis 38, Theoc. 5.94–
5); the wood preferred for making the plough-tree (Hes. *Op.* 429, 436),
and for burning (Ar. *Ach.* 668, *Ran.* 859), is particularly that of the holm

oak; it is the leaves of the kermes oak that are prickly (1122) and are browsed on by goats (1122, Eup. 14). Even the more scientific Theophrastus uses πρῖνος for both species. For example in *HP* 3.16.1 the description δένδρον μέγα, καθάπερ ἡ δρῦς is appropriate only to the holm oak, whereas only the kermes oak can be said to produce κόκκον τινὰ φοινικοῦν. As far as the weather lore is concerned, there is no indication that the acorn crop of one species is significantly different from that of the other, and it is perhaps best to regard the πρῖνος as one kind of tree and call it the evergreen oak.

δ' αὖ Introducing the next topic by way of a contrast; cf. B 198.

καρποῖο Cf. Thphr. *HP* 3.16.1 καρπὸν δὲ ἔχει βαλανώδη· μικρὰ δὲ ἡ βάλανος. Gen. as after verbs of fullness; cf. S. *OT* 83, *El.* 895–6.

καταχθέες Perhaps coined by A. as a variation of ἐπαχθής. Cf. Nicander's imitation in *Alex.* 322 καταχθέος ἕρματα γαστρός.

1045 σχῖνοι The mastich, *Pistacia lentiscus*, an evergreen shrub particularly prized for its gum (Theophr. *HP* 9.1.2). See Polunin & Ever. 120, Polunin & Hux. 119, plate 97. The epithet μέλαιναι refers to the dark green colour of its leaves; Call. *H.* 3.201.

ἀπείρητοι In passive sense, with negative, as always in Homer. A. may be particularly recalling β 170 with its context of prophecy, οὐ γὰρ ἀπείρητος μαντεύομαι. Cf. M 304, P 41.

πολλός Cf. 953 πολλὴ στρέφεται. The idea of the farmer being constantly on the look-out for signs (sch. ὁ σπουδαῖος γεωργὸς καὶ ἀροτρεύς) is emphasised by the verbal accumulation πάντη ... πολλὸς ... αἰεί and the verb παπταίνει itself; cf. 20, 1049.

ἀλωεύς Cultivator of an ἀλωή (816), a piece of land for growing grain or fruit trees. Cf. A.R. 3.1401 ἀλωήων πόνος ἀνδρῶν. The name Aloeus appears in E 386 as father of Otus and Ephialtes; cf. Hes. fr. 19.

1046 παπταίνει Cf. 128, 297, where the verb also suggests anxiety. Here the use with a fearing clause recalls N 649 πάντοσε παπταίνων, μή τις χρόα χαλκῷ ἐπαύρῃ.

θέρος The sense of 'harvest' occurs particularly in the metaphor τἀλλότριον ἀμῶν θέρος (Ar. *Eq.* 392), ἀμᾶσθε τῶνδε δύστηνον θέρος (E. fr. 423.4), and is implied in Agath. *AP* 11.365.3 θέρος αἴσιον.

ἐκ χερὸς ἔρρῃ An imaginative metaphor, apparently not found elsewhere, but based on such literal uses as κ 393 ἐκ μὲν μελέων τρίχες ἔρρεον, N 539 κατὰ δ' αἷμα νεουτάτου ἔρρεε χειρός. The opposite is διὰ χειρὸς ἔχειν, of keeping control, e.g. Ar. *V.* 597, Arist. *Pol.* 1308a27. ἔρρῃ is emphatic, suggesting complete disappearance; cf. κ 72 ἔρρ' ἐκ νήσου θᾶσσον, S. *OT* 560 ἄφαντος ἔρρει. The alliteration in the second half of this line seems to draw attention to the envisaged loss.

1047 θαμινῆς The epithet refers to the closely-set nature of this crop, which in this case is only moderately heavy, as opposed to the excessive crop of 1049. There is no question of successive crops here, as is implied by Mair's 'frequent' or Martin's 'à plusieurs reprises' or Erren's 'häufig ansetzenden'. It is the mastich that has successive crops (1051–9), and sch. 1051 must be the source of the garbled comment here: θαμινῆς δὲ τῆς συνεχῶς φυομέμης· τρίτον γὰρ τοῦ χειμῶνος φύει. Plu. fr. 17 refers to the normally light nature of the crop: φησὶν οὖν ὁ Θεόφραστος ὅτι ὁ πρῖνος καὶ ἡ σχῖνος αὐχμηρὰ τῇ κράσει καὶ ξηρότερα τῶν ἄλλων πεφυκότα πολὺν καρπὸν οὐ φέρει, ἐὰν μὴ εἰς βάθος ὑγρανθῇ. εἰκότως οὖν τῇ τούτων εὐφορίᾳ [Sandbach: ἀφορίᾳ codd.] καταμαντεύονται περὶ τῶν σπερμάτων οἱ γεωργοί, μιᾶς αἰτίας οὔσης δι' ἣν ἀμφοτέροις ἡ πολυκαρπία· εἰ δ' ὑπερβάλλει τοῦ καρποῦ τὸ πλῆθος, οὐκ ἀγαθὸν σημεῖον· ἄμετρον γὰρ ἐπομβρίαν καὶ πλεονασμὸν ὑγρότητος ἡ περὶ τὸν ἀέρα ἄνεσις καὶ θηλύτης δηλοῖ.

ἀκύλου Once in Homer, κ 242 πάρ ῥ' ἄκυλον βάλανόν τ' ἔβαλεν. Theophr. *HP* 3.16.3 καλοῦσι δέ τινες τὸν μὲν τοῦ πρίνου ... καρπὸν ἄκυλον, τὸν δὲ τῆς δρυὸς βάλανον. The former is the smaller, and Hort translates 'mast'. Cf. Amphis 38 ὁ πρῖνος ἀκύλους [φέρει].

κατὰ μέτρον ἔχουσαι Sch. συμμετρῶς ἔχουσαι τῶν καρπῶν. Cf. Hdt. 1.32 πολλοὶ δὲ μετρίως ἔχοντες βίου εὐτυχέες. This intransitive use of ἔχω offers the simplest explanation of the dependent genitive. Mair and Martin appear to take ἔχουσαι transitively ('with moderate crops', 'portent ... une charge modérée') and have to understand an appropriate noun as object. It is perhaps possible to take κατὰ ... ἔχουσαι *in tmesi*, and let the genitive depend on μέτρον, and this may be what Erren has in mind when he translates 'das rechte Mass haben'. But κατὰ μέτρον is a phrase that A. uses again (1099), and the run of words is very similar here. πρῖνος is feminine also in Theophr. *HP* 3.6.4, but masculine in 3.16.1 and *D.S.* 45 and 49.

1048 χειμῶνος *Gp.* 1.4.1 πρῖνοι καὶ δρύες τὸν καρπὸν πολὺν φέρουσαι ἐπὶ πλεῖον ἔσεσθαι τὸν χειμῶνα δηλοῦσι (≈ Anon. Laur. 11.47). Mair translates 'heavy storm to come' and Martin 'que la tempête va l'emporter', but vegetation can only give seasonal signs, and the reference is to a severe winter. So Erren, 'dass der Winter noch härter werden wird'. Cf. sch. 1044 αἱ μὲν οὖν πρῖνοι μὴ ὑπὲρ τὸ δέον εὐφοροῦσαι μακρὸν ἐσόμενον τὸν χειμῶνα σημαίνουσιν.

λέγοιεν A variation for verbs of predicting, especially associated with divine warning: cf. 7, 8, 732, 1071, 1148.

ἐπὶ πλέον ἰσχύσοντος Cf. Th. 1.9.3 ναυτικῷ ἅμα ἐπὶ πλέον τῶν ἄλλων ἰσχύσας. Here the point of the comparison is left to be understood, 'more than usual': cf. Theoc. 3.47 ἐπὶ πλέον ἄγαγε λύσσας. The verb is not elsewhere used of weather, but here it reflects *D.S.* 49 ἰσχυρόν (cited on 1044).

1049 μή A warning expressed as negative hope; cf. 287, 413, 824.
ἄδην Cf. 703. In Homer and other writers before A. this adverb expresses sufficiency, here with another adverb its sense is closer to 'very'; cf. Latin *satis*. The preceding μιν in M may have come from N 315.

ἔκπαγλα The adjective and its adverbs are frequent in Homer, of what is surprisingly, sometimes frighteningly, excessive; for this adverb cf. Γ 415 ἔκπαγλα φίλησα. The word is mostly used of human action, but cf. ξ 522 χειμὼν ἔκπαγλος. Here the adverb is a poetic hyperbole in a line designed to stress the sense of a heavy crop. Eustath. 68.18 derives the word from ἐξεπλάγη, and perhaps an intervening *ἔκπαγλος may be assumed. See Frisk 1.477, and Kirk on Γ 415.

περιβρίθοιεν The simple verb itself can describe a heavy crop; cf. 1082, and τ 112 βρίθησι δὲ δένδρεα καρπῷ, Θ 307 (μήκων) καρπῷ βριθομένη, Σ 561 σταφύλησι μέγα βρίθουσαν ἀλωήν. Here the prefix, a variation of Homer's μέγα, intensifies the meaning. It is imitated, with participles in the same metrical position, by Nic. *Ther.* 851, *Alex.* 143, 180. According to Plu. fr. 17 (cited on 1047) an excessively heavy crop is due to excessive rain, and farmers take this as a prediction of a heavy winter rainfall still to come.

ἀπάντη Cf. 22, 539, 824, also at line-ends, as in Homer (Η 183, 186, θ 278). The adverb, adding the further detail that the heavy crop is 'all over' the tree, forms a climax to the accumulation of meaning in this line. Cf. 1045 πολλός.

1050 τηλοτέρω The superlative occurs once in Homer (η 322), in the literal sense; the figurative use appears only here. What A. means is that with luck there will not be an excessively heavy crop of mast and a consequential drought in the grain-fields.

αὐχμοῖο After 1047–8 we would expect to be told that a very heavy crop predicts a very heavy rainfall, and in fact this is what Plutarch says (fr. 17, quoted on 1047). But instead A. chooses the second alternative found in *D.S.* 49, ἐνίοτε δὲ καὶ αὐχμούς φασι γίνεσθαι. The weather lore here represents what people have observed and interpreted on the principle of *post hoc, ergo propter hoc*. Avien. 1781ff. ignores the drought alternative and follows Plutarch, even to the extent of including his note on the arid nature of this tree. Virgil appears to be recalling these lines in *G.* 1.187ff. (Avien. 1780 borrows *induit* from 188), but his prediction of grain failure depends more reasonably on an overabundance of foliage (and therefore a poor crop of nuts): *at si luxuria foliorum exuberat umbra, | nequiquam pinguis palea teret area culmos* (191–2).

συνασταχύοιεν Only here; but cf. υ 212 ὑποσταχύοιτο, and A.R. 3.1354 ἀνασταχύεσκον ἄρουραν, 4.271 ἀνασταχύουσιν ἄρουραι. The force of the prefix is to link the prediction closely with the sign; cf. 967

σὺν ὕδατος ἐρχομένοιο. A. also has the noun ἀσταχύς in a similar context (150).

1051 τριπλόα N.pl. as adverb only here and 1054. It is a variation for the more usual τριχθά (1060), and a quaint contrast to the contracted τριπλῇ, which occurs once in Homer (A 128). It was perhaps chosen as a punning echo of νειὸν τρίπολον (Σ 542, ε 127, Hes. *Th.* 971). *D.S.* 55 ὁ τῆς σχίνου καρπὸς σημαίνει τοὺς ἀρότους· ἔχει δὲ τρία μέρη καὶ ἔστιν ὁ πρῶτος τοῦ πρώτου ἀρότου σημεῖον, ὁ δεύτερος τοῦ δευτέρου, ὁ τρίτος τοῦ τρίτου· καὶ ὡς ἂν τούτων ἐκβαίνῃ κάλλιστα καὶ γένηται ἀδρότατος, οὕτως ἕξει καὶ ὁ κατὰ τοῦτον ἄροτος, Cic. *Prog.* fr. 5 *iam uero semper uiridis semperque grauata | lentiscus, triplici solita grandescere fetu, | ter fruges fundens tria tempora monstrat arandi.* Pliny quotes these lines in *Nat.* 18.228, and develops the topic in 244 *ergo haec aratio duas habebit notas, lentisci primum fructum ostendentis ac piri florentis. erit et tertia in bulborum satu scillae, item in coronamentorum narcissi; namque et haec ter florent primoque flore primam arationem ostendunt, medio secundam, tertio nouissimam, quando inter sese alia aliis notas praebent.* Cf. *Gp.* 11.12 ἡ σχῖνος χαίρει μὲν καθύγροις χωρίοις, φυτεύεται δὲ ἀπὸ καλανδῶν Ἰανουαρίων. τρεῖς δὲ καρποὺς φασι φέρειν, καὶ εἰ μὲν ὁ πρῶτος καρπὸς καλὸς γένηται, τὸν πρῶτον σπόρον καλῶς καρποφορεῖν σημαίνει· ὁμοίως δὲ καὶ ἐπὶ τῶν ἄλλων. There appears to be no botanical foundation for this lore of triple fruiting and triple flowering, and no ancient writer indicates at what intervals these crops are supposed to occur. Jermyn (58) quotes an opinion of the Director of the Royal Botanic Gardens, Kew, that the flowerings of the squill might be attributed to different species flowering at different times, but that no such explanation is possible for the fruiting of the mastich. A. S. Pease on Cic. *Div.* 1.15 refers to these predictions as 'hints drawn from coincidences in the habits of plants'. Perhaps they also represent attempts to relate the growth of plants in this way to the well-established system of triple ploughing: see note on 1054.

σχῖνος Cf. 1045. Plu. fr. 18 ὅσα γὰρ τὴν σχῖνον ἐκ τοῦ ἀέρος ὠφελεῖ, ταῦτα καὶ τὸν σῖτον.

κυέει Twice in Homer, of human and animal pregnancy (Τ 117, Ψ 266), in Theophrastus of swelling buds, e.g. *HP* 4.2.4 ὁ ἕτερος (καρπὸς) εὐθὺς φανερὸς κυούμενος, 6.4.8 τὸ μὲν κυοῦν, τὸ δὲ ἀνθοῦν, τὸ δὲ σπέρμα τίκτον. Cf. Bion fr. 15.17 εἴαρι πάντα κύει.

τρισσαί Used in the plural to denote a significant groups of three, e.g. divinities (*h.Hom.* 5.7, S. *OT* 164, E. *Hec.* 645), libations (S. *OC* 479), Plato's τριττὰ εἴδη ψυχῆς (*R.* 504a). A natural triad of events in the growth of a plant could be the budding, the flowering, and the fruiting; cf. the successive stages in the growth of the sow-thistle in Theophr. *HP* 6.4.8 (cited in the preceding note). It is possible that this natural sequence played some part in the development of this piece of farming-lore.

αὖξαι A rare noun, favoured especially by Plato, e.g. *Phlb.* 42d.

1052 καρποῖο The berries are pea-sized and very aromatic, red then black (Polunin & Ever. 120, Polunin & Hux. 119).

ἑκάστη Sc. αὖξη.

1053 ἀρότῳ Ploughing times are foreshadowed in the proem 7–9; cf. also 267. Ploughing was not necessarily accompanied by sowing (see note on 1054), but in this passage sowing is implied.

ἀροτήσιον Only here; cf. βουλύσιος ὥρη, which also occurs only in A. (825, 1119).

1054 τριπλόα μείρονται On τριπλόα cf. 1051; on μείρονται cf. 657, and *D.S.* 55 τρία μέρη (cited on 1051). This tradition of triple ploughing is hard to identify. It seems to look back to the νειὸν τρίπολον of Homer and Hesiod (Σ 541–2, ε 127, *Th.* 971); cf. [Theoc.] 25.25, Call. fr. 24.4. But τρίπολος probably refers to the breaking-in of fallow land in three successive stages as a preliminary to sowing (see Armstrong, *CR* 47, 1943, 3–5, for a different interpretation). Cf. Varro, *RR* 1.29.2 *terram cum primum arant, proscindere appellant, cum iterum, offringere dicunt ... tertio cum arant, iacto semine,* etc. *D.S.* and A., however, seem to mean three ploughings, each accompanied by a sowing, at different times of the year, and yet there is no general adherence to a system of three ploughings in the Greek writers: the number varies according to the type of land and the kind of crop to be grown. Hes. *Op.* 462 recommends only two: ἔαρι πολεῖν· θέρεος δὲ νεωμένη οὔ σ᾿ ἀπατήσει. X. *Oec.* 16 prefers spring (12), but also multiple ploughings in summer (14). Theophr. *CP* 3 suggests ploughing in summer for heavy, wet soil, in winter for light, dry soil (20.2), and reploughing for both in spring (7.8). Roman farmers may have regarded three ploughings as normal, since they used as technical terms the verbs *arare, iterare, tertiare* (e.g. Col. 2.4.4). But Virgil prefers four in *G.* 1.48 *bis quae solem, bis frigora sensit*; cf. Plin. *Nat.* 18.181. Columella on the other hand gives a variety of different dates for different kinds of soil (2.4.2–11). See *RE* 1.268–9, West on Hes. *Op.* 462–3, A. F. V. Jardé, *Les céréales dans l'antiquité grecque* (1925) 22–5, R. Billiard, *L'agriculture dans l'antiquité* (1928) 49–55.

ἄκρας Sc. ὥρας, in conformity with μέσσην (ὥρην); the transmitted ἄκρα is a corruption due to the influence of ἀμφότερα. The language here is drawn from mathematics: cf. Pl. *Ti.* 36a δύο εἶναι μεσότητας, τὴν μὲν ταὐτῷ μέρει τῶν ἄκρων αὐτῶν ὑπερέχουσαν καὶ ὑπερεχομένην, Arist. *EN* 1106a30 τοῦ μὲν πράγματος μέσον τὸ ἴσον ἀπέχον ἀφ᾿ ἑκατέρου τῶν ἄκρων.

1055 ἄροσιν In Homer used of the land itself (Ι 580, ι 134); cf. A.R.

1.826. A. follows the practice developed by Ionian writers, and particularly notable in Sophocles, of using the suffix -σις for action nouns: see, for example, Palmer 137.

1056 ἀπαγγέλλει The sense of foretelling may have been suggested by P 409 ἦ οἱ ἀπαγγέλλεσκε Διὸς μεγάλοιο νόημα.

πυμάτην Cf. 448.

ἔσχατος ἄλλων Cf. K 434 ἔσχατοι ἄλλων, Z 295 νείατος ἄλλων, and with longer superlatives A 505, Ψ 532, ε 105, A.R. 1.180, Theoc. fr. 3.4, Call. *H.* 4.156. The genitive is ablatival, expressing comparison by indicating those from which this is distinguished. See Chantraine 2.151, Schwyzer 2.100, Kirk on A 505.

1057 κάλλιστα Taken unaltered from *D.S.* 55.

λοχαίη From λοχεία 'child-birth', hence 'prolific'. Cf. Theophr. *CP* 3.21.5.

ἄρηται The short α indicates ἄρνυμαι, aor. ἀρέσθαι, meaning 'win'; e.g. M 435 μισθὸν ἄρηται, Σ 121 κλέος ἐσθλὸν ἀροίμην, Hes. *Op.* 632 κέρδος ἄρηαι, Pi. *N.* 9.46f. ἄρηται κῦδος. Cf. 640. The meaning is extended to accommodate δίκας (S. *El.* 34), λώβας (E. *Hec.* 1073), δειλίαν (S. *Aj.* 75); but in Υ 247 ἄχθος ἄροιτο, and S. *Aj.* 247 ποδοῖν κλοπὰν ἀρέσθαι, the sense of 'take up' properly belongs to αἴρομαι (<ἀείρομαι), aor. ἄρασθαι, with α long. Either there is a confusing of the two verbs, or a conscious poetic borrowing of meaning. Here the translators have usually given the verb the sense of simply 'bearing', though this is not a possible meaning for ἄρνυμαι, nor does it appear that αἴρομαι is ever so used. On the other hand A. seems to be consciously imitating M 435 and possibly also the phrases of Hesiod and Pindar cited above, and in view of κάλλιστα the sense of 'achieving' a bumper crop is both imaginative and appropriate. For a discussion of these two verbs see Jebb, S. *Aj.*, Appendix 217ff. The pure subjunctive in an indefinite clause is common in A., especially after εἰ; see note on 858. Voss's κεν for γάρ is unnecessary.

1058 κείνῳ Sc. καρπῷ. A. means that the most productive of the three ploughings will be the one that was done when the mastich produced the best of its three crops.

ἐξ ἄλλων With comparative sense, as in 95; cf. Σ 432 ἐκ μέν μ' ἀλλάων ἁλιάων ἀνδρὶ δάμασσεν, where the idiom provides a variation of ἐκ πασέων in the preceding line. The extension of meaning is similar to that in ἔσχατος ἄλλων (1056). Here ἐξ ἄλλων balances κάλλιστα in 1057. The almost word-for-word correspondence (varied only by the inversion of adjective and noun in 1058) in these two lines reinforces the correspondence in the meaning. Plutarch relates it to the Stoic notion of sympathy in nature (fr. 19): οὐ μόνον ἐν τοῖς ζῴοις συμπάθειά ἐστι ἀλλὰ καὶ ἐν τοῖς φυτοῖς. ὁσαοῦν [Sandbach: ὅταν οὖν codd.] κεκραμένην ὑγρότητι ἢ ψυχρότητι παραπλησίως ἔχει τὴν ἕξιν, καὶ [ἢ codd.] τρέφεται ἀπὸ τῶν ὁμοίων καὶ τοῖς αὐτοῖς εὐθηνεῖ καὶ μαραίνεται. διὸ πολλὰ μετ' ἀλλήλων συνακμάζει καὶ καρποφορεῖ, τὰ μὲν θέρει τὰ δὲ χειμῶνι τινὰ δὲ καὶ ἔαρι. τῶν μὲν οὖν αἱ κράσεις διάφοροι, τῶν δ' ὅμοιαι καὶ συγγενεῖς σφόδρα· τῶν οὖν τὴν ὁμοίαν κρᾶσιν ἐχόντων εἰσὶ πρῖνος, σχῖνος, σκίλλα, πυρός.

πολυλήιος Once in Homer, but of a man, Ε 613 πολυκτήμων πολυλήιος; cf. *h.Hom.* 4.171. Of a place, Hes. fr. 240.1 πολυλήιος ἠδ' εὐλείμων. The adjective is formed from λήιον 'standing crop', e.g. Β 147.

εἴη For the pure optative see note on 76. Voss's κ' for γ' is unnecessary.

1059 δέ γ' After 1057–8 γε indicates the obvious converse, 'and of course'; cf. Denniston 155 for similar examples. The v.l. is probably due to the influence of δέ τε later in the line.

ἀφαυροτάτῳ In Homer and Hesiod only of human beings, e.g. Ο 11, υ 110, *Op.* 586; elsewhere in A. of faint stars (227, 256, 277, 569).

1060 αὔτως Cf. 825, 869.

ἀνθέρικος 'Flowering stalk'; cf. Theophr. *HP* 7.13.2, of the asphodel, ὁ γὰρ ἀνθέρικος μέγιστος.

τριχθά Homeric adverb, e.g. Γ 363 τριχθά τε καὶ τετραχθά. A. also has its equivalent once, τρίχα (624).

σκίλλης The squill is a bulbous plant with several different varieties. A.'s source here is Theophr. *HP* 7.13.6 ποιεῖται δὲ (ἡ σκίλλα) τὰς ἀνθήσεις τρεῖς, ὧν ἡ μὲν πρώτη δοκεῖ σημαίνειν τὸν πρῶτον ἄροτον, ἡ δὲ δευτέρα τὸν μέσον, ἡ δὲ τρίτη τὸν ἔσχατον· ὡς γὰρ ἂν αὗται γένωνται καὶ οἱ ἄροτοι σχεδὸν οὕτως ἐκβαίνουσιν. In this respect it is compared to the asphodel (ibid. 3): τὴν ἄνθησιν ποιεῖται κατὰ μέρος, ὥσπερ καὶ ἐπὶ τῆς σκίλλης, ἄρχεται δὲ πρῶτον ἀπὸ τῶν κάτωθεν. As Martin observes, A.'s use of Theophrastus as a source here seems to suggest a Theophrastean origin for the *D.S.* Pliny (*Nat.* 18.244, after the passage cited on 1051) compares the squill in this respect with the narcissus: *namque et haec ter florent primoque flore primam arationem ostendunt, medio secundam, tertio nouissimam.* This triple flowering is not confirmed by botanists, but may be explained by the fact that different varieties flower at different times: cf. *RE* 1.268 'die verschiedenen Scillen-Arten zu verschiedenen Zeiten, vom Frühling bis in den Spätherbst blühen', Jermyn 58. On the squills see e.g. Polunin & Hux. 214. plate 23.

ὑπερανθεῖ First attested here; the prefix as in Th. 4.19.4 ὑπεραυχοῦντα, Ar. *Pl.* 354 ὑπερπλουτεῖν.

1061 σήματ' ἐπιφράσσασθαι Cf. 1103 σήματ' ἐπιγνῶναι. The infinitive is very loosely attached to the preceding clause; it expresses purpose, and requires a different subject to be understood with it: the squill flowers thrice so that the farmer can observe the signs. Cf. α 136–8 χέρνιβα δ' ἀμφίπολος προχόῳ ἐπέχευε φέρουσα | ... | νίψασθαι, λ 75–6 σῆμά τέ μοι χεύαι ... | ἀνδρὸς δυστήνοιο καὶ ἐσσομένοισι πυθέσθαι.

ὁμοίου Homeric adjective, used especially in the formula ὁμοιίου πολέμοιο (Ι 440, al.), but also with γῆρας (Δ 315), νεῖκος (Δ 444), and θάνατος (γ 236). Cf. Theoc. 22.172 with νεῖκος: see Gow's note on the uncertainty of the Homeric meaning. A. N. Athanassakis, *Rh.M.* 119 (1976) 4–7, suggests 'making equal', 'levelling'; cf. Kirk on Δ 315. Hesiod, however, takes the adj. as equivalent to ὅμοιος in *Op.* 182 πατὴρ παίδεσσιν ὁμοίιος, and A. has followed Hesiod here: the similarity lies in the relative abundance of the squill flowers and the grain. Cf. Opp. *H.* 2.233 πέτρῃσιν ὁμοίιοι ἰνδάλλονται, Nonn. *D.* 2.148 ὁμοίιον υἷα τοκῆι.

ἀμήτοιο Once in Homer, Τ 223 ἄμητος δ' ὀλίγιστος. Cf. 1097. In Hesiod it is used of the action of farming (*Op.* 384, 575).

1062 ἐπί Voss corrected the ἐπὶ σχῖνον of earlier editors, but needlessly adopted ἐνί, and has been followed by all later editors except Maass (Martin mistakenly reading ἐνί in M). A. elsewhere uses ἐπί with the phenomenon in which a sign is observed, e.g. 434 ἐπὶ παμφανόωντι Θυτηρίῳ, 801 ἐπὶ χροιῇ.

ἐφράσσατο Cf. 374, 745, 1149. The v.l. shows the influence of the compound verb in 1061. A. repeats the sense of 1060–1 in 1062–3, thus concluding his botanical passage with an emphatic chiasmus.

1063 τόσσα καὶ ἐν There is no reason to alter the transmitted text here, with ἐν varying ἐπί in the preceding line. This whole line illustrates A.'s skill in combining balance with variation. The balance of the lines is also marked by rhyme; it is difficult to say whether this is intentional here, but cf. 190–1, 266–7, 888–9, 1115–16.

ἄνθεϊ λευκῷ Cf. Polunin & Hux. 214 on the squill (*Urginea maritima*): 'in the late summer when the tall spikes of white flowers grow leafless from the dry ground'.

1064–1093 Warnings of winter from animal life and of drought from comets
Most of the examples are taken from everyday observation on the farm: the swarming of wasps (1064–7), the mating of pigs, sheep and goats (1068–74), the migration of cranes (1075–81), cattle and sheep digging the ground (1082–90); also comets presaging drought (1091–3). All the material is to be found in *D.S.*, each item occurring in a different passage: 47, 25, 54, 38, 41, 34.
1064 σφῆκες *D.S.* 47 ἔστι δὲ σημεῖον χειμώνων μεγάλων καὶ

ὄμβρων καὶ ὅταν γένωνται ἐν τῷ μετοπώρῳ πολλοὶ σφῆκες. Cf. Μ 167 σφῆκες in same metrical position.

μετοπωρινόν Adv. (see note on 943 ἄπληστον), in same *sedes* as in Hes. *Op.* 415. The season called μετόπωρον or φθινόπωρον came after the late summer when the fruits ripened (ὀπώρα). Its beginning was traditionally marked by the MR of Arcturus in mid-September: cf. Gem. *Cal.* Virgo 20 (= 15 Sept.) Ἀρκτοῦρος Εὐκτήμονι ἐκφανής· μετοπώρου ἀρχή, Hp. *Vict.* 3.1. Q.S. adds to his Homeric simile of angry wasps (11.146ff.) the season ἐν ὀπώρῃ.

ἤλιθα Cf. 254, 611, 1011.

1065 βεβρίθωσι Properly of weight (cf. 1049, 1082), here denoting the compactness of the swarm. For the perfect cf. Φ 385, o 334, Hes. *Op.* 234. For the pure subjunctive after ὅτε see note on 828 περιτέλλῃ.

1065–1066 ἑσπερίων ... Πληϊάδων Sch. τῶν ἀπὸ ἑσπέρας ἀνατελλουσῶν. So Avien. 1792–3 *uespertinus primo cum commouet ortus | Vergilias pelago.* But the ER of the Pleiades (see notes on 265 and 266) occurred about the beginning of October (Gem. *Cal.* Libra 8), and this is much too early for the start of winter. Soubiran on Avien., p. 285 n. 6, is therefore mistaken in accepting the explanation of sch., and Mair, Martin and Erren are correct in pointing out that winter began with the Pleiades' MS in the first half of November: cf. Gem. *Cal.* Scorp. 19 Εὐδόξῳ Πλειάδες ἑῷαι δύνουσι. A. himself denotes the same time of year with the juxtaposition of χειμῶνα and κατερχόμεναι in 1085, and here too he means the MS. Therefore ἑσπερίων means not 'in the evening' but 'in the west', as in other contexts of sun and stars setting (407, 710, 858, 890–1). On Theocritus' apparent imitation in 7.53 ἑσπερίοις Ἐρίφοις see Introd. p. 40.

προπάροιθε C. gen., of time; cf. 938, 1010.

1066 ἐπερχόμενον χειμῶνα The context makes it clear that this is the onset of winter, whereas in 1136 χειμῶνος ἐπερχομένοιο is a storm at any time of the year. The latter is presumably the source of the v.l. here. The normal reliability of the signs set in the sky by Zeus (cf. 13) can thus be modified by the observation of local signs, and winter can begin even (καί) before its official calendarial date.

1067 οἷος Voss and Mair take this as relative, comparing a winter storm to the whirling movement in the swarm of wasps, and also bringing out the suddenness as well as the form of the movement. But χειμῶνα is the season of wintry weather, and it is difficult to see why A. should add such an obscure and inappropriate simile at this point. Kaibel proposed to understand δῖνος as the wind itself, suddenly coming on at the time when (ἐπί) the wasps' sign occurs, and took οἷος as an indirect exclamation. Martin accepts this interpretation of δῖνος, but, insisting here as elsewhere that αὐτίκα expresses a contrast, takes ἐπί in its additional sense, and understands the blast of wind as a second sign of winter, supplementing the sign from the wasps. I think the key to the problem certainly lies in Kaibel's interpretation of οἷος. It eliminates the awkwardness of the supposed comparison, and is very Aratean: see note on 143 οἷος, also 1007 οἷα. Similarly here, after εἴποι τις, οἷος explains why one can so confidently predict the onset of winter: the sight of the swirling mass of wasps is so striking, and the fact that it happens so quickly (αὐτίκα as in 199, 307, 903) adds to the impressiveness of the spectacle. A. characteristically rounds off his four-line sentence with a variation of the first line (cf. 1013–16).

ἐπὶ σφήκεσσιν Cf. 1062 ἐπὶ ... καρπῷ.

δῖνος A. chooses the form made familiar by fifth-century cosmologists and Ar. *Nub*. 380, instead of Homeric δίνη.

1068 θήλειαι Cf. ξ 16 θήλειαι τοκάδες (σύες), ι 439 θήλειαι δ' ἐμέμηκον (after ἄρσενα μῆλα), Υ 222 θήλειαι (ἵπποι), all in same *sedes*.

μῆλα *D.S*. 26 καὶ ὅταν πάλιν ὀχεύωνται πρόβατα ἢ αἶγες, χειμῶνος μακροῦ σημεῖον (Hort thinks the text is probably defective), *Gp*. 1.4.2 καὶ αἶγες καὶ οἶες ὀχευθεῖσαι, καὶ πάλιν ὀχεύεσθαι βουλόμεναι μακρότερον σημαίνουσι χειμῶνα (≈ Anon. Laur. 11.5 with ὕες for οἶες). A. appears to have added the sows to the traditional weather sign.

1069 ἀναστρωφῶσιν Once in Homer, but transitive, of Odysseus turning his bow in every direction (φ 394); here intransitive, with the sense of ἀναστρέφω 'return' (cf. X. *An*. 1.4.5, 4.3.29).

ὀχῆς Only here in the sense of 'mating', because of its similarity to the normal ὀχεία: see J. Wackernagel, *Kleine Schriften* 1 (1953) 729. At first sight the genitive appears to express separation (cf. Voss), but withdrawal is a strange way of referring to the first mating. Maass therefore translates 'ad coitum reuertuntur', and Martin agrees, explaining the gen. as 'marquant l'objet du désir, ce qui est un tour très aratéen'. The gen. of purpose is mostly restricted to τοῦ with an infinitive, but cf. Dem. 18.100 ἃς ἁπάσας ἡ πόλις τῆς τῶν ἄλλων Ἑλλήνων ἐλευθερίας καὶ σωτηρίας πεποίηται, 19.76 πᾶσ' ἀπάτη καὶ τέχνη συνεσκευάσθη τοῦ περὶ Φωκέας ὀλέθρου. Alternatively the genitive may be regarded as simply defining the reference of the verb. A. has several other idiosyncratic uses of the genitive, e.g. 82, 430, 758, 1048.

τὰ δέ γ' ἄρσεσι πάντα The reading best attested by the MSS, restored by Maass in place of the readings of earlier editions with ἄρρενα or ἄρσενα. The corruption is easily explained by the proximity of τὰ πάντα, and Homer's ἄρσενα μῆλα (ι 438) may have had some influence. Maass does not indicate how he construes the dative; but Martin takes it with ὀχέωνται, punctuating after ἄρσεσι and δεξάμεναι, and reading ταὶ δ' for τὰ δέ γ'. Keydell 583 disallows the former punctuation, and the emendation is also unconvincing because the demonstrative article with δέ is not normally used to continue the same subject, but to take up a noun that is not the subject of the preceding clause or sentence (cf. 284, 298, etc.). The simplest solution is to take ἄρσεσι with δεξάμεναι: δέχομαι c. dat. is regularly used in the sense of receiving a favour from someone (see Monro HG 136), e.g. B 186 δέξατό οἱ σκῆπτρον, Ο 87–8 Θέμιστι δὲ καλλιπαρήῳ | δέκτο δέπας, Ρ 207–8 νοστήσαντι | δέξεται: cf. Hes. Th. 479, Pi. P. 4.21–3, 8.5, A. Ch. 762, S. El. 442–3, E. Hec. 535. Then τὰ δέ γ' ... πάντα is an amusingly emphatic reference to all that is implied in ὀχῆς.

1070 πάλιν αὖτις Cf. Ε 257 in same sedes.

ἀναβλήδην Variation of Homeric ἀμβλήδην (Χ 476 with γοόωσα), where the sense is usually based on ἀνα- meaning 'up', e.g. 'with deep sobs' (Leaf, comparing Φ 364 ἀμβολάδην of a boiling cauldron). Here the force of the prefix has been otherwise and variously interpreted. Voss, comparing Call. H. 3.61 ἀμβολαδὶς τετύποντες, supposes that the females 'sich selbst einander besteigen'. Martin relates the adve b to ἀναβάλλω in the sense of 'delay', and translates 'au delà du temps normal', ignoring πάλιν αὖτις. But the meaning suggested by the context here is 'repeatedly', with ἀνα- in the sense of 'again', as in ἀναγιγνώσκω, ἀναμιμνήσκω, and such special cases as Α 236 ἀναθηλήσει and Hp. Aer. 8 ἀναμετρεῖν τὸ ὕδωρ. Cf. LSJ 'afresh'. Here the adverb reinforces πάλιν αὖτις (cf. Ar. Nub. 975 αὖ πάλιν αὖθις), with an accumulation of meaning as in 20, 1045, 1049. It is the repetition that makes the animals' behaviour both noticeable and significant as a weather sign. It is possible that Homer's ἀμβλήδην has the same meaning. Cf. Max. 287.

ὀχέωνται Only here in the sexual sense, as a variation of ὀχεύω. For the passive cf. Arist. HA 575a24 ὀχεύει δὲ τὰ ἄρρενα καὶ ὀχεύεται τὰ θήλεα.

1071 αὔτως κε σφήκεσσι Cf. 1077 with γεράνοισι. This dative is common with ὁ αὐτός, e.g. A. Ch. 543 τὸν αὐτὸν χῶρον ἐκλιπὼν ἐμοί, but rare with the adverb: cf. Anacr. PMG 388, 11–12 σκιαδίσκην ... φορεῖ γυναιξὶν αὔτως, S. Tr. 372 συνεξήκουον ὡσαύτως ἐμοί. As Voss noted, the καί of the MSS does not make sense: it would have to be followed by a nominative corresponding to θήλειαι κτλ., as in S. fr. 563 ὁμοῖα καὶ βοῦς ἐργάτης. κε is not actually necessary with λέγοιεν, since the pure optative can express a possibility, as in 1066 εἴποι, but καί and κε are regularly confused, and καί is inappropriate here.

1072 ὀψὲ δὲ μισγομένων D.S. 54 πρόβατα ὀψὲ ὀχευόμενα εὐδιεινὸν ἀποτελοῦσι τὸ σημεῖον, 40 πρόβατα ἐὰν πρωὶ ὀχεύηται, πρώϊον χειμῶνα σημαίνουσι, sch. ἐν τοῖς αὐχμηροῖς τε καὶ ἀνόμβροις ἔτεσι τὰ ζῷα ἀπρόθυμα πρὸς συνουσίαν διὰ τὴν τῶν σωμάτων ὑγρότητα ὀλίγην οὖσαν. So Apollinarius ap. sch. 1068 ἡ ὑγρότης ἢ ἡ τοῦ ἀέρος κίνησις εἰς χειμῶνα γόνιμος καὶ κινητικὴ σπερματικῆς δυνάμεως. διαχυθὲν γὰρ τὸ σῶμα καὶ τὸ πνεῦμα τῇ ἀνέσει εὔρουν γίνεται καὶ ὑπόθερμον εἰς ὁρμὰς ἀγωγοὺς ἐπὶ τὸ τῆς γενέσεως ἔργον.

μισγομένων Only here of animals, so that the rural scene seems to be elevated into a heroic setting. In Homer this verb is normally used of either the men or the women (e.g. χ 445 μίσγοντό τε λάθρῃ of the latter), and here similarly of the females (1074 βιβαιόμεναι), which are the important ones for the farmer's produce.

αἰγῶν κτλ. The nouns of 1068 in reverse order and in a different case.

1073 ἄνολβος In tragedy of luckless men, e.g. A. *Eu.* 551, S. *Aj.* 1156. Cf. Hes. *Op.* 319 αἰδώς τοι πρὸς ἀνολβίῃ.

ὅ Homeric conjunction; cf. 32. See Monro *HG* 244, Chantraine 2.285-6. Here A. is probably recalling λ 540 γηθοσύνη ὅ οἱ υἱὸν ἔφην ἀριδείκετον εἶναι, since both lines express joy and both are suitably dactylic.

θαλπιόωντι Once in Homer τ 319 εὖ θαλπιόων. A. responds with an ironical οὐ μάλα, contrasting the poverty of the farmer with the wealth of Penelope.

1074 βιβαιόμεναι Only here, a poetic form of βιβάζομαι, used by Aristotle, e.g. *HA* 577a30 τεκοῦσα δὲ βιβάζεται ἑβδόμῃ ἡμέρᾳ ... ταύτῃ βιβασθεῖσα τῇ ἡμέρᾳ. The verb is not listed in LSJ, but there seems to be no reason for rejecting it. A. alone has διχαιόμενος (495, 807) for διχαζόμενος, and is the first to attest κεδαιόμενος (159, 410).

ἐνιαυτόν The relevant 'season', in this case winter; cf. 1093, 1100. This use is not given by LSJ, but it may be a farmers' idiom, as we talk of a good year for the grapes, etc.

1075 γεράνων *D.S.* 38 γέρανοι ἐὰν πρωῒ πέτωνται καὶ ἀθρόοι, πρωῒ χειμάσει, ἐὰν δὲ ὀψὲ καὶ πολὺν χρόνον, ὀψὲ χειμάσει. This passage comes from the section on storm signs, from which A. has already taken one aspect of the flight of cranes (1031-2). But the reference to the beginning of winter makes this sign more appropriate to his section on seasons. The southward migration of cranes before the onset of winter had been a familiar theme since Homer (Γ 3-4 ἠΰτε περ κλαγγὴ γεράνων πέλει οὐρανόθι πρό, | αἵ τ' ἐπεὶ οὖν χειμῶνα φύγον καὶ ἀθέσφατον ὄμβρον), and A. now adds the association with ploughing-time from Hes. *Op.* 448ff. εὖτ' ἂν γεράνου φωνὴν ἐπακούσῃς | ... ἥ τ' ἀρότοιό τε σῆμα φέρει καὶ χείματος ὥρην | δεικνύει ὀμβρηροῦ. Cf.

Ar. *Av.* 710 σπείρειν μὲν, ὅταν γέρανος κρώζουσ' ἐς τὴν Λιβύην μετα-
χωρῇ, Triph. 353ff. χείματος ἀμφίπολοι γεράνων στίχες ἠεροφώνων |
... | γειοπόνοις ἀρότῃσιν ἀπεχθέα κεκληγυῖαι, Opp. *H.* 1.621 ὑψι-
πέτης γεράνων χορὸς ἔρχεται ἠεροφώνων.

ἀγέλαις In Homer only of cattle (e.g. Λ 678, in same *sedes*), but cf.
1094 and S. *Aj.* 168 πτηνῶν ἀγέλαι.

ὡραῖος Sch. 1075 ὁ ἐπιθυμῶν γεωργὸς ἐν τάχει τοὺς καρποὺς ἀκμάσαι, 1076 ὁ βουλόμενος καθ' ὥραν τῶν ἔργων ἅπτεσθαι γεωργός.
A. extends the normal sense of being ready (i.e. at the right age) for some
event, e.g. marriage or death, to that of being ready (by choice) for the
season's work, the latter being implied by the noun following. There
seems to be no parallel for this meaning, and it is not given by LSJ.

ἀροτρεύς A Hellenistic variation of ἀροτήρ, repeated in 1117 and
(gen. pl.) 1125. Cf. A.R. 1.1172, [Theoc.] 25.1 and 51, Nic. *Ther.* 4, all
at line-ends. Nicander's πολύεργος ἀροτρεύς seems to be a conscious
echo of A.

1076 ὥριον The rare adverb is a variation of Hesiod's adjective in
Op. 543 κρύος ὥριον ἔλθῃ. The adjective occurs once in Homer (ι 131),
the adv. in Antip. Thess. *AP* 6.198.1 = *GP* 633 ὥριον ἀνθήσαντας, Nonn.
D. 7.31 ὥριον ἀμώουσα.

ἀώριος Sch. ὁ δὲ βουλόμενος ὀψίστερον σπείρειν ταῖς ὀψιμωτέραις
(χαίρει), 1075 ὅταν δὲ βραδύτερον διαίρωνται, ὁ βουλόμενος βράδιον
ἀκμάσαι τὴν θερείαν γεωργὸς γέγηθεν. The argument for ἀώροις was
based on the scholia and Avien. 1801-2 *gaudebit tardus arator | agmine pi-
grarum*, but these passages support ἀώριος equally well. Moreover ὁ δ'
by itself is unsatisfactory, and αὐτίκα μᾶλλον (sc. ἐρχομέναις) gives the
reference to the late appearance of the cranes. Voss and Martin appear
to take μᾶλλον with χαίρει, but this is not required by the context. For
αὐτίκα μᾶλλον see note on 199.

1077 αὕτως C. dat.; cf. 1071.

χειμῶνες Cf. Suda s.v. χειμὼν ὀρνιθίας· ὁ ἐπὶ τὴν γῆν τὰ ὄρνεα
στορεννὺς ὑπὸ τῆς πνοιῆς, τουτέστιν ὁ σφοδρός, ἐν ᾧ τὰ ὄρνεα φθείρ-
εται. λέγεται δὲ καὶ ἄνεμος ὀρνιθίας. ἢ ὅτι τὰ ὄρνεα χειμῶνος φαίνεται, ὡς Ἄρατός φησι. Cf. Nonn. *D.* 14.332, of cranes, φυγοῦσαι χει-
μερίην μάστιγα.

1078 πρώϊα Homer has πρώϊον adv. once (Ο 470). A. varies with
plural form and seasonal reference. *Gp.* 1.3.12 γέρανοι θᾶσσον ἐρχόμεναι χειμῶνα εὐθέως ἔσεσθαι δηλοῦσι.

ὁμιλαδόν In Homer only of men (as ὅμιλος), Μ 3, Ο 277, Ρ 730, all
in same *sedes*. A. extends the usage to birds, [Opp.] *C.* 2.199 to deer.

ἐρχομένῃσι Ionic variation of 1076; cf. 235-6.

1079 πρώϊον Sc. χειμῶνες ἐπέρχονται. The singular form gives sufficient variation to provide an effective balance to πρώϊα, and there is nothing to be gained by emending to the adjective, whether singular (Voss) or plural (Maass).

ὀψέ With reference to the season, as in 585, 1072. Erren aptly draws attention to Hesiod's advice on late planting in *Op.* 479–90.

ἀγεληδά Cf. 965.

1080 πλειότερον Cf. 644 of size, 1005 of numbers. When the birds fly in small groups, the migration naturally takes longer.

οὐδ' ἅμα πολλαί A. repeats the sense of οὐκ ἀγεληδά, perhaps to emphasise the significance of this phenomenon. The variant in M may be due to the influence of ἀμβολίη following, and also to the frequency of such phrases at line ends, e.g. in 188, 503, 520.

1081 ἀμβολίη Cf. 886.

ὀφέλλεται Cf. 771. The association of this verb with the beneficence of Zeus is explicit there, and is probably implied here also. Cf. Theoc. 17.78 λήϊον ἀλδήσκουσιν ὀφελλόμεναι Διὸς ὄμβρῳ. A. extends the application of this verb from the actual crops to the work that is done to produce them. This form of the verb occurs in the same *sedes* in γ 367, as also ὀφέλλετο (ξ 233), ὀφέλλετε (Τ 200).

ὕστερα ἔργα A suitable footnote to this passage would be Hes. *Op.* 490 οὕτω κ' ὀψαρότης πρωιηρότῃ ἰσοφαρίζοι.

1082 βόες καὶ μῆλα *D.S.* 41 μετοπώρῳ ἐὰν πρόβατα ἢ βόες ὀρύττωσι καὶ κοιμῶνται ἀθρόοι πρὸς ἀλλήλους ἔχοντες τὰς κεφαλάς, τὸν χειμῶνα χειμέριον σημαίνει. ἐν δὲ τῷ Πόντῳ φασίν, ὅταν Ἀρκτοῦρος ἀνατείλῃ, ἐναντίους τῷ βορρᾷ νέμεσθαι, *Gp.* 1.4.3 καὶ ἐὰν τὰ βοσκήματα τὴν γῆν κατορύσσῃ, καὶ τὰς κεφαλὰς πρὸς βορρᾶν τείνῃ, χειμῶνα μέγαν προαγορεύουσιν (≈ Anon. Laur. 11.13), Ael. *NA* 7.8 πρόβατα δὲ ὀρύττοντα ταῖς ὁπλαῖς τὴν γῆν ἔοικε σημαίνειν χειμῶνα.

μετὰ βρίθουσαν ὀπώρην A verbal echo of Σ 561 μέγα βρίθουσαν ἀλωήν, and at the same time a poetic version of μετόπωρον. See note on 1064. On βρίθουσαν cf. 1049 περιβρίθοιεν, 1065 βεβρίθωσι.

1083 ὀρύσσωσιν In Homer and mostly elsewhere of men digging; but cf. Ar. *Eq.* 605, of horses, ταῖς ὁπλαῖς ὤρυττον εὐνάς.

1084 ἀντία C. gen.; cf. 917.

χείμερον Cf. 797. The word-play with χειμῶνα brings out the double meaning of these words.

αὐταί The pronoun signifies the importance of the Pleiades, which is further emphasised by being placed first in the following line. Cf. 322, 561, 630 αὐτός.

1085 Πληιάδες Cf. 255, 1066. Here the setting is specified in κατερχόμεναι, and the ms is implied by the time of year: see note on 1065–1066. The sentence concludes with an impressive four-word line, reminding the reader again of the influence of Zeus (cf. 265) in everyday human life. Cf. 333.

1086 μηδὲ λίην Cf. 1049 μὴ μὲν ἄδην. The notion of the severity of the winter being proportional to the violence of the digging is an amusing conceit of the poet's. The variant εἰ comes from sch. 1090 εἰ γὰρ λίαν ὀρύχοιεν.

ὀρύχοιεν A poetic variation of ὀρύσσω, probably formed on the analogy of ὀρυχή, and perhaps influenced by the future form in Ar. *Av.* 394, where the metre requires κατορυχησόμεσθα. Voss suggests that it is a variation of normal perfect, in view of sch. (K) 1090 μὴ οὖν ὀρωρύχοιεν (Buhle).

οὐ κατὰ κόσμον Cf. 654, 913; but here the adverbial phrase goes with μέγας.

1087 φυτοῖς Vines and other fruit trees (cf. ω 246–7), as opposed to grain; cf. 9, Ξ 122–3, Call. *H.* 3.156. This line partly recalls ι 108 οὔτε φυτεύουσιν χερσὶν φυτὸν οὔτ' ἀρόωσιν, partly 122 (see below on ἀρότοισιν).

φίλος A rare use of the metaphor with dative of things, no doubt implying the Stoic view of organic nature as sharing the cosmic life-force.

ἀρότοισιν Once in Homer, ι 122 οὔτ' ἄρα ποίμνῃσιν καταΐσχεται οὔτ' ἀρότοισιν.

1088 χιών Sch. explain why snow is desirable: καὶ γὰρ αὕτη κατ' ὀλίγον τηκομένη καὶ ποτίζουσα τὴν γῆν τρόφιμός ἐστι τοῖς ἐσπαρμένοις.

ἐν ἀρούραις The transmitted ἐπ', followed by ἐπὶ ποίῃ, is both clumsy and unclear. It does not make sense to hope that snow will lie 'on the fields on the corn', and even a comma after 'fields' does not make it convincing. The point of the sentence is that the snow will cover the young corn, and the fields are introduced merely as the location. For this sense the variant ἐν is clearer and more apt: cf. τ 205 ὡς δὲ χιὼν κατετήκετ' ἐν ἀκροπόλοισιν ὄρεσσιν. It is easy to explain ἐπ' as due to the influence of ἐπί in the next line. Voss and Mair read ἐν, but both needlessly punctuate after ἀρούραις, and in consequence translate rather freely.

1089 κεκριμένη In the regular Homeric *sedes*, particularly echoing Κ 417 οὔ τις κεκριμένη. Here the participle describes the young corn before it has become distinguishable as separate stalks; cf. 376 of stars taken individually.

μηδέ Lengthening with ictus before initial plosive + liquid (Hilberg 76, West *GM* 38). Cf. 1092, same *sedes*, as frequently in Homer, e.g. Α 210, Γ 434, Δ 302, β 231, κ 177, π 459.

βλωθρῇ In Homer of trees, Ν 390 πίτυς, ω 234 ὄγχνην. Cf. A.R. 4.1476 (poplar), Opp. *H.* 4.293 (fir). Q.S. 8.204 (pine or fir). The point here is that if the corn-stalks are too high, they will be broken by the weight of the snow, as the scholia explain.

ποίη Aptly chosen to describe the young corn, and perhaps derived from farming usage, since the new shoots look like a covering of grass when they first appear. Cf. sch. ἰσχὺν λαβούσῃ πόᾳ and εἰς πολὺ τῆς πόας ηὐξημένης.

1090 εὐεστοῖ An imitation of A. *Ag.* 647 χαίρουσαν εὐεστοῖ πόλιν. Cf. ibid. 929 and *Th.* 187 ἐν εὐεστοῖ φίλῃ, Call. fr. 112.7 σὺν εὐεστοῖ δ' ἔρχεο, Max. 534 πολλήν τ' εὐεστὼ φερέμεν. Hsch. εὐθηνία· ἀπὸ τοῦ εὖ εἶναι. Εὐεστώ, in the sense of εὐδαιμονία, was the title of a work by Democritus (D.L. 9.45).

ποτιδέγμενος Homeric present participle, usually with object, e.g. Κ 123 ποτιδέγμενος ὁρμήν, ι 545 ἡμέας ποτιδέγμενοι αἰεί, in same *sedes*. In Call. *H.* 3.147–8 it is followed by a clause, εἴ τι φέρουσα | νεῖαι. Here it is used absolutely, recalling 762 αἰεὶ πεφυλαγμένῳ ἀνδρί, in the sense of knowing what weather to expect. This is the only instance of Doric ποτί in A.

1091 οἱ δ' Anticipatory use of the article in introducing a new topic; cf. 19, 239, etc. The variant μηδ' is presumably due to the influence of the next line: the context requires the positive sense. A. seems to have inserted this sign at this point because in *D.S.* 34 the reference to drought is followed immediately by a reference to snow; see also note on κομόωντες.

καθύπερθεν A common Homeric *sedes*, e.g. Β 754. The adverb is not superfluous: it redirects the observer's attention from the ground to the sky.

ἐοικότες ἀστέρες Cf. 903, and 168, 433 ἐοικότα σήματα. If all the fixed stars are recognisably visible in their constellations, and that is a sign of good weather.

1092 Tripartite line with repeated negative; cf. *h.Hom.* 4.363, also Call. *H.* 6.5 with Hopkinson's note and his suggestion that this line may have inspired that of Callimachus.

μηδ' εἷς μηδὲ δύω μηδ' is necessary, to provide a connective contrasting the negative with the preceding positive. The corruption of μηδ' to μήθ' before an aspirate is easy (cf. 992 μήθ' A), and μήτε would have been a consequential change. It appears unlikely that μήτε is ever used after μηδέ in a reciprocal relation: see K–G 2.289 οὐδέ ... οὔτε.

κομόωντες *D.S.* 34 οἱ κομῆται ἀστέρες ὡς τὰ πολλὰ πνεύματα σημαίνουσιν, ἐὰν δὲ πολλοί, καὶ αὐχμόν. A. uses the familiar Homeric participle (e.g. B 323, 542) to represent the technical κομῆται. Aristotle also uses the latter as an epithet (e.g. *Mete.* 345b35), but more frequently treats it as a substantive. Both *D.S.* and A. clearly mean comets, but as visible comets appear only at intervals of several years, there is no real possibility of seeing two or more at any one time, and there is obviously a confusion here with meteors (cf. 926). Aristotle discusses comets at length in *Mete.* 1.6–7. He refutes earlier speculations, that comets are formed by a conjunction of planets (Anaxagoras and Democritus), that they are one planet reappearing at long intervals (Pythagoreans), that the *coma* is merely the reflection of moisture, which this collects in its passage through space (Hippolytus of Chios and Aeschylus). Aristotle's own explanation is that a comet is formed in the uppermost level of the air, which consists of a hot, dry exhalation, either when an exhalation from below or when a star or planet from above comes into contact with it. For a full account see Heath 243–7.

On this theory comets are closely related to meteors, and in fact Aristotle defines one category of comet as a kind of shooting star (344a33). This explains why he can envisage a plurality of comets appearing at the same time: cf. 343a26 πλείους ἑνὸς ἅμα γεγένηνται πολλάκις. Aristotle then introduces, as something already well known, the association of comets with drought, and cites this fact as a proof of their fiery origin: περὶ δὲ τοῦ πυρώδη τὴν σύστασιν αὐτῶν εἶναι τεκμήριον χρὴ νομίζειν ὅτι σημαίνουσι γιγνόμενοι πλείους πνεύματα καὶ αὐχμούς (344b19). On this basis he formulates a general rule: ὅταν μὲν οὖν πυκνοὶ καὶ πλείους φαίνωνται, καθάπερ λέγομεν, ξηροὶ καὶ πνευματώδεις γίγνονται οἱ ἐνιαυτοὶ ἐπιδήλως (ibid. 27). He gives no actual instance of more comets than one being seen at the same time. He does, however, refer to the sighting of single comets at different times (343b2 and 6, 345a3), and notes that in the year of the one known as the great comet (373/2) ξηρὸς ἦν ὁ χειμὼν καὶ βόρειος (344b35). The winter drought in this year may well have been the event that initiated this new piece of weather-lore. It may also explain why A. has included this item in his section on winter predictions.

The scholia give the gist of Aristotle's discussion, and add a note on the later cometary theory of Posidonius (F 131a, b EK), which also supports the belief in an ensuing drought, ὅπερ καὶ ὁ Ἄρατος λέγει, αὐχμῶν αὐτοὺς σύμβολα παραδιδοὺς ὑπάρχοντας. Cf. Ptol. *Tetr.* 2.14.10 αἱ μὲν τῶν κομητῶν συστροφαὶ ὡς ἐπίπαν αὐχμοὺς καὶ ἀνέμους προσημαίνουσι.

557

1093 αὐχμηρῷ ἐνιαυτῷ On the prediction of drought see note on 1092. For ἐνιαυτός denoting the season cf. 1074, 1100.

1094–1103 Predictions of summer
The only signs are drawn from bird life (1094–1100), after which A. marks the conclusion of the whole section with another comment on the relevance of weather signs to human life (1101–3).

1094 ἠπειρόθεν Only here, as 995 χειμωνόθεν. The adverb is attached to the noun with the force of an adjective, a simple extension of the normal prose usage with the definite article. The use is commonest with adverbs in -θε: e.g. Theoc. 24.111 Ἀργόθεν ἄνδρες, Call. *H.* 4.284 Δωδώνηθε Πελασγοί, Nic. fr. 74.2 ἄνθε' Ἰαονίηθε. But cf. also Z 450 ἄλγος ὀπίσσω, [Theoc.] 9.34 ἔαρ ἐξαπίνας (where see Gow's note).

1095 ἐκ νήσων *D.S.* 17 καὶ θέρους ὅταν πολλοὶ ἀθρόοι φανῶσιν ὄρνιθες οἳ βιοτεύουσιν ἐν νήσῳ, ὕδωρ σημαίνουσιν· ἐὰν δὲ μέτριοι, ἀγαθὸν αἰξὶ καὶ βοτοῖς, ἐὰν δὲ πολλοὶ ὑπερβολῇ, αὐχμὸν ἰσχυρόν. Sch. (MA) quote from Aristotle (fr. 252 Rose): ὅταν μὲν ὑγρὸς ᾖ καὶ ψυχρὸς ὁ ἀήρ, τὸ τηνικαῦτα καὶ αἱ νῆσοι βρεχόμεναι ἀναφύουσι, καὶ τὰ ἐν αὐταῖς ὄρνεα τρέφουσιν. ὅταν δὲ αὐχμώδης ᾖ καὶ ξηρός, τότε παντελῶς τῶν νήσων μὴ ἀναφυουσῶν ἐπὶ τὴν γῆν τὰ ἐν ταῖς νήσοις ὄρνεα φεύγουσιν, εἰς ἣν δύνανται κἂν ἐξ ὀλίγου τρέφεσθαι. Plu. fr. 20 Sandbach ξηρότεραι γὰρ αἱ νῆσοι τῶν ἠπείρων ὑπάρχουσαι ὥς φησι Πλούταρχος, θᾶττον καὶ ῥᾷον τοῦ αὐχμηροῦ καταστήματος ἀντιλαμβάνονται. διὸ καὶ τὰ ὄρνεα φεύγει καὶ ταῖς ἠπείροις ἐπιπελάζει.

ἐπιπλήσσωσιν C. dat., as in M 211 ἀεὶ μέν πώς μοι ἐπιπλήσσεις, but there of verbal attacks. Here the choice of verb may suggest recurring strikes by the birds.

1096 θέρεος A. makes it clear that the topic has changed from winter to summer.

περιδείδιε Cf. Κ 93 αἰνῶς γὰρ Δαναῶν περιδείδια, Ν 481 δείδια δ' αἰνῶς, and c. dat. Ρ 242 ἐμῇ κεφαλῇ περιδείδια. Q.S. 5.217, 8.430 imitates with verb in same *sedes*.

1097 ἀμήτῳ Cf. 1061.

κενεός Cf. 150, in similar context. The form is common in Homer, e.g. κ 42, Β 298; cf. Call. *H.* 6.105, *E.* 32.1.

ἀχύρμιος Only here, formed from ἀχυρμιαί, which appears once in Homer (Ε 502).

1098 ἀνιηθείς Cf. γ 117, in same *sedes*, πρίν κεν ἀνιηθεὶς σὴν πατρίδα γαῖαν ἵκοιο. A. again applies to organic nature a word normally used of personal feelings; cf. 1087 φίλος.

χαίρει κτλ. A chiastic arrangement responding to 1094–6, with the unusual feature of an additional clause intervening between the two contrasting elements.

αἰπόλος ἀνήρ Δ 275, Nonn. *D.* 29.158; cf. 935 ναυτίλος ἀνήρ, Ψ 845 βουκόλος ἀνήρ. The addition of ἀνήρ gives the humble goatherd a certain dignity, as also the shepherd in S. *OT* 1118 νομεὺς ἀνήρ. Contrast the contemptuous use in Theoc. 6.7 αἰπόλον ἄνδρα. A. has ἀνήρ in this position three times in the last nine lines, evenly spaced at intervals of four lines.

1099 αὐταῖς I.e. the birds from the islands (1093–4). For the meaning 'same' expressed without the article cf. 928 αὐτὴν ὁδόν (= θ 107), 1031 αὐτὰ κέλευθα (= M 225), 1131 αὐτήν.

κατὰ μέτρον Cf. 1047, and Hes. *Op.* 720, of the tongue, κατὰ μέτρον ἰούσης. Here the moderateness applies to the numbers of the birds.

1100 ἐλπόμενος C. gen., a favourite construction of A. with verbs of expecting, e.g. 559 δεδοκημένῳ, 795 δειδέχθαι, 813 δοκεύειν. A. probably has in mind Σ 260 ἐλπόμενος νῆας αἱρησέμεν, since the participle has the same *sedes* and follows χαίρεσκον (259), while the variation of the construction is characteristic. This four-word line concludes a topic, as in 1074, 1085. It is worth noting that the incidence of four-word lines increases towards the end of the poem: there are seven in the next section (1104–41).

μετέπειτα Cf. in same *sedes* Ξ 310, Call. *H.* 1.45, 3.248.

πολυγλαγέος Variation of Π 642 περιγλαγέας (Apollon. *Lex.* πολυ-); cf. Nonn. *D.* 9.176 πολυγλαγέων ἀπὸ μαζῶν. On the lengthening before initial vowel here, Hermann 703 'hoc habet excusationem longioris uocabuli'.

1101 μογεροί The recurring theme of human suffering is here related particularly to men on land, as earlier to men at sea (419). It is repeated here in order to remind us of the benevolence of Zeus in providing helpful signs.

ἀλήμονες A. recalls a similar sentiment spoken by Odysseus as a beggar: τοιοῦτοι πτωχοὶ καὶ ἀλήμονες ἄνδρες ἔασι (τ 74). The line also carries a verbal echo of ρ 376 ἀλήμονές εἰσι καὶ ἄλλοι.

1102 ζώομεν A rare instance of the first person, whereby the poet identifies himself with the human condition he describes. The phrase glances back to 1–5 ἐῶμεν, κεχρήμεθα, εἰμέν, 769 γινώσκομεν.

πὰρ ποσί Cf. 167, N 617, Ξ 411, Pi. *O.* 1.74. Here the sense is extended to include a wider environment. It introduces the next section on signs from everyday life. The alliteration reflects O 280 πᾶσιν δὲ παραὶ ποσὶ κάππεσε.

πάντες ἑτοῖμοι A.'s normally sympathetic attitude to human life is suddenly sharpened by the recollection of Democritus' satirical comment in fr. B 147 (cited on 1123). Thus ἑτοῖμοι has the sense of 'only too ready'.

1103 ἐπιγνῶναι Cf. ω 217 αἴ κέ μ' ἐπιγνώῃ, in same *sedes*.

ἐς αὐτίκα Cf. 770.

ποιήσασθαι Cf. 379, 565, 777, and Democr. fr. B 147 σημεῖα ποιουμένους.

1104–1141 Local signs from animals
A. began his catalogue with universal signs in the sky (773), and now concludes it with signs observable locally on the ground, in the behaviour of animals on or near the farm: sheep (1104–12), cattle (1113–21), goats and sows (1122–3), a lone wolf (1124–31), mice, dogs, crab, pigs (1132–41). All signs are warnings of bad weather, and the material, except for the lines on sheep, is mostly to be found in *D.S.* 38–49, the section already referred to on 1013–1043.

1104 ἀρνάσι The Attic form, as opposed to the Epic ἄρνεσσι (Π 352); cf. ἀνδράσι (932), but also ἄνδρεσσι (732). The word is here a general term for 'sheep', since it must include the rams and lambs specially mentioned in 1106.

χειμῶνας The weather theme for this section, repeated with the variations χειμῶνος (1114), negative ἀχείμεροι (1121) and εὔδιοι (1123), χειμῶνα (1128), χείματος (1130), with a return to χειμῶνος ... χειμῶνα ... χειμῶνος in 1136–9.

ἐτεκμήραντο The variant in M is unlikely, since ἐπιτεκμαίρομαι c. acc. means 'identify' (cf. 229, 456), c. gen. 'predict' (1038).

νομῆες Homeric plural, e.g. Σ 525 = ρ 214 δύω δ' ἅμ' ἕποντο νομῆες.

1105 ἐς νομόν A. chooses not to imitate Homeric νομόνδε (Σ 575, ι 438), but later (1119) adopts the rarer σταθμόνδε from ι 451.

μᾶλλον Sc. τοῦ εἰωθότος (e.g. *D.S.* 41 μᾶλλον ἐσθίοντες τοῦ εἰωθότος); cf. 1132 and Homeric κηρόθι μᾶλλον (Ι 300, ο 370).

ἐπειγόμενοι The choice of participle and its placing in this position carries an amusing reminiscence of the heroic chariot-race in Ψ 437, 496 ἐπειγόμενοι περὶ νίκης.

τροχόωσιν Cf. 27.

1106 ἄλλοι δ' ... ἄλλοι δέ This use of double ἄλλοι is unusual, in that each pronoun is specifically identified by a noun in apposition. I do not know of a parallel instance, but the scholia make the meaning clear by simplifying, ὅταν κριοὺς ἢ ἀμνούς ... ἴδωσι, i.e. 'some of the flock, either rams or lambs'. There is no need to emend to double ἄλλη (Voss and Maass), since the transmitted text gives the required sense.

ἐξ ἀγέλης The point of the preposition is that the sportive animals stand out from the rest of the stolid flock: it does not mean that they somehow become separated (Mair 'behind the flock', Martin 'quittant le troupeau'); cf. 95 ἐξ ἄλλων, Σ 431 ἐκ πασέων. ἀγέλη is properly a flock being herded (ἄγω), hence on the move, as opposed to being in pens or grazing. Cf. 1110, and, by analogy, of birds in flight (1075, 1094).

1107 εἰνόδιοι Once in Homer, in same *sedes*, Π 260 εἰνοδίοις. Cf. 132.

παίζωσιν This sign is not in *D.S.*, but appears in *Gp.* 1.3.9 ποίμνια σκιρτῶντα χειμῶνα ἐσόμενον δηλοῦσι. Cf. Plin. *Nat.* 18.364 *pecora exultantia et indecora lasciuia ludentia*, and the opposite prognosis in Ael. *NA* 7.8 ἄρνες δὲ ἄρα καὶ ἔριφοι ἀλλήλοις ἐμπηδῶντές τε καὶ ὑποσκιρτῶντες φαιδρὰν ἡμέραν ὁμολογοῦσιν ≈ *CCAG* 8.1.137, 6 ≈ Anon. Laur. 11.4. A. again attributes human behaviour to animals.

ἐρειδόμενοι Reciprocal sense, as in Ψ 735 μηκέτ᾽ ἐρείδεσθον. *D.S.* 41 μαχόμενα πρόβατα is combined with birds fighting over their food, and is probably not relevant here.

1108 ἀναπλήσσωσι Voss, Maass, Martin and Erren have adopted J. Schneider's emendation, proposed on the basis of ζ 318 εὖ δὲ πλίσσοντο πόδεσσιν. But the basic use of πλίσσομαι is to describe position or movement with the legs wide apart, i.e. straddling or striding. The mules in Homer stretched their legs to trot at a good pace, and Amphitheos in Ar. *Ach.* 218 (ἀπεπλίξατο) fled with long strides. At S. *Tr.* 520 Pearson conjectured ἀμφίπλικτοι, but for -πλεκ-, not -πληκ-. For fuller discussions and notes on other uses of this verb see Frisk 2.563, Gow on Theoc. 18.8 περιπλίκτοις, and sch. on ζ 318 and Ar. *Ach.* 218. The derivation is uncertain. The verb and related adv. accommodate the prefixes ἀπο-, ἐκ-, δια-, κατα-, ἀμφι-, περι-, but ἀνα- is not attested, and indeed ἀνα- does not go easily with the sense of this verb. On the other hand it goes very well with the idea of animals kicking up their legs, which the context here requires: cf. sch. 1104 τινὰς δὲ τοῖς ποσὶν ἀλλομένους, 1107 τοῖς τέτρασιν ἀλλόμενοι ποσί, and Avien. 1840 *persultans aries*. For this meaning the reading of the manuscripts is more promising, especially as the simple verb is used by Homer of horses kicking in Ε 588 ἵππω πλήξαντε χαμαὶ βάλον ἐν κονίῃσι. Cf. χ 19–20 τράπεζαν ὦσε ποδὶ πλήξας. There the participles imply an object, but here the verb will have to be taken intransitively, a reasonable extension of the normal usage, since the animals do not actually kick anything. As to the imitation of ζ 318, it should be noted that there is a variant (ἐ)πλήσσοντο, of which A., whose work on the text of the *Odyssey* is referred to as a διόρθωσις (see *SH* 118), was probably well aware. He may have deliberately chosen the variant for his imitation, as the Alexandrians sometimes did: see Giangrande, *CQ* 17 (1967) 85ff. In any case A. was quite capable of varying his Homer with a similar but slightly different word (cf. 412, 1112).

1109 τέτρασιν I.e. with all four feet off the ground. The chiastic pattern of this line reinforces the contrast between the young and the mature sheep.

κοῦφοι The sense of nimble movement appears first in the adverb, e.g. N 158 κοῦφα ποσὶ προβιβάς, then the adjective is used of the feet, e.g. S. *Ant.* 224 κοῦφον ἐξάρας πόδα, and now A. extends it to the animals. Theocritus keeps to the traditional idiom in ποδὶ κούφῳ (2.104).

κεραοί Cf. δ 85 ἄρνες ἄφαρ κεραοί.

ἀμφοτέροισιν Sch. 1104 τοῖς ἐμπροσθίοις. Cf. 236, 1136.

1110 ἐξ ἀγέλης A. repeats the phrase from 1106, but gives the preposition a different sense.

ἀεκούσια Normally of acts or their consequences (LSJ), e.g. Theogn. 1343 ἀεκούσια πολλὰ βίαια, only here of animals, like ἀέκων of persons. Since all the sheep are now involved, A. changes to the generalising neuter, perhaps with πρόβατα or μῆλα in mind. Hence τὰ δέ (1111), which Bernhardy (430) sees as imitating Ε 140 τὰ δ᾿ after ὀΐεσσι in 137.

κινήσωσι Sc. νομῆες. For the pure subjunctive see note on 828.

1111 δείελον Normally either adjective, as in δείελον ἦμαρ (ρ 606, [Theoc.] 25.86), or substantive (Φ 232, Call. fr. 260.55). The adverbial use here may be compared with the adverbial phrase in 1119, A.R. 3.417–18 δείελον ὥρην | παύομαι ἀμήτοιο. The time is late afternoon, the third division of the day: cf. Φ 111 ἔσσεται ἢ ἠὼς ἢ δείλη ἢ μέσον ἦμαρ.

εἰσελάοντες Cf. κ 82–3 ποιμένα ποιμὴν | ἠπύει εἰσελάων, A.R. 2.80 ἐλάοντες, Call. *H.* 5 ἐξελάοισα.

ὅμως I.e. despite the recalcitrance of the sheep; ὁμῶς, 'all alike' (cf. 19, 264, 891), has no relevance here.

πάντοθι Cf. 743. The exaggeration suggests how much the sheep are out of control ('all over the place'), and the alliteration reinforces it.

ποίης Cf. σ 372 (βόες) κεκορηότε ποίης.

1112 δάκνωσιν A surprising choice of a word usually associated with harmful effects (cf. 975). A more normal expression for sheep grazing is βόσκετο ποίην (*h.Hom.* 4.232). Perhaps A. means to imply an element of aggressiveness in their nibbling, which is in accord with their recalcitrant behaviour.

πυκινῇσι ... λιθάκεσσιν Imitation of ξ 36, ψ 193 πυκνῇσιν λιθάδεσσιν. Cf. A.R. fr. 12.21 (*CA* p. 8) θαμινῇσιν ἀράσσοντες λιθάδεσσιν. The form πυκν- in Homer is used only with the first syllable *in arsi*, and it is therefore unlikely that the reading of M here is correct: no doubt it is due to the influence of ξ 36. For πυκιν- in the same *sedes* as here cf. Λ

576 πυκινοῖσι βιαζόμενον βελέεσσι. The noun λιθάκεσσιν is a deliberate variation, but it has a Homeric source in the adjective λίθακι ποτὶ πέτρῃ (ε 415). Eustath. 1749.51 says that λιθάδες are smaller than λίθακες. **κελευόμενα** The sense of 'urging on' with gestures, not words, is an early use of this verb, e.g. ὣ 326 ἵπποι, τοὺς ὁ γέρων ἐφέπων μάστιγι κέλευε. Cf. the related meanings in 631 and 775. For the lengthening before initial λ cf. 719, Mosch. 2.34.

1113 ἀρόται A variation of ἀροτήρ (132, 1062), ἀροτρεύς (1075, 1117, 1125); cf. Pi. I. 1.48, Hdt. 4.2.

βουκόλοι ἄνδρες An exact imitation of N 571; cf. Ψ 845 βουκόλος ἀνήρ. See note on 1098 αἰπόλος ἀνήρ.

1114 κινυμένου Cf. 915.

χηλάς D.S. 15 βοῦς τὴν προσθίαν ὁπλὴν λείξας χειμῶνα ἢ ὕδωρ σημαίνει. Cf. Gp. 1.3.10 καὶ βόες πρὸς μεσημβρίαν ὁρῶσαι, ἢ τὰς χηλὰς περιλειχόμεναι, καὶ μετὰ μυκηθμῶν ἐπὶ τὴν βουστασίαν ἐρχόμεναι ὄμβρους δηλοῦσιν (≈ Anon. Laur. 11.12).

1115 ὑπωμαίοιο Cf. 144.

περιλιχμήσονται See note on χηλάς (1114), and cf. Plin. Nat. 18.364 seque lambentes contra pilum. A. may be recalling Hes. Th. 826 γλώσσῃσι ... λελιχμότες. Cf. [Theoc.] 25.226 γλώσσῃ δὲ περιλιχμᾶτο γένειον, Opp. H. 1.786 δέμας περιλιχμάζουσιν. The scholia offer an explanation: ἐπειδὴ ἐν τῇ ἀρχῇ τοῦ χειμῶνος ψυχρὰ ἡ γῆ γίνεται, ὁ βοῦς ψυχιζομένην τὴν χηλὴν τὴν ἐμπροσθίαν τῇ περιλιχμήσει πειρᾶται θερμαίνειν.

1116 κοίτῳ Cf. 1005, of birds roosting. Mair and LSJ, following Ceporinus' version stabulo, take this to mean the actual 'stall'. But κοῖτος in Homer (nine times in the Odyssey) means 'rest' or 'sleep' or 'going to bed', and in Hesiod 'lying in bed' (Op. 574), never the bed itself or an animal's lair or stall, which is κοίτη. Voss, Martin and Erren translate as 'rest' or 'sleep', but take the dative as expressing purpose. This is a rare use of the dative, and it tends to go with nouns, e.g. A. Pers. 1022 θησαυρὸν βελέεσσιν. Cf. Hes. Sc. 215, Theoc. 28.10 and Gow's note. It is more likely that κοίτῳ is a locative, 'at rest', 'when resting', comparable with the adverbial κύκλῳ (e.g. 401, 1040), and such uses as B 863 ὑσμῖνι μάχεσθαι, Κ 472 χθονὶ κέκλιτο, S. OT 65 ὕπνῳ γ' εὕδοντα.

πλευρὰς ἐπὶ δεξιτερὰς D.S. 41 βόες ... ἐπὶ τὸ δεξιὸν κατακλινόμενοι χειμέριον. A. has combined this storm sign with the rain sign in 15. Cf. Ael. NA 7.8 ὅτι δὲ βοῦς, ἐὰν μέλλῃ ὕειν ὁ Ζεύς, ἐπὶ τὸ ἰσχίον τὸ δεξιὸν κατακλίνεται, ἐὰν δὲ εὐδία, πάλιν ἐπὶ τὸ λαιόν, θαυμάζει ἤ τις ἢ οὐδείς, Anon. Laur. 11.8 βόες ὁπότε μέλλει [μέλειν cod.] ὕειν ἤγουν βρέχειν, ἐπὶ τὴν δεξιὰν πλευρὰν κατακλίνονται, CCAG 8.1.137, 8 βόες, ὁπόταν μέλλῃ ὕειν, ἐπὶ τὴν δεξιὰν πλευρὰν κατακλίνονται· ἐὰν δὲ ἐπὶ τὴν λαιάν, τὸ ἀνάπαλιν.

τανύσωνται Cf. ι 298 κεῖτ' ἔντοσθ' ἄντροιο τανυσσάμενος διά μήλων. For the end-rhyme see note on 191 στιχόωσιν.

1117 ἀμβολίην Cf. 886, 1081.

ἀρότοιο Cf. 267.

γέρων I.e. the experienced veteran; cf. Theogn. 1351 γέροντι δὲ πείθεο ἀνδρί.

ἐπιέλπετ' Epic form of ἐπέλπομαι, twice in Homer c. inf. (Α 545–6 ἐπιέλπεο μύθους | εἰδήσειν, φ 126 ἐπιελπόμενος). Α. varies the use with an accusative, perhaps recalling Ο 539 ἔτι δ' ἔλπετο νίκην.

1118–1121 This passage was misunderstood at least by late antiquity, and its sense and structure have only gradually been re-established by the successive insights of editors after Voss. There were two main obstacles to the understanding of these lines. One was the remoteness of οὐδ' from ἀχείμεροι, although Α.'s fondness for this double negative structure has already been illustrated in 845–7, 866–8, 869–71. The negative was replaced by ἠδ', and this created a problem in the interpretation of 1121. The other obstacle was that the ὅτε clause was seen to run on to the end of 1120, and this made it difficult to explain βόες and πόριες as both subjects of ἀγέρωνται, to interpret the genitives after σκυθραί, and to determine the subject of τεκμαίρονται.

The movement back to explaining the original text without emendation began with Bekker's restoration of οὐδ'. But Maass, to eliminate βόες and so leave πόριες as subject of the clause, replaced it with βοῶν, citing in support Anon. Laur. 11.12 ἐπὶ τὴν βουστασίαν and A.R. 2.1 σταθμοί τε βοῶν. But βοῶν is superfluous, and πόριες in the general sense of 'sheep' is unparalleled. Then Mair restored the structure of the passage by punctuating after 1119, thus giving the two clauses two lines each and making πόριες the subject of τεκμαίρονται. But he construed the genitives in 1120 with σκυθραί, translating 'reluctant to leave'. He was perhaps influenced by sch. 1120 σκυθρωπαὶ ἀπὸ τοῦ λειμῶνος κτλ. It is a doubtful meaning for the Greek, but in any case the heifers are sullen because of their presentiment of bad weather. Finally Martin completed the restoration by taking the genitives with ἐμπλήσεσθαι.

1118 οὐδ' With ἀχείμεροι in 1121, another variation in negative form; cf. 845–7, 867–9.

μυκηθμοῖο The status of the ordinary farm animals in enhanced by this reminiscence of Achilles' shield (Σ 575) and the cattle of the Sun (μ 265). Cf. A.R. 3.1297.

περίπλειοι Epic form of περίπλεως, only here; cf. 1006 ἔμπλειοι. A.R. 1.858 has περίπλεον c. dat.

ἀγέρωνται Homeric form, e.g. Β 94 οἳ δ' ἀγέροντο, in same *sedes*.

Cf. λ 36, β 385, θ 321, υ 277, also A.R. 3.895. A. also uses ἀγείρωνται (976), ἀγειρομένη (105), as Β 52 etc.

1119 σταθμόνδε Once in Homer, ι 451 πρῶτος δὲ σταθμόνδε λιλαίεαι ἀπονέεσθαι.

βουλύσιον ὥρην Cf. 825. The adverbial accusative denoting a point of time is a standard usage with this noun: e.g. A. *Eum.* 109 ἔθυον ὥραν οὐδενὸς κοινὴν θεῶν, Ε. *Ba.* 723-4 τὴν τεταγμένην | ὥραν ἐκίνουν θύρσον, Arist. *Mete.* 371b31 πᾶσαν ὥραν γίγνεται ('at any time'), A.R. 3.417-18 δείελον ὥρην | παύομαι ἀμήτοιο. Cf. 1111 δείελον. See K-G 2.314-15. Martin's dative is therefore unnecessary.

1120 σκυθραί Cf. Men. 10 σκυθρός, πικρός. The regular adjective is σκυθρωπός, because the feelings are judged from the facial expression. The word describes a look that is 'worried' (e.g. Men. *Epit.* 230 Sandbach) or 'surly' (e.g. E. *Alc.* 774) or 'sad' (e.g. E. *Ph.* 1333). The related verbs σκύζομαι (e.g. Δ 23) and σκυδμαίνω (Ω 592) denote anger, σκυθράζω rather a scowling look (e.g. Ar. *Lys.* 7). These words are used normally of human beings, only here of animals, which explains A.'s choice of the simple adjective without -ωπός. Animals show their feelings rather by their behaviour, which in this case could be called 'dispirited'. The point is that only the young can give this weather sign, because they are naturally frisky, and an unusual lack of spirit shows there is something wrong.

πόριες Once in Homer, κ 410 ἄγραυλοι πόριες περὶ βοῦς ἀγελαίας, where it is the young animals that show their feelings, in that case feelings of joy.

βουβοσίοιο In Call. *H.* 2.50 ῥεῖά κε βουβόσιον τελέθοι πλέον this noun means a herd of cattle, and Williams ad loc. suggests that it was formed on the analogy of συβόσιον (Λ 679, ξ 101). A., however, uses the word in the sense of 'cattle-pasture', so that he may also have had in mind the Homeric adjective βούβοτος (ν 246), of Ithaca as good for grazing cattle. Cf. Str. 12.4.7 χώραν ἀρίστην βουβοσίοις. The phrase λειμῶνος καὶ βουβοσίοιο is a hendiadys, the genitives depending on ἐμπλήσεσθαι.

1121 αὐτίκα 'In due course'; cf. 761, 770, 774, 1103. Martin specifies 'demain', but the storm could come the day after: cf. 1131.

ἀχείμεροι Only here, a variation of ἀχείμαντος (Alc. *PMG* 319), ἀχείματος (A. *Supp.* 136). Cf. 797. 1084 χείμερος.

ἐμπλήσεσθαι The *spondeiazon* recalls σ 45 κνίσης τε καὶ αἵματος ἐμπλήσαντες.

1122 αἶγες This sign is not in *D.S.* or *Gp.*, but cf. Ael. *NA* 7.8 αὗται μὲν [sc. αἱ αἶγες] καὶ μέλλοντα ὑετὸν προδηλοῦσιν. ἐπειδὰν γὰρ προἔλθωσι τῶν σηκῶν, δρόμῳ καὶ μάλα γε ὤκιστα ὁρμῶσιν ἐπὶ τὸν χιλόν, *CCAG* 8.1.137, 3 αἶγες ἐπειδὰν προσέλθωσιν τῷ σηκῷ δρόμῳ ≃ Anon. Laur. 11.1.

πρίνοιο See note on 1044.

περισπεύδουσαι Not attested before A. The verb describes the urgency of the goats' feeding, not as LSJ 'go in search of'.

ἀκάνθαις Cf. Theophr. *HP* 1.10.6, on leaves, τὰ δὲ καὶ παρακανθίζοντα καὶ ἐκ τοῦ ἄκρου καὶ ἐκ τῶν πλαγίων, οἷον τὰ τῆς πρίνου κτλ. Leaves of the kermes oak are 'toothed and spiny' (Polunin & Hux. 56), but also leaves of sucker shoots of the holm oak are 'prickly, holly-like' (Polunin & Ever. 52). The dative is explained by the prefix περι-, as with the preposition in β 245 μαχήσασθαι περὶ δαιτί.

1123 σύες φορυτῷ ἔπι μαργαίνουσαι A quotation from Democritus (B 147) ap. Plu. 129A ἄτοπον γάρ ἐστι κοράκων μὲν λαρυγγισμοῖς καὶ κλωσμοῖς ἀλεκτορίδων καὶ "συσὶν ἐπὶ φορυτῷ μαργαινούσαις", ὡς ἔφη Δημόκριτος, ἐπιμελῶς προσέχειν, σημεῖα ποιουμένους πνευμάτων καὶ ὄμβρων, τὰ δὲ τοῦ σώματος κινήματα καὶ σάλους καὶ προπαθείας μὴ προλαμβάνειν μηδὲ προφυλάττειν μηδὲ ἔχειν σημεῖα χειμῶνος ἐν ἑαυτῷ γενησομένου καὶ μέλλοντος. Cf. Clem. Al. *Protr.* 92.4 (1.68.7 St.) οἱ δὲ σκωλήκων δίκην περὶ τέλματα καὶ βορβόρους τὰ ἡδονῆς ῥεύματα καλινδούμενοι ἀνονήτους καὶ ἀνόητους ἐκβόσκονται τρυφάς, ὑώδεις τινὲς ἄνθρωποι. ὕες γάρ, φησίν, ἥδονται βορβόρῳ μᾶλλον ἢ καθαρῷ ὕδατι καὶ ἐπὶ φορυτῷ μαργαίνουσιν κατὰ Δημόκριτον, *D.S.* 49 τὸ πανταχοῦ δὲ λεγόμενον σημεῖον δημόσιον χειμέριον, ὅταν σύες [Maass p. xxvi, μύες codd.] περὶ φορυτοῦ μάχωνται καὶ φέρωσιν. Cf. V. *G.* 1.399–400 *non ore solutos | immundi meminere sues iactare maniplos.* Plin. *Nat.* 18.364 *turpesque porci alienos sibi manipulos feni lacerantes.*

φορυτῷ Sch. πρὸς τὸν φορυτόν, ὅ ἐστι βόρβορον. But here it is rather straw and other rubbish blown in by the wind; cf. Ar. *Ach.* 72 παρὰ τὴν ἔπαλξιν ἐν φορυτῷ κατακείμενος, 927 δός μοι φορυτόν, ἵν' αὐτὸν ἐνδήσας φέρω.

μαργαίνουσαι Once in Homer, E 882 μαργαίνειν ἀνέηκεν ἐπ' ἀθανάτοισι θεοῖσι, of a hero's rage. Voss's suggestion of ἔπι is supported by the earlier uses of the simple verb with ἐπί, and by the fact that the compound is not elsewhere attested.

1124 λύκος *D.S.* 46 λύκος ὠρυόμενος χειμῶνα σημαίνει διὰ τριῶν ἡμερῶν. λύκος ὅταν πρὸς τὰ ἔργα ὁρμᾷ ἢ εἴσω χειμῶνος ὥρα, χειμῶνα σημαίνει εὐθύς, Ael. *NA* 7.8 λύκοι δὲ φεύγοντες ἐρημίας καὶ εὐθὺ τῶν οἰκουμένων ἰόντες χειμῶνος ἐμβολὴν μέλλοντος ὅτι πεφρίκασι μαρτυροῦσι δι' ὧν δρῶσι, *Gp.* 1.3.11 ὁμοίως καὶ λύκος πλησίον τῶν οἰκημάτων θρασυνόμενος, *CCAG* 8.1.138, 13 λύκοι φεύγοντες τὰς ἐρημίας καὶ τὰ οἰκούμενα διώκοντες χειμῶνα πεφρίκασιν (= Anon. Laur. 11.30).

μονόλυκος The lone wolf was thought to be particularly strong and savage; cf. Arist. *HA* 594a30 ἀνθρωποφαγοῦσι δ' οἱ μονοπεῖραι τῶν λύκων μᾶλλον ἢ τὰ κυνηγέσια, Ael. *NA* 7.47 ὁ δὲ τέλειος καὶ μέγιστος καλοῖτο ἂν μονόλυκος, Antip. Thess. *AP* 7.289.3 = *GP* 223 μούνιος ἐκ θάμνοιο θορών λύκος, Luc. *Tim.* 42 μονήρης δὲ ἡ δίαιτα καθάπερ τοῖς λύκοις, *Ep. Sat.* 34 μόνον ἐμπίπλασθαι ὥσπερ τοὺς λέοντάς φασι καὶ τοὺς μονίους τῶν λύκων, Eustath. ad ζ 133 κέλεται δέ ἑ γαστήρ· ὡς γὰρ τὸν λέοντα ἡ γαστὴρ πείθει καὶ ἐς πυκινὸν δόμον ἐλθεῖν κατὰ τὸν παρὰ τῷ Ἀράτῳ μονόλυκον. Demosthenes' striking metaphor for Alexander is recorded by Plutarch: Ἀλέξανδρον δὲ τὸν Μακεδόνα μονόλυκον προσηγόρευσεν (*Dem.* 23.4). A.'s use of this word as an epithet of λύκος brings out the unusual phenomenon of such a creature coming so close to human habitation. A similar compound is μουνολέων (Leon. *AP* 6.221.3 = *HE* 2293). For the lengthening of a syllable before initial λ cf. 719, 1112.

ὠρύηται Especially of wolves and dogs howling; see Call. fr. 725 καὶ ὡς λύκος ὠρυοίμην, and Pfeiffer's note. Cf. Theoc. 1.71 τῆνον λύκοι ὠρύσαντο, 2.35 κύνες ... ὠρύονται, Q.S. 12.518 ἐν δὲ λύκοι καὶ θῶες ἀναιδέες ὠρύσαντο.

1125 ὅτ' Buttmann's ὅ γ' is adopted by Maass and Mair. But A. uses ὅ γε mostly to introduce a new sentence after αὐτάρ (21, 49, 250, 278, 285, 339, 537, 591) or οὐδέ (214, 714), or in adding a phrase (772, 842). The present passage is not comparable. Here the wolf is given two alternative signs, and the conjunction is repeated in a different form for variation; cf. 1105ff. ὁππότε ... ἢ ὁπότ' ... ἢ καὶ ὅτ'.

ἀροτρήων Cf. 1075, 1117.

πεφυλαγμένος C. gen., as in 48.

1126 ἔργα An old usage, of farm land worked by men, e.g. Μ 283 ἀνδρῶν πίονα ἔργα, Π 392 ἔργ' ἀνθρώπων, κ 147 ἔργα ἴδοιμι βροτῶν. Cf. Tyrt. 5.7, Sol. 13.21, B. 10.44, Call. *H.* 3.125 (with Bulloch's note); also in prose, Hdt. 1.36, *D.S.* 46. See 1030, of bees' work in the hives.

σκέπαος Cf. 857.

χατέοντι C. gen., as once in Homer, γ 48 θεῶν χατέουσ' ἄνθρωποι. Cf. Agath. *AP* 5.302.20 Λαΐδος οὐ χατέων, 7.583.8 χθονὸς οὐ χατέεις.

1127 ἐγγύθεν ἀνθρώπων Cf. Λ 723 ἐγγύθεν Ἀρήνης.

λέχος Sch. οἱ δὲ "λόχος", ἀντὶ τοῦ ἐνέδρα· ἵνα τι ἁρπάσῃ. Voss prints λόχος as more suited to αὐτόθεν, which he takes in a temporal sense, 'sogleich'. Martin rightly notes that αὐτόθεν simply echoes ἐγγύθεν, but he still accepts λόχος, translating 'pour leur arracher du butin'. This gives the word an unparalleled verbal force. In any case it is not food that is in question here, but shelter (1126 σκέπαος) from the anticipated storm: cf. 857, Hes. *Op.* 529ff. Erren also reads λόχος, but translates somewhat ambiguously 'ein Versteck finde'. The transmitted λέχος, supported by Avien. 1855 *lectumque laremque*, suits the required meaning better; it is not normally used of an animal's lair, but cf. A. *Ag.* 51, S. *Ant.* 425, of birds' nests. The description of animal and bird life in human terms is a feature of A.'s style: cf. 1005–6.

αὐτόθεν   The use with εἶναι is perhaps influenced by the preceding ἐγγύθεν, which is elsewhere so used adverbially by A., e.g. 247, 480. Cf. ζ 279 ἐγγύθεν εἰσίν.

1128 τρὶς περιτελλομένης ἠοῦς   Sch. ἀντὶ τοῦ τρίτον τῆς ἡμέρας παρελθούσης, τουτέστι μετὰ τρεῖς ἡμέρας. Hence Mair 'when the third dawn comes round', Martin 'au troisième lever du jour', Erren 'nach dreimal umlaufendem Tageslicht'. But the paraphrase with an aorist participle changes the sense, and what A. really means is shown by 1131: the storm may come at any time during the three days. The genitive expresses 'time within which'. Moreover περιτέλλομαι has the sense of circling, not rising, and ἠώς here is the period of daylight, not just dawn; cf. 739.

δοκεύειν   Cf. 813, 908.

1129 ἐπὶ σήμασι   Cf. 429, 801, 1154.

1130 ἀνέμων ἢ χείματος ἢ ὑετοῖο   The three traditional categories of bad weather: see note on 909–1043, and cf. *D.S.* 1 σημεῖα ὑδάτων καὶ πνευμάτων καὶ χειμώνων.

1131 αὐτήν   Adv. acc. denoting a point of time; cf. 1111 δείελον, 1119 βουλύσιον ὥρην. For αὐτός 'same' without the article cf. 928, 1031, 1099. This line clarifies the sense of 1128: the storm may come at any time during the three days. It is probably the period implied by αὐτίκα in 1121; cf. 761–4. *CCAG* 8.1.140, 5 = Anon. Laur. 12.2 ἢ αὐθημερὸν ἢ τῇ ἐρχομένῃ ἢ εἰς τὰς ἐπομένας β' ἡμέρας.

μετὰ τήν   Cf. 545, 549 ἐπὶ τῷ.

1132 μύες   *D.S.* 41 καὶ μῦες τρίζοντες καὶ ὀρχούμενοι χειμέριον. Ael. *NA* 7.8 γαλαῖ δὲ ὑποτρίζουσαι καὶ μύες ἐκείναις δρῶντες τὰ αὐτὰ χειμῶνα ἔσεσθαι συμβάλλονται ἰσχυρόν, *Gp.* 1.3.13 καὶ μύες τετριγότες χειμῶνα σημαίνουσιν (≈ Anon. Laur. 11.18), *CCAG* 8.1.137, 13 γαλαῖ καὶ μῦες τρίζοντες ἰσχυρὸν χειμῶνα σημαίνουσιν. The scholia give two explanations: καὶ γὰρ οὗτοι τῆς τοῦ ἀέρος πιλήσεως αἰσθανόμενοι τοῦτο ποιοῦσιν (ΜΔΚUAS), ἢ ὅτι ἀσθενὲς καὶ λεπτὸν τὸ δέρμα ἔχοντες, ἐπειδὰν ψυχρὰν γενομένην πατήσωσι τὴν γῆν, μὴ φέροντες τὸ κρύος ἅλλονται (ΜΚΑ).

τετριγότες   An onomatopoeic verb expressing high-pitched sounds, e.g. of bats (ω 7 τρίζουσαι), nestlings (Β 314 τετριγῶτας), ghosts (Ψ 101 τετριγυῖα, ω, 5 τρίζουσαι), a creaking axle (Call. fr. 260.68 τετριγώς).

μᾶλλον   Cf. 1105.

COMMENTARY: 1133–1137

1133 ἐσκίρτησαν Especially of horses, e.g. Υ 226 ὅτε μὲν σκιρτῷεν
ἐπὶ ζείδωρον ἄρουραν, E. *Ph.* 1125 πῶλοι δρομάδες ἐσκίρτων φόβῳ.
Cf. 282 μετασκαίροντα ('Ίππον). But of goats in Theoc. 1.152. The
verb is associated with dancing in Ar. *Pl.* 761 ὀρχεῖσθε καὶ σκιρτᾶτε καὶ
χορεύετε.

ἐοικότα ἐοικότες is unsatisfactory, since the mice cannot be said to
look like dances. Hence the recourse of translators to either a free version (e.g. Mair 'and seemed to dance') or a meaning that the words or
the syntax will not bear (e.g. Martin 'semblables à des troupes de dan-
seuses', Voss and Erren 'gleich wie im Reihntanz', 'wie in Reigen-
tänzen'). Either the mice are likened to dancers, or their movements are
likened to dance movements. Emendation to ὀρχησταῖσιν would be too
forced to be acceptable, especially as ὀρχηθμοῖσιν seems intended to
echo Homeric ὀρχηθμοῖο, three times in the same position (Ν 637, θ
263, ψ 134). The application of this Homeric and essentially human
word to mice is another humorous touch. Maass may well be right with
ἐοικότα, comparing 1007 βοόωσι λιγαινομένοισιν ὁμοῖα (but 939 is not
parallel). This also has the advantage of eliminating the awkward clash
with τετριγότες in the same clause. And if A. did write ἐοικότα, the
corruption was almost inevitable. For the hiatus cf. 962.

1134 ἄσκεπτοι 'Unobserved', i.e. as a weather sign. Cf. 1045 ἀπείρητοι, also with preceding negative, and similarly 2, 180 ἄρρητον, 277
ἀφαυροῖς, 586 ἀεικής, 608 ἄφραστοι, 868 ἄρραντοι, 1121 ἀχείμεροι.

παλαιοτέροις The comparative is the more likely form in A.'s reference to traditional lore; cf. 442 πρότεροι ἐπεφημίξαντο, 637 προτέρων λόγος. The phrase echoes Ψ 788 παλαιοτέρους ἀνθρώπους, also
a four-word line.

1135 κύων ὠρύξατο *D.S.* 42 κύων τοῖς ποσὶν ὀρύττουσα ... χειμέριον, *Gp.* 1.3.11 κύνες ὀρύσσοντες τὴν γῆν χειμῶνα δηλοῦσι (=Anon.
Laur. 11.28). The same sign is attributed to sheep in 1082–3. The scholia explain both this reading and its variant: τινὲς γράφουσιν "ὠρύξατο". φιλόψυχρος γὰρ ὢν ὁ κύων, χαίρων ἐπὶ τῷ ἐσομένῳ χειμῶνι
σκάπτει τὴν γῆν παίζων. τινὲς δὲ "ὠρέξατο", ἀντὶ τοῦ ἐξέτεινεν. ἀρχομένου γὰρ τοῦ σώματος αὐτοῦ ὑπὸ τοῦ ψύχους πυκνοῦσθαι, ὄντος
κατὰ φύσιν ψυχροῦ, βουλόμενος τὸ σῶμα διαλύειν ἐκτείνει αὐτό, ὡς
ἡμεῖς μετὰ τὸν ὕπνον. Another scholion, however, claims that the dogs
are digging a hole as a shelter, ἀπὸ τῆς τοῦ ἀέρος ὑγρασίας ὥσπερ
κατάδυσίν τινα ζητοῦντες.

1136 ἀμφοτέροις Sch. τοῖς ἐμπροσθίοις ποσί. Cf. 1109.

1137–1141 The manuscript tradition shows lines 1138–41 either before or after 1137 or omitted altogether. The scholia have no comment
on them, they are not translated by either Avienius or *Arat. Lat.* and

569

their subject-matter is not to be found in either *D.S.* or any of the later extant lists of weather signs. Some editors have therefore taken these lines, and 1137 with them, to be spurious.

At least 1137 should be above suspicion. Its subject-matter is covered by the scholion on 1132 (χειμῶνα σημαίνουσι), it is translated by *Arat. Lat.*, and M has a marginal note on it. It is also a necessary conclusion to the chiastic pattern of 1132ff., which begins by introducing mice and dogs simply as weather prophets (1132–5), and concludes by specifying the weather that dogs and mice predict (1135–7): see Maass p. xxix. Line 1137 is therefore authentic and must follow 1136.

The problem of 1138–41 is more difficult. If the lines are authentic, their displacement and omission can be explained by the assumption that they were omitted in an early copy, then added in the margin, and later inserted in the wrong place by one copyist, and omitted completely by another. To account for the omissions in the scholia and the Latin translations, the original omission must have occurred in antiquity, and this would also explain the absence of the subject-matter in the later lists of weather signs. Martin (*HT* 288) suggests a different explanation, which he prefers, namely that these lines were relegated to the margin by a Byzantine scholar, when he learned from the discovery of an earlier copy that they were not authentic. If Martin means simply that the lines were not present in that text, this hardly constitutes a proof that they are spurious. If they are to be so regarded, some explanation is required of how they came to be inserted into the text. They are not in themselves unsatisfactory, like the obvious interpolations 138 and 613, or clumsily composed, like the Planudean substitutions for 481–96, 501–10, and 515–24. And their style is certainly Aratean, for example in their Homeric echoes, alliteration, and ascribing of human feelings to animals (see the following notes). Failing more cogent evidence to the contrary, it is reasonable to retain them as authentic.

There is still, however, the problem of 1140–1. It seems curious that this couplet on the behaviour of mice is separated from the earlier lines on the same subject by a couplet on a very different animal. To remove this inelegance R. F. Thomas, *HSCPh* 90 (1986) 91–2, proposes σύες for μύες, citing in support *D.S.* 49 with σύες (Maass p. xxvi: see note on 1123), *V. G.* 1.399–400 and Plin. *Nat.* 18.364. But this creates other difficulties. The passages just cited are more obviously related to 1123 (see note ad loc.), and it is unlikely that A. would have added a similar reference to pigs here. The point of these ten lines (1132–41) is that even the lesser animals can be useful as weather prophets, e.g. mice, dogs, crabs. Pigs, on the other hand, rank among the more important farm animals and have their proper place in 1068–74 and 1123. It is tempting to put 1140-1 after 1137, where it would also enhance the chiasmus with three lines on mice to balance the initial three (1132-4). This would leave the crab couplet as a surprise conclusion, aptly introduced by the lively καὶ μήν (cf. Procyon at the end of the constellations (450)). But, as Maass has observed (p. xxix), there is a possible reason for leaving 1140-1 slightly detached from the preceding lines. All the other signs in this section predict storm (cf. 1104, 1114, 1121, 1128, 1136, 1137, 1139), but the final item is a sign of rain, which is always distinguished from storm in A., as in the traditional weather-lore. The purpose of 1140-1 could therefore be to show that mice can predict rain as well as storm. And since there is no evidence of textual disruption within these four lines, it seems best to leave them undisturbed.

1137 καὶ κεῖνοι A. elsewhere uses κἀκεῖν- (81, 129, 197, 359), but καὶ κ. is more Homeric (e.g. κ 437). The pronoun refers back to 1132, as τότε to 1132-3; cf. M^mg πρώην εἰρημένοι, οἳ εὐδεινοὶ ἐσκίρτησαν.

μαντεύονται Cf. A 107, β 180 μαντεύεσθαι. An impressive human power is humorously attributed to animals, perhaps with the implication that their predictions are reliable; cf. [Theoc.] 21.45 πᾶσα κύων ἄρτον μαντεύεται, Ael. VH 1.11 ἦσαν ἄρα μαντικώτατοι τῶν ζῴων καὶ μύες, of houses about to collapse; cf. NA 11.19, Plin. Nat. 8.103, Aus. Techn. 13.12 Green, and the association of mice with Apollo: see Roscher IV 1086.

1138 καὶ μήν Introducing a new item in a series, e.g. λ 582 (Denniston 351-2). Here it is a different kind of animal that is introduced, and it also concludes the long catalogue of storm signs. Cf. 450 ναὶ μὴν καί.

καρκίνος Not elsewhere mentioned as a weather sign. Arist. HA 525b7 has a note on crabs that run very fast on the beach, and Ael. NA 7.24 gives an account of crabs on land. There is a curious association of crabs with mice in Bat. 299, but A. has no verbal echo of that passage. A. may have added this detail from his own knowledge of folk-lore, having in mind that the crab has some prominence in the earlier part of the poem as a small but important constellation.

ᾤχετο The imperfect from is sometimes used as aorist, e.g. Ψ 564 ὁ δ᾽ ᾤχετο καί οἱ ἔνεικεν, and without augment ν 415 οἴχετο πευσόμενος μετὰ σὸν κλέος, α 260 οἴχετο γὰρ καὶ κεῖσε (with the force of pluperfect); cf. Hdt. 5.43 ἐς Δελφοὺς οἴχετο χρησόμενος τῷ χρηστηρίῳ. See Veitch 427. The rarity of this form explains the two variants οἴχεται and ᾤχετο.

χέρσον The accusative is necessary, since the point is that the crab comes out of its natural habitat on to the dry land.

1139 ἐπαΐσσεσθαι ὁδοῖο Rarely middle, but cf. Ψ 627-8 χεῖρες | ...

ἐπαΐσσονται [v.l. ἀπ-] ἐλαφραί, 773 ἔμελλον ἐπαΐξασθαι ἄεθλον. The active verb is used c. gen., e.g. N 687 of Hector σπουδῇ ἐπαΐσσοντα νεῶν. For the present infinitive after μέλλω expressing strong probability cf. B 116 οὕτω που Διὶ μέλλει ὑπερμενέϊ φίλον εἶναι. Voss, Martin and Erren construe as an infinitive of purpose depending on οἴχετο.

1140 καὶ μύες A different kind of weather sign from mice (see note on 1137–1141). This single rain-sign at the end of the long catalogue reads almost as an afterthought. A. has not attempted a climax at this point, perhaps because the next thirteen lines provide an effective conclusion to the whole poem.

ἡμέριοι The portent is recognisable because an activity normally associated with evening occurs during the daytime. This sense is more commonly given by ἡμερινός, as in 851; but cf. 509 χειμέριος 'in winter'. The variation is characteristic of A.

στιβάδα στρωφῶντες A verbal echo of η 105 ἠλάκατα στρωφῶσιν, ρ 97 ἠλάκατα στρωφῶσα. The alliteration draws attention to a remarkable portent.

1141 ἱμείρονται Cf. Ξ 163 εἴ πως ἱμείραιτο in same *sedes*, and c. gen. α 41 ἧς ἱμείρεται αἴης.

φαίνει The transmitted text favours the optative, but in the many temporal clauses in which A. describes weather signs the MSS offer mostly indicative and subjunctive (see note on 828 περιτέλλῃ). Here the former seems the more likely, since -ει and -οι are often confused in the MSS (e.g. in 825 and 905), the indicative is the prevailing mood from 1132, and the clause for once follows the main verb.

The subject of φαίνει is not clear. Ceporinus takes it to be σήματα, translating 'cum pluuiae signum appareat', and so Martin, 'lorsque apparaissent des signes de pluie'. This makes good sense, but 'appear' is an unparalleled meaning for φαίνω, which in its intransitive use means 'shine': cf. φαείνω 148, 450, 789, 905, and the name Φαίνων for the planet Saturn (Gem. 1.24); see Diggle *Studies* 41–2 on E. *El.* 1234 and S. *El.* 1359. The alternative is to take σήματα as object of φαίνει, which is the most natural interpretation here in view of 772 (and perhaps 433), and σήματα φαίνων in Β 353, Δ 381, φ 413 and Hes. fr. 141.25, in which Zeus is the subject. Hence Voss understood Zeus as the implied subject here, comparing ὕει and similar weather verbs. So Maass, Mair, Erren ('when Zeus shows signs of rain' etc.). A. certainly makes frequent reference to Zeus throughout the poem, but we would expect him to be explicit here if this is what he meant. Moreover Zeus is the provider of signs for men, not for mice, and in this case the sign is the behaviour of the mice. It may therefore be better to regard φαίνει as purely impersonal, as weather verbs frequently are, e.g. 430 ἀπαστράψαντος, 933 ἀστράπτησιν. Cf. σημαίνει in *D.S.* e.g. 46 ὅταν μέλιτται ... πέτωνται, χειμῶνα ἐσόμενον σημαίνει, Arist. *Pr.* 941b2 ἐπὶ πᾶσι μὲν σημαίνει τοῖς ἄστροις, Hdt. 6.27 φιλέει δέ κως προσημαίνειν. I know of no other instance of impersonal φαίνει, but for a similarly rare use cf. Χ 319 ἀπέλαμπε.

It is worth noting that A. uses a syntactical variation here. Instead of expressing the sign in a subordinate clause and the weather inference in the main clause (e.g. 1124–8), he now puts the sign in the main clause and the inferred weather in a temporal clause, which is thus parallel to the genitive absolute in the preceding couplet.

1142–1154 CONCLUSION

The thirteen lines of conclusion balance the fourteen lines of the proem before the invocation. They sum up the lessons of all parts of the poem, but recall especially the star calendar (1145–8) and the lunar phases (1148–52). This contrasts with Hesiod's very brief conclusion (*Op.* 822–8), which rounds off only the section on the days. The didactic character of the *Phaenomena* is emphasised with a varied sequence of imperatives and 2nd pers. verbs, encouraging the reader to profit by the instructions given. But the Stoic message is strangely absent here, and there is no final reference to the benevolent Zeus.

1142 κατόνοσσο Only one group of the manuscripts gives this reading, but it is supported by Avien. 1864 *non spernenda tibi sunt talia*, sch. μηδὲν καταμεμψάμενος παροδεύσῃς, sch. (E) μὴ μεμψάμενος παρέλθῃς, and Eˢˡ μὴ μεμψάμενος παρέλθε. Cf. Theoc. 26.38 μηδεὶς τὰ θεῶν ὀνόσαιτο. The variant κατόνησο does not make sense, and is probably to be explained by the influence of ὄνησο in τ 68, while κατόκνησο is an emendation of it in the direction of the required meaning. The simple verb ὄνομαι is Homeric, e.g. Ι 55 οὔ τίς τοι τὸν μῦθον ὀνόσσεται, and -σσ- here reflects that future form. The old imperative middle in -σο is revived here in imitation of epic ὄνησο, κεῖσο (Φ 122), ἵστασο (Hes. *Sc.* 449); cf. 758 πεπόνησο, 930 πεφύλαξο. The compound verb occurs in Herodotus, e.g. 2.172.

καλόν Sc. ἐστι. Cf. S. *Ph.* 1155–6 καλὸν | ἀντίφονον κορέσαι στόμα, Ar. *Pax* 278 νῦν ἐστιν εὔξασθαι καλόν, and again 292, in the same sense of 'now is a good time to'.

ἐπὶ σήματι σῆμα Cf. 962 ἐπὶ ὕδατι ὕδωρ.

1143 δυοῖν The variant δυεῖν is a late Attic form, which appears especially in inscriptions from the last quarter of the fourth century: see Meisterhans–Schwyzer, *Grammatik der attischen Inschriften*³ (Berlin 1900) 157, 201. It occurs as a variant in some literary texts, e.g. *Th.* 1.20.3, E.

El. 536, Theophr. *Char.* 2.3, but is authentic in Men. *Dys.* 327. It is an unlikely reading in the Homeric style of the *Phaenomena*.

εἰς ταὐτὸν ἰόντων Cf. 243, 459. For εἰς see note on 995. In Attic ταὐτόν is used for ταὐτό when metrically convenient; cf. S. *OT* 325 ταὐτὸν πάθω, E. *Tr.* 684 ἐς ταὐτὸν ἥκεις συμφορᾶς. Barrett on E. *Hipp.* 1178–9 sees a preference for -ον in dramatists, but Mastronarde on E. *Ph.* 499, praef. 20(5), thinks scribes often altered ταὐτό to ταὐτόν.

1144 ἐλπωρή Homeric only in ἐλπωρή τοι ἔπειτα (β 280, ζ 314, ψ 287).

τελέθοι Potential optative without κε or ἄν; see note on 76. It is not necessary to read κε for δέ in 1143, as Martin suggests. In this line the use of κε with the second optative, which has the same force, may be seen as a deliberate variation, or taken ἀπὸ κοινοῦ with τελέθοι.

θαρσήσειας Cf. *Gp.* 1.3.14 ὅταν δὲ ἅμα πλείω σημεῖα ἐπὶ τὸ αὐτὸ συντρέχῃ, βεβαιότερα τὰ ἐλπιζόμενα, Hdt. 3.76 τεθαρσηκότες τοῖσι ὄρνισι.

1145 παριόντος The scholion on this line paraphrases with an aorist participle and introduces the notion of comparing last year's signs with this year's: παρατηρητέον δὲ καὶ τὰ τοῦ παρελθόντος ἐνιαυτοῦ σημεῖα πρὸς τὰ τοῦ ἐνεστῶτος. Cf. Avien. 1867–8 *et transactorum sollers componere mensum | signa laborabis*. Among modern translators Voss and Schott also make the participle refer to the previous year. But the present participle can only denote the current year, and this is all that A. means in this line. The comparison involved is explained in 1146. Martin would construe αἰεί with παριόντος, but it is more natural to take it with ἀριθμοίης, since it is the observing that should go on all the time (cf. 762, 1046).

ἀριθμοίης The optative with ἄν in the sense of a mild command (cf. 300–2) is post-Homeric, e.g. S. *El.* 637 κλύοις ἄν ἤδη, 1491 χωροῖς ἄν εἴσω. But the verb itself is Homeric, e.g., in same *sedes*, δ 411 φώκας μέν τοι πρῶτον ἀριθμήσει, ν 215 τὰ χρήματ' ἀριθμήσω. Here the significance of the present tense is not made clear by some translators, e.g. Erren's 'die Zeichen ... zählen', while Mair's 'add the signs' does not even make sense. What A. means is that the weather signs to be expected are known from the parapegmata (cf. 752), and one must 'keep count of' them as they appear successively in the sky.

1146 σήματα Since we are concerned here with watching the sky day by day, Rehm proposed ἤματα on the basis of the Miletus parapegma fr. M 1 (*Sitzungsb. Akad. Berlin* 1904, 98–9) and *CCAG* 8.1.140, 6 = Anon. Laur. 12.3 ἐξετάζων δὲ καὶ τὰς κατ' ἐνιαυτὸν ἡμέρας. But it is strictly not the days that are to be observed, but the signs, and the σήματα in this context are the constellations, which give warnings of seasonal weather changes by their annual risings and settings (cf. 1146–7). The Greek word can mean both signs and constellations (like Latin *signa*), and A. has both senses in mind here, looking back to 10–11. The usual translation 'signs' is therefore inadequate, possibly even misleading, since A. is not referring to the 30° arcs of the ecliptic (see note on 555), but to the visible constellations (cf. 559ff.). For the sake of clarity it therefore seems best to translate 'constellations'.

συμβάλλων The comparing involves checking the actual weather against the observed phenomena; sch. ἐάν που καὶ ἐπὶ ἀστέρι ἀνατέλλοντι ἢ δύνοντι τοιαύτη γενήσεται ἡ ἡμέρα οἷαν λέγει καὶ τὸ σημεῖον, Anon. Laur. 12.3 ἐπισκοπῶν εἴ που ἀνατολὴ ἄστρων ἢ δύσις ἐκείναις ταῖς ἡμέραις γίνεται ἐν αἷς καὶ σημεῖα τινὸς χειμῶνος προδηλοῦται (= *CCAG* 8.1.140, 7 with ἐν ἐκείναις and σημάδιά τινος).

1147 φαείνεται The reading is supported by sch. 1145 εἰ πρὸς τῷ σημείῳ τοῦ ἀστέρος τοιαύτη καὶ ἡ ἡμέρα φαίνεται. The variant κατέρχεται does not make sense, and may have its origin in 689 κατέρχεται ἀντέλλοντι.

1148 ὁπποίην Required by the sense; cf. sch. (MKA) 1146 τοιαύτη γενήσεται ἡ ἡμέρα οἷαν [ΚΑ, οἷον Μ] λέγει καὶ τὸ σημεῖον, sch. (ΜΔKUA) ὁποία λέγει τὸ σημεῖον ἡ ἡμέρα ἔλθῃ. The corruption can be explained by the influence of σῆμα.

λέγοι The optative contrasts the hypothetical character of the prediction with the actual weather experienced, which is expressed in the indicative (φαείνεται). Cf. such mixed constructions as ζ 286 ἄλλη νεμεσῶ, ἥ τις τοιαῦτά γε ῥέζοι, τ 510–11 κοίτοιο τάχ᾽ ἔσσεται ἡδέος ὥρη, | ὅν τινά γ᾽ ὕπνος ἕλοι, S. *Ant.* 666 ὃν πόλις στήσειε, τοῦδε χρὴ κλύειν.

μάλα δ᾽ ἄρκιον εἴη μάλα has almost superlative sense; sch. πρὸ πάντων. Hence the variant μάλιστα. Cf. V. *G.* 1.432 *namque is certissimus auctor*, *Gp.* 1.3.15 μάλιστα δὲ παραφυλάττειν. For ἄρκιον expressing certainty, cf. 741, in a context of reliable signs, and Ο 502–3 νῦν ἄρκιον ἢ ἀπολέσθαι | ἠὲ σαωθῆναι. The whole phrase echoes the rhythm of πολὺ κέρδιον εἴη (Η 28, Χ 108); but in the Homeric phrases the optatives are used with κεν and ἄν, whereas A. follows the rarer idiom, as in 1144.

1149 φράζεσθαι In the sense of observing, as ρ 160–1 οἰωνὸν ... ἐφρασάμην, but c. gen., as in 744–5 and Theoc. 2.84. A. also has ἐπιφράζεσθαι in this sense (40, 76, 1061).

φθίνοντος ... μηνός A. recalls Homeric τοῦ μὲν φθίνοντος μηνός, τοῦ δ᾽ ἱσταμένοιο (ξ 162, τ 307), and Hesiod's φθίνοντός θ᾽ ἱσταμένου τε (*Op.* 798). But the contexts are all different. Homer is referring to a time of year marked by the ending of one lunar month and the beginning of the next; cf. κ 470 μηνῶν φθινόντων. Hesiod is concerned with specific days of the month and their character (for purely superstitious reasons) as lucky and unlucky. He uses mainly a triple division, whereby days are labelled ἱσταμένου or μέσση or φθίνοντος (though he also has the overall numbering for the 20th and 27th). A. on the other hand is thinking of the natural lunar month, as in 778-810, in which the days are determined by observation of the moon's phases. It is a bipartite month, waxing (781, 800) and waning (800, 809), with the main division at full moon (799, 808) and subdivisions at the half-moon phases (799, 807, 809). The actual observation of the moon is in keeping with that of the stars elsewhere in the poem and with the poet's theme of identifying signs established by Zeus. With ἐφισταμένοιο cf. 782 ἐφεσταότος.

1150 τετράδας ἀμφοτέρας D.S. 5 αἱ σύνοδοι τῶν μηνῶν χειμέριοί εἰσιν, ὅτι ἀπολείπει τὸ φῶς τῆς σελήνης ἀπὸ τετράδος φθίνοντος μέχρι τετράδος ἱσταμένου, Gp. 1.3.15 μάλιστα δὲ παραφυλάττειν χρὴ αὐξούσης καὶ φθινούσης τῆς σελήνης τὰς τετράδας, τὴν τοῦ ἀέρος κίνησιν τρεπούσας. It is not clear whether Hesiod in Op. 798 is counting τετράδ' ... φθίνοντος forwards from the 20th or backwards from new moon, but the latter procedure seems, on the face of it, likely to have been an old one. Certainly the days of the third decad were so reckoned in the Athenian civil calendar: see the reckoning of days in Dem. 19.58-60, and the count-down in Ar. Nub. 1131 πέμπτη, τετράς, τρίτη, μετὰ ταύτην δευτέρα. The context here and in 809-10 shows that A. too is using this method of reckoning. The two fourths are significant because they represent the visible boundaries (πείρατα 1151) of the old moon and the new, between which the nights are moonless. It is true that the crescents can sometimes be sighted on the third and third last days, and A. allows for the former in 781 and 810, but they are normally too faint and too low in the sky to be seen.

ἄμυδις Cf. 581, 838, 1153.

συνιόντων Strictly speaking the months meet in the day the Athenians called ἕνη καὶ νέα (cf. Ar. Nub. 1134), when the moon comes into conjunction with the sun (cf. Th. 2.28), and the last day of the old month becomes the first of the new. But from the point of view of weather signs it is realistic to regard the whole period of the moon's invisibility as the change-over time.

1151 πείρατ' A. transfers to time the Homeric use with reference to place, e.g. δ 563 Ἠλύσιον πεδίον καὶ πείρατα γαίης.

σφαλερώτερος The comparative is more appropriate than the variant superlative, because the period of moonless nights is being compared with the rest of the month. Voss calls this corruption 'das gewöhnliche Schicksal der Comparative': cf. 1134.

1152 ὀκτὼ νυξί The eight nights include the two τετράδες (cf. D.S. 5 ἀπὸ τετράδος φθίνοντος μέχρι, τετράδος ἱσταμένου), but since the crescents then are visible for only a short time in the morning and evening twilights, the nights before and after the respective twilights can reasonably be described as moonless. Strictly speaking, of course, there should be only seven such nights, if the 24-hour period within which the conjunction occurs is to be regarded as shared by both the old month and the new.

χήτει Disyllabic also in π 35 χήτει ἐνευναίων, probably trisyllabic in Z 463 and T 324.

χαροποῖο See note on 394. Cf. also Plu. 934D, of the moon in eclipse: πρὸς ἔω λαμβάνει χρόαν κυανοειδῆ καὶ χαροπήν, ἀφ' ἧς δὴ καὶ μάλιστα γλαυκῶπιν αὐτὴν οἱ ποιηταὶ καὶ Ἐμπεδοκλῆς [fr. B 42] ἀνακαλοῦνται. Here a greater degree of brightness must be intended in view of the contrast with the moonless sky. Cf. A.R. 1.1280 χαροπὴ ὑπολάμπεται ἠώς.

1153 ἄμυδις Emphatic: it is only by taking all the available signs together that the observer can make a reliable forecast of the weather.

ἐσκεμμένος εἰς ἐνιαυτόν A. concludes with a reference back to the proem, ἐσκέψατο δ' εἰς ἐνιαυτόν (11), with some word-play on the different meanings of the verb. A. normally uses this verb c. acc. and in the sense of 'observe' (159, 428 etc.), but c. gen. only here and in 560 meaning 'watch for'. The observer must make a point of looking out for all these signs, not just notice them casually.

1154 σχεδίως I.e. without having sufficient evidence to make a more accurate forecast. The meaning seems to be derived from σχεδόν in the sense of 'approximately'; cf. σχεδιάζω of saying something on the spur of the moment, e.g. Pl. Sis. 387e σχεδιάζοντα λέγειν ὅτι ἂν τύχῃ. Sch. ἀντὶ τοῦ προσφάτως, ἀσκόπως, παρέργως, προπετῶς καὶ ὡς ἔτυχεν.

ἐπ' αἰθέρι τεκμήραιο Cf. 801 ἐπὶ χροιῇ τεκμαίρεο, 1129 ἐπὶ σήμασι τεκμήραιο.

INDEXES

1 GREEK

INDEXES

ὁπότε in a Herodotean usage, 120
ὁππῆμος, *hapax*, 568
ὀργυιή, Ionic form, 69
ὀρνιθέης, *hapax*, 274
ὀρύχοιεν, *hapax*, 1086
ὀρχίλος, 1025
ὅτινι, 65
ὀτλήσαντες, Hellenistic form, 428
οὖλος, Ionic form, 717
οὐραῖα, form and meaning of, 243
οὖτα, epic aorist, 643
ὀχέομαι = ὀχεύομαι, *hapax*, 1070
ὀχῆς, gen. of ὄχεα, *hapax*, 956
ὀχῆς, gen. of ὄχεια, *hapax*, 1069
ὀψὲ δύοντι, 585

πάγχυ, Ionic form, 406
παλιμπετές, 1032
παλίνορσος, 54
παλίνωρα, *hapax*, 452
παλιρρόθιος of a ship, 347
πανσυδίη, meanings, 649
πάντη, adverb, 4
πάντοθεν + gen., 455
παραθλίβω, first instance of, 993
παρακλίνω, meaning of, 738
παρβολάδην in geometry, 318
παρελαύνεται, middle use, 675
παρέξ, compound prep., 988
παρήλια, 881
παρηορίαι of the River, 600
πειραίνω, 24
πενθέριος, first instance of, 252
πεπλήγοντες, Aeolicism, 193
πεπονήαται, 82
πεπόνησο, *hapax*, 758
πεπτηώς, meanings of, 167
περάτη = 'horizon', 499
πέρι, adverb, 830
περιαγή, *hapax*, 688
περιβρίθω, first instance of, 1049
περιγληνής, *hapax*, 476
περιδνοφέομαι, *hapax*, 876
περιελίσσω, meaning of, 531
περιηγής, 401
περιλιχμάομαι, 1115
περιμεμφής, *hapax*, 109
περιμήκετος + gen., 250
περίπλειος, *hapax*, 1118
περιπολλά, adv., *hapax*, 914
περισπεύδω, first instance of, 1122
περιστέλλω of securing ship, 766

περιστέφω, meaning of, 567
περιτέλλεται of stars and sun, 215
περιτέμνεται of stars, 50
περιτροχάομαι of haloes, 815
πέτηλος, 271
πεφασμένος from φαίνω, 328
πεφυλαγμένος + gen., 48, 1125; acc.,
    973; abs. 762
πεφύλαξο, 930
πίσυρες, Aeolic, 478
πλειότερος, meaning of, 644
πνευμάτιος, *hapax*, 785
πόδας ... ποδός ... πόδα, 185
ποικίλλω of colour, 822; sound, 1001
πόλος, meanings of, 24
πολυγλαγής, first instance of, 1100
πολύκλαυτος, 360
πολυλήϊος of crops, 1058
πολυρρόθιος, first instance of, 412
πολύσκεπτος, meaning of, 136
πολυτειρής, only in A., 604
πομφόλυγες, 980
πόρσω, post-Homeric form, 298
ποτήν, adverbial acc., 278
ποτιδέγμενος, abs., 1090
πρῖνος, 1044
προμολῇσι, preferred variant, 239
προφερέστερος, meaning of, 240
πρυμνόθεν, 343
πρώϊα, adv., *hapax*, 1078
πρῶτόν τε καὶ ὕστατον, 14
πτερὰ πυκνά, meaning of, 969
πυγούσιον, adv., 896
πυριβήτης, *hapax*, 983
πυρώτερα, *hapax*, 798

ῥαθάμιγγες, 889
ῥάχις of a fish, 572
ῥηγνύατο as sg., 817
ῥυμοί of meteors, 927

σειριάω, extended meaning of, 331
σεληναίη, noun, 818
σημαίνετον of parhelia, 891
σκαρθμός = πόδες, 281
σκέπτομαι suggesting concern, 11
σκιόωνται, extended meaning of, 600
σκυθρός of animals, 1120
σπίνος, 1024
σταλαγμούς†, 966
στιχάω, transitive, 191
στροφάδες as participle, 1032

2 PASSAGES DISCUSSED

References are to page numbers.

2 PASSAGES DISCUSSED

3 SUBJECTS

References are to page numbers.